The History and Antiquities of the Counties of Westmorland and Cumberland, Volume 1

Isaac Mitchell
1874

THE

HISTORY

AND

ANTIQUITIES

OF THE COUNTIES OF

WESTMORLAND AND CUMBERLAND.

By JOSEPH NICOLSON, Esq; and RICHARD BURN, LL.D

IN TWO VOLUMES.

VOL. I.

LONDON:
PRINTED FOR W. STRAHAN; AND T. CADELL, IN THE STRAND.
MDCCLXXVII.
1777

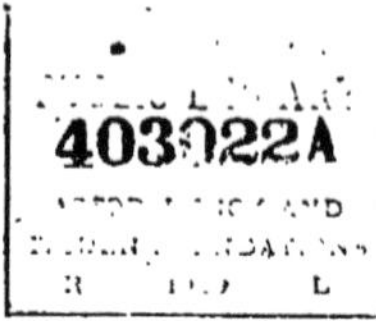
403022A

PREFACE.

VARIOUS collections have been made from time to time by inquiſitive and learned men, concerning the hiſtory and antiquities of the Counties of Weſtmorland and Cumberland, ſome with an intention of publication, others to gratify private curioſity.

By the favour of the preſent proprietors, theſe are now collected, digeſted, and offered to the public view: it being judged more eligible that the following work ſhould come abroad in its preſent ſtate, however imperfect, than to wait for further information, whilſt the preſent materials are periſhing.

The right reverend Dr. WILLIAM NICOLSON lord biſhop of Carliſle (whom we mention in the firſt place) made a collection of materials towards a general hiſtory of the ſaid two counties; conſiſting of, 1. A topographical deſcription and hiſtory of the county of Cumberland. 2. A collection from books, manuſcripts, and records for an hiſtory of the biſhops, priors, deans, and chapter of Carliſle. 3. Collections for a monaſticon of the ſaid dioceſe. 4. Hiſtory of all the rectories and vicarages in the dioceſe of Carliſle, extracted chiefly from the regiſters of the ſeveral biſhops at Roſe. 5. Miſcellany account of the ſtate of the churches, parſonage and vicarage houſes, and other things remarkable, in the ſeveral pariſhes within the dioceſe of Carliſle, taken in his parochial viſitation in the year 1703. All theſe are now at Hawkſdale in the poſſeſſion of his nephew Joſeph Nicolſon eſquire. Tranſcripts of ſeveral of theſe in four folio volumes, the ſaid learned prelate cauſed to be depoſited in the library of the dean and chapter of Carliſle.

Towards the eccleſiaſtical part of ſo much of the two counties as lies within the dioceſe of Cheſter, we have received aſſiſtance from biſhop GASTRELL's manuſcript account of the ſaid dioceſe of Cheſter, with continuations by the late commiſſary STRATFORD: Now in the poſſeſſion of Mr. James Collinſon of Lancaſter.

Mr. JOHN DENTON of Cardew made large extracts from the Eſcheators books for Cumberland, and from the records in the Tower and other public offices; containing accounts of fines levied, pleas of lands, inquiſitions *poſt mortem*, grants of fairs and markets, parks, free warren, and many other particulars. Copies of which extracts are now at Rydal hall, in the poſſeſſion of Sir Michael le Fleming baronet. From the ſaid extracts Mr. Denton compiled his manuſcript hiſtory of Cumberland, which is in ſeveral hands.

Sir DANIEL FLEMING of Rydal baronet, great grandfather of the ſaid Sir Michael, made very large collections relating to both counties; and from his family evidences, which have been accumulating almoſt ever ſince the conqueſt, he formed a manuſcript hiſtory of his own family (and incidentally of divers other families) in two volumes quarto. Amongſt his other collections (beſides the aboveſaid copies from Mr. Denton) are many pedigrees of ancient families, marriage ſettlements, inquiſitions *poſt mortem*, extracts from the records at London and from the Bodleian library at Oxford, and decrees in courts of equity on matters ariſing within the ſaid two counties. He alſo writ a ſmall manuſcript hiſtory of Weſtmorland; one copy whereof is at Rydal, and another in the ſaid Bodleian library.

The right honourable ANNE counteſs dowager of PEMBROKE, DORSET, and MONTGOMERY, at a vaſt expence, procured from all the publick offices copies of every thing that could be found relating to any of her anceſtors the Veteriponts and Cliffords, lords of Weſtmorland and hereditary ſheriffs of the ſame; and cauſed the ſaid copies to be ingroſſed in three large folio volumes, and lodged in her caſtle at Appleby, where they now remain. In making this collection, ſhe employed that learned antiquary Mr. Roger Dodſworth, who left a large collection of manuſcripts to the univerſity of Oxford. From theſe records ſhe cauſed to be compiled an hiſtory of her anceſtors, from the firſt Robert de Veteripont in the reign of king John, down to her own time: In the digeſting of which memoirs ſhe employed that great and learned lawyer Mr. *Hale*, afterwards lord chief juſtice.

The reverend THOMAS MACHEL, M. A. ſometime fellow of Queen's College in Oxford, and rector of Kirkby Thore, from his firſt entrance in the univerſity to the day of his death, employed himſelf with unwearied aſſiduity in collecting materials for an hiſtory of Weſtmorland; and as his collections multiplied, an hiſtory alſo of

Cumberland. At his death, he left his collection to the aforesaid bishop Nicolson, with a request (if it might easily be done) that his papers should be put into form and published. This collection, the bishop says in a prefatory introduction, was all in loose papers; and so imperfect and indigested, that he could not think of compleating the design. But he gathered all the scattered fragments together, and bound them up in six volumes in folio, and lodged the same in the library of the dean and chapter of Carlisle, that they might be made use of, if any person afterwards should undertake an history of the said two counties. This collection of Mr. Machel consists, first, of extracts from the evidences at Appleby castle and at Skipton castle (another seignory belonging to the lords of Westmorland). Next, Mr. Machel by himself, and by divers amanuenses, made many extracts from the records in the Rolls chapel and in the Tower; unto which he had free access by the friendship of Sir Joseph Williamson, secretary of state, who had formerly been fellow of the aforesaid college. He also made extracts from the private evidences of several ancient families; which extracts are become more valuable, as many of the originals are now lost. Mr. Machel had also consulted the records in the heralds office, and the separate collections of several particular heralds, and especially of Sir William Dugdale his intimate friend. It was usual in ancient time for the heralds to perambulate the several counties at certain intervals, where they received and examined the pedigrees of the several families, approved the genuine, rejected the spurious, and respited the doubtful for further consideration, blazoned their arms, granted new bearings to new families, or new marks of distinction to different branches of the same ancient family. The last visitation of that kind in Westmorland and Cumberland was made by the same Sir William Dugdale in the years 1664 and 1665; and Mr. Machel received copies from him of all the particulars. But above all, the said Sir William Dugdale had made a collection in 62 volumes in folio and quarto of matters relating to different parts of the kingdom. From thence Mr. Machel hath copied all that related to the said two counties.

The reverend HUGH TODD, D. D. vicar of Penrith and prebendary of Carlisle, composed an historical description of the diocese of Carlisle, in a large folio manuscript, and intended the same for publication, but was prevented by the most obvious of all reasons, namely, waiting for further materials. Hence it hath happened, that there is no account in his manuscript from what fountains he derived his information: and in fact, many of his accounts, when compared with the records of ancient times, appear to have wanted a reconſideration. Nevertheleſs, he was a gentleman of ability and learning, and there are many things in his collection both curious and inſtructive. Copies of this work are in ſeveral hands.

Sir THOMAS CARLETON of Carleton hall made divers extracts from the public offices relating to Cumberland and Weſtmorland, and writ large notes on ſome of Mr. Denton's extracts; and particularly, there is a large and curious collection of letters, which he ſays were found in the library at Carleton hall after his grandfather's death, relating to the Border ſervice, during the time that lord Dacre was warden of the Weſt Marches in the reign of king Edward the ſixth: Which particulars make part of the valuable collection at Rydal hall.

CHRISTOPHER RAWLINSON of Cark hall in the county of Lancaſter eſquire left a large collection of manuſcripts, in which are many particulars relating to the counties of Weſtmorland and Cumberland: Copies of theſe alſo are at Rydal.

JAMES BIRD of Brougham eſquire, who had been ſteward at Appleby caſtle, made a collection in alphabetical order of matters relating to the ſeveral townſhips or manors in Weſtmorland holden of the ſaid caſtle, from the ſame materials which Mr. Machel had made uſe of before: And there are in Mr. Bird's collection ſome inquiſitions and other evidences, which had not fallen under Mr. Machel's inſpection. This Mr. Bird appears to have had a moſt ample repoſitory of old evidences; but after the ſtricteſt inquiry, nothing hath been found now remaining, ſave only the above mentioned alphabetical digeſt, preſerved from oblivion by the aforeſaid Sir Daniel Fleming.

To all theſe we may add the original CHARTULARIES of the ſeveral religious houſes of HOLME CULTRAM, WETHERAL, and LANERCOST; the firſt of theſe at Hawkſdale, the ſecond in the library of the dean and chapter of Carliſle, and the third at Naward caſtle belonging to the right honourable the earl of Carliſle. As alſo the *Regiſters* of the ſeveral biſhops of Carliſle at Roſe, from the year 1293 to the preſent time, but with ſeveral intermiſſions, eſpecially during the long and dreadful conteſt between the two houſes of York and Lancaſter: Theſe eccleſiaſtical Regiſters are extremely uſeful even on a temporal account, in helping to rectify the heraldic pedigrees of ancient families; for as moſt of the great men were patrons of advowſons,

ſons, the hiſtory of the incumbents helps to elucidate the ſucceſſion of their patrons.

But our greateſt curioſity is a folio manuſcript (at Hawkſdale) of RICHARD BELL in the reign of queen Elizabeth warden clerk of the Weſt Marches of England over againſt Scotland; which, above all our other materials, affords the fulleſt and moſt ſatisfactory account of the ancient ſtate of the Borders, and conſequently of that remarkable and extraordinary tenure of Border ſervice, with which the cuſtoms of every manor throughout both the counties are moſt intimately connected.

It would be tedious to recount all the aſſiſtances we have been favoured with from individuals; Theſe will more properly be noticed in their reſpective places.

INTRO-

INTRODUCTORY DISCOURSE

OF THE

ANCIENT STATE OF THE BORDERS.

THE hiſtory of the two counties of WESTMORLAND and CUMBERLAND is ſo connected with the Border laws and ſervice againſt Scotland, that ſome account thereof ſeems to be neceſſary, before we come to treat of the particular places in each county. Nor will it, we truſt, be uſeleſs; ſince it will exhibit to us, as it were in a mirror, the miſerable ſtate of our anceſtors in theſe parts, and incline us to reflect with gratitude on the ineſtimable bleſſing of the union of the two kingdoms under one monarch and government. And of this we will treat in the order following:

CH. I. *Of the commencement of Border ſervice; with the authority and power of the lord warden of the Marches.*
CH. II. *Of the Border laws.*
CH. III. *Of the manner of keeping warden courts.*
CH. IV. *Of the ſtate of the Borders from the reign of king* Edward *the firſt to the reign of king* Richard *the ſecond incluſive.*
CH. V. *Of the ſtate of the Borders from the reign of king* Richard *the ſecond to the reign of king* Henry *the eighth.*
CH. VI. *Of the ſtate of the Borders during the reign of king* Henry *the eighth.*
CH. VII. *Of the ſtate of the Borders during the reign of king* Edward *the ſixth.*
CH. VIII. *Of the ſtate of the Borders during the reigns of queen* Mary *and queen* Elizabeth.
CH. IX. *Of the ſtate of the Borders during the reign of king* James *the firſt.*
CH. X. *Of the ſtate of the Borders from the reign of king* James *the firſt to the preſent time.*

CHAP-

CHAPTER I.

Of the commencement of Border service; with the authority and power of the lord warden of the marches.

THERE seems to be no doubt but that the Border service against the Scots, as distinct from the general military service throughout the kingdom, is as ancient as the distribution of the several seigniories and manors amongst the Norman adventurers by William the Conqueror or his grantee Ranulph de Meschiens. And the tenants of the several manors were obliged all along, upon firing of beacons or other warning, to attend their lord in the service of the Borders at their own expence; which attendance might be prolonged for forty days. And according to the value of their respective tenements, some were obliged to serve on horseback, and others on foot, with their proper accoutrements. Hence there were *nag tenements* and *foot tenements*; the owners whereof were obliged to furnish their stipulated number respectively, on pain of forfeiting their estate to the lord. Within the manor of *Bewcastle* in particular, they seem to have been all *nag tenements*; for in the reservation of an heriot to the lord upon the death of the tenant, there is an exception of the riding horse of every such tenant, kept by him for the lord's service, according to ancient custom.

But the regulation of the Borders by distinct laws, under the rule of lords wardens of the marches, seems to have commenced in the reign of king Edward the first of England, at the time when he affected the sovereignty over Scotland. Hostilities then became inveterate. The Scots ill brooked a claim, frivolous in itself, and supported by violence. Happy indeed had it been for both kingdoms, if Edward, bad as his cause was, had finally prevailed. It would have spared much blood, treasure, misery, and desolation which ensued; and, as experience hath at length instructed us, instead of two jealous, wrangling, contentious neighbours, distinguished by no natural boundary, would have made us many ages sooner, one great, opulent, and flourishing kingdom.

The first lord warden of the marches, of whom we have had any authentic account, was *Robert de Clifford* lord of Westmorland, and hereditary sheriff of the same; of whom the countess of Pembroke's memoirs take notice, that "in the 25th year of king Edward the first, viz. 1296, the said Robert, "being then about 23 years of age, was made the king's captain and keeper "of the Marches in the north towards Scotland;"—which was the very year in which Edward subdued that kingdom. And in the 27th year of the same king, amongst the records of writs, there is a letter of request from Robert de Clifford captain of the counties of Cumberland, Westmorland, and Lancastre, to the treasurer and barons of the exchequer, desiring them to excuse Sir William de Molecastre, Sir Thomas de Felton, Robert de Molecastre, and Richard de Molecastre, from appearing in the court of exchequer according to their summons, by reason of their attendance upon him, in aid and defence of the Marches: Dated at Lockmaben, July 4, in that year †.

'Tis

† Trin. 26 and 27 Ed. 1. Rot. 29. b.

'Tis true there is an account of laws made by commissioners of both kingdoms for the Borders, of an earlier date, namely in the year 1249, which was the 33 Hen. 3. purporting to be laws of March, made and recognized by the sheriff of Northumberland on the part of the king of England, and the sheriff of Berwick and Roxbrough on the part of the king of Scotland, upon the oaths of 12 knights of England, and 12 knights of Scotland. But this seems to have been a manifest forgery of the Scots; not only because the names neither of the kings nor of the sheriffs are set forth (which yet affords some argument of suspicion), but chiefly because Robert de Clifford is the first knight mentioned on the English side; and this was just five and twenty years before Robert de Clifford was born. Edward, it is well known, destroyed all the public records of Scotland; and hence it is not unaccountable, that the Scots (though their cause needed no such helps) might contrive this instrument to shew, that before the time of Ed. 1. they treated with England upon equal terms, as a sovereign and independent kingdom. The laws differ not much from several bodies of laws that followed afterwards. The preamble to the same runs thus:

Anno gratiæ millesimo ducentesimo quadragesimo nono, ad festum sanctorum Tiburtii *et* Valeriani, *ad leges Marchiarum condendas et observandas convenerunt ad Marchias, vicecomes* Northumbriæ *ex parte domini regis* Angliæ, *et vicecomes de* Bervico *et* Roxbrugh *ex parte domini regis* Scotiæ, *ad recognoscendas leges et consuetudines Marchiarum, per duodecim milites* Angliæ, *et duodecim milites* Scotiæ *firmiter juratos. Et hæc sunt nomina militum regis* Angliæ.

Robertus *de* Clifford Robertus *filius* Radulphi Robertus Malefante Robertus *de* Ulfester Willielmus *de* Burnvile Willielmus *de* Scremeston Willielmus *de* Herington Robertus *de* Glendale Sampson *de* Coupland Willielmus *de* Cookperte Henricus *filius* Godfridi	*Milites* Angliæ.
Adam de Earth Radulphus de Boucle Willielmus de Nothinton Robertus Bernham major de Berwick Adam de Norham Henricus filius Walden Henricus de Brade Richardus Holkerton Robertus de Durham Aymerus de Emsley Adam de Newbiggin	*Milites* Scotiæ †.

† Nicolson's Border Laws, p. 1.

To

To the other suspicions of forgery we may add, that not one of the names of the English knights, except Robert de Clifford only, is to be found (so far as we can recollect) in any authentic instrument of those times. (Of the Scots we have not sufficient knowledge to pronounce with so much certainty.) And instead of twelve knights, as above expressed, here are only eleven mentioned on each side.

Note, The word *March* is not derived, as many have supposed, from the hostile situation of the place, where parties were constantly or frequently *marching* to and fro; but it is a genuine old English word signifying boundary. So the Germans use the word *Margrave, marchiarum comes*, to denote the governor of a district. So in a like signification we use the word *landmark*.

The power of the lords wardens of the Marches was not always exactly the same, but varied in different reigns according to circumstances, some being more limited in their commissions than others; but their power in general was of necessity very great. This will best appear from the general tenor of their commission, which was as followeth:

" ELIZABETH by the grace of God of England, France, and Ireland queen, defender of the faith, and so forth: To all to whom these presents shall come, greeting. Know ye, that we, of our special grace, certain knowledge, and mere motion, fully trusting and having special confidence in the fidelity, valour, discretion, and provident circumspection, of our trusty and well beloved Henry lord Scroope of Bolton, by the advice of our council, have constituted and appointed and by these presents do constitute and appoint him the said lord Scroope our keeper or warden and governor general of the West Marches of our kingdom of England against the parts of Scotland, and captain of our city of Carlisle, and head steward of all our lordships, manors, lands, and tenements within the West Marches aforesaid: Giving and granting to the said lord Scroope full power and special commandment to do and execute all and every thing which therein doth appertain to the office of warden and keeper aforesaid, as heretofore by authority as well of the lord Richard the second late king of England, as also of Henry the fourth, Henry the fifth, Henry the sixth, Edward the fourth, Richard the third, Henry the seventh, Henry the eighth, our most dearly beloved brother Edward the sixth late king of England, and our dearest sister Mary late queen of England, in this behalf hath reasonably been used and accustomed to be done:

And all and every thing, by whatsoever our lieges and subjects, as well our officers as others, against the form of whatsoever trewes between us or our keepers or commissioners lawfully authorized and the commissioners of Scotland also lawfully authorized, concluded or to be concluded according to the form of the same trewes, to correct, reform, and amend; and the offences in that behalf, according to their deservings, as well by imprisonment of their bodies, as by distresses of their lands and tenements, goods and chattels, wheresoever they shall be found, as well within liberties as without, to chastise and punish:

And

And alſo to take cognizance of all plaints, pleas, and debates, as well in impriſonments, ſpoils, and reifs, as other whatſoever hoſtile acts, there moved or to be moved, and the ſame to hear and determine:

And alſo to hold warden courts and ſeſſions in whatſoever places of the Weſt Marches aforeſaid, as well within liberties as without, to inquire of whatſoever perſons offending againſt the form of the trewes or ordinances made or to be made by our commiſſioners and the commiſſioners of the realm of Scotland, and them according to the quantity of their offence to correct, and as well in their goods as in their perſons to puniſh, as to the ſaid lord Scroope or his deputy in that behalf, for the preſervation of the ſaid trewes and ordinances, and the ſafety of our Marches aforeſaid ſhall ſeem expedient:

And whatſoever ſums of money or other obligations, which for the breach of ſuch trewes and ordinances any of the officers aforeſaid ſhall incur, to levy and by his deputies and miniſters cauſe to be levied; and whatſoever perſons who ſhall in the execution aforeſaid be diſobedient or refuſe to obey, to chaſtiſe and puniſh, by all ways and means which to the ſaid lord Scroope ſhall ſeem expedient; or otherwiſe, if any perſiſt in their diſobedience, to certify to us and our council, to the end we may provide and give indelayedly equal remedy:

Alſo we have aſſigned the ſaid lord Scroope to inquire of all and every perſon and perſons, who ſhall preſume or take upon them any practices with our enemies, in prejudice of our realm, howſoever or by whatſoever colour the ſame ſhall be done; and the ſame perſons accordingly, and our traytors whatſoever in this behalf offending, conforme to their demerits, to chaſtiſe and puniſh:

And alſo the ſaid plaints, pleas, and debates to hear, diſcuſs, and duly to end and determine, according to the law and cuſtom of the parts of the Marches and dominions aforeſaid:

And alſo, at the coſts of our liege ſubjects of thoſe parts, by their own aſſent and good will as heretofore hath been reaſonably done, to ſet and appoint watchmen and others to explore and give notice to us and our faithful ſubjects for the defence of us and our realm, againſt the hoſtile incurſions of our enemies of Scotland, if any ſhall be made againſt us, our realm, or our faithful ſubjects:

And for the ſafety and defence of our town and caſtle of Berwick and our city of Carliſle, ſo often as any aſſault or ſiege of the ſaid town and caſtle or city ſhall be propoſed or made by the Scots or any other our enemies, all fencible men between the ages of ſixteen and ſixty within the ſaid Marches to cauſe to be muſtered; and all men at arms, armed billmen, and archers, every of them according to their eſtate, degree, and condition, to be armed and defended with fit and competent armour; and to be marſhalled in thouſands, hundreds, and twenties; and the ſame ſo arrayed and appointed to be holden and kept, ſo as all men at arms, armed billmen and archers, be ready and prepared to march to the defence and ſafe-keeping of our town and caſtle of Berwick, or our city of Carliſle aforeſaid, ſo often as any peril, aſſault, or

ſiege,

ſiege, by the incurſions of our enemies ſhall happen to be; and to be compelled upon ſummons or warning of the ſaid lord warden or his deputy, in our name and behalf, to proceed, march, and be led, remain, and continue, for the defence of our Marches aforeſaid, and our realm and faithful ſubjects, and the reſcue, defence, and ſafe cuſtody of the town, caſtle, and city aforeſaid, by impriſonment of their bodies, and by other ways and means as to the ſaid lord warden or his deputy reſpectively ſhall ſeem expedient.

And we give and grant to the ſaid lord Scroope and his deputy or deputies in this behalf, full power and authority for us and in our name to appoint, conclude, and agree upon abſtinences of war between us our lieges and ſubjects, and the governors, miniſters, and ſubjects of the realm of Scotland, from week to week, from two weeks to two weeks, from three weeks to three weeks, and from month or months to month or months.

And furthermore, that the ſaid lord Scroope may be the better enabled to execute the ſaid office and every thing thereunto appertaining, we will and by theſe preſents do give and grant to the ſaid lord Scroope power and authority to name and aſſign, make, ordain, and ſubſtitute under him in the ſaid office of wardenſhip two deputies or ſubſtitutes, and alſo two other officers under him called warden ſerjeants, and alſo all and all manner of other miniſters and officers under him neceſſary and expedient to the ſaid office or for the exerciſe of the ſame and all and ſingular the premiſſes in his place and ſtead to be done and executed, which by the keepers or wardens of the Weſt Marches aforeſaid from time to time have been accuſtomed to be done, as to him ſhall be thought expedient: Ratifying and confirming hereby all and every thing by the ſaid lord Scroope, his deputies or ſubſtitutes, in form aforeſaid to be done in the premiſſes or any part thereof.

To have and to hold, occupy and enjoy, the office of keeper or wardenſhip aforeſaid, and all and ſingular the premiſſes above expreſſed and ſpecified, with their appurtenances, liberties, commodities, advantages, profits, and all other appendages, to the ſaid lord Scroope, his deputy or deputies, ſubſtitute or ſubſtitutes, in as ample manner and form in all things, as any other perſon or perſons before this time have had or received, from the feaſt of the Annunciation of the bleſſed virgin Mary laſt paſt, ſo long as it ſhall pleaſe us.

And further we grant to the ſaid lord Scroope, for the exerciſe of the office of wardenſhip aforeſaid; ſo long as in that office he ſhall remain, the fee and wages of 600 marks by the year, for himſelf, and for his two deputies aforeſaid under him in the ſaid office of the Weſt Marches aforeſaid, that is to ſay, for either of them by the year 10*l*, and alſo for the ſaid two officers called warden ſerjeants of the Weſt Marches, for either of them yearly 40*s*, during our pleaſure aforeſaid; to be paid at the feaſts of St. Michael the archangel and the Annunciation of the bleſſed virgin Mary, by equal portions, out of our treaſury, at the receipt of our exchequer at Weſtminſter, by the hands of the treaſurer and chamberlain there for the time being.

And further we command all and ſingular our miniſters, lieges, and ſubjects whatſoever, that in the execution of all and every the premiſſes to the aforeſaid lord Scroope, and alſo to his deputies and miniſters whatſoever, from time to to time, they be helping, obedient, and conforming in all things as appertaineth.

In witness whereof, we have caused these our letters to be made patent. Witness ourself at Westminster the sixth day of April in the fifth year of our reign."

CHAPTER II.

Of the Border laws.

The Border laws, agreed upon by commissioners of both kingdoms specially appointed, received many alterations from time to time; which to set forth in the order as they were made, would cause frequent repetitions, and would be withal perplexing; it is therefore thought fit to reduce the same into one regular uniform code as followeth.

1. The wardens yearly at the first day of Trewes after Midsummer, to be holden within four days at the furthest after the said feast, shall shew their commissions either of them to other interchangeably; and give and receive reciprocally their solemn oath, in presence of the inhabitants of both the Marches, and swear by the high God that reigneth above all kings and realms, and to whom all christians owe obedience, That he shall, in the name of God, do, exercise, and use his office, without respect of person, malice, favour, or affection, diligently and undelayedly, according to his vocation and charge that he beareth under God and his prince; and shall do justice upon all complaints presented unto him, upon every person complained upon under his rule; and that, when any complaint is referred unto him, to swear, speir, and deliver upon his honour, he shall search, inquire, and redress the same at his uttermost power; and that, if it shall happen him in so doing to acquit and absolve the persons complained upon as clean and innocent, yet if he shall any ways get sure knowledge of the very offender, he shall declare him foul of the offence, and make lawful redress and delivery thereof, albeit the very offender be not named in the complaint. Wardens oath of office.

And all such persons as shall be adjoined to the said wardens, or be chosen upon any inquest for the trying complaints, shall make in like manner one solemn oath for the due execution of their duties.

2. And for prevention of such great enormities and mischiefs as have frequently undone the Borders, and disquieted the peace between the realms, the sovereigns on either side shall in all humility be intreated, to chuse and establish a council in every Marche, of the most sufficient and discreet borderers inhabiting the bounds thereof, who shall conveen twice in the year, for such effect and at such time and place, as by the particular commissioners shall be appointed unto them. Which Border council as aforesaid, at their conveenings and meetings, shall make diligent inquiry and trial of all notorious thieves and robbers within their wardenry; and such as they find to be of that quality, Assistant council to the wardens.

quality, they shall inrol them under their hands, and deliver a copy of the same unto their warden; who shall, upon the first attempt that shall be truly tried and fouled * upon any of them hereafter, put the said offender immediately to death; or, in case he be fugitive, shall cause him to be proclaimed such, according to the order and custom of the Borders, and his house immediately to be demolished and destroyed, that it serve him no more for receipt within that wardenry.

Murder.

3. If any subject or subjects of the kingdom of England do violently kill any subject or subjects of the kingdom of Scotland, the warden of the marches of the kingdom of England aforesaid, or his deputy or deputies, with all care and diligence, all fraud, favour, male-engine, and guile set apart, shall prosecute (and every of them shall follow and prosecute) that such murderer or murderers may be taken and brought by the wardens of both Marches or their deputies to the day of Trewes, to be assigned by the said wardens; where if he or they be lawfully convicted by the laws of Marche, then the warden of the marches of England shall deliver or cause to be delivered such murderer or murderers so convicted, to the warden of the Marches of Scotland, to be punished by death.

And if it happen any subject or subjects of the realm of Scotland violently to kill any subject or subjects of the realm of England, within the Marches of England or the Marches of Scotland, the warden of the Marches of Scotland aforesaid, or his deputy or deputies, with all care and diligence, all fraud, favour, male-engine, and guile set apart, shall follow (and every of them shall follow and prosecute) that such murderer and murderers may be taken, and that they may be brought by the wardens of both the Marches, or their deputies, to the day of Trewes, by the said wardens or their deputies to be appointed: Where if by the laws of March he or they be lawfully convicted, then the warden of the Marches of Scotland shall deliver or cause to be delivered such murderer or murderers as abovesaid, so convicted, to the warden of England; which warden of England, the said murderer or murderers, so as abovesaid convicted, assigned, and delivered as a murderer, shall punish by death.

And the wardens shall do justice therein precisely within fifteen days after they shall be required thereto by their opposites, under the pain of 10*l* sterling, to be paid by the warden making default, to the party grieved, for every month during his delay of justice.

Wounding or maiming.

4. If any of the subjects of either realm shall unlawfully bodily hurt or wound any of the subjects of the other realm, the person or persons so hurt or wounded shall make a bill of complaint upon the person so offending at the days of Trewes; and the party offender to be arrested to answer such bill, and be compelled to answer thereto after like manner as is used for robbers, thieves,

* Fouled] This word is promiscuously written *fouled* or *fyled*. *Foul* and *clean* are synonymous with *Guilty* and *Not Guilty*.

and ſpoilers; and ſuch like proof and trial to be had, in every behalf, until either the bill be acquitted or fouled; and the damage thereof to be ſet down by ſix gentlemen of worſhip and good name of Scotland to be named by the warden of England, and other ſix like gentlemen of England to be named by the warden of Scotland, and by the diſcretion of both the wardens or their deputies then being preſent; and the damage ſo being ſet and eſteemed, to be two doubles *, as in caſe of theft and ſpoil is uſed; and deliverance to be made to the warden of the Marche where the party grieved inhabiteth, to be kept with him until redreſs be made thereof accordingly.

And if the party ſo hurt and wounded be mutilate and maimed, the warden where the offender inhabiteth ſhall be bound thereby to do his uttermoſt diligence, without fraud, favour, or deception, to apprehend the ſaid offender, and deliver him to the warden of the oppoſite Marche, to be puniſhed by him in ſtrayte priſon by the ſpace of ſix months for the ſame offence.

5. If any of the ſubjects of either of the ſaid realms ſhall wilfully or maliciouſly raiſe fire within the other oppoſite realm, in burning of houſes, corn, or hay in ſtacks; the perſon or perſons ſo offending, being lawfully thereupon fouled, ſhall not only anſwer to the other party thereby, to all his damages cauſed by the ſaid fire, with a double and *sawſey* [the Scotch copy ſays, with a double of all his damages] according to the laws and cuſtoms uſed in the Borders of both realms, but alſo the warden of the Marches where ſuch offender or offenders do inhabit, ſhall do his uttermoſt diligence, without fraud, favour, or deceit, to apprehend ſuch offenders, and to deliver him or them to the warden of the Marche where the offence was done, to be grievouſly puniſhed by the ſpace of ſix months, over and above the redreſs and ſatisfaction of the party grieved. Fire raiſing.

6. For maſterful and violent theft and reiſe, by night or day, and for ſecret ſtealing wherewith is joined either bodily hurt of men, women, and children, or violent reſiſtance againſt the followers in hot and freſh purſuit of their goods; it is ordered, that beſides the ordinary redreſs to be made of the goods, any one of the offenders, whom the complainant ſhall chuſe, ſhall be delivered to the oppoſite warden, to be puniſhed at his diſcretion, according to the quality of the offence. Violent theft.

7. If it fall out, that any deadly feud be born againſt any of the oppoſite realm, for executing of any thief by juſtice, or killing him with red-hand where he findeth him ſtealing or clad with ſtolen goods, or for purſuing him to death by whatſoever lawful means; the warden to whoſe office he appertaineth, upon ſignification made to him of the ſaid feud, ſhall apprehend the ſaid party ſo bearing feud, and either cauſe him preſently to renounce the ſaid feud by writing under his hand, or ſhall deliver him to the oppoſite war- Deadly feud.

* That is, fourfold (according to the Jewiſh law of reſtitution).

den,

den, to be kept by him until he have renounced the ſaid feud as aforeſaid, and found ſurety to that effect to the content of the party complainant.

Cutting down trees.

8. Foraſmuch as the inhabitants of the Marches aforeſaid, with great numbers of men, have been accuſtomed to cut down other mens trees, and to carry them away, to the uſe of their houſes, without the good-will and conſent of the owner thereof, which hath been a matter of diſſenſion and diſcord upon the Borders; therefore to remove all occaſions of contention, it is concluded, that no ſubject of the princes aforeſaid, dwelling either in the Marches aforeſaid, or in the *Debateable Ground*, or in any other place elſewhere, ſhall commit or do ſuch or the like things, or ſhall conſent to be done or committed; nor ſhall cut down or carry away any trees or wood whatſoever; out of the Marches of either prince, by any means or colour, except that he or they have covenanted and agreed with the owner thereof for the ſame; and if any thing hath been done or committed contrary to the premiſſes, it ſhall be reformed according to the laws of Marche.

[Note, The *Debateable Ground* was a tract of land claimed by both kingdoms, which was the occaſion of infinite troubles and vexations. The boundary of it in an old roll is thus deſcribed: "Beginning at the foot of the "White Scyrke running into the ſea, and ſo up the ſaid water of Scyrke, till "it come to a place called the Pyngilburne foot running into the ſaid water "of Scyrke, and up the Pyngilburne till it come to Pyngilburne Know, from "thence to the Righeads, from the Righeads to the Monke Rilande Burne, "and from thence down Harvenburne till it fall in Eſke, and through Eſke "to the foot of Terras, and ſo up Terras to the foot of Reygill, and up "the Reygill to the Tophous, and ſo to the ſtanding ſtone, and to the Mearburne head, and down Mearburne to it fall in Lyddal at the Rutterford, "and down Lyddal to it fall in Eſke, and down Eſke to it fall in the ſea." It was in length eight computed miles of the country, and in breadth four miles. The ſubjects of both kingdoms commonly depaſtured their cattle upon it in the day-time, but were to remove them before ſun-ſet on the peril that ſhould thereof enſue *.]

Sowing corn in the oppoſite realm.

9. If any ſubject of either realm ſhall manure, occupy, or ſow with corn any ground within the oppoſite realm; it ſhall be lawful to the owner of the ground or warden to deſtroy the ſame, if he think ſo convenient; or elſe to make bill, or complain thereupon to the oppoſite warden, and if the party be fouled, he ſhall forfeit his corn to the complainant, and ſhall pay four times the value of the corn ſown, and further ſuffer impriſonment by the ſpace of three months.

* The ſtory of king James's favourite cow is well known, that not liking her accommodations in England, ſhe found her way back to Edinburgh; which the king ſaid he did not ſo much wonder at, as how ſhe got through the Debateable Ground without being ſtolen.—Had the ſingularity of the event been remarked upon, that ſhe was the only one of the king's train that had any thought of returning; it would have been not unlike him to have anſwered, with the ſame kind of humour, that "ſhe was a brute, and knew no better."

10. The

Depasturing cattle.

10. The inhabitants of the said realms respectively shall feed and depasture their cattle within the limits and bounds of their own realm: And if any inhabitants of either the said realms willingly and customably depasture and feed with his cattle or sheep, or staffherd the same, within the bounds of the other realm; it shall be lawful for the owner of the ground so depastured, or to the warden of the Marches in his default, to cause the said cattle to be taken and impounded, and in pound kept, until the owner thereof shall have paid, at the first time, for every cattle or nolt a penny sterling, and for every sheep a penny Scots. And if, upon any deliverance thereof, the party will not reform his wrong depasturing, but eftsoons attempt like injury in depasturing or feeding his cattle or sheep within the other's realm; then it shall be lawful to the owner or warden as aforesaid to cause the said cattle or sheep to be taken and impounded, and so to be kept, till he have paid a double poundage after the rate above written; and so, upon the iterating and continual new offending again in depasturing within the other realm, it shall be lawful to the owner continually to cause the cattle so offending to be taken and impounded, and so kept, until he be satisfied of a double poundage, until the poundage extend for every nolt to 2*s* sterling, and for every sheep to 6*d* sterling, and no higher; but that to stand unto the beginning of a new year's day, that is, the first day of January, after the first impounding.—And after the new year's day, to begin the poundage of every nolt a penny sterling, and every sheep a penny Scots. And for the next impounding, double of the first, and so to extend until the sum amount to the foresaid sum of 2*s* sterling for every nolt, and 6*d* sterling for every sheep, and no higher; but there to stand until another new year begin, and continue until such offenders shall be compelled (by occasion of distress, and the charge of so great and grievous poundage) to keep his cattle within the limits and bounds of his own realm, and not wrongfully to depasture or feed his cattle within the other opposite realm, to the incroaching of the ground, and disinheriting of the owner thereof.

And if the keeper of the goods so depasturing in the opposite realm, or any other for or with him, will not permit the owner of the ground or the warden to use the aforesaid order of impounding, but will make let, trouble, or impediment against the pounding or keeping of the cattle until they be redeemed by paying of the poundage; in that case the cattle and sheep shall be lawfully forfeited, and taken to the use of the owner of the ground or warden, for the contempt and resistance made against the order of justice.

Hunting in the opposite realm.

11. No man, of one part or the other, shall enter the lands, woods, forests, warrens, places, demesnes, or lordships of any other person in the opposite realm, for the sake of hunting, fishing, fowling, disporting, or solace in the same, or for any other cause, without the licence of him or them whose the lands are, or person deputed by them, first had and obtained. [This law came in first in the reign of Hen. 6. perhaps occasioned by the tragical exploit which was the subject of the famous ballad of Chevy Chace.]

Goods stolen may be followed into the opposite realm.

12. If any the subjects of the princes aforesaid have stolen any thing, or committed any attempts within the Marches or land to which he is subject; it shall be lawful for him against whom it hath been so done and attempted, freely (within six days to be accounted from the time of the said fault so committed or attempted) by authority of this ordinance without any other letter of safe conduct, to follow the same offender, and (him so following) to enter safely and surely the Marches or land into which the same evil doer is gone; so that so soon as he hath entered the said Marches or land for that cause, he go unto some honest man, being of good name and fame, inhabiting within the Marches which he hath entered, and declare unto him the cause of his entry, that is to say, to follow his goods stolen; and shall declare what goods or things he hath been spoiled or robbed of; and further shall require the same, that so long as he shall make the search he go with him, that he may (when he shall be thereunto required upon the same) give testimony of truth of his behaviour in time of his search.

Pursuit of hot trod.

13. If it shall happen the warden of either realm, for the apprehending of fugitives, or punishment of offenders, in the execution of justice, to pursue any fugitive or offender through the realm where he beareth rule unto the Marche, and the fugitive or offender flee into the opposite realm; it shall be lawful to the said warden to pursue the chace in hot trod with hound and horn, with hue and cry, unto such time and place as the fugitive or offender be apprehended, and to bring them again within their own jurisdiction, to be punished for that offence as appertaineth; and that, without let, trouble, or impediment to be made or done unto him by any of the inhabitants of that realm wherein he pursueth. And if any person shall make resistance, let, or impediment, to the said warden in the foresaid pursuit, he shall be billed for, and delivered to the warden whom he offended, to be punished for his offence at the discretion of the said warden. And in the following of the said chase in manner aforesaid, it is thought convenient and ordained, that the pursuer shall, at the first town he cometh by of the opposite realm, or to the first person he meeteth with, give knowledge of the occasion of his chase, and require them to go with him and assist him in the said pursuit.

And if it shall happen the said warden, pursuer, or any of his company, to do injury or unlawful harm within the opposite realm, in the time of their being there; the offender shall be delivered to the opposite warden to be tried of the offence, and be punished therefore at the discretion of the said warden and other 12 persons of that realm to be nominated by the opposite warden.

Receiving fugitives.

14. Every warden within his own jurisdiction shall take care and rule upon the inhabitants under him, to keep them in due obedience; and if it shall happen any person to be disobedient, escape, run away, and be fugitive from any of the said wardens; the warden so disobeyed shall certify the opposite warden, requiring him to take, apprehend, and deliver the offender with all possible speed: Which warden so required shall be bound not only at the uttermost

termoſt of his power to ſearch for, apprehend, and deliver the offender being within his juriſdiction; but alſo ſhall make proclamation throughout his wardenry, by the ſpace of ſix days after, of the ſaid fugitive; and ſhall ſo certify the other two wardens of that realm to proclaim the foreſaid fugitive throughout all the bounds of their wardenry, within the ſpace of ſix days after they be ſo certified in the manner aforeſaid.

And if the ſaid fugitive ſhall after that be received, kept, aided, or comforted by any ſubject of that realm; the ſame ſubject ſhall be delivered to the warden complainant, and ſhall have the ſame puniſhment that was due to the fugitive, in caſe he do not preſent and deliver the fugitive to ſuffer for his own offence.

And if it ſhall happen the foreſaid fugitive to fly with his foreſaid goods, and carry them into the oppoſite realm; the warden thereof, delivering the fugitive to be puniſhed for his offence, ſhall retain the goods to himſelf for his labour: And if the fugitive be not apprehended, then the goods to be reſtored to the warden of the realm they came from.

15. The wardens ſhall take good heed in every Marche, that none of the broken borderers [that is, not of any known clan] be ſuffered to keep in their companies any idle perſons, not employed in any honeſt ſervice or trade; and likewiſe that no idle perſons be ſuffered to remain in the Border villages or alehouſes, certifying ſuch as ſhall receipt them upon their ground, that they ſhall be billable for their ſo doing, as if they had actually receipted the goods by them ſo ſtolen. Loiterers.

16. No letters of ſafe conduct ſhall be granted by either prince to the rebels of the other; nor to any other the ſubjects of either of them, of what eſtate, dignity, or condition ſoever they be, under the great or privy ſeal of either of them, nor by word of mouth or other ways, unleſs the one of them by the other be expreſsly required thereunto by writing. And in caſe the one of the ſaid princes hath required the other by writing, to grant ſuch letters of ſafe conduct to any of their ſubjects, it ſhall be notwithſtanding at the liberty of the prince ſo required, whether he will or not grant any ſuch letters of ſafe conduct. Safe conduct.

Provided, that if any of the ſubjects of the one prince come to the kingdom of the other under ſafe conduct, and be ſo vehemently ſick, that he cannot return into his country again before the day of the expiration of his ſafe conduct; he may continue in that place in which it chanced him to fall ſick, until he be amended: and from thenceforth it ſhall be lawful for him, with letters of teſtimonial to be granted and delivered to him by the mayor, bailiff, conſtable, or any other officer of the place where it may ſo happen him to be ſick, to depart into his own country without moleſtation.

17. The wardens of the marches muſt keep their days of Marche often, and in proper perſon ſo far as may be, and not by their deputies without juſt Days of trews to be kept.

 and

and great occaſion; and ſhall not ſlip nor diſappoint any day of trewes appointed; ſo that at the leaſt every month one day of trewes be kept at every Marche by the officers thereof, and oftner if need require; and at every ſuch meeting to keep there ſitting, day by day, until all former attempts complained upon be fully ordered and anſwered according to the treaties: So that the ſaid wardens ſhall not have reſpect to make redreſs of value for value, or bill for bill, but for all offences complained upon to them.

And albeit, for the more ſpeedy redreſs and furtherance of juſtice, it is ordained, that the warden ſhall proceed upon all complaints and attempts, by ſpeiring, fouling, and delivering upon his honour, together with ſix honeſt and famous men of that wardenry adjoined to him for the trial thereof, to be named by the oppoſite warden; yet it is not thereby intended to make derogation or aboliſhment of the laws and cuſtoms of the Marches of old ordained, but as well providing the parties grieved to follow their lawful purſuit of hot trod, and all other accuſtomed manner of freſh purſuit, for the recovery of their goods ſpoiled, as otherwiſe to uſe the order and trial of a jury and lawful inqueſt and of lawful proof to be uſed at the election and choice of the complainant.

And whereas in times paſt there have been different forms of judgment, every warden having a form and manner of proceeding different from the other; ſome redreſſing the attempts with the ſingle only, and ſome other redreſſing with the ſingle and two doubles; ſome redreſſing with a low price and value of goods, and other with an higher price; ſome permitting the party to value and eſteem as well his cattle and ſheep, as his other goods ſpoiled, by his oath, and ſome by the contrary; and ſo having different cuſtoms at ſundry Marches, which was altogether inconvenient; therefore from henceforth there ſhall be one uniform order of juſtice, according to the laudable laws and cuſtoms of the Marches heretofore uſed.

Fouling of bills.

18. All complaints ſhall be inrolled by the warden of the Marche where the complainant doth inhabit; and the roll ſhall be ſent to the oppoſite warden, who ſhall receive the ſaid roll, and ſhall do his uttermoſt power and endeavour to ſpeire, ſearch, and inquire the truth and verity of thoſe attempts contained in the ſaid complaints, and to cauſe ſuch perſons as be there complained upon to be arreſted by his ſerjeant to anſwer thereunto if they be preſent; and if they then ſhall happen to be abſent, then they are to be arreſted to anſwer at the next day of trewes; where and when, the warden and the jury ſhall either foul the ſaid bills, or give another lawful anſwer at their next meeting after the laws and cuſtoms of the Marches, whereof ſix to be of the ſaid warden's appointment, and the other ſix to be appointed by the ſaid complainant, or ſuch as purſue the bill.

Swearing of bills.

19. For eſchewing of perjury in ſwearing of bills in time to come, it is ordained, that every man ſwear his own bill; otherwiſe to have no delivery for the ſame.

20. And

20. And becauſe baughling and reproving at the aſſemblies of juſtice between the ſaid realms giveth great occaſion of trouble and inconvenience, it is ordered, that no perſon of either the ſaid realms ſhall, at any day of trewes or other convention or aſſembly between the officers of both the ſaid realms, bear, ſhew, or declare any ſign or token of reproof or baughling, againſt any ſubject of the oppoſite realm, unleſs he be thereunto licenſed by the wardens of both the realms: And if any attempt, or do contrary hereunto, the offender in that behalf to be attached by the warden of the Marches, and delivered to the other warden of the oppoſite Marche, to be puniſhed by impriſonment at his diſcretion by the ſpace of one month; and nevertheleſs the ſaid offender to forfeit and loſe his cauſe and matter, for that he (at an inconvenient time) baughled and reproved, and the other party to be therefore acquitted and diſcharged for ever. Baughling.

21. And conſidering how that perjury uſed upon the Borders moſt commonly is the root and ground of the hindrance and perverting of all juſtice, and the occaſion and cauſe of great diſorders; it is agreed and ordered, that if any of the ſubjects of either realm acquit himſelf by his oath taken in form of law before the wardens or their deputies, and after be tried and found foul and guilty of the ſame bill whereof he ſo acquitted himſelf by his oath, and thereupon ſhall appear plainly perjured to both the ſaid wardens: Then, over and above the juſt reward and recompence of the party grieved, the ſaid perjured perſon ſhall be attached and taken by the warden of the Marche where he inhabiteth, and delivered to the warden of the oppoſite realm, to be puniſhed as a grievous offender by ſtrait impriſonment during the ſpace of three months; and at the next day of trewes, and after the ſaid three months ended, the ſaid offender ſhall be brought before the wardens or their deputies, and there openly be denounced and proclaimed a perjured man; after which time, he ſhall not be reputed to be a man able to give further faith or teſtimony in any caſe or matter. Perjury.

22. If it ſhall happen any perſon unmeaſurably or outragiouſly to ſwear the number and value of his goods to be more and greater than of truth they were, to the great loſs and damage of the adverſe party; the wardens of both the realms, or their deputies then preſent, without any hindrance, ſtop, or delay in juſtice in any wiſe, ſhall take unto them 12 of the moſt worſhipful and credible perſons of both realms then being preſent, whereof ſix of the realm of Scotland to be of the denomination of the warden of England or his deputy then preſent, and the other ſix of the realm of England to be likewiſe at the denomination and appointment of the warden of Scotland or his deputy then preſent; and the ſaid wardens, with their deputies and the ſaid twelve, ſhall have power to moderate, diminiſh, or qualify the number or price of the goods or cattle ſo overſworn by the party above rehearſed. Overſwearing.

23. And becauſe it hath often happened, that the offender may be fouled in bills, being delivered to the oppoſite warden for the redreſs of the attempt committed Offender reſcuing himſelf.

committed by him, would make resistance to them that lead or should lea him away, and suddenly escape and return into his own country; whereby, in so doing, both the parties grieved lack redress, and trouble is raised between the companies of both realms being together at days of trewes: For avoiding whereof, it is ordained, that the offender so delivered shall quietly pass and remain with the party he is delivered unto, during all the time of their said assembly, and two hours after their departure; and if the said offender shall do the contrary hereof, he shall be punished by death or otherwise, at the discretion of the wardens, as a breaker of the assurance: And this to have place for offenders that are not delivered to be put to death.—For such persons as should be executed by death, we will that the strait hold and keeping shall be used, until justice shall be executed on them.

Bill cleared may be preferred again.

24. If it shall happen any of the wardens of either realm, in default of knowledge, to acquit any bill upon his honour in form aforesaid, which is indeed foul; it shall nevertheless be lawful to the complainant to pursue a new bill again, requiring justice to be done to him for the said attempts, upon better information and knowledge, unto the said warden, or any other succeeding in that office; and that justice be done to him for the said attempts, upon his said second complaint, by a jury and lawful proof to be had and received, and thereupon his bill to be fouled or acquitted after the laws and customs of the Borders heretofore used, notwithstanding the same bill was once acquitted by any warden upon his honour in form aforesaid.

Against retaliation.

25. Item, It is covenanted and agreed, that if any subject of either the princes aforesaid hath sustained any robberies or spoils by the subjects of the other prince, and by his own authority hath made for the same other robberies or spoils, or taken distresses of men or goods in the self same act; he shall lose his cause, and yet nevertheless shall be punished according to the desert of his trespass.

Thrice foul to suffer death.

26. Finally; Forasmuch as it hath appeared, by experience of time past, that thieves and evil doers have not ceased nor forborn from committing of offences and attempts against the treaties of peace, albeit they were compelled to make redress by payment of the principal with two doubles; it is ordained, that from henceforth, if it shall happen any of the subjects of either realm to be fouled upon bills for three several offences and attempts to be committed hereafter against the peace and amity, he shall for the third fault incur the pain of death, as a common offender against the laws of the Marches. So that above the satisfaction and redress of the attemptate, with the payment of the singles and two doubles to the party complainant; the warden of the foresaid offender shall, to the uttermost of his power, search for, take, and apprehend the said offender, and bring him to the next day of Marche, and deliver him to the opposite warden to be executed to death: So that by this example, all other shall take fear to offend or violate the amity between the two realms.

5 Provided

Provided always, that the intent of this article is to be taken, that the second of the foresaid three offences shall be understood to be committed after the offender be once found foul of the first offence; and the third offence likewise to be taken an offence to be committed after the offender be found foul of the second offence †.

CHAPTER III.

Of the manner of keeping warden courts.

A BRIEF *declaration of the special heads, orders, and forms of the laws of Marches of ancient time used upon the Borders, by the lords wardens of* England *and* Scotland *at their meetings and days of trewes; composed by* RICHARD BELL *clerk of the West Marches of* England.

As

In the time of wars denounced by the princes of both realms, the lords wardens are to use both by policy, fire, and sword, or martial forces of their office, for to make invasion and take hostile revenge upon and against the inhabitants of either of the other's Marche reciprocally as time and occasion may best afford, for the exploits of service tending to the honour of their realms and harm of their enemies:

So

In time of peace, by sending over their clerks, interchanging of bills containing the offences severally attempted, appointing and keeping of days of trewes, fouling of bills, and making of delivery, with all other good offices, for to entertain the peaceable amity betwixt the realms to the defence and comfort of all true subjects, the daunting of the insolent and disobedient under their rules, agreeable to the good concordance of the princes treaties of peace, and to the use and custom of the Borders, bills of faults are interchanged, days of trewes agreed on, bills fouled and delivery of principal offenders made, without respect of person or surname.

Days of Marche so appointed, proclamation is to be made, and straite letters of commandment directed in the queen's majesty's ‡ name, for all lords, knights, esquires, gentlemen, and several officers, with convenient numbers of their charge and tenants (as time and service require) for to repair the night before, and give their attendance upon the lord warden unto the said day of Marche, defencibly arrayed, with their best horses and nags, the morrow next following.

† Nicolson's Border Laws, *passim*.

‡ Richard Bell, author of the curious manuscript from whence this account is taken, appears to have been warden clerk during the greatest part of the reign of queen Elizabeth. His unaffected, circumstantial, and minute detail cannot fail to give pleasure to every reader.

Which

Which done,

The lord warden, attended with the gentlemen, officers, ſervants, and their powers, is to ride from the place where he inhabiteth, unto the Marche bank, all ſtaying there without riding any further, or going over the ſtream if there be water, or bounds if it be dry land:

Until

The lord warden of England firſt of all (the oppoſite warden known to be come to the place appointed) doth ſend either his deputy, or ſome other ſpecial gentleman of good worth whom it pleaſeth him for to make choice of, with a convenient number of the beſt horſed and moſt ſufficient gentlemen of his company, unto the warden of Scotland, ſignifying his repair thither, and craving aſſurance during their meeting until the ſun-riſing of the next day following.

Which aſſurance being required by England and granted by Scotland; the Scotch warden, holding up his hand, engages for performing thereof in all reſpects.

Then the deputy and other gentlemen of England, returning back to the lord warden of England, are to make relation of the aſſurance granted, and conſent for the preſervation of the amity.

Forthwith after,

The lord warden of Scotland ſendeth his deputy, or ſome other ſpecial gentleman, accompanied with others of the beſt ſort of horſemen, unto the lord warden of England, ſhewing that the lord warden of Scotland yieldeth to allow and confirm the aſſurance demanded for Scotland, craving the like for England; which the warden of England, holding up his hand, granteth.

That done,

The deputy of Scotland and his company return back to the warden of Scotland, declaring the granting of the aſſurance by England.

The lord warden of England, before he or any of his company enter into Scotland, cauſeth proclamation to be made for obſervation of the peace, for old feeds † and new, word, deed, and countenance, from the time of the proclaiming thereof, until the next day at the ſun-riſing, upon pain of death.

And

The like proclamation, after their return forth of England, by the Scotch warden made before meeting.

The lord warden of England with his company entereth into Scotland, riding to the place where the lord warden of Scotland is, and lighting off horſeback ſtands ſtill, until the Scotch warden comes to him then and there, in all friendly and orderly manner, mutually embracing the one the other.

After meeting and conference had between the lords wardens, they draw themſelves remote to ſome quiet place, interchangeably calling the rolls and bills of both ſides, in the preſence of the gentlemen of the beſt ſorts of both the countries.

† Feuds.

Whereof,

Whereof,

If any doubt arise touching the fouling of the said bills, then the same is to be tried either by the lord warden's honour, or a jury of six gentlemen of England and six of Scotland, or by a vower publique †.

The oath for the jurors is,

You shall clean no bills worthy to be fouled, you shall foul no bills worthy to be cleaned, but shall do that which appeareth with truth, for the maintenance of the peace, and suppressing of attempts: So help you God.

The ancient oath for excusing bills:

You shall swear by heaven above you, hell beneath you, by your part of Paradise, by all that God made in six days and seven nights, and by God himself, you are whart out sackless of art, part, way, witting, ridd, kenning, having, or recetting of any of the goods and cattels named in this bill; So help you God.

The oath of swearing of bills fouled:

You shall leile price make, and truth say, what your goods were worth at the time of their taking to have been bought and sold in a market taken all at one time, and that you know no other recovery but this. So help you God.

The lords wardens having proceeded to the calling, fouling, and making delivery of bills; concluding, cause proclamation to be made by three Oyes's:

We do you to wit, That the lords wardens of England and Scotland, and Scotland and England, have at this day of trewes well agreed, conform to the laudable custom of the law of Marche, and have made answer and delivery, foul or clean, of all the bills inrolled. And so the proclamation holds on according to the lords wardens agreements and directions.

Proclamation made, and leave taken by the wardens in all kindly sort, they with their companies depart and return homeward.

Which done,

The warden of England calleth upon the gentlemen, demanding their opinions and good likings of the proceedings and conference had betwixt him and the lord warden of Scotland that day. Whereunto the gentlemen give answer, and their opinions. Which done, the gentlemen take their leave; the warden yielding them thanks for their attendances and readiness of service.

These meetings by both wardens at the days of trewes were for the mutual redress of grievances between the subjects of the one kingdom and the other: Next follows the order of keeping a warden's court for the punishment of offences within his own jurisdiction:

† A person agreed upon by both parties, who was to be of the country of the party accused.

THE *order of keeping a warden court in cases of* MARCH TREASON:

First, The warden serjeant to make an Oyes, pronouncing the words following:

All men keep silence, and hear the queen's majesty's commission of wardenry read.

After the commission is read, the warden serjeant must return his precept with the panel.

That done, call, *All gentlemen that be summoned to serve the queen's majesty in this court, come and make your appearance, and every man answer to your names at the first call.*

Then, when as many have appeared as will form a jury, give them the oath; first, to the foreman in the words following:

Ye shall truly inquire, and true presentment make of all things that shall be given unto you in charge; the queen's counsel, your fellows, and your own, you shall keep and not disclose. So help you God at his holy dome.

Then call the rest to the book, by four at once or more, giving them their oath in this wise:

Heard you the oath your foreman hath taken: All such oath as your foreman on his behalf hath made, you and every of you on your behalfs shall make. So help you God.

Then say aloud,

Gentlemen that be sworn, come near and hear your charge.

Then read them the charge distinctly as follows:

"First, Ye shall inquire of March Treason, that is to say, where any "Englishman trists or intercommoneth or bringeth in any Scotsman to come "into this realm, in time of peace or war, to do any slaughter, to burn, to "rob, steal, or do any other offence within this realm.

"Also, ye shall inquire, if any Englishman aid, receipt, accompany, or "ride with any Scotsman coming into this realm, in doing any slaughter, "burning, robbing, stealing, or doing any other offence.

"Also, if any Englishman do give harbour, receipt, or convey any Scots-"man, after he hath slain, robbed, burned, or stolen within this realm, in "body, goods, or otherwise.

"Also, ye shall inquire if any Englishman put forth or support any "Scotsman, in time of peace or war, with any armour or artillery belonging "to war, as jacks, splents, breastplates, brigandens, coats of plate, bills, "halberds, battle-axes, bows, arrows, spears, darts, or any manner of guns, "as serpentines, half-hawks, harquebuzes, curryes, colyvers, handguns or "daggs, or any other armour, artillery, or engines belonging to the war, by "reason and means whereof destruction of any of the queen's subjects "might the rather ensue and follow, without the special licence of the lord "warden for the time being in writing.

"Also, if any Englishman hath given, sold, or put forth any manner of "victuals, as bread, or corn, that is to say, wheat, rye, bigg, beans, pease, "oats, oatmeal, malt, or any other corn; or barked leather, wool-fell, iron,

"or

" or any other merchandiſe belonging to armour or artillery, either by water " or by land, but only to ſuch as have licence of the lord warden.

" Alſo, you ſhall inquire if any Engliſhman hath ſold or put away any " horſes, mares, geldings, or nags, at any time in fairs, markets, or " otherwiſe, to any Scotſman or woman, without ſpecial licence of the lord " warden in writing.

" Alſo, if any Engliſhman foreknown do of intent and purpoſe ſell any " horſe, mare, gelding, or nagg, unto any other Engliſhman, that uttereth " or ſelleth the ſame to any Scotſman.

" Alſo, ye ſhall inquire, if any Engliſhman hath attempted or done any " thing to the breaking of the truce or peace taken between the queen's " majeſty and the Scots queen, or the commiſſioners or wardens, to the " ſubjects and liegemen of the ſaid Scots queen, as in killing any of them, " aſſaulting, forreying, or robbing of any of them, within the realm of " Scotland.

" Alſo, if any Engliſhman have murdered, aſſaulted, affrayed, or robbed " any Scotſman within this realm of England, coming in by the authority of " the ſafe conduct of the ſaid lord warden, his deputy or deputies.

" Alſo, if any Engliſhman, in the time of war, hath given knowledge " or intelligence of any exploit of ſervice or inroad intended or put in ure by " the lord warden, his officers, or any other Engliſhman in time of war.

" Alſo, if any Engliſhman hath married with any Scotſwoman, or confe- " derate in friendſhip, without the lord warden's licence.

" Alſo, if any Engliſhman, hath ſold, felled, led, or carried away into " the realm of Scotland forth of England, any manner of timber to build " houſes withal.

" Alſo, if any Engliſhman hath conveyed into the realm of Scotland any of " the coin of ſilver or gold currens in this realm, plate, or bullion, above " 40*s* at one time.

" Alſo, if any Engliſhman hath bewrayed the counſel of any other Eng- " liſhman, in doing any annoyance to Scotland in time of war, of malice to " the party, and commodity to himſelf.

" Alſo, ye ſhall inquire, if any Engliſhman do convey or make appoint- " ment with any Scotſman, or that triſteth or intercommoneth with them by " any manner of means, rideth or goeth with any of them, and raiſeth no " fray upon them, without licence of the warden, his deputy or deputies; " or with their licence, to the prejudice of this realm; and what hurt cometh " thereby from time to time.

" Alſo, ye ſhall inquire, if any Engliſhman receive or put forth any " Scotſman, pilgrim or other, and them with their writings and money " recetteth and keepeth, without knowledge of the ſaid lord warden or his " deputy, or otherwiſe than is accuſtomed by order of the law of Marche.

" Alſo, if any perſon inhabiting within the office of the wardenry, hath " not obediently and well obſerved and kept all watches made and appointed " by the lords wardens or their deputies from time to time, in defence of her "highneffes's fubjects, againft the incourfe as well of the riders of Scotland "as of England.

"Alfo, if any Englifhman hath not rifen and gone, or ridden forward, at "any commandment, warning, cry, or fray, of the lord warden or his de-"puty, or of the fearchers or watchers, fo often as hurt or prejudice hath "been likely to enfue unto this realm or Marches, or to any fubject within "the fame.

"Alfo, if any Englifhman hath receipt any Scotfman or fugitive or rebel "to Scotland, or any their goods or chattels, by any manner of means, con-"trary to the laws of Marches, or proclamation made in that behalf.

"Alfo, if any Englifhman hath unjuftly fouled any Scots bill upon any "Englifhman, or falfely avowed the fame, without good matter, but either "for profit unto himfelf, or difpleafure to the party billed.

"Alfo, if any man hath ftopped or letted the trods of any Englifhman, in "purfuing of his goods ftolen and carrying into Scotland, to the hindrance "of the followers.

"Alfo, if any man hath fet at liberty any Scotfman taken red-hand and "with the manner, without fpecial licence of the lord warden.

"Alfo, if any Englifhman hath paid any Blackmail † either to Englifh-"men or Scots, or any Englifhman hath taken or received any fuch Black-"mail."

And he that is clerk of this court muft have forefight and fpecial regard, to fearch and learn, what new laws, orders, and ftatutes are made from time to time, by any act of parliament, or at any day of Marche, between the lords wardens of England and Scotland, concerning any law of Marches, or any other caufe inquirable in this court, and add the fame to the charge.

Then let the jury go apart. And then make an Oyes, faying, *All men that have any complaints or bills concerning matters triable in this warden court, come and put them in, and ye fhall be heard.*

Then call your recognizances, if you have any; and take fureties.

When the jury are returned, call them by name, and receive their bills.

Then let the prifoners be brought to the bar, and calling one of them by his name, fay on this wife:

A. B. Thou art here indicted, for that thou, &c. (and read forth the indict-ment)—*How fayeft thou by this March-treafon, art thou guilty, or not guilty?*

If he fay, Not guilty; then fay, *How wilt thou be tried?—By God and the country.*

And fo proceed with another, until all be arraigned.

Then call a jury of gentlemen, giving the prifoners leave to challenge. And when you have a full jury, befides the challenged, give them their oath in this manner;

† Blackmail was a certain rent of money, corn, cattle, or other confideration, exacted by divers powerful men in the Borders, on pretence of protecting the payers thereof from fpoil and rapine.

Ye ſhall truly inquire, and true delivery make, between the queen's majeſty and the priſoners here at the bar, according to the evidence that ſhall be given in this court: As God ſhall help you at his holy dome.

Then arraign them all again, reading their indictments, ſaying, *Thou that haſt been indicted, &c. and arraigned, whereunto thou haſt pleaded Not guilty, and put thyſelf upon God and the country, who be theſe; What canſt thou ſay for thyſelf?* And ſo through them all.

Then make an Oyes, and ſay, *Gentlemen that be ſworn for delivery between the queen's majeſty and the priſoners at the bar, come near and hear your charge. Your charge is, to inquire and find, whether A. B. priſoner at the bar be guilty or not guilty of the March-treaſon he ſtandeth indicted and arraigned of, and whether he fled upon the fact done or not, and if you find him guilty, then what lands, goods, and tenements he was ſeiſed of at the committing of the ſaid treaſon or flying, in the ſhire or elſewhere within this realm, and of what value they were.*

Then make an Oyes, ſaying, *If there be any man that will give evidence for the queen's majeſty againſt A. B. priſoner at the bar, come into the court, and you ſhall be heard; for the priſoner ſtandeth upon his deliverance.*

That done, after they have been apart, and be agreed, call the jurors names, ſaying, *Who ſhall ſay for you? What ſay you to A. B. is he guilty or not guilty?* And ſo take their verdict.

Then when the verdict is given, if any perſon be found guilty, the lord warden muſt call him by name, and bid him hold up his hand; then ſay:

Foraſmuch as thou A. B. haſt been indicted of March-treaſon, and thereupon arraigned, and pleaded not guilty, and put thyſelf upon God and the country, and they have found thee guilty; wherefore this court doth award thou ſhalt be had hence unto the place from whence thou came, and from thence to the place of execution, and there to have thy head ſmitten from thy body, according to the law of the Marches.

After judgment given, my lord warden muſt call upon him whoſe office is to ſee the priſoner ſuffer, and ſay:

I command you in the queen's majeſty's name, that ye ſee execution done upon theſe perſons, according to the law of Marches, at your peril.

Then my ſaid lord warden, if it pleaſe him, may exhort the priſoner (or more, if there be more than one) in this wiſe; or let ſome godly man inſtruct them:

"Ye that are adjudged by order of law of this realm to die, remember "that ye have but a ſhort time to live in this world; therefore earneſtly call "to God, with penitent hearts, for mercy and forgiveneſs of your ſinful "lives. Repent ye have broken God's commandment, and be ſorry there-"fore; and for that ye did not fear the breach and danger of the laws, "therefore your bodies muſt ſuffer the pains of death provided to ſatisfy the "reward of your fact in this world; yet the ſalvation of your ſoul's health, "for the world to come, ſtands in the great mercy of almighty God. "Wherefore do ye earneſtly repent, and aſk mercy for your ſins, now when "ye are living, put your truſts to be ſaved by the merits of Chriſt's paſſion; "and think in your hearts, if ye were able to recompence them ye have "offended,

"offended, ye would do it; and where you are not able, aſk forgiveneſs. "And thus I commit you to the mercy of God, wiſhing your deaths may be "example to all parents to bring up their children in the fear of God, and "obedience to the laws of this realm."

And ſo command to take the priſoners from the bar; and adjourn the court by proclamation, ſaying:

All manner of men that have more to do at this court before my lord warden, keep your day here upon a new warning; and ſo for this time depart in God's peace and the queen's:

God ſave the Queen.

THE proper buſineſs of the trewes, when the lords wardens of both ſides with their companies met together at the days of Marche (and withal the ſad condition of the country, even when it was peace between the two kingdoms), will be beſt underſtood from an example, as here ſubjoined, from a minute of the proceedings at a meeting at Berwick, in the year 1587.

A breviate of the attempts of England committed upon the Weſt Marches by the Weſt borders of Liddeſdale, and fouled by the commiſſioners of Berwick for lack of appearance.

Weſt Marches againſt Liddeſdale.

June 1581.

Sir Simon Muſgrave knight, with Thom of the Toddhill and his neighbours, complain upon	Robin Ellot of the park, Sim Ellot, Clemie Croſer, Gawen's Jock, and their complices, for	60 kie and oxen, a horſe, and the taking of Thome Rootledg priſoner.

July 1581.

James Foſter of Symwhaite complains upon	Will. Ellot of the Redhughe, Adam of the Shawes, Archie of the Hill, and John Ellot of Heughouſe; for	50 kine and oxen, and all his inſight *.

June 1582.

Matthew Taylor, and the poor widow of Martin Taylor, complain upon	Old lard of Whitaugh, young lard of Whitaugh, Sim's Thom, and Jock of Copſhawe, for	140 kie and oxen, 100 ſheep, 20 gate, and all their inſight, 200*l* ſterling: and the ſlaughter of Martin Taylor, John Dodgſhon, John Skelloe, and Matthew Blackburne.

* Viz. houſehold goods.

Oct.

Oct. 1582.

Thomas Muſgrave deputy of Bewcaſtle and the tenants, againſt	Walter Scott lard of Buckluth, and his complices; for	200 kine and oxen, 300 gaite and ſheep.

15 Nov. 1582.

Sir Simond Muſgrave knight complains upon	The lard of Mangerton, lard's Jock, Sim's Thom, and their complices; for	burning of his barns, wheat, rye, oats, bigg, and peas; worth 1000*l* ſterling.

St. Andremaſs 1582.

Andrew Taylor complains upon	Robin Ellot, Will. his brother, George Simpſon, and their complices; for	60 kie and oxen, 100 ſheep, all his inſight, and money 60*l*.

July 1586.

Thomas Muſgrave deputy warden of Bewcaſtle, complains upon	The lard's Jock, Dick of Dryupp, and their complices; for	400 kine and oxen, taken in open forrie from the Dryſike in Bewcaſtle.

Sep. 1587.

Andrew Rootledge of the Nuke, complains upon	Lard's Jock, Dick of Dryupp, Lancie of Whiſgills, and their complices; for	50 kine and oxen, burning his houſe, corn, and inſight, 100*l* ſterling.

Nov. 1587.

Clemie Taylor, complains upon	Archie Ellot, Gibbie Ellot, and their complices; for	50 kine and oxen, all his inſight, 100 marks ſterl.

Martinmaſs 1587.

The poor widow and inhabitants of the town of Temmon, complain upon	Lard of Mangerton, lard of Whitaugh, and their complices; for	the murder of John Tweddel, Willie Tweddel, and Davie Bell; the taking and carrying away of John

Thirlway, Philip Thirlway, Edward Thirlway, John Bell of Clowſegill, David Bell, Philip Tweddel, Rowye Corrock, Thomas Alliſon, George Lyvock, and Archie Armſtrong, ranſoming them as priſoners; and the taking of 100 kine and oxen, ſpoil of houſes, writings, money, and inſight, 400*l* ſterling.

Commiſſioners.

John Forſter	Carmigell
John Selbie	Alexander Hume of Hutton Hall
Richard Lowther	Mr. George Yonge.

Liddeſdale againſt Weſt Marches.

A breviate of the Liddeſdale Bills fouled of the inhabitants of the Weſt Marches by the commiſſioners at Berwick; with the names of ſuch perſons noted in the Marches, as my lord Scroope had ready to deliver.

Lard of Mangerton complains upon	Cuddie Taylor, John Taylor, and their complices; at two times,	200 kie and oxen, inſight 20 *l* ſterling.
Lard of Mangerton complains upon	Mr. Humfrey Muſgrave, captain Pikeman and his ſoldiers; for	taking him priſoner, oxen, kie, horſes, mares, ſheep and gaite, inſight, 1500 *l* ſterling.
Lard of Mangerton, complains upon	Adam's Jamie Foſter, Matthew Taylor, Skailbies Hutchin, and Geordie Hetherton;	200 kie and oxen, 800 ſheep and gaite, 6 horſes and mares, from Tunden.
Thom Armſtrong of Tinniſburne, complains upon	Enſign Knap, Jamie's Adam Rootledge, John Taylor, Geordie Hetherton, and Mark's Tom's Geordie; for	300 kie and oxen, 6 horſes and mares, 800 ſheep and gaite.
Lancie of Whitaugh complains upon	Sim Taylor, John Taylor, Cuddie Taylor; for	inſight, ſilver coined and uncoined, 4000 *l* ſterl.
Sim Armſtrong of Whitaugh	John Taylor, Adam's Jamie, for	800 ſheep.
Robin Ellot of the Redheugh, complains upon	Thomas Carleton, for	60 kie and oxen, 400 ſheep, inſight 200 *l* from the ſteile.
Hob Ellot of Ranſgill	Thomas Carleton, and Riche of the Moat	60 kie and oxen, 6 horſes and mares, three priſoners, inſight, 400 marks.
Bramche of the Burnhead	Mr. Humfrey Muſgrave, and Thomas Carleton	200 kie and oxen, 40 horſes and mares, from the Ellots of Burnhead.

John

John Ellot of the Haugh-houſe, and Gaven of Rarſ-gill	Captain Carvell and his band, with the clans of Leven	200 kie and oxen, 30 horſes and mares.

The names of ſuch of the perſons complained upon as my lord Scroope had ready to deliver:

John Taylor	Sim Taylor
Mr. Humfrey Muſgrave	Paite's Cuddie
Geordie Hetherton	Adam's Jamie
Geordie Grame ſon to Mark's Thomie	Thomas Carlton
	Richie of the Moate.

Subſcribed by the Commiſſioners:

John Forſter	Carmighell
John Selbie	Alexander Hume of Hutton Hall
Richard Lowther	Mr. George Yonge.

Weſtmarches of England
againſt
Weſtmarches of Scotland.

A breviate of the bills of England fouled at Berwick upon the Weſtmarches of Scotland, by the commiſſioners according to the indenture.

Jan. 1582.

Thomas Rootledge of Todholes, and his neigh-bours complain upon	Kynmont Jock, Eckie of Stubholme, Jock of Calf-hill, and their complices	40 kine and oxen, 20 ſheep and gaite, a horſe, inſight 300*l* ſterl.

Jan. 1582.

Dick's Rowie Rootledge, complains, upon	Kynmont Jock, Jock of Calfhill, and their com-plices	30 kine and oxen, a horſe, inſight and ſpoil 60*l*.

Sept. 1582.

James Rootledge and his neighbours, complain up-on	Geordie Armſtrong of Calfhill, and Jock his brother, with their com-plices; for	100 kie and oxen.

Date	Complainant	Against	Loss
March 1586.	Chriſtopher Burtholme of Breckonhill, complains upon	John Armſtrong ſon to Sandie, Eckie's Richie, Willie Grame called Will with the Silk	60 kine and oxen, a bull, a horſe, inſight 200 marks ſterling.
June 1586.	Geordie Taylor of the Bone Riddings	Will Bell Redcloak, Wat Bell, Richie Bell, with their complices, for	30 kine and oxen, inſight 100*l* ſterling.
June 1586.	Walter Grame, William Grame, and the tenants of Eſk;—againſt	Will Bell Redcloak, Wattie Bell and the ſurnames of the Carliells; for	burning of their mills, houſes, corn, inſight 400*l*
18 June 1586.	William Grame, of Sleddells	Will Bell Redcloak, Tom Bell, and their complices; for	30 kine and oxen, 60 ſheep, 3 horſes, inſight 100*l* ſterling.
26 June 1586.	James Grame, and Hutchin Grame of Peretree	Will Bell Redcloak, Tom Bell, and their complices	60 kine and oxen, 100 ſheep, and the ſpoil of their houſes 100*l*.
Nov. 1586.	Cuddie Taylor and his neighbours of Hullethirſt	Young Chriſtopher Armſtrong of Awghing gill, Jock of Calfhill, Eckie's Richie, Willie Cany (Gait warden)	60 kine and oxen, 4 horſes, armour, and inſight 200*l* ſterling.
8 Nov. 1586.	Rowie Forſter, John Birnie, and their neighbours	Richie Maxwell of Cavens, and the ſoldiers of Langholme	200 kine and oxen, 200 ſheep and gaite.
Dec. 1586.	The poor widow of Watt's Davie's Fargie	John of Hollas, Willie Cany, Eckie's Richie, and their complices	Slaughter of her huſband, 40 kine and oxen, 2 horſes, inſight 100*l* ſterl.
May 1587.	James Taylor of the Croſrigg	Jock of Calfhill, Kynmont's Jock, with their complices; for	30 kine and oxen 2 nags, 40 gaite, 100*l* ſterling.

July 1587.

Thomas Mufgrave, deputy of Bewcaftle, and the tenants there	Geordie of Calfhill, Patie of the Hairelowe, Willie Cany, Eckie's Richie, and their complices	200 kie and oxen.

Dec. 1587.

Thomas Grame called Watt's Davie's Thome.	Echie's Richie of the Stubbholme, Willie Cany, John of the Hollas, with their complices	30 kine and oxen, 2 horfes, infight 100 *l*, and the taking of Will Grame and Patie Gramie prifoners.

Subfcribed by the commiffioners:

John Forfter	Carmighell
John Selbie	Alexander Hume of Hutton Hall
Richard Lowther	Mr. George Yonge.

Weftmarches of Scotland
againft
Weftmarches of England.

An abftract of the attempts fouled by the commiffioners upon the Weftmarches of England committed to the Weftmarches of Scotland.

Walter Scott of Branxholme, and the tenants of Ettrick houfe, complain upon	Will Grame of the Rofetrees, and Hutchin's Richie of the Balie, with their complices	80 kine and oxen, 40 nolt, 160 fheep, one horfe.
John Wood and others of Revells, tenants to the lord of Cookepoole, complain upon	Richie Grame of the Moate, Fargie's Chriftie, Rob Grame fon to Fargie's Chriftie, Richie of the Balie, with their complices	40 nolt, 160 fheep, one horfe.
Alexander Kirkpatrick	Thom's Geordie Grame and his complices	80 kine and oxen, 6 horfes and mares, 60 ftolts.

The

The tenants of Smallhame	Braid Jock's Jonie, Fergie of Meadupp	100 kine and oxen, 30 horses and mares, insight 400 marks.
Walter Scott of Branxholme and his tenants of Eldinghope	Will Grame of the Fold	2000 sheep, 200 kine and oxen, 24 horses and mares, insight 300*l*.
The lard of Cowhill, James Maxwell of Poltrack, and others of the water of Neith.	Walter Grame, Davie Grame, Will Grame brother to the said Walter, Rob of the Fald, Richie's Will	Burning of Cowhill, Poltrack, Dinhowe; 1000 kine and oxen, 500 sheep, 200 horses and mares, prisoners ransomed to 30000*l* Scots.
John lord Maxwell and his tenants of Dunhowe, Querelwood, Cowhill, and other places	Walter Grame of Netherbie, Rob of the Fald, Alie's Willie's Johnie, Dick's Will	Burning of 800 onsets (3000*l* Scots), 800 kie and oxen, 300 horses and mares, 3000 sheep, prisoners and ransomers 500*l* sterling.
Robert Maxwell of Castle Milk and his tenants	Walter Grame of Netherbie, Rob Grame of the Fald, and their complices	Burnt houses and corn 4000 marks Scots, 120 kine and oxen, 180 sheep, insight 500 marks.
Friends of Adam of Carliells and the Bells	Walter Grame of Netherbie, Davie and Willie his brother, Richie's Will, Rob of the Fald	Burning of Goddesbrigg, 3000 kine and oxen, 4000 sheep and gate, 500 horses and mares, estimated to 40000*l* Scots.
Sir Robert Maxwell of Dunwoddie knight	Walter Grame, Davie and Willie his brother, Rob of the Fald, Richie's Will, and others	Burning of Tinwell, Rawshawe and Mickle Woodside, 600 kine and oxen, 60 horses and mares, insight 10000*l* Scots.
James Douglass of Drumlangrig	Walter Grame, Rob of the Fald, Will his brother	Burning the Laithes at Rose 20000 marks, Cumrew 2000 marks, 20 kine and oxen, 40 horses and mares, 500 sheep.

Executors

Executors of the lard Johnston	Hutchin's Andrew, Hutchin's Richie, Will of the Rosetrees, Francie of the Moate, and others	Burning of Loughwood 5000*l* Scots, 600 kine and oxen, 80 horses and mares, 500 sheep and gaite.
The earl of Morton, and Herbert of Cavens	—— Grame of the Fald, Walter Grame of Netherby, George Grame son to Little Tom, and others	Burning of Langholme, 400 kine and oxen, 1000 sheep, 200 horses and mares, 300*l* Scots.
Warden of Scotland, complaining upon	Walter Grame, Richie of the Moate, and others	For bigging houses, and depasturing their cattle in Scotland, and sowing corn to the value of 40 chalders of corn for ten years by-past, estimating the hard corn every Bow 30*s* Scots, pasturing of 2000 head of nolt and horse, every head 30*s* Scots, 2000 sheep, every head 3*d* Scots.

Subscribed by the commissioners:

John Forster	Carmighell
John Selbie	Alexander Hume of Hutton Hall
Richard Lowther.	Mr. George Yonge.

Estimate of the bills fouled:

Westmarches of England against Liddesdale — —	3230*l*	4770*l* in surplus.
Liddesdale against Westmarches of England — —	8000*l* unde	
Westmarches of England against Westmarches of Scotland — —	6470*l*	27130*l* in surplus.
Westmarches of Scotland against Westmarches of England —	33600*l* unde	

Sum total for England 9700*l*.
Sum total for Scotland 41600*l*.

Sum

Sum total to the surplus what England hath to answer to Scotland, viz.	To Liddesdale — 4770*l*	31900*l*.
	To Westmarches — 27130*l*	

CHAPTER IV.

OF *the state of the Borders from the reign of king* EDWARD THE FIRST, *to the reign of king* RICHARD THE SECOND, *inclusive.*

ROBERT DE CLIFFORD, whom we took notice of as the first officer with a special commission for the wardenship of the marches, was slain at the battle of Bannock's-bourn in Scotland, June 24, 1314; which was in the latter end of the 7th year of the reign of king Edward the second. And in the 8 Ed. 2. *Andrew de Harcla* was made warden of the Marches †; and soon after, governor, and afterwards, earl of Carlisle. On whose attainder, this office, together with divers of the estates of the said earl, were granted to *Nevil* baron of Raby. And in the 8 Ed. 3. there is a special commission to *Henry de Percy* and *Ralph de Nevil*, jointly and severally, to execute the office of head wardens of the Marches in the counties of Northumberland, Cumberland, and Westmorland; with power to them, and their deputy wardens, to chastize and punish all who shall go about to break the peace, by arrest, imprisonment, and detention of their bodies, at the king's will; and also to raise the whole power of the counties of the Marches, as often as shall be needful; with an injunction to all the king's liege subjects within the said Marches, on pain of forfeiture and confiscation, to be obedient and assisting to the said wardens, as often as they shall be summoned thereunto §.

In the 33 Ed. 3. *Gilbert Welton* bishop of Carlisle, and *Thomas de Lucy* lord of Cockermouth were constituted, jointly and severally, wardens of the western marches ǂ.

In the 40 Ed. 3. a commission for wardens of the western marches was granted to *Thomas Appleby* bishop of Carlisle, *Roger de Clifford*, *Anthony de Lucy*, and *Ranulph de Dacre* ‡.

In the 44th of the same king, a like commission issued to the aforesaid bishop *Appleby*, *Roger de Clifford*, *Thomas de Musgrave*, *Alan de Heton*, and nine others*

In the 47th of the same king, a like commission was granted to *Thomas* bishop of *Durham*, *Thomas* bishop of *Carlisle*, *Edmund Mortimer* earl of *March*, *Roger de Clifford*, *Ralph de Dacre*, *Richard de Stafford*, *Henry le Scrope*, *Thomas de Musgrave*, and *John de Appleby* dean of St. *Paul's* (probably the bishop's brother) ‖.

† 2 Dugd. Bar. 97.
§ Nicolson's Border Laws, 372.
ǂ Registr. Welton.
‡ Registr. Appleby.
* Rymer, tom. 6. p. 657.
‖ Registr. Appleby.

In

In the 8 Ric. 2. Mar. 15. A day of trewes for the Weſt Marches was agreed upon by indenture between *Henry Percy* earl of *Northumberland*, and *Archibald de Douglas* lord of *Galway*, at the water of Eſk beſide Salom to be holden on the 19th day of April then next following, with continuation of days, to take full redreſs and execution of all things done between their reſpective bounds on the Weſt Marche from the 14th of October to Candlemaſs day then laſt paſt: But in communication together, it ſeemed to them, that it would be more for the common profit of both realms, that a longer time of Trewes ſhould be appointed, and a day of Trewes appointed for the Eaſt March likewiſe, if the wardens of the ſaid Eaſt Marche ſhould aſſent thereto; they therefore came to the following agreement, that is to ſay, the earl of *Northumberland* for himſelf and the lord *Nevill*, and the lord of *Galway* for himſelf and the earl of *Douglas*, that ſpecial trewe and aſſurance ſhall be betwixt them and their bounds, from that time to the firſt day of July next enſuing; and that during the ſaid time, none of the ſaid lords nor any within their bounds, ſhall do harm to the bounds of the other party, but they ſhall cauſe it to be redreſſed as law of Marche requires. And if it happens any great power of the one realm or the other to ride with hoſt, each of the ſaid lords ſhall do all they can to hinder it; and if they cannot hinder it, they ſhall give warning to the other part not to be at that riding, but to hinder the ſame as much as they can without fraud or guile. And if the ſaid earl of *Northumberland* or the lord *Nevill* ſhall like or miſlike the ſaid covenants, they or one of them ſhall certify the ſame by letter, on Black Monday that next cometh, before noon, at the chapel of *Salom*, by the water of *Eſke*: And in the ſame manner, if the ſaid earl *Douglas* or lord of *Galway* ſhall like or miſlike the ſaid covenants, they or one of them ſhall certify the ſame by letter, at the place, day, and hour aforeſaid. And in caſe they certify that this agreement ſtand, that day that ſhould have been holden on the 19th of April ſhall be holden on the 15th of May next coming, and the day on the Eaſt Marche ſhall be holden on the 29th of the ſame month of May. Alſo it is accorded, that all priſoners taken on both ſides ſhall be freely delivered, and all their pledges diſcharged. And if any ſtealeth, either on one party or on the other, he ſhall be hanged or headed. And if any company ſteal any goods within the trewes, one of that company ſhall be hanged or headed, and the remnant ſhall reſtore the goods ſtolen in the double †.

CHAP.

† To ſhew the orthography of the Engliſh tongue at that time, we here ſubjoin the record in its own words and ſpelling:

Yis endenture madé at ye water of Eſke, beſid Salom ye xv day of Marcz, ye zher of our Lord $\frac{i}{m}$ ccc$\frac{xx}{iiii}$ and iiii: Betwixt noble lardes and meghty, Siris Henry Percy erle of Northumbr' of theta part, and Archibald of Douglaſs lord of Galway on ye toyir parte, contenys and berres witnes, that day of radreſs ſal be halden betwixt yam in propre perſons at the place beforeſaide, ye xix day of Averill next for to cumme, wht ye continuation of days for to do and tak full radreſſe and execution of all things don betwixt yair boundes apan the Weſt Marche, begynande ye xiiii day of Octobr' to Candlemaſs day laſt paſſyt: And yan it fell in ſpech betwixt the forſayd lords, That in entent of common profit of bathe reaumes, gif hit meght happen of langer trewe,

on

CHAPTER V.

OF *the state of the Borders from the reign of king* RICHARD THE SECOND *to the reign of king* HENRY THE EIGHTH.

THE first thing remarkable that we meet with in this period, is a body of laws in the 28 Hen. 6. by *Robert* bishop of *Durham*, *John Beamond* lord high constable of England, *Thomas Stanley* comptroller of the host, *Richard Andrew* the king's secretary and doctor of laws, *James Strangwaies* knight, and *Robert Dobbies* doctor of the canon law, on the part of the king of England; and *Andrew* abbot of *Mellross* king's confessor and treasurer of Scotland, *Andrew* lord *Grey*, *John Methine* master of the rolls, and *Thomas Grafton* esquire provost of Edinburgh, on the part of the king of Scotland †:—Which, with the alterations made in several subsequent conventions, make up the Code of Border laws as above rehearsed.

In the 5 Ed. 4. there was another like convention, by the commissioners *Andrew* bishop of *Glasgow*, *Colin* lord *Campbell* earl of *Argyle*, *Archibald* abbot

or els of pees (gif God vald vouche saufe), and als for the time is to schort to make full redrass beforsayd, the forsayd lordes are accordit in specialte, as efter folowes; yat is for to say, the erle of Northumbr' for hym and for the lord Nevill, and the lord of Galway for the erle of Douglas and for hymselfe, yat speciall trew and assurance sall be betwixt thaim and thair boundes, betwixt this and the first day of July next for to come, contenant and havand the force and effect in all poyntez as the next trew gangand before. Also it is accordit, that durant the tyme beforesayd, nane of the lords beforsayd, ne nane of their boundes, sal do skathe to tha of the boundes of the tothir partie; bot tha sal ger it be redressit, als lawe of Marche will enterchaungeably. And gif it happins that any gretter awir of the ta reaume or of the tothir, schapes for to ride wht Oste, ilken of the lordes beforsayd, enterchaungeably sall set let thairin at thair powar; and in cas tha ma noght let it, thai sall ger warne the tother part of xv days, and thai sall noght be at that rydyng, bot thay sall lely let thaim of thair boundes at thair power, for owten fraude or gile. And also it is accordit, that this condition of speciall trewe and assurance sall stand and be kephit fullely by see als well as for theis boundes be lande, as the trewes beforesayd askys. And also hit is accordit, that gift hir specialx trewes likes to the Erle of the Marche to be compriset whtin, thanne that thei sall stand furght for hym and his boundes, and he sall stand for hym and his boundes under the samen condition anentys thaim and thair boundes. And gif thir covenantz beforesayd likis or mislikis to the forsayd erle of Northumbr' or to the lord Nevil', thay sall certifie be thair letters, or be on of thaires, opon Black Monday that next commis befor none, at the chapell of Salom, be the water of Eske; and in the samen manere, gif it likis or mislikis to the erle of Douglas or to the lord of Galway, thai or ane of thaim sall certifie be letter, at the place, day, and oure beforesayd. And in case gif thai certifie that this specialtie stand that day that chuld be halden, the xix day of Averill chall be chot to the xv day of May next to cumme, to be halden in all force and effect as the xix day of Averill; and the day on the East Marche sall be delayed in the samen maner as it is indentit to be halden the xxix day of May. And also it is accordit, that all prisoners taken on both the sidis, sall be freely deliverid, and all their boros frethit. Also it is accordit, gif ony stellis authir on the ta part or on the tothyr, that he sall be henget or hesdit; and gif ony company stellis any gudes whtin the trieux beforesayd, ane of that company sall be hengit or heofdit, and the remanent sall restore the gudys stollen in the double. In the witnes of the wische thinges, lely to be halden and fulfillyt, the foresayd erle of Northumbr' and the lord of Galway has sett thair signetz enterchangeably, in absens of thair selles, day and the yer beforesayd.

† Nicolson's Border Laws, 9.

of

of *St. Cross* in Edinburgh, Master *James Lindsey* provost of the collegiate church of *Lincluden*, and *Alexander Boyd* of *Drumcol* knight, on the part of the king of Scotland; and *George* bishop of *Exeter* chancellor of England, *Richard* earl of *Warwick* and *Salisbury* great chamberlain of England and warden of the West Marches of England against Scotland, *Ralph* lord of *Graystock*, *William de Hastings* the king's chamberlain, Master *Thomas Keate* doctor of both laws, *James Strangwaies* and *Robert Constable* knights, on the part of the king of England †.

In the 9 Ed. 4. (1468) there is a collection of Border laws made for Scotland only, for the regulation of their own men in making inroads, taking prisoners, and the like: But which, most probably, mutatis mutandis, were also used in England; for we find a copy thereof in Mr. Bell's manuscript, who was warden clerk as aforesaid of the West Marches of England.—Which laws are as follows:

Be it remembered, that on the 18th day of December 1468, earl *William Douglas* assembled the whole lords, freeholders, and eldest borderers, that best knowledge had, at the college of *Lincluden*; and there he caused those lords and borderers bodily to be sworn, the holy gospel touched, that they justly and truly, after their conning, should decrete, decern, deliver, and put in order and writing, the statutes, ordinances, and uses of Marche, that were ordained in *Black Archibald* of *Douglas*'s days, and Archibald his son's days, in time of warfare; and they came again to him advisedly with these statutes and ordinances which were in time of warfare before. The said earl *William*, seeing the statutes in writing decreed and delivered by the said lords and borderers, thought them right speedful and profitable to the borderers; the which statutes, ordinances, and points of warfare he took, and the whole lords and borderers he caused bodily to be sworn, that they should maintain and supply him, at their goodly power, to do the law upon those that should break the statutes underwritten. Also the said earl *William* and lords and eldest borderers made certain points to be treason in time of warfare to be used, which were no treason before his time, but to be treason in his time and in all time coming.

1. It is founded and ordained by the law of Marches, that no manner of person, man nor woman, of any degree, shall intercommon with any English man or woman, either in Scotland or England, except the prisoners shall come in Scotland; without special licence of the warden or his deputy asked and obtained in time of warfare, under the pain of treason. *Intercommoning with Englishmen.*

2. It is statute and ordained, that when it happens that the warden or lieutenant, with any fellowship, do pass in England, that what person for covetise of goods, or singular profit to himself, departs and passes from his fellowship, *Of him who passeth from his company.*

† Nicolson's Border Laws, 36.

all the goods that he happens to take ſhall be taken from him, and be eſcheat, and by the governor of the hoſt or company ſhall be diſpoſed among the fellowſhip as to him ſhall ſeem ſpeedful; and he ſhall be noted as a traytor for his deed, and puniſhed for open treaſons.

That all men fight on foot.

3. Item, It is ordained, that what time it is ſeen ſpeedful that the hoſt light down and array themſelves, that each man light down at commandment, and no man bide on horſe, but as many as are ordained by the chieftain; and whoſo does not, to be puniſhed in like manner as is before ſaid: And if he happens to win any priſoner or goods, that bides on horſe without commandment; two parts ſhall be his majeſty's, and the third part the chieftain's of the hoſt.

Arraying the hoſt.

4. Item, That no man make obſtacle or letting to them that are ordained to array the hoſt; and that each man ſhall anſwer and obey under the ſame pain.

Taking another man's horſe.

5. Item, It is ſtatute and ordained, that if there happens any chaſe, either fleeing or following, whatever he be that takes his fellow's horſe, if he wins any goods on him, either priſoner or other goods; he that owed the horſe ſhall have the half of it, and he ſhall bring the horſe again to the ſtake: and failing thereof, he ſhall be noted as a traytor and puniſhed. And if it happens him to fly on that horſe, as ſoon as he comes home, he ſhall paſs to the market of the ſhire, and proclaim him, and immediately deliver him to the ſheriff or ſteward of the land: and if he does not this he ſhall be puniſhed as a traytor.

Taking of priſoners.

6. Item, When it ſhall happen us to win any field, whoever he be that arreſts any priſoner, and then follows off the field, and he will ſwear, when he comes home, that he did that for ſafety of his priſoner's life; that condition ſhall be of no avail: And whoever he be that ſlays his fellow's priſoner after he be arreſted, ſhall pay his ranſom to his taker, if he be of power; and if he be not of power, he ſhall die therefore.

Alſo it is found ſtatute and uſe of Marche, that it is lawful to any man to take as many priſoners as he may, both on foot and horſe: ſo that he lead them with the ſtrength of Scotſmen: And to take a token of his priſoner with him, that he may be ſufficiently known; and to leave his token with his priſoner. And ſo many as he takes in ſuch like manner, to be his priſoners; and the determination thereof to be decided by the warden or his deputy, if there be any complaints.

Rieving of other men's priſoners.

7. Item, It is found, ſtatute, and ordained, that any man being complainant of reif of his priſoner or his goods, ſhall find a borgh (pledge) in the hands of the warden-ſerjeant, upon the party that he is plaintiff of; which party ſhall be arreſted to bring the priſoner or the goods to the next warden court; and the priſoner there to be challenged by his party, and both their

7 witneſſes

witnesses shall be heard and examined: And it shall be at the will and discretion of the judge and his sworn counsel, when both the parties are heard, to give his decree, who has reason to the prisoner or to the goods: And the party found in the wrong shall pay 10*l* to the judges.

And if it happens any man to complain in the field to the chieftain, that his prisoner is reft from him; as soon as he may be gotten, he shall be delivered to the warden or lieutenant, to be put in even hands, that neither of the parties induce him to their will, that it may be determined and judged who has most reason to him.

8. Item, If it happens a prisoner to be taken, and divers persons contend about him, he shall be, at the command of the warden, delivered in even hands, or else in the warden's hands, at the will of the parties which they had rather; and the warden shall cause the prisoner to be brought to the warden court, and there the parties shall challenge, and he that is found arrester shall challenge first: And if he has any Scotsmen to witness that he took him prisoner, and first arrested him, the witnesses of the first arrester shall be of value, what Scotsmen that ever they be; the arrester and his witnesses being bodily sworn, that they shall truth say, without dread or favour of any person. And failing of this, the action of any other claimer shall be put to the oath of the Englishman, he being bodily sworn, and in even hands, that he shall truth say, without regard to profit or loss to himself, and without fraud or favour of any other parties. Contention for a prisoner.

9. Item, It is statute and found use of Marche, whatever he be that takes any prisoner who may lead an hundred men; he shall not be by him letten to pledge, nor yet ransomed for 15 days in time of war, unless he have leave of the warden. Ransoming officers.

10. Item, It is statute and found use of Marche, whatever he be that strikes down a man off horseback in the chase, suppose he be yielded thereafter to another man, or that strikes him down through justing of war; he that strikes him down shall have half his ransom, so that it be proved. Proportioning of ransom.

11. Item, It is statute and found use of Marche, that whatever he be that brings a traytor to the warden or his deputy, he shall have for his reward an hundred shillings: And he that puts him away fraudfully, shall underlie the pain of death for his so doing, like as the traytor should have done. Takers or concealers of traytors.

12. Item, It is found statute and used in time of warfare, with respect to bails burning and keeping, for coming of an English host into Scotland, there shall a bail be burned on *Traillrow-hill*, and another on the *Penchat-hill*, and on the *Bail-hill* above the *Hame-ends*, one on the *Cowdens* above *Castlemilk*, one on *Quitsoun*, one on *Drysdail*, and on the *Burraw Skenton* in *Applegarth* parish, one on the *Browan-hill*, and one on the *Bleis* in the tenement of *Wamphray*, one on the *Kindol-knok* in the tenement of *Johnstoun*, one on the *Gallow-hill* of *Moffat* Beacons to be sustained.

Moffat parish, and five in *Nithisdale*, one on the *Wardlaw*, one on the *Rabeckstoun*, one on *Barloch*, one on the *Pittarra* hill, one on the *Malow* hill, one on *Corswinton*, one on the *Corsell*, one on the fell above *Dowlbark*, and one on the *Watchfell*: And to cause these bails to be kept and made, the sheriff of *Nithisdale*, the stewart of *Annandale*, and the stewart of *Kirkudbright* in *Galloway* shall be debtors; and whoso keepeth not the bails, shall pay for each default one mark *.

Pursuit on firing the beacons.

13. Whoever he be, an host of Englishmen coming in the country, the bails being burned, that follows not the host on horse or on foot, ever till the English men be passed off Scotland, and that they have sufficient witnesses thereof; all their goods shall be escheat, and their bodies at the warden's will, unless they have lawful excuse for them.

Prisoners not to pass without safe conduct.

14. Item, It is ordained, if there be any Englishman taken in Scotland, they shall have no freedom to pass in the country farther than the place of their entry, and the streight way from England to the place, on no man's conduct, except only our sovereign lord's, or the warden's proper self; and that they shall come on another conduct to the very day and place of their entry and payment: And if they happen to be without conduct, or any Scotsman with them in name of their taker, he shall be prisoner to any Scotsman that may get him.

Suffering prisoners to escape.

15. Item, That no Scotsman, after any host be ridden, or ready to ride in England, let his prisoner pass home, or that an host of English be come in Scotland and Scotsmen gathering against them; under the pain of treason.

Parting of goods.

16. Item, Whoever he be that comes to the host without bow and spear, and there be any parting of goods, two of them shall be to one bow part.

Deserting.

16. Item, Whoever he be, after that they come in the field, that flees from the lord his master and his fellows, and bides not to the uttermost; all his goods shall be escheat, and his person punished as a traitor at the next warden court thereafter to be holden.

Rieving of prisoners or goods.

18. Item, whoever he be that rieves from any man his horse, prisoner, or goods, after that they be known unto him; he shall restore them again, and his person punished therefore as for open treason.

HERE end the laws and constitutions made by the earl Douglas †.

* In Cumberland, the places appointed for beacons were *Blackcomb*, *Boothill*, *Mulcaster* fell, *St Bees* head, *Workington* hill, *Moothay*, *Skiddaw*, *Sandale* top, *Carlisle* castle, *Lingy close* head, *Beacon* hill, *Penrith*, *Dale Raughton*, *Brampton* Mote, and *Spade-Adam* top. In Westmorland, upon the top of *Stanemore*, *Orton* scar, *Farleton* knot, *Whinfell* fell, and *Hardknot*.

† Balfour's Practicks, p. 590.

CHAPTER

CHAPTER VI.

Of the state of the Borders during the reign of king Henry *the eighth.*

IN this king's reign there was another commission of Border laws and regulations; the commissioners were *Thomas Audley* knight high chancellor of England, *Thomas Cromwell* secretary of state, *Edward Fox* almoner, *John Treymevell* privy counsellor, and *Richard Givente* official principal of the metropolitical church of Canterbury, on the behalf of the king of England; and *William* bishop of *Aberdeen* great treasurer of Scotland, and *Adam Otterburne* knight privy counsellor, on the behalf of the king of Scotland *.

Also in this king's reign, Sir *Thomas Wharton* (afterwards lord *Wharton*) became eminent and in high trust with the king as a most active and vigilant warden of the Marches. He first signalized himself when deputy warden of the West Marches under the lord Scroop, in the memorable rencounter at Sollom Moss, of which there is scarce a parallel in history. Being then governor of Carlisle, he (together with Sir William Musgrave) with 300 horsemen [according to the common account, but from the fragments of a letter hereafter following they seem to have been 1400 horse and foot] attacked an army of 15000 Scots, and with very little resistance took prisoners almost every person of distinction in the Scotch army, with 800 common soldiers, and all their baggage and artillery. The reason was, the Scots being disgusted that Oliver Sinclair the king's favourite and an upstart was made commander in chief, would not fight under him. Historians say, that the Scots fled, because they supposed Wharton's men to be the van of the duke of Norfolk's army coming against them. But most probably, Wharton had some private intimation from the Scots of what they intended; otherwise his enterprise would not have been courage but madness. It broke the Scotch king's heart, and he died within a month, leaving his infant daughter Mary.

After the Scotch king's death, king Henry meditated a marriage between his son prince Edward and the said Mary; and in order to prepare the way to it, sent for the chief of the Scotch prisoners up to London. And there is yet extant a copy of a letter from Sir Thomas Wharton to the king, giving an account of the prisoners sent up by him, with the names of their takers; and an original letter from the king to the said Sir Thomas Wharton about the ransom of said prisoners to be given to their takers; together with a copy of Sir Thomas Wharton's answer to the same; which are as here follows:

Copy *of a letter from Sir* Thomas Wharton *to the king's most excellent majesty, the tenth of* December (1542).

Please your most excellent majesty to be advertised, that your gracious and most noble letters of the date at your highness's honour of Hampton court the

* Nicolson's B. L. 62.

last

laſt day of November, was delivered unto me at Newcaſtle the 4th of December, being repaired thither with divers noblemen and gentlemen Scottiſh priſoners, according to the right honourable my lord of Hertford's letters of commandment unto me ſo to do: Humbly advertiſing your majeſty, that the contents of your highneſs's ſaid gracious and moſt noble letters ſhewed by me and read in that part to the gentlemen your highneſs's ſervants and humble ſubjects there preſent, we all have received the ſame in our hearts with moſt joy and comfort, for that our fortune by the favour of almighty God, to ſerve your majeſty to your highneſs's moſt noble contentation. In ſuch wiſe we ſhall moſt humbly pray with our hearts, that we may ſerve your majeſty to the continuance of the ſame, which is all our worldly comfort to do to our lives end. It may alſo pleaſe your majeſty to be advertiſed, that herewith I do ſend unto your highneſs the names of the noblemen and gentlemen priſoners, which I delivered at Darnton to my lord Scropp, and the names of their takers in the ſame. I do ſend alſo to your majeſty the order of that fortunable ſervice done by the power of almighty God to your highneſs againſt your majeſty's enemies, and the names of ſuch gentlemen, and the numbers with them, in that your majeſty's ſervice; together with ſuch communication in effect as I have had with the lord Maxwell and Oliver Synclere. I ſhall attend your majeſty's moſt noble commandment for all the other priſoners, according to my moſt bounden duty. And yet there are divers good priſoners upon the Marches here, as I am informed. Your majeſty hath not a little comforted us all to ſerve, for that your highneſs's moſt noble goodneſs ſignified for the ward of Robert Bryſco *, which ſhall be employed to the widow and ward accordingly. I ſhall attend to annoy and aſſail the enemy, with all vigilance, diligence, and circumſpection, according to your ſaid moſt noble letters, and all other your highneſs's ſervices, to the beſt I can or may unto my life's end, as I am moſt bounden; and ſhall daily pray to almighty God, that your majeſty may moſt long in proſperous health reign over us. At Carliſle the 10th of December.

The names of the noblemen and gentlemen of Scotland, priſoners, to be ſent unto the king's majeſty from Sir Thomas Wharton knight, with the names of their takers, as followeth:

The earl of Caſſill.	Batill Routlege his taker: John Muſgrave claimeth a part for the loan of his horſe to the ſaid Routlege.

* It appears from Sir Thomas Carleton's memoirs, that this Robert Briſco was ſlain at Sollom Moſs, and the king here remits the profits of the wardſhip of his heir, for the benefit of his widow and the ſaid heir; which widow the ſaid Sir Thomas Carleton afterwards married.

In

In plea amongst them.	The earl of Glencarne, otherwise called the lord of Gilmawres.	Willye Grame called Watt's Willye, Willye Grame of the Balie, Sir Thomas Wharton, and Thomas Dacre.
In plea between them.	The lord Flemynge, one of the king of Scots privy council.	George Pott and Stephen James claimeth to be the taker.
In plea between them.	The lord Maxwell, admiral of Scotland, warden of the west Marches of the same, and one of the king of Scots privy council.	Edward Aglionby or George Foster his taker.
	The lord Somervell.	Richard Brysco his taker.
In plea between them.	The lord Olivaunt.	Thomas Denton or James Alenson his taker.
	The lord Graye.	Thomas Whyte, Willie Storye, and George Storye his takers.
	Oliver Synkeler, one of the king of Scots privy council.	Willie Bell his taker.

LETTER *from the king to Sir* Thomas Wharton *concerning the ransom of the Scotch prisoners.*

To *our trusty and right well beloved counsellor Sir* Thomas Wharton *knight, deputy warden of our West Marches for anempst* Scotland, *and captain of our town and castle of* Carlisle.

By the King.

Trusty and right well beloved, we greet you well: Letting you wit, that forasmuch as we consider that the takers of the prisoners which do now come up may perease by reason of the taking of them out of their hands fear lest they should not be recompensed for the same as appertaineth; our pleasure is, that you shall call them together, and assure them on our behalf, that their repair hither shall be nothing to their loss or hindrance: Nevertheless, forasmuch as we purpose to prosecute our enterprize with Scotland, whereby the wars cannot shortly be determined, but be like to have a long continuance, during the suspence whereof they can have no recompence for the same; to the intent they may be the better satisfied, and that they may also have wherewith to furnish themselves against the next year with all things necessary and convenient for them, our pleasure is, that of yourself you shall commune with the said takers of all the prisoners which do now come up, and know what they

they would demand for them; promising to do what you can, if they will be reasonable, to get them ready money for them, which ſhall be moſt their commodity, ſeeing the long tract of time that muſt be before they ſhall elſe get any thing for them. Which well compaſſed by your dexterity and wiſdom, we might take ſuch order touching the deliverance of the ſaid priſoners either in redemption of our men in Scotland, or otherwiſe as ſhall be thought moſt convenient.

Finally, foraſmuch as many of our ſubjects of thoſe marches do now repair hither, we deſire and pray you to take order that none of them, as much as you can, do in any wiſe depart from thence, whereby the ſame ſhould be in any wiſe disfurniſhed, but that every of them may be on his guard both to defend and annoy as the caſe ſhall require.

Given under our ſignet at our honour of Hampton Court, the 11th day of December the 34th year of our reign.

SIR Thomas Wharton's *anſwer to the ſame.*

To *the king's moſt excellent majeſty, in haſte, with poſt haſt.*

Pleaſed your moſt excellent majeſty to be advertiſed, that this 16th of December, at five of the clock aforeday, I have received your majeſty's moſt noble letters of the date at Hampton Court the 11th of the ſame; commanding me to call together the takers of the priſoners now ſent to your highneſs, and to aſſure them in your majeſty's behalf, that the conveying of the priſoners to your highneſs ſhall be no loſs nor hindrance unto them; and by this your majeſty's enterprize, the wars cannot ſhortly be determined, your highneſs's pleaſure is that of myſelf I ſhall commune with them to know what they would demand for them, and that I ſhould promiſe to do what I can to get them money, which ſhall be their moſt commodity, that your majeſty may thereupon take convenient order; and that as nigh as I can to take order, that none of your majeſty's ſubjects ſhall depart from hence for disfurniture here; as your majeſty's moſt noble letters at length ſignifieth: I ſhall with all dexterity, according to your highneſs's commandment, attend for the accompliſhment of all the ſame.

Advertiſing your majeſty, that I have not been privy and conſenting to the repair of any perſons from theſe Marches, except one Thomas Denton gentleman, who hath to his power ſerved your majeſty honeſtly ſince mine entry in office; and he hearing that a ſervant of the lord Dacre's was repaired againſt him for the taking of the lord Olivaunt, then he deſired me that he might depart for his trial thereof, wherewith I was content.—The repair from theſe Marches, and uſe of priſoners, by divers the lord Dacre's * ſervants and tenants, hath perplexed divers perſons here, conſidering their delivery of priſoners unto me according to your majeſty's commandment, and theſe others not ſo doing,

* There appears to have been all along a jealouſy and rivalſhip between Sir Thomas Wharton and the lord Dacre.

nor alſo making me privy of their paſſages to any other part from theſe marches, and I have had earneſt requeſts made by others that hath not ſo done.

It may alſo pleaſe your majeſty to underſtand, that there are yet here upon theſe marches divers good priſoners better than ſundry that I have ſent; amongſt which there is one William Grame lord of Sentre, which married the Cardinal's ſiſter; he ſaith to me he may ſpend in land 300 marks Scotiſh; he is taken amongſt the Grames, they bear him the more favour for his name. I intend of myſelf to practice with their takers, your majeſty to have them accordingly. All the others . . . . good priſoners gone for ſmall ranſoms from evil men upon the Borders [without my] knowledge, and againſt all commandments given. Advertiſing [alſo there] was many good priſoners in the hands of your highneſs's ſubjects, after . . . . and more in number taken than I have hitherto written . . . . And in all of your majeſty's ſubjects there was xiiii [ſpace of about three words torn off] horſe and foot. Advertiſing alſo, that at the arrival of your majeſty's moſt noble letters, I had preſently written a letter unto the right honourable my lord warden; I have with theſe ſent a copy thereof to your majeſty. And as I am moſt bounden, I ſhall ſerve your majeſty, and pray daily to almighty God to continue your grace, with moſt perfect health, moſt long to reign over us. At your majeſty's caſtle of Carliſle the 16th of December at five of the clock aforeday *.

In the next place, within a quarter of a year after this, we meet with a liſt of the gentlemen of both counties called out by Sir Thomas Wharton upon ſome further ſervice of the borders; which ſhews who were the principal gentlemen of that time ſubject to border ſervice, and what was the proportionable value of their reſpective eſtates: *viz.*

The names of ſuch as were ſent for by Sir Thomas Wharton's *letter* 34 Hen. 8. 1543.

Sir *William Muſgrave*, 60 horſe and 40 foot (beſides Bewcaſtle).
Sir *Thomas Curwen*, horſe at his pleaſure.
Sir *John Lowther*, 100 horſe and 40 foot.
William Pennington, all his tried horſemen.
John Lamplough for his father, ten horſe.
John Leigh (beſides Burgh horſe and foot) 10 horſe.
John Thwaites, houſhold ſervants.
John Skelton of Branthwaite, 4 horſe.
Thomas Dykes, 4 horſe.
Richard Egleſfield, 6 horſe.

* For the communication of theſe letters, we are obliged to the reverend Mr. Watſon of Middleton Tyas, Yorkſhire.

Alexander Appleby, 2 horſe.
Mr. *Latus* for the lord of *Millum*, 60 horſe.
William Porter, 2 horſe.
Thomas Salkeld of the Whitehall, 4 horſe.
Anthony Barwis, 2 horſe.
John Senhouſe, 4 horſe.
William Aſmotherley, 2 horſe.
John Swinburne, houſhold ſervants.
Anthony Highmore, 2 horſe.
Robert Ellis, 2 horſe.
Robert Lamplough, houſhold ſervants.
William Sands and *Edward Berdeſey*, for the lord of St. Bees, 10 horſe.
Robert Briſco, horſe and foot.
Cuthbert Hutton, 6 horſe and 10 foot.
Edward Aglionby, horſe and foot.
Thomas Dacre of Grayſtock, horſe and foot.
William Skelton, 6 horſe.
Thomas Dalſton (beſides Carliſle) 10 horſe and 20 foot.
Thomas Blenerhaſſet for Gilſland, horſe and foot.
Chriſtopher Threlkeld, 4 horſe and 6 foot.
John Muſgrave, for Bewcaſtle, horſe and foot.
William Pickering, for Barton, Martindale, Paterdale, and his own tenants, 20 horſe and 20 foot.
William Vaux, 4 horſe and 6 foot.
Richard Blencow, 6 horſe.
Richard Hutton, 4 horſe.
Richard Warwick, horſe and foot.
Lancelot Lowther for Derwentwater, all horſemen.
Tenants of the Biſhop and College, all horſe.
The lordſhip of Holme, all tried horſe.

Weſtmorland:
Sir *James Leyburne*, 20 horſe.
Walter Strickland, 200 horſe.
The ſon of Sir *Jeffrey Middleton*, 20 horſe.
Anthony Ducket, 20 horſe.
John Preſton, houſhold ſervants.
William Gilpin, 6 horſe.
Thomas Sandford, 80 horſe and 20 foot.
John Warcop, 6 horſe.
Lancelot Lancaſter, 20 horſe and 20 foot.
Chriſtopher Crackenthorp, 10 horſe.
Hugh Machel, 4 horſe.
Henry Shaw, 2 horſe.
James Pickering, 6 horſe.
Thomas Blenkinſop, 120 horſe.

Robert

Robert Hilton, 2 horſe.
Robert Pullen, 2 horſe.
Richard Salkeld of Roſgill, 20 horſe and 20 foot.
Richard Dudley, 6 horſe and 6 foot.
Thomas Wybergh, 6 horſe and 6 foot.
Thomas Fallowfield, 4 horſe.
Robert Cleburne, 6 horſe and 10 foot.
Barnaby Warcop, 2 horſe.
Ambroſe Machel, 2 horſe.
Simon Slingſby and *Thomas Lambert* for Culgaith, 6 horſe.
Edward Birkbeck, 2 horſe.
Thomas Lough, 4 horſe.
Henry Barton, 2 horſe.
Robert Warcop, 4 horſe.
Lancelot Wharton, 10 horſe.
Richard Salkeld of the Grange, 4 horſe.
Thomas Rooſe, 2 horſe *.

What kind of atchievements they performed in this peculiar kind of warfare in the Borders, we are informed from Haines's ſtate papers; p. 51, 54. The total amount whereof in one inroad or *forray*, from the 2d of July to the 17th of November in that ſame year, is thus computed:

Towns, towers, ſtedes, barnekyns †, pariſh churches, baſtel houſes ‡ caſt down or burned — — — —	192
Scots ſlain — — — — —	403
Priſoners taken — — — — —	816
Nolt (i. e. horned cattle) taken — — —	10,386
Sheep — — — — —	12,492
Nags and geldings — — — —	1,296
Goats — — — — — —	200
Bolls of corn — — — — —	890
Inſight (i. e. houſhold furniture) not reckoned.	

In the next year, in a forray made by the earl of Hertford, between the 8th and 23d of September 1545, the ſum total of miſchief is thus ſet down:

Monaſteries and friar houſes, burnt or deſtroyed — —	7
Caſtles, towers, and piles — — — —	16
Market towns — — — — —	5
Villages — — — — — —	243
Milns — — — — — —	13
Hoſpitals — — — — — —	3

* Fleming. † *Barnekin* was the outermoſt ward of a caſtle; within which were the barns, ſtables, and cow-houſes. ‡ *Baſtel houſes* ſeem to have been monaſteries or hoſpitals.

CHAPTER VII.

Of the state of the Borders during the reign of king Edward *the sixth.*

IN the beginning of this reign, in 1547, in the month of February in that year, is a manuscript account by Sir *Thomas Carleton* of Carleton hall of a forray in Scotland conducted by himself, who commanded a party under the (then) lord Wharton.

" The first day (he says) we made a road into Tevidale, and got a great booty of goods, and that night we lay in the old walls of Wawcop Tower, and builded to-falls; but for lack of housing both for ourselves and horses, we could not remain there the weather was so sore; and so we came to Canonby, where we lay a good space, and then went to Dumfries, and lay there, who submitted themselves to become the king's majesty's subjects of England. And the morrow after my coming hither, I went into the Moot hall, and making a proclamation in the king of England's name, that all manner of men should come in and make oath to the king's majesty, every man at his peril, they all came and swore, whereof I made a book and sent it to the lord Wharton. And I so continued about ten days. And so making proclamation, that whoso would come in and make oath, and lay-in pledges, to serve the king's majesty of England, he should have our aid and maintenance, and who would not, we would be on them with fire and sword; many of the lards of Nidsdale and Galloway came in and laid-in pledges. But the town of Kirkobree, being 24 miles from Dumfries, refused: insomuch that the lord Wharton moved me, if it were possible, with safety, to give the same town of Kirkobree a preiffe † to burn it. And so we rode thither one night, and coming a little after sun-rising, they who saw us coming barred their gates, and kept their dikes: For the town is diked on both sides, with a gate to the water-ward, and a gate in the over end to the fell-ward. There we lighted on foot and gave the town a sharp onset and assault, and slew one honest man in the town with an arrow; insomuch that one wife came to the ditch, and called for one that would take her husband and save his life. Anthon' Armstrong being ready said, Fetch him to me, and I'll warrant his life. The woman ran into the town, and fetched her husband and brought him through the dike, and delivered him to the said Anthon'; who brought him into England, and ransomed him.—The tutor of Bombye, near adjoining the said town, impeached us with a company of men; and so we drew from the town and gave Bombye the onset, where was slain of our part Clement Taylor; of theirs three, and divers taken, and the rest fled.

And so we returned, seized about 2000 sheep, 200 kye and oxen, and 40 or 50 horses, mares, and colts, and brought the same towards Dumfries. The country beyond the water of Dee gathered, and came to a place called the Forehead ford. So we left all our sheep, and put our worst horsed men

† Proof, trial.

before

before the nowte and naggs, and sent 30 of the best horsed to preeke at the Scots, if they should come over the water, and I to abide with the standard in their relief. Which the Scots perceiving, stayed and came not over. So that we passed quietly that night to Dumfries, leaving the goods in safety with men and good watch. In the morning we repaired to the goods, a mile beyond Dumfries, of intent to have divided and dealt the booty; and some claimed this cow, and some that nagg, to be under assurance, and ran through the goods. Above all, one man of the laird of Empsfielde came amongst the goods, and would needs take one cow, saying he would be stopped by no man, insomuch that one Thomas Taylor, called Tom with the bow, being one of the garrison, and being charged with keeping of the goods, struck the said Scotsman on the head with his bow, so that the blood ran down over his shoulders. Going to his master there, and crying out, his master went with him to the Master Maxwell. The Master Maxwell came, with a great rout after him, and brought the man with the bloody head to me; saying, with an earnest countenance, "Is this, think ye, wele; both to take our goods, and thus to shed our blood?" I, considering the Master at that present to be two for one, thought best to use him and the rest of the Scots with good words, and gentle and fair speeches, for they were determined even there to have given us an onset, and to have taken the goods from us, and to have made that their quarrel. So that I persuaded him and the rest to stay themselves; and for the man that hurt the other man, he should be punished to the example of all others to commit the like, giving him that gave the stroke sharp words before them; and the goods should all be stayed, and none dealt, till the next morrow, and then every man to come that had any claim, and upon proof it should be redressed; and thus willed every man quietly for that time to depart. Upon this we all agreed, and so we left the goods in safe keeping, and came to Dumfries about one of the clock in the afternoon, giving every one of the garrison secret warning to put on their jacks, and bridle and saddle their horses, and to meet me immediately at the bridge end, and so they did. I sent 42 men for the goods, and to meet me at a ford a mile above the town, where we brought the goods over, and so came by Lochmaben, and divided them that night, and brought them to Canonby where we remained before: And thus with wiles we beguiled the Scots."

Afterwards, he goes on: "Considering Canonby to be far from the enemy, for even at that time all Annerdale, Liddisdale, and a great part both of Nidsdale and Galway, were in assurance, and entred to serve the king's majesty of England, saving the lard of Drumlanricke, who never came in nor submitted himself, and with him continued Alexander Carlell lard of Bridekirk, and his son the young laird,—I thought it good to practise some way we might get some hold or castle, where we might lie near the enemy, and to lie within our own strength in the night, where we might all lie down together, and rise together. Thus practising, one Sander Armstrong, son to ill Will Armstrong, came to me and told me he had a man called John Lynton, who was born in the head of Annerdale, near to the Loughwood, being the laird Johnston's chief house, and the said laird and his brother (being the abbot of

 Salside)

Salside) were taken prisoners not long before, and were remaining in England. It was a fair large tower, able to lodge all our company safely, with a barnekin, hall, kitchen, and stables, all within the barnekin, and was but kept with two or three fellows and as many wenches. He thought it might be stolen in a morning at the opening of the tower door; which I required the said Sandee to practise, and as he thought good, either myself to go to it, or that he would take a company and give it a priefe, with as much foresight to make it sure as was possible; for if we should make an offer, and not get it, we had lost it for ever. At last it was agreed that we should go with the whole garrison. We came there about an hour before day; and the greater part of us lay close without the barnekin: But about a dozen of the men got over the barnekin wall, and stole close into the house within the barnekin, and took the wenches and kept them secure in the house till day-light. And at sun-rising, two men and a woman being in the tower, one of the men rising in his shirt, and going to the tower head, and seeing nothing stir about, he called on the wench that lay in the tower, and bad her rise and open the tower door, and call up them that lay beneath. She so doing, and opening the iron door, and a wood door without it, our men within the barnekin brake a little too soon to the door; for the wench perceiving them, leaped back into the tower, and had gotten almost the wood door to, but one got hold of it that she could not get it close to; so the skirmish rose, and we over the barnekin and broke open the wood door, and she being troubled with the wood door left the iron door open, and so we entred and wan the Loghwood; where we found truly the house well purveyed for beef salted, malt, big, havermeal, butter, and cheese. Immediately, taking a short survey of the house, leaving the same in charge with Sandee Armstrong, and giving strict command no man to imbezil or take away any manner of thing, until my lord Wharton's mind and pleasure should be known, I rid to his lordship to Carlisle, who willed me in the king's majesty's name to keep that house to his grace's use; and to ride to Moffet 4 miles off, and make proclamation according to the effect of the proclamation made before in Dumfries; and whoso did others wrong, either by theft, oppression, or otherwise, that I should order it amongst them, and in all weighty causes to refer it to his lordship and his council: which I accomplished to the utmost of my power, and so continued there for some time in the service of the king's majesty as captain of that house, governor and steward of Annerdale under the lord Wharton. In which time, we rode daily and nightly upon the king's majesty's enemies; and amongst others, soon after our coming and remaining there, I called certain of the best-horsed men of the garrison, declaring to them I had a purpose offered by a Scotsman which would be our guide, and that was, to burn Lamington, which we did wholly, took prisoners, and won much good both malt, sheep, horse, and insight, and brought the same to Moffet in the head of Anerdale, and there distributed it, giving every man an oath to bring in all his winnings of that journey, wherein truly the men offended so much their own conscience, very many layning [concealing] things which afterwards I speired out, that after that time my conscience would never suffer me to minister an oath

oath for this, but that which could be ſpeired or known to be brought in, and every man to have a ſhare accordingly.

After that, I made a road in by Crawfurth caſtle to the head of Clyde, where we ſieged a great vaſtil houſe of James Douglaſs, which they held till the men and cattle were all devoured with ſmoke and fire: And ſo we returned to the Loughwood. At which place we remained very quietly, and in a manner in as civil order both for hunting and all paſtime, as if we had been at home in our own houſes. For any man within Annerdale, being within 12 or 16 miles of the Lowghwood, would have reſorted to me to ſeek reformation for any injury committed or done within the ſaid compaſs, which I omitted not, but immediately after the plaint either rode myſelf and took the party complained upon, or ſent for him, and puniſhed or redreſſed, as the cauſe deſerved. And the country was then in good quietneſs: Annerdale, Nidſdale, and a great part of Galway all to the water of Dee, were come in and entred pledges; for then was Kirkobree come in and entred their pledges alſo."

Here next follows, from Mr. Bell's Manuſcript, *An abſtract of the names of the gentlemen and principal headmen of the West Marches of* Scotland, *taken in aſſurance by the lord* Wharton *lord warden of the Weſt Marches of* England, *who made oath and delivered pledges to ſerve the king's majeſty with ſuch number and perſons as are named in their ſeveral bills as followeth*:

ANNERDALE.

Lard of Kirkmighell —	222
Lard of Roſe — —	165
Lard of Hempsfield —	163
Lard of Home Ends —	162
Lard of Wamfrey —	102
Lard of Dunwoddie —	44
Lards of Newby and Gretney	122
Lard of Tinnell —	102
Patric Murray — —	203
Chriſtie Urwen of Coveſhaw	102
Cuthbert Urwen of Robbgill	34
Urwens of Sennerſack —	40
Wat Urwen —	20
Jeffrey Urwen —	93
Thomas Johnſton of Crackburne	64
James Johnſton of Coites	162
Johnſtons of Craggyland	37
Johnſtons of Drieſdell —	46
Johnſtons of Malinſhawe —	65
Gawen Johnſton —	31
Will Johnſton the lard's brother	110
Robin Johnſton of Loughmaben	67
Lard of Gillerſbie —	30
Moffits — —	24
Bells of Toſtints —	142
Bells of Tindells —	212
Sir John Lawſon —	32
Town of Annan —	33
Roomes of Tordephe —	32

ANNERDALE AND GALLOWAY.

Lord Carliſle —	101

ANNERDALE AND CLIDSDALE.

Lard of Applegarth —	242

NIDSDALE.

Mr. Maxwell (and more)	1000

Lard

Lard of Closeburne —	403	Lard of Orcherton —	112
Lard of Lagg —	202	Lard of Carlisle —	206
Lard of Cransfield —	27	Lard of Loughenwarr —	45
Mr. Edward Creighton	10	Tutor of Bombie —	150
Lard of Cowhill —	91	Abbot of New Abbay —	141
Maxwells of Brackenside and vicar of Carlaverick —	310	Town of Dumfries —	201
		Town of Kirkubrie —	36

Lidsdale and Debatable Lands.		Tividale.	
Armstrongs — —	300	Lard of Drumlire —	364
Elwoods — —	74	Caruthers' —	71
Nixons — —	32	Trumbells —	12

Galloway.		Eskdale.	
Lard of Dawbaylie —	41	Batisons and Thomsons	166

Sum of these persons Scotsmen, bound by oath and pledges to serve the king's majesty of England — — 7008

Next *follow divers letters that same year, whilst lord Wharton continued warden.*

Lord Wharton *to lord* Eure.

To the right honourable my very good lord, my lord *Eure* lord warden of the East Marches of England for anempst Scotland, and captain of Berwick:

RIGHT honourable and mine especial good lord, after my most hearty commendations unto your good lordship, advertising in the same, that the 13th of June I received your letters of the 12th of the same, signifying the news from out of Scotland, of the governor and queen's advancing towards Pebles; with others, as your friendly letters purporteth; for which I right heartily thank your lordship: And to advertise you such news as I have from out of Scotland. I am informed by sundry intelligence, that the governor and queen came to Pebles upon Sunday night. The captains of their garrisons, with many other gentlemen, were summoned to be afore the governor yesterday forenoon. I am also informed, that certain guns was set forth of Edinburgh upon Sunday last at afternoon, and intended to be at Pebles yesternight. If they proceed without let or stop, I esteem they may be at Langholme upon Thursday or Friday. Advertising further your lordship, that upon Saturday last afore day, John Maxwell (the lord Maxwell's brother), the lards Drumlangerk, young Loughenwar, and others, with their garrison lying at Loughmaben, and the countrymen thereabouts, to the number

number of 1000 men or thereupon, assembled themselves and came to a place called Tordofe in Scotland, near to the water bank which divideth the realms over against the lordship of Burgh; and being there, sent 100 light horsemen in the day breaking to a town called Glassen upon the water bank in England, and laid the rest in an ambush at the said Tordofe. And the country, being in good watch, escried and encountered their horsemen, where was a sharp skirmish. They have slain one Wattie Bell servant to John Maxwell, two or three of their geldings, and taken one notable borderer; and (thanks be to God) no damage done to any Englishman, town, or goods, except a gelding slain under a servant of mine.—These are such news as I have at this present; and I shall, as I can, attend to advertise your lordship from time to time, requiring semblable from you; knowing well that your honourable wisdom will consider these my said letters and the present affairs of his majesty better than I can advertise or declare the same. I shall notwithstanding endeavour myself to the accomplishment of all things to the best I may, according to my duty. And almighty God send your good lordship good health and prosperous success in honour. At Carlisle the 14th of June 1547.

A PROCLAMATION *made at* Penrith, June 14, 1547, *for raising the power of the Borders.*

FORASMUCH as the governor of Scotland, their queen, and others noblemen of that realm, repaired to Pebles upon Sunday at night last, and also their ordnance coming from Edinburgh, of intent with a great army of the whole body of the said realm of Scotland to do some enterprize against the king's majesty's possessions and subjects upon these West Marches: Therefore, Thomas Wharton knight, lord Wharton, lord warden of the West Marches of England for anempst Scotland, captain of the king's majesty's city of Carlisle, and one of his highness's most honourable council, strictly chargeth and commandeth, in his majesty's name, That all his highness's subjects, horsemen and footmen, within the bounds of the said West Marches, prepare their arrediness and come forward, with ten days victuals, as hath been appointed, so as they may be at Carlisle upon Thursday next at noon, not failing hereof upon pain of death. Written at Carlisle this Tuesday the 14th of June 1547. God save the King.

LETTER *from lord* Wharton June 15, 1547, *to the Gentlemen West Marchers.*

AFTER my hearty commendations unto you, when yesterday I wrote as well proclamations to be made at Penrith, as otherwise in the parts of Westmorland and Cumberland, for the beacons to burn, and the subjects to come forwards to be at Carlisle to-morrow at noon, for the defence and power of Scotland; and forasmuch as I am credibly informed this Wednesday by intelligence from out of Scotland, that the governor, their queen, ordnance, and munition, came to Pebles upon Saturday night last, as I wrote; where, and in those parts, they continue, and as yet the governor hath not so great an army as he looked to have at this present time, and therefore hath determined with a power to come to the town of Dumfries upon Saturday next as is appointed, and to levy the garrisons in all parts over against these West Marches, until they may levy a greater army to do the annoyance they may against the king's majesty's realm and possessions upon these Marches: Trusting, with the leave of God, to put the borderers in these outward parts of these Marches in such watch and areadiness, as we shall be able to defend their sudden enterprizes; and that I would all his majesty's subjects under my rule should live in as much quiet and preservation of themselves and victual, until the occasion shall come by the enemies (for intelligence whereof I shall do so well as I can, the weightiness of this the king's majesty's service considered), I require you to repair home to your own houses, with hearty thanks for your arreadiness and diligence, and also desire you in his majesty's name, to continue at your houses in like arreadiness, with watch of beacons to come forwards, with ten days victuals, upon warning; and that none of his majesty's loving subjects fail hereof, upon pain of death. Be the more earnest for your arreadiness, for that the governor continueth on their Borders for anempst these Marches. And cause these be read openly to all the king's majesty's subjects, every gentleman and officer under his several rule, for their better knowledge of the same. And right heartily fare you well. From Carlisle this Wednesday the 15th of June at four of the clock afternoon, 1547.

Your loving friend
THOMAS WHARTON.

LORD Wharton *to the privy council, the 16th of* June 1547.

To the right honourable the lords of the king's majesty's most honourable privy council:

IN my lawlye and due manner, it may please your most honourable lordships to be advertised, that upon Sunday night the 12th of June the governor and queen of Scots came to the town of Pebles, and no great power with them; the earl of Cassills and George Douglass came with the governor, and then were they his chief counsellors. The same Sunday afternoon was set forth of Edinburgh towards Pebles a demiculverin, and two facons, which came to Pebles upon Monday night. The morrow after, it is said, there shall more ordnance come from Hamilton, whereupon I have espial. The governor had sent letters to the great number of noblemen and gentlemen of the east and west parts of Scotland bysouth the water of Forthe, and also for the captains of the garrisons had against these Marches, to be afore him at Pebles the said Sunday night and Monday aforenoon. I am informed, that the lord Hume and the lard of Bukclugh would not come at his commandment. He sent again, the said Monday in the morning, John Maxwell (the lord Maxwell's brother), the lard Drumlanrick, and young Loughenwar, and other captains of the

‡ garrisons

garrisons which did lie at Loughmaben and Moffet, who came to Loughmaben the said Monday night. And upon Tuesday the morrow after, had afore them the garrisons, and delivered the pledges to the countrymen again, and therewith said that the governor would come himself in person to the town of Dumfries, and bring a sufficient power with him to defend those countries, and in those parts would continue, until he should have his purpose for their relief. The governor and queen appointed to hunt on this side Pebles the 15th and 16th of this instant. I have espial there, to see the manner of their hunting. I am informed that the queen intendeth to return homewards by Hamilton; and that the governor hath appointed to be at Moffet the 17th at night towards Dumfries. And he being in great fear to come in those parts, John Maxwell hath undertaken with others at the governor's appointment to watch and ward his body *. The same John Maxwell made great brags afore the governor and queen at Pebles of his truth to that realm, and his service lately shewed against England, shewing his last enterprise upon Saturday last, whereof I wrote to your lordships in my letters of the 12th, where he got neither honour nor profit, but his chief man Wattie Bell there slain, and the others done as I wrote. The earl of Angus and many others, noblemen of that realm, work in all they may against the Lang-holme and these marches. I trust they dare not enterprise against the same, or any his highness's possessions, without the power of an army, ordnance, and munition for the same. The Scotsmen inhabiting upon his majesty's possessions, which served in these last wars, continue and serve at my commandment, notwithstanding all these great countenances of the enemy's approaching towards them. The old lard of Mangerton, his son, and of the Liddisdales and others, once or twice a week are with me, and shew themselves very willing to serve the king's majesty, and desire that I will appoint with them where their goods shall be relieved, and stand at this present in appearance to me very serviceable men, and well deserving reward. The poor entertainment I can make, I use with them. For they have been, and yet are, continually doing displeasure to the enemies, which has the more appearance to me for their service to be well done. Sundry espials say, that they will levy their army against Langholme and these parts; which if they do not, many the Westmarchers of Scotland will yield themselves to serve the king's majesty at your lordship's most honourable commandment, to the great annoyance of that realm; and that the governor and council know right well.

I did advertise my lords wardens of the East and Middle Marches, by my letters of the 14th, as well of the governor and queen's coming to Pebles, as of the ordnance set forth of Edinburgh, with other news as I had presently then; of intent the rather they might, with their own intelligence, be the more ready to advance the king's majesty's service, according to your lordships

* Dr. Robertson speaking of this governor (James Hamilton earl of Arran) says, Timidity and irresolution were his predominant failings; the one occasioned by his natural constitution, and the other arising from a consciousness that his abilities were not equal to his station. With these dispositions he might have enjoyed and adorned private life; but his public conduct was without courage, or dignity, or confidence. Hist. Scot. i. 83.

 letters

letters unto me the 27th of May.—And almighty God preſerve your lordſhips in health. From Carliſle the 16th of June 1547 ‡.

The truth was, the privy council, or rather the duke of Somerſet who had ſet himſelf at the head of them as lord protector, was meditating an invaſion of Scotland, which in September following the ſaid duke entred with an army of 18000 men, and defeated the Scots at Muſcleburgh. But the next year he was unſucceſsful, and was obliged to abandon Haddington.

About this time the lord Wharton was removed from the wardenſhip. The emoluments which he received from the ſaid office will appear from the following ſchedule;

Offices, fees, and ſervices which the lord Wharton had with the wardenry of the West Marche and captainſhip of the city and caſtle of Carliſle: viz.

For the wardenry *per annum* 600 marks.
Two deputies at 10 *l per annum* each.
Two warden ſerjeants 40 *s per annum* each.
For the captainſhip *per annum* 100 marks.
Three porters at 26 *s* 8 *d per annum* each.
One trumpeter at 16 *d per diem.*
One ſurgeon at 12 *d per diem.*
The receipt of the queen's lands called the Queen's Hames, and foreſt of Englewood, with the ſtewardſhip of the foreſt there.
The demaines of Carliſle.
The office of cuſtome paying yearly the rent of 20 marks to the exchequer.
The ſtewardſhip of the Holme, with the fees of 18 *l* and odd money *per annum.*
The ſtewardſhip of the biſhop's lands; the fees *per annum* 40 *s.*
The ſtewardſhip of the College lands; the fees 26 *s* 8 *d.*
The ſtewardſhip of the late cell of Wetheral, that is annexed to the college; the fee 26 *s* 8 *d.*
The tithe corn of Peareth, Langanby, Scotby, Bochardby, Stainton, Mickle Croſbie, Little Croſbie; paying the old rent to the biſhop and college.
The half fiſhing at Cowgarth, of the college; without rent.
The caſualties belonging to theſe offices, uncertain.

The lord Wharton was ſucceeded by William lord Dacre; during whoſe wardenſhip, there is a collection of letters in manuſcript, from September 1559 to October 1560, which Sir Thomas Carleton ſays was found in the library at Carleton hall after his grandfather's death; ſix other great books of like writing being ſpoiled (he ſays) by rain and wet, and even this greatly damaged †.

‡ Communicated by the reverend Mr. Watſon aforeſaid.

† Now at Ridal Hall.

Out

Out of which we ſhall report the correſpondence of about one month, to ſhew the alertneſs and activity wherewith matters were tranſacted at that time.

THE *lord Protector (the Duke of* Somerſet) *to the lord* Dacre.

To our very good lord the lord Dacre, warden of the Weſt Marches for anempſt Scotland, in haſte, haſte, poſt haſte, for thy life, for thy life, for thy life.

AFTER our hearty commendations to your good lordſhip, By your letters of the 21ſt of this inſtant, we underſtand your opinion on the country there in Scotland about Dumfries; nevertheleſs we let your lordſhip underſtand the ground and circumſtances of our opinion, which is, that the border thereabouts may, and of conſequence muſt be inlarged and incroached upon the enemy, and therefore we would you conformed your ſole purpoſe and intent of ſervice thereto; which thing can no way be better brought to paſs than in this manner: The Almains, in number two thouſand, very valiant ſoldiers, which ſhall be ſent to you ſhortly from Newcaſtle together with Sir Thomas Holcroft, with the force of your wardenry (which we would were advanced to the moſt ſtrength of horſemen that might be), ſhall make the attempt to Loughmaben, being of no ſuch ſtrength but that it may be ſkailed with ladders, whereof beforehand we would ye cauſed ſecretly ſome number to be provided, or elſe undermined with the pyke axe; and ſo taken, either to be kept for the king's majeſty, or otherwiſe to be defaced and taken from the profits of the enemy. And in like manner the houſe of Carlaverok to be uſed. During which time Dumfries may be either burned or taken, as occaſion ſhall require. For this we are aſſured, that the thing being kept ſecret, this power ſhall well be able to attempt any enterprize in all thoſe parts, if it be to Douglaſs; eſpecially ſince the French power, for lack of victual, ſhall not be able to come thither being ſo far diſtant, and the country not able to find them it. Wherefore, firſt of all, your lordſhip muſt of neceſſity give your ſole ſtudy hereunto, and receive our direction having ſo good ground and reaſon. And for this purpoſe ye muſt with all ſpeed make proviſion of victual all manner of ways ye can poſſibly deviſe, and in ſuch manner as the preparation thereof diſcloſe not the purpoſe; for therein we think the advantage ſhall be great, to have the matter ſuddenly attempted. And next this, your wardenry muſt be put in arreadineſs to be preſt at one hour's warning, not revealing unto any of them the purpoſe. For your lack of things pertaining to the munition, we ſhall take order the ſame ſhall be ſent to you. And to the anſwer of this letter we pray your lordſhip make convenient ſpeed. And ſo we bid the ſame heartily farewell. From our houſe at Odyham the 27th of September 1549.

Your loving friend,

E. SOMERSET.

P. S. This enterprize we would the rather were advanced at this time, becauſe now at the abandoning of Haddington we may keep our credit in Scotland.

land. And for the number of Almains, if ye shall desire to have the more number; signify it, and we shall answer thereunto.

Lord Dacre *to Sir* Thomas Holcroft.

Right worshipful, in my most hearty manner I commend me unto you: And having received letters from my lord protector's grace, for a service to be done on these borders, wherein I trust you shall be party; and knowing your inclination is to have things done with such wisdom and circumspection, as they may redound to the advancement of the king's majesty's service and affairs, and to the comfort of yourself and such as shall go about them; Therefore I have sent unto you this bearer my servant, to shew you the present state of things here, and to have such further conference with you in these affairs as it shall please you. To whom I pray you give credit therein. And thus I bid you heartily farewell. Fr m the king's majesty's castle of Carlisle the 3d of October.

Your loving friend assuredly,
W. Dacre.

Lord Dacre *to the lord Protector.*

To my lord Protector's grace, in haste, haste, post haste, for thy life, for thy life, for thy life, haste, haste.

May it please your grace to be advertised, that this present day I received your grace's letter of the 27th of September last, whereby your grace seemeth not to allow mine opinion touching the affair on these borders, presently to be put in use against Scotland, but declaring the ground and circumstance of your grace's opinion to be, that the border may and of congruence must be inlarged, and that with the number of 2000 Almains to be sent hither with Sir Thomas Holcroft and the power of this wardenry, your grace's purpose towards Loughmaben, Carlaverok, and Dumfries may be atchieved, your pleasure is that I should conform my whole purpose and intent of office thereto, and that I shall receive your grace's direction in that behalf; willing me further to make provision of victuals and ladders, and to put the power of the wardenry in arreadiness; and all this to be done in such manner, as the preparation thereof disclose not the purpose: May it please your grace to understand, that according to my duty and charge committed unto me, my whole study is and always hath been applied, to inlarge the borders here, and incroach, and annoy the enemy; and so according to my simple knowledge, I have as well before, as in my last letters declared to your grace, the most easy and ready way and least chargeable that I could imagine for that intent. And now albeit your grace shall in this and all other find me (for the advancement of the king's majesty's honour and service, and the accomplishment of your grace's direction) neither to spare my body, lands, nor goods, nor the bodies of my children, kinsfolk, nor friends; yet I consider my duty is, is, to open all such things, as either may hinder or frustrate any your grace's purposes of service enterprized, to the intent that the cause may be by your grace's politic wisdom foreseen and provided for, and that the declaration thereof may be my discharge. First, As in my former letters for victuals, I have conferred with discreet and expert gentlemen (not disclosing the purpose, nor no semblable thereof), and grains be here at this instant so skant, that wheat is presently sold for 40*s* the quarter, malt for 26*s* the quarter, and other corns of excessive prices, yet the soil unapt for these kinds of grains, it is not to be had in the country for money; so that the provision for that purpose must needs be had in some other parts, and either transported hither by sea, or carried by land, and that with a great foresight, or else there shall neither be sufficient for the people that be here already, nor yet the country cannot be able to serve soldiers at reasonable prices as their wages shall leave them: And for this purpose, if it shall please your grace to appoint some convenient man to provide it where it may best be had, he shall have my assistance, advice and counsel as appertaineth. Also, the nature of the ground and country is such, that we shall be able to have few or none other carriages but only upon horses; and the winter is here so fallen already, that it can be no worse; divers waters which we have to pass having no bridges over them, so that all our speed in that point must hang upon fair weather. And yet if these and divers other were put out of doubt, the country of Scotland standing as it doth at this present, it shall be very like that the powers of Frenchmen and Scots shall be at us before we can finish our enterprise. Nevertheless, as prest at commandment to all assays, if it please your grace to appoint the provision of grains, and other such victuals as be necessary, and give order that the strangers come not hither, nor that their coming be not bruited (which is most danger of revealing the enterprise), till all things may be brought in the best arreadiness that can be; I shall in the mean time endeavour me to have the whole power of the wardenry (advancing as much horsemen as I can) in arreadiness, and such other things as I am able to do here, for the furniture of the purpose, with as much diligence as I can use. The grains that were provided here be utterly lost *, and will serve for no purpose, as the keepers thereof have informed me.—Whereas your grace seemeth by this enterprize now at the abandoning of Haddington, the rather to keep credit in Scotland; I suppose the garrisons named in my former letters should annoy the enemy, renew credit, and bring the borders in such plight this winter season, that the provision being made ready, your grace in the spring of the year should bring to pass such things as cannot now well be done. And this, under correction, I think, as I have before declared, to be the least charges and most commodity to the service. As knoweth almighty God, who grant your grace long life

* This seems to be intended as a slur upon the lord Wharton. In some following letters, lord Dacre advises the council to sell those decayed provisions to several persons at a price then proposed; To which the council returned in answer, that the lord Wharton would take those provisions in his own hands, that so the king might be no loser.

and

and good health, with good and honourable succeſs in all affairs. At the king's majeſty's caſtle of Carliſle, the 3d of October, 1549.

A LETTER of the ſame effect and date was ſent to my lord great maſter (Saintjohn); with all the conſiderations before expreſſed fully declared; requeſting his lordſhip to be the meane, that the importance thereof might be pondered, and preparation and proviſion had, before the attempting of any enterpriſe.

THE *earl of* Rutland *(lord warden of the Eaſt and Middle Marches) to the lord* Dacre.

MY very good lord, after my right hearty commendations; Becauſe I am informed that the power of Scotland, with the French, are minded to invade this realm, about the 20th day of this month, to devaſt the borders, whereby the king's majeſty ſhould be unable to keep garriſons to annoy them this winter; and foraſmuch as I am uncertain in what part they mind to attempt their enterprize, either upon your charge or mine, therefore I thought good to admoniſh your lordſhip of the ſame; to the intent that if they ſhall approach and purpoſe to annoy upon your part, I having knowledge of the ſame may forthwith repair to aid and aſſiſt you; and upon the contrary, if the enemy ſhall come towards me, your lordſhip receiving warning thereof may likewiſe ſupply me with the power of your charge; which I pray your good lordſhip may be put in ſuch arreadineſs, as upon one hour's warning the ſame may be ready to advance forwards in the ſervice of the king's majeſty. And where heretofore your lordſhip hath written unto me, for munition and ordnance lacking at Carliſle, I ſhall deſire your lordſhip to ſend hither the clerk of the ordnance there, with a note of all ſuch munition and ordnance as remain within his charge; to the intent I may take order for the ſupply thereof accordingly. Thus fare your lordſhip right heartily well. From the camp beſide Roxborough the 4th of October 1549.

Your lordſhip's aſſured friend,

H. RUTLAND.

THE 9th of October the lord Dacre ſent to my lord of Rutland the clerk of the ordnance with letters for ſupply of the lack of munition and ordnance, according to his book thereof made, referring credit to the bearer for the neceſſity of the premiſſes, and ready diſpatch of the ſame: Declaring further, that upon like intelligence, he had given order for the arreadineſs of the power of his wardenry, before the arrival of my lord of Rutland's letters.

Which order was taken, as well by proclamation generally, as by ſpecial letters to all the gentlemen and officers within his wardenry as by a copy of the ſame hereafter written appeareth:

A Pro-

A Proclamation.

At the king's majesty's castle of Carlisle the 5th of October, Anno Regis Edwardi sexti tertio, 1549.

Whereas the lord warden of these West Marches foranempst Scotland is informed by credible spials, that the queen and governor of Scotland have presently assembled a great army toward some part of the king's majesty's dominions; for the resistance whereof it is meet and requisite to put the country in perfect arreadiness: Wherefore the said lord warden strictly chargeth and commandeth, in the king our sovereign lord's name all and every his majesty's subjects within the limits and precincts of the said wardenry of West Marches, between 16 and 60, as well footmen as horsemen, to be in arreadiness furnished as appertaineth, and victualled for ten days, to set forwards upon one hour's warning, by writing, beacons burning, or otherwise, upon pain of death. And that all such as have charge of keeping and watching any beacons within the precincts aforesaid, have vigilant respect and regard unto their charge, upon like pain; so as in due time they may give warning by the same as occasion shall require.

A LETTER *to the same effect to the gentlemen West Marchers.*

After my hearty commendations, Forasmuch as I am credibly informed that the governor of Scotland doth presently assemble a great army, to invade some part of these the king's majesty's dominions, for the resistance whereof it is meet to put the country in arreadiness; wherefore these shall be strictly to charge and command you in the king our sovereign lord's name, that ye and every of you, upon sight hereof, take such order and direction, that all your servants, tenants, and others within your rowmes (rooms), rules, and offices, between 16 and 60 years, as well horsemen as footmen, be in arreadiness fully furnished as appertaineth, and victualled for ten days, to set forwards upon one hour's warning, by writing, burning of beacons, or otherwise; so that the contrary do not hinder the king's majesty's service, as occasion thereof shall require. Fail not hereof, as ye tender the advancement of the same, with the quietness of the country, and will answer to the contrary at your peril. I bid you heartily farewell. At the king's majesty's castle of Carlisle, the 8th of October 1549.

Your loving friend,
W. DACRE.

SIR Thomas Holcroft *to lord* Dacre.

Pleaseth your lordship to be advertised, that I have received your letters by this bearer your servant. And where my lord Protector's grace is minded of an exploit upon the West borders and the attempting of Loughmaben, for

 the

the which I doubt not your lordſhip ſhall do it with much honour, ſo that we may be well furniſhed with victual and carriages: And as I know the weſt borders to be a ſtraite country, and now in the winter-time full of moſſes, moraſſes, and waters; I do not know how we ſhall attempt the thing, unleſs we carry with us victual to endure the time we ſhall lie without; and how ſuddenly waters will be up, your lordſhip knoweth it beſt. And as the whole matter reſteth upon your lordſhip's hands, ſo I doubt not there ſhall be a good proviſion of victual and carriages for the ſame. For otherwiſe I ſhall aſſure your lordſhip, having Almains and ſtrangers with you, ye ſhall have more buſineſs with them lacking their victuals and their carriages, than ye ſhall have trouble with the enemy. And as your lordſhip is able to proceed, ſo to advertiſe my lord's grace; and if ye be not able to fulfil theſe things, let the matter be referred to the ſpring-time of the year; and in the mean time to provide all things for the ſame, as my lord's grace ſhall think convenient. And as your lordſhip is in towardneſs of the ſame, I pray you that I may be advertiſed from time to time. For if your lordſhip ſhall be furniſhed with the neceſſaries for the ſame, I doubt not your lordſhip ſhall do it and more with much honour. Before the 20th of this inſtant, your lordſhip may not look for me; becauſe there is a purpoſe pretended by the Scots for the invading of this realm. But as ſoon as I ſee to what end their purpoſe is, I ſhall not fail to come unto your lordſhip; truſting your lordſhip will put all things in arreadineſs. And if their purpoſe be towards your lordſhip, I ſhall not fail to be with you with an honeſt power, leſt they be able to attempt any thing there. And thus praying to God to ſend your lordſhip good health with much honour. From Berwick the 7th day of October 1549.

Your lordſhip's to command,
THOMAS HOLCROFT.

LORD Dacre *to the lord Protector.*

To the right honourable my lord Protector's grace; in haſte, haſte, poſt haſte, for thy life, for thy life, haſte, haſte.

PLEASE it your grace to receive here incloſed ſuch news and intelligence as this day I received forth of Scotland, from a ſpial of mine who was in Edinburgh on Friday laſt; and I have made him repair thither again and bring me further word of their enterprize, as ſoon as he can ſurely perceive where they intend the ſame. And whereas I lately advertiſed your grace of the decay of the walls of the city and caſtle of Carliſle, yeſterday 14 yards of the city wall on the ſide towards Scotland, by reaſon that it ſtood on a ſpring, the weather being wet, and the wall old and in ruin, did ſhoot and fall to the ground the one ſide from the other, and divers parts of the wall is like to do the ſame, which cannot be repaired and made up this winter; wherefore I ſhall be forced to cauſe the watch be ſtronger laid in that place: Humbly beſeeching your grace that I may know your grace's pleaſure, as well in the premiſſes, as in my late letters to your grace concerning the ſame. And thus almighty

God preserve your grace in health, with most increase of honour. From Carlisle the 8th of October 1549.

Your grace's humble at commandment,
WILLIAM DACRE.

THE *intelligence sent in the same letter.*

Honerable Sir,

Efter right hertie commendationes please it your worshipe to wit, I was in Edynburghe this last Friday the fourte of Octobre; and for tidings, there is an galyon cumyt owt of Fraunce, and twa ships with mekle money, whilk causes this army to ryse of Scotland, and charged all manner of men to be in aredines on 24 houres warninge. And the erle of Huntley and the erle of Argyll hais promised to bring fyve thousand ma men nor ever ther faders dyd. And therle of Angwish getts Arboth againe to taike the lieutenantship upon hyme. As I am advertised, ther is writting comyt to the quene and the governor, owt of Fraunce, that ther shall cum within 15 days 10 thousand men of warr. Ther is an advertisement cumyt, that an host will be in at this border in this light. And please your worship that I and the gentlemanne mak yow further service, advertise us with this bearer, whilk shall let for no expences or travaile when time cumys. And the gentleman and I be syker where we ryde or gang, goods and servands. And I pray your worship's answer of the premisses. For I purposed to have cumyt to yow and durst not for fear of my life. And as ye wold have me doande in all things, advertise with this berer, which shal be at power, God willande, wha everlastinge have your worship in keaping. By your servant,

Ye wait wha.

FROM *my lord Great Master.*

To my very good lord the lord Dacre, &c.

I commend me heartily unto your good lordship, and have perceived by your letters of the 3d of October the discourse the duke of Somerset made to you, and what enterprize he would have had you to have made upon that discourse, and your answer made thereto, and what was your further advice, albeit my said lord was not contented therewith but willed you to advance his device, to the doing whereof ye lack victuals and carriages, which must needs be considered, and so shall be by my lords of the council, who mind to be privy of all the proceedings of the borders, and to give their advices to the order of the same, as you shall further perceive in short space*: Thinking your lordship take good heed, the mean while, of the earl Bothwell and other

* This is an intimation of the meditated downfal of the lord Protector, who is here styled barely *duke of Somerset.*

assured

assured men; by whom for trust ye may soonest be deceived, as you know well. And I pray you devise with me by your letters, what way ye think best to increase the king's borders into strength, and then how ye may win and hold of the enemy's ground that may do you service, evermore making your own borders strong for the defence of yourself and of that you win, and that manner of increase shall strengthen the king's borders and inrich his people, and give them courage to march upon the enemy for gaining of ground and cattle, wherein I would gladly learn how it might best be done. Thus fare you heartily well. Written the eighth of October 1549.

Your lordship's loving friend,

W. SEINCTJOHN.

THE *earl of* Rutland *to lord* Dacre.

To my very good lord the lord Dacre, &c. in haste, haste, post haste, for thy life, for thy life, for thy life.

MY very good lord; After my most hearty commendations, understanding the gathering of the Scots purposing to invade this realm, and doubting yet which way they will draw, I thought good to signify the same unto you; praying you in case they winne this way, ye send some relief out of your office; and if they repair towards you, I shall be ready to send that way such a company as I doubt not but ye will be satisfied. Thus I am the more earnest, because as ye know the state of the realm, it is wisdom to foresee the worst, and to defend these parts for our own discharge, which as far as my power will extend shall not be lacking to do, that shall be most and best for the service of the king's majesty; and so I trust your lordship will do the like. And thus I wish your lordship well to fare. From Berwick the 18th of October 1549.

Your good lordship's assured friend,

HERRY RUTLAND.

LORD Dacre *to the earl of* Rutland.

To the right honourable the earl of Rutland, &c. in haste, haste, post haste, with all diligence possible.

Right honourable and my very good lord, after my right hearty commendations; I have received your letters of the 18th of this instant, and like as I look if the army of Scotland should march towards these borders to have competent supply of your lordship; even so if they come to your marches, I have already taken order, how such relief as may be furnished within this office shall repair unto you. Assuring your lordship further, that ye shall not fail to find me in all things both ready and willing to my power, to advance the king's majesty's service as shall appertain; and so much the rather, considering the state of the realm, as in your said letters is expressed. And yet, as I have advertisement, all things (thanks to God) be in such case at this present, that neither we need

† greatly

greatly to doubt the sequel thereof, nor our enemies thereby take any hope of advantage, but all to be well and quiet, which I pray God send. Thus, advertising your lordship that ye lose much time in my letters to Newcastle, but that the post of Morpeth should convey them to Hexham *; I commit your lordship to the tuition of almighty God. At the king's majesty's castle of Carlisle the 22d of October 1549.

Your good lordship's own assured,

W. Dacre.

THE *Council to the lord* Dacre.

To our very good lord the lord Dacre, lord warden of the West Marches, in haste, haste, for thy life, post haste.

After our most hearty commendations unto your good lordship, Understanding by your letters of the 8th of this instant, that the Scots have made proclamation for assemblies of men, minding as they bruit to invade England; albeit we doubt not but your lordship doth so consider all things, as you will be ready to the defence of your charge as much as may be in you, yet for that ye write that some part of the walls of Carlisle be fallen down, we have thought good to put your lordship in remembrance, both to cause the dyke be cleansed, and all other things foreseen and done as may be most for your surety: And also to advertise you for your better aid, you may have 800 Almains, which be now in their journey northward; for whom, if ye mind to have their service, you must cause victuals to be provided; and advertising us with speed what ye will do therein; we will give undelayed order for their coming to you. In the mean time, we effsoons pray you foresee your things with your accustomed diligence. And in case of any such need you may confer by letters with our very good lord the earl of Rutland, for having or giving succours the one to the other, as the case shall require. Thus fare your good lordship most heartily well. From Windsor the 13th of October 1549.

Your lordship's assured friends,

Thomas Cant', R. Rich Canc', W. Seinctjohn, W. Northe, John Warwyke, F. Shrewsbery, Thomas Southampton, Anthony Wentworthe, Thomas Cheyne, William Paget, William Petre.

P. S. We wrote of late unto you of our doings touching the duke of Somerset; wherein albeit the said duke, for maintenance of his former and ill doings, travailed as much as he might to stir the people and make tumults, yet the king's majesty's person (thanks be to God) is in surety, and the duke committed to ward according to his deservings, without any stir. Which things being thus well begun, shall, we trust, turn to the great quiet and commodity of the whole realm.

As for the device of an enterprize upon Loughmaben, *&c.* ye may defer it to a more proper time.

* Dispatches of the utmost importance appear all along to have been intrusted to the ordinary conveyance of the post.

EARL

Earl *of* Rutland *to the lord* Dacre.

To our very good lord the lord Dacre, lord warden of the West Marches; haste, haste, post haste, for thy life, for thy life, for thy life.

After our most hearty commendations unto your lordship, Where we are presently advertised that the enemy intendeth to attempt some of the king's majesty's places or to invade his realm, and in such a readiness for the same as they have taken all the oxen of Howdyam for drawing of their artillery, and to set forward towards us upon Monday next: Wherefore this shall be to require your lordship to put your whole power in such a readiness, as they may draw themselves to be at Warke upon Tuesday night next coming, whereby to defend and safeguard the king's majesty's realm and places in Scotland. We think it good ye gave knowledge unto my lord Bothwell, so as he may join together with your powers, and to come forward. And if the enemy do alter his purpose, and come towards you, your lordship shall be sure we will not fail to come unto you for your better relief. And thus we desire your lordship to use a great diligence for the better service of the king's majesty in the same. And thus we bid your lordship heartily well to fare. From Berwick the 25th of October 1549.

Your loving friends,

Herry Rutland, Thos Holcroft, John Harrington, Francis Leek.

P. S. We are informed the stay of the enemy hitherto hath been, for that the earls of Huntley and Argyle as yet be not come on this side Sterling; and that the earl of Argyle hath lost a great number of his company by water.

Lord Dacre *to the earl of* Rutland.

To the right honourable and my very good lord the earl of Rutland, lord warden of the East and Middle Marches for anempst Scotland; in haste, post haste, with all possible diligence, haste, haste.

Right honourable and my very good lord, after most hearty commendations, This present day at eight of clock at night I received your letters of the 25th of this instant, having no little marvel, that letters of such importance should come with so small speed, the default whereof were meet to be examined amongst the posts as convenient leisure should serve thereunto: Advertising your lordship, that having spials about the Scottish army, who I trust will bring me word and knowledge what way they draw, as soon as they proceed in the purposed enterprize; if they come towards your charge, I shall supply you with all the tried horsemen within this wardenry, whom I have appointed to wait on my son George for the same, being the power on these borders that are able to do you any service, which I trust shall be addressed thither in such sort as they may be with you in good time. And as for the footmen, they

they dwell ſo far off, that firſt coming hither by general warning, and then to repair unto you, they ſhould neither come in due time, nor yet upon their arrival be able to ſerve after ſuch ſore travel, without furniture of victuals, being uncertain as yet what way they will draw. And beſides that the country of the enemy adjoining, as I am informed by my ſpials, be very few ſtirred or called off the borders, I have thought it not convenient utterly to disfurniſh theſe frontiers. Not doubting if they ſhall make their enterpriſe upon the ſame, but your lordſhip will remember me with a ſupply as ſhall appertain. And according to your letters, I have given knowledge to the earl Bothwell this night by poſt. Thus I beſeech the living Lord preſerve your lordſhip in health, with proſperous ſucceſs in all affairs. At the king's majeſty's caſtle of Carliſle the 27th of October 1549.

Your good lordſhip's own aſſured,
WILLIAM DACRE.

THE *earl of* Rutland *to the lord* Dacre.

To our very good lord the lord Dacre, lord warden of the Weſt Marches for anempſt Scotland; in haſte, haſte, poſt haſte, for thy life, for thy life, haſte, haſte.

AFTER our hearty commendations, This day we received your lordſhip's letters of the 27th of this inſtant, wherein we perceive the ſlowth of the poſts, which indeed hath continued now for a long time, and ſurely we will be glad to remedy the ſame as we may, if your lordſhip will for your part do the ſemblable. As for the arreadineſs of your horſemen, we like well; and the coming of the footmen, as you ſay they ſhould be to ſmall purpoſe, therefore we be in opinion that for them to remain for the defence of that border, order be taken. Neverthelesſ, perceiving the enemy have deferred their purpoſe, we believe they will not come at all into England; but if they come forwards, they will no further than Lauder. Howbeit, becauſe we be uncertain of them, and doubting as yet which way they will draw; if they come towards you, we ſhall relieve you both with horſemen and footmen, praying your lordſhip in caſe we come that way, ye will take order for a ſufficient maſs of victuals; and upon their drawing towards us, we truſt ye will ſend your power as ſhall appertain. And as you hear of the enemy, ſo we pray you advertiſe us with ſpeed. Thus fare your good lordſhip right heartily well. From Berwick the 29th of October 1549.

Your good lordſhip's own aſſured,
Herry Rutland, Thomas Holcroft, John Harrington,
Francis Leeke, James Crofte.

The truth was, the privy council, after their reaſſuming the reins of government, laboured hard for a peace, which was then well nigh effected, between England and France, in which Scotland was included.

But

But the ordering of the DEBATEABLE LAND happening not to be provided for in the treaty; it became a further bone of contention between the two ſnarling parties, as will appear from ſome few other of the lord Dacre's letters as followeth:

Lord Dacre *to the lord* Maxwell.

To the right honourable the lord Maxwell, warden of the Weſt Marches of Scotland anempſt England.

After my lawful commendations unto your lordſhip, Whereas the ſame hath heretofore written as well unto me as to my ſon in mine abſence, for a meeting on the Marches to redreſs injuries committed ſince the concluſion of the peace, for the better confirmation and performance of the ſame, which I am ready on my part to accompliſh accordingly upon any convenient day to be appointed thereunto; nevertheleſs, ſince my return into the country, I am informed that ye go about, contrary to the effect of your ſaid letters, to levy a power to devaſt the batable land, miniſtring thereby ſuch occaſion of pik as I would wiſh your wiſdom ſhould foreſee, and conſider to what inconvenience and end the ſame may grow: Aſſuring your lordſhip, that like as I never thought to attempt or procure any matter to the violation or breach of the peace, but rather to travel with my little power to continue the ſame to the glory of God and the preſervation of the common wealth, whereunto every good man ought to have ſpecial regard; even ſo, foraſmuch as I know not the king my ſovereign lord and maſter's pleaſure therein, for the which I have preſently written, looking for ſuch advertiſement in that behalf as ſhall ſtand with the concluſion of the peace and your lawful contentation, by which concluſion all forts and pieces comprehended within the ſame have been delivered and not taken by force, I am determined by God's grace according to my duty of allegiance (if ye proceed to your preteneed purpoſe) to reſiſt your violence and force as occaſion ſhall require; truſting that as my cauſe, ſo ſhall I be able to defend the ſame as appertaineth. Thus I commit your lordſhip to the tuition of almighty God. From the king's majeſty's caſtle of Carliſle, the 7th day of Auguſt 1550.

Your lordſhip's lawfully,
William Dacre.

Lord Maxwell *to the lord* Dacre.

To the right honourable my lord Dacre lord warden of the Weſt Marches of England.

After my leſul commendations, This is to certify your lordſhip I am commanded by my lord governor and lords of the ſecret council to advertiſe you, there is a power of men to be raiſed for ſuppreſſion of ſuch fugitives, themſelves, houſes, and goods, as do now preſently inhabit the batable ground, contrary

contrary to the virtue of the peace, and the ancient custom that hath been used on these borders, as the said fugitives do daily trouble the true subjects of this realm, and as far as in them lies give occasion to break the peace. My lord, our repairing to the batable land is for no annoyance nor molestation of the king your sovereign's realm nor subjects, neither are we minded to proceed in any sort farther than we have been accustomed to do in the late peace. And what will be your part with the subjects under your charge in these the premisses above written, I desire you to give me advertisement in writing by this bearer John Ireland. Thus I beteich you to God. From Loughmaben this 9th of August 1550.

Yours lawfully,
ROBERT MAXWELL.

LORD Dacre *to the lord* Maxwell.

To the right honourable the lord Maxwell, lord warden of the West Marches of Scotland.

AFTER my leful commendations unto your lordship, Perceiving by your letters that ye are determined according to the council's direction (as you say) to proceed to your purposed enterprize, without respect to what inconvenience the same may grow, whereof I do not a little marvel, that their wisdoms will minister such occasion of breach of the peace which I would be loth should happen, especially on these marches where I have charge. And therefore I have already required you by my last letters to spare your proceedings therein, with consideration of the sequel of the same, till I may know the king's majesty my master's pleasure in the premisses, which I look for within these eight days, and thought ye would have done accordingly; assuring your lordship that my lords our fathers have used (which I have seen) in time of war to take abstinence till the king their master's pleasures were known, sometimes by the space of two months, for matters of weightier importance than this is. Not doubting but ye will conform yourself thereunto accordingly. And thus I commit your lordship to God. From Carlisle the 9th of August 1550.

Your lordship's lefully,
W. DACRE.

LORD Dacre *to the Privy Council.*

To the right honourable and my singular good lords, the lords of the king's majesty's most honourable privy council; haste, haste, post haste, for thy life.

MAY it please your honourable lordships to be advertised, that since my late arrival in these parts, I have been credibly informed by my spials, that the governor and council of Scotland go about to levy a power to destroy and burn the batable land; whereupon I addressed my letters unto the lord Maxwell,

well, a copy whereof I ſend your lordſhips herewith, which he hath ſent to the governor by poſt, but as yet hath received no anſwer again, as he hath advertiſed me by his meſſenger who brought me the letters here incloſed; whereby, and by my ſpials, I do perceive that they intend indelayedly to proceed to their purpoſed enterprize; whereunto, as I have written to him, I am determined with God's grace and the power of theſe borders to make ſuch reſiſtance as I can, according to your late letters to me directed for the ſame, bearing date the 22d of May laſt, if upon my further requeſt they do not deſiſt and forbear: Humbly beſeeching your lordſhips to advertiſe me of your determinate pleaſure herein with all poſſible haſte.—I am credibly informed, that certain of the brethren and ſons of Richard Greyme, and divers others dwelling upon the batable land, are determined to become Scotchmen, if England do not reſiſt the enemy, and aid them as occaſion ſhall require; and ſo they have declared to their friends of England. As knoweth almighty God, who proſper your honourable lordſhips with increaſe of honour. From the king's majeſty's caſtle of Carliſle the 9th of Auguſt 15;0.

Your honourable lordſhips at commandment,

William Dacre.

Lord Dacre *to the Privy Council.*

To the moſt honourable and my ſingular good lords, the lords of the king's majeſty's moſt honourable privy council; haſte, haſte, poſt, for thy life haſte.

May it pleaſe your honourable lordſhips to be advertiſed, that on the 12th of this inſtant in the morning, the lord Maxwell with the lord Johnſton and a band of 400 horſemen, with a power of Scotland to the number of 2000, came to the batable land, to a houſe of Sandie Armſtrang; which houſe I had cauſed, for fear of raſing with gunpowder, to be filled with peats and turves, and fire to be put to them, ſo that no powder could be put to it. And having no knowledge from your lordſhips, nor anſwer of my ſeveral letters for this purpoſe, whereof I am much amarvelled, the juſtices of aſſize being here preſent I could not well know what ſhould beſt be done, either to reſiſt them with force (which ſeemed your pleaſure in your former letters), and ſo to have adjourned the aſſizes, which ſhould have been inconvenient, conſidering that in three years before there was none aſſize nor gaol delivery here, and alſo thereby to put in danger the peace lately concluded, or elſe to ſuffer ſuch as have uſed themſelves as ſubjects to the king (whom by your letters I was commanded to defend) to be devaſted. Yet as the things ſtood, thinking to do good both ways, I ſent my ſons and Sir Thomas Dacre with a company of horſemen and footmen with them to the Borders, commanding them without great occaſion not to paſs the bounds of England; and I remained in Carliſle with the reſt of the power, ready to ſet forth as I ſhould be occaſioned, and willed the judges to proceed to the aſſizes. And as in all my former letters to the lord Maxwell, I declared that I muſt defend the king's ſubjects, even ſo

5 now

now I caufed my fon to fend a meffage to him (either power looking upon the other) that I was amarvelled of his ufage of any fuch force, confidering the peace; and that the councils of both realms had not concluded any fpecial appointment for that purpofe. Whereupon feeing they could not rafe the houfe, by reafon of the fire that was put in and about it by my commandment, and thinking by likelihood they fhould not work all their will without refiftance, they returned without doing any harm, fave the burning of a thatched cote houfe that the Frenchmen burnt. And no Englifhman had to do with them, either in pricking or otherwife; but they of the debatable land pricked with them and have taken three or four of them. Befeeching your lordfhips, that as well in this for the time to come, as alfo in all fuch matters of importance coming upon a fuddenty, I may be anfwered and know your pleafures, with more expedition than I have had heretofore; otherwife I fhall be driven in fuch things, either to jeopard the violation of the peace (if they intend to pick it), or elfe the difhonour of the king's majefty and the harm of thefe his marches. It fhall be moft neceffary I know your pleafures in the batable land, fpecially now at our meeting for redrefs. For neither I will fuffer the warden of Scotland to anfwer for it, becaufe I will not affirm it to be Scotland; nor will they on the contrary confent that it fhall be England: which unprovided for, fhall bring the marches in great miforder, and be occafion that no redrefs fhall be had, nor punifhment for them which be the notable offenders. And thus I commit, *&c.* From the king's majefty's caftle of Carlifle the 13th of Auguft 1550.

Your honourable lordfhips at commandment,

W. Dacre.

Lord Dacre *to the Privy Council.*

To the right honourable and my fingular good lords, the lords of the king's majefty's moft honourable privy council; hafte, poft hafte, with all poffible diligence.

May it pleafe your honourable lordfhips to be advertifed, that having in my former letters declared the ftate of the batable land, and the doings of the Scots againft the inhabitants thereof; now, fince the return of the faid Scots, Sandye Armftrang hath been with me, and faith how that he perceiveth the Scots to be fo bent in malice, that they will yet more purfue him, and defireth me either to promife him aid of thefe marches when he fhall need thereof, or elfe he muft be forced to take fuch appointment with Scotland, as he and other dwelling there heretofore for their fafeguard have ufed to do. Wherein I deferred any anfwer, confidering I cannot aid him (except there be fome other conclufion in this peace for the bateable land, than hath been in other treaties before) without the plain violation of the fame. And if he fhall turn him for his fafeguard to Scotland, then the king's majefty fhall lofe his fervice, who hath ferved very dutifully all the time of thefe wars, and the habitation of that ground where he and his band dwelleth fhall be very noifome to this realm.

 Wherefore

Wherefore I most humbly beseech your lordships, that I may know your pleasures herein, with such expedition as the importance thereof doth require. Furthermore, Monsieur De Fermes the lieutenant of the Frenchmen was at the time of this assembly at the Armitage my lord Bothwell's house, and there hath caused hay to be won, to the intent (as it seemeth) for the furniture of some horsemen that they purpose to place there this winter season. And thus I commit your lordships to the tuition, &c. From the king's majesty's castle of Carlisle the 15th of August 1550.

Your honourable lordships at commandment.

WILLIAM DACRE.

THE *Privy Council to the lord* Dacre.

To our very good lord the lord Dacre, lord warden of the West Marches of England for anempst Scotland, haste, with all possible diligence.

AFTER our right hearty commendations to your good lordship; Upon the advertisement given us by your last letters of the preparation made by the Scots to invade the batable ground, we have certified the French ambassador of it, who hath also received letters out of Scotland conformable to your said advertisement. And nevertheless he hath dispatched in post a servant of his into Scotland with letters, to see whether he can stay them of their purpose. And although we would your lordship should provide as much as lieth in you, that no occasion be given them on your behalf to attempt any such thing, yet in case they will needs go through with it, we think it meet (as we wrote to your lordship before) that you resist and lett them by force again, if you find and perceive yourself strong enough and able to do it. And likewise we require you to take good heed to all other the king's places committed to your charge, lest the Scots might bear you in hand one thing and mean another. Aug. 17, 1550.

Your lordship's loving friends,

W. Wilteshire, J. Warwick, E. Clynton, G. Cobham, A. Wingfield, N. Wotton.

P. S. After the signing of these letters, we received your lordship's packet, with letters of yours dated the 13th of this instant; and your wise handling of the matter being so agreeing with that we determined here, we commend the same very much, giving you our hearty thanks for the same. Whereas ye find fault with the slack arrival of our letters for your address in this matter, ye shall perceive by the contents of this letter, what occasion hath been of this leisure taken.

PRIVY

PRIVY *Council to the lord* Dacre.

To our very good lord the lord Dacre, lord warden of the West Marches anempst Scotland; haste, haste, post haste, with all diligence possible.

AFTER our hearty commendations unto your good lordship, we have received your letters of the 15th of this instant; and as for Sandy Armstrang, for the considerations by your lordship rehearsed, we think it meet to comfort him to continue faithful and true towards the king's highness, and that you promise to assist and succour him, as far forth as he himself (as the king's subject) attempt nothing contrary to the comprehension of the Scots made in the last treaty with France. And as for the debatable ground, your lordship hath been advertised ere this, that by the last treaty the king's highness is only to redeliver certain forts which are already redelivered, and to rase two other, the Scots doing the like for their parts, which things are already performed. And as for the rest, seeing no mention is made of it, the king's highness ought to remain in peaceable possession of all that whereof he was in possession at the date of the said treaty: and so may you declare unto them, when you shall have any occasion so to do. In the mean season ye shall do well to defend the debatable ground, as far as ye shall be able to do it; having consideration to the king's honour. Thus fare your lordship heartily well. From Oking the 21st of August 1550.

Your lordship's assured friends,
J. Warwick, E. Clynton, G. Cobham, A. Wingfield, N. Wotton.

LORD Maxwell *to the lord* Dacre.

To the right honourable my lord Dacre, warden of the West Marches of England:

AFTER my lawful commendations; It would please your lordship to be advertised, that among other gentlemen of this country, I am commanded for one to go with the queen into France, and seeing our passage is so shortly that I may not have the time to meet your lordship at a day of Marche, for the reforming of such attempts as are done on both the Borders, I am desirous, if it be your pleasure, to wait upon you on Friday next, to come to Tordawath at eight o'clock before noon, in quiet manner, with fifty horse, to the intent that we may commune together for the better stay of both the princes subjects. My lord, it is not unknown to you, as I trust, that there is a conduct granted for 200 horse of the queen's company to go through England; and as ye know it is a far way to me to send my horse about by Berwick, wherefore I will desire, if it be your pleasure, that ye will suffer four horse of mine and two servants to go in at Carlisle hand, and meet with the rest of the queen's horse at Borrowbriggs. And what your pleasure is in these the premisses, I pray you

you give me advertisement with speed; for I must shortly depart, it requires no less. And thus I beteich you to God. From Dumfries this Wednesday at night the 27th of August, 1550.

Your lordship's lefully.
R. MAXWELL.

LORD Dacre *to the lord* Maxwell.

To the right honourable lord Maxwell lord warden of the West Marches of Scotland.

AFTER my lefull commendations to your lordship, these shall be to advertise the same, that I am very well contented (according to your request) to meet you with such like company as your letters do purport on Friday next at Tordawath, for reformation of injuries, and establishing of quietness, as need shall require. And herein inclosed ye shall receive a conduct to Borrowbriggs, according to your letters. Committing your lordship thus to almighty God. From Naward the 28th of August 1550.

Your lordship's lefully,
W. DACRE.

A PROCLAMATION.

THE 29*th of* August, *Anno Regis* Edwardi *sexti quarto* 1550, *on* Roucliffe *sands.*

WE do you to wit, this day it is agreed between us the lords wardens of the West Marches of England and Scotland and of Scotland and England, that either of them shall send to the other on Sunday come eight days, being the 7th of September next, such plaints as the inhabitants of either wardenry have to exhibit against the other, for any matter committed since the last comprehension of the peace; the bills of England to be sent the same day to Loughmaben, and the bills of Scotland to Carlisle. And for the ordering and redress of the same, they have appointed Tuesday the 16th day of September, to meet at Loughmaben Stone, either in their own persons, or their sufficient deputies. And in the mean time, the said lords wardens do strictly charge and command in both the princes names, all and every person and persons within their several wardenries, that they observe and keep the peace according to the said comprehension.

LORD Dacre *to the Privy Council.*

To the right honourable and my singular good lords, the lords of the king's majesty's most honourable privy council; haste, post haste, with all possible diligence.

MAY it please your honourable lordships to be advertised, that this day the lord Maxwell and I met at Gotewath for communication of matters requiring redress,

redreſs. And foraſmuch as the country had no perfect warning of the ſame, becauſe it was ſuddenly appointed upon the requeſt of the lord Maxwell, becauſe he is commanded to wait upon the queen, we took order that we ſhould make proclamation in our ſeveral charges, that all ſuch as had cauſe of complaint for injuries committed ſince the concluſion of the peace, ſhould make ready and deliver their bills before Sunday the 7th of September to the ſaid wardens or their deputies: And either of us to ſend them interchangeably to other; that the defendants may be commanded to anſwer the ſame as appertaineth, the 16th day of September next, being a day appointed for redreſs of the ſame. Amongſt which, the lord Maxwell demanded, what anſwer I had from your lordſhips for the batable land; whereunto I made anſwer according to your letters to me addreſſed for that purpoſe, and that I would anſwer and do as well for the king's majeſty's ſubjects inhabiting upon the ſame, as for the reſt of this wardenry. Which he ſeemed to take ſtrangely, ſeeing that he would make no redreſs again to any of them. And according to the ſame, I have learned by a truſty ſpiall of mine, that their intent is either to have the batable land uſed as it hath been in other times of peace, and the Cawe milns reſtored again, or elſe to break the peace (yet ere Martinmaſs). And further he ſaith there are ſix gallies come for the Scottiſh queen, which have been ſo ſore driven and troubled with weather, that they were forced to caſt a great number of ſlaves overboard, and one of the gallies driven from the reſt was yeſterday unſeen or heard of. At Carliſle the 29th of Auguſt 1550.

Your honourable lordſhips at commandment,

W. Dacre.

Lord Dacre *to the Privy Council.*

To the right honourable and my ſingular good lords, the lords of the king's majeſty's moſt honourable privy council; haſte, haſte, poſt haſte, with all poſſible diligence, haſte, haſte.

May it pleaſe your honourable lordſhips to be advertiſed, that yeſterday, according to the late appointment between the lord Maxwell and me, my ſon in my place, and John Maxwell deputy for the lord Maxwell, met at Loughmaben Stone to keep the day of March. And before their meeting, according to the cuſtom, ſent for aſſurance of peace interchangeably. And whereas it hath been uſed in times paſt, that the ſaid aſſurance was aſked and granted on both parts, before the lord warden of England paſſed over the water; I thought it meet now, for the better maintenance of the king's title and intereſt of the debatable land to go over the water unto the ſame batable, before we either demanded or granted any aſſurance; where the ſame was accompliſhed accordingly, and ſo proceeded to the place prefixed. Where divers bills of injuries were exhibited by both parties, and put to the juries to inquire upon. And becauſe they refuſed to make redreſs to Sandy Armſtrang and others dwelling upon the batable, mine officers there preſent thought it not meet to grant nor take any redreſs of other bills; and ſo condeſcended to appoint another

another day, the 2d of October next, further to proceed in those bills already exhibited, and all other then as occasion shall require. Wherefore I humbly beseech your lordships to advertise me of your pleasures in the mean time, whether I shall take or give any redress for other bills, unless I may have also redress of the injuries committed to the inhabitants of the batable land, for they will grant no redress of the same. And I, on the other part, am so persuaded by your late letters for that matter, that I determine to take nor grant no redress of the rest, unless I may have redress for the same accordingly. I am informed by a credible spiall, that the French king hath written unto the governor of Scotland, that rather than the Scots shall lose any part of their possessions, or suffer either the batable land aforesaid, or the lands called the Threpelands between Bowbent and the Ryding burne on the East March, to be otherwise used than hath been in times past, he will spend the revenues not only of Scotland but also of the crown of France in defence of the same; wherein I perceive the Scots take great courage. And thus almighty God, &c. At the king's majesty's castle of Carlisle the 17th of September 1550.

Your honourable lordships at commandment,

W. Dacre.

THE *Privy Council to the lord* Dacre.

To our very good lord the lord Dacre, lord warden of the West Marches for anempst Scotland; haste, post haste, for thy life, for thy life.

After our right hearty commendations unto your good lordship, we have received your letters of the 17th of this instant, by the which we do understand the manner of your doings at the last appointment with the lord Maxwell. And where they refuse to make redress to Sandy Armstrang and others dwelling upon the debatable ground, we do like very well your answer therein. And if they shall remain of the same mind at the next meeting, you shall for answer say unto them, that by the treaty between the king's majesty and the French king, both the debatable ground, and such others as be not otherwise specially provided, be and ought quietly to remain in the king's majesty's subjects possession and occupation. And forasmuch as the said treaty was made with France, and the Scots only comprehended, the consideration thereof ought to be with France; wherein we doubt not but such end shall be taken, as is agreeable both with the meaning of the treaty and with reason, either at the coming of the Scottish commissioners, which (as we have heard) be in journey hitherwards, or shortly after, in conference between the king's majesty's commissioners and the French king's: In the mean time, if they will offer injuries to Armstrang or any other dwelling upon the debatable ground, ye must and will defend the same; and if they will forbear, and do justice to them and all others the king's subjects, then will ye likewise do the semblable, otherwise you may say you will not. And then if any inconvenience shall ensue by this their refusal, the fault must be imputed to them. And this answer we think good

good to be made at your said next meeting. And thus fare you heartily well. From Oteland the 25th of September 1550.

Your loving friends,
E. Somerset, W. Wilteshire, W. Northe, A. Wingefield,
W. Petre, W. Cecylle.

These commissioners brought about a compromise and partition. And on the 8th of March following there is a commission to the aforesaid lord Wharton and Sir Thomas Challoner on the part of the king of England, and a like commission was granted to Sir James Douglas of Drumlangrig and Richard Maitland of Lethington on the part of the queen of Scotland, for the partition of the said debatable land (in order to prevent contentions); who made their award Sept. 24, 1552, setting forth, that whereas the inhabitants of the western part inclined more to be subjects of England, and the inhabitants of the eastern part inclined more to be subjects of Scotland, they therefore award the western part of the said debatable land to the king of England, and the eastern part thereof to the queen of Scotland; to be divided by a line drawn across from Esk to Sark, and a square stone set up at each end with the arms of England on the west thereof, and the arms of Scotland on the east side. And lest the stones by length of time or evil practice should be destroyed or removed, they describe the places where the stones were to be set, *viz.* the stone upon Esk to be where the course of that river bends at the western side of a field called Dymmisdaill, where Dymmisdaill syke comes in; and the stone upon Sark to be at a red cliff in Kirkrigg, where also the water of Sark makes a turn *.

But after all these treaties of accommodation and concord, there was no peace to the Borders. The inhabitants on both sides continued their ravages unintermittedly as before; for they had been inured to no other kind of living. And the queen of Scotland being gone into France, there was a sort of anarchy in that kingdom, by reason of the contentions and competitions amongst the nobility; and the English borderers no less availed themselves of those times of confusion. The aforesaid Mr. Bell hath exhibited lists of some hundreds of the English side that were complained of by the Scots for depredations (and, no doubt, there were as many on the other side). Out of the said Mr. Bell's list, we shall present the reader with the following specimen:

Cumberland and Westmorland. } The collection of the names of the principal offenders, that were present with their complices, at the incursions, murders, burnings, mutilations, and spoils committed presently after the queen's majesty's departure, and contained in the bills of complaints exhibited to the lord bishop of Carlisle.

Simon Musgrave of Firbank.
Lard of Pattinson.
Jock of Kinmont.

* Appendix, No. I.

Will's Arthur.
Richie Grame of Bailie.
Will's Jock Grame.
Richard Grame of Akesha-hill.
Adam Grame of Hall.
Richie of Bushe.
Fargue's Willie Grame.
Geordie's Christie.
Black Jock's Johnie.
George Grame of Sandhills.
Dick's Davie's Davie.
Georgie Armstrong of Catgill.
Hector of Harelawe.
Emie of Gingles.
Mickle Willie Grame.
Richie's Geordie.
Will Grame of Rosetrees.
Will Grame brother to Hutchin.
John Musgrave of Catterlen.
Gib's Jack's Johnie.
Tom's Robbie.
Patie's Geordie's Johnie.
Young John of Woodhead.
Richie Grame son of Goodman of Breckonhill.
Young lard of Graitney.
Archie of Gingles.
Jock of Gingles.
Black Jock's Johnie.
Black Jock's Leonie.
Will's Jock.
Richie Grame younger of Netherby.
Sandie's Rinyon's Davie.
Gibb's Geordie's Francie.
George of the Gingles, *alias* Henharrow.
John Nelson curate of Bewcastle.
Jock of the Lake's Christie.
John Noble, *alias* Langfoot.
Wat Grame flaughtail.
Will Grame (nimble Willie).
Will Grame (Mickle Willie).
Will Patrick priest of Bewcastle.
Black Will Storie of Bewcastle.
John of the Side (Gleed John).
Red Rowy Forster.

With about 400 more.—The reason why they are styled in this extraordinary manner is very evident: Abundance of them having the same surname (as (as the Grames, for inftance), where it happened that feveral of thefe had alfo the fame chriftian name, fome other diftinction became neceffary.

About this time, the lord Dacre was removed from the wardenfhip, and the lord Wharton came in as deputy warden general of all the three marches, under the duke of Northumberland head warden; the lord Eure, lord Ogle, and Sir Thomas Dacre (of Lanercoft), being then deputy wardens under him of the Eaft, Middle, and Weft Marches.

Upon his acceffion to the office, he took order for watches to be kept all along throughout all the three marches from fea to fea; together with other regulations as followeth:

Articles devifed at Newcaftle the 12th and 13th of September, in the 6th year of the reign of our fovereign lord king Edward the fixth.

At confultation there, it was thought good by the lord *Wharton*, lord deputy warden general, the three deputy wardens, with the captains of *Carlifle*, *Norham*, *Wark*, and others, wife and moft expert gentlemen of all the three marches, for better fervice of the king's majefty, and the peace and quiet of the frontiers, that thefe articles fhould immediately be put in execution.

Firft, that watches be appointed for the inhabitants of the faid marches, and the places, with the numbers of the watches, with fetters, fearchers, and overfeers, according to the ancient cuftoms of the marches.

Alfo, That every man do rife and follow the fray, upon blowing of horn, fhout, or outcry; upon pain of death.

Alfo, That no man receive, harbour, lodge, or by any means aid or comfort any rebel, fugitive, felon, murderer, Englifhman or Scotchman, or practife with them; upon pain of death.

Alfo, That every gentleman and fubject give information of any thief or receivers of theft, to their knowledge, to my lord deputy warden general, or to the deputy wardens of the Weft marches, or to the fheriff of the county where the gentleman or fubject dwelleth.

Alfo, That no man practife with rebel, thief, nor murderer; but that the fame be opened to my faid lord deputy general.

Alfo, That all days of marches appointed be kept; and none to be broken nor put over of any thefe three marches of England; and all the marchers to attend their deputy wardens at the fame, and other their commandment, according to their duties.

Alfo, that every deputy warden fhall within feven days give in writing all the attempts committed as well againft Scotchmen as againft Englifhmen, to my lord deputy warden general, or one of the wardens within their own offices.

Alfo, That all other officers, captains, and gentlemen fhall abide and dwell upon their own offices, and at their own houfes.

Alfo, That no fubject fpeak with any Scotchman, except upon licence fo to do, of my lord deputy warden general, or of the deputy wardens within their own offices.

Alſo, That every captain and every officer and gentleman ſee their ſoldiers and tenants, and ſuch as are under their rule, be well horſed, according to their duties and powers.

Alſo, That every officer and gentleman ſhall give knowledge to their ſoldiers, tenants, and every ſubject under their rules, of theſe orders, to the intent every ſubject may uſe himſelf accordingly, and not for want of knowledge run into ſuch pain as ſhall enſue thereon.

THE orders of the Watches upon the Weſt Marches made by the lord *Wharton*, upon the inſtructions aforeſaid, as the deputy warden of the ſame, at Carliſle, in the month of October, in the ſixth year of the reign of our ſovereign lord king Edward the ſixth.

Beginning at the foot of *Levin*, and ſo up *Eſk* to *Liddiſdale*; in *Eſk*, eight ſeveral watches to be appointed, and in every watch two men.

From the foot of *Liddiſdale*, to *Haithwayte* burn fall into *Liddell*, three ſeveral watches; and in every watch two men: *Richard Graham* and his aſſociates, having the king's highneſs's grants in theſe places, nightly to appoint the grounds and places moſt needful to be watched within the ſaid bounds; and theſe watches nightly to be ſearched by the appointment of the ſaid *Richard* and his aſſociates, by two men.

From *Hathwate* burn foot unto the foot of *Cryſſop*, five ſeveral watches, and four men in every watch: And theſe watches nightly to be ſearched by two men appointed at the aſſignment of *John Muſgrave*, the king's highneſs's ſervant.

From the foot of *Cryſſop* unto the head of *Cryſſop*, three ſeveral watches, and in every watch four men; whereof one to be at *Craighill* foot, and the other two beneath: and the ſearchers for every watch nightly to be appointed by the ſaid *John Muſgrave*.

A watch to begin at the head of *Kirkbeck* and go to the foot of *Kirkbeck*, four ſeveral watches, and in every watch two men; the dwellers on both ſides of *Kirkbeck* to watch theſe four watches: and two ſearchers, one thereof nightly to be appointed by the land ſerjeant of *Gilſland* for the time being, and the other by the above named *John Muſgrave*.

From *Kirkbeck* down *Levin* to *Harperhill*, four ſeveral watches; two men in every watch, one half of either ſide *Levin* water, nightly to be appointed by the ſaid land ſerjeant and *John Muſgrave*, and two ſearchers for the ſame.

From *Harper hill* till *Raborn* fall into *Levin*, two ſeveral watches, and two men in every watch: with ſearchers likewiſe to be appointed by the land ſerjeant and *John Muſgrave* aforeſaid.

Aglionby, *Holmend*, and *Warwick*, to watch nightly, three perſons: *Warwick* watch, ſearchers thereof nightly to be appointed by the bailiffs.

Wetheral, *Cotbill*, *Corby*, and *Combynton*, to keep nightly three fords, called *Brokelwath*, *Granywath*, and *Monkwath*; four nightly at *Brokelwath*, and two nightly of either of the other two watches: and two ſearchers nightly to be appointed by the bailiffs and conſtables, *Thomas Salkeld* overſeer of the ſaid watch and ſearcher there.

Corby

Corby Minor, and *Brigend*, to watch nightly *Warwick bridge*, and the ford beneath the bridge: and two searchers nightly to be appointed by the bailiffs and constable, to set and search the same watch.

Ormesby and *Meretbwaite* nightly to keep *Longstroble* watch, and *Dorestreme*; with two persons.

Ainstable, *Armathwaite*, *Nunclose*, and *Flodelcruke*, to keep nightly *Paytwath*, with four persons: *William Skelton*'s bailiffs and constables to appoint nightly to set and search the said watch.

Four fords upon *Raven*, to be watched by *Kirkoswald*, *Laisingby*, *Glassenby*, *Little Salkeld*, *Ullesby*, *Melmorby*, *Ranwyke*, and *Harskew*; at every ford nightly four persons: And the searchers to be appointed by the bailiffs and constables, upon the oversight of *Christopher Threlkeld* the king's highness's servant.

Upon *Blenkarn* beck are five fords, to be watched by *Blenkarn*, *Culgaith*, *Skyrwath*, *Kirkland*, *Newbigging*, *Sourby*, *Milburn*, *Dufton*, *Marton*, *Kirkbythore*, *Knock* and *Milburn Grange*; bailiffs and constables to appoint searchers: Overseers, *Christopher Crackenthorp*, and *Gilbert Wharton*, the king's highness's servants.

From the head of *Cardewmire* to *Little Dalston* bars, the lordship of *Dalston* to watch and keep the Bishop-dyke, according to their ancient custom in the same.

From *Little Dalston* bars, to the mill dam head of *Carlisle*; *Blackell*, *Blackelwood*, *Brounelston*, and two *Comersdails*, to keep the bounds and fords thereabout: *Thomas Dalston* the king's highness's servant, to oversee and set the watch and search.

From *Laurence-Holme* to the *Morehouse*, *Laurence-Holm* and *Ulton* to keep watch nightly.

From *Westwample* bridge, to the foot of *Shanks*; *Rosswen*, *Murethwait*, *Woodside*, and *Kirkwath*, at every place four men: To be appointed nightly by *Robert Brisco* the king's highness's servant, and *Richard Studholme*; and in like wise the search to be appointed by them.

From *Morehouse* to *Westwample* bridge, *Morehouse* and *Dockwray* to watch.

From *Raburn* down to the foot of *Levin*, six several watches, and four men in every watch, to be charged to keep that watch, *Kirklinton*, *Hothersgill*, *Soulby*, *Austenby*, and those that dwell on the outside of *Levin* to help them in those watches: The searcher thereof to be appointed by *Richard Philipson* ruler of *Scaleby*, *Edward Story* warden serjeant, *George Hetherington* the king's bailiff, and proud *Dick Grame*.

From the foot of *Irding* to the foot of *Gelt*, four several watches, and four men in every watch; *Over Crosby*, the *Wall*, *Lyversdale*, and *Irdinton* to keep these watches nightly, at most doubtful and needful places; the bailiffs and constables to appoint searchers for these watches: Overseer thereof, *Thomas Blennerhasset* the king's highness's servant.

From *Irdington* upon *Irding* unto *Poutross*, ten several watches, and in every watch four men; with searchers nightly, to be appointed by the land serjeant of *Gilsland* for the time being, to be watched by the inhabitants near thereabouts.

The foot of *Gelt* unto *Castle Carrick*, three several watches, and four men in every watch; to be watched by *Felton* and *Hayton*: And the searchers nightly to be appointed by the land serjeant, the bailiffs and constables there.

From *Castle Carrick* to *Stamford*, above *Braunybank*, four several watches, and three men in every watch; to be watched by *Talken*, *Castle Carrick*, *Cumrew*, *Newbiggin*, and *Abbyfield*: Searchers to be appointed nightly by the said land serjeants and bailiffs there.

Etterby watch, and the watch at the *Hogill*, to be watched by *Stainton*, *Heriton* houses, *Caldyate*, and *Etterby*, and four nightly to keep these watches. The bailiff and constables to set and search the said watch; overseer, *William Mulcastre*.

Stanwix and *Richargate*, nightly to be appointed two men to watch *Eden* bridge, and the watch beneath the bridge: The bailiffs and constables to set and search the said watch nightly.

Houghton, *Terreby*, and *Brunsketh*, nightly to watch from *Brunsketh* beck to *Gosling* sike, with four persons by night: The bailiffs and constables to set and search the said watch nightly.

Richardby, to watch nightly *Richardby* and the *Stanyholme* watch with two persons: The bailiffs and constables whereof to set and search the said watch nightly.

Lynstoke, *Walbie*, and *Amersholme* nightly to watch *Lynstoke* watch and the ford at *Bishopgarth*, with four persons: Searchers thereof nightly to be appointed by the bailiffs and constables.

Item, *Nether Crosby* to keep the fords to *Warwick* watch, with two persons nightly.

The barony of *Burgh*: *Cardronock* shall watch to *Bowness*;

Bowness to watch to *Glasson*,
Glasson to *Drumburgh*,
Drumburgh to *Eston*,
Eston to *Burstedhill*,
Burstedhill to *Langburgh*,
Langburgh to *Dykesfield*,
Dykesfield to *Burgh*,
Burgh to *Beaumont*,
Beaumont to *Kirkanders*,
Kirkanders to *Grymsdale*,
Grymsdale to the *Hogill* and *Grymesdale* watch.
Aikton to *Whytrigg*,
Whytrig to the *Lathes* and *Wampoll*,
Wampoll to *Finlarigg*,
Finlarig to *Little Bampton*,
Little Bampton to *Ughterby*,
Ughterby to *Kirkbampton*,
Kirkbampton to *Thurstenfield*,
Thurstenfield to the *Morehouse*,
The *Morehouse* to *Wylmerby*,

Wylmorby

Wylmorby to the *Borow*,
The *Borow* to *Little Orton*,
Little Orton to *Mekle Orton*,
Mekle Orton to *Ortonrigg*,
Ortonrigg to *Bawdingholme*,
Bawdingholme to the *Meklehouse*,
The *Meklehouse* to *Thursby*,
Thursby to *Whynno*,
Whynno to *Croftone*,
Croftone to *Mekelthwayte*,
Mekelthwayte to *Parton*,
Parton to *Drumlyning*,
Drumlyning to *Gamelsby*,
Gamelsby to *Acton*,
Acton to *Wygynby*,
Wygynby to *Thornby*,
Thornby to *William Carudders*, with the *Woodhouses*, to keep that between them and the *Woodhouses*; and the Flat between them and the *Woodhouses*: Bailiffs and constables to set and search these watches within the barony of *Burgh*. Overseers, *John Leigh*, the king's highness's servant and steward, with *William Threlkeld* bailiff there.

Brunsketh beneath *Rocliff*, to keep and watch the *Stainwath* and *Irelandwath*: Bailiffs and constables to set and search, at the oversight of *Robin Grame*. *Peter Grame* and his servants to keep the *Layngrake*, and the ford of the *Esgarth* there nightly.

Roclyff to keep between them and *Cargo*, and *Garwath*: *John Leighe* the king's highness's servant, and *William Threlkeld*, overseers thereof.

The lordship of *Holme Cultrayne*: *Augerton* to keep watch from *Kirkbryde* to *Augerton*. *Newton* to keep watch from the *Moss side* to the town, and from the town to the sand.

The *Sallcotes* to keep watch from the *Sallcott* to the water of *Waver*: *Moss side* and *Sletholme* to keep watch from the *West Myer* to the *Salcotts* nightly.

Raby to keep watch from *Raby Rigg* syke to *Wetholme* gate.

Swynsty to keep watch from *Cromock* bridge.

Sutterfield to keep watch.

And the *High Laws* to keep watch at the *New-couper* causey.

Dubmylne, *Satbowe*, and *Old Mawbray*, to keep watch from the *Dubmylne* to the east end of *Old Mawbray* lands.

New Mawbray to keep watch from *Frankhill* to *Mawbray beck*.

Mawbray beck and the *Godyhills* to keep watch from *Mawbray beck* to *Ulsty*.

Ulsty and the *Fernes* to keep watch from *Ulsty* to the *Leys*.

Blatter Leys to keep watch from the *Leys* to *Selythe*.

Selythe, *Harrigge*, and *Dryholme*, to keep watch from *Selythe* to the *Estcote*.

Skynburneyes and *Pellathow* to keep watch from the *Estcote* to St. *John*'s of the Green.

7

Sulwath,

Sulwath, *Dalway*, and the *Foalsyke* to keep watch from the *Sulwath* to *Troderfyke*.

Myrchide, and *Christopher Harifke* with his neighbours of *Whinnyclose*, to keep watch from the *Starybill* to *Troderfyke*.

Brownrigge and *Sewell* to watch from the *Brownrigge* kiln to the *Starybill*.

Sauden house and the *Albay Cowper* to keep watch from *Brownrigge* kiln to the *Castlebill*.

Also, upon the water of *Pettrel*: From *Carlisle* to *Pettrelwray*; bailiffs and constables there, with the oversight of the gentlemen of the late prior of *Carlisle* for the time being, or the steward of the lands.

And from thence to *Plompton*; overseer of the search and watch nightly, *John Skelton* of *Appletreetbwayt*, and *Thomas Herrington*.

Ednel and *Dolphenby*; Sir *Richard Musgrave* knight overseer, his deputy or deputies.

Skelton and *Hutton* in the Forest; overseers thereof *William Hutton* and *John Sutbake*.

Newton and *Caterlen*; *John Vaux* overseer nightly.

Gaytskaile and *Raughton*; overseer thereof *Christopher Musgrave*.

Ivegill, *Braythwaite*, *Myddleskew*, with the Closes; overseers thereof *Lancelot Lowther* constable of *Ivegill*, and *John Hutton* steward of *Middleskew*, or their deputies: And for the search of the watches of all the king's highness's lands, called the *Queen's Hames*, the steward there, his deputy or deputies, nightly.

From *Dalston* to *Caldbeck*; *Richard Bewley* overseer: And from *Caldbeck*, the steward there, his deputy or deputies, overseers.

From the barony of *Graystock*; the lord *Dacre*, his steward, deputy or deputies, overseers.

And down between that and the water unto *Wampoll*; the steward, Mr. *Foster* of the Forest, their deputy or deputies.

And between *Waver* and *Aill*, as those waters join with the lordship of the *Holme*; *Thomas Salkeld*, *William Porter*, and *Gabriel Heymoor* deputy bailiff of *Allerdale*, overseers; and *Richard Eglesfield* the king's highness's servant overseer of them and all that.

Between *Aill* and *Darwen*, as they fall in the sea; *Thomas Dykes* and *Alexander Appleby* the king's highness's servants, overseers: Appointers and searchers of that watch, by the advice of *John Leigh* and *John Thwaytes* the king's servants.

This watch to begin the first night of October, and to continue until the 16th day of March; and the same sooner to begin, or longer to continue, at the discretion of the lord warden general or his deputy for the time being.

Also, all this watch notwithstanding, every township aforenamed, to appoint and have a man to watch their town nightly, as well to raise frays from other watches as occasion shall be, as for safeguard of other towns; to be searched by those persons aforenamed for the other watches.

Also

Alſo, all the other towns not aforenamed, every of the ſaid towns next together, to deviſe and ſet their watch without their towns, at moſt needful places, as the bailiffs and conſtables ſhall appoint.

Alſo, every ſuch perſon or perſons as ſhall take any offenders, Engliſhman or Scotſman, within this realm; he or they which ſo doth ſhall have reward of the lord warden general or his deputy, or of them both, as the worthineſs of ſuch good ſervice deſerveth.

Alſo, if any perſon or perſons, at the coming in, or forth going, ſuffer any offender to eſcape, if they may in any wiſe take them; he or they that ſo doth, to be brought by the officers, bailiffs, conſtables, and ſearchers of that watch, to the king's gaol within that county where the ſame ſhall be done; there to be puniſhed according to the laws of this realm, which is felony.

Alſo, if any perſon or perſons come within any of the watches, in the time of their watching; if they be true men known, and that proved, the ſaid watchers ſhall ſuffer them to depart; and if they be unknown, the ſaid watchers ſhall bring them to the bailiffs and conſtables to be tried: And if the ſaid perſon or perſons ſo brought before the ſaid bailiffs and conſtables, cannot try or prove them to be true men, labouring in their true and lawful buſineſs, that then the ſaid bailiffs and conſtables bring the ſaid ſuſpected perſons to the king's highneſs's gaol, there to remain until ſuch time as he or they be lawfully tried by due examinations of the lord warden general, or his deputy, or by the juſtices of peace of that county.

Alſo, the night watch to be ſet at the day-going, and to continue until the day be light; and the day watch, where the ſame is, to begin at the day light, and to continue until the day be gone. And if any perſon or perſons diſobey any of the ſaid watchers, bailiffs, conſtables, ſetters, ſearchers, or overſeers, in or for the execution of the ſaid watch, in any manner of wiſe; he or they ſo diſobeying to be brought to the king's highneſs's gaol, there to be puniſhed at the diſcretion of the lord warden general or of the deputy warden for the time being, where ſuch offence ſhall be done †.

CHAPTER VIII.

Of the ſtate of the Borders during the reigns of queen Mary *and queen* Elizabeth.

THE firſt thing remarkable within this period, was an act of parliament in the 2 & 3 Ph. & M. c. 1. which was in force for ten years, and afterwards continued by an act of queen Elizabeth (with ſome alterations) during queen Elizabeth's life: whereby, for the better habitation, reſtoring, and re-edifying of the caſtles, fortreſſes, and fortelets, villages and houſes decayed, within the counties of Northumberland, Cumberland, Weſtmorland, and Durham,

† Nicolſon's Bord. L. 215. 319.

within twenty miles of the Borders, and for the better manuring and improving the grounds within the same, and for the more increase of tillage; commissioners were to be appointed under the great seal, with power to inquire, what and how many castles, fortresses, and fortelets, villages, houses, and habitations were decayed, and by whom, and by what occasions, and how many of them were meet to be re-edified, and what new ones were meet to be made, and where most meet to be situate, and what parts within the said limits were most apt to be inclosed and converted to tillage, and who were the lords, owners, or farmers of the same, and what estate, term, or interest they had therein; and to take order for the execution of the premisses, by laying assessments, by arresting and taking carts, oxen, or other instruments necessary, as also workmen and labourers, paying a competent stipend for the same; and also taking as many trees, woods, underwoods, quicksets, stone, and timber, and other necessaries, as should be sufficient, paying for the same reasonable prices, according to their discretion.—And the said act of queen Elizabeth recites, that the queen had been informed by report and certificate of her principal officers having charge of her borders, that the force of her said borders both of horsemen and footmen was greatly decayed, and like daily to grow weaker by many occasions, and among others by decay and ruin of sundry the habitations of those borders, whereby the number of the ancient inhabitants able for service had been diminished; and part of the same habitations, tenancies, and farms had been reduced rather to pasturing of cattle, than to the maintenance of men of service; and that also in some parts the tenants and inhabitants themselves had diminished their own strength, by dividing their houses and farms, which were meet only for one able housholder and family, into the occupation of sundry persons commonly being their children or other kinsfolk, so as by the smallness and meanness of the holding no one of them was able to furnish a man for service; and also that divers owners and tenants had, for more gain than they could have of natural subjects, letten their lands or feedings or some part thereof to Scottishmen, thereby not only weakening the strength of her majesty's natural subjects, but strengthening foreigners: And therefore enacts, that the said commissioners shall inquire, as well by the oaths of 12 men as otherwise by their discretions, what tenancies since the 27 Hen. 8. have been decayed, and not held by men able to serve as horsemen or footmen according to the ancient duties of those tenancies, and of the causes of such decays, and of the wants or evil furnitures of the said horsemen and footmen, and give order for the reformation thereof. And if it shall appear that the fault hath been in the lords or their officers, or in the officers or farmers of her majesty's manors, lands, or tenements; they shall injoin such lords, or such her majesty's officers or farmers, to re-edify or repair the said tenements and houses of habitation, and specially the capital houses and barnekins, at their own charges, and restore like quantities of lands thereunto as had been occupied therewith in the said 27th year of king Henry the eighth: And if they shall find default of furniture of the tenements with horse, weapon, or armour, according to their duties; they shall injoin the said lords and others to give such help as to the said commissioners shall seem meet, towards the enabling of the tenants respectively, to be furnished according to the ancient duty of such tenant, so that thereby the said tenant be furnished and able for service. And if the unableness of the said tenants shall be found to have grown by their own default or wilfulness without just occasion; the said commissioners shall order the same tenants to furnish themselves with horse, armour, and weapon, or with armour and weapon, according to their ancient usage, and their utmost reasonable ability, at their own charges, without any contribution of the lords but at their own wills †.

Some commissions were granted, and inquisitions made, in pursuance of these statutes; but nothing seems further effectually to have been done, to carry the same into execution.

The next thing that hath occurred within this period, is, An abstract of the musters of horsemen and footmen within the counties of Westmorland and Cumberland, taken by the earl of Huntingdon lord president of the north, in September and October 1584, by virtue of a commission to him and the lord Hunsden for that purpose:

Westmorland.

Able men mustered:	
Light horsemen amongst the gentlemen and their houshold servants, furnished according to the use of the Borders	100
Archers furnished — — — —	1400
Billmen furnished — — — —	1300
Able men unfurnished — — — —	1342
	4142

Cumberland.

Able men mustered:	
Light horsemen amongst the gentlemen and their houshold servants, furnished according to the use of the Borders —	100
Light horsemen furnished;	
Burgh barony — — — —	100
Gilsland — — — —	60
Holm Cultram — — — — —	40
Leven, Kirklinton, Solport — — —	30
Sarke debatable ground — — —	18
Eske — — — — —	100
Queen's Hames — — — —	40
Forest of Englewood — — —	30
The office of Bewcastle — — —	50

† Rustal.

 Archers

Archers furniſhed — — — —	1100
Billmen furniſhed — — — —	1200
Able men unfurniſhed — — —	1340
	4208

Weſtmorland	4142	8350 *.
Cumberland	4208	

ANOTHER account of muſters given us by Mr. Bell, taken in ſeveral places:

Weſtmorland.		
At Sandford moor — —	1981	
Strickland head — —	1269	— — 5919
Greenholme — — —	2669	
Cumberland.		
Allerdale above and beneath Derwent — —	5405	
Leeth Ward — — —	1590	— — 9153
Cumberland Ward — —	2158	
	Sum total	15072

This latter account ſeems to have been upon a general muſter of all between 16 and 60.

UPON the death of the old lord Scroope, his ſon was appointed to ſucceed him in the wardenſhip of the Weſtern Marches. Whereupon, in the year 1593, he propoſed divers matters to be conſidered of by the gentlemen of both counties, as followeth:

" HEADS to be conſidered upon and reſolved, as ſhall be thought moſt commodious for the common quietneſs of theſe countries, delivered by the right honourable lord Scroope, lord warden of the Weſt Marches of England towards Scotland, unto the gentlemen of Cumberland and Weſtmorland.

Firſt, Foraſmuch as it is conjectured that divers diſorders grow, and infinite outrages are committed upon her majeſty's good ſubjects on the frontiers, and more inwards in the country, as well by the remiſs dealing of the officers and negligence of watches and watchers, as by the ſervants, tenants, and dependers of divers gentlemen, freeholders, and heads of ſurnames, on and near the frontier, and likewiſe by triſtes, aſſurances, and alliances between the Engliſh and Scots on the Borders; which ſort of people, beſides their own filcheries, do (as it is thought) to the great oppreſſion of others, either guide or accompany Scotſmen in their day or night roads, for ſtealth from her ma-

* Bell.

jeſty's

jesty's subjects, and to share the Englishmens goods between them and the Scots; or at least, if they lay not the plot, do willingly and wittingly tolerate and suffer the Scots to pass and repass by them and through their strengths, for and with Englishmens goods, without causing of hue and cry, fray, or following of the thieves, in such sort as they are bound to do, both by the statute laws and ancient custom and constitutions of the Borders, and by the common curtesy of good neighbourhood they should: In reformation whereof, first, it would be considered and resolved, what course can be taken with the head and under officers under the lord warden's commandment, to assure the bringing in of any offenders within their charge, unto the lord warden at his lordship's direction of the same.

Secondly, Whether it will not be convenient that the order for watches resolved by the late lord Scroope, Sir John Forster, and Sir Simon Musgrave, be now again renewed, and with severity observed; namely, that whereas any goods should pass through any of the watches, without hue and cry made by them of the watch, those said watchers should answer the goods so driven and carried throughout or within the precinct or compass of the same.

Thirdly, Whether it will not be very needful duly to put the statute for hues and crys in execution, in such sort, that whosoever shall be proved before the lord warden not to have risen and followed the fray according to the same law; the same person or persons presently to answer and satisfy for the goods reived or taken away: and consideration to be had, how the penalty of the same statute may best and most readily be levied for the relief of the party damnified.

Fourthly, It would fall in consideration how the marriages between the English and the Scottish nations in these frontiers may be from henceforth restrained, and heretofore hath been enacted, though too remissly executed; and what bonds and assurance can be taken of all such as are already allied, for their demeanor towards the rest of her majesty's subjects, and for like good behaviour of all their branches, servants, and dependents.

Fifthly, It would moreover be considered, what bonds and security can be taken of every particular gentleman, freeholder, and head of surnames, so to become answerable for their servants, tenants, and followers or dependents, as they either bring in unto the lord warden, and upon his lordship's call, such servants, tenants, followers and dependers, as have or are suspected to have committed any transgression against the Marche or common laws, for to abide a trial according to their demerits; or, failing thereof, to satisfy the party offended for his harm done by any of the abovesaid persons so belonging or depending unto them.

Sixthly, Because the surnames of the *Grames* have no commander under the lord warden; what courses are therefore most meet to be taken for good order amongst them and their branches, as well for themselves, as the evil-doers un derthem.

Lastly, How the resort of Lowlands men into the inland may best be restrained, seeing that under colour of their errands to gentlemen and others, many evil offices are effected by them in their passages.

THOMAS SCROOPE.

THE

The answer and opinions of the gentlemen of Cumberland and Westmorland made to the heads propounded and demanded by the right honourable Thomas lord Scroope of Bolton, lord warden of the West Marche of England towards Scotland.

To the first, We think it very convenient for reformation of offenders, that the lord warden, upon complaint made unto him, do direct his warrant to the officer within whose office such offenders shall dwell and remain, to apprehend and bring before the lord warden the said offender; and where the offender dwelleth in such place wherein there is no known officer over them, that then the lord warden to direct his letters to the landlords of whose lands the offenders dwell, that he the said landlord shall in like manner apprehend and bring the said offender before the said lord warden at the day limited in the said letter. And if any default be either in the said officer or landlord in the execution of the said letters, that then the said officer or landlord to be punished at the discretion of the said lord warden. And if the said offender make default of his appearance, either by flying from his officer or landlord, or any other contemptuous course of himself; that then it may please the lord warden, of his authority, not only to restrain the said offenders or any to their use from the enjoying of the inhabitations, tenements, and goods, but also if there be any that after the said felony do maintain and assist or recett the said offenders, that his lordship will accordingly write for the said offenders to their officer or landlord, and minister punishment unto them according to their deserving.

To the second; As concerning keeping of watches, we all think that your lordship hath very well and effectually considered of the same, and do think it very meet that watches throughout the whole wardenry be continued. And for that the place of watching by many occasions is known to be more meet for some time in one place and some time in another, and one place to be stronger, and one place to be weaker, and not to continue always in one certainty; therefore that it would please your lordship to give charge to all justices and gentlemen to meet together at some places convenient, as well both for the one part of the wardenry as for the other, calling to them officers and other some discreet men to every quarter, to consider and set down, as time now serveth, where or in what place watches are most needful to be established, and to make a book thereof to be preferred to your lordship; and that thereupon your lordship will make your several commissions to as many of the said gentlemen and others, as your lordship shall think convenient from time to time, some in one place, some in other, to see the said watches duly established and continued; and that if any default be certified unto your lordship of any of the said watches, that your lordship would see the same punished as the case shall require.

To the third; Concerning the execution of the statute of hue and cry, commonly called in this country following the fray, We all think it meet the same be duly put in execution. And if there be any that do fail in following of the same, or who wilfully will stop or resist any person so following; that such offender be called before your lordship, and punished according to the offence, as heretofore hath been accustomed by the warden. And yet nevertheless,

theless, those who are offended may further seek their redress therein according to the statute or the common laws in that behalf provided.

To the fourth; We think that concerning marriages commonly used between Scots and English borderers, whereof your lordship hath most wisely considered that the same may breed great inconveniences and hurts to England; yet nevertheless we think it meet, before your lordship shall establish any order thereagainst, that your lordship do know her majesty's pleasure or council's therein. And as concerning taking of bonds of them already married, we do think it fit that your lordship not only call them, but all the rest of the principal headsmen of the *Grames*, *Hetheringtons*, *Taylors*, and other names, to enter bond unto your lordship to be of good behaviour, and to be answerable for the appearance of all such as they take to be under them; and if they will not so do, then to commit them until such time as they be willing so to do.

To the fifth; We all think, that for all other persons brought before your lordship upon suspicion of felony, whether they belong to any gentleman, or to any other, that they be safely kept and continued, until they be either justified of the said offence, or otherwise bailed by the due course of law.

To the sixth: As your lordship hath considered, that the *Grames* have no proper officer over them, as we ourselves also do think, that so long as they have not one specially appointed over them, we take it that both your lordship as warden, and by express words of your lordship's letters patent, standeth officer over them; and that they ought to be obedient to your lordship; and that your lordship from time to time by your letters call the principal men before you, to answer for themselves and those under them; and if any of them make default, your lordship may apprehend them, according to the authority of your lordship's letters patent, and punish as you shall think convenient.

To the seventh; We think it were good that warning by proclamation were given by your lordship, that no Scottishman or suspected Border man under any colour do repair into Westmorland or Cumberland above Carlisle, without your lordship's licence; upon pain of punishment at your lordship's consideration: And that every justice or other officers or persons in England do apprehend any such and bring them before your lordship upon the occasion of their repairing thither. And that no gentleman shall receive into his service any Scotsman or Borderman, but such as before his departure from his service he will make known to your lordship, so as he may be answerable what any man can say against him.

Cumberland.

William Musgrave of Hayton esquire, Sheriff of Cumberland.

John Dalston, Joseph Pennington, John Lamplughe, Nicholas Curwen, Wilfride Lawson, Thomas Lampleugh — esquires.

Christopher Dalston, Henry Blencowe, John Denton, John Richmond, Gerard Lowther — esquires.

Westmorland.

Thomas Strickland, James Bellingham — esquires †.

† Bell.

In

In the same year, articles were proposed and agreed upon at Newcastle, by the earl of Huntington lord lieutenant of the North, with the consent of Thomas lord Scroope of Bolton lord warden of the West Marches, and of Sir Robert Cary knight deputy warden of the said West Marches, and others.

First, Whereas the lord warden, for the more easy subduing of the bad and most vagrant sort of the great surnames of the Borders, namely, of the *Grames*, *Armstrongs*, *Fosters*, *Bells*, *Nixons*, *Hethertons*, *Taylors*, *Rootlidges*, with other very insolent members appertaining to them; his lordship concluded with himself, to call the principal and chief of every branch of every several surname before him, and to constrain them to enter bond in good security for their own appearance before him when they shall be called upon, and also to give his lordship a perfect note of all such as any way depend upon them by blood or otherwise, and of that number to signify for how many he the chief and principal would undertake by sufficient bond or by pledge to make answerable for any matter to be laid to their charge. Which course his lordship hath begun and entered with *William Grame* of Rosetrees and *Rob of the Fald*, and intendeth to proceed till his lordship hath likewise gone through with every several branch and sirname.

And because his lordship hath not yet begun nor resolved upon any course against those, which the principal or chief shall refuse to undertake to make answerable, being of their blood, dwelling on their land, serving or depending upon them; it is considered, that these unreasonable persons be sent for by the lord warden's letter or summons, to be delivered at the house where the party dwelleth, or for the most part maketh his abode or resorteth; and if the party so summoned having habitation by himself shall refuse and do not appear at the day and place appointed; that then at any time after, upon the precept and mandate of the lord warden, the chief lord of the manor or lordship where the transgressor dwelleth shall, with a competent number of men within his rule, be bound on pain of imprisonment at the warden's pleasure to repair to the house of the offender, and if the party be fled, to seize the tenement, with all the goods there or thereon, to her majesty's use, and shall utterly expel and put out from the same the wife, children, servants, and friends of the offender, and shall restrain him or any of them to his or their use, from taking or enjoying by any means any benefit of the said tenement and goods belonging and found his at the time of the seizure thereof: And whosoever, after the same seizure, shall abet, harbour, recett, or any way relieve the said offender; the same abbettor, harbourer, recettor, or reliever, to be apprehended and brought by the bailiff or other head officer before the lord warden, and shall receive such punishment as in case of accessaries of felonies is appointed.

But if the contemptuous person be not fled, then the said head officer to make seizure of the house and goods, and to apprehend and bring in safety to the lord warden the offender, to answer his contempt. And if the contemptuous person have no certain place of dwelling, then the party that giveth him receipt or relief is to be charged to bring the offender within 20 days to the lord warden; wherein if he fail, the offender shall be proclaimed a fugitive, and so used of all men. And whosoever at the proclamation shall be

 found

found to have given him any relief or comfort, ſhall receive puniſhment as in caſes of acceſſaries of felonies are provided. And this law likewiſe in all reſpects to be uſed againſt all felons and other malefactors whatſoever within this weſt wardenry. And if the bailiff or other officer appointed to this ſervice ſhall find the power under his own command inſufficient to perform the ſame, he ſhall ſignify his weakneſs to the warden, and require further aſſiſtance at his hands; which if he obtain not, he ſhall be excuſed.

AND whereas within Bewcaſtle and other places, the head officer challengeth to have the eſcheat of all offenders under them, by which means the ſheriff perceiving that the goods and chattels do go to the officer, and that himſelf ſhall have only his labour for his travel; therefore the ſheriff forbeareth to make an arreſt and to apprehend any offenders, when he ſeeth that he may not with the party make ſeizure of his goods alſo; ſo is the felon reſerved by that means to do miſchief, without further puniſhment than by appeaſing his own officer with a part of the things ſtolen (as ſome inform), the officer not caring how many evil men live under him, ſeeing that by them groweth ſo great benefit unto him; the remedying whereof the lord warden wholly referreth to wiſer conſideration.

ALSO, the evil men at theſe days uſe this policy, namely, to ſteal goods from their neighbours, and indelayedly before the thief can be ſpeired out, the felon himſelf, or ſome other for him, will go to the party rieved, and will ſeek to draw him to compound for the redelivering of his own goods; ſo remaineth the thief unrevealed, and eſcaping unpuniſhed thus cunningly fyleth his hands with his neighbour's goods: Which courſe alſo how to reform, the lord warden referreth to better conſideration.

MOREOVER, that the heatheniſh cuſtom of deadly feud in theſe countries may be avoided, a matter intolerable amongſt the barbarous heathen, much more in chriſtian civil policy; the lord warden thinketh it meet, without favour and in greateſt ſeverity, to puniſh with death and confiſcation of lands and goods, all ſuch as ſhall hereafter ſo commit murder within this office; and to call all thoſe perſons betwixt whom feuds do now remain, and labour the taking up of them, and whoſo refuſeth to come to agreement, that ſuch perſons be cauſed to do the ſame by warding and binding to the good abearing.

ALSO, that all perſons which ſhall openly ſhore or threaten any other for any cauſe whatſoever, from henceforth may be bound to good abearing, notwithſtanding a pecuniary puniſhment laid and ſet down for every ſuch tranſgreſſor.

ITEM, That no priſoner being a Scotſman, whether driven into England by due courſe of Marche law, or elſe taken by any Engliſhman howſoever, be ſuffered to ride abroad in the country, nor above a mile from the place where he is priſoner; upon the pain of impriſonment to the priſoner's keeper, for every time it can be proved the priſoner hath been otherwiſe.

ALSO, That no Scots felon or murderer be permitted to have any receipt or relief in England, at any Engliſhman's hands; upon pain of impriſonment at the lord warden's pleaſure, beſides the puniſhment he is to ſuffer by the laws of Marche in that caſe provided.

Item, That whatsoever subject shall be proved hereafter to pay Blackmaile (as it is commonly termed), either to Englishman or Scotsman; the giver to be fined at the sum of 5*l* and imprisonment, and the broker and taker (being an Englishman) to be apprehended and punished at the discretion of the warden †.

Also, That whoever shall from henceforth compound with any Englishman for his own goods stolen from him, and do not first acquaint the lord warden, and obtain his lordship's assent to the same, shall be punished as in case of accessary for the stealing of his own goods.

Item, That for all defaults in night or day watches, and the setters and searchers of them, together with the defaults in repair to the Plump watches, and other necessary services commanded by the warden; forfeitures and good fines may be imposed upon every transgressor, according to the demerit of the offence, besides the corporal punishment to be inflicted by the warden.

Item, That there may be a good reward appointed and set down to be paid to every one, that will publickly and privately inform and prove any disorder, disobedience, or negligence, in any person touching the execution of these or any other orders or good rules to be thus constituted by the lord lieutenant and the said justices.

Item, That recognizances for appearance of persons before the lord warden be kept in a perfect record; and that forfeitures of them or any of them be duly collected by a collector appointed, and the money delivered to the treasurer of the country for the money for hurt soldiers or mariners. Which

† By an act of parliament some few years after, viz. 43 Eliz. c. 13. this offence is made felony: Which act recites—" Forasmuch as now of late years, very many of her majesty's subjects dwelling " within the counties of Cumberland, Northumberland, Westmorland and Duresme, have been " taken, some forth of their own houses, and some in travelling by the highway, or otherwise, " and carried out of the same counties, or to some other places within some of the said counties, " as prisoners, and kept barbarously and cruelly, until they have been redeemed by great ransoms; " and where now of late time there have been many incursions, roads, robberies, and burning " and spoiling of towns, villages, and houses within the said counties, that divers and sundry of " her majesty's loving subjects within the said counties, and the inhabitants of divers towns there, " have been forced to pay a certain rate of money, corn, cattle, or other consideration, commonly " there called by the name of Blackmail, unto divers and sundry inhabitants upon or near the " Borders, being men of name, and friended and allied with divers in those parts, who are commonly known to be great robbers and spoil-takers within the said counties, to the end thereby " to be by them freed, protected, and kept in safety, from the danger of such as do usually rob " and steal in those parts; by reason whereof, many of the inhabitants thereabouts, being her " majesty's tenants, or other good subjects, are much impoverished, and theft and robbery much " increased, and the maintainers thereof greatly encouraged, and the service of those borders and " frontiers much weakned and decayed, and divers towns thereabouts much dispeopled and laid " waste, and her majesty's own revenue greatly diminished; which heinous and outrageous misde" meanors there, cannot so well by the ordinary officers of her majesty in those parts be speedily " prevented or suppressed, without further provisions of law."—And therefore enacts, that the said offence shall be felony without benefit of clergy: But not to abridge or impeach the jurisdiction or authority of the lords wardens of any the marches of England for and anenst Scotland.

Note, the word *maile* imports a tribute or rent in general. *Black maile* seems to have been commonly paid in cattle, as *white maile* was paid in silver, vulgarly (but improperly) styled *quit rent.*

money

money of forfeitures to remain with the treasurer, until order and warranty come to him for disposing thereof. And likewise all other fines and forfeitures for any of the causes abovesaid, or for any other thought meet to be set down, or which are already set down and not here expressed; the money of all to be paid by the appointed collectors to the said treasurer as before is said.

AND forasmuch as the lord warden of himself is very loth to be the author of invasion or innovation for any use and custom of the Borders, thereby drawing to himself the hatred of the country, as also for other causes, he prayeth that these, or as many of them as shall be thought necessary, with such further orders as shall be thought meet to be added, may be the whole deed, and as proceeding from the lord lieutenant and the justices of assize, and may be set down in writing under their hands, and the justices of peace of the country, with the gentlemen, to be made acquainted therewith, and to signify their assent by subscription to the same.

THE names of the gentlemen that were present at this meeting at Newcastle:

Sir *Robert Cary* knight, deputy warden of the West Marches.
William Musgrave esquire, sheriff of Cumberland.

George Salkeld *John Dalston* *Francis Lamplugh* *Wilfride Lawson* *Thomas Carleton*	esquires.
Lancelot Carleton *Leonard Musgrave* *Richard Tolson*	gentlemen †.

THE aforesaid Sir ROBERT CARY (afterwards earl of *Monmouth*) according to a laudable custom of many in those times, wrote certain memoirs of his own life, which in the year 1759 were from his manuscript presented to the public by the right honourable John earl of Cork and Orrery. A few extracts of which will further shew to us the state of the Borders at that time.

" Upon the death of the old lord Scroope, the queen gave the West wardenry to his son, that had married my sister. He having received that office, came to me with great earnestness, and desired me to be his deputy, offering me that I should live with him in his house; that he would allow me half a dozen men, and as many horses, to be kept at his charge; and his fee being 1000 marks yearly, he would part it with me, and I should have the half. This his noble offer I accepted of, and went with him to Carlisle; where I was no sooner come, but I entered into my office. We had a stiring time of it, and few days passed over my head but I was on horseback, either to prevent mischief, or to take malefactors, and to bring the Border in better

† Bell.

quiet

quiet than it had been in times paſt. One memorable thing of God's mercy ſhewed unto me was ſuch, as I have good cauſe ſtill to remember it.

I had private intelligence given me, that there were two Scottiſh men, that had killed a churchman in Scotland, and were by one of the *Grames* relieved. This *Grame* dwelt within five miles of Carliſle. He had a pretty houſe, and cloſe by it a ſtrong tower for his own defence in time of need. About two o'clock in the morning I took horſe in Carliſle, and not above 25 in my company, thinking to ſurprize the houſe on a ſudden. Before I could ſurround the houſe, the two Scotts were gotten into the ſtrong tower, and I could ſee a boy riding from the houſe as faſt as his horſe could carry him, I little ſuſpecting what it meant. But *Thomas Carleton* came to me preſently, and told me, that if I did not preſently prevent it, both myſelf and all my company would be either ſlain or taken priſoners. It was ſtrange to me to hear this language. He then ſaid to me, 'Do you ſee that boy that rideth 'away ſo faſt? He will be in Scotland within this half hour, and he is gone 'to let them know, that you are here, and to what end you are come, and 'the ſmall number you have with you; and that if they will make haſte, on 'a ſudden they may ſurprize us, and do with us what they pleaſe.' Hereupon we took advice what was beſt to be done. We ſent notice preſently to all parts to raiſe the country, and to come to us with all the ſpeed they could; and withal we ſent to Carliſle to raiſe the townſmen, for without foot we could do no good againſt the tower. There we ſtayed ſome hours expecting more company; and within ſhort time after, the country came in on all ſides, ſo that we were quickly between three and four hundred horſe: And after ſome little longer ſtay, the foot of Carliſle came to us, to the number of three or four hundred men; whom we ſet preſently at work to get up to the top of the tower, and to uncover the roof, and then ſome twenty of them to fall down together, and by that means to win the tower. The Scots ſeeing their preſent danger offered to parley, and yielded themſelves to my mercy. They had no ſooner opened the iron gate, and yielded themſelves my priſoners, but we might ſee 400 horſe within a quarter of a mile coming to their reſcue, and to ſurprize me and my ſmall company; but of a ſudden they ſtayed, and ſtood at gaze. Then had I more to do than ever. For all our borderers came crying with full mouths, 'Sir, give us leave to ſet upon them; for 'theſe are they that have killed our fathers, our brothers, our uncles, and 'our couſins; and they are come thinking to ſurprize you, upon weak graſs 'nags, ſuch as they could get on a ſudden; and God hath put them into 'your hands, that we may take revenge of them for much blood that they 'have ſpilt of ours.' I deſired they would be patient a while, and bethought myſelf if I ſhould give them their wills, there would be few or none of the Scots that would eſcape unkilled (there were ſo many deadly feuds among them); and therefore I reſolved with myſelf, to give them a fair anſwer, but not to give them their deſire. So I told them, that if I were not there myſelf, they might then do what pleaſed themſelves; but being preſent, if I ſhould give them leave, the blood that ſhould be ſpilt that day would lie very heavy upon

upon my confcience. And therefore I defired them for my fake to forbear; and if the Scots did not prefently make away with all the fpeed they could upon my fending to them, they fhould then have their wills to do what they pleafed. They were ill fatisfied with my anfwer, but durft not difobey. I fent with fpeed to the Scots, and bade them pack away with all the fpeed they could; for if they ftayed the meffenger's return, they fhould few of them return to their own home. They made no ftay, but they were turned homewards before the meffenger had made an end of his meffage. Thus by God's mercy I efcaped a great danger, and by my means there were a great many mens lives faved that day."

Afterwards, the faid Sir *Robert Cary* was made deputy warden of the Eaft Marches, under his father the lord *Hunfdon*. On his entry upon that office, he fays.—"I wrote to Sir *Robert Ker*, who was my oppofite warden; a brave, active, young man, and defired him that he would appoint a day, when he and myfelf might privately meet in fome part of the border, to take fome good order for quieting the borders, till my return from London, which journey I was fhortly of neceffity to take. He ftayed my man all night, and wrote to me back, that he was glad to have the happinefs to be acquainted with me, and did not doubt but the country would be better governed by our good agreements. I wrote to him on the Monday, and the Thurfday after he appointed the place and hour of meeting.

After he had filled my man with drink, and put him to bed, he and fome half a fcore with him got to horfe, and came into England to a little village. There he broke up an houfe, and took out a poor fellow, who (he pretended) had done him fome wrong, and before the door cruelly murdered him, and fo came quietly home and went to bed. The next morning he delivered my man a letter in anfwer to mine, and returned him to me. It pleafed me well at the reading of his kind letter, but when I heard what a bravo he had put upon me, I quickly refolved what to do, which was, never to have to do with him, till I was righted for the great wrong he had done me. Upon this refolution, the day I fhould have met with him, I took poft, and with all the hafte I could, rode to London, leaving him to attend my coming to him as was appointed. There he ftayed from one till five, but heard no news of me. Finding by this, that I had neglected him, he returned home to his houfe; and fo things refted (with great diflike the one of the other) till I came back, which was with all the fpeed I could, my bufinefs being ended. The firft thing I did after my return, was to afk juftice for the wrong he had done me, but I could get none. The Borderers feeing our difagreement, they thought the time wifhed for of them was come. The winter being begun, there were roads made out of Scotland into the Eaft March, and goods were taken three or four times a week. I had no other means left to quiet them, but ftill fent out of the garrifon, horfemen of Berwick, to watch in the fitteft places for them; and it was their good hap many times to light upon them, with the ftolen goods driving before them. They were no fooner brought before me, but a jury went upon them, and being found guilty, they were prefently hanged: a courfe which had been feldom ufed; but I had no way to keep

keep the country quiet but to do ſo. For when the Scotch thieves found what a ſharp courſe I took, with thoſe that were found with the bloody hand, I had in a ſhort time the country more quiet. All this while we were but in jeſt as it were, but now began the great quarrel between us.

There was a favourite of his, a great thief, called *Geordie Bourne.* This gallant, with ſome of his aſſociates, would in a bravery come and take goods in the Eaſt Marche. I had that night ſome of the garriſon abroad. They met with this *Geordie* and his fellows, driving of cattle before them. The garriſon ſet upon them, and with a ſhot killed *Geordie Bourne*'s uncle; and he himſelf, bravely reſiſting till he was ſore hurt in the head, was taken. After he was taken, his pride was ſuch, as he aſked, Who it was that durſt avow that night's work? but when he heard it was the garriſon, he was then more quiet. But ſo powerful and awful was this Sir *Robert Ker* and his favourites, as there was not a gentleman in all the Eaſt Marche that durſt offend them. Preſently after he was taken, I had moſt of the gentlemen of the Marche come to me, and told me, that now I had the ball at my foot, and might bring Sir *Robert Ker* to what condition I pleaſed; for that this man's life was ſo near and dear unto him, as I ſhould have all that my heart could deſire for the good and quiet of the country and myſelf, if upon any condition I would give him his life. I heard them and their reaſons; notwithſtanding, I called a jury the next morning, and he was found guilty of marche-treaſon. Then they feared, that I would cauſe him to be executed that afternoon. Which made them come flocking to me, humbly intreating me, that I would ſpare his life till the next day; and if Sir *Robert Ker* came not himſelf to me, and made me not ſuch proffers as I could not but accept, that then I ſhould do with him what I pleaſed. And further they told me plainly, that if I ſhould execute him before I had heard from Sir *Robert Ker*, they muſt be forced to quit their houſes and fly the country; for his fury would be ſuch againſt me and the Marche I commanded, as he would uſe all his power and ſtrength to the utter deſtruction of the Eaſt Marche. They were ſo earneſt with me, that I gave them my word he ſhould not die that day. There was poſt upon poſt ſent to Sir *Robert Ker*, and ſome of them rode to him themſelves, to advertiſe him in what danger *Geordie Bourne* was; how he was condemned, and ſhould have been executed that afternoon, but by their humble ſuit I gave them my word that he ſhould not die that day; and therefore beſought him, that he would ſend to me with all the ſpeed he could to let me know, that he would be the next day with me, to offer me good conditions for the ſafety of his life.

When all things were quiet, and the watch ſet at night, after ſupper about ten o'clock, I took one of my mens liveries, and put it about me, and took two other of my ſervants with me in their liveries, and we three as the warden's men came to the provoſt marſhal's where *Bourne* was, and were let into his chamber. We ſate down by him, and told him, that we were deſirous to ſee him, becauſe we heard he was ſtout and valiant, and true to his friend; and that we were ſorry our maſter could not be moved to ſave his life. He voluntarily of himſelf ſaid, that he had lived long enough to do ſo much as he had done, and withal told us, that he had lain with above forty mens wives, what in England, what in Scotland; and that he had killed ſeven Engliſhmen with his own hands: that he had ſpent his whole time in whoring, drinking, ſtealing, and taking deep revenge for ſlight offences. He ſeemed to be very penitent, and much deſired a miniſter for the comfort of his ſoul. We promiſed him to let our maſter know his deſire; who, we knew, would preſently grant it. We took our leaves of him, and preſently I took order that Mr. *Selby*, a very worthy honeſt preacher, ſhould go to him, and not ſtir from him till his execution the next morning: for after I had heard his own confeſſion, I was reſolved no conditions ſhould ſave his life; and ſo took order, that at the gates opening the next morning, he ſhould be carried to execution, which accordingly was performed.

In the ſame morning I had one from Sir *Robert Ker* for a parley, who was within two miles ſtaying for me. I ſent him word, I would meet him where he pleaſed, but I would firſt know upon what terms and conditions. Before his man was returned, he had heard, that in the morning very early *Geordie Bourne* had been executed. Many vows he made of cruel revenge, and returned home full of grief and diſdain; and from that time forwards ſtill plotted revenge. He knew the gentlemen of the country were altogether ſackleſs, and to make open road upon the Marche would but ſhew his malice, and lay him open to the puniſhment due to ſuch offences. But his practice was, how to be revenged on me or ſome of mine.

It was not long after, that my brother and I had intelligence that there was a great match made at football, and the chief riders were to be there. The place they were to meet at was *Shelſey*, and that day we heard it, was the day for the meeting. We preſently called a council, and after much diſpute it was concluded, that the likelieſt place he was to come to, was to kill the ſcouts. And it was the more ſuſpected, for that my brother (who was deputy warden before my coming to the office), for cattle ſtolen out of the bounds, and as it were from under the walls of *Berwick*, being refuſed juſtice upon his complaint, or at leaſt delayed, ſent of the garriſon into *Liddeſdale*, and killed there the chief offender which had done the wrong.

Upon this concluſion, there was order taken, that both horſe and foot ſhould lie in ambuſh in divers parts of the bounds, to defend the ſcouts, and to give a ſound blow to Sir *Robert* and his company. Before the horſe and foot were ſet out, with directions what to do, it was almoſt dark night, and the gates ready to be locked. We parted; and I was by myſelf coming to my houſe: God put it into my mind, that it might well be, he meant deſtruction to my men that I had ſent out to gather tithes for me at *Norham*; and their rendeſvous was every night to ſup and lie at an alehouſe in *Norham*. I preſently cauſed my page to take horſe, and to ride as faſt as his horſe could carry him, and to command my ſervants (who were in all eight) that preſently upon his coming to them they ſhould all change their lodging, and go ſtraight to the caſtle, there to lie that night in ſtraw or hay. Some of them were unwilling thereto, but durſt not diſobey; ſo all together left their alehouſe, and retired to the caſtle. They had not well ſettled themſelves to ſleep, but

but they heard in the town a great alarm. For Sir *Robert* and his company came ſtreight to the alehouſe, broke open the doors, and made inquiry for my ſervants. They were anſwered, that by my command they were all in the caſtle. After they had ſearched all the houſe, and found none, they feared they were betrayed, and with all the ſpeed they could, made haſte homewards again. Thus God bleſſed me from this bloody tragedy.

All the whole Marche expected nightly ſome hurt to be done; but God ſo bleſſed me and the government I held, as, for all Sir *Robert*'s fury, he never drew drop of blood in all my Marche, neither durſt his thieves trouble it much with ſtealing, for fear of hanging, if they were taken."

Afterwards, Sir *Robert Cary* being advanced to the head wardenſhip of the Middle Marche, he came to the place of the warden's reſidence at Alnwick Abbey: Where being arrived, he ſays, "The thieves hearing of my being ſettled there, continued ſtill their wonted courſe in ſpoiling the country, not caring much for me, nor my authority. It was the beginning of ſummer, when I firſt entred into my office; but before that ſummer was ended, they grew ſomewhat more fearful. For the firſt care I took was, to cleanſe the country of our inbred thieves, for by them moſt miſchief was done. For the Scotch riders were always guided by ſome of them in all the ſpoils they made. God bleſſed me ſo well in all my deſigns, as I never made journey in vain, but did that I went for.

Amongſt other malefactors, there were two gentlemen thieves, that robbed and took purſes from travellers in the highways (a theft that was never heard of in thoſe parts before). I got them betrayed, took them, and ſent them to Newcaſtle gaol, and there they were hanged.

I took not ſo few as 16 or 17 that ſummer and the winter following, of notorious offenders, that ended their days by hanging or heading. When I was warden of the Eaſt Marche, I had to do but with the oppoſite Marche, which Sir *Robert Ker* had; but here I had to do with the Eaſt, Middle, and Weſt Marches of Scotland. I had very good juſtice with Sir *Robert Ker* and the laird of *Farneherſt* (that had charge over the eaſt part of the Middle March); but the weſt part, which was *Liddeſdale* and the Weſt Marche, kept me a great while in cumber. The firſt thing they did was the taking of *Haltweſell*, and carrying away of priſoners and all their goods. I ſent to ſeek for juſtice for ſo great a wrong. The oppoſite officer ſent me word, it was not in his power, for that they were all fugitives, and not anſwerable to the king's laws. I acquainted the king of Scots with his anſwer. He ſignified to me that it was true, and that if I could take my own revenge without hurting his honeſt ſubjects, he would be glad of it. I took no long time to reſolve what to do, but ſent ſome two hundred horſe to the place where the principal outliers lived, and took and brought away all the goods they had. The outlaws themſelves were in ſtrong holds, and could no way be caught. But one of the chief of them, being of more courage than the reſt, gate to horſe and came pricking after them, crying out and aſking, What he was that durſt avow that mighty work? One of the company came to him with a ſpear, and

and ran him through the body, leaving his ſpear broken in him, of which wound he died. The goods were divided to the poor men, from whom they were taken before.—The next ſummer after, I fell into a cumberſome trouble, but it was not in the nature of thieves and malefactors. There had been an ancient cuſtom of the borderers, when they were at quiet, for the oppoſite border to ſend to the warden of the Middle Marche, to deſire leave, that they might come into the borders of England, and hunt with their greyhounds for deer, towards the end of ſummer, which was never denied them. But towards the end of Sir *John Forſter's* government, when he grew very old and weak, they took boldneſs upon them, and without leave aſking would come into England, and hunt at their pleaſure, and ſtay their own time. And when they were hunting, their ſervants would come with carts, and cut down as much wood, as every one thought would ſerve his turn, and carry it away to their houſes in Scotland. Sir *John's* imbecility and weakneſs occaſioned them to continue their miſdemeanor ſome four or five years together, before he left his office. And after my lord *Euers* had the office, he was ſo vexed and troubled with the diſorders of the country, as all the time he remained there he had no leiſure to think of ſo ſmall a buſineſs and to redreſs it; ſo that now they began to hold it lawful to come and go at their pleaſures, without leave aſking. The firſt ſummer I entered, they did the like. The *Armſtrongs* kept me ſo on work, that I had no time to redreſs it. But having over-maſtered them, and the whole Marche being brought to a good ſtay and quietneſs, the beginning of next ſummer I wrote to *Farnehurſt*, the warden over-againſt me, to deſire him to acquaint the gentlemen of his Marche, that I was no way unwilling to hinder them of their accuſtomed ſports to hunt in England as they ever had done, but withal I would not by my default diſhonour the queen and myſelf, to give them more liberty than was fitting. I prayed him therefore to let them know, that if they would, according to the ancient cuſtom, ſend to me for leave, they ſhould have all the contentment I could give them; if otherwiſe they would continue their wonted courſe, I would do my beſt to hinder them.

Nothwithſtanding this letter, within a month after, they came and hunted as they uſed to do, without leave; and cut down wood, and carried it away. I wrote again to the warden, and plainly told him, I would not ſuffer one other affront; but if they came again without leave, they ſhould dearly abide it.

For all this, they would not be warned, but towards the end of the ſummer they came again to their wonted ſports. I had taken order to have preſent word brought me; which was done. I ſent my two deputies, with all the ſpeed they could make; and they took along with them ſuch gentlemen as were in their way, with my forty horſe, and about one of the clock they came to them and ſet upon them. Some hurt was done, but I gave eſpecial order they ſhould do as little hurt, and ſhed as little blood, as poſſibly they could. They obſerved my command, only they broke all their carts, and took a dozen of the principal gentlemen that were there, and brought them to me to Witherington where I then lay. I made them welcome, and gave them the best entertainment that I could. They lay in the castle two or three days, and so I sent them home; they assuring me, that they would never hunt there again without leave, which they did truly perform all the time I stayed there; and I many times met them myself, and hunted with them two or three days: and so we continued good neighbours ever after. But the Scots king complained to queen Elizabeth very grievously of this fact. The queen and council liked very well of what I had done; but to give the king some satisfaction to content him, my two officers were committed to the bishop of Durham's, there to remain prisoners during her majesty's pleasure. Within a fortnight I had them out again, and there was no more of this business."

[This naturally reminds one again of the famous adventure of Chevy Chase: On which, the noble editor of these memoirs justly observes, that Mr. Addison in his celebrated criticism on that ancient ballad (Spect. No. 70.) mistakes the ground of the quarrel. It was not any particular animosity or deadly feud between the two noble earls the principal actors, but was a contest of privilege and jurisdiction between them respecting their offices as lords wardens of the Marches.]

THE next thing that occurs in order of time is a petition of the *Grames*, in Mr. Bell's manuscript, to the lord *Scroope*, dated Sep. 19, 1600.

To the Right honourable *Thomas* lord *Scroope*, lord warden of the West Marches of England towards Scotland:.

RIGHT Honourable,

We her majesty's tenants and faithful subjects, whose names are hereunder written, do in all humble sort beseech your good lordship to stand our good lord: Whereas we understand that the destruction of ourselves and our posterity is intended, by colourable practice of some of the gentlemen of the country, whose cunning hath drawn in a number of simple gentlemen to join with them; for preventing thereof, and to lay the presumption of their dangerous plot more open, we thought good, in discharge of our duties, first to our lord God, next to her majesty, and lastly to your good lordship, so much in expressing our dutiful obedience, as we do trust either your good lordship will crave at our hands, or that we ought any way to perform.

First, in shewing our obedience and affection to the favouring of justice: we will stand bound unto your good lordship, every man particularly for himself, his children, servants, and tenants, that if your good lordship have any cause against them in time to come, they shall be answerable to underlie her majesty's laws at the general sessions.

Secondly, we shall all be ready, as becometh good subjects, to rise and assist your lordship's officers, servants, and all her majesty's subjects, in following hue and cry, and aiding them to our uttermost power.

Lastly, if any offence be committed within your lordship's Marche by any of Scotland, we shall be ready to serve your good lordship truly in seeking revenge,

revenge, not respecting kindred or favour, but serve our prince and our country, as becometh true and faithful subjects to do.

Most humbly craving your lordship's favour, in having an honourable care of these our offers, and thoroughly to consider, how cruelly our lives are sought, and our utter destruction intended, by these gentlemen confederates of this new league lately erected amongst us, the like never heard of in these parts before. What cause we have to fear to answer law, how clear soever our causes shall be, God and your lordship may judge, when these gentlemen sit on the bench and at the gaol delivery as our judges, and are known to thirst for our bloods, and would cut our throats with their hands if they durst, but only that your good lordship will have an honourable care in preventing their wicked attempts, having openly avowed our destruction, knowing us not to depend on any subject but only her majesty and your good lordship her majesty's officer; not to be drawn from our loyalty, although our lives and destruction is one of the first marks they openly aim at.

We pray that the meaning may prove to her majesty's good, but sure the presumption is dangerous;

First, in convening such a multitude together that is joined in bond and oath, in such a league as they are bound and sworn in:

Secondly, in joining all together to disgrace Mr. *Lowther* her majesty's officer under your good lordship, knowing his fidelity to her majesty could not be withdrawn:

Thirdly, in seeking our destructions, who they know do only depend of God, her majesty, and your good lordship her majesty's officer;

Fourthly and lastly, in presuming to nominate your lordship's deputy, wherein they have laid open all their practices against Mr. *Lowther*, which if they can get obtained, then all is at their own will and pleasure, being all birds of one nest, and feathers of one wing; for first having all the gentlemen convened together thereby to be strong, then to have the whole county in their hands in your lordship's absence, thereby to have Carlisle castle her majesty's key in this part at their own commandment: Whether the presumption is perillous or not, we refer that to your lordship's honourable care. But who have read stories have found, that such a presumption in such a multitude hath often proved a dangerous event. And especially in this case, Mr. *Thomas Salkeld* and Mr. *William Hutton*, two principal men of this new league, and not only themselves but as well men of their convenors, standing deeply affected many ways, both in favour, kindred, and alliance to Mr. *Francis Dacre*, a man whom we do hold no good subject to her majesty, who lieth here most part within 20 miles, and some of their friends resorting unto him; and for that we do owe our faithful zeal to her majesty, in fearing the worst of their convenings, will still aggravate the gentlemen to their former purpose.

We humbly crave, that your good lordship will vouchsafe that honourable favour, as to send this our humble petition and offer of dutiful service to the lords of her majesty's most honourable privy-council; to whom, and to your good lordship, we hold ourselves, lives, and livings. And wherein we have not offered our duties in every degree, as becometh faithful and true subjects, to amend it in any thing we can to their lordſhips, as to your lordſhip's ſelf ſhall be thought fitting for us to do: referring our cauſes, and the preventing of the gentlemens wicked intentions, to God and her majeſty's moſt honourable privy council and your lordſhip's ſelf, whom we will ſerve with unfeigned hearts during our lives.

Subſcribed by
Walter Grame.
John Grame.
William Grame of Moate.
Richard Grame of Breckinhill.
William Grame of Roſetrees.
Alexander Grame of Kirkanders.
David Grame of Bankhead.
William Grame of Fald.
Hutchin Grame the younger.
With the reſt of our friends.

THE Gentlemens anſwer to the ſlanderous aſſertions of the *Grames*, Sep. 25, 1600.

THE Gentlemen do affirm, that the *Grames* and their clans, with their children, ſervants, and tenants, are the chiefeſt actors in the ſpoil and decay of our country; and do think that your lordſhip is ſo perſuaded. And therefore they do well to remember, that it is over heavy a burden for them to be bound to be anſwerable for their offences done. And ſo for their three offers, they are good ſo far as they do extend, if they may be performed; for better it is to amend hereafter, than to hold on as they have done: but of what validity their bonds are, experience may declare.

The cauſes wherefore they are drawn to make their offers to your lordſhip are moſt ſlanderous, and wrongfully imputed by them to the gentlemen, as it is well known to your honour: unleſs they account their reſtraints of liberty from wronging her maſeſty's ſubjects, and yielding their obedience to authority, to be the deſtruction of them and their poſterity.

We truſt, our uſages and demeanor in the country to be ſuch, as no true man will affirm or judge, that we thirſt after their blood, would cut their throats, or avow their deſtruction. For it is far from our thoughts to imagine any ſuch wicked practice. But we know that theſe untrue ſuggeſtions came from *Lancelot Carleton* to enrage the Grames againſt the gentlemen; who, as party with the Grames, came to prefer the ſaid petition, and uſed unbecoming ſpeeches therein before your lordſhip; a man known to be contentious, and a practiſer of lewd actions, as in part was openly manifeſt before the lord biſhop of Carliſle, your honour, and other juſtices of peace, at a ſeſſions, in his accuſation againſt *John Muſgrave* her majeſty's land ſerjeant of Gilſland; where, by *Carleton*'s own witneſſes, the ſaid land ſerjeant was cleared, and by them it was upon oath confeſſed, that he the ſaid *Carleton* would have ſuborned them to have depoſed againſt the ſaid land ſerjeant; which he in ſome manner openly confeſſed, to his own diſgrace, if he had any reſpect to his credit. And now by him are theſe ſlanders inſerted in the ſaid petition, and the whole drift thereof contrived to prevent by his untruths, ſo far as he can, the

the good means now in hand for the reformation of the ſpoils and outrages in our country, greatly thereby decayed; not reſpecting his neighbours harms, he himſelf living in ſafety; being allied to the *Grames* by ſeveral marriages of his kindred to them, both upon the borders of England aud Scotland, and thereby not only protected, but imboldened to proſecute his unchriſtian devices.

They are againſt themſelves in alledging, that their not anſwering to the law is becauſe the gentlemen which are their judges thirſt after their blood; for they will not anſwer their offences done already before any judge, be he never ſo indifferent. And ſo their refuſals are in reſpect of their guiltineſs of the offences, and not in reſpect of the judges: And this appeareth forth of their own offers. Neither have they had any cauſe to complain upon any gentlemen for any injuſtice offered to any of them; and therefore their aſſertion is very weak.

For the four cauſes which draw a dangerous preſumption to diſquiet the land:

Firſt, they anſwer and do deny any unlawful joining together, or any joining at all, but ſuch as was allowed by your lordſhip's deputy in your abſence, and confirmed by your lordſhip at your home coming. Of which company ſo joined together, Mr. *Lowther* and his ſon and heir were two; only done for the better repreſſing of theft, then and yet commonly uſed in our country; which draweth no dangerful preſumption of diſquiet to the land, for then by their own confeſſion Mr. *Lowther* could not have been drawn to it if there had been any ſuch appearance.

To the ſecond, they do anſwer, that the gentlemen had no intention to diſgrace Mr. *Lowther*; but, upon his too great bearing with thieves, to the hurt of our country, and contrary to that which he had undertaken before in his joining with the gentlemen, they upon juſt cauſe did complain againſt him: which hath been deliberately heard, and the truth of the whole cauſes known to your Honour and the reſidue to whom the hearing and determining thereof was referred. Wherein Mr. *Lowther* will not think himſelf wronged, neither commend the *Grames* in alledging the doings betwixt him and the gentlemen as any cauſe to draw any peril to the diſquiet of the land.

To the third; It is untrue, and the ſame with all the reſidue are frivolous: They ſeek not their lives.

To the laſt: They are not ſo void of diſcretion, as to appoint your lordſhip's deputy; whereof they have no authority nor power. But in regard of the troubles within your wardenry, which are great, the gentlemen in all true humbleneſs have intreated your Honour to appoint a deputy for better furtherance to your lordſhip to redreſs the wrongs and oppreſſions of our country; and upon juſt cauſe they did commend to your lordſhip a gentleman of good worth and ability, well experienced, and one who fears God, generally loved, and thought fit for that place, with whom the gentlemen with heart and hand will willingly join for her majeſty's ſervice; whereby the good of her ſubjects, and the ſafety of our country, is rather to be expected.

And for that the ſaid *Carleton* and the *Grames* do fear, that the gentleman ſo commended as fit to be your lordſhip's deputy, if he ſhould be allowed, would look into their doings, and ſomewhat reſtrain their former liberty of offending, they labour to prevent your lordſhip of your good and honourable purpoſe therein, by preferring that doubt before your eyes as touching *Francis Dacres*, whom the gentlemen do favour, as they alledge, who lieth within 20 miles. As though your lordſhip did not know the diſpoſition of the gentleman commended to your honour, or of the gentlemen who do commend him. This is not the firſt time that the ſame hath been preferred againſt the gentlemen, and particularly againſt ſome of them, not of any danger which might thereby enſue to the quiet of the land, but as an help to prefer their own private cauſes by their ſuggeſtings thereof. In which their allegation, the gentlemen who have hitherto lived without any ſuſpicion of diſloyalty to her majeſty or the ſtate, do think themſelves wronged, to be charged with any favour or affection towards Mr. *Dacres*, but as true and faithful ſubjects may and ought to do; and ſo moſt humbly deſire, that your lordſhip will examine the ſaid *Carleton* and the *Grames* (who preferred this petition), of their further knowledge, which be thoſe friends of the gentleman who reſorted to Mr. *Dacres*; that if any ſuch be, they may receive their puniſhment therein according to their deſerts.

And for concluſion: As often before, ſo now we humbly beſeech your Honour, to be the means, that the *Grames* and the reſidue of our Borderers may be drawn in obedience to your lordſhip's authority, and may be compelled to anſwer her highneſs's laws from time to time in ſome reaſonable manner for their offences, the better to ſtay their common robberies and ſpoils of our country, whereof the *Grames* are not blameleſs; and that this our anſwer may be ſent with their petition to the lords of her majeſty's moſt honourable privy council, if your lordſhip do think fit to ſend their petition.

NEXT follows in the ſaid Manuſcript of Mr. *Bell*,

A NOTE and abſtract of the ſeveral names of the clans of all the *Grames*, ſeverally given in to the right honourable *Thomas* lord *Scroope* of *Bolton*, lord warden of the Weſt Marches of England towards Scotland, preferred by them the eighth day of October 1602; whom they ſeverally bound themſelves to be anſwerable for to the ſaid lord *Scroope*.

Theſe following belong to the Goodman of Netherby:

Walter Grame himſelf
Richie Grame his ſon
Arthur Grame his ſon
William Grame his brother
John Grame his uncle
Francis Grame his uncle
John Grame his brother
John Grame of Sleylands

Richie

Richie Grame
Dick Grame
Thomas Grame } his brether.
Arthur Grame
Andrew Grame

Their tenants;

Thomas Taite
Alexander Grame
John Gibson

Richard Grame
Richie Armstrong
Herbert Johnston
Willie Bailie
Andrew Little
Christopher Calvert
John Baytie
John Armstrong
John Gibson
Matthew Watson.

These following are they which John Grame of Anghouse-well will be answerable for:

John Grame himself
Richie Grame } his sons
Walter Grame
Geordie Grame
William Grame } his brether
Arthur Grame
Thomas Grame

Tenants belonging to them;

Willie Grame
Henry Grame of Skaleby
William Blacklock miller
Reyne Grame
Cuddie Glesby
(And 25 more, by name.)

These following are the names that I Fargus Grame of Sowport will be answerable for:

Fargus Grame myself
Willie Grame } my sons
Jamie Grame

My tenants and dependers are these;

John Wilson
James Davieson
James Browne
Thomas Browne
John Hope
Robert Carrudders
James Philip
James Litle
Herbert Whittie
John Grame of the Ley
Christie Grame of the Ley
Davie Moffett
Richard Urwen

These are the names that I Davie Grame of the Millens do undertake for:

Davie Grame myself
John Blawett
John Batie
John Turner
John Grame
Davie Batie
William Grame
Matthew Urwen
John Tynning
John Baitie

John Grame of the Peretree for myself and my brother Wattie.

These

Theſe are they following that appertain to the Goodman of the Moate; for which he and Breckinhill do undertake for:

William Grame of Moate
Richie Grame of Breckinhill
George Grame of Langtown
Richie Grame junior of Breckinhill
Arthur Grame of Moate
William Grame of Langtown
Fargue Grame of ſame
Richie Grame of ſame
John Grame of Sandhills
George Grame of ſame
Fargue Grame
Robert Grame
George Grame
Richie Grame of Bailie
William Grame } his ſons
Francis Grame } his ſons
Thomas Storie of Howend
Florie Storie
Richie Bell
(With 84 more, by name.)

Now hereafter follows young Hutchin's clan and gang. And firſt the names that Geordie anſwers for, being brother to young Hutchin:

John Litle
Gordie Edger
William Litle
Andrew Elwood
Jock Anderſon

Theſe are the names that I William Grame brother to young Hutchin anſwer for:

William Mark
Arthur Grame
John Waughe
Simon Urwen
Cuthbert Mounſey
Matthew Moffett
Matthew Henderſon
Davie Baitie
Chriſtie Wilkin
John Archerſon

Theſe are the names that I William Grame ſon to Robbie anſwer for:

Andrew Linton
Jock Linton
Jock Coutert
Andrew Glendoning
Thomas Scott
Matthew Browne
John Waugh
Davie Browne
Thomas Coutert
Thomas Pott
Willie Pott
John of Scotland
Wattey Murrey
Jock Urwen
Chriſtie Halliday
John Pott
John Croſſer

Theſe are the names that I Willie Grame brother to Hutchin do anſwer for:

Jamie Bell
Jock Turner
Willie Philip
Wattie Stoope
Chriſtie Byers

Followeth

Followeth Jock's Johnie, and his;

Jock's Johnie and his
Jock Storie
Thomas Grame his man.

These following are young Hutchin's mens names:

Thomas Urwen
Willie Twedopp (And 21 more).

These are the names of Robert Grame's men son to Hutchin's Davy and Andrew his brother:

John Armstrong
Willie Sarkbriggs
Edie Waughe
William Turner
John Glendonning
John Armstrong
Davie Carrudders
George Sarkbriggs
John Bell
Jamie Grame

For these following Hutchin's Arthur doth answer:

Hutchin Grame son to Arthur
William Grame son to Hutchin's Arthur (And 20 more).

These following be the names of those that I William Grame of the Fauld will answer for:

William Grame of the Fauld
Walter Grame
Matthew Grame
William Grame
Robert Grame
Hutchin Grame

Their tenants;

Adam Glendonning
John Michelson
Herbert Blakeburne
Geordie Kennedie
George Carne
William Coutert
Wattie Bell
Herbert Martin
Rinyon Grame
John Mayburne.

These following are those that William Grame of Rosetrees will answer for:

William Grame of Rosetrees
William Grame } his sons
Wattie Grame }
Geordie Grame } his brether
Walter Grame }
Andrew Grame son to Geordie

Juſtice Grame
Francie Grame }
Geordie Grame } his brether (with 46 more).

Theſe are they that Davie Bankhead undertakes for:

Davie Grame
Thomas Grame his ſon
William Grame
Regnald Grame (And 24 more).

Theſe are they following that Jock of the Lake doth undertake for:

Jock Grame of the Lake
George Grame }
Richie Grame }
Chriſtie Grame } his ſons
Arthur Grame }
Francis Grame }
Robert Grame of Akeſhawhill
Fargus Grame }
John Grame } his ſons
Richie Grame of Akeſhawhill
Walter Grame
Will Grame his brother
With his tenants, in number 13.

Theſe following are thoſe that Dick's Davie will undertake for:

Davie Grame
Davie his ſon
Wattie his nephew
Richie Purdon
John Litle
William Pott
Robert Foſter

Theſe are they that Will Grame goodman of Medop, his eames [uncles], ſons, and friends will anſwer for:

Francie Grame
Robert Grame
Walter Grame
Arthur Grame
Richie Blakeburne
Hobbie Blakeburne
Jock Anderſon
Archie Halliday
William Taite
William Parke
Richie Anderſon
Robert Wright
John Glendoning.

The whole number of theſe names given in to my lord as aforeſaid, 439.

CHAP.

CHAPTER IX.

Of the state of the Borders, during the reign of king James *the first.*

FROM the acceffion of king James the firft, when the two kingdoms came to be governed by one monarch, we begin to eftimate the *modern* ftate of the borders; as matters then began to incline, though but very flowly, towards a reformation.

The firft thing king James did after his acceffion was, to publifh a proclamation for union between the two kingdoms, May 19, 1603, as followeth:

FORASMUCH as the king's majefty, in his princely difpofition to juftice, having ever a fpecial care and regard to have repreffed the flaughters, fpoils, robberies, and other enormities, which were fo frequent and common upon the Borders of thefe realms, and to have reduced and fettled the faid Borders unto a perfect obedience, to the comfort of his highnefs's peaceable fubjects, the courfe whereof hath been heretofore impeded by the difference of the Borders, Englifh and Scottifh; till it hath now pleafed almighty God, in his great bleffing to this whole ifland, by his majefty's lawful fucceffion to the imperial crown of England, not only to remove this difference, but alfo to furnifh his highnefs with power and force fufficient to profecute that his majefty's royal and worthy refolution, as his highnefs hath already begun; intending that the bounds poffeffed by thofe rebellious people, being in fertility and all other benefits nothing inferior to many of the beft parts of the whole ifle, fhall be no more the extremities, but the middle, and the inhabitants thereof reduced to perfect obedience; yet notwithftanding, his majefty is informed, that certain difordered and wicked perfons of both Marches, enemies to peace, juftice, and quietnefs, pretending ignorance of his majefty's refolution for the union of the two realms already fettled in the hearts of all his good fubjects, and feeding themfelves with a finifter conceit and opinion that no fuch union fhall be eftablifhed and take effect, ftill continue in all kind of robbery and oppreffion; whereunto they are encouraged by the receipt and harbour granted unto them, their wives, children, goods, and gear in the inland and peaceable parts of both the realms, highly to his majefty's contempt, and fruftrating his highnefs's commiffion granted to the effect aforefaid: And therefore his majefty, for the better fatisfaction of all his good fubjects who may ftand in any doubt of the faid union, and to take away all pretence of excufe from wicked and turbulent perfons, hath hereby thought good to publifh and make known to all thofe to whofe knowledge thefe prefents fhall come, that as his majefty hath found in the hearts of all the beft difpofed fubjects of both the realms of both qualities, a moft earneft defire that the faid happy union fhould be perfected, the memory of all preterite difcontentments abolifhed, and the inhabitants of both the realms to be the fubjects of one kingdom, fo his highnefs will with all convenient diligence with the advice of the eftates and parliament of both the kingdoms make the fame to be perfected.

 And

And in the mean time, till the ſaid union be eſtabliſhed with the due ſolemnities aforeſaid, his majeſty doth hereby repute, hold, and eſteem, and commands all his majeſty's ſubjects to repute, hold, and eſteem both the two realms as preſently united, and as one realm and kingdom, and the ſubjects of both the realms as one people, brethren and members of one body; and in regard thereof, that every one of them abſtain and forbear to commit any kind of robbery, bloodſhed, or any other inſolence or diſorder, or to receive and harbour the perſons, wives, children, or goods of the fugitives and outlaws of either of the realms, but to contain themſelves in peace and quietneſs and all ſuch dutiful behaviour as becometh good and loyal ſubjects: certifying all and every perſon who ſhall do, practiſe, or attempt any thing to the violating of theſe preſents, that they ſhall incur the puniſhment due to the ſaid rebels, and that the ſame ſhall be executed againſt them, with all rigour and extremity to the terror of others.

Given under our ſignet at our manor of Greenwich the nineteenth of May †.

In the ſame year, July 8, the king publiſhed another proclamation for concord and amity between the two nations; as follows:

We have, ſince our entry into this realm of England, had ſpecial care to make all our ſubjects know, with how equal affection we reſolved to proceed in all things which ſhould concern the ſafety or honour of our kingdoms, for both which we know we are to make one and the ſelf-ſame account to almighty God, under whom we hold all earthly things; in which reſpect we were very curious to prevent at our firſt coming all manner of offences or affronts which naturally ariſe between ſeveral nations at their firſt joining in ſociety and converſation; never ceaſing to lay ſevere commandment upon our greateſt ſubjects that came in with us, to ſuppreſs any injurious actions of any their ſervants or train, towards the meaneſt ſubject of Engliſh birth, in whom from the higheſt to the loweſt we have obſerved ſo great love and general obedience to us and our commandments; and whenſoever it hath come to our ears, that any offence hath been done by any of them, we have made them know how much it hath diſpleaſed us.

Nothwithſtanding, becauſe we do hear of many inſolences reported to be committed by our nation of Scotland to our Engliſh ſubjects, with this addition further, that the magiſtrates and juſtices are thought to be remiſs towards ſuch, in doubt leſt the ſame ſhould be offenſively reported to us; we have thought it convenient, as well for the ſatisfaction of the one ſort, as for admonition to the other, to publiſh by open ſignification, that ſeeing it hath pleaſed almighty God to call us to the ſupreme power over both, we are purpoſed to be an univerſal and equal ſovereign to them both, and to adminiſter juſtice where there ſhall be occaſion without any worldly reſpect to either of them; and therefore do hereby enjoin all lieutenants, deputy lieutenants, juſtices of peace, and all other our officers and miniſters of this kingdom, that whenſo-

† Rymer, v. 16. p. 506.

ever complaint ſhall be made to any of them, that breach of peace is committed by thoſe of our nation of Scotland, upon the ſubjects of England, or by the ſubjects of England upon thoſe of the nation of Scotland, in both which kinds we hear of many great abuſes, though ſometimes aggravated according to humour of the reporters, they ſhall carefully upon every complaint examine with all indifferency the particulars of every ſuch action, and cauſe puniſhment to be inflicted upon the party offending, without reſpect of nation, according to the laws of this realm.

And to the end they may not doubt to proceed to the execution thereof, as we do hereby not only aſſure them that we will ſtrengthen and maintain all officers and magiſtrates in the execution of their offices for the preſervation of the public peace of this realm, ſo if we ſhall ſee at any time that any magiſtrate ſhall be ſlow to redreſs ſuch grievances or puniſh the offenders, we ſhall have cauſe to think that they are willing to furniſh ſome cauſe of ſuch rumours, the rather to ſerve for colour or cauſe of further alienation, and ſo by conſequence of ſedition amongſt our people, and an hindrance to that union between both ſtates, which is one of the greateſt benefits that we bring with us to our people for their ſtrength and ſafety; in governing of whom, though we muſt uſe, as all other princes do, the miniſtry of ſubordinate miniſters, yet God almighty knoweth that in our own mind there is not a thought of partiality towards either of them, but an internal deſire and reſolution to afford indifferent grace and juſtice to all: For demonſtration whereof, we have been forced to publiſh thus much, leſt the iniquity of factious and unruly ſpirits might blemiſh the innocency and integrity of our heart towards all our ſubjects, whom we hold dearer than our own life.

Given at our caſtle of Windſor the 8th day of July 1603, in the firſt year of our reign of England, France, and Ireland, and of Scotland the ſix and thirtieth †.

In the ſame year, Dec. 4. the king iſſued a proclamation reſpecting the Grames in particular; againſt whom he ſeems to have had a peculiar averſion, the *Grames* having generally adhered to the Engliſh intereſt, and by reaſon of their number and vicinity having been a great annoyance to his ancient ſubjects of Scotland:

By the King.

Forasmuch as all our ſubjects in the north parts, who have felt the ſmart of the ſpoils and outrages done upon them at our firſt entry into this kingdom, by divers borderers, but ſpecially by the *Grames*, cannot be ignorant what care we have had, that puniſhment ſhould be done upon the offenders, having for that purpoſe to our charge maintained our forces to apprehend them and commiſſioners to try them according to the law; by whoſe travel, namely, of our couſin the earl of Cumberland our lieutenant there, with the aſſiſtance of other commiſſioners, things are brought to that point, that the offenders

† Rymer, v. 16. page 526.

are

are all in our mercy, and do all (but ſpecially the *Grames)* confeſs themſelves to be no meet perſons to live in thoſe countries, and therefore have humbly beſought us that they might be removed to ſome other parts, where with our gracious favour they hope to live to become new men, and to deſerve our mercy; although we do confeſs, we have rather inclined to this courſe of mercy, as a thing more agreeable to our nature, than the taking of ſo much blood as would be ſhed, if we ſhould leave them to the juſt cenſure of the law: Nevertheleſs, leſt our good ſubjects, ſeeing no ſuch execution preſently follow of our ſaid commiſſion, ſhould make other conſtruction thereof than is cauſe; we have thought good to make known to them, that this courſe for the preſent proceedeth from no alteration of our former deteſtation of ſuch injury, nor from want of care and affection to our good ſubjects oppreſſed by ſuch heinous offenders, but only for lack of means to provide preſently for the tranſplantation of theſe *Grames* elſewhere, to the intent their lands may be inhabited by others of good and honeſt converſation; we have thought it not amiſs, for better effecting thereof, and for eaſe of the priſons, to diſmiſs the vulgar ſort of them; retaining their heads and principals for pledges, not only to be anſwerable for their forthcoming when they ſhall be called for, but for their good behaviour alſo in the mean ſeaſon. Of all which our reſolution, we require all perſons to take notice, and to comfort themſelves with full aſſurance, that they ſhall find the effects at all times of our promiſes in all things tending to the weal of our people.

Given at Wilton the fourth day of December in the firſt year of our reign of England, France, and Ireland, and of Scotland the 37th.

Upon this occaſion, Mr. Bell gives an account of "The tax aſſeſſed and "received for tranſplantation of the *Grames* in the year 1606; *viz.*

	l	s	d
The earl of Cumberland for Eſke	4	0	0
The lord William Howard for Gilſland	5	0	0
Dalſton lordſhip	4	10	0
Sir Edward Muſgrave	4	0	0
Mr. Salkeld of Corby	2	0	0
Mr. Harrie Dacre	2	0	0
Mr. Richard Fletcher	1	0	0
Mr. Briſkoe of Crofton	0	10	0
Mr. Thomas Middleton	1	0	0
Mr. Thomas Clyburne	0	6	8
Mr. John Borehead	0	5	0
Mr. Richard Kirkbryde	0	6	8
Part of Cumberland Ward by Dr. Studholme	16	13	6
Itonfield	0	8	0
Rockliffe	0	12	0
Bowneſs	0	8	5
The townſhips of Burgh pariſh	4	4	4
Armathwaite	1	10	0

Nuncloſe

	l	s	d
Nuncloſe	0	10	0
Petterel Crooke	0	4	6
Cargo and Stainton	0	15	0
Thurſtonfield	0	18	8
Kirkanders	0	6	3
Petterel Banks	0	4	5
Aykton	3	15	0
Great Orton	2	10	0
Kirkbanton	1	13	0
Lytle Banton	0	16	0
Kirkbryde	0	15	0
Sebraham	0	2	0
Houghton	0	12	0
Linſtock and Millhouſe	0	10	5
Skailby	0	19	4
Over Heſkett	0	7	0
Richardby	0	9	6
Blencogo	0	0	4
Dundraw	0	1	5
Wigton	1	7	1
Brunſketh	0	6	2
Upper Croſby	0	7	6
Nether Croſby	0	5	0
Waverley	0	4	2
Thureſby	2	5	0
Kirklinton pariſh	1	13	10
Stanwix pariſh, Etterby, and Terreby	1	6	4
Mr. Ralph Hilton	0	11	10
Botcherby	0	6	0
Warwick	0	10	0
Aglionby	0	5	0
Botchargate	0	6	0
Carlton	0	10	0
Allerdale Ward by Mr. Pearſon	97	0	0
Sir Harry Curwen	2	0	0
Mr. Cleter of Ravenſkarr	0	3	4
Leeth Ward	59	1	8
Mr. John Threlkeld	0	2	0
Buſkebeck in Sourby	0	13	0
Kirkoſwald in part	0	5	4
Mr. Thomas Waughe	0	3	0
Lamonby and Ainſtable	0	0	5
Wethermelock	0	2	8
John Skelton of High houſe	0	1	0

Weſtmorland.

Weſtmorland.

	l	s	d
Kendal Ward — — — —	96	13	0
Eaſt Ward — — — — —	50	0	0
Weſt and Middle Ward — — — —	28	0	0
Mr. Harry Brougham — — — —	0	6	0
Total	408	19	9

Money diſburſed to the Grames for their tranſplantation:

Aug. 30th, 1606.

	l	s	d
To Sir Ralph Sidley — — — —	300	0	0

Money diſburſed at their ſecond going over, Apr. 23. 1607.

	l	s	d
To Arthur Grame of Netherby — — —	2	0	0
To old Dick's Davy — — — —	2	0	0
To young Davy his ſon — — —	2	0	0
To Will's Walter — — — —	2	0	0
To Mickle Willie — — —	2	0	0
To William Grame of Cockplay — — —	6	13	4
To David Grame of Bankhead — — —	2	0	0
To William Grame of Langtown — — —	2	0	0
To Grame of Nuke — — — —	3	0	0
To Richard Grame of Moathead — — —	1	0	0
To Hugh's Francie Grame — — —	2	0	0
To George Grame of Meadop — — —	2	0	0
To William Grame of Blackford — — —	2	0	0
To Richy Purdom — — — —	1	0	0
To Stephen Blackburne — — —	0	10	0
To Walter Grame of Milles — — —	1	0	0
To John Foſter — — — —	1	0	0
To George Grame of Hetherick — — —	0	10	0
To Thomas Grame of Sleylands — — —	0	5	0
To Thomas Robinſon for fraught and victuals for theſe into Ireland	13	6	8
More for fraught and victuals of another ſhip —	3	10	0
Expence of horſe and men in attending them at Workington	1	4	6
Horſes and carts from Carliſle — — —	0	6	2
Boats to ſea with men and luggage — —	0	5	0
To a footman with money and letters from the ſheriff of Weſtmorland	0	2	6
Money bags for all the taxes — — —	0	3	4
	53	16	6

Money

Money disbursed to the Grames at their third going over, Sep. 11. 1607.

	l	s	d
To Hutchin Grame — — — —	2	0	0
To Richy Grame of Breas — — — —	0	10	0
To Thomas Baty — — — —	0	10	0
To Arthur Grame of the Lake — — —	1	0	0
To William Grame of Hetherſgill — —	0	10	0
To Peter Grame — — —	0	10	0
To Flory Story — — —	2	0	0
To Thomas Sanderſon — — — —	1	0	0
To Thomas Grame of Logan — — —	1	0	0
Wife of William Grame of Medop — — —	1	0	0
Wife of young Bletherbye — — — —	2	0	0
Wife of Walter Carliſle — — —	4	0	0
Wife of William Langtowne — — —	2	0	0
To Fargus Grame of Langtowne — —	1	10	0
To Archie Grame of Mill hill — — —	2	0	0
James Maingie his charges in ſeeing theſe ſhipped at Workington	1	10	0
George Clay, in regard of his expences and travel, collecting of the money, and helping to get them in that were to be ſent into Ireland, and ſeeing proviſion made for them for all their ſeveral paſſages — — — — —	12	1	5
	35	1	5
Sum total diſburſed — — — — —	388	17	11
So remained of the ſum collected — — —	20	1	10
Unto which a ſmall ſum being added, out of the ſame was allowed to be paid to William Grame of Mote — — —	10	0	0
Arthur Grame of Mote — — — — —	3	6	8
Richard Grame of Breckinhill — — — —	3	6	8
John Grame of Whole Shields — — — —	3	6	8
Edward Grame of Mills — — — —	3	6	8

Examined by us, Hen. Carliol'.
Wilfr. Lawſon.

In the mean time the king was very ſolicitous for an union between the two kingdoms, and for that purpoſe, in his wonted manner, iſſued a proclamation; for he was fond of proclamations, eſpecially when they were of his own compoſing, as the following from the ſtyle and manner thereof undoubtedly was, and which therefore we inſert chiefly as matter of curioſity.

By the King:

A Proclamation for the union of the kingdoms of England and Scotland.

As often as we call to mind the most joyful and just recognition made by the whole body of our realm, in the first session of our high court of parliament, of that blessing which it hath pleased God to reserve many years in his providence to our person, and now in the fulness of time of his disposition to bestow upon us, namely, the blessed union or rather reuniting of these two mighty famous and ancient kingdoms of England and Scotland under our imperial crown; so often do we think it our duty to do our uttermost endeavour for the advancement and perfection of that work which is of his beginning, and whereof he hath given so many palpable signs and arguments, as he that seeth them not is blind, and he that impugneth them doth but endeavour to separate that which God hath put together. For to omit those things which are evident to sense, that the isle within itself hath almost none but imaginary bounds of separation, without but one common limit or rather guard of the Ocean sea, making the whole a little world within itself, the nations an uniformity of constitutions both of body and mind, especially in martial processes, a community of language (the principal means of civil society), an unity of religion (the chiefest band of hearty union, and the surest knot of lasting peace); what can be a more express testimony of God's authority of this work, than that two mighty nations, having been ever from their first separation continually in blood each against other, should for so many years immediately before our succession be at peace together, as it were to that end, that their memory being free from sense of the smart of former injuries, their minds might in the time of God's appointment more willingly come together, that it hath pleased him so to dispose that this union is not inforced by conquest and violence, nor contracted by doubtful and deceivable points of transaction, but naturally derived from the right and title of the precedent princes of both kingdoms concurring in our person, alike lineally descended from the blood of both through the sacred conjunction of wedlock; an union which is the work of God and nature, and whereunto the works of force or policy cannot attain.

We may add hereunto, that which we have received from those that be skilful † in the laws of this land, that immediately upon our succession divers of the ancient laws of this realm are *ipso facto* expired. As namely, that of Escuage, and of the naturalization of the subjects; and that there is a greater affinity and concurrence between most of the ancient laws of both kingdoms, than is to be found between those of any other two nations:

As namely,

In estates of inheritance and freehold, as fee simple, fee tail, tenant for life, by curtesy, dower, and such like.

† This was Sir Francis Bacon (afterwards lord Verulam) who prepared a draught of a proclamation on this occasion; which the editor of Bacon's works, vol. 2, p. 144. says was not used.

In

In cafes of defcents of inheritance, in tenures of lands, as of knight's fervice, focage, frankalmoin, burgage, villenage, and fuch like.

In writs and forms of procefs.

In cafes of trial by juries; grand juries.

And laftly, in officers and minifters of juftice, as fheriffs, coroners, and fuch like; which we leave to be further confidered by the commiffioners of both realms.

All which, being matter prepared only by the providence of almighty God, and which by human induftry could not have been fo ordered; we and all our fubjects ought firft with all reverence to acknowledge his handy-work therein, and to give him our moft humble thanks for the fame, and then to further by our endeavours that which his wifdom doth by fo many figns point out to be his will, whereof many particularities depending upon the determinations of the ftates and parliaments of both realms, we leave them there to be difcuffed, according to the commiffions granted by the feveral acts of both parliaments; and fome other things refting in our own imperial power, as the head of both, we are purpofed, towards the building of this excellent work, to do by ourfelf that which juftly and fafely we may by our abfolute power do: And for a firft ftone of this work, whereupon the reft may be laid, feeing there is undoubtedly but one head to both peoples which is ourfelf, and that unfeignedly we have but one heart and mind to communicate equally to both ftates, as lines iffuing from one center, our juftice, our favours, and whatfoever elfe, dependeth upon the unity of our fupreme power over both, God having miniftred to us fo juft caufe to embrace them both with equal and indifferent love, inafmuch as our birth and firft part of our life hath been in the one, and the latter part thereof is like to be for the moft part in the other: we think it unreafonable that the thing which is by the work of God and nature fo much in effect one, fhould not be one in name, unity in name being fo fit a means to imprint in the hearts of people a character and memorial of that unity which ought to be amongft them indeed.

Wherefore we have thought good to difcontinue the divided name of England and Scotland out of our royal ftyle, and do intend and refolve to take and affume to us, in manner and form hereafter expreffed, the name and ftyle of king of Great Britain, including therein, according to the truth, the whole ifland, wherein no man can imagine us to be led by any humour of vain glory or ambition, becaufe we fhould in that cafe rather delight in a long enumeration of many kingdoms and feigniories, whereof in our inheritance we have plenty enough, if we thought there were glory in that kind of ftyle, but only that we ufe it as a fignification of that which in part is already done, and fignificant prefiguration of that which is to be done hereafter, nor that we covet any new affected name devifed at our pleafure, but out of undoubted knowledge do ufe the true and ancient name, which God and time have impofed upon this ifle, extant and received in hiftory, in all maps and charts wherein this ifle is defcribed, and in ordinary letters to ourfelf from divers foreign princes, warranted alfo by authentical charters, exemplifications under feals, and other records of great antiquity, giving us precedent for our doing,

 not

not borrowed out of foreign nations, but from the acts of our progenitors kings of this realm of England both before and ſince the Conqueſt, having not had ſo juſt and great cauſe as we have.

Upon all which conſiderations, we do by theſe preſents, by force of our kingly power and prerogative, aſſume to ourſelf, by the clearneſs of our right, the name and ſtyle of king of Great Britain, France, and Ireland, defender of the faith, &c.* as followeth in our juſt and lawful title, and do hereby publiſh, promulge, and declare the ſame, to the end that in all our proclamations, miſſives foreign and domeſtical, treaties, leagues, dedicatories, impreſſions, and in all other cauſes of like nature, the ſame may be uſed and obſerved.

And to the end the ſame may be ſooner and more univerſally divulged both at home and abroad, our will and pleaſure is, that the ſtyle be from henceforth uſed upon all inſcriptions upon our current monies and coins of gold and ſilver hereafter to be minted.

And for that we do not innovate or aſſume to us any new thing, but declare that which is and hath been evident to all, our will and pleaſure is, that in ſuch appellations or nominations as ſhall be hereafter made by force of theſe preſents, the ſame ſhall be expreſſed in ſuch and the ſame manner and form, and after ſuch computation, as if we had aſſumed and declared the ſame the firſt day of our reign of our realm of England; forbearing only for the preſent, that any thing herein contained do extend to any legal proceedings, inſtrument, or aſſurance, until further order be taken in that behalf.

Given at our palace of Weſtminſter the twentieth day of October †.

In the 4th year of the ſaid king's reign, the parliaments of both kingdoms repealed all hoſtile acts that had been made in former reigns againſt each other: And commiſſioners were appointed to treat of an union; but after ſome progreſs, it was ſilently dropped by the Engliſh parliament, chiefly (as it ſeemeth) from an abſurd policy of the king, in overvaluing his native kingdom, eſtimating the ſame as one third part of the whole iſland; whereas, in about a century after, when ſuch union actually took effect, the Scots were better informed, being contented that in the parliament of Great Britain they ſhould not exceed an eleventh or twelfth part, and in the land-tax ſhould bear ſcarce a fortieth part.

All this while, outrages in the Borders continued unremitted. Special commiſſions were iſſued again and again to try and puniſh delinquents; which

* Lord Coke, in his comment upon Littleton, ſpeaks ſomewhere in high terms of encomium of an &c, as containing certain excellent points of learning: perhaps this inſtance before us exhibits matter of more curious obſervation than any of thoſe on which that learned commentator hath deſcanted. If this &c. had been expreſſed in full, it muſt have run—*of the church of England and alſo of Ireland in earth the ſupreme head* (omitting Scotland; and which, if Scotland had been inſerted, the Scots would never have aſſented to). And from this time forward, the king's ſtyle hath moſt commonly run in this abbreviated form, *defender of the faith, and ſo forth.*

† Pat. 2. J. 1. Rymer. v. 16. p. 603.

com-

commiſſions differing little in form one from another, we here inſert one only as a ſpecimen of all the reſt:

JAMES by the grace of God, &c. To our truſty and well beloved Sir William Selby, Sir Robert Dallavell, Sir Wilfrid Lawſon, Sir William Seton, and Sir William Howme, knights, Joſeph Pennington, Edward Grey of Morpitte, Patrick Chermeſide of Eſtneſbitt, Robert Chartrons of Amisfield, and Gideon Murraye of Elybank, eſquires, and every of them, greeting.

Whereas by the happy union of the kingdoms of England and Scotland in ſubjection and allegiance by the providence of almighty God under our imperial crown in our royal perſon, the laws or uſages of the late marches or borders inſtituted or tolerated while they ſtood ſeparate or divided under ſeveral kings for the peace and tranquillity thereof are utterly fruſtrated and expired, and yet many of both nations dwelling near the late borders or marches (of ſuch force is cuſtom) do continue their former godleſs, looſe, and diſordered courſe of life; who by the ordinary and ſeparate proceeding of either country cannot, as the neceſſity of the cauſe requireth, be either ſo ſpeedily brought to the knowledge of God, and to obedience to us and to our laws (which we chiefly deſire), or ſuch as will not be reclaimed ſo ſoon cut off by the ſword of juſtice leſt they infect others, as by joining certain of our loving ſubjects of both nations in one commiſſion for that purpoſe, whom God hath already conjoined as members of one body under one head:

And foraſmuch as one of the greateſt cauſes of their offences is hope of impunity; and the greateſt motive of their hope is, after murders, felonies, riots, routs, unlawful aſſemblies, or other offences committed in either country, to eſcape puniſhment by flying into the other:

And foraſmuch as the ſaid laws and uſages of the late borders and marches are vaniſhed and delete, and for that it appertaineth to our kingly office to care and provide that all our loyal and obedient ſubjects may live in peace and tranquility, without fear of rapine and ſpoil and danger of their lives, and that murderers, felons, and other delinquents may be puniſhed according to our laws reſpectively in that behalf:

We have therefore thought good, as well to remove all occaſions of ſtrangeneſs and marks of diviſions between the ſaid nations, as alſo to take away all ſubterfuge and quench all the ſparks of any hope of eſcape from puniſhment in ſuch as ſhall offend, to join together in one commiſſion certain of either nation, for the eſtabliſhment and preſervation of our peace in thoſe parts, and for the utter ſuppreſſing and preventing of all ſuch exorbitant offences and diſorders, or elſe for the apprehending and ſending of ſuch offenders as ſhall perſiſt in their wickedneſs, to the country and place where they offended, to receive their condign puniſhment for their demerits according to law and juſtice reſpectively in that behalf.

Know ye therefore, that we, truſting in your wiſdoms, fidelities, and diſcretions, have conſtituted, authorized, and appointed you the ſaid Sir William Selby, Sir Robert Dallavell, Sir Wilfrid Lawſon, Sir Robert Seton, Sir William

liam Howme, knights, Joseph Penington, Edward Grey, Patrick Chermeside, Robert Chartrons, and Gideon Murraye, esquires, to be our commissioners, and by these presents we do give full power and authority unto you and every six or more of you, to convene and assemble together and consult, when, where, and as often as you or any six or more of you shall think fit, using therein all the possible expedition that may be, how and by what means our peace may be established and preserved, in the several counties, shires, shiredomes, and stewarties hereafter following, being about the middle part of our kingdom of Great Britain: That is to say, in the counties of Northumberland, Westmerland, and Cumberland, and in the shires or parishes of Norham, the Holy Island, and Bedlingdon, parcel of the county palatine of Durham, and in the sheriffdoms and towns of Berwick, Roxburgh, Selkrigg, Pebles, Dumfreys, and in the stewarties of Kirkoubriche and Annerdale; and how and by what means the said murders, felonies, riots, routs, unlawful assemblies, offences, and disorders may be prevented, and the offenders according to law and justice respectively in that behalf punished.

And further, our will and pleasure is, and by these presents we give unto you our said commissioners, and every one or more of you, full power and authority from time to time and at all times, by all lawful ways and means, and with all possible expedition, as well to establish, preserve, and keep our peace within the said counties, shires, sheriffdoms, and stewarties, and each and every of them, and also to apprehend all such malefactors and delinquents within the said counties, shires, sheriffdoms, and stewarties, or any of them, and to commit them to prison or to other safe custody, and further to send or deliver them to such place and places, within any of our said counties, shires, sheriffdoms, stewarties, towns, and parishes, in either of our said countries, where they may receive justice according to their demerits and our laws and statutes respectively in that behalf.

And further, for the speedy suppressing of the said offenders, we do by these presents charge and command the several sheriffs of every of the said counties and shires for the time being, to whom the charge and custody of the same respectively appertaineth, to assist you and every of you, according to our laws respectively in that behalf, with the powers of the several counties, shires, sheriffdoms, stewarties, towns, and parishes aforesaid, as often as you, or any one or more of you, as is aforesaid, shall require the same.

And also to assist and strengthen yourselves, or any one or more of you as is aforesaid, with such forces of men and horsemen, as we shall from time to time as occasion shall serve assign unto you in that behalf, and to use the same as often as you or any one or more of you shall think fit, as well for the preservation of our peace in the counties, shires, sheriffdoms, stewarties, towns, and parishes aforesaid, and each and every of them, as for the apprehending of any of the malefactors or delinquents within the same, to the end they may be conveyed and brought to the ordinary trial and judgment of our laws respectively made and provided in that behalf.

And that our will and pleasure herein expressed may take the more speedy effect; we do by these presents give full power and authority unto you or any one

‡

one or more of you, to do and execute all and every other lawful or necessary act and acts, thing and things whatsoever, which you or any one or more of you as is aforesaid shall think fit and necessary for the doing and speedy execution of this our commission.

And whatsoever you or any one or more of you shall do or cause to be done by virtue of this our commission, and according to the tenor and effect of the same, touching the execution of the premisses or any part thereof; these presents shall be to you, and every one or more of you, a sufficient warrant and discharge in that behalf, against us, our heirs and successors.

And further we will and command all and singular our sheriffs, justices of the peace, bailiffs, constables, headboroughs, and all other our officers, ministers, and subjects, to whom it shall or may appertain, that they and every of them shall not only by all possible ways and means use their uttermost endeavours and have special care in and about the due execution of their several authorities and powers, according to the duties of their several places and the trust we have reposed in them, for suppressing and preventing the said inconveniences, offences, and disorders, but also that they and every of them be helping, aiding and assisting you and every one or more of you as aforesaid in the execution hereof, as they and every of them tender our pleasure, and will answer to the contrary at their utmost perils.

And our further will and pleasure is, that these our letters of commission shall be in due manner made and settled as well under our great seal of England as under our great seal of Scotland, without any other or further warrant from us to be had or obtained in that behalf.

In witness whereof we have caused these our letters of commission, as well under our great seal of England as under our great seal of Scotland to be made patent.

Witness ourself at Westminster the 25th day of February (1605) †.

Next followeth a copy of the condescendings of the said commissioners, as well English as Scottish, touching the execution of their said commission, Apr. 9. 1605.

First, it is agreed, that Sir Wilfrid Lawson knight shall be convener of the rest of the commissioners, according to the articles thereanent contained in his majesty's instructions, and so continue for the space of three months next coming.

Item, It is agreed, that concerning old feuds between the low countries there shall be a general assurance.

Item, It is agreed, that old feuds shall be put to agreement, or else the party offending to lie by it, viz. Englishmen in Edinburgh, and Scottishmen in Newcastle, until they will agree; and in the mean time the parties to be bound to keep the peace: And for new feuds, that justice shall be executed upon the offenders according to the law reciprocally.

† Rymer, v. 16. p. 609.

Also,

Alſo, It is agreed, if any Engliſhman ſtrike a Scottſman, or contrariwiſe if any Scotſman ſtrike an Engliſhman, without weapon; the party offending ſhall be committed to the next gaol, there to remain 3 days without bail: And if the ſaid parties ſhall ſtrike with weapons, then to lie in gaol for 20 days without bail. And if the party be hurt, then he ſhall not be delivered at the 20 days end, until he make ſuch further ſatisfaction to the party as the commiſſioners that committed him ſhall think fit. But if the hurt fall out to be a maiming or mutilation; then the party offending ſhall not be delivered after the 20 days impriſonment, until he perform the order of two of his majeſty's commiſſioners for ſatisfaction of the party maimed. And if death follow, then the offender to receive his puniſhment according to his majeſty's laws reciprocally.

Item, It is agreed, that if any Engliſhman ſteal in Scotland, or any Scotſman ſteal in England, any goods or cattels amounting to the value of 12*d*; he ſhall be puniſhed by death: And that all acceſſaries to ſuch felonies, viz. outputting, or reſetting, ſhall likewiſe ſuffer death for the ſame.

Alſo, It is agreed, that proclamation ſhall be made, that all inhabiting within Tindale and Riddſdale in Northumberland, Bewcaſtle dale, Wilgavey, the north part of Gilſland, Eſk, and Leven in Cumberland, Eaſt and Weſt Tevidale, Liddeſdale, Eſkdale, Ewſdale, and Annerdale in Scotland (ſaving noblemen and gentlemen, unſuſpected of felony or theft, and not being of broken clans) and their houſhold ſervants, dwelling within thoſe ſeveral places before recited, ſhall put away all armour and weapons, as well offenſive as defenſive, as jacks, ſpears, lances, ſwords, daggers, ſteelcaps, hagbuts, piſtols, plate ſleeves, and ſuch like; and ſhall not keep any horſe, gelding, or mare, above the price of 50*s* ſterling, or 30*l* Scots; upon like pain of impriſonment.

Item, That proclamation be made, that none of what calling ſoever, within the countries lately called the Borders, of either of the kingdoms, ſhall wear, carry, or bear any piſtols, hagbuts, or guns of any ſort, but in his majeſty's ſervice; upon pain of impriſonment, according to the laws of either kingdom.

Item, That proclamation be made, that all landlords or officers within the bounds above contained ſhall, at the firſt ſeſſion, gaol delivery, or general meeting of the ſaid commiſſioners, to be holden within the ſeveral bounds either Engliſh or Scotiſh, come to the ſaid juſtice courts provided to give up in writing a ſpecial account upon their oaths, of the number, quantity, and names of all their tenants or inhabitants, and their ſons dwelling with them or under them, and what manner of form or trade of life they relieve or maintain themſelves by; that ſuch may be known which are not able to maintain themſelves but by evil practice: whereby they may be either puniſhed, or otherwiſe provided for, as the ſaid commiſſioners ſhall think meet and convenient.

Finally, It is ordered, that the bills of complaints which are to be exhibited to the ſaid commiſſioners, ſhall be orderly placed, viz. as the offence was

was done, according to the time; and those which were latest done to be first heard: and so orderly to be redressed as they shall be called for.

William Seton	Robert Dallivell
William Hume	Wilfride Lawson
Patrick Chirnside	John Charters
Joseph Pennington	Edward Grey.

Here next followeth "A Proclamation, July 22, 1614, for apprehending the Grames returned from transportation."

By the King.

IT always hath been and is our natural disposition, and the temper of our government to purge our dominions of malefactors, and nevertheless draw as little blood as may be, and rather to prevent offences than suffer them to go on to the hurt of the innocent subjects, and the final destruction of the malefactors themselves: According to which mixture of clemency and good policy, we did in the first year of our reign proceed against the Grames, being the principal and most violent disturbers of the peace and quiet of the middle shires. For notwithstanding that numbers, by barbarous spoils, slaughters, and outrages were fallen under the sword of our justice to be capitally inflicted upon them; yet we were pleased to extend mercy unto them, and upon their own suit and humble prostrating of themselves by submission, to remove them and transplant them into our realm of Ireland, there to become new men, and to put off their wicked and desperate course of life formerly continued in blood and rapine. For which purpose we did at that time publish our royal proclamation, and also direct our commission, for the effecting of the same; which, not without the great charge of us and the country thereabouts in their shipping and removing, was executed accordingly. But now being given to understand, that divers of them are of late returned into the said middle shire, and begin to revive their old courses of robbing, riding armed, and other heinous disorders, to the great terror of our loving subjects there inhabiting, and to the manifest contempt of our former grace and mercy, and to the renewing of former troubles and dangers in those parts, which at this time by our politick and peaceable government enjoy equal benefit of peace and security with the rest of our counties.

We do therefore hereby strictly forbid, That none of the said Grames hereafter do presume to return into our realms of England or Scotland, out of Irelend, or the cautionary towns of the Low Countries whereunto some of them are sent, and are since returned into Ireland, without the special licence of out deputy of Ireland for the time being, which licence we intend to be according to such directions, and with such cautions, as we have already prescribed unto our said deputy.

And further we do, in like strict manner command and ordain, that if any of them shall be taken within these middle shires within the space of 40 days after this our proclamation, or any other time after such limitation of stay as may be given to them in any their licences, that forthwith with all search and diligence they be apprehended and committed to prison, and further proceeded with, as well upon any their former crimes, as upon the contempt of this our royal commandment, according to the uttermost severity of our law, and according to the directions formerly given by us and our council for the government of those parts; and that as well our right trusty and right well beloved cousin the earl of Cumberland, and our right trusty and well beloved the lord Weldein our lieutenant in those parts, as also all our other commissioners, justices, and ministers for the middle shires, do take special care and order for the due and strict executing of this our proclamation, observing in all other points not here mentioned their former instructions.

Given at Royston the two and twentieth day of July, in the twelfth year of our reign of England, &c.

Next follows a warrant for *slough dogs*, for pursuing offenders through the *sloughs*, mosses, and bogs, that were not passable but by those who were acquainted with the various and intricate by-paths and turnings. These offenders were peculiarly styled *moss troopers:* And the dogs were commonly called *blood hounds*; which were kept in use till within the memory of many of our fathers. And all along, the pursuit of *hot trod (flagrant delicto*, with *red hand*, as the Scots term it) was by *hound* and horn and voice. And the following warrant ascertains by whom and where those dogs were to be kept.

Sep. 29. 1616. Sir Wilfride Lawson and Sir William Hutton knights, two of his majesty's commissioners for the government of the middle shires of Great Britain, To John Musgrave the provost marshall and the rest of his majesty's garrison (of Carlisle) send salutations. Whereas upon due consideration of the increase of stealths daily growing both in deed and report among you on the borders, we formerly concluded and agreed, that for reformation therefore watches should be set, and slough dogs provided and kept, according to the contents of his majesty's directions to us in that behalf prescribed; and for that, according to our said agreement, Sir William Hutton at his last being in the country did appoint how the watches should be kept, when and where they should begin, and how they might best and most fitly continue. And for the bettering of his majesty's service, and preventing further danger that might ensue by the outlaws, in resorting to the houses of Thomas Routledge, alias Baylihead, being near and next adjoining to the marches (he himself being fled to amongst them, as is reported) order and direction was likewise given that some of the garrison should keep and reside in his the said Thomas Routledge's houses, and there to remain till further directions be given them, unless he the said Thomas Routledge shall come in and enter himself answerable to his majesty's laws as is convenient: Now we further, by virtue of our authority from his majesty so as directed touching the Border service, do command you, that the said watches be duly searched as was appointed, and presentments to us or one of us to be made, of every

7 fault,

fault, either in conſtables for their neglect in not ſetting it forth, or in any perſons ſlipping or neglecting their duties therein; and that you likewiſe ſee that ſlough dogs be provided according to our former directions, and as this note to this warrant annexed particularly ſets down.

A note, how the ſlough dogs are to be provided and kept, at the charge of the inhabitants, as followeth:

Imprimis, beyond Eſke by the inhabitants there to be kept above the foot of Sarke	1 Dogge.
Item, by the inhabitants the inſide of Eſke to Richmont's Clugh, to be kept at the Moate	1 Dogge.
Item, by the inhabitants of the pariſh of Arthered, above Richmont's Clugh, with the Bayliffe and Black quarter; to be kept at the Bayliehead	1 Dogge.
Item, Newcaſtle pariſh, beſides the Baylie and Black quarters; to be kept at Tinkerhill	1 Dogge.
Item, the pariſh of Stapylton	1 Dogge.
Item, the pariſh of Irdington	1 Dogge.
Item, the pariſhes of Lanercoſt and Walton	1 Dogge.
Item, Kirklington, Skaleby, Houghton, and Richarby	1 Dogge.
Item, Weſtlinton, Roucliff, Etterby, Stainton, Stanwix, and Cargo; to be kept at Roucliff	1 Dogge.

The ſheriff, officers, bailiffs, and conſtables, within every circuit and compaſs wherein the ſlough dogs are appointed to be kept, are to take care for taxing the inhabitants towards the charge thereof, and collect the ſame, and for providing the ſlough dogs; and to inform the commiſſioners if any refuſe to pay their contribution, ſo as thereby ſuch as refuſe may be committed to the gaol till they pay the ſame.

CHAPTER X.

Of the ſtate of the Borders, from the reign of king James the firſt to the preſent time.

DURING the reign of king Charles the firſt, we meet with no regulations in particular relating to the Borders. The ruling powers were moſt commonly otherwiſe employed. And towards the end of that unhappy prince's reign, the whole kingdom became Borderers, that is, acted the part of Borderers one againſt another.

Soon after the Reſtoration of king Charles the ſecond, the Marches became again an object of public attention, when the act of the 13th and 14th Cha. 2. c. 22. (1662), was made, intitled, "An act for preventing of theft and rapine upon the Northern Borders of England;" which was explained by two ſubſequent

ſubſequent acts, 18 Cha. 2. c. 3. and 29 and 30 Cha. 2. c. 2. all of which are in force at this day, and are in ſubſtance as follows:

"WHEREAS a great number of lewd diſorderly and lawleſs perſons, being thieves and robbers, who are commonly called *Moſs-troopers*, have ſucceſſively for many and ſundry years laſt paſt, been bred, reſided in, and frequented the Borders of the two reſpective counties of Northumberland and Cumberland, and the next adjacent parts of Scotland; and they, taking the opportunity of the large waſte ground, heaths and moſſes, and the many intricate and dangerous ways and by-paths in thoſe parts, do uſually, after the moſt notorious crimes committed by them, eſcape over from the one kingdom into the other reſpectively, and ſo avoid the hand of juſtice, in regard the offences done and perpetrated in the one kingdom cannot be puniſhed in the other:

And whereas ſince the time of the late unhappy diſtractions, ſuch offences and offenders as aforeſaid have exceedingly more increaſed and abounded, and the ſeveral inhabitants of the ſaid reſpective counties have been for divers years laſt paſt neceſſitated, at their own free and voluntary charge, to maintain ſeveral parties of horſe for the neceſſary defence of their perſons, families, and goods, and for bringing the offenders to juſtice; and whereas moſt part of the inhabitants of the ſaid counties being more remote from the Borders than other parts, and conſequently not ſo much expoſed to imminent dangers as others, are therefore unwilling to contribute their proportionable parts of the aforeſaid charge, and yet notwithſtanding, it cannot probably or poſſibly be avoided, but that thoſe inhabitants of the reſpective counties who hold themſelves moſt ſecure, muſt certainly ſuſtain much damage and detriment in their goods and eſtates, in caſe the aforeſaid *moſs-troopers* be not timely ſuppreſſed, but ſuffered to grow numerous, ſtrong, and potent, which they muſt needs do in caſe there be no reſtraint upon them:

It is therefore enacted, that the juſtices of peace in ſeſſions ſhall have power to order an aſſeſſment on every of the inhabitants of the ſaid counties, for the ſafeguard of the ſaid ſeveral counties and inhabitants thereof, from all injury, violence, ſpoil, and rapine of the *moſs-troopers* aforeſaid; ſo as Northumberland be not charged above 500*l* a year, nor Cumberland above 200*l*.

And the ſaid juſtices ſhall have power to employ any perſon, to be choſen by them yearly or every two years at the furtheſt, to have the command of a certain number of men, not exceeding 30 in Northumberland and 12 in Cumberland, whereby the malefactors may be ſearched out, apprehended, and brought to trial: And ſuch malefactors being convicted of theft in the ſaid counties reſpectively, ſhall not have the benefit of clergy.

And the ſaid juſtices ſhall take ſecurity of the perſon by them employed in the ſaid ſervice, to anſwer the damages ſuſtained by any perſon by his neglect or default, and to pay the ſame within four months after proof thereof made on oath at the ſeſſions; ſo as the goods ſtolen be entred in one of the books to be kept for that purpoſe, within 48 hours after the ſame ſhall be ſtolen or gone: which books ſhall be kept for that end in every market

† town

town of the respective counties, and at such other convenient places therein, and by such persons, as the said justices in sessions shall appoint."

FINALLY: In the 5th year of queen Anne, 1706, Articles of UNION were agreed upon, by commissioners of both kingdoms respectively, and confirmed by their respective parliaments; that from thenceforth the two kingdoms of England and Scotland should be for ever united into one kingdom, by the name of *Great Britain*; and that the ensigns armorial of the said united kingdom shall be such as her majesty shall appoint; and the crosses of St. George and St. Andrew be conjoined in such manner as her majesty shall think fit, and used in all flags, banners, standards, and ensigns, both at sea and land:

That the succession to the monarchy shall be and remain to the princess Sophia, electoress, and duchess dowager of Hanover, and the heirs of her body, being protestants; and that all papists, and persons marrying papists, shall be for ever excluded:

That the crown, scepter, and sword of state, the records of parliament, and all other public records, continue to be kept in Scotland as they were before the Union:

That the kingdom shall be represented by one and the same parliament:

That 16 peers of Scotland shall sit in the house of lords; and 45 commoners in the house of commons:

That when the land tax for England shall be 1,997,763*l* 8*s* 4½*d*; Scotland shall pay 48,000*l*.

With many regulations respecting trade and navigation, excise, customs, duties, subsidies, and administration of justice:

With confirmation of two acts of parliament; one for securing the church of England as by law estalished, the other for securing the presbyterian church government in Scotland.

From this blessed period, hostilities in the Borders have by degrees subsided; and as the then generation, which had been brought up in rapine and misrule, died away, their posterity on both sides have become humanized; the arts of peace and civil policy have been cultivated; and every man lives safe in his own possessions; felonies and other criminal offences are as seldom committed in these parts, as in most other places of the united kingdom; and their country, from having been the outskirt and litigated boundary of both kingdoms, is now become the center of his majesty's British dominions †.

Neverthelefs, the old wounds have left some scars behind. Much common and waste ground remains, which will require a length of time to cultivate

† There is now remaining only one species of theft peculiar to the borders; and that is, where a man and woman steal each other. They hasten to the Borders. The kindred of one side or the other sometimes rise, and follow the fray. But the parties fugitive most commonly outstrip them; pass over into the opposite Marche, without any hostile attempt; get lovingly married together, and return home in peace.

and

and improve. The churches near the Borders are many of them in a ruinous condition, and very meanly endowed. In many of the pariſhes there is not ſo much as an houſe for the incumbent to live in, and in ſome pariſhes no church. And ſome defects there are in the civil ſtate, which nothing but the legiſlature can ſupply. Whilſt the laws of marche ſubſiſted, criminal offences were ſpeedily redreſſed by the power of the lords wardens or their deputies; and after the abolition of the laws of marche, the ſaid offences were redreſſed by ſpecial commiſſioners appointed for the Borders: And matters of property of any conſiderable conſequence were moſt commonly determined in the court at York for the Northern parts. The judges in their circuit came only once in the year, and ſometimes much ſeldomer. They ſtill come only once in the year into the bordering counties; which cauſes determinations of civil rights to be dilatory, and confines criminals (or perhaps innocent perſons) in priſon ſometimes near a twelvemonth before they can come to their trial.

THE

DURHAM
Teas R.
R. Lune
Rerecross
Maiden Cast.
Dale
Stanemore Chapel
Greata R.
Spittle House

THE HISTORY AND ANTIQUITIES OF THE COUNTIES OF WESTMORLAND AND CUMBERLAND.

OF WESTMORLAND IN GENERAL.

WESTMORLAND, *Westmoreland*, or as it is anciently written *Westmerland*, hath its name, according to common acceptation, from its being a *western moorish* country. The learned archbishop Usher, in his Antiquities of the British churches, page 303, quotes several authors as deriving it from *Marius* a king of the Britons, who in the first or second century defeated Roderic or Rothinger a Pictish general from Scythia, upon the mountain now called Stanemore; in memory whereof (he says) Reicross or Rerecrosse (a red, or royal cross) was erected: and from him that part of the kingdom was called *Westmerland*. But Mr. Camden treats this notion as chimerical, and says, it is only a fancy that some people have taken in their sleep *, and is positive that the county hath received its name from the barren, mountainous, uncultivated, *moorish* land (as he is pleased to represent it). Neverthelefs, there is not one ancient record that we have met with, wherein it is not expressly called *Westmerland*, and not *Westmorland*, or *Westmoreland*; which doth not altogether favour Mr. Camden's supposition:

* Quia tota inter montes alte pertingentes sit sita, et magna ex parte inculta jaceat, hoc nomen in nostra lingua invenit. Loca etenim inculta, et quæ non facile agricultura sublevari possint, *mores* Angli septentrionales vocant, et *Westmorland* nihil aliud est nobis, quam inculta ad occasum regio. Ex venerandæ igitur antiquitatis schola illud de *Mario* rege ejiciatur somnium, quem Pictos contudisse, et de suo nomine hanc regionem denominasse, resupini nostri historici per quietem viderunt.

the Latin termination is *Westmaria*, sometimes *Westmeria*, which hath still less resemblance of the *moor*. If the county had bordered upon the *western sea*, it might have been conjectured that it had received its name from thence; but as Cumberland lies between this county and the sea on the west, it can scarcely admit of that derivation. Therefore we must be content to leave it in the same uncertainty as we found it.

This county is *bounded* on the East by the counties of Durham and York; on the South, by the counties of York and Lancaster; on the West, by the counties of Lancaster and Cumberland; and on the North, by the counties of Cumberland and Durham.

The *length* of this county, from Heron-sike in the parish of Burton on the South, to where it adjoins to the counties of Cumberland and Durham on the North, is about forty miles; and the *breadth* thereof is nearly the same, from the top of Stanemore on the East, to Great Langdale on the West; according to the English standard, of 1760 yards to a mile, and not according to the customary measure of the country, which is after the proportion of about two computed miles to three measured ones. From what source this difference in the length of miles did arise, we have not been able to discover. It hath no reference to the Roman mile. Theirs was somewhat short of the English statute measure, in the proportion (according to Mr. Horsley) of about 13 to 14. Mr. Horsley further observes, that through the most part of England, three computed miles make four in the Itinerary (that is, Roman miles). Near Wales, and in the western as well as northern parts of England, two English computed miles make three Roman. It is nearly the same also in Scotland, and in some cross-roads. About London and 20 miles round, they are near equal, or not above one or two in twenty different. *Horsl.* 382, 383.

There is also in the counties of Westmorland and Cumberland a mensuration of *acres*, called customary measure, which varies from the statute measure, and is itself also diverse in different places. The most general customary measure is that of 6760 square yards to the acre, whereas the statute measure is only 4840. In some parts of Westmorland, the customary acre is measured to 7840 yards *; as if where the land is bad, they were willing to give so much the greater measure. And there was good reason for this, inasmuch as they proportioned the military duty according to the number of acres that a man possessed. But this could be no rule as to the miles: there being no reason, where the road was bad, that therefore they should make the miles so much the longer.

The AIR in this county (especially in winter) is somewhat sharp and severe, but withal very healthful; and people live commonly to a very great age. And whereas in cities and great towns, scarce above one third part of those

* And this is also the measure of the Irish plantation acre. *Smith's* County of Down, p. 7.

that

that are born do ſurvive the age of two years, in this county generally not above one in thirteen or fourteen dies within that age.

The SOIL of this county is in many places, as Mr. Camden deſcribes it, barren and unfruitful; there being much uncultivated waſte ground, and much of it incapable of cultivation. Yet there are many fruitful and pleaſant vallies; and the bottom of Weſtmorland (as it is called) hath a conſiderable quantity of level ground, though ſurrounded on every ſide with high mountains.

Lying near the weſtern ocean, it is much expoſed to RAIN, brought by the South-weſt winds, which blow in this part for above two thirds of the year. Hence their crops are later by three, four, and in ſome places ſix weeks, than in ſome other parts of the kingdom.

This county abounds with MOUNTAINS, which in the language of the country are called *Fells*, this being the genuine Saxon appellation, and the word is yet retained as an epithet in our language, to ſignify ſomething that is wild and boiſterous, as we ſay a *fell* tempeſt, a *fell* tyrant, or the like.

Yet theſe mountains are not altogether unprofitable. Beſides that they fan the air, and render it ſalubrious, they feed large ſtocks of SHEEP, of the wool whereof the farmers make great advantage. And the ſheep being very ſmall, and fed for the greater part of the year upon the ling, their mutton is moſt excellent, eſpecially that which is killed in ſummer and autumn from off the common. The wool of the ſheep is coarſe and thick, ſuitable to the climate; and, which is very remarkable, where larger ſheep, with finer and thinner fleeces, have been introduced, the breed gradually diminiſhes, and the fleece grows thicker, as if nature intended to adapt the animal to its ſituation. So the ſame ſheep, or other cattle, removed to a more favourable climate, grow larger and finer.

Theſe mountains alſo produce plenty of GROUSE, or moor-game; which are nouriſhed in like manner chiefly by the ling. And when that ſhrub is in flower, about the middle of September, it attracts the induſtrious BEE; ſo that the heath at that ſeaſon ſeems to be covered as it were with one large ſwarm. This ſhrub in Latin is called *bruera*, and in Domeſday-book *bruaria*.

The ſaid mountains alſo abound with RIVULETS, which water the vallies beneath: inſomuch that in almoſt every little village there is water ſufficient to carry a mill; which renders the precarious help of windmills ſuperfluous: though, if need ſhould be, there are few countries better ſituate for ſuch like conveniences.

Nor are theſe mountains inconſiderable in reſpect of the MINERALS they contain. The Reverend *Thomas Robinſon*, rector of Ouſby, who was a con-

 noiſſeur

noiſſeur in that branch of ſcience, in an Eſſay towards a Natural Hiſtory of Weſtmorland and Cumberland, publiſhed in the year 1709, treats of the ſame in the following manner: he firſt takes notice of the mineral productions along the ridge of mountains on the North, beginning from Stanemore, aſcending gradually to the top of Croſs-Fell, and from thence deſcending by the like gradation to Gilſland in Cumberland. "The firſt elevation of this " ridge (he ſays) is called *Hilton Fell*; the mineral productions whereof are " lead and coal: which being of a diſagreeing nature, the one renders the " other of little value. The proſpect of lead upon this fell, is only from the " appearance of ſeveral veins of ſpar, ſoil, and vein-ſtone, breaking out " upon the ſurface; and theſe being oftentimes either unripe or dead veins, " cheat the miners with vain hopes.—The ſecond elevation of this ridge is " called *Dufton Fell*; the mineral productions whereof are chiefly lead: of " which there is ſuch plenty got, as keeps a lead mill for the moſt part ſmelt-" ing down the ore. That which is here moſt remarkable is, that all the ore " got upon this mountain is not found in natural veins, which run down " perpendicularly or ſloping (which is moſt uſual), but in ſeams like coal, " which run parallel, being incloſed within the ſtrata of an hard and ſolid " limeſtone ſill, without any conſiderable depreſſion from the horizon. This " we generally call flat ore, being the overflowing of a rich vein; and doubt-" leſs, if the miners would be at the charge of croſs-cutting the riſe of this " limeſtone-ſill, they would diſcover the vein from whence this ore doth flow. " Upon this mountain there is a petrifying ſpring, which turns moſs, or any " other porous matter, that either falls into the water and ſucks it up, or " comes within the ſteam and vapours that ariſe from it, into ſtone; inſomuch " that upon the mouth of the well there is raiſed a conſiderable hill of ſuch " petrefactions.——The third elevation of this ridge of mountains is called " by the name of *Silverband*; ſo called from the richneſs of the ore, which " when refined by art yields a valuable product of ſilver.——The fourth ele-" vation is called *Blencarn-Fell*: the mineral productions, by the veins of ſpar " and ſoil which appear at day, ſeem to be lead; there having been as yet no " trials made.——The fifth elevation is *Kirkland-Fell*; which, as well as the " other mountains, hath its veins of ſpar: but as yet no trials have been " made.——The ſixth and higheſt elevation is *Croſs-Fell*. From whence " deſcending the firſt depreſſion is *Green-Fell*; the mineral productions whereof " are lead, copper, coal, and oker. The copper is very rich, but ſo inter-" mixed with the lead ore in the ſame vein, that it requires ſome labour to " ſeparate them. In this fell there is a large vein of copperiſh ſulphur, two " yards wide, which is diſcovered by the rivulet. I doubt not, but if this " vein were ſunk down, till it got its natural feeder, it would turn to a rich " vein of copper; for it is very uſual in the kingdom of Peru, that the richeſt " veins are ſulphur at the top, and as they get more moiſture, turn to copper, " and when ſunk deeper into the veins, turn to ſilver. The coal lieth upon " the inſide of the mountain, and is ſo broken and disjointed that it turns to " no account.——The ſecond depreſſion is *Melmerby Fell*; the mineral pro-" ductions are lead, of which ſome quantities have been got; the veins are

" very

"very hopeful, but no thorough trials have been made.——The third de-
"pression is *Gamelſby Fell*, known by the name of *Hartſide*. The mineral pro-
"ductions are chiefly coal. There is ſome appearance of veins of glaſſy ſpar
"and float copper, but no trials of either have been made. Here the
"metallic claſs changeth into a claſs of coal; and as the lead gradually goes
"off, ſo the ſeams of coal do gradually come in and increaſe. The ſeam of
"coal at Hartſide colliery is about half a yard thick.——The fourth de-
"preſſion is *Buſk Fell*, where no trials have been made.——The fifth de-
"preſſion is *Renwick Fell*, where the ſeam of coal is increaſed to three quarters
"thick.——The laſt and loweſt depreſſion is *Coal Fell*, ſo called from the
"colliery. Here the coal claſs is in full ſtrength and perfection, the ſeams
"being at their full height and growth.——All the ſolid ſtrata upon theſe
"mountains have their horizontal depreſſions, which the miners call dibbing
"and riſing; and they dib moſt commonly to the north."

He then proceeds to the inner parts of the county of Weſtmorland, and obſerves, "At *Reagill* and *Sleagill* we meet with ſome ſmall ſeams of coal, the "main body of the coal lying upon Stanemore-heath; ſo that if the miners "ſhould ſink there for a lower coal and a thicker ſeam, they would run a "hazard of loſing both labour and money. For as in all claſſes of coal, the "ſeams gradually increaſe in thickneſs till they come to their full height and "growth; ſo they gradually decreaſe till they dwindle out into ſmall ſeams, "and then the covers change, and the coal goes out."——So in Cumberland he ſhews, how the vein of coal comes in at Sourby paſture about eight or nine inches thick, then advances to fourteen inches, then at Warnel Fell to half a yard, then in the manor of Weſtward to a yard, where alſo a ſmall ſeam of canel coal comes in; then in the manor of Bolton it is increaſed to ſeven quarters or two yards, and the canel ſeam to a yard, and the craw coal to three quarters. And here it is come to its full growth and perfection, and ſpreads over a great part of the level country to the Scotch ſea.

He then proceeds to the mountains which are the boundaries of Weſtmorland on the South and Weſt: and obſerves how the ſeam of coal diminiſhing from Stanemore (where the ſeam is about a yard and a quarter thick), comes in at *Hartley Fell*; ſo alſo we may add, at *Nateby*, *Mallerſtang*, *Ravenſtondale*, and other places. The weſtern fells, he obſerves, are of a quite different nature from the others above-mentioned, conſiſting of a blue crag and continued rock, without any horizontal flat beds. And the mineral productions of all of them are lead, copper, and iron; there is no proſpect of coal in any of them, for where there are no flat and pinguid ſtrata, there can be expected no coal. From theſe mountains fine blue ſlate is got, which ſupplies ſeveral parts of the kingdom.

The ſame author further obſerves: "Though we cannot hope to make any "diſcovery of veins either of gold or ſilver in theſe two counties, yet we have "rich veins of ſilvery lead, in which we frequently meet with ſtones richly "imboſſed with cluſters of diamonds, as bright and ſparkling as any we have "from Briſtol. We have alſo in our rich lead veins great variety of ſpar; "ſome

"ſome white, and as tranſparent as fine chryſtal. We have others green, "blue, red, and of a violet colour; which if they could be ſo ſoftened as to "be cut into figures, might be of uſe and value."

Dr. Woodward, in his Natural Hiſtory, ſays, "That near Ambleſide, and "in the ridge of mountains leading from thence to Penrith, there is marble "of a duſky green colour, veined with white; and in Knipe Scar, are ſeveral "talky fibrous bodies, which might be employed for the making wicks for "lamps, as they will burn very long without any ſenſible diminution; they are "opake, and of an aſh colour. Foſſils of various kinds are found in different "parts of this country; as at Threapland the *entrochi* and *trochitæ* of various "kinds, ſome of which are compreſſed and flatted, others raiſed and trun-"cated, ſome hollow in the middle, and filled with grey ſtony matter. Of "the ſame are thoſe found near Strickland-head on the banks of the rivulet "which runs down from Shap, and by the inhabitants called Fairy-ſtones. "Here alſo are found the *mycetites*. *Coralloid* bodies are found in great "quantities, and differently variegated, near the river Lowther: they will "bear a poliſh, and are about the hardneſs of Genoeſe marble. Some of the "ſame kind are found at Helsfell nigh Kendal, and appear beautifully varie-"gated, of a brown ſandy colour, but ſo interſperſed with different colours, "that they are little inferior to Syena marble."—Specimens of all theſe are to be found in the collection left by Dr. Woodward to the univerſity of Cambridge.

Of ſome of the more ſcarce and curious PLANTS growing in this county, we have inſerted a catalogue in our Appendix, No. 40.

The RIVERS in this county are but ſmall; for as the mountain tops are for the moſt part the boundary, the rivers all ſpring within the county; and only three, that can properly be called rivers, carry their name to the ſea; to wit, *Eden*, which ſprings in Mallerſtang, and having received in its courſe (beſides many leſſer ſtreams) the conjoined rivers of Lowther and Eamont, enters Cumberland, and running the whole length of that county, empties itſelf into the ſea at Rowcliff. The ſecond river is *Lune* or *Lon*, which hath its ſource in Ravenſtondale, and runs down the vale which from the name of the river is called Lonſdale, where it enters the county of *Loncaſter* (as it was anciently called), and a little below the town of Lancaſter falls into the ſea. The third is *Kent*, which riſes in Kentmere, and waſhes the vale which from thence receiveth the name of Kendale, and empties itſelf into the ſea below Levens.

In the hollows amongſt the mountains are formed divers large LAKES, having ſmall rivulets running through them, which preſerve the water clear, the lakes having commonly a pebbly or rocky bottom; as Windermere, Ulleſwater, Haws-water, Ridal-water, Elter-water, Greſmere-water, and other leſſer lakes which go by the name of Tarns, as Sunbiggin Tarn, Ravenſtondale Tarn, Whinfell Tarn, and others. Which lakes and tarns abound with divers ſpecies of fiſh, as trout, eel, baſs, perch, tench, roach, pike, char, and divers others.

The southern part of this county is also pretty well furnished with SEA FISH, caught near the Kent and Levens sands, and other places upon the sea coast. Which heretofore were brought weekly to Kendal market, insomuch that upon a market-day there have been sometimes five and thirty different sorts of fish. But since the great improvement of the town and port of Lancaster, the market for fish is considerably drawn that way.

There is no very great plenty of WOOD in this county; it seems to have been industriously destroyed, to prevent its affording shelter to the Scotch invaders. It is very certain, that long after the conquest, this county was over-run with wood; we read of nothing but forests, and chases, and parks, and mastage, and pannage, and vert, and venison, and greenhue, and regarders, and foresters, and verderers, and an hundred other names and titles respecting the keeping or preservation of the woods and game therein. In almost all the mosses, there are large trees of oak, fir, birch, and other wood, covered now four, five, or six feet in depth, with that kind of earth that the people dig up for fuel, many of which have the marks of the stroke of the ax upon them, and are lying near to their root, which is at the bottom of the moss; and the tops and leaves, by their stoppage of the water draining into the vacuities, seem to have contributed towards increasing the growth of the peatmoss, which in some places, it is very observable, acquires a new covering every year. The water, weeds, moss, straws, grass, ling, and other matter, which collect in the winter and stagnate, are dried up in summer, and effect a new crust upon the former mass.

Upon many of the commons are ridges and furrows, which evidently bear the signature of the plough. The tradition amongst the country people is, that this was done in the reign of king John, when the kingdom was under an interdict from the Pope, and the inhabitants thereby prohibited from tilling their improved ground. But besides that an interdict doth not imply any such prohibition, being only an hinderance of the celebration of divine offices, it seemeth that the true reason of these ploughings which now appear upon the common hath been, that these places happened to be first cleared from wood, and afterwards were deserted for more favourable situations, as the wood became gradually cleared away.

In these mountains, towards the north-east part of the county, is a very remarkable phenomenon, such as we have not found any account of elsewhere in the kingdom, except only about Ingleton and other places bordering upon the mountains of Ingleborrow, Pendle, and Penigent, in the confines of the counties of York and Lancaster. It is called a HELM-WIND. A rolling cloud, sometimes for three or four days together, hovers over the mountain tops, the sky being clear in other parts. When this cloud appears, the country people say the *helm* is up; which is an Anglo-Saxon word, signifying properly a covering for the head, from whence comes the diminutive *helmet*. This helm is not dispersed or blown away by the wind, but continues in its station, although a violent a violent roaring hurricane comes tumbling down the mountain, ready to tear up all before it. Then on a sudden ensues a profound calm. And then again alternately the tempest: which seldom extends into the country above a mile or two from the bottom of the mountain.

In the modern part of the Universal History, vol. xv. p. 519. we find an account of exactly the like appearance on some of the hills near the Cape of Good Hope, thus described by those elegant authors: "In the dry season, a "white cloud hovers over the top of the mountains; from which cloud issue "the south-west winds with incredible fury, shattering houses, endangering "shipping, and greatly damaging the fruits of the earth. Upon discovery of "which cloud, the sailors immediately prepare for a storm."

This county, together with the counties of Cumberland, Northumberland, Durham, York, and Lancaster, was anciently the country of the Brigantes, who were subdued by the Romans; and there are remaining many ancient monuments of the Romans in this county to this day.

The great Roman causeway went quite through this county, entering upon Stanemore, and going out at Brougham castle. Until the turnpike road was made, which destroyed a considerable part thereof, it was very conspicuous almost the whole length of its course. It was carried in a direct straight line, over hills and dales, through mosses and tarns, as if nothing should be able to interrupt their progress. It was about six yards in breadth, and on the level ground appears to have been made of three courses of large square stones, the lowest course being the largest, and the other two diminishing gradually, the whole three courses being of the depth of a yard or somewhat more; and consequently it was able to sustain an immensely greater weight of carriages than any that are now in use. And the earth which was cast forth to make room for the pavement was laid on the outside, to form the whole into a proper rotundity.—But this was not in all places the form and manner in which they made their roads. In some places stone was not to be had but at a very great distance, in which case they made use of gravel, flint, or other materials which the country furnished. And where they had not solid stone, they made the road so much the higher and broader. From the general elevated form of the Roman roads, Mr. Horsley conjectures that the denomination of *high-way* given to all publick roads derives its original.

There was also a Roman way, called Maiden way, branching out from the other at Kirkby Thore, and stretching northwards over the low end of Cross-Fell, to where it joined with the Picts' wall in Northumberland. From whence it received this name we know not. At its first entrance upon Stanemore, it passeth by a place called *Maiden castle*, which was a small square fort of Roman structure, as appeared by the mortar found therein. (*Machel.*)

In modern military language, a *Maiden* fort signifies one that has never been taken, by reason of its extraordinary strength. But that could never be applicable to this small fortification upon Stanemore. It rather seems to be derived of the Anglo-Saxon *Mai (maigan, magan, magnum)* great, and *Dun* a hill.

hill. In Northumberland, this ſame military road bears the ſame name of the *Maiden way*. Under the caſtle of Wark in the ſaid county, there is a walk called the *Maiden walk*. And at Cattle Well near Wooler in the ſame county, is an intrenchment called by this ſame name of the *Maiden caſtle*. Wallis's Northumberland, ii. 21. 466. 486. So, nigh Dorcheſter there is a camp of a ſquare form, called *Maiden caſtle*, which takes in the whole ſummit of a great hill, having a double ditch and rampart, and in ſome places treble. *Horſl.* 461.

There are no fewer than eight good TURNPIKE roads in this county, ſeven of which terminate at, or paſs through, the town of Kendal. One of theſe roads goes through the bottom of Weſtmorland, and follows (but with ſome variations) the direction of the Roman way, from the top of Stanemore where it comes in from Yorkſhire, through Brough, by Appleby, to Eamont bridge, where it enters Cumberland.

Another, from Kendal, through Kirkby Lonſdale to Keighly in Yorkſhire.

The third, from Kendal to Sedbergh in the county of York, and from thence branching out to Kirkby Stephen on one ſide, and to Aſkrigg in the county of York on the other ſide.

The fourth, from Kendal, branching out nigh Tebay, through Ravenſtonale and Kirkby Stephen to Brough on one ſide; and through Orton to Appleby on the other ſide.

The fifth, from Heron Sike, where the road comes in from Lancaſhire, through Burton, Kendal, and Shap, to Eamont bridge.

The ſixth, from Kendal, by Ambleſide and Dunmal Raiſe, to Keſwick in Cumberland, with a branch from Plumbgarths Croſs nigh Kendal to Windermere Water.

The ſeventh, from Kendal, by Ulverſton, to Kirkby Irelith in Lancaſhire.

And the eighth, from Kendal to Milthorp, and from thence communicating with the turnpike road coming from Heron Sike.

The INHABITANTS of this county are generally a ſober, ſocial, humane, civilized people; owing in ſome meaſure to the inſtitution of ſmall *ſchools* in almoſt every village. And in the larger towns, as Appleby, Heverſham, Kendal, Bampton, Kirkby Lonſdale, and Kirkby Stephen, there are free ſchools handſomely endowed. Inſomuch that it is a rare thing in this county, to find any perſon who cannot both read and write tolerably well.

Barren as the ſoil is in many places, the county is very POPULOUS, perhaps more populous in proportion to the value of the lands than any other county in the kingdom. Every man lives upon his own ſmall tenement, and the practice of accumulating farms hath not yet here made any conſiderable progreſs. Here are large remains of the ancient feudal policy, which was kept up in theſe parts after it had ceaſed elſewhere, by reaſon of the particular military ſervice againſt the Scots. The lands at firſt were granted out in large diſtricts by William the conqueror and his ſucceſſors to certain great Norman barons. Theſe parcelled them out to inferior lords; who again granted the fame to individuals, each man having a portion of land affigned to him for the fuftentation of the military character. And they feem to have extended this regulation as far as it would go. The foldier's eftate, from the number of ancient tenements in the feveral manors, appears to have been fmall, as what perhaps would now let for about ten or twelve pounds a year. And befides the general military fervices in the King's wars at home and abroad, thefe tenants in the borders were liable (as hath been obferved before) to be called out in the particular fervice againft the Scots, at the command of the lords wardens of the marches.

All the ancient manor houfes and other BUILDINGS in this county appear to have been formed, not fo much for ornament, or even utility in other refpects, as for defence againft the Scotch incurfions. The larger houfes had areas or yards ftrongly walled about, with turrets and battlements; within which inclofures they fhut up their cattle in the night-time, or otherwife occafionally as they had notice given to them by the firing of beacons or other intelligence.

The leffer houfes were fecured with ftrong doors and gates, having the windows very fmall, and croffed with ftrong bars of iron. And many of the country houfes, for the greater fafety, had the cow-houfe and ftable underneath the dwelling-houfe.

Even the very diverfions of the children had a reference to this border enmity. The boys to this day have a play which they call *Scotch and Englifh*; which is an exact picture in miniature of the RAID, that is, of the *inroad* by plundering parties. The boys divide themfelves into two companies, under two captains, who chufe their men alternately. Then they ftrip off their coats, the one party calling themfelves Scots, the other Englifh. They lay their cloaths refpectively all on an heap, and fet a ftone as it were a bounder mark between the two kingdoms, exactly in the middle between their heaps of cloaths. Then they begin to make incurfions into each other's territories; the Englifh beginning with this reviling expreffion, "Here's a leap in thy land, dry-bellied "Scot." And fo they plunder and fteal away one from another all that they can lay their hands on. But if they can take hold of any invader within their own jurifdiction, either before or after he catcheth his booty, which they call a *wed*, (the fame being a Saxon word, *waed*, *weda*, *wead*, not yet quite out of ufe, fignifying *cloathing*) unlefs he efcape clear into his own province, they take him prifoner, and carry him to the *wed* or heap of cloaths, from whence he is not to remove till fome of his own party break in, and by fwiftnefs of foot lay hold of the prifoner, before he himfelf be touched by any of the adverfe party; which if the adverfary do, he hath refcued his man, and may carry him off without moleftation. And thus fometimes one party will fo far prevail over the other, what with plundering, and what with taking prifoners, that the other fhall have nothing at all left. It is a very active and violent recreation.

The

The BREAD used by all persons of condition in this county is made of *wheat*, but the common people eat *oaten* bread (as they do also in Scotland, hence the abovementioned sarcastical expression of *dry-bellied Scot*); for the supply whereof in this county, there is not a sufficient quantity of oats grown within the county, but they receive many loads thereof every week out of Cumberland, and some out of the counties of Lancaster, York, and Durham: The land in Westmorland yielding better for grazing. And therefore they breed a large number of *cattle* yearly, and sell them out at three or four years of age.

And they make a considerable advantage by the sale of *butter*, especially since the turnpike road was made over Stanemore, whereby a communication by land-carriage is opened to the sea-port towns, from whence they supply the London markets. Westmorland *hams* also, which are cured in the smoke of peat fewel, are much preferable to those cured elsewhere in the coal fire chimnies.

In the article of CLOATHING, they have departed of late years from their ancient simplicity. Their forefathers were wont to cloath themselves with their own wool manufactured at home, which wool is now bought up for the use of the manufacturers at Kendal and in the West Riding of Yorkshire. Clogs, instead of shoes, the labouring people still wear; the upper part whereof is made of strong curried leather, and the sole of wood shod and bound about with iron.

The LANGUAGE of the country people hath large remains of the ancient Saxon. Which shews, that although William the conqueror granted the lands to some of the principal leaders amongst his Normans, and they to other mesne lords their countrymen; yet they did not dispossess the ancient inhabitants entirely, but granted to them lands to hold under the respective mesne lords, or otherwise kept them in a state of villenage.

THIS county is divided into two great baronies; the BARONY OF KENDAL, and the BARONY OF WESTMORLAND: this latter is sometimes called the barony of *Appleby*, but most commonly in ancient times the barony of *Westmorland*. Indeed the barony of Kendal seemeth not formerly to have been deemed a part of Westmorland, but rather of Lancashire. In the Domesday-survey, an account is taken of many places within this barony of Kendal, together with the adjoining places in Lancashire and Yorkshire *; whereas of Westmorland properly

* Thus, in Oustewic and Heldetune there are 12 manors recited which had belonged to Torfin, viz. Clapeham, Middletun, Manzerge, Chercebу, Lupetun, Prestun, Holme, Bortune, Hotune, Warton, Clactun, Catun: And two thirds of these clearly are in Westmorland, viz. Middleton, Mansergh, Kirkby (Lonsdale), Lupton, Preston, Holme, Burton, and Hutton (probably that part now called Hutton Roof). Hæc habuit Torfin pro 12 maneriis.

Amongst the possessions of Tosti earl of Northumberland, where mention is made of Leck, Ingleton, Sedberg, and other adjoining places, we find these following; Castertune, Berebrune, and Tiernebi; that is, Casterton, Barbon, and Thirneby (now corruptly called Thrimby). Omnes hæ villæ pertinent ad Witetune: Tosti comes habuit.

in

properly so called no survey was made, being all wasted and destroyed, and worth nothing. And the barons of Kendal, we find, contested the right of jurisdiction of the sheriff of Westmorland within their boundaries. And so late as the reign of king Henry the eighth, this barony of Kendal comprehended a considerable part of Lancashire. Warton is often mentioned as being within this barony; and there is a record in the Dutchy office, which determines many other places to be within this barony †.

And it exended a good way into that part which is now called the Bottom of Westmorland; particularly into almost all the western part, comprehending tke greatest part of the parishes of Barton, Lowther, and Morland. And the barons of Kendal were patrons also of the church of Kirkby Stephen, and gave it and also the church of Morland to the abbey of St. Mary's York. But now the boundary of the barony of Kendal, as distinguished from the Bottom of Westmorland, is the same nearly as the boundary of the several parishes of Gresmere and Kendal on one side, and Barton, Shap, and Orton, on the other.

The HUNDREDS in this county are distinguished by the name of WARDS, and are four in number; being the districts of the like number of High Constables, who presided over the *wards* to be sustained at certain fords and other places,

In Stercaland: Cherchebi, Helsingtun, Staintun, Hotun, Patun; viz. Kirkby (in Kendal), Helsington, Stainton, Hutton, and Patton. Hæc habuit Gilemichel.

Amongst the lands of Roger of Poictou: Beidun, Fareltun, Prestun, Hennecastre, Eureshaim, Lefuenes; viz. Betham, Farleton, Preston, Hincaster, Heversham, and Levins.

† In the first year of king Henry the eighth, it was found, by inquisition in the county of Lancaster, that Margaret late countess of Richmond and Derby, the said king's grandame, was seised in her demesne as of fee for the term of her life of the third part of the lordship or town of Whittington, and the lordship or town of Warton, and of 20 *l* fee farm going out of the manors of Ashton and Berneforth, and of the moiety of the lordship or manor of Nether Wyresdale, and of the third part of the old lordship of Scotford in the said county; the reversion to Henry the eighth in right of his dutchy of Lancaster, and as parcel of our county palatine of Lancaster. Since which, by another office taken by virtue of a commission, it is found, that our noble progenitor king Henry the sixth was seised of the lordships, towns, and hamlets of Nether Wyresdale, Whytington, Scotford, Warton, Moreholm, Asheton, and Kerneford in the said county of Lancaster, in his demesne as of fee, as members and parcel of the manor, lordship, or barony of Kendal in the county of Westmorland. The which lordships, towns, and hamlets, specified in the said later office, we understand to be the same manors, lands, tenements, rent, fee farms, and other the premises named and specified by the said other names in the said first office, and be all one, and not diverse. And further it was found by the said later office, that king Henry the sixth gave all the premises to Edmund then earl of Richmond and to the heirs of his body lawfully begotten, by the name of his manor and lordship of Kendale, and manor and lordship of Wyresdale, with the appurtenances, in the counties of Westmorland and Lancaster, and of other lands and tenements, and of other things, as more plainly appeareth by the said second office; and so descended to our father, son and heir in tail to the said Edmund late earl of Richmond; and that Henry the seventh gave all the said premisses to our said grandame for term of her life, by the name of the third part of the lordship and manor of Kendale, and of the lordship and manor of Wyresdale, with the appurtenances, in the counties of Lancaster and Westmorland. Whereupon we perceive they were not Dutchy land, but members of our barony of Kendale in the county of Westmorland. Whereupon the king now commands to make frustrate the said first office found by the escheator of Lancashire. Dated at Westminster the first day of December in the 4th year of the reign of king Henry the 8th. *From the Dutchy Rolls at the Savoy.* (Machel from Dugdale.)

places, for repelling plundering parties out of Scotland. Two of these *wards* are in the barony of Kendal, to wit, Kendal and Lonsdale Wards; and two in the Bottom, called East and West Wards: There was anciently a Middle Ward between these two last; but since watching and warding ceased, that hath fallen into and been absorbed by the other two.

The barony of Kendal is in the DIOCESE of *Chester*; and therein are two rural deanries, the deanry of Kendal, and the deanry of Kirkby Lonsdale, both of which extend also into the adjoining parts of Lancashire. The Bottom of Westmorland is in the diocese of Carlisle, and is all one rural deanry, called the deanry of Westmorland. This office of rural dean had anciently a large jurisdiction annexed to it, but by degrees hath fallen into disuse. But so late as the year 1571, we find Robert Pearson dean of Westmorland receiver of the subsidy granted to the crown by the clergy, and also of the procurations and synodals paid to the bishop.

It is a vulgar mistake, that this county paid no *subsidies* during the existence of the border service, as supposing it to be exempted from such payment merely upon that account. For we find all along such and such persons collectors of the subsidies in this county, granted both by clergy and laity. The LAND TAX succeeded into the place of subsidies; being not so properly a new tax, as an old tax by a new name. From the reign of Edward the third downward, certain sums and proportions were fixed upon the several townships within the respective counties, according whereunto the taxation hath constantly been made *. In process of time this valuation may be supposed to have become unequal, especially since by the increase of trade and manufacture in some large towns much wealth is accumulated within a small compass, the tax upon such division continuing still the same. And hence a new valuation hath often been suggested to render this tax more adequate, which nevertheless from the nature of the thing must always be fluctuating according to the increase or diminution of property in different parts of the kingdom. But in reality this notion proceeds upon a very narrow and partial principle. An *equal tax*, according to what a man is worth, is one thing; and an *equal land tax*, all the other taxes being unequal, is quite another. Setting aside

* In Cumberland, the manner of laying public taxes and assessments is somewhat peculiar, by a rate called the *Purvey*; which originally was a composition in money for the king's *purveyance*, or providing for his houshold, when he went on a progress into different parts of the kingdom. In some places it was paid in cattle, or other provisions in kind: Hence in Lancashire they have a manner of laying assessments still called *an-lay*. Against king James's return out of Scotland through the county of Cumberland in September 1617, the justices of the peace were ordered to compound for the king's purveyance at the rate of 108 *l*, or thereabouts; which sum being laid through the whole county, became afterwards a rule for laying most of the other assessments, calling it one purvey when 108 *l* was raised, two purveys when 216 *l* was raised, and so on. In the year 1665, for the more ease and convenience, the purvey was fixed at the precise sum of 100 *l*; so that where the sum of 100 *l* is wanted, it is called one purvey; where 200 *l* two purveys; and so on: and the same was proportioned amongst the several wards, as it still continues. Thirty-seven purveys and an half nearly make up one land tax, when the land tax is at 4 *s* in the pound. *Flem.*

the

the populous manufacturing towns, let us take the county of Westmorland in general (in which there is no such manufacturing town, Kendal only excepted); and we shall find that this county, upon the whole, taking all the taxes together, pays more to the government, in proportion to the wealth of the inhabitants, than perhaps any other county in the kingdom. And that is by reason of its comparative populousness. Suppose a township (which is a common case in Westmorland) worth about 400*l* a year. In this township there are about 40 messuages and tenements, and a family in each messuage. And at the proportion of five persons to a family, there are 200 inhabitants. These, by their labour and what they consume, are worth to the public double and treble the value of the land tax in its highest estimation. These 40 messuages or dwelling-houses, at 3*s* each, pay yearly 6*l* house duty; and so many of them perhaps have above seven windows, as will make up 6*l* more. Now let us advance further South. An estate of 400*l* a year is there frequently in one hand. There is one family of perhaps 15 or 20 persons; one house duty of 3*s*, some few shillings more for windows; and a tenth part of the consumption of things taxable, as salt, soap, leather, candles, and abundance of other articles. Now where is the equality? One man for 10*l* or 5*l* a year, pays as much house duty, as another person for 400*l* a year. In Westmorland many persons (and the clergy almost in general) dwell in houses that pay more house and window duty than the house itself would let for. And in other respects, the public is as much benefited by three or four families occupying ten or twenty pounds a year each, as in the other case by one family occupying ten times as much.

It hath been computed by political calculators, that every person, one with another, is worth to the public 4*l* a year. On that supposition, the inhabitants in one case are estimated at 800*l*, in the other case at 80*l*. So if we reduce the sum to half, or a quarter, or any other sum; it will always come out the same, that the one and the other are of value to the public, just in the proportion of ten to one.

In short: Populousness is the riches of a nation; not only from the consumption of things taxable, but for the supply of hands to arts, manufacture, war, and commerce. A man that purchaseth an estate, and lays it to his own, making one farm of what was two before, deprives the public of a proportionable share of every tax that depends upon the number of houses and inhabitants. A man that gets a whole village or two into his possession by this means, consisting of an hundred ancient feudal tenements, evades ninety-nine parts in an hundred of such taxes, and throws the burden upon others, who by reason of the smallness of their property are proportionably less able to bear it; for a man of an hundred pounds a year can better spare twenty pounds, than a man of ten pounds a year can spare forty shillings; for the one has eighty pounds left, and the other only eight.

The general military tenure of the lands in this county was by *homage*, *fealty*, and *cornage*; which *cornage* drew after it *wardship*, *marriage*, and *relief*. And the service of this tenure was *knight's service*.

Homage

HOMAGE (according to Littleton) was the most honourable service, and most humble service of reverence, that a free tenant can do to his lord. For when the tenant was to do homage to his lord, he was to appear ungirt of his sword, with his head uncovered, and the lord was to sit, and the tenant kneel before him on both his knees, and hold his hands extended and joined together, between the hands of his lord, and was to say thus: "I become your "man, from this day forward, of life and limb and earthly honour, and unto "you will be true and faithful, and faith unto you will bear for the tenements "that I claim to hold of you; saving the faith that I owe to our sovereign "lord the king." And then the lord so sitting was to kiss him. *(Littleton's Tenures, sect. 85.)*—It had its name from *homo*; I become your *man*,—Jeo deveigne vostre *home*.

FEALTY is the same as *fidelitas* in latin. And when a free tenant was to do fealty to his lord, he was to hold his right hand upon a book, and say thus: "Know ye this, my lord, that I will be faithful and true unto you, and faith "to you will bear for the tenements which I claim to hold of you, and that "I will lawfully do to you the customs and services which I ought to do at "the terms assigned: So help me God and his Saints." But he was not to kneel nor make such humble reverence as in homage; and fealty might be done before the steward of the court, but homage could only be done to the lord himself. *(Litt. sect. 91, 92.)*

CORNAGE we will speak of by and by, when we have explained the three incidents thereof, *wardship*, *marriage*, and *relief*.—WARDSHIP and MARRIAGE was thus: When the tenant died, and his heir male was within the age of 21 years, the lord was to have the land holden of him until the heir should attain that age; because the heir by intendment of law was not able to do knights service before his age of 21 years. And if such heir was not married at the time of the death of his ancestor, then the lord was to have the wardship and marriage of him. But if the tenant died leaving an heir female, which heir female was of the age of 14 years or upwards, then the lord was not to have the wardship of the land, nor of the body; because a woman of that age might have a husband able to do knights service. But if such heir female was under the age of 14 years and unmarried at the time of the death of her ancestor, the lord was to have the wardship of the land holden of him until the age of such heir female of 14 years; within which time the lord might tender unto her covenable marriage without disparagement: And if the lord did not tender such marriage within the said age, she might have entred into the land, and ousted the lord. *(Litt. sect. 103.)*

RELIEF was a certain sum of money that the heir, on coming of age, paid unto the lord, on taking possession of the inheritance of his ancestor; by payment whereof, the heir *relieved*, *(relevabat)* that is, as it were raised up again the lands, after they had fallen into the hands of the superior. And on payment of the relief, the heir had LIVERY of the lands, that is, the lands

 were

were to be *delivered* to the heir; and in caſe of refuſal, the heir might have a writ to recover the ſame from the lord, which recovery *out of the hands of the lord*, was called *ouſter le main*.

And for the fuller execution of theſe purpoſes, in caſe of the king's tenants *in capite*, an officer was appointed, called the Eſcheator, to whom a writ iſſued on the death of ſuch tenant, to take the lands into the king's hands, and to inquire by a jury, how much land ſuch tenant held of the king *in capite*, what was the yearly value thereof, who was his heir, and of what age: Which writ was called a writ of *Diem clauſit extremum* (from theſe words contained in the writ); and the finding of the jury was called an *Inquiſition poſt mortem* *. For the more certain and regular proceedings in which matter, a *court of Wards and Liveries* was erected by act of parliament in the reign of king Henry the eighth.

All theſe circumſtances of *homage*, *fealty*, *wardſhip*, *marriage*, and *relief*, were common to the military ſervice in general. CORNAGE ſeems to have been peculiar to the Border ſervice againſt the Scots. Sir Matthew Hale in his comment (hereafter ſet forth) upon king John's charter to Robert de Veteripont of Appleby and Burgh, and the ſheriffwick and rent of the county of Weſtmorland, juſt takes notice of it, and ſays, it is a tenure not known to the ſouthern parts of England. And judge Littleton, in his book of tenures, in the chapter concerning Grand Serjeanty, ſpeaks of this ſervice only upon hearſay. "It "is ſaid," he obſerves, "that in the marches of Scotland, ſome hold of the "king by *cornage*, that is to ſay, to wind a horn to give the men of the coun"try warning, when they hear that the Scots or other enemies are come or "will enter into England; which ſervice is grand ſerjeanty. But if a tenant "hold of any other lord than of the king by ſuch ſervice of *cornage*, this is "not grand ſerjeanty, but is knights ſervice; for none may hold by grand "ſerjeanty but of the king only. And it draweth to it ward and marriage."

Sir Edward Coke, in his comment on the ſecond chapter of Magna Charta, which aſcertains what *relief* ſhall be paid by the military tenants of the crown, ſaith, (2 Inſt. 9.) that tenure by *cornage* is not within this ſtatute of Magna Charta, becauſe Littleton ſaith, that it draweth unto it *wardſhip* and *marriage*,

* Edwardus Dei gratia, rex Angliæ, dominus Hiberniæ, et dux Aquitaniæ, dilecto clerico ſuo Willielmo de Boyvill eſcaetori ſuo ultra Trentam, ſalutem. Quia Robertus de Ros de Werke, qui de nobis tenuit in capite, *diem clauſit extremum*, ut accepimus, vobis mandamus, quod omnes terras et tenementa, de quibus præfatus Robertus fuit ſeiſitus in dominico ſuo ut de feodo in balliva veſtra, die quo obiit, videlicet, tam de hæreditate Margaretæ uxoris ejus, quam de hæreditate propria, ſine dilatione capiatis in manum noſtram, et ea ſalvo cuſtodiatis donec aliud inde præceperimus; et per ſacramentum proborum et legalium hominum de balliva veſtra, per quos rei veritas melius ſciri poterit, diligenter inquiratis, quantum terræ præfatus Robertus tenuit de nobis in capite, tam de hæreditate prædictæ Margaretæ uxoris ſuæ, quam de hæreditate propria, et quantum de aliis, et per quod ſervicium, et quantum terræ illæ valeant per annum in omnibus exitibus, et quis propinquior hæres ejus ſit et cujus ætatis; et inquiſitionem diſtincte et aperte factam nobis ſub ſigillo veſtro et ſigillis eorum per quos facta fuerit ſine dilatione mittatis et hoc breve. Datum per manum W. de Merton cancellarii noſtri apud Weſtminſter xx° die Aprilis anno regni noſtri ſecundo.

and ſpeaketh nothing of *relief*. But it is very evident from many of the inquiſitions *poſt mortem* of the Cliffords and others, that this ſervice of *cornage* did draw unto it *wardſhip*, *marriage*, and *relief*. And it is obſervable, that Littleton, though he expreſſeth only *wardſhip* and *marriage*, yet he doth not exclude *relief*, and ſpeaketh of the whole matter, not as of his own knowledge, but by the report of others. And the ſame learned commentator recites a very notable record in the eighteenth year of the reign of king Edward the firſt, between John de Graiſtoke plaintiff, and Idonea de Leyburn defendant, concerning a *relief* to be paid to her by the ſaid John, for the manors of Duſton, Brampton, Yanewich, and Bolton (for thoſe were the manors he poſſeſſed, tho' from the copy it ſeems that the names were not very legible in the record) which he as meſne lord held of the ſaid Idonea. In which diſpute it was admitted by both parties that a *relief* was due, and they differed only about the quantum. Idonea had diſtrained his goods for a *relief* to be paid for his lands at the aforeſaid places, which he held of her by *homage* and *cornage*, and which were worth by the year 100 *l*. And ſhe ſaid, that the cuſtom in Weſtmorland is ſuch, that the heirs after the death of their anceſtors ought to *relieve* their lands from the lords of whom they are holden, by paying for *relief* as much as the lands are worth by the year, unleſs they can agree with their lords for leſs. Whereupon ſhe avows the taking of the diſtreſs for a relief according to the ſaid cuſtom. John de Graiſtoke denies that there is ſuch cuſtom, but admits that he holds his tenements aforeſaid by the *cornage* of 25 *s* 6 *d*; and ſaith, that his anceſtors in time paſt doubled the ſaid *cornage*, by paying to the anceſtors of the ſaid Idonea 51 *s*. She replies, that foraſmuch as the ſaid John admits that he holds the tenements aforeſaid by *cornage*, ſuch *relief* is incident thereunto by virtue of the ſaid cuſtom; and ſaith, that the ſaid John and his anceſtors for time immemorial have required the like relief againſt his tenants in the ſame county. And concerning the cuſtom, they both put themſelves upon the country. Moreover the ſaid Idonea ſaith, that there is a twofold tenure in the county of Weſtmorland, to wit, one by *White rent* [which was a rent paid in ſilver, vulgarly, but improperly, called a quit-rent] and another by *cornage*: And that the tenants by *White rent*, after the death of their anceſtors, ought to double their rent only; and the tenants by *cornage*, after the death of their anceſtors, ought to pay the value of their lands for one year. And John ſaith on the contrary, that the cuſtom of the country is, that the heirs ſhall not pay but by doubling the cornage *.

The

* Inter Johannem Graiſtoke querentem, verſus Idoneam de Leybourne, quæ diſtrinxit ipſum per averia pro relevio dando pro terris in *Dunſton*, *Brampton yane which*, *Eſeclyve* † et *Boulton*, quæ valeat *C. li. per annum*, qui tenet de ea per homagium et cornagium. Et ipſa dicit, quod talis eſt conſuetudo patriæ de Weſtm' quod hæredes poſt mortem anteceſſorum ſuorum debent relevare terras ſuas dominis de quibus, &c. ſcilicet, ſolvendo pro relevio quantum terræ valent per annum, quæ de ipſis dominis tenentur, niſi de minori ipſis dominis poſſunt ſatisfacere: Unde ipſa advocat captionem pro relevio ſecundum prædictam conſuetudinem, &c. Johannes negat talem eſſe conſuetudinem, ſed concedit, quod tenet tenementa prædicta per cornagium xxv *s* vi *d*; et dicit, quod anteceſſores ſui prius duplicarunt anteceſſoribus ipſius Idoneæ, ſolvendo li *s*. Ipſa dicit, quod cum Johannes cogn', quod

† This ſeems to be what is now called *Keiſley*, being part of the manor of Duſton.

The *perſonal* ſervice of *cornage*, if ever it was in actual exerciſe, ceaſed very early, and was converted into a pecuniary payment; which was accounted for to the crown, and paid yearly into the exchequer. And perhaps from the firſt it might be a ſtipulated payment, for the finding of ſcouts and horners, and procuring intelligence. And by reaſon of the ſcarcity of ſilver (for gold coins were not in uſe till long after) it ſeemeth that this *cornage* rent was at firſt paid in cattle, which kind of payment was called *noutegeld*, and under that name was accounted for in the exchequer, in the reign of king Henry the ſecond. (Denton, from the Red Book in the exchequer.) And to this day, in the Bottom of Weſtmorland, the *cornage* rent is paid under the name of *neatgeld*. This rent, together with the ſheriffwiek, was granted by king John as aforeſaid to Robert de Veteripont, by the name of the rent of the county of Weſtmorland; and the poſterity of the ſaid Robert ſtill enjoy the ſame. But the *noutegeld* within the barony of Kendal was not included within that grant; the ſame having been quitted before and extinguiſhed by grant from king Richard the firſt to Gilbert ſon of Roger Fitzreinfred.

Theſe *cornage* tenants were bound, in their moſt defenſible array for the wars, to be ready to ſerve their prince and the lord of the manor, upon horſeback or on foot, at their own proper coſts and charges; and when the king's army paſſed into Scotland, they had the poſt of honour to march in the vanguard; and on their return, in the rereguard ‡. And for good reaſon: becauſe they beſt knew the paſſes and defiles, and the way and manner of the enemy's attacking and retreating.

The *White rent*, or payment in money, above mentioned, was what is now called the LORD'S RENT. And hereupon we may obſerve, that in thoſe days, on the death of the tenant, the lord required only that rent to be doubled; and in the caſe of *cornage*, it was demanded to have one year's value of the lands, which on the other ſide was conteſted, inſiſting only to pay double of the cornage. Whereas in ſucceeding ages, the lords have advanced to eight or ten and in ſome places to twenty times the ancient rent, and in other places to two years improved value of the lands. The crown tenants in the barony of Kendal continue neareſt to the ancient eſtabliſhment, paying only double

ipſe tenet prædicta ten' de ipſa per cornagium, ad hoc hujuſmodi relevium mere eſt acceſſor', ratione conſuet' prædictæ: Et dicit, quod idem Johannes exigit tale relevium verſus tenentes ſuos in eadem patria, a tempore quo non, &c. Et de conſuet' uterque ponit ſe ſuper patriam. Ideo ven' jur' in Cra. S. Johannis Baptiſtæ, &c. Inſuper Idonea dicit, quod duplex eſt tenura in Com. Weſtmerl. ſcilicet, una per Albam firmam, et alia per cornagium: Et quod tenentes per Albam firmam, poſt mortem anteceſſorum ſuorum, debent duplicare firmam ſuam tantum; et tenentes per cornagium, poſt mortem anteceſſorum ſuorum, tenentur reddere valorem terrarum ſuarum unius anni. Et Johannes e contra dicit, quod conſuetudo patriæ eſt, quod hæredes non ſolvant niſi duplicando cornagium, &c.

‡ Omnes ſupradicti (ſc. tenentes per cornagium) ibunt ad preceptum regis in exercitu Scotiæ, in eundo in antegardia, et redeundo in retrogardia. *(Denton, e libro rubro vetuſto in Scaccario.)*

Omnes tenentes per cornagium ibunt ad præceptum regis in exercitu Scotiæ, in eundo in anteguard, et redeundo in retroguard: Quod quidem ſervicium adjudicatur Magna Serjeantia. *(Dugd. apud Machel: E libro Feodorum in Com. Cumbr. ſub titulo de Teſta de Nevill.)*

and in ſome places treble of the lord's rent, for a FINE on the death of the tenant; whereas the other tenants in divers parts of the ſaid barony have been required to pay two years value of the lands: notwithſtanding that until after the death of William de Lancaſtre the third in the reign of king Henry the third, the tenure throughout the ſaid barony was intirely the ſame, under one and the ſame lord.

Beſides the aforeſaid military ſervices, we find another ſervice often mentioned, called SCUTAGE, or *eſcuage*; from the latin word *ſcutum*, a ſhield: which was a compenſation in money, inſtead of perſonal ſervice againſt the Scots. This ſervice by eſcuage was indeed no part of the border ſervice, for in the border ſervice perſonal and immediate attendance was abſolutely neceſſary to repel ſudden and deſultory incurſions; but eſcuage was when a royal army marched, not againſt the borders particularly, but againſt the kingdom of Scotland. Concerning which, Littleton expreſſeth himſelf in the like cautious manner as before: "It is ſaid, that when the king makes a voyage "royal into Scotland to ſubdue the Scots, he which holdeth by the ſervice "of one knight's fee ought to be with the king forty days, well and conveniently arrayed for the war; and he which holdeth his land by the moiety "of a knight's fee, ought to be with the king twenty days; and he which holdeth his land by the fourth part of a knight's fee, ought to be with the king "ten days: and ſo he that hath more, more; and he that hath leſs, leſs. "And after ſuch voyage royal into Scotland, it is commonly ſaid, that by "authority of parliament, the *eſcuage* ſhall be aſſeſſed and put in certain, that "is, a certain ſum of money, how much every one which holdeth by a whole "knight's fee, who was neither by himſelf nor by any other with the king, "ſhall pay to his lord of whom he holds his land by *eſcuage*. As put the "caſe that it was ordained by parliament, that every one which holdeth by a "whole knight's fee, who was not with the king, ſhall pay to his lord 40*s*; "then he which holdeth by the moiety of a knight's fee, ſhall pay to his lord "but 20*s*; and he which holdeth by the fourth part of a knight's fee, ſhall "pay 10*s*; and he which hath more, more; and he which hath leſs, leſs." *Litt. ſect.* 95. 97.

There hath been great diverſity of opinions concerning the value of a KNIGHT'S FEE, that is, how much land was deemed ſufficient for the maintenance of a knight. Sir Edward Coke ſays, "Some hold, that a knight's "fee conſiſted of 8 hides, and every hide contained 100 acres; and ſo a "knight's fee ſhould contain 800 acres: others ſay that a knight's fee contained 680 acres. But I hold," ſays he, "that a knight's fee doth not contain any certain number of acres; but is properly to be eſtimated according "to the quality, and not according to the quantity of the land, that is to ſay, "by the value, and not by the number of acres." (1 *Inſt.* 69.) Nevertheleſs, in theſe northern parts, it appears from an entry made in the Regiſter of the priory of Wetheral, that the knight's fee was eſtimated, not according to the quality, but quantity of the land. And this ſeems to account for the large meaſure of an acre before mentioned, in order to compenſate for the deficiency

ciency in goodneſs. There we find explicitly, that ten acres make one ferndell, four ferndells one virgate (which is half a carucate), four virgates one hide, and four hides one knight's fee *. So that the knight's fee in this caſe will amount to 640 acres. The value of theſe appears to have been aſcertained at the time of Magna Charta; which fixes the *relief* to be paid for a knight's fee at 5 *l*; and as the *relief* in all the caſes there ſpecified was after the rate of one fourth part of the yearly value of the fee, it follows that a knight's fee was then eſtimated at 20 *l* a year.

All theſe particulars are neceſſary to be known, in order to the underſtanding of the ancient ſtate of this county. But happily now moſt of this knowledge is only matter of curioſity, all the tenures by knights ſervice with all the incidents and conſequences thereof having been aboliſhed by act of parliament ſoon after the reſtoration of king Charles the ſecond. For by the act of 12 C. 2. c. 24. it is enacted as followeth: Whereas it hath been found by experience that the court of wards and liveries, and tenures by knights ſervice, and the conſequents thereupon, have been much more burdenſome, grievous, and prejudicial to the kingdom, than beneficial to the king; be it enacted, that the court of wards and liveries, and all wardſhips, liveries, primer ſeiſins, and ouſterlemains, values and forfeitures of marriages, and all fines for alienations, ſeizures and pardons for alienations, tenure by homage, and all tenures by knights ſervice of the king or of any other perſon, and by knights ſervice in capite, and by ſocage in capite of the king, and all the incidents and conſequences thereof, ſhall be and are hereby taken away and diſcharged; and all tenures of any honours, manors, lands, or any eſtate of inheritance at common law, held either of the king or any other perſon, ſhall be turned into free and common ſocage, and ſhall ſtand and for ever be diſcharged of all tenure by homage, eſcuage, voyages royal, and charges for the ſame, wardſhips incident to tenure by knights ſervice, and values and forfeitures of marriage, and all other charges incident to tenure by knights ſervice. Provided, that this ſhall not be conſtrued to take away any rents certain, heriots, or ſuits of court, belonging to any former tenure now taken away or altered by this act, or the fealty and diſtreſſes incident thereto; and that ſuch relief ſhall be paid in reſpect of ſuch rents, as is paid in caſe of the death of a tenant in common ſocage. And provided, that this ſhall not take away any fines for alienation due by particular cuſtoms of particular manors and places, other than fines for alienations of lands or tenements holden immediately of the king in capite. And alſo provided, that this ſhall not be conſtrued to take away any tenures in frankalmoign, or to ſubject them to any greater or other ſervices than now are; nor to alter any tenure by copy of court roll, or any ſervices incident thereunto; nor to take away the honorary

* Sciendum eſt, quod x acræ terræ faciunt unam ferndellam; et iiij ferndellæ faciunt unam virgatam, ſive dimidium carucatæ; et ſic iiij virgatæ faciunt unam hidam, ſive duas carucatas; et iiij hidæ, viii carucatas; quod eſt feodum militis.

Item, Sciendum eſt, quod quando dabitur ad ſcutagium pro magno feodo militari xl *s*, tunc pro una hida terræ x *s*; pro una virgata ii *s* vi *d*; et pro dimidio virgatæ xv *d*; et pro ferndella vii *d* ob.; et pro una acra ob. q^a.

ſervices

ſervices of grand ſerjeanty, other than of wardſhip, marriage, and value of forfeiture of marriage, eſcuage, voyages royal, and other charges incident to tenure by knights ſervice.——And in conſequence of the premiſſes, power is given by the ſaid act to the father, by his deed or will, to diſpoſe of the tuition of his children till their ages of 21 years.

So much concerning the military tenure.—But beſides all this, there was another tenure in Weſtmorland, which hath greatly puzzled antiquarians to explain or underſtand. It was called Drengage. Sir Matthew Hale, in his expoſition aforeſaid of the Veteripont charter, takes notice of it, and ſays, that there is no ſuch tenure in the ſouthern parts of England, and obſerves from the records before him that it drew wardſhip and relief. Sir Henry Spelman in his Gloſſary, on the words *Drenches*, *Drenges*, *Drengagium*, ſays, theſe words had perplexed him a long time: *(Voces altius ſopitæ, et quæ me diu torſere.)* He recites ſeveral records, wherein theſe words had occurred to him, and conjectures upon the whole, that the *Drenges* were free tenants holding by military ſervice. But there are other records, which had not fallen under the inſpection of that learned author, that deſtroy this notion intirely. Mr. Denton, from the Red Book in the exchequer, obſerves, that Sir Hugh Morvil in Weſtmorland changed *drengage* into free ſervice *; which implies, that it was not free before. At Brougham in this county, Gilbert de Burgham gave one half of the village of Brougham to Robert de Veteripont of whom he held in *drengage*, that the other half might be free from that ſervice. At Clifton alſo in this county, and other neighbouring parts, there were *drengage* tenants; and in the 31 Ed. 3. Gilbert de Engain of Clifton granted by indenture to Roger de Clifford lord of Weſtmorland the ſervices of divers perſons there by name, with their bodies and all that belonged to them *(cum eorum corporibus et eorum ſequelis)*, during the life of the ſaid Roger. So that they ſeem to have been drudges, to perform the moſt ſervile and laborious offices. And of theſe Roger had great uſe at Brougham; for of him the counteſs of Pembroke's memoirs take notice, that he was a lover of building, and a great repairer of his ancient caſtles, the ſeats of his anceſtors. They ſeem to have been tenants in pure villenage, who were bound to the lord as members of and annexed to the manor, and were uſually ſold with the farm to which they belonged.

And it was in contradiſtinction to theſe, that the others were called *free*. Which obſervation ought eſpecially to be noted, otherwiſe we ſhall fall into great confuſion in abundance of inſtances. For wherever *free* men, *free* tenants, or *free* holders are mentioned of old time, by theſe are not to be underſtood what we now call *freeholders*, but only that they were not *villains* or *bondmen*. All our military anceſtors within the ſeveral cuſtomary manors are ſtyled *free tenants*, but the lands were not freehold, according to the modern acceptation of that word.

* Drenga vertitur in liberum ſervicium per Hugonem Morvil in Com' Weſtmerl.'

And

And the very identical record, on which Sir Henry Spelman grounds his opinion, seems to make against him. "Behold," says he, "the very origin "of the matter (if I do not deceive myself) from an old manuscript of the "family of Sharnburn in Norfolk, which I some time ago fortunately met "with. Edwin de Sharnburn, and some others, who were ejected out of "their lands, went to the Conqueror and told him, that never before the "conquest, nor in the conquest, nor after, were they against the king in "counsel and aid, but held themselves in peace. And this they are ready to "prove, as the king shall ordain. Whereupon the said king caused inquiry "to be made all over England, if it was so. Which was proved. Where- "fore the king commanded, that all they who so held themselves in peace in "form aforesaid, should have again all their lands and possessions, as perfectly "and in peace as ever they had or held the same before his conquest. And "that thereafter they shall be called *Drenges*."—From which, the most natural inference seemeth to be, that they should hold their lands, not by knights service, for they had done no act of military atchievement in the Conqueror's behalf, as his faithful Normans had done; but that they should hold their lands by tenure of villenage, in peace and without disturbance, but not in the same degree of confidence and military employment, as those who had exerted themselves for his cause in the field †.

Also in the tenures of many of the manors, there were certain services respecting the FORESTS; as, to keep aireys of hawks for the lord's use, to herd the lord's hogs during the mastage season, to watch with nets or dogs at such a station: More particularly, there are two services that occur frequently, to wit, to find *puture* of the foresters, and *witnesman*.

PUTURE, Sir Edward Coke explains as signifying *poture*, or drinking. It was a demand made by the officers of the forest, within the circuit of their perambulation, of all kinds of victuals for themselves, their servants, horses, and dogs. Others, who call it *pulture*, explain the word as signifying a demand in general; and derive it from the monks, who before they were admitted, *pulsabant*, that is, knocked at the gates for several days together.

Of the word WITNESMAN, no etymologist, or other author that we have met with, hath given any account. It is frequently found by the inquisitions, that such a man, being lord of a manor, was obliged *to find to the foresters witnesman*. And amongst the privileges granted to the mesne lords or their tenants, mention is made of *freedom from finding to the foresters witnesman*.

In order to form a probable conjecture concerning this matter, it seemeth that we must go back to the statute of Magna Charta. Before that statute, by the abuses of the King's officers and others, people were put to their waging

† Mr. Hume, in his history of England, vol. i. p. 179. says, that although this record was able to impose on such able antiquarians as Spelman and Dugdale, yet Dr. Brady has proved it to be a forgery. But whether it is a forgery or not, is not material as to the supposed meaning of the word *drenges*.

of

of law, upon the bare furmife of fuch officers, without other teftimony. This waging of law was, that the defendant fhould clear himfelf by the oath of 12 perfons, viz. himfelf abfolutely, and 11 others, of their belief that what he fwore was true. Now by the ftatute of Magna Charta, c. 28. it is enacted, "That no bailiff (or other officer) fhall put any man to his open law, nor to "an oath, upon his own bare faying, without faithful witneffes brought in "for the fame." In purfuance hereof, the lords of the forefts, making a virtue of neceffity, granted to the mefne lords holding under them, that they would not put any man upon his trial by waging of law for offences within the foreft, upon the fole accufation of the verderers or other officers without other teftimony. But at the fame time, they had no power to fummon any perfons either as witneffes or jurymen that inhabited out of the limits of the foreft; for by the ftatute of Charta de Forefta, chap. 2. (which was made in the fame year as the other called Magna Charta) "Men dwelling out of the "foreft were not to be fummoned before the juftices of the foreft, unlefs ac- "cufed of fome trefpafs therein, or as fureties for other offenders;" therefore the lords of the foreft required at the fame time of the faid mefne lords, that they fhould caufe the tenants within their jurifdiction to appear in the foreft courts, and give teftimony to the truth either as jurors or witneffes, or in other words *to find unto the forefters witnefman.*

Thus John de Veteripont, fon of the firft Robert, grants to the lords of the manors of Sandford, Burton, Helton, and Warcop, and their tenants, freedom from pulture of the forefters; and from all things that he or his heirs, or his forefters, by occafion of the faid pulture, might demand by the tefti-mony of his verderers or other officers in the foreft: And if any forfeiture fhould happen by reafon of any trefpafs within the foreft; that the forefters fhould apply to the lords of the faid manors, and demand of them *witnefman*: And that the lords fhould find unto the forefters *witnefman*: And that every forefter fhould fwear, upon the entrance into his office, that he would hurt no man by the occafion of fuch teftimony *.

In reality, the holding of foreft courts, the faid forefts being in the hands of fubjects, was intirely an ufurpation; and the lords of Weftmorland, being alfo fheriffs of the county, drew the foreft caufes into their county court. Thus the fame John de Veteripont grants to the men of Kirkby Thore, that they fhall be free from pulture of the forefters, and from finding teftimony to the forefters, which is called *witnefman*: And if the forefters fhall find within their bounds a manifeft offence of vert or venifon; the offenders fhall not be

* Sciant præfentes et futuri, quod ego Johannes de Veteriponte, pro me et hæredibus meis, conceffi et quietum clamavi in perpetuum, dominis de Sandford, de Burton, de Helton, et de Warthecop, ex utraque parte aquæ, et Willielmo filio Willielmi de Goldington, et hæredibus eorum, et hominibus eorum, quietantiam de pultura foreftariorum, et de omnibus quæ ego vel anteceffores mei, vel hæredes vel foreftarii mei, aliquo tempore, occafione dictæ pulturæ capere vel exigere potuimus vel poterimus, teftimonio veredariorum vel venatorum. Ita tamen, quod fi forisfactum fuerit de forefta mea, vel de venatione, vel de viridi, vel de foreftar'; inde venient ad fupradictos dominos prædictarum villarum, et petent ab eis *wytnefman*: Et ipfi domini facient foreftariis *wytnefman*. Et omnes foreftarii mei jurabunt invicem qui facti fuerint foreftarii, quod nemini nocebunt occafione illius teftimonii. *(Machel.)*

called

called to account for the ſame, but only in his county court of Weſtmorland *. Upon which grant Sir Matthew Hale's obſervation is very remarkable: He ſays, it was altogether an incroachment of the great lords to draw theſe cauſes into the foreſt courts; for they were not enabled by law to hold ſuch courts, theſe foreſts in the hands of ſubjects being but chaſes. And he ſays, treſpaſs of vert and veniſon were determinable either by a ſpecial commiſſion, or by action at common law: But the lords of Weſtmorland, having their own county court, and not being enabled to hold ſwainmote courts, drew the preſentments for theſe offences into their county court.

In ſome places, this obligation of *finding to the foreſters witneſman* was converted into a pecuniary compenſation. Thus in the 7 Hen. 7. in a rent roll of the crown lands within the barony of Kendal, whereof Sir Thomas Strickland was then ſteward, there is a payment of 2 *s* yearly by the tenants of Thornton, to the bailiff of the manor of Burton, by the name of *witneſs-ſilver*.

By cuſtom within the barony of Kendal, the WIDOW enjoys the whole cuſtomary eſtate during her widowhood; or, as others ſay, during her *chaſte* viduity. Whether ſuch diſtinction ought to be admitted, cuſtom hath not eſtabliſhed. To the honour of the ſex, there is no inſtance upon record, that we know of, wherein that matter hath been conteſted. And in the ſurvey which was made by order of queen Elizabeth in the 16th year of her reign (as will hereafter appear) this diſtinction is not taken notice of; it being there expreſſed, that "ſhe ſhall enjoy her huſband's tenement *during her widow's* "*eſtate*." And in the decree which ſettled the cuſtoms in all the crown manors in the reign of king James the firſt, the words are, that "ſhe ſhall enjoy "her huſband's cuſtomary eſtates *during her widowhood*."

And for this widow's eſtate is due to the lord an HERIOT; which, as the widow could not go to war, was a recompence, in order to provide things neceſſary for the marching of the army; as the word *heriot* imports, being of Saxon original, derived of *here*, an army, and *yate* or *gate*, a march or expedition. And this *heriot* was anciently the beſt beaſt of the deceaſed. In ſome manors cuſtom hath obtained, for the lord to have the beſt of the quick or dead goods at his option.

* Omnibus hoc ſcriptum viſuris vel auditutis, Johannes de Veteriponte ſalutem in domino. Noverit univerſitas veſtra me conceſſiſſe et præſenti charta mea confirmaſſe hominibus de Kirkby Thore, et eorum hæredibus et aſſignatis, et eorum tenentibus, ut quieti ſint de pultura foreſtariorum meorum in Weſtmerland: Et quod quieti ſint in perpetuum de teſtimorio inveniendo foreſtariis meis quod appellatur *witneſman*: Et quod ſi iidem foreſtarii manifeſtum invenerint delictum verſus prædictos homines de Kirkby Thore, de venatione aut de viridi, infra diviſas ſuas; in nulla curia quæ ad me vel hæredes meos pertineat trahantur in placitum, de aliquo placito aut querela, niſi tantum in comitatu Weſtmerland. Et ut hæc mea confirmatio, conceſſio, et quieta clamatio perpetuam obtineat firmitatem, præſens ſcriptum ſigilli mei impreſſione roboravi. Hiis teſtibus, Thoma filio Johannis nunc vicecomite meo, Henrico de Suleby, Roberto de Hellebeck, Roberto de Aſkeby, Johanne Mauchael, Richardo Baliſtario, Alano Pincerna, Adamo de Soureby, Willielmo Anglico de Aſkeby, Waltero de Meburne, Alano do Berwys, et multis aliis. (*Machel.*)

In ſome places alſo are claimed *parcel heriots*, that is, an heriot for every parcel of land acquired to the original eſtate. This perhaps ſhould mean, for every ancient military tenement, upon this reaſon, that if a man purchaſeth two tenements, which before paid two heriots, the lord ſhall not loſe his benefit by thoſe tenements coming into one perſon's hands. This diſtinction of tenements, though ſeveral of them be now enjoyed by one perſon, yet is ſtill kept up in many places, thoſe eſtates being called emphatically by the name of *Ancients*, which reſpects particularly the ancient manſion-houſe, or place where that houſe ſtood; for which the owners ſerve ſeparately and diſtinctly the office of conſtable, and other like offices. But in none of the inquiſitions or other evidences that we have met with, is this diſtinction taken notice of; but they run all in the ſtyle of one heriot to be paid by one perſon. In the ſurvey of the Marquis Fee, made by order of the Marchioneſs of Northampton, in the 14th year of the reign of queen Elizabeth, the words are, "By the death "of the tenant, the wife payeth *a heriot*." In queen Elizabeth's ſurvey of the Richmond Fee, in the 16th year of her reign as aforeſaid, the commiſſioners return, that "on the death of the tenant, the lord is to have the *beſt beaſt* being "upon the tenement, of which beaſt the tenant died ſeiſed as of his own pro"per goods, in the name of *the heriot*." And in the ſettlement of the cuſtoms in the reign of king James the firſt abovementioned (for the confirmation of which cuſtoms the tenants paid a valuable conſideration, as will hereafter appear) the words are, "Upon the death of every tenant dying ſeiſed of a tene"ment, leaving a widow behind him, *an heriot* (ſhall be paid); for which ſhe "is to enjoy her huſband's *cuſtomary eſtates* during her widowhood only." And in all antiquity we have not met with more than one heriot paid by one perſon. On the contrary, the ſecond beſt horſe was due to the church, and was carried, by the name of mortuary or corſe preſent, before the corps, and delivered to the prieſt at the place of ſepulture *.

In the bottom of Weſtmorland, the widow has in ſome places half, and in others only one third, of her huſband's cuſtomary eſtate; and in that part of the county not many heriots are paid: for in thoſe caſes there is an heir at law, who enters immediately; and conſequently the lord did not want a ſoldier, or if the heir was under age, the lord had the wardſhip of his lands.

* In the dioceſe of Carliſle it ſeemeth that the church was to be firſt ſerved, and the lord had only the ſecond beſt; as appears from the following entry in the regiſter of Wetheral priory: "Be "it knawen to all manner of men that this preſent wrytinge ſhall ſe or here, That I Thomas Bamp"ton of Threpland within the pariſh of Torpenhowe, 89 years and more of age, ſaw and had "knowledge, that Robert Heghmore, lord of Bowaldeth, preſumptuouſly tooke, in the name of "a herriot, a horſe called a mare, of the goods of John Overhowſe of Bowaldeth, afore the kyrke "took the mortuary. Wharfore he ſtoode accurſed thowro the dioces of Carlil, and was cited to "apper at Aſpatry affore Mayſter William Barowe biſhoppe of Carlil, and doctor of both laws; "whar he aſked penance and abſolution. And thare he made reſtitution of the ſayde horſe to Sir "Robert Ellergill vicar of Torpenhowe. And in remembrance, the ſayde Robert Heghmore "gaffe to the ſayde vicar ſix akes beſte in his wodde; the whilk the ſayde Thomas Bampton fellid "and carred to Torpenhowe; and there the biſhopp oppynly gaffe a decre and a ſentence to all "thayme that aftyrward and from thensforthe tooke the herriot, affore the holy kyrke war poſ"ſeſſed, God's curſe, and his, and all holy kyrkes."

In a small manuscript by one *Isaac Gilpin*, whose father had been steward of several manors within the barony of Kendal, and died about the year 1630, at the age of 92 years; he says, he had heard of his father, and had observed the same himself, that by general custom within the said barony, if a woman hath an estate and marries, hereby the estate is so far vested in the *husband*, that he may sell it in his lifetime; but if in his lifetime he doth not alter the property, then it shall continue to her and her heirs.

And Mr. Machel says, he heard this custom proved at the assizes at Appleby before judge Dolben, Aug. 29, 1690; that if a man marries an heiress, or a woman who hath purchased lands before marriage, he is intitled thereupon to be admitted tenant, and may aliene the land to whom he pleaseth. But it did not appear (as the judge observed) that it was so, where lands fall to a feme-covert or are given to her after marriage.

The said Mr. Gilpin observes further; that generally a *fine* is due upon change of the lord by death, and change of the tenant by death or alienation: The one called a general, the other a special or dropping fine.

But as to the general fine, there is this exception, where a man purchaseth the manor and dieth, the former lord being yet living. In that case, there is no fine due upon the death of the purchasing lord, nor of his son or other descendent or assignee, so long as the last general admitting lord is living; but upon the death of the last general admitting lord, it hath been determined that a fine shall be paid to the lord then in possession.

A fine arbitrary or uncertain (he says) is lost, if the tenant dies before it is assessed by the lord, and demand thereof made.

But in most of the manors, to prevent endless altercations, the fines have been reduced to a certainty; and in others extinguished, and the estate purchased to freehold.

Besides rent, fines, heriots, suit of court, and the like dependencies, there are likewise BOONS, which vary in the several manors; as, to pay a hen or capon; to plow, harrow, mow, reap, for a certain number of days; to carry coals; to repair the lord's mill race; and such like. The very word *boon* implies a benignity or voluntary kindness; but length of time hath riveted these services, and they are become matters not of choice, but of necessity.

In the barony of Kendal the customary lands are *devisable by will*; but not so in the bottom of Westmorland.

As for such as have been EARLS of this county, Sir Daniel Fleming observes, that although it be generally affirmed, that king Richard the second created the first earl of Westmorland, yet there seem to have been some earls of this county before; for he finds Humphrey de Bassingburne one of the knights of the earl of Westmorland about the time of the conquest. As to the rest, the said king Richard the second created Ralph Nevill of Raby earl of Westmorland, a man of the greatest and most ancient birth of English nobility, as descended

descended from Uchtred earl of Northumberland; whose heirs successively flourished in that honour, until Charles Nevill, casting off his allegiance to queen Elizabeth, and covering treason under pretext of religion, dishonoured that noble house, and in the year 1599 was forced to fly into the Low Countries, where he ended a miserable life. The aforesaid earl Ralph, by his wife Catharine daughter of John of Gaunt duke of Lancaster, had so fair issue, and the name of Nevill became thereby so greatly multiplied, that almost at one and the same time there flourished, besides the earls of Westmorland, an earl of Salisbury, an earl of Warwick, an earl of Kent, a marquis Montacute, a duke of Bedford, a lord Latimer, and lord Abergavenny, all Nevills. Francis Fane, eldest son of Mary lady Despencer, descended from the Nevills earls of Westmorland, was by king James the first created earl of this county; in which family the honour still continues.

Sheriffs of this county, before the grant of the sheriffwick in fee to Robert de Veteripont, so far as we have been able to trace them, are as follows:

In the reign of king Hen. 2. in a trial between Robert de Musgrave and the abbot of Byland in the county court at Appleby, *William Fitz-Hugh* was sheriff.

In the 22 Hen. 2. *Elias* son of *Gilmichael* accounted in the exchequer for several fines paid for delivering up Appleby castle to the king of Scots, viz. Gospatrick son of Orme 500 marks, Ralph de Cundal 40 marks, Odard de Burgham 20 marks, Humphrey Malchael 15 marks, John de Morvilla (sc. Morton) 20 *l*, Robert son of Colman 15 *l*, Richard de Cotesford 10 *l*, Robert dapifer (steward of the houshold) of Hugh Morvill 5 *l*, Gilbert de Engain 5 *l*, Robert de Broy 40 *s*, William de Colby 40 *s*, Robert Ribble 2 marks, William Despencer 20 *s*, William Clerk of Appleby 10 marks, Walter Plummer 2 marks, Stephen de Ebor' 20 *s*, John Perimpter 20 *s*, Odard Rufus 2 marks, Bernard Cook son of Wilfrick 4 marks, Robert de Ebor' 2 marks, Adam de Mercher 5 *l*, Geoffrey de Bolton 20 *s*, Gregory le Pinder 20 *s*, Ravenchill Molendarius 2 marks, and Richard English 2 marks. *(Denton, from the Red Book in the exchequer.)*

In the 25 Hen. 2. *Ranulph de Glanvill*, sheriff of Westmorland, accounted in the exchequer (amongst other particulars) for the rent of the county of Westmorland, received by him of Hugh de Morville of Hoff. *Id.*

In the 2 Ric. 1. *Osbert de Longchamp* was sheriff. *Id.*

In the 8 Ric. 1. *Hugh Bardulphe*, sheriff, accounted in the exchequer. *Id.*

In the 9 Ric. 1. *Adam de Deepdale.* Id.

In the 1 Joh. *Gilbert* son of *Reinfred* passed his accounts in the exchequer, for fines paid by Henry de Weshington for lands in Crosby, by Gamel de Clifton for lands at Clifton, for a relief of 13 *s* 4 *d* paid by Walter son of Durand, for 3 *l* paid by Hugh de Cottesfurth for lands at Asby after the death of his uncle, and other particulars. *Id.*

In the 2 Joh. *Geoffrey Fitz Peter* and *Roger de Bellocampo* were sheriffs of Westmorland. In their account mention is made of Richard Pippard constable of Appleby, and John Mathon constable of Burgh; and that the castles

 of

of Appleby and Burgh were repaired, and the repairs viewed and approved by Thomas ſon of Goſpatric, and Evo de Johnby. *Id.*

In the 3 Joh. *William Stutevil* and *Philip Eſcrope* were ſheriffs. *Id.*

In the 4 Joh. Robert de Veteripont was ſheriff; and in the next year the ſheriffwick was granted to him in perpetuity, in whoſe poſterity the ſame continues to this day.

This county ſends two members to parliament; a liſt whereof is inſerted in the Appendix, N° XXXIII.

——So much concerning Weſtmorland in general. In treating of the two great diviſions thereof, it ſeemeth requiſite to begin with the barony of Kendal, not only as this was held by the more ancient grant, but alſo becauſe heretofore it extended to ſeveral places within the bottom of Weſtmorland; and conſequently what we ſhall have to ſay of thoſe places, will be better underſtood, after we have treated of that barony unto which they originally belonged.

A GENE-

A GENERAL VIEW of the SUCCESSION to the BARONY of KENDAL.

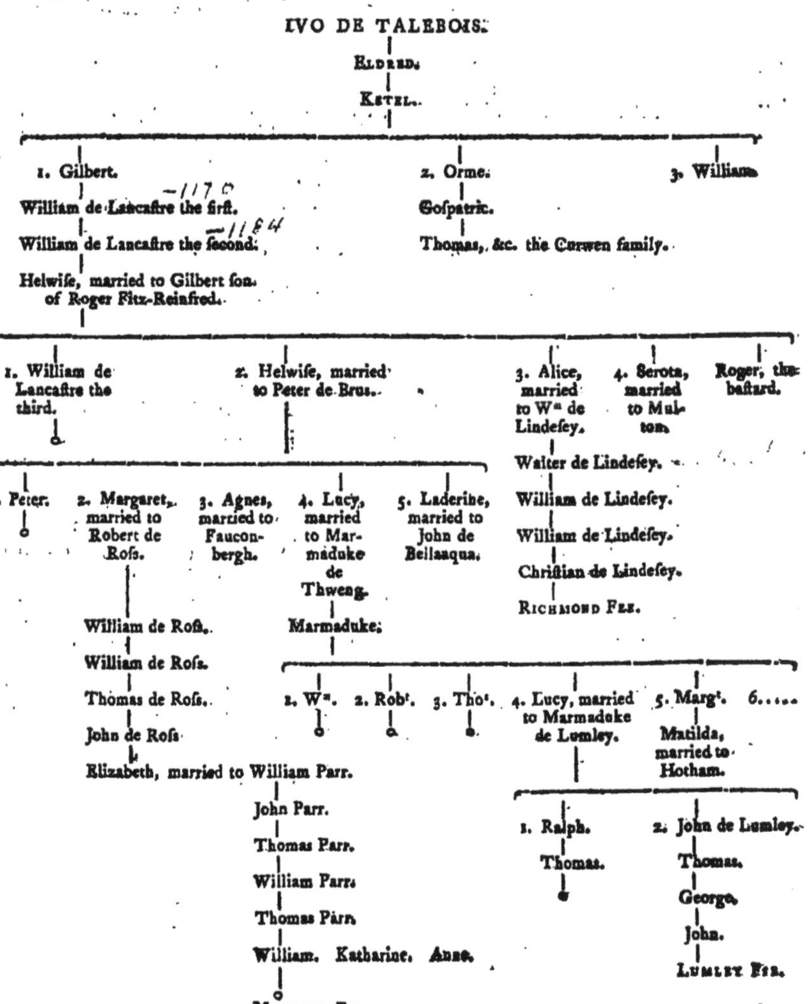
IVO DE TALEBOIS.
Eldred.
Ketel.
1. Gilbert.
2. Orme.
3. William.
William de Lancastre the first.
Gospatric.
William de Lancastre the second.
Thomas, &c. the Curwen family.
Helwise, married to Gilbert son of Roger Fitz-Reinfred.
1. William de Lancastre the third.
2. Helwise, married to Peter de Brus.
3. Alice, married to Wm de Lindesey.
4. Serota, married to Multon.
Roger, the bastard.
1. Peter.
2. Margaret, married to Robert de Ross.
3. Agnes, married to Fauconbergh.
4. Lucy, married to Marmaduke de Thweng.
5. Laderine, married to John de Bellaaqua.
Walter de Lindesey.
William de Lindesey.
William de Lindesey.
Christian de Lindesey.
Richmond Fee.
William de Ross.
William de Ross.
Thomas de Ross.
John de Ross.
Elizabeth, married to William Parr.
Marmaduke.
1. Wm.
2. Robt.
3. Thos.
4. Lucy, married to Marmaduke de Lumley.
5. Margt.
6.....
Matilda, married to Hotham.
John Parr.
Thomas Parr.
William Parr.
Thomas Parr.
William.
Katharine.
Anne.
Marquis Fee.
1. Ralph.
Thomas.
2. John de Lumley.
Thomas.
George.
John.
Lumley Fee.

CHAPTER I.

Of the BARONS *of* KENDAL *before the division of the inheritance.*

CHAP. I.

I. IVO DE TALEBOIS, brother to *Fulk* earl of *Anjou*, came in with William the conqueror: Unto whom the conqueror gave that part of Lancashire which adjoins unto Westmorland, and so much of the county of Westmorland as is now called the barony of Kendal. And hence this *Ivo* is styled the first baron of Kendal. His estate extended into several parts of the bottom of Westmorland. He gave the church of *Kirkby Stephen* to the abbey of St. Mary's York. The manors of *Barton*, *Patterdale*, *Hackthorp*, *Melkanthorp*, and *Morland*, appear to have belonged to that family. He gave also all the churches in the barony of Kendal to the said abbey *.

II. ELDRED, or ELTHRED, son of *Ivo*, the second baron of Kendal.

III. KETEL, son of *Eldred*. Unto whom, *William Meschiens*, brother to *Ranulph de Meschiens* lord of Cumberland, gave several places in Cumberland; and, amongst the rest, a place which from him received the name of *Kelton* (or Ketelton). Whether the division of the manor of *Strickland* in the barony of Kendal was made in his time, or afterwards, hath not appeared. The denominations of *Strickland Ketel* and *Strickland Roger* most probably were received from this family.

This *Ketel* son of *Eldred* gave to the abbot and convent of St. Mary's York the church of *Morland*, and two carucates of land there; which grant was confirmed by Athelwold and Hugh bishops of Carlisle. (*Register of Wetherel.*)

The said *Ketel* had three sons; *Gilbert*, the eldest, who succeeded as baron of Kendal: Another son *Orme*, who was founder of a family that is not yet extinct. Which *Orme* had a son *Gospatric*, who had a son *Thomas*, which *Thomas* son of *Gospatric* was founder of Shap abbey; and from him are descended in a regular succession of the male line (taking in collaterals sometimes to exclude the female descent) the present family of the *Curwens* of Workington. All the pedigrees of the *Curwen* family that we have met with do express, that *Orme* was son of *Ketel*, son of *Eldred*, son of *Ivo*. But none of these take notice that he was a younger son; which hath caused some confusion. That he was son of *Ketel*, there seems to be no doubt. So he is expresly styled in the record of a plea in the 6 Ed. 1. wherein it is set forth, that *Gospatric* son

* Most of the particulars relating to these barons are taken from Sir William Dugdale's 62 volumes of records, as extracted by Mr. Machel, and from Sir Daniel Fleming's copies or extracts of records and other evidences.

Ingulf, speaking of the depredations made or permitted by the Conqueror, says, that Ivo de Taillebois plundered the monastery of Croyland of a great part of its lands, and no redress could be obtained. (Hume's Hist. of Engl. vol. i. p. 179.)

of *Orme* son of *Ketel* gave Salter in Cumberland to the abbey of St. Mary's York. And that he was not the eldest son is very clear; for the inheritance of the barony of Kendal descended to Gilbert son of *Ketel* son of *Eldred* son of *Ivo*.—The name of *Ketel's* other son was *William*, as appears from the attestation of his grant of the church of Morland aforesaid to the said abbey; from which also appears that his wife's name was *Christian*: "*Testibus, Christiana* "*uxore mea, Willielmo filio meo, et multis aliis.*"

IV. Gilbert, son of *Ketel*, fourth baron of Kendal.

V. William de Talebois, son of *Gilbert*, was the first who (by licence of king Henry the second) took the name de Lancastre. He was a great benefactor to many religious houses; as, to St. Bees, Furness, Cockersand, St. Leonard's nigh Kendal, and others. And he founded the priory of Conyngshead. He married Gundred countess of Warwick, daughter of William earl of Warrene; and by her had issue,

VI. William de Lancastre the second. He was steward to king Henry the second.

This William gave to one Hugh the hermit, a certain place called Afsclesus and Croc, to look to his fishing in the river Loyn.

The said William son of William gave to the King 30 marks, that he might have a duel with Gospatric son of Orme; which sum was accounted for in the exchequer by the sheriff Elias son of Gilmichael aforesaid.

He married Helwise de Stutevile, by whom he had only a daughter, named after her mother *Helwise*. So that here the direct male line failed, and the inheritance was transferred by a daughter into another family.

VII. This Helwise, daughter and heir of the said *William de Lancastre* the second, was married to Gilbert son of Roger Fitz-Reinfrid. Which *Roger Fitz-Reinfred* was one of the judges of the court of king's bench, and likewise justice itinerant, and sheriff of Sussex from the 23d to the 33d of Hen. 2. and of Berks in the 34 Hen. 2. and 1 Ric. 1.

To this Gilbert, king Richard the first, in the first year of his reign, granted the whole forest of Westmerland and of Kendale and of Furneise, to hold to him and his heirs as fully and freely as William de Lancastre and Nigel de Albiny had held the same: And granted also, that what had been waste in the woods of Westmorland and Kendale, in the time of the said William, should be so still; except the purpresture made by licence and consent of the lords of the fee of Kendale and of Westmorland.

The said king granted to him also in the same year a quittance, through all his lands of Westmerland and of Kendale, from *noutegeld*, and from suit to the shire, hundred, or trithing courts, and aid to the sheriff or his bailiffs †.

This

† Ricardus Dei gratia, &c. Sciatis nos concessisse et dedisse et praesenti charta confirmasse, Gilberto filio Rogeri filii Renfredi, et haeredibus suis post eum, quietantiam per totam terram suam de Westmerland.

CHAP. I.

This Gilbert alſo procured from the ſaid king a charter for a weekly market at Kendale on Saturday. Another grant he had from the ſaid king of lands in Levenes, Farleton, Detene, Preſton, Holme, Berton, Henecaſtre, and Loppeton, with the fiſhery belonging to the ſaid lands, and all other liberties and privileges *.

The ſaid Gilbert granted to Thomas ſon of Goſpatric certain lands in Holme, Preſton, and Hoton. Witneſſes of which grant were, Roger ſon of Reinfred, Hugh de Morville, Gilbert de Lancaſtre, Gervaſe de Aincourt, Roger de Bellocampo, and others.

The firſt witneſs to the charter of Robert de Veteripont of the ſite and demeſne lands of the abbey of Shap, is this ſame Gilbert ſon of Roger Fitz-Reinfred.

The ſaid Gilbert adhered ſo far to the rebellious barons in the time of king John, that he was forced to pay a fine of 12,000 marks in the 17th year of that king. Upon which he obtained a pardon, as alſo that William de Lancaſtre his ſon, Ralph de Aincourt and Lambert de Buſſy his knights, ſhould be freed from their impriſonment, having been taken in Rocheſter caſtle by the king. Nevertheleſs, he was not ſo far truſted, as to be at liberty without giving divers hoſtages for his own future fidelity, and for the fidelity of William his ſon; viz. Benedict ſon and heir of Henry de Redman, the heir of Roger de Kirkby his daughter's ſon, the ſon and heir of William de Windleſore, the daughter and heir of Ralph d'Eincourt, the daughter or ſon and heir of Roger de Burton, the daughter and heir of Adam de Yelond, the ſon or daughter of Thomas de Bethun, the ſon or daughter and heir of Walter de Stirkland, the daughter of Richard de Coupland, and the ſon of Gilbert de Lancaſtre.

He died in the fourth year of king Henry the third, leaving one ſon, who ſucceeded him, and three daughters.

VIII. William de Lancastre the third; ſon of the ſaid Gilbert ſon of Roger Fitz-Reinfred, by his wife Helwiſe de Talebois daughter of William

Weſtmerland et de Kendale de *noutegeld*, ſc. de 14*l* 16*s* 3*d*, quas ipſe Gilbertus ſolebat reddere per annum pro *noutegelde* de præfata terra. Conceſſimus etiam eidem Gilberto et hæredibus ſuis quietantiam per totam præfatam terram ſuam de ſchiris, et de wapentac, et de trithinga, et de auxiliis vicecomitum et omnium ballivorum ſuorum. Hanc quietantiam ei conceſſimus et confirmavimus et hæredibus ſuis, per ſervitium unius militis quod nobis facere debet ipſe Gilbertus et hæredes ſui poſt eum, et hæredibus noſtris, pro prædicto *noutegelde*. Pro hac autem quietantia et conceſſione dedit nobis ſupradictus Gilbertus viginti marcas argenti. Quare volumus et firmiter præcipimus, quod prædictus Gilbertus, et hæredes ſui poſt eum, habeant et teneant prædictam quietantiam de nobis et hæredibus noſtris, per prædictum ſervitium, bene et in pace, libere et quiete, integre, plenarie, et honorifice, in boſco et plano, in viis et ſemitis, in pratis et paſturis, in vivariis et ſtagnis, in nundinis et feriis, in mercatis et extra, et infra burgum et extra, et in omnibus aliis locis. Et prohibemus ne quis eundem Gilbertum vel hæredes ſuos de præfata quietantia diſturbet. Teſte Willielmo Comite Arundel (et multis aliis).——Is erat tenor chartæ noſtræ in primo ſigillo; quod quia aliquando perditum fuit, et dum capti eſſemus in Alemannia in aliena poteſtate conſtituti mutatum eſt, hujus innovationis teſtes ſunt hii, H. Sar. Epiſc. &c.

* .... in burgo et extra burgum, et in omnibus locis, liberas et quietas de geld, et denegeld, et neutegeld, et horngeld, et de blodwitha, et frithwitha, et de leirwitha, et ferdwitha, cum ſoca et ſaca, et tol et theam, et infangtheif, et cum omnibus aliis libertatibus et liberis conſuetudinibus, quæ ad eas terras pertinent.

de

de Lancaſtre the ſecond. He took the name *de Lancaſtre*, together with the inheritance, from his mother. CHAP. I.

He married Agnes de Brus: by whom he had no iſſue.

He was juſtice itinerant for the county of Cumberland, in the 10th year of king Henry the third; and was ſheriff of Lancaſhire from the 18th to the 30th year of that king.

This William confirmed to Patric ſon of Thomas ſon of Goſpatric the aforeſaid grant made by Gilbert father of the ſaid William, of lands in Holme, Preſton, and Hoton. Witneſſes of which confirmation were, Gilbert de Kirketon then ſheriff of Weſtmorland (that is, under-ſheriff to the then Robert de Veteripont), Matthew de Redeman then ſeneſchal (that is, ſteward, or recorder) of Kendal, Ralph de Aincourt, Alexander de Windeſore, Richard de Preſton, Robert de Laiburne, Robert de Kerneford, Gilbert de Witeby clerk, and others †.

For the health of his ſoul, and the ſoul of Agnes his wife, he gave to the monks of Furneſs one boat to be uſed on Wynender-mere, for carriage of timber and other commodities; and one other boat, to fiſh in that mere.

The ſaid William de Lancaſtre the third gave to one Laurence de Cornewall and his heirs the mills at Ulverſton and certain lands there. Which Laurence begat John, and John begat Laurence, which Laurence (becauſe he had no heirs of his body) gave the ſame to Edmund Nevill and his heirs. Which

† The ſheriff is often mentioned as a witneſs to ſuch ancient grants, together with divers of the principal gentlemen of the county. And the reaſon is, becauſe theſe matters, for the greater notoriety thereof, were frequently tranſacted in the county court; which in ancient time was the court for almoſt all buſineſs. And every freeman was bound to attend, and the meſne lords holding under the lords of Weſtmorland, who alſo were ſheriffs of the county, were obliged by their tenure to attend monthly, and did regularly attend, at the ſaid court. And the law to this day, in many inſtances, ſuppoſeth this general concourſe and attendance: For there the knights of the ſhire are elected, as alſo coroners; and outlawries are there pronounced, as being the place moſt likely for the offenders to come to the knowledge thereof. Subſcribing witneſſes were not uſual in thoſe days, nor till many ages after. And therefore the writing only mentions ſuch and ſuch perſons as witneſſes, who were generally the principal perſons for rank and diſtinction there preſent. The truth is, very few people could then write, not even perſons of the higheſt rank and eminence. Many charters are yet extant, granted by kings and other great perſons, from which it appears that they could not ſubſcribe their names, but they ſigned the charters with a croſs, as thus, "Ego "Athelwaldus + ſubſcripſi;" which croſs was affixed with their own hands, *propter ignorantiam literarum* (as Du Cange expreſſeth it); and it is remarkable, that even to this day, perſons who cannot write uſually mark the writing with this ſame ſignature of a croſs. So late as the fourteenth century, Du Gueſclin, conſtable of France, the greateſt man in the ſtate, and one of the greateſt men of his age, could neither read nor write. Nor was this ignorance confined to laymen; the greater part of the clergy was not many degrees ſuperior to them in ſcience. Many dignified eccleſiaſtics could not ſubſcribe the canons of thoſe councils, in which they ſat as members. Alfred the great complained, that from the Humber to the Thames there was not a prieſt who underſtood the liturgy in his mother tongue, or who could tranſlate the eaſieſt piece of Latin; and that from the Thames to the ſea, the eccleſiaſtics were ſtill more ignorant. This was owing, beſides the ferocity of the times, to the great ſcarcity of books before the invention of printing. (1 Robertſon's Hen. 5. p. 232.)——Such an one *Clericus*, doth not mean a clergyman, for thoſe they expreſſed by *perſona* or parſon of ſuch a church; or if not beneficed, they ſtyled him *capellanus*: But *Clericus* ſeems moſt commonly to denote the perſon who wrote the inſtrument. *Gilbert de Watsby*, as we find from abundance of inſtruments, was a common conveyancer in thoſe times.

 Edmund

CHAP. II.

Edmund begat William, William begat John, John begat Thomas (then living, *viz.* in the year 1409, when that entry was made in the register of Furness abbey).

He confirmed to one Alward de Broghton and his heirs the manor of Broghton; to be holden by knights service and rent.

His arms on several of these grants are, Argent, two bars Gules: In a quarter Gules, a lion passant Or.

In the 11th year of king Henry the third, there was a contest between Robert de Veteripont sheriff of the county, and this same William de Lancastre lord of Kendale, concerning suit to be made to the county court by the said William and his tenants. And by a fine levied thereupon in that year, William grants suit for his lands to the county, by himself or his attorney; and if any pleas be attached touching the tenants of William, whereof by the law the barons ought to have their courts, then upon demand thereof he shall have it: Martin Patishull, John de Saul, William de Insula, and Richard Duckett, being then justices itinerant.

By his will he bequeathed his body to be buried in the quire of the abbey of Furness, near to the tomb of William his grandfather.

Agnes de Brus his wife survived him; and had, for part of her dower, an assignment of the manors of Gresmere, Langedon, Crossethwait, and Lyth.

IX. The male line failing again in this William de Lancastre the third; we pass to his three sisters, daughters of Gilbert and Helwise aforesaid. These were, HELWISIA, married to PETER DE BRUS; ALICIA, married to WILLIAM DE LYNDESAY; and SEROTA, married to ALAN DE MULTON, who died without issue of her body.

And therefore the inheritance descended to the two sisters HELWISE and ALICE, and was divided between them; one of whom received for her share what was afterwards called the RICHMOND FEE; the other, what was afterwards called the MARQUIS and LUMLEY FEE.

ALICE was the younger sister. But as her share was kept more intire, there will be less confusion if we dispatch that first; and then proceed to the other, which became afterwards further divided.

CHAPTER III.

Of the RICHMOND FEE.

ALICE, sister of the last William de Lancastre as aforesaid, was married to WILLIAM DE LINDESAY; and brought with her in marriage one moiety of the barony of Kendal.

They

They had a son Walter de Lyndesay; who died in the 56 Hen. 3. at which time he held, as found by inquisition, of the king *in capite*, a moiety of Kirkeby in Kendale.

He had a son and heir William de Lyndesaie; on whose death in the 11 Ed. 1. the inquisition finds, that he died seised of the forest of Gresmere, Langden, Troutbeck forest, Applethwaite, Wynandermere, Eclesall, Skandall, Lyith, Crosthwayte, Stirkland Ketell, Kirkeby in Kendale, Helsington, Kent fishery, and Hoton in the Hay.

This William had a son and heir William de Lyndesay; concerning whom we find nothing particular, save only that he died without any male heir of his body, leaving issue only a daughter and heir, *viz.*

Christian de Lyndesey, who was married to Ingelram de Guisnes lord of Coucy in France. They had a son *William*, born in France, who after his father's death inherited his estate there. They had a second son Ingelram, born in England, who died without any heir of his body. And his brother *William* being an alien, and thereby not capable to inherit, the estate escheated to the crown.

The aforesaid elder brother *William* had two sons; *Ingelram* the elder, and William, both of them born in France, in the ligeance of the king of France. *Ingelram* enjoyed the paternal estate there; and the king granted to *William* the younger brother his grandmother *Christian's* estate in England. Which *William* also died without issue of his body, and the estate again escheated to the crown.

After which, the said king, namely, king Edward the third, in the 21st year of his reign, granted the same to John de Coupland (of Coupland nigh Wooler in the county of Northumberland, and captain of Roxbrough castle) and Johan his wife, during their lives, and the life of the longer liver of them: As follows,——" The king, to whom these presents shall come, greet" ing. Know ye, that whereas we, lately considering the acceptable and " laudable services done unto us by our beloved John de Coupland, and the " good state which he hath held in our wars, and also the valiant behaviour " of the said John in the battle of Durham, where God by his divine power " conferred upon our faithful subjects of the northern parts a glorious victory " over our enemies the Scots, in which battle the same John took David de " Bruys, who caused himself to be called king of Scotland, and delivered him " up unto us, and being willing to reward the said John for his fidelity and " valour, in such wise that others in time to come may take example from " thence, have advanced him to the state of a baneret, and for maintenance " of the said state have for us and our heirs granted to the said John 500 *l*, " to be received by him every year, to wit, 400 *l* out of the issues of our

CHAP. II.

" customs in the port of our city of London, and 100*l* out of the issues of " our customs in the port of the town of Berewic upon Tweed, until we should " make a competent provision for him of 500 librates of land, or a compe- " tent yearly rent; and now being willing that our said grant may be effec- " tually carried into execution, we have given and granted for us and our heirs, " to the said John, the manor of Coghull with the appurtenances in the " county of York, and a moiety of the manor of Kirkeby in Kendale with its " members and other appurtenances in the counties of Westmerland and Cum- " berland, and a moiety of Ulverston with the appurtenances in the county of " Lancastre: And we have also granted to the said John the manors of Mor- " holme, Warton, Carnford, and Lyndheved, with the appurtenances, to " hold of us at our will at the yearly rent of 78*l* 5*s* 11*d*. All which said " premisses belonged to William de Coucy, and which after the death of the " said William came into our hands as escheats." And then he goes on and makes provision for Johan, in case she survive her husband. " Dated at our " Tower of London the 21st day of May, in the 21st year of our reign."

It hath been observed above, that the last William had an elder brother Ingelram, who inherited the Coucy estate in France. This Ingelram had a son Ingelram lord of Coucy, who married ISABEL daughter of king Edward the third of England. And the king granted unto them the reversion of the English estate, after the death of the said John de Coupland and Johan his wife, to them and the heirs of their bodies; except the reversion of the moiety of the manor of Ulverston, which he gave to the abbey of Furness.

And all this appears from an inquisition taken at Lancaster for the Lancashire estates (for in every different county where they had estates there were different inquisitions) in the 49 Ed. 3. after the death of the aforesaid Johan de Coupland. By which it is found, that William son of William de Coucy deceased was of the kingdom of France, that he died seised in his demesne as of fee of the manor of Moorholme, a moiety of the manor of Wiresdale, a moiety of the manor of Eston, a third part of the manor of Whittington, all holden of John duke of Lancastre by knights service and several rents; and of a moiety of the manor of Ulverston, holden of the abbot of Furnese by the like service and rent. The jurors further find, that the said William son of William died without any heir of his body, and that he had no heir within the kingdom of England, or within the dominion of the king of England. But they say, that Ingelram de Coucy, who was of the ligeance of the king of France, was brother and next of kin by blood to the said William son of William; which Ingelram is dead. And they say, that Ingelram de Coucy, lord of Coucy that now is, who is of the parts of France and of the ligeance of the king of France, is son and next heir of the said Ingelram. And they say, that our lord the king that now is, after the death of the said William son of William, seized into his hands all the said lands and tenements as escheats, for that he died without any heir or heirs within the kingdom of England or dominion of the king of England. And that the said king granted all the said lands and tenements to John de Coupland and Johan his wife for their lives; and the reversion

reversion thereof to Ingelram de Coucy that now is, and Isabel his wife, and the heirs of their bodies; and the reversion of the said moiety of Ulverston to the abbot of Furneys and his successors.

And there is a licence in the exchequer, 31 Ed. 3. for the abbot of Furneys to take the reversion of the moiety of the manor of Ulverston, and to enter upon the same after the death of John de Coupland and Johan his wife, for the fine of 40 marks.

The Westmorland inquisition after the death of the said Johan is as follows:

" An inquisition indented, taken before John Savill escheator of our lord " the king in the county of Westmerland, at Kirkby in Kendale, on Saturday " next after the feast of Corpus Christi, in the 49th year of the reign of king " Ed. 3. by the oath of Thomas de Redeman, Roger de Levens, Roland de " Thornburgh, John de Chambre de Kendale, Robert de Docura, Richard " Carous, William Danny, Richard Walker, William de Gilpin, Roger de " Stirkland, Henry de Gnype, and John de Stirkland; who say,

" That *Johan*, who was the wife of *John de Coupland*, held for the term " of her life, by the grant of our lord the king, the manor of *Wynandermere*, " with its members and appurtenances, to wit, the hamlet of *Langden*, " *Lougbrigge*, *Grismer*, *Hamelside*, *Troutbeck*, *Appletbwate*, *Crostbwate*, *Stirk-* " *land Ketell*, and *Hoton*; and the manor of *Casterton* with the appurtenances; " and also a moiety of the manor of *Kirkby* in *Kendale* with the appurte- " nances: The reversion thereof (after the death of the said *Johan*) to the " lord *Ingelram de Coucy* earl of *Bedford*, and *Isabel* his wife daughter of our " said lord the king, and the heirs of their bodies.

" Extent of the knights fees which the wife of *John de Coupland* deceased " had for the term of her life.

" The same jurors say upon their oath, that *Ralph de Betbome*, knight, held " of the same Johan the manor of *Betbome* with the appurtenances, by ho- " mage and fealty, and the service of 32*s* a year, as of her manor of Kirkeby " in Kendale: And *Nicholas de Haverington* held of *Ralph de Betbome* the ma- " nor of *Farleton*, by homage and fealty, and the service of two marks a " year, as of his manor of *Betbome*.

" *William Windlesore* held of the said Johan the manors of *Haversham*, *Mor-* " *land*, and *Grarigge*; by homage and fealty, and the service of 13*s* 4*d* a " year as of her said manor of Kirkeby.

" *Matthew de Redman* held of the said Johan the manors of *Levens* and " *Lupton*, by homage and fealty, and the service of two marks a year, as of " her manor aforesaid.

" *Thomas Adamson* held divers tenements in *Middleton* of the said Johan, by " homage and fealty, and the service of 4*s* a year, as of her manor afore- " said.

" *Ralph Lascells* held of the same the manor of *Barburne*, by homage and " fealty, and the service of 30*s* 7*d* a year, as of her manor aforesaid.

" *Hugh de Moresby* held of the same Johan the manor of *Hoton Roose*, by " homage and fealty, and the service of 8*s* a year, as of her manor aforesaid.

" *Thomas*

CHAP. II.

"*Thomas de Redman* held of the same divers tenements in *Kirkslack*, as of "the inheritance of *Sturnel*, by homage and fealty, and the service of 3*s* 4*d* "a year, as of her manor aforesaid.

"*William de Bourdale* held of the same divers tenements in the town of "*Kirkeby*, by homage and fealty, and the service of 16*d* a year, as of her "manor aforesaid.

"*Simon de Haversham* held of the same divers tenements in *Hoton Roofe*, by "homage and fealty, and the service of 3*s* 4*d* a year, as of her said manor "of Kirkeby.

"The prior of *Watton* and *Johanna de Haverington* held of the same the "manor of *Thornby*, by homage and fealty, and the service of five marks a "year, as of her manor of Kirkeby.

"*Margaret* who was the wife of *Roger de Lancastre* held of the same divers "tenements in *Bravandesdale*, by homage and fealty, and the service of 2*s* a "year as of her manor of Kirkeby.

"*Robert de Bellingham* held of the same Johan divers tenements in *Stirkland* "*Ketell*, by homage and fealty, and the service of 8*d* a year, as of her má-"nor of Kirkeby.

"*Robert de Stirkland* held of the same divers tenements in *Stirkland Ketell*, "by homage and fealty, and the service of 8*d* a year, as of her manor of "Kirkeby.

"*Robert de Docura* held of the same divers tenements in *Kirkeby Kendale*, "by fealty, and the service of 2*s* a year, as of her manor of Kirkeby.

"*Adam Thurstanson* held of the same one tenement in *Stirkland Ketell*, by "fealty, and the service of 20*d* a year, as of her manor of Wynandermere.

"Also they say, that the same Johan died seised for the term of her life as "aforesaid of the advowson of the chapel of *Grisemere*, which is taxed at 10*l*; "and of the advowson of the chapel of *Wynandermere*, which is taxed at 100*s*; "and of the advowson of the chapel of *St. Mary Holme*, within the lake of "*Wynandermere*, which is worth nothing, because the land which the said "chapel enjoyed of old time, hath been seised into the hands of the king, "and lies within the park of *Calvgarth*.

"The reversion of all the premisses wholly belongs to *Ingelram de Coucy* earl "of *Bedford*, and *Isabel* his wife, and the heirs of their bodies, by the grant "of our lord the king, as appeareth by his charter.

"In witness whereof the jurors aforesaid have set their seals."

The said INGLERAM DE COUCY, and ISABEL his wife, daughter of the king of England as aforesaid, had a daughter named PHILIPPA, married to *Robert de Vere* earl of *Oxford* and duke of *Ireland*; from whom, in the reign of king Richard the second, she was divorced for lack of children.

She died in the 13 Hen. 4. and by an inquisition in that year it was found, that *Philippa* who had been the wife of *Robert de Vere* late duke of *Ireland* died seised of a moiety of the manor of Kirkeby in Kendale.

And the same having reverted again to the crown for want of heirs of the body of the said *Philippa*, the said king Henry the fourth granted the pre-missès miffes to his third fon JOHN duke of BEDFORD. And by an inquifition of knights fees in Weftmorland taken at Appleby in the 6 Hen. 6. it was found, that the lord *John* duke of *Bedford* then held of the king *in capite* a moiety of the manor of Kirkby in Kendale, by the fervice of one knight's fee; and that the fame lately belonged to dame *Philippa* duchefs of *Ireland*. The faid *John* duke of *Bedford* died in the 14 Hen. 6. as appears by the inquifition after his death, in which he is ftyled uncle of the faid king.

The faid king Henry the fixth, in the 22d year of his reign, granted the fame to JOHN DE BEAUFORT duke of SOMERSET and of KENDAL, and his heirs male, with remainder to the crown: Which John duke of Somerfet was fon of John de Beaufort earl of Somerfet, fon of John of Gaunt duke of Lancafter, fon of king Edward the third. The faid duke of Somerfet died in the fame year in which his grant was made, without iffue male; and the premiffes reverted again to the crown.

And the king thereupon granted the fame by letters patent to MARGARET daughter and heir of the faid *John* duke of *Somerfet*, by the name of MARGARET countefs of RICHMOND, fhe having been the wife of *Edmund* late earl of *Richmond*, and being then (by her fecond marriage) wife of *Henry Stafford* fon of *Humphrey* late duke of *Buckingham*. The grant was to her and the faid *Henry*. And there is a private act of parliament, 3 Hen. 7. c. 2. confirming to her the faid grant.

And this feems to have firft given to the faid moiety of the manor of Kendale the name of RICHMOND FEE, which it retains to this day.

In the feventh year of king Henry the feventh fhe caufed a rental to be made of the faid moiety, of which the particulars were as follows:

	l.	s.	d.		l.	s.	d.
Grefmere - - - -	11	1	11	Fifhery of Kent - - -	1	0	0
Langden - - -	6	0	0	Burgage of Kendal - -	2	2	8
Loughrigg - - - -	2	3	9½	Toll of Kendal - - -	4	10	0
Amelfide - - - - -	26	14	8½	Whittington - - - - -	6	0	0
Troutbeck - - - - -	4	4	1	Cafterton - - - - - -	3	10	0
Aplethwait - - - -	30	4	0	Thornton - - - - -	12	12	1
Undermilnbeck - - -	8	10	6	Whierfdall - - - - -	49	12	1
Crofthwait - - - - -	16	7	6	Scotforth - - - - - -	6	1	0
Hutton - - - - -	17	4	6	The office of land ferjeant	10	6	7
Stirkland Ketell - - -	1	8	1½	Warton - - - - - -	60	3	9
Frofthwait - - - - -	1	6	8	Kneton and Middleton - -	6	13	4

Fees and penfions paid forth of the fame.

	l.	s.	d.
To the Steward - - - - -	5	0	0
To the land ferjeant - - - - -	10	0	0
Fees to the forefters of Troutbeck - -	2	3	0
To Reignal Bray knight, general receiver, - -	4	11	0
To Richard Berwick bowbearer of Troutbeck - -	3	1	6
Unto St. Mary Holme - - - -	6	0	0

2 The

The aforesaid *Margaret* countess of *Richmond* was mother to the said king Henry the seventh; and from her this *Richmond fee* came again to the crown.

King Henry the eighth, in the 23d year of his reign, granted the same to his natural son HENRY duke of RICHMOND and SOMERSET; who dying without any issue of his body, the same reverted the eighth time to the crown.

The MARQUIS FEE escheated not long after, first by attainder, and afterwards for want of heirs of the body of the last grantee; and both have continued in the crown ever since, and have commonly passed together by temporary grants; as will appear in due course, when we have brought up the *marquis fee* through the several possessors till its return into the hands of the crown.

CHAPTER III.

Of the MARQUIS FEE.

HAVING deduced the *Lindsey* moiety of the barony of Kendal, which came to that name and family by the marriage of *Alice* one of the sisters and coheirs of the last William de Lancastre baron of Kendal; we proceed to the other sister and coheir before mentioned, namely, HELWISE who was married to PETER DE BRUS, son of *Peter de Brus*, son of *Adam de Brus*, son of *Adam de Brus*, son of *Robert de Brus* knight, who came in with William the Conqueror. Unto which *Robert*, for his extraordinary services, the conqueror gave 43 lordships in the East and West Ridings of the county of York, and 51 in the North Riding. Of the younger branch of this family was *Robert de Brus* (or *Bruce*), who in the reign of king Edward the first was competitor with *John Baliol* for the crown of Scotland.

This PETER DE BRUS, of whom we speak, being the second of that name, had by his said wife *Helwise* a son PETER DE BRUS, who succeeded his father and mother in their inheritance; and four daughters, *viz.* 1. *Margaret*, married to *Robert de Ross*. 2. *Agnes*, married to *Walter de Fauconberge*. 3. *Lucy*, married to *Marmaduke de Thweng*. 4. *Laderine*, married to *John de Bellew* (or *de Bella-aqua*).

PETER DE BRUS the third, son of *Peter* and *Helwise*, after his mother's death, succeeded to a moiety of the barony of Kendal.

This *Peter* confirmed to the free burghers of his moiety of Kirkby in Kendale, all the liberties and free customs which they had of the gift of William de Lancastre his uncle.

In the 44 Hen. 3. he granted to William de Pickering the manor of Killington.

He died in the 7 Ed. 1. seised, as the inquisition finds, of a moiety of the manor of Kirkeby in Kendale; and as parcel thereof, of the castle, with the parks, vivaries within the parks, and herbage therein of the yearly value of ten

ten marks. And the jurors further find, that he died without any heir of his body; and that *Margaret*, *Agnes*, *Lucy*, and *Laderine*, were his sisters and coheirs.

The arms of *Brus* were; Or, a saltire Gules, a chief of the last.

Upon his death, a partition of the Lancastre and Brus estates was made amongst the said four sisters. And in the 11 Ed. 1. there is a writ to the escheator beyond Trent, to take the inheritance of Peter de Brus back into the king's hands, till another partition be made, if Walter de Fauconberghe (husband of Agnes), who was absent at the time of the partition, is not satisfied therewith.

The share of *Margaret* the eldest sister is that only which we are concerned with at present. *Agnes*, the second sister, had no share in Westmorland. *Lucy*, the third sister, had that which is now called the Lumley-fee. And *Laderine*, the fourth sister, had Kentmere, and nothing else in Westmorland.

Margaret's share upon the partition is thus described, *viz.* Kendal castle, with all in Kendale which had been Peter's, and whatsoever belonged to the said Peter in demesnes, villenages, rents, and services of free men and others; except the vill of Kentmere, which was assigned to Laderina. And there was a dispute whether the advowson of the church of Warton in Kendale belonged to Margaret by virtue of this partition of the estate; and it was determined for her, in the 17 Ed. 1.

This MARGARET DE BRUS was married as aforesaid to ROBERT DE ROSS (or, as it was most commonly written, *Roos*). He was younger son of *Robert* lord *Roos* of Hamlake and Werke, by his wife Isabel daughter of the king of Scots. The elder brother was *William* lord *Roos* of Hamlake and Werke, father of *William* lord *Roos*, father of *John* lord *Roos*, father of *William* lord *Roos* of Belvoir, one of whose daughters and coheirs, *Elianor*, was married to Sir *Robert Manners* ancestor of the present duke of *Rutland*, who still retains amongst his other titles that of baron *Ross* of Hamlake.

This *Robert de Roos*, husband of *Margaret*, died in the 2 Ed. 1. before her brother *Peter*. Hence the partition of the estate is set forth to have been between *Margaret de Ross* and the *husbands* of the three other sisters; *viz.* *Walter de Fauconberghe*, *Marmaduke de Thweng*, and *John de Bella-aqua*.

She appears to have been living many years after the death of her husband; for in the 29 Ed. 1. she conveyed by fine to her son *William de Ros* 2 messuages, 31 carucates, and 45 acres of land, 5 mills, and a moiety of 3 mills, in Helsington, Scaleghwayt Rig, Hoton, Hay, Strikeland Randolphe, Greenerigg, Hogayl, Patton, Dilaker, and the advowson of the hospital of St. Leonard in Kirkebie in Kendale, the castle of Kirkebie in Kendale, and the fourth part of the manor of Kirkebie in Kendale, and 10*l* 2*s* 0½*d* of rent, also the rents of one sparhawk, of 3 pounds of pepper, 2 pounds of cumin, 1 pound of wax, and 12 arrows; and two parts of one knight's fee in Burton, Manserghe, Preston Richard, Lupton, Hencastre, Killington, Frittebank, Berghes, Sockbrede, Tereghe, Stirkeland Roger, Slegill, Bannandesdale, Little Styrkeland, Conyngeswyke, Bratha lake, Tranthewayte, Barton, Melkanthorpe, Middleton, Stainton, Libberghe, Haverbrake, Stirkeland Ketell, Crook, Patton, Ulne-

 thwayte,

CHAP. III. thwayte, Asthewayt, and Stirkeland Randolfe, in the county of Westmerland; and the 100th part of one knight's fee in Leighton and Yelond Coygners in the county of Lancastre: To hold to the said William and the heirs of his body; and in defect thereof, to (her nephew) Marmaduke de Thweng, and his heirs.

This *William de Roos*, son and heir of Margaret, died probably before his mother. For the inquisition after his death bears date in the 3 Ed. 2. And in that year we find that *Margaret de Ros* held the manor of Molcanthorp. How long she lived after this, we have not found.

The said *William* had a son WILLIAM DE ROOS, who in the 2 Ed. 3. obtained a charter for a market at Staveley on the Friday weekly; and a fair yearly, on the eve, day, and morrow of St. Luke the evangelist. He was succeeded by his son,

THOMAS DE ROOS knight, who died in the 14 Ric. 2.

This *Thomas* had a son JOHN DE ROOS, who died before his father, leaving an infant daughter: For among the escheats in the 32 Ed. 3. we find, that *John* son of *Thomas Roos* of Kendal died in that year, and that ELIZABETH was his daughter and heir, aged two years. Which daughter was afterwards married to *William del Parre* knight. And by an inquisition upon *Thomas*'s death, in the 14 Ric. 2. as aforesaid, it was found, that he died seised of one fourth part of the manor of Kirkeby in Kendale; and that Elizabeth wife of *William del Parre* knight was his kinswoman and heir. The mother of *Elizabeth* lived a long time after: For in the 6 Hen. 6. it is found by inquisition, that *Katherine* widow of *John Roos* of Kendal died in that year, seised of the manor of Carghow in Cumberland (which of a long time had belonged to the barons of Kendal, and this probably was part of her jointure).

The arms of *Roos* were; Gules, three water budgets Sable.

ELIZABETH as aforesaid, heiress of the family of *Roos*, was married to WILLIAM DEL PARRE knight. She died before him. For in the 20 Ric. 2. we find the said *William del Parre* holding by the curtesy of England [*per legem Angliæ*] the fourth part of Kirkby in Kendale of the king *in capite*, by the service of one knight's fee. He died in the 6 Hen. 4. seised (as the inquisition finds) of the said fourth part of the right of *Elizabeth* his late wife, kinswoman and heir of *Thomas de Roos* knight, and daughter of *John de Roos* son of the said *Thomas*. And the jurors find, that *John Parre* was his son and heir.

JOHN PARRE knight, son and heir of *William*, did not long survive his father; for the inquisition after his death bears date in the 9 Hen. 4.

He was succeeded by his son THOMAS PARRE knight; who by an inquisition of knights fees in the 6 Hen. 6. appears to have held one fourth part of the manor of Kirkby in Kendale, by the service of the fourth part of one knight's fee. This *Thomas* died in the 4 Ed. 4. having two sons, 1. *William*, who succeeded him. 2. *John*, to whom king Edward the fourth, in the 2d year of his reign, granted the sheriffwick of Westmorland during his life, with power to exercise the office by a deputy or under-sheriff; the young Henry lord Clifford, hereditary sheriff of the county, being then deprived of his ho-

nours.

nours and estate, by reason of his father having sided with the house of Lancaster in the then civil wars. Which king also granted to the said *John* and his brother *William* all the lands of Sir Henry Bellingham of Bourneshead, who was attainted on the like account.

Sir William Parr knight, son and heir of Sir *Thomas*, married Elizabeth one of the three sisters and coheirs of Henry lord Fitz-Hugh. He was made knight of the garter by king Edward the fourth. He was knight of the shire for Westmorland in the 6th, and again in the 12th of Ed. 4. He appears have been living in the 22d year of that king. In what year he died we have have not found.

He had two sons, *Thomas* the elder; and a younger son Sir *William Parre* of Horton in Northumberland, who married a daughter and coheir of Roger Salisbury. This younger son Sir William was buried in the parish church at Horton, June 21, 1546; leaving only a daughter, married to Sir Thomas Tresham.

The elder son Sir Thomas Parr knight succeeded his father. He was master of the wards and comptroller to king Henry the eighth. He married *Maud* daughter and coheir of Sir Thomas Green. By her he had one son and two daughters. The elder daughter *Katherine* was married first to Edward Borough, secondly to John Nevil lord Latimer, thirdly to king Henry the eighth (being his sixth wife), and lastly to Thomas lord Seymour of Sudley, one of the uncles of king Edward the sixth; and she died in the 2 Ed. 6. The other daughter *Anne*, was married to William Herbert earl of Pembroke.

In the 3d year of the said king Henry the eighth, this Sir *Thomas* had a grant of free warren in his manor of Kendale, and in all his lands within the county of Westmorland.

In the same year he took to farm of Henry lord Clifford the profits of the shrievalty arising within the barony of Kendal, for the rent of 4*l* a year. At the same time there was a payment out of the barony of Kendal into the exchequer called *Herbert silver*, which probably was so styled from this same Herbert earl of Pembroke; which being left in arrear and unpaid by Sir Roger Bellingham when he was under-sheriff, a writ was issued, on behalf of the lord Clifford, for the payment thereof.

The said Sir *Thomas* died in the 9 Hen. 8. and by his will dated the 7th of November in that year, he ordered his body to be buried, according to his degree, without pomp or pride, in the Black Friers London, if he should die within 20 miles thereof: All his manors, lands, and tenements within the realm of England, which descended to him as heir from his father Sir *William Parr* knight, he gave to his wife *Maud* during her life; 800*l* betwixt his two daughters *Katherine* and *Anne* towards their marriages; 100 marks to the chantry of Kendal; to his son *William Parr* his chain of gold worth 140*l* and his signet which the king gave to him the testator.

By an inquisition after his death of his lands in Westmerland, in the 10 Hen. 8. the jurors find, that he was seised of the manor of Kendale, with 1000 acres of pasture, and 400*l* rent, with the appurtenances, in Hutton,

 Hay,

CHAP. III.

Hay, Strickland, Hugill, Greenrigge, Ullerthorne, and Kirkby in Kendale; and that *William Parr* esquire was his son and heir, aged then five years.

His wife *Maud* survived him; and by her will, the probate of which bears date 14 Dec. 23 Hen. 8. she orders her body to be buried in the Black Friers church in London, where her husband lieth, if she die in London, or within 20 miles thereof. She mentions therein her son and heir *William Parr* as to be married to the lady Bourchier, daughter and heir apparent to the earl of Essex. One of the witnesses to the same is Sir *William Parr* of Horton, called the brother of the testatrix.

And by an inquisition taken at Shap 28 Oct. 24 Hen. 8. the jurors find, that *Thomas Parr*, knight, late husband of the said *Maud*, was seised of and in the manor of Kendale, to wit, Grenehede, Skalthwaitrig, Strickland Roger, Grenerig, Ullathorne, Riston, and Kirkeby in Kendale: That a fine was levied thereof in Michaelmas term 23 Hen. 7. That they had two daughters *Katherine* and *Anne*: And that *William Parr* is son and heir of the said *Maud*, and was 19 years of age on the 14th day of August last.

William Parr, esquire, succeeded his father Sir *Thomas*. It hath not appeared that this *William* was ever knighted. His steward's accounts in the 24 Hen. 8. style him only *William Parr*, esquire. In which accounts, amongst other particulars, is the following Item: "In money paid to the abby and "convent of St. Mary's York, for the tithes of corn and hay of all the de-"mesne lands of the castle of Kendal, called Myntesfeete, Gallobar, Kirke-"fielde, and 20 acres of inclosure at Staneecrosse lying contiguous, 44 *s.* 8 *d.* "as allowed in accounts of preceding years."

In the 30 Hen. 8. he was created *lord Par and Ross* of Kendal; and in the 35th of the same king he was made *baron of Hart* in Northamptonshire, to him and his heirs male. And having married Helena daughter and heir of Henry Bourchier earl of Essex, he was in the same year (as it were in her right) created *earl of Essex*, to him and his heirs male, and knight of the most noble order of the garter. And finally, in the 1 Ed. 6. he was created Marquis of Northampton; and from hence that part of the barony which he held received the name of the Marquis fee, which it still retains.

In the first year of queen Mary he was attainted of high treason, for taking part with William Dudley duke of Northumberland and the lady Jane Grey married to Guilford Dudley his son. Whereby his estate became forfeited to the crown. But he was soon after pardoned, and the estate (or at least a great part of it) restored to him.

For by a charter bearing date 8 Jan. in the 1 and 2 Ph. and Mary, the said king and queen grant to *William Parre* the whole demesne, manor, castle, and park of Kendale, parcel of the possessions of *Thomas Parre* knight, father of the said *William Parre*, late Marquis of Northampton. And all those free rents of the free tenants of the fourth part of the barony of Kendale, parcel of the possessions aforesaid. And all those demesne lands without the walls of the said park of Kendale, and the mill and burgages in the vill or burgh aforesaid, parcel of the said manor of Kendale. And all those improvement rents as well nigh Kendale as in the country, extending to the clear yearly value of 50 *s.* 5 *d.* Also the tallage, market, fairs, toll, stallage, weights and measures in Kendale, demised to Christopher Sadler. And also Cargo in Cumberland [with divers other possessions elsewhere] parcel of the possessions aforesaid. To hold to him the said *William* late marquis of Northampton and the heirs of his body lawfully begotten, of the king and queen *in capite*, by the service of one knight's fee.

The said *William* died in the 13 Eliz. and was buried at the upper end of the quire of the collegiate church at Warwick, where his body was dug up (Sir William Dugdale says) in the reign of king James the first, to make room for the burial of an ordinary gentlewoman. It was found perfect, with the skin intire, dried to the bones, with rosemary and bays lying in the coffin fresh and green. All which were so preserved by the dryness of the ground wherein they lay, it being above the arches of that fair vault which is under the quire, and of a sandy condition, mixed with rubbish of lime. All which, Sir William Dugdale says, was related to him by those who were eye-witnesses thereof. 2 Dugd. Bar. 380.

By an inquisition taken at Kendal, 14 Mar. 14 Eliz. the jurors find, that he died seised in his demesne as of fee tail (the reversion thereof belonging to the said queen) of all the possessions as in the aforesaid grant, and of and in all those manors of Gresmere, Langden, Greenrigge, Skallthatrigge, Strickland Rogers, Hoton, Hay, Hewgill, and Grenehead: And that the said *William Parr*, late marquis of Northampton, married one Helena, late marchioness of Northampton, yet living: That he died on the 28th of October, in the 13th year of the reign of the said queen. Of his heir they find nothing.

But by an inquisition taken at Leicester Ap. 12. in the same year, the jurors find, that he died without any heir of his body.——His arms were; Argent, 2 barulets Azure, within a bordure ingrailed Sable.

It was observed before, that he had only two sisters; *Katherine*, wife of king Henry the eighth, who died before her brother, and without issue; and *Anne*, who was married to William Herbert earl of Pembroke, ancestor of the present earl of Pembroke, who hath still, amongst his other titles, that of baron *Ross* and *Parr* of Kendal.

His widow Helena had dower assigned to her by letters patent of the queen, of which she the said Helena caused a survey and rental to be made as follows:

"The rental and survey of the fourth part of the manor and barony of "Kendal, and other lands and possessions in the counties of Westmorland "and York, limited and assigned by the letters patent of our sovereign lady "queen Elizabeth, for the dower of the right honourable Ellen lady marquis "of Northampton; and now taken and renewed, July 12, 1572, by Tho-"mas Whalley and Fowlk Obell esquires, by virtue of the warrant and com-"mission of the lady marquis to them in that behalf directed as followeth:

"Com' Westmorl'.

"Baronia sive manerium de Kendal.

"Freeholders there, who hold of the barony or manor of Kendal and the "castle of the same certain lands and tenements, viz. by rent payable at Pen-"tecost and Martinmass, &c. The earl of Derby, for tenements in Burton,

"payeth

CHAP. III.

" payeth yearly 3 s. George Middleton esquire, for tenements holden by " him, a spar-hawk or 12 d." And so in like manner of many others. " Total of the free rent per annum, 9 *l* 5 *s* 4 *d*.

" The *castle* of Kendal is situate on the knowl of an hill within the park " there, and on the east side of the town of Kendal, with a fair and beautiful prospect, both of wood, pasture, and running water. The out walls " embattled 40 foot square. And within the same no building left, saving " only on the north side is situate the front of the gate-house, the hall, with " an ascent of stairs to the same, with a buttery and pantry at the end thereof; one great chamber, and two or three lesser chambers and rooms of ease " adjoining to the same: being all in decay, both in glass and slate, and in all " other reparations needful. Under the hall are two or three small rooms of " cellars. In the south side is situate a dove coat, in good repair. The " yearly rent of the demesne and one fourth part of the toll, 64 *l* 14 *s* 0 *d*. " Yearly rent of the tenants at will in New-biggin in Kendal, 4 *l* 3 *s* 0 *d*. " Yearly rent of the burgage lands there, 10 *l* 15 *s* 6 *d*. Fourth part of the " fishing of Kent, 1 *l* 2 *s* 4 *d*. Memorandum, That the said liberty of fishing " in the said water of Kent extendeth from St. John's Cross beneath Milnthorp unto Gilthroughton above Staveley; wherein are taken salmon, trouts, " eels, and other small fish: And the royalty of the said fishing is limited as " followeth; viz. half to the queen, a fourth part to my lady marquis, and " a fourth part to Mr. Bellingham. The rents of the improvements and intacks taken off the wastes of Kendal, called Dob Freer, the Barks, and " Cross-Bank, 3 *l* 12 *s* 5 *d*.

" Reprizes: The yearly fee to the keeper of Kendal park, 3 *l* 6 *s* 8 *d*. To " the collector of the rents of the land serjeanty, 10 *s*. And to the clerk of " the courts in Kendal, 20 *s*.

" There is a wood in Kendal park of the value of 400 *l*; in Saprigg, of the " value of 100 *l*.

" Memorandum, that the whole barony of Kendal, since the attainder of " the late marquis in queen Mary's time, is divided, half to the queen, and the " other half to the lady marquis and Mr. Bellingham.

" Besides the other wastes and commons, there is a parcel of waste ground " lying by the water side, containing one acre, belonging to the castle, called " Tenterholme or Goosehulme, and used of long time by the inhabitants of " Kendal for the place of their tenters, without any rent paying for the " same.

" There is also kept a three weeks court, and two leets, viz. on the Monday after Low-Sunday, and the week after Michaelmass. And the said " courts are also kept in the name of the queen, lady marquis, and Mr. Bellingham, and the profits divided amongst them as above. And likewise " all other royalties, waifs, estrays, felons goods, fines, amerciaments, are to " be divided amongst them accordingly.

" Concerning the custom of the burgage land and tenant right, the tenants " which claim the same have neither copy nor other evidence to shew for " their titles; but by continuance of time, and by prescription, do hold the " same

"same to them and their heirs. By the said custom, at the change of lord or "tenant, every tenant payeth double his rent; and by the death of the te-"nant, the wife payeth a heriot. The tenant is to have timber for reparations, "firebote, plowbote, and cartbote, to be assigned him by the lord's officer "within the manor, and four sworn men; but they cannot fell any wood of "warren without the lord's licence.

"All the tenants are bound to serve at the west marches at Carlisle, upon "their own costs and charges, without the queen's wages."

Then the rental goes on and particularizes the several other manors within the said Marquis Fee, which we shall take notice of when we come to treat of those places respectively *.

By the abovesaid rental it seemeth, that the said late marchioness had the whole Marquis Fee assigned to her for dower (for her husband had other large possessions). But not long after this, queen Elizabeth made an exchange with her for this Marquis Fee, giving her other lands in lieu thereof; whereby both the Marquis and Richmond fees came into the queen's hands. And in the 16th year of her reign, she issued a commission to inquire of the following articles; viz. "Articles to be inquired upon, for and touching the survey of "divers manors, lands, and tenements, demised to Henry late earl of Cum-"berland for the rent of 335*l*." (of which queen Mary had granted to him a lease for 21 years); "and also of all the manors, lands, and tenements late "assigned for the jointure of the lady Helen marchioness of Northampton, "and now delivered into the queen's majesty's hands by the said lady marquis "for other lands. 1. To view and survey the estate of every castle or fort "upon the premisses. 2. To make a perfect terrier or rental of every several "manor or township, dividing therein the rents of the freeholders, farmers, "customary tenants, and tenants at will, and what ground every of them "holdeth, with their several rents. 3. To enquire of all decays, intrusions, "incroachments, and whether any such have been made upon the said pos-"sessions, and who hath done the same. 4. To inquire of all the customs, "services, and royalties, belonging to any of the said manors, or other the "premisses or any parcel thereof. 5. For the better service of her majesty "in all and every the articles above mentioned, to call before them all and "singular the freeholders, customary tenants, and other inhabitants, within "any of the said manors or townships, by whom they may have knowledge "of the premisses, and to take copies of their leases and other writings, "whereby they claim the lands and tenements holden by them." The return of the commissioners bears date 7 Sept. 16 Eliz. whereby they certify as follows:

"The NAMES of the manors, lordships, hamlets, and townships, belonging "to the lands called *Richmond* lands, viz. Gresmyer, Langdon, Loughrigge, "Crosthwaite and Lyth, Troutbecke, Amylside, Applethwaite, Undermil-"becke, New Hutton, Casterton, Strickland Kettle, Helsington.

* The said rental was copied by Sir Daniel Fleming from a book belonging to Mr. Thomas Sands of Kendal in the year 1672.

4 "CUSTOMS:

CHAP. III.

"Customs:

"*Customary admittances.* The jury find and present upon their book oaths, "that every person and persons in the aforesaid manors, lordships, hamlets, "and townships, having a just and lawful title to the tenant right of any te-"nement of the aforesaid lands commonly called Richmond lands, and com-"ing to the court holden there by the lord of the same lands or his lawful "deputy or officer, and paying there in open face of the court, at the ex-"change of lord or tenant, one penny of silver, commonly called a God's-"penny, thereby is or ought to be admitted tenant of his said tenement, with "all its appurtenances, according to the ancient custom of the barony of Ken-"dale called Tenant right.

"*Customary fines.* Item, that every such person and persons, upon his and "their admittance and allowance to be tenant or tenants of any tenements of "the said Richmond lands, in any the places aforesaid, and being an old "tenant before, is and ought to pay, at the exchange of lord and tenant, for "his or their fine or gressome of his or their tenement, to the lord of the "same, or to his lawful deputy or officer, two years rent of the same tene-"ment with the appurtenances, whereof he or they ought to be admitted "tenant or tenants: Saving only every old tenant within the forest of Amyl-"side and Troutbecke; who is and ought to pay, at every exchange of lord "and tenant, one year's rent of his tenement. Item, that every such person "and persons, upon his and their admittance and allowance to be tenant or "tenants of any tenement of the aforesaid Richmond lands in the places afore-"said, and being made a new tenant, is and ought to pay, at the exchange "of lord and tenant, for his or their fine or gressome of his or their tenement "or tenements, to the lord of the same, or to his lawful deputy or officer, "three years rent of the tenement or tenements whereof he or they is or ought "to be admitted tenant or tenants: Saving only every new tenant within the "forest of Troutbecke and Amylside; who is and ought to pay, at every "exchange of lord and tenant, two years rent of his tenement, at customary "rent days.

"Item, that every such tenant or tenants so admitted and allowed of any "tenement or tenements of the aforesaid Richmond lands, is and ought to "pay their several annual *rents* of the same, at two term days in the year, by "equal and even portions, due and of old accustomed, to the lord of the same, "or his lawful deputy or officer.

"*Heriots.* Item, that at the decease of every or any such tenant or tenants "being so admitted and allowed, the lord of the same is and ought to have "the best beast being upon the tenement, of which beast the said tenant or "tenants did die seised, as of his own proper goods and chattels, in the name "of the heriot; for which the wife and wives of such tenant or tenants so "dying as aforesaid is or ought to have the possession and occupation of her "and their husband's said tenement or tenements, during her or their widow "estates; yielding and paying the several annual rents thereof, and doing all "other duties, suits, and services, therefore of old time at days due and "accustomed.

"*Customary*

"*Customary allowances.* Item, that every such tenant or tenants, so admitted and allowed as aforesaid, is and ought to have, by the lord's lawful deputy or officer unto him or them to be delivered, sufficient timber, to be taken within the same lands, for reparations of their buildings and other necessaries for husbandry, so often as occasion shall require. Item, that every such tenant or tenants, so admitted and allowed as aforesaid, is and ought to have and take all *Ramell woods* †, growing within any their several tenements, to the reparations and maintenance of their hedges and fences and other their necessaries; timber trees and coppyes of woods excepted.

"SERVICES:

"*Customary services.* The jury aforesaid find and present upon their book oaths, that every person and persons, being admitted and allowed tenant or tenants of any tenements within any of the several places above specified, from the age of 16 years till 60, hath been always accustomed, and so still owe to be, at all times, in their most defensible array for the wars, ready to serve their prince, on horseback and on foot, at the west borders of England for anent Scotland, on their own proper costs and charges, and so to be ready night and day, at the commandment of the lord warden of the said west marches, being warned thereunto by beacon, fire, post, or proclamation; and there so to continue during the said lord warden's pleasure.

"Item, that every such person or persons, so being admitted and allowed tenant and tenants as is aforesaid, owe unto the lord of the said lands, at the court holden within the manor, lordship, or township, where such person or persons is tenant and tenants, yearly lawful suit and service, as heretofore hath been accustomed.

"ROYALTIES:

"*Court leet.* The jury aforesaid find and present, upon their said book oaths, that for the Richmond lands there be kept within the town of Kirkby Kendale a three weeks court and two leets in the year; *viz.* on Monday after the first Sunday after Easter, commonly called Low Sunday, and the week next after Michaelmas day. At which two leets and head courts the lands called Richmond lands find six freeholders to serve in the same, the Marquis lands find three freeholders for that quarter, and Mr. Alan Bellingham finds other three freeholders for his quarter of the barony; and that all such fines, forfeitures, profits, and commodities, coming at the said two head courts and leets, are divided and estreated unto all the said quarters, *viz.* to the Richmond lands one moiety thereof, to the Marquis lands one quarter part, and to Mr. Bellingham one other quarter part.

"TOLLS AND STALLAGES.—Item, the same jury find and present likewise, that tolls and stallages of all the fairs and markets kept within the said town of Kirkby Kendale, being all together of old time demised and let for the rent of 20*l*, are likewise belonging and appertaining to the said quarter

† Perhaps from the Latin *ramus*, a bough: It signifies little branches or loppings of trees cut off or blown down.

CHAP. III. "parts or quarter barons of the barony of Kendale aforesaid, *viz.* to the "Richmond lands one moiety, to the Marquis lands one quarter part, and to "Mr. Bellingham one other quarter part.

"FISHINGS. Item, the same jury find and present in like manner, that "the fishing of the water of Kent, bearing the rent of old of 40 *s.* is likewise "belonging and appertaining to the said quarter parts or quarter barons of "the barony of Kendale aforesaid, and is divided unto them all by like pro- "portions as the profits of the said two head courts."

Queen Elizabeth, in the 23d year of her reign, granted to Ambrose earl of Warwick a part of the demesne lands belonging to the castle, by the name of the Park of Kendal, with divers edifices, buildings, lands, tenements, and other premisses to the same appertaining: To hold in socage, as of the manor of East Greenwich.

What became further of the castle and other demesne or park lands (for there were two parks, as was observed before) we have not found, until the reign of king Charles the second, when the same appear to have been in the hands of Sir *Francis Anderton* of Lostock in the county of Lancaster, baronet. His son and heir Sir *Charles Anderton*, on his marriage with dame Margaret his wife, in 1685, settled the same to the use of himself for life, remainder to his first and other sons in tail male, with divers remainders over. Sir *Charles* died in 1691, and left issue, *Charles*, *James*, *Laurence*, *Francis*, and *Joseph*, and three daughters. *Charles* the son succeeded his father, and died without issue. Upon whose death, *James* entered, and died without issue. *Laurence*, the third son, became a monk. And thereupon *Francis* the next brother assumed the title, and possessed himself of the family estate; but being engaged in the rebellion in 1715, and taken prisoner at Preston, he was tried and attainted of treason: He was pardoned as to his life, but the commissioners of forfeited estates seized all his real estate. And thereupon *Laurence* the monk claimed it, insisting before the commissioners that his brother had no right. *Laurence*, on his examination before the commissioners, confessing himself a monk, they decreed for the crown; for that by *Laurence*'s profession he was dead in law, and by consequence incapable to take, and therefore the estate must immediately vest in the brother, who being attainted of treason, the estate must be forfeited. And thereupon a decree was made for the king; from which *Laurence* appealed to the Delegates, who reversed the decree so far as to order that the appellant might bring an ejectment, and try his title at law; and that the decree should not stand in the way. But afterwards *Laurence* conformed, and became a protestant, and so enjoyed the title and estate without any further trial. In 1723, *John Huggins* esquire purchased the premisses of the said *Laurence*. And the said *John Huggins* dying in 1735, the same descended to his brother and heir *William Huggins* esquire. Which *William Huggins*, by his will in 1761, devised the premisses to his two sons in law, Sir *Thomas Gatehouse* knight, and the reverend Dr. *James Musgrave*, in trust to sell the same for the purposes in the said will mentioned; who accordingly sold the premisses in the year 1765 to the present owners *Thomas Holme* and *James Dowker* of Kendal, esquires, and *Benjamin Hall* of Newton in the parish of Cartmell, gentleman.

As to the rest of the Richmond and Marquis fees, king *James* the first, in the 12th year of his reign, granted the same to his son *Charles* prince of Wales, for the better maintenance and supportation of his princely estate. And in this prince's time there was a decree in chancery, ascertaining the customs of the several manors within the Richmond and Marquis fees. The history of which is curious and important, not only with respect to these particular manors, but to other manors in the several counties of Westmorland and Cumberland, and even to the publick affairs of the nation in general at that time. And therefore it is hoped the reader will indulge us in going to the bottom of this affair, and deducing the same according to the materials now in our power, several of which, at this distance of time, and especially by reason of the confusions that ensued, are probably not to be met with elsewhere.

It is well known, that king James, after he had formed the resolution of laying aside parliaments, was distressed for want of money, and took all methods that he or his courtiers could contrive for the obtaining of it. One scheme, amongst the rest, was, to take all the crown lands in the counties of Westmorland and Cumberland into his own hands, upon the pretence, that as border service had then ceased by the union of the two kingdoms in his royal person, the estates were determined likewise, which the tenants held by that service. And (to keep himself in countenance, as it were) he encouraged all the other lords of manors within the said counties to take to themselves the absolute estate of the several tenants within their respective manors, and refuse to admit the heirs to their ancestors estate.

In consequence of this doctrine, the prince of Wales, in the 16th year of the said king, exhibited his bill in chancery, complaining, that the tenants claimed by colour of a tenant-right estate, under certain yearly rents, to have an estate of inheritance in the respective tenements; whereas it was conceived, that their estates in the premisses were of no such force in law as they pretended. The tenants put in their answer. But from the hazard of contesting with the king, who had the judges both of law and equity, in a considerable degree, at his devotion, and Sir Francis Bacon lord Verulam presiding then in the court of chancery (who, notwithstanding his greatness in other respects, was as tame, submissive, and obedient to orders, as any courtier could be), and at the same time, a good round sum in hand appearing to be not unacceptable to the prince, the matter was compromised, and for the sum of 2700 l. he agreed to confirm unto them their custom, as set forth in their answer: Which was in these words,——" That they and their ancestors, and all those whose estates they " severally and respectively had or claimed to have in the several messuages, " lands, tenements, meadows, pastures, closes, improvements, milnes, woods, " mosses, commons, grassings, and other hereditaments, with the appurte- " nances, had, from time whereof the memory of man was not to the con- " trary, been severally seised to them and their heirs, of a good and lawful

 " customary

CHAP. III.

"customary estate of inheritance, to them and their heirs respectively, commonly called tenant-right, according to the custom of the barony of Kendal and lands called Richmond Fee and Marquis Fee, in the several lordships, towns, hamlets, and places following; *viz.* Gresmere, Langdall, Loughrigg, Clappersgate, Rawthy bank, Ambleside, Briggraffe, Troutbecke, Hallinge, Applethwaite, Undermilbecke, Windermere, Winster, Hugill, Riston, Riston meadows, Over Staveley, Nether Staveley, Strickland Roger, Laithead, Strickland Ketel, Garnett house, Mirkslacke, Helsington, Greenrigg, Underbarrow, Grigghall, Brathwaite close, Crooke, Crosthwaite, Lyth, Cawmire, Sipling meadows, New Hutton, Hay, Hutton in the Hay, Skalthwaite Rigg, Nethergraveship, Gilthwaite Rigge, Greenhead, Casterton, Kirkby Kendal, Long Sleddall, and Sadgill, and elsewhere in the barony of Kendal. Which their customary inheritance is descendible after the course of descents at common law; save only where a customary tenant dieth, having no heir male of his body, his customary lands descend to the eldest daughter, sister, or cousin, and not to all the daughters, sisters, or heirs female, as coparceners. For which premisses they had been accustomed to pay certain yearly rents or fines, namely, two years old rent only for a fine certain, upon change of lord by death, and three years old rent only for a fine upon change of every tenant by death or alienation: Except the tenants of Ambleside and Troutbeck aforesaid, who paid fines certain, *viz.* one year's rent upon change of lord by death, and two years rent upon change of tenant by death or alienation. And upon the death of every tenant dying seised of a tenement, leaving a widow behind him, an heriot; for which she was to enjoy her husband's customary estates, during her widowhood only. And also by all the time aforesaid, they the said tenants, by the custom of the said barony respectively, had yearly made suit to the several courts holden for his highness's said barony and lands called Richmond Fee and Marquis Fee, where they were and are called tenants, and being found by the jury, and paying their God's-penny for their several entries, were and are admitted tenants, and entered in the court rolls upon every such charge as tenants, upon such fines as aforesaid paid respectively." And on the 14 Nov. in the 17th year of the said king, it was decreed accordingly, "that they shall hold and enjoy all the premisses aforesaid, and all other easements, profits, commodities, and hereditaments, with the appurtenances whatsoever; together with all their ancient customs, usages, and liberties, to them, their heirs and assigns for ever: Yielding and paying the said fines, heriots, suit of court, and services aforesaid; and being subject to such other customs as in his highness's said barony, and the several manors or lordships and lands within the same, have been anciently used and accustomed."

But as to the other manors, the matter did not rest here; but the lords in several places ejected the tenants, and decrees both in chancery and in the exchequer were obtained against them. The tenants still would not submit. Though the service had ceased, the Border spirit remained. And they combined to defend each other even by force, if no other course should be effectual. Particularly,

Particularly, on the 2d of January following, there was a meeting at Staveley, by order of James Smith high constable, under colour of viewing a bridge; where they came to the following resolutions:

"We, and every of us, whose names are hereunder subscribed, having "taken into consideration the danger of the times, do therefore, for ourselves, "our heirs, executors, and administrators, severally agree, covenant, assume, "and promise unto and with each other, to observe and perform in every re-"spect, part, and behalf, all and every article, clause, matter, and thing "hereafter expressed, according to the true meaning of the same; *viz.*

"1. That we and every of us, as in conscience we are bound, will stand to "the general protestation by us taken, to the utmost of our and every of our "abilities in every point.

"2. Also, that to the utmost of our power we and every of us, at all times "hereafter, will defend our own persons, families, and estates, and the per-"sons, families, and estates one of another, as far as lawfully we may.

"3. Also, if any person or persons shall plunder, or go about in violent "manner, without due course of law, to take away the persons, families, or "goods of any of us; it shall be reputed as done unto all of us: And that "upon notice given thereof to us, and every or any of us; every man, having "notice, and able to do service, shall and will, with all speed and expedition, "repair to the persons or places so plundered, pillaged, or restrained of their "liberty, and shall to our utmost power rescue such persons and goods.

"4. Also, that if any of our goods or estates, real or personal, shall hap-"pen to be violently taken away contrary to law as aforesaid, if satisfaction "cannot be gotten out of them who so took them, the loss thereof shall be "equally born, and restored to them so plundered, by us all who have here-"unto subscribed, who shall be equally rated according to every man's abi-"lity, by such persons or committees in every town, hamlet, and village, as "shall be agreed upon by the more part of us or them who have subscribed "to these presents, according to the true meaning hereof."

And they chose one Samuel Knipe to be their agent and manager. They preferred a petition to the king, to be allowed their custom of tenant-right. They also procured a bill to be brought into the house of commons for the same purpose; which bill was rejected by the commons. And on the 28th of July following, the king published the following proclamation:

"By the King,

"A Proclamation against Tenant rights.

"WHEREAS it hath been oftentimes by decrees and judgments at law "declared and settled, that tenant rights since the most happy union of these "two renowned kingdoms of England and Scotland in our person are utterly, "by the ancient and fundamental rule of law of this our own kingdom of "England, extinguished and abolished, being but dependencies of former "separation and hostility; and that there is like settled rule and constant

"practice

CHAP. III.

"practice in Scotland since the union; and yet neverthelefs divers fuits are "continually raifed and profecuted in our courts of juftice here in England, "grounded upon the faid claim of tenant-right or cuftomary eftate of inheritance, under that pretence, whereby not only the memory of the faid "tenant-right is continued, which ought to be damned to a perpetual oblivion, but alfo both parties do fuftain needlefs charge and impoverifhment, "in queftioning of that which is beyond all difpute, which may alfo (in regard of combination of tenants, and general taxes to purfue their landlords "upon a common purfe) open a way to turbulent and feditious attempts: "We, out of our princely and never-intermitted care to avoid thefe maintainings aforefaid, have both recommended the matter to all our judges, "to fupprefs and furceafe ftrifes and fuits of this nature, and have alfo given "an exprefs charge and commandment to all the principal officers and minifters of ourfelf and our deareft fon the Prince (near or bordering upon Scotland where fuch tenant-rights have been claimed) that they do let all eftates, "whether for lives or years, be it for fine or improvement of rent, by indenture only, and not otherwife, to the end to ceafe and difcontinue the faid "claim. And further, to the end the fame courfe may be uniform and general amongft all our loving fubjects; We do by thefe prefents wifh and "expect from all our loving fubjects in thofe parts, that they fhall follow and "conform themfelves to the fame example, for leafing fuch lands in manner "aforefaid. But herewithal we do ftrictly command, that no entry in any "court roll hereafter, either of our own honours or manors, or of the Prince's, "or of any of our fubjects, do mention any eftate termed of tenant-right or "cuftomary eftate pretended for border fervice. On the other fide, our exprefs pleafure is, that good and dutiful tenants, who fhall willingly fubmit "themfelves to fuch eftates, be ufed with all favour and moderation, as we "doubt not but the landlord will do: Yet if any fhall be found to do the "contrary, our courts of equity fhall ever be open, and ready to over-rule "fuch landlords; as, on the other fide, both our courts of law and equity "fhall be, to bridle and eject all fuch unreafonable tenants as fhall with"ftand it.

"Given at our court at Charlton, the 28th day of July, in the 18th year "of our reign of Great Britain, France, and Ireland, 1620.

"God fave the King."

We have recited this proclamation *verbatim*, as it is perhaps one of the moft flagrant exertions of defpotifm that is to be met with in the Englifh hiftory. However, the tenants did not defpond. They drew up and publifhed a remonftrance againft the claim of the lords; complaining therein, that the landlords intended "to pull the fkins over their ears, and bray their bones "in a mortar: That having peaceably enjoyed their tenements fo long, it "would be hard that fome greedy eagle or devouring vulture fhould violently "pull them out to miferies. The poor bird and weaker cattle" (fay they) "are taught and encouraged, for maintenance of their ancient poffeffion, to "refift others even to death, though more able and ftrong by far than they "are."

" are." And it was a common saying amongst them—" If the devil be lord, " I'll be tenant."

Upon this, the lords exhibited a bill against them in the star-chamber for a libel; the minutes for the draught whereof were in these words:

" The names of the persons against whom the bill is to be drawn for the libel " for tenant-right:

" Anthoine Wedtherell, vicar of Kirkby Stephen, to be charged with the " making of the libel.

" Samuel Knipe, James Smithe, John Cartemell, Thomas Pricket, John " Beck, Rowland Harrison, Robert Mawson, Francis Washington, Edward " Tarne, and many other unknown persons to the number of one hundred or " above, to be charged with a riotous assembly at Stavely chapel in the county " of Westmorland, the 2d of January 1620: And there the said libel first read " and divulged by the said Knipe; and so immediately after, read and pub- " lished by the rest, and put forth, and many copies made thereof.

" James Smith the high constable to be further charged, for summoning " the petty constables.

" Robert Rawes, William Ducket, Francis Washington, Thomas Wash- " ington, Edward Tarne, Rowland Harrison, Richard Helme, Arthur Briggs, " and many others, for combining and making a common purse.

" Principal actors in the stage plaie, Richard Helme, Henry Ward, and " Thomas Ducket."

Against the assizes in the next year, a letter was written by the king to the bishop of Carlisle (and the like probably to some other principal persons in the country) as followeth:

" JAMES *Rex.*

" Right trusty and right well beloved, we greet you well.—Whereas we " were pleased to declare our princely care which we had of our subjects and " of the public good and quiet of these our kingdoms, by our proclamation " against tenant-right set forth in the 18th year of our reign; and that not- " withstanding our favour and moderation in that used towards dutiful and " good tenants, we have understood that some tumultuous and evil disposed " persons have in those parts not only used liberal speeches, but made unlaw- " ful assemblies, and published seditious libels, in maintenance of their said " pretended custom of tenant-right, to veil it under the name of customary " estate of inheritance, the punishment of some of which their offence, though " it be prosecuted in a due course in the Star-chamber; nevertheless, we " foreseeing what inconvenience may in the mean time happen, if care be not " had to suppress the insolency of such people, have now again given strait " charge and command to our judges of assize for those counties, in all their " proceedings to hold themselves strictly to the tenor of our proclamation, " and by no means to give countenance to any estate claimed to be of cus- " tomary, which shall any way appear to have reference to the maintaining " of border service, or where the parties themselves or those from whom they

" claim

CHAP. III.

"claim have been tied to border ſervice, and that accordingly they make the "people generally to underſtand it, without giving any hope to the contrary "(which we thought good to intimate to you) that you may confer with the "judges about the ſame, and that in your actions both you and they proceed "in conformity to theſe our directions. And if any thing ſhall be practiſed "to the contrary, we require you to give us preſent notice of it, who expect "at your hands a ſtrait account of your proceedings herein.

"Given at our court at Whitehall, the 26th day of July, in the 20th year "of our reign of England, France, and Ireland, and of Scotland the 55th.

"To the reverend father in God our truſty and right "well beloved the lord biſhop of Carliſle."

The aforeſaid remonſtrance of the tenants was rather warm than judicious, deriving their title from king Brute, with other like abſurdities; never touching upon the diſtinction (which undoubtedly is the proper and true one) that they held their eſtates by a double tenure, namely, by border ſervice in particular, and moreover by the general military tenure by which all other tenants *in capite* were obliged. And there are abundance of inſtances, when at the ſame time that they were ſubject to be called to the border ſervice, they were required to attend their lord in a military capacity into other parts of the kingdom, and not ſeldom into France.

But what the event was in that arbitrary court of the Star-chamber, the reader (no doubt) will have the curioſity to inquire. And as to that, a copy of the record will give ample ſatisfaction; which is as follows:

"In Camera Stellata coram conſilio ibidem, ſeptimo die Novembris, anno "viceſimo primo Jacobi regis.——This day, as alſo the laſt ſitting day, were "ſpent in opening and hearing of the matters of complaint here exhibited by "Mr. Attorney General plaintiff, againſt Samuel Knipe, James Smith, John "Cartmell, Thomas Prickett, John Robertſon, Humphrey Bell, Thomas "Lucas, and Richard Helme, defendants, for unlawful aſſemblies, and pub-"liſhing a libellous book, and other contempts and practices to oppoſe his "majeſty's proclamation for aboliſhing of the tenure and name of border ſer-"vice in the county of Weſtmorland. Upon the opening of which cauſe, "and ſome depoſitions read, of the plaintiff's part only, it appeared to the "court, that the king's moſt excellent majeſty publiſhed his proclamation.—
And ſo ſetting forth the ſubſtance of the proclamation, the record goes on: "For the contempt and neglect of which ſaid proclamation, and many miſ-"demeanors to maintain the tenants in their ſaid oppoſition, his majeſty's at-"torney general hath exhibited this information againſt the defendants and "divers other tenants of certain tenant right and cuſtomary eſtates, charging "them with ſundry combinations and attempts to oppoſe the ſaid proclama-"tion. Unto which the ſaid defendants plead and anſwer, that they hold "their lands and ſeveral tenements by cuſtomary eſtate of inheritance, deſcend-"able from anceſtor to heir, by the payment of cuſtomary fines, heriots, rents, "boons, and ſervices, and not by border ſervice; and have pleaded *Not*

"*guilty*,

"*guilty* to the several misdemeanors charged by the information. Whereupon "the court conceived, that the matter of title will much aggravate or extenuate the criminal offence therein complained of, if any such be. And the "court taking it into gracious consideration, that the same concerned many "poor people, thought it convenient for the ease, peace, and quiet of the "country, that the said differences between the landlords and tenants of the "country, concerning the said tenant right or customary estate, should be considered by the lords judges, to settle the same between them, if it may be; "and if they shall by mediation end that part, and the tenants appear before "them to be peaceable and well disposed to quietness, then the court doth "incline, upon the judges certificate, to refer likewise unto them the compounding of the misdemeanors, which as yet doth remain in the consideration and cognisance of this court. And for that purpose, the court hath "respited the further hearing of the cause in the mean time. And therefore "the court hath ordered, that the lord chief justice of the king's bench, "the lord chief justice of the common pleas, Mr. justice Hutton, and Mr. "justice Chamberlaine, (all now present) shall call the parties before them, "both landlords and tenants, and such whom it may concern, and consider "of the title and claim of both sides, and to mediate and settle a final end, "rule, and order therein, if they can, that there may be an absolute peace, "agreement and quietness hereafter amongst them: And for default thereof, "to certify the court of their opinions and judgments therein; that then the "court may proceed to take such further consideration of the criminal offences here complained of, as cause shall require." (And this accounts for the special charge given by the king to his judges against the next assizes, as set forth in his letter to the bishop of Carlisle above recited.) Then the record goes on,—"Camera Stellata 19no Junii, 1625." (Note, king James was then dead.) "The certificate of the right honourable James lord Lee lord treasurer of England, Sir Henry Hobart knight and baronet lord chief justice "of his majesty's common pleas; between the king's attorney plaintiff, and "Samuel Knipe and others defendants: According to two several orders of "this honourable court, the one bearing date the 17 Nov. 21 Ja. and the "other bearing date the 22d day of May last past; we did by three several "letters require the lords and tenants of the several manors of the barony of "Kendal mentioned in the said orders, to come before us at certain times by "our said letters appointed; at which several times the said tenants by some "authorized for them always appeared, but of the lords none appeared, nor "gave answer to us, neither by themselves nor by any other, saving only Sir "James Bellingham knight and John Preston esquire, for whom we heard "Mr. Downes, being of their counsel; Sir Henry Bellingham, son and heir "of the said Sir James Bellingham, authorized by his said father, being also "present; and Samuel Knipe and John Cartmell, two of the tenants on the "behalf of themselves and all other the said tenants being authorized for that "purpose, with whom Mr. Holt was of counsel, being likewise present: "Whereupon we thought good to proceed with them and for themselves, "according to the said orders. In the handling of which said cause we find

CHAP. III.

"plainly, that the case of all the said lords and tenants in all the said manors "is in effect the same. The questions between them concerning their estates "being but two; the first, Whether the said estates themselves, which they "hold, be sufficient customary estates in law, descendable from ancestor to "heir? the second, Whether the fine payable to the lords upon death or alien-"ation of the tenants, and also upon death of the lords (for in that case also "these tenants pay fines), be certain, or arbitrary at the will of the lord? And "upon hearing of this cause, and the allegations and proofs of both sides, we "are of full opinion, that the estates of the tenants are estates of inheritance "at the will of the lord, descendable from ancestor to heir, according to the "several customs of the several manors whereof they are holden; as the copy-"hold estates of inheritance in these parts are, though they want divers for-"malities that are used in copyholds in these parts; as they have also some "customs that are not used here, as in fining upon death of the lord, which "is very beneficial to their lords, and is not used in these parts. And though "it be true, that these tenants did border service in former times; yet we are "of opinion, upon all that we have seen, that the border service was no spe-"cial part of their services reserved, or in respect of the tenure of their lands, "but a duty and readiness required of them to tend those occasions, as the "lords themselves and all other freeholders, great and small, of the whole "country, did and ought to do, by virtue of their allegiance and subjection; "not by order and direction of their lords, but of the lord warden of those "parts. Neither was there ever any mention of their border service in their "admittances or other entries touching the said estates; and we think fit that "for ever hereafter there be no mention of tenant right or border service in "any admittances or other writings or incidents of this kind, but a perpetual "oblivion made thereof according to the meaning and prescript of his maje-"sty's proclamation in that behalf. And touching the matter of fines, whe-"ther the same be arbitrary or no, because we conceive that point not to be "directly referred unto us by the said orders, we forbear to deliver any opi-"nion of it; and yet nevertheless, because it appears by the said orders, that "the court has a desire to settle an universal peace betwen the lords and te-"nants being very many and poor, and that we conceive, if this point be "left at large still as it is now, it will breed endless suits amongst them, and "leave them at no more quiet than they were before; we have thought fit "to move this honourable court, to recommend the settling of the fines at "some certain rate, either to some court of justice, or other way of mediation, "as shall seem good to their great wisdom."——Afterwards: "In Camera "Stellata coram consilio ibidem vicesimo nono die Junii anno secundo Caroli "regis—This day Sir Heneage Finch knight, recorder of London, of counsel "with Samuel Knipe and other the tenants of the several manors of the ba-"rony of Kendal defendants, at the suit of his majesty's attorney general, "informed this honourable court"—of the said certificate, setting forth the substance thereof; "and thereupon humbly prayed the confirmation of the "same certificate, concerning the point of the said tenants customary estates, "by the decree of this court, and the further direction of this honourable

"court

" court concerning the determination of the said other point of the said " fines. Whereupon the court hath ordered and decreed, that the point of " the tenants customary estates of inheritance be absolutely ratified, confirmed, " and for ever settled, according to the tenor and intent of the said certificate: " And that the counsel learned both of lords and tenants of those several " manors do attend this honourable court, upon the fourth sitting day after " All Saints Day in the next term, for the settling of the rates of the fines " likewise, as to equity and justice shall appertain *."

What was further done about ascertaining the fines, doth not appear. Probably nothing further was done. But in many of the manors in this county (as appears by the several dates) compositions were made about that time between the lords and tenants, for reducing the tenements to a fine certain. And in several of the compositions, which were made *flagrante bello*, as it were, during the time of king James, (who seems to have been in effect both judge, jury, plaintiff, and counsel in the cause) there are clauses assuring and confirming to the tenants their estates, descendable from ancestor to heir, as if the same before had been nothing but a pretence.—Others purchased their tenements to freehold.

——But to proceed with the Marquis and Richmond Fees.

King Charles the second granted the same in jointure to his wife queen Katherine, and from her they received the name of QUEEN'S LAND; and not from queen Katherine, wife of king Henry the eighth, for she never had them, her father and brother enjoying the Marquis Fee all her time, and the Richmond Fee being then in grant to others.

In the 28 Cha. 2. a rental was made of these fees by Sir John Otway, deputy steward of the queen, and a jury of the respective fees, containing the names of the tenants within the several manors, and their respective rents.

In the Marquis Fee:

They set down the free and other dry rents of the several tenants throughout the said Fee, amounting in the whole to 20*l* 17*s* 4½*d*. Amongst the rest, there are several items for lands in Great and Little Strickland, and Boredale in the parish of Barton.

	l.	*s.*	*d.*		*l.*	*s.*	*d.*
Burgage rents in Kendal	9	17	11	Overknots, or Nethergrave ship - - -	10	16	8
Customary rents in and about Kendal - -	4	0	0	Skalthwaite Rigge - -	12	5	0¼
				Hay - - - -	13	3	3
Customary and other dry rents in				Hutton in the Hay - -	8	18	2¼
Grasmere - - -	11	6	2	Strickland Roger - -	13	14	11
Langdale - - -	5	4	11	Greenhead - - - -	10	16	10
Underbarrow - - -	20	8	1	Hugill - - - -	3	19	9
Stavely and Hugill - -	9	3	7½	Crosthwaite - - -	0	15	0

* From an exemplified copy taken out by Samuel Knipe, James Smith, John Cartmell, Thomas Prickett, John Robertson, Humphrey Bell, Thomas Lucas, and Richard Helme, bearing date 28 July, 2 Cha.

CHAP. IV.

In the Richmond Fee:

Free and other dry rents of ſeveral tenants throughout the ſaid fee, 36 *l* 10 *s* 8¾*d*. Amongſt the reſt there is a charge for certain lands in Thrimby.

Cuſtomary and other dry rents in

	l.	*s.*	*d.*		*l.*	*s.*	*d.*
Greſmere - - -	11	11	3	Croſthwaite and Lyth	19	3	7
Langdale - - -	7	12	5¾	New Hutton - - -	10	9	9½
Loughrigg - -	2	16	1	Caſterton - - -	12	9	4
Ambleſide - -	26	17	0	Strickland Ketel and Helſington - - -	3	10	10
Undermilbeck - -	13	8	0	Thornton, Weſthouſe, and Mayſinghill - - -	12	14	10
Troutbeck - - -	27	0	10				
Applethwaite - - -	24	10	10½				
Fiſhing and ferry of Windermere water - -	6	0	0				

After the deceaſe of queen Catherine, they were granted to the Lowther family, in which family they ſtill continue by a renewal of the leaſe from his preſent majeſty to Sir James Lowther baronet.

CHAPTER IV.

Of the LUMLEY FEE.

HAVING thus deduced the *Richmond* and *Marquis Fees*, which comprehend near three fourths of the ancient barony of Kendale; we proceed to inveſtigate the remaining part, moſt of which goes by the name of the LUMLEY FEE.

From *Margaret* the eldeſt of the four ſiſters of the laſt *Peter de Brus*, we have deduced the *Marquis Fee*.

The ſecond ſiſter and coheir was *Agnes*, married to *Walter de Fauconbridge*. She had nothing in Weſtmorland; her whole ſhare being in Lancaſhire and Yorkſhire.

The third ſiſter and coheir was LUCY, who had for her ſhare what is now called the *Lumley fee*. She was married to MARMADUKE DE THWENG, lord of Kilton caſtle and THWENG, with divers other manors in Yorkſhire, Lancaſhire, and Weſtmorland.

They had a ſon, MARMADUKE DE THWENG; who in the 3 Ed. 2. together with his couſin-german *William de Roſs*, obtained a grant of a market and fair at Kirkby in Kendale. He died in the 10 Ed. 2. ſeiſed, as the inquiſition finds, of the fourth part of the barony of Kendale.

He was ſucceeded by his ſon WILLIAM DE THWENG, who in the 2 Ed. 3. obtained a grant for a market at Staveley on Friday weekly, and a fair yearly on the eve, day, and morrow of St. Luke. And in the 9th of the ſame king, he obtained a grant of free warren in Stavely. He died in the 14 Ed. 3. and by the inquiſition taken after his death, it appears what was then the *Thweng* ſhare of the barony. Which inquiſition is as follows:

"An

"An inquisition taken at Kirkby in Kendale, before Thomas de Metham "escheator of our lord the king in the counties of York, Northumberland, "Cumberland, and Westmorland, on Saturday being the feast of St. Hilary, "in the 14th year of the reign of Edward the third after the conquest, by the "oath of Matthew de Redman, Robert de Layburn, Simon de Gnype, John "de Patton, Walter de Schepesheved, Robert de Romondeby, Roger de "Kendale, Benedict Garnet, Alan de Kaberghe, John de Shepesheved, John "de Tonstal, and Adam de Stanyford; who say upon their oath,

"That *William de Thwenge* held in his demesne as of fee, on the day on "which he died, the manor of *Helsington* with the appurtenances, together "with certain lands and tenements in *Kirkeby in Kendale*, *Crossthwait*, *Stavely*, "*Sapgill*, *Hugill*, *Respton*, *Gresmer*, and *Langden*, to the same manor apper"taining, of our lord the king *in capite* as of his crown, by the service of a "moiety of three parts of one knight's fee, and by the service of doing suit "at the county court of Westmorland from month to month.

"And there is at *Helsington* the site of one capital messuage, which is worth "nothing by the year, because it is altogether waste.

"And there is there of the rent of free tenants and tenants at will by the "year 15*l* 0*s* 8*d* at the terms of Martinmass and Pentecost.

"And there is at *Crossetwait* of the rent of free tenants and tenants at will "by the year 13*l* 16*s* 0*d* at the same terms.

"And there is at *Stavely* and *Sapgil* of the rent of free tenants and tenants "at will by the year 8*l* 0*s* 0*d* at the same terms.

"And there is at *Stavely* a certain park, the herbage whereof is worth by "the year in summer 53*s* 4*d* and nothing in winter.

"And there is there one fulling mill, and it is worth by the year 10*s*.

"And there is at *Hugill* and *Respton* of the rent of free tenants and tenants "at will by the year 9*l* at the terms aforesaid.

"And there are at *Respton* 7 acres and 1 rood of meadow, which are worth "by the year 29*s*.

"And there is there one water mill, which is worth by the year 30*s*.

"And there are at *Gresmer* and *Langden*, of the rent of free tenants and te"nants at will by the year 12*l* at the terms aforesaid.

"And there is there a certain fishery called the *Fors*, which was wont to "pay by the year 36*s* 8*d*, and now is worth by the year only 20*s*.

"And there is there a certain pasture called the *Hay*, the herbage whereof "in summer is worth 12*d*, and nothing in winter.

"And there is there a certain pasture called *Mosertwayt*, the herbage where"of is worth in summer 2*s* 6*d*, and nothing in winter.

"And there is a certain fishery called the *Keent*, and is worth by the year 2*s*.

"And there is a certain herbage called *Wodmale*, and is worth by the year in summer 12*s* 2*d*, in winter nothing.

"And there is there a certain place called *Roger Holme*, the rent whereof "by the year is 6*s* 8*d* at the feast of the nativity of St. John Baptist for the "whole year.

"And

CHAP. IV.

"And there is at *Kirkeby in Kendale* of the rent of free tenants by the year "6*l* at the terms of Easter and Michaelmass.

"And there is there a certain fee farm issuing out of divers free tenements "in *Kendale* and elsewhere in the county of Westmorland of 60*s* by the year, "at the same terms of Easter and Michaelmass.

"Also they say, that the perquisites of court in the manor and tenements "aforesaid are worth by the year 6*s* 8*d* and no more, by reason of the po-"verty of the tenants.

"Also they say, that the said *William* held no other lands or tenements on "the day on which he died, in the said county of Westmorland.

"Also they say, that *Robert de Twenge*, parson of the church of Warton, "brother of the said *William*, is his next heir, and of the age of 40 years and "upwards.

"In witness whereof, the jurors aforesaid to this inquisition have set their "seals."

Robert de Thweng therefore, parson of the church of Warton aforesaid, succeeded his brother *William*. Which *Robert* died in the 18 Ed. 3. seised of the premises aforesaid, Thomas de Thweng, parson of the church of Betham, being his brother and heir.

This Thomas de Thweng died in the 48 Ed. 3. having three sisters coheirs; the youngest of whom had no portion in Westmorland; the other two sisters, Lucy and Margaret, had this *Tweng* share of the barony between them.

Lucy, the eldest of the three sisters, was married to Marmaduke de Lumley, and from hence came the denomination of the Lumley Fee. She had for her part the manors of *Helsington*, *Crosthwaite* and *Lyth*, and one fourth part of the town of *Kirkby in Kendale*, together with the turbary of *Sampool*.

This *Marmaduke de Lumley* seems to have been succeeded by Ralph de Lumley; for in the 6 Hen. 4. one fourth part of the manor of Kirkby in Kendale was taken into the king's hands by the death of *Ralph de Lumley* knight, and by reason of the minority of *Thomas Lumley* son and heir of the said *Ralph*. And it was found that *John de Lumley* was brother to the said *Ralph*.

Thomas de Lumley, son and heir of *Ralph*, died without issue, and was succeeded by

John de Lumley knight (his uncle); which *John* died in the 10 Hen. 5. seised (as the inquisition finds) of one eighth part of the manor of Kirkby in Kendale, *Thomas* his son and heir being then under age.

Concerning which *Thomas*, by an inquisition of knights fees in Westmorland in the 6 Hen. 6. it was found, that Thomas Lumley then in ward to the king, son and heir of *John Lumley* knight deceased, held of the king *in capite* a moiety of all those lands and tenements in Kendale, which sometime belonged to *Thomas de Thweng* who was parson of the church of Betham, by the service of one fourth part of one knight's fee; and that *Walter Pennardine* and *John Ellerker* held of the king *in capite* the other moiety, which formerly be-

longed

longed to the said *Thomas de Thweng*, by the service of the eighth part of one knight's fee: And that *Thomas de Stirkland* knight held the third part of a knight's fee of the said *Thomas Lumley*, in Helsington, Haversham, Burton, Lowther, Whale, Hackthorp and Stirkland Ketel. CHAP. IV.

In the 6 Hen. 8. John Fleming of Ridal esquire, escheator for the king in the counties of Cumberland and Westmorland, accounted that year in the exchequer for *115l 17s 7d* of the issues of the manors of Kirkby in Kendale, of which GEORGE LUMLEY knight was seised; and for *1224l 9s 10½d* of the issues of the moiety of the barony or lordship of Kendale (viz. the Richmond fee) of which the said king was seised.

Finally, JOHN LORD LUMLEY in the 23 Hen. 8. exchanged his part of the barony with the king, for certain lands in the South. And the said king granted the same, together with the Richmond fee aforesaid, to his natural son the duke of Richmond and Somerset; on whose death, the same came again into the hands of the king, who in the 36th and 37th years of his reign granted the same to ALAN BELLINGHAM esquire and his heirs, in as large and ample manner, as the duke of Richmond and John lord Lumley or any of his ancestors held or enjoyed the same.

MARGARET the second daughter of MARMADUKE DE THWENG aforesaid had a daughter named MATILDA, who was married to *John de Hotham*; who had with her in marriage the other moiety of the *Thweng* share of the barony, in *Stavely* and other places; being the same which was held by *Walter Pennardine* and *John Ellerker* aforesaid, as trustees probably on a settlement. A descendant of *Hotham* in the 12 Eliz. granted this moiety to ALAN BELLINGHAM esquire, grandson of the foregoing *Alan Bellingham*; which coming into the same name and family with the *Lumley* part before mentioned, the whole, though improperly as to this latter part, hath since commonly gone under the name of the LUMLEY FEE.

By an inquisition after the death of this later Alan Bellingham esquire, in the 20 Eliz. it is found, that he died seised of the manor of Over Stavely, and divers messuages and tenements and other hereditaments in Over Stavely, Nether Stavely, Hugill, Sadgill, Respton (with the moiety of Respton mill), Fairbank, Gresmyre, Langden, Potter fell, Vowflatt, Ulthwaite, Ratherhead, Sabergh, Crookfell, West Wood, and Roger Holme (an island in Winandermere), with a fishery in the waters of Winandermere, Skelefwater, and Gresmyre.

This *Alan Bellingham* had a son Sir *James Bellingham*, who had a son Sir *Henry Bellingham*, who was succeeded by his brother *Alan Bellingham* esquire; who sold this Lumley fee to Colonel *James Grahme*, whose daughter and heir *Katherine* was married to *Henry Bowes Howard* earl of Berkshire, whose grandson *Henry Howard* earl of Suffolk and Berkshire now enjoys the same.

CHAPTER V.

Of LADARINA'*s share of the Barony.*

CHAP. V.

THERE remains yet one other of the four sisters of the last *Peter de Brus* to be accounted for, namely, LADARINA, married to JOHN DE BELLA-AQUA in Yorkshire. It hath been shewed before, that this *Ladarina* had *Kentmere* assigned to her; and this was all that she had in Westmorland.

She had by her said husband *John de Bella-aqua* only two daughters; *Sibilla*, married to *Milo de Stapelton*; and *Johan*, married to *Aucberus* son of *Henry*. In the 5 Ed. 2. a partition was made in chancery of their mother's inheritance between these two daughters or their representatives, to wit, *Nicholas de Stapelton* son and heir of *Sibilla*, and *Johan* the wife of *Aucberus* then living. And amongst the particulars, the manor of *Kentm.re* was to remain to *Nicholas*; and all the rest of the manors, messuages, lands, and tenements, are set forth to be in Lancashire and Yorkshire.

This family of *Stapelton* continued owners of *Kenimere* till the reign of king Charles the first, when it was sold by them, as will hereafter appear.

CHAPTER VI.

Other descendents of the LANCASTRES.

CHAP. VI.

WE have now deduced the whole Talebois family in the barony of Kendal, so far as our materials will admit; except what relates to one ROGER DE LANCASTRE, who is often mentioned, and was founder of a very considerable family.

Who this *Roger* was, is matter of curious disquisition. It hath been shewed, that *William de Lancastre*, the third and last of that name in the direct line, died without issue, leaving his sisters coheirs. And yet nevertheless, this *William* had a brother; which was this same *Roger*: So *William* calls him in one of his grants to Furness abbey—*Teste Rogero fratre meo.* And from hence it hath been concluded, that this *Roger* was a brother of the half blood. And so indeed he was. But (whether by design, or through inadvertency) it hath not been expressed what kind of half brother he was. The register of Furness abbey will inform us—"*Rogerus* bastardus *frater Willielmi.*" This circumstance is not taken notice of in any of the pedigrees, which derive the name and family of the *Lancastres* from this same *Roger*; which name and family flourished and long continued in this county, at Ridal, Sockbridge, Howgill castle, and other places, and by intermarriages was connected with most of the considerable families in the county, and probably is not yet extinct, many of the name yet remaining, though the estates are passed into other hands.

This

This *Roger de Lancastre* held, in what is now called the Bottom of Westmorland, the manor of Barton, by the gift of William his brother; as also Patterdale. And in the 3 Ed. 1. he obtained of that king a confirmation to him of the forest of Ridal, as also of Amelsate and Loughrigge, which before had been granted to him by Margaret de Brus. He was sheriff of Lancashire in the 49 Hen. 3. He married Philippa, one of the four daughters and coheirs of Hugh de Bolebeck in the county of Northumberland, and died in the 19 Ed. 1. leaving issue,

John de Lancastre, who was summoned in the 22 Ed. 1. amongst divers other persons of note, to attend at Portsmouth, well provided with horse and arms, and thence to sail with his majesty to France. In the 25th of the said king, he was employed in the expedition against the Scots, being in the retinue of Brian Fitz-Alane of Bedal in Yorkshire. He was summoned to parliament from that year to the 3 Ed. 2. and died in the 8th year of king Edward the third. Amora his wife survived him: For in the 11 Ed. 3. she appears to have held the manor of Ridal for the term of her life, remainder to *John de Lancastre* of Holgill and his heirs, he being the next heir male of this family.

This *John de Lancastre* of Howgill had a son *William*; who had a son *William*; who had a son *John*; who had another *John*, who died without issue male in the reign of Hen. 6. leaving four daughters; 1. *Christian*, married to Sir Robert de Harrington, knight. 2. *Isabel*, married to Sir Thomas le Fleming of Coniston, knight. 3. *Margaret*, married to Sir Matthew de Whitfield, knight. 4. *Elizabeth*, married to Robert de Crackenthorp, esquire.

There was another branch of the *Lancastres* at Sockbridge; which continued in the direct male line till the reign of king James the first; and then became also extinct in daughters.

There were others in other places; all of whom will be particularly considered in their respective places.

PARISH AND TOWN OF KENDAL.

THE parish of *Kirkby in Kendale* is very extensive, comprehending 24 townships or constablewicks, *viz.* Kendal, Helsington, Natland, Scalthwaite-Rigg (including Hay and Hutton in the Hay), New Hutton, Old Hutton and Holme Scales, Docker, Lambrigg, Grayrigg, Whinfell, Fawcet Forest, Whitwell and Selside, Skelsmergh and Patton, Burneshead, Strickland Roger, Strickland Ketel, Long Sleddale, Kentmere, Crook, Winster, Over Staveley, Nether Staveley, Hugill, Underbarrow and Bradley Field; and some of these, for convenience, have been subdivided:—And 15 chapelries, *viz.* Kendal, Helsington, Natland, New Hutton, Old Hutton, Grayrigg, Selside, Burneshead, Long Sleddale, Kentmere, Crook, Winster, Staveley, Ings, and Underbarrow.

This parish was anciently larger; for *Windermere* and *Gresmere* were parts thereof, though now they have obtained by reputation the name of distinct parishes, and are the only rectories within the barony of Kendale.

CHAP. VI.

It is bounded on the Eaſt by the pariſhes of Shap, Orton, Sedberg, and Kirkby Lonſdale; on the South, by the pariſhes of Kirkby Lonſdale, Burton, and Heverſham; on the Weſt, by the pariſhes of Heverſham and Windermere; and on the North, by the pariſhes of Windermere, Greſmere, and Orton.

The TOWN of *Kendal* is the chief town in this county, for largeneſs, neatneſs, buildings, populouſneſs, and trade; and is pleaſantly ſituate on the weſtern bank of the river *Kent*, which ſprings in *Kentmere*, and gives name to this town and pariſh.

It deals largely in the woollen and cotton manufactures. So early as the 11th of king Edward the third, the king's agents having ſolicited a great many men from the Low Countries, well ſkilled in cloth-making, ſent a colony of them (amongſt other places) to Kendal. And in the reigns of Ric. 2. and Hen. 4. ſeveral regulations were made by act of parliament for the making of Kendal cloths. Before this, all the wool of the country was exported; which, being manufactured in the Netherlands, was ſuch a ſource of riches, as to occaſion the duke of Burgundy to inſtitute the order of the Golden Fleece.

The people of Kendal are generally induſtrious, ſo that it is a very rare thing to ſee any perſon ſtanding idle, as is too uſual in other thorough-fare towns, or other places of public reſort.

The largeneſs of their trade may be eſtimated from the quantity of goods brought into and carried out of this town weekly, by the pack-horſe carriers, before the turnpike roads were made, when waggons came in uſe, whoſe contents are not ſo eaſily calculated.

	Horſes.
One gang of pack-horſes to and from London every week, of about	20
One gang from Wigan weekly, about — — —	18
One gang from Whitehaven, about — — —	20
From Cockermouth, — — — —	15
Two gangs from Barnard caſtle — — —	26
Two gangs from Penrith twice a week, about 15 each gang, —	60
One gang, about 15, from Settle, twice a week, — —	30
From York weekly, about — — —	10
From Ulverſton, — — — —	5
From Hawkſhead, about 6, twice a week, — —	12
From Appleby, about 6, twice a week, — — —	12
From Cartmell, — — — —	6
Two waggons from Lancaſter twice a week, computed at 60 horſe load,	60
Carriages 3 or 4 times a week to and from Milnthorp, computed at 40 horſe load, — — — —	40
From Sedbergh, Kirkby Lonſdale, Orton, Dent, and other neighbouring villages, about — — — —	20
Total	354

Beſides 24 every ſix weeks from Glaſgow.

Here

Here is a very large market on Saturday weekly, which was granted by king Richard the first to *Gilbert* son of *Roger Fitz-Reinfred* before mentioned †.

Afterwards, in the third year of Edward the second, *Marmaduke de Thweng* and *William de Ross* (as is aforesaid) obtained a charter for a market and fair at Kirkby in Kendale.

And in the 7 Ed. 3. another grant of a market and fair at Kirkby in Kendale was obtained by *Christian* wife of *Ingelram de Gynes*.—Or rather, these last were confirmations of the former grant.

And these were again confirmed by the charter of incorporation of queen Elizabeth in the 18th year of her reign; and by a further charter in the 11th of Charles the first, confirming that of queen Elizabeth, and granting more ample privileges. The substance of which two charters put together is as followeth: "That in the town of Kirkby in Kendale there shall be a body politic "and corporate, consisting of one mayor, 12 aldermen, and 20 capital bur-"gesses, by the name of mayor, aldermen, and burgesses of the borough of "Kirkby in Kendale; to have a common seal; with power to take lands not "exceeding 100*l* a year.

"The mayor to be chosen out of the number of aldermen, on Monday next "before Michaelmass day yearly, by the mayor and aldermen, or the major "part of them (of whom the mayor to be one), to continue for one whole "year, and from thence until another be chosen and sworn.

"The aldermen to be chosen by the mayor and aldermen, or the major "part of them, to continue during life, or until amoval from the office for "reasonable cause.

"The capital burgesses to be chosen by the mayor and aldermen, or the "major part of them (of whom the mayor to be one), to continue in the "office during their good behaviour.

"One man learned in the laws to be recorder or seneschal; to be chosen by "the mayor and aldermen, to execute the office during their pleasure.

"They shall also appoint a clerk of the recognizances (or town clerk); and "a sword-bearer, and two serjeants at mace.

"The mayor shall be clerk of the market; and the mayor and senior alder-"man shall be coroners for the said borough.

"If the mayor die within the year, or be lawfully amoved from his office, "another shall be chosen for the residue of the year. And no mayor shall "serve again till after four years from the expiration of his office.

"If an alderman live out of the borough, another shall be chosen.

† Ricardus Dei gratia, rex Angliæ, &c. Omnibus fidelibus et ministris suis, salutem. Sciatis nos dedisse et concessisse, et præsenti charta nostra confirmasse, Gilberto filio Rogeri filii Renfredi et hæredibus suis, forum per diem Sabbati in Kirkeby in Kendale. Tenendum in feodo et hæreditate de nobis et hæredibus nostris. Et pro hac donatione et concessione nostra, dedit ipse Gilbertus nobis viginti marcas argenti. Quare volumus et firmiter præcipimus, quod prædictus Gilbertus et hæredes sui prædictum forum habeant et teneant de nobis et hæredibus nostris in feodo et hæreditate, bene et in pace, libere et quiete, et honorifice, ita quod nullus præsumat illud impedire, super forisfacturam decem librarum argenti. Test. &c. (*Machel.*)

CHAP. VI.

"There ſhall be two fairs yearly; one, on the eve, day, and morrow of "the feaſt of St. Mark; the other, on the eve, day, and morrow of the feaſt "of St. Simon and Jude.

"On Thurſday from 3 weeks to 3 weeks, the mayor, recorder (or deputy "recorder), and two ſenior aldermen, or three of them (whereof the mayor, "recorder, or deputy recorder in the abſence of the recorder, ſhall be two), "ſhall hold a court of record, and view of frankpledge, and ſhall have cog-"nizance of pleas of matters ariſing within the borough, amounting to any "ſum not exceeding 20 *l.*

"And they ſhall have power to make by-laws, for the good rule and go-"vernment of all officers, artificers, burgeſſes, inhabitants, and reſiants in the "ſame borough, ſo as they be reaſonable, and not contrary to the laws of the "land.

"And the mayor, aldermen, and burgeſſes, may appoint ſearchers and "inſpectors of woollen cloth and cottons, and impoſe fines for offences in the "manufacturing thereof.

"And no petty chapman or artificer, not free of the borough, ſhall, ex-"cept in open fair or market on the market day, put to ſale any wares or "merchandizes (except victuals) without licence of the mayor and aldermen "under their ſeals.

"The mayor, recorder, and two ſenior aldermen, ſhall be juſtices of the "peace; and they, or any three of them (whereof the mayor and recorder "ſhall be two), may hold ſeſſions, and hear and determine offences; except "treaſon, murder, felony, or any other matter touching the loſs of life or "limb, in which they ſhall not proceed without the king's ſpecial command. "And the juſtices of the county ſhall not intromit, unleſs in defect of the "juſtices of the borough.

"Provided, that nothing herein ſhall derogate from the right of the here-"ditary ſheriff of the county, with reſpect to any goods or chattels of felons "and fugitives, waifs, deodands, eſtrays, views of frankpledge, tourns, and "county court, or execution of proceſs.

"And provided, that the mayor, recorder, aldermen, and town clerk, "ſhall not be put or impanelled in any jury at the aſſizes; and the ſheriff ſhall "not impanel them, nor ſhall they forfeit any iſſues for not appearing."

——With reſpect to this laſt clauſe, the regulations as they ſtand at preſent by law for ſerving upon juries, being made by acts of parliament ſubſequent to theſe charters, without any ſaving of ſuch like exemptions; this privilege by charter (if ever it was legally in force) ſeemeth now to be vaniſhed and gone.

As to the reſt, amongſt other charters in many other parts of the kingdom, which were ſurrendered to the crown in the latter end of the reign of king Charles the ſecond, and in the reign of king James the ſecond, theſe two charters ſuffered the ſame fate. The hiſtory of which is as follows: In the laſt year of the reign of king Charles the ſecond, the lord chief juſtice Jeffreys was ſent judge of aſſize on the northern circuit. And all along as he proceeded, he laboured this ſurrender of the charters in every corporation where he came. At Kendal he ſucceeded; and there are ſome copies of letters yet extant,

extant, very characteriftic of that judge and of thofe times, in relation to the obtaining a new charter for this corporation: Particularly that which here next follows; CHAP. VI.

To the right honourable Sir George Jeffereys knight and baronet, lord chief juftice of England:

My Lord,

IN the performance of our duty, when your lordfhip was here, in giving up our charter, whenfoever his majefty fhould be pleafed to call for it, your lordfhip was pleafed to give us not only your word but your oath to become a buxome and beneficial member of this corporation. This, my lord, we mention with all due refpect and thanks to your lordfhip, for the great honour then done us. We have now fent up our charter, in order to lay it at his majefty's feet, and hope by your lordfhip's beneficence to obtain his majefty's royal charter, with fuch privileges and benefits *de novo* as your lordfhip fhall approve of. 'Tis not much we would defire, nor fhall defire any thing which your lordfhip fhall judge unfitting either for us to afk, or his majefty to grant. But in fuch things as are feifible, we humbly beg your lordfhip's advice and affiftance. My lord, we know we cannot apply ourfelves to any perfon more defervedly happy in his prince's favour, and in the love and honour of all good and loyal men. Long may your lordfhip live and enjoy this happinefs, whilft we think ourfelves happy in having fo worthy a member of our poor corporation. We beg leave to fubfcribe ourfelves, as we really are,

Your lordfhip's moft obliged humble fervants.

Another letter was addreffed to the lord keeper:

To the right honourable Francis lord Guilford, lord keeper of the great feal of England.

May it pleafe your lordfhip,

IN obedience to his majefty's defires, intimated to us by the right honourable the lord chief juftice of England, we are now upon furrendering our charter into his majefty's hands; and as your lordfhip was pleafed to honour us fo far as to become a member of this corporation, fo we humbly requeft your lordfhip's favour in relation to our new charter, and fuch privileges and benefits as we hope his majefty will be pleafed to grant us. This, we muft confefs, is a great prefumption in us, but beg your lordfhip's favourable acceptance hereof, from

Your lordfhip's moft obedient fervants.

Another letter was fent to Sir Chriftopher Mufgrave, one of the knights of the fhire.

Honoured Sir,

SINCE you were pleafed to be our reprefentative to yield up our old charter, we do not queftion but you will fairly reprefent us to his majefty in order to the getting a new one, with fuch alterations and additional benefits,

as

CHAP. VI.

as shall be approved of by yourself and the lord chief justice, whose advice and assistance we have likewise desired. Be pleased, Sir, to consider us as a poor corporation, whose yearly revenue will scarce defray the yearly charges thereof; insomuch that we are hard put to it to raise money for the ordinary fees for renewing our charter. So that if the thorough-toll, or any other thing we have desired, shall meet with any difficulty or obstruction, we must rather desist, than be put to the charges of petitions, references, reports, and the like: But all we can hope for (besides the confirmation of our old charter) must be from yours and the lord chief justice's immediate intercession to his majesty without further charge; for really we are not in a condition to do as may be expected from us on this account, being rich in nothing but as having so worthy members and friends as yourself. This we humbly offer to you, and subscribe ourselves

Your most obliged and humble servants.

The matters we desire may be humbly offered to his majesty's consideration are these:

1. That his majesty would be graciously pleased to grant us his royal charter *de novo*, humbly submitting to whatever alterations his majesty in his great wisdom shall think fit to make therein.

2. We enjoy the tolls of the market here, which we hold by lease from the crown, under the yearly rent of 15 *l.* We have all along managed the said tolls to the best advantage we could, and yet never made above 17 *l per annum* of them. So that the yearly profit will not answer the charge of renewing our lease (as we ought to do) once in ten years. Wherefore if his majesty would be pleased to grant us the said toll in fee farm, under the said yearly rent of 15 *l*, it would be a great ease to the corporation, and not prejudicial (we think) to his majesty's interest.

3. These tolls have been anciently, almost time out of mind, received by us; yet of raw hides and apples no toll was ever taken here, in regard (as we conceive) that heretofore they were not worth the taking notice of. But now the trade in leather and fruit being grown very considerable, if by our charter or otherwise such power were given us as might justify our taking toll thereof, it would be a benefit to the corporation, and no less to his majesty, nor burden to the people but what they are liable to in other markets.

4. There is adjoining to the town a parcel of waste ground, called Dob Freer, which is all the common of pasture that is belonging to the town, and is no more than a hill full of rocks and stones. The fee and soil thereof doth belong to the crown, but is of little or no advantage to his majesty, neither is it worth to the town above 5 *l per annum*, but might be of greater use and benefit to us, if his majesty were pleased to grant us the soil and inheritance thereof.

5. We repair and uphold two large bridges, and the half part of a third bridge, at our own proper costs and charges, which is a burden too heavy for us to bear. But if, in consideration thereof, his majesty would be graciously pleased to grant us a thorough-toll of one penny or halfpenny only for each pack

pack of goods passing into or out of the town, it would be some ease and benefit to us; and is no more than what Carlisle enjoys in a much greater measure throughout the whole county of Cumberland, for all sorts of goods and chattels passing into or out of the said county.

These are the things we humbly offer, and if it might not be thought too great presumption in us, we would humbly pray in aid the right honourable the lord keeper of the great seal of England and the lord chief justice of England; who as they have done us the honour of being made members of our corporation, so we hope will do us the favour of interceding with his majesty on our behalf, whilst we shall desire nothing which may be thought in the least prejudicial to his majesty's interest, or which he cannot willingly and easily grant us, but shall thankfully acquiesce in his majesty's good-will and pleasure, whatsoever it shall be.

Finally, a new charter was obtained, and on its being brought from London was ushered in with much solemnity. On the 26th of December 1683, the town clerk Mr. Richard Rowlandson, who brought the charter, was met at Burton by a large number of horsemen from Kendal. And at the extremity of the town liberty, he was met by Mr. Lancelot Forth then mayor, the aldermen, burgesses, and many gentlemen out of the country; where the mayor, kneeling and bareheaded, received the charter; from whence it was conveyed to the town hall, many hundreds of the people huzzaing at the first delivery thereof, and all the way through the town, the mayor and aldermen being in their robes, with maces, sword, trumpets, musick, bells ringing, and other rejoycings. After the charter was read, the mayor began the king's health at the cross, commonly called the Cold Stone; and then treated the gentlemen nobly at his own house.

This new charter of king Charles the second doth not grant any of the particulars above petitioned for, but is copied for the most part *verbatim* from that of king Charles the first, with a few alterations, *viz.* that the *mayor* shall be chosen by the mayor, aldermen, and capital burgesses;—that on a *vacancy* of the mayoralty within the year, one of the two senior aldermen shall serve during the remainder of the year;—that they shall hold pleas for any matter arising within the borough for any sum not exceeding *forty pounds*;—and that the *deputy recorder* shall be a justice of the peace (and may act as such in the absence of the recorder): With a clause, as in all the new charters of those times, of reservation to the crown of a power to displace and remove the mayor, recorder, aldermen, or any other corporation officers at pleasure.

But here a question arises, of importance, not only to this, but to many other boroughs in the kingdom; namely, Which of the charters are in force? From what hath been already observed, it should seem, that the two former charters on their surrender became totally void; and that the charter of Charles the second is the only charter now valid and effectual. And the practice in this borough, and in many other corporations, goeth accordingly. But perhaps

haps it may be doubted, whether the reverfe of this be not the cafe, namely, that the former charters are in force, and the laft void. And the reafon of the doubt is this: When king James the fecond found matters declining, and that this garbling of corporations was one particular heavy charge againft him, he publifhed a proclamation, thereby revoking the new charters, and re-eftablifhing thofe which had been furrendered; fetting forth, that whereas feveral of the deeds of furrender of corporations which had been lately made were not recorded and inrolled, and the rules for judgment which had been obtained againft other of the corporations upon Quo Warrantos or informations in the nature of Quo Warranto were not yet entered upon record; which faid deeds of furrender, or rules for judgment, being not recorded, do not amount to a furrender in law, nor diffolve the corporation; the king therefore reftores all the faid corporations into the fame ftate and condition as they were before fuch furrender, or rule for judgment obtained; and revokes all the new charters granted in the reign of his brother or of himfelf *. And the rule of law feems to be, that the furrender of a charter without inrollment is void, and a new charter granted in confideration of a void furrender is alfo void. As was refolved in the cafe of *Bully* and *Palmer*, *Mich.* 10 *Will.* 3. And the fame doctrine was held by the court in the cafe of *Piper* and *Dennis* in the fame term †.

Amongft the tradefmen in this corporation, there are feven *companies*; viz. of mercers, fhearmen, cordwainers, tanners, fkinners, taylors, and barbers; each of which companies hath two wardens chofen yearly, and fworn to fee the rules and orders of the refpective companies duly obferved.

They have a very elegant town hall, lately repaired by the corporation at a confiderable expence, where they hold their courts; and the quarter feffions of the peace are likewife commonly held there by adjournment from Appleby at Michaelmafs, Chriftmafs, and Eafter; and originally, at Midfummer every fecond year.

They have a *court of confcience* by virtue of an act of parliament of the 4th year of the reign of king George the third, for the recovery of debts under 40*s*, which extends to the whole parifh, and fuch debts are not to be fued for in any other court. But the fame doth not extend to debts for rent, nor to any contract where the freehold doth come in queftion, nor to any matter cognizable by the ecclefiaftical court, or before juftices of the peace.

Adjoining to the town of Kendal on the South, is *Kirkland*, which is commonly reckoned part of Kendal, but it is a diftinct townfhip, feparated from

* This proclamation we have inferted in the Appendix, N° xxxix.

† 12 Modern Rep. 247. 253. Viner's Abridgment, Tit. Corporations. (J. 3.) 15. and (M.) 3.

the

the town of Kendal by a little brook, which having but a ſmall current, and as it were ſeeking a paſſage, is called *Blindbeck*.

This place, being out of the mayor's liberty, is much reſorted to by tradeſmen that are not free of the corporation.

The CHURCH of Kendal ſtands in *Kirkland*, from whence the place hath received its name. It is a very large, neat, and handſome building, and contains every Sunday as large a congregation, as almoſt any pariſh church in the kingdom. It is 180 feet long, and 99 feet in breadth; with five alleys, each of them being parted by a row of 8 fair pillars; and with a ſtrong ſquare ſteeple, wherein are 6 large and very tunable bells.

It is a vicarage, in the patronage of Trinity college in Cambridge; valued in the king's books at 99*l* 5*s* o*d*, in Henry the eighth's time; which is a very high valuation, and the reaſon ſeems to be, becauſe a conſiderable part of the vicar's revenue conſiſts of preſcriptive payments in money, which were the ſame then as they are now; whereas where the revenue depends upon the prices of the produce of land and of other things tithable, the valuation betwixt that time and the preſent will be more diſproportionate. The great tithes, and alſo the tithes of wool and lamb, belong to the college.

This church, together with divers others, was given by Ivo de Talebois, firſt baron of Kendal after the conqueſt, to the abbey of St. Mary's York. And the grant thereof was confirmed by Gilbert ſon of Roger Fitz-Reinfred *. And afterwards, the ſame was appropriated to that abbey, as appears by an inquiſition of *Ad quod damnum*, taken at Appleby before the ſheriff on Thurſday next after the Epiphany in the 30 Ed. 1. whereby it was found, That it is of no damage to the king or any other, to appropriate the church of Kirkby in Kendale to the abbot and convent of St. Mary's York: That the ſaid church is in the patronage of the ſaid abbot and convent; but that its chapels, viz. of Greſmere and Windermere, are in the patronage of Sir Ingram de Gynes and Chriſtian his wife as heireſs, who hold the ſame of the king *in capite*. *(Machel from Dugd.)*

After the diſſolution of the monaſteries, this rectory (with the advowſon of the vicarage) was granted to the ſaid college by queen Mary in the firſt year of her reign: Who having called together the chief of the popiſh clergy that were then about the court, conſulted with them concerning publick prayers

* Omnibus ſanctæ matris eccleſiæ filiis ad quos præſens ſcriptum pervenerit, Gilbertus filius Reinfredi et Elewiſa uxor ejus ſalutem in domino. Noverit univerſitas veſtra nos intuitu charitatis conceſſiſſe et hac præſenti charta noſtra confirmaſſe Deo et eccleſiæ ſanctæ Mariæ Eborum et monachis ibidem Deo ſervientibus, eccleſias de Clapham, et de Kirkeby in Loneſdale, et de Borton in Kendale, et de Biethum, et de Everſheim, et de Kirkeby in Kendale, et de Morland, et de Brunefeld, et de Wirkington. Has autem prædictas eccleſias confirmamus eis, cum capellis, molendinis, terris, paſturis, poſſeſſionibus, libertatibus, et omnibus aliis pertinentiis ſuis, ſicut chartæ anteceſſorum noſtrorum teſtantur. Hiis teſtibus, Ricardo de Mariſco, Adamo de Biethum, Rogero de Heverſheim, Nicolao de Kendale, Johanne de Loneſdale, Magiſtro Hugone Ruffo, Gervaſio de Aincurt, Henrico de Redeman, Waltero de Bovington, Johanne de Haverington, Petro Bleyn, Johanne Bleyn, Roberto Bachel, Magiſtro Gregorio de Ebor', Roberto Mure, Johanne et Waltero Cocis, Waltero de Piſtr', Oſberto Janitor', Turgis Granetar', Samſone Clerico, et multis aliis. *(Regiſtr. Wetherel.)*

CHAP. VI.

to be made for the soul of her father king Henry the eighth, conceiving his case not to be so desperate, but that his soul might be benefited thereby. They possessed her of the impossibility thereof, and that his Holiness would never consent such an honour to be done to one dying so notorious a schismatic. But they advised her, in expression of her private affection to her father's memory, to add something to Trinity college in Cambridge, as being the best monument he had left; whereon, chiefly at the instance of John Christopherson bishop of Chichester who had been master there, she bestowed this and other advowsons upon the said college, together with an annual sum of 376*l* 10*s* 3*d*, part of which sum did arise from the rectory of this church. (*History of Cambr. Univ.*)

But it seems that the college did not immediately come into possession of this advowson; for the same appears to have been in other hands so late as the latter end of the reign of king James the first, by grant probably of some long term, either by the abbot and convent before the dissolution, or by the crown afterwards. For by an indenture leading the uses of a fine, in the 15th year of the said king, between Thomas Lyttelton of Frankley in the county of Worcester esquire, and Katherine his wife (daughter and sole heir of Sir Thomas Crompton of Driffield in the county of York knight), among other estates therein recited, and which the said Thomas Lyttelton was then possessed of in the right of his wife, the following occur; viz. "The chantry of Kirkby "Kendale: Three messuages, three gardens, and three orchards; 80 acres of "arable land, 80 acres of pasture, 40 acres of meadow, 20 acres of wood, "and 40 acres of furze and heath, in Kirkby Kendale aforesaid. Also all "tithes whatever arising and growing in Kirkby Kendale; together with the "advowson of the church there, in the county of Westmorland †.

What the chantry above mentioned was, doth not particularly appear; for there were several chantries in this church. In the 24th year of queen Elizabeth, there was a grant made by the said queen to Sir Christopher Hatton and his heirs of the chantry of *St. Anthony* in the church of Kirkby in Kendale, and the chantry of *Thomas a Becket* in the said church; out of which, together with other particulars in his purchase, he was to pay 7*l* 11*s* 4*d* a year to the Schoolmaster of Burgh. In the general return of the commissioners appointed to inquire of colleges, chantries, hospitals, and free chapels, in the reigns of king Hen. 8. and Ed. 6. it was certified, that in Kirkby in Kendale there was the chantry of *Our Lady*; *Becket*'s chantry; *Trinity Guild*; a stipendiary in the chapel; and four other stipendiaries.

Near unto the church, towards the North, is an house called *Abbot-Hall*; which undoubtedly belonged heretofore to the said abbey. It was rebuilt by the late owner George Wilson esquire at the expence of about 8000*l*, who sold the same to John Taylor esquire the present possessor.

And nigh unto the said Abbot-Hall was a *chapel*, near the head of *Well-sike*; from which place there is a lane which leads to the great street, called *Capel-lane* (having received its name from the *chapel*) now corruptly called *Capper-lane*.

† From the original remaining among Lord Lyttelton's evidences at Hagley in Worcestershire.

There

There was another chapel called *St. Anne's chapel*, which is supposed to have been situate near Dockwray hall; and at this place there was an house in Mr. Machel's time, which from the form of the windows and the fabrick thereof seemed to have been this same chapel.

William Gilpin, steward to Alan Bellingham of Levens esquire, purchased of the said Alan certain rents belonging to the said chapel of *St. Anne*, of 3*l* 7*s* 8*d* a year, at 30 years purchase; and by his will, dated in the year 1561, bequeathed the same to two Gilpins his relations, and to others of the nearest of his kindred successively, to distribute the same to the poor in Kendal of his name and family for ever.

There was another chapel at the head of the Bank, upon an hill called *Chapel-Hill*, now demolished; and an house erected upon the site thereof, where the arms of Roos are very apparent in the front.

There was also a chapel called *All-Hallows chapel* at the east end of Strammongate bridge now converted to a dwelling.

There was also an *hospital of lepers* at Kirkby in Kendale; the patronage whereof was given by William de Lancastre to the priory of Conyngesheved in Lancashire. This hospital was dedicated to *St. Leonard*; and was valued at the dissolution at 11*l* 4*s* 3*d* a year. It was granted in the 38 Hen. 8. to Alan Bellingham and Alan Wilson esquires, being the same which is now called *Spittle*, and belongs at present to Sir James Lowther baronet.

There are in the church four iles or quires, appropriated to distinct families and houses in the neighbourhood. The outermost on the south side is called *Parr's*; the inner on the same side, *Strickland's*; the outermost on the north side, *Bellingham's*; the inner on the same north side, called the *Aldermens*, because the aldermen were formerly wont to sit there.

In the ile called *Parr's*, which belonged to the *Parrs* of Kendal castle, Sir *Thomas Parr* knight is commonly supposed to have been interred, under a large tombstone without any inscription, there having been in the glass window over it (until demolished by Cromwell's soldiers) the following distich,

" Pray for the soul of Sir Thomas Parr knight,
" Who was squire of the body to king Henry the eighth."

But it hath evidently appeared before, that he was not buried here, but in the Black Friers church in London. Therefore, most probably, that inscription was in memory only of his having caused that window to be made of painted glass. These windows were of considerable expence: And they who caused them to be put up, were solicitous oftentimes of having not only their names, but their arms also painted thereon. An instance parallel to this, but more explicit, was in the church of Burgh in this county: " Orate pro anima Do-" mini Thomæ Rud, qui istam fenestram fieri fecit." Most probably, under this stone lies interred the body of Sir *William Parr* father of the said Sir *Thomas*; for the arms on the said tombstone are incircled with the garter, and no other of the family besides this Sir William, and his grandson *William* marquis of Northampton, was dignified with that honour; and the latter, we have found, was buried at Warwick.

CHAP. VI.

Nigh unto the said tombstone lies the body of Sir Augustine Nicols knight, one of the justices of the court of common pleas, who sitting as judge of assize in this town (the assizes being held here at that time, by reason of some differences between Francis earl of Cumberland the then sheriff and the town of Appleby *) died Aug. 3. 1616, in the 57th year of his age, and was buried here, over whom is a very fair monument, with an inscription.

Next adjoining to this ile, is that belonging to the *Stricklands* of Sizergh; in which, five of the sons of Sir *Thomas Strickland* knight lie buried with a rich marble monument over them.

The *Bellingham* ile was so called from the *Bellinghams* of Over Levens; in which is an handsome tomb, wherein lies interred *Alan Bellingham* esquire (great grandfather of the last *Bellingham* of that place), and over it his effigies cut in brass with an inscription.

The *Aldermens* ile is that which was anciently *Our Lady's chapel.* It is said to have been re-edified by Sir *Roger Bellingham* of Burneshead knight, who lies there interred, with his wife, in a goodly tomb, with an inscription in brass under their effigies.

In the same place lies dame *Thomasin Thornburgh*, wife of *William Thornburgh* of Selside knight, and grand-daughter of the said Sir *Roger Bellingham*, with an epitaph over her in white marble.

In the high chancel or quire of this church lies the body of the right reverend *Robert Dawson*, bishop of Clonfert in Ireland; who in the time of the Irish rebellion returned, with much difficulty, to his native country, and died in his father's house in Kendal. Over his grave is this epitaph inscribed on a brass plate:

"Hic jacet reverendus in Christo Robertus Dawson, episcopus Clonfertensis et Ducensis Hibernicus. Qui obiit die 13 Apr. 1643."

Near him divers vicars of Kendal lie buried. Among whom is Mr. *Ralph Tyrer*; whose epitaph, composed by himself, was afterwards engraved in brass, as followeth:

"Here lieth the body of Ralph Tyrer, late vicar of Kendal, B. D. who died June 4th, A. D. 1627.

London bred mee, Westminster fed mee,
Cambridge sped mee, my Sister wed mee,
Study taught mee, Living sought mee,
Learning brought mee, Kendal caught mee,
Labour pressed mee, Sickness distressed mee,
Death oppressed mee, the Grave possessed mee,
God first gave mee, Christ did save mee,
Earth did crave mee, and Heaven would have mee."

Other vicars of Kendal, of whom we have found any remembrance, were as follows:

In 1312, *Roger de Kirkeby*, vicar of the church of Kirkeby in Kendale, was witness to an exchange of lands at Sizergh.

* Machel.

In

In 1366, one *Thomas de Leynesbury*, vicar of Kendal, was a trustee of certain lands granted by Sir Thomas de Strickland knight.

In 1432, *Richard Garsdale*, vicar of Kendal, was one of the trustees in a settlement of Sizergh estate.

In 1495, *William*, abbot of St. Mary's York, was vicar of Kendal; who in that year granted a lease of part of the tithes to Sir Thomas Strickland.

In 1597, *Ambrose Hetherington*, S. T. B. vicar of Kendal, had a grant of the next avoidance of the rectory of Skelton by Philip earl of Surrey and the lady Anne his wife, and William Howard otherwise William lord Howard and the lady Elizabeth his wife.

We find one Mr. *Stanford* vicar in the reign of king Charles the second; of whom there is the following monumental inscription:

Hic in proximo situs est
Michael Stanford.
Erat ornamentum literarum et decus:
Veritatis cultor eximius:
Fidei propugnator strenuus:
Ecclesiæ Anglicanæ Hookerus alter;
Et fanaticorum malleus:
Et quicquid vel cupiunt vel debent esse viri.
Is adeo omni laude major,
Cœlo maturus,
Suum ad triumphum evectus est,
Quinto Nonas Martii,
Anno { Salutis reparatæ 1682.
Ætatis suæ 48.
Animarum hic curæ } 10.
Hoc
Willielmus Rawlinson
De Gilthwaite Rigge, armiger,
Summus ei amicus,
In memoriam
Posuit.

And within our own memory was *William Crosby*, M. A. who left behind him an extraordinary character of sanctity, charity, and other amiable qualities. He was succeeded by *Richard Cuthbert*, M. A. On whose tomb-stone at the east end of the church-yard is the following inscription:

Here lies buried
The Rev[d] Richard Cuthbert, M. A.
Vicar of Kirkby Kendale:
In whose character
The christian, the scholar, and the gentleman,
rendered each other more illustrious.
His zeal was happily tempered

with

CHAP. VI.

with knowledge and moderation.
His publick labours and private conduct
agreed to demonstrate the integrity of his life.
Stranger, suspect not this epitaph of flattery;
His praises are more fully inscribed
on the hearts of all who knew him.
And his master's presence
will reward and perfect his virtues,
By a more intimate converse
with the great exemplar.
Ob. Nov. 7. A. D. 1744. Ætat. 48. Cur. huj. Par. 11.

On Mr. Cuthbert's death, the present vicar *Thomas Symonds*, M. A. (now D. D.) succeeded.

In this church is a neat *organ*, with a very handsome and large gallery, erected about the year 1702. The organist has a pretty decent salary arising partly from the seats, and partly from contributions, together with the rent of a field in Park lands called Haverbrack or Organist close, now let at 12*l* a year; which was given by Janet the wife of Alderman Wilson. The organist to be chosen by the mayor, recorder, two senior aldermen, the vicar, and the master of the free grammar school, or the major part of them.

On the 3d pillar in the south ile of the church, is the following inscription:

Here lyes Frances late wife of Jacob Dawson Gent. who departed this life 19th June 1700, in the 25th year of her age: Who by a free and chearful resignation of herself, even *in the midst of this world's affluence*, has left us just grounds to hope she is now happy.——This epitaph we only take notice of, as it hath occasioned a display of the droll humour of the people, who upon any particular occasion of festivity have from hence framed a proverb, "We "live as Jacob Dawson's wife died."

On the 4th pillar in the same ile, on a brass plate:

To the memory

Of the most religious and orthodox christian, the most loyal subject, and most ancient and most serviceable member of this corporation, William Guy of Water-Crook, Gent. who died the 25th day of December, in the year of our lord 1683. Aged 84.

Had loyalty been life, brave Guy, thou had then
Stood Kendal's everlasting alderman.
Nay, could the joint united force of all
That's good or virtuous over death prevail,
Thy life's pure thread no time or fate could sever,
And thou'd still liv'd to pray, King live for ever!
But thou art gone; a proof such virtue is
Too good for earth, and only fit for bliss,
And blissful seats; where if bless'd spirits do
Concern themselves with any thing below,

Thy

Thy prayers the ſame, thou ſtill doſt ſupplicate
For Charles's life, for England's church and ſtate.
Whilſt to thy juſt eternal memory
Envy and malice muſt in this agree
None better lov'd or ſerv'd his prince than Thee.

In the middle ile pillar neareſt to the chancel on a braſs plate:

Nigh to this pillar lies the body of Mrs. Frances Strickland, late wife to Mr. John Strickland of Strickland, and daughter to Edward Backhouſe of Moreland eſquire.

She was born } 24 June { 1690
Married } 24 June { 1708
Buried } 24 June { 1725

Emblem of temporal good, the day that gave
Her birth and marriage ſaw her in her grave.
Wing'd with its native love her ſoul took flight,
To boundleſs regions of eternal light.

At the eaſt end of the churchyard is the following:

Here lieth the body of Joſeph Hall, M. A.
Sometime fellow of Queen's College, Oxford;
And late rector of Weyhill, Hants.
Who,
By the help of good natural talents,
and a conſtant application to literature,
acquired, to a maſterly perfection, the knowledge
of various languages, ancient and modern;
of Philoſophy, thro' all its branches;
of Divinity, his principal profeſſion.
Such uncommon attainments,
With an open, ingenuous temper,
and the firmeſt integrity of heart,
rendered him a moſt faithful and valuable friend,
an uſeful and ornamental member of ſociety,
an excellent college-tutor,
an accompliſhed and reſpectable pariſh miniſter.
He departed this life in Kendale July 13th 1756,
on a piouſly intended viſit to his aged parent,
Mr. Nicholas Hall of Lazonby in Cumberland:
Who cauſed this moument to be erected
in memory of
ſo deſerving and ſo dutiful a ſon.

The *vicarage houſe* is moſt pleaſantly ſituate, on the ſouth ſide of the church, and is in fine and neat condition, having been greatly improved by the preſent

2 incumbent.

CHAP. VI.

incumbent. Though it ſtands low, it has a beautiful proſpect of the river, the caſtle, the park lands, and country adjacent.

About the middle of the town was erected in the year 1754 a *chapel* of eaſe, which was conſecrated on the 24th day of June 1755, by biſhop Keene, by the name of *St. George's chapel in Kendale.* The executors of the will of the late Dr. Stratford. commiſſary of the archdeaconry of Richmond, contributed 600*l.* towards the building and endowment thereof, beſides 11*l* and upwards for a ſet of communion plate for the ſame. The ſame Dr. Stratford gave alſo by his will 50*l* to the poor of Kendal, 20*l* to the poor of Killington in this county, and upwards of 3000*l* more in ſpecific charities elſewhere; and bequeathed the reſiduum of his perſonality, amounting to 9390*l*, to be laid out by his executors in buying good books, to be diſpoſed of to proper perſons within the archdeaconry of Richmond or elſewhere, in relieving poor houſekeepers, putting out poor children apprentices, cloathing poor old people and poor boys and girls, and in any publick charity or charitable uſes which his executors ſhould approve of. Out of which they augmented 58 ſmall livings and curacies, in the counties of Weſtmorland, Cumberland, Lancaſter, York, and Cheſter; ſeveral of them with 200*l*, others with other ſums, but moſtly with the ſum of 100*l* conditionally that the inhabitants, incumbents, or others, would contribute another 100*l*, whereby to obtain the augmentation of queen Anne's bounty; which increaſed the charity quadruple. The remainder they beſtowed in other charities, according to the intention of the donor.

There is alſo in this town a *preſbyterian diſſenting meeting-houſe*, with other meeting-houſes of different denominations; particularly a large *quaker meeting-houſe*, ſeveral of the conſiderable tradeſmen of the town being of that perſuaſion. The quakers alſo have lately built an elegant ſchool-houſe for the inſtruction of youth.

On the weſt ſide of the churchyard ſtands the *free grammar ſchool*; being a pretty large building, and conſiderably endowed by king Edward the ſixth, king Philip, queen Mary, and queen Elizabeth.

In the 20 Eliz. on the ſale of the rectory of Burton in this county by the crown, there was a rent reſerved to the ſchoolmaſter of Kendal of 9*l* 5*s* 8*d* a year.

And in the 24th year of the ſame queen, an order was made in the exchequer, ſetting forth, that whereas it appeared from the accounts of the receiver of the crown revenues in Weſtmorland, that there had been yearly allowed out of the ſame, the ſum of 9*l* 5*s* 8*d*, for the maintenance of two curates (viz. 4*l* 12*s* 10*d* each) to ſerve within the pariſh church of Kendal and to be aiding and aſſiſting to the vicar there; which ſum, ſince the death of ſuch chantry prieſts as were admitted to ſerve there at the firſt diſſolution of chantries, hath been otherwiſe employed, as to the finding of ſinging men, and ſometimes to other uſes, according to the directions of the pariſhioners there; it was therefore ordered by the court (on petition of the inhabitants) that the ſaid ſum for the future be paid, towards the augmentation of the ſalary of the ſchool-maſter of the grammar ſchool there, over and beſides 10*l* a year already allowed him by the crown.

Other

Other benefactors to this ſchool were, Dr. *Airay* and Mr. *Richard Jackſon*. Which laſt had been ſchoolmaſter here, and removed to Appleby: He gave 100*l*, the intereſt thereof to be applied to the benefit of the ſchoolmaſter. In 1717, it was certified, that the maſter's ſalary is 28 *l* 13 *s* 4 *d* yearly; *viz*. 19 *l* 5 *s* 4 *d* out of the crown rents, and 9 *l* 8 *s* 0 *d* paid by the chamberlains of Kendal; and that there is likewiſe 8 *l* a year to an uſher paid by the ſaid chamberlains, which was given by Mr. Johnſon formerly uſher himſelf. Both which ſums, to the ſchoolmaſter and uſher, are paid by the chamberlains out of lands given to them for that purpoſe. Both maſter and uſher are nominated by the mayor and aldermen.

Dr. *George Fleming*, 6 March 1627, gave 40 *s* yearly to poor ſcholars of the burgh of Kendal going to Queen's college in Oxford, to be paid by the mayor and aldermen.

Mr. *Henry Park*, alderman, by his will dated 8 Apr. 1631, gave to the aldermen of Kendal 100 *l*, upon truſt, that the intereſt thereof be given to a poor ſcholar from Kendal ſchool to Oxford, without mentioning any college, for four years: The ſaid ſcholar to be of the pariſh of Kendal, Millom, or Heverſham.

Mr. *Joſeph Smith* gave 20 *s* a year for a poor boy from the ſaid ſchool, to Queen's College in Oxford, to be paid to him by the mayor and aldermen.

Mr. *Sands* gave 100 *l* to the ſaid college, in truſt to pay 5 *l* yearly for 7 years, to ſuch boy going from Kendal ſchool, as the mayor and aldermen ſhall appoint.

Mr. *Jopſon* gave an exhibition of 40 *s* a year to a boy going from Kendal ſchool to the ſaid college.

Mr. *Henry Wilſon* gave three exhibitions for poor boys going from Kendal ſchool to the ſaid college, to be paid out of the tithes of Farleton; together with four exhibitions from Kirkby Lonſdale: which then were 35 *l* for the whole, or 5 *l* a year each.

There is alſo an *hoſpital* or *charity ſchool*, of the foundation as followeth; *viz*. By indenture, bearing date Sept. 6. 1670, between *Thomas Sands* of Kirkby Kendal gentleman of the one part, and the mayor, aldermen, and burgeſſes of the borough of Kirkby Kendal aforeſaid of the other part; reciting, that whereas the ſaid Thomas Sands hath gained a conſiderable ſhare of his temporal eſtate by buying and ſelling of woollen cottons, commonly called Kendal cottons, and being mindful to ſet apart one convenient dwelling-houſe within Kirkby Kendal aforeſaid, for the uſe of eight poor widows, to exerciſe carding and ſpinning of wool, and weaving of raw pieces of cloth for cottons called Kendal cottons; and for the uſe of a ſchoolmaſter to read prayers to the ſaid widows twice a day, and to teach poor children till prepared for the free ſchool of Kendal or elſewhere: He therefore the ſaid Thomas Sands grants to the ſaid corporation certain meſſuages and lands for the purpoſes aforeſaid. The widows to be of the age of 52 years or upwards; three of them to be choſen out of Stricklandgate, three out of Strammongate and Highgate, one out of Strickland Roger and Strickland Ketel, and one out of Skelſmergh and Patton. The overſeers of the poor of the reſpective places, to nominate (on a vacancy)

 two

CHAP. VI.

two to the said trustees, out of which they to chuse one. On default of the overseers, the mayor, senior alderman, vicar, and schoolmaster of Kendal, or the major part of them (of whom the mayor to be one), shall have power to appoint: Who shall also in like manner appoint the schoolmaster. The widows to have each four marks a year, and the schoolmaster the residue of the rents and profits of the estates.

In the body of the church, upon the 4th pillar in the 2d north side alley, is a fair marble monument, with an inscription, in memory of the said Thomas Sands: and the arms thereupon of the family of Sands in Lancashire. Unto which arms, Mr. Machel (who was a staunch royalist) observes, that the said Thomas Sands had no title, being of mean extraction, and having no arms but what he took up against the king. And he adds, that Mr. Sands's charities would have been more laudable, if what he gave had not been obtained by sequestrations.

In the year 1671, the trustees for sale of the fee farm rents of the crown, for the sum of 1640*l* 11*s* 6*d*, conveyed to the aforesaid Thomas Sands of Kendal gentleman, his heirs and assigns, the several fee farm rents following, *viz.* 95*l* 6*s* 8*d* reserved and issuing out of and for the park of Kendal, then or late payable by Henry lord Herbert (and this was the *Herbert-silver* above mentioned); 1*l* 6*s* 8*d* reserved and issuing out of the town of Apulby, and payable by the burgesses of the same; 20*s* reserved and issuing out of the borough of Kirkby in Kendal, payable by the mayor, aldermen, and burgesses.

Dorothy Brathwaite, widow of Thomas Brathwaite of Burneshead esquire, by her will in 1623, gave 50*l* to be laid out in land, and the profits thereof to be given to poor housholders in Kendal, at the discretion of her son Richard Brathwaite and his heirs owners of Burneshead, and the aldermen of Kendal for the time being.

Rowland Wilson, of the city of London esquire gave 1*s* weekly to the poor of Kirkby Kendale for ever, to be laid out in bread, and distributed every Sunday at the discretion of the minister and churchwardens.

Mr. *John Robinson* of Lane-foot in Strickland Ketel by his will gave 1*s* weekly to be distributed in the church at the like discretion of the minister and churchwardens.

Mr. *Janson* gave some fields in the park lands, and some burgage rents in Kendal; out of which, 6 poor men of 50 years of age or upwards receive 20*s* a year each; and the remainder is laid out in cloth, which furnishes about 40 new coats yearly to other poor men belonging to the town.

There is also the sum of about 13*l* a year, given by Mr. *Towers* and Mr. *Parks*, to be laid out in cloth, and distributed amongst the poor at Christmass.

And the interest of 120*l* given by *John Prissoe*; to be distributed yearly at Christmass to poor housekeepers: With which money two inclosures were purchased within the Church fields, now let to farm for 8*l* 5*s* 0*d* a year.

And 6*l* 10*s* yearly, given by Mr. *Fleming*; to be distributed amongst the poor on Good Friday.

Mr.

Mr. *Bryan Lancaster* gave an estate to the society of Quakers; out of which, six poor men (not Quakers) receive 20*s* a year each, and six poor women 10*s* a year each.

Also the rents and profits of an house in the possession of Mr. John Sleddale and William Lawn were given by Mr. *Stephenson* of Dodding-Green, to trustees for the use of the poor; which are yearly distributed.

And 30 *blue-coat boys* are cloathed and educated chiefly by voluntary subscriptions.

And Dr. *John Archer* late of Oxenholme deceased gave a field in the Park lands, the profits whereof are yearly to be applied to the cloathing of 6 poor men and 6 poor women; and the surplus to the charity school.

There is a stipend also of 15*l* 12*s* 0*d* a year for an afternoon lecturer in the church, to be chosen by the mayor and aldermen, and paid by them.

In the 7th year of the reign of king George the third, an act of parliament was obtained for inclosing a parcel of ground within the borough of Kirkby in Kendal, called *Kendal-fell*, for the use of the poor there; and for cleansing and enlightening the streets of the said borough: And on the credit of the said act, money was borrowed, wherewith at the north end of the town was erected a neat, airy, pleasant building, large enough to contain 80 poor persons, who have a master and mistress that preside over them, and employ them in such work as their age and infirmities will admit of.

In the 50 Ed. 3. there was a grant of pontage for five years, for repairing the *bridge* at Kendal. At present there are three bridges over the river Kent: Two of which are repaired by the corporation; and the third, to wit, Strammongate bridge, is repaired one fourth by the corporation, and three fourths by the county.

Eastward from the town, on the opposite side of the river, stands the *castle*, situate on an hill, with a fair and beautiful prospect. It was old and decayed even in Camden's time, and hath been never since repaired.

There was a large demesne belonging to the castle, and a park with deer, which was disparked in the 8th year of queen Elizabeth. The administration of the affairs and revenues thereof seems to have been divided into two distinct stewardships, bearing the name to this day of Upper Graveship and Nether Graveship.

Opposite to the castle, on the other side of the town, is a large artificial mount, called *Castle bow-hill*; which, from its name, seems to have been intended as a fort: It is within sight of the Roman station at *Water-crook*; and is very like the exploratory mounts, Mr. Horsley observes, which are to be seen in other places, especially near the military ways: But whether it is Roman, and relates to the station; or more modern, and erected with a view to the castle; he doth not take upon him to determine. *Horsl.* 484.

CHAP. VI.

In this town was born Dr. *Barnaby Potter*, bishop of Carlisle; and Dr. *Christopher Potter*, provost of Queen's college in Oxford; and Dr. *Thomas Shaw*, principal of Edmund Hall, and author of a learned and ingenious book of travels, which bears his name.

There hath been also at this place a respectable family of the name of CHAMBRE *(De Camera)*, for many generations. The first of which name that hath occurred to us, was,

1. *Hugh de Chambre*; who, towards the beginning of the reign of king Henry the third, was assessed 16 *d* for the 20th part of one knight's fee at Kendal.

2. The next that we meet with was *John de la Chamber*; who, together with Sybil his wife, in the 9 Ed. 1. conveyed by fine certain lands in Skelsmergh, Sizergh, and Stirkland Ketel, to Nicolas de Laybourne and Margaret his wife. And the said John and Sybil purchased of William son of Robert de Stirkland knight the demesne lands of Houwys, which to this day bear the name of Chambre Hawes.——This John had issue,

3. *John del Chambre*; who in the 36 Ed. 3. had some remaining parts of the said Hawes from Richard Carus and Agnes his wife in exchange for his lands in Watchfield. And in this same year, he was a juror in the king's bench at Westminster, in a cause between the abbot of St. Mary's York and Walter de Helton concerning a messuage in Colby. And in the 49 Ed. 3. he was one of the jurors upon the inquisition after the death of Johan de Coupland aforesaid.

4. Probably about this time comes in another *John*; for in the 15 Ric. 2. we find *John Chambyr* executor of the will of *John* de Helsington. And in the 6 Hen. 4. *John del Chambre* was one of the jurors upon the inquisition after the death of William Parr. And in the 9 Hen. 4. after the death of John Parr.

5. *Thomas Chamer*, in the 24 Hen. 6. was a witness (together with John Pennington knight, and Richard Redman and John Betham esquires) to the grant of an house in Kirkland.

6. *Thomas Chammer*, son of Thomas, was party and witness to several deeds in the reign of king Henry the seventh.

7. *Walter Chamber* was witness (and sometimes obligee) in several bonds in the reign of Hen. 8. In the 20th year of that king, he purchased for his son the marriage of Jane one of the 4 daughters and coheirs of Thomas Wessington of Hallhead-hall esquire.

8. *Robert Chambre*, son of Walter, in the 22 Hen. 8. appears to have had the site of Hallhead hall, in virtue of the said marriage. It is a demesne in Strickland Ketel, and still enjoyed by that family. In the next year, a division was made of Wessington's whole estate; whereby other lands were assigned to his other three daughters, Catherine wife of Miles Beck, Elizabeth wife of William Gilpin, and Margaret wife of Thomas Carus.

9. *Walter Chamber*, son of Robert, was a minor at his father's death, attaining only his full age in the 3 Eliz. He married Anne daughter of ——— Traves of Naitby in Lancashire esquire; and was drowned in passing over the sands in that county.

10. *Alan Chamber*, son of Walter. He also was a minor at the death of his father, and was granted in wardship to Sir Thomas Boynton in the 23 Eliz. being then only 16 years of age. The lands named in the grant are Hawes and Hallhead-hall, held by knight's service; three messuages and tenements in Staveley, held of the queen in socage; one messuage and tenement in Sedgwick, by knight's service; and 6 burgages in Kendal by socage. This Alan married Anne daughter of John Carlton of Beeforth near Birdlington in Yorkshire; whose mother was daughter of Walter Strickland of Sizergh esquire.

11. *Walter Chamber*, son of Alan. He sued out a general livery of his lands in the 18th of James the first. He married Elizabeth daughter of William Pricket of Natland gentleman. He died at the age of 69 years, and was buried in Kendal church, Oct. 2. 1665.

12. *Alan Chamber*, his son, lived most of his time in Yorkshire; where he married Dorothy second daughter of James Moor of Angram Grange gentleman, by Anne his wife daughter and coheir of Michael Askwith of the same place gentleman. He was buried in the parish church of Coxwold in Yorkshire, where a monument was erected to his memory, in 1690.

13. *Alan Chambre*, son of Alan. He varied in writing his sirname from several of his late ancestors, reducing it to the original orthography. He was barrister at law; and married Mary the elder daughter and coheir of Marmaduke Trueman of Marderby Grange in the county of York, and by her had issue, (1) *Walter*. (2) *Alan*, who died unmarried. (3) *Jane*, married to William Symson esquire, senior alderman of Kendal, now living; unto whose son and heir apparent, Mr. Joseph Symson, we are obliged for several of the above particulars relating to the town of Kendal. Which William Symson was son of Joseph Symson esquire, senior alderman of Kendal; son of Robert Symson, M. A. rector of Marton in this county.

14. *Walter Chambre*, barrister at law, married Mary daughter of Jacob Morland of Capplethwaite esquire; and by her had issue, (1) *Alan*. (2) *Jacob*, a clergyman. (3) *Walter*, a merchant in Whitehaven. (4) *Mary*, as yet unmarried.

15. *Alan Chambre*, barrister at law; now living, and unmarried.

The bearings of this family are, 1. Or, a cross erminee, 4 martlets rising Sable: And for an augmentation, on a chief Azure, a snake coronee, devouring a child Proper, betwixt two roses Gules. By the name of *Chambre*. 2. Argent, a cheveron Gules, between ten cross croslets Sable. By the name of *Wessington*. 3. Ermine, on a bend Gules, three elephants heads Or. [It doth not appear to whom this quartering belongs; perhaps it was one of the bearings of Wessington: For upon the marrying an heiress, it was usual to take not only the arms of that family, but the other arms also which that family quartered.] 4. Three asses Sable passant. By the name of *Askwith*. 5. Argent, a cheveron between 3 escallop shells Azure. By the name of *Trueman* †.

† The above account of this family is taken partly from an extract made from the family writings by Alan Chambre esquire, grandfather of the present Alan, of which he gave a copy to bishop Nicolson; and partly from other evidences, as they occurred to us in the course of our investigations.

Earls

CHAP. VI.

Earls of Kendal there have been feveral. *John* duke of *Bedford*, third fon of king Henry the fourth, was advanced to that dignity by his brother king Henry the fifth. *John* duke of *Somerfet* was created Earl of Kendal by king Henry the fixth. And by the fame king Henry the fixth, *John de Foix*, of a family of that name in France, for his faithful fervices in the French wars, was preferred to that dignity; fince which time, thofe of that family write themfelves earls of Longueville and Kendal. *George*, prince of *Denmark*, hufband of queen Anne, was by king William created earl of Kendal.

There hath been alfo one *duke* of Kendal; namely, *Charles* third fon of king James the fecond when duke of York; but he died young.

And finally, *Erengard Melofina Schulenberg*, a German lady, who came into England with king George the firft, was by him honoured with the dignity of *duchefs* of Kendal.

Having thus finifhed what we had to fay concerning the town of *Kendal* and its environs; we proceed to the other parts of this extenfive parifh, beginning with *Helfington* on the South, and fo travelling Eaftward through the feveral townfhips and manors, and from thence going about by the North and Weft, until we arrive where we firft fet out.

HELSINGTON.

Helsington, below Kendal, on the Weft fide of the river Kent, is part of the *Lumley Fee*; and in the 14 Ed. 3. by inquifition after the death of *William de Thweng*, it appears, that the faid *William* died feifed in his demefne as of fee of the manor of *Helfington* with the appurtenances, and of the rent of free tenants and tenants at will there of 15 *l* 0 *s* 8 *d* a year, and that the capital meffuage or manor-houfe there was worth nothing by the year, becaufe it was totally in ruins: For the Thweng family, having other and better eftates elfewhere, probably never refided at *Helfington*.

After this, we have found no further particular account of the manor of *Helfington*, till the reign of king Henry the eighth; when it appears to have been in the poffeffion of a family of the name of Bindlose; who had alfo *Borwick-hall* in Lancafhire, and finally fettled there.

And from them it feems to have been purchafed by the Bellinghams, who continued there till the laft century, when this manor (and alfo *Over Levins*) was fold to Colonel *James Grahme*, whofe great grandfon Henry earl of Suffolk and Berkshire now enjoys the fame.

There is a pedigree of Bindlose, which was delivered in at an herald's vifitation, in the 4th year of the reign of king Charles the firft; which is as follows:

1. *William Byndlofe* of Haylfton in Weftmorland, who lived in the reign of king Henry the eighth, had a fon,

2. *Robert Byndlose* esquire, whose wife's name was Agnes Harrison. They had issue 8 children. Amongst whom were, *Robert* the eldest, and *Agnes* married to William Fleming of Ridal esquire, and another daughter *Dorothy* married to Sir Thomas Brathwaite of Burneshead knight.

3. Sir *Robert Byndlose*, knight, married to his first wife Alice daughter of Lancelot Dockwray of Dockwray-hall in Kendal; and by her had two daughters, *Anne*, married to Henry Denton of Cumberland, and *Alice* married to Henry Banks of Bank Newton in Yorkshire. By his second wife, Mary daughter of Edmund Ekost of Churchill in Yorkshire, he had 5 children. The first, *Robert*; who died young. The second succeeded his father, *viz.*

4. Sir *Francis Byndlose* of Borwick knight. He was first married to Dorothy Charnock of Ashley in Lancashire; by whom he had Mary, of the age of 5 years, at the visitation aforesaid in 1628. His second wife was Cicely daughter of Thomas West lord Delawar; and by her he had 4 children: The eldest was,

5. *Robert*, who had issue only a daughter, *Cicely*, married to William Standish of Standish in Lancashire.—And here ended the family of *Bindlose*, of which we have thought proper to give this account, as it is often mentioned in the transactions of those times.

Their arms were; Quarterly, parted per fess indented Or and Gules, on a bend Azure a cinquefoil between two martlets of the first. The Crest; a demihorse couped, with a ducal flourished collar Azure †.

It was in the time of the first or second of the above series, that ALAN BELLINGHAM esquire purchased the manor of Helfington. Which *Alan* was of a younger house of the *Bellinghams* of *Burneshead*, and whose posterity finally settled at *Levins*. And therefore his pedigree more properly belongs to *Burneshead* until the separation of this younger branch; and afterwards to *Over-Levins*, which was their last place of residence. Intermediately, they frequently resided at *Helsington Laithes*, the manor-house of *Helsington*.

In *Helsington* there hath been a family at SIZERGH HALL, much more ancient than any of the name of *Bindlose* or *Bellingham* as lords of the manor. Which family came from STRICKLAND (or rather STIRKLAND, which was the pasture ground of the young cattle called *stirks* or steers) in the parish of Morland in this county; in which part they had considerable possessions, as well as at *Sizergh* and other adjacent places, generally holden under the barons of Kendal. For the barony of Kendal, as we observed before, extended further than the present division thereof, and especially into the western part of what is now called the Bottom of Westmorland.

It is somewhat extraordinary, that amongst the pedigrees of almost all the other ancient families in this county, we have met with no satisfactory account of this family; but by the indulgence of the late worthy owner of Sizergh-hall, Charles Strickland esquire, we have been enabled to make out a regular and

† Machel. Fleming.

authentic

CHAP. VI.

authentic deduction of this family from the clearest and most undeniable evidence, namely, the family writings. From whence, and from other informations as they have occasionally fallen in our way, our history of this family proceeds as follows:

1. The first of the name of *Stirkland* that we have met with, was in the reign of king John; when Gilbert son of Roger Fitz-Reinfred, falling under the displeasure of that prince for his having sided with the rebellious barons, was required in the 17th year of that king to give hostages for his future good behaviour; which hostages were the sons or daughters and heirs of divers of the principal mesne lords holding under the barons of Kendal: amongst whom was the son and heir of WALTER DE STIRKLAND.

In the time of Hugh bishop of Carlisle, who came to the see towards the beginning of the reign of king Henry the third, this *Walter de Stirkland* knight had a licence to keep a domestic chaplain in his family within the parish of Morland, so as it should be no prejudice to the mother church. For the assurance whereof, he gave juratory caution, that his chaplain should not injure the mother church in her revenues or in any other respect *.

The same *Walter de Stirkland*, knight, granted to the church of St. Mary's York, and to the prior and monks of Wederhal (which was a cell of the abbey

* Omnibus Christi fidelibus, ad quorum notitiam præsens scriptum pervenerit, Walterus de Styrkeland, miles, æternam in domino salutem. Noveritis, me promisisse pro me et hæredibus meis indemnitatem matricis ecclesiæ de Moreland in omnibus, pro cantaria habenda in capella mea quam habeo in curia mea de Stirkelaund; quam cantariam tam R. abbas et conventus Sanctæ Mariæ Eborum, patroni ejusdem ecclesiæ, quam Michael tunc temporis vicarius ejusdem, mihi concesserunt. Ita quod capellanus meus, quicunque pro tempore deserviet illi capellæ, jurabit fidelitatem et obedientiam vicario matricis ecclesiæ de Morelaund et rectoribus ejusdem ecclesiæ qui pro tempore fuerint, et illis præsentabitur, et per eos in capella serviet. Ita tamen quod ego et hæredes mei tam capellæ, quam capellanis, in omnibus competenter providebimus. Jurabit autem capellanus meus, in capella mea ministrans, quod nullum parochianorum de Morelaund, nec aliquem extraneum, recipiet ad confessionem, vel ad alia divina officia, vel sacramenta, in prejudicium matricis ecclesiæ de Morelaund et rectorum ejusdem qui pro tempore fuerint; et quod omnes oblationes et obventiones qualescunque fuerint, et undecunque provenerint, fideliter et integre sine aliqua detentione matrici ecclesiæ persolvet, et fidelis tam matrici ecclesiæ prædictæ quam rectoribus ejusdem in omnibus existet.—Præterea, Ego Walterus juravi, pro me et hæredibus meis, quod (sicut prædictum est) nullum parochianorum vel aliorum permittam admitti ad divina officia; vel oblationes, vel obventiones, a capellano meo ibidem detineri.—Præterea juravi, pro me et hæredibus, quod fideliter persolvemus matrici ecclesiæ omnes decimas domus meæ, tam majores quam minores, tam animalium quam servientium.—Præterea juravi, quod ego et uxor mea, cum familia mea, debitis et consuetis solemnitatibus, sc. die Natali, Purificationis, Resurrectionis, et Assumptionis, cum debitis et consuetis oblationibus et obventionibus, matricem ecclesiam prædictam visitabimus.—Præterea juravi, pro me et hæredibus meis, quod si ego, vel hæredes mei, vel capellanus noster, aliquando contra aliquem articulum in hoc scripto insertum in aliquo excesserimus, et post primam admonitionem competenter non satisfecerimus super prædicto excessu, licebit rectoribus vel vicariis matricis ecclesiæ qui pro tempore fuerint, me et capellanum meum per sententiam excommunicationis sive suspensiouis in me et capellanum meum et etiam in capellam meam ferendam, omni appellatione et cavillatione sive quolibet juris remedio remotis, ad condignam compellere satisfactionem.—Juravi etiam, pro me et pro dictis hæredibus meis, quod nunquam aliquid impetrabimus contra matricem ecclesiam, quo minus hoc præsens scriptum ratum et stabile permaneat in perpetuum: Quod si aliquo casu impetratum fuerit, authoritate præsentis scripti irritum sit et inane.—Insuper autem, præter prædictam juratoriam cautionem, per sigillum meum huic scripto appositum me et hæredes meos ad omnia supra scripta fideliter observanda in perpetuum obligavi. Hiis testibus, &c. *(Regist. Wetheral.)*

of

of St. Mary's York) four acres of land in the territory of Stirkeland (specifying the particulars), with liberty to grind the corn growing thereupon at his mill of Stirkeland moulter-free. Witnesses of which grant were, Ralph prior of Carlisle, Master G. (that is, Gervase Lowther) archdeacon, Sir W. official of Carlisle, Richard Brun and Thomas son of John sheriffs of Cumberland and Westmorland, Robert de Castelkairoc brother of the said Walter, Adam son of the said Walter, Walter dean (rural) of Westmorland, Michael vicar of Morlaund, John son of William, Thomas de Lowther, Thomas Frances, Adam and Robert his sons, Hugh Frances, Adam de Slegyle, Stephen and Robert de Newby, and others. *Regist. Wether.*

The names of the sheriffs here mentioned nearly ascertain the time of this grant. For in the 15 and 16 Hen. 3. Walter bishop of Carlisle was sheriff of Cumberland, and Thomas son of John his deputy. The sheriffwick of Westmorland was then become hereditary in the Veteripont family, so that either of these persons could only be under-sheriff there.

Another thing also we learn from hence, that this Sir *Walter de Stirkland* had a son *Adam*, perhaps the same that was delivered to king John as an hostage. And this helps to compleat our pedigree. For in the 20 Ed. 1. *William de Stirkland* knight confirmed this grant, which he styles the grant of Walter de Stirkland his *great grandfather*. This *William* is mentioned as son of *Robert*. And if we suppose *Robert* to be son of *Adam*, we have then a compleat series from *Walter* down to the said *William*. Therefore we assume as second in our pedigree,

2. ADAM DE STIRKLAND, son of *Walter*.

3. ROBERT DE STIRKLAND knight. This *Robert*, by deed dated at his manor of Great Strickland on the eve of St. John Baptist in the 23 Hen. 3. granted to *William* his son and *Elizabeth* daughter of Ralph Daincourt knight, on their marriage, his whole manor of Great Strickland, with the services of free tenants there, together with the mill, woods, pastures, and other appurtenances; to hold to them and the heirs of their bodies, remainder to his own right heirs. Witnesses, Sir Thomas de Hellebeck, William de Warthecop, Henry Tyror, and others.—This Ralph Daincourt had a son Ralph, who died without issue; and Elizabeth succeeded to the inheritance.

The said *Robert* was witness to a grant of lands at Thrimby to the abbey of St. Mary's York, together with Thomas de Musgrave then sheriff of Westmorland, and other witnesses. Which Thomas was under-sheriff to Robert de Veteripont in the latter end of the reign of king Henry the third.

4. WILLIAM DE STIRKLAND knight, son of *Robert*. In the 4 Ed. 1. he was under-sheriff of the county.

In the 6 Ed. 1. we find *William de Strikeland* in possession of a third part of the manor and advowson of the church of Lowther.

By deed without date, John son of Thomas de Levens grants to *William de Stirkland* knight, son and heir of *Robert de Stirkland* knight, lands in the Howes, which lands he had from his mother Alice del Howes. Witnesses, Roger de Burton, Richard de Preston, knights; William de Windshover, Matthew de Redman,

CHAP. VI.

Redman, John and Benedict Garnet, John de Camera (or Chambre), and others.

In the 17 Ed. 1. the said *William* granted to John de Camera and Sybil his wife the demesne lands of Howes, adjoining to those of Sizergh. Witnesses whereof were, John de Rosgill, Robert le Englays, Roger de Burton, Richard de Preston, knights; William de Windeshovere, Gilbert de Culwen, Jeffrey de Melcanthorp, Alan Clericus, and others.

The said *William de Stirkland* married as aforesaid Elizabeth sister and heir of Ralph D'Aincourt. And in the 20 Ed. 1. there is a letter of attorney from *William de Stirkland* to Baldwin de Schepsheved to deliver seisin to *Walter* his son, of lands that had been his mother's, and other lands at Howes and Brigsteer.

In the same year, this *William de Stirkeland*, knight, grants and confirms as is aforesaid, to God and St. Mary and the abbot of St. Mary's York, and the monks of Wederhal, and of St. Beg's in Coupland, all the lands which they then had, of the gift and grant of *Walter de Stirkland* knight his great grandfather, and all other his ancestors, in the village and territory of Great Strikeland. Dated at Appilby on Thursday next after the feast of St. Wylfrid the archbishop, in the year of grace 1292, and in the 20th year of the reign of Edward the king. Witnesses, Michael de Hardclay, Thomas de Derwentwater, Hugh de Multon, knights; Robert de Warthwic, William de Wyndesover, William his son, Adam de Haverington, and many others *.

In the 27 Ed. 1. *William de Stirkland* was collector of the fifteenths in the county of Westmorland †.

By deed without date, Peter de Brus grants to the said *William* freedom from pulture of his foresters, as well horsemen as footmen, and also from witnesman, in all their lands of Hakethorp, Natland, Syresergh, and other places. Witnesses, William de Pickering seneschal, John de Burton, Roger de Barton, Henry Stanley, knights; Robert de Hormesayt, Geoffrey de Wateby, Thomas de Lancastre constable, and others.

In the 32 Ed. 1. there was an agreement between Sir *William de Stirkland* and *Walter* his son, touching waste and destruction in the lands that had been *Elizabeth*'s (mother of the said *Walter*) in Haversham, Barton, and Hakethorp; which waste and destruction were released by *Walter*, and thereupon Sir *William* releases to *Walter* his right to *Elizabeth*'s inheritance in Barton, with the services of freemen therein; and all lands, possessions, and services of free tenants, in the vills of Lowther and Lowther Quale, which he held of his wife's inheritance; rendering yearly 10*l.* to Sir William at Stirkland during his life, with power of distress and driving it to Stirkland.

This *William* granted to the priory of Cartmel the chapel of Croskrake in Stainton, which had been founded and endowed by Anselm de Furness; with all its rights, members, and appurtenances.

The said *William*, by deed without date, releases to William de Morland certain lands at Great Stirkland, which had been granted in trust to Sir Richard

* Registr. Wetheral.

† Machel from Dugdale.

de

de Agneta vicar of the church of Morland, for the use of Robert Timpleman, to hold of the said Robert by the yearly rent of one pound of ginger: The said *William* also grants, that the said lands shall be free from suit to his mill at Stirkland. Witnesses, Richard de Musegrave, Adam de Haverington, Hugh de Sourby, Geffrey de Milkanthorp, Robert de Newby, Robert de Hodelston, Thomas de Magna Stirkland, Adam de Helebek, and others.

5. WALTER DE STIRKLAND, knight, son of *William*. This *Walter* seems to have had a brother *William*: for there is a release from Margaret late wife of Hugh de la Vale, in her chaste widowhood, to this *Walter*, of lands in Stainton, which had been given by *William de Stirkland* to *William de Stirkland* her first husband. Witnesses, Hugh de Louther, Walter de Wessington, Robert de Swinburne, Thomas de Wessington, and others.

He had also a sister *Johan*; to whom, together with her husband Robert de Wessington, he gave 9 messuages, 5 oxgangs, and 40 acres of land, in frank marriage.

In the 35 Ed. 1. the king grants to his trusty and well beloved *Walter de Stirkeland* knight, free warren in all his demesne lands of Helsington, Heversham, and all other his lands in the county of Westmorland, for his good services in the parts of Scotland.

About the same time there was an agreement between the abbot and convent of St. Mary's York, and *Walter de Stirkland* knight, concerning a way in Helsington in the territory of Sizergh, for leading the tithe belonging to the church of Kendal. Witnesses whereof were, Nicholas de Layburn, Thomas de Pickering, Robert de Asleby, knights; Henry de Warthecopp, Patric de Culwen, and others. The original of which is yet extant at Sizergh, under the abbey seal, very fair.

This Sir *Walter* was knight of the shire for Westmorland, in the first, and again in the sixth year of Edward the second.

In the 15 Ed. 2. *Walter de Stirkland* was appointed sheriff of the county of Westmorland, from the 10th of February in that year, *quamdiu se bene gesserit* *.——And this most probably was, upon the attainder of Roger de Clifford in that year, for adhering to Thomas earl of Lancaster.

In the next year, there is an indenture, reciting that a *Quare Impedit* had been depending in the common pleas, between *Walter de Stirkland* plaintiff, and the prior of Watton defendant, concerning the advowson of the church of Lowther, in Hilary term in the present year, and that they accorded that the prior should have the presentation for the then turn, vacant by the death of William del Chappell, according to a composition before the justices in Eyre at York in the 8 Ed. 1. between this prior's predecessor complainant, and William de Stirkland defendant, concerning the advowson of the said church: And it is agreed, that Walter and his heirs and the prior and his successors shall present by turns. In the same year, and again in the 17 Ed. 2. he was knight of the shire.

* Machel from Dugdale.

CHAP. VI.

In the 6 Ed. 3. there is an indenture between William de Thweng knight and *Walter de Stirkland* knight, whereby it is agreed, that the said *Walter* shall inclose no more of the waste belonging to Brigsteer, but what was already inclosed should so remain. The said William de Thweng reserving to himself and his heirs, and to his fishermen of the Fors a bridle way through the lands so inclosed, to and from his fishery of the Fors at all seasons: And confirming to the said *Walter* his right of common, and liberty to cut down timber and underwood in all the woods there specified, for the use and service of his manor of Syresergh and tenants of Helsington. Reserving also to the said William and his heirs their free chase.—In the same year he was knight of the shire.

In the 7 Ed. 3. Sir *Walter Stirkland* grants to his son *John* all his lands of Whinfell, with the services of his free tenants there, remainder to his son *Thomas*, remainder to his son *Ralph*, in tail male, remainder to his own right heirs. Witnesses, Ralph de Betham, Roger de Brunolesheved, knights; Thomas de Roos, Richard de Preston, Matthew de Redman, and others.

In the 9 Ed. 3. he obtained a grant to inclose his wood and demesne lands at Sirefergh, and to make a park there, and hold the same so inclosed to him and his heirs for ever.

This Sir *Walter*, on the marriage of his eldest son *Thomas*, with Cecilia daughter of Robert de Wells, settled the manor of Hackthorp and his lands in Over Winder, Croftormont, and Thorp in Barton, and a messuage and 9 acres of land in Great Strickland, on the issue of that marriage, remainder to the heirs of the body of the said *Thomas*, with remainders to *John* and *Ralph* his other two sons. Witnesses, John de Stirkland, Hugh de Lowther, John de Rosegill, Gilbert de Lancastre, knights; William Lengleys of Askolm, Robert de Cliburn, Henry de Cundall, John son of Robert de Stirkland, and others.—The said *John* the son was knight of the shire in his father's life-time in the 1 Ed. 3. And in the 10 Ed. 3. he was sheriff of the said county.

In the 17 Ed. 3. this Sir Walter was again knight of the shire, and soon after died.

6. THOMAS DE STIRKLAND knight, son of *Walter*.—In the 23 Ed. 3. he was witness to a grant of lands by the abbot and convent of Shap to Sir Hugh de Lowther. Sir *John de Stirkland*, son of *Robert* was another witness.

In the 31 Ed. 3. Roger de Clifford (on his going over with the king into France, as it seemeth) assigns to Sir *Thomas de Stirkland* knight and Hugh de la Course, in trust, all his lands in England and Ireland, and also the reversion of the lands which his mother Isabella de Clifford was then in possession of. Dated at his castle of Appleby. The seal of this instrument is very perfect.

In the 35 Ed. 3. a patent was granted to *Thomas de Strikeland* to impark his woods in Helsington, Levenes, and Hackethorp, containing 300 acres; for his good service done in the parts of France *.

* Machel from Dugdale.

In the ſame year, Katharine de Roſs, daughter of the ſaid Sir Thomas, and widow of John de Roſs of Kendal caſtle, in her lawful and chaſte widowhood, aſſigns over to her ſaid father the wardſhip and marriage of her daughter Elizabeth de Roſs then in her cuſtody. Which Elizabeth was afterwards married to William del Parr knight.

In the 36 Ed. 3. there is an indenture of covenant between Sir *Thomas Strickland* knight and Ranulph de Dacre lord of Gilſland, concerning the marriage of *Walter* ſon and heir of the ſaid Thomas, with Margaret de Latham niece to the ſaid Ranulph; and Ranulph was to pay, in conſideration of the ſaid marriage, 20 *l* a year out of his lordſhips of Halton and Kellet in the county of Lancaſter (to be paid at Halton), till 240 marks ſhould be diſcharged.

In the 40 Ed. 3. this Sir *Thomas* made a ſettlement of lands at Siggeſwick and Levins, upon his younger ſons *John*, *Peter*, and *Thomas*, ſucceſſively, for life; remainder to his own right heirs.

In the 46 Ed. 3. he preſented *Walter de Wells* (probably a relation of his wife) to the rectory of Lowther.

He died about the laſt year of that king's reign, and his youngeſt ſon *Thomas* was his executor; as appears by a receipt from the abbot of St. Mary's York, of 4 *l* due from his father to the ſaid abbot.

7. Sir Walter de Stirkland knight, ſon and heir of *Thomas*.—In the 1 Ric. 2. this *Walter*, by an indenture dated at Lowther, becomes bound to John de Arleton and Alexander Walker, in the penal ſum of 100 *l*, to preſent to the next vacancy of the church of Lowther, John ſon of the ſaid Alexander and Agnes his wife; and if John ſhall not accept the ſame, then they were to forfeit to the ſaid *Walter* the ſum of 20 marks. (From the biſhop's regiſter it appears, that this John was not preſented.)

The ſaid *Walter* had no iſſue by his firſt wife Margaret aforeſaid, daughter of Sir Thomas de Latham.—He married, to his ſecond wife, Iſabella, daughter of John de Olney; which John, in the 5 Ric. 2. ſettled upon the iſſue of that marriage, a tenement in London, known by the name of the Great Place, ſituate in the pariſh of St. Mary at Hyll, with the advowſon of the ſame church; with all his other lands, tenements, and houſes within the liberties of London; as alſo a moiety of the manor of Compton Chamberlyn in the county of Wilts, with the advowſon of the church of Berford.

In the 14 Ric. 2. he was eſcheator for the king on the inquiſition *poſt mortem* of Thomas de Roos; and at the ſame time *John de Stirkland* (his brother) ſtands firſt in the liſt of jurors.

In the 18 Ric. 2. he was knight of the ſhire for Weſtmorland.

In the 6 Hen. 4. he was one of the jurors on the inquiſition *poſt mortem* of William del Parre.

He ſeems to have had a third wife Alice; for in the 9 Hen. 4. there is a releaſe from Alice late wife of *Walter de Stirkland* knight, to Sir *Thomas de Stirkland* knight and Mabel his wife of all her right of dower in the lands and tenements of which they were then infeoffed.

[A re-

CHAP. VI.

[A relation of this family was *William de Strickland*, who in the latter end of the reign of king Richard the second was chosen bishop of Carlisle; but being then opposed, he was again elected, and consecrated, in the first year of king Henry the fourth. He built one of the towers at Rose Castle, which still beareth the name of Strickland Tower. And at his own charges he caused a channel for a watercourse to be made for the use of the town of Penrith, out of Petterill a small river in Cumberland.]

8. Sir THOMAS DE STIRKLAND knight, son and heir of *Walter*.—In the 5 Hen. 5. he conveyed his whole estate to trustees, that if he should die in his voyage to serve the king, they should enfeoff Mabel his wife therein, during her chaste viduity; and if she should die before his son *Walter* should come of age, then they were to receive the profits during his nonage, delivering the same to William de Tunstall and John de Wessington.

In the 5 Hen. 6. the said Sir *Thomas* and Nicholas de Crofte esquire enter into articles and mutually bind themselves in the penal sum of 400*l* for the solemnization of a marriage between *Walter* son and heir apparent of the said Sir *Thomas*, and Douce daughter of the said Nicholas, when he the said *Walter* should attain his age of 14 years. Which marriage was in due time solemnized accordingly.

In the 6 Hen. 6. on an inquisition of knights fees in Westmorland, it appears, that Sir *Thomas Stirkland* knight held the third part of a knight's fee of Thomas Lumley then in ward to the king in Helsington, Haversham, Barton, Lowther, Whale, Hackthorpe, and Strickland Ketel.

In the next year he represented the county of Westmorland in parliament.

In the 9 Hen. 6. Sir *Thomas* went to London, and joined in the solemn cavalcade that was to attend the young king to Paris in order to his coronation. At Sandwich he made his will, and sent it down to Mabel his wife; which was as follows:

"In Dei nomine. Amen. In the year of the reign of Hen. 6. after the "conquest of England the nent. I *Thomas Styrkland* knight, in gud prosperity and hale mind, dispose my will in the maner and form that followys. "First, I betake my saule to almighty God and to his moder Mary, and to "all the holy court of heoven. And my body to be buryt in some haly kirke "or seyntwary quan almighty God shall see best tyme my saule to pass fro this "warde. Also it is my will that Mable my wife be my hale exectrixe, and have "hale ministracion on all my gudys, with the helpe and consel of Nyander "and John Wilson if it like her. And if ought come to me but gude, I "will that my wiffe have all my landys, tentys, rents, and dues, with their "appurtenances, with all my gudys muvable and immuvabyll, during the "nonage of *Wat* my son, to the quiting of my detys, and marrying and "helping of my two doghtyrs, and finding a prist to syngge for me and my "ancestors at Synt Kattin's auter in Kirkby Kendale thre years. Also it is "my will that quan my son comys to full age, that he have his londys de-"livert to him, aw to have, except my wiffes joynter and her dower; also "what the deeds thereof make mencyon, except the lands and rents I have

I "given

" given to *Robert* my ſon for term of life, in the quilke Richard Broughton and " Thomas Broughton priſts ſtand enfeoffed. Praying yow endeavour to think " on *Robert* and hald him to the ſkole. Alſo it war my will, that ye take " none huſbond, te my two doghters were maryt or holpyn. And after my " dettes quitt and my doghters maryt, the ſurplus of guds demiſe ye me at " your awne will. Praying you to have me excuſſett yff I write ſo ſhortly, " for it was writen in gret haſt at my ſchiping in Sandwightith. And this " pray you be dune als my moſt intire truſt is in you of all other creaturs " levyng."

In the 10 Hen. 6. Pope Eugenius the fourth granted to him and Mabel his wife licence for a domeſtic chapel and portable altar; which bull is yet extant, with the ſeal of lead very fair, about the breadth and ſomewhat more than double the thickneſs of an Engliſh half crown; with a croſs on one ſide, and underneath, EVGENIVS. PP. IIII. On the reverſe, two faces of venerable old men, and above, the letters SPASPE *.

10. WALTER STRICKLAND eſquire, ſon of Sir *Thomas*.—In the 15 Hen. 6. he had a grant of the office of keeper of the park of Calgarth: In the next year, the king appointed him receiver general of all his rents in and about Kendal, with a fee of 10*l* *per annum*, and 2*s* a day when upon the king's buſineſs. And after, in lieu of theſe, the king granted to him the pannage and herbage of the ſaid park, the fiſhing of Windermere, and all his lands and tenements in the hamlets of Applethwaite and Undermilbeck, for term of life, he paying to the king 5 marks yearly.

In the 18 of Hen. 6. he releaſed to the king the demand and claim of 1000 marks due to the ſaid *Walter* from the ſaid lord the king, for taking of Henry Talbot, a moſt notorious traytor *(proditoris excellentiſſimi)* of our lord Henry the fifth late king of England, by virtue of the proclamation of the ſaid late king; in conſideration of the king's granting to him the ſaid *Walter* the office of maſter of the king's dogs called *Heirers* †.

About the ſame time, he had a grant of certain alien abbey lands in the counties of Suſſex and Southampton for a term of years.

He ſeems to have been active and ſtrenuous in the Lancaſtrian cauſe, amongſt the civil diſſenſions of thoſe times: And of the forces he was able to raiſe,

* Eugenius epiſcopus, ſervus ſervorum Dei. Dilecto filio nobili viro Thomæ Stirkland militi, et dilectæ in Chriſto filiæ nobili mulieri Mabilæ ejus uxori, Eboracenis dioceſeos, ſalutem et apoſtolicam benedictionem. Sinceræ devotionis affectus, quem ad nos et Romanam geritis eccleſiam, non indigne meretur, ut petitionibus veſtris, illis præſertim quas ex devotionis fervore prodire conſpicimus, quantum cum Deo poſſumus, favorabiliter annuamus. Hinc eſt quod nos, veſtris devotis ſupplicationibus inclinati ut liceat vobis et cuilibet veſtrum habere altare portatile cum debita reverentia et honore, ſuper quo in locis ad hoc congruentibus et honeſtis poſſitis per propium vel alium ſacerdotem ydoneum miſſam et alia divina officia, ſine juris alieni præjudicio, in veſtra ac familiàrum veſtrorum domeſticorum præſentia facere celebrari, devotioni veſtræ tenore præſentium indulgemus. Nulli ergo omnino hominum liceat hanc paginam noſtræ conceſſionis infringere, vel ei auſu temerario contraire. Si quis autem hoc attemptare præſumpſerit, indignationem omnipotentis Dei et beatorum Petri et Pauli apoſtolorum ejus ſe noverit incurſurum. Datum Romæ apud ſanctum Petrum, anno incarnationis dominicæ milleſimo quadringenteſimo triceſimo primo, viii Kal. Julii, Pontificatus noſtri anno primo.

† Machel from Dugdale.

with

CHAP. VI.

with their proper habiliments, we have a muster roll yet extant, which seems to have been made out chiefly in respect of the border service. And an excellent method it was, in order to know what strength every lord of a manor could bring into the field on any emergency. And as such muster roll contained the names of all persons able to bear arms, we may from thence discover the increase or diminution of the number of people within the respective districts: And the account will turn out not much in favour of population. In some of the manors specified in the aforesaid muster roll, the numbers are decreased more than double *.

In

* The booke off Walter Strykelande esquier & depute steward off Kendal, his servants, tenants, and inhabitants within the countie of Westmerland of his inheritance thayre.
The *howsholde servants* of the said Walter Strykelande:
Rowlande Becke, horse harnes and a bowe.
Richard Atkinson, horse harnes and a bowe.
(And so, in like manner, nine servants more; with each, horse harnes and a bowe.)

Natland.

Thomas Macareth, horse harnes and a bowe.
Edward Macareth, horse harness and a bowe. (With 7 more.)
Bylmen within the same:
Thomas Waryner, horse harnes and a byll.
Thomas Syll, horse harnes and a byll. (With 11 more.)
Foytmen, with some harnes, others none:
Thomas Spence; a jak, a sallet, and a bowe.
Rowlland Myles; harnes, and a bowe.
Hew Hodson, a bowe.
Bryan Hyggyn, a bowe.
Bylls:
Jhon Atkynson, a jake and a byll.
Nycall Spyght, a sallet and a byll.
Robert Strykland, a sallet and a byll.
Henry Grenebanke, a byll.
James Kowper, a byll.
Edward Syll, a byll.
William Shipert, a byll.
Yongmen, bowys:
Nycholes Scherman, a bow, &c.
Yongmen, bylls:
George Bowman, a byll, &c.
Total in Natland, 55.

In *Stainton*, in like manner, 79.
In *Hencaster*, 16.
In *Syggysfwyke*, 48.
In *Whynfell* (that is, the moiety of it) 34.
In *Wynder*: Jhon Smyth; a horse, a jake, and a bowe.
Robert Walker; a horse, stel coyt, and a bowe.
William Lawson; a horse, stel coyt, and a bowe.
Jhon Busher, and 6 others, with each a horse, a jake, and a bowe.
Bylls:
Thomas Smyth, and 4 others; a horse, a jake, and a byll.
Footmen, without harnes:
Jhon Wynder, and 5 more; a bowe, or byll.
Yongmen:
William Smyth, and 6 others, each a bowe.
Total in Wynder 28.

In

In the 20 Hen. 6. he was knight of the shire for Westmorland.

In the 27 Hen. 6. he was retained (according to the custom of those times) by Richard earl of Salisbury to serve him in peace and war. The original instrument of which retainer is yet preserved at Sizergh hall, and is as follows: "This endenture made bitwen Richard Erl of Salisbury on the tone partie, "and Waultier Strykland son and heir of Sir Thomas Strykland knyght on "the tothre, bereth witnesse, that the same Waultier is beheste [*retained*] and "with-holded with the said Erl, for terme of his life, ayenst al folkes, sav"ying his ligeance, And the said Waultier shal bee wele and couvenably "horsede, armede, and arrayede, and alway redy to ride, come, and go with, "to, and for the said Erl, at al tymes and into al places on this sid and be"yond the see, as wele in tyme of paix as of werre, that he bee warned by "the said Erl on his behalve, at the wages and costes resonnables of the same "Erl. Takyng the said Waultier yerely for his fee of the said Erl ten markes "of money of thissues and profitts of the lordship of Penreth, with thappur"tenances; Givin by the handes of the receivor there beeing for the tyme; "at the festes of Martynmesse and Whitsonday by even porcons. And the "said Waultier shall take of the said Erl in tyme of werre suche wages as then "he yeveth to othre of his degree rebatyng of suche wages of werre thaffer-

In *Hacktborp*:
Thomas Wyllen; a horse, a jake, and a spere.
Henry Danson; a horse, a jake, and a bowe.
Jhon Chappelhow; a horse, a jake, and a bowe.
Bylls:
Christopher Wyllen, horse harnes and a byll.
Rychard Mylne; a horse, a jake, and a byll.
Robert Taylyer; a horse, a jake, and a byll.
Christopher Chappelhow; a horse, a jake, and a byll.
Jhon Banke; a horse, a jake, and a byll.
Jhon Dobson, a horse, a jake, and a byll.
William Hudson, a horse and a byll.
Footemen, with parte harnes:
Thomas Chappelhow, a jake and a bowe.
Renald Water, a jake and a byll.
Thomas Stevenson, a jake and a byll.
Footemen, without harness:
Rychard Willen, a byll.
Hew Sands, a byll.
Yongmen:
Henry Sawkelt, a bowe.
Rolland Willen, a bowe.
Jhon Taylyer, a bowe.
Robert Myllne, a bowe.
Edward Ayray, a byll.

The hoole noumber: Bowmen horsyd and harnassed, lxix.
Bylmen horsyd and harnassed, lxxiiii.
Bowmen without hors harnasse, lxxi.
Bylmen without hors harnasse, lxxvi.
Totalis numerus CCLXXXX.

Note, The *jack* was a coat of mail, scale-wise, covered with leather, and in that respect differed from the steel coat. *Sallet* was an helmet of iron.

CHAP. VI.

"rance of his wages in tyme of paix. And the said Erl shal have the thrid of "al wynnyngs of werre to bee wonne or geten by the said Waukier or eny of "his men that he shal have at the costes and wages of the same Erl. And if "eny captaigne or man of estate bee taken by the said Waultier or eny of "his said men, the said Erl shal have him, dooying to the taker resonnable "rewarde for him. In witnesse of which thing, the parties aforesaid to the "partes of this endenture have entrechangeably set their seals. Yeven the "furst day of Septembre the xxvii yere of the reign of king Henry sexe sith "the conquest."

On the house of York prevailing, there was a reverse of fortune to the friends and partizans of the house of Lancaster. Accordingly, in the 1 Ed. 4. we find a charter of pardon granted to *Walter Strickland*, son and heir of Sir Thomas Strickland knight, of all trespasses, treasons, murders, and other offences, committed before the 4th day of November last.

In the 4 Ed. 4. *Walter Strickland* esquire settles on Agnes wife of his son *Thomas* his manor of Wynder, with all his lands in the parish of Barton, and other lands in Kendale; remainder to the said *Thomas* in fee.

This *Walter* had also a daughter *Margaret*, married to William son of Richard Redman, whose marriage portion was 200 marks. For which marriage a dispensation was obtained from Vincent Clement the pope's nuncio.

10. Sir THOMAS STRICKLAND knight, son and heir of *Walter*.—In the 1 Ric. 3. he grants to Thomas Chambre a messuage and 25 acres of land in Siggiswick, paying to the said Sir Thomas yearly two farthings for all services.

In the 6 Hen. 7. he infranchised 82 tenants in the vills of Kirkby in Kendale, Seggiswick, Hencaster, Brigster, Levens, Sizergh, and Stainton.

In the 9 Hen. 7. he settles divers lands on *Walter* his son and heir; whose wife's name was Elizabeth.

In the 10 Hen. 7. The right reverend father in God William abbot of St. Mary's York, and parson of the parish church of Kirkby in Kendale, together with the convent, demise and lease to Sir *Thomas Strickland* knight all the tithes of Natland and the tithes of a moiety of Whinfell, for nine years.

11. WALTER STRICKLAND esquire, son and heir of Sir *Thomas*.—In the 13 Hen. 7. he gave a letter of attorney to *Gervase Strickland* to take livery of all his lands in Westmorland.

In the same year, there is an indenture between this *Walter* of the one part, and John Preston of Preston-hall esquire and Elyn late wife of Richard Redman of Thornton of the other part; whereby it is covenanted, that *Walter* son and heir of this *Walter* shall, within ten years after the execution of the said indenture, marry Agnes daughter of the said Richard Redman.

In the 16 Hen. 7. he granted all his lands to Sir Thomas Dacre knight, Thomas Parr, Thomas Middleton, John Pennington, esquires, and *Thomas Strickland*, rector of the church of Gosford; together with the manors of Sizergh, Stainton, Siggiswick, Hencastre, Natland, Whinfell, Hackthorp, Winder, with all the burgages in Kirkby in Kendale, with an acre and an half

of

of land in Lowther, with the advowson of the church there; in trust for the purposes of his will. CHAP. VI.

12. Sir Walter Strickland knight.—In the 19 Hen. 7. he was constituted by George lord Lumley his seneschal (or steward) of Kendal for life.

In the 10 Hen. 8. he had a charter of pardon for all trespasses and neglect of homage, with a renewal of the grant of all the manors and lands which his father Walter was found seised of at his death, and were held of the king *in capite*.

This Sir *Walter* was much afflicted with an asthma, which gave occasion to the following indenture: "This indenture made 26 Apr. 18 Hen 8. between "Sir Walter Strickland knight, of one part; and Alexander Kenet, doctor of "physic, on the other part: Witnesseth, that the said Alexander permitteth, "granteth, and by these presents bindeth him, that he will, with the grace "and help of God, render and bring the said Sir Walter Strickland to per-"fect health of all his infirmities and diseases contained in his person, and "especially stomach, and lungs, and breast, wherein he has most disease and "grief; and over to minister such medicines truly to the said Sir Walter "Strickland, in such manner and ways as the said Mr. Alexander may make "the said Sir Walter heal of all infirmities and diseases in as short time as "possible may be, with the grace and help of God. And also the said Mr. "Alexander granteth he shall not depart at no time from the said Sir Walter "without his licence, unto the time the said Sir Walter be perfect heal, with "the grace and help of God. For the which care, the said Sir Walter Strick-"land granteth by these presents, binding himself to pay or cause to be paid "to the said Mr. Alexander or his assigns 20*l* sterling monies of good and "lawful money of England, in manner and form following; that is, 5 marks "to be paid upon the first day of May next ensuing, and all the residue of the "said sum of 20*l* to be paid parcel by parcel as shall please the said Sir Wal-"ter, as he thinks necessary to be delivered and paid in the time of his dis-"ease, for sustaining such charges as the said Mr. Alexander must use in me-"dicine, for reducing the said Sir Walter to health; and so the said payment "continued and made, to the time the whole sum of 20*l* aforesaid be fully "contented and paid. In witness whereof, either to these present indentures "have interchangeably set their seals, the day and year above mentioned."—Sir Walter, nevertheless, died on the 9th of January following, as appears by inquisition.

By his wife Agnes Redman he had no issue. He married a second wife Catharine daughter and heir of Sir Ralph Nevell of Thornton Briggs in the county of York knight, by his wife daughter and coheir of Sir Christopher Ward knight; by whom he had issue a son *Walter* who succeeded him, and two daughters, namely, *Elizabeth* married to Sir William Strickland of Boynton on the Would in the county of York knight, and *Agnes* married to Sir Thomas Curwen of Workington knight.

The said Catharine survived her said husband, and was afterwards married to Henry Brough esquire, and after him to William Kniut esquire; as appears by

CHAP. VI.

by feveral fines levied by the faid Catharine late wife of Sir Walter Strkland knight, and her faid hufbands refpectively.

13. WALTER STRICKLAND of Sizergh, and alfo of Thornton Briggs, efquire. He was a minor at his father's death, and in ward to the king till the 29th of Hen. 8. when he had livery of his lands: In the fchedule whereof, mention is made of an uncle of the faid *Walter* by the name of Sir *Thomas Strickland* knight, who lived at Sizergh during the minority of his nephew.

In the 29 Hen. 8. the king, on appointing Sir Thomas Wharton deputy warden of the Weft Marches, and Sir Thomas Wentworth captain of the town and caftle of Carlifle, fent a fpecial commiffion to *Walter Strickland* efquire, commanding him to affift with his perfon and power the faid warden and captain in the execution of their office, in the adminiftration of juftice, and keeping of the peace in the borders. For which, and in confideration of paft fervice, the king granted him a penfion for life.

In the 5 Eliz. he was knight of the fhire.

He married Alice daughter of Nicholas Tempeft of Holm in the county of Durham efquire, and relict of Chriftopher Place of Halnaby in the county of York; and died in the 11 Eliz. as appears by inquifition.

14. Sir THOMAS STRICKLAND, knight of the Bath, fon and heir of *Walter*. He was under age at the time of his father's death; and his mother Alice Strickland of Halnaby in the county of York widow, for the fum of 700 *l*, purchafed of the crown the cuftody, wardfhip, and marriage of the faid Thomas.

In the 15 Eliz. there is an indenture between Alice Strickland widow and *Thomas* her fon and heir apparent, and *Alice* her daughter, reciting part of the will of Walter Strickland efquire her late hufband, and that fhe had the wardfhip and marriage of her fon.—In the 23 Eliz. he came of age, and had livery of his lands.

His mother married again to her third hufband Sir Thomas Boynton, whom alfo fhe furvived. For in the 29 Eliz. there is a deed, whereby lady Boynton, after recital of her two laft widowhoods, and that fhe was devifee for life from the late *Walter Strickland* of Sizergh efquire, of the parks of Sizerh, Lawkrig, Brigftere, and Natland, and of lands in Helfington, releafes her right thereof to her fon *Thomas Strickland* efquire.—In the fame year there is a releafe from the faid *Thomas* to Alice lady Boynton his mother.—And in the 31 Eliz. there is a releafe from Francis Boynton efquire to his brother-in-law Thomas Strickland efquire.

In the 43 Eliz. he was knight of the fhire; and again in the firft year of king James; which king on the 24th of July, being the day preceding his coronation, created him knight of the Bath.

He married to his firft wife Elizabeth Symon of Briftol, and had iffue by her *Alice* married to Sir William Webb knight, equerry to prince Henry.

To his fecond wife he married Margaret daughter of Sir Nicholas Curwen of Workington knight, and by her had iffue *Robert*, *Thomas*, *Walter* (from whom

whom descended the Stricklands of Catterick in Yorkshire), *Dorothy* third wife of John Fleming of Ridal esquire, and *Margaret* second wife of George Preston of Holker in the county of Lancaster esquire.

He died about the 12th year of king James the first, and was succeeded by his son and heir,

15. Sir ROBERT STRICKLAND, knight. In the 21st year of king James, he represented the county of Westmorland in parliament.

In the civil wars, in the reign of king Charles the first, he embarked early in the royal cause. In the year 1638, he received a colonel's commission from the lord viscount Wentworth lord lieutenant of the county of York, to command 900 militia in the North Riding for the king's service. And in 1640, he received the king's commission from Algernon earl of Northumberland to regiment, accoutre, and march the same to Newcastle upon Tyne. After this he received a third commission to command a troop of horse. Which horse and foot he is said to have supported in a great measure at his own expence. At the battle of Edgehill, he himself commanded the horse, and his son Sir *Thomas Strickland* commanded the regiment of foot.

His wife was Margaret eldest of the three daughters and coheirs of Sir William Alford of Bylton in Cleveland in the county of York knight; by whom he had issue, besides his eldest son Sir *Thomas Strickland*, another son *Walter Strickland* esquire.

In the year 1646, there is an indenture between Sir *Robert Strickland* knight and *Margaret* his wife, Sir *Thomas Strickland* knight their son and heir apparent, *Thomas Strickland* second brother of Sir Robert, and *Walter Strickland* third brother of Sir Robert, of the one part; and Sir John Mallory and Richard Aldbrough esquire, of the other part; containing covenants of an intended settlement upon the marriage of Sir *Thomas*, with Jane widow of Sir Christopher Dawney baronet.

This Sir *Robert* lived till after king Charles the second's restoration: for in the next year after the said restoration, he was constituted by Thomas viscount Falconbergh one of the deputy lieutenants of the North Riding of the county of York.

At Sizergh hall there is a valuable portrait of this Sir Robert in armour*.

* At this time was *Walter lord Strickland* one of the 43 peers created by Oliver Cromwell, who was second son of Sir William Strickland of Boynton. He was one of the commissioners in this county, for putting in execution an ordinance of Cromwell's parliament in 1656, for levying an assessment of 60000*l* a month in nature of a land-tax. The commissioners for Westmorland were these: Lord Richard Cromwell, Sir Thomas Widdrington knight speaker of the parliament, Philip lord Wharton, Charles lord Howard, Walter lord Strickland, Christopher Lister, Thomas Burton, George Downing, Thomas Lilburn, Robert Branthwaite, Francis Sisson, Edward Briggs, John Archer, and Roger Bateman, esquires: Edmund Branthwaite, Robert Atkinson, James Cock, William Garnet, Richard Burton, Robert Skaife, and John Lowson gentlemen. [Those for Cumberland were, Col. Charles Howard, Sir George Fletcher baronet; Sir Wilfrid Lawson knight; George Downing, William Brisco, John Barwis, Lancelot Fletcher, esquires; Thomas Graister, Cuthbert Studholm, Arthur Foster, Thomas Langhorn, John Hudson, Gawin Wren, William Thompson, Henry Tolson, Thomas Lamplugh, William Orfeur, John Salkeld, esquires; Robert Brisco, Robert Hutton, Thomas Sewel, Nicholas Studholm, Thomas Laiths, gentlemen.]

16. Sir

CHAP. VI.

16. Sir THOMAS STRICKLAND knight, and alſo banneret, being ſo created in the field by the king in perſon.

In 1661, he was knight of the ſhire for Weſtmorland.

He married to his firſt wife Jane daughter and coheir of John Moſeley of Ulſkelfe in the county of York eſquire, and relict as aforeſaid of Sir Chriſtopher Dawney of Cowick in the ſaid county baronet, and by her had iſſue ſeveral children, all of whom died in their infancy.

After her deceaſe he ſettled his eſtate on his younger brother *Walter*, who married Barbara daughter of the lord Falconbergh; but *Walter* dying without iſſue, the eſtate reverted, and Sir *Thomas*, at the age of 53, married to his ſecond wife Winifred daughter and heir of Sir Charles Trentham of Roceſter in the county of Stafford knight; and by her had iſſue, (1) *Walter*. (2) *Robert*, who died at Sizergh unmarried, and lies interred in the family burying-place in Kendal church. (3) *Roger*, who was page to the prince of Conde when he went from France to be elected king of Poland, and died unmarried about the 24th year of his age. (4) *Thomas*, who dedicated himſelf to the church, and was for many years biſhop of Namur, where he made great additions to the cathedral, built an epiſcopal palace, and founded and endowed a ſeminary; and alſo within 3 or 4 miles of the city built the ſhell of a country houſe, but did not live to finiſh it. He was ſent ambaſſador to England by the emperor Charles the ſixth. He died at Namur in the year 1743, and was buried in his own cathedral.

This Sir *Thomas* was one of the privy council to king James the ſecond, whoſe fortunes he followed into France and died there, and was buried in the church of the Engliſh nuns at Roan in Normandy, where an handſome monument was erected to his memory. His lady alſo died abroad, and was interred in the ſame church.

17. WALTER STRICKLAND eſquire ſucceeded his father Sir *Thomas*. He married Anne daughter of Gerard Salvin of Croxdale in the county of Durham eſquire, and by her had iſſue, (1) *Thomas*. (2) *Gerard* (now living, in 1770) who married firſt Mary Bagnal, and by her hath iſſue one ſon and two daughters; to his ſecond wife he married the lady Gaſcoign relict of Sir Edward Gaſcoign baronet. (3) *Mary*, who died at Roan in Normandy, at the age of 15 and unmarried.

18. THOMAS STRICKLAND eſquire, ſon of the ſaid *Walter*, married Mary daughter of Simon Scroop of Danby eſquire; and by her had iſſue, beſides three children who died young, (1) *Walter*. (2) *William*, now living, who embraced a religious life in the Romiſh church. (3) *Charles*.

The ſaid Mary died in 1737, in the 30th year of her age, and lies buried in Kendal church. Her huſband married to his ſecond wife the widow of John Archer of Oxenholme eſquire, but by her had no iſſue.

19. WALTER STRICKLAND eſquire ſucceeded his father, and married Margaret daughter of Michael James Meſſenger of Fountain-abbey in the county of

of York esquire, and died in the year 1761, without issue. He was succeeded by his brother.

20. CHARLES STRICKLAND esquire, who married Cecilia only daughter of William Townley of Townley in the county of Lancaster esquire, by his wife Cecilia daughter and sole surviving heir of Ralph Standish of Standish in the county of Lancaster esquire (by the lady Philippa Howard his wife second daughter of Henry duke of Norfolk), and died in 1770, leaving issue *Thomas*, *William*, *Mary*, and *Charles*.

21. *Thomas Strickland* esquire, now an infant.

The ARMS of *Strickland* are; Sable, three escalops within a bordure ingrailed Argent.

Sizergh hall is a venerable old building, in a pleasant situation, formed like the rest in ancient time, for a place of defence. The tower is a square building, defended by two square turrets and battlements. One of them is over the great entrance, and has a guard-room capable of containing ten or a dozen men, with embrasures. The winding stair-case terminates in a turret, which defends the other entrance.

There is in this house an apartment called the Queen's, with the royal arms therein. From whence it hath been vulgarly imagined that this place belonged to the crown; and it is said that these arms were put up by queen Katherine Parr, widow of king Henry the eighth. This perhaps may be true, that the said queen might be admitted to retire to this place after the king's death; but it did not then belong to the crown, but to the Strickland family, as it had done long before. Nor could the queen reside here long; for she married again so soon after the king's death, that had she then proved pregnant, it was said that it would be doubtful to what husband the child should belong, and she died in the year following.

The CHAPEL of Helsington, in point of situation and neatness of building is inferior to few of the chapels within this parish; affording a beautiful and romantic prospect, of the sea, woods, rocks, and a fertile valley below. It was founded in the year 1726, by John Jackson of Holeslack gentleman; who gave an estate called Scar-house in Helsington, towards a yearly stipend for a teaching curate: so as a chapel, with vestry or school-house annexed, should be erected, and a chapel yard sufficiently fenced out; with all ornaments and conveniences belonging to the same. All which was accordingly effected, by contribution of the inhabitants, and his own further donation.

Afterwards he gave another estate, called Chamber tenement, within the said chapelry, on condition that the inhabitants should raise 100*l* towards obtaining an augmentation from the governors of queen Anne's bounty. In pursuance whereof, the sum of 44*l* 12*s* 0*d* was subscribed by the inhabitants; and the remainder, being 55*l* 8*s* 0*d*, was given by Mr. Mason the curate. In consideration of which estate, and of the said sum of 100*l*, the governors of the

2

CHAP. VI.

the said bounty gave 200*l*: With which sum of 200*l*, a field was purchased called Kirkbarrow, within a place called Churchfield, adjoining to Kirkland; and the remaining sum of 100*l* was laid out in a parcel of land called Rawnrigg in Barbon in this county.

And in the year 1745, the said chapel was consecrated by bishop Peplowe, by the name of the chapel of St. John.

In the year 1762, the late bishop of Chester, Dr. Keene, procured 200*l* from the countess dowager Gower, towards a further augmentation; which augmentation being obtained from the said governors, the whole sum of 400*l* was laid out in the purchase of an estate at Scarfoot in Underbarrow. And the whole revenue of the chapel, from the several estates above mentioned, amounts to about 80*l* a year; which renders it worthy of the acceptance of a clergyman of liberal education. The present curate is the reverend John Wilson, M. A. fellow of Trinity college in Cambridge; to whose learning, industry, and knowledge, we are indebted for several useful informations in this part of the county.

And to this chapel, being of so late foundation, the vicar hath undoubted right of nomination; whereas in many of the other chapelries, the inhabitants prescribe to nominate by custom for time immemorial.

The said Mr. Jackson gave also a small parcel of land called Jack Parrock for the use of the chapel clerk: and 13*s* 4*d* yearly, being one moiety of the rent of a shop in Kendal, for teaching three poor boys or girls of the said township, in reading, writing, and arithmetic; to be named by the curate, and the executrix of the said John Jackson, her heirs or assigns for ever.

NATLAND.

Advancing Eastward from *Helsington*, we come to NATLAND, which is a small manor or lordship, containing only about 30 families. It seems to have had its name from the *Nativi* or bondmen probably placed there, as attendent upon the capital lord at Kendal castle to do servile offices, like as the inhabitants of *Bondgate* nigh Appleby, or the *Drengage* tenants nigh Brougham castle. The chapelry also of Natland is commensurate to the manor.

It is of the Marquis Fee, and hath of a long time been the property of the *Strickland* family of Sizergh.

Upon the death of *Walter Strickland* esquire, in the 11 Eliz. the inquisition finds, that he held of the heir of Thomas Parr knight the manor of Natland, with the appurtenances, as of the fourth part of the barony of Kendale, by knights service; and that it was worth by the year 26*l* 9*s* 10*d*. And that he held in Natland 16 acres of pasture ground, and 30 acres of wood called Natland Park; of the yearly value of 16*s* 8*d*.

His great grandson Sir *Thomas Strickland* knight sold to the tenants their estates to freehold, except some few fields and a cottage or two, which continue of arbitrary tenure and heriotable, of which the owners at that time probably were not able to purchase the infranchisement.

The

The park aforefaid hath been long ago difparked.

At the time of Mr. Machel's furvey, there was at Natland a ruinated *chapel*, 9 yards long and near 5 yards wide; without any chapel-yard, or any falary belonging to it. About the year 1735, the inhabitants rebuilt the fame, and gave the profits of two inclofures belonging to the townfhip, together with an annual fubfcription, to a perfon who fhould teach their children, and read prayers in the chapel on Sundays.

In the year 1746, an augmentation of 200 *l* by the governors of queen Anne's bounty came to this chapel by lot, with which an eftate was purchafed in Skelfmergh. And in 1749, it received a further augmentation by lot of 200 *l*; and in 1754 was again augmented with 400 *l*, viz. 200 *l* from the faid governors, 100 *l* from the truftees of archbifhop Bolter late primate of Ireland, and 100 *l* from the executors of the late Dr. Stratford; which whole fum of 600 *l* was laid out in the purchafe of two eftates, one in Old Hutton and the other in Barbon. And the whole revenue now amounts to about 33 *l* a year.

The moft remarkable place within this chapelry is *Water-Crook*, half a mile north from the chapel, and about as much fouth from Kendal church. It is fo called from a remarkable turn in the water, the river Kent almoft furrounding it, in the fhape of an horfe-fhoe. The area inclofed by the turn of the water is about eight acres.

The Romans, obferving the advantage of the fituation, placed a fort or ftation here, which feems to have been the *Concangium* of the *Notitia*. Mr. Machel, on a perfonal furvey, fays, That there have been dug up here fragments of Roman urns, bricks, and cement; and an oven was found under ground, being built with bricks or tiles on the infide fixed one into another, run over with cement half a foot thick, and the bottom paved with bricks one foot broad and three inches thick.

Amongft the ruins was found a Roman floor 16 inches deep, of three courfes, the loweft courfe being a cement of lime and fand with fome pounded brick about 9 inches deep, then a courfe of gravel and pebbles about 4 inches, then a courfe of true Roman cement with great ftore of pounded brick in it about 3 inches.

There were refervoirs of water made of the fame cement. And a femicircular courfe of vacuities like ovens, divided by a thin brick between each.

Within the area, there are marks of trenches about 140 yards fquare, with many foundations of buildings.

The angles of the fquare fort appear to have been rounded after the Roman fafhion.

Mr. Horfley takes notice of feveral coins and feals that have been found here, and fome broken altars and ftatues. One infcription of the fepulchral kind he hath in part preferved, fo far as he was able to make it out, which is as follows:

Publius Ælius Publii filius Sergia tribu Baffus Quæftor defignatus legionis vicefimæ valentis victricis vixit annos ...... et Publius Rivatus liberti et Hero ...... miles legionis fextæ victricis faciendum curarunt. Si quis in hoc fepulchrum alium mortuum intulerit inferet fifco dominorum noftrorum ......

CHAP. VI. Above the station, nearer unto Kendal, a little below the bridge, is a place very suitable for the purpose, which still bears the name of *Watch-field*; in a most delightful situation, now belonging to Mr. John Lambert.

SCALTHWAITE RIGG, HAY, AND HUTTON IN THE HAY.

Scalthwaite Rigg is variously written of old time: It seems to be derived from *scale*, a *shelter*, shed, or hut for habitation; from whence comes also the word *shield*; so the *shell* of a fish, or of a nut, is by the common people still pronounced *skell*.——*Hutton*, adjoining, is of the same import; being the place where they had erected *huts* or cottages in the forest or hunting ground, now distinguished by the names of *Old* and *New Hutton*.——Within the *inclosed* hunting ground or park, which the word *Hay* imports, the scales or huts there erected, by way of further distinction, were denominated *Hutton in the Hay*. And this distinction seems to have been made, upon the division of the estate between the two sisters before mentioned of William de Lancastre the third. For *Old* and *New Hutton* are of the Richmond Fee; and *Scalthwaite Rigg*, *Hay*, and *Hutton in the Hay*, are of the Marquis Fee.——*Thwaite*, the other component of the word first above mentioned, means a parcel of ground where the wood has been grubbed up and cleared away.

In the 15 Eliz. part of the dower assigned to the widow of William Parr, marquis of Northampton, was as follows:

"Manor of *Skaltwaitrigg*: Every tenant by ancient custom is to pay yearly "to the lord at the keeping of his court for his greenhew 2 *d*, or else 1 *d* and "an hen.—Total of the yearly rent of the demesnes, 10 *l* 16 *s* 8 *d*. Of the "tenantrights, 12 *l* 5 *s* 0¼ *d*. And of the greenhews, 3 *s* 2 *d*. In all, 23 *l*. "4 *s* 10¼ *d*.

"The manor of *Hey*: Total of the tenantright there, 13 *l* 6 *s* 5½ *d*.

"The manor of *Hutton*: Total of the tenantright there, 9 *l* 2 *s* 7¼ *d*."

In the 28 Cha. 2. by the survey made by order of queen Catherine aforesaid, there were found, of the Marquis Fee, customary rents;—*Skalthwaite Rigg*, for 9 tenements, 12 *l* 5 *s* 0¼ *d*.—*Hay*, for 23 tenements, 13 *l* 3 *s* 3 *d*.—*Hutton in the Hay*, for 19 tenements, 8 *l* 18 *s* 2½ *d*.

OLD HUTTON, NEW HUTTON, AND HOLME SCALES.

At first there was only one general name of Hutton. The distinction between Old and New Hutton seems to have come in about the beginning of the reign of king Edward the first.

Holme Scales is in the parish of *Burton*; being, as the name imports, *scales* or huts belonging to *Holme* in that parish. But for the sake of vicinity and convenience, *Holme Scales* hath for a long time been annexed to *Old Hutton*, and is now deemed part of that township or constablewick.

About the time of the reign of king Richard the first, *Gilbert son of Roger Fitz-Reinfred* granted to *Thomas son of Gospatric*, who was founder, or at least a great benefactor to the abbey of Preston (which was afterwards removed to Shap), all his lands in Kendale, to wit, *Holme*, *Preston*, and *Hoton*, with the appurtenances, to hold of him and his heirs, by the service of the fourth part of one knight's fee; and by this service, that the said Thomas and his heirs should be quit against him the said Gilbert and his heirs of 43 *s*, which the said Thomas and his ancestors had paid yearly for the farm and cornage of the said land *. And at the dissolution of the said abbey, it appears that the abbot and convent had lands in Hutton; which without doubt had been given to them by the said Thomas.

In the next generation, *William de Lancastre* granted and confirmed to *Patric* son of the said *Thomas son of Gospatric* and his heirs, the charter which *Gilbert* son of *Roger Fitz-Reinfred*, father of the said *William*, granted to the said *Thomas*, of the lands in Kendale which he held of the said *Gilbert*, in *Preston*, *Holme*, and *Hutton*; described by these boundaries: As the water of Ebakerdale falls into the water of Hoton; and so going up to the rivulet running from Surthwaite to the way under Surthwaite; and so going up that way to the higher parts of Stamburild; and so across to Raiseherling; and from Raiseherling to below the Dubbs eastward; and from the Dubbs to the ancient boundaries of Luptoun to Hordpotrig. And for this grant and confirmation Patric granted to the said William, that he the said Patric would find *puture* to two of William's foresters, being on foot, in the vills of Hoton and Preston, as other his neighbours do, when it shall so happen, and as they are bound; and that the said Patric's men of the said vills shall find to the same foresters *witnesman*, in matters appertaining to the said forest †.

In the 25 Ed. 1. *John de Culwene* grants and confirms to *Patric de Culwene* his brother and the heirs of his body, all his land at Old Hoton and Holme Scales, with the mill and services of his free tenants there; except the wood of Hoton, in which nevertheless the said Patric shall have estovers for housboote and hayboote; and shall have his hogs there free from pannage. Rendring to him the said *John* one penny of silver yearly at the Nativity of our Lord, for all services ‡.

And in the 7 Ed. 3. *Gilbert de Culwene*, lord of Wirkington, releases and quitclaims to *Thomas de Culwene* son of *Patric de Culwene* knight his uncle, all his lands of Old Hutton and Holme Scales in Kendale, with the mill and homages of the free tenants there; to hold to the said Thomas and the heirs of his body. Rendring to the said Gilbert and his heirs yearly one penny of silver at the Nativity of our Lord, for all services. Witnesses: Ralph de Bethome, Roger de Layburne, Roger de Bronnolsheved, knights; Richard de Preston, John de Washington, John de Haverington de Threnby, Thomas Warde, and others. Dated at Penrithe on Wednesday next after the feast of Pentecost, in the year aforesaid ‖.

The manor of Old Hutton hath been infranchised of a long time. In a bundle of Escheats, towards the beginning of the reign of king Charles the first,

* Rawlinson. † Id. ‡ Id. ‖ Id.

CHAP. VI. first, the tenements in Old Hutton and Holme Scales appear to have been held of the king as of his manor of Kirkby in Kendale called the Richmond Fee, in socage, by payment of certain rents. This manor, together with many freehold rents, after several mesne conveyances, is now the property of Sir Michael le Fleming of Rydal baronet.

In New Hutton, which also is of the Richmond Fee, there are only about two tenements of freehold.

The *chapel* of *Old Hutton* was built about the year 1628, and rebuilt in 1699. The original chapel salary, like as of many of the rest, seems to have been twenty nobles, or 6 *l* 13 *s* 4 *d*; of which, four nobles were paid by the inhabitants of Holme Scales (as certified in 1717), who had seats in the chapel; but they afterwards with-held the payment on pretence of their being within another parish. The remaining sixteen nobles were then reduced to somewhat less than fifteen, *viz.* 4 *l* 17 *s* 10 *d*: And the ancient salary is now only 4 *l* 12 *s* 0 *d*. Mr. Henry Bateman devised lands to this chapel, which in 1717 were certified at 5 *l* 10 *s* 0 *d* yearly. And in the year 1706, one Thomas Robinson of Old Hutton gave by his will 5 *l* a year to this chapel for an afternoon sermon. About 30 years ago, this chapel received an augmentation by lot of 200 *l*. from the governors of queen Anne's bounty. The executors of the will of the late Dr. Stratford gave 100 *l*, unto which was added another 100 *l* by other benefactors, and therewith a further augmentation of 200 *l* was procured from the said governors. With all which sums lands have been purchased.

Nigh unto the chapel is the *school*, which was built at the expence of Edward Milner of Kendal yeoman; and endowed by him, in 1613, with nigh 20 *l* a year. It was rebuilt and rendered more commodious by contribution of the inhabitants and others in 1753. In this school there is a considerable parochial library, established in the year 1757.

Belonging to this township is an estate given by Roger Ward of Old Hutton, now of the value of 8 *l* a year; to be distributed among the poor housholders of Old Hutton and Holme Scales.

There is also a rent charge of 26 *s* 8 *d* issuing out of an estate at Bendridge in the said township, to be applied to the like purposes.

The aforesaid Thomas Robinson gave 12 loaves weekly to be distributed amongst 12 poor housholders. And Joseph Dawson, alderman of Kendal, gave other 12, to be distributed in like manner.

The *chapel* of *New Hutton* was built in the year 1739, and endowed by contribution of the inhabitants of New Hutton, Hay, and Hutton in the Hay, with 200 *l*; whereby an augmentation of 200 *l* was procured from the governors of queen Anne's bounty, and an estate purchased therewith in Killington. In 1756, a further augmentation of 200 *l* by lot fell to the said chapel, wherewith an estate was purchased at Grayrigg.

The rents of these two estates make up the whole revenue of the chapel.

DOCKER.

DOCKER.

This manor belonged to the hoſpital of St. Peter's, afterwards called the hoſpital of St. Leonard's, in York. This hoſpital had divers poſſeſſions in Weſtmorland, as at Aſby, Croſby Ravenſworth; Newby, Meburn, and Hoff. And particularly, Ketel ſon of Eldred, ſon of Ivo de Talebois, gave to the ſaid hoſpital certain lands in Kirkeby, and William de Lancaſtre the firſt gave to the ſame divers lands in High Barton: In exchange for which lands, William de Lancaſtre the ſecond by his charter granted to the ſaid hoſpital the manor of Docker, by the metes and bounds therein ſpecified *.

Which grant was confirmed by Gilbert ſon of Roger Fitz-Reinfred, and afterwards by king Edward the firſt. The ſaid Gilbert further granted to the ſaid hoſpital, that they might have their horſes and hogs going in his foreſt, with two folds wherein to take them; and that they might have one of their own brethren, together with one ſecular perſon, to tend the horſes and hogs within the foreſt, without bow, arrows, or dog: and if their cattle ſhould ſtray out of the above granted limits into the foreſt, that they ſhould be driven back quietly and without hurt or damage to the brethren of the ſaid hoſpital †.

This place claims, and in ſome reſpects exerciſeth, a privilege of exemption from eccleſiaſtical juriſdiction; but by whom, or in what inſtances, the ſame hath been granted, we have not found.

After the diſſolution of the religious houſes, this manor ſeems to have been granted to one Richard Waſhington; for in the 35 Hen. 8. there is a licence of alienation to *Richard Waſhington*, to convey the manor of Docker to *Richard Ducket* of Grayrigg eſquire: Whoſe deſcendent *Anthony Ducket* eſquire, about

* Notum ſit omnibus, tam præſentibus quam futuris, quod ego Willielmus filius Willielmi de Lancaſtre conceſſi et hac præſenti charta confirmavi, Deo et pauperibus hoſpitalis beati Petri Ebor', totam terram quæ dicitur Dockerga, cum omnibus pertinentiis ſuis, viz. per rivulum qui eſt inter Dockerga et Grarig, et Dockerga et Lambrig, et Dockerga et Wynfel, et Dockerga et Pattun; et ſicut idem rivulus deſcendit in Mimed, et inter Docharke et Falbek, uſque ad deſcenſum ejuſdem rivuli in Mimed, et a deſcenſu ejus ſicut aſcendit uſque ſubter wardas, et a wardis uſque ad Knotermild, et a Knotermild ex tranſverſo uſque ad Brunehou in aquilonari parte a Lickegile ubi crux poſita eſt, et exinde ex tranſverſo verſus orientem uſque ad aliud Brunehou juxta ſailis ubi altera crux poſita eſt, et deinde directe ex tranſverſo ultra Lickegile verſus orientem uſque ad magnam fraxinum verſus ſupercilium montis ubi tertia crux poſita eſt, et deinde ex tranſverſo verſus orientem uſque Blabec qui deſcendit in Warlaheſhayth et cadit in moſſam ad Baitingſted; et extra hos terminos, communem paſturam uſque ad Lon. Hanc præſatam terram ego et hæredes mei dedimus et conceſſimus prædictis pauperibus in eſcambium pro terra de Kirkeby quam Ketellus filius Eltredi eis dederat in eleemoſynam, et pro terra de Bartonheved quam Willielmus pater meus eis dederat. Hanc præſatam Dockergam, cum omnibus predictis terminis, prædictis pauperibus ego et hæredes mei contra omnes homines warrantizabimus imperpetuum. Teſtibus, Helwiſa ſponſa mea, Gilberto de Lancaſtre, Patricio filio Bernardi, et aliis. 2 Dugd. Mon. 395.

† .... Præterea conceſſi eiſdem quod habeant equos et porcos ſuos infra foreſtum meam, et habeant duas faldas in foreſta mea, unam ſcilicet in Capelthwaite et aliam in Roakerdale, ad capiendum equos et porcos ſuos cuſtodiendos infra foreſtam. Conceſſi etiam eiſdem fratribus, quod habeant unum fratrem et unum ſecularem ad equos et porcos ſuos cuſtodiendos infra foreſtam meam, ſine arcu et ſagittis, et ſine cane. Si vero animalia eorum extra terminos prænominatos in foreſta mea reperta ſuerint, cum omni manſuetudine et ſine læſione et damno fratrum ejicientur. Teſtibus, Domino H. decano, et capitulo Sancti Petri Ebor'. Ibid.

CHAP. VI. the year 1690, sold the same, together with the manors of Grayrigg and Lambrigg, to Sir John Lowther baronet; in whose name and family the same still continues in the person of Sir James Lowther baronet.

This manor pays a quit rent of 13 *s* 4 *d* yearly to the duke of Leeds, whose ancestor in the reign of king Charles the second purchased this and many other fee farm rents of the crown in this county.

LAMBRIGG.

This perhaps might be the place to which they carried their *lambs* at certain seasons. For many places received their name of distinction from such like circumstances; as, Sheepshead, Ramsbottom, Ewbank, Stirkland, Cowbrow, Oxenholme, and the like.

In the 11 Ed. 1. *Thomas de Chenays* granted to *Gilbert de Bronolesheade* all his lands at Lambrigg (reserving only to himself the park); all which he had of *Lambert de Bussey*.

By the heiress of *Burneshead* the same came to *Bellingham*; and by one of the daughters and coheirs of the last *Bellingham* of *Burneshead*, to *Anthony Ducket* of Grayrigg esquire, whose descendent *Anthony Ducket* esquire sold the same as aforesaid to Sir John Lowther, in whose family it still continues.

Lambrigg is of the Marquis Fee, and was holden of the king *in capite* by knights service.

There is no remembrance or tradition of any deer having been kept in Lambrigg park, or any other place belonging to the *Duckets*; although so considerable a family in ancient time was seldom without.

Within this manor there is a vein of copper, which was wrought by the late viscount Lonsdale. But the water being very troublesome, and the vein withal not very rich, he desisted.

DILLAKER.

Adjoining to Lambrigg on the East, is the hamlet of DILLAKER; of which we have met with no particular account. It is in the parish of Kendal, but in Lonsdale Ward; and perhaps hath been anciently part of the manor of Killington and Firbank. It is freehold; and in the survey of the Queen's lands in the 28 Cha. 2. stands charged with a free rent of 3 *s*, of the Marquis Fee.

GRAYRIGG.

Having now advanced to the Eastern extremity of the parish of Kendal, we incline Northwards to the manor of GRAYRIGG; so called probably from being frequented by badgers, brocks, or *grays*; as on the east side of the river Lune, opposite thereto, is a place which yet bears the name of *Brockholes*. The hollow

low between is called *Grayrigg-hause*, from *haustus* perhaps, which signifies a draught; even as yet a throat or gulley is by the common people called a *hause*.

This manor of Grayrigg, like as the rest, belonged to the barons of Kendal, and was granted by *William de Lancastre* the first in marriage with his daughter *Agnes*, to *Alexander de Windesore*, son and heir of *William de Windesore* *.

The said *Alexander* had a son *William de Windesore*; who was a juror on several inquisitions *post mortem* in the reign of king Edward the first. Which *William* had a son *Alexander*, who levied a fine of the manors of Grayrigg and Morland in the 11 Ed. 2.

This last *Alexander* had a son *William de Windesore*, who was knight of the shire for Westmorland in the 28 Ed. 3. and was sheriff of Cumberland in the 41st and 42d of the same king.

By the inquisition *post mortem* of *Joan de Coupland* aforesaid in the 49 Ed. 3. he appears to have held of the said *Joan* the manors of Heversham, Morland, and Grayrigg.

Which *William* had a daughter and heir *Margery*, who in the reign of king Richard the second was married to *John Ducket* esquire, son of *Hugh*, son of *Richard*, son of *William*, son of *Richard Ducket* of Fillingham in the county of Lincoln esquire; and hence came the *Duckets* to the manor of Grayrigg and other possessions in Westmorland, who enjoyed the same for 12 generations following, with this peculiar felicity, that none of the issue male, possessors of the family estate, was ever in ward, every ancestor living until his heir was above 21 years of age.

The arms of *Windesore* were; Gules, a saltier Argent, between 12 cross crosslets Or.

The succession of the said family of *Ducket* of Grayrigg was as follows:

1. *John Ducket* aforesaid, who married the heiress of Windesore, had a son and heir,

2. *Richard Ducket* of Grayrigg esquire; who married a daughter of Sir Richard Redman of Over Levins knight: And by her had issue,

3. Sir *Richard Ducket* of Grayrigg knight; who married Mabel daughter of Sir Roger Bellingham of Burneshead knight. In the 5 Hen. 4. he represented the county of Westmorland in parliament. He had issue,

* Willielmus de Lancastre, omnibus amicis et omnibus probis hominibus suis, tam futuris quam præsentibus, salutem et amorem. Sciatis me concessisse, et cum assensu Willielmi de Lancastre filii mei et hæredis præsenti charta confirmasse, Alexandro de Windesore simul cum Agnete filia mea et hæredibus suis, in liberum maritagium, quicquid habeo in Haversham, Grayrigge, et Morlande, cum omnibus pertinentiis suis: Concessi etiam præfatis Alexandro de Windesore simul cum Agnete filia mea, et hæredibus eorum, libertatem firmandi stagna et molendina super meum dominicum, ubicunque locum competentem invenient ad usum suum; ac etiam libertatem assartandi et faciendi et habendi assarta sua in boscis suis ubicunque voluerint infra divisas suas. Quare volo quatenus prænominati Alexander et Agnes filia mea et hæredes sui habeant et teneant prædictas terras et prænominatas libertates, cum omnibus aisiamentis, de me et hæredibus meis, sicut liberum maritagium, in feodo et hæreditate, bene et in pace, libere et quiete, et honorifice, et plenarie, in bosco et plano, in pratis et pasturis, in viis et semitis, in mossis et mariscis et montanis, in molendinis et stagnis, in pannagiis et assartis, et in omnibus libertatibus, sicut hac charta mea confirmavi. (*Rawlinson.*)

CHAP. VI.

4. *Thomas Ducket* esquire; who married Elizabeth daughter of Thomas Middleton of Middleton-hall esquire, by Isabel daughter of Sir Richard Musgrave of Hartley castle. This Thomas was slain at Edgcote field in the reign of king Henry the sixth. He had issue,

5. *Richard Ducket* esquire; who married Eleanor daughter of William Harrington, who had considerable possessions both in Lancashire and the barony of Kendal. He had issue, Richard, Robert, Anne married to Thomas Wessington of Hallhead in Westmorland, and Mabel married to John Whittington of Barwick.

6. *Richard Ducket* esquire, son and heir of Richard, married Agnes daughter of John Fleming of Ridal esquire. He seems to have had a second wife of the name of Katherine Culwen. He had issue, Anthony, James, Walter, Randolph, and two daughters Elizabeth and Dorothy, the latter of whom was married to Salkeld of Rosgill.

7. *Anthony Ducket* esquire, son and heir of Richard, married Dorothy one of the daughters and coheirs of Sir Robert Bellingham of Burneshead, and by her had issue Richard, Charles, Jasper, William, and Gabriel.—To his second wife he married Alice daughter of Thomas lord Dacre of Gilsland, and by her had issue Lionel, Alan, and Agnes married to John Myller of the Temple, London. This Lionel was fellow of Jesus College in Cambridge, and a great benefactor to that college: At which place there is an elegant monument of him, with this inscription;

Lionell Duckett,

Westmorlandiensis, e generosis ortus parentibus; Collegii Divi Johannis olim alumnus; Academiæ Cantabrigiensis quondam Procurator; Sanctæ Theologiæ Baccalaureus; et nuper hujus Collegii Jhesu senior socius. Obiit Aprilis 5°, *Anno Domini* 1603. *Ætatis suæ* 39.

8. *Richard Ducket* of Gragrigg esquire, son and heir of Anthony, married Catherine daughter of Sir James Leyborne of Cunswick knight; and by her had issue Francis, and Margery married to Ralph Brackenburgh of Denton in the county of York.

9. Sir *Francis Ducket* of Grayrigg knight, son and heir of Richard, married Marian daughter of Alan Bellingham of Helsington esquire, and by her had issue two sons, Anthony and William; and four daughters, Alice married to John Fleming of Ridal esquire, whose marriage portion was 666 *l* 13 *s* 4 *d* (a large sum in those days): She had no issue. The other 3 daughters Frances, Catherine, and Jane, all died unmarried.

Sir Francis to his second wife married Jane one of the daughters and coheirs of John Bradley of Bradley-hall in Lancashire esquire, and widow of William Leyborne esquire.

He died in the 12th year of king Charles the first. And the inquisition thereupon finds, that he died seised of the manor of *Grayrigg*, holden of the king *in capite* as of his manor of Kendal called the Richmond Fee, worth by the year 10 *l*: And of the manor of *Docker*, holden of the king *in capite*, by the service of the 20th part of one knight's fee, worth by the year 3 *l* 6 *s* 8 *d*: And

And of the manor of *Lambrigg*, holden of the king as of his manor of Kendal called the Marquis Fee, by knights service, worth by the year 4 *l*: And of the rectory of *Beethom*, holden of the king as of the manor of East Greenwich, in free socage, and by the rent of 25 *l* a year: And of one messuage, with 20 acres of land in Whinfell, worth by the year 2 *s* 6 *d*: And of 3 burgages in Kendal, and 4 acres of land thereto belonging, holden in socage; worth by the year 5 *s*: And that Anthony Ducket was his son and heir, of full age.

10. *Anthony Ducket* esquire, son of Sir Francis and Marian Bellingham. He married Elizabeth daughter of William Leyborne of Cunswick esquire; and died in 1661: leaving issue,

11. *James Ducket* of Grayrigg esquire, who was of the age of 50 years at Dugdale's visitation in 1664.

He was thrice married. His first wife was Magdalen daughter of Sir Henry Curwen of Workington knight; by whom he had Anthony his eldest son and heir, and a daughter Margaret married to John Girlington of Thurland castle in Lancashire esquire. To his second wife he married Mary daughter of William Sanders of Sutton Court in the county of Middlesex esquire, and by her had William, Richard, Elizabeth, and Bridget. He had to his third wife Elizabeth daughter of Christopher Walker of Workington, and by her had Thomas, John, Christopher, Marian, Ellen, and Anne: After his death, she married to her second husband Thomas Hilton, a younger son of Hilton of Murton.

12. *Anthony Ducket* esquire, son and heir of James. He married Elizabeth daughter of John Dalston of Acorn Bank esquire; and at Sir William Dugdale's visitation aforesaid was 28 years of age.

In the time of this Anthony, there was a suit in chancery between him and the tenants of Grayrigg, Lambrigg, and Docker; the tenants setting forth in their bill, that in the 11 Cha. 1. a decree had been obtained in the court at York for the northern parts by the tenants against Anthony Ducket esquire son of Sir Francis, whereby the tenants were to pay one year's moderate value for a fine both general and special; and that the widows were to pay the general fine, but no fine upon their admission but only the best beast; that fines not assessed and demanded before the tenant died should be lost; and that all boons and duties to the king were to be reprized: That the said Anthony was succeeded by his son James; and that the like decree was obtained against him in the court of chancery in 1662: That James was succeeded by the present Anthony his son; and they claimed in like manner, according as had been determined by the aforesaid decrees. They claimed likewise underwood, and wood for all necessary boots, and loppings of timber trees and other wood, for which they paid greenhew. And it was decreed, in the year 1670, that they should pay for a fine one clear yearly value that the tenement would let for, above the lord's rent and other reprizes. The determination concerning the wood was referred till York assizes.——The reason why these lords stood not to the former decrees, as they alledged, was, because they were not bound thereby, for that they came in by intail, and not by descent *.

* A copy of this decree, and several other documents relating to our history, were found among the writings of the late John Kitching of Cowperhouse, gentleman.

CHAP. IV.

Not long after this, the said Anthony sold the estate to Sir John Lowther, and died without issue. All his brothers also died without issue male; and the name and family in Westmorland is now extinct.

The arms of Ducket are; Sable, a saltier Argent.

About the year 1695, the said Sir John Lowther infranchised the tenants of Grayrigg, Lambrigg, and Docker; except some few who were not able to purchase.

Grayrigg-hall, being the ancient manor house, was a strong old building, in a quadrangular form, adapted for defence more than for convenience. It is now totally in ruins, most of the lead and timber thereof having been removed to Lowther.

The CHAPEL of Grayrigg is common to the several townships of Grayrigg, Lambrigg, Docker, Whinfell, and Dillaker. The ancient salary is 20 nobles. In the year 1708, this chapel was rebuilt at the expence of the inhabitants; and soon after made parochial.

In 1723, Anthony Lowther esquire, brother to Henry viscount Lonsdale, gave 100*l* to this chapel, unto which the governors of queen Anne's bounty added another 100*l*, wherewith an estate was purchased in Dillaker.

And in 1751, the sum of 200*l* was advanced to the said governors, and with other 200*l* allowed by them, an estate of 400*l* value was purchased in Whinfell. An inscription on the wall in the inside of this chapel will inform posterity to whom they stand indebted for this estate: which is as follows,

"This chapel obtained the Queen's bounty in the year 1751, by the liberal "benefactions of Mr. William Rudd late of Kendale deceased, the worship-"shipful William Stratford Commissary, and the reverend John Haistwell "Curate.

"The first	gave	120*l*
2d	——	20
3d	——	60
		200*l*.

"Zeal for the house of God here you do see,
"Shining with brightest beams even to futurity,
"May Heav'n be th' reward of all such boundless charity*."

The whole revenue of this chapel, arising from the premises, is now about 42*l* a year.

* Unto which triplet a wag of our acquaintance proposes a line to be added, to make it run upon all four: viz.

"And the D—— take the authors of all such Poetry."

Robert

Robert Adamson of Blacket Bottom in Grayrigg, gentleman, gave 30*l* to a school in Grayrigg, with which sum two fields, containing 11 acres, in Dillaker, were purchased in the year 1723.

There is a meeting-house in Grayrigg belonging to the *Quakers*, and also an estate of 8*l* a year, purchased with 100*l* given to them by John Dicconson of the said township.

WHINFELL.

From Grayrigg, travelling northwards, along the eastern extremity of the parish, we come to WHINFELL; which carries its own derivation along with it.

This manor appears to have been early divided into moieties, or separate shares; as were many other manors, sometimes by purchase, and not seldom by the marriage of coheirs.

In the 49 Ed. 3. after the death of Joan de Coupland, the inquisition finds, that *Matthew de Redman* (of Over Levins) held of the said Joan, on the day on which she died, a moiety of the vill of Quinfell. Who held then the other moiety, is not certain: In the reign of Hen. 6. it appears to have been in the Stricklands of Sizergh. And amongst the escheats in the 11 Eliz. it is found, that *Walter Strickland* esquire held of the queen *in capite* by knights service the *manor* of Whinfell (which probably means only a moiety thereof; for it was very usual in like cases to express the whole instead of a part: So when they come to sell such part, they express the manor in general, meaning thereby so much thereof as belonged to the vendor). And amongst the Escheats in the 3 Cha. 1. it appears that *William Thornebrughe* esquire held of the heirs of *Richard Redman* in socage, a moiety of the manor of Whinfell (that is, the *Redman* moiety aforesaid): And he held also in Whinfell, Selsyde, and Patton, divers lands and tenements of the clear yearly value of 6*l* 4*s* 4*d*. And at the same time *Richard Ducket* esquire held three messuages and tenements in Whinfell in socage of the clear yearly value of 41*s*.

In the year 1670, Sir *Thomas Strickland* of Thornton Briggs in the county of York knight, and *Walter Strickland* of Rippon esquire, conveyed to Robert Stephenson and three others, trustees for the inhabitants and land-owners, parcel of the said manor, by the general name of all that the manor, seigniory, township, or lordship of Whinfell, with all its rights, members, and appurtenances. And the said trustees conveyed to the several land-owners; Yet so, that the mines and quarries upon the wastes, the waifs and estrays, and fishings in the ponds or tarns on the wastes or commons, were to remain in the trustees, for the use of the tenants at large.

And in 1723, by indenture quadripartite, between *Jane Thornburgh* of Kendal, widow of *Rowland Thornburgh* of Methop esquire, of the first part; *John Trafford* of Crofton in the county of Lancaster esquire, aud *Elizabeth* his wife, sister and heir of *Thomas Thornburgh* esquire deceased, son and heir of the said *Rowland*, of the second part; *Thomas Townley* of Royle in the county of

CHAP. VI.

of Lancaster esquire, and *John Knipe* of Flodder in Lyth gentleman, of the third part; and Henry Wilkinson and seven others in trust for the tenants and land-owners, of the fourth part; they the said Jane Thornburgh, John Trafford and Elizabeth his wife, Thomas Townley, and John Knipe, for the sum of 1040*l* 3*s* 4*d*, convey to the said trustees, the manors or reputed manors, lordships, or seigniories, of *Whinfell* alias *Whinfield*, *Selside*, *Skelsmergh*, and *Patton*; with all royalties, deodands, ponds, waifs and estrays: paying thereout yearly 9*s* 1½*d* to the king; and a yearly rent of 1*s* to the lord viscount Lonsdale. And the trustees conveyed severally to the tenants: The fishery in Whinfell tarn to remain amongst the tenants undivided.

The learned Dr. John Pearson, bishop of Chester, was descended of a family of that name in this township.

FAWCET FOREST.

Pursuing our course northwards, we come to FAWCET FOREST, at the utmost extremity of the parish towards the east and north. It was anciently called *Fauside*, and belonged to the abbey of Byland in Yorkshire, having been given thereto by William de Lancastre the first. *Burton's Mon. Ebor.* 332.

After the dissolution of the monasteries, it was purchased by Alan Bellingham esquire, a younger son of the Bellinghams of Burneshead, who also purchased Helsington and Levins. The last of whose family at Levins sold this, together with the other estates, to Colonel James Grahme, from whom it hath descended to the present earl of Suffolk and Berkshire.

It is within the chapelry of Selside.

Forest-hall is the ancient manor house; and one half of the forest still lies in demesne.

WHITWELL AND SELSIDE.

Inclining westward, we come to WHITWELL and SELSIDE, which though separate divisions, yet make but one constablewick, and seem to have been originally but one manor. When they were first separated, doth not appear. They became united afterwards in the ancient family of *Thornburgh*, which came from *Thornburgh* in Yorkshire, afterwards removed to *Hampsfell* in Lancashire, and finally settled in Westmorland.

The first account we have of *Whitwell* is in the 25 Ed. 3. in which year we find that *Gilbert de Burnesheved* held of *William de Coucy* the hamlet of *Whitwell*, by the service of cornage, wardship, and relief. (Where we may observe, by the way, that though the king had acquitted them of *cornage*, yet he did not thereby alter the tenure, but only remitted the payment.)—The heiress of *Burneshead* was married to *Bellingham*, and one of the daughters and coheirs of the last *Bellingham* of *Burneshead* brought *Whitwell* by marriage into this family of *Thornburgh*.

2 OF

Of Selside we have met with no early account. In the 49 Ed. 3. *Matthew de Redman* held of *Joan de Coupland* divers tenements in *Selsat*, but the manor itself seems even then to have been in the hands of the *Thornburghs*, for they were many years before that time a considerable family in the county.

The first of the name of *Thornburgh* that hath occurred, was *Rowland de Thornburgh*; who in the 11 Ed. 1. was one of the jurors on the inquisition *post mortem* of William de Lindesey.

The next that we meet with was *William de Thornebergh*; who in the 20 Ed. 3. is first in the list of jurors on the inquisition *post mortem* of William de Coucy.

In the 29 Ed. 3. and again in the 34th of the same king, we find *Rowland de Thornburgh* knight of the shire for Westmorland. In the 47 Ed. 3. *Rowland de Thornburgh* and *William de Thornburgh* were chosen to represent the said county in parliament. In the 15th and in the 17th of Ric. 2. and again in the 2 Hen. 4. *William de Thornburgh* was knight of the shire. In the 5 Hen. 4. *Rowland de Thornburgh*. In the 2 Hen. 5. *William de Thornburgh*. And in the 3d, and again in the 5 Hen. 5. *Rowland de Thornburgh*. All these respectively were chosen to represent the said county in parliament—But what connexion these had with the present family, doth not certainly appear.

The family pedigree (as copied from one remaining at Selside hall, by Sir Daniel Fleming in the year 1670, which also agrees in the main with a pedigree certified at an herald's visitation in 1628) begins with,

I. WILLIAM DE THORNBURGHE of THORNBURGHE in the county of York esquire; who married a daughter of Sir John Croker of the city of London knight, and had issue,

II. Sir WILLIAM THORNBURGH of Thornburgh knight: He married Anne daughter of Richard Maleverer esquire, and by her had issue, *William* who died without issue, *John* who resided at *Hamsfeld* in Lancashire, and *Anne* married to Christopher Curwen esquire.

III. JOHN THORNBURGH of Hamsfeld, esquire; married Elizabeth daughter of Sir Henry Pierpoint knight. They had issue, *William*, *Thomas*, *John* dean of York, and *Margaret* married to William Easton of the county of Lancaster.

IV. WILLIAM THORNBURGH esquire, son and heir of John. He married Catherine daughter of William Hilton esquire; and had issue *Thomas*, *William*, and *Henry*; and a daughter *Mary*, married to Thomas Coatsworth; and another daughter *Catherine*, married to John Balderstone.

In the 20 Ric. 2. there was one *William de Thornburgh*, who had a daughter Margaret married to William Machel of Crackenthorp gentleman. But whether she was daughter of this William that we now speak of, doth not appear from the pedigree.

Indeed, besides those of this name above mentioned which are not taken notice of in the pedigree, there are other confusions in this, as in almost all other ancient pedigrees, which seldom agree in all points with the inquisitions *post mortem* (where such can be found), or other authentic instruments. Which is not at all to be wondered at after such a length of time, in which also there

have

CHAP. VI. have been so many revolutions by the contests between the houses of York and Lancaster, the civil wars in the reign of king Charles the first, and especially in these northern parts by the burnings and desolation made by the Scots.

In one of the genealogies of this family, we find about this time *William de Thornburgh* who is said to have married Eleanor daughter of one *Selsed* of *Selsed* gentleman (and hence Sir Daniel Fleming observes, that this place in king Richard the second's time came by marriage to the *Thornburghs*); which *William*, by his wife *Eleanor Selsed*, had issue *William*, *Rowland*, *Edward*, and *Leonard*: That *William* the eldest married Margaret daughter of John Washington of Washington in the county of Lancaster esquire, and by her had issue *William* who married Eleanor daughter of Sir Richard Musgrave hereafter mentioned. But in all our disquisitions we have never met with any other person of the name of *Selsed*; and the family of *Thornburgh* undoubtedly had possessions in Westmorland long before this time. Therefore probably here must have been some mistake. And their own family pedigree goes on thus:

V. Thomas Thornburgh esquire, son and heir of William by his wife Catherine Hilton, married Jane daughter of Sir John Dalston knight; and had issue *Henry*, *Thomas*, *Richard*, and *Robert*.

VI. Henry Thornburgh esquire, son and heir of Thomas, married Elizabeth daughter of Matthew Boothe esquire; and by her had issue, *William*, *John*, *Henry*, *Jane* married to William Bradshaigh, *Catherine* a nun, and *Elizabeth* married to Pierce Starkey.

VII. William Thornburgh of Hamsfeld esquire. He lived in the reign of king Henry the sixth. He married Elianor daughter of Sir Richard Musgrave of Musgrave knight; and had issue,

VIII. William Thornburgh of Hamsfeld esquire, who married Elizabeth daughter and heir of Thomas Broughton of Broughton in Lancashire esquire. They had issue, *Rowland*, *Anne* married to Thomas Preston of Levins, *Thomas*, *Nicholas*, *Elizabeth* married to William Kirkby of Radcliff in Lancashire, and *Dorothy* married to William Clifton of Westby in the said county.

IX. Rowland Thornburgh of Hamsfeld esquire. He married Margaret daughter of Sir Geoffrey Middleton of Middleton-hall knight; and by her had issue, *William*, *Rowland*, *Elianor* married to Robert Beck gentleman, *Elizabeth* married to Thomas Warcop of Smerdale esquire, *Anne* married to Thomas Roos gentleman, and *Alice* married to Thomas Kellet of Winder in the county of Lancaster.

X. Sir William Thornburgh of Hamsfeld knight. He married Thomasin one of the four daughters and coheirs of Sir Robert Bellingham of Burneshead knight. In the 15 Eliz. we find that Thomasin Thornburgh held 15 messuages and tenements in Whitwell of the said queen as of her barony of Kendal. She died in the 26 Eliz and there is a monument of her in Kendal church. By her last will and testament she devised to her eldest son William all her right, title, and estate, in the several holdings of divers tenants in the lordships of Whittington in Westmorland and Poulton in Lancashire. And to her second surviving son Nicholas she gives her farmhold estate at Whitwell for ever; and her tenants with their appurtenances in Whitwell, Patton, Lambrigg, Long Sleddale, Dalefoot, and the tithes of Selside and Whitwell, during his life, remainder to her son William in fee*.

The said Sir *William*, by his wife Thomasin Bellingham had issue, 1. *William*. 2. *Rowland*, who died without issue. 3. *Margaret*, married to Richard Fallowfield of Melcanthorp. 4. *Nicholas*, from whom the present family of the Thornburghs of Selside are descended, who thererefore bear a crescent by way of distinction of a younger house. 5. *Thomasin*, married to Hugh Dicconson of the county of Lancaster. 6. *Cicely*, married to John Wharton of Kirkby Thore. 7. *Dorothy*, married to Henry Middleton of Threlkeld.

And here in the course of our investigation it being necessary, in order to deduce the present family of Selside-hall, to pursue the younger branch; we will first derive the descent of the elder branch until failure of issue, and then take up the pedigree from Nicholas aforesaid, and bring the same down to the present time.

WILLIAM THORNBURGH of Hamsfeld esquire, eldest son of Sir William and Thomasin Bellingham, married Etheldred daughter of Thomas Carus of Halghton in Lancashire, one of the justices of the court of king's bench. They had issue *Rowland*, *Anne*, and *Thomasin*.

ROWLAND THORNBURGH of Hamsfeld esquire, son of William and Etheldred Carus, married Jane daughter of Thomas Dalton of Thurnham in Lancashire esquire; and had issue *William*, *John*, *Rowland*, and *Francis*; and four daughters, *Etheldred* married to John Gregson of Moor-hall, *Jane* married to John Knipe of Ramside, *Anne* married to Henry Bigland of Grange in Lancashire, and *Thomasin*.

* During her widowhood she kept a book of acccount of her receipts, expences, and disbursements; from whence it appears that wool sold for 10s a stone, an immense price, compared with the prices of other things. The account of her servants wages for one year is as follows:—" Anno
" Domini 1579. The holle yeare waigs of Dame Thomasyne ladye Thornburgh of all her ser-
" vants at Selsatt;

" Imprimis Edward Bowman - - -	40s
" Item, Andrewe Rogersone - - -	26s 8d
" Item, Henrie Gylpine - - - -	30s
" Item, Michael the miler - - - -	26s 8d
" Item, Peter Langhorne - - - -	21s
" Item, Thomas Sowelbye - - - -	14s
" Item, John Bowman the Pleugh boy - -	10s
" Item, George Bownesse - - - -	12s
" Item, Thomas Thompson - - -	21s
The Maydes.	
" Imprimis, Agnes Waterfurthe - - -	8s
" Item, Elizabeth Becke - - - -	8s
" Item, Genett Bowman - - - -	10s
" Item, Agnes Warrener - - - -	10s
" Item, Genett Pepper - - - -	8s
" Item, Margaret Baxter - - - -	8s
" Item, Margaret Hodgesone - - -	10s
" Item, Mrs. Isabel - - - - -	26s 8d"

CHAP. VI.

William Thornburgh esquire, son and heir of Rowland married Catharine daughter of Edward Langtree in the county of Lancaster esquire; and had issue *Rowland*, *Elizabeth*, *Richard*, *Charles*, and *Catherine*. This William, in the 16 Cha. I. sold part of the manors of Whitwell and Selside to Henry Wilson esquire, who was succeeded by his brother Thomas Wilson, who had a son Henry Wilson, who in the year 1656 had a chancery suit with the tenants concerning the fines and services; which in the end was referred to Thomas Brathwaite of Ambleside esquire, and John Otway of Gray's Inn esquire, who awarded that the tenants who had not before purchased their tenements to freehold, should pay 13 years ancient rent to be reduced to an eightpenny fine certain, that is, eight times the ancient rent, on death of the lord, or change of the tenant by death or alienation; the rent hens, capons, and boons, to be purchased and sold at 16 years value *. The said William also sold the hall and demesne to William Thornburgh son of Nicholas aforesaid.

Rowland Thornburgh of *Methop* esquire, son and heir of William by his wife Catharine Langtree, married a daughter of Hugh Dicconson of Raseham in Lancashire. They had issue *Rowland*, *James*, and *William*.

Rowland Thornburgh of Methop esquire, son and heir of Rowland, married Jane Brokeld of Clayton in Lancashire, and had issue (besides several other children who came not to maturity) a son *Thomas* who died unmarried, and a daughter *Elizabeth* married to John Trafford of Croston in the county of Lancaster esquire, and had no issue.

The elder branch failing here, we recur to the younger branch in the person of the aforesaid Nicholas.

XI. Nicholas Thornburgh of Whitwell esquire, third son of Sir William Thornburgh knight by his wife Thomasin Bellingham, married Isabel daughter of Robert Salkeld of Thornemonby, and had issue *William*, *Thomas*, *Dorothy*, and *Thomasin*.

XII. William Thornburgh of Whitwell esquire, son and heir of Nicholas. This is that William who purchased Selside as aforesaid of his cousin William. He married Catherine daughter of Jerome Hawley of Brentford in Middlesex esquire; and had issue (besides several other children) *James* and *Francis*.

James the elder sold the estate in Selside and Whitwell to his brother *Francis*, from whom is descended the present family of Selside-hall, and whom therefore we must assume as next in succession after we have done with *James*.

The said *James* married a sister of Walter Nicholson of Grisedale and Whelpside; and had issue two sons, *Nicholas* and *John*; and four daughters, Frances, Catharine, Elizabeth, and Mary.

Nicholas, the elder of these two sons, married Barbara daughter of John Pickering of Bowbank; and had issue two sons and two daughters, all of whom died unmarried, except Agnes who was married to Mr. James Singleton of Kendal, but hath no issue. *John*, the younger son of James, married Margaret another of the daughters of the said John Pickering, and had issue a son who died unmarried, and several daughters, some of whom are now living and have issue.

* Kitching.

We

We now recur to *Francis* younger brother of *James* aforesaid, *viz.*

XIII. FRANCIS THORNBURGH of Selside esquire, who purchased the inheritance as is aforesaid. He married Frances daughter of Mr. George Waite of Leyburne nigh Middleham in Yorkshire; and had issue *William*, *George*, *Catharine*, *Agnes*, *Margaret*, and *Isabel*. All which daughters died unmarried, except *Agnes* who was married to Thomas Ratcliffe of Dilston in Northumberland.

George the second son married Rebecca daughter of Thomas Thornburgh of Wilson-house in Lancashire, and had issue *John* and *Susanna*. *John* married Mary sister of William Newman of Froyle in Hampshire; and had issue *Francis*, and *Margaret* married to Gaspar Conti professor of the Italian tongue in the French military school at Paris: Of this branch there is no issue.—*Susanna*, sister of *John*, was married to one Canter a Spaniard, engineer at Minorca in the reign of queen Anne, and had issue a son *James* now living, by profession a painter in perspective.

XIV. WILLIAM THORNBURGH of Selside esquire, elder son of *Francis*, married Mary only daughter of captain William Huddleston of Hale, a younger son of Andrew Huddleston of Hutton-John esquire; and by her had issue 1. *Francis*. 2. *William*, president of the English college at Douay. 3. *George*, who married Mary daughter of John Dalton of Thurnham in Lancashire; and had issue *Francis* who died unmarried in 1769, and *Mary* now inheritrix of the family estate. 4. *Frances*, married to Ferdinando Johnson of Middleton in Teasdale in the county of Durham; and to him had issue *Robert* now living, a clergyman of the church of Rome; and *Catherine* married to Robert Pringle of Richmond in Yorkshire, M. D. and hath a son *James*. 5. *Agnes*, who died a nun at Antwerp. 6. *Mary*, married to one Mr. Huntback in Essex. 7. *Ellen*, married to Joseph Tufton chymist in London. These three last had no issue.

XV. FRANCIS THORNBURGH of *Layburn* and *Selside* esquire, son and heir of *William*, married Katharine daughter of Thomas Sudell of Wanlass Park and West Witton in Yorkshire esquire, and died in 1774 without issue.

The *Thornburghs* bear 6 coats quarterly: 1. Ermin, a frette and chief Gules, by the name of *Thornburgh*. 2. Argent, two bars; and on a canton Gules, a cross Argent; by the name of *Broughton*. 3. Argent, two bars and a canton Gules, over all a garter (or cost) Sable; by the name of *Copeland*. 4. Sable, a frette Argent; by the name of *Harrington*. (Which two last were probably quarterings of Broughton, and came by the heiress of Broughton into this family.) 5. Argent, three bugles Sable, garnished Or, stringed Gules; by the name of *Bellingham*. 6. Argent, three bendlets, on a canton Gules a lion rampant Argent; by the name of *Burneshead*: (which, by the same reason, was a quartering of Bellingham)—The crest: A martin seiant (or a leopard passant Proper).—Motto: "Through thankfulness taken."

The halls and demesne of Whitwell and Selside still continue in this branch of the family. The manor was sold off by degrees; part thereof to the Wilsons aforesaid; part to the Bellinghams of Levins, who sold the same to Colonel

CHAP. VI.

lonel James Grahme, from whom it descended to the present earl of Suffolk and Berkshire, whose grandfather sold part of the tenements to freehold, and the present earl all or most of the rest. What remained to the Thornburghs was sold (as is aforesaid) in 1723, to the use of the tenants, by John Trafford esquire and Elizabeth his wife, daughter and heir of the aforesaid Rowland Thornburgh of Methop.

The corn tithe, after the dissolution of the monasteries, was granted to the Bellinghams of Burneshead. From the lady Thomasin above mentioned it came to her eldest son William Thornburgh, from whom it descended to the last Rowland Thornburgh of Methop, whose widow Jane sold it to William Cock of Redbank in Selside, from whom it came to his nephew and heir the present owner.

The CHAPEL of Selside was heretofore in the hall or manor house. Which being inconvenient to the owners, who were all along Roman catholicks, the late William Thornburgh esquire gave to the inhabitants a parcel of ground, at about 200 yards distance, for a chapel and chapelyard, in a beautiful situation; and a new chapel was accordingly erected and consecrated and made parochial. And on the chapel becoming vacant, a dispute happened between the vicar of Kendal and the inhabitants concerning the appointing of a curate; the vicar claiming as of common right, especially this being a new chapel; and the inhabitants claiming by custom for time immemorial of chusing their curate. But in regard of the great expence of a suit in chancery, the vicar gave it up. It was certified to the governors of queen Anne's bounty at 3*l* 19*s* 0*d* being the ancient chapel salary. In 1717, it was certified at 8*l* 5*s* 0*d*, *viz.* 4*l* charged upon the estates of the inhabitants; 4*l* given by Miles Birkbeck and issuing out of an estate of Robert Harrison; and 5*s* interest of money given by Thomas Nelson. In 1721, Peter Shepherd gave 40*l*, the interest thereof to go to the curate. In 1722, it was augmented by 100*l* given by lady Moyer, 100*l* given by Colonel James Grahme and the inhabitants, and 200*l* by the governors of queen Anne's bounty; with which, and other parish money, two estates in Whinfell called Harrod and Stonegarth were purchased for 525*l*. There is also another estate in Firbank called Beckstones, which was purchased with 100*l* given by the executors of the late Dr. Stratford, 100*l* given by the late curate the reverend William Atkinson, and 200*l* by the governors of queen Anne's bounty. The whole revenue of the chapel is now about 60*l* a year.

In the year 1730, John Kitching of Cowper-house in Selside gentleman, gave an estate in Selside called High Biggersbank, for the use of a schoolmaster, to be chosen by the major part of the inhabitants of the chapelry of Selside, and to be approved of by the vicar and first schoolmaster of Kendal for his ability and qualification. To teach *gratis* all the children of the farmers or inhabitants of the said messuage and tenement of High Biggersbank and of Cowperhouse tenement, and all poor children within the chapelry. The said estate to be in four feoffees; and on the death of any of them, the survivors to chuse another. The value of the estate then was about 16*l* a year.

SKELS-

SKELSMERGH AND PATTON.

SKELSMERGH and PATTON are both one conftablewick, but they have been feparate divifions for a long time.

SKELSMERGH belonged to the *Laburns* for upwards of 400 years; the principal refidence of which family was at Cunfwick.

It was granted in the reign of king Henry the third to *Robert de Leyburne* by *William de Lancaftre* the third, by the metes and bounds in the grant fpecified: Saving to the faid William his hunting therein; but with permiffion to the faid Robert and his heirs to take within the fame wild goats, foxes, and and hares, without hindrance of the faid William or his heirs. Rendering for the fame yearly a pair of gilt fpurs at the feaft of St. Michael, for all fervices. Witneffes whereof were, Sir Roger de Leyburne, Sir Ralph de Aincourt, Sir Richard de Copeland, Sir Matthew de Redeman, Sir Richard de Winewick, Sir Richard de Bereburne, Thomas de Levins, Thomas the Tax-gatherer (*Thoma Talliatore*), Gilbert de Wateby, and many others *.—It is called in the faid grant, and many other ancient evidences, *Skelfmerefergh*.

In the 30 Ed. 1. there was a grant of free warren in *Skelfmerefergh* to *Nicholas de Leyburne* grandfon of the faid *Robert* ‡.

The *Leyburns* in queen Elizabeth's time, being great fufferers for popery, fold the manor to *Bellingham* of Levins and *Braithwaite* of Burnefhead, who infranchifed moft of the tenants. But the hall and demefne continued to the *Laburns* till the year 1715, which being then forfeited, they were purchafed by Thomas Crowle efquire, and by him fold to *Daniel Wilfon* of Dallam Tower efquire, grandfather of *Daniel Wilfon* efquire the prefent owner.

There was heretofore a CHAPEL in Skelfmergh, dedicated to St. John Baptift; with the ftream of a well, called St. John's well, running through it from Eaft to Weft. Mr. Machel fays, part of it was ftanding in his time, and the current of water was planked over, and there were fome feats remaining in the quire. There was one Sir Uter Gilpin chaplain here before the reformation, as appears by his will written with his own hand.

There were fome lands and tenements in Skelfmergh, which belonged to the abbey of St. Mary's York, given probably by Ivo de Talebois or fome of his fucceffors.

In the 4 and 5 Ph. and Mary, there was a grant of two fulling mills nigh Sprent-bridge in Skelfmergh, and divers lands there called *Kirkfields* (probably the fame that had belonged to the abbey), to Walter Northcourt and John his fon, to hold of the crown by fealty only, in focage, as of the manor of Eaft Greenwich.

PATTON feems anciently to have belonged to a family of that name. In the 15 Hen. 3. *Ralph de Patton* was one of the witneffes to the grant of Killington, by Peter de Brus to William de Pickering.

* Rawlinfon. ‡ Denton.

CHAP. VI.

In the 7 Ed. 1. a fine was levied, between Symon Crook and Agnes his wife and Elias de Sandford and Alice his wife of the one part, and *Ralph de Patton* of the other part, of lands in Patton.

In the fame year, *Ralph de Patton* was one of the jurors on the inqufition after the death of Peter de Brus.

In the 3 Ed. 2. *Rowland de Patton* was one of the jurors after the death of William de Rofs.

In the 17 Ed. 2. *Michael de Patton*, after the death of Ingelram de Guifnes.

In the 14 Ed. 3. *John de Patton*, after the death of William de Thweng.

In the 20 Ed. 3. *John de Patton*, after the death of William de Coucy.

After this, we find no more of the name *de Patton*. But not long after, Patton appears to have belonged to the *Bellinghams* of Burneshead; and with *Thomasin* one of the daughters and coheirs of the laft *Bellingham* of Burneshead, to have come to the *Thornburghs* of Methop and Selfide. And accordingly, in the 3 Cha. 1. after the death of *William Thornburgh*, the inquifition finds, that he held the manor of Patton of William late marquis of Northampton, and afterwards of the king, as of his caftle of Kendal, by the fervice of one red rofe at the feaft of St. John Baptift yearly, if demanded; and it was worth by the year 20*s*. In which family it continued till the year 1723, when it was fold, together with part of Whinfell and Selfide as is aforefaid, to truftees for the ufe of the tenants.

A moiety of the lands in Patton (which probably had come by the marriage of a daughter and coheir) was granted to the priory of Coniefhead in Lancafhire; as appears from a confirmation by king Edward the fecond of grants made to the faid priory, amongft which there is a recital of the grant which John fon of Richard de Coupland made to the canons of the faid priory of all the lands of the faid John, with the appurtenances, in Patton; namely, a moiety of the faid vill, except one acre which was holden by Bertlot de Bofchefley †.

BURNESHEAD.

This name is varioufly written of ancient time, but moft commonly Burneshead, and feems intended to fignify the *head* of the *burn* or river which fprings a little above in Kentmere.

The manor belonged anciently to a family of the name de Burneshead; of which family we have only the laft of the name, before it ended in a daughter. And this was *Gilbert de Burneshead*; of whom mention is firft made, in any writing that we have found, in the 11 Ed. 1. who in that year purchafed Lambrigge of Thomas de Chenaye.

About feven years after this, in a conteft between the two daughters of Robert de Veteripont concerning the fheriffwick of Weftmorland, one of the daughters prefented this fame *Gilbert* to the barons of the exchequer, to be fworn into the office of under-fheriff.

† 2 Dugd. Mon. 424.

This *Gilbert* had an only daughter and heir *Margaret*, who was married to *Richard de Bellingham*, whose ancestors received their surname from a place called *Bellingham* in Tindale in the county of Northumberland; in which family this manor of Burneshead continued a long time.

The arms of *Gilbert de Burneshead* were; Argent, three bendlets Gules, on a canton of the second a lion rampant of the first.

Some of the BELLINGHAMS have attempted to derive their descent from an ancient family in this county and elsewhere *de Bello-campo*; but as they do not make out the connexion, this can be looked upon only as matter of conjecture, and the conjecture itself seems to be founded on a mistake; for the surname *de Bello-campo*, when divested of the Latin idiom, is not *Bellingham*, but *Beauchamp*, commonly pronounced *Beecham*.

The first of this family of *Bellingham*, of whom we can pronounce with certainty, was,

1. WILLIAM DE BELLINGHAM, father of the aforesaid *Richard*; who in the 2 Ed. 1. was under-sheriff to William de Swineburne in the parts of Tindale.

2. RICHARD DE BELLINGHAM, who married (as aforesaid) *Margaret* daughter and heir of *Gilbert de Burneshead* knight; and thereupon came to Burneshead, in the reign of king Edward the 2d. They had a son,

3. ROBERT DE BELLINGHAM of Burneshead, whose wife's name was Margaret Salkeld. In the 49 Ed. 3. after the death of Joan de Coupland, the jurors find, that *Robert de Bellingham* held of her divers tenements in Strickland Ketel. This *Robert* had a son,

4. RICHARD DE BELLINGHAM; who married Anne daughter of John de Barburne; and had issue,

5. Sir ROBERT BELLINGHAM of Burneshead knight. In the 10 Hen. 5. he was one of the jurors on the inquisition *post mortem* of John de Clifford. He married Elizabeth daughter of Sir Thomas Tunstall of Thurland in the county of Lancaster; and by her had issue, (1) *Henry*, his eldest son and heir. (2) *Richard*, from whom descended the Bellinghams of Lincolnshire. (3) *Robert*, who married a daughter of Sir Robert Aske by Elizabeth his wife daughter of the aforesaid John de Clifford, lord of Westmorland and hereditary sheriff of the same. (4) *Thomas*, from whom descended the Bellinghams of Sussex and Surry. (5) *Alexander*. (6) *Nicholas*, who married a sister of lord Ogle. (7) *William*. (8) *Alan*, who married a Gilpin, and was ancestor of the Bellinghams of Helsington and Levins.

6. Sir HENRY BELLINGHAM knight. He married Katherine daughter of James Leyburn of Cunswick esquire; and by her had issue, *Roger*, *Nicholas*, *Gilbert*, *John* (from whom descended the Bellinghams of Berkshire and Wiltshire), *Walter*, *Anne*, *Mabel*, and *Margaret*.

7. Sir ROGER BELLINGHAM of Burneshead, knight and banneret. He married Mabel daughter of Thomas Middleton of Middleton-hall esquire; and had issue by her, *Robert*, and a daughter *Margaret* married to Sir Christopher Curwen of Workington. This is that Sir *Roger* who lies buried and hath a monument in Kendal church.

8. Sir

CHAP. VI.

8. Sir ROBERT BELLINGHAM of Burneshead knight. He married Anne daughter of Sir James Pickering of Killington knight; and had issue only four daughters, (1) *Dorothy*, married to Anthony Ducket of Grayrigg esquire. (2) *Thomasin*, married to Sir William Thornburgh of Hampsfel knight. (3) *Katherine*, married first to Richard Ashton of Middleton, and afterwards to Davenport father of judge Davenport. (4) *Elizabeth*, married to Cuthbert Hutton of Hutton-John in Cumberland *.

And thus ended the eldest male line of the *Bellinghams* from Bellingham in Northumberland. They bore for their arms; Argent, a bugle or hunting horn-Sable, stringed Gules.

This last Sir *Robert* sold Burneshead to Sir *Thomas Clifford*. And by the inquisition after the death of the said Sir Thomas Clifford knight, the jurors find, that he died seised in his demesne as of fee of the manor of Burneshead, and of one corn mill parcel of the said manor: Out of which manor, by his deed dated Nov. 26. in the 33 Hen. 8. he granted to Marmaduke Wyvell esquire and dame Mabel his wife (late wife of Roger Bellingham deceased) an annuity of 13 *l* 6 *s* 8 *d* during her life (that is, in lieu of her dower, as it seemeth): And the jurors find that he died 26 March, 34 Hen. 8. and that *Elizabeth Clifford* his daughter was his next heir, then of the age of 15 years †.

Sir Daniel Fleming says, that Sir Thomas Clifford sold this estate to one *Fitzwilliam*. To reconcile which account with the aforesaid inquisition, we must suppose that *Fitzwilliam* (which is not improbable) married the said daughter and heir of Sir Thomas Clifford, and that Sir Thomas settled the estate in consideration of that marriage to be solemnized.

Fitzwilliam (Sir Daniel says) sold the same to one *Machel* of Kendal; who sold it to *Robert Brathwaite* of Ambleside esquire, and this brought in the family of BRATHWAITE to Burneshead.

The ancestor of the *Brathwaites* both of Ambleside and Burneshead, and also of Warcop, was,

1. RICHARD BRATHWAITE of Ambleside esquire; who by his wife Anne Sandys had issue,

2. ROBERT BRATHWAITE of Ambleside esquire; who purchased, as aforesaid, the manor of Burneshead. He married Anne daughter of John Williamson of Under-Skiddow in Cumberland, and by her had issue *Thomas* and *James* (besides several other children). To his second son *James* he gave Ambleside; and was succeeded at Burneshead by his eldest son, *viz.*

3. THOMAS BRATHWAITE of Burneshead esquire; who married Dorothy daughter of Robert Bindloss of Borwick esquire, and by her had issue, (1) *Thomas Brathwaite* of Burneshead, afterwards of Warcop. (2) *Richard*; who, on removal of his elder brother to Warcop, remained at Burneshead. (3) *Agnes*, married to Sir Thomas Lamplugh of Dovenby knight. (4) *Alice*, married

* The principal part of this pedigree, as also of that of the Brathwaites hereafter following, we have from Sir Daniel Fleming and Mr. Machel.

† Dugdale.

ried to Thomas Barton of Whenby in the county of York esquire. (5) *Dorothy*, married to Francis Salkeld of Whitehall esquire. (6) *Mary*, married to John Brisco of Crofton esquire. (7) *Anne*, married to Alan Askoughe of Richmond in Yorkshire gentleman.

4. RICHARD BRATHWAITE of Burneshead esquire, second son of Thomas by his wife Dorothy Bindloss, married to his first wife Frances daughter of James Lawson; and by her had issue, *Thomas*, *Robert*, *James*, *Richard*, *John*, *Philip*, *Agnes*, *Dorothy*, and *Alice*.

To his second wife he married Mary daughter of Roger Croft; and by her had issue Sir *Strafford Brathwaite* knight, who was killed in the ship Mary commanded by Sir Roger Strickland, in an engagement with an Algerine man of war called the Tyger, which ship Sir Roger took in that engagement.

5. Sir THOMAS BRATHWAITE knight, son and heir of Richard, married Ursula daughter of Sir Jordan Mettam; and by her had issue, *Thomas* who died unmarried, *Richard*, *Francis*, *Edward*, *Anthony*, *John*, *Mark*, *Lewis*, *Ursula*, and *Margaret*.

To his second wife he married Elizabeth Nicolson; and by her had issue, *Philip*, *Robert*, *Dorothy*, *Elizabeth*, *Frances*, *Alice*, *Agnes*, and *Catharine*.—In all, 18 children.

He died in 1683, leaving these last eight young children in a great measure unprovided for, except what he could leave to them out of his personalty. For he had before made a settlement of his estate for payment of debts and provision for his younger children, being supposed to be then a widower: for he had not then acknowledged his second marriage, although he had been for some time married to his second wife, who was daughter of one of his servants. And after his death, his son and heir *Richard*, by various devices and suits at law, attempted to deprive them of all provision and their mother of dower, which he in a great measure effected.

6. RICHARD BRATHWAITE of Burneshead esquire, son and heir of Sir Thomas, married Anne daughter of Sir Henry Waldegrave baronet. What issue he had we have not certainly found. In Betham church there is a monument, which seems to point out the next in succession, *viz.*

7. HENRY BRATHWAITE of Burneshead esquire, who seems to have received his christian name from the said Sir Henry Waldegrave. The inscription on the said monument is this: "Here lies the body of Henry Braithwaite of "Burneside esquire, who departed this life the 11th of August 1703. An "instance of this world's mutation, this gentleman (against all the strokes of "adverse fortune or the thick clouds of the world) behaved himself with a "constant loyalty to his prince. An affectionate husband, a kind and indul-"gent father, a just and faithful friend. In all his actions religiously cha-"ritable, sober, reserved, prudent, and circumspect."

We are equally uncertain as to his immediate successor; most probably it was,

8. RICHARD BRATHWAITE of Burneshead esquire; who sold the estate to Mr. *Thomas Shepherd*, and died in Wales about 25 years ago.

The

CHAP. VI.

The arms of Brathwaite are; Gules, on a cheveron Argent 3 cross crosslets fitchy Sable.

The said THOMAS SHEPHERD sold several of the customary tenements to freehold, reserving the rent. All the other estate at Burneshead descended to his son *Thomas Shepherd* esquire, a gentleman of wit and learning, and eminent in his day in the exercise of the office of justice of the peace. He sold the hall, and part of the demesne, and corn tithe, to *Christopher Wilson* of Bardsea in Furness esquire, who settled the same upon his daughter *Sarah* on her marriage with John Gale of Whitehaven esquire. Another part of the demesne, called Cowen Head, he sold to lady Fleming (relict of Sir William Fleming of Ridal baronet), who sold part thereof to Mr. Thomas Ashburner of Kendal, who has now thereupon a paper mill. Burneshead mills were sold by the said Thomas Shepherd esquire to Mr. Roger Wakefield of Kendal, from whom the same descended to the present owner his son Mr. John Wakefield. And finally, he sold the manor to the present owner thereof Sir James Lowther baronet.

The *hall* is in a very pleasant situation, on a plain, at the foot of an hill which rises with an easy ascent. At the time of Mr. Machel's survey, in the year 1692, there was a court, with a lodge and battlements, through which the ascent was into the hall. Before the court was a large pond, on each side of the passage up to the gate; and on either side a little island, with a tree planted in it. And in the windows of the gallery and dining-room were the Brathwaite arms, with impalings of the several families to which they were related.

The CHAPEL of Burneshead is common to Burneshead, Strickland Roger, and Strickland Ketel.

To what saint it was dedicated, we have not certainly found. There is a well called the *Miller's*, formerly St. *Oswald's* well, about 30 yards north-east from the chapel, which probably leads to the name of the tutelar saint. The bell was anciently called St. *Gregory's*; but at the consecration or benediction of the bells in old time, they had not always the name of the saint of the church or chapel given to them, but of other saints occasionally: a well near the place, bearing the name of any particular saint, is a more certain indication of the name of the saint to which the church or chapel was dedicated; the water whereof was reputed sacred, and resorted to for the cure of divers maladies, for which an offering was made at the church or chapel, at the altar of the tutelar saint.

The original salary belonging to this chapel was 20 nobles; raised from the inhabitants at so much a seat. This indeed was the ancient way of raising salaries to most of the chapels, but now the sum is by length of time become settled upon the estate. It comes indeed much to the same thing; for the house and seat by law are inseparable. But this may create a difficulty sometimes, where new houses are erected, or old houses are suffered to go down; but

but in this latter case it seemeth that the seat shall belong to the owner of the ground where the ancient house stood.

The present revenue of the chapel is as follows:—Ancient salary (being part of the said 20 nobles, the rest by some means or other being lost) 5*l* 17*s* 6*d*.—Five marks yearly out of three parcels of land in Staveley, which were purchased in the reign of king Charles the first with money given by Mr. Robert Kitchin alderman of Bristol, born in Strickland Ketel, and by Mr. Rowland Kitchin of Underbarrow: (The residue of the rents of the said lands goes to the poor.)—A rent charge of 20*s* yearly out of an estate in Strickland Ketel, given by Mr. Thomas Atkinson of Coppackhow.—An estate in Skelsmergh purchased with 200*l* given by the governors of queen Anne's bounty, 100*l* given by lady Moyer, ancient chapel money 65*l*, subscriptions in the neighbourhood 91*l* 5*s* 0*d*; and to make up the whole purchase money, which was 531*l*, there was added 20*l* school money given by Mr. Alan Bracken, and 31*l* ancient poor stock, and the curate Mr. John Towers made up the rest, *viz.* 23*l* 15*s* 0*d*. Afterwards, Mr. James Hodgson gave 20*l* to the chapel, and 10*l* to the school, to which the curate added 20*s*, and therewith paid back the poor money. And for the 30*l* school money, the schoolmaster receives a proportionable part of the rent.—Another augmentation of 200*l* was given by the said governors; towards the obtaining whereof, the late Dr. Stratford's executors gave 100*l*, and 50*l* was raised by wood sold off from the Skelsmergh estate, and the inhabitants advanced 50*l*, which sum they borrowed. With which whole sum of 400*l*, an estate was purchased in Dent in the county of York; and the present curate the reverend William Smith applied the mesne profits as they became due, to discharge the said sum of 50*l*. And the two estates at present clear to the curate yearly about 40*l*. So that the sum total of the curate's revenue is about 50*l* a year.

STRICKLAND ROGER AND STRICKLAND KETEL.

STRICKLAND anciently was always written *Stirkland*, being no other than the pasture ground of the *stirks* or steers and other young cattle.

At what precise time this *Stirkland* was divided into moieties, and so denominated from the several owners, hath not appeared to us. It seems to have been about the reign of king Henry the first, in the time of *Ketel*, son of Eldred, son of Ivo de Talebois first baron of Kendal.

Roger de Lancastre above mentioned, bastard brother of William de Lancastre the third, had large possessions given to him by his said brother, but he had not Strickland Roger, for that continued in the legitimate line; therefore Strickland Roger had not its name from him, but from some other probably before his time.

The family *de Stirkland*, which finally settled at Sizergh, had not their name from this *Stirkland* of which we now speak, but from *Stirkland* (which in after times was divided into *Great* and *Little Stirkland*) in the bottom of Westmor-

 land.

CHAP. VI.

land. They had indeed certain tenements in Stirkland Ketel holden under the lords of the manor, but they were never lords of the manor themselves.

By the inquisition aforesaid after the death of Joan de Coupland in the 49 Ed. 3. it is found, that she held of the crown the hamlet of Stirkland Ketel, as parcel of the manor of Wyandermere; and that others held divers lands there of her, as parcel of the manor of Kirkby in Kendale.

In the 9 Hen. 8. Sir Thomas Parr by his will devised to his wife for life the manor of *Strykelond Rogers*; being of that which was afterwards called the Marquis Fee.

And in the 14 Eliz. William Parr, marquis of Northampton, died seised thereof: And the same was assigned to his widow for dower, and the particulars in the rental made thereof were as follows; "Manor of Strickland Roger: Freeholders there; Edward Lancaster esquire 26*s* 8*d*. John Master esquire 11*s* 9*d*. William Gilpin 9*s* 9*d*.—Total of the (customary) rent of this manor 15*l* 14*s* 5*d*. Ten shillings paid yearly by Mr. Lancaster's tenants, to be free of their grist from the lord's mill, being part of the said sum."

In queen Catherine's rental in the 28 Cha. 2. the particulars stand thus: "There are held of the said queen, of the *Marquis Fee*, divers tenements in *Strickland Roger*, of the yearly free or dry rent of 6*s* 8*d*. And divers tenements also in *Strickland Kettle*, paying yearly a certain free or dry rent" (specifying the particulars): "And in *Strickland Roger* 12 tenements paying yearly a finable rent.——And of the *Richmond Fee*, 9 tenements in *Strickland Kettle* and *Helsington*, of the yearly customary or other dry rent of 3*l* 10*s* 10*d*."

At the hamlet of *Strickland Ketel* it happened, in the arbitrary times we before mentioned when speaking of king James's proclamation against tenant-right, that another remarkable instance of the oppressive measures of the crown glared forth, with respect to the court of wards and liveries. And these things we the rather take notice of, as being supplemental to the general history of those days. On the death of one Henry Kitchen of Strickland Ketel, a writ of *Diem clausit extremum* was issued as usual, in the 14 Cha. 1. The escheator summoned a jury; who found, that the said Henry Kitchen, whose heir was within age, died seised of two closes in Strickland Ketel, which were held of the king *in socage*.

The escheator William Briscoe esquire, and the feodary Robert Curwen gentleman, not being satisfied with this finding, certified to the court of wards and liveries, that they apprehended the said closes were holden of the king by *knights service*, and not in *socage*. (The difference was, if the lands were holden of the king by *knights service*, the king had the profits of the lands during the minority, and the wardship and marriage of the heir; if by *socage*, the king had not this right.) Upon this, it was ordered by the court, that a *Melius inquirendum* should issue; and if the escheator or feodary should perceive the jury inclinable to find against his majesty, that then they should forbear to take

take their verdict, and adjourn them over to a further day, and bind three or four of the most refractory of them to appear at a day certain at London, and receive their evidence at the bar of the court.

Accordingly, a writ of *Melius inquirendum* was issued; and a jury impanelled and sworn. And upon hearing the cause, the jury seeming inclinable to find against the king, the escheator and feodary did not take their verdict, but certified to the court, that it appeared upon the inquest, that the lands mentioned in the former office were holden of the king as of his manor of Kirkby in Kendale called the Marquis Fee, by certain yearly rents and services; that the said Marquis Fee (and also the Richmond Fee), before it came into the crown, was holden of the crown in chief by knights service; that the lands in question were anciently parcel of the lands of one John Burghe; and that there did not appear any tenure in socage held of the Marquis Fee; that therefore they adjourned the jury to appear again at Kirkby Kendal on the 19th day of December following, and bound over three of the jury to appear in the mean time in Michaelmass term in the court of wards and liveries, and receive their evidence at the bar.

And accordingly, in the said Michaelmass term, Miles Sill gentleman, and Thomas Strickland, two of the said jurors bound over, appeared in court. And upon hearing the evidence at the bar, touching the tenure of the said two closes heretofore John Burghe's lands, the court did conceive, that all the lands of the said John Burghe were holden of the king as of the said Marquis Fee by knights service: It was therefore ordered by the court, that if it shall not be made appear by those that oppose the tenure, that the lands in question are none of the lands in either office found of Burghe's lands, or if the prosecutor for the crown shall make it appear that rent hath been paid for the same as part of the rent of Burghe's lands; then the jury shall find a tenure by knights service: And it is further ordered by the court, that no evidence as touching the tenure of Burghe's lands shall be given to the contrary.

On the 19th of December, the jurors met at Kendal according to their adjournment. And the order of the court was read unto them. And upon further hearing, they still persisted in their former opinion. Wherefore their verdict was not received. And the escheator and feodary further certify to the court as follows; *viz.* That proof was made before them, of a free rent having been paid for the said lands by the said Henry Kitchen to the king as of Burghe's lands: But that some deeds without date being produced of lands in Strickland Ketel held in socage of the Marquis Fee, the jury were inclined to find against the king: Whereupon, they the said escheator and feodary, inasmuch as the case concerned divers other freeholders holding of the Marquis Fee by knights service, adjourned the jury again to appear before them at Kendal on the 13th day of March following.

This certificate being delivered to the court, and the attorney-general being heard on behalf of the king, the said court on the 6th of February did order, that if at the said next meeting the jurors should not find the tenure according to the direction of the aforesaid order and decree, the escheator or feodary should bind over two of the jurors to appear in court, at their own proper

 charges,

CHAP. VI.

charges, at a day certain this term, to receive the further order of the court thereupon; and that the payment of 10 *l* ordered to Miles Sill and Thomas Strickland two of the jurors, for their attendance to receive the evidence at the bar the last term, be suspended until the office be found.

At the said next meeting on the 13th of March, the jurors refusing to find for the king; the escheator and feodary adjourned them again, and bound over Henry Fisher and James Awdland, two of the said jurors, to appear in the court as above ordered: Who appearing accordingly, on the 16th of May, the court did finally order and decree, That the jurors at their next meeting shall find the lands in question to be holden by knights service, without hearing any evidence at all to the contrary *.

——We shall make no observation upon this; but only felicitate our country, that juries are not treated in this manner in our days; and that this court of wards and liveries, and all the incidents thereof, were abolished by act of parliament soon after the restoration of king Charles the second. It cost the nation dear, if any thing could be dear for such a purchase; for they gave the excise for it. And bishop Burnet observes, that the exchange was made, before either party knew or had considered thoroughly what it was they parted with.

Thomas Brathwaite of Burneshead esquire, by his will dated 18 Feb. 1606, gave 10 *l* for a stock for relieving poor housholders in Strickland Ketel and Strickland Roger; to be lent to them without interest yearly, by the churchwardens and overseers of the poor respectively, and the owner of Burneshead Hall for the time being.

The abbey of Cockersand had lands in Strickland Roger, called *Hundbow*; where anciently was a chapel called *Chapel le wood*: but there are now scarce any footsteps thereof remaining.

In Strickland Roger was heretofore a family of the name of *Godmond*, who gave name to an ancient tower house, which still bears the name of Godmond-Hall; and is now the property of John Burn esquire. Part of the house hath been rebuilt, but the tower remaineth in its original form, having been intended as a place of security and defence. The walls are two yards in thickness or upwards, and firmly cemented. The windows small, and crossed with strong bars of iron. The lowest floor is arched over, and the next above that laid with massy boards or planks grooved into each other, to prevent assaults from above. For the predatory parties did not proceed by way of sap or undermining; but, by a compendious method, strove to unroof the building, and let themselves down by ropes and ladders.

* Fleming.

LONG

LONG SLEDDALE.

LONG SLEDDALE, like the reft, belonged to the ancient barons of Kendale. They granted in fee divers tenements there to feveral perfons, and finally granted the manor to the *Thornburghs* of Hamsfel and Selfide, who fold the fame to *Bellingham*, who fold to Colonel *James Grahme*, from whom the fame hath defcended to the prefent earl of Suffolk and Berkfhire.

In the reign of king Henry the third, *William de Lancaftre*, baron of Kendal, enfeoffed *Rowland de Renegill* of 29 acres of arable land in Sleddale, and pafture there to the value of 100*s*. He alfo enfeoffed *Gilbert de Bereburn* of 20 acres of land there. And he enfeoffed *Robert de Leyburne* (to whom alfo he gave Skelfmergh) of three acres and an half in Sleddale of meadow ground, and pafture there alfo.

Amongft the Efcheats in the 3 Cha. 1. it is found, that William de Thorneburghe efquire held 20 meffuages or tenements with two fulling mills in Sleddale of the late marquis of Northampton, and then of the king; as of his caftle of Kendal, in focage, by fealty and the rent of 6*d* a year for all fervices; and that the fame were of the clear yearly value of 12*l* 4*s* 4*d*.

The tenements have been from time to time all or moft of them enfranchifed.

Here is no manor houfe, for the lords of the manor, fo far as we have found, never refided at this place. When the *Thornburghs* had the manor, the tenants attended the court at Selfide Hall.

The moft confiderable houfe in the dale was *Ubery-hall*, having an ancient tower, and the walls two yards thick. This feems to have been part of that which was granted to *Robert de Leyburne* aforefaid, and came with a daughter of *Leyburne* to a younger brother of *Harrington* of Wreyfham in Lancafhire, in whofe name and family it continued for feveral generations. In the 28 Cha. 2. one of the *Harringtons* paid to queen Katherine a free rent of 1*s* for Ubarrow Hall.

The *chapel* ftands about the middle of the dale, and was made parochial by bifhop Dawes in 1712. The ancient falary thereof is 5*l* 2*s* 10*d*.

In the year 1713, four fifters of Henry Holme of Long Sleddale deceafed gave 5*l* each, and Anthony Dennifon heir at law to the faid Henry Holme gave 60*l*, wherewith an eftate in Long Sleddale was purchafed, which was a cuftomary eftate; and the infranchifement thereof was purchafed by the then curate out of the mefne profits: And the eftate is now worth about 10*l* a year.

In 1746, an augmentation of 200*l* of queen Anne's bounty by lot fell to this chapel, which was laid out in the purchafe of a freehold eftate in Long Sleddale, now worth 12*l* a year or upwards.

So that the whole annual revenue is about 27*l* a year.

Sleddale Beck, commonly called *Spret*, fprings in Wrangdale-head in this dale (a place famous for fine blue flate got there), runs fouthward all along the

CHAP. VI.

the dale on the west side of the chapel and Ubarrow Hall, from thence on the east side of Burneshead Hall, and about half a mile below falls into the river Kent.

KENTMERE.

This place hath its name from the river *Kent*, which springs there, and from a *mere* or lake therein called *Kentmere*; which said river gives name not only to this particular district, but to all the south-west part of this county, called *Kendale*. It springs about 3 miles north from the chapel, and from thence runs southward through Kentmere, Staveley, Strickland, the township of Kendal, by Natland, Helsington, Levins, and from thence into the sea. It receives in its course two small rivers, *Sprit* and *Mint*. The former springs in Long Sleddale, and runs in at Burneshead. The other springs in Fawcet Forest, and in its course meets with Grayrig water which springs above the hall, and falls into Kent about a mile above Kendal.

Kentmere is bounded on the East by the chapelry of Long Sleddale, on the South by the chapelries of Staveley and Ings, on the West by the top of Garburne Fell, and on the North by Patterdale in the parish of Barton and Mardale in the parish of Shap.

In the partition of the *Brus* estate, amongst the four sisters and coheirs of the last *Peter de Brus*, about the 11 Ed. 1. *Margaret* the eldest had that which is now called the Marquis Fee; *Agnes* the second had no share in Westmorland (her portion being assigned to her in Lancashire and Yorkshire); *Lucy* the third sister had that which is now called the Lumley Fee; and *Ladarine* the fourth sister had *Kentmere*.

This *Ladarine* was married to *John de Bella-aqua*, and had issue two daughters coheirs; *Sibil* married to *Miles de Stapleton*, and *Johan* married to *Aucherus* son of *Henry*.

The said *Miles de Stapleton*, by *Sibil* his wife, had a son *Nicholas de Stapleton*, between whom and the said *Johan* (his aunt) in the 5 Ed. 2. a partition was made in chancery of the inheritance; by which partition, the manor of *Kentmere* (besides divers estates in Yorkshire therein mentioned) were to remain to *Nicholas*.

The said *Nicholas* had a son and heir *Miles de Stapleton*, who in the 21 Ed. 3. paid his fine to the king for his relief; and amongst other particulars, for a certain *chase* called *Kentmere*, which *Nicholas* father of the said *Miles* held of the king *in capite*, by hereditary descent after the death of *Miles Stapleton* grandfather of the present *Miles*, as the third part of the inheritance of *Peter de Brus* in the barony of Kendale, being that part which had belonged to *Ladarine* fourth daughter and coheir of *Peter de Brus*, which came to the said *Miles* the grandfather in right of *Sibilla* his wife first daughter and heir of the said *Ladarine*.

In the 47 Ed. 3. on the inquisition *post mortem* of *Thomas de Stapleton*, the jurors find, that the said *Thomas* died seised of the manor of Kentmere to him and the heirs male of his body; remainder to *Brian de Stapleton* knight; remainder

mainder to *Miles de Stapleton* son of *Miles*; remainder to the right heirs of the said *Thomas*. And the jurors say, that the said *Thomas* died without heir male of his body, and that the said *Brian* is heir of the said *Thomas* of the manor aforesaid by the intail aforesaid: And that *Elizabeth* wife of *Thomas de Metham* knight is sister and heir of the said *Thomas de Stapleton*, and of the age of 24 years and upwards.

The said *Brian* had a son *Thomas de Stapleton*, who lived in the reign of king Henry the sixth. And on an inquisition of knights fees in the sixth year of that king, it was found, that *Thomas de Stapleton* (then in wardship of the king), son and heir of *Brian de Stapleton*, held of the king *in capite* Kentmere in Kendale with the appurtenances, by the service of the 4th part of one knight's fee *.

This manor of Kentmere continued in the name and family of *Stapleton* till the reign of king Charles the first; when *Gilbert Stapleton*, in the year 1626, sold the same to *Nicholas Fisher* of Stanebank Green gentleman.

The *arms* of Stapleton were; Argent, a lion rampant Sable.

Henry Fisher, a descendent of the said *Nicholas Fisher*, devised the manor of Kentmere to be sold; and the same was accordingly purchased, in the year 1745, by *Thomas Wilson* of Kendal gentleman, by whom it was devised to his younger son the present owner *Thomas Fenwick* esquire; which name of *Fenwick* he took by act of parliament, in pursuance of the last will and testament of *Robert Fenwick* of Burrow-hall in the county of Lancaster esquire.

The whole number of tenements originally in this manor was sixty; that is, the lands were apportioned and set out for the sustentation of sixty soldiers: and the vestiges of this establishment yet remain. The manor is divided into four quarters; each quarter into fifteen tenements; each tenement consists of a proportionable quantity of inclosed ground, with pasture for ten cattle in a common pasture lying within each quarter respectively, and privilege for 80 sheep in another pasture common to the whole manor; and for each tenement a man serves the office of constable, pays 2*s* a year to the curate of the chapel, and 13*s* 4*d* rent to the lord of the manor. So where a man has two tenements, he serves the office of constable two years; or if he has half a tenement, he joins with another who has also half a tenement, for the finding a constable for one year. And so of the rest in like proportion. One of which ancient military tenements, at the present improved value, may be deemed to be worth about 10*l* a year.

Having deduced this manor of Kentmere, from its first separation from the barony of Kendal at large to the present time, we find no room for a family which hitherto hath been supposed to have been lords of this manor for several generations. Inhabitants within Kentmere they undoubtedly were, and had a considerable estate there; but lords of the manor they could not be.— These were of the name of GILPIN.

* All this concerning the Stapletons Mr. Machel had from Dugdale's MSS.

Bishop

Bishop Carleton, in his life of that eminent preacher *Bernard Gilpin*, begins his account of this family with *Richard Gilpin*, who (he says) in the time of king John had Kentmere given to him by one of the barons of Kendal, for his extraordinary services both in war and peace. And this is that *Richard* (he says) who signalized himself in killing a wild boar, which had infested the neighbouring parts, and done much mischief. In memory whereof, the *Gilpins* bear in their arms a boar to this day.

That there was some person of this name who performed such exploit, is very probable, as well from the said bearing on their escutcheon, as from universal tradition. But that the baron of Kendal at that time gave Kentmere unto him, cannot be asserted. Gilbert son of Roger Fitz-Reinfred had then the whole barony, and it continued intire for many years after that. And when Kentmere at last was separated from the rest, it passed to a grand-daughter of the said Gilbert, in whose posterity it continued (as hath appeared) till the reign of king Charles the first, and then passed into other hands. So that the *Gilpins* never had the manor of Kentmere. The mansion-house, which is called Kentmere-hall, they had, and also a considerable estate in land; but not so early (as it seemeth) as the reign of king John. The learned prelate above mentioned observes, that *Richard* was the sixth ancestor in the ascending line from the said *Bernard* who flourished in the reign of queen Elizabeth, which comprehends the space of about 350 years; and it will scarcely be found in any instance that so few descents have happened in so long a tract of time. The highest that we can reasonably ascend in the sixth degree upwards from the said Bernard, is to about the reign of king Edward the third, and the evidences that have occurred to us seem to favour this calculation.

1. The first in their own family pedigree is the aforesaid RICHARD GILPIN, who is supposed to have killed the wild boar above mentioned. He had a son,

2. WILLIAM GILPIN; who married a daughter of Thomas Ayray bailiff of Kentmere. In the 48 Ed. 3. this William was one of the jurors on the inquisition *post mortem* of Thomas de Thweng: And in the next year, after the death of Joan de Coupland, he had issue,

3. RICHARD GILPIN; who married a daughter of Fleming of Coningston, and by her had issue, *William*, *John*, *Robert*, *Margaret*, and *Isabel*. From *John* and *Robert* many Gilpins about Kendal are descended.

4. WILLIAM GILPIN, son and heir of Richard. He was a man eminent in his time. He married Elizabeth daughter of Thomas Lancaster of Sockbridge; and had issue, *Richard*, *Thomas*, *Edward*, *Oliver*, and three daughters married to Bellingham, Askew, and Aglionby. He flourished in the reign of king Edward the fourth.

5. RICHARD GILPIN, son and heir of William. He married Dorothy Thornburgh; and had issue, *William*, *Edwin*, *Sabergh*, *Caber*, *Giffiat*, *Giles*, *Ambrose*, and four daughters married to Lancaster, Dickson, Bateman, and Birkhead. He died in the reign of king Richard the third.

6. WILLIAM GILPIN, son and heir of Richard. He was a captain at the battle of Bosworth-field, and was there slain. And having died without issue, he was succeeded by his brother,

7. EDWIN

7. EDWIN GILPIN; who married Margaret daughter of Thomas Layton of Dalemain, and by her had issue, *William*, *George*, *Randolph*, *Bernard*, *Richard*, and three daughters, *Cicely*, *Mary*, and *Margaret*, married to Maud, Wharton, and Selthorp. He married a second time, and had issue by that second marriage, *Randolph*, *Christabel*, and *Helen*.

George, the second son above mentioned, was ambassador of queen Elizabeth to the States of Holland.

Bernard, the fourth son, was the famous preacher above mentioned, whose life was set forth by his cotemporary Dr. Carleton bishop of Chichester. He was entered in Queen's college in Oxford in the 25 Hen. 8. and was afterwards removed to Christ-Church in that university, being one of the first scholars upon that foundation. He was collated by Tunstal bishop of Durham (who was his mother's uncle) to the rectory of Houghton. He was learned, pious, charitable, and indefatigable in preaching and doing good. On the death of Oglethorp bishop of Carlisle, the queen offered to him that see, which he refused, though strongly solicited to accept it by his kinsman Edwin Sandes bishop of Worcester, afterwards archbishop of York. He published a sermon which he had preached before king Edward the sixth, concerning the robbery of the churches.

8. WILLIAM GILPIN, son and heir of Edwin, married Elizabeth daughter and coheir of Thomas Washington gentleman; and had issue *George* and six other sons, and seven daughters, married to Gilpin, Layton, Wharton, Cowper, Carus, Benson, and Mallory.

9. GEORGE GILPIN, son and heir of William, was twice married, to two of his tenants daughters; and had issue,

10. WILLIAM GILPIN, who married to his first wife Dorothy daughter of Sir Richard Sandford of Howgill, and by her had a son *George*. To his second wife he married Magdalen daughter of Danby of Masham, and by her had issue, *Christopher*, *John*, *Elizabeth*, *Mary*, *Margaret*, and *Anne*.

11. GEORGE GILPIN married Catharine daughter of Robert Philipson of Hollinghall gentleman; but had no issue. He was succeeded by his half-brother as next in tail, *viz.*

12. CHRISTOPHER GILPIN, in whom the direct male line ended. He had a daughter and heir married to *Nathanael Nicholson* of Hawkshead-hall; who had a son *Daniel Nicholson*; who had issue two daughters coheirs, 1. *Beatrix*, married first to Mr. Sands of Graythwaite attorney at law, to whom she had a child that died young; to her second husband she married Mr. John Copley attorney at law, nigh Egremont, to whom she had children. 2. *Judith*, married to Mr. George Carus of Sellet nigh Kirkby Lonsdale.—But the estate was sold to Sir *Christopher Philipson* of Crooke.

The *arms* of Gilpin were; Or, a boar passant Sable, armed Gules.

The said Sir *Christopher Philipson* had three daughters coheirs; who sold the estate to Sir *Daniel Fleming* of Ridal baronet. Which Sir *Daniel* devised the same to his son *Richard Fleming* esquire; from whom it hath descended to his

 three

three daughters and coheirs, *Catherine* wife (now widow) of George Cumpſtone of Ambleſide gentleman, *Barbara* and *Iſabella*, both now living and unmarried.

The *hall* is an old building, with a tower, ſtanding under a vaſt craggy mountain.

The *chapel* is erected nigh the hall, about 12 miles north from the pariſh church. The ancient ſalary thereof is 6*l* a year, being an aſſeſſment after the rate of 1*s* for every noble of rent paid to the lord.

Beſides which, about 30 years ago, an allotment of 200*l* of queen Anne's bounty fell to this chapel; with which an eſtate was purchaſed in Strickland Ketel, now let for 12*l* a year.

Towards a further augmentation, the executors of the will of the late Dr. Stratford gave 100*l*, and the inhabitants added thereto another 100*l* being moſt of it charity money given by divers perſons to the ſaid chapelry; whereby having procured 200*l* from the governors of the ſaid bounty, an eſtate in Whitwell and Patton called Patton Folds was purchaſed for the ſum of 400*l*, now let for about 20*l* a year.

Dr. Ayray, provoſt of Queen's College in Oxford, was born in this chapelry; and bequeathed to the ſame 40*s* a year for a monthly ſermon.

STAVELEY AND HUGILL.

Having now advanced to the furtheſt extremity of the pariſh towards the north-weſt, we turn ſouthwards to Staveley and Hugill.

In the diviſion of the *Brus* moiety of the barony of Kendal amongſt the ſiſters of *Peter de Brus*, a great part of what we now ſpeak of was given to the third ſiſter *Lucy* who was married to *Marmaduke de Thweng*, who had two daughters *Lucy* and *Margaret*, betwixt whom the inheritance was divided; one of which daughters was married to *Lumley*, and the daughter and heir of the other married to *Hotham*. But the eldeſt ſiſter of *Brus* had ſome ſhare herein likewiſe, from whom it deſcended to the *Parrs*, being part of the Marquis fee.

Staveley and *Hugill* are bounded on the eaſt by Long Sleddale, being divided therefrom by the ridge of Potter Fell; on the ſouth by Underbarrow, being divided by the top of Ratherhead; on the weſt by Crook, being divided by the ridge of Brackenthwait Fell; and on the north by Kentmere, being divided by Blackbeck which runs by Milrigg.

After the death of *William de Thweng*, in the 14 Ed. 3. the inquiſition finds, that he died ſeiſed of the park of Staveley, the herbage whereof was worth 53*s* 4*d* in ſummer, and in winter nothing; of the fulling mill there, worth by the year 10*s*; of certain lands at Reſpton, worth yearly 29*s*; of the rents of free tenants and tenants at will at Staveley and Sapgill 8*l* a year, and at Hogill and Reſpton 9*l*.

Amongſt

Amongst the Escheats in the 1 Hen. 5. it is found, that *John Hothame* knight held the manor of Staveley; and that *John Hothame* was his son and heir. And in the 12 Eliz. the *Hothams* sold their share to *Bellingham*.

In the assignment of dower to Helena marchioness of Northampton in the 15 Eliz. amongst other particulars are these following:—*Hewgill:* Total of the customary rent there, parcel of Kendal castle, by the year, 3*l* 19*s* 9*d*.—*Staveley:* Freeholders there, James Harrington gentleman for lands in Sleddale 12*d*. The heirs of Thomas Washington 18*d*. The heirs of Rounthwat and Gilping for lands in Staveley 22*d*. Rowland Philipson gentleman for lands there 12*d*.—*Staveley and Hewgill late Ducket's lands:* Agnes Ducket widow holdeth the manor place of Ducket's lands called Gilthwait Rigg, consisting of a dwelling-house and out-houses and 58 acres of land, and payeth yearly 40*s*.—*Total of the rent of Staveley and Hewgill:* Tenant-right 12*l* 11*s* 9*d*. Intacks 12*s* 0½*d*. Concealed rents 3*s*. Greenhue 5*s* 8*d*. Improved rent in Staveley 8*s* 6*d*.

In the 20 Eliz. after the death of *Alan Bellingham* esquire, it is found, that he died seised of the manor of Staveley, and of divers lands, tenements, and hereditaments in Over Staveley, Nether Staveley, Sadgill, Respton, Fairbank, Hewgil, Grismere, Langden, Potterfell, Vowflatt, Ulthwaite, Raderhead, Saberghe, Crookefell, Westwood, and Rogerholme, and a fishery in Winandermere and the lakes of Skelleswater and Grismere, and a moiety of the watermill in Respton: And that he held the same of the queen by knights service.

In the same year it was found, that *William Gilpin* held the manor of Over Staveley: That is, he held *part* of the manor; for a jury upon an inquisition in the like cases were seldom very exact in setting forth what particular part every person held.

In the 38 Eliz. it is found, that *Robert Bindlose* esquire and *James Bellingham* esquire held of the queen as of her barony of Kendale, in free socage and not *in capite*, in Nether Staveley, one capital messuage called Asawaythall, and two other messuages called Brackenthwait and Headhouse, and divers other messuages and tenements there.

In the 6 Cha. 1. *Rowland Philipson* gentleman held in Staveley, by fealty, and 12*d* rent, one capital messuage called Hollinghow, and a parcel of land and wood called the Outwoode, of the king as of his castle of Kendal.

In the 11 Cha. 1. one capital messuage called Ashes, with 31 acres of land, in Staveley-Godmond (so called from Godmond who had estates there), were holden of the king as of his manor of Kendal called the Marquesse fee, by the yearly rent of 16*d* for all services, by *Christopher Philipson*; his heir being within age.

In the 28 Cha. 2. there were holden of Katherine queen consort in Staveley and Hugill of the Marquis Fee, 6 freehold tenements of the yearly rent of 4*s* 7*d*. Thirteen customary tenements of the yearly rent of 5*l* 17*s* 4½*d*. Fulling mills and lords acres, of the rent of 1*l* 8*s* 4*d*. And 15 cottages, of the rent of 1*l* 13*s* 4*d*. Four other tenements in Hugill, paying a free or dry rent of 3*l* 19*s* 9*d*. Ulthwaite mill in Hugill, 1*s* 2*d*.

Several

CHAP. VI.

Several courts are held by the several lords, and the tenements lie intermixed.

In the 2 Ed. 3. *William de Thweng* obtained a grant of a market on Friday weekly at Staveley, and a fair yearly on the eve, day, and morrow of St. Luke *.

And in the 9th year of the same king, the said *William* obtained a charter of free warren in Staveley †.

The *chapel* of Staveley is a fair building, with an handsome steeple and three good bells. To what saint it was dedicated is not certain: From the inscription on one of the bells, it seems to have been St. Margaret; viz.

Margaretam
Concrepat illa divam
Voce sonoram.

On another of the bells is inscribed "In the name of God. Amen."

The ancient salary was 20 nobles. And Henry Nicholson of Pick'd-how in Over-Staveley gave 10*s* for a sermon to be preached on St. Thomas's day yearly.

Belonging to the same are also two estates, one of them at New-house in Patton, and the other at Crow Park in Natland, purchased with the sum of 400*l*; of which 100*l* was lady Moyer's, procured by Dr. Gastrel bishop of Chester, 100*l* by the inhabitants and other benefactors, and 200*l* by the governors of queen Anne's bounty: which estates are now worth to the present curate George Myers, B. A. 26*l* 10*s* 0*d* yearly.

There are also two tenements called Low Scroggs and Elfhow, worth about 30*l per annum*, which were given by George Jopson of Staveley in the year 1696, to a preaching minister that shall officiate as curate at Staveley, provided he shall teach and instruct children, and perform the office of a schoolmaster within the said chapelry.

Staveley and *Hugill* were originally one chapelry. But afterwards a separate chapel was erected at INGS in Hugill, so called from a long Ing or watery meadow, at the head of which it stands. But the inhabitants of Hugill still pay a salary of 40*s* a year to the chapel of Staveley, and have seats, and christen and bury there.

The ancient salary of this chapel is 7 nobles. Which was augmented with 5 marks a year paid by the king's auditor. And 12*l* a year was given to this chapel, in the year 1655, by Mr. Rowland Wilson of the Low hall in Grasgarth, where he was born. He had been a poor boy, and going to London acquired there a considerable fortune. He gave this augmentation for the curate to teach the children of the chapelry *gratis* ‡.

There are also belonging to this chapel two estates; one of them in Middleton, purchased with 200*l* which came by lot from the augmentation of queen Anne's bounty; and the other in the parish of Aldingham, purchased with

* Denton. † Id. ‡ Machel.

the

the Sum of 400*l*, being 200*l* given by Mrs. Mary Foster of Kendal, and 200*l* bounty-money: both together worth yearly 23*l* 15*s* 0*d*.

Also a place called Chapel-house, built for the curate's residence, of the yearly value of 9*l*.

Robert Bateman esquire, merchant at Leghorn, by his will charged an estate belonging to him called Rifton-hall, with the payment of 12*l* a year to this chapel, and 8*l* to the school; but this devise being since the mortmain act of the 9 Geo 2. is deemed to be void.

The said Mr. Bateman gave 1000*l* for the benefit of the poor of Ings, which he ordered to be laid out in purchasing an estate within the township, and 8 cottages to be built thereon for the reception of so many of the most necessitous families belonging to the said township. Accordingly an estate was purchased at Grasgarth, and houses erected thereon, the expence of which purchase and building amounted to 810*l*, and the remainder hath part been laid out in a purchase, and part out at interest. And when all this is done, it is doubted by many, whether this charity is beneficial to the township, as it draws to it a number of poor, striving to get settlements.

There is a sum of 50*s* yearly to be given on Good Friday to the poor housholders of Nether Staveley chiefly, charged upon Broadfoot there; and 10*s* yearly to the poor of the Brow and Gate, charged upon Langclose; by Mr. Fleming.

At Gasgarth there was anciently a chapel called St. Anne's, about a quarter of a mile north-west from the present chapel of Ings.

CROOK AND WINSTER.

These two, in like manner as Staveley and Ings, were originally one chapelry; but now they are two distinct chapelries.

The tenants in CROOK are intermixed, in like manner as those in Staveley and Hugill, being part of the Marquis fee under the crown, and part of the Lumley fee under different lords.

In the 3 Ed. 2. after the death of *William Roos*, the inquisition finds, that *Simon de Gnype* held of the said *William* the 4th part of the hamlet of Crok, by the cornage of 5*s* 11½*d*, and for puture of the foresters 6*s*.

In the 15 Eliz. part of the jointure of *Helena* widow of *William Parr* marquis of Northampton was, The rent of Crook and improvements there 15*s* 7*d* a year.

In the 41 Eliz. it was found, that in Crook 17 messuages or tenements in the several tenures of divers customary tenants were holden by *William Knype* gentleman, of the queen as of her barony of Kendal, by knights service, *viz.* the 50th part of one knight's fee, and were worth by the year 4*l* 18*s* 4*d*.

Crook *hall* was anciently called Thwatterden hall, and for several descents belonged to the *Philipsons*; a younger branch of which family settled here, the elder remaining at Calgarth.

The

CHAP. VI.

The firſt of the ſaid younger branch that ſettled here, was,

1. MYLES PHILIPSON of Thwatterden-hall eſquire, ſecond ſurviving ſon of *Chriſtopher Philipſon* of Calgarth eſquire; which *Chriſtopher* died in the 7th year of queen Elizabeth. The ſaid *Myles* married Barbara ſiſter and coheir of Francis Sands of Coniſhead in Lancaſhire, and by her had iſſue, (1) *Robert.* (2) *Francis.* (3) *Chriſtopher Philipſon* of Coniſhead, who married Bridget daughter of Roger Kirkby of Kirkby eſquire, and had iſſue Myles, Thomas, and Chriſtopher. (4) *Thomas.* (5) *John*, fellow of Merton college in Oxford. (6) *Myles*, a captain; who married Anne daughter of John Wharton of Kirkby Thore eſquire. (7) *Elizabeth.* (8) *Jane.* (9) *Anne*, married to Thomas lord Arundel of Wardour, count of the Holy Roman empire. (10) *Mary*, married to Samuel Knype of Fairbank in Weſtmorland.

2. ROBERT PHILIPSON of Thwatterden-hall eſquire, ſon and heir of Myles, married Anne daughter of Ralph Latus of Beck-hall in Cumberland; and by her had iſſue, (1) *Chriſtopher.* (2) *Elizabeth*, married to George Corham of Barton in the county of Southampton.

3. CHRISTOPHER PHILIPSON of Thwatterden hall eſquire, ſon and heir of Robert. He married Mary daughter of William Huddleſtone of Milholme-caſtle in Cumberland eſquire, and by her had iſſue, (1) *Huddleſton Philipſon.* (2) *Robert*, who was major of a regiment in the ſervice of king Charles the firſt, and for his military atchievements was diſtinguiſhed by the ſtyle and title of Robin the Devil: He married Anne daughter of Thomas Knype, and had iſſue a ſon Robert. (3) *Elizabeth*, married to Latus.

This Chriſtopher died in the 7 Cha. 1. and by inquiſition it was found, that he died ſeiſed of one capital meſſuage and tenement in Helsfell, with 60 acres of land; one meſſuage called Crook-hall, with 24 acres of land; and ſix other meſſuages in Crook; holden of the king as of his manor of Kendal called the Marquis Fee, by knights ſervice: And that Huddleſton Philipſon his ſon and heir was then within age.

4. HUDDLESTON PHILIPSON of Crook-hall, eſquire, married Elizabeth daughter of Alan Aſcough; and by her had iſſue, (1) *Chriſtopher.* (2) *Alan*, who married Mary widow of Arthur Beſt, but had no iſſue. (3) *Robert.* (4) *Miles.*

5. CHRISTOPHER PHILIPSON of Crook-hall, eſquire, was knighted by king Charles the ſecond in the year 1681, being then repreſentative of the county of Weſtmorland in parliament. He married Clara widow of Francis Topham eſquire, and daughter of Samuel Robinſon of Cowton-grange in Yorkſhire; and by her had iſſue three daughters, *Frances*, *Elizabeth*, and *Clara*. Theſe three daughters ſold the eſtate to major Pigeon, natural ſon of king Charles the ſecond; whoſe daughter was married to Ralph Day eſquire the preſent owner.

The *chapel* of Crook is a fair building, with a tower ſteeple, and one bell. The ancient ſalary is 3*l* 16*s* 6*d*. It received an augmentation of 200*l* of queen Anne's bounty by lot in 1751, with which an eſtate was purchaſed in Stainton, now of the yearly value of 10*l*. In 1767, it received another augmentation of of 200*l* by lot, with which an estate was purchased in the chapelry, of the yearly value of 7*l*. There is also another estate at Lane-head in Crook belonging to this chapel, of the yearly value of 5*l*, but by whom given is not known.

WINSTER, though it is in the parish of Kendal, yet is said to be in the constablewick of Undermilbeck in the parish of Windermere; probably because the tenements were holden of the Philipsons of Calgarth in Undermilbeck. The last Philipson of that place left four daughters, Mary, Frances, Jane, and Clara; who sold the manor in 1717, to John Taylor and Miles Birket both of Winster, who conveyed to the several tenants respectively, subject only to the payment of a free rent to the crown.

The *chapelry* of Winster was anciently a part of the chapelry of Crook; and the inhabitants of Winster still pay towards the repairs of Crook chapel.

The original salary of Winster chapel was certified in 1717, at 3*l* 19*s* 0*d*. To which also belongs an inclosure of meadow ground lying in Winster, given by Mr. Knipe in the year 1617. Also to the said chapel belongs an estate in Cartmel Fells, purchased with 200*l* which came to it by lot from queen Anne's bounty in 1720. And an estate in Dent, purchased in 1760, with 400*l*; of which sum 200*l* was contributed by the governors of the said bounty, 100*l* by Dr. Stratford's executors, and 100*l* by divers other benefactors. The whole yearly revenue of the said chapel now amounts to about 25*l* a year.

Part of Cartmel Fells, though in another parish and county, pays to the curate of this chapel, as part of the chapelry, for the ease and convenience of those parts, being far distant from their mother church.

This place gives name to the rivulet called Winster Beck; which almost from head to foot divides Westmorland from Lancashire.

UNDERBARROW AND BRADLEY FIELD.

This is the last division that remains to be spoken of in the parish of Kendal.

UNDERBARROW hath its name from its situation under the *barrow*, hill, or scar, which extends from north to south all along in this division.

That part which is called BRADLEY FIELD received its denomination from a family of the name of *Bradley*, which came from *Bradley* in Lancashire. They had also possessions in the parish of Betham. The last of whom, *viz. John Bradley* married Anne daughter of Robert Brathwaite of Ambleside esquire; and by her had issue three daughters coheirs: 1. Elianor, married to John Osbaldeston of Osbaldeston in the county of Lancaster esquire. 2. Elizabeth, married to Thomas Talbot of the county of York esquire. 3. Jane married to William Laborne of Conswick esquire.——The arms of Bradley are; Sable, a fess; and above that a mullet between two cross crosslets fitche, Or.

CHAP. VI.

This family of *Layburn* at *Consfwick* in this divifion hath been very ancient, and a very confiderable family in the county. The fucceffion whereof in a chronological feries, fo far as we have been able to make it out (though we cannot vouch for it as a regular pedigree all along from father to fon), is as follows:

1. *Robert de Leyburne* is the firft we find mentioned; to whom, in the reign of king Henry the third, William de Lancaftre, baron of Kendal, granted Skelfmergh. He had a fon,

2. *John de Leyburne*; who had a fon,

3. *Nicholas de Leyburne*, whofe wife's name was Margaret; for in the 9 Ed. 1. a fine was levied, between Nicholas de Laybourne and Margaret his wife, and John de la Chamber and Sibil his wife, of certain lands in Skailfmer, Syzar, and Strickland Ketell; to hold to the faid Nicholas in fee. In the 33 Ed. 1. he was knight of the fhire, together with Sir Hugh de Lowther.

4. *Robert de Leybourne*, in the 8 Ed. 2. was elected to reprefent the county of Weftmorland in parliament.

5. *Thomas de Layborn*, in the 48 Ed 3. was one of the jurors on the inquifition *poft mortem* of Thomas de Thweng.

6. In the 14 Ric. 2. *John de Layborn* was one of the jurors on the inquifition after the death of Thomas de Roos. And again in the 9 Hen. 4. after the death of John Parr.

7. In the 6 Hen. 4. and again in the 12 Hen. 4. *Robert de Leybourne* was one of the knights of the fhire for Weftmorland.

8. *John de Leyborne*, in the 13 Hen. 4. was one of the jurors on the inquifition *poft mortem* of Philippa daughter of Ingelram de Coucy.

9. *Philip de Leyborn*, in the 10 Hen. 6. was a juror on the inquifition *poft mortem* of John de Clifford.

10. *Robert de Leyborne*, in the 1 Hen 6. was chofen knight of the fhire for Weftmorland. This Robert had a daughter married to a younger brother of Harrington, who brought with her in marriage Ubery-hall in Long Sleddale to the family of Harrington.

11. *Nicholas Layborn*, in the 14 Hen. 6. was one of the jurors on the inquifition *poft mortem* of John duke of Bedford the king's uncle.

12. *James Laiborne* of Cunfwick efquire, in the reign of king Hen. 7. married Katherine daughter of Sir Henry Bellingham of Burnefhead.

Of this family probably was Roger Leybourne, who was fellow of Pembroke-hall, and afterwards confecrated bifhop of Carlifle in the 19 Hen. 7.

The faid James Laiborne, by his wife Katherine Bellingham, had a fon,

13. *Thomas Laiborne* of Cunfwick efquire; who married Margaret daughter of Sir John Pennington of Moncaftre knight.—Befides their fon and heir *James*, they had a daughter *Janet*, married to Robert Philipfon of Hollinghow efquire.

The faid Thomas died Aug. 5. in the 2 Hen. 8. and by an inquifition on the 16 Jan. following, it appears, that he died feifed of the manors of Confwyk, Bradley, and Skelfmergh: And that James his fon and heir was then of the age of 20 years.

2 14. Sir

14. Sir *James Layborn* of Cunfwick was knight of the fhire in the 33 Hen. 8. He was twice married: Firft, to Elena daughter of Sir Thomas Curwen knight; and by her had (1) *Nicholas*. (2) *Catherine*, married to Richard Ducket of Grayrigg efquire. His fecond wife was Elinour daughter of Sir Thomas Prefton knight; by whom he had (1) *Thomas*. (2) *Elizabeth*, married to Thomas lord Dacre, and after his death to Thomas duke of Norfolk. (3) *Anne*, married to Sir William Stanley lord Mounteagle, fon and heir of Sir Thomas Stanley, fon and heir of Sir Edward Stanley the firft lord of that title.

15. *Nicholas Layborne* of Cunfwick efquire. He married Elizabeth Warcop [widow, as it feemeth, of Thomas Warcop the laft of that name] of Smerdale. They had iffue, (1) *James*, who married Bridget daughter and heir of Sir Ralph Bulmer, but died without iffue, for any thing that appeareth. (2) *William*, who fucceeded to the inheritance. (3) *Bridget*, married to Arthur fecond fon of James Philips of Brignall in the county of York efquire. (4) *Elizabeth*. (5) *Julian*. (6) *Dorothy*.

16. *William Layborn* of Cunfwick efquire, fecond fon of Nicholas by his wife Elizabeth Warcop. [And with him, and not before, begins the pedigree certified at Dugdale's vifitation in 1664. *] He married Jane one of the three daughters and coheirs of John Bradley of Betham. They had iffue, (1) *John*. (2) *George Layborn*, D. D. prefident of the college at Douay. (3) *Nicholas*, vice-prefident of the fame. (4) *Charles*. (5) *Thomas*, who married Mary Bradley of Arnfide. And feveral daughters; one of whom, *Elizabeth*, was married to Anthony Ducket of Grayrigg efquire.

17. *John Leyburne* of Cunfwick efquire. He married to his firft wife Catherine daughter of Sir Chriftopher Carus of Halghton in Lancafhire; and by her had (1) *William*, who died in his father's lifetime, without iffue; being flain in a fkirmifh at Sheriff Hutton in Yorkfhire in the year 1642, being then cornet of horfe in the queen's regiment. (2) *Thomas*, who fucceeded to the inheritance. (3) *James*, an officer in the French fervice. (4) *John*, a bifhop of the Romifh church. And three daughters; (1) *Jane*, married to Richard Sherburne of Heyfham in Lancafhire. (2) *Elizabeth*, married to Henry Wifeman in Maryland. (3) *Lucy*, married firft to Thomas Kitfon of Killington, afterwards to Robert Weftby of Winder in the county of Lancafter.

The faid John married to his fecond wife Mary daughter of William Croft of Claughton in the county of Lancafter efquire; and by her had *George*, *Nicholas*, *Roger*, *Charles*, *William*, *Frances*, and *Catherine*.

In the time of this John, the family removed to Witherflack, having purchafed the hall and demefne there, during the diftreffes of the Derby family.

John died in the year 1663; and was fucceeded by his fecond fon as aforefaid, *viz*.

18. *Thomas Leyburn* of Witherflack efquire. He married Dorothy daughter of William Lafcells of Brackenburgh in the county of York efquire; and by her had (1) *John*, who was of the age of 11 years at Dugdale's vifitation aforefaid.

* Machel.

CHAP. VI.

aforesaid. (2) *Catherine*, married to Dr. Marmaduke Witham of Cliff in the county of York. (3) *Elizabeth*. (4) *Anne*.—The said Thomas died in 1672.

19. *John Leyburn* of Witherslack esquire. He died unmarried in 1679; and was succeeded at Witherslack by his three sisters coheirs. But Cunswick and the other intailed estates came to the then next surviving heir male, *viz.* George Leyburn of Neatby in Lancashire, son of John at N° 17. by his second wife Mary Croft.

20. *George Leyburn* of Cunswick esquire, married Anne Stanley of Dalegarth in Cumberland: And by her had issue, *John*, *George*, *Nicholas*, *James*, and four daughters.

21. *John Leyburn* of Cunswick esquire, married Lucy only daughter of Thomas Dalston of Hornby esquire, counsellor at law; and died without leaving issue. His brothers *George*, *Nicholas*, and *James*, all died unmarried. Of his sisters, two only were married. The eldest sister *Mary* was married to Marmaduke Tunstall of Barningham, and died without issue. The other sister was married to Mr. Walton of Winder nigh Cartmell, and left issue a daughter; which daughter was married first to Thomas Cholmondeley of Brandsby in Yorkshire, to whom she had no child. To her second husband she married George Ann of Burwallis, to whom she had only a daughter, who died young.—So that the family is now totally extinct.

The said John, having been engaged in the rebellion in 1715, this estate became forfeited, and was purchased of the crown by *Thomas Crowle* gentleman, from whom it descended to his son George Crowle gentleman; after whose decease in 1753 the same was sold to the present owner Sir James Lowther baronet.

The *arms* of Leyburn are; Azure, 6 lioncells rampant, 3, 2, and 1, Argent, langued and membred Gules. The crest: On a wreath Argent and Azure, an hawk regardant Azure.

Underbarrow is part of the Marquis Fee, and part of the Lumley Fee. That part which is of the Marquis Fee, in the survey made in the 28 Cha. 2. stands charged, for 26 tenements, with the customary rent of 19*l* 5*s* 7*d*. The fulling mill rents 1*l* 0*s* 8*d*. Cunswick stands charged with a free or dry rent of 18*d* for one pound of pepper; and Bradley Field with 4½*d* for a quarter of a pound of pepper.—That part which is of the Lumley Fee belonged to the Bellinghams, and was by them sold to Colonel James Grahme, from whom the same hath descended to the present earl of Suffolk and Berkshire.

There was an ancient chapel at this place, and the salary belonging to the same was 6*l* 4*s* 2*d* a year: Or rather perhaps 6*l* 13*s* 4*d*; part of which hath been lost probably, as is not unusual in like cases. For twenty nobles was the stipulated sum at the foundation of many of the chapels to be settled for the maintenance of a curate: Which sum, considering the continual decrease in the value of money, was equal to 30, 40, or 50*l* a year now.

In the year 1708, this chapel was rebuilt at the expence of the inhabitants of Underbarrow only (for Bradley Field is not in the chapelry). And in 1732, an an estate in Killington called High Bendrigg was purchased for the use of this chapel, with the sum of 400*l*, whereof 200*l* was given by the said Colonel Grahme and lady Moyer, and the other 200*l* by the governors of queen Anne's bounty.

There is also belonging to the said chapel a rent charge of 30*s* yearly issuing out of a field in the said township. And a small estate called Chapel House (which house is situate about 100 yards from the chapel) now let for 7*l* a year; out of which is paid 35*s* yearly to the poor housholders of the township, in consideration of 35*l* poor stock laid out in the purchase of the said estate.

The whole revenue of the chapel arising from the premisses, amounts at present to about 34*l* a year.

PARISH OF GRESMERE.

I. *Gresmere church and manor.*

II. *Rydal and Lougbrig.*

III. *Langdale and Baisbrow.*

I.

GRESMERE CHURCH AND MANOR.

GRESMERE is supposed by some to have had its name from the *grassy mere* or lake there. But anciently it was never written *Grasmere* (much less *Grasmire*); but most commonly *Gresmere*, sometimes *Grismere*. From whence one might conclude, that it received its name from the *grise* or wild swine, with which this country formerly abounded. In like manner as in the adjoining parish of Barton, there is *Grisedale*, *Boardale*, *Stybarrow*, and such like. In Kentmere, Richard Gilpin is supposed to have signalized himself as aforesaid for killing a wild boar, which infested all the neighbouring parts.

The parish of Gresmere is bounded on the East by Patterdale in the parish of Barton, from which it is divided by the very ridge or top of the mountains; on the South, by the parish of Windermere, from which it is divided in part by Stockbridge water; on the West, by Furness Fells in Lancashire, from which it is divided by the river Brathey; and on the North, by part of Cumberland, from which it is divided by the ridge of mountains called Langdale Fells, as the water runs off to each side of the mountain.

The church is dedicated to St. Oswald, as is supposed, from a well called St. Oswald's near unto the church.

It is rated in the valuation in the king's books in the 26 Hen. 8. at 28*l* 11*s* 5½*d*.

This parish (as also that of Windermere) was originally a chapelry only within the parish of Kendal; but by length of time, and little or no commu-

 nication

CHAP. VI.

nication with the mother church by reason of the distance, it hath acquired the reputation of a distinct parish. When the church of Kendal was appropriated to the abbey of St. Mary's York, a pension was appointed to be paid out of Gresmere to the said abbey of 1 *l* 13 *s* 4 *d*. But the chapel continued in the patronage of Ingelram de Gynes and Christian his wife, in the 30 Ed. 1.

Accordingly, in the 49 Ed. 3. after the death of Joan de Coupland, the inquisition finds, that she died seised of the advowson of the *chapel* of Grismere, which was then valued at 10 *l*.

In the 3 Hen. 8. the king nominated to the abbot and convent of St. Mary's near York walls, under the great seal, *John Frost* to be presented unto the *chapel* of Gresmere, being then void by the resignation of *Hugh Ashton*.

And in the 16 Hen. 8. the king nominated *William Holgill* to the said *chapel*.

After the dissolution of the monasteries, the patronage of this chapel was granted to the *Bellinghams*. And in the 16 Eliz. *Alan Bellingham* esquire, for the sum of 100 *l*, sold the same to *William Fleming* of Ridal esquire, in whose family the advowson thereof still continues.

The church of Gresmere is situate in the midst of a large plain, encompassed almost round with high mountains. It is a pretty large building, with a strong steeple and three good bells. The owners of Ridall-hall have a peculiar burying-place in the said church.

The *parsonage-house* stands about 40 yards west from the church, on the north side of the river Raisbeck, which runs by the church, near the end of the parsonage house. It was rebuilt by Dr. *Henry Fleming*, rector thereof, in the year 1691.

At the north-east corner of the church-yard, there is a *school*, which was built about the year 1685, at the expence of the inhabitants, and endowed by Mr. *Ambrose* then rector with 50 *l*. Anthony Dawson of Gresmere gave 7 *l*. The interest thereof to go towards the support and maintenance of a schoolmaster.

The MANOR of Gresmere is now esteemed a distinct manor, like as the chapelry hath obtained the name of a parish. But heretofore the manor was parcel only of the manor of Windermere.

Thus in the 49 Ed. 3. after the death of Joan de Coupland aforesaid, the inquisition finds, that the said Joan died seised of the manor of Wynandermere, with its members and appurtenances; and, amongst the rest, the hamlet of *Grismer*.

In the 14 Eliz. after the death of William Parr, marquis of Northampton, the inquisition finds, that he died seised of and in the manor of Gresmere, and of divers messuages, lands, and tenements there.

And in the rental of dower assigned to his widow, the particulars as to Gresmere stand thus: *Manor of Gresmere*. Total of the yearly rent there 11 *l* 10 *s* 0½ *d*. The inhabitants of Gresmere hold one parcel of pasture ground, as an improvement of the common waste there called the Forest, and pay yearly for the moiety of the same (the other moiety to the queen) 3 *l* 6 *s* 8 *d*.

The

The ſaid inhabitants pay alſo for the rent of four water-mills now decayed 23*s* 4*d*. And for lands unknown 2*s* 6*d*.

That which belonged to the queen is of the Richmond fee: For Greſmere ſeems to have been near equally divided; as by the inquiſition in the 28 Cha. 2. when queen Catherine was in poſſeſſion of both the Marquis and Richmond fees, it appears, that in Greſmere there were 39 cuſtomary tenements of the Marquis fee, of the yearly rent of 11*l* 6*s* 2*d*; and 35 tenements of the Richmond fee, of the yearly rent of 6*l* 12*s* 4*d*.

In a rental (now at Sizergh-hall) of the crown lands in the barony of Kendal, in the 7 Hen. 7. whereof Sir Thomas Strickland was then ſteward, amongſt the particulars of rents for two parts of the ſaid lands, due to (the king's mother) Margaret counteſs of Richmond and Derby (the third part belonging to the ducheſs of Bedford in right of dower), there was iſſuing out of Greſmere a rent called *foreſt ſilver* 44*s* 5*d ob.* a rent called *brewefarme* 8*d*, and a rent called *goldewether* 7*d ob. q.*—So, out of Langden; *foreſt ſilver* 33*s* 4*d*, *goldewether* 4*d*.—In like manner, Loughrigg paid *foreſt ſilver* 8*d*, *goldewether* 3*d q.* and a rent called *walking ſilver* 4*s* 5*d ob.*——The *foreſt ſilver* was for agiſtment of cattle in the foreſt. *Walking ſilver* ſeems to have been a compoſition for puture of the foreſters or other officers whoſe buſineſs it was to perambulate and ſurvey. *Brewefarm* by ſome is underſtood to be a rent paid for licence to *brew* and ſell ale and beer; for the lord of the manor in moſt places had juriſdiction of the aſſize in that reſpect: But as the word *bruer* ſignifies alſo heath or ling, perhaps this might be a payment for the privilege of getting ling for fuel. As to *goldwether*, we have not found any account of it, except in this and ſome other rentals of the ſame lands about that time: poſſibly, as the *foreſt ſilver* was for the agiſtment of cattle, ſo *goldwether* might be for the agiſtment of ſheep.

Within this manor there are ſeveral *tarns* or *meres*; of which, the moſt conſiderable is *Greſmere-water*, into which the river *Raiſbeck* empties itſelf, after a courſe of about three miles, from Raſegill-head where it ſprings, down by *Dunmal Raiſe*, and thence weſtward down the dale, and ſo by the ſide of the church and parſonage as aforeſaid. Out of which water of Greſmere, runs a river, which taking its courſe through Rydal water, maketh the river *Rowthey*; and ſo paſſing by Ambleſide, it loſeth itſelf, with the river *Brathey*, in Windermere water.

Dunmal Raiſe aforeſaid is a large mountain, a great part whereof is in this pariſh, over which the highway leadeth from Keſwick by Ambleſide unto Kendal. It is ſo called from a great heap or *raiſe* of ſtones, by the highway ſide, which divides Cumberland from this county, thrown together in ancient time, either by *Dunmaile* ſometime king of Cumberland, as a mark of the utmoſt border of his kingdom, or by ſome other in remembrance of his name, for ſome memorable act done by him there, or ſome victory obtained over him.

II. RYDAL.

CHAP. VI.

II.

RYDAL AND LOUGHRIG.

Rydal, Sir Daniel Fleming supposes to be a contraction of *Rowthey-dale*, from the river of that name running down there.

This manor was granted to *Roger de Lancastre* before mentioned, by Margaret de Brus, widow of Robert de Ross of Werk, and sister and one of the coheirs of Peter de Brus who married Helwise sister and coheir of William de Lancastre the third of that name, baron of Kendal. In which grant, the boundaries are described in this manner: "Incipiendo del Dovecragg per altiora montis inter Rydal et Scandal, sicut aqua se dividit, sequendo altiora montis illius usque ad Scandendestay in le Swythene; et sic descendendo de Swythene, per quandam semitam quæ vocatur le Waythesti, usque ad parcum de Amelsate; et sic sequendo parcum dexterius usque in Scandelbec; et sic sequendo Scandelbec usque in Routha; et sic sequendo Routha, ascendendo usque in Routhemere; et sic sequendo Routhemere usque ex opposito del Brokestay, et sic linealiter usque le Brokestay, et de le Brokestay usque ad summitatem de la Nab; et sic ascendendo per altiora, sicut aqua se dividit, usque Laverdkrag; et de Laverdkrag per superiora ascendendo per altiora usque le Ernekrag; et inde ascendendo per altiora illius montis usque ad divisas Westmerlandiæ; et sic per divisas Westmerlandiæ usque ad summitatem del Dovecrag prædicti."—She granted to him also all her part of Amelsate and Louthrigg, with common of pasture in Gressmere for all kinds of cattle, and that the inhabitants within the bounds aforesaid shall have common with her tenants in Gresmere wheresoever: To enjoy the same, with free chase in the forest of Rydal, as peaceably as Peter de Brus her late brother, or William de Lancastre her late uncle, did possess the same. Witnesses, Thomas de Musgrave then sheriff of Westmorland, Ranulfe de Dacre, Michael de Harcla, knights; and many others.

The said Roger in the 3 Ed. 1. obtained a confirmation from the king, under the great seal, of the said grant of Margaret de Brus, reciting the same *verbatim*; so as the said Roger and his heirs have and hold the said forest, and the aforesaid part of Amelsate and Lochrigg, and all other things in the said grant contained, with the appurtenances, of the king and his heirs, *in capite*, by doing for the same the service of the fourth part of one knight's fee for all services for ever.

The said Roger had likewise a deed from William de Lindesey (there having been some contentions between the said Roger de Lancastre and William de Lindesey) concerning what should be taken by the said Roger, for goods found by eschape in his forest of Rydal, belonging to the said William's tenants; and concerning an inclosure to be made by the said William, adjoining upon Rydal park.

This Roger procured a charter for a market weekly on Thursday at his manor of Ulverston, and a fair yearly on the eve, day, and morrow after the feast of the Nativity of our Lady; the said manor having been granted unto him by by Walter de Falconbergh, Marmaduke de Thweng, and William de Lindesey and his wife. CHAP. VI.

This *Roger* had three sons, *John*, *William*, and *Christopher*. From *Christopher* the youngest came the Lancastres of Sockbridge. *John* the eldest died in the 8 Ed. 2. without issue male; and the inheritance was transferred by intail to *John de Lancastre* of Howgill-castle the next heir male, being son and heir of the second brother *William*. This *John de Lancastre* of Howgill and Rydal died in the 25 Ed. 3. leaving issue,

Sir *William de Lancastre*; who dying in the 22 Ric. 2. was succeeded by his son,

Sir *William de Lancastre*, who died in the 8 Hen. 4, leaving a son and heir,

Sir *John de Lancastre*; who appears to have been living in the 6 Hen. 6. for in that year, upon an inquisition of knights fees in Westmorland, it was found, that *John de Lancaster* of Howgill knight held of the king *in capite*, *Ridall* in Kendale, by the service of the fourth part of one knight's fee. How long he lived after this, we have not found. He died without issue male; leaving four daughters coheirs, 1. *Christian*, married to Sir *Robert de Harrington* knight. 2. *Isabel*, married to Sir *Thomas le Fleming* of Coniston knight, with whom he had *Rydal*. 3. *Margaret*, married to Sir *Matthew de Whitfield* knight. 4. *Elizabeth*, married to *Robert de Crackenthorp* esquire.

RYDAL being thus brought into the name and family of FLEMING, we proceed to deduce the history of that ancient family; for which we are furnished with ample materials, by the large and valuable collection made by Sir *Daniel Fleming* baronet; whose account of his own family is extracted from the family evidences and other authentic documents.

There seems to be no doubt, that the first of the name who had possessions in England came in with William the conqueror, out of Flanders.

I. The first *Fleming* that hath appeared to us, by any record or other authentic instrument, was MICHAEL LE FLEMING knight, in some writings called *Flandrensis*: Unto whom William de Meschiens, brother to Ranulph de Meschiens who lived in the time of the conqueror, gave Beckermet, Frisington, Rotington, Weddikar, Arlochden, Kelton, Salter, and Brunrigg, in Cumberland.

This *Michael* and his posterity had commonly in records and writings *le* prefixed to their surname, until the time of king Edward the fourth: which helps to confirm the observation of Camden, that *de* and *le* were strictly observed in some local names, until about that time.

When Stephen earl of Boulogne (who was afterwards king of England) founded the abbey of Furness in the year 1126, he granted to the said abbey whatsoever was in Furness, except the land of *Michael Flameng*. Which grant was confirmed by pope Eugenius, with the like exception.

This Sir *Michael* resided commonly at Beckermet, where was a castle anciently, called by the common people Caernarvon castle. He was also lord of the manors of Aldingham and of Gleston in Furness in the county of Lancaster.

CHAP. VI. caster. And as he sometimes also resided at Gleston, he received from thence the name of *Michael de Furness:* On the contrary, he gave the name of *Mitchel-land* (or Michael-land) to a great part of Furness, which continues to be so called to this day.

In the 19th year of king Stephen, he granted Fordebote to the said abbey of Furness; and soon after died, and was buried in the said abbey, wherein most of the nobility and gentry in those parts were interred, as was very usual also in other places, many bequeathing their bodies, together with a legacy, to the religious houses; and others desiring not only to be buried near the monks habitations, but also in their very habits.

He had issue five sons and one daughter.

1. *William*, to whom he gave the manor of Aldingham and castle of Gleston, with other possessions in the county of Lancaster.

2. *Richard*, to whom he gave his castle of Caernarvon and manor of Beckermet, with the homage and service, wards and reliefs, of all the freeholders in Frisington, Rotington, Weddikar, Kelton, Salter, Arlochden, and Brunrigg aforesaid, with other possessions in that county and in the county of Lancaster, which are yet enjoyed by his posterity and issue male, lineally for the most part, and sometimes collaterally for want of issue male in the elder branch.

3. *Daniel*, a clergyman; who had the church of Urswic reserved to him, upon his father's exchange of Ros and Crinelton for Bardsey and Urswick, with the abbot of Furness.

4. *Anselm*, who assumed the surname *de Furness*. He was living in the 13th year of king John. He married Agnes daughter of Alice wife of Edgar, and had half of Yanewith with her in marriage.

5. *Jordan*, who also took the name *de Furness*.

6. *Godith*; with whom her father gave in marriage 3 carucates of land in Adgaresslith.

The present family at Rydall proceed from *Richard* the second son, who (as aforesaid) was settled in Cumberland. And it is this branch that we are chiefly to pursue. The elder branch, who enjoyed the Lancashire estate, continued owners thereof in a regular hereditary succession of males and females, till it arrived as it were at the foot of the throne, in the person of Henry Grey marquis of Dorset and afterwards duke of Suffolk, father of the lady Jane Grey. Which branch we will first briefly deduce; and then return to the younger branch, with which we are more particularly concerned.

The eldest son of Sir *Michael* aforesaid was (1) *William le Fleming* of Furness knight, who after the death of his father enjoyed the manor of Aldingham, the castle and manor of Gleston, with other lands in the county of Lancaster and elsewhere, which had belonged to the said Michael his father; and he inhabited for the most part at Gleston castle. (2) Sir *Michael le Fleming* of Furness knight, son and heir of William. He had a son, (3) *William le Fleming*; who had issue, (4) Sir *Michael le Fleming* knight, who in the reign of king Henry the third was drowned in Leven, and died without issue, and left his whole estate to (5) *Alice*, his only sister and heir. She married *Richard de de Cancefield*, and had iſſue a ſon and daughter. (6) *William de Cancefield*, ſon and heir of Richard and Alice, died without iſſue; and was ſucceeded by his ſiſter and heir, (7) *Agnes de Cancefield*, who was married to *Robert de Harrington* of Harrington in Cumberland, in the reign of king Edward the firſt, and carried the eſtate to that family. Though the family of Harrington at firſt aſſumed their ſurname from that place, which they had held of long time, and continued to poſſeſs, till the heir female thereof married to the lord Bonvil; yet after this marriage, their chief ſeat was at Gleſton caſtle and Aldingham. The ſaid Agnes de Cancefield to her huſband Robert de Harrington had iſſue (8) *John de Harrington*, who in the 34 Ed. 1. was knighted; and having been ſummoned to parliament as a baron from the 18 Ed. 2. to the 21 Ed. 3. he died in that year. This John had a ſon (9) *Robert de Harrington*, who died before his father, having married Elizabeth one of the ſiſters and coheirs of John de Multon of Egremont, and by her had a ſon and heir (10) *John de Harrington*, who ſucceeded his grandfather, and died in the 37 Ed. 3. leaving iſſue (11) *Robert de Harrington*, his ſon and heir, who reſiding at Aldingham in the firſt year of king Richard the ſecond, was knighted at his coronation. He married Iſabel daughter and coheir of Sir Nigel Loring knight of the garter, and left iſſue by her (12) Sir *John Harrington* knight, his eldeſt ſon and heir; who died in the 5 Hen. 4. without iſſue, and was ſucceeded by his brother and heir (13) Sir *William Harrington* knight; who married Margaret daughter of Sir Robert Nevil of Hornby. He was ſummoned to parliament from the 8 Hen. 5. to the 15 Hen. 6. He had an only child (14) *Elizabeth Harrington*, who was married to *William lord Bonvile*, who died in his father's lifetime, leaving a ſon (15) *William Bonvile* junior, commonly called *William lord Harrington*; who married Catherine one of the daughters of Richard Nevil earl of Saliſbury, and was ſlain in the battle of Wakefield on the part of the houſe of York in the 39 Hen. 6. leaving only a daughter, *viz.* (16) *Cecilie*, married to Thomas Grey marquis of Dorſet, and afterwards to Henry Stafford earl of Wiltſhire. She had to the ſaid marquis of Dorſet a ſon (17) *Thomas Grey*, marquis of Dorſet; who married Margaret daughter of Sir Robert Wotton knight (widow of William Medley), and died in the 22 Hen. 8. leaving iſſue (18) *Henry Grey*, marquis of Dorſet; who married Katherine, daughter of William Fitz-Alan earl of Arundel, but had no iſſue by her. Afterwards he married the lady Frances, eldeſt daughter of *Charles Brandon* duke of Suffolk by his wife Mary the French queen. And foraſmuch as the lady Frances's two brothers died without iſſue, this Henry her huſband was created duke of Suffolk. By her he had three daughters, Jane, Katherine, and Mary. The lady *Jane*, the eldeſt, was proclaimed queen, after the death of king Edward the ſixth, and ſoon after beheaded. Her father, for countenancing the ſaid proclamation, was beheaded on Tower-hill in the ſecond year of queen Mary; and the whole eſtate, in Cumberland, Lancaſhire, and elſewhere, became forfeited to the crown, and was granted out to divers perſons, whoſe poſterity or aſſignees enjoy the ſame to this day.

CHAP. VI.

Having thus given an account of the said Sir *William le Fleming* and his heirs, and of the several owners of Glefton castle, Aldingham, and the rest of his estate, we proceed to his next brother, *viz.*

II. Sir RICHARD LE FLEMING of Beckermet in Cumberland knight, second son of Sir Michael. This Sir Richard had also some lands in Lancashire given to him by his father; for Sir Michael had other estates there, besides those of Michel-land, Aldingham, and Glefton, which he gave as aforesaid to his eldest son.

To this Sir Richard, William de Skelsmeresergh by several deeds without date granted divers lands in Lancashire, with the fishery of Thurstan-water: to which deeds his elder brother William de Furness is a witness.

He died in the reign of king John, and was buried with his father and brother in the abbey of Furness; and was succeeded by his only son and heir,

III. Sir JOHN LE FLEMING of Beckermet knight. By a deed without date, this John conveyed to his son Richard, all the land of the said John which his father had given him in Coupland, with the homage and service of certain freeholders which then held of the said John, *viz.* the homage and service of Sir Alan de Peninton and his heirs for Rotingen, of Sir Robert de Lamplogh for half of Harlofden and for Brunrigg, of William de Wedacre for two parts of Wedacre, of Sir Adam de Haverington for the third part of Wedacre, and of Ralph de Frisington for Frisington, with wards and reliefs, and all other liberties thereunto belonging. And by several other deeds, he conveyed to him other lands in Cumberland. Witnesses to which deeds (amongst others) were, Robert prior of St. Bees, Sir Patrick de Wirkington, Sir Adam de Millum, Sir Richard de Coupland, and Sir Hugh de Morriceby.

He gave also the patronage of the rectory of Arloghden, and land in Great Beckermet, to the abbey of Caldre, in the 26 Hen. 3.

And the rectory and advowson of the church of St. John Baptist of Beckermet was granted to the said abbey either by him or his father; which was confirmed by the archbishop of York, about the year 1262. And the archbishop at the same time annexed the church of St. Michael of Arlokedene to the archdeaconry of Richmond.

He also conveyed other lands in Lancashire to divers persons: Witnesses whereof were, the prior of Kertmel, John prior of Cuningsheved, Sir William de Furnas, William son of Orme, Matthew de Redeman, Thomas de Bethun, Richard de Preston, Adam son of Gamel, John de Cancefield, Michael de Hurswic, and others.

He died in the reign of king Henry the third, and was buried in the abbey of Calder, to which he had been a benefactor. Sir Daniel Fleming says, there was to be seen in his days at the said abbey a very ancient statue in free stone of a man in armour, with a frett (of six pieces) upon his shield, lying upon his back, with his sword by his side, his hands elevated in a posture of prayer, and his legs across; being so placed probably from his taking upon him the

cross,

crofs, and being engaged in the holy war. Which ftatue was placed there moft probably in memory of this Sir John le Fleming. CHAP. VI.

He left a fon and heir,

IV. Sir RICHARD LE FLEMING of Beckermet, knight. He married *Elizabeth* fifter and heir of *Adam de Urfwick* and *John de Urfwick* her two brothers; whofe father was Adam de Urfwick, fon of Gilbert, fon of Adam, fon of Bernulf. By which marriage, the faid Richard got the manor of *Coningfton* [King's-town]; and other poffeffions in the county of Lancafter; which have continued in his heirs male to this day.

By a deed without date, John brother of the faid Elizabeth granted to the faid Sir Richard le Fleming and the faid Elizabeth all the lands which had been Adam de Urfwick's his brother, in Urfwick, Coningfton, Claughton, and Kerneford, in exchange for other lands. Witneffes; Roger de Lancaftre, John de Cancefield, John de Kirkby, Richard de Kirkby, and others.

In the 52 Hen. 3. a writ of trefpafs was brought by Ifabel de Fortibus countefs of Albermarle, againft Roger de Lancaftre, *Richard le Fleming*, Gilbert de Culwen, Ranulph de Dacre, and others.

After this marriage, the caftle of Caernarvon was fuffered to go to decay, and at laft demolifhed, and the demefne lands let to cuftomary tenants: And the family removed to *Coningfton* hall, where they refided for feveral generations.

He died, leaving a fon and heir,

V. JOHN LE FLEMING of Coningfton; who in the 28 Ed. 1. was in the expedition then made into Scotland, being with the king when he was in perfon at Carlaveroke, fituate upon the very mouth of Solway, accounted an impregnable fortrefs; which king Edward, accompanied with the flower of the Englifh nobility and gentry, befieged, and with difficulty took. During his abfence out of the kingdom, John had a protection from the king, dated at Carlaveroke 10 July, 28 Ed. 1. of his people, lands, goods, rents, and other poffeffions, and freedom from all fuits and plaints, until Eafter following.

He had iffue two fons, Raynerus and Hugh: Which Hugh had a daughter Mary, married to Ralph de Frifington.

VI. RAINERUS LE FLEMING of Coningfton. He gave to the abbot of St. Mary's York, two oxgangs of land in Rotington, and alfo one villein in the fame town: Which was confirmed by king Edward the fecond, in the firft year of his reign.

Raynerus had the appellation of *dapifer* added to his name; perhaps as being purveyor of the king in thefe northern parts.

He left iffue,

VII. Sir JOHN LE FLEMING of Coningfton, knight. By an inquifition *poft mortem* of Thomas de Multon of Egremont, in the 15 Ed. 2. it appears, that Richard de Hodlefton and Gilbert de Culwen did then hold Millum and Work-

 ington

CHAP. VI.

ington of the said Thomas; and that John son of Rayner le Fleming held of the said Thomas the hamlets of Beckermet, Frisington, Rotington, Wedacre, and Arlocden, by homage and fealty and suit of the court of Egremont, and by the service of the ninth part of one knight's fee, and 5*s* 6*d* a year for cornage, and 2*s* 5*d* for watch of the sea, and by the puture of two serjeants of the said Thomas every ninth day at his manor of Egremont.

The lords of the manor of Beckermet do yet pay yearly 3*s* 4*d* of the free rents above mentioned, to the owner of Egremont castle: And all the residue of the aforesaid rents are yearly paid by the freeholders of Frisington, Rotington, Wedacre, and Arlocden.

That this John le Fleming was lord of Beckermet in the 19 Ed. 2. and was related to Hugh le Fleming above mentioned, and to the Frisingtons, appears by an intail of the manor of Frisington made by Hugh le Fleming unto Ralph de Frisington and Mary his wife for their lives, and then to Thomas their son and the heirs of his body, and then to Alice and Agnes their daughters and the heirs male of their bodies; and for want of such, then to John le Fleming lord of Beckermet and his heirs.

He had issue two sons; and one daughter Joan, who was married to John le Towers of Lowick, whose arms were, Argent, on a bend Gules, three towers Or.

VIII. The elder son of the said Sir John was WILLIAM LE FLEMING of Coningston. He died without issue, either before his father, or soon after. For,

Sir JOHN LE FLEMING of Coningston knight, second son of the last Sir John, appears to have been heir to his father in the 7th year of king Edward the third.

By an inquisition taken at Ulverston, after the death of this Sir John, it appears, that he died in the 27 Ed. 3. and that on the day on which he died he held of the king *in capite* (which had been of the fee of William de Coucy) the manor of Coningston with the appurtenances, and a certain fishing there in Thurstan water; that he had two marks rent issuing out of Claughton, holden of John de Croft; forty acres of land at the Water-end, holden of John de Haverington by a pair of white gloves for all services; and that Richard le Fleming was his son and heir, then of the age of 30 years.

Besides this son Richard, he had also Robert le Fleming a second son.

IX. Sir RICHARD LE FLEMING of Coningston knight, son and heir of the last Sir John, married Catherine daughter (or sister) of Sir John de Kirkby in the county of Lancaster knight; whose arms were, Argent, two bars Gules, on a canton of the second a cross moline Or.

By his said wife he had issue, *Thomas*, *John*, *James*, and a daughter *Joan*. Which Joan in the 44 Ed. 3. released unto her father all her lands in Cumberland and Lancashire, which had been her grandfather's; which deed she concludes thus, "And because my seal is not known to many, I have procured "to be set to these presents the seal of the official of the deanry of Coupland, "together with the seals of William de Cleter and Thomas de Lamplowe."

In

In the 6 Ric. 2. Nicholas de Bowenefs, parfon of the moiety of the church of Ayketon, granted to William del Dykes all his lands in Diftington in Coupland which he had of the feoffment of John fon of Hugh de Dyftyngton. One of the witneffes to which grant was Richard le Fleming knight.

He appears to have been witnefs afterwards to feveral deeds; the lateft of which was in the 16 Ric. 2. at which time, by the above accounts, he was of the age of 69 years. He died at Coningfton-hall not long after, and was fucceeded by

X. Sir THOMAS LE FLEMING of Coningfton knight, his eldeft fon and heir. This Sir Thomas married firft Margaret daughter of William de Berdefey, as appears by a deed in the 47 Ed. 3. whereby Sir Richard, father of the faid Thomas, grants to him and to Margaret his wife daughter of William de Berdefey and to the heirs of their bodies the manor of Beckermet, remainder to his own right heirs. The Berdefey's arms are, Argent, two bars Gules: On a canton of the fecond, a march of the firft. By her he had no iffue.

He afterwards married Ifabel daughter of Sir Thomas Layburne knight; and had iffue by her, *Thomas le Fleming* his fon and heir, and *John le Fleming* his fecond fon.

Sir Thomas Layburne in the marriage articles did covenant to give with his faid daughter for her portion 80 marks in filver and fufficient rayment; whereupon the manor of Beckermet and lands in Urfwick were intailed upon the faid Sir Thomas le Fleming and Ifabel his wife and their heirs male; and for want of fuch, then upon John le Fleming his brother.

There appears a releafe to have been executed by him in the 12 Hen. 4. How foon after he died, is not known. But it appears he was dead in the 6 Hen. 5. his wife Ifabel being then a widow.

XI. Sir THOMAS LE FLEMING of Coningfton knight, fon of Sir Thomas by his wife Ifabel Layburne. He married, in his father's life-time, *Ifabel* daughter and coheir of Sir *John de Lancafter* of *Rydal* and *Howgill* caftle; and this was the firft introduction of the *Flemings* into Weftmorland. In the marriage articles it was covenanted, that Sir John her father fhould pay 80 marks for his daughter's portion, and that Sir Thomas father of the faid Thomas fhould fettle the manor of Coningfton and all other his lands on his faid fon and his heirs male; and for defect of fuch, then upon John le Fleming younger brother of the faid Thomas and his heirs male; and for want of fuch, then upon the right heirs of the faid Sir Thomas: And that if the faid Thomas the fon fhould die without heirs of the body of the faid Ifabel, then that John his younger brother aforefaid fhould marry another daughter of the faid Sir John de Lancafter, without any other portion or fettlement.

But the faid Thomas and Ifabel had children; and the other three daughters of Sir John de Lancafter married other perfons (as is above mentioned), and after his deceafe his eftate was divided amongft them; in which divifion, the manor of Rydal and all the faid Sir John's lands and tenements in Rydal and Loughrigg acceded to the two daughters, Margaret wife of Sir Matthew Whitfield,

CHAP. VI. field, and Isabel wife of the said Sir Thomas le Fleming. They afterwards purchased the Whitfield moiety; and Rydal from henceforth became the chief seat of the Fleming family, and their posterity have ever since enjoyed it.

The said Sir Thomas, by his wife Isabel de Lancaster, had issue *John*, and a younger son *William*.

XII. JOHN FLEMING of Rydal, esquire. After the death of the said Sir Thomas le Fleming and dame Isabel de Lancaster his wife, the aforesaid demesnes and manors of Beckermet, Coningston, and Rydal, and all their other estate in Cumberland, Lancashire, and Westmorland aforesaid, came unto this John their son and heir.

This John, in the 7 Ed. 4. was retained by indenture, according to the custom of those times, to serve the lord of Graystock, who was often employed in the king's service against Scotland: The form of which retainer was as follows: "This indenture made the 9th day of December in the 7th year "of the reign of king Edward the 4th, betwixt Rauff lord Graystock and "Wemm on the ton party, and John Fleming esquire on the todir party, "Witness, that the said John is reteined and behest * with the said lord for "terme of his life, as well in were as in peace, against all manner of men, "except his legeance: The said John taking yearly of the said lord 4 *l* of "lawful money of England. And in the time of were, such wages as the "king gyffs to such men of such degree, and [*i. e.* if] he go with the said "lord. And the said John to take his said fee be the hands of the receiver of "Graystok that is or shall be, that is to say, at Whitsunday and Martynmes. "And if the said John go with the said lord over the sea, or into Scotland, "and then it happen the said John Fleming or any of his servants to take any "prisoners, that then the said lord to have the third, and the third of thirds. "And if it happen that the said lord send for the said John to come to him, "and to ryde with him to London or for any other matter, that then the said "lord to pay for his costs, and to give him bouche-court † for him and his "feliship. In witnes hereof ayther party to the partyes of these indentures en-"terchangably hath set to their seales. Wretyn the day and yere aforesaid."

This John married Joan daughter of Broughton of Broughton Tower; by whom he had issue *John Fleming* his son and heir. The paternal coat of the Broughtons is, Argent, two bars Gules, on a canton of the second a cross Or.

He had a second wife Anne, by whom he had no issue.

He appears to have been dead in the 2 Ric. 3. for in that year there was an award, whereby it was ordered, that Anne late wife of John Fleming should enjoy for her dower lands in Claughton in Lonsdale, and one tenement in Coningston,

* It is an Anglo-Saxon word, from *hest*, a command; as much as to say, he had put himself under his command. So *behight* signifies promised or engaged.

† Meat and drink (from *bouche*, a mouth) scot free. For so is the French *avoir bouche a court*, to be in ordinary at court. And this extended as well to the court of noblemen who were subjects, as to the king's court.

ningſton, and yearly during her life, one buck or doe out of Coningſton-park; and that John Fleming ſon and heir of the ſaid John deceaſed enjoy all the reſt of his father's lands.

XIII. JOHN FLEMING of Rydal eſquire, ſon and heir of John. He married a daughter of Sir Hugh Lowther of Lowther knight, whoſe name was *Joan*; yet after his death we find his widow called *Janet*. For the reconciling of which, it is to be obſerved, that according to Camden, in late years ſome of the better and nicer ſort, miſliking *Joane*, have mollified the name into *Jane*; for *Jane* is never found in old records, and (as ſome will have it) not before the time of king Henry the eighth. In the 32 Eliz. it was agreed by the court of king's bench, that *Jane* and *Joan* are all one. *Janet* is a diminutive of *Joan*, as little or pretty *Joan*.

This John had iſſue *Hugh Fleming* eſquire, his ſon and heir. And five daughters, (1) *Agnes*, married to Richard Ducket of Grayrigg eſquire. (2) A daughter married to Richard Kirkby of Kirkby eſquire. (3) *Margaret*, married to Thomas Stanley of Dalegarth in Cumberland eſquire; whoſe arms are, Argent, on a bend Sable three ſtags heads caboſhed Or, with two cotices Vert. (4) A daughter married to William Bardſey of Bardſey in Lancaſhire eſquire. (5) A daughter married to ——— Thwaites of Thwaites in Cumberland eſquire; whoſe arms are, Argent, a croſs Sable, fretty Or.

In the 4 Hen. 8. there was an award between Alexander abbot of Furneſs of the one part, and this John Fleming of the other part, made by Brian Tunſtal, John Lowther of Lowther, John Lamplogh of Lamplogh, and William Redmayne of Thwyſil-towne, eſquires; which was, that they ſhould each ſhew their writings to the next judge of aſſize at Lancaſter, who ſhould determine, whether the ſaid John Fleming held the manor of Coningſton by knights ſervice and a certain rent of the ſaid monaſtery; and alſo that the ſaid abbot ſhould pay to the ſaid John Fleming, for all ſuch titles and tenant-rights as the ſaid abbot claims in Furneſs-fells, except Crag-houſe, the ſum of 40 *l.*

In the 6 Hen. 8. this John was eſcheator for the counties of Cumberland and Weſtmorland.

Before the 24 Hen. 8. this John Fleming died; and was buried at Greſmere church, in the burying-place belonging to the lords of Rydal.

XIV. HUGH FLEMING of Rydal eſquire, ſon and heir of John. He married *Joan* (or *Jane*) one of the two ſiſters and coheirs of *Richard Hodleſton* eſquire, being alſo one of the daughters and coheirs of Sir *Richard Hodleſton* of Millum-caſtle in Cumberland knight. Margaret Hodleſton the other daughter was married to Lancelot Salkeld of Whitehall in the ſaid county, eſquire.

The paternal arms of the *Hodleſtons* of Millum-caſtle are, Gules, a frette Argent. And the ſaid Sir *Richard Hodleſton* and *Richard Hodleſton* his ſon quartered the arms of *Millum*, *Boyvell*, *Fenwick*, *Stapleton*, *Faulconbridge*, *Fitz-Alan*, *Maultravers*, *Ingham*, *De la Pool*, and *Chaucer*. All which arms, together with their eſtates which were not intailed upon the males of that family,

CHAP. VI. came to the ſaid *Hugh Fleming* and *Lancelot Salkeld* in the right of their wives, and deſcended upon their heirs; and the ſaid arms have been ever ſince quartered by the two families of *Fleming* and *Salkeld* aforeſaid until this day.

The ſaid Hugh outlived his wife; for in the 30 Hen. 8. there is an award between the ſaid Hugh Fleming and Lancelot Salkeld, made by Richard Redman, William Pickering, Gilbert Wharton, and Ambroſe Machel, that the ſaid Hugh ſhould have during his life (which he held by the curteſy after the deceaſe of his wife) half the rents and profits of Bowes, alſo 4 nobles and 40 pence out of the lands of Perote, alſo half the rents and profits of Blenerhaſſet, half of Hakemanby, and that the ſaid Lancelot ſhould have other lands in the ſaid award mentioned.

In the 33 Hen. 8. he was made eſcheator for the counties of Cumberland and Weſtmorland.

He died in the 4 Phil. and Mar. being then an old man, and having ſurvived moſt of his children: Which were as follows,

1. *Anthony*, his eldeſt ſon.

2. *Thomas*, who had iſſue, (1) *Richard*, who married the heireſs of Troughton-hall, and by her had ſeveral children, who ſpread out into many branches. (2) *John*, who had iſſue *Thomas*, *John*, *Richard*, *Roger*, *Jane*, *Margaret*, *Agnes*, *Bridget*; moſt of whom married and had children.

3. *David*, who was ſteward to the lord William Parr, marquis of Northampton; and married a daughter of Sir John Lamplugh, by whom he had iſſue (1) *John*, who had a ſon Richard. (2) *Thomas*. (3) *Henry*, who had iſſue John. (4) *Elinour*. (5) *Nicholas*, who had iſſue Roger, Thomas, and Ralph. (6) *Robert*, who had a ſon John. (7) *David*, who was one of queen Elizabeth's falconers. (8) *Adam*.

4. *Daniel*, who died without iſſue.

The ſaid Hugh had alſo a daughter *Joan*, who was married to Lancelot Lowther of Sewborwens in Newton Regney in the county of Cumberland gentleman; and by their marriage articles, May 30, in the 29 Hen. 8. it was ſtipulated, that each of the parties ſhould pay for their own marriage apparel, that the meat and drink ſhould be at the charge of the ſaid Hugh, and alſo the licence; that the ſaid Hugh ſhould give to the ſaid Lancelot and Joan bedding and inſtyghe, as ſhall ſtand with his worſhip to give; and that the portion ſhould be 66*l* 13*s* 4*d*, to be paid at the pariſh church of Lowther.

XV. Anthony Fleming of Rydal eſquire, ſon and heir of Hugh. He married firſt a daughter of Sir Geffrey Middleton of Middleton-hall knight, by whom he had no iſſue. Secondly, he married Elizabeth daughter of William Hoton of Hoton in the foreſt eſquire; and by the marriage articles, 28 May, 24 Hen. 8. it was covenanted, that each party ſhould buy their own wedding cloaths; that the marriage ſhould be in Hoton church; and that the ſaid William ſhould find meat, drink, and other things neceſſary for the marriage feaſt; that whereas the ſaid Anthony and Elizabeth were of couſinage in the fourth degree, a diſpenſation ſhould be purſued and obtained for the ſame at the equal charge of the ſaid Hugh and William; that the whole eſtate

7 ſhould

should be intailed upon the issue of the said marriage; and that in consideration thereof, the said William should pay 120*l.* at several days; and if the said Elizabeth should die without issue before any of the said days respectively, so much was agreed not to be paid. There was issue born of this marriage, an only son *William*, heir both to his father and grandfather; for his father died in the lifetime of the aforesaid Hugh the grandfather. This Anthony Fleming had also a third wife, Jane daughter of John Rigmaden of Weddicre in the county of Lancaster esquire; by whom he had issue, *Thomas* and *Charles*.

XVI. WILLIAM FLEMING of Rydal esquire, after the decease of the said Anthony his father, and of Hugh Fleming his grandfather, became heir to the whole estate.

In the 3 Ed. 6. Gabriel Croft, parson of Gresmere, in consideration of the sum of 58*l* 11*s* 5½*d*, granted a lease of the rectory and tithes of Gresmere to Marian Bellingham of Helsington widow, for the term of 97 years, paying yearly to the parson there 18*l* 11*s* 7*d*. Which lease was confirmed by John bishop of Chester as ordinary, and by Alan Bellingham of Helsington esquire son of the said Marian as patron.—For until the disabling statute of the 13 Eliz. the incumbents of livings, with the consent of patron and ordinary, might grant such leases, and they were valid in law: but by the said statute they are restrained (although with such consent) from granting such leases for a longer term than 21 years or three lives.

In the 16 Eliz. the said Alan sold to this William Fleming, for the sum of 500*l*, his interest in the said lease, which had come to him as executor to his said mother deceased.

There had some little time before been a suit between the said Alan and William concerning the tithes of the demesne of Rydal, wherein the said William obtained a verdict for a prescription of 20*s* a year to be paid at Easter or upon demand, for all manner of tithes for the said demesne; which verdict was exemplified under the great seal, 8 Feb. 18 Eliz.

In the same year, the said William sold some tenements at Loghrigg into freehold.

He married, to his first wife, Margaret daughter of Sir John Lamplugh of Lamplugh knight; and to his second wife he married Agnes daughter of Robert Bindloss of Borwick in the county of Lancaster esquire.

He had issue by his former wife, 1. *Jane*, married to Richard Harrison of Martindale gentleman. 2. *Margery*, married to Nicholas Curwen of Clifton in Cumberland gentleman. 3. *Elizabeth*, married to William Carter of Broghton in Lancashire gentleman.

By his second wife, he had, 1. *John*, his eldest son and heir. 2. *Thomas*, who died without issue. 3. *William*, who died also without issue; he was a stout man, being above six feet high; and was in the ship which first descryed the Spanish armada in the year 1588, and therein behaved gallantly. 4. *Daniel*, whose son succeeded as heir in tail, after failure of heirs male from his eldest brother John. 5. *Joseph*, who died without issue. 6. *Dorothy*, mar-

 ried

CHAP. VI.

ried to John Ambrofe of Lowick in Lancafhire efquire. 7. *Mary*, married to John Senhoufe of Seafcales-hall in Cumberland efquire. 8. *Grace*, married to Anthony Barwife of Hyldekirk in Cumberland efquire. 9. *Eleanor*, married to Sir John Lowther of Lowther knight, one of his majefty's counfel at York for the northern parts; with whom her mother, being then a widow, gave 1000*l* for her portion.

XVII. JOHN FLEMING of Rydal efquire, fon and heir of William. He had three wives, 1. Alice, eldeft daughter of Sir Francis Ducket of Grayrigg knight; whofe portion was 666*l* 13*s* 4*d*. By her he had no iffue. 2. Bridget, daughter of Sir William Norris of Speke in Lancafhire knight; who died alfo without iffue. 3. Dorothy, daughter of Sir Thomas Strickland of Sizergh knight of the Bath; by whom he had iffue, (1) *William*, his fon and heir. (2) *Bridget*, married to Sir Jordan Crofland of Haram-how in the county of York knight. (3) *Agnes*, married to George Collingwood of Elfington in the county of Northumberland efquire.

In the 4th year of king James, his mother Agnes purchafed the manor of Skirwith, and one third of the manor of Brougham; with divers lands in Skirwith, Owfeby, Crosfell, Langwathby, and Culgaith. And in the 8th year of the fame king, fhe entailed the fame upon her fon Daniel and his iffue male.

She alfo purchafed Monk-hall, and divers other meffuages and tenements in the county of Cumberland; all of which, after her deceafe (or before) came into the family eftate.

This John was a juftice of the peace for Weftmorland from the 7 Jac. (which is the firft time that the rolls of feffion make mention of him) until the 22 Jac. about which time he turned Roman catholic.

In the 5th year of Charles the firft, he procured a fuperfedeas for his recufancy; and an acquittance for his knighthood money.

In the 7th year of the fame king, he obtained a licence (being a popifh recufant convict) to travel above five miles from Rydal.

In the fame year he paid to the king for his recufancy, after the rate of 30*l* a year; and two years after, according to the proportion of 50*l* a year.

He died in the 18 Car. aged about 68; and was buried in Grefmere church, in the burying-place belonging to the lords of Rydal.

He gave by his will 2000*l* each to his two daughters for their portions.

WILLIAM his fon and heir was only 14 years of age at the time of his father's death, and died of the fmall-pox before he was 21, and unmarried, in the year 1649. By whofe death without iffue, his two fifters portions became augmented to 10000*l* each; but the family eftate went over to his uncle *Daniel* the next heir male.

Young as this William was, he appeared in arms on the king's party. And after his death, the fequeftrators put both his and his father's name into their bill of fale, in the year 1652. Which put his heirs male to great charge and trouble afterwards, to get the eftate cleared from the then commonwealth's title.

title. Sir Wilfred Lawson of Isel, one of Cromwell's party, plundered and ftripped Rydal-hall of all that was valuable, and tore up the floors to fearch for hidden treafure.

THE direct male line failing on the death of this William, we go back to his father's eldeft furviving brother, DANIEL FLEMING of Skirwith efquire; who married Ifabel daughter of James Brathwaite of Amblefide efquire; by whom he had iffue, 1. *William*, who fucceeded to the whole inheritance as heir in tail. 2. *John*, who died without iffue, and was buried in the chancel of Kirkland church, May 30, 1662, as appears by the infcription on his tombftone there. 3 *Thomas*. 4. *Jofeph*. 5. *Daniel*, who was lieutenant of a troop of horfe in the fervice of king Charles the firft, under the command of the earl of Newcaftle: he died without iffue. 6. *Agnes*, married to Chriftopher Dudley of Yanewith efquire. 7. *Dorothy*, married to Andrew Huddlefton of Hutton John efquire. 8. *Mary*, married to Thomas Brougham of Scales-hall in Cumberland efquire.

In the 9 Jac. he purchafed one third of the manor of Kirkland, and in the next year another third of it.

He died Aug. 2, 1621, and was buried in the quire of Kirkland church, as appears by an infcription ingraved in brafs on his tombftone there.

XVIII. WILLIAM FLEMING of Skirwith and Rydal efquire, fon and heir of *Daniel*. On the death of the laft William without iffue as aforefaid, this William fon of Daniel fucceeded as next heir male to the whole family eftate.

He married Alice daughter of Roger Kirkby of Kirkby in Lancafhire efquire; by whom he had iffue, 1. *Daniel*. 2. *Roger*. 3. *William*, major of a regiment of militia in the county of Lancafter. 4. *John*, who died young. 5. *John*, who was loft at fea on the coaft of Africa, on a trading voyage. 6. *Alexander*, a merchant at Newcaftle, who died without iffue. 7. *Ifabel*, who died unmarried.

In 1642, he had a commiffion from the earl of Newcaftle to be major of a regiment of foot whereof Sir Henry Fletcher of Hutton baronet was colonel, and William Carleton of Carleton-hall efquire was lieutenant colonel. And this William Fleming raifed in the neighbouring parts a very good company, *viz.* at Ainftable 12, Croglin and Newby 6, Kirk Ofwald 18, Renwick 6, Melmerby 12, Oufeby 12, Glaffonby 6, Gamelfby 6, Little Salkeld 6, Hunfonby and Winfkell 6, Skirwith 6; in all 98: Which he commanded as captain until the latter end of the year 1644, when the counties of Weftmorland and Cumberland were totally fubdued, except the city of Carlifle, which furrendered to David Lefley in about 9 months after, having firft endured all the extremities of famine.

Upon the coming in of duke Hamilton, he again accepted a commiffion of lieutenant colonel of a regiment of horfe, whereof John Lamplugh of Lamplugh efquire was to be colonel. But before they could get their troops raifed, the king's party were routed by Cromwell near Prefton in Lancafhire.

 He

He died at Coningston-hall in the year 1653, in the 44th year of his age; and was buried in the chancel of the church of Gresmere, in the same place where his grandmother Agnes had been buried about 20 years before. His epitaph is on a square piece of brass fixed in the wall near his grave in the east end of the church. And on an oblong piece of glass in the east window was put up this inscription:

Deo trino et uni
Sacrum.
Secundum Christi Redemptoris
Adventum hoc templo expectat
Gulielmus Fleming
Armiger.
Qui pie in Christo expiravit
Conistoniæ, et quicquid mortale
habuit hic deposuit,
25° Maii,
Anno Epochæ Christianæ
MDCLIII.

And underneath, the paternal arms of Fleming and Kirkby impaled. And above, in the same window, the several coats in colours quartered by the family of Fleming.

XIX. Daniel Fleming of Rydal esquire, afterwards knight and baronet, son and heir of William; author of the aforesaid memoirs, from which this account is chiefly taken.

He entered commoner in Queen's college in Oxford in 1650, under the reverend Thomas Smith afterwards bishop of Carlisle. Christopher Musgrave esquire, second son of Sir Philip Musgrave baronet, was then of the same college. And Dr. Gerard Langbaine was provost. Daniel had for his servitor Joseph Williamson second son of the reverend Joseph Williamson vicar of Bridekirk in Cumberland, who afterwards became fellow of the said college, was recommended by the said Mr. Smith to Sir Edward Nicholas, and afterwards was knighted, and promoted to the office of secretary of state; he was one of the king's plenipotentiaries at Colen; and married one of the blood royal, namely, Catherine only sister to Charles Stuart duke of Richmond, widow of Henry lord Obrian, son and heir of Henry earl of Thomond in the kingdom of Ireland. At the same time Sir George Fletcher of Hutton baronet was a student and fellow commoner in that college.

In the year 1653, this Daniel got possession of the manors of Rydal, Conningston, and Beckermet, which had hitherto been under sequestration; Rydal having been leased out by Mr. John Archer and other committee-men at Kendal to Walter Strickland esquire, uncle to the two daughters of John Fleming esquire sisters of William aforesaid, who died without issue; those two daughters claiming as heirs to their father and brother, against this collateral branch who claimed by virtue of the intail. But he did not get the whole compleated till the latter end of the year 1654.

In 1655, he married Barbara sister of Sir George Fletcher aforesaid, eldest daughter of Sir Henry Fletcher of Hutton baronet (who was killed on the king's party at Routon-heath battle near Chester in 1645) and of the lady Catherine Fletcher his wife, eldest daughter of Sir George Dalston of Dalston in Cumberland knight.

In the same year he purchased the remaining part of the manor of Kirkland, which had not been compleated by his father.

He was the first sheriff of Cumberland after the restoration of king Charles the second; and was knighted by that king in the year 1681, for which he paid as the usual fees to the officers 78 *l* 13 *s* 4 *d*.

He continued in the interest of that family till the reign of king James the second; when finding the established religion to be in danger, he joined with the party that opposed that king's measures; and being one of the two burgesses in parliament for Cockermouth in the first year of the said king, he voted against the court. His election to that borough was contested, yet such was the moderation of those times, that his whole expences in that contest did not amount to 20 *l*.

Towards the latter end of that king's reign, Sir Daniel in the aforesaid memoirs gives a very curious account of the attempt made by the court for taking away the penal laws and test. He begins with a letter to himself from Sir John Lowther of Lowther (who, as representative for Westmorland, had voted in parliament for the bill of exclusion, and was strenuous in opposing the measures then carrying on for introducing the popish religion and arbitrary power). There had in the former reign been some differences between the two families of Lowther and Rydal, which Sir John Lowther first endeavours to reconcile, in order that they might join together in the same common cause. And Sir Daniel's narrative proceeds as follows:

Letter from Sir John Lowther of Lowther to Sir Daniel Fleming.

SIR,

HAVING had the pleasure of late to understand from several hands, but especially from Sir John Lowther [of Whitehaven], that you still retain a friendship for our family; and since I am willing to hope, that whatever misunderstanding was betwixt us happened rather by mistake, or for reasons which are now removed, than for any thing else: I would no longer forbear assuring you, that I have no greater pleasure than to live well with all people, and especially with my relations and ancient friends. And since you have formerly shewed yourself such upon many occasions, I cannot but wish that there may be the same mutual good offices as formerly. And if whilst Sir John Lowther is here, who hath always been a friend of yours, you please to visit this place, you shall be sure to find that hearty welcome that you were wont to receive from,

Sir,

Lowther, Aug. 24.
1687.

Your most affectionate kinsman
and humble servant,
JOHN LOWTHER.

At

CHAP. VI.

At the ſame time Sir John Lowther of Whitehaven writ to Sir Daniel by the ſame meſſenger as followeth:

SIR,

I CANNOT leave the country without returning you my acknowledgments for your great civilities to both me and my ſon at the aſſizes, and for the continued teſtimonies of your friendſhip upon all occaſions; and if our whole family have not had of late the ſame advantages thereof that I have enjoyed, it is not unknown how great a trouble it has been to me, nor how often I have wiſhed to be the happy inſtrument of reſtoring the good correſpondence betwixt ſo near relations. This, Sir, not I alone, but the whole country, I find, and all good men, have equally deſired, and I doubt not to ſee the wiſhed ſucceſs; ſince I can aſſure you, the ſame friendſhip that ever was on our ſide we do deſire may be renewed and continue as long as the families: which, by the freedom wherewith you were pleaſed to declare yourſelf to me at Carliſle upon this ſubject, is, I hope, what will be moſt welcome to you. The incloſed from Sir John himſelf will ſpare me the adding any more, and I hope bring you over whilſt I ſtay, which will be till Monday next. And I pray bring your ſon with you, that the young men may fix their acquaintance.

I am, Sir,
Lowther, Aug. 24, 1687.
Your moſt affectionate kinſman
and humble ſervant,
JOHN LOWTHER.

Theſe two letters arriving at Rydal late in the evening, and Sir Daniel Fleming's two ſons being gone two days before to viſit their ſiſters in Lancaſhire, and Sir Daniel thinking it neceſſary to ſpeak with Sir Chriſtopher Muſgrave (who was lately come into the country from London, and had writ to Sir Daniel to meet him at Carliſle the week following), he returned the following anſwers to the ſaid two letters by the meſſenger who brought them, rather than go forthwith unto Lowther. His anſwer to the former letter was thus:

SIR, Rydal, Aug 24, 1687.

I THANK you for your very obliging letter, which I have this evening received, and for your kind invitation unto Lowther; and I ſhould now have waited upon you and Sir John Lowther according to your deſires, had not my two ſons (William and Daniel) been gone into Lancaſhire with my ſervants and horſes. I do concur with you, that whatever miſunderſtanding was betwixt us, happened rather by miſtake than for any thing elſe. For I ever had a friendſhip for yourſelf and family; and without taking any further notice of what is paſt, upon my part ſhall be performed the ſame mutual good offices as formerly. My humble ſervice unto my good lady and all my couſins.

I am, Sir,
Your very affectionate kinſman,
and moſt humble ſervant,
DAN. FLEMING.

In

In anſwer to Sir John Lowther of Whitehaven, he writ as follows:

SIR, Rydal, Aug. 24, 1687.

I HAVE even now received yours, with one from Sir John Lowther; and I have made him ſuch a return as I hope will be ſatisfactory unto you both. I am troubled that I cannot wait on you before your leaving this country, and that my ſon is no better acquainted with my couſin Lowther. I ſhall ever acknowledge my great obligation unto you for your conſtant friendſhip, and for the many favours which I have received from you. And if I may be any way ſerviceable unto you here in the country, I hope you will favour me with your commands. My humble ſervice unto yourſelf and my couſin your ſon, heartily wiſhing you both a ſafe return unto London. My ſon William and his brother Daniel are now in Lancaſhire, which hinders me now from telling you in perſon that I am, Sir,

Your very affectionate kinſman
and moſt faithful ſervant,
Dan. Fleming.

In the mean time, Sir Daniel Fleming had an interview with Sir Chriſtopher Muſgrave; who had been diſplaced ſome little time before from the office of lieutenant of the ordnance for refuſing (as it was ſaid) to promiſe the king to give his vote for taking away the teſt and penal laws. About the ſame time, the king had removed the earl of Derby from being lord lieutenant of the county of Lancaſter, and put into his place the lord Molineux; and had alſo removed the earl of Thanet from being lord lieutenant of the counties of Weſtmorland and Cumberland, and put into his place the lord Preſton.

And that the king's declaration for liberty of conſcience might the more eaſily paſs into a law, the council agreed on the three queſtions following:

1. If in caſe you ſhall be choſen knight of a ſhire, or burgeſs of a town, when the king ſhall think fit to call a parliament; whether you will be for taking off the penal laws and teſts?

2. Whether you will aſſiſt and contribute to the election of ſuch members, as ſhall be for taking off the penal laws and teſts?

3. Whether you will ſupport the king's declaration for liberty of conſcience, by living friendly with thoſe of all perſuaſions, as ſubjects of the ſame prince and good chriſtians ought to do?

The ſeveral lords lieutenants were ordered to deſire the anſwers of all deputy lieutenants and juſtices of the peace within their reſpective lieutenancies, to each of the aforeſaid queſtions in particular.

And the lord Mollineux at Lancaſter, in the beginning of November following, having propoſed the ſaid queſtions to the juſtices there; they anſwered ſeverally as followeth: *viz.* Mr. Girlington, that he would have thoſe laws damned, with the contrivers of them. Mr. Preſton agreed to take away the ſanguinary laws only. Mr. Carus was for having thoſe laws burned, as the Scotch covenant was. Mr. Curwen Rawlinſon anſwered, No. Captain Kirkby and his uncle William Kirkby were for the affirmative; and ſo were colonel

CHAP. VI.

Roger Sawry and Mr. Henry West. But Mr. Cole, Mr. Bradil the son, Mr. Knipe of Broghton, Mr. Copley, Mr. Joseph Fletcher, and others, were negatives. Sir Robert Bindloss appeared not, writing a letter negatively, and afterwards another letter otherwise. Edward Wilson junior esquire answered, that he would speak by his representative in parliament; and when the king should please to call one, he would do his endeavour to chuse a loyal man; and was of opinion that none ought to suffer for mere matters of religion. At Liverpool, only four or five, who were custom-house officers, were for the affirmative. At Wigan, two only; and no more at Preston, where colonel Rigby, colonel Rawstorne, and many more, were negatives. At Clitheroe, all were also for the negative.

The lords lieutenants of divers counties having not met with that success they expected, occasioned the printing the following declaration:

Whitehall, Dec. 11, 1687.

His majesty, having by his gracious declaration of the 4th April last, granted a liberty of conscience to all his subjects; and resolving not only to maintain the same, but to use his utmost endeavours that it may pass into a law, and become an established security to after ages; hath thought fit to review the lists of the deputy lieutenants and justices of the peace in the several counties: that those may be continued, who shall be ready to contribute, what in them lies, towards the accomplishment of so good and necessary a work; and such others added to them, from whom his majesty may reasonably expect the like concurrence and assistance.

The lord Preston's occasions would not give him leave to make such haste into the country, as many other lords lieutenants did. But in January following, he writ letters to every deputy lieutenant and justice of the peace within the counties of Westmorland and Cumberland as followeth:

SIR,

I DESIRE you will meet me at Penrith upon Tuesday the 24th of this month, about ten of the clock in the morning; I having some matters to impart to you by his majesty's command. I am, Sir,

Your most humble servant,

PRESTON.

To the letter sent to Sir Daniel Fleming, his lordship added this postscript with his own hand:

I should be very glad to see you at Hutton, before the meeting at Penrith. I hope to be there on Thursday come se'nnight. My humble service to Mr. Fleming; and believe me to be, Sir,

Your most affectionate and humble servant,

PRESTON.

Sir Daniel Fleming having received lord Preston's letter, and his son another letter from his lordship, and Sir Daniel having not yet visited Lowther since Sir John Lowther and he were made friends (although he was much pressed to make that journey by Sir John Lowther of Whitehaven), Sir Daniel thought

thought it not amiss for him to take Lowther in his way to Penrith, which he did on Jan. 21, being accompanied thither by his two sons William and Daniel, and by his cousin John Brougham; where they were all very kindly entertained by Sir John Lowther and his lady; and where Sir John and Sir Daniel did agree upon their answers to the aforesaid questions.

On the 23d, Sir Daniel Fleming, his son Daniel, and his cousin Brougham, went early to Hutton; where they dined, and would have returned that evening unto Lowther, but the lord Preston would not permit them, obliging them to stay there all night; from which place they waited (with some other gentlemen) the next day upon his lordship who rode on horseback unto Penrith; whither came Sir John Lowther, in his coach with six horses, attended by Sir Daniel Fleming's eldest son, and the rest of the deputy lieutenants and justices of the peace for the counties of Cumberland and Westmorland, save some who were so indisposed in health that they could not safely travel so far from home.

The lord Preston having desired the gentlemen then present to take their places at a long table in the George inn at Penrith, and his lordship in a short speech having acquainted them with his majesty's appointing him to be lord lieutenant of the two counties, and with the reasons of his lordship's desiring them to meet him there; he desired them in his majesty's name, either to deliver their several answers unto the three questions aforesaid in writing, or that they would permit his lordship to call in his secretary to write the same. Upon which, all being silent a good while, Sir John Lowther stood up, and acquainted his lordship, that he conceived it would be more for his lordship's ease, to permit every gentleman to write his own answer: Which was seconded by Sir Daniel Fleming, adding, that if his lordship would give leave to the gentlemen there to withdraw into some other place for about one hour's time, then every one would come to his lordship with their several answers in writing under their hands. Which was forthwith assented unto. And the protestant gentlemen did go into one room, and the papists into another.

Within an hour's time all were ready with their answers; and then returning to his lordship, and taking again their places at the table, Sir George Fletcher stood up and read aloud his answer, which was pretty long, consenting to indulge tender consciences; but as to the test, referring it to the debate of the house: and declaring that he would stand for a knight of the county of Cumberland. Sir William Pennington read also his answer, consenting to indulge tender consciences, and to take away the tests, so far as it shall not be prejudicial to the church of England. Then Sir John Lowther read his answer, which was as followeth:

1. If I be chosen a member of parliament, I think myself obliged to refer my opinion concerning the taking away the penal laws and tests, to the reasons that shall arise from the debate of the house.

2. If I give my interest for any to serve in the next parliament, it shall be for such as I shall think loyal and well affected to the king and the established government.

3. I will live friendly with those of several persuasions, as a loyal subject and a good christian ought to do.

After

CHAP. VI.

After whom, Sir Daniel Fleming, Sir John Ballantine, Edward Stanley, William Fleming, John Senhouſe, Miles Pennington, Chriſtopher Dalſton, Anthony Hutton, Edward Muſgrave, Henry Brougham, Thomas Denton, Chriſtopher Richmond, and Edward Haſſel eſquires, gave in the ſame anſwers verbatim as Sir John Lowther did, only with the change of their ſeveral names thereunto. Francis Howard, Thomas Brathwaite, William Fletcher, and John Skelton, eſquires (papiſts), gave in ſeveral anſwers, but all were for taking off the penal laws and teſts; and ſo did Thomas Warwick, Henry Dacre, John Aglionby, ——— Orfeur, and Thomas Dalſton, eſquires, (eſteemed proteſtants), the laſt of them abominating the teſt laws. Richard Patrickſon anſwered particularly, conſenting to indulge tender conſciences, and referring the teſt to the conſideration of the parliament. All theſe anſwers were delivered to his lordſhip, before Sir Richard Muſgrave of Hayton-caſtle arrived; who anſwered afterwards to the effect of Sir John Lowther's anſwer.—All which being done (our author adds) his lordſhip treated all the gentlemen very kindly and nobly, with wine, ale, and a good dinner.

Soon after this meeting, the lord Preſton writ to every of the abſent gentlemen thus:

SIR,

NOT meeting you with the reſt of the gentlemen at Penrith, I take this way of communicating to you the three following queſtions, to each of which in particular I am from his majeſty to deſire your anſwer.

I am, Sir,
Your moſt humble ſervant,
PRESTON.

Sir Chriſtopher Philipſon, Edward Wilſon, Thomas Fletcher, John Lamplugh, and Richard Lamplugh, eſquires, anſwered affirmatively. Edward Wilſon the younger eſquire had no letter ſent to him, he living in Lancaſhire, and having anſwered the ſame queſtions in that county *.—So far Sir Daniel Fleming's narrative of the proceedings of that time.

In

* As the above account manifeſts the diſpoſition of moſt of the principal gentlemen of the two counties at that critical juncture, ſo the following addreſs indicates the ſentiments of the corporation of Carliſle upon the ſame occaſion:

" To the king's moſt excellent majeſty,

" The humble addreſs of the mayor, aldermen, bailiffs, and citizens of the city of Carliſle.

" Dread Sovereign,

" Being now at liberty by the late regulation made here, to addreſs ourſelves unto your majeſty " we beg leave to return our late but unfeigned thanks for your majeſty's moſt gracious declaration " of indulgence, which we will endeavour to maintain and ſupport againſt all oppoſers. We like- " wiſe thank your majeſty for the royal army, which really is both the honour and ſafety of the " nation, let the Tikelites † think and ſay what they will. And when your majeſty in your great " wiſdom ſhall think fit to call a parliament, we will chuſe ſuch members as ſhall certainly concur " with your majeſty in repealing and taking off the penal laws and teſts, and not hazard the election " of any perſon who hath any ways declared in favour of thoſe Cannibal laws. Surely they do not

† Count Tekeli was at the head of the proteſtant malecontents in Hungary, who were then attempting to throw off the yoke of the houſe of Auſtria.

" conſider,

In the fourth year of queen Anne he was created baronet.

His lady died before him, and on an oblong piece of brass fixed in the wall at the east end of Gresmere church, he caused the following inscription to be ingraved: CHAP. VI.

Barbaræ Fleming,

Henrici Fletcher de Hutton in comitatu Cumbriæ baronetti, et Catharinæ uxoris ejus (filiæ primogenitæ Georgii Dalston de Dalston in eodem comitatu equitis aurati) filiæ natu maximæ, et Danielis Fleming de Rydal in comitatu Westmerlandiæ armigeri, amantissimæ, amabilissimæ, fidelissimæque conjugi, in ipso ætatis flore morte immatura præreptæ;

Quæ
ob fælicissimam indolem, insignem pietatem,
ingentem charitatem, singularem modestiam,
summam probitatem, generosam hospitalitatem,
vigilantem bonæ parentis curam,
moresque suavissimos,
magnum sui apud omnes desiderium relinquens,
Corpus humo, amorem sponso et amicis,
Benedictionem quatuordecim liberis,
(decem nempe pueris ac quatuor puellis,)
Cœloque animam legavit.
Monumentum hoc, amoris et mœroris perpetuum testem,
Charissimus posuit maritus.
Nata est apud Hutton 25 Julii, A. D. 1634.
Nupta ibidem 27 Aug. A. D. 1655.
Confirmata apud Witherslack 22 Junii, A. D. 1671.
Mortua apud Rydal (de XV^a prole) 13 Apr. A. D. 1675.
Lector,
Si lugere nescias, (quod præstat) æmulare.

The issue which he had by his said wife were as follows:

1. *William*, the eldest son and heir.

2. *Catherine*, married to Edward Wilson son of Edward Wilson of Dalham-Tower esquire.

3. *Alice*, who died unmarried.

4. *Henry Fleming*, D. D. rector of Gresmere and of Asby; who married Mary daughter of John Fletcher of Hunslet esquire, and had issue one daughter Penelope married to John Keate esquire, lieutenant in the Scotch horse grenadier guards.

" consider, what a sovereign prince by his royal power may do, that oppose your majesty in so " gracious and glorious a work; a work, which heaven smiles upon, and with no less blessing " (we hope) than a prince of Wales; that there may never want of your issue to sway the scepter, " so long as the sun and moon endure. That your majesty's reign may be long and prosperous, " and blessed with victories over all your enemies, are the daily prayers of,

Gracious Sir,

Your majesty's most obedient and dutiful subjects."

CHAP. VI.

5. *Daniel*, who died unmarried.

6. *John*, who died at the age of three years.

7. *Barbara*, married to John Tatham of Overhall esquire.

8. *Mary*, married first to Henry (or Anthony) Bouch of Ingleton esquire, afterwards to Edward Wilson of Casterton esquire.

9. *George Fleming*, D. D. bishop of Carlisle; who after the death of *William* without issue male, succeeded to the intailed estate.

10. *Michael*, whose posterity, after failure of issue male from *George*, succeeded as tenants in tail, and still enjoy the inheritance aforesaid.

11. *Richard*, who married Isabel only daughter and heir of William Newby of Cawmire gentleman, and by her had issue one son Daniel, who married but had no issue; and four daughters, Barbara, Anne, Isabel, and Catharine, the last of whom was married to George Cumpston of Ambleside gentleman.

12. *Roger Fleming*, M. A. vicar of Brigham; who married Margaret Moorhouse a Yorkshire gentlewoman, and by her had issue one son Daniel, now land-surveyor of the port of Whitehaven; which Daniel married Mary daughter of Joseph Dixon of Whitehaven gentleman, by whom he hath one son Roger and three daughters.

13. *James*, who was a captain in the militia, and died unmarried.

14. *Thomas*, who died at the age of four years.

15. *Fletcher*, who married Elizabeth daughter of Mr. Thomas Brathwaite of Windermere; and by her had issue a son Fletcher, who married Isabella daughter of Mr. William Herbert of Kendal, and had issue one son Fletcher; and three daughters, Agnes, Isabella, and Barbara.

XX. Sir WILLIAM FLEMING of Rydal baronet, son and heir of Sir Daniel. In 1695, on Sir John Lowther's being made a lord, he was chosen to represent the county of Westmorland in parliament, and again in 1698, 1702, 1705, and 1707.

He married Dorothy daughter of Mr. Thomas Rowlandson of Kendal, and by her had three daughters, 1. *Dorothy*, married to Edward Wilson of Dallam-Tower esquire. 2. *Barbara*, married to Edward Parker of Broosholm esquire. 3. *Catharine*, married to Sir Peter Leicester of Tabley baronet.

And here, on the death of Sir *William*, the direct male line failing, the next surviving heir male of the family was

Sir GEORGE FLEMING baronet, fourth brother of the said Sir *William*; which *George* was bishop of Carlisle as aforesaid. He married Catherine daughter of Robert Jefferson (and one of the coheirs of Thomas Jefferson) of the city of Carlisle gentleman, and by her had issue,

1. *William Fleming*, M. A. archdeacon of Carlisle; who married Dorothy daughter of Daniel Wilson of Dalham-Tower esquire, and by her had issue one daughter Catherine, married to Thomas Ascough esquire. This *William* died in the life-time of his father, without other issue; whereby the inheritance became transferred to another collateral male branch.

2. *Mary*, married to Humphrey Senhouse of Netherhall esquire.

3. *Barbara*, who died young.
4. *Catherine*, married to Joseph Dacre Appleby of Kirklinton esquire.
5. *Mildred*, married to Edward Stanley of Ponsonby esquire.
6. *Elizabeth*, who died in her infancy.

The direct male line failing again upon the death of *George*, we have recourse to his next brother *Michael*, who was tenth child as aforesaid of Sir *Daniel*. This *Michael* was major of a regiment of foot. He married Dorothy Benson a Yorkshire gentlewoman; and, dying before his brother *George*, he left issue a son *William*, who succeeded as heir in tail, and a daughter *Susan* married to Michael Knott of Rydal gentleman.

XXI. Sir WILLIAM FLEMING of Rydal baronet, son of *Michael*, succeeded as next heir male upon the death of *George*. He married Elizabeth daughter of Christopher Petyt of Skipton gentleman, and had issue, 1. *Michael*. 2. *Amelia*. 3. *Barbara*. 4. *Elizabeth*. 5. *Dorothy*.—This Sir *William*, from his veneration for antiquity, was desirous to restore the primitive orthography of the family name, by inserting the particle *le*; and (in this instance) effectually performed it, by incorporating the particle with his son's christian name at his baptism: who thereby bears the same name with the first founder of the family after the conquest, *viz.*

XXII. Sir MICHAEL LE FLEMING of Rydal baronet, now knight of the shire for the county of Westmorland, and as yet unmarried.

——In deducing this pedigree, which is one of the clearest we have, and most indubitable, we have attended particularly to the course of generation rather than of succession; from whence, so far as it may be reasonable to form a general conclusion from a particular instance, we may conjecture, that the number of generations since the conquest hath been about one or two and twenty.

The ARMS of Fleming, with their several quarterings, in Sir Daniel's time, were as follows: 1. The paternal arms of *Fleming*; Gules, a frett of six pieces Argent. 2. Argent, on a bend Sable, three lozenges of the first charged each with a saltier Gules; by the name of *Urswic*. 3. Argent, two bars Gules, on a canton of the second a lion passant guardant Or: *Lancaster*. 4. Gules, frettee Argent: *Hodleston*. 5. Argent, a bend between two mullets Sable: *Millum*. 6. Argent, a cheveron between three bulls heads caboshed Sable: *Boyvill*. 7. Parted per fess Gules and Argent six martlets counterchanged: *Fenwick*. 8. Argent, a lion rampant Sable, armed and langued Gules: *Stapleton*. 9. Argent, a lion rampant Azure, armed and langued Gules: *Fauconberge*. 10. Barry of eight pieces Or and Gules: *Fitz-Alan*. 11. Sable, a frett Or: *Maltravers*. 12. Parted per pale Or and Vert, a cross moline Gules: *Ingham*. 13. Azure, a fess between three leopards heads Or: *De la pole*. 14. Parted per pale Argent and Gules, a bend counterchanged: *Chaucer*.

The

CHAP. VI.

The *Crest*: An helmet, and thereupon a mantle Gules, doubled Argent. Above the same, a torce Argent and Gules. Thereon a serpent nowed, with a garland of olives and vines in its mouth; all proper.

Motto, underneath: *Pax, Copia, Sapientia*; all relating to the crest, as *peace* to the olive branches, *plenty* to the vine, and *wisdom* to the serpent.

All after *Hodleston*'s coat are quartered by virtue of that match; viz. *Hodleston* married *Millum*'s (who had married *Boyvell*'s) heir; then *Hodleston* married *Fenwick*'s heir, and afterwards *Stapleton*'s. *Stapelton* had married *Falconberge*'s heir, and *Fitz-Alan*'s. *Fitz-Alan* had married the heir of *Maltravers*. Then *Stapleton* married *Ingham*'s heir and *De la pole*'s. *De la pole* had married the heir of *Chaucer*. (All which we the rather take notice of, as it affords an eminent example of heiresses carrying over the arms of their family into that with which they intermarry.)

Sir *Daniel* impaled *Fletcher*; viz. Argent, a cross ingrailed Sable, between four ogresses, each charged with a pheon of the first.

RYDAL HALL is a large old building, which hath been erected at several times. It is intended by the present owner to be rebuilt. It is situate on the side of an hill, with a pleasant prospect over most of the vale, and over part of Winandermere, which is said to be the greatest standing water in England.

Nigh to the hall runs a rivulet on the east side called the *Gill*, which exhibits a natural cascade; and a little below it on the south side, the river *Rowtha* taketh its course, which probably gave name to this dale, and runneth by Ambleside into Winandermere.

This country abounds with *wood*, which is much used in the iron works.

The *demesne* belonging to the lord of the manor is very considerable; in which is a large park, for which a charter was obtained in the reign of king Edward the first, but it hath now no deer in it. Here was also another park called the Low-park, but that hath been disparked a long time ago.

Upon the top of a round hill, on the south side of the highway leading from Keswick to Kendal, was anciently placed the manor-house or hall near to the said Low-park. But upon the building of the other hall, on the north side of the said highway, near unto the High-park, the said manor-house became ruinous, and got the name of the Old Hall, which it still beareth; where is now to be seen nothing but the ruins of buildings, walks, and fish ponds; and the place where the orchard was, is now a large inclosure without ever a fruit tree in it, now called the Old Orchard.

In the highway at the end of the old orchard, was a causway, which was charitably made by John Bell, curate and schoolmaster of Ambleside; every Thursday and Saturday in the afternoon causing his scholars to gather stones for the paving thereof, and he did then pave the same himself.

The tenants are chiefly customary and heriotable.

LOUGHRIG evidently derives its name from the *loughs* or lakes with which this country abounds. It is an hamlet of itself, opposite to Rydal on the other side

ſide of the water: which being conjoined with a bridge, makes as it were one intire village, yet they are two manors.

There is a place in Loughrig called Fold-houſe, which is freehold, and heretofore belonged to the family of *Benſon*. The laſt of which name, *Bernard Benſon*, married a daughter of Gilpin of Kentmere, and had four daughters coheirs; of whom, one was married to judge Hutton, another to James Brathwaite of Ambleſide eſquire, a third to Mr. Davies of Winder in the pariſh of Barton, and the fourth to Mr. Michael Benſon of Coat-how.

III.

LANGDALE AND BAISBROW.

LANGDALE is divided into *Great Langdale* and *Little Langdale*; the former being held under the crown as parcel of the manor of Windermere; the latter hath been granted off, and hath for a long time been enjoyed by the Penningtons of Moncaſter, who ſold moſt of the tenements to freehold about the year 1692; of the reſt, the ſeigniory was purchaſed by John Philipſon of Calgarth eſquire.

In the 49 Ed. 3. after the death of Joan de Coupland aforeſaid, the inquiſition finds, that ſhe died ſeiſed of the manor of Winandermere with its members and appurtenances, and amongſt the reſt the hamlet of Langden.

In the 14 Eliz. the inquiſition finds, that William Parr marquis of Northampton died ſeiſed to him and his heirs male of the manor of Langden, and of divers meſſuages and tenements in Langden.

And in the particulars of the dower aſſigned to his widow, one Item is, "*Langden:* Total of the yearly rent there, 3 *l* 6 *s* 10 *d*. The tenants and inhabitants of Langden pay for a parcel of waſte ground for their common unto the lords of the ſame 5 *l*; whereof to the queen 50 *s*, to my lady marquis 37 *s* 6 *d*, and to Mr. Gilpin 12 *s* 6 *d*. The ſaid tenants pay yearly to the lord for greenhue at his court 2 *d*, or elſe 1 *d* and an hen, amounting in all to 11 *s* 10 *d*."

The *chapel* ſtands in Great Langdale, but it belongs alſo to Little Langdale and Baiſbrow. The ancient ſalary thereof is 6 *l* 4 *s* 3 *d*, which ſeems originally, like as in many other of the chapelries, to have been 20 nobles, or 6 *l* 13 *s* 4 *d*. There is alſo an houſe and ſmall parcel of ground belonging thereto, of the yearly value of 2 *l*. In 1743, queen Anne's bounty of 200 *l* fell to it by lot, with which an eſtate was purchaſed in the pariſh of Ulverſtone, with the addition of 51 *l* 4 *s* poor ſtock, for which the poor receive one fifth part of the rent. In 1767, another lot of 200 *l* fell to the ſaid chapel, wherewith an eſtate was purchaſed in Little Langdale. The whole revenue of the chapel amounts to about 21 *l* a year.

In Little Langdale is a place called *Chapel mire*, where it is ſaid a chapel formerly ſtood, which was removed and united to that of Great Langdale.

In

CHAP. VI.

In Langdale are two high hills, in the road from Cumberland to Gresmere, called *Hardknot* and *Wreynose*, the latter being so denominated from its crookedness. Upon the latter of which mountains are placed the shire stones, being three little stones, near the highway, of about a foot high, and a foot from each other, set in a triangle, where the counties of Westmorland, Cumberland, and Lancaster do all meet together in a point, each of the said stones being in one of the three counties aforesaid.

In Little Langdale is got fine blue slate; large quantities of which are sent off to London and other places.

BASEBROWNE (as it was anciently called) is within the constablewick of Langdale, which was given by William de Lancastre baron of Kendal, to the prior and convent of Coningshead in Lancashire. The principal estate therein was made up of several tenements purchased by Mr. Gawen Brathwaite, and so made into a demesne. The tenants belonged to the Bensons, and were sold by John Benson to Thomas Brathwaite of Amblesíde. In which name they continued, till they came into the hands of Miles Atkinson, by his marriage with Dorothy daughter and heir of Robert Brathwaite of High-house in Hugill, brother and heir of Thomas, son and heir of Gawen, son of Thomas the purchaser.

Eagles and ravens sometimes build in this chapelry.

AMBLESIDE is part in this parish, and part in the parish of Windermere; and we defer to treat thereof until we come into that parish. Which here next follows.

PARISH OF WINDERMERE.

THE parish of WINDERMERE hath received its denomination from the famous *mere* or lake therein. From whence the lake itself hath derived its name, is not certain. Some have imagined it to be so called from the great *winds* which pour down upon it from the mountains; others from its *winding* and turning; but Sir Daniel Fleming's conjecture seems to be most probable, that it hath received its name from the proper name of a man, as well as that of Thurstan water (now called Coningston water) in Lancashire, and that of Ulfs's water (now called Ulswater) in the confines of Westmorland and Cumberland.

This parish is bounded on the East by Kentmere in the parish of Kendal; on the South, by Crooke and Winster in the said parish of Kendal, and by Cartmell-fell in the county of Lancaster; on the West, by the bailiwick of Hawkshead in the said county of Lancaster (so that the whole lake is in this parish); and on the North, by the parish of Gresmere.

The church is dedicated to St. Martin; and is a rectory, valued in the king's books at 24*l* 6*s* 8*d*. It was certified to the governors of queen Anne's bounty at 78*l*: *viz*. parsonage house and land 30*l*; compositions, tithes of wool

wool and lamb, and other small tithes 44 *l*; surplice fees 4 *l*. But the deductions reduced the same to 71 *l* 7 *s* 2 *d*; amongst which deductions were, to the receiver of the crown rents 1 *l* 13 *s* 4 *d*, and to the vicar of Kendal 13 *s* 4 *d*. CHAP. VI.

Anciently, this parish, in like manner as that of Gresmere, was part of the parish of Kendal; but by length of time it hath obtained the reputation of a distinct parish.

At the appropriation of the church of Kendal to the abbey of St. Mary's York, the patronage of this *chapel* (as it was called) was not given to the said abbey as was that of the church of Kendal, but the same remained to Ingelram de Gynes and Christian his wife, grantees of the crown. But there was a pension of 38 *s* 4 *d* paid out of this chapel to the said abbey.

By the inquisition *post mortem* of Joan de Coupland in the 49 Ed. 3. it is found, that she held by grant of the king during her life the advowson of the *chapel* of Wynandermer, valued at 100 *s*. And in token of subjection, the rector of Windermere pays to this day an annual pension of 13 *s* 4 *d* to the vicar of Kendal.

The patronage and advowson of this church seems to have continued in the crown till the 7th year of queen Elizabeth, when the same was granted to William Herbert and John Jenkins, to hold of the queen in free socage by fealty as of the manor of East Greenwich. And after several mesne conveyances, the same was purchased by the late Sir William Fleming baronet, who by his last will and testament devised the same to his four daughters.

There are four townships or constablewicks in this parish; *Undermilbeck*, *Applethwaite*, *Troutbeck*, and *Ambleside*, part of which last (as aforesaid) is in the parish of Gresmere.

I.
UNDERMILBECK.

UNDERMILBECK is divided from Applethwaite by the brook which carries a *mill* there, from whence it receiveth its name; as Applethwaite may be styled *Overmilbeck*.

This most commonly goes by the name of the *manor* of Windermere. But the manor originally was much larger, extending through several townships which were parcels thereof.

Thus after the death of Joan de Coupland aforesaid the inquisition finds, that she died seised of *Wynandermer*, with its members and appurtenances, to wit, the hamlets of Langden, Loughrigge, Grismer, Hamelside, Troutbeck, Applethwaite, Crosthwaite, Stirkland Ketel, and Hoton.

It is of the Richmond fee; and in the 4 Ed. 3. Christian de Lindesey obtained a charter of free warren in Windermere. And in the 14th year of the same king, William de Coucy obtained a like charter of free warren there.

CHAP. VI.

On the survey made of the queen's lands, in the 28 Cha. 2. it was found, that in Undermilbeck there were 81 tenements of the Richmond fee, of the yearly rent in the whole of 13*l* 8*s* 0*d*.

There are some few tenements in this division which pay rent and fine to other persons besides the king, by grant probably from the crown in former times.

At the dissolution of the monasteries, there was a tenement in Winandermere which belonged to Shap abbey, then in the possession of Isaac Dixon; and for which the owners of Thornborrow-hall paid a yearly rent of 5*s* to the lord Wharton, whose family had a grant from the crown of the possessions of the said abbey.

Part of Undermilbeck is called *Bowness*, anciently *Balness*; in which stands the *church*; which is an handsome large building, with two rows of pillars, a square tower with 3 bells and a saint's bell. Anciently there was an organ; but it was demolished in the civil wars in the reign of king Charles the first. There is a large quire window, with excellent coloured glass therein, which glass (it is said) belonged to Furness abbey, and after the dissolution of the said abbey was purchased by the parishioners of Windermere, and placed here in their church. The window consists of seven compartments or partitions. In the third, fourth, and fifth, are depicted, in full proportion, the crucifixion, with the Virgin Mary on the right, and the beloved disciple on the left side of the cross: Angels are expressed receiving the sacred blood from the five precious wounds: Below the cross, are a group of monks in their proper habits, with the abbot in a vestment: Their names are written on labels issuing from their mouths; the abbot's name is defaced, which would have given a date to the whole. In the second partition, are the figures of St. George and the dragon. In the sixth is represented St. Catharine, with the emblems of her martyrdom, the sword and wheel. In the seventh are two figures of mitred abbots, and underneath them two monks dressed in vestments. In the middle compartment, above, are finely painted, quarterly, the arms of England and France, bound with the garter and its motto, probably done in the reign of king Edward the third. The rest of the window is filled up by pieces of tracery, with some figures in coats armorial, and the arms of several benefactors, amongst whom are Lancaster, Urswiek, Harrington, Kirkby, Preston, Middleton, and Millum *. The Flemings paternal coat (*viz.* Gules, a frett of six pieces Argent) is in divers parts of this window, some of them with a file of five points or lambeaux; which began to be used about the reign of king Edward the first, as a difference for the eldest son, the father being living.

The *parsonage house* is called the *hall*; there being no other gentleman's house in the village of Bowness. It stands in a pleasant situation, which is rendered more agreeable by Windermere water on the north and west sides thereof, upon the banks of which the glebe land lies for near half a mile in length,

* West's Furness Abbey, p. 95.

being

being about 40 acres, reaching from the house to the water side. It is a good house: Part of it was rebuilt by Mr. Richard Archer, formerly fellow of Queen's college in Oxford, rector thereof; and another part by Mr. William Wilson taberdar of the said college: And it hath received considerable improvements by the present worthy rector Mr. Giles Moore, elder son of John Moore of Grimeshill in this county esquire.

The *school* also is situate in the village of Bowness, at a small distance from the church. There was a stock of 200 *l* raised for the support of a schoolmaster by contribution of the inhabitants of Undermilbeck and Applethwaite. A school-house also was erected by a like contribution, about the year 1637. It is governed by four trustees and ten feoffees. In 1677, the trustees were Robert Philipson of Calgarth esquire, William Wilson rector of Windermere, Thomas Dixon of Orrest-head, and Robert Birket of Lickbarrow; whose respective heirs or successors are to succeed in this office for ever. The feoffees are to be chosen out of the rest of the most substantial inhabitants in both the said hamlets, and when one half of them is dead, the survivors chuse others to fill up the number, and then new security is drawn between the trustees and feoffees. And an estate was purchased with the contribution money, which is now worth about 15 *l* a year.

By a further agreement in 1762, it was settled, that the rector, and the owners of Rayrigg, Lickbarrow, and Berkthwaite estates, for the time being, shall be trustees of the said school.

Thomas Dixon of Fulbarrow, in the year 1730, gave 20 *s* yearly issuing out of the said estate, for books to be distributed to poor children taught at the said school: and also 20 *s* to the use of the poor of Undermilbeck.

John Kirkby of Lindeth gave 5 *l*, the interest whereof to be distributed in like manner.

Francis Bonack of Bought in this parish, in the 14 Cha. I. gave by his will 100 *l* to the poor of this parish, wherewith an estate was purchased in Natland, now of the yearly value of 11 *l* 18 *s* 0 *d*, to be disposed of in the following proportions, *viz.*

	l	*s*	*d*.
Undermilbeck - - - -	4	1	10
Applethwaite - - - -	4	1	10
Troutbeck - - - - -	2	9	6
Ambleside - - - - -	1	4	9

Robert Dixon and ——— Shaw, in 1731, gave 14 *l*, the interest thereof to be distributed yearly to the poor of the said parish.

Edward Bellman, Thomas Collinson, and Robert Dixon gentleman, in the year 1742, gave 22 dozen of loaves of bread to the poor of the said parish yearly.

CHAP. VI.

II.

APPLETHWAITE.

APPLETHWAITE expresseth its own derivation. It is a long straggling hamlet, like many of the rest, or rather a number of single houses, each house being situate as is most convenient for the lands about it. And in this respect these dales have the advantage of towns and villages, where the lands are frequently intermixed, and some of them at a considerable distance. It is an intire constablewick. The river Troutbeck runs at the high end of it, on the west side thereof. The great road from Kendal to Keswick goes through it; and near this road, at a place called St. Catharine's Brow, was an ancient chapel, now converted into a dwelling-house, but it may yet be distinguished, standing east and west, and having an end window (as in other chapels) now walled up.

Applethwaite is of the Richmond fee; and on the survey made of the queen's lands in the 28 Cha. 2. it appeared, that in Applethwaite there were 62 tenements, of the yearly lord's rent in the whole of 24 *l.* 10 *s.* 10½ *d.*

Sir Daniel Fleming takes notice of a custom in this hamlet which is somewhat extraordinary. Every tenant's wife below the said highway pays 5 *d* yearly, and every other woman above 16 years of age 2 *d*, to the king, as lord of the manor. Above the said highway, every tenant's wife or widow pays 3 *d* yearly, and every other woman dwelling there 1 *d*. What might be the foundation of this custom, or what the reason of the diversity, we have not been able to conjecture. And the custom itself seems to be now vanished and gone.

Within this township of Applethwaite is *Calgarth* (anciently written *Calfgarth*), a good old house and tenements, near the side of Windermere water; which for a long time was the chief seat of the *Philipsons*, an ancient family in this neighbourhood.

The ancientest house in this county belonging to the *Philipsons*, some say was *Hollinghall*; others affirm that *Thwatterden* or *Crook-hall* was the ancienter house, though it was afterwards given to a younger brother.

This family, by a traditionary account, derive their descent from *Philip* a younger son of *de Therkwall* in Northumberland; whose heir, from his father, took the name of *Philipson*.

The first in their family pedigree * is,

I. ROBERT PHILIPSON of Hollinghall, who married a daughter of one Dockwray of Dockwray-hall in Kendal; who, as the pedigree sets forth, lived in the reign of king Henry the third. Which probably is a mistake; for the next in the pedigree lived in the reign of king Henry the sixth, and died not until the 8 Hen. 8. So that by this account there must have been near 200 years intervening between these two persons. So indeed it might be, and the

* As copied both by Sir Daniel Fleming and Mr. Machel.

account

account of the intermediate persons be lost. But in all the inquisitions *post mortem*, and other evidences during that period, we have not found the name of *Philipson* in this county earlier than the person who stands second in the said pedigree in the reign of king Henry the sixth as aforesaid. Possibly, Hen. 3. may have been mistaken for Henry 4. (as the mistake might easily be made in the numeral letters in old writings); and then the difficulty vanisheth. And we shall scarcely find the termination *son* at the end of a name much earlier than that period. Upon this supposition, this Robert may stand as father to the person who next follows in the Philipson pedigree, *viz.*

II. ROWLAND PHILIPSON of Hollinghall esquire; who married Katherine daughter of Richard Carus of Astwait. He had two sons, *Edmund* and *Robert*. And by a deed bearing date in the 20 Ed. 4. it was agreed between him and Thomas Layburne of Cunswick esquire, that the said Edmund should marry Janet daughter of the said Thomas Layburne; and if the said Edmund should die before such marriage, then Robert the second son should marry her. Edmund died before his age of consent; and Robert afterwards married her. —This Rowland died (as is aforesaid) in the 8 Hen. 8. and was succeeded by his surviving son and heir,

III. ROBERT PHILIPSON of Hollinghall esquire: He died in the 31 Hen. 8. leaving issue, by his wife Janet Layburne aforesaid,

IV. CHRISTOPHER PHILIPSON of Calgarth esquire; who married Elizabeth daughter of Robert Briggs of Helsfell-hall. From which Robert, colonel Briggs seems to have descended, who was an eminent commander under Oliver Cromwell, and a justice of the peace for Westmorland during the time of the commonwealth.—This Christopher was receiver to king Edward the sixth of his rents in Westmorland. He died in the 7 Eliz. and had issue 5 sons and 2 daughters:

1. *Robert*, who was a bencher in the Middle Temple, London.
2. *Nicholas*, who died without issue.
3. *Francis*, who also died without issue.
4. *Rowland*, who succeeded to the inheritance after the death of Robert, his other two brothers Nicholas and Francis being then also dead.
5. *Myles Philipson* of Thwatterden-hall esquire, from whom descended the Philipsons of Crooke. He married Barbara sister and coheir of Francis Sandys of Conishead in Lancashire; by whom he had *Robert Philipson* of Thwatterden-hall; who had *Christopher Philipson* of Thwatterden-hall; who married Mary daughter of William Huddleston of Milholme Castle in Cumberland, and by her had *Huddleston Philipson* esquire his eldest son and heir, who was colonel of a regiment in the service of king Charles the first; another son *Robert Philipson*, who was major in the said king's service, and for his martial atchievements (as is aforesaid) was surnamed Robin the Devil; and a daughter *Elizabeth* married to Latus.

The said *Huddleston Philipson* married Elizabeth daughter of Alan Askeugh of Skeughsby in Yorkshire esquire; and by her had issue (1) Sir *Christopher Philipson* knight, who married Clara daughter of Lionel Robinson of Cowton Grange nigh Richmond in Yorkshire. (2) *Alan*, who was a captain of foot

CHAP. VI. in Flanders at the siege of Mons. (3) *Robert*, captain of a privateer in the West Indies. (4) *Miles*.

Robin surnamed the Devil aforesaid, brother of *Huddleston*, married Anne daughter of Thomas Knype of Burblethwaite in Lancashire near Witherslack; and had issue *Robert*, *Christopher*, and *Clare*.

6. *Anne*, married first to Cristopher Carus, and secondly to John Richardson of Ramside-hall in Lancashire.

7. *Janet*, married to Thomas Ward of Rigmaden.

V. ROBERT PHILIPSON of Calgarth esquire, eldest son of Christopher, died without issue in the year 1631; and there is in the wall of Windermere church a monument of him in black marble. He was succeeded by his next surviving brother,

VI. ROWLAND PHILIPSON of Calgarth esquire, fourth son of Christopher. He married Catharine daughter and heir of Nicholas Carus of Kendal; and by her had issue, (1) *Christopher*, who married Elizabeth daughter of Sir Marmaduke Wyvil of Constable Burton in the county of York baronet, and died without issue. (2) *Robert*, who succeeded his father: During his brother's lifetime, he resided at Melsonby in Yorkshire. (3) *Rowland*, who married Elizabeth Mohun, and had a daughter Elizabeth married to Hugh Fisher of London.

To this Rowland son of Christopher the heralds confirmed the arms of Therlwall, and granted him a crest to the same, as follows: "To all and "singular as well nobles, gentles, as others, to whom these presents shall "come, to be seen, heard, read, or understood; Robert Cooke esquire, "alias, Clarencieulx king of arms, of the east, west, and south parts of this "realm of England, sendeth greeting: Forasmuch as Rowland Philipson, "alias, Therlwall, of Calgarth in the county of Westmorland, and Miles "Philipson alias Therlwall of Thwatterden hall in the county aforesaid, bro-"thers, sons to Christopher, son to Robert, son to Rowland Philipson alias "Therlwall of Thwatterden-hall aforesaid, which Rowland was descended of "a younger brother forth of the house of Therlwall in the county of North-"umberland, which said Rowland by reason of the christian name of one of "his ancestors was called Philip, the younger son of the said Philip was called "Philipson, and so continueth the same surname, which Rowland their an-"cestor was the bearer of these arms, which likewise to them by just descent "and prerogative of birth are duly received, unto the which no crest or cog-"nizance is known properly to belong, as unto many ancient coats of arms "there be none,—have therefore required me the said Clarencieulx king of "arms, to assign unto their ancient arms not only a crest, but such difference "of the crests, as also a difference to the arms of Miles Philipson (younger "brother as aforesaid to Rowland) which may be meet and lawful to be born, "without prejudice or offence to any other person or persons. In considera-"tion whereof, and at their instant request, I the said Clarencieulx king of "arms, by virtue of my office, and by the power and authority to me com-"mitted by letters patent under the great seal of England, have assigned, "given, and granted unto the said Rowland Philipson alias Therlwall his

"ancient

"ancient arms, being Gules and a cheveron between three boars heads coopey "Ermine, tusked d'Or, and for his crest or cognizance upon the helme, five "ostretch feathers, three Argent, two Gules, set in a crowne murall d'Or: "And to Miles Philipson alias Therlwall (younger brother to the said Row- "land) the same coat of arms, with a border Gold, the crest to the same coat "as the other crest, differing only in the feathers; that is to say, three Gules "and two feathers Argent, mantelled Gules, doubled Or, lyned White. "Which arms and crests or cognizances, and every part and parcel of them, "I the said Clarencieulx king of arms do by these presents ratify, confirm, "give, and grant unto the said Rowland Philipson and Miles his brother, "gentlemen, and to their issue and posterity for ever. They and every of "them the same to have, hold, use, bear, enjoy, and shew forth, at all times "and for ever hereafter, at their liberty and pleasure, with the distinctions "and differences due according to the laudable usage and custom of bearing "arms, without the impediment, lett, or interruption of any person or per- "sons. In witness whereof, I the said Clarencieulx king of arms have here- "unto subscribed my name, and set the seal of my office, the 18th day of "May in the year of our Lord God 1581, and in the 23d year of the reign "of our most gracious sovereign lady Elizabeth, by the Grace of God queen "of England, France, and Ireland, defendress of the faith, and so forth."

VII. ROBERT PHILIPSON of Melsonby and Calgarth esquire, married Anne daughter of Geoffrey Gourley of the city of London; and by her had issue *Christopher*, *Robert*, *Rowland*, *Carus*, *John*, *Anne*, *Mary*, and *Catharine*.

VIII. CHRISTOPHER PHILIPSON of Calgarth and Melsonby esquire, eldest son of Robert, married to his first wife Mary daughter of Thomas Percehay of Riton in Yorkshire esquire. To his second wife he married Anne daughter of Richard Burghe of Eseby in Yorkshire, coheir of Lancelot her brother. He was barrister at law, and major of a regiment in the service of king Charles the first. He died without issue, and was succeeded by his eldest surviving brother,

IX. JOHN PHILIPSON of Calgarth and Melsonby esquire; who married Dorothy daughter of Christopher Crackenthorp of Newbiggin esquire.

In the year 1652, this John was one of those delinquents (as they were called) whose estates were confiscated by an act of Cromwell's parliament. He died in 1664, and had issue *Robert*, *Christopher*, *John*, *Rowland*, *Carus*, *William*, *Miles*, *Mary*, *Anne*, *Margaret*, *Dorothy*, and *Barbara*.

X. ROBERT PHILIPSON of Calgarth esquire, son and heir of John. He sold the Melsonby estate, the family having been greatly impoverished by sequestrations and heavy compositions. He married Barbara daughter of William Penington of Seaton in Cumberland esquire, and had issue *John*, *Christopher*, *Robert*, *Miles*, *Rowland*, *William*, *Beatrice*, *Dorothy*, and *Judith*. He died beyond the seas.

XI. JOHN PHILIPSON of Calgarth esquire, his eldest son and heir, was born in 1665; and in 1688 was married to Mary youngest daughter of Sir Robert Patton of the city of London knight. He had issue only four daughters, who sold the estate of Calgarth, and the same is now in the possession of William

CHAP. VI.

Penny of Penny bridge esquire during his life, and after his decease to go to the male heirs of Miles Sandys of Graythwaite esquire late deceased.

CALGARTH-HALL is a fair old building. Its situation is very pleasant, being upon a level, within twelve score yards of Windermere-water, on the east side of the said water.

In the hall windows Mr. Machel observed the following arms, some of which are yet remaining:

1. *Philipson* (sc. Gules, a cheveron between three boars heads couped Ermine tusked Or); impaling, Azure, a cheveron between 10 cinquefoils, 4, 2, 1, 2, 1, Argent, charged with 3 mullets Gules, by the name of *Carus*.

2. *Philipson* impaling *Laburne*, sc. Azure, 6 lioncells rampant Argent.

3. Barry of ten, Or and Sable, a canton of the second; by the name of *Briggs*.

4. *Philipson* impaling *Wyvil*, sc. Gules, 3 chevronells braced vaire; on a chief Or, a mullet pierced of 5 points Sable.

5. *Carus* impaling *Wyvil*; and also *Philipson* single.——Both of these also are in plaister-work over the hall chimney very compleat; and over Philipson this motto, "Fide non Fraude."

Here was anciently a park: And in the 21 Hen. 6. the king granted to Walter Styrkland esquire the office of keeper of the park of Calgarth for the term of his life; and a like grant was soon after made to Sir Thomas Styrkland knight his son. But it hath been long since disparked.

The large lake called WINDERMERE-WATER is in this division. The islands within it are all in Windermere parish. The rector hath for time immemorial had a pleasure-boat upon it; and he hath a prescription of so much a boat, in lieu of all the tithe fish that are caught in the lake.

This lake is from one to two miles broad, and extends with crooked banks for the space of about 13 miles, but in a streight line drawn from one end to the other perhaps not above 8 or 9 miles, being in some places of a wonderful depth, and of a clear pebbly bottom; breeding good store of fish, as eels, trouts (both common and grey trouts), pikes, bass or perch, skellies, and particularly char, which is a fish generally about nine inches long, the rareness of which fish occasions many pots of chars to be sent to London and other places yearly as presents. There are three sorts of chars; first, the male, being large, with a red belly, but the fish thereof somewhat white within, having a soft roe, and these are called milting chars; secondly, the female, being also large, with not so red a belly, but the fish thereof very red within, having its belly full of hard roes or spawn, called roneing chars; thirdly, the female being not so large, nor so red on the outside, but the reddest within, having no roes in its belly, and these are called gelt chars *.

* Fleming.

Sir

Sir Daniel Fleming says, there are no chars to be found save only in this lake and Coningston water. Some other waters (he says) pretend to have chars in them, as Buttermere in Cumberland, and Ulleswater (which is between Westmorland and Cumberland); but these are generally esteemed by knowing persons to be only case, a kind of fish somewhat like unto a char, but not near so valuable, but the owners of the fishery in Ulleswater do not assent to this position.

The fishery in the lake is farmed by several persons, who all together pay to the king's receiver for fishing 6*l* a year, or for the fishing and ferry together 6*l* 13*s* 8*d*. And so it descends to their executors or administrators.

The fishing is divided into three cables, as they call them: 1. The high cable, from the water head to the char bed, half a mile above Calgarth. 2. The middle cable, from thence to below the ferry. 3. The low cable, from thence to Newby. And in each cable there are four fisheries.

Out of this lake there yearly pass up the river Routhey many very large trouts, and up the river Brathey great store of case (which are like the char, but spawn at another season of the year). And although these two rivers do run a good way together in one channel before they disembogue into Windermere water, and are both very clear and bottomed alike, yet scarce ever any trouts are found in Brathey, or case in Rowthey. Some few salmon also, at the spawning season, come from the sea through the lake and up the river Rowthey, but none ever up Brathey.

Water fowl in great plenty resort to this lake, especially in winter; such as wild swans, wild geese, duck, mallard, teal, widgeons, didappers, gravyes (which are larger than ducks, and build in hollow trees), and many others.

In this lake are several *islands*; the largest of which is now called *Long-holme*, but anciently it was called *Wynandermere island*.

Amongst the Escheats in the 21 Ed. 3. there is an order, that the wood in the *island of Wynandermere* called *Brendwood* (that is, fire-wood, from the Saxon *brenne*, to burn) shall not be several, but common to all the free tenants of Kirkby in Kendale, and of Stirkland, Crosthwaite, Croke, and others, as well to depasture with all their cattle, as to take housebote and heybote, at their will, without the view of the foresters.

Unto whom this island was first granted in fee by the crown, we have not found. It belonged in after times to the *Philipsons* of Crooke; and was sold by Frances daughter and sole heir of Sir *Christopher Philipson* aforesaid son of *Huddleston Philipson* to Mr. *Thomas Brathwaite* of Crooke, who sold the same to one Mr. *Floyer*, who sold to Mr. *Thomas Barlow*, whose brother and heir Mr. *Robert Barlow* sold the same to the present owner *Thomas English* esquire.

This island contains about 30 acres of ground, most of it arable; and had an handsome neat house in the middle of it called the Holme-house; which in the civil wars was besieged by colonel Briggs for eight or ten days, until the siege of Carlisle being raised, Mr. Huddleston Philipson of Crooke to whom it belonged, hastened from Carlisle and relieved his brother Robert in Holme-house. The next day, being Sunday, Mr. Robert Philipson, with three or four more, rode to Kendal, to take revenge of some of the adverse party

 there;

CHAP. VI.

there; paſſed the watch, and rode into the church, up one iſle and down another, in expectation to find one particular perſon there whom they were very deſirous to have met with (our author, Mr. Machel, who was a royaliſt, out of delicacy did not chuſe to name him, as he was then living, but probably it was colonel Briggs). But not finding him, Robert was unhorſed by the guards in his return, and his girths broken, but his companions relieved him by a deſperate charge; and clapping his ſaddle on without any girth, he vaulted into the ſaddle, killed a ſentinel, and galloped away, and returned to the iſland by two o'clock. Upon the occaſion of this and other like adventures, he obtained the appellation aforeſaid of Robin the Devil. He was killed at laſt in the Iriſh wars, at the battle of Waſhford.

Upon this iſland there is a remarkable echo; and for hearing the ſame in perfection, Mr. Barlow provided two ſmall cannon, on the exploſion whereof towards the rock on the weſt ſide of the water, there is firſt a burſt of the ſound upon the rock exactly ſimilar to the firſt exploſion by lightning, then after an intermiſſion of about three ſeconds a ſudden rattling of thunder to the left. And after another intermiſſion, when one imagines all to be over, a ſudden rumbling to the right, which paſſes along the rock and dies away not diſtinguiſhable from diſtant thunder.

St. Mary Holme, otherwiſe called *Lady Holme*, is another iſland in this lake, ſo denominated from a chapel built anciently therein, and dedicated to the bleſſed virgin.

By the inquiſition aforeſaid after the death of Joan de Coupland, the jurors find, that ſhe died ſeiſed of the advowſon of the chapel of St. Mary Holme within Wynandermere, which was valued at nothing, becauſe the land that had belonged to the ſame had of old time been ſeiſed into the lord's hand, and laid within the park of Calvgarth.

Amongſt the returns made by the commiſſioners to inquire of colleges, chapels, free chantries, and the like, in the reigns of king Henry the eighth and Edward the ſixth, there is the "Free chapel of Holme and Winandermere."

This iſland belonged to the Philipſons of Calgarth, and ſtill goes along with the Calgarth eſtate. There are no ruins of the chapel remaining. It is a very ſmall iſland. The chapel would cover near half of it. It is a rock, with ſome few ſhrubs growing upon it, in the middle of the lake, wonderfully adapted to contemplation and retirement.

There is another iſland, anciently called *Roger Holme*, which is of the Lumley fee; whereof William de Thweng died ſeiſed in the 14 Ed. 3. It was granted by king Henry the eighth, with the reſt of the Lumley fee, to Alan Bellingham eſquire; and now belongs (with the other Bellingham eſtates in Weſtmorland) to the preſent earl of Suffolk and Berkſhire.

About the year 1634, there were 47 perſons drowned in this lake in paſſing the ferry, coming homewards from Hawkſhead market, on a ſtorm ariſing.

6 III.

III.

TROUTBECK.

TROUTBECK is bounded on the East by Kentmere, on the South by the mother church division, on the West by Amblesside, and on the North by Patterdale in the parish of Barton.

It receives its name from the rivulet, which springs in the head of the dale, and running along the east side of this division, empties itself below Calgarth in Windermere water.

It is of the Richmond fee; and on the survey made as aforesaid of the Queen's lands in the 28 Cha. 2. there appeared to be 48 tenements, of the yearly rent of 27*l* 0*s* 10*d*.

There was here an *ancient park*, which was disparked and divided amongst the tenants. At which apportionment, they who had lands without wood were to have a share (though in other men's allotment) where wood grew. Hence it is, that some tenants have dalts of wood in other men's grounds *.

The *new park* was granted by king Charles the first to Mr. Huddleston Philipson aforesaid, for his good service in the civil wars. And the same was afterwards confirmed by king Charles the second to Christopher Philipson son of the said Huddleston, afterwards Sir Christopher.

In Troutbeck there is a *chapel*, which was consecrated by bishop Downham in the year 1562, by the name of Jesus Chapel, for the use of the inhabitants of Troutbeck and Applethwaite: With a saving (as is usual in like cases) of the rights of the mother church of St. Martin in Winandermere.

There was an ancient salary raised by the inhabitants at so much an house, which at present amounts to 4*l* 12*s* 3*d*; the rest was paid out of a chapel stock, that is, a fund raised gradually by donations of the inhabitants or others, the produce of which was generally applied to the use of a schoolmaster who should teach their children, and read prayers to them on Sundays.

Out of this stock a school-house was erected, nigh unto the chapel. And by licence of the bishop in 1639, 5*l* a year of the produce of this stock was settled on the school, to be enjoyed by the curate, if he should chuse to teach according to the canon; or if he shall refuse, then to be given to whom the parson and churchwardens shall nominate and the bishop approve. Out of the aforesaid stock, 3*l* 12*s* 6*d* yearly is now given to the curate; and 7*l* 7*s* 6*d* to a schoolmaster.

In the year 1747, an allotment of 200*l* of queen Anne's bounty fell to this chapel; and in 1756, another allotment of 200*l*: with which sum of 400*l* an estate was purchased in Dent, of the present clear yearly value of 13*l*. And in 1773, the countess dowager Gower gave 200*l*, and the governors of the said bounty other 200*l*, wherewith an estate was purchased at Marthwaite Foot in the parish of Sedbergh, of the present yearly value of 14*l*.

* Machel.

CHAP. VI.

There is an hill in this township called *Gallow How*; which seems to argue, that anciently the steward of the manor under the crown exercised a jurisdiction over capital offences.

At a place called *Spying How* in this constablewick, there was an heap of stones called the *Raise*, which the inhabitants took away to make their fences withal, and found therein a chest of four stones, one on each side, and one at each end, full of dead men's bones. There is another called *Woundale Raise*, a very large heap. They are supposed to have been British sepulchres †.

IV.

AMBLESIDE.

AMBLESIDE, from the similitude of the name, is supposed by Camden to have been the *Amboglana* in the Itinerary. But anciently it was written *Hamelside*, which hath not so much resemblance of the word *Amboglana*, but may seem rather to have been derived from the name of the owner. And Mr. Horsley makes it appear clearly, that the *Amboglana* of the Romans was Burdoswald in Northumberland. That there has been a Roman station here there is no doubt; and Mr. Horsley, from the distances, supposes it to be the *Dictis* in the *Notitia*. Sir Daniel Fleming, speaking of it, says; at the upper corner of Windermere water, not far from the present town of Ambleside, lies the carcase (as it were) of an ancient city, with large ruins of walls; and without the walls, the rubbish of old buildings in many places. Adjoining to which, and opening to the water, there hath been a fort, the dimensions whereof are yet very distinguishable, being of an oblong figure, in length about 165 yards, and in breadth 100. It hath been fortified with a ditch and rampire. That it was a work of the Romans, the British bricks, the mortar tempered with small pieces of bricks, the little urns, the glass vials, the Roman coins which have been often found there, the round stones like millstones (of which soldered together they were wont to make pillars), and the paved ways leading to it, are undeniable testimonies.—And to this place Mr. Horsley supposes the military ways to have gone, which pass by Pap-castle, and through Graystock park.

Ambleside is all within the manor of Windermere, but only part of it within the parish. It is of the Richmond fee; and on the aforesaid survey in the 28 Cha. 2. it was found, that there were 43 tenements, yearly rent of 26*l* 17*s* 0*d*.

At Ambleside there is a small *market*, which is kept in that part which is in Windermere parish; the boundary being at a place called the Stock. All below the Stock is in the parish of Windermere; above the Stock, in the parish of Gresmere.

In the year 1650, the keepers of the liberty of England by authority of parliament, setting forth a writ of *ad quod damnum* issued, and an inquisition

† Many of the particulars relating to this parish we have from Mr. Machel, who received the same from the reverend Mr. Wilson then rector of Windermere.

and return made thereupon by Anne lady Clifford, countess of Dorset, Pembroke, and Montgomery, sheriffess of the county of Westmorland, do grant, that within the vill of Ambleside in the county aforesaid, there shall be a market weekly on Wednesday, and two fairs yearly, on Wednesday in Whitsunweek, and the 18th of October, with a court of pie-powder and other incidents thereunto.

And in the year 1688, July 25, king James the second granted to Brathwaite Otway esquire, Francis Topham esquire, Reginald Brathwaite, George Mackerath, Thomas Mackerath, George Dixon, Matthew Mackerath, William Fisher, and George Kelsick, their heirs and assigns, a market weekly at the vill of Ambleside, at the place called the Stock, on Wednesday; and two fairs yearly, one on the Wednesday next after Whitsunday and the day next following, the other upon St. Luke's day and the day next following, unless St. Luke's day be Sunday, then to be on Monday and the day next following; and a fair every fortnight on Wednesday, from the Whitsuntide fair to St. Luke's fair; with a court of pie-powder, to be holden before their steward; with reasonable toll, tallage, piccage, fines, amercements, and other profits to the same appertaining, to the use and behoof of the poor inhabitants of the town of Ambleside.

In that part which is in Gresmere parish, stands the *chapel*, endowed by the inhabitants, and made parochial by bishop Pearson in 1675. The ancient salary was about 14*l* a year (which is now reduced to 12*l* 4*s* 11*d*) which the inhabitants voluntarily charged upon their estates, by proper deeds for that purpose; which the said bishop ordered to be lodged in the hands of such person and at such place, as that the inhabitants and other persons concerned may come at the same when required.

In 1726, 200*l* of queen Anne's bounty fell to this chapel by lot. And in 1746, Dr. Stratford's executors gave 100*l*, Sir William Fleming baronet 30*l*, unto which was added 40*l* 10*s* chapel stock, and 29*l* 10*s* given by Isaac Knipe M. A. the present curate; wherewith another sum of 200*l* was procured from the governors of the said bounty. With which whole sum of 600*l*, an estate was purchased in Grayrigg, of the present yearly value of 26*l*.

The curate, Mr. Machel says, is recommended by the majority of persons paying the said salary, and approved by the rector. But Sir Daniel Fleming, who was patron of the church of Gresmere, says, the curates of this chapel have been nominated by the patrons of the advowson of Gresmere, in which parish it is seated. The truth is, these chapels originally by law were in the patronage of the incumbent of the mother church, unless it was otherwise ordered at the foundation and consecration thereof. By the decrease in the value of money, the revenues became so inconsiderable, that the incumbents of the mother churches could not procure, or consented that the inhabitants might procure, persons able to officiate; until at length the inhabitants obtained a custom against them; which custom, in the eye of the law, having been for time immemorial, is valid and effectual. In the present case, the patrons of the mother church, by acquiescence of their presentees the rectors, seem to have obtained the like custom.

In

CHAP. VI.

In the year 1723, John Kelsick of Ambleside gentleman devised to John Mackereth yeoman, George Cumpstone yeoman, and Tomas Knott clerk, all of Ambleside aforesaid, and to the survivors and survivor of them, their heirs and assigns for ever, all his lands at Ambleside, in trust, to sell part thereof for payment of debts and legacies, and to let the rest to farm, and with the profits and rents of the same to build a school-house as near the chapel in Ambleside as conveniently may be, and afterwards to pay the rents and profits to a schoolmaster to be chosen by them the said trustees, and the survivors and survivor of them, their heirs or assigns, and the feoffees of the chapel salary for the time being, and their successors or the major part of them.—The said lands produce to the schoolmaster at present about 40*l* a year.

In Ambleside is the ancient house belonging to the family of the *Brathwaites* in this country, who possibly might have received their name from some *thwaite* or woody ground nigh the river Brathey.

There was a very ancient family of this name in Yorkshire; but it doth not appear that these Brathwaites had, or claimed, any connexion with them. The first in their pedigree is,

I. RICHARD BRATHWAITE of Ambleside; who married Anne daughter of William Sandys of East-thwaite in the county of Lancaster, and had issue,

II. ROBERT BRATHWAITE of Ambleside; who married Alice daughter of John Williamson of Under-Skiddow in Cumberland. He purchased the manor of *Burneshead*, which he gave to his eldest son Thomas, afterwards Sir Thomas; unto which place the said Sir Thomas removed, and was founder of the families of that name both at *Burneshead* and *Warcop*. Ambleside he reserved to his second son, *viz.*

III. JAMES BRATHWAITE of Ambleside; who married Joyce daughter of Bernard Benson of Loughrigg, and by her had issue two sons, *Thomas* and *Gawen*, and three daughters, *Dorothy*, *Isabel*, and *Anne*, the second of which daughters was married to Daniel Fleming of Skirwith esquire.

IV. THOMAS BRATHWAITE of Ambleside, son and heir of James. This Thomas in the last year of queen Elizabeth obtained a grant and confirmation of arms by William Segar, Norroy king of arms on the north of Trent; setting forth, "That whereas Thomas Brathwaite of Ambleside, son of James, "son of Robert of the same place, who bore for their ancient seals of arms "(to very many old deeds before him the said Norroy produced) a horn "within an escutcheon, having inscriptions of their name thereabout, and not "knowing certainly what colour the said horn or shield should be, had re-"quested him the said Norroy as well to blazon and set forth the same in co-"lours, as to appoint him a crest; therefore he the said Norroy grants to him "for his coat of arms, Or, a horn Sable, with a banderick of the same: And "for his crest, on a wreath of his colours a greyhound jacent Argent, collared "Sable, studded Or."

It is remarkable, that this coat of arms is the same with that of the Brathwaites in Yorkshire, which may seem to argue that the horn upon the seal came from that family, though these Westmorland Brathwaites at that time

were

were not aware of it. And Sir Thomas Brathwaite of Warcop, great uncle to this Thomas, twenty years before this, had a grant and confirmation of other arms, which the Brathwaites both of Warcop and Burneshead always bore, and which the said grant sets forth to be the ancient arms of their family, *viz.* Gules, on a cheveron Argent, three cross crosslets fitchee Sable.

It hath not appeared, whether this Thomas Brathwaite of Ambleside was ever married: However, he died without issue, and was succeeded by his brother,

V. GAWEN BRATHWAITE of Ambleside; who married Elizabeth daughter of Sir John Penruddock of Hale; and by her had issue, 1. *Thomas*, 2. *James*. 3. *John*, who married Elizabeth Hudson, and by her had a daughter and heir Elizabeth married to Sir John Otway of Ingmire-hall knight. 4. *Robert*, who married Bridget daughter of Henry Fletcher of Moresby in Cumberland, and by her had a daughter. 5. *William*, who married Elianor daughter of Edwin Nicolson, and had issue Dorothy. 6. *Dorothy*, married to Samuel Sands of East-thwaite, and had issue five sons and four daughters. 7. *Francis*. 8. *George*. 9. *Jane*, married to Edward Wilson of Nether Levins. 10. *Catharine*. 11. *Edward*.

This *Gawen*'s will bears date in 1653, and by it we may perceive what was then the family estate. He therein deviseth his lands at Brimham Park, Revyhill, Fellbeck, Bowler Shaw, North pasture houses, and Warsell, in the county of York; his lands at Ambleside, Clappersgate, Gresmere, and Langdale, in Westmorland; at Lancaster, Brathey, Freermoss, and Parkamoor, in Lancashire; and a tenement and forge at Hockbert, and a finery hearth and forge at Consey. He mentions lands that he had purchased for his son Robert at Hugill and Baysebrowne. He gives therein 10*l* to the chapel stock of Ambleside. Five pounds to be put forward so as the use of it yearly may go to the opening and cleansing the watercourses in the highway, especially in Ambleside town street. And he orders the bridge which he built at the Pull, to be repaired for ever by the owners of his tenements at Pullbeck and Brathey *.

VI. THOMAS BRATHWAITE of Ambleside, son and heir of Gawen, married Margaret daughter of Piers Leigh of Lime. He had no child. His brother *James* also died without issue. His brother *John* died leaving a daughter *Elizabeth* as aforesaid, unto whom the inheritance descended: She was married to Sir *John Otway*, and to him had issue a son *Brathwaite Otway* esquire, and three daughters.

This *Thomas*, in the year 1670, conveyed by deed to his sister Dorothy Sands, his lands at Ambleside above the stock late purchased of Edward Forest, also a pasture ground called Scandal-close, and divers parcels late purchased of Hugh Jackson; upon trust, if Brathwaite Otway of Ingmire esquire pay to her 300*l*, then she to convey to him; which if she should refuse, then the said lands to be sold to raise the said 300*l*; to be disposed of as follows: 50*l* thereof, to the use of eight or ten of the poorest householders born in Ambleside, not being customary tenants; to be put out by the overseers of the poor, with the advice and assistance of the rectors of Gresmere and Windermere;

* Flem.

and

CHAP. VI.

and the interest to be paid to the said poor householders on the 24th day of December yearly: 100*l* thereof to go in temporary charities: and the remaining 150*l* to the uses of his will.

In the year following, *viz.* in 1671, he conveyed to his said sister certain other parts of his estate at Amblesside, in trust, that if the said Brathwaite Otway should pay to her 1000*l*, then she to convey the same to him; if he should refuse to pay the same, then the said lands to be sold to raise the said sum of 1000*l*, to be applied to the uses of his last will and testament.

And by his will bearing date in the year 1674, he deviseth his lands at Low Wray in Furness Fells, and at Pulbeck and Brathey in the bailiwick of Hawkshead, to his brother Robert, in trust, that if his niece the lady Elizabeth Otway pay to the said Robert 700*l*, then Robert to convey to her; if not, then the said lands to go to Robert and his heirs charged with the said 700*l*; of which, 250*l* to go towards the maintenance of two scholars at St. John's college in Cambridge, going from the schools of Kendal and Hawkshead, and for want of such, then to any others going out of either of the said counties.—Amongst other bequests in the said will, he gives to the chapel stock of Ambleside 10*l*, and other 10*l* for buying two silver chalices; and 10*l* to the mayor and aldermen of Kendal to be laid out for a piece of plate for the use of their corporation *.

The lady Otway and her son Brathwaite Otway esquire refused to pay the aforesaid several sums, amounting in the whole to 2000*l*; insisting upon a marriage settlement, whereby the said Thomas Brathwaite covenanted that the lands should descend to the said lady Otway, chargeable with 500*l* and no more. The matter was brought into the court of Chancery; and the allegation on the other hand was, the insufficiency of the supposed settlement in point of form, and particularly as it was only by deed-poll. But by the court it was decreed, in the 31 Cha. 2. that the said agreement, though by deed-poll only, should bind the lands; and the heir at law recovered the same chargeable only with 500*l* †.—The consequence of which would be, that the first charge of 300*l* by the deed in 1670 would be good; and the lands being sold to raise that sum, it was decreed on a commission of charitable uses at Kendal, Feb. 8, 1679, that the lands should stand chargeable with the same in the hands of the vendee, being a purchaser with notice ‡. The second charge of 1000*l*, by the deed in 1671, would be good only as to 200*l* thereof, to the uses of the will. And the charge of 700*l* upon the lands in the will would be also void.

During the course of this contest, the statute of frauds and perjuries was made (in the 29 Cha. 2.) in order to a more perfect declaration what contracts of the like kind should be valid, and what not: and it is said, that the circumstances of this particular case gave rise to that act.

Thomas Brathwaite son of James aforesaid made a considerable collection of ancient coins; which upon his death came to *Gawen* his brother, who added

* Flem. † Finch. Reports, 405. ‡ Flem.

many

many more unto them; and after his death, the ſame coming to this laſt *Thomas* of whom we have been now ſpeaking, he increaſed the ſame to the number of 322, and gave them in the year 1674 to the univerſity of Oxford; being 6 of gold, 66 of ſilver, and 250 of braſs and copper; moſt of them being coins of the Roman emperors.

In the year 1658, Feb. 25, Robert Jackſon of Kendal, mercer, deviſed his lands at Ambleſide (the ſeigniory or lord's right whereof, as the will ſets forth, he had lately purchaſed of John Archer eſquire) to his eldeſt daughter Jane and the heirs of her body; in defect thereof, to his younger daughter Grace and the heirs of her body; remainder to two collateral relations and the heirs male of their bodies reſpectively; remainder to his own right heirs. And out of the ſame he deviſeth 3 *l* a year to be paid by his heir either lineal or collateral, to the churchwardens and overſeers of the poor of Ambleſide, and they to diſtribute out of the ſame every lord's day at Ambleſide chapel 1 *s* in bread to the poor people of Ambleſide, and the remaining 8 *s* they ſhall have for their pains. And if the heirs of the bodies of his two daughters ſhall fail, then he gives 5 *l* a year out of the premiſſes to a preaching miniſter at Ambleſide for ever. And he gives 5 *l* out of his perſonalty towards the repairing of the fleſh-houſe or weighing-houſe in the market place at Ambleſide; and makes his wife executrix.

Grace the younger daughter died without iſſue. Jane the elder was married to Lionel Topham eſquire. On a commiſſion of charitable uſes at Kendale in the year 1680, Lionel Topham and his wife, and alſo the widow who was executrix, appeared before the commiſſioners; and Mr. Topham alledged, that the lands were cuſtomary, commonly called tenantright, and were held of his late majeſty of bleſſed memory king Charles the firſt, according to the confirmed cuſtom of the manor of Windermere, under the payment of 26*s* 8*d* yearly finable rent, 8 *d* wood rent, and 8 *s* briggegraſſe rent, with a fine certain of 33 *s* 4 *d* upon the death or alienation of the tenant: And that the ſaid John Archer, who in the time of the late rebellion claimed by purchaſe under the then uſurpers, and before the making of the will, did under colour of the ſaid title ſell the ſame to the ſaid Robert Jackſon. The commiſſioners (*viz.* Chriſtopher Redman eſquire mayor of Kendal, Sir John Otway knight, Daniel Fleming and Edward Wilſon eſquires, and Michael Stanford clerk vicar of Kendal) upon full hearing, and proof being made before them, that the premiſſes were of the clear yearly value of 30 *l* and upwards, and that the premiſſes are by the cuſtom of the ſaid manor [excluſive of the ſaid pretended infranchiſement] deviſable by will, and being of opinion that the ſame is a good gift, limitation, appointment, and aſſignment of the ſaid ſums of money to the charitable uſes aforeſaid, do decree the ſaid ſum of 3 *l* to be paid yearly to the poor as aforeſaid, and 54 *l* arrears thereof then run to be laid out by the churchwardens and overſeers upon ſecurity, and the intereſt thereof to be diſtributed in bread every lord's day proportionably at Ambleſide chapel, to the poor people of Ambleſide for ever. And they do decree the ſaid 5 *l* out of the perſonalty, together with 6 *l* 6 *s* being the arrears thereof then run, to be paid

paid by the executrix, to the use and repair of the flesh-house or weighing-loft aforesaid, according to the direction of the said will. And the 5*l* a year to the curate of the chapel, to await the event of the failure of issue of the body of Jane aforesaid ‡.

Mr. George Mackereth gave 100*l*, the interest whereof is to be laid out on the feast of St. Martin yearly in cloaths for the poor of Ambleside.

At a place called *Borrans* in this lordship, there was a square fort called Borrans Ring, surrounded with a bulwark and trench. The inner part of the square had been walled about, and buildings in the midst; amongst the ruins of which much hewn stone hath been found, and divers of the aforesaid coins which Mr. Thomas Brathwaite gave to the university *.

PARISH OF HEVERSHAM.

THIS is one of those places in Westmorland which is mentioned in Domesday, and therein is written *Eureshaim*; probably from the name of the owner, *Eure* being a name not yet out of use.

This parish is bounded on the east by Preston Patrick in the parish of Burton, divided from it by Betha, otherwise Hutton Beck or Lilly Beck; on the South, by the parish of Betham; on the West, by the chapelry of Witherslack in the said parish of Betham; and on the North, by Cartmell Fells, being divided therefrom by the river Winster.

About 200 yards north-west from the church, there is a well which bears the name of St. *Mary*'s well; from whence it hath been conjectured that the church was dedicated to that Saint.

It is a vicarage, valued in the king's books at 36*l* 13*s* 4*d*. The advowson whereof belongs to Trinity college in Cambridge.

This church, amongst many others in this county, was granted by Ivo de Talebois, first baron of Kendal after the conquest, to the abbey of St. Mary's York; and afterwards confirmed to the said abbey, by the name of the church of *Eversheim*, by Gilbert son of Roger Fitz Reinfred †.

And in the year 1459, it was appropriated to the said Abbey by William Boothe archbishop of York, reserving out of the fruits thereof a competent

‡ Flem.

This event hath not yet happened, but in all probability will happen on the death of the present countess of Litchfield. The said Lionel Topham and Jane his wife had issue Francis, Lionel, Robert, Jane, and Dinah. The four first named died without issue. Dinah was married to Sir Thomas Frankland baronet, and had issue Elizabeth and Dinah. Elizabeth died without issue, and Dinah her sister (the only surviving descendent of Jane Jackson) was married many years ago to George-Henry earl of Litchfield, and hath no issue. (From an account of the late Dr. Topham, judge of the prerogative court at York, who was son of Edward the younger brother of Lionel husband of the said Jane).

* Machel. † Registr. Wetheral.

portion for a vicar; and also in consideration of the repairs of the cathedral church of York, reserving to himself a pension annually of 3*s* 4*d*, to the dean and chapter 3*s* 4*d*, to the archdeacon of Richmond 5*s*, and to the poor of the said parish 3*s* 4*d*.—And in the next year he set out the portion of the vicar by a special endowment as followeth; *viz*. That there shall be in the said church a perpetual vicar, presentable by the said abbot and convent, who shall have for his portion 20*l* a year, with a manse and garden. For which said sum of 20*l*, he shall have assigned to him, out of the fruits of the church, the annual sum of the third part of the mill of Milnthorp anciently belonging to the said church, also the tithes of the demesne lands of the same, and the quadragesimal tithes of all the parishioners, and the tithes of lambs, and wool, and hay of the whole parish, and all sorts of tithes of fishings, mills, foals, calves, pigs, brood geese, hens, ducks, bees, eggs, pigeons, lint, hemp, leeks, onions, and garden fruits of the whole parish, with all other small tithes of the same, and mortuaries as well quick as dead, and all other kinds of oblations made within the parish church or elsewhere. For which the said vicar shall find bread, wine, and wax, in the said church for ever, and shall pay yearly to the abbot and convent 106*s* 8*d* out of his part of the fruits of the church, and shall repair the chancel of the said church, and bear all archiepiscopal and archidiaconal charges, and other charges ordinary and extraordinary.

After the dissolution of the monasteries, queen Mary in the first year of her reign granted the rectory and advowson of this church to the said college, with other possessions in Westmorland, in exchange for the church of Wymeswold in Leicestershire, late belonging to the monastery of Beaucliff in the county of Derby *. (Except the corn tithes of Crosthwaite, which king Edward the sixth in the third year of his reign had granted to John Southcoat and Henry Cheverton.)

The fabric of the CHURCH is not ancient; for the old church was burned down by accident in the year 1601, whereby all the monuments, seats, bells, organ, and other ornaments were utterly destroyed. It was soon after rebuilt (at the expence of the parishioners), and restored to its pristine state; as appears by certificate entered in the parish book, as follows: "Memorandum, "That upon Sunday, commonly called Low Sunday, being the 15th day of "April 1610, the right worshipful Sir Thomas Strickland and Sir James Bellingham knights, according to a certain agreement set down between the "inhabitants of Crosthwaite and Lithe on the one part, and the churchwardens of Heversham parish on the other part did survey and view the parish "church of Heversham, which was newly repaired and re-edified: And "upon their sight and view, they found the same church to be very sufficient, "and in as good estate as the same was before the ruinous decay, to their "knowledge."

Since the said fire, the bells have been cast at different times. The third bell has an inscription in 1605.

Me pulsante, preces O vos effundite gentes,
Et laudes nostro psallite usque Deo.

* Dugd. MS.

The

The firſt or largeſt bell was caſt in 1662, with this inſcription:
Dulcedine vocis cantabo tuo nomine.

The ſecond bell bears date in 1669, and is thus inſcribed:
When I do ceaſe,
Remain in peace.

In 1609, they had a new organ, which was made at York; the whole expence whereof amounted to 29*l* 10*s* 5*d*. Which, amongſt others of the ſame kind in other places, was probably demoliſhed in the civil wars; for the preſbyterian party profeſſed open hoſtility againſt organs equally as againſt monarchy.

In the ſouth wall of the church, a few yards eaſt from the porch, is an arch juſt appearing with its top above the ſurface of the ground on the outſide; which, on new ſeating the church a few years ago, appeared on the inſide at large; and under it were ſeveral human bones. For under theſe arches in ancient time were interred ſome of the principal perſons, as the lord of the manor, the patron of the church, or the incumbent. And from the arch having ſunk ſo deep, or rather the ground being raiſed on the outſide, it ſeemeth that the church was not totally rebuilt, but raiſed on the old foundation.

Between two arches in the north ile of the chancel, belonging heretofore to the Bellinghams, and now to the earl of Suffolk and Berkſhire, is an elegant monument with the following inſcription;

M. S.

Here lyeth the body of the Lady Dorothie Bellingham, daughter to Sir Francis Boynton of Barmſton in the county of Yorke knight, and wife to Sir Henry Bellingham of Helſington in the county of Weſtmorland knight and baronett. Shee dyed the 23 of January 1626. Ætate ſua 32.

Thriſe ſixe yeares told brought up by parents deare,
Duely by them inſtructed in God's fear;
Twice ſeaven yeares more I liv'd to one betroth,
Whoſe meanes yea life were comon to us both.
Seaven children in that ſpace to him I browght,
By nature perfect, and of hopeful growght.
His parents unto mee deare as myne owne,
Theire loves were ſuch as to the world's well knowne.
But ere that one yeare more her courſe had runne,
God in his mercie unto me hath ſhowne,
That all theiſe earthly comforts are but toyes,
Being compar'd with thoſe celeſtiall joyes,
Which thro' the blood of Chriſt are kept in ſtore
For thoſe in whom his word has rul'd before.
To labour borne I bore, and by that forme
I bore to earth, to earth I ſtraight was borne.

In the year 1765, Sir Griffith Boynton of Burton Agnes in the county of York baronet, lineally deſcended from the ſaid Sir Francis, repaired and beautified the ſaid monument.

In

In this ile the Bellingham arms are cut in ſtone, with the year 1602 (which ſeems to have been done at the rebuilding of the church).

In the ſouth ile of the chancel, belonging now to Daniel Wilſon of Dallam-Tower eſquire, but formerly to the Preſton family, is the pew of Sir Thomas Preſton, with his arms cut in wood in the ſame year 1602. In the middle of which pew, raiſed about half a yard from the floor, on a plain black marble is this inſcription:

Hic jacet Domina Maria Preſton,
Filia
Illuſtriſſimi Domini Carilli Molineux
Vicecomitis de Maryborough;
Conjux
Nobiliſſimi Domini Thomæ Preſton
Baronetti. Quæ obiit
Die VI Julii
Anno Domini MDCLXXIII.

In the eaſt window of this ſouth ile are the arms of Buſkell, with the year 1601. And underneath is part of the name yet remaining of Richard Buſkell.

In this ſame ile lies interred the body of Mrs. Crowle of Froyſton in the county of York, great grandmother of the preſent Daniel Wilſon of Dallam-Tower eſquire; over whom is raiſed an handſome monument of free-ſtone, but without an inſcription.

In the north ile, affixed to the wall, nigh the little door, is a ſmall marble monument in memory of the reverend and learned Mr. Thomas Watſon a celebrated ſchoolmaſter of Heverſham, with this modeſt inſcription:

Juxta hoc marmor
S. E.
Rev^{dus} Thomas Watſon,
Annos prope quinquaginta ludimagiſter
Haud inutilis,
Obiit Nov. 22. { Ætat. 81.
Salut. 1753.

In the ſouth ile, adjoining to the chancel, is an inſcription in memory of Mary wife of Richard Chamber, who died in the year 1684. Which Richard was father of Ephraim Chamber, author of the celebrated Dictionary of Arts and Sciences.

In 1761, was erected by John Maychel and Edward Johnſon eſquires, Richard Crampton, John Dickinſon, John Preſton, and Joſeph Backhouſe, gentlemen, a new and handſome gallery, adjoining to the belfrey, containing ten ſeats or pews, ſufficient to hold about 60 perſons.

Vicars, ſince the burning of the church, have been as follows:

Mr. *Whitmell* probably was vicar when the church was burned; for in 1605, a legacy given by him was paid for whitening the chancel.

Mr. *Calvert*, in 1617.
Mr. *Bigge*, 1638.
Mr. *Cole*, 1645.
Mr. *Tatham*, 1654.
Mr. *Wallace*, 1658.
Mr. *Bigge* restored, 1663.
Mr. *Milner*, 1678.
Mr. *Ridley*, 1686.
Mr. *Farmer*, 1692.
Mr. *Williams*, 1723.
Mr. *Murgatroyd*, 1727.
Mr. *Smyth*, 1733.
Mr. *Wilson*, the present very learned and worthy vicar, in 1757. To whom our acknowledgments are due, for many of the particulars relating to this church and parish.

About 200 yards from the church towards the north-east stands the SCHOOL, which was built at the cost of Mr. Edward Wilson of Nether Levins in the year 1613, and endowed by him with several burgage messuages and tenements in Kendal, 26 in number, of the then yearly value of 21*l* 3*s* 10*d*; together with a yearly rent-charge of 3*l* issuing out of a field in Strickland Ketel called Dawson's Close.

The said Edward Wilson, by his will in 1651, gave to his kinsman Thomas Wilson of Heversham-hall the rectory of Tunstal, and capital messuage and tenement at Sellet, to hold to him the said Thomas, and to Edward his eldest son, and every other son successively in tail male: and charged upon the tithes of Lecke, parcel of the said rectory, two pensions of 6*l* 13*s* 4*d* each, to two colleges, *viz.* Queen's college in Oxford and Trinity college in Cambridge, for the maintenance of two poor scholars, in each college one, who shall be taught at and sent to the university from Heversham school, to be nominated by the said Thomas Wilson and the heirs male of his body, and in their default, by the several colleges, for four years and no longer, unless for want of other scholars properly qualified, and in such case they may hold the same two years longer; and if none be qualified, then the same to go to poor scholars at the school till fit to be sent. He charges also upon the same the sum of 10*l* yearly, to the poor, lame, and impotent people of the parish of Heversham, dwelling on the east side of the moss lying between Sinderbarrow and Crosthwaite and Lyth.—Which said sums having been neglected to be paid for several years, a commission of charitable uses was issued out of the Dutchy court of Lancaster in the 24 Cha. 2. Whereupon the same were decreed to be paid, together with 500*l* arrears and interest, to be employed as by the direction of the said will *. Which said exhibitions now amount to about 20*l*. a year each; and the annuity to the poor of 30*l* a year.

There is also an exhibition of 20*l* a year from this school to Magdalene college in Cambridge, called Milner's exhibition; to be held four years. The scholar intitled is to enter pensioner.

* Flem.

There

There are alſo two ſmall exhibitions of about 4*l* a year each, called Rigg's exhibitions, to Queen's college in Oxford, in the diſpoſal of the college.

This ſchool alſo is intitled to ſend a ſcholar to be examined for one of the exhibitions of the lady Elizabeth Haſtings to Queen's college in Oxford aforeſaid: which will be treated of more at large when we come to Appleby in this county.

The ſeveral manors, or other diviſions, in this pariſh are as follows:

I.

MANOR OF HEVERSHAM.

This manor, or part thereof, in the time of William the Conqueror, belonged (together with many others) to *Toſti* earl of *Northumberland*; and at the time of Domeſday ſurvey in that king's reign, in order to a taxation, it belonged to *Roger of Poictou* *.

Afterwards it appears to have been in the hands of the barons of Kendal. For *William de Lancaſtre* the firſt of that name, baron of Kendal, gave with his daughter *Agnes* in frank marriage to *Alexander de Windeſore* ſon and heir of *William de Windeſore* the manors of Heverſham, Grayrigg, and Morland. Which *Alexander*, in the 8 Ed. 1. obtained a grant of a market and fair at Heverſham; which are now, and all along ſeem to have been held at Milthorp: for Milthorp ſeems originally to have been parcel only of the manor of Heverſham.

This *Alexander de Windeſore* had a ſon *William*, who had a ſon *Alexander*, who had a ſon *William*, who after the death of Joan de Coupland in the 49 Ed. 3. was found by inquiſition to have held of the ſaid Joan, on the day on which ſhe died, the manors of Heverſham, Grayrigg, and Morland.

This laſt *William de Windeſore* had iſſue only a daughter *Margery*, married to *John Ducket* of a Lincolnſhire family, which firſt brought the name and family of *Ducket* into Weſtmorland, which continued at Grayrigg for many generations; but the manor of Heverſham did not go to the *Duckets*, or did not continue long in their poſſeſſion; for it appears afterwards, or a great part thereof, to have belonged to the abbey of St. Mary's York.——The Stricklands alſo of Sizergh had ſome lands here; for in the 35 Ed. 1. Walter de Stirkland obtained a grant of free warren in his lands in Heverſham, Helſington, and Barton.

After the diſſolution of the monaſteries, king Philip and queen Mary, in the 4th and 5th years of their reign, granted the manor of Everſham to *Edmund Moyſes*, *Richard Foſter*, and *Richard Bowſkell*; and *Bowſkell*'s ſhare, by

* In Biedun habuit comes Toſti 6 carucatas terræ ad geldum: Nunc habet Rogerus Pictavienſis et Eruvin preſbyter ſub eo. In Jalant 4 carucatas. Fareltun 4 carucatas. Preſtun 3 carucatas. Berewic 2 carucatas. Hennecaſtre 2 carucatas. Eureſhaim 2 carucatas. Leſuenes 2 carucatas. *Domeſd.*

an

an inquisition in the 13 Eliz. is thus described; viz. *Richard Bowskell* held of the queen *in capite* one capital messuage of the manor of Eversham, with 6 cottages, 72 acres of land, and all the works of the tenants of the said manor called *bond days*, if any there be of right accustomed to the said capital messuage appertaining. Which said capital messuage and other the premisses were assigned to the said *Richard Bowskell* and his heirs, in full recompence of the whole part and portion which he or his heirs might claim of the said manor of Eversham by the release of *Edmund Moyses* and *Richard Foster*. And the jurors further find, that the said *Richard Foster* released to the said *Edmund Moyses* all his right in the residue of the said manor: And that the said *Edmund Moyses* sold the whole residue of the said manor to the said *Richard Bowskell*; except one tenement sold by them the said *Edmund Moyses* and *Richard Foster* in Rowel to *Gabriel Croft*, another in Leesgill sold by them to *Thomas Smith*, one in Woodhouse to *John Preston* esquire, one in Aughtinwhaite to *Walter Strickland* esquire, one in Milnethorp then in the tenure of *Thomas Moyses* brother of the said *Edmund*, and one in Rowel late in the tenure of *Edmund Moore*; and also several other tenements granted severally to *William Wilson*, *Christopher Holme*, *John Jackson*, *Henry Holme*, *John Helme*, *John Atkinson*, *Thomas Holme*, *Christopher Wilson*, *Walter Parke*, *Robert Wilson*, and *William Benson*, parcel of the premisses in Eversham, Milnethorp, Aughtinwhaite, Rowel, and Woodhouse.

This is that *Richard Buskel* whose arms are put up in one of the church windows above mentioned. He was second son of *Buskell* of Milnhouse in the parish of Kirkby Lonsdale; and, by his wife Catherine Bindloss, had issue *Thomas*, *Robert*, and *James*, and four daughters, one of whom was married to Rigg of Strickland.

By indenture tripartite, Aug. 8. in the 24 Eliz. between *Richard Buskell* of Heversham gentleman of the first part, *Jasper Cholmlay* of Highgate in Middlesex esquire of the second part, and *Thomas Buskell* of Gray's Inn son and heir apparent of the said *Richard* of the third part, he the said *Richard Buskell*, in consideration of a marriage to be had between the said *Thomas Buskell* and *Frances* one of the daughters of the said *Jasper Cholmlay*, settles the manor of Heversham on the issue of that marriage *.

The said *Thomas Buskell* died before his father, having had issue, by his said wife Frances Cholmlay, 1. *Jasper*. 2. *John*, who died unmarried. 3. *Ralph*, who had issue Margaret, Anne, Thomas, and Jasper. 4. *Thomas*, who died unmarried.

Richard the father died in the 44 Eliz. as appears by inquisition taken at Kendal in that year, before Thomas Strickland and Thomas Brathwaite esquires, Thomas Atkinson esquire feodary of our lady the queen in the county of Westmorland, and William Hutton gentleman, commissioners in the nature of a writ of *Diem clausit extremum* to inquire after the death of *Richard Buskell* gentleman lately deceased; whereby it is found, that the said *Richard Buskell* long before his death was seised in his demesne as of fee of and in the manor of Eversham with the appurtenances, one capital messuage called Ever-

* Rawlinson.

sham-

ſham-hall, 6 cottages, 72 acres of land, and of and in one burgage or meſſuage in Kendal; that on the marriage of his ſon *Thomas*, he ſettled the ſame upon the iſſue of that marriage; that the ſaid Thomas died before his father; and that *Jaſper*, ſon of the ſaid Thomas, is heir to the ſaid *Richard*, and is of the age of 15 years and 2 months †.

This *Jaſper Buſkell* in the 11 Jac. ſold Heverſham-hall and the demeſne, with all that the manor of Heverſham with the appurtenances, to Edward Wilſon of Nether Levins gentleman, whoſe deſcendent Daniel Wilſon eſquire now enjoys the ſame.—The ſaid *Jaſper* was counſellor at law, and died unmarried.

But notwithſtanding the aforeſaid inquiſitions, the whole manor of Heverſham did not go in the manner above ſpecified. For the inquiſitions *poſt mortem*, or other like evidences, did not uſually with minute exactneſs diſtinguiſh particular ſhares or portions, but oftentimes expreſſed the whole inſtead of ſome particular part. And we find ſeveral parts of the manor of Heverſham at large (including Milnthorp, Aughtinwhaite, Rowel, and Woodhouſe) to have been in other hands.

In the 25 Eliz. Sir Thomas Cecil knight (probably one of the purchaſers from the crown) and Dorothy his wife conveyed by fine to Thomas Bradley eſquire the manor of Everſham and Milnethorpe, with 100 meſſuages, 20 tofts, one mill, 100 gardens, 1000 acres of land, 600 acres of meadow, 1000 acres of paſture, 100 acres of wood, 600 acres of heath and furze, 200 acres of turbary, 20*s* rent, and one fair and market; to hold of the queen *in capite*. Which Thomas Rradley died in the 29 Eliz. his ſon and heir William Bradley being then 13 years of age.

Jaſper Buſkell aforeſaid, beſides what he ſold to Edward Wilſon, ſold a part of the ſaid manor to Sir *James Bellingham* of Upper Levins, the laſt of whoſe name there ſold the ſame to colonel *James Grahme* anceſtor of the preſent owner *Henry* earl of *Suffolk* and *Berkſhire*.

Robert Gibſon of Atkenthwaite, by his will in 1701, gave 40*s* yearly out of certain tithes in Stainton and other places, for putting out ſuch poor children apprentices to trades, as ſhall be born within the towns, hamlets, and precincts of Heverſham, Milnthorp, Atkenthwaite, Rowell, and Woodhouſe.

II.

MILTHORP.

The name of Milthorp ſhews the antiquity of a mill there. In Mr. Machel's time, about 80 years ago, there was a paper mill a little above the bridge; and before that, at the ſame place was an iron forge. There are now two paper-mills at this place.—It is a market town, having a market weekly on Friday, and a fair yearly on Old May-day.

† Rawlinſon.

The river Betha, coming from Betham, runs by this place; over which there is a good ſtone bridge: Which river makes this to be a convenient little port, being the only ſea-port in the county.

III.

HINCASTRE.

Within this pariſh is the village of HINCASTRE, called in Domeſday-book *Hennecaſtre*; which name ſeems to import that a caſtle hath been anciently there; for *hene* ſignifies old, and *caſtre* a caſtle. But as there is no tradition, nor any remains or appearance of there ever having been a caſtle at this place, perhaps it may have received its denomination from ſome ancient *camp* there (which the word *caſtre* doth alſo denote).

King Richard the firſt granted to Gilbert ſon of Roger Fitz-Reinfred and his heirs, one carucate of land in *Henecaſtre*, to hold of the king by knights ſervice.

In the reign of king Edward the firſt, there was one *Adam de Henecaſtre*, who had a daughter *Avicia* married to Sir Thomas de Hellebeck, and brought with her divers lands into the Helbeck family. She ſeems to have been an heireſs; for after this, we find no more of the name *de Henecaſtre*.

IV.

LEVINS.

LEVINS, in Domeſday *Leſuenes*, at the time of the conqueſt or ſoon after was part of the poſſeſſions of *Toſti* earl of Northumberland; and, at the time of Domeſday ſurvey, belonged to *Roger of Poictou*. In the reign of king Henry the ſecond, we find the ſame in the poſſeſſion of *Ketel* ſon of *Uchtred*, which *Uchtred* poſſibly might be deſcended from the ſaid *Roger*. This *Uchtred* had large poſſeſſions in this part of the county. That which was afterwards called *Preſton Richard*, was at this time called *Preſton Uchtred*. *Ketel* ſon of this *Uchtred*, in the 34 Hen. 2. ſold a moiety of *Levins* to *Henry* ſon of *Norman de Redeman*, as appears from a fine paſſed in that year *.

And from that time *Levins* hath continued divided, the one part called *Upper* or *Over Levins*, the other part *Under* or *Nether Levins*.

We will begin with

* Henricus filius Normanni de Redeman debet unam marcam; ut finis, factus inter eum et Ketellum filium Uchtredi de terra de Levenes, recordetur in curia regis, de dominatione illius terræ, quam Ketellus conceſſit Henrico et hæredibus ſuis. Cujus medietatem Henricus tenebit in dominico ſuo; et Ketellus tenebit aliam medietatem de Henrico, per idem ſervicium quod Henricus inde facit capitali domino. *(Dugd. MS.)*

UPPER

UPPER OR OVER LEVINS.

This being granted as aforesaid to *Henry* son of *Norman de Redeman*, the name and family of *Redeman* continued there for many generations, and had large possessions as well at *Levins* as in other parts of the county.

The *Redemans* that we meet with, were probably not all of Levins: But this was the place where the principal family resided.

In the 13th year of king John, *Henry de Redeman* (probably the same *Henry* son of *Norman* aforesaid) seneschal of Kendal, was witness to Robert de Vetripont's grant to Shap abbey.

In the 17th year of the same king, *Benedict* son and heir of *Henry de Redeman* was one of the hostages for the future fidelity to that king of Gilbert son of Roger Fitz-Reinfred.

In the reign of king Henry the third, *Matthew de Redeman*, seneschal of Kendal, was witness to a confirmation of a grant of lands at Preston, Holme, and Hutton, by William de Lancastre the third to Patric son of Thomas son of Gospatric. He was also a witness to the grant of Skelsmergh by the said William to Robert de Leyburne.

In the 25 Ed. 1. *Matthew de Redeman* was witness to a grant of lands at Old Hutton and Holme-Scales by John de Culwen to Patric de Culwen his brother.

In the 7 Ed. 2. *Matthew de Redman* was representative in parliament for the county of Westmorland.

In the 17 Ed. 2. *Matthew de Redman* was one of the jurors on the inquisition *post mortem* of Ingelram de Gynes.

In the 18 Ed. 3. *Matthew de Redmane* was a juror on the inquisition *post mortem* of Robert de Clifford.

In the 31 Ed. 3. *Matthew de Redeman* represented the county of Westmorland in parliament.

In the 49 Ed. 3. after the death of Joan de Coupland, the inquisition finds, that *Matthew de Redman* held of her, on the day on which she died, the manors of Levins and Lupton, by homage, and the service of two marks yearly, as of her manor of Kirkby in Kendale: And that he held also of her a moiety of Quinfell, and divers tenements in Selfat. And that *Thomas de Redman* held of her divers tenements in Kirkeslack: Which *Thomas* was one of the jurors on the said inquisition.

In the 9 Hen. 4. *John de Redmane* was a juror on the inquisition *post mortem* of John Parr knight.

And in the 13 Hen. 4. *James Redmane* was one of the jurors on the inquisition *post mortem* of Ingelram de Coucy.

In the 20 Hen. 6. *Richard de Redman* was chosen one of the knights to represent the said county in parliament. He married Margaret daughter of Thomas Middleton of Middleton-hall esquire.

In the 22 Ed. 4. it was found by inquisition, that the manor of Levins was holden of William Parre as of the barony of Kendale; and that *Richard Redmayne* knight had a son *Matthew* who died in the lifetime of his father, who had a son *Richard*, who had a son *William* who died without issue, whose heir was *Edward* his younger brother then of the age of 27 years.

This *Edward* appears to have been living in the reign of Hen. 7. For in the 4th year of that king, after the attainder of the Harringtons, the inquisition finds, that Thomas Harrington held a messuage and tenement in Lupton of *Edward Redman* esquire. And this is the last of the name of *Redman* that we have met with at Levins. And the estate appears to have been sold about this time.

The arms of *Redman* were; Gules, 3 cushions Ermine, tasselled Or.

At this time there was a flourishing family of the name of BELLINGHAM at Burneshead. Of a younger branch of which family, one *Alan Bellingham* esquire purchased Levins, of one *Redman* by name, who then lived at Thornton nigh Egleston in Yorkshire. Which family therefore of *Bellingham* of Levins we proceed next to deduce.

1. ALAN BELLINGHAM the purchaser was eighth son of Sir *Robert Bellingham* of Burneshead knight; son of *Richard*; son of *Robert*; son of *Richard*, who married the heiress of Burneshead, and thereby came to that inheritance; son of *William de Bellingham* of *Bellingham* in Northumberland, who was under-sheriff in that county in the beginning of the reign of king Edward the first.

This *Alan* purchased not only *Levins*, but also *Helsington* (where the family frequently resided), *Gaythorn*, and *Fawcet forest*, and divers lordships in Lancashire and Northumberland. And finally he had a grant from king Henry the eighth, in the last year of his reign, of the fourth part of the barony of Kendal, which is called the Lumley Fee.

He was treasurer of Berwick, and deputy warden of the marches.

Of him this rhyme was made, alluding to his social, and at the same time martial disposition:

" Amicus Amico Alanus,
" Belliger Belligero Bellinghamus."

He married Elizabeth daughter of William Gilpin of Kentmere; and by her had issue,

2. THOMAS BELLINGHAM of Helsington esquire, who married Marian daughter of Thomas Beck of the barony of Kendal.

This Thomas was dead before the 3 Ed. 6. for in that year Marian Bellingham of Helsington widow had a lease granted to her of the rectory of Gresmere for 97 years, which came to her son Alan afterwards as executor to her, who sold his term and interest therein to William Fleming of Rydal esquire in the 16 Eliz. This Alan, during his mother's life, lived at Forest-hall, and after her death removed to Helsington.

Besides this son *Alan*, who was the elder, there was another son *Thomas*, who lived at Gaythorn, and married a daughter of Thomas Blenkinsop of Helbeck esquire.

3. ALAN BELLINGHAM of Helsington esquire. He was a bencher of the Inner Temple, and one of the king's council at York for the northern parts. In the 13 Eliz. he was knight of the shire for Westmorland.

He

He married to his first wife Catherine daughter of Anthony Ducket of Grayrigg esquire, by whom he had no issue. To his second wife, he married Dorothy daughter of Thomas Sandford of Askham esquire, and by her had issue, 1. *Thomas*, who died an infant. 2. *James*, who succeeded to the inheritance. 3. *Henry*. 4. *Robert*. 5. *Alan*. And seven daughters; amongst whom were, *Grace*, married to Clyburn of Clyburn. *Marian*, married to Francis Ducket of Grayrigg esquire. *Thomasin*, married to Thomas Salkeld of Corby esquire. And *Dorothy*, married to William Burrow of Biggins.

This is that *Alan* who lies interred in the chancel of Kendal church.

4. JAMES BELLINGHAM of Helsington esquire. He was knighted by king James the first at Durham, at his first coming into England in the year 1603.

He married Agnes daughter of Sir Henry Curwen of Workington knight.

In the year 1617, this Sir James presented *William Willaine* to the vicarage of Crosby Ravensworth, the advowson thereof being appendent to his manor of Gaythorn.

He died in 1641; leaving issue, 1. *Thomas*, who died unmarried. 2. *Henry*, who succeeded to the inheritance. 3. *Alan*, who succeeded as heir in tail, after failure of issue male from his elder brother Henry. And six daughters; 1. *Mary*, married to Christopher Crackenthorp of Newbiggin esquire. 2. *Alice*, married to William Mallory of Studley in the county of York. 3. *Dorothy*, married to Sir Ralph Ashton of Whalley in Lancashire baronet. 4. *Frances*, married to Sir William Chaytor of Crofte in the county of York knight. 5. *Agnes*, married to Sir William Ingleby of Ripley in the county of York knight. 6. *Elizabeth*, who died unmarried.

5. Sir HENRY BELLINGHAM of Helsington baronet was knight of the shire in every parliament that was summoned in the reign of king Charles the first. He married Dorothy daughter of Sir Francis Boynton of Bramston in the county of York knight: And by her had issue seven children (as appears from her epitaph above mentioned, but of these three only arrived to maturity, *viz.*) 1. *James*, who married a daughter and coheir of Sir Henry Willoughby of Risley in the county of Derby knight, but died before his father without issue. 2. *Dorothy*, married to Sir Henry Griffith of Burton Agnes in the county of York knight. 3. *Elizabeth*, married to John Lowther of Lowther esquire.

And here the male issue failing in the line of primogeniture; *Alan*, the next brother of Sir Henry, entered as heir in tail, paying 3000*l* to Sir Henry's two daughters and coheirs.

6. ALAN BELLINGHAM of Levins esquire, brother of Sir Henry, and third son of Sir James by his wife Agnes Curwen.

In 1661, he represented the county of Westmorland in parliament.

In 1668, he sued for a general fine; and an issue out of chancery was directed to be tried at the assizes at Appleby, whether as the said Alan came in by purchase, and not by descent, a general fine was due to him upon the death of the said Sir Henry: And a verdict was given for the defendants. The same issue was tried over again at the next York assizes, and a verdict was given for the plaintiff *.

* Fleming.

He

He married Susan daughter of Marmaduke Constable of Masham in the county of York esquire; and died in 1672; leaving issue *James*, *Henry*, and *Thomas*; and two daughters *Mary* and *Dorothy*, the latter of whom was married to Henry son and heir of Sir John Marwood of Little Buskby in the county of York.

7. James Bellingham of Levins esquire, son of Alan. He married first Barbara daughter of Sir Christopher Dalston of Acorn Bank, and by her had a daughter *Elizabeth*. To his second wife he married Elizabeth daughter of Sir Francis Leke of Newark upon Trent, and by her had *Alan*, *Henry*, *William*, *Roger*, *Mary*, *Agnes*, and *Bridget*. He was of the age of 42 at Dugdale's visitation in 1664; and died in 1680.

8. Alan Bellingham of Levins esquire, son and heir of James. He was 9 years of age at the time of the said visitation. He was chosen knight of the shire in 1681, and again in 1685. And this was the last of the Bellinghams at Levins; of whom the reverend Thomas Machel gives this eulogium, that he was an ingenious but unhappy young man. He consumed a vast estate, and sold Levins, together with the rest of his lands in Westmorland, to colonel *James Grahme*, privy purse to king James the second, younger brother of Sir *Richard Grahme* of Netherby in the county of Cumberland baronet, afterwards created viscount Preston.

These *Bellinghams* bore for their arms; Argent, 3 bugles or hunting horns Sable, garnished and furnished Or. The crest (in Dugdale) a buck's head couped Or.

The said James Grahme married *Dorothy* daughter of *William* earl of *Berkshire*, son and heir of *Thomas* earl of *Berkshire*, second son of *Thomas* earl of *Suffolk*, second son of *Thomas* duke of *Norfolk*, who in the reign of queen Elizabeth was beheaded for aspiring to the marriage of Mary queen of Scots. He represented the county of Westmorland in the several parliaments chosen in the years 1708, 1710, 1713, 1714, and 1722.

By his said wife Dorothy, he had a daughter and heir *Katharine*, married to *Henry-Bowes Howard* earl of *Berkshire*, and thereby brought the inheritance into that family.

Henry-Bowes Howard, earl of Berkshire, was son of *Craven Howard*, son of *William* aforesaid, father of the aforesaid *Dorothy*. So that Henry-Bowes and his lady were first cousins, both being descended from the same grandfather *William* earl of *Berkshire*. He had the appellation of *Bowes* from his mother, who was daughter and sole heir of *George Bowes* of Elford nigh Litchfield in the county of Stafford esquire.

He had issue by his said wife Katherine Grahme, *William* viscount *Andover*, who married the lady Mary Finch, second daughter of Heneage earl of Ailesford, and died in the lifetime of his father; leaving issue,

Henry Howard the present earl of *Suffolk* and *Berkshire*; which title of *Suffolk* came to this family by failure of issue male from the elder branch of Thomas earl of Suffolk aforesaid, second son of the aforesaid Thomas duke of Norfolk.

folk. Which *Henry* earl of Suffolk and Berkſhire married Maria Conſtantia ſole daughter of the preſent lord Trevor, and hath iſſue Maria Conſtantia his only child, of whom her mother died in child-birth.

The *Suffolk* arms are: Gules, a bend between ſix croſs croſslets fitchy Argent; with an augmentation in the midſt of the bend, on an eſcutcheon Or, a demi-lion rampant pierced through the mouth with an arrow, within a double treſſure counterflory Gules. The creſt: On a chapeau Gules, turned up Ermine, a lion guardant, his tail extended, Or; gorged with a ducal coronet Argent.—Supporters: On the dexter ſide, a lion guardant Or, gorged ducally Argent; on the ſiniſter, a lion Argent.—Motto: "Non quo, ſed quo-"modo."

The manor-houſe is Upper Levins Hall; which is a venerable old building, on the ſouth ſide of the river Kent; with extenſive gardens, bowling-green, wilderneſs, and green-houſe (now well furniſhed with curious plants), on the ſouth ſide thereof; and on the north, a large court, fine gravel walks, and handſomely paliſaded towards the river.

The arms in the hall, at the time of Mr. Machel's perambulation in 1692, were as follows:

In the glaſs of the large north window in the great hall; *Bellingham* and *Burneſhead* quarterly, impaling *Sandford* quartered with *Engliſh*.

Alſo, *Bellingham* and *Burneſhead* quarterly; impaling *Curwen*, with another coat, *viz.* Azure, a lion rampant Argent, langued Gules, debruiſed on the ſhoulder with three billets (the name not mentioned).

In plaiſter: *Bellingham* and *Burneſhead*; impaling, a wild boar leaning againſt a tree, the name not mentioned (probably, *Gilpin*).

Bellingham and *Burneſhead*; impaling *Sandford*, with its three quarterings, *Engliſh*, *Crackenthorp*, and *Lancaſtre*.

In the parlour window: *Bellingham* quartering *Burneſhead*; and on a ſcroll on one ſide, *Amicus Amico Alanus*, on the other ſide, *Belligerus Belligero Bellinghamus*.

In the bow window: Impalings of *Barburne*, *Tunſtall*, *Gilpin*, *Becke*, *Sandford*, *Salkeld*, all by name.

The park adjoining is well ſtored with fallow deer. The river Kent runs through the middle of it, over which there is a fair ſtone bridge, and a waterfall at the head where they catch ſalmon, called Levins Force (the ſame which in ſeveral ancient writings is called The Fors) *. Mr. Camden mentions two

catadupæ

* The accounts of the growth and migration of this fiſh in the two counties of Weſtmorland and Cumberland are very different, and not eaſy to be reconciled. The ſalmon come up into the freſh water to ſpawn, in the months of October, November, and December. The fiſhermen at King Garth near Carliſle, which is one of the largeſt ſalmon fiſheries in England, hold, that the fry, which appear in all the rivers in vaſt plenty in the ſpring following, do all go down to the ſea in the firſt floods that happen in the ſucceeding months of May and June, and return the next ſpring full ſalmon, that is, breeding fiſh, but far from the ſize they afterwards attain, which it is ſuppoſed may require ſeveral years. And the late Mr. John Carnaby, who occupied this fiſhery for many years, and who was deemed an intelligent man and of great veracity, has been often heard to ſay, that he had many times marked fry as they went down, and taken them again in the next year full ſalmon as aforeſaid.—On the other hand, the fiſhermen in Weſtmorland and at Lancaſter in the

6 river

catadupæ or water-falls in this river; but the other is not in Kent, but in the river Betha nigh Betham. The water at these places falls with a mighty noise; which to the neighbouring inhabitants is a prognostication of the weather. When that which is north from them sounds more loud and clear, they look for fair weather; when that on the south side doth the same, they expect rain. The philosophy of which is no more than this; that the south west winds, blowing from the sea, bring the vapours along with them, and generally produce rain; consequently, blowing from the north or north-east, they have the contrary effect.

On the west side of the Force was erected, some few years ago, by Thomas Holme esquire and other gentlemen in Kendal, a forge for beating out pigs of iron, and other iron work, which employs several families, who have dwelling-houses and offices near adjoining.

And at Sedgwick, on the east side of Kent, is lately erected by Mr. John Wakefield of Kendal and others a mill for making of gunpowder.

In the park of Levins, on the south side of the river, are the ruins of an ancient round building now called Kirkstead, which is said to have been a temple dedicated to Diana; near whereunto are to be seen the ruins of another building, which it is supposed belonged to that place.

In the same park, on the other side of the river, is a spring called the dropping well; which is of a petrifying quality, and in a short space of time will turn moss, wood, leaves, and the like, into stone.

A little below Levins, the river Kent enters upon the Sands, from which they are denominated Kent Sands; and though it is larger than the river Betha, yet no vessels can come up.

William de Lancastre, the first of that name, granted to the priory of Conishead the fishery of *Levene*, with a seyn and boat, from the place where Craike falls into Levene, as the said William used to fish there; reserving to himself liberty to fish there in person, and saving the view of his men which they had used to have in the said fishery †.

river Lune, say, the produce of the salmon is six years before it comes to be full grown salmon, and they distinguish the same in the following manner; First year, pinks; second year, smelts; third year, sprods; fourth year, morts; fifth year, fork tails; sixth year, salmon. Whereas the Carlisle fishermen distinguish these as different species: The pinks and smelts being their fry or young salmon; the sprods and morts they call the fresh water whiting; and the fork tails they distinguish by the name of gilse; and will not allow, that any of these three last sorts will ever come to be salmon. However, this is certain, (and the author of this note speaks from his own knowledge as an angler,) that in the higher parts of the river Lune, where the salmon usually resort to spawn, there are in the beginning of the spring two different sizes of young salmon, the one somewhat less than two inches in length, and the other commonly between four and five inches. This larger sort goes down in the latter end of April or beginning of May. The smaller sort remain the whole summer in great abundance, and grow to the size of four inches or upwards, and make much diversion to the angler. This brood goes down the next spring, and leaves the last autumn spawn remaining as before.

† 2 Dugd. Mon. 424.

NETHER

NETHER OR UNDER LEVINS.

After a moiety of Levins was ſold as aforeſaid by *Ketel* ſon of *Ughtred*, it doth not appear how long *Ketel* and his poſterity continued in poſſeſſion of the other moiety: Probably not long; for in the next generation we find ſeveral perſons of rank and note in this part of the county of the name *de Levins*, and ſome of them expreſsly ſtyled of Levins-hall.

Their arms were; Argent, on a bend Sable 3 eſcalops of the field. The creſt; a ſlip of a *vine* (in alluſion to the name) Proper.

In Betham church windows in Mr. Machel's time there were ſeveral defaced coats of arms; amongſt which were to be ſeen inſcribed ſeveral times the name of *Lewins*.

Next to this family, and perhaps purchaſers from them, we find the *Preſtons* of *Preſton*. In the 15 Hen. 8. by an inquiſition after the death of *Thomas Preſton*, it is found, that he died ſeiſed of the manors of Preſton, Holme, Heverſham, Nether Levins, and other places. This family of *Preſton* ending in daughters, Nether Levins came by marriage of one of the two coheirs of Sir *Thomas Preſton* to the lord *Montgomery*, who ſold the ſame to *Edward Wilſon* of Dallam Tower eſquire, about the year 1694.

On the ſurvey of the queen's lands in the 28 Cha. 2. Sir Thomas Preſton ſtands charged with a free rent of 20 *s*, and James Bellingham eſquire 10 *s*, for a fiſhing in the river Kent.

The *manor-houſe* is Under-Levins-hall, on the north ſide of the ſaid river; which has two demeſnes, one of which is called Naynſergh, on the oppoſite ſide of the river.

Mr. Machel's account of the arms which he found at Under-Levins-hall is as follows:

In the dining-room;

Preſton, ſingle.
Preſton impaling *Curwen*.
Preſton impaling *Preſton* of a younger houſe.
Preſton impaling *Thornburgh*.
Preſton impaling *Redman*.
Preſton impaling *Bradley*.

V.
STAINTON.

This place, at the time of the conqueſt, belonged to *Gilemichel* *, but ſoon after belonged to the *Flemings*, and ſo early as the reign of king Edward the firſt or before to the *Stricklands* of Sizergh, of which family Sir *Thomas Strickland* about the year 1674 ſold the tenements to freehold.

* Domeſday.

The *chapel* in Stainton commonly goes by the name of *Croscrake* chapel, from two farm houses of the name of *Croscrake*, nigh which it stands.

It was founded and endowed by *Anselm de Furnass*, son of the first *Michael le Fleming*, about the time of king Richard the first; and in the reign of king Edward the first was granted by Sir *William de Stirkland* knight to the priory of Cartmell: Witnesses of which grant were; Henry de Redman and Roger de Burton knights, Master Roger de Warwick rector of Hersam, William de Windeshover, Richard de Preston, Thomas de Derlay, Roger de Levins, and others *.

After the dissolution of the religious houses, this chapel had gone to decay, and Mr. Machel describes it in his time as an ancient chapel rebuilt; having a chimney in the north-west corner; the lintel thereof lying about a yard from the ground; and a yard above that, the funnel going out at an hole in the wall; without any bell, or any salary belonging to it, or any service performed. But it was made use of for the purpose of a school.

The chapel having long remained in the same sorry condition, the late bishop of Chester (Dr. Keene) procured it to be put in the list of chapels to be augmented by the governors of queen Anne's bounty, whereby it became intitled to 400*l*. about the year 1757. Since that time it hath been again augmented with the said bounty, procured by 100*l* given by the said bishop, being part of a legacy in his lordship's hands to augment poor chapels; 60*l*. given by the executors of the late Dr. Stratford; and 40*l* advanced by the present curate the reverend John Wilson, who is also master of the free grammar school of Heversham aforesaid. With the above sums, two estates were purchased, one at Dilaker, and the other in Killington; both of which together amount to the yearly value of about 30*l*. And in the year 1773, by the help of a charity brief this chapel was rebuilt.

VI.

PRESTON RICHARD.

PRESTON, of very ancient time, appears to have been divided into two parts; long before those two parts obtained the names of *Preston Richard* and *Preston Patrick*. At the Domesday survey, *Torfin* had one part of *Preston*, and *Roger of Poictou* the other. And even at the time of the distribution of parishes, they seem to have been separate; for *Preston Richard* is in the parish of *Heversham*, and *Preston Patrick* in the parish of *Burton*: And it was usual that a man's whole intire estate in the neighbourhood should belong to one and the same parish. Hence we see that Farleton, which extends almost quite through the parish of Burton, yet belongs to the parish of Betham.

There was a long succession of persons of the name of *Richard de Preston*, from the reign of king Henry the second to the reign of king Edward the third, both inclusive; comprehending the space of upwards of 200 years: from

* Amongst the evidences at Sizergh-hall.

the first of whom probably this part of *Preston* of which we now speak received the name of *Preston Richard*. At which time also, the other part of *Preston* belonged to *Patrick de Culwen*, from whom it seems to have received the name of *Preston Patrick*.

Before the time of the said first *Richard de Preston*, this part was called *Preston Ughtred*; from another owner probably of the name of *Ughtred*, who (as we have shewn) was in possession of the whole manor of Levins at that time; and, as he sold a moiety of the manor of Levins to Redman, so it is most likely that he sold this moiety of Preston to the said *Richard*.

After this *Richard de Preston* (the first of the name) we find, in the reign of king Henry the third, *Richard de Preston* knight, who was witness to divers grants of lands in Lancashire by Sir John le Fleming knight; together with Sir William de Furnes, William son of Orme, Matthew de Redeman, Thomas de Bethun, Adam son of Gamel, and divers others.

He was also witness to a grant and confirmation of lands in Preston, Holme, and Hutton, by William de Lancastre the third to Patric son of Thomas son of Gospatric.

In the 11 Ed. 1. *Richard de Preston* was one of the jurors on the inquisition *post mortem* of William de Lindesey.

In the 20 Ed. 1. Sir *Richard de Preston* was one of the jurors in a cause between the king and the abbot and convent of St. Mary's York, concerning the advowson of the two churches at Appleby.

In the 7 Ed. 2. *Richard de Preston* appears to have held lands at Preston.

In the 7 Ed. 3. *Richard de Preston* was witness to a release of lands at Old Hutton, by Gilbert de Culwen to Thomas son of Patric de Culwen.

In the 15 Ed. 3. *Richard de Preston* held lands in Preston Richard of Thomas de Ross.

In the 17th, and again in the 27th of Ed. 3. *Richard de Preston* knight represented the county of Westmorland in parliament.

In the 42 Ed. 3. *Richard de Preston* had a licence to impark 500 acres of land.

After this, we come to a family pedigree of the Prestons, which family finally settled at Preston Patrick, and the name became extinct in daughters in the reign of king Charles the second. The first in the said pedigree is *John de Preston*, who several times in the reign of king Edward the third represented the county of Westmorland in parliament.

The second in the said pedigree is *Richard de Preston*, who in the 14 Ric. 2. appears to have held the manor of Preston Richard of Sir William Parr knight.

This Sir Richard (according to the Pennington pedigree) died without issue male, leaving daughters coheirs; of whom Margaret was married to Alan Pennington lord of Moncaster, whereby a moiety of the manor of Preston Richard came to that family in which it still continues. The other moiety belonged to the Hudlestons of Hutton John, which was taken from them by Oliver Cromwell, whereby it came to the *Bensons* of Hugill, and by marriage of one of the coheirs came back into the *Preston* family, whose pedigree is further

further deduced as followeth.—The last mentioned Sir *Richard Preston* had a brother (as it seemeth) Sir *John Preston* knight, who was brought up to the law, and was one of the judges of the court of common pleas; who had issue *Richard*; who had issue *Thomas*; who had issue *John*; who had issue Sir *Thomas Preston*; who had two sons, *John* who continued at Preston Patrick, and a younger son *Christopher Preston* of Holker esquire, from whom did descend the Prestons of Holker.

Which *Christopher Preston* married Margaret Southworth, and by her had issue, (1) *John*. (2) *Thomas*, who married the lady Wandesford of Kirklinton in Yorkshire widow. (3) *Anne*, married to Christopher Laton of Sexey in Cleveland.

John Preston of Holker esquire, son and heir of Christopher, married *Mabel* one of the daughters and coheirs of *William Benson* of Hugill; and with her received a moiety of the manor as aforesaid of Preston Richard. They had issue,

George Preston of Holker esquire; who married to his first wife Elizabeth daughter of Ralph Ashton of Lever in Lancashire, and by her had issue, (1) *Thomas*. (2) *Christopher*. (3) *Frances*, married to Robert Duckenfield of Duckenfield in Cheshire. To his second wife he married Anne daughter of Sir Thomas Strickland of Sizergh, and by her had issue, (1) *George*. (2) *Anne*, married to Sir George Middleton of Leighton baronet. (3) *Margaret*, married to Francis Biddulph of Biddulph in Staffordshire. (4) *Elizabeth*, married first to John Sayer of Yarm: Secondly, to Nathanael West esquire: And thirdly, to George Layburne gentleman.

Thomas Preston of Holker esquire, son and heir of George, married Katharine daughter of Sir Gilbert Houghton of Houghton-Tower baronet, and by her had issue, (1) *George*. (2) *Thomas*, who married first Mary daughter of George Dodding esquire, and by her had no issue; to his second wife he married a daughter of Sir Roger Bradshaigh of Haigh in Lancashire baronet, and by her had issue Katharine married to Sir William Lowther of Mask baronet.

George Preston of Holker esquire, son and heir of Thomas, married Mary daughter of John Lowther of Lowther esquire; and had issue *Elizabeth*, married to Sir Wilfrid Lawson baronet.

And here ended the name of *Preston* of *Holker*.

The arms of *Preston* were; Argent, two bars Gules. On a canton of the second, a cinquefoil Or, pierced of the first. The Prestons of Holker had a crescent, by way of distinction of the younger house.

On failure of issue male, their moiety of the manor was sold to Sir John Lowther, from whom it hath descended to the present owner Sir James Lowther baronet.

Part of the Lowther tenants pay annually a free rent of 11*l* 14*s* 11½*d*, whose tenements were purchased to freehold of Sir John Lowther baronet in 1679; the rest pay a customary and finable rent of 8*l* 4*s* 9*d*.—And part of the Pennington tenants pay a free rent of 1*l* 13*s* 8*d*; and a customary and finable rent of 23*l* 4*s* 9*d*. (But in 1772 about one third of them purchased their

their tenements to freehold.)—The customary lands pay a fine arbitrary, but no boons or other like services.

Both lords have waif and estray upon the common, as they come first to them; or upon the other lands in the manor, as they happen to be in the grounds of their respective tenants.

This whole manor, according to Mr. Machel, is holden of the earl of Derby as paramount or chief lord, and formerly paid to him a noble rent yearly. The Penningtons, he says, purchased their moiety free; but the other half, *viz.* 3 *s* 4 *d* yearly continues to be paid by the Lowther tenants.

The ancient manor-house was at the place which is now called *Old-Hall*, and belongs to *Edward Johnson* esquire, a gentleman eminent for his love of gardening and botany, and deservedly esteemed for other accomplishments of more general and public utility. It was purchased in the year 1603, by his ancestor William Johnson of Stub gentleman.

Adjoining to Old-Hall and Stub estates was the ancient *deer-park*, but it hath been long ago disparked. And in the north-east part of Preston Richard is a place called *Birkrig-park*, within which is a place called the *Sepulchre*, where many Quakers have been interred; but it is now seldom used, they having a commodious meeting-house and burying-place in Preston Patrick.

At End-Moor in this township, in a place belonging to *John Savage* gentleman, in digging the foundation of a building some few years ago, the workmen found a curious hammer-head of stone, which undoubtedly must be extremely ancient, as it hath in all probability been formed before the use of iron in this island. It is of the exact form and size of a smith's striking hammer. The worthy vicar of this parish sent it to Trinity college in Cambridge; and in the year 1770, the learned Mr. Lort, fellow of the said college, and greek professor in that university, exhibited it to the Antiquarian Society. He observed thereupon, that "a weapon of this size and shape is figured in the "Museum Danicum; and that in the same Museum there is an account of an "urn dug up in Holsatia in 1686, containing ashes, bones, and the head of a "spear made of flint, and another stone like an hatchet: That the famous old "northern poem, called the Edda, makes frequent mention of the *malleus* of "the god Thor, or god of thunder, which, in the original, is called *hammaren* "*miolnar*, and, in the latin translation, *malleus contusor*, and is particularly celebrated as fatal to enemies, giants, and dæmons."—To which may be added the sentiments of a learned Frenchman on the same subject, from the History of Arts and Sciences in 3 volumes printed at Edinburgh, vol. i. page 156. "A kind of thunder stones, as they are commonly called, are still preserved "in a great many cabinets. They have the shape of axes, plough-shares, "hammers, mallets, or wedges. For the most part they are of a substance "like our gun-flints, so hard that no file can make the least impression upon "them. They are almost all pierced with a round hole, in the place most "proper for receiving a handle, and this hole is made in such a manner, that "the handle being once forced in, will not come out again, but with great "difficulty, as is with our hammers. It is well known, that tools of stone "have been in use in America from time immemorial. They are found in the

6 "tombs

"tombs of the ancient inhabitants of Peru, and ſeveral nations uſe them to "this day. They ſhape and ſharpen them upon a kind of grindſtone; and, "by length of time, labour, and patience, form them into any figure they "pleaſe; and uſe them nearly in the ſame manner as we do our tools of iron." Mr. Robinſon of Newby-bridge in Lancaſhire, in draining ſome low grounds, at a good depth below the ſurface, met with a ſtone hammer-head like this above deſcribed. And the late biſhop of Carliſle, Dr. Lyttelton, exhibited ſuch another to the Antiquarian Society, found in the pariſh of St. Cuthbert's Carliſle.

Miles Greenwood, a native of Crooklands in this townſhip, by his will in 1637, gave 20*s* yearly iſſuing out of an houſe at Grantham in Lincolnſhire, to be diſtributed to the poor people dwelling nigh unto Crooklands.

VII.

CROSTHWAITE AND LYTH.

This is a large diviſion, conſiſting part of the Richmond and Marquis fees, and part of the Lumley fee.

By the inquiſition aforeſaid of the lands belonging to queen Katharine in the 28 Cha. 2. it was found, that in Croſthwaite and Lyth there were 63 tenements of the Richmond fee, of the yearly cuſtomary rent of 19*l* 3*s* 7*d*. And two tenements of the Marquis fee, of the rent of 15*s*.—Of the Lumley fee there are about 50 tenements.

The *chapel* of Croſthwaite is about five miles north weſt from the pariſh church. It ſeems to have been of ancient foundation, but was not made parochial till the reign of Philip and Mary. For in the year 1556, Cuthbert biſhop of Cheſter, reciting the petition of the inhabitants of the vills or hamlets of Croſthwaite and Lyth, ſetting forth their great diſtance from the pariſh church, ſo that they cannot carry their dead to be buried without great charge and inconvenience, nor carry their children to be baptized without great danger to the ſaid children both of ſoul and body, nor attend the church for divine ſervice and ſacraments without great charge and labour, and therefore praying that he would vouchſafe to conſecrate a certain chapel of theirs commonly called Croſthwaite chapel, and grant licence for a chaplain to officiate therein, to be maintained by their own ſalary and charge, and not otherwiſe; he the ſaid biſhop, with the aſſent of the maſter and fellows of Trinity college in Cambridge, patrons of the pariſh church of Heverſham, grants licence, that in the chapel or oratory aforeſaid called Croſthwaite chapel, in honour of the bleſſed virgin Mary, ſituate in the hamlet of Croſthwaite aforeſaid, maſs ſhall be celebrated, the canonical hours rehearſed, the bodies of the dead buried, and the ſacraments adminiſtred, by fit prieſts canonically ordained, having firſt been approved by the vicar of Heverſham for the time being: Yet ſo, that no prejudice thereby ariſe to the mother church in tithes, oblations, obventions, or other eccleſiaſtical rights. With a proviſo, that this licence once in three years be brought by the chaplain or three other principal inhabitants of the ſaid hamlets to the pariſh church, and there on the ſecond Sunday after Pentecoſt be

read

read at the high altar after reading the gospel by the minister there officiating, if by the vicar or churchwardens of the said church of Heversham they be thereunto required.

Afterwards, about the year 1580, on some disputes between the inhabitants of the chapelry and the rest of the parishioners, an award was made. Which award being destroyed by the burning of the church as aforesaid, a memorial thereof was put into writing, and registred in the parish book as followeth: " Whereas it fortuned, through negligence of a careless workman, being a plumber, in the year 1601, on Wednesday being the first day of July, the parish church of Heversham was utterly consumed with fire, and all implements, ornaments, books, monuments, chests, organs, bells, and all other things were perished; amongst which things, there was an award indented, the date whereof we have not in perfect memory, yet we think that it was about the year of Christ 1580, made between the inhabitants of Crosthwaite and Lyth, being a hamlet of the said parish, on the one part, and the inhabitants of the other hamlets of the said parish on the other part, awarded by the right worshipful Sir Thomas Boynton knight and Rowland Philipson esquire, touching certain questions, articles, suits, and controversies then depending amongst them. The articles whereof, we whose names are hereunto subscribed thought meet and convenient to express and set down, so near as our memories do extend unto. First, ordered and awarded, that the said inhabitants of Crosthwaite and Lithe, by their churchwardens and sworn men, shall yearly upon New Year's even make their accounts and reckonings at Heversham church, for all matters and receipts for the benefit of the said church, and yearly pay such sums of money as shall fall due to the church, to the then churchwardens of Heversham. And also shall pay towards the stipend and wages of the parish clerk of Heversham yearly, on New Year's even, the sum of 17*s*. And also shall pay for every corpse being buried above the Quire wall at Crosthwaite 3*s* 4*d*; and for every corpse buried beneath the Quire wall 1*s* 8*d*. Also ordered and awarded, that when any assessment, cuilibet, or proportion shall be laid and imposed for the necessary repairs of the church of Heversham, the said inhabitants of Crosthwaite and Lithe shall answer, bear, and pay a full quarter or fourth part of the same, so oft as need shall require. Also ordered and awarded, that the said inhabitants of Crosthwaite and Lithe shall appoint and name two sufficient men within their hamlet, to serve as churchwardens at Heversham church yearly, and six others to be sworn men as assistants, to make up the number of 24 sworn men. And the said churchwardens and sworn men to join with the other churchwardens and sworn men of the said parish, in all things needful and necessary for the said church; and always to be appointed on New Year's even; and to take their oaths on the fifth day of January, being the twelfth even, at the said church of Heversham, according as hath been accustomed."—The substance of which oath is, to maintain and support the benefit of the mother church.

The chancel and steeple of this chapel were built by one William Gilpin, who also contributed largely towards the three bells, in 1626. On which

bells

bells are the following inscriptions: On the first bell; *Jesus, be our speed.* On the second bell; *Soli Deo gloria.* On the third bell;

A young man grave in godliness,
William Gilpin by name,
Gave fifty pounds, to make these sounds,
To God's eternal fame.

The curate's revenue consists of 5*l* 8*s* 10*d* ancient chapel salary, paid by the inhabitants; who also in the year 1716 raised 200*l* by subscription, and thereby obtained 200*l* from the governors of queen Anne's bounty: With which an estate was purchased in Dent in the county of York, of the present yearly value of about 17*l*. There is also a small cottage belonging to the curate of about 40*s* a year; and the interest of 158*l* contributed by divers benefactors, amounting to 8*l* a year. The whole amounting to about 32*l per annum.*

In the year 1756, Agnes widow of William Burns bequeathed by her will 15*l* for a flagon to be used at this chapel; which was accordingly purchased, with her name ingraved thereon.

In 1665, George Cock of Brow-head in Lyth gave by his will 20*l* to the poor of this chapelry; the interest thereof to be distributed on New Year's day yearly: And 10*l*, whereof the interest to go to the use of a schoolmaster at Crosthwaite; and when there is no schoolmaster, then to go towards repairing the highways in Lyth quarter: And 20*l*, the interest whereof to go to the curate at Crosthwaite: And 10*l*, of which the interest to be applied for the repair of the highways in Lyth quarter: Also 50*l* to his trustees, referring it wholly to them to bestow so much thereof as they please towards building a school-house convenient for the whole hamlet. In 1671, Janet his widow by her will gave 10*l* to the poor stock.

By other like benefactions, they have now a poor stock of 215*l*, and a school stock of 70*l*. Besides which, there was the sum of 60*l* school stock laid out in the purchase of a cottage and two small parcels of land called Elie Parrocks, which yielded 3*l* a year. But the tides having washed away great part of the land, the inhabitants (with the consent of the lords of the manor) laid part of the common to the said lands to make up the deficiency; and the cottage also being gone to decay, they repaired the same with the 10*l* highway money, and the tenant of the cottage to pay 10*s* yearly for the repair of the highways in Lyth quarter.

In a meadow within this chapelry, belonging to John Robinson of Watermillock esquire, are three pits; the largest of which is immensely deep, and commonly said to be unfathomable. One thing very remarkable is, that when there is much rain on the west side of Whitbarrow, in Witherslack or Cartmell Fells, the water in the pits will rise and overflow the meadows. And, in the season of salmon smelts, these pits abound with those smelts, at the same time that they are to be seen in the river Kent; which argues, that they arrive from thence in subterraneous passages. The water from the pits runs under Thorpel bridge, and the course thereof is called Thorpel Dike.

In

In this hamlet is a large mofs, known by the name of Lyth-mofs; where feveral large trees, as oak, fir, and birch, are frequently dug up. One oak was lately taken up, quite found, which contained 2000 feet of wood.

And at a place called High in Crofthwaite, belonging to Mr. Thomas Robinfon, was a remarkable large beech tree; whereof one fingle branch, broken off by a violent hurricane Oct. 8, 1756, meafured 193 feet. The remaining part, about two years afterwards, was cut down, which meafured 605 feet. Befides which, there were four cords and an half of fmall wood.

PARISH OF BETHAM.

I. *Parifh of Betham.*
II. *Manor of Betham.*
III. *Haverbrack.*
IV. *Farleton.*
V. *Witherflack.*

I.
PARISH OF BETHAM.

BETHAM feems to have had its name from the river *Betha*, which runs through the village, and fo by Milnthorp into the fea; as much as to fay, the *hamlet* or village on the river *Betha*. This river is now called *Bela*, by corruption as it feemeth; for in Mr. Machel's account it is invariably written *Betha*, without any intimation of its having any other name. And Mr. Leland who travelled through this country in the reign of king Henry the eighth, fays, "By *Bytham* runneth *Byth* water, a pretty river." And efpecially, in a grant of lands and other poffeffions to the priory of Conifhead (as hereafter mentioned), it is exprefsly called *the water of Betha.*

Sometimes the name of the place is written *Bethom*; in which refpect it may be underftood to fignify the *holme* ground adjoining to the river.

This parifh is bounded on the Eaft by the parifh of Burton (indeed it runs almoft quite through and interfects the faid parifh of Burton, which part is called *Farleton)*; on the *South*, by the parifh of Warton in the county of Lancafter; on the Weft, by the fea; on the North-weft by the parifh of Cartmell in the faid county of Lancafter; and on the North, by the parifh of Heverfham.

The church, according to Mr. Machel's account, is dedicated to St. *Leoth* or *Lyth*, otherwife called *Lioba* or *Liobgytha*; but according to Mr. Brown Willis it is dedicated to St. *Michael*. It is a vicarage, in the patronage of the

 crown,

crown, and in the presentation (under the crown) of the chancellor of the duchy of Lancaster. It is rated in the king's books at 13*l* 7*s* 6*d*; and the clear yearly value, as it was certified to the governors of queen Anne's bounty 19*l* 6*s* 8*d*.

Ivo de Talebois gave this church and certain lands at *Halfrebeck* (now called *Haverbrack*) to the abbey of St. Mary's York; to which abbey this church was afterwards appropriated. And Gilbert son of Roger Fitz Reinfred and his wife Helwise daughter and heir of William de Lancastre the second confirmed the same to the priory of Wetherall in Cumberland which was a cell of the said abbey *. And the same Gilbert son of Roger Fitz Reinfred gave to St. Peter's hospital in York liberty for their horses and swine to be within his forest; and to have two folds therein, one in Capelthwaite and the other in Roakerdale, for the taking of them; and that one person of the said hospital, and one other person, may keep the same within his forest, so as it be done without any bow, arrows, or dog †.

This church paid a pension of 40*s* a year to the said abbey.

After the dissolution, the rectory of this church continued in the hands of the crown till the 9th year of king James the first (the crown leasing it from 21 years to 21 years, under the fee farm rent of 25*l* a year, the lessee paying also 13*l* a year to the vicar). Which said king, in the year aforesaid, granted the same to Sir Francis Ducket of Grayrigg knight, reserving the ancient rent and payment to the vicar.

From Sir Francis it descended to James Ducket esquire; who sold the great tithes of Farleton to the Wilsons of Underley; the great tithes of Helslack and Storth to Hugh Tomlinson, who sold the same again to Mr. Ralph Buskell: Whatside great tithes he gave to William his eldest son by his second wife, who sold the same to John Girlington of Thurland-castle in Lancashire esquire.

The residue of the rectory he settled in trustees to be sold for raising portions for his three daughters which he had by his third wife, who was afterwards married to Thomas Hilton esquire, and the overplus to go to their mother. One of these daughters, *Mariana*, died unmarried; *Anne* the second daughter was married to one Mr. Gandy; and the third daughter *Elianor* was married to Mr. *Thomas Shepherd*, who purchased the other sisters shares, and his son the late *Thomas Shepherd* of Kendal esquire sold the same about the year 1730 to *Daniel Wilson* of Dallam-Tower esquire, grandfather of the present owner thereof.

The small tithes by the said settlement came to their mother, in whose family they continued till after the death of her son George Hilton. And in the year 1756 the same were purchased to the church for the use of the vicar, for the sum of 120*l*; of which the late commissary Stratford gave 40*l*, and the parish subscribed 80*l*. The whole crown rent of 25*l* a year remains upon these small tithes, and they only produce to the vicar upon an average about 4*l* 10*s* a year: But if they shall happen to fall short, so as to be insufficient to satisfy the crown rent, undoubtedly the other tithes before sold off will be liable to make it up.

* Regiſtr. Wetheral. † Dugd. MS.

The whole revenue of the vicarage at this day is as follows: Pension as aforesaid reserved out of the rectory 13*l.* Small Tithes 4*l* 10*s.* Three inclosures at Kellet purchased by Mrs. Dorothy Wilson in 1707, 4*l* 10*s.* In 1722, Edward Colston of Mortlake in Surrey esquire gave 100*l*, Mr. James French of London another 100*l*, and the reverend Mr. Smith vicar 60*l*, unto which the governors of queen Anne's bounty added 200*l*, wherewith an estate was purchased at Priest Hutton: And in 1731, Mrs. Elizabeth Palmer gave 200*l*, and the governors of the said bounty 200*l*, wherewith an estate was purchased at Yelland: Which two estates are worth yearly about 27*l*.—So that the total of the vicar's revenue is about 49*l per annum.*

There is no vicarage-house, nor glebe-land, not even so much as the churchyard, belonging to the vicar.

Vicars, since the accession of king James the first, have been as follows:

Edward Halstead died in 1612, and was succeeded by *Edward Fisher.*

On the death of *Edward Fisher* in 1642, *George Bennison* succeeded.

In 1665, *George Bennison* resigned, and *John Brockbank* was instituted.

On his resignation in 1670, *William Jackson* was instituted, who continued vicar 39 years.

On the death of *William Jackson* in 1709, *James Smith* was instituted, and continued vicar 43 years.

In 1753, on the death of *James Smith, Daniel Wilson*, M. A. was instituted.

Upon whose resignation in 1762, the present vicar *William Hutton* succeeded, unto whom we are obliged for several of the particulars relating to this parish. This gentleman, by an example worthy of imitation, hath made a large folio collection of matters curious and useful concerning his said parish, and hath lodged the same in the vestry of the church for the information of posterity, desiring that the same may never be removed from thence upon any account whatsoever; with vacant pages to be filled up from time to time, as materials shall occur. And this undoubtedly is the proper method to render such a work compleat; for it is impossible in the nature of the thing, for one person, or during the course of one man's life, to collect all things that may be useful in such an undertaking, and time will add many other particulars.

The *parsonage* or rectory-house stood at the north-east corner of the churchyard, and was formerly called the college of St. Mary's; and the old *vicarage-house* stood behind it, adjoining to the churchyard wall.

Nigh to the place where the old rectory-house stood, the aforesaid *Thomas Hilton* esquire erected a fair-house, which was afterwards improved and rendered more commodious by his son and heir *George Hilton* esquire. Which said George Hilton, being a Roman catholic, joined the rebels in 1715, and making his escape was pardoned amongst the rest by the act of grace in the year following. He ever afterwards lived private, and built an house at the south end of Betham park, unto which he retired. The reverend Mr. Hutton aforesaid takes notice, that some few years ago there was found in an old chest a journal of his life, which unfortunately hath been since lost or mislaid. It appeared to have been an account of his life taken by himself every night, or sometimes at the end of the week. "On Sunday," says he in one place, "I

 vowed

"vowed to abstain from three things during the course of the ensuing week" [which was in Lent], "*viz.* the use of women, eating flesh, and drinking "wine. But, alas, the frailty of good resolutions! I broke them all, laid "with a girl at the Sandside, was tempted to eat the wing of a fowl, and "got drunk at Milnthorp."

The three sisters aforesaid of the Ducket family dying one after another, and the furniture which was divided amongst them having been sold at different sales, the goods came into the hands of divers housekeepers within the parish. At Hangbridge there is now an ancient picture of one of this family which had been drawn on a table or board, and now converted into a clock-case. The venerable face of this ancestor is in front, and an inscription partly in front and partly on the side, having been cut through by the saw. As near as it can be made out the inscription is thus:

Quos fortuna premit, patientia tollit in altum.
Non nisi mentis inops nimboso turbine cedit.
Sic mea vita fuit: Sed nunc donabitur ætas,
Et placido vento sulcabit æquora tutò,
Sicut acu demptâ pannus contexitur inde,
Sic cælesti ardens depellit amorque timorem.
Et velut omissis multis, nugisque relictis,
Grandia concurrunt (demptis florentibus annis)
Sic mea sors repetit, repetet pars optima vitæ.

At the bottom appears his age and the year of our lord; viz. Ætatis 74. Anno 1597.

The purport of the inscription is, "That having been tossed in troubles and "vanities in his youth, now he is become old he is engaged in greater and "more important concerns."

According to the course of chronology, this must be the picture of *Anthony Ducket* esquire, grandfather of Sir Francis; which Anthony had a son Lionel Ducket at that time fellow of Jesus college in Cambridge, who (most likely) accommodated his father with this inscription.

The longevity of this family was remarkable; for during the course of 12 successions, being the whole time that they lived at Grayrigg-hall, not one of them (as we observed before) was ever in wardship, the heir being always of the age of 21 or upwards, at the time of the death of his ancestor.

The *church* is in fair and neat condition, with a tower steeple and three bells. It stands in a fine vale (or holme ground), and the situation is rendered very pleasant by the variety of wood, water, and rocky cliffs in prospect.

On a pillar nigh the rails of the communion-table is the following monumental inscription:

Juxta hanc columnam,
jacent reliquiæ
Viri admodum pii ac reverendi J. Smyth,
Hujus ecclesiæ 43 annos vicarii,

Qui vitæ jam actæ recordatione lætus,
et futuræ spei plenus,
Animam Deo reddidit die Maii 14°
Anno Dom. 1753. Ætat. 69.
In vita, labor et periculum:
In moriendo, pax et resurgendi securitas.

In the south ile, on a broad pillar, the late Daniel Wilson esquire caused a fair monument of white marble to be erected in memory of his grandfather and father, on which is the following inscription:

Ad pedem hujus columnæ,
Conduntur reliquiæ Edwardi Wilson de Dallam Tower
Armigeri,
Qui, amici fidelis, boni civis, et integri magistratus
Muniis diu et feliciter perfunctus,
Tandem octoginta novem annis fractus,
Requievit mense Julii, A. D. 1707.
Duas sibi adscivit uxores,
Elizabetham * *filiam Thomæ Braithwaite* de Ambleside,
Per quam filium unum reliquit Edwardum armigerum:
Huic successit Dorothea filia Ricardi Kirkby de Kirkby
in agro Lancastriensi armigeri,
Ex qua,
Unicum suscepit filium Rogerum Wilson de Casterton
in hoc comitatu.
Hic etiam cum paterno miscetur cinis
Edwardi Wilson armigeri, filii et hæredis;
sinceri, æqui, eruditi:
Uxorem duxit Catherinam,
filiam Danielis Fleming de Rydale militis,
Fœminam, seu conjugem seu matrem spectes, lectissimam:
Et annum agens 69, e vivis discessit 5° die Febr. A. D. 1719.
Superstites reliquit Danielem et Catherinam:
Hæc
paulo post paternas exequias,
ex hac vita demigravit innupta,
et apud Tunstal juxta matrem sepulta est.
Daniel Wilson armiger,
Avo patrique optime merentibus pie parentavit.
Juxta quoque jacent, secundo et tertio geniti,
Daniel et Gulielmus, hujus filii;
optimæ spei pueri.

* Her name was *Jane* daughter of *Gawen Braithwaite*.

On

On the north side of the said pillar is another monument, with this inscription:

Near this pillar
are interred the remains
of Daniel Wilson esquire of Dallam-Tower;
who departed this life
the 31st of May, A. D. 1754, aged 74.
He married Elizabeth daughter
of William Crowle of Hull esquire in Yorkshire;
By whom he had issue 6 sons and a daughters.
He represented the county of Westmorland
in parliament near 40 years, with the
strictest honour and integrity.
In private life,
he was an affectionate husband,
an indulgent parent,
a sincere friend,
an hospitable neighbour;
and in all stations of life,
his conduct was uniform and consistent.
His son Edward Wilson esquire
erected this monument
to his memory.

The *seats* in this church (according to the ancient laudable custom in churches) are in common to the parish; except where special faculties have been obtained.

On a seat in the passage from the middle to the north ile, are the following lines, in the genuine style of inscription poetry:

"This seat gave Thomas Kendal, we say,
"To Witherslack, Methop, and Ulva."

(It was given in the year 1636, to the inhabitants over the sands.)

Belonging to this church are two silver *chalices* for the communion; upon one of which is this inscription. *Ob pæn. mulct. dedicat. huic ecclesiæ* 1716. It was purchased by the late commissary Stratford with money paid in commutation of penance for adultery and fornication. (But it doth not seem to have been of any necessity at all to inscribe this upon the cup.)

About 60 yards from the church is a *school-house*, which was built out of the parish stock about the year 1663; and there remained the interest of 100*l* yearly towards a salary for the schoolmaster. There have been some benefactions to it since, but none very considerable.

They have also a *poor stock* of 100*l*, contributed by about 13 different persons.

About

About 40 yards distant from the place where the school-house now stands, there was anciently a *chapel*, which is said to have been dedicated to St. John, and near it many human bones have been dug up in a place which is now converted into a garden. A mole some few years ago cast up a large amber bead, and with it an oval piece of silver near the bigness of a shilling. It had an hole through it, and on one side of it was impressed our Saviour crucified, with these letters above the crucifix J. N. R. J. ||. On the right thereof there was a crescent, and on the left a rising sun. At the bottom, the Virgin Mary in a weeping attitude. On the reverse, a lamb, with the standard and St. Andrew's cross.

Nigh to the school-house is a neat elegant dwelling-house, with large and pleasant gardens adjoining, belonging to John Benson gentleman.

II.

MANOR OF BETHAM.

In the parish of Betham there are three divisions (exclusive of *Witherslack*) which seem anciently to have been all one manor or lordship, to wit, *Betham*, *Haverbrack*, and *Farleton*. They all belonged to the family of Talebois, barons of Kendal; and were holden (except what was given away to religious houses) under the barons of Kendal by one and the same lord. And this most probably is the reason, why the parish of Burton is intersected as aforesaid by Farleton; for in the distribution of parishes, a man's whole estate or manor was commonly annexed to that church where he usually resided, and of which indeed in many places the lord of the manor was founder and patron.

At the time of the conquest this was part of the possessions of *Tosti* earl of *Northumberland*, and at the time of the Domesday survey belonged to *Roger of Poictou*, and under him to *Eruvin* the priest *; whose successors (as was usual) took their name from the place.—In the 17th year of king John, the heir of *Thomas de Bethun* (amongst other sons or daughters and heirs of divers mesne lords holding under the barons of Kendal) was delivered as an hostage to the said king, for the future fidelity of Gilbert son of Roger Fitz-Reinfred and of William his son, who had sided with the rebellious barons.

In the 30 Ed. 1. and again in the 2d, 4th, and 5th of Ed. 2. *Thomas de Betham* was knight of the shire for Westmorland.

In the 4 Ed. 2. *Thomas de Betham* obtained a charter for a market and fair in Betham †.

In the 8 Ed. 3. *Ralph de Betham* had a grant of free warren in Betham ‡.

|| i. e. Jesus Nazarenus Rex Judæorum.

* In Biedun habuit comes Tosti 6 carucatas terræ ad geldum: Nunc habet Rogerus Pictaviensis, et Eruvin presbyter sub eo.—In Fareltun 4 carucatas. (*Domesd.*)

† Denton. ‡ Idem.

In

In the 20 Ed. 3. writs were directed to *Ralph de Betham* and Thomas de Ross of Kendal castle, to send their prisoners from their castles to the Tower of London.

In the 49 Ed. 3. *Ralph de Bethame* knight held of Joan de Coupland the manor of Bethome with the appurtenances, by homage and fealty and the service of 32*s* a year, as of her manor of Kirkby in Kendale.

In the 8 Hen. 4. *John de Bethom* represented the county of Westmorland in parliament.

In the 3 Hen. 5. a commission of array was issued and directed to *Thomas de Betham* to muster and array all the men at arms.

In the 3 Hen. 6. *Thomas de Betham* was representative in parliament for Westmorland.

And this is the last of the Bethams of Betham that we have met with.

In Betham church, on the south side of the communion-table, in that part which is repaired by the owner of the manor of Betham, are two effigies of stone raised near a foot and an half from the floor, which tradition reports to be the monuments of the last Sir *Thomas de Betham* and his lady. He is laid in a coat of armour, with his sword by his side. His lady is in a shroud, with her hands clasped upon her breast. On the north side are the following arms quarterly, 1. A raguled cross. 2. Six annulets, three, two, and one. 3. Three escalops, two and one. 4. A saltier ingrailed.

The same tradition goes, that this manor was forfeited in consequence of the battle of Bosworth-field, wherein the house of York received their final overthrow; and that thereupon it was granted to the Stanleys. It seemeth indeed to have come into that family about that time, perhaps by purchase from the former possessor, rather than by any grant from the crown upon attainder; for in the other grants to the Stanleys by king Henry the seventh of the forfeited estates of Farleton, Witherslack, and the rest, we have not found any mention of the manor of Betham. And it seemeth that either the abovesaid monument is not the monument of the last Thomas de Betham, or that he was not attainted; otherwise it would scarcely have been permitted that his monument should be ornamented with his armorial ensigns, nor indeed would he have been suffered to be interred there at all, after having forfeited his right of sepulture in that place, and the property thereof transferred into other hands, and those also of the opposite and prevailing party.

This manor is of the *Richmond Fee*; and by the survey made in the 28 Cha. 2. amongst the free rents then paid to queen Catharine, the earl of Derby stands charged with the annual payment of 2*l* 13*s* 4*d* for Bethom park.

The *hall* or manor-house at Betham was anciently a large handsome building, but is now in ruins. It is in a delightful situation, having the prospect variegated with woods, water, and champion ground. It hath been built castle-wise, and by Leland and others is called a castle. Like all the other old houses in the northern parts, it hath been built for defence as well as ornament.

ment. In all of them there was one large room called the *hall*, where they transacted all business, and according to the laudable practice of hospitality entertained and feasted their friends and dependents; hence came the proverb,

'Tis merry in the hall,
When beards wag all.

College halls, and halls of trading companies, have some remains of these ancient customs.

The following is a description of the castle and ruins, as surveyed by the present worthy vicar aforesaid.—By an easy ascent from the river, we come to a gateway, being the grand entrance into the castle-yard. Entering there, we find ourselves in a fine large open area, 70 yards long by 44 in breadth. On the right appear to have been some buildings as low as the walls of the yard to the length of 98 feet, like barracks for the soldiers. On the left we have a charming view of the castle, standing at the south end of the area. The walls of the yard are 3½ foot thick, with loop-holes for the archers, at proper distances. They are 12 foot high below the parapet. The loop-holes are about 3 foot from the ground, 2 foot and an half in height and breadth, sloping outward to 3 inches and an half. The front of the house is in length 87 feet, of which the east wing is 22, and the west 26. The remaining space of 39 feet makes the hall, which is in breadth 25 feet. The windows in the hall are high up in the wall, and small in proportion to the room, with much Gothic work about them. Indeed, in all the old houses in the country the windows (for the sake of defence) have been small, and strongly secured with cross bars of iron. The doors of the rooms are all little, and one above another through each story. Up one pair of stairs there hath been a chapel, with a back staircase to it, whereby the tenants and neighbours might come to the chapel without disturbing the family. Southward from the castle, there is a fine descent, at the foot of which is a good spring that supplies two large ponds with water.

Behind the house was the *park*, and in one of the walks there are the remains of a lodge, and near it a spring of good water, which Camden says had a petrifying quality, but there is little or no appearance of such quality at present.

Within this division is *Capplefide* demesne, where anciently was an hall of considerable dimensions; containing in front, including the two wings, 117 feet. It may seem, from its name, to have belonged to the *chapel*; for anciently this word was founded *Capel*, in like manner as the Latin *capella*. This demesne belonged to the Prestons, and by marriage of one of the coheiresses came to the Cliffords, and in the year 1767 was sold by the present lord Clifford to Daniel Wilson of Dallam Tower esquire for 2560 *l*.

Within this manor also is *Helslack Tower*, now in ruins. Hellslack mosses are remarkable for the ant or pismire: About the middle of August, when they take wing, a thousand sea-mews may be seen here catching these insects: The neighbours call them the pismire fleet. In these mosses are found likewise, as in many others, large trees lying in all directions at five foot depth.

In this division likewise is *Arnside Tower*, having the walls thereof not yet much decayed. These towers seem to have been erected to guard the bay; as there are on the opposite side the vestiges of Broughton tower, and Bazin tower; so there is Castle-head upon the island in Lindal Pow; and higher up, the mosses of Methop, Ulva, and Foulshaw, were inaccessible. In the center of the bay is Peel castle.

In the river Betha is one of the two *catadupæ* or water-falls mentioned by Camden. The rock which crosses the bed of the river 66 foot in breadth is 16 feet perpendicular, down which the water falls with a mighty noise. But in the summer season the whole of the river is employed in carrying two corn-mills, one on each side; one of which mills, belonging to the earl of Derby, has two thirds of the water; and the other, belonging to Mr. Wilson, has one third.

In the 7 Ed. 1. there is a patent for a free *fishery* in the water of Methop in Westmorland ‡.

The fishery in the river Betha belongs at present to the earl of Derby, the earl of Suffolk and Berkshire, and Mr. Wilson. The two last claim from St. John's cross upon the sands, up to another cross of the same name above Betham bridge.

III.

HAVERBRACK.

This division, like as the rest, belonged to the barons of Kendal, and seems to have been a part only of the ancient manor of Betham. The church itself, which was given by Ivo de Talebois as aforesaid to the abbey of St. Mary's York, stands in Haverbrack; and he and his successors gave certain lands therein to divers religious houses. Particularly, Margaret de Ross gave the capital messuage and divers demesne lands there to the priory of Conishead in Lancashire. And William de Haverbrec gave to the same priory a messuage in Haverbrec, with the gardens thereto belonging, and two acres of land adjoining to the same; also the land called Blacket Croft, with the messuages there; which Blacket Croft lies between the water of Betha and the demesne of the said William; with half an acre of turbary which lies without the ditch, and one perch of land between the gate of Betha and the land of the church, and seven acres of land with a messuage below Bethegate. Also Elias de Gyle granted to the canons of the said place, all his lands at Haverbrec, and the fourth part of the mill of Haverbrec, with all the suit belonging to the said fourth part, and a moiety of the garden which had belonged to William de Haverbrec. And Thomas son of Elias de Gyle granted to the said canons all his lands at Haverbrec, with the appurtenances *.

‡ Denton. Dugd. MS.

* 2 Dugd. Mon. 424.

In

In the 37 Hen. 8. Haverbrack-hall, manor, and capital messuage, with divers appurtenances, late belonging to the priory of Conishead, were granted by the crown to *William Thornburgh* gentleman; to hold of the king *in capite* by the 20th part of one knight's fee, and a yearly rent of 18 *s* 3 *d*. †

And by an inquisition after the death of the said William, in the 7 Ja. 1. it is found, that he died seised of one capital messuage called *Dallam* (Daleham) *Tower*, with 60 acres of land; six other messuages, with 100 acres of land, in Betham, Patten, and Lupton; the moiety of one corn-mill called Heron mill in Haverbrack; two messuages and 40 acres of land in Methope; and two messuages and 40 acres of land in Ulvey. ‡

Another part of Haverbrack belonged to the Prestons. The said manor was afterwards purchased by three mine adventurers in prospect of a lead mine *. Afterwards it was sold to *Henry Parker* second brother of lord *Morley*; and by *Edward Parker* esquire was sold to Mr. *Edward Wilson*, great grandfather of the present owner *Daniel Wilson* esquire.

The ancient *hall* stood at the high end of what is now called Dallam Tower garden, which the said William Thornburgh removed to the place where the ancient tower stood, out of the ruins whereof he built a commodious dwelling-house, which in the year 1720 was rebuilt in a beautiful and elegant manner by the late *Daniel Wilson* esquire. The park was made about the same time. Behind it is a grove of fine oak wood.

In the park, a little eastward from the hall, is a small hill, on the top of which formerly was a castle, of a circular form; and the hill is yet called Castle-hill, and the side thereof Castle-bank.

In the turn of the river, opposite to the north part of the house, is *Dallam-wheel*, where formerly was a very rapid eddy. Three brothers, grown up to man's estate, were bathing in this place; the circling water sucked in one of the brothers, the second going to his relief likewise perished, and the third in the attempt to preserve both met the same fate.

The first person of note of this family of *Wilson* was *Edward Wilson* of Nether Levins in the reign of king James the first. He was only farmer there, but acquired a very considerable estate; and it was said of him, that though he had many houses, he never lived in a house of his own.

He was succeeded by his kinsman and heir *Thomas Wilson* gentleman; who had a son and heir,

Edward Wilson esquire, who married to his first wife Jane daughter of Gawen Brathwaite of Ambleside esquire, and by her had issue Edward his son and heir. To his second wife he married Dorothy daughter of Richard Kirkby of Kirkby-hall in the county of Lancaster esquire, by whom he had issue Roger Wilson esquire, ancestor of the late Roger Wilson of Casterton esquire.

Edward Wilson esquire, son and heir of Edward, was commonly denominated of Parkhouse, because he resided there during the lifetime of his father; which was an house in the park belonging to Thirland castle nigh Tunstal in

† Rawlinson. ‡ Idem. * Machel.

Lancashire,

Lancashire, purchased by the first Edward. He married Katherine daughter of Sir Daniel Fleming of Rydal baronet, and by her had issue,

Daniel Wilson of Dallam Tower esquire, who married Elizabeth daughter of William Crowle of Hull in the county of York esquire, and sister of Richard Crowle a very eminent counsellor at law. By her he had issue six sons and two daughters; and at his death in 1754, there were living four sons, viz. 1. *Edward*, the eldest. 2. *George*. 3. *Thomas*, counsellor at law. 4. *Daniel*, a clergyman. And one daughter, *Dorothy*, married to William Fleming archdeacon of Carlisle, only son of Sir George Fleming of Rydal baronet, lord bishop of Carlisle.

Edward Wilson of Dallam Tower esquire, son and heir of Daniel, married Dorothy eldest daughter of Sir William Fleming of Rydal baronet, and by her had issue 4 sons and 7 daughters; and at his death in 1764, had living 3 sons, *Daniel*, *William*, and *Edward*; and 6 daughters, *Dorothy*, *Elizabeth*, *Catharine* (since dead), *Barbara*, *Margaret*, and *Charlotte*.

Daniel Wilson of Dallam Tower esquire, son and heir of the last Edward, as yet unmarried.

The arms of Wilson are; Argent, 3 wolves heads Sable, couped Sanglante. Crest, a blazing ball.

By the aforesaid survey in the 28 Cha. 2. Edward Wilson esquire stands charged 2*s* for Haverbrack, of the *Marquis Fee*.

IV.

FARLETON.

This division includes also Overthwaite and Akebank.

King Richard the first granted to Gilbert son of Roger Fitz-Reinfred and his heirs 4 carucates of land in Farleton; and at the same time released to him the rents of all his lands in Westmorland and in Kendale; and (amongst the rest) the rents of the market of Kendale, the forest of Kendale, and the lands of Preston, Farleton, and Lupton.*

In the 49 Ed. 3. at the same time that Ralph de Bethome held the manor of Bethome of Joan de Coupland as of her manor of Kirkby in Kendale, *Nicolas de Haverington* held of the said Ralph the manor of Farleton as of the manor of Bethome.

The said *Nicolas de Haverington* had 2 sons; the elder, Sir *James Harrington* knight, from whom descended an elder branch of Harringtons; the younger son was Sir *William Harrington* knight, who married Margaret daughter and heir of Sir Robert Nevill, and by her had issue, 1. Sir *John Harrington*, who was slain a day before his father at the battle of Wakefield in the 39 Hen. 6.—2. Sir *James Harrington*, who succeeded to the manor of Farleton, and was attainted in the 1 Hen. 7. for having sided with the house of York. 3. Sir *Robert Harrington*, who was also attainted for the same cause †.

* Dugd. MS.

† Flem.

On

On this attainder, the eſtates being confiſcated, king Henry the ſeventh granted the ſame to Sir *Edward Stanley* knight, a younger ſon of the firſt earl of Derby, for his perſonal ſervices in the Lancaſtrian cauſe.

Thus in the 4 Hen. 7. there is a grant by that king to *Edward Stanley* knight, *pro corpore ſuo*, of the manor of Farleton in Louneſdale in the county of Lancaſter, and the manor of Farleton in Kendale in the county of Weſtmorland, (with other places elſewhere) which lately belonged to *James Harrington* knight, and which by reaſon of the forfeiture of the ſaid *James* came to the hands of the king: To hold to the ſaid *Edward* and the heirs male of his body, of the king and his heirs for ever; without any account to be made to the king for the ſame *.

And in the 5 Hen. 8. after the death of the ſaid *Edward Stanley* lord *Monteagle* (which title he had given to him by king Henry the eighth for his ſervices in war, having reference particularly to a *mount* or hill which he won in attacking the Scots at the battle of Flodden-field, and thereby obtained the victory, and alſo to the creſt of his anceſtors, in which they bore an eagle)—the inquiſition finds, that in the firſt year of king Henry the ſeventh, one *James Harrington* knight, for certain horrible treaſons on the firſt day of Auguſt in the ſaid year by him committed, was convicted and attainted, and thereby forfeited to the king all his poſſeſſions; whereupon the ſaid king granted to the ſaid *Edward Stanley* lord *Monteagle*, by his letters patent bearing date the 8th day of March in the 4th year of his reign, the manor of Farleton in Lonſdale in the county of Lancaſter, and the manor of Farleton in Kendale in the county of Weſtmorland: And that the ſame ought to deſcend to the heirs male of the ſaid *Edward*, and the reverſion thereof to the ſaid king Henry the ſeventh, which now is in our lord the now king, ſon and heir of the ſaid king Henry the ſeventh †.

The arms of Harrington were; Sable, a frette Argent.

After this, we find the manor of Farleton in the hands of Sir *Richard Hutton* of Gouldſborough in Yorkſhire knight, one of the juſtices of the court of common pleas, whoſe deſcendents in the year 1693 ſold the tenements to freehold, there being then 19*l* 17*s* 5*d* cuſtomary rent; and now remains only a free rent of 24*s* yearly to the earl of Derby as ſuperior lord.

At a ſmall diſtance from the village of Farleton, is an high hill called *Farleton Knot*; on which, in the time of the Scotch incurſions, a beacon was ſuſtained for communicating intelligence.

The abbot and convent of *Shap* had certain lands at Farleton, which at the time of the diſſolution were in the poſſeſſion of John Gibbonſon and the wife of John Hutton.

* Dugd. MS. † Idem.

W. WITHER-

V.

WITHERSLACK.

WITHERSLACK, METHOP, and ULVA, are included within a peninſula (as it were) between Winſter beck, Brigſteer moſs, and the Sands. *Methop* and *Ulva*, though diſtinctly named in the title and deſcription of this manor, yet make but a ſmall part of it, containing only about ten families in the whole: Whereas *Witherſlack* alone contains near 40 families.

This manor did alſo belong to the *Harringtons*; and in the 10 Ed. 3. a fine was levied thereof to *John de Haverington* for life, remainder to *Michael* his eldeſt ſon in tail male, remainder to *Thomas* his ſecond ſon in tail male, remainder in like manner to *John* his third ſon, remainder to his own right heirs *.

In the 14 Ed. 3. the ſaid *John de Haverington* obtained a charter of free warren in his manor of Witherſlack †.

On the attainder of the *Harringtons* as aforeſaid, the ſaid manor was granted by king Hen. 7. to Sir *Thomas Broughton* of Broughton Tower in Lancaſhire; and on the attainder of Sir Thomas, for having been concerned in the affair of Lambert Simnel, was granted by the ſaid king to *Thomas* lord *Stanley* the firſt earl of *Derby*.—And here it may not be amiſs to rectify a miſtake in lord Bacon's hiſtory of that king, who ſaith, that this Sir *Thomas Broughton* was ſlain at Stoke near Newark on the part of the counterfeit Plantagenet Lambert Simnel; whereas Sir *Thomas Broughton* eſcaped from that battle hither into Witherſlack, where he lived a good while *incognito*, amongſt thoſe who had been his tenants, who were ſo kind unto him as privately to keep and maintain him, and who dying amongſt them was buried by them, whoſe grave Sir Daniel Fleming ſays in his time was to be ſeen there.

The *Derby* family were great ſufferers in the civil wars in king Charles the firſt's time. The hall and demeſne were conveyed to *John Laybourn* of Cunſwick eſquire for about 130 *l*, which was ſuppoſed to have been a mortgage; but the defeiſance, if there was any, did not appear. The *Laybourns* continued at Witherſlack in poſſeſſion, till the direct male line failed in coparceners; one of whom was married to Dr. *Marmaduke Witham* of Yorkſhire: And the other coparceners died without iſſue. This eſtate was ſettled on the iſſue of that marriage, and on failure thereof, remainder to the right heirs of *Witham*. Dr. *Witham* had by that marriage a ſon *John Witham*. Againſt this *John Witham* the preſent earl of *Derby* claimed the eſtate, by virtue of a ſettlement by act of parliament, firſt upon the Stanleys of Eynſham in the ſouth, and then upon the Stanleys of Lancaſhire; and that branch in the ſouth being all extinct, and the late earl James being dead without iſſue, he claimed as next of kin in remainder of the Lancaſhire branch. At the aſſizes at Appleby in 1743, a ſpecial verdict was found, upon this point, Whether a recovery ſuf-

* Denton. † Idem.

fered

fered by one of the *Labourns* was properly executed or not. And on appeal to the house of lords, the question was determined in favour of his lordship. In about 12 years afterwards, an ejectment was brought against his lordship by the heir at law on the *Labourn* side, in order to have the same point tried over again, and a jury was summoned from Westmorland to try the cause at the bar of the court of king's bench in 1759, and whilst in pursuance thereof the jury were attending, the original settlement was found, whereby it appeared that the estate was settled and limited as aforesaid to the *Withams* and not to the *Labourns*, and the cause thereupon on that issue was at an end. And the said earl having levied a fine, which by the statute had run, all claim under the settlement was precluded.

The *park* at Witherslack, when the Labourns inhabited there, was well stocked with fallow deer.

At this place there is a remarkable range of rocks called *Whitbarrow Scar* (from *white* the colour of the stone, and *barrow* a hill), which affords a romantic prospect to the country all about.

The tenants are most of them customary, arbitrary, and heriotable.

By reason of their great distance from the parish church, a *chapel* was anciently erected, about 20 yards south from the hall; and endowed with a salary of 20 nobles, part of which was paid by divers of the inhabitants of the parish of Heversham, for their convenience of resorting to the said chapel: But since the building of the new chapel, the said payment hath ceased. Which new chapel was erected by Dr. John Barwick, dean of St. Paul's, who was born near the place where the chapel now stands. It was consecrated by bishop Wilkins in the year 1671, by the name of the chapel of St. Paul in the town of Witherslack in the parish of Betham; with a clause, as is usual in like cases, that the same shall be in no wise prejudicial to the mother church. It hath an handsome steeple, with three bells.

In the east window, which is very ornamental, having five double lights, are two coats of arms: The first is the *Derby's*, quarterly of eight. 1. Argent, a bend Azure charged with 3 bucks heads caboshed Or. 2. Gules, three arms, legs, and feet in triangle Argent. 3. Gules, four bars Argent, and a chief Or, charged of all with a lion rampant Or. 4. Quarterly, Gules and Argent, in a quarter of the first a mullet of the second. 5. Or, a cheveron Gules, between three eagles displayed Azure. 6. Azure, three flower de lis Or. 7. The same, with a battoon Gules. 8. Or, a serpent Azure devouring a child from the feet upwards: Impaling; Azure, an eagle volant Or. The crest; On a chapeau Gules, turned up Ermine, an eagle Or, preying upon a child in a cradle Proper.—Motto; Sans changer.

The second is: The *Deanry of St. Paul's*; Gules, 2 swords in saltier, with points to the points of the escutcheon, hilted Or. Impaling *Barwick*, viz. Argent, a red rose between three bears heads erased Proper, bridled Gules. Motto, Adversis servata fides.

The curate's houſe is about 30 yards ſouth from the chapel, deſigned alſo for a ſchool-houſe, the curate being required by dean Barwick's eſtabliſhment to teach the children of the inhabitants *gratis*.

The earl of Derby, lord of the manor, allowed ground upon the common for a chapel-yard and for the ſchool-houſe.

The curate is to be appointed by feoffees in truſt, and by them to be nominated to the biſhop.

For the ſupport and maintenance of which curate, the ſaid Dr. John Barwick, by his will bearing date Oct. 21, 1664, reciting, that whereas the village or hamlet of Witherſlack is four or five miles diſtant from the pariſh church, and is cut off from it by an interpoſition of an arm of the ſea twice every day, and is both troubleſome and dangerous for paſſage, eſpecially for burial of the dead from the ſaid village, doth therefore deviſe the impropriate rectory or parſonage of Lazonby in the county of Cumberland (to which his brother Peter Barwick, M. D. phyſician in ordinary to king Charles the ſecond, added the capital meſſuage or demeſne eſtate of Hareſkeugh nigh Kirk Oſwald) for the purpoſes of building a chapel, and allowing to the curate thereof 26*l* a year, 40*s* yearly to the vicar of Lazonby, 4*l* yearly for the repairs of Witherſlack chapel and providing utenſils and ornaments for the ſame, and 10*l* yearly to the binding out poor apprentices or marrying poor maids within the ſaid chapelry, and the reſidue of the rents and profits (if any there be) to be diſpoſed of to any of the ſaid uſes as the truſtees ſhall agree.

And from the above donation appears in part the inconvenience of limiting a certain ſum of money on the like occaſions; which though agreeable to the intentions of the donor at that particular juncture, yet ſoon becomes inadequate by the alteration of circumſtances. And this would have been the caſe here, if proviſion had not been made for diſpoſal of the ſurplus. The ſum of 26*l* a year was then deemed a competent proviſion for the maintenance of a curate, being at that time at leaſt double the value of the like ſum at this day; that is, it would purchaſe as much of any of the accommodations of life, as double the ſum will purchaſe at preſent. At the foundation of the ancient chapel at this place, twenty nobles were ſet apart for the curate's ſtipend. And more anciently, by a canon of the church in archbiſhop Sudbury's time, the general ſalary for curates was limited to 16 nobles a year; and before that, by a canon of archbiſhop Iſlip, to 12 nobles. All theſe proviſions and limitations did intend one and the ſame thing; and the incompetency hath ariſen from the progreſſive continual diminution of the value of money. In the preſent caſe, over and above the limited ſums, the aforeſaid demeſne and impropriate rectory produce annually a clear ſum of about 100*l*. Out of which, the truſtees have been inabled to contribute towards procuring augmentations to the chapel from the governors of queen Anne's bounty, and in future times may be inabled to raiſe competent diſtinct ſalaries both for a curate and ſchoolmaſter, if the curate ſhall deſire to be exempt from that charge himſelf. In the mean while, a court of equity probably would direct the ſurplus to be diſtributed according to the reſpective proportions eſtabliſhed by the donors, as being leaſt liable to the objection of partiality or miſapplication of any kind.

Besides the above dispositions, the said Dr. John Barwick by his will aforesaid gave 300*l* to St. John's college in Cambridge; 100*l* towards the repair of St. Paul's cathedral; 20*l* to Sedbergh school; the works of king Charles the martyr in two volumes folio to Sir John Otway, as a memorial of his thankfulness for the great pains and hazard Sir John underwent at his intreaty, towards the restoration of king Charles the second. And after divers other legacies to his relations and others, he gave the residue to the poor.

His said brother Dr. Peter Barwick gave to Witherslack chapel rich and elegant furniture for the pulpit and communion table: and caused a monument of white marble to be put up, with the following inscription;

REVERENDUS admodum et primævæ pietatis vir,
JOHANNES BARWICK, S. T. D.
Hic in vicinia natus,
Qui post operam indefesso studio navatam,
Afflictiones infracto animo toleratas,
Res tandem, licet summe arduas, feliciter gestas,
Pro collapso regni et ecclesiæ statu,
Ad curam et dignitatem Decanatus,
Primo Dunelmensis, deinde Paulini,
Merito evectus,
Hanc ædem
In Dei honorem et suorum gratiam,
Structam et dotatam voluit,
Et bonorum residuum egenis legavit.
A. D. 1668 *.

The present salary of the curate of this chapel (including the schoolmastership) is as follows:—Of the ancient salary, after the deduction made as aforesaid by the inhabitants of the parish of Heversham, there remaineth 4*l* 16*s* 8*d*. A cottage-house, garden, and peat-moss, worth yearly about 3*l*. Dean Barwick's augmentation 26*l*. And in 1749, an augmentation of 200*l* was procured from the governors of queen Anne's bounty; towards the obtaining whereof, the aforesaid trustees of dean Barwick contributed 120*l*, the late commissary Stratford 30*l*, and the present curate 50*l*. And in 1759, another like augmentation was procured; towards the obtaining whereof the aforesaid trustees contributed 100*l*, and the executors of the said commissary another

* Mr. *Walker*, in his *Sufferings of the Clergy*, Part 2. page 20. says of him, that after being deprived of his prebend of Durham and of his fellowship of St. John's college in Cambridge, though he was then in a very weak and sickly condition, he both undertook and managed successfully many matters of the greatest difficulty and danger in the cause of the king and of the church, and for that reason was shut up in a dire and loathsome prison, where he suffered inhuman and barbarous usage, and was near famished, being fed only with bread and water for several years: Which, however, had an effect much beside that which his prosecutors intended; as conducing in a surprizing manner to the recovery of his health; which the learned Dr. Sydenham takes notice of as a thing very well worth remark, in these words, "In languido hoc statu, cum vir egregius, "regiis partibus tunc temporis tyrannide oppressis, favisse deprehensus est, ac in arctissimum car- "cerem conjectus, loco potus ordinarii meram aquam biberet, præter omnem spem et expectationem "revaluit."

100 *l*. The lands purchased with the said benefactions yield 28 *l* a year. So that the sum total of the present income is 61 *l* 16 *s* 8 *d*.

The present worthy curate, the reverend John Hunter, hath executed the office of schoolmaster for many years, with honour to himself, and much advantage to the publick.

About a mile from the chapel, there is a well called *Holy-well*, which about the year 1656 was discovered to be medicinal. Unto which many persons resort in the summer season for the cure of scorbutic and other disorders. It is ranked by Dr. Short in the class of laxative and purging chalybeats.

Below Methop, there is an island called *Holme*, between Arnside and Cartmell, which is sometimes in Westmorland and sometimes in Lancashire. The reason is, because the water called Pow (Pool), which is the boundary, sometimes runs on one side of it, and sometimes on the other.

PARISH OF BURTON.

I. *Parish of Burton.*
II. *Manor of Burton.*
III. *Holme and Holme Scales.*
IV. *Preston Patrick.*

I.
PARISH OF BURTON.

ADVANCING from the parish of *Gresmere* in the north-western extremity of the barony of Kendal, by the parishes of *Windermere*, *Heversham*, and *Betham*, we are now arrived at the furthest extremity towards the south, and turn in the next place eastward along the southern boundary to the parish of Burton, which is part in Kendal Ward, and part in Lonsdale Ward: from whence we shall afterwards proceed through the rest of Lonsdale Ward; which will finish the barony of Kendal.

Burton is sometimes called *Burton in Kendale*, to distinguish it from another Burton which is in Lonsdale in the county of Lancaster.

It is pronounced by the natives and neighbouring inhabitants *Borton*, as in Domesday-book it is written *Bortun*, which seem to point out the true derivation; not from *burgh*, which signifies a fortified place; but from the ancient *boro*, which is no other than the district of the frankpledge or tithing.

The parish of Burton is bounded on the East by the parish of Kirkby Lonsdale; on the south by the parish of Warton in Lancashire; on the West, by the parishes of Betham and Heversham; and on the North, by the parish of Kendal.

This

This parish consists of five divisions, *viz.* Dalton (which is in Lancashire), Burton, Holme, Holme Scales, and Preston Patrick; which two last join no where on any of the other divisions, being separated by Farleton in the parish of Betham: And it is said there is a small parcel of land, not belonging to this parish, which is surrounded with the township of Burton.

The church is said to be dedicated to St. *Helen*, indicated by a well about 60 yards north-east from the church, which bears the name of that saint.

It is a vicarage, valued in the king's books at *15l 17s 3½d*. The clear yearly value as certified to the governors of queen Anne's bounty *31l 6s 8d*.

This church was given (amongst the rest), together with one carucate of land, by Ivo de Talebois to the abbey of St. Mary's York, and confirmed to that abbey by Gilbert son of Roger Fitz-Reinfred.

In 1359, it was appropriated to the said abbey, reserving a pension of *40s* yearly to the archdeacon of Richmond, *3s 4d* to the archbishop, and *3s 4d* to the dean and chapter of York. In 1460, the vicar's portion was set out as follows; *viz.* *20l* a year, consisting of an house and garden, and a close called Kirk-Butts, with all small tithes, oblations, and mortuaries living and dead: he paying thereout *10l 3s 4d* yearly to the said convent, repairing the chancel, and bearing all burdens ordinary and extraordinary.

After the dissolution of the monasteries, the rectory of this church and advowson of the vicarage were granted by queen Elizabeth in the 20th year of her reign to Edward earl of Lincoln and Christopher Gough gentleman; with reservation of a rent to the crown of *9l 7s 8d*; to the schoolmaster of Kendal *9l 5s 8d*; to the curate of Hewgill *3l 6s 8d*; and to the bishop of Chester *2l*.

The advowson appears soon after to have been in the hands of the Middletons of Leighton in Lancashire. The last of whom, Sir George Middleton baronet, had a daughter and heir Mary, who by marriage carried the same to the Oldfields of Somerforth in Cheshire, who sold the same (together with the manor of Burton and demesne of Claythorp-hall) to Mr. Benison of Hornby attorney at law; whose daughter, the present Mrs. Fenwick of Hornby, sold the advowson to Mrs. Hutton of Kirkby Lonsdale, who sold the same to Mr. Lancaster of Sedgefield in the county of Durham, who sold the same to the present patrons Mr. Thomas Hutton of the parish of Kirkby Lonsdale, and Mr. Jeffrey Tenant of the parish of Bentham in Yorkshire.

The *rectory* or great tithes appear to have been in the name and family of the Prestons of Preston Patrick; the last of whom had two daughters, married to the lords Montgomery and Clifford, between whom the inheritance was divided; lord Montgomery had the tithes of Burton, Holme, and Dalton, which came by purchase to colonel Francis Charteris grandfather of the present owner the honourable Francis Charteris; and lord Clifford had the tithes of Preston Patrick and Holme Scales, which the present lord Clifford sold some few years ago to Mrs. Gibson of Lancaster.

In the year 1732, in a cause between the parishioners and the vicar Mr. John Benison, the vicarial tithes and revenues of the church were ascertained, and decreed in chancery; in which decree there are specified divers parcels of

 land

land holden in fee farm of Thomas Benison lord of the manor of Burton; and, amongst others, the following remarkable particulars; for burial in the church or churchyard shall be paid 1*s*, except of women that die in childbed, for whom nothing is due; the modus for tithe lambs shall be double for the two first years after induction of a new vicar; and every person keeping a plough shall pay yearly 1*d*, in lieu and full satisfaction of agistment of barren cattle, which last article seems contrary to the general rule of law, which doth not allow of one tithe being paid in lieu of another, and it should seem to follow from hence that if a man doth not keep a plough he shall pay tithe of agistment.

The present vicarage-house and glebe were purchased with queen Anne's bounty money. The aforesaid inclosure called Kirk-Butts hath been seised by the lords of the manor, who were for some time patrons also of the advowson.

The *church* is a pretty good old building, with two rows of pillars; and a square tower, with three bells. There are two iles; one on the north side, belonging to Dalton-hall; and the other on the south side belonging to Preston-hall.

Nigh to the churchyard wall on the east side, is the *school*; with a small endowment, being the interest of several sums of money contributed by the inhabitants, to the amount of about 117*l*. The ground on which it is situate was given by Mr. John Hutton of Burton, ancestor of the present worthy vicar the reverend John Hutton. Another gentleman of the same name, a native of Burton, by his will dated in the year 1657, gave 40*s* yearly to the poor of the parish of Burton, and 20*s* to the poor of the parish of Cockfield in the county of Durham, out of his estate at Hindon in the said parish of Cockfield. The residue of the rents and profits of the said estate he gave to a schoolmaster at Burton, who should be master of arts of Oxford or Cambridge, and officiate every Sunday as curate at Preston chapel. The said schoolmaster to be chosen by a majority of housholders within the parish. In defect of such schoolmaster, then the said residue to go to the poor of the parish of Burton and the poor of the parish of Betham, to each an equal share. It is probable he expected some larger benefactions to the school: for this whole estate at present yields no more than 13*l* a year. The chapel, as it seemeth, had then no curate, and he intended this as a kindness to the inhabitants, and not as thinking to impose a curate by his own authority. Though this happened to be the occasion of some doubt afterwards concerning the manner of appointing the curate.

II.

MANOR OF BURTON.

Burton is mostly of the Marquis Fee, and the lord thereof pays a yearly quit rent of 1*l* 11*s* to the crown.

King Richard the first granted to Gilbert son of Roger Fitz-Reinfred two carucates of land in Borton, and four carucates in Preston and Holme.

The manor seems to have been then or soon after granted to a family of the name *de Burton*: for when this same Roger Fitz-Reinfred was obliged to give hostages for his fidelity to king John, one of the said hostages was the heir of *Roger de Burton*.

In the 25 Ed. 1. *Roger de Burton* knight (probably grandson of the former) was one of the witnesses, together with *Richard de Preston* and *Matthew de Redman* knights, to a grant of lands at Old Hutton and Holme Scales, by John de Culwen to Patrick de Culwen his brother.

In the 26 Ed. 1. *Roger de Burton* represented the county of Westmorland in parliament.

After this, we have found nothing more concerning the family *de Burton*; most probably it ended in daughters: for in the 4 Hen. 7. after the attainder of Sir James Harrington, the inquisition finds, that he was seised of a *moiety* of the manor of Burton in Kendale.

This manor appears to have been some time after in the hands of the Middletons of Leighton, whose heir female was married to Oldfield, who sold the manor to Thomas Benison of Hornby esquire, whose daughter and heir carried the same by marriage to John Fenwick of Borrow-hall esquire, whose brother and heir Thomas Fenwick esquire, in pursuance of an act of parliament for that purpose, sold the same to Thomas Pearson esquire, the present owner.

The hall or manor-house is about a quarter of a mile south from the church, and is now converted to tenancy.

The tenants only pay a twopenny fine, that is, doubling the rent; and no heriot.

The town of Burton is tolerably well built, and a pretty good thoroughfare between Kendal and Lancaster. It was procured to be a market-town in 1661, by Sir George Middleton aforesaid; the market-day to be on Tuesday in every week, and two fairs yearly on April 23, and Whitsun-Monday. It is said to be the largest corn market in the county, the corn being brought chiefly out of Lancashire, and sold to the dealers at Kendal, Sedbergh, and other places.

To the west of Burton and Holme is a large tract of marshy ground, consisting chiefly of peat moss. The inhabitants are at present occupied in draining these mosses, having expended some hundreds of pounds therein. The main drain is between two and three miles long, about four yards broad, and two yards deep: besides several smaller, and many private drains. At the bottom of the peat moss, is a bed of whitish earth, which is neither sand, nor clay, nor marl, and yet in some respects resembles each of them. It every where abounds with innumerable small shells of the snail and periwinkle kind, and such as appear sometimes in limestone and marble. There are also trunks of large trees, both of fir and oak.

III.

III.

HOLME AND HOLME SCALES.

About a mile and an half north from the church is the village of HOLME; which was anciently divided between two lords, of the names of Preston and Tunſdal: And hence one half of the tenants are heriotable, and the other not. The Tunſdal tenants were free from heriots, but deeper charged in their rents. They lie interſperſed, and are only diſtinguiſhable by their rentals.

Here is no manor-houſe, but a large park, called Holme-Park, about three miles in circumference; which in Sir Thomas Preſton's time was well repleniſhed with fallow deer.

HOLME SCALES belonged anciently to Holme, and is in the pariſh of Burton; but it is in the chapelry and conſtablewick of Old Hutton. This alſo belonged to the Tunſdals and Preſtons, and after came to the Preſtons only.

The preſent lord of theſe manors is the aforeſaid Francis Charteris eſquire.

IV.

PRESTON PATRICK.

It is moſt likely, that *Preſton Patrick* received its preſent denomination from the ſame perſon who gave name to *Bampton Patrick*. *Bampton* and *Preſton Patrick* belonged both to the ſame family, deſcended from Ivo de Talebois firſt baron of Kendal after the Conqueſt. And the individual perſon of that family, from whom both theſe places received their denomination was, very probably, *Patricius de Culwen*, anceſtor to the *Curwens* of *Workington*, who was grandſon of Thomas ſon of Coſpatrick who gave lands and poſſeſſions to the abbey at Preſton about the year 1119, which abbey was afterwards removed to Shap. Which Coſpatrick was ſon of Orme, ſon of Ketel, ſon of Eldred, ſon of Ivo de Talebois aforeſaid.

Preſton is by ſome ſuppoſed to have been ſo called from the abbey aforeſaid, as much as to ſay *Prieſt-town*: But if it had this name upon any ſuch religious account, it was before the foundation of the abbey many years; for at the time of the Conqueſt it was called *Preſtun*.

The grant of *Thomas* ſon of *Coſpatrick* to the ſaid abbey was to the following effect: "To all ſons of our holy mother the church, as well preſent as to "come, who ſhall ſee or hear this preſent writing, Thomas ſon of Coſpatrick "ſendeth greeting. Know ye, that I have given and granted, and by this "my preſent charter have confirmed to God and St. Mary Magdalene and the "canons of Preſton who are of the order of Præmonſtratenſes, in free, pure, "and perpetual alms, for the health of the ſoul of myſelf, and my wife, and "all my anceſtors, one portion of my land in Preſton in Kendale, to make a

"manſion

" mansion of canons, to wit, my whole demesne park below Lackslost, and " in Lackslost, to the way which comes from Preston Uchered; and from " thence following the way, unto the way which comes from Holme; and so " following the way from Holme, unto the sike which comes from Hasald- " mire; and by the same sike to the water which is the division between the " two Prestons; and so going up to the aforesaid way of Lackslost. More- " over I have given to them all the land below the way of Wathsudden unto " Stainebrigge, and all the land of Stainbrigge unto Brackenthwaite, as the " wood and the plain divide; and so to the land of Richard son of Sigith; " and so to the way which comes from Stainbrigge to the boundary of Farle- " ton; that is, all the land which belonged to Michael son of Helene. And " so following the division of Farleton, to the boundary between the two " Prestons; and so going up to the aforesaid way of Wathsudden: Except " half of the meadow of Miresbrigge, and ten acres of land [not legible " where]. And all that land from above Wathsudden, namely, where the " chapel of the Infirmary stood. They shall have also of my wood, as much " as they will, and as they now have, without the view of my foresters; and " the bark also of the wood which they shall cut down. Also, I grant unto " them free common within the boundaries of Preston, with all other easments " and liberties which belong to the aforesaid village of Preston; in wood and " in plain, in ways and in paths, in waters and in mills; and feeding also or " pannage for their hogs, and the tithe of my pannage. And they shall grind " at my mill without multure, whensoever they shall come, and as soon as " the mill shall be empty. And I will that the said canons shall have and hold " the same peaceably, fully, and honourably, in free, pure, and perpetual " alms, without any secular service, custom, or payment. And I and my " heirs will warrant to them this donation against all men for ever *."

After the dissolution of the monasteries, these possessions coming into the hands of the crown, were granted by king James the first to Philip lord Wharton, in whose posterity they continued till the late duke of Wharton's time, when they were purchased by Robert Lowther of Mauls Melburn esquire; father of the present owner Sir James Lowther baronet.

How long Preston Patrick (exclusive of what was given to the abbey aforesaid) continued in the Talebois family, after the said *Patricius de Culwen*, hath not appeared to us. After some intermission, we find this, as well as Preston Richard, and many other places both in Westmorland and Lancashire, in the name and family of Preston, who seem to have been first possessed of Preston Richard, and from thence to have removed, and finally settled at Preston Patrick. Which family we have deduced at Preston Richard, through a long succession of persons of the same individual name of *Richard de Preston*, until we come down to a family pedigree, which is as follows:

I. JOHN DE PRESTON knight; who in the 36th, 39th, and 46th of Ed. 3, was one of the knights chosen to represent the said county in parliament.

* 2 Dugd. Monast. 594.

II. Richard de Preston, in the 14 Ric. 2. held the manor of Preston Richard of Sir William Parr knight. He died without male issue, and was succeeded at Preston Patrick by his brother (as it seemeth) *viz.*

III. Sir John Preston knight, who in the reigns of king Hen. 4. and Hen. 5. was a justice of the court of common pleas; and being grown very old and infirm, he resigned his office in the 6 Hen. 6.—He had issue, 1. *John*, a clergyman; who in the 2 Hen. 5. had a grant of the church of Sandal from the prior of St. Pancrass. 2. *Richard*, who succeeded to the inheritance.

IV. Richard Preston esquire. He married Jacobine, a daughter of Middleton of Middleton-hall. And in the 30 Hen. 6. he and his said wife obtained a licence from the archdeacon of Richmond, to have an oratory within the manors of Preston and Levens.

V. Thomas Preston esquire, son of Richard, married a daughter of Redman of Twisleton; and had issue,

VI. John Preston esquire, who married a daughter of Redman of Harwood; and had issue,

VII. Sir Thomas Preston knight; who married Anne daughter of William Thornburgh of Hampsfeld esquire, and by her had issue, 1. *John*, who succeeded as heir at law. 2. *Christopher Preston* of Holker, from whom did descend the Prestons of Holker. 3. *Anne*, married to William Banister of Bolland in Lancashire. 4. *Elianor*, married to Sir James Labourn of Cunswick. 5. *Jane*, married to William Lamplugh of Dovenby esquire. 6. *Dorothy*, married to William Travers of Nateby in Lancashire. 7. *Elizabeth*, married to Robert Cansfield of Robert-hall in Lancashire. 8. *Catharine*, married to judge Carus.—This Sir Thomas died in the 15 Hen. 8. and by inquisition after his death the jurors find, that he died seised (in Westmorland) of the manors of Preston, Holme, Nether Levins, and Heversham; and that *John Preston* was his son and heir, and was then of the age of 12 years.

VIII. John Preston (of the manor in Furness), esquire, married Margaret daughter of Sir Thomas Curwen of Workington; and had issue, 1. *Thomas*. 2. *Margaret*, married to Roger Kirkby of Kirkby esquire. The said John married to his second wife the widow of Redman of Levins.

IX. Thomas Preston, son and heir of John. He married Margaret daughter of John Westby of Mowbreck in Lancashire; and had issue,

X. John Preston esquire; who married Frances daughter and heir of Richard Holland of Denton in Lancashire, and by her had issue, 1. *Thomas*, who died young. 2. *John*, who succeeded his father in the inheritance. 3. *Anne*, who died young. 4. *Margaret*, married to Sir Francis Howard second son of the lord William Howard of Naward. 5. *Agnes*, married to Anderton of Lostock. 6. *Elizabeth*, married to Frances Downes of Wardley in Lancashire.

In the 13 Cha. 1. this *John Preston* settled the manors of Preston Patrick, Nether Levins, and Holme, and other his hereditaments in Westmorland, on the issue of the marriage of his son John with Jane one of the daughters and coheirs of Thomas Morgan of Moston in Wales esquire.

XI. Sir

XI. Sir JOHN PRESTON baronet, by his ſaid wife Jane Morgan, had iſſue 1. *John*. 2. *Thomas*. 3. *Anne*, married to William Gerard of Brin eſquire. 4. *Elizabeth*, married to William Stourton eſquire, ſon and heir of baron Stourton.

XII. Sir JOHN PRESTON baronet, ſon and heir of the laſt Sir John, died unmarried; and was ſucceeded by his brother,

XIII. Sir THOMAS PRESTON baronet, who was a prieſt of the Romiſh church; but on the death of his brother, he married Mary daughter of Carill viſcount Molineux of Maryburgh in Ireland; and by her had iſſue, 1. *Mary*, married to William Herbert viſcount Montgomery, ſon of William marquis of Powis. 2. *Anne*, married to Hugh lord Clifford. His ſaid wife the lady Mary died before him in the year 1673, and was buried in the ſouth ile of the chancel of Heverſham church, whoſe monument remaineth there to this day. And Sir Thomas becoming a widower, was perſuaded by the Romiſh prieſts to return to his former function. Upon which, he ſettled his Weſtmorland eſtate on his two daughters, and went beyond the ſeas; having firſt ſettled his Lancaſhire eſtate, called The Manor, upon the Jeſuits. On which grant there was a trial in the exchequer, and the eſtate was adjudged forfeited to the king; who ſeized upon the ſame, and granted a leaſe thereof to Thomas Preſton of Holker eſquire.

As to the reſt, in the partition of the eſtate, the manor of Preſton Patrick was aſſigned to the elder ſiſter, in whoſe family it continued till the year 1717, when William Herbert eſquire commonly called duke of Powis and Mary his wife, and William Herbert commonly called lord Montgomery (their ſon and heir apparent), conveyed to *Francis Charteris* of Hornby-caſtle eſquire the manors of Preſton Patrick and Holme, with the capital meſſuage or manſion-houſe called Preſton-hall; and fee farm rent of 15*s* 4*d*, being the tithe hay ſilver of Preſton Patrick aforeſaid; and alſo all thoſe parks or lands commonly known by the names of Holme Park, Lodge Park, and Wood Park, containing by eſtimation 185 acres; and the tithes and tithe barns of Dalton, Holme, and Burton; and the lands called Hutton Park, containing by eſtimation 137 acres, and cuſtomary rents of 42*l* 8*s* 3*d*, with fines and heriots.

Finally, in 1773, *Francis Charteris* of Hornby-caſtle eſquire, grandſon of the aforeſaid Francis Charteris, granted the infranchiſement of the ſaid manor, for the ſum of 5130*l*, to William Bateman, Thomas Cartmell, and Richard Wright, in behalf of themſelves and as many other of the tenants as ſhall chuſe to purchaſe.

The ſaid manor-houſe of *Preſton-hall* is an old building, in a low, damp, and moiſt ſituation, but now converted into a good farm-houſe: Part of the ancient fabric ſtill remains, particularly two large arched rooms, which ſeem to have been cellars.

On the weſt ſide of the hall is the *park*; in the north end whereof is the keeper's houſe; and in the time of the Preſtons the ſaid park was well repleniſhed with fallow deer.

Next to Preſton-hall, the moſt conſiderable place is *Challen-hall*, belonging to Mr. Roger Dickinſon, who hath lately rebuilt the ſame in a neat and hand-

 ſome

some manner. In which anciently have been, and are still kept, the courts for the Lowther tenants in this manor. It was anciently called *Chanon-hall*, probably from its having belonged to the canons or monks of the abbey *.

In the middle of the park stands the *chapel*, about a quarter of a mile from the hall. It is a neat, handsome building, standing on an eminence, with a fine prospect every way. There is a well about 200 yards distant from the chapel eastward, called St. Gregory's well; which leads probably to the name of the saint, to whom the chapel is dedicated.

Mr. Machel takes notice of a yew tree in the chapel-yard, which he says was very old and decayed (*viz.* in the year 1692); which shews, he observes, the antiquity of the chapel. The yew tree is there yet, which shews also the longevity of that species of wood. These yew trees in church and chapel yards seem to have been intended originally for the use of archery; the best bows being made of that wood, and our ancestors having remarkably excelled in that kind of exercise. But this is only matter of conjecture; antiquity having not furnished any account (so far as we have been able to find) of the design of this kind of plantation.

There is no dwelling-house belonging to the curate; but an ancient salary of five marks a year, payable out of the respective tenements within the chapelry. By the smallness of which salary, this seemeth not to have been the oratory for which Richard Preston obtained a faculty in the 30 Hen. 6. for at that time no chapel seems to have been allowed without setting apart for the curate just double the salary of five marks, *viz.* 20 nobles (the reason of reckoning by marks and nobles was because their coins were of that denomination).—So that the foundation of this chapel seems to have been much earlier than the reign of king Henry the sixth. But the faculty for an oratory which Richard Preston obtained, was probably a licence to keep a domestic chaplain, which it was not lawful to do without licence from the ordinary, lest it might be the occasion of heresy, and also lest injury might arise to the incumbent of the mother church in oblations or otherwise.

There is also belonging to this chapel an estate of about 18*l* a year purchased by queen Anne's bounty, 100*l* given by lady Moyer, and subscriptions in the neighbourhood, for the obtaining of that bounty.

In the reign of king George the second, there was a long dispute between Mr. John Benison vicar of Burton and the inhabitants of this chapelry concerning the appointing a curate; the vicar claiming as of common right, and the inhabitants as by custom for time immemorial. And at length it was determined in favour of the inhabitants. And this is the case in most of the old chapelries; where the salaries having been very small, it was rather a burden than an advantage to the incumbents of the mother churches to provide a curate: And therefore they voluntarily gave up their claim to the inhabitants; who having made choice of a person, such as they liked (who generally by the terms of the contribution from the inhabitants towards a salary was required to teach a school also), the said inhabitants presented the person

* Bishop Nicolson.

elected by them to the incumbent, to be by him presented to the bishop for his licence. And from hence chiefly hath arisen the claim, and by length of time the legal right, of the inhabitants and landowners within the chapelries, chusing their own curate.—Generally, indeed, that which is deemed a privilege, is a real inconvenience. Popular elections are often conducted by prejudice, and perpetuate party-distinctions from one generation to another. And a clergyman's situation must needs be uncomfortable, who comes in against the opposition of perhaps a considerable part of his hearers. And there is often great irregularity in this kind of election. In order to make such election valid, it is not the fittest method for a few persons to go about in the neighbourhood, and get the electors to set their hands to a nomination; but there ought to be a meeting, after previous notice for that purpose (which notice the chapel-warden, as having charge of the chapel during the vacancy, seems the properest to give), and at such meeting the curate to be chosen by a majority of votes. And it is not a canonical election, unless it be by a majority of the whole number; as if there be nine electors (for instance) and four vote for one candidate, and three for another, and two for another, none of those candidates is elected, inasmuch four cannot present against five. And it seemeth that persons absent cannot vote by proxy for any particular candidate, signified by letter, or *viva voce* evidence; but there ought to be, upon stamp, a power of attorney, generally, to act in the election for the absent party, ratifying and confirming what such proxy shall do in the premisses. And the general custom is, that all persons chargeable to pay chapel salary have a right to vote; which includes widows, and infants also of whatever age (as infants, even of tender years, may present to a rectory or vicarage).

PARISH OF KIRKBY LONSDALE.

I. *Parish and Manor of Kirkby Lonsdale.*

II. *Casterton and Hutton Roof.*

III. *Lupton.*

IV. *Barborn and Mansergh.*

V. *Middleton.*

VI. *Killington and Firbank.*

I.

PARISH AND MANOR OF KIRKBY LONSDALE.

KIRKBY LONSDALE, that is the *kirk-town* in Lonsdale, hath its name from the *dale* in which it is situate, through which the river *Lon* (corruptly called *Lune*) runs all along from north to south; which river also gives name

 to

to the town of *Lancaster*; at which place the said river runs into the sea. Which dale also gave title to the noble family of Lowther, until the title became extinct on the death of the late *Henry* viscount *Lonsdale*.

Kirkby Lonsdale is the largest town in the county, next unto Kendal; and is beautifully situate upon the banks of the river, over which there is a large stone bridge of three arches; for the repair of which bridge, there was a grant of pontage in the third year of King Edward the first.

The *parish* of Kirkby Lonsdale is bounded on the East by the limits of the county of York; on the South, by the county of Lancaster and the parish of Burton in the county of Westmorland; on the West, by the said parish of Burton and the parish of Kendal; and on the North, by the parish of Kendal, and the parish of Sedberg in the county of York: and contains within it the several townships of Kirkby Lonsdale, Casterton and Hutton Roof, Lupton, Barbon and Manserghe, Middleton, Killington and Firbank.

The *church* is dedicated to St. Mary; and was given by Ivo de Talebois to the abbey of St. Mary's York, and confirmed to the same by Gilbert son of Roger Fitz-Reinfred *.

The *impropriation*, and *patronage of the vicarage*, after the dissolution of the said abbey, were granted to Trinity college in Cambridge by queen Mary in the first year of her reign. The vicarage, in the valuation of the 26 Hen. 8. was rated at 20*l* 15*s* 5*d*. The clear yearly value, as certified to the governors of queen Anne's bounty, 49*l* 13*s* 8*d*.

The *manor* also of Kirkby Lonsdale was given to the said abbey, and after the dissolution was granted to the family of *Carus*, which family had been of considerable note in this county; of whom we find, particularly in the reign of king Hen. 8. one *Richard Carus*, who had a daughter Catharine married to Rowland Philipson of Holling-hall esquire. He had a son and heir,

Thomas Carus, who married Margaret daughter of William Wilson of Staveley gentleman: and by her had issue,

William Carus, who married Isabel daughter of Thomas Leyburne of Cunswick esquire; and by her had issue, Thomas, Adam, Robert, Christopher, Richard, Elizabeth, Margaret, Anne, Helen, and Jane.

Thomas Carus, son and heir of William, married Catherine daughter of Sir Thomas Preston of Preston Patrick.—In the 4 and 5 Ph. and Mary, this Thomas Carus, who was then a lawyer of the Middle Temple London, and afterwards one of the justices of the court of king's bench, purchased of the crown the manor and demesne of Kirkby Lonsdale, with the water mill there, and divers lands and tenements in Kirkby Lonsdale, Hegholme, Kesthwaite, Mansergh, Middleton, Biggins, Underley, and Tarnside; late parcel of the possessions of the monastery of St. Mary's York: To hold of the crown *in capite*, by the service of the 40th part of one knight's fee. He had issue, by his wife Catherine Preston, Thomas, Richard, Christopher, and William; and four daughters, of whom Mary was married to Edward Middleton of Middleton-hall esquire, and Etheldred married to William Thornburgh of Hamsfield in

* Registr. Wetheral.

the

the county of Lancaster esquire.—To his third son Christopher, afterwards Sir Christopher, he gave Halton in Lancashire.

Thomas Carus, son and heir of judge Carus, married Anne daughter and heir of Wilfrid Preston of Over Biggins esquire; and had issue only a daughter *Elizabeth*, married to Sir Nicholas Curwen of Workington, being his second wife. She had issue three daughters, (1) *Mary*, married to Sir Henry Widdrington knight. (2) *Anne*. (3) *Jane*, married to Lambton.

In the 29 Eliz. the aforesaid Christopher Carus of Halton (probably next in the intail) and Katherine his wife, and Nicholas Curwen and Elizabeth his wife, did by fine convey to William Thornburgh esquire and Thomas Curwen gentleman, the manor of Kirkby Lonsdale with the appurtenances, late belonging to the monastery of St. Mary's York: To hold of the crown *in capite* by knights service.

In the south ile of Kirkby Lonsdale church, there is a monument with this inscription: "Felici memoriæ Elizabethæ Carus, filiæ et hæredis Thomæ "Carus, Nicolai Curwen equitis aurati uxoris. Matri suæ meritæ mærens "filia Maria Henrico Witheringtono nupta, hoc sacrum posuit. 1611."

The arms of Carus were; Azure, a cheveron Argent, charged with three mullets Gules, between ten cinquefoils of the second, 4, 2, 1, 2, 1, Argent.

The manor was afterwards sold to the *Prestons* of Holker; who sold the same to Sir John Lowther of Lowther, whose descendent Sir James Lowther baronet now enjoys the same.

Of the tenants, about a third part have been sold free, the rest are some copyhold, some customary at fine arbitrary, and some of them also heriotable.

The *market* and *fair* at Kirkby Lonsdale were granted in the 11 Hen. 3. And in the 20 Ed. 1. a *Quo warranto* was brought against the abbot of St. Mary's York, to shew, why he claimed a market, fair, assize of bread and beer, tumbrel, pillory, infangthief, and gallows. Unto which he answered, that he claimed a market and fair as parson of the church there, by a charter of king Henry the third, dated in the 11th year of his reign; by which charter, the said king granted to *John de Kirkeby*, parson of the church in Kirkeby in Lonesdale, that he and his successors, parsons of the church aforesaid, shall have for ever a fair at Kirkeby in Lonesdale, upon the land of the said church, every year for three days, to wit, on the eve, day, and morrow of the nativity of the blessed virgin Mary [viz. Sep. 7, 8, and 9.], and that they shall have one market there, on Thursday in every week. Infangthief and gallows he claimeth not; but the assize of bread and beer, tumbrel, and pillory he claimeth, as annexed and appurtenant to the said market and fair. And because it appeared, that the said king Henry was under age at the time of the said grant, the said market and fair were taken into the king's hands. Afterwards, it was accorded, that the said abbot should enjoy the said liberties, namely, the market and fair, and other things appurtenant to the said market and fair *.

* Registr. Wetheral.

But

But though the abbot disclaimed the infangthief and gallows, yet it seemeth that his successors did not intirely give up all jurisdiction of pleas of the crown; for the lord of the manor to this day claimeth and exerciseth a power of appointing a coroner within the said manor.

The *church* stands in a pleasant situation, upon the banks of the river; in a large, level, and beautiful churchyard. It is 120 feet in length, and 102 feet in breadth, and hath 3 rows of pillars. The steeple is about 68 foot high, and hath six good bells.

At the east end of the north ile is Middleton quire, where in Mr. Machel's time were the ruins of a fine monument in alabaster of a duskish red colour; having been formerly the effigies of a man in armour, with his sword girt to his side, lying on his back, with his hands elevated, and his head resting upon an helmet; and the figure of a woman lying by him. And amongst several coats of arms defaced, the two first remained almost intire; the former was Middleton single, and the latter Middleton impaling Tunstal. Which seem plainly to indicate the same to have been the monument of John Middleton of Middleton-hall esquire, son of Sir Geoffrey Middleton who lived in the reign of king Henry the eighth; which John married a daughter of Tunstal of Thurland castle.

The south porch or quire was built by one Mr. Baynes of Hegholme-hall, as by these verses over the door (of which Mr. Machel makes mention) did appear, but which all-devouring time hath effaced:

This porch by Baynes first builded was,
  Of Hegholm-hall they were:
And after sold to Christer Wood,
  To keep in good repair.
And is repaired as you see,
  And kept in order good;
By the true owner now thereof,
  The foresaid Christer Wood.

In the year 1486, Oct. 20, a chantry was founded in this church, by the name of Middleton chantry in the church of St. Mary in Kirkby Lonsdale, by William Middleton; unto which he appropriated a pension of 7 marks yearly, issuing out of lands in Garsdale in the parish of Sedbergh. The said William to have the nomination of the priest there during his life; and after his death, his son Richard and his heirs †.—This William was not of the direct line either of Middleton-hall or Leighton; but probably was a collateral of the same family.

In the reign of king Charles the first, one *George Buchanan*, a Scotchman, was vicar of this church, having been driven out of Scotland (where he had the living of Moffet, then worth 800 *l* a year) for refusing the covenant. He first applied himself to archbishop Laud, who gave him a living in Essex,

† Dugd. MS. from the register of Furness abbey.

which

which he afterwards exchanged for Kirkby Lonſdale, as being nearer to his own country, where his Scotch pronunciation would be leſs offenſive, and better underſtood. During the progreſs of the rebellion, he ſuffered greatly; being perſecuted by two of his pariſhioners, who were captains in the parliament army, and got him not only ſequeſtred, but alſo ſeveral times hurried to Lancaſter gaol, once out of the church, another time out of his bed from his wife then big with child, the laſt of which times he ſuffered near three years impriſonment. After which, being ſet at liberty, he fled into Yorkſhire, where he obtained a ſmall living of about 20 *l* a year, and on the reſtoration came back to his vicarage at Kirkby Lonſdale, where he did not long continue, being made prebendary of Carliſle, and inſtituted to a living in that neighbourhood.—It was obſerved, that one of the two captains, who had been the chief inſtruments in his ſufferings, grew very rich, and purchaſed a field and built a very fine houſe with the wages of iniquity, but before his death he became miſerably poor, and was caſt into gaol, where he was daily relieved from the table of one of Mr. Buchanan's ſons ‡. [Which ſon, probably, was James Buchanan, who was made vicar of Appleby in 1661.]

There was heretofore a chapel at Tarnſide in this lordſhip, which was demoliſhed about 100 years ago.

At the eaſt corner of the church-yard, is a place called *Abbot-hall* (which is now only an ordinary houſe). It belonged to the abbey aforeſaid, and is ſaid to have been the place where they kept their courts.

There is alſo a place in this lordſhip called *Dean's Bigging*. This alſo belonged to the abbey; and perhaps might be the ſeat of the Rural Deanry, which from this place ſtill retains the name of the deanry of Kirkby Lonſdale.

About 100 yards eaſtward from the church, nigh the river ſide, ſtands the *ſchool-houſe*; the foundation whereof was as follows: One Godſalve of Newton in the pariſh of Whittington, gave 100 *l* to be diſpoſed of towards a free-ſchool, at the diſcretion of the then rector of Whittington, one Mr. Bland, a native of Kirkby Lonſdale. The ſaid Mr. Bland, in conſideration that the town of Kirkby Lonſdale was the principal market town of thoſe parts, and only one mile diſtant from Whittington, propoſed that the ſaid 100 *l* ſhould be laid out towards the eſtabliſhment of a free grammar-ſchool at Kirkby Lonſdale, provided that the inhabitants of the town or pariſh would add another 100 *l* to the ſame uſe. Which was accordingly done. And queen Elizabeth, in the 33d year of her reign, granted letters patent for the foundation of a free grammar-ſchool at Kirkby Lonſdale, and therein appointed 24 governors of the ſaid ſchool. The lady Curwen before mentioned, heireſs of the family of Carus, gave the ground upon which the ſchool-houſe was erected; and alſo gave certain parcels of land to the ſame, lying near to a place called the Biggins. And in conſideration of the ſaid ſum of 200 *l*, one Mr. Tenant granted a rent charge upon the manors of Bedal and Scotton in Yorkſhire of 20 *l* a year to the governors for the uſe of a ſchoolmaſter for ever (that being the legal intereſt for the ſame at that time).

‡ Walker's Sufferings of the Clergy, Part 2d, page 211.

The

The ſchool-houſe at firſt being but an indifferent building, one Mr. Henry Wilſon of Blackwell-hall London, a native of Kirkby Lonſdale, did in the year 1628 cauſe the ſame to be taken down, and at his own expence rebuilt the ſame in a more ſpacious and convenient manner. And in regard the former ſalary was applied to the ſole uſe of the maſter, he gave 120*l* for the ſupport of an uſher; which, together with other charity money, was charged upon the demeſne lands of Thurland caſtle in the pariſh of Tunſtal.

Mr. Thomas Wilſon, a clergyman in Norfolk, brother to the ſaid Henry, gave 200*l* to be laid out in land, the produce whereof was to go to the maſter and fellows of Chriſt's college in Cambridge, to be by them applied as exhibitions for 3 poor ſcholars going from this ſchool to the ſaid college, at 5*l* a year each, till they be of ſtanding to commence maſters of arts. Which ſum was laid out in a meſſuage and tenement at Bulbank in the pariſh of Melling.

And the aforeſaid Henry Wilſon gave 400*l*, ſecured upon the tithes of Farleton, for exhibitions for 7 poor ſcholars, 4 of them from the ſaid ſchool of Kirkby Lonſdale, and 3 from the ſchool of Kendal, to Queen's college in Oxford, the ſaid ſcholars to be natives of Weſtmorland or Cumberland. He gave alſo 500*l* to the poor of Kirkby Lonſdale; with many other charities to other places.

The ſaid Henry Wilſon alſo erected a ſmall library in the church, at the eaſt end of the north ile, over the veſtry; and gave ſeveral books to it.

This family of Wilſon had conſiderable poſſeſſions in the townſhip of Kirkby Lonſdale about that time. For among the Eſcheats in the 10 Ja. it is found by inquiſition, that *Henry Wilſon* (probably of the eldeſt branch of the family) held, on the day on which he died, 12 meſſuages and tenements in Keaſthwaite, Manſerghe, Dean's Bigging, and other places, of the king *in capite*, as of the Richmond fee: and that Jane wife of Nicolas Borrett, and Mary wife of Thomas Gibſon, were his daughters and coheirs.

And in the 13 Ja. Nicolas Borret and Jane his wife conveyed her moiety in fee to Edward Burrow and ſeven others; conſiſting of ſix meſſuages and tenements, and divers other parcels of land, all in the lordſhip of Kirkby Lonſdale.

One male branch of this family continued at Underley till about the year 1730, when Mr. Thomas Wilſon ſold Underley to Hugh Aſhton gentleman, from whom the premiſſes deſcended to his ſon James Aſhton eſquire, who died unmarried, leaving 4 ſiſters coheirs; *viz.* Elizabeth married to Mr. Joſeph Burrow of Whitehaven, Frances married to Mr. Arthur Burrow of Lupton, Anne married to Mr. William Birdſworth of Kirkby Lonſdale, and Eleanor married to Mr. Thomas Carus of Kirkby Lonſdale.

II.

CASTERTON AND HUTTON ROOF.

CASTERTON and HUTTON ROOF, although ſeparated by the river, have commonly been conſidered as one manor only; and perhaps ſo they might be originally: but ſo far back as we have now any account, they have been ſeparate and diſtinct.

Caſterton (which lies on the Eaſt ſide of the river) did probably receive its name from ſome *caſtle* erected there; of which nevertheleſs there are now no veſtiges remaining.—*Hutton Roof* ſeems to be no more than the top or higher part of *Hutton*; which name of *Hutton* was frequently given to places, where a number of *huts* or ſmall houſes of habitation were ſet up: And particularly in theſe parts, which were appendent to Kendal caſtle, beſides *Hutton Roof*, there was *Old Hutton*, *New Hutton*, and *Hutton in the Hay*.

In the 12 Ed. 2. the manor of Caſterton appears to have been in the poſſeſſion of *Ingelram de Gynes* and *Chriſtian* his wife.

In the 25 Ed. 3. we find one third part of the manor of *Caſterton* holden by *Gilbert de Burneſhead* of *William de Coucy* grandſon of the ſaid *Ingelram*, by cornage, wardſhip, and relief.—And at the ſame time, the manor of *Hutton Roof* was holden of the ſaid *William*, by *John de Hutton Roofe* and *Agnes* who had been the wife of *John Dursfleete*, by the like ſervice of cornage, wardſhip, and relief.

In the 49 Ed. 3. after the death of *Joan de Coupland*, the inquiſition finds, that ſhe died ſeiſed of the manor of *Caſterton*, with the appurtenances.—And that *Hugh de Moreſby* held of her the manor of *Hutton Roofe*, as of her manor of Kirkeby in Kendale; by homage, fealty, and the ſervice of 8 *s* a year: And that *Simon de Heverſham* held of her divers tenements there, of the yearly rent of 3 *s* 4 *d*.

In an old rental, 7 Hen. 7. when Sir Thomas Strickland was ſteward, for two parts of Caſterton were paid 60 *s* 2 *d* rents and farms; 8 *s* 7 *d* free rent of aſſize paid by four different tenants by name; 5 *s* 6 *d* free rent for the lands called Symington's lands; 4 *d* new rent of Chriſtopher Symſon for licence of putting a grindſtone in Caſterton beck, to be turned by the water thereof; for the fulling mill, nothing, becauſe it was in the lord's hands for want of repair.

Amongſt the Eſcheats in the 13 Cha. 1. it is found, that *George Stockdale* held 3 meſſuages and tenements in *Caſterton*, late purchaſed of *William Davenport* knight (father of judge *Davenport*), of the king as of his manor of Kirkby in Kendale, late called Richmond Fee, by the 100th part of one knight's fee; and that he held alſo one water corn mill there, of the king as of his manor of Eaſt Greenwich in Kent, in free ſocage, and by the rent of 20 *s*.

By an inquiſition in the 28 Cha. 2. it is found, that Catherine queen conſort, in the 21ſt year of the ſaid king, for 50 *l* fine paid, granted to *Edward Wilſon* of *Caſterton* gentleman, all thoſe lands and tenements in *Caſterton* (except great trees, and all woods and underwoods, mines, and quarries) for 93 years, if *Edward*, *Thomas*, and *Roger Wilson*, sons of the said *Edward*, should so long live; paying the yearly rent of 12 *l* 6 *s* 8 *d*.

In *Hutton Roof* there was anciently a *park*, and there is an house which is yet called the Park house; which in the reign of Ed. 6. belonged to judge *Carus*; after that, was purchased by the *Bellinghams* of Levins; then by the *Prestons*; and finally, by Colonel *Francis Charteris* (together with divers other of the *Preston* estates), and by him devised to his grandson *Francis Charteris* esquire, the present owner, second son of the earl of Wemyss in Scotland.

The tenants of *Casterton* are about half free, and half customary, paying a fine certain of 3 years ancient rent, and a prescription of 40*s* for an heriot.

The tenants of *Hutton Roof* are all free, paying a quit-rent to the crown. And they have been so long free, that there hath appeared to us no memorial or remembrance when or by whom they were infranchised. Some part of Hutton Roof belonged to the abbey of St. Mary's York, being given thereto by Ivo de Talebois; and the free tenure of this is easily accounted for, inasmuch as the religious generally held their lands free from all secular exaction and service.

The *chapel* of *Hutton Roof*, so far as one may judge by the smallness of the original salary, which is 12 nobles, seems to be very ancient. It hath now belonging to it three estates purchased by queen Anne's bounty and other augmentations, of the yearly value of about 40*l*.

In *Casterton* there are two houses called *Chapel houses*, and a place near unto them called *Chapel head close*, where a chapel formerly stood, but the ground is now ploughed up. And there is a well nigh unto it, called St. Coumes [St. Columbe's] well; to which saint the chapel probably was dedicated.

Amongst the particulars made out in the reign of king Charles the first, for the sale of the Richmond fee and other crown lands in Westmorland, there is mentioned a *coal mine* in Casterton, of which Roger Bateman proposed to be purchaser.

III.

LUPTON.

LUPTON (called in Domesday *Lupetun*) belonged, like as the rest, to the barons of Kendal; and was holden under them for a long time by the *Redmans* of Levins. In which family it continued till the reign of king Henry the seventh. For by an inquisition in the 4th year of that king, it is found, that Thomas Harrington esquire (then attainted) held lands in Lupton of *Edward Redman* esquire, but by what services the jury did not know.

This *Edward* seems to have been the last of that branch of the family, and their Westmorland estates were sold soon after. Unto whom Lupton immediately

diately was granted, we have not found. The *Bellinghams* purchased Levins, and probably Lupton likewise. For Lupton, like as most of the rest of the Bellingham estates, is of the Lumley fee.

Afterwards it appears to have belonged to Sir *Richard Hutton* of Goldsborough in Yorkshire, one of the justices of the court of common pleas; one of whose daughters was married to Sir *Philip Musgrave* of Hartley castle baronet, whose son and heir Sir *Christopher Musgrave* knight (afterwards baronet) in the year 1681 purchased the same of the trustees of the said Sir Richard; whose descendent Sir *Philip Musgrave* baronet is now owner thereof.

There are only about two freehold tenements in the whole manor: All the rest are customary.

IV.

BARBON AND MANSERGH.

BARBON and MANSERGH are said to have been originally one manor; and only broken into separate divisions for convenience, by reason of the river Lune running between. But so early as the Domesday survey they appear to have been separate; for *Tosti* earl of Northumberland held *Berebrune* (as it is there called), and *Torfin* held *Manserge*.

In the reign of king Henry the third, *Richard de Bereburne* knight was one of the witnesses to the grant of Skelsmergh by William de Lancastre to Robert de Leyburne.

In the reigns of Ed. 1. and Ed. 2. we find divers others of the name. In the 18 Ed. 3. the manor of Barborne and divers lands in Middleton were conveyed to *Roger Lassels* and *Elianor* his wife, but by whom was not legible when the copy of the record was taken *. Possibly it might be some settlement on Lassels's marrying the heiress of Bereburne.

In the 25 Ed. 3. *Ralph Lassels* held the manor of Berburne of William de Coucy; by cornage, wardship, and relief.

In the 49 Ed. 3. *Ralph Lascells* held the manor of Barburne of Joan de Coupland, by homage and fealty, and the service of 30*s* 7*d*, as of her manor of Kirkby in Kendale.

We find nothing further in particular relating to this manor till the 23 Eliz. when it appears to have been in the name of *Vaughan*. For in that year *Francis Vaughan* esquire conveyed the same to Sir Thomas Boynton knight and Francis Boynton esquire, in trust, for the use of the lady Anne Knyvett for life, remainder to Francis Vaughan and his heirs.

About 30 years after this, the manor was purchased of Vaughan, by *John Middleton* of Middleton-hall esquire; who sold the same not long after to serjeant (afterwards judge) *Shuttleworth*; who gave the same to his nephew *Richard Shuttleworth* of Gauthorp esquire, whose son *James Shuttleworth* esquire now enjoys the same. The said *Richard*, in the year 1716, sold all the tenements to freehold, reserving an annual free rent of 15*l* 8*s*.

* Denton.

The ancient *chapel* salary of Barbon was 2 *l* 10 *s* 0 *d*; in lieu of which the inhabitants gave a valuable consideration, wherewith in conjunction with an allotment of 200 *l* from queen Anne's bounty an estate was purchased in Barbon now let at the yearly rent of 11 *l*. And with a further allotment of 200 *l* an estate was purchased at Kellet in Lancashire, now let at the yearly rent of 7 *l* 4 *s*. So that the whole revenue is 18 *l* 4 *s* 0 *d*.

John Garnet of Barbon gave some lands which were sold for 105 *l*; one half of the interest whereof is paid to the curate or schoolmaster for teaching 4 poor children of the chapelry, and the other half to the poor.

MANSERGH seems anciently to have been in the name of a family *de Mansergh*. Amongst the fines in the 12 Ed. 2. we find that *Thomas de Mansergh* purchased certain lands in Barbourne. And especially, in the 7 Ric. 2. *John de Mansergh* was chosen knight to represent the county of Westmorland in parliament.

Nevertheless *Rigmaden hall*, which is said to have been the ancient manor-house, was in the hands of a family of the name *de Rigmaden*. It is possible, the Manserghs residing there might assume the name *de Rigmaden*. Their arms were; Argent, 3 stags heads couped Sable.

After the *Rigmadens*, this place came into the name and family of *Ward*, who continued there for a considerable time, and had possessions also in Killington, Firbank, and other places. The last of whom, Henry Ward, sold the same to Mr. *Thomas Godsalve* merchant, who had a son *Thomas Godsalve* gentleman, whose daughter *Margaret* widow of the reverend Thomas Maudesley now enjoys the same.

The *chapel* of Mansergh was built by Mr. Jacob Dawson on his estate called Nether Hall; towards defraying the expence whereof, the inhabitants agreed to pay for their seats. To make a revenue for the said chapel, the said Mr. Dawson and the inhabitants gave 120 *l*, and Oliver Martin esquire from a charity in his disposal 80 *l*, whereby a benefaction of 200 *l* was procured from the governors of queen Anne's bounty. Another augmentation of 200 *l* from the said bounty came by lot. And a third augmentation of 200 *l* from the said bounty was procured by a benefaction of 100 *l* from lady Gower, wood sold off from one of the purchased estates 28 *l*, and 72 *l* advanced by Mr. William Sedgwick the present curate. The whole amounting to 1000 *l*. Wherewith one estate was purchased in Old Hutton, another in Casterton, and another in Dent; of the clear yearly rent in the whole of 41 *l* 5 *s* 0 *d*.

V.

MIDDLETON.

MIDDLETON is bounded on the East, by Dent in the parish of Sedbergh; on the South, by Barbon; on the West, by Killington, from which it is parted by by the river Lune; and on the North, by the river Rowthey, which ſeparates it from Howgill and Bland in the pariſh of Sedbergh.

It is part of the ancient barony of Kendal; and ſeems to have been given (with divers other poſſeſſions) by *Ketel*, the third baron of Kendal, to his younger ſon *Orme*, father of *Coſpatrick*, father of *Thomas* who was founder of Shap abbey. The elder branch of the Talebois family enjoyed divers poſſeſſions in Cumberland. And the ſaid *Orme*, having married Gunild ſiſter of Waldieve firſt lord of Allerdale, ſon of Coſpatrick earl of Dunbar, received with her large poſſeſſions in Cumberland; and his ſon Coſpatrick (ſo called after the name of his mother's father the aforeſaid earl of Dunbar) made an exchange of Middleton in Lonſdale, and ſome manors which he had in Cartmell, with *William de Lancaſtre* his couſin german, for the manors of Workington and Lamplugh, lying contiguous to ſome of his other eſtates in Cumberland: Reſerving to him the ſaid Coſpatrick and his heirs, the homage of Middleton, and a quit-rent of 6*d* yearly, or a pair of gilt ſpurs *: And the ſaid *Coſpatrick* to diſcharge the foreign ſervice of him the ſaid William for the premiſſes in Cumberland, due to the barony and caſtle of Egremont †. And the poſterity of this *Coſpatrick* have continued at Workington to this day.

Middleton having thus came back to the elder branch of the Talebois family; it ſeems to have been firſt granted by them to the *Preſtons*, and by the *Preſtons* to others. For amongſt the fines in the 7 Ed. I. *Richard de Preſton* conveys to *Henry de Kennet* and *Euphemia* his wife, the manor of Middleton in Lonſdale. Poſſibly this might be a daughter of Preſton.

Whether this family of *Kennet* took afterwards the name *de Middleton* (as was not unuſual in like caſes), or how otherwiſe the *Middletons* came to this manor, doth not appear; however, certain it is, the *Middletons* not long after were in poſſeſſion of this manor, in which name and family it continued for ten generations, and then ended in daughters. The firſt that we find was,

1. THOMAS MIDDLETON of Middleton-hall, in the reign of king Edward the third. He had 6 children; amongſt whom were 3 daughters, *Agnes* married to John Chambre, *Margaret* married to John Morley, and *Joan* married to John Manſergh.

2. JOHN MIDDLETON, ſon and heir of Thomas. He married a daughter of John Medcalf. They had 6 children. One of whom was *Jeffrey Middleton*, the third ſon, who was anceſtor of the Middletons of *Leighton* in Lancaſhire, a very eminent family, whoſe male line failed near the ſame time with this elder branch at Middleton. Another of their children was *Jacomin*, who was married to Richard Preſton.

3. THOMAS MIDDLETON, ſon and heir of John, married Mabel daughter of Sir Richard Muſgrave of Hartley caſtle, in the reign of king Henry the ſixth.

* This reſervation of a pair of *gilt ſpurs* in many ancient grants had a particular meaning, becauſe they were peculiarly uſeful to the grantor; every knight (who ſerved on horſeback) being obliged to wear gilt ſpurs: hence they were called *equites aurati*.

† So ſays Mr. Denton. But ſome of the pedigrees of the Curwen family ſay, that *Orme* himſelf made this exchange.

They

They had 13 children; amongst whom were, *Elizabeth*, married to Thomas Ducket of Grayrigg esquire, *Margaret* married to Richard Redman of Over Levins esquire, and *Mabel* married to Sir Roger Bellingham of Burneshead knight.

4. THOMAS MIDDLETON, son and heir of Thomas, married Margaret daughter of Roger Lascells; and by her had nine children, of whom the eldest was,

5. GEOFFREY MIDDLETON, who married Margaret daughter of George Kirkham of Northamptonshire. And to his second wife he married a daughther of Kirkby in Lancashire.

With this Geoffrey begins the pedigree confirmed by Sir William Dugdale at his visitation in 1664. Nevertheless, the above account (which is taken from a pedigree in 1628), so far as we can judge from the intermarriages with Musgrave, Ducket, Redman, and Bellingham, seems to be sufficiently authentic.

This Geoffrey was knighted by king Henry the eighth; and was major general in that king's expedition to Bulloign.

Besides his eldest son *John*, he had a son *Thomas Middleton* of Applegarth; upon whom William Par, marquis of Northampton bestowed that tenement for his faithful service. The said Thomas married Katherine fourth daughter of William Conyers of Marske esquire, who was buried in the church at Marske in the year 1569; as appears from her epitaph there, setting forth the above particulars. He had also one daughter, which daughter was married to Anthony Fleming of Rydal esquire.

6. JOHN MIDDLETON, son and heir of Sir Jeoffrey. He married Anne daughter of Tunstal of Thurland-castle in Lancashire; and by her had eight children. Amongst whom was *Frances* married to Richard Lowther of Lowther esquire; and another daughter married to Lancaster of Sockbridge.

7. EDWARD MIDDLETON, second son and heir of John (for Christopher the eldest died before his father without issue). He married Mary daughter of Sir Thomas Carus knight, one of the justices of the court of king's bench; and by her had issue eight children. He died about the year 1599.

8. JOHN MIDDLETON, son and heir of Edward, married Jane daughter of Thomas Ashton of Crofton in Lancashire esquire. They had six sons; and one daughter, which daughter was married to one Alexander in the county of Chester. The sons were (1) *Edward*. (2) *Thomas*, who died without issue. (3) *John*, who was major general in the king's service, and was slain at the battle of Hopton-heath in 1642. (4) *William*, who was colonel of horse and foot in the said king's service. This William married Dorothy Moore of Middleton, and by her had eight sons and four daughters, all living at the time of Dugdale's visitation aforesaid. (5) *Richard*, slain in the civil wars in the said king's service. (6) *Christopher*, slain also fighting in the said king's cause.

9. EDWARD MIDDLETON, son and heir of John, by his wife Jane Ashton. He married Bridget daughter and heir of Robert Byndlose of Borwick-hall in Lancashire. He died just about the beginning of the civil wars. For by an

an inquisition in the 17 Cha. 1. it is found, that Edward Middleton esquire died seised of the manor and demesne of Middleton, with one capital messuage called Middleton-hall, and one water corn miln, which he held of the king as of his castle of Kendal called Marquis fee, in free socage, by fealty and the free rent of 26*s* 8*d*; and that *John* Middleton is his son and heir, aged 19 years and 6 months. And the said Edward had no other child.

10. JOHN MIDDLETON, son and heir of Edward. He married Mary Cole of Coat near Halton in Lancashire; and was of the age of 42 at Dugdale's visitation aforesaid in 1664; and had issue then five children, *Edward*, *David*, *Robert*, *Bridget*, and *Mary*.

The three sons died without issue; and the inheritance descended to the two daughters. And here ended the direct male line of the Middletons of Middleton-hall.

The *arms* of Middleton were; Argent, a saltier ingrailed Sable.

Of the two daughters; *Bridget*, the elder, was married to Joshua Heblethwaite of Dent, and to him had five children, John, Edward, Joshua, Bridget and Agnes. Of the three sons there are no descendents remaining. Bridget was married to Thomas Fawcet father of the present James Fawcet of Kirkby Stephen attorney at law. And Agnes was married to John Fawcet, brother of the said Thomas, who hath several children now living.

The other daughter *Mary* was married to James Cragg of Dent, and had eight children, John, James, David, Agnes, Mary, Rebecca, Bridget, and Isabel. Of this branch also there is no issue male remaining of the name of Crag. Mary, the second daughter of James Cragg, was married to Giles Moore of Grimeshill esquire; and to him had issue John, James rector of Tatham, Agnes, George, Mary married to Edward Johnson of Old Hall esquire, and Giles.

Part of the demesne remains to John Moore esquire eldest son of Giles aforesaid; the hall, the manor, and the remaining part of the demesne, were sold to one Benjamin Middleton (who doth not appear to have been of kindred to this family), whose son Adolphus Middleton sold the same to Dr. Adam Askew of Newcastle upon Tyne, son of Dr. Anthony Askew of Kendal, and father of Dr. Anthony Askew of London, all three very eminent and able physicians.

This family of *Askew* (*Akeskeugh*, which word signifies an hilly ground covered with oaks) was of long continuance in the county of Cumberland, deriving their descent from *Thurston de Bosco* (a name of the same import, *boscus* signifying a *wood*), who lived in the reign of king John, and had feoffment from the Boyvills, lords of Kirksanton, of a place there called Aikskeugh, within the lordship of Millum; whence his posterity, according to the custom of those early ages, have assumed their surname.

For several generations this family resided at Graymains in the parish of Moncaster and county aforesaid. Of which family was Sir Hugh Askew, to whom king Henry the eighth, in the 33d year of his reign, gave Seaton in the said lordship of Millum, which had been an house of Benedictine nuns.

Of

Of which Sir *Hugh*, there is a curious anecdote in a manuſcript account of Cumberland (a copy of which is in the ſixth volume of Mr. Machel's collection) written by Mr. Edmund Sandford a gentleman of the houſe of Aſkham. Speaking of Moncaſter and the country thereabouts, he ſays, "Four "miles ſouthward ſtands Seaton, an eſtate of 500*l* a year, ſometime a religious houſe, got by one Sir Hugh Aſkew yeoman of the cellar to queen "Katherine in Henry the eighth's time, and born in this country. And "when that queen was divorced from her huſband, this yeoman was deſtitute. "And he applied himſelf for help to the lord chamberlain for ſome place or "other in the king's ſervice. The lord chamberlain knew him well, becauſe "he had helped him to a cup of the beſt, but told him he had no place for "him but that of a charcoal carrier. Well, quoth Aſkew, help me in with "one foot, let me get in the other as I can. And upon a great holiday, the "king looking out at ſome ſports, Aſkew got a courtier, a friend of his, to "ſtand beſide the king; and he got on his velvet caſſock and his gold chain, "and a baſket of charcoal on his back, and marched in the king's ſight with "it. O, ſays the king, now I like yonder fellow well that diſdains not to do "his dirty office in his dainty cloaths; what is he? Says his friend that ſtood "by on purpoſe; it is Mr. Aſkew that was yeoman of the cellar to the late "queen's majeſty, and is now glad of this poor place, to keep him in your "majeſty's ſervice, which he will not forſake for all the world. The king "ſays, I had the beſt wine when he was in the cellar: he is a gallant wine "taſter: let him have his place again. He afterwards knighted him, and "gave unto him Seaton. At laſt he ſold his place, and came to Seaton, and "married the daughter of Sir John Huddleſton, and ſettled this Seaton upon "her. And ſhe afterwards married Mr. Pennington lord of the manor of "Moncaſter, and had a ſon Joſeph, and a younger ſon William Pennington, "to whom ſhe gave Seaton."

Of this ſame Hugh, Mr. Denton alſo, in his manuſcript hiſtory of Cumberland, makes honourable mention; where, ſpeaking of the ſaid nunnery of Seaton or Lekeley, he ſays, "When by the ſuppreſſion of abbies it came to "the crown, king Henry the eighth gave the ſite and lands there to his ſervant Sir Hugh Aſkew, who was deſcended from Thurſton de Boſco, and "was raiſed to great honour and preferment by his ſervice to the ſaid king "in his houſe ordinary, and in the field at the ſiege of Bologne and wars of "France."

He ſeems to have continued in his office of yeoman of the cellar to queen Anne Boleyn, and afterwards to king Edward the ſixth.

In the firſt year of Edward the ſixth, he ſerved in the expedition againſt Scotland under Edward duke of Somerſet, and for his bravery and conduct at the battle of Muſſelborough was created knight banneret under the royal ſtandard in the camp of Roqueſborough *.

In the 3d year of queen Elizabeth he was ſheriff of Cumberland; and in two years after died: as appears from the following inſcription on a braſs

* Hollingſhead. Grafton.

plate

plate upon his tomb-ſtone, "Here lieth Sir Hughe Aſketh knyght, late of "the Seller to kinge Edward the VI; which Sir Hughe was maid knyght at "Muſkelbroughfelde, in the yere of oure Lord 1547, and dy'd the ſecond "day of Marche in the yere of oure Lord God 1562."

The ſaid Sir *Hugh* was ſucceeded by his ſon (or rather perhaps his nephew) *Hugh Aſkew* of Graymains; who had a ſon *Henry*, who died, according to the pariſh regiſter of Moncaſter, in the year 1621. Which *Henry* had a ſon *William*, who ſold the eſtate of Graymains, and purchaſed an eſtate at Kirkby in the county of Lancaſter. The ſaid *William* died in 1641, leaving a ſon *John Aſkew* of Kirkby. Which *John* had two ſons; of whom, the younger was,

Anthony Aſkew of Kendal, M. D. who married Anne only daughter and heir of Adam Storrs of Storrs-hall in the county of Lancaſter eſquire, by his wife Jane daughter of William Rawlinſon of Grathwaite in the ſaid county eſquire, and ſiſter to Sir William Rawlinſon knight, one of the lords commiſſioners of the great ſeal in the reign of king William the third. He had iſſue, by his ſaid wife Anne Storrs, Adam, Anthony, and Margaret.

Adam Aſkew of Newcaſtle upon Tyne, M. D. ſon and heir of Anthony, married Anne younger daughter and coheir of Richard Crackenthorp of Newbiggin in the county of Weſtmorland eſquire; and by her had iſſue four ſons, and one daughter *Anne*. The ſons were, (1) *Anthony*. (2) *Adam Aſkew*, M. A. rector of Plumbland in the county of Cumberland, and now by his father's will owner of Middleton-hall, unmarried. (3) *Henry Aſkew* of Redheugh in the county of Durham eſquire, who married Dorothy only daughter of Adam Boulby of Whitby in the county of York gentleman. (4) *John Aſkew* of Pallinſbourn-houſe in the county of Northumberland eſquire, who married Bridget, daughter and heir of Thomas Watſon of Goſwick in the ſaid county of Northumberland eſquire.

Anthony Aſkew of London, M. D. late deceaſed, ſon and heir of Adam, married firſt Margaret only daughter of Cuthbert Swinburn of Long Witton in the county of Northumberland eſquire, by whom he had no iſſue. To his ſecond wife he married Elizabeth younger daughter of Robert Holford eſquire late maſter in chancery, by whom he had living in 1771, five ſons and four daughters; namely, Adam, Anthony-Linacre, Anne-Elizabeth, Sarah, Deborah, John, Henry, Amy, and Elizabeth.

The Arms of Aſkew are; Sable, a feſs Or, between three aſſes paſſant Argent.

Middleton hall is an old caſtle-like building, and is now made uſe of only as a farm-houſe. There was anciently a chapel in it, but that went to decay many years ago. When Mr. Machel made his ſurvey in the year 1692, the arms in the hall were then ſo much defaced, that he could only make out one ſingle coat, which was an impaling of Middleton and Lowther. The deer in the park were deſtroyed about the year 1640. And the family were great ſufferers in the civil wars that followed.

The tenants purchased their estates to freehold at different times, most of them of *John Middleton* in the reigns of queen Elizabeth and king James the first.

Next to the hall, the most considerable place in Middleton is *Grimeshill*, belonging to *John Moore* esquire aforesaid; a gentleman of most respectable character, as an active, able, and uncorrupt magistrate, a zealous and sincere friend, a promoter of piety and virtue by his own example and encouragement thereof in others, and an abhorrer of every thing that is vicious, mean, scandalous, or dishonourable.

His father *Giles Moore* esquire, by the mere force of genius and application, without the help of an university education, was profoundly learned, not only in the history and antiquities of our own country, but in the ancient Grecian and Roman literature, and was critically skilled even in the Hebrew language.

The next remarkable place, after *Grimeshill*, is *Hawkin-hall*; which was built by Dr. *Christopher Bainbridge* master of Christ's college in Cambridge in the reign of king Charles the first. It is a pretty large house, and yet is so contrived, that it hath but one pair of principles. Dr. Bainbridge was born at this place; and married at 60 years of age, and by his wife had 19 children.

At *Beckside-hall* in this township was born Sir *John Otway* knight, an eminent counsellor at law. He was admitted fellow of St. John's college in Cambridge in the year 1635; and was amongst the first of those that were ejected by the earl of Manchester in 1643. After his removal from the university, he became one of the readers in Gray's Inn. He was greatly instrumental in bringing over to the royal cause two officers who commanded each a regiment under Cromwell, *viz.* colonel Redman who married Mr. Otway's sister, and colonel Clobery who married his wife's sister. On king Charles the second's return, he was knighted and made one of the king's counsel, vicechancellor of the dutchy of Lancaster, and chancellor of the county palatine of Durham. He acquired a considerable estate, and settled at Ingmire hall, nigh unto his own paternal estate, but situate in the edge of Yorkshire, in the parish of Sedbergh. His descendents were as follows:

1. The said Sir *John Otway* married first Mary Rigg of Winchester, and by her had issue (1) *John*, who died unmarried. (2) *Charles Otway*, LL. D. many years fellow of the aforesaid college, where he died in 1621. (3) *Anne*, married into Ireland. (4) *Mary*, married to Posthumus Wharton of Sedbergh clerk, to whom she had issue Mary married to John Cawthorne esquire, and Margaret married to Samuel Saunders of Sedbergh, D. D.

To his second wife he married Elizabeth daughter of John Braithwaite and niece and heiress of Thomas Brathwaite of Ambleside gentleman, and by her had issue, (1) *Brathwaite*. (2) *Elizabeth*, married to Byram. (3) *Margaret*, married to Fothergill. (4) *Catherine*, married to Upton.

He

He died at Ingmire-hall in 1693, and was interred in the parish church of Sedbergh; where, on a marble monument, is the following inscription:

In pious memory
of the worshipful
Sir John Otway, knight;
Vicechancellor of the dutchy of Lancaster,
and chancellor of the county palatine of Durham,
late one of the readers of Gray's Inn,
and one of his majesty king Charles the 2d's counsel
learned in the law:
To whom he was very instrumental
in his happy restauration.
He lived much beloved,
and died much lamented,
the 15th of Oct', 1693.
In the 74th year of his age.
In memory of him,
his sorrowful lady
hath caused this monument
to be erected.

2. *Brathwaite Otway* of Ingmire-hall esquire, only surviving son of Sir John Otway, was sometime fellow-commoner of the aforesaid college, and afterwards a student in Gray's Inn. In his time a dispute happened between Thomas Strickland esquire lord of the manor, and the tenants of Sedbergh, which cause he took up in behalf of the tenants, and managed at his own expence; as appears from the following inscription upon a brass plate in the church, which the tenants put up in his life-time, but without his knowledge:

"In the year 1744.
" Gratitude obliged the parishioners of Sedbergh to erect this monument, in " memory of *Brathwaite Otway* esquire, their generous benefactor; whose " singular humanity, beneficence, and integrity, ought never to be forgotten. " When *Bluecaster* was inclosed, with an intent to take it from them, and " many impositions took place; he voluntarily defended their cause at his own " expence, and with great assiduity recovered their rights, and firmly esta- " blished them in their ancient properties. A judicious and noble patriot of " his country, a strenuous defender of the poor, and an ardent lover of jus- " tice; a bright and shining example to the rich and potent, whose amiable " conduct justly merits their imitation."

He died unmarried, and was succeeded by his sister,

3. *Catherine*, who was married to *John Upton* of Upton in the county of Devon esquire, and had issue *William*, *Catherine*, *John*, *Arthur*, and *Elizabeth*. The two sons *William* and *Arthur* died unmarried; *Catherine* married Egerton, and died without issue; *Elizabeth* (now living, in 1771) married Fennyhough, and hath no issue.

 4. *John*

4. *John Upton* of Ingmire-hall esquire, the surviving son of Catherine, married Elizabeth Boucher, by whom he had issue, (1) *Elizabeth*, married to Thomas Swettenham of Swettenham in the county of Chester, now Thomas Willis, esquire, and hath no issue. (2) *John*.

5. *John Upton* of Ingmire-hall esquire, son and heir of the last John. In the year 1761, he was chosen to represent the county of Westmorland in parliament.

He married Mary Noble of Westoe in the county of Durham, by whom he hath issue a son and two daughters now living, *viz. Mary, John*, and *Jane*.

The Arms of Upton are; Sable, a cross moline Argent. Crest, an horse caparisoned upon a ducal coronet.

The *chapel* of Middleton was built by the inhabitants in the year 1634, upon ground given by the aforesaid Dr. Bainbridge, who also gave 40 *s* towards the building. It was consecrated by bishop Bridgman in the year following, by the name of the Chapel of the Holy Ghost, reserving to the bishop of Chester the nomination of a preaching minister, and 1 *s* synodals, and 1 *s* 4 *d* for procurations. It was made parochial by bishop Pearson in 1671. The chapel-yard was inlarged by land given to Giles Moore of Grimeshill esquire, and in 1712 a licence was obtained to bury therein. The revenue thereof arises, first, from an estate in Middleton purchased with 106 *l* ancient stock, by sale of some wood upon the said estate, and divers contributions, now let at 12 *l* a year. Afterwards 200 *l* came to this chapel by lot, with which and with divers benefactions called chapel stock, an estate was purchased in Middleton of the yearly value of 12 *l*. In the year 1756, the executors of the late Dr. Stratford gave 100 *l*, the present curate Mr. Garnet and the inhabitants gave other 100 *l*, whereby an augmentation of 200 *l* was procured from the governors of queen Anne's bounty, and two estates purchased therewith, one in Middleton and the other in Garsdale, of the yearly rent of 7 *l* each. The whole revenue of the estates together being 38 *l*.

Mr. John Moore of Grimeshill, grandfather of the present John Moore esquire, gave 60 *l*, wherewith land was purchased now let for 3 *l per annum*; one third whereof is paid to the curate; one third to the schoolmaster to teach four poor children; and one third to the poor of Middleton, as also 30 *s* being the rent of some lands purchased with money given by John Bailiff.

Mr. Giles Moore of Borwens left 40 *l*, the interest thereof to be given one half to poor householders in Middleton, one fourth to the schoolmaster, and one fourth towards placing out poor children of the said township apprentices.

John Bainbridge of Middleton gave 10 *l*, the interest thereof to be applied towards buying bibles and common-prayer books for poor children who repeat the church catechism in Middleton chapel.

Jeffrey Hadwen gave 10 *l*, the interest whereof to be given yearly to poor widows of the said chapelry.

John Hawden gave 10 *l*, the interest whereof to be given every Good Friday in wheaten loaves to the poor of the township. And his widow gave 10 *l*; the

the intereſt whereof to be applied towards buying cloaths for the poor children of the ſaid townſhip.

The abbey of Cockerſand in Lancaſhire had ſome lands in Middleton, given by Edmund de Nevil knight.

VI.

KILLINGTON AND FIRBANK.

KILLINGTON and FIRBANK were anciently one manor. The latter was not ſo called as having heretofore been planted with fir trees; for the ancient name of it univerſally was *Frithbank*, from the Saxon *frith* or *frid* which ſignifies *peace*, and is transferred to places incloſed which are *free* from annoyance or purpreſture, and are kept clear from cattle at certain ſeaſons of the year: of which ſort is a ſtinted paſture, where ſeveral perſons have cattle-gaits; and the perſon who looks after the paſture and ſtint is to this day called the *frithman*.

The river Lune is the Eaſtern boundary of both theſe diviſions. Killington adjoins on the ſouth to the other parts of Kirkby Lonſdale pariſh. On the weſt of Killington, lies Old Hutton; and on the weſt of *Firbank* lies Lambrigg. And the northern boundary of Firbank is Dillaker.

There are between 30 and 40 families in each of theſe diviſions, all freehold; the manor having been purchaſed from the meſne lords by the tenants, who therefore hold immediately of the crown as of the marquis fee by the yearly free rent (jointly) of 6*s* 8*d*, as found by inquiſition 28 Cha. 2.

In the reign of king Edward the firſt, we find one *William de Frithbank* a juror on ſeveral inquiſitions *poſt mortem* of the Talebois family: But the manor at the ſame time was in the name and family of PICKERING.

I. The firſt of the name of *Pickering* that came to Killington, was WILLIAM DE PYKERINGE ſon of *Thomas*, in the reign of king Henry the third. For in the 44th year of that king, *Peter de Brus* the third grants to *William de Pykeringe* the manor of Killington: To hold to the ſaid William and his heirs, and to his aſſigns (except Jews and religious perſons), of him the ſaid Peter and his heirs in fee, with all the game * thereof, and other appurtenances whatſoever. Saving to him the ſaid Peter, during his life, freedom of chaſe for himſelf or his men, at their pleaſure, within the boundaries of the ſaid manor; yet ſo, that neither he nor any for him ſhall have entry into the incloſed grounds to make chaſe. Rendering for the ſame yearly a pair of gilt ſpurs, or ſixpence, at the Feaſt of Pentecoſt; and doing ſervice of the 20th part of one knight's fee when occaſion ſhall be, for all ſervices, ſuits of court,

* *Cum omnium ſalvagina*:—*Salvaginus catus*, in ſome old writings, ſignifies a ſavage or wild cat. From the circumſtances of this grant it ſeemeth, that the word *ſalvagina* here is to be underſtood of the beaſts fit for hunting, as deer, hares, marterns, foxes, and in general all the wild beaſts of the foreſt.

and

and other customs. He grants moreover to the said William, his heirs and assigns, that they shall have the same liberty in pursuing the game out of the boundaries of Killington, as far as the limits of that part of the forest of the Hay, which belongs to Walter de Lindesay, and in driving back the same with their men and dogs, which he the said Peter himself had: So nevertheless, that they shall claim no such liberty in the said Peter's part of the forest of the Hay. Witnesses whereof were, John de Burton knight, Gilbert de Bereburne, Thomas de Lancastre, Ralph de Patton, Nicolas de Ninesergh, Thomas de Derlay, Richard de Crok, and others *.

II. THOMAS DE PICKERING, son of William.—By a charter in the 32 Ed. 1. the king grants to *Thomas de Pickeringe* free warren in all his demesne lands of Killington and Millehope in the county of Westmorland; so as those lands be not within the limits of the king's forest. So that no person shall enter those lands to make chase therein, or take any thing which belongs to the warren, without the licence and will of the said *Thomas* and his heirs, on pain of forfeiture of 10 *l.* to the king. Witnesses whereof; the reverend father W. bishop of Coventry and Litchfield, Henry de Lacy earl of Lincoln, Henry de Percye, Hugh de Veer, William de Vavasor, and others †.

In the 3 Ed. 2. after the death of William de Roos, the inquisition finds, that *Thomas de Pykeringe* held the hamlet of Kyllington, Frethebank and the Berghes, by the service of the tenth part of one knight's fee, and the rent of 9 *s* yearly.—And the said Thomas was one of the jurors in taking the said inquisition, and is styled *Thomas de Pykeringe* knight.

King Edward the third, in the 10th year of his reign, confirms to *Thomas de Pykering*, son of *William de Pykering*, the manor of Killington; for the fine of 40 *s* paid into the exchequer ‡.

III. The next that we meet with was JAMES PICKERING; who in the 36th and again in the 39th of Ed. 3. was knight of the shire for Westmorland.

This *James*, in the 38 Ed. 3. granted by fine to Richard Carus and Agnes his wife certain lands in Kirkby, Helsington, and Stirkland: To hold to them and the heirs of their bodies; and in defect thereof, to revert. So that this was probably a settlement on the marriage of his daughter.

Six years after this, Richard de Wisbitche conveys to *Alexander* son of *Alice de Pickering* a moiety of the manor of Preston Patrick, with a reversion to the said Richard in fee.—This *Alice* possibly might be widow of the said *James*; and this conveyance, a settlement on the marriage of her younger son.

IV. Sir JOHN PICKERING of Killington knight, married Elianor daughter of Sir Richard Harrington; and by her had issue, 1. *James*. 2. *Margaret*, married to Robert de Roos knight. And another daughter who was a nun at Watton.

V. Sir JAMES PICKERING knight, in the 1 Ric. 2. and again in the 2d and 6th years of the same king, was chosen knight of the shire for Westmorland. He married to his first wife, Mary daughter of Sir Robert Lowther of Lowther knight; and by her had issue *James* his son and heir. To his second wife

* Dugd. MS. † Idem. ‡ Idem.

he

he married Margaret daughter and heir of Sir John Norwood knight; and by her had issue Sir *Edward Pickering*, comptroller of the king's houshold; which Sir *Edward* had a son Edward who died without issue.

VI. Sir JAMES PICKERING knight, son and heir of Sir James by his wife Mary Lowther, married Margaret daughter and heir of Lassels of Eskrigg; and had issue *James* and *John*.

VII. Sir JAMES PICKERING knight, married Anne daughter and heir of Sir Christopher Moresby of the county of Cumberland knight; and by her had six children; 1. *Anne*, married to Sir Robert Bellingham of Burneshead knight. 2. *Christopher*, his eldest son and heir. 3. *Margaret*, married to Sir William Stapleton knight. 4. *Thomas*, who had a son Thomas that married Margaret daughter of Nicolas Starkey. 5. *James*, who married Elizabeth one of the three daughters and coheirs of Sir Lancelot Threlkeld of Threlkeld by his wife the baroness Vesey widow of John lord Clifford. 6. *William*, who married Winifred another of the said daughters and coheirs.

VIII. Sir CHRISTOPHER PICKERING knight, by his wife, whose name was Elizabeth, had an only child *Anne*, who was heir both to the Pickering and Moresby estates. She was thrice married: First, to Sir *Francis Westby*, upon whose issue by that marriage the Cumberland estates seem to have been settled. Her second husband was Sir *Henry Knevitt* of East Horseley in the county of Surrey: To whom she seemeth to have had no issue: He appears to have been dead in the 6 Eliz. For in that year there was a presentation to the church of Asby by virtue of a title derived from her (as heiress of Moresby) by the name and title of the lady Anne Knevet widow of Sir Henry Knevet. Nine years after this, there was a presentation to the same church by *John Vaughan* of Eskrigg in the county of York esquire and the lady *Anne* his wife. This *John Vaughan* was her third husband, and to him it is probable she had issue. For the person who sold the manors of Killington and Firbank to the tenants was *Francis Vaughan* in all likelihood her son.

This *Francis Vaughan*, styled *Francis Vaughan* of Sutton upon Derwen in the county of York esquire, in the 27 Eliz. conveyed the said manors to trustees for the use of the tenants; which trustees conveyed to every of the tenants their own tenements, with a proportionable part or portion of the moors, wastes, common of pasture, perquisites, and profits of courts, and of all other privileges, liberties, and franchises, parcel of or belonging to the said manors, according to their then annual rent; and to every individual, the wood growing upon his own tenement.—The king, as paramount, claims waif and stray within the respective liberties; and they pay to the lessee of the crown the ancient quit rent of 6*s* 8*d*, which comes nearly to the sum of one penny for each house.

What became of the further descendents of the lady *Anne*, we have no particular account.

The *arms* of *Pickering* were; Ermin, a lion rampant Azure, crowned Or.

Killington *hall* is an ancient tower-house. It was sold, together with the demesne, by the said Mr. Vaughan to *Robert Wadeson* gentleman. Mr. *Wade-*

son, about five years after, sold the same to *Radcliffe Ashton* of Preston in Lancashire gentleman. Mr. *Ashton* in the 15 Ja. 1. sold the premises to *Thomas Kitson* of Warton in Lancashire gentleman; on whose death in the 15 Cha. 1. the inquisition finds, that he died seised of one capital messuage called Killington-hall, and the demesne thereof, and one other messuage and tenement, and one water corn mill in Killington, late purchased of the heir of Christopher Pickering knight, holden of the king as of his manor of Kirkby in Kendale, late called the Marquis fee, by the 60th part of one knight's fee; his son and heir *Thomas* being of full age.

Which *Thomas* the son died without issue. And the estate came to his sister *Elizabeth*, who was married to *Robert Hebblethwaite*; who had a son *Thomas Hebblethwaite* esquire, who devised the same to trustees to be sold, and the same was accordingly purchased by *Jacob Morland* of Caplethwaite esquire, whose grandson Jacob Morland esquire now enjoys the same.

There is a *park* belonging to the hall, which anciently had deer in it; but none, probably, after the death of Sir *Christopher Pickering*, the last resident of the family there.

These two divisions had originally but one *chapel*; which stood in a close called Chapelgarth; adjoining to which are two closes called Priest fields, lying in Killington. And both the divisions jointly paid a chapel salary; which seems to have been the usual limited sum of 20 nobles: for now when the salary is divided between the two chapels, Firbank chapel has appropriated to it near half that sum: the ancient chapel salary indeed of Killington is larger, but that seems to have been by reason of an addition made to it on establishing a separate chapel in Killington.

In or about the year 1585, on the petition of the inhabitants of Killington and Frithbank to bishop Chadderton, setting forth, that by reason of their distance from the parish church (some of them being distant ten miles and none less than six), and by reason of inundations and of storms frequently raging in those parts in the winter season, they cannot carry their dead to be buried without great trouble and inconvenience, nor their children to be baptized without great peril both of soul and body, nor resort thither to hear divine service and receive the sacraments as becometh christians and by right they are bounden: He the said bishop, in consideration of the premisses, grants unto them his faculty and licence, that in the chapel situate within the territory, hamlet, or lordship of Killington and Frithbank aforesaid, commonly called Killington chapel, by a minister or curate lawfully ordained, or sufficiently approved from time to time, to be hired at the costs and charges of the said inhabitants [*sumptibus et expensis dictorum inhabitantium conducendum*], divine service shall be performed, the sacraments and sacramental rites administred, matrimony solemnized, and the dead buried in the said chapel or chapel-yard thereof, as freely and in as ample manner and form, as then they were, or lately had been obliged to perform the same at their said parish church.

The present revenue of Killington chapel is somewhat more than 40*l* a year; arising from an ancient chapel salary of 9*l* 6*s* 8*d*; a rent-charge of 20*s* out of of ſome lands in Killington called Lord's holme, formerly part of the demeſne (in conſideration whereof the demeſne pays no chapel ſalary); another rent-charge of 20*s* given by William Walker out of an eſtate in Old Hutton called Bendrigg; an eſtate in Killington purchaſed with an allotment of 200 *l* of queen Anne's bounty and an ancient chapel ſtock given by different perſons, now let for 12 *l* 12 *s*; another eſtate in Dent purchaſed with 200 *l* given by Dr. Stratford's executors, and 200 *l* queen's bounty, now let for 14 *l* 14 *s*; and the intereſt of 55 *l* (whereof 40 *l* was given by Thomas Heblethwaite eſquire, 10 *l* by Hugh Bowman, and 5 *l* by Jacob Morland eſquire) amounting to 2 *l* 9 *s*.

The ſaid Thomas Heblethwaite gave a legacy to the uſe of the *poor*, wherewith lands were purchaſed, now let for 3 *l* 11 *s*. Alſo the ſaid William Walker gave a rent-charge of 40 *s* out of the ſaid eſtate at Bendrigg. And there is another eſtate in Firbank belonging to the poor of Killington, now let for 11 *l* 10 *s*, and it is not known who was the donor (probably it was purchaſed with ſome ancient poor ſtock).

Alſo there is a *ſchool* ſtock of 65 *l*; whereof 40 *l* was given by the ſaid Thomas Heblethwaite eſquire, 5 *l* by the ſaid Jacob Morland eſquire, and 20 *l* by Thomas Sharpe.

The ancient chapel *ſalary* of Firbank is nine nobles or 3 *l*. Anthony Ward of Whinny How gave an eſtate called Green in Lambrigg then of the yearly value of 8 *l*, and alſo the ſum of 50 *l* in money, in conſideration whereof the governors of queen Anne's bounty gave 200 *l*. Alſo 200 *l* came twice by lot to this chapel. With all which ſums lands were purchaſed in Firbank, Strickland Roger, and Strickland Ketel. And the whole revenue of this chapel at preſent (including the chapel ſalary) is 37 *l* 10 *s* 0 *d*.

OF THE BARONY OF WESTMORLAND.

HAVING finiſhed the *barony of Kendal*, which is one of the two great baronies of which the county of Weſtmorland doth conſiſt; we now proceed to the other, which is emphatically ſtyled the *barony of Weſtmorland*, conſiſting of the honours or ſeignories of Appleby and Burgh, which contain under them all the ſubordinate manors holden of the lords of Weſtmorland, and indeed all that ſeems anciently to have been deemed within the county of Weſtmorland; the barony of Kendal (as we obſerved before) being conſidered as part of Lancaſhire and Yorkſhire, and in Domeſday ſurvey inſerted under the title *Agemundreneſſe*.

In order to deduce the hiſtory of this barony, it is neceſſary to obſerve in the firſt place, that in the diſtribution of the provinces by William the conqueror, the earldom of CHESTER was granted to HUGH DE ABRINCIS ſurnamed LUPUS, ſon of a ſiſter of the ſaid *William*, whoſe huſband's name was *Richard*

 viſcount

viſcount of Aurenches ſurnamed *Gez*. This *Hugh* received the appellation of *Lupus* probably from his martial ſpirit, and for the ſame reaſon was appointed to that important ſtation againſt the Britons then driven into Wales. And the king granted him a ſort of royal power, *tenere ita libere ad gladium, ſicut ipſe rex tenebat Angliam per coronam* *. Where we may obſerve, by the way, the delicacy of expreſſion: the conqueror did not chuſe to affirm expreſsly that he held the kingdom by the right of conqueſt, but rather ſpeaks in ambiguity and with reſerve; but the meaning could be no other, than to hold the earldom by the ſword, as he himſelf held the kingdom.

At the ſame time, the county of Cumberland, and ſo much of Weſtmorland as was not included within the barony of Kendal, were granted to *Ranulph de Meſchiens* another Norman; who, in the year 1088, granted the two churches of St. Michael and St. Laurence of his caſtle of Appleby, to the abbey of St. Mary's York †.

The ſaid *Ranulph de Meſchiens* married *Lucia* ſiſter of *Hugh Lupus* aforeſaid, by whom he had iſſue a ſon and daughter. The ſon, *Ranulph de Meſchiens*, ſo called after his father's name, ſucceeded to the Cumberland and Weſtmorland eſtates (except what his father had before granted away to his brother *William de Meſchiens* and others); and afterwards, upon the death of *Richard* brother of the ſaid *Hugh Lupus*, the ſaid *Ranulph* the ſon was, in his mother's right, being next heir in blood, and by the favour of the king, made earl of Cheſter. For the king propoſing to him to make war upon the marchers in Cheſhire, who had invaded a great part of that country, he undertook the charge, and drove them out. Whereupon the king gave him all that province, and made him count palatine of it, as he had made the earl *Hugh* before. And having obtained of the king to confirm the grants that he had made in Cumberland, he thenceforth left that earldom, and ſettled himſelf in Cheſhire ‡.

Whereupon the eſtates which he left behind him in Cumberland and Weſtmorland, came by his appointment and diſpoſition to his ſiſter, who was married to (another Norman) *Robert d'Eſtrivers*, or *Trevers*.

This *Robert de Trevers* had a daughter and heir *Ibria Treverz*, who was married to *Ranulph Engain*; who had a ſon and heir *William Engain*; who had a daughter and heir *Ada Engain*, married to *Simon de Morville* (who alſo was of Norman extraction).

The ſaid *Simon de Morville* had a ſon and heir *Roger de Morville*; who had a ſon and heir *Hugh de Morville*, and a daughter *Maud* married to *William de Veteripont* father of *Robert de Veteripont* whom we ſhall often have occaſion to mention in the ſequel, with whom the ſaid *William de Veteripont* had that part

* Fleming.

† R. Meſchiens omnibus catholicæ fidei cultoribus, ſalutem. Notum ſit omnibus, quod ego Ranulphus dedi abbatiæ ſanctæ Mariæ Eboraci eccleſiam ſancti Michaelis et eccleſiam ſancti Laurentii caſtelli mei de Appelbi, cum omnibus quæ ad eas pertinent, ſicut Radulphus capellanus meus tenuit, quietas et liberas ab omni terreno ſervicio. Teſte uxore mea Lucia, et Willielmo fratre meo, et Gilberto Tyſun, et Godardo. *Regiſtr. Wetheral.*

‡ Fleming.

 of

of Meburn in Westmorland, which from her still bears the name of Mauld's Meburn (Meburn Matildæ).

This same *Hugh de Morville* was one of the four knights that assassinated Thomas a Becket archbishop of Canterbury in the reign of king Henry the second. Whereupon the said *Hugh*'s estates in Westmorland were seized into the king's hands; as appears by an inquisition taken at York in the 3 Ed. 1. whereby it is found *(inter alia)* that the castles of Apelby and of Burgh under Stanemore were seized into the king's hands, by reason of the trespass committed *(propter transgressionem factam)* by *Hugh de Morville*.

After this forfeiture, it seemeth that the said king Henry the second granted the custody of Appleby castle to *Gospatric* son of *Orme*; for amongst the fines in the exchequer in the 22 Hen. 2. it appears, that *Gospatric* son of *Orme* was fined 500 marks, because he delivered the castle of Appleby to the king of Scots; Ralph de Cundale for the same fact was fined 40 marks; Odard de Burgham 20 marks; John de Morevil 10 *l*; Gilbert de Engaine 5 *l*; and others other sums.

This family of *Gospatric* had very considerable possessions, not only in Cumberland, but also in Westmorland. *Ormes-head* nigh Appleby had probably its name from them. Thomas son of this Gospatric son of Orme was founder of Shap abbey; and Thomas son of this Thomas confirmed his father's grants. Nevertheless the barony of Westmorland and custody of the castles was not granted to them in fee; for by the said inquisition in the 3 Ed. 1. it is found, that after the forfeiture thereof by Sir *Hugh de Morville*, they continued in the hands of the crown, till king John granted the same to ROBERT DE VETERIPONT before mentioned.

The said ROBERT DE VETERIPONT was a descendent of a family in Normandy *(de Veteri Ponte)* lords of Curvaville. His father's name was *William de Veteripont*, and his mother was *Maud* sister of Sir *Hugh Morville* aforesaid. King John, in the 4th year of his reign, granted to this *Robert* the custody (as probably he had granted to Gospatric before) of Apelby and Burgh, and also the sheriffwick of Westmorland, to hold during the king's pleasure.

In the very next year, the said king granted to him in perpetuity, as follows: *viz.* " Appleby and Burgh, with all their appendages, with the sheriffwick " and rent of our county of Westmorland, and the services of all our tenants " who hold not by knights service; to hold of us and our heirs to him the said " Robert and his heirs by his espoused wife, by the service of four knights " fees. Saving to us and our heirs our pleas of the crown, and royal dignity. " And saving that the said Robert or his men shall not commit waste in the " woods of Whinfell, and that his servants shall not hunt there during our life " without the bodily presence of the said Robert *."

And

* Johannes, Dei gratia, rex Angliæ et dominus Hiberniæ, dux Normanniæ, Aquitaniæ, et Andegaviæ, &c. Archiepiscopis, episcopis, abbatibus, comitibus, baronibus, vicecomitibus, et omnibus ministris et fidelibus nostris, salutem. Sciatis nos dedisse, et præsenti charta nostra confirmasse, dilecto et fideli nostro Roberto de Veteriponte, Apelby et Burk, cum omnibus appendiciis suis,

And becaufe much depends upon this charter, it is thought fit here to fubjoin Sir Matthew Hale's learned comment thereon.

Appleby and Burgh] Thefe are all the particulars that are mentioned in this charter, and thefe only barely Appleby and Burgh, and not the caftle, manor, or the like; but they include the fame, and indeed all the reft of the barony of Weftmorland.

With all their appendages] Thefe words carry, firft, the feveral parts of thefe caftles and manors, which are particularly fpecified in the inquifitions after the death of the feveral poffeffors; as Langton, Brougham, Kirkby Thore, Kirkby Stephen, Winton, Mallerftang, and the reft: all of them being appendant either to Appleby or Burgh, and both together making up the barony of Weftmorland. The words carry alfo the franchifes to the fame belonging, that are appendant to the fame by prefcription; as liberties of free chafe, free warren, affizes of weights and meafures, of bread and beer, and fuch like.—And befides thefe ordinary tenures and fervices, we find in the records mention of three kinds of rents and tenures, which the fouthern parts of England are not acquainted with: 1. *White farms* of the tenants; but this feems to be their ordinary rents. 2. A fervice called *cornage*, paid by the knights and free tenants; which drew wardfhip and relief. 3. A fervice or tenure called *drengage*; which was not a knight's fervice, yet it drew wardfhip and relief.

With the fheriffwick and rent of the county of Weftmorland] This paffed the fheriffwick, which was parcel of the barony of Weftmorland. And whereas this whole barony was held by four knights fees, the fheriffwick was eftimated at one.

With the fervices of all our tenants there, who hold not by knights fervice] By the general words, knights fees would have paffed, if they had not been particularly excepted. But here they are excepted, and no knights fervice tenure paffed, though other tenure which had relation to the wars and had the fame effect with knights fervice as to the point of wardfhip did pafs, namely, cornage. And in propriety, none were in thofe times accounted tenants by knights fervice, but fuch as held by a knight's fee or part thereof.

To him and his heirs by his wife] This at common law was a fee fimple conditional. So that before iffue had, the donee by his alienation might bar his iffue; and by his alienation after iffue had, might bar the donor. If no alienation was made mefne between the grant and the 13 Ed. 1. then this eftate in

fuis, cum ballivato et reditu comitatus Weftmerlandiæ, cum ferviciis omnium inde tenentium de nobis qui non tenent per fervicium militare: Habenda et tenenda de nobis et hæredibus noftris, fibi et hæredibus fuis qui de ipfo et uxore fibi defponfata exierint, per fervicium quatuor militum pro omni fervicio. Salvis nobis et hæredibus noftris placitis omnibus quæ ad coronam regiam pertinent, et falva dignitate regali; et falvo, quod dictus Robertus vel fui vaftum neque exitium facere poterint in brulliis de Whinfell, vel in ipfis venari quamdiu vixerimus fine corpore ipfius Roberti. Quare volumus, et firmiter præcipimus, quod ipfe Robertus vel hæredes fui poft ipfum habeant et teneant omnia prædicta de nobis et hæredibus noftris ut dictum eft, in bofco et plano, in viis et femitis, in pratis et pafturis, in moris et marifcis, in ftagnis et vivariis, in aquis et molendinis, et in omnibus locis et libertatibus fuis et liberis confuetudinibus, ficut prædictum eft. Teftibus, &c. Datum per manum Hugonis de Wells vicefimo octavo die Octobris anno regni noftri quinto. *(Dugd. MS.)*

fee

fee simple, by the statute *De Donis* made in that year, turned into an estate tail, and a reversion settled in the crown. But if there were an alienation mesne, then the said statute works not this into an estate tail. But this continued unaltered; and therefore by the statute aforesaid is turned into an estate tail, with the reversion in the crown.

By the service of four knights fees] And accordingly was this service answered by the said Robert and his successors. And it is to be noted, that the barony always accompanied the possessions, and they were never severed, and relief was answered for it accordingly. Yet the charter is not to hold *per baroniam*, but only *per quatuor milites*. So that it is not necessary, that a barony by tenure be held *per baroniam*. But if a large possession be granted to be held by an honourable person, this intitled him in those ancient times to a particular summons to parliament as one of the *barones regni*.

Saving our pleas of the crown] This, if it had not been provided for expresly in this charter, had been provided for before by the Great Charter, ch. 17. "Nullus vicecomes, vel alii ballivi nostri, teneant placita coronae "nostrae."

And our royal dignity] This also was no more than the law had said, had this saving been omitted. And therefore as incident to this royal dignity, the kings placed constables in the castles, and had a superintendency over their judicate proceedings. So, in the 19 Ed. 2. we find a writ directed, "The "king, to his constable of his castle of Appleby."

Shall not commit waste in the woods of Whinfell] This imports two things, 1. That the woods did pass; which afterwards came to be called the *forest* of Whinfell, as also in like manner the *forest* of Mallerstang. These nevertheless, in the hands of subjects the patentees, are in right not forests, but only chases. 2. That here is a special exception, restraining the liberty of the grantee from what he might otherwise have done. And here we see the wisdom and care of the ancient times, in preserving of timber. And indeed the preservation of forests, and the game of deer, was principally in order to the preservation of timber, which by inclosure (though otherwise more profitable) would have been more subject to destruction.——So much concerning the charter.

This *Robert de Veteripont* was a man of great parts and employments.

He was trusted with the custody and disposal of much of the king's treasure.

He was intrusted with the custody of the prisoners taken in the wars in France; as appears by the several writs for their deliverances upon several occasions.

He was trusted with the education and custody of the king's niece, daughter of William Longspee; as also of the king's son Richard, who was afterwards earl of Cornwall.

He was employed in offices of great trust and importance; was sheriff of Caen in Normandy; was eleven times sheriff of several counties in England, as appears by the pipe rolls of those times.

He was employed to publish the treaties at Winchester, between the king on the one hand, and the pope and clergy on the other.

He

He had the cuſtody of many caſtles and towns of note at different times; as namely, Windſor, Bowes, Saliſbury, Carliſle, and divers others.

He was juſtice in eyre, and ſate in commiſſion with Martin de Patiſhull and others.

He purchaſed of Maud daughter of Torphin, and of Philip de Burgo, their lands in Weſtmorland.

He purchaſed of Walter Morvil divers lands at Brampton and elſewhere.

He purchaſed of Adam ſon of Waldeve the advowſon of Kirkby Thore, together with the chapels of Sourby and Milburn.

He purchaſed of Nicholas Stutevill all the lands of the ſaid Nicholas in Weſtmorland; and, amongſt the reſt, Milburn Grange, which he gave to the abbey of Shap, together with the tithes of all his mills in Weſtmorland, and the tithes of the renewal of all the beaſts taken by him or his men in all his foreſts in Weſtmorland.

And he confirmed unto the ſaid abbey the grants which had been made to the ſaid abbey by Thomas ſon of Goſpatric and Thomas his ſon; and the grant of Renegill which had been made to the ſaid abbey by Maud his mother and Ivo his brother.

He was one of thoſe, who in the reign of king Henry the third took the croſs in the holy land. His arms then (as appears by his ſeal) were, a lion paſſant, with a coronet upon his head; and his brother Ivo's, a lion paſſant without any crown. So that the ancient arms of the Veteriponts ſeem to have been a lion paſſant, and that the coronet was added upon the advancement and promotion of Robert to his honours and dignities; for he had not only thoſe places and poſſeſſions in England which have been hitherto ſpoken of, but his brother's alſo in Normandy (who ſeems to have been the elder brother, and to have inherited the family eſtate there) which were given to the ſaid Robert by king John, on Ivo's ſiding with the king's enemies in Normandy. [Their ſeals Mr. Machel ſays he found amongſt the Blenkinſop papers at Helbeck relating to Shap abbey.] Howbeit, though this was their bearing then, yet not long after (by what occaſion appeareth not) their arms were changed; for John, ſon of this ſame Robert, bore annulets: and the coat which is now owned by his poſterity, is this; *viz.* Gules, ſix annulets Or, 3, 2, and 1. And their ſeal is an armed man on horſeback, bearing a ſhield charged with annulets, and the horſe trapped with the ſame. And here perhaps it may not be amiſs to obſerve, how ſeveral ancient families do agree in their arms; ſome borrowing probably their arms of the lords of whom they held in fee; others by taking the arms (as they duly might) of thoſe perſons to whom they were related, or moſt devoted. Therefore as the Veteriponts bore ſix annulets, 3, 2, and 1; ſo alſo do the Muſgraves and Lowthers: varying only in colour, for diſtinction ſake.

This *Robert de Veteripont* married Idonea, daughter and heir of John Builly, ſon and heir of Richard de Builly, ſon and heir of Jordan de Builly, ſon and heir of Arnold, uncle and heir of Roger, ſon of Roger, that in the reign of king Henry the firſt was lord of the caſtle and manor of Tickhill in Yorkſhire; and by that title Robert de Veteripont and Idonea his wife demanded the ſame in in a writ of right, againſt Alice counteſs of Ewe, in the 4 Hen. 3. which ended in a compromiſe and partition.

The ſaid *Robert de Veteripont*, having been 24 years ſheriff of Weſtmorland, died in the 12th year of king Henry the third, and was buried in the Middle Temple in Fleetſtreet London; to the brethren whereof he gave his moiety of the manor of Wycum in Buckinghamſhire.

Idonea his wife died about 7 years after, in the 19 Hen. 3. and was buried at Rupe or Roch abbey in Yorkſhire, which her grandfather Richard de Builly aforeſaid had founded and endowed.

They had iſſue a ſon *John de Veteripont*; and a daughter *Chriſtian*, married to Thomas, ſon of William, ſon of Ralph baron of Grayſtock, the wardſhip of which Thomas had been granted by the king to the ſaid Robert.

JOHN DE VETERIPONT, ſon and heir of *Robert de Veteripont* and *Idonea* his wife, was the ſecond lord of the honour of Appleby, baron of Weſtmorland, and ſheriff by inheritance; but not of the caſtle, honour, and manor of Tickhill; for his father and mother in the 6 Hen. 3. paſſed the ſame away by fine to the aforeſaid Alice counteſs of Ewe.

In the time of this John, Walter de Stirkland and Robert de Hellebeck, collectors of the aids of the crown, rendered an account of eight marks for four knights fees of John de Veteripont for his barony of Weſtmorland; of four marks for two knights fees of William de Lancaſtre for his barony of Kendale; of two marks for one knights fee of Ralph de Aincourt and Patrick ſon of Thomas of the ſaid barony of Kendale; of four ſhillings for the tenth part and twentieth part of one knight's fee of Roger de Lancaſtre of the ſame; and of ſeveral other ſmall ſhares of knights fees in ſeveral hands parcelled out in the ſaid barony of Kendale.

The ſaid John de Veteripont ſold off ſome part of the lands of the barony of Weſtmorland.

He married Sibilla daughter of William Ferrars earl of Derby, and by her had iſſue a ſon *Robert*. He died young, after he had been about 12 or 14 years lord of Weſtmorland, about the 26th year of king Henry the third.

His widow Sibilla was married afterwards to Francis de Bohune, lord of Midhurſt in Suſſex, who founded Cowdry-houſe there.

ROBERT DE VETERIPONT, ſon and heir of John, was very young at his father's death, and conſequently was a long time ward to the king, and in the cuſtody of the prior of Carliſle; who ſuffered great waſte to be made in his eſtate, his houſes at Appleby and other places to go to decay, his game to be deſtroyed, and his woods cut down; as appears by an inquiſition thereof taken at that time.

He married Iſabella Fitz Peter, ſecond ſiſter and afterwards one of the coheirs of Richard ſon of John Fitz Geofrey ſon of Geofrey Fitz Peter, baron of Berkhamſtead, and chief juſtice of England.

This Robert, after he came of full years, was one of thoſe who ſided with Montfort earl of Leiceſter and Humphrey de Bohun and other lords barons againſt king Henry the third. He died of the wounds he had received

in

in the battle of Lewes in Suffex or that of Evefham in Worcefterfhire. And after his death, the king feized all his lands, but afterwards reftored them to his children. For the faid king, at the interceffion of Edward his fon, by letters dated at Oxford, Apr. 26, in the 50th year of his reign, remitted to *Ifabella* and *Ivetta*, daughters and heirs of Robert de Veteripont deceafed, who held of the king *in capite*, the trefpafs which the faid Robert committed by adhering to Simon de Montford heretofore earl of Leicefter and his fautors the king's enemies; fo that the faid *Ifabella* and *Ivetta* be not troubled nor molefted by any action to be brought by the king in refpect of the lands and tenements defcended to them from the faid Robert: Yet fo, that if it fhall happen that the faid *Ifabella* and *Ivetta* fhall die without heirs of their bodies, the faid lands and tenements fhall remain to the king for the forfeiture of the faid Robert.—Upon this Sir Matthew Hale obferves, that there was no attainder in this cafe, and confequently that this was not a reftitution, but a pardon of a feizure, which was ufually made in the faid times in fuch cafes, as well after the death, as in the life-time of the offender. So that now *Ifabella* and *Ivetta* were feifed by force of the eftate granted to their great grandfather Robert.

[Note, This is the only record wherein we have found the younger daughter called by the name of *Ivetta*; elfewhere, fhe is called *Idonea.*]

When the wife of this laft Robert died, is not known; but probably before him.

The elder daughter *Ifabella* was not much above ten years of age at the death of her father; and the other daughter *Idonea* was fix or feven years younger. So that by reafon of their non-age the king had them in wardfhip, and committed them to the cuftody of two great men *Roger de Clifford* of Clifford-caftle in Herefordfhire, and *Roger de Laybourne* of the county of Kent; who married them, after they became of proper age, to their two fons and heirs, *Roger de Clifford*, and *Roger de Leybourne*.

In the 51 Hen. 3. there was an agreement between the two Rogers the guardians, touching a partition to be made between them. And afterwards, Roger de Clifford the father having married Ifabella to Roger his eldeft fon, they came to a new partition or agreement, not much differing from the former. By which, Roger de Clifford and Ifabella his wife were to have the manor of Brougham; a moiety of the manors of Merton, Appleby, Winton, and Burgh; a moiety of the forefts of Whinfell and Mallerftang; three parts of the manor of Meburn Regis; and a moiety of the profits of the fheriffwick: and Idonea was to have the caftle of Burgh; a moiety of the manors of Merton, Appleby, Winton, and Burgh; the manor of Kirkby Stephen; the caftle of Mallerftang; a fourth part of the manor of Meburn Regis; a moiety of the forefts of Whinfell and Mallerftang; and a moiety of the profits of the fheriffwick. All which appears by the inquifitions after the death of the two Rogers the hufbands, the one in the eleventh, and the other in the twelfth years of king Edward the firft *.

* Dugd. MS.

The two sisters being then become widows, it is said that Isabella the elder sate personally in court and executed the office of sheriff. But the *profits* of the sheriffwick, it is evident from the above inquisitions, were divided between the two sisters, and the office during their lives was generally executed by an under-sheriff. Nevertheless Isabella, as the elder sister, claimed the sole right of appointing the under-sheriff; which Idonea contested: and it ended in a compromise, that Isabella should present, and Idonea should approve. Thus, in Michaelmass term, 15 Ed. 1. Isabella de Clifford sheriffess of Westmorland presented to the barons of the exchequer Robert Morevill her under-sheriff by her letters patent which the said Robert produced before the said barons; who was admitted, and took the oath faithfully to execute his office, and *to answer to her and Idonea her sister parcener of the inheritance.*

And in the Michaelmass term in the 18th year of the said king:—Whereas Isabella de Clifford, eldest daughter and coheir of Robert de Veteripont heretofore sheriff of Westmorland in fee, to whom belongeth the office of sheriff of Westmorland according to an ordinance before the barons of the exchequer by common assent made between the said Isabella and Idonea her sister, hath presented to the barons Gilbert de Brundesheved to do for the said Isabella what belongeth to the said office; and in the same ordinance it is contained, that the said Idonea ought to consent to such presentation made or to be made by the said Isabella her sister: the king, for that it hath not appeared that the said Idonea hath consented to such presentation, and that the said Idonea may not be prejudiced in this behalf, hath deferred for this time to take the oath of the said Gilbert for the faithful execution of his office. And day is given till the octaves of St. Hilary next following.

And in Michaelmass term in the 23d year of the said king, Isabella being then dead, her son Robert de Clifford presented Ralph de Manneby, requesting him to be admitted; and the said Robert, being demanded what he had to say concerning Idonea younger daughter and coheir of Robert de Veteripont heretofore sheriff of Westmorland in fee, with respect to her consent to the presentation aforesaid, who ought to consent to the same according to a composition heretofore made between the said Isabella and Idonea, said, that he had the letters patent of the said Idonea, giving her consent, which he produced in court; *viz.* "To the venerable men and discreet lords the treasurer "and barons of the exchequer of our lord the king, Idonea de Leyburne "wisheth health in the lord: Know ye, that whereas Robert de Clifford and "I are sheriffs of Westmorland in fee, and to him belongeth the presentation "of an under-sheriff of the same county, and to me the assent, (as in a certain "composition between Isabella de Clifford mother of the said Robert whose "heir he is and me some time ago in the same exchequer made more fully is "contained) I have assented in my beloved in Christ Ralph de Manneby, so "that the same Ralph may be under-sheriff thereof under the said Robert and "me, so long as it shall please us. In witness whereof, I send unto you "these my letters patent. Dated at Kymbreworth in the county of York, "on the Lord's day next after the feast of St. Michael the apostle in the 23d

 "year

" year of the reign of our lord Edward the king." And thereupon the said Ralph was admitted and took the oath in that behalf accustomed *.

The said *Isabella* survived her husband about eight years, and never married again. *Idonea* lived many years after, and married to her second husband John de Crombwell of a Northumberland family, but died without issue. After whose decease the whole Veteripont inheritance became vested in the heirs of *Isabella* by her husband *Roger de Clifford* aforesaid, whose family therefore we proceed next to deduce.

He was descended of a noble family of the *Cliffords* of Clifford-castle in the county of Hereford; which had its name from being placed on a rock or *cliff*, near a *ford* upon the river Wye.

Before their coming to Clifford-castle, the surname of this family was *Pons*, and they were of Norman extraction. For this Roger who married Isabella was descended of Roger second son of Walter de Clifford and Margaret de Tony his wife, daughter and heir of Ralph de Tony lord of Clifford-castle (with whom he had the said castle); which Walter, who was the first that assumed the surname *de Clifford*, was son to *Richard Fitz Pons*, son of William earl of Argues in Normandy, second son of Richard duke of Normandy surnamed *Ponz*.

This Walter de Clifford was father of the fair but unfortunate *Rosamond*, whose tomb is to be seen at Godstow in Oxfordshire, to which place her father became a benefactor after her decease. And from her descended (by king Henry the second) the family of the Longspees earls of Salisbury; the last of which name, to wit, William grandson of the first earl, married Maud daughter and sole heir of Walter de Clifford, grandson of the first Walter, father of the said Rosamond; and they had only a daughter, whose name was Margaret. So that this match put a period to both these families of Clifford and Longspee in the direct male line.

Roger, younger brother of the said last Walter, married Sibilla daughter and heir of Robert de Ewias, lord and baron of Ewias-castle in Herefordshire, and widow of lord Robert Tregos. They had issue *Roger* of whom we speak, who married *Isabella de Veteripont* as aforesaid. And here beginneth the

1st Generation of the Cliffords, in Westmorland.

The first of the name of Clifford, that came to be seated in Westmorland, was ROGER DE CLIFFORD surnamed the younger, by reason of his father (whose name also was Roger) being cotemporary with him; for he outlived his son five years.

* All this concerning the sheriffwick was transcribed by Mr. Machel from the copies of records in Sir William Dugdale's collection: Which records it is probable had not occurred to the compilers of the countess of Pembroke's memoirs; notwithstanding that all the public offices seem to have been searched with great diligence by the order and at the expence of the said countess. What here follows, concerning the Cliffords, is taken chiefly from the said valuable memoirs.

Both

Both he and his father were chief commanders, for 20 years together, in the wars of England, Ireland, and France, in the reigns of king Henry the third and Edward the first.

His paternal inheritance was the manor of Temedbury, which is part in Worcestershire and part in Herefordshire; but his estate was largely augmented by the donation of king Hen. 3. who gave to this Roger the younger, in the 48th year of his reign, 100 marks in land, with the appurtenances, in the vale of Monmouth, for the service of one knight's fee. His paternal estate of Temedbury continued in the family till the reign of queen Elizabeth, when it was sold by Henry lord Clifford. The other estate, in the vale of Monmouth, was given back to the crown in exchange for Skipton-castle.

But the greatest advancement of estate and honour was brought unto him by the marriage of his wife, namely, a moiety of the whole Veteripont estate as above set forth and described.

He built the greatest part of Brougham-castle, and over the inner door placed this inscription, "This made Roger:" which, by reason of the ambiguity, caused some to question whether it was to be understood from thence that Roger made the castle, or the castle made him, that is, augmented his estate by that large accession of fortune which came to him by his wife.

He was slain at the age of 40, in the isle of Anglesey, in the king's service against the Welch.

2d Generation.

ROBERT DE CLIFFORD, son and heir of Roger and Isabella, was about eight years of age at his father's death.

In the 20 Ed. 1. before Hugh Cressingham and his associates, justices itinerant at Appleby, the king demanded against Idonea de Layburne, 1600 acres of wood and 1000 acres of pasture in Kirkby Stephen and Burgham, the castle of Burgh, the manors of Appleby, Meburn Regis, and other places; and set forth seisin thereof in king Henry the second. She alledged, that Robert de Veteripont her ancestor died seised of the premisses, and they descended to her and Robert de Clifford within age: She prayed aid of him, and that for his non-age the plea might demur. The truth of the allegation was found by the jury, and thereupon the plea stayed.—Hereupon Sir Matthew Hale observes, that this no way impeached the title; nothing being more common in eyre, than when they found at any time a seisin in the crown, to put in informations of *Quo warranto* to make the tenants set forth their title.

In the same eyre, an information of *Quo warranto* was presented against the same Idonea, to shew by what right she claimeth to have free chase in Newbiggin, Milneburne, Kirkeby Thore, Merton, Crakenthorp, Appleby, Langeton, Morton, Helton, Wardecop, Sandford, Harcla, and Nateby; and free warren in all her demesne lands of Appleby, Merton, King's Meburne, Kyrkeby Stephan, Langeton, Ormesheved, Great Askeby, Little Askeby, Tebay, Soulby, Nateby, Sandford, Harcla, Kabergh, Wateby, Crosseby Gerard, Dryebeck, Great Musegrave, Little Musegrave, Morton, Helton, Overton, Bruham, Morland, Askham, Lowther, Meburne Maud, Kyrkeby Thore, Wynanderwath, Clifton, Crakenthorp, Hepp, Crosbyravenswart, Clyburne, Milneburn, Newbiggin, Helton Flechan, Rossegill, Bampton Patrick, Querton, Smerdale, Hellebeck, Warthecop, and Colleby; and the assize of ale, and weyf in the vills aforesaid; which belong to the crown and dignity of the king; without the licence of the said king and his progenitors. And Idonea cometh and saith, that she claimeth to have free chase as in the writ is contained; and free warren in Appelby, Merton, King's Meburne, Kyrkeby Stephan, and Langeton, but not in the other vills. Also she claimeth to have the assize of ale and weyf in Merton, King's Meburne, Kyrkeby Stephan, and the moiety of the vill of Overton; except in the lands of the abbot of St. Mary's York. And as to the other vills, she claimeth to have the aforesaid liberties in common with Robert son and heir of Isabella sister of the said Idonea, of the inheritance of Robert de Vespunt, father of the said Idonea and grandfather of the said Robert son of Isabella, whose heirs they are. Which Robert de Vespunt died seised of the aforesaid tenements which the said Idonea and Robert son of Isabella now hold; and of the aforesaid liberties in like manner, as appurtenant and annexed to the aforesaid tenements. Which Robert son of Isabella is under age, without whom she cannot answer. And the jurors find, that the said Robert de Vespunt the ancestor died seised of the aforesaid liberties, and that the said Idonea hath not seised any of the same as of her own proper fee, and that Robert son of the aforesaid Isabella is under age. Therefore let the plea remain till his full age.

This Robert de Clifford is said to have been the greatest man of all this family, being of a most martial and heroic spirit. In the 25 Ed. 1. when he was about 23 years of age, he was made the king's captain, and keeper of the marches in the north towards Scotland, and made several inroads into that kingdom. In the 26th of the said king, he was summoned to come with his horse and arms to Carlisle against the Scots.

He was one of the four guardians appointed by king Edward the first, for Edward his son and successor: And was justice of the king's forests on the north of Trent.

He was made admiral of England in the first year of Edward the second; and lord marcher also about the same time: And in respect of his great and laudable service, had the honour of Skipton castle in Craven in Yorkshire bestowed upon him, at first for life, and afterwards (in consideration of giving back to the crown the lands above mentioned in the vale of Monmouth) to him and his heirs for ever. The confirmation of the grant bears date Sept. 7. in the 4 Ed. 2.

He married Maud de Clare, daughter of Thomas de Clare, younger brother of Gilbert de Clare earl of Gloucester and Hereford, whose wife was Johan de Acres, one of the daughters of king Edward the first. The said Gilbert dying without issue, Maud became one of his coheirs.

This lord Robert was slain at the battle of Bannocks-burn or Striveling in Scotland, on the 24th of June 1314, being on a Sunday, in the 7 Ed. 2. in the

the 40th year of his age. His body was ſent to king Edward at Berwick, but where it was buried is not certainly known.

By agreement with his aunt Idonea and her ſecond huſband, this Robert enjoyed the whole Weſtmorland eſtate. And what that was, appears fully by the inquiſition taken after his death, which is the moſt compleat of any of the inquiſitions *poſt mortem* of the Clifford family. The jurors find, firſt of all, what he held of the king *in capite*, *viz.* the barony of Weſtmorland by the ſervice of four knights fees, ſetting forth the particulars, at Appleby, Burgh, Stanemore, Brough Sowerby, Winton, Mallerſtang, Langton, Brougham, Temple Sowerby, and Kirkby Thore; ſpecifying the quantities and quality of the demeſne lands, and of what value; meſſuages, cottages, ſervices of tenants, and the like: Next, they ſet forth the ſeveral free tenants who held (as meſne lords) under him by the ſervice of cornage, at Helbeck, Aſcham, Kaber, Hartley, Great Muſgrave, Little Muſgrave, Murton, Soulby, Sandford, Rookby, Warcop, Wateby, Orton, Croſby Gerard, Helton Bacon, Helton Flechan, Clifton, Brougham, Dufton, Yanewith, Bolton, Brampton, Knock, Clibburn, Colby, Hoff, Ormſhead, Newbiggin, Milburn, Kirkby Thore, Crackenthorp, Kirkber, Lowther, Meaburn Maud, Whale, Burton, Croſby Ravenſworth, Nateby, Shap, Knipe, Bampton, Aſby, Bretherdale, and Wharton; with the advowſons of Kirkby Thore, Marton, and Brougham. All which are hereafter particularly ſet forth in their reſpective places. The ſum total of the cornage amounted to 27 *l* 15 *s* 9 *d*. The wardſhips alſo, when they ſhould happen, were reſpectively valued.

The lady Maud outlived her huſband, and married again about four years after to one Robert de Wells, and died in the firſt year of king Edward the third.

The iſſue which ſhe had to lord Robert de Clifford were,

1. *Roger*, who ſucceeded his father.

2. *Robert*, who ſucceeded his brother Roger.

3. *Idonea de Clifford*, who was married to Henry lord Piercy, and by him had iſſue that Henry lord Piercy who married Mary daughter of Henry Plantagenet earl of Lancaſter, and had iſſue by her Henry lord Piercy firſt earl of Northumberland.

3*d Generation.*

ROGER DE CLIFFORD, ſon and heir of Robert, was about 15 years of age at his father's death. He was attainted of treaſon in the 15 Ed. 2. (being then about 23 years of age) for adhering to Thomas earl of Lancaſter.

And during the time of his eſtate being in the king's hands, there is a writ in the 19 Ed. 2. to the conſtable of the king's caſtle at Appleby, to pay four marks yearly out of his cornage or horngelt to Shap abbey, which abbey had been endowed therewith by Robert ſon of John de Veteripont; which ſeems to have been then behind and unpaid, ſince the forfeiture of Roger aforeſaid.

And the king granted to Sir Andrew de Harclay the caſtles and manors of Brougham, Mallerſtang, King's Meaburne, Kirkby Stephen, and Langeton, with

with the wood of Whynnefeld, together with the sheriffwick; reserving to himself the cornage*. Which being again forfeited by Sir Andrew, the same, together with the rest of the estate, lands, and honours were restored to the said Roger by king Edward the third in the first year of his reign. But he enjoyed them not above a month, until he died.

He was never married; so that his brother Robert succeeded to his honours and estate.

He had some illegitimate children by one Julian of the Bower; for whom he built a little house hard by Whinfell, which still bears her name.

ROBERT DE CLIFFORD, second son of Robert, succeeded his brother Roger. This Robert received a great addition to his estate by the death of his great aunt Idonea de Veteripont, who had been married, as is aforesaid, to Roger de Layburne (to whom she had issue a son *John*, who died an infant); and after that, to John de Crombwell, to whom she had no issue. She died in a good old age, about the 8th year of king Edward the third, after having survived her father about 70 years. By whose death the estate of the Veteriponts, which had been divided between the two sisters for want of male issue, became again united in the same family.

This Robert lived for the most part a country life; no martial atchievements being recorded of him, further than that he accompanied the earl of Warwick and other lords with an army into Scotland.

He married Isabella de Berkeley, daughter of Maurice lord Berkeley, of Berkeley-castle in Gloucestershire: And had for her portion 1000*l* and 50 marks, with a gown of scarlet cloth having a cape furred with the best miniver; and for the honour of the bride, her brother the lord Berkeley and his lady were attired in the like apparel. The bride-saddle cost 5*l* (that is about 50*l*, according to the present diminished value of the coin). All the lands of Skipton, and a great part of the lands in Westmorland, were settled upon her by way of jointure.

He died, May 20, in the 18 Ed. 3. in the 39th year of his age or thereabouts, having possessed his estate about 17 years; and was buried in Shap abbey, as most likely several of his ancestors had been before.

His wife survived him; and married again, about two or three † years after his decease to Sir Thomas Musgrave knight, whom she left surviving.

The issue which lord Robert had by his said wife were,

1. *Robert*, his eldest son and heir.

* 2 Dugd. Bar. 97.

† So say the countess of Pembroke's Memoirs. But here seems to be a small mistake (not very material) concerning the time of the said Isabella's widowhood. For there is an account of a fine paid into the exchequer on the 9th of June, in the 19th of Edward the third, of 200*l*, by Thomas de Musgrave, for the trespass which he committed in marrying Isabella who had been the wife of Robert de Clifford. (*Dugd. MS.*)—The former husband died the 20th of May, and the fine was paid into the exchequer within a little more than a year after, and the marriage must have been some time before the payment of the fine. So that it is most probable that she married *intra annum luctus* (within the year of mourning); which by the civil law, then much in use in England, it was not lawful to do, without a special dispensation from the prince.

2. *Roger*, who succeeded his brother Robert.

3. *Thomas*; from whom descended Richard de Clifford, who was bishop of Worcester, and afterwards of London.

4th Generation.

ROBERT lord CLIFFORD, son of Robert and Isabella de Berkeley, was 13 years and 6 months old at the death of his father, and consequently was ward to the king 7 years and 6 months. And notwithstanding his being so young, he was married before his father's death, to Euphemia one of the daughters of Ralph de Nevill lord of Middleham-castle in Yorkshire, and sister of Ralph de Nevill the first of that family who was created earl of Westmorland.

He served king Edward the third in his wars in France, and was with the Black Prince in the battle of Cressy, when he was but 16 years of age.

The said king by his letters patent granted to this Robert, for his good and laudable service, 12*l* 14*s* 8½*d* of lands which were Christopher Seaton's, the king's enemy, in Cumberland.

He had the least estate of any of the lords Cliffords either before or after him, by reason that his mother had all the lands in Skipton, and great part of the lands in Westmorland in her jointure during his life, and she outlived him two months.

He died, in France as is supposed, about the 32d year of his age, without any issue.

His widow was afterwards married to Sir Walter Hazlerton, and died in the 18 Ric. 2.

ROGER DE CLIFFORD second son of lord Robert and Isabella de Berkeley, was accounted one of the wisest men of his time. He was a man of much gallantry and valour, being often in the wars both in France and Scotland; particularly, in that remarkable sea voyage of the earl of Arundel, when he transported a great army to assist the duke of Britanny against the French king. He was a lover of building, and took great care to repair the ancient castles, the seats of his ancestors.

In Michaelmass term, 3 Ric. 2. he presented to the treasurer and barons of the exchequer William de Lancastre (baron of Kendal) to be his under-sheriff, during his pleasure. Whereupon a mandate was issued to the abbot of Shap to administer to him the oath of office, and notify the same to William de Warthecop the late under-sheriff, requiring him to deliver over to the said William de Lancastre by indenture the writs and other things belonging to the said office.

One Robert de Herle, knight, released and quit-claimed to this Roger, his heirs and assigns, all his right and claim in one messuage and tenement in Fleet-street, next to St. Dunstan's church, which is now one of the inns of chancery, and still called by the name of Clifford's Inn.

He

He married Maud de Beauchamp, daughter of Thomas earl of Warwick, by Katherine his wife, who was daughter of Roger Mortimer earl of March.

He died in peace at home, which few of his anceftors or fucceffors did, in the 15 Ric. 2. juft 100 years after the death of his great grandmother Ifabella de Veteripont, in the 57th year of his age.

His wife died in the 4 Hen. 4. having lived his widow about 12 years.

They left iffue,

1. *Thomas*, their eldeft fon and heir.

2. Sir *William Clifford*, governor of Berwick; who married Anne daughter and coheir of Thomas lord Bardolph, and died without iffue.

3. Sir *Lewis Clifford*, who in the 47 Ed. 3. accompanied the duke of Lancafter into France. He was chofen one of the knights of the garter. In the 9 Ric. 2. he was commander in chief of the city of Carlifle, when the Scots and French attacked it, which he valiantly defended, and forced them to retire. The faid duke of Lancafter was a favourer of the doctrines of Wicliff, which induced feveral of the followers of that duke to efpoufe thofe doctrines. Amongft whom was this Sir Lewis Clifford: But he afterwards renounced the fame, and confeffed his error to the archbifhop of Canterbury. And this explains fome remarkable paffages in his will, the probate whereof bears date Dec. 5, 1404. "The fevententhe day of September, the yere of our lord "Jefu Chrift a thoufand foure hundred and foure, I Lowys Clyfforth, fals and "traytor to my Lord God and to all the bleffed company of hevene, and un-"worthi to be clepyd a Chriften man, make and ordeine my teftament and "my laft will in this manere. At the begynning I moft unworthi and Goddis "traytor recommaunde my wrechid and fynfule foule hooly to the grace and "to the grete mercy of the bleffed trynytie, and my wrechid careyne to be "beryed in the ferthest corner of the chirche-zerd, in which pariche my "wrechid foule departeth fro my body. And I prey and charge my furvivors "and myne executors, as they wollen anfwere to fore God, and as all myne "hoole truft in this matere is in him, that on my ftinking careyne be neyther "leyd clothe of gold, ne of filke, but a black clothe, and a taper at myne "hed, and another at my fete, ne ftone ne other thing, whereby eny man "may witt where my ftynkyng careyne liggeth. And to that chirche do "myne executors all thingis, which owen duly in fuch caas to be don, with-"out eny more coft faaf to pore men. And alfo I prey my furvivors and "myne executors, that eny dette that eny man kan axe me by true title, that "hit be payd. And yf eny man kan trewly fay, that I have do hym eny harme "in body or in good, that ye make largely his gree, whyles the goodys wole "ftreeche. And I wole alfo, that none of myne executors meddle or mynyftre "eny thinge of my goodys, withoutyn avyfe and confent of my furvivors or "fum of hem. I bequethe to Sire Phylype la Vache knight my maffe book "and my porhoos, and my book of tribulacion to my daughter his wyf."— All the reft of the will is in latin, in which he gives the refidue of his goods to Phylype la Vache, John Cheynee, and Thomas Clanvow, knights; and conftitutes

conſtitutes executors John Andrew, John Carleton, Walter Gaytone, and Thomas Barbowe *.

From all which circumſtances put together, it ſeems not improbable that the above recited Engliſh part was dictated by the archbiſhop by way of penance for his (ſuppoſed) hereſy. And no doubt care would be taken after his death, that the ſame (for the example ſake) ſhould be ſufficiently made public.

This Lewis was anceſtor of the preſent lord Clifford of Chudleigh in Devonſhire.

4. *Margaret*; married to Sir John Melton.

5th Generation.

THOMAS, ſon and heir of Roger, was about 26 years of age at the death of his father. In his youth, he was much at court, and in great favour with king Richard the ſecond, and ſomewhat wild and extravagant; for he was one of thoſe that were baniſhed the court by authority of parliament in the year 1387.

He married Elizabeth Roſs, daughter of Thomas lord Roſs of Hamlake-caſtle in Yorkſhire.

He went with Thomas of Woodſtock, duke of Glouceſter, into the country of Spruce in Germany, againſt the infidels; where he was ſlain, on the 4th of October 1393, in the 17 Ric. 2. In which year his wife's father died in the city of Paphos in the iſle of Cyprus, as he was returning from the holy land.

She outlived her huſband about 31 years, remaining a widow.

They had iſſue,

1. *John*, who ſucceeded to the inheritance.

2. *Maud*; who was married, as ſecond wife, to Richard Plantagenet earl of Cambridge; which Richard was beheaded at Southampton in the 3d year of Hen. 6. and left no iſſue by her. But by his former wife, Anne Mortimer, he had iſſue Richard Plantagenet duke of York, which Richard was father to king Edward the fourth. This Maud lived to a very great age.

6th Generation.

JOHN, ſon and heir of Thomas, was ward to the king when only two years of age, by reaſon of the untimely death of his father.

On the 16th of November next after the ſaid Thomas's death, the king granted the ſheriffwick of Weſtmorland to his queen conſort; and the queen granted the ſame to Elizabeth mother of the ſaid John, with the king's conſent and confirmation †.

* Dugd. Bar. 341. † Dugd. MS.

This John when he grew up, was highly favoured (by reafon of his valour and good experience in martial affairs) by king Henry the fifth, by whom he was made knight of the garter. In that king's wars in France, the faid John was by articles between the faid king and him, to carry over a number of men at arms, to wit, 3 knights, 47 efquires, and 150 archers, one third of them on foot, and the reft on horfeback. To himfelf was allowed 4*s* a day, to the knights 2*s*, to the efquires 1*s*, and to the others 6*d*.

King Henry the fifth, at the coronation of his wife queen Katharine, who was daughter of Charles the fixth of France, honoured him with the office of butler at that folemnity.

He married Elizabeth Piercy, only daughter of Henry lord Piercy, furnamed Hotfpur, by Elizabeth Mortimer his wife; which Elizabeth Mortimer was daughter of Edmund Mortimer third earl of March, by Philippa Plantagenet fole daughter and heir of Lionel duke of Clarence.

This John lord Clifford was flain at the fiege of Meaux in France, by the quarrel (or nutt) of a crofs-bow, in the 10 Hen. 5. being of the age of 32 years or thereabouts.

His mother Elizabeth was then living; for the inquifition after his death finds, that he died poffeffed of the fheriffwick of Weftmorland, except a third part of the faid office, which his mother had in dower. But fhe died foon after.

His wife married again about four years after his death, to Ralph Nevil, fecond earl of Weftmorland, and had by him one fon only, which was John lord Nevil, who died before he came to be earl of Weftmorland, being flain at the battle of Towton-field in Yorkfhire. The misfortunes of the wars between the houfes of York and Lancafter fo purfued her, that in her time her grandfather the earl of Northumberland was beheaded, and her father flain in battle, her hufband the faid John lord Clifford was flain, and after her death her fon Thomas lord Clifford and her fon John lord Nevil were both flain, and fo was her grandfon John lord Clifford. She died in the 14 Hen. 6. and was buried at Staindrop in the county of Durham, where fome of the Nevil family lie interred.

The iffue which fhe had by John lord Clifford were as follows:

1. *Thomas*, the eldeft.

2. *Henry*, who died without iffue.

3. *Mary*, married to Sir Philip Wentworth, of a younger branch of the family of Wentworth Woodhoufe.

7th Generation.

THOMAS, fon and heir of John lord Clifford, was not much above feven years of age when he fucceeded to the inheritance (by reafon of the untimely death of his father, who was flain as aforefaid), and was in ward 13 years by reafon of his minority.

It

It is evident by Hollingshead, Stowe, and other chronicles and records, that this Thomas lord Clifford did brave service as a chief commander in the wars of France. At the assault of Poictiers, he and his men, it being then snow, cloathed themselves in white, and by that means surprized the town, about the year 1438, which he strongly defended in 1440, being the 18 Hen. 6. against the assaults of the French king, who endeavoured to retake it. He was also an eminent commander in the civil wars of that age in England. With much courage and activeness, he took part with Henry the sixth against Richard Plantagenet duke of York. In which wars also his young son John was a leading man and commander, for two or three years together during his father's life; whereupon Thomas was called Old lord Clifford, though he was then under 40 years of age.

He married Johanna daughter of Thomas lord Dacre of Gilsland by Philippa his wife; which Philippa was daughter of Ralph de Nevil first earl of Westmorland. She died before her husband.

He was slain in the first battle of St. Alban's in the 40th year of his age, where he died fighting in his sovereign's behalf, together with his uncle Henry Piercy second earl of Northumberland, May 22, 1455. And they were buried, together with a great many other persons of quality, in the abbey church there.

He left nine children; four sons, and five daughters.

1. *John*, the eldest son and heir.

2. *Roger*, who married the sister and heir of one of the Courtneys in Devonshire, and had one son; but the family in two or three descents became extinct in daughters.

3. *Robert*, who married one of the Berkeleys, who was then widow of one alderman Joscelin of London; by whom he had issue; and from them did lineally descend George Clifford of Lincolnshire, who married Ursula Digby. He left behind him a daughter, whose name was Ursula. This Robert was deeply engaged in Henry the seventh's time in the business concerning Perkin Warbeck.

4. *Thomas*, who was a brave man, and died aged in the reign of Hen. 7. having born many offices. He died without issue.

5. *Elizabeth*, who was the eldest daughter, and indeed the first child. She was married first to one Plompton, in Skipton castle, when she was but six or seven years of age; but he dying before she was twelve years of age, she was married to his second brother, by a dispensation from the pope, which is still to be seen in Skipton-castle.

6. *Maud*, married to Sir Thomas Harrington knight, and after his death to Sir Edward Dudley knight; to both of which husbands she had issue.

7. *Anne*, married first to Sir Richard Tempest knight, and after that to Sir Richard Conyers knight, to both of whom she had issue.

8. *Joan*, married to Sir Richard Musgrave of Hartley-castle knight, from whom the present Sir Philip Musgrave baronet is descended.

9. *Margaret*, married to one of the Carres of Lincolnshire.

8th Generation.

JOHN, at the death of his father, was 20 years and 23 weeks old; whereupon he became ward to the king for half a year and three weeks, although he had been a commander in the king's army for three years before that.

After his father's death, he continued active in the king's service in the civil wars, which were then very hot between the houses of York and Lancaster.

In Grafton's and Speed's account of those times it is recorded, that this John lord Clifford was one of the chief leaders of the queen's army in December 1460 (the king being then a prisoner), together with lord Nevil and lord Rosse and in effect all the northern nobility, at Wakefield battle; where the duke of York amongst many nobles was slain, with his young son the earl of Rutland, who fell in flight by the hands of lord Clifford, in part of revenge; for the earl's father had slain his. A deed which worthily blemished the author (saith Speed); but who (as he adds) can promise any thing temperate of himself in the heat of martial fury? chiefly, when it was resolved not to leave any branch of York line standing (for so one maketh this lord to speak *).—And the earl was no child, as some writers would have him, but able to bear arms, being 16 or 17 years of age, as is evident (say the countess of Pembroke's memoirs) from this, that he was next child to king Edward the fourth that his mother had by Richard duke of York, and that king was then 18 years of age: And for the small distance betwixt her children, see Austin Vincent in his book of Nobility, page 622; where he writes of them all, being 12 in number. The lord Clifford was then 25 years of age.

The said lord John was at the second battle of St. Albans, where king Henry the sixth was brought into his tent on the 17th of February, and met his wife there, with his son prince Edward, to his exceeding great joy. But it lasted not long; for on the 28th and 29th of March following, the latter of those days being Palm Sunday, was the great battle fought between Towton and Saxton in Yorkshire, where king Henry's party was totally overthrown, and this lord John slain, between Ferrybridge and Castleford by the river Aire,

* Grafton's account of this matter is thus: "While this battaile was in fighting, a priest called Sir Robert Aspall, chaplaine and scholemaster to the yong erle of Rutland, the second son to the above named duke of York, scarce of the age of 12 years, a fayre gentleman, and a maydenly person, perceiving that flight was more savegard than tariyng both for him and his master, secretly conveyed the erle out of the field, by the lord Cliffordes bande, toward the towne; but or he could enter into a house, he was by the sayde lord Clifforde espyed, folowed, and taken, and by reason of his apparell demanded what he was. The yong gentleman, dismayde, had not a word to speak, but kneeled on his knees cravyng mercy and desiring grace, both with holdying up his hands and making a dolorous countenance, for his speeche was gone for feare. Save him, said his chapleyn, for he is a prince's sonne, and paradventure may do you good hereafter. With that worde, the lord Clifforde marked him, and sayde, By God's blood, thy father slue mine, and so will I do thee and all thy kinne; and with that worde strake the erle to the hart with his dagger, and bad his chapleyn beare the erle's mother and brother worde what he had done and sayde. In this act, the lord Clifforde was accompted a tyraunt and no gentleman."

where

where he was feeking for a paffage; for having put off his gorget a little before, either through pain or heat, he was fhot into the throat with a headlefs arrow.

It is remarkable, that he, his father, and great-grandfather, all died in the wars; the two former beyond the feas, and the two latter at home.

His wife was Margaret Bromflett, by birth baronefs of Vefcy, and the firft who brought that title to the Cliffords. She was daughter and fole heir of Henry Bromflett, by Elinour daughter of lord Henry Fitz Hugh. Her father was created baron of Vefcy by king Hen. 6. or rather indeed reftored thereunto, for he had title by right of his mother from William lord Vefcy of Alnwick. Her paternal coat was, In a fhield Or, a plain crofs Sable. She outlived her faid hufband 32 years; for he was flain (as aforefaid) March 29, 1461, in the 26th year of his age, and interred with many other knights and gentlemen of quality to the number of 4 or 5000 perfons in a pit by the river Aire, near to the place where the battle was fought, where a chapel (now decayed) was built, and did for fome time remain their monument.

His widow was afterwards married to Sir Lancelot Threlkeld of Threlkeld in Cumberland, who proved a very kind hufband to her, and helped to conceal her two children, which fhe had by her faid former hufband the lord Clifford, from the fury of king Edward the fourth and the houfe of York, to which their father and grandfather had been very active and mortal enemies. She had feveral children to Sir Lancelot; one of whom named Anne was married to Sir Hugh Lowther of Lowther. She died at her own houfe of Loufbrough, Apr. 12, 1493; whofe monument remaineth in the church there to this day.

The iffue which the faid John lord Clifford had by the faid Margaret his wife were,

1. *Henry*, the eldeft.

2. *Richard*; who, together with his brother, was concealed by their mother; and for the more fecurity, fhe conveyed him over the feas; where he died young, in the Low Countries, without any iffue.

3. *Elizabeth*, married to Sir Robert Afke; from whom defcended the Afkes of Yorkfhire, and the lord Fairfax of Denton in the fame county *.

9th Generation.

HENRY, fon of John lord Clifford and Margaret his wife, was 7 years old or thereabouts at the death of his father. He was deprived of his lands and honours during the fpace of 24 years, from the firft year of Edward the fourth to the firft year of Henry the feventh. All which time he lived as a fhepherd, in Yorkfhire, or in Cumberland about Threlkeld where his father-in-law's eftate was, and fometimes in the borders of Scotland. During which time,

* The inquifition *poft mortem* of the faid John is very laconic and concife: The jurors find, That he was attainted of high treafon by virtue of an act of parliament in the 1 Ed. 4. That he died on Palm Sunday in that year; and held nothing in any county. (*Dugd.* & *S.*)

we

we find ſeveral grants of the Cliffords eſtates to divers perſons; and, amongſt the reſt, one to Richard duke of Glouceſter, who was afterwards king Richard the third. And the ſaid Richard, when king, granted the ſheriffwick to Sir Richard Ratcliffe during his life, for his good ſervices; the ſaid ſheriff to appoint an under-ſheriff yearly *.

But when king Henry the ſeventh obtained the crown, the good ſervices of the anceſtors of this Henry lord Clifford were called to remembrance, and he was reſtored (by an act of parliament made in the firſt year of the ſaid king Henry the ſeventh, intitled, "An act for Henry lord Clifford") to his eſtate and honours. Which act was the principal ground of the lady Anne Clifford's title to the ſame, in thoſe ſuits which were managed in her behalf during her infancy, againſt her uncle Francis lord Clifford earl of Cumberland.

From henceforth the ſaid Henry lord Clifford became baron of Weſtmorland, and hereditary ſheriff of the ſame, lord alſo of the honour of Skipton, and baron of Veſcy.

Before this time, he was not able to write any thing at all, by reaſon of his obſcurity and illiterate education. He now learned to write his name, but no more †. When called to parliament, he behaved nobly and wiſely; but otherwiſe came ſeldom at London or the court; and rather delighted to live in the country, where he repaired ſeveral of his caſtles which had gone to decay during the late troubles. He was about 31 years of age when he came to his eſtates, and enjoyed the ſame about 37 years.

He was twice married; firſt, to Anne daughter of Sir John St. John of Bletſo; which wife of his was couſin-german by the half blood to king Henry the ſeventh; for her father was half brother to Margaret counteſs of Richmond

* Denton.

† There is yet extant a grant under the ſignature of this Henry lord Clifford, which was found amongſt the evidences belonging to the lords of the manor of Ormeſhead, dated Nov. 4. in the 20 Hen. 7. whereby the ſaid Henry lord Clifford, Weſtmorland, and Veſcy, in conſideration of the releaſing by Robert Barton lord of the manor of Ormeſhead all right and title to an Intack called Luckmanflat, grants and releaſes to the ſaid Robert Barton and his heirs, all that ground, feeding, paſture, and common, from the ſaid Intack dike nuke over the ſtreet england ‡ Stanbarr leas dike, joining to a paſture at the head of Stanbarr gill, and from thence england the ſame to Ravenſtandale way, and over it ſtill england the outſide of Bradmyre, as the ſike deſcendeth from towards the Rutter unto a great ſtone lying without the dike, where the lands of the aforeſaid lord and the lands of the ſaid Robert and the Rutter bounders meet. In witneſs whereof, the ſaid lord patteth both his ſeal and *ſign manual* (thus):

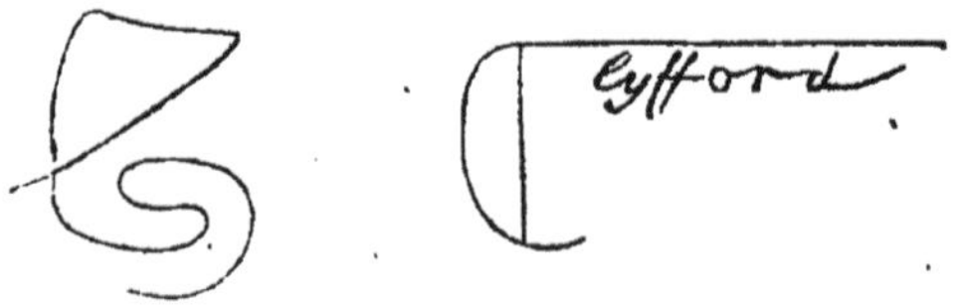

The letters *lyfford* (well written) ſeemingly by another hand.

‡ *England*, an old word, ſignifying *over againſt*.

and

and Derby, who was mother to the ſaid king Henry the ſeventh. She died in the 21ſt year of the ſaid king, and was buried in Skipton church vault, having been his wife 21 years.

He was married the ſecond time to Mrs. Florence Pudſey; who outlived him, and was afterwards married to Richard lord Grey, one of the younger ſons of Thomas the firſt lord marquis of Dorſet which was of that family.

He died in the 15 Hen. 8. in the 70th year of his age; and was buried either at the abbey of Shap, or at the abbey of Bolton in Craven in the county of York; for ſo he requeſted in his laſt will. But at which of them he was buried, is not certainly known.

The iſſue which he had by his two wives (beſides ſeveral illegitimate children) are as follows:

By his firſt wife Anne St. John,

1. *Henry*, who ſucceeded him.

2. *Thomas*, who married Lucy daughter of Sir Anthony Brown, who was governor of Berwick caſtle, and enjoyed divers other places of truſt, under king Hen. 8. The ſaid Thomas died without iſſue.

3. *Mabill*, who married William Fitz-William earl of Southampton; by whom he had iſſue two ſons, who lived to be men, but died without iſſue.

4. *Elianore*, married to one Markenfield.

5. *Anne*, married to Robert Medcalf, from whom a family of the Medcalfs is deſcended.

6. *Johan*, married to Sir Ralph Bowes; from whom deſcended the family of Bowes in Yorkſhire.

7. *Margaret*, married to Cuthbert ſon and heir of Sir Edward Ratcliffe of Corington in Northumberland. They had Derwentwater ſettled upon the marriage, and her portion was 500 *l.*

By Florence his ſecond wife, he had two or three ſons, who all of them died when they were very young. And a daughter *Dorothy*, married to Sir Hugh Lowther of Lowther; whoſe grandfather Sir Hugh was he who married Anne Threlkeld daughter of Sir Lancelot Threlkeld by the baroneſs Veſcy.

10*th Generation.*

HENRY, ſon and heir of Henry lord Clifford and Anne St. John his wife, was about 30 years of age when his father died. So that he was immediately thereupon poſſeſſed of his father's lands, titles, and honours; unto which were added, the earldom of Cumberland, and order of the garter. For about two years after his father's death, he was created earl of Cumberland by king Henry the eighth; and ſome years after, knight of the garter. He was alſo made by the ſame king lord preſident of the north parts of England, and many times lord warden of the marches. And he was employed in all the armies ſent into Scotland in the ſaid king's reign, and ever behaved himſelf nobly and valiantly. But the greateſt inſtance of that king's favour towards him was, the marrying his niece Elianor Brandon, daughter of his youngeſt ſiſter the ducheſs of Suf-

folk,

folk, to the eldeſt ſon of this ſame Henry lord Clifford. He was one of the moſt eminent lords of his time, for nobleneſs and gallantry; through which he waſted ſome part of his eſtate.

He was twice married; firſt, with Margaret Talbot eldeſt daughter of George earl of Shrewſbury the fourth of that family: But ſhe died very young, within two or three years after their marriage, and left no iſſue.

His ſecond wife was Margaret Piercy, daughter of Henry Piercy fifth earl of Northumberland. She had for her portion all thoſe lands in Craven, which are called Piercy's fee.

He died at Skipton caſtle in the 34 Hen. 8. in the 49th year of his age; having been poſſeſſed of his lands of inheritance about 19 years; and was buried with ſeveral of his anceſtors in Cliffords vault there.

Margaret his wife ſurvived him about two years, and died alſo at Skipton as is ſuppoſed, and was buried next unto him in the ſame vault.

They had iſſue,

1. *Henry*.

2. *Ingelram*; who married Anne, daughter and ſole heir of Sir Henry Ratcliffe, knight; and they had iſſue two daughters only, who died in their infancy.

3. *Katharine*, married to John lord Scroope of Bolton caſtle in Yorkſhire; and afterwards to Sir Richard Cholmeley.

4. *Maud*, married to Sir John Conyers, eldeſt ſon to lord Conyers of Hornby caſtle in Yorkſhire.

5. *Elizabeth*, married to Sir Chriſtopher Medcalf of Napper in Yorkſhire knight. She ſeems to have been unmarried at the time of her father's death: For by his will, which bears date only 20 days before his death, he orders, that the lady Elizabeth his daughter ſhall have, for her marriage preferment and neceſſary living, 1000 *l*, if ſhe be married to a man of honour, being an earl, or an earl's ſon and heir or heir apparent, his lands being unherited; and if ſhe be married to a baron, or a baron's ſon and heir apparent, having his lands not herited, 1000 marks; and if ſhe be married unto a knight, having his lands unherited, 800 marks.

6. *Jane*, married to Sir John Huddelſton of Millum knight.

11th Generation.

HENRY CLIFFORD, ſecond earl of Cumberland, ſon and heir of Henry the firſt earl by Margaret Piercy his wife, was in his father's lifetime made knight of the Bath, at the coronation of queen Anne of Bullen, being then in the 16th year of his age. And when he was about 25, by the death of his father he became poſſeſſor of his lands and honours. He waſted ſome part of his eſtate, and ſold the manor of Temedbury before mentioned, given by Walter the ſecond lord Clifford and Agnes de Condy his wife to their younger ſon Roger, after it had continued in the name and family 326 years. In the latter end of his time, he retired and lived a country life.

He

He was twice married: Firſt, to the lady Elinour Brandon, youngeſt daughter of Charles Brandon duke of Suffolk, by his wife Mary who was the French queen.

His ſecond wife was Anne, youngeſt daughter of William lord Dacre of Gilſland and Grayſtock, by Elizabeth Talbot daughter of George fourth earl of Shrewſbury. They were married in Kirk Oſwald caſtle, about the latter end of the reign of king Edward the ſixth. She outlived her huſband, and died at Skipton 11 years after, and was buried in the vault there, in the 48th year of her age; leaving this note of her good houſwifry behind her, that ſhe never came at London in all her life, but employed herſelf wholly in domeſtic affairs.

By his firſt wife he had ſeveral ſons, who all died in their infancy: And one daughter *Margaret*, married to Henry Stanley lord Strange, afterwards earl of Derby.

By his ſecond wife, the lady Anne Dacre, he had,

1. *George*, his elder ſon.

2. *Francis*; who was made knight of the Bath by king James the firſt, when his ſon Charles was made duke of York. By the death of his brother George without male iſſue, he ſucceeded to the title of earl of Cumberland. He married Griſſel Hughes daughter of Mr. Thomas Hughes of Uxbridge, and widow of Edward Nevill lord Abergavenny. By whom he had ſeveral children, (1) George, who died an infant. (2) Henry, who lived to be the fifth earl of Cumberland, the laſt heir male of the northern Cliffords; for though he had five children, three ſons and two daughters, yet they all died young, except one daughter Elizabeth married to Richard Boyle earl of Cork, and afterwards of Burlington. (3) Margaret, married to Sir Thomas Wentworth, afterwards earl of Strafford, who was beheaded in 1641. She was his firſt wife, and had no iſſue to him. (4) Frances, married to Sir Gervaſe Clifton.

3. *Frances*; who was married to Philip lord Wharton, and had ſeveral children to him. She died at Wharton-hall in 1592, and was buried in Kirkby Stephen church.

4. *Mary*, who died an infant.

5. *Elianore*, who alſo died unmarried about 14 or 15 years of age.

12th *Generation*.

GEORGE, the third earl of Cumberland, ſon and heir of Henry by his wife the lady Anne Dacre, was born in Brough caſtle in the laſt year of queen Mary. His father died before he was 12 years of age; ſo that he became ward to queen Elizabeth during his minority, which wardſhip ſhe beſtowed on Francis earl of Bedford, whoſe daughter he married.

He ſtudied ſome time at Oxford, under the tuition of Dr. Whitgift, afterwards archbiſhop of Canterbury. And here he obtained ſome knowledge in the arts, and eſpecially in mathematicks, which did not only incline him thereto, but rendered him more fit for maritime employment, in which he

 excelled.

excelled. For he undertook 11 or 12 expeditions; his first putting out being in 1587, with a design against the duke of Parma; the second against the Spanish armada in 1588; the third against the isles of Terceres and Azores, where he took the town of Fyall, being dangerously wounded in the assault. The rest were performed with equal valour and success. His last expedition was against St. John de Porto Rico, where he won the town, and returned victorious in 1598. He was a man of great quickness of wit, activity of body, and affable disposition. Queen Elizabeth made him knight of the garter; and he was her champion in all the tilting, from the 31st year of her reign till the time of her death. And in that he excelled all the nobles of his time. For he was so much addicted to tilting, horsecoursing, shooting, and other active (but expensive) exercises, that these recreations, next to his sea voyages, many of which were sustained and managed at his own proper cost, were the great occasion of his selling of lands; and he is said to have consumed more than any one of his ancestors besides. The armour which he wore is yet to be seen in Appleby castle.

He was one of the forty peers, who (together with five of the judges) were commissioned to try Mary queen of Scots; and after her attainder, was one of the four earls who were sent down to Fotheringay castle, to be present at the execution.

His wife was the lady Margaret Russel, youngest daughter of the earl of Bedford aforesaid, by Margaret his wife daughter of Sir John St. John baron of St. John of Bletso in Bedfordshire. She outlived her husband ten years, and died at Brougham castle, and was buried in Appleby church, where her stately monument remains to this day.

He died in 1605, in the 48th year of his age, and was buried in the vault at Skipton. Whither also afterwards his brother Francis's body was brought, and also the body of Henry son of the said Francis: Which Henry was the last earl of Cumberland, and the last heir male of this family of the Cliffords. And it is remarkable, that when the body of Henry was brought thither, there was but one vacancy left, so that he filled up the last space in that vault called Clifford's.

He had issue by his said wife,

1. *Francis*, who died about the age of five years.

2. *Robert*, who also died in his infancy.

3. *Anne*, married first to Richard Sackville lord Buckhurst, afterwards earl of Dorset; and afterwards to Philip Herbert earl of Pembroke and Montgomery.

And having thus no issue male surviving, the said George, for the preservation of his name and family, in the 33 Eliz. levied a fine, and cut off an intail of the estate which had been made by his father, and settled the same to himself and his wife for life, then to the heirs male of his body, then to his brother Francis and the heirs male of his body, in default of these to the heirs (general) of his own body, and in default of these to his own right heirs for ever.

For

For further assurance, in the 3 Ja. he executed a deed to corroborate the same.

And in the same year, by his will he devised the same to the purposes aforesaid; giving to his daughter, besides the said reversion, the sum of 15000*l* for her portion. He devised also the sheriffwick to his brother: which not being in the aforesaid intail, his brother took possession thereof during the widow's life.

13th Generation.

ANNE, sole daughter and heir of George earl of Cumberland, by his wife the lady Margaret Russel. Upon her father's death, she (by the advice and under the direction of her mother) contested the settlement; grounding her claim, on the intail by king John upon Robert de Veteripont and the heirs of his body by his then wife; on the like grant by king Edward the third to the two daughters of the second Robert upon the forfeiture by their father; and on the aforesaid act of parliament in the 1 Hen. 7.

Upon this, king James (who commonly made himself a party in any cause of considerable consequence depending in his courts either of law or equity) in order to strengthen the earl Francis's title, in the fifth year of his reign, granted to the said Francis, his heirs and assigns, to the effect following; to wit, "All our castles, demesnes, and manors, of Appleby and Burgh; and also the whole bailiwick or office of sheriff of the county of Westmorland, and the rents of the county of Westmorland aforesaid, and the services of all our tenants within the same county who do not hold of us by knight's service; and all and singular rights, jurisdictions, liberties, profits, commodities, advantages, emoluments, and hereditaments whatsoever, to the said office of sheriff or bailiwick belonging or appertaining: And all that whole estate whatsoever, which the said Francis's ancestors had held, in the counties of Westmorland and York. To hold by the service of six knights fees and an half." With all the usual non obstante's, and particularly with a non obstante of the act of parliament of the 23 Hen. 6. (which enacts, that no sheriff shall abide in his office above one year; with an exception, nevertheless, of such persons as had then an inheritance in the office.)

The king also took much pains to get himself made arbitrator of these differences.

During the course of the contention, the said Anne was married to her first husband the lord Buckhurst. This lord, together with her uncle and his son, agreed to accept of the king's arbitration; and the king took upon him to make an award, although the said Anne, when she was brought into his presence, utterly refused to submit to his arbitration. And his majesty's award (which was in her disfavour) was confirmed in the court of chancery. And judgment was given against her in the same year in the court at York for the northern parts. Her uncle obtained possession of the estate, and he and his son after him kept the same till the death of the said son as aforesaid without

 issue

issue male. By whose death, the said Anne became undeniably intitled, both as heir to her father, and as next also in the intail.

Her said husband died in the year 1624, in the 35th year of his age: who had issue by her (besides three sons who died very young) two daughters *Margaret* and *Isabella*; the latter of whom was married to James Compton earl of Northampton, to whom she had six children, who all died without issue, and most of them very young. So that after the death of *Isabella* and her children, *Margaret* remained sole heir of the Clifford family.

About six years after the death of her said first husband the lord Buckhurst (who at the time of his death was become earl of Dorset), the lady Anne married to her second husband Philip Herbert earl of Pembroke and Montgomery, and had to him only two sons, who died soon after they were born.

About this time, whilst earl Francis was in possession of the estate, a dispute happened about the cornage, commonly called nowtgelt, and the serjeant oats or bailiff corn. The tenants of the several manors denied to pay the same; and, supposing the same to be payable, they complained of divers grievances in the manner of collection. On the 23d of May 1634, (10 Car.) it was decreed by the lord keeper Coventry, That the said duties did of right belong to the said earl of Cumberland as lord of the fee and seigniory of Westmorland: but that, for prevention of abuses, the oats shall be gathered yearly between St. Andrew's day and Candlemass: That upon 8 or 10 days warning to be given to every town by the lord's bailiff for the time being, the same shall be brought to one place certain in the town, by the said bailiff likewise to be made known at the same time of warning, that the bailiff may know where to demand and expect the same: That such town as shall not have their proportion ready, shall within one month after bring them home to the said earl's officer, or otherwise the township so failing to be subject to a distress for the same, or the earl to take such other course for recovery thereof as he shall think fit: That the said oats shall be good and marketable according to the season of the year, not putting the worst and refuse upon the officer, but such as shall be of the better sort. And Sir John Lowther was desired to examine and certify concerning the measure; who having examined two old pecks, one containing 8, and the other 10 striked quarts, both of which had been paid upheaped (which was reckoned one third part more), he, to avoid uncertainty, recommended, and so it was decreed, that instead of the old peck upheaped, they should pay 13 quarts striked; and the nowtgeld to be paid in money as before *.

In

* The sums and quantities on each township or place agreed to by both parties were as follows: (Unto which are added here the pout-hens usually demanded and received by the land serjeant at the same time, which were not mentioned in the aforesaid dispute.)

	cornage.			oats.		
	l	*s*	*d*	bush.	pecks.	hens.
Appleby	0	2	0			
Asby Cotesforth	0	9	2	-	-	11
—— Grange	1	6	8			
—— Little	0	2	10	-	-	9

Asby

In the year 1649, died the lady Anne's fecond hufband, the aforefaid earl of Pembroke and Montgomery. She lived his widow about 27 years; all which

	cornage.			oats.		
	l	s	d	b.	p.	h.
Afhy Winderwath	1	0	8			16
Afkham	2	15	0	11	0	28
Bampton Patrick	0	17	2			25
——— Cundale	0	18	3			
Bolton	1	0	0			28
Bondgate						19
Brampton	1	0	0			13
Bretherdale	0	5	0			
Brough	0	9	0	27	0	9
Brougham	0	16	5			
Brown clofe	0	4	0			
Burton	0	13	4			7
Clibburn Harvey	0	8	10			19
——— Talebois	0	12	4			
Clifton	1	4	4			22
Colby	0	14	6			26
Crackenthorp	0	16	0			19
Crofby Gerard	0	8	6	55	0	
——— Ravenfworth	0	13	4	44	3	10
Croftormount	0	1	0			
Drybeck	0	17	6			12
Dufton	1	5	6			
Gilts						9
Hackthorp	0	3	2			13
Harberwain						6
Hartley	0	12	4			
Helbeck	0	10	0			
Helton Bacon	1	13	8			12
——— Flechan	0	3	4	16	1	
Kaber	1	4	4	63	0	12
Kirkber	0	2	0			
Kelleth	0	4	0			
King's Meaburn						30
Knipe				8	0	
Knock	0	3	4			21
Kirkby Thore	4	3	0			
Lowther and Whale	2	0	0			
Marton	0	8	6			15
Mauls Meburn	1	0	2	70	1	36
Melcanthorp	0	5	0			15
Milburn	5	5	8			
Morland	0	4	2			8
Murton	0	15	2			11
Mufgrave, Great	0	11	4			
——— Little	0	11	2	16	0	
Nateby	0	13	7	19	0	
Newbiggin	1	6	0			
Newby						22
Oddendale						7
Ormfide, Great	0	17	0			16
——— Little	0	3	4	12	0	6
Orton	0	5	2			

Prifedale

which time she employed in repairing her castles, which had gone to decay, or been ruinated in the civil wars; and in many other publick and private works of charity.

For a further account of this extraordinary person, it is thought proper to insert here the substance of a very curious manuscript written by one Mr. Sedgwick, intitled, "A summary or memorial of my own life, written by me, "to the honour and glory of God, and in a thankful commemoration of his "manifold goodness and mercies to me, in the whole course thereof."

"I was born at Capplethwaite in my father's house in Killington, the 10th "of January 1618. My father was then possessed of a competent estate in "land, of about 80 acres, lying between the old and new bridge, by the side "of the river Lune. He had also a considerable portion (in those times) "with my mother, viz. 320 *l*; she being one of the daughters of Mr. Tho-"mas Benson of Hugill in the barony of Kendal. But my father having "contracted large debts, particularly by suretiship (having paid 600 *l* on "that account for his brother in law), sold the estate of Capplethwaite for "about 1100 *l*, to Mr. John Ward of Rigmaden, he buying it for a younger "son of his.

	cornage.			oats.		
	l	*s*	*d*	b.	p.	h.
Prisedale *	0	7	0			
Raisbeck	0	5	8			
Rookby	0	3	1			
Rosgill	0	5	5	16	1	
Rounthwaite	0	1	8			
Sandford	0	19	4			17
Scattergate						9
Shap	0	5	5	61	1	
Sleagill	0	9	0			16
Smardale	0	13	6	15	0	
Sockbridge	0	1	11			
Soulby	0	14	4	63	0	
Sowerby (Brough)						28
Strickland, Great	0	3	6			
——— Little	0	6	8			13
Sunbiggin	0	4	0			
Tebay	0	9	4			
Thrimby	0	5	2			
Tirrel	0	1	2			
Warcop	1	3	6			19
Wateby	0	14	10	20	0	18
Wharton	0	6	0			
Wickerslack	0	2	6			8
Winder	0	5	0			
Winton	1	0	9			50
Yanewith	0	6	0			
Total of cornage	52	1	6	oats 517	3	hens 684

* There is no place of this name. So that either the name of the place hath been since changed, or the name is mistaken in the record.

"Capplethwaite

"Capplethwaite being fold, my father then bought a fmall eftate a mile "above Sedbergh; from whence I and my fecond brother went every day to "the fchool there, being then of great note and eminence, under Mr. Gil- "bert Nelfon the worthy fchoolmafter; who out of his love and affection to "me, when my father began to decay in his eftate, took me into his own "houfe, and gave me diet and lodging for a year and above, with other "fcholars then boarders there.

"A great honour I had for the memory of fo worthy a perfon; and though "God did not prolong his life till my coming into the north in 1652, yet I "had the means and opportunity, by the favour of my moft honoured lady "the countefs of Pembroke, to place his widow (then in a low condition) "mother of her ladyfhip's alms-houfe in Appleby, then newly built and en- "dowed by her; where fhe had a convenient chamber, a garden, and 8 *l* a "year, during her life; taking a daughter of hers at the fame time into her "fervice, from whence fhe was after well married.

"When I had fpent fome years at Sedbergh fchool, I was fent to St. John's "college in Cambridge, fubfizer to George Brathwaite of Warcop efquire, "fellow commoner of that college. My tutor was Mr. Thomas Fothergill" [who was born at Brounber in Ravenftondale, and was afterwards mafter of the faid college.]

Then he relates, how not being able to fupport himfelf at the univerfity any longer, he removed to London, where his father had got into fome fmall bufinefs; and after recounting feveral adventures there, the narration proceeds as follows:

"My good father, ftudying all ways and means to provide for me, God "put into his mind to make ufe of a letter which many years he had care- "fully kept, written from the lady Margaret countefs of Cumberland, to my "grandfather Mr. Jeffrey Sedgwick, giving him many thanks for his upright "dealing as a juror at York, in the great caufe there tried, between her "daughter then countefs of Dorfet, and Francis earl of Cumberland her "uncle; with which letter fhe alfo fent my faid grandfather half a buck, and "a gold ring, with this motto, *Truth is crowned.*

"My father one morning taking that letter and me along with him, went "to the court at Whitehall, to wait upon the faid countefs of Dorfet, then "countefs of Pembroke, Dorfet, and Montgomery, by her marriage with "Philip earl of Pembroke and Montgomery, then lord chamberlain of his "majefty's houfhold.

"As foon as that lady faw that letter of her dear mother, whom fhe loved "with an entire affection, fhe feemed very glad of a prefent opportunity fhe "then had to do me good. So fhe fent forthwith for one of her lord's fecre- "taries, whom fhe called coufin, who was then deftitute of a young clerk, "and immediately preferred me to him. And with him I continued five or "fix years very happily and contentedly.

"In the year 1639, the troubles in Scotland began; and the king's ma- "jefty raifed a gallant army againft them: And feveral of the great nobility "fupplied the king with money. Among the reft, the lord chamberlain ad-

" vanced twenty thousand pounds. And in further testimony of his forward-
" ness in the king's service, he then raised a regiment of 600 horse, being
" six troops compleat, for the guard of his majesty's person; consisting of
" the king's servants, and the servants of the noblemen and gentlemen volun-
" teers, his lordship's friends. The commanders of these six troops, being
" persons of great rank and quality, are fit to be remembered; *viz.* Philip
" earl of Pembroke and Montgomery, colonel; the earl of Caernarvon, his
" son-in-law; Philip lord Herbert, his eldest son; Sir Ralph Hopton, knight
" of the Bath, afterwards lord Hopton; Sir Bevil Greenvill, father of the
" now earl of Bath; Sir Foulke Hunkes, a Low Country colonel. Colonel
" Thomas Carew, deputy governor of the isle of Wight, was commissary
" and muster-master. And I was appointed by them to make their and their
" under-officers commissions, and to be the paymaster of the regiment.

" In the beginning of the long unhappy parliament in 1640, my master the secretary was chosen burgess of Salisbury; who thereupon quitted his relation to his lordship, and he was pleased to accept of my service in his place.

" I thought myself then in a very good condition. But by reason of a falling out between my lord and master the lord chamberlain and the lord Mowbray and Maltravers, in the house of peers; they were both sent prisoners to the Tower of London, there to remain during the pleasure of the two houses of parliament, where they continued eight days. And during my master's imprisonment, the king took away his chamberlain's staff. And shortly after, he retired into the country; where he kept a noble house, entertaining his friends, neighbours, and tenants, with great freedom. Then was I reduced only to the employment for his lordship's private affairs and estate, which notwithstanding was considerable. And thus I lived with him till the time of his death, which was in January 1649.

" Though he had 18000*l* a year, yet through the vast charge in keeping hounds, hawks, and hunting horses, his great hospitality, and other ways and means, he died 55000*l* in debt, which by the care of his honourable executors was all paid within four years time.

" In how noble and splendid a manner he lived, may in part appear from this; that his family in London was for the most part about 80, in the country double that number. And he was always attended by persons of good note and quality.

" He was second son of Henry Herbert earl of Pembroke and lord president of Wales. His mother was lady Mary Sidney, sister to the famous Sir Philip Sidney, author of the Arcadia.

" His father left him 10,000*l* in money, and 300*l* a year in quit rents. Upon his father's death, he applied himself to the court, where in two years time he had spent all his money. But by his pleasing king James in his hunting exercises, he got soon into great favour with him, so as that king in a short time heaped honours and riches upon him. He first knighted him; then he created him baron of Shurland; shortly after, earl of Montgomery, and lord chamberlain of his houshold; giving him 2000*l*

" a year lands in the isle of Sheppey; and Enfield-house, park, and chase, " worth as much more. And upon the death of his elder brother, he came " to the family inheritance of 14000*l* a year, besides 6000*l* a year more that " belonged to his brother's widow, which he held during her life, she being " a lunatic.

" This earl Philip could scarce either write or read; not that he wanted " good breeding and education, but he would never be brought to mind his " book, being addicted to all manner of sports and recreations.

" Yet this very person, upon the death of archbishop Laud, was chosen by " the university of Oxford for their chancellor. Strange, that an illiterate " man (as he was) should be elected with so general applause, and so unani- " mous a consent by them. And it was more strange, that in a few years " after, when he was sent by the parliament with some gentlemen, members " of the house of commons, as visitor of that university, they not only re- " fused to submit thereunto, but received him with all the contempt and de- " rision imaginable, and writ in red letters over the doors of the colleges and " schools, LORD HAVE MERCY UPON US, FOR WE ARE VISITED!—as is usual " in places infected with the plague.

" He was very temperate in eating and drinking, but much given to wo- " men, which caused a separation between him and his virtuous lady Anne " countess of Pembroke, several years before his death.

" His greatest delight was in hunting; lying every dry summer in the New " Forest in Hampshire (whereof he had the command under the king) six or " eight weeks together, hunting the stag daily, keeping 24 couple of hounds " always for that purpose.

" He was also an excellent bowler; keeping in his house one or two ser- " vants the best in that quality about London: so as he would oftentimes " make bowling matches for 500*l*, which for the most part he won.

" Upon his death, his eldest son Philip, then earl of Pembroke, was de- " sirous to have me continue with him in the same employment I had under " his father. So I staid.

" At my first coming to him, he became, or at least he counterfeited him- " self, a quaker. But I rather believe he was not really one, being assured, " that for several years he sent his majesty that now is, in his exile, 2000*l* a " year. However, he was of such a disposition, that he never minded his " own business, but shifted it off from time to time. So that after I had " been with him about two years, I grew weary of any longer attendance " upon him.

" I believe this earl wasted his estate; for though he lived but in a private " manner, no way comparable to his father, yet he lost great sums of money " at bowls and dice. One time, before I left him, he lost at Greenwich above " 300*l* in money, and his coach and six horses.

" About that time, Sir Thomas Bendish being to go ambassador leiger to " the court of the grand Seignor at Constantinople, I had some honourable " good friends that recommended me to attend upon him as secretary to the " embassy. But at this juncture of time, the countess dowager of Pembroke,

" being then at her castle of Skipton, and hearing of my intention, dissuaded " me by letters from so long a voyage, and invited me to come down to her, " to write all her post letters, make all her leases, and receive and pay all " her money, offering me a liberal allowance for the same. This course I " rather embraced, being near my friends, and the place of my nativity, " which all sorts of people love; rather than run the hazard perhaps of ending my life, among pagans and infidels in a foreign climate.

" So in August 1652, I came down to Skipton, where I began to do her " ladyship the best service I could. Where after I had continued to my great " contentment about four years, her ladyship then proposed to me her earnest " desire for me to go over sea, into France, Flanders, and the Low Countries, with her grandson Mr. John Tufton, since earl of Thanet deceased. " I was to take charge of him abroad some two years in those parts, and " to order his exercises and expences, for which she promised to give us good " allowance.

" I must confess I had no great inclination to it; but by reason of the manifold favours I had received from her, and the desire I had to see foreign " countries, I could not in gratitude deny her ladyship the best service I was " able to perform.

" According to her promise, she was pleased to assign us 400 *l* a year for " our expences, for Mr. Tufton, his man, a footman, and myself. Besides " 50*l* more for Mr. Tufton's cloaths yearly, and 20 *l* for my own. All which " money she took punctual order to be duly returned to us, by bills of exchange from London, to what place soever we were then at abroad."

Our author then proceeds to give an account of their travels. When they were at Utrecht, in the year 1656, he observes;

" At that time England being full of trouble, a great number of our English nobility and gentry were resident in that city. Some of the chief of " whom were Dr. Bramhall afterwards archbishop of Armagh and primate " of Ireland; Dr. Honeywood, now dean of Lincoln; Dr. Edward Martin, " master of Queen's college in Cambridge; Dr. Bargrave, whose father was " dean of Canterbury; William Howard lord Stafford, uncle to the duke of " Norfolk who was lately beheaded at London; lord Gerard of Lancashire; " lord Culpepper; lady Elizabeth Obrian, daughter of the earl of Inchiquin; " a daughter of the lord Berkeley; Sir Francis Coventry; Mr. Edward Russel, " brother to the earl of Bedford; Mr. John Digby, second son to the earl of " Bristol; Mr. William Paulett, eldest son to Edward lord Paulett; Sir Edward Brett and his lady; Dr. Creighton; a son of Sir George Carterett; " Sir Ralph Verney baronet; Sir John Denham; Sir William Swan and his " lady; Sir John Ogle and his lady; Sir William Juxon baronet, nephew and " heir to the archbishop of Canterbury; Sir Francis Mackworth baronet; Sir " John Holland and colonel Wheeler, two secluded members of the English " parliament; and captain Penruddock, brother to colonel Penruddock who " was beheaded for his rising in Wiltshire for the king.

" Also the latter year of our sojourning there, the duke of York came " thither *incognito*, with three or four servants, from the king his brother at

" Colein,

"Colein, in some disgust (as it was said); where after he had been private some "two days, the marquis of Ormond, the lord Craven, and John lord Berkeley came thither in quest of him, and to attend him back to his brother at "Coleine. As soon as it was publickly known that he was in the city, all "the English went to wait upon him and to kiss his hand; and amongst the "rest, myself had that honour. And that was the last time I saw his highness; whom God preserve."

After their return, with respect to his own particular circumstances, he proceeds as follows:

"Before my going over sea, my lady gave me a rent charge of 20*l* a year "for 21 years, and 50*l* in gold. At our return also 100*l* in money, and "another rent charge of 20*l* a year for 21 years, both which I enjoyed till "the expiration of those terms.

"After 18 years service with this good lady, she began to mind me of myself and my future well-being in the world; often repeating to me a verse "of Mr. Samuel Daniel the famous poet and historiographer, who had been "her instructer in her childhood and youth:

"To have some silly home I do desire,
"Loth still to warm me by another's fire.

"She further declared her noble intention to me, that when I met with some "small habitation, she would give me 200*l* towards the purchase, which she "punctually performed.

"Within a while God directed me to Collinfield, a small estate held under "queen Katherine, as part of her jointure, by a moderate rent and fine, "convenient for the church and market, freed from all assizes and sessions; "where by God's blessing I enjoy a quiet and retired life to my contentment; "having oftentimes the society of several of my worthy friends and neighbours from the town of Kendal; having lived here above 14 years at the "writing hereof," (*viz.* in December 1682.)

As to the aforesaid countess of Pembroke he says,—"Her father died "when she was about ten years of age, leaving her under the tuition of her "good mother, but her chief breeding was under her aunt the countess of "Warwick, chief lady of the bed-chamber to queen Elizabeth: Her instructer in her younger years being the learned Mr. Daniel the historiographer and poet.

"She was first married to Richard Sackville earl of Dorset, to whom she "had Thomas lord Buckhurst, who died young; and two daughters, Margaret married to John Tufton earl of Thanet, and Isabella married to James "Compton earl of Northampton.

"After the earl of Dorset's death, she continued a widow five years; having a large jointure of 3400*l* a year.

"In her first widowhood (as I have heard her say) she resolved, if God ordained a second marriage for her, never to have one that had children, and "was a courtier, a curser and swearer. And it was her fortune to light on "one with all these qualifications in the extreme.

" She was of an undaunted ſpirit, worthy the daughter of ſo gallant a father. " A high conteſt ſhe had with king James, who would have forced her " to accept of 10,000 *l* from the earl of Cumberland, and in lieu thereof to " paſs away all her right and future claim to the inheritance of her father. " This ſhe abſolutely refuſed to do, nor could be induced to it by any threats " or perſuaſions whatſoever.

" Her ſecond huſband the earl of Pembroke dying in the year 1649, ſhe " came down into the north, where ſhe continued till her death in 1675, be- " ing 26 years, in great honour and proſperity; a year or two in Yorkſhire, " and a year or two in Weſtmorland, to the great benefit of both counties, " expending not only the rents and fines ſhe had in theſe counties, but alſo " for the moſt part the rents of her two great jointures in the ſouth in Suſſex " and Kent.

" At her coming down, ſhe found five of her caſtles and the tower of Bar- " den demoliſhed and thrown down in the late unhappy wars: Skipton-caſtle, " that had been a ſtately building, ſcarce affording lodging for herſelf and " her family; ſo that ſhe was reſolved to build ſome lodging rooms in it, " notwithſtanding the malignancy of the times. Some gentlemen of that " neighbourhood, her friends and well-wiſhers, diſſuaded her from it; al- " ledging (and probably enough) that as faſt as ſhe built up Oliver Crom- " well would order it to be pulled down. She replied, If they do not take " my eſtate from me, as long as I have money or credit, I will repair my " houſes, though I were ſure to have them thrown down the next day. This " being reported to Oliver,—Nay, ſays he, let her build what ſhe will, ſhe " ſhall have no hindrance from me.

" Thereupon ſhe began with Skipton-caſtle, and in a year's time made it a " very convenient houſe, though not ſo ſtately and large as it was before it " was demoliſhed. The ſteeple alſo of Skipton church, having been for the " moſt part beaten down, when Sir John Mallory kept the caſtle for the king, " ſhe cauſed it to be new built as good as it was before.

" The tower of Barden alſo ſhe re-edified; and repaired the chapel there, " and furniſhed it with ſeats for her neighbours and tenants of that dale, they " being far from the pariſh church."

Our author next ſets forth, how ſhe repaired her caſtles of Appleby, Brougham, Brough, and Pendragon; her ſeveral charities at Mallerſtang, Appleby, and Brougham; her repairing the churches of Appleby and Bongate, the church and chapel of Brougham, and the chapel of Mallerſtang: All which particulars we have noted in their proper places. Mr. Sedgwick then proceeds thus:

" All theſe buildings and repairs could not be computed at leſs than 40,000 *l*, " as may be made appear by the yearly books of account.

" She was at a vaſt charge in law-ſuits to vindicate her rights. Her uncle " Francis earl of Cumberland, and his ſon the lord Clifford, being but te- " nants for life, raiſed great ſums of money from the tenants in Craven to " make them a fine certain, which was not in their power to do. The fine

" certain was 7*d* fine. She demanded only 8*d* fine, for making them arbi-
" trary as before, which the said tenants refused to pay. Thereupon the long
" law-suit began between them, which lasted several years both in common
" law and chancery, and cost 4000 *l* on each side; and in the conclusion her
" ladyship recovered against them. During that suit, Oliver Cromwell, then
" protector of the commonwealth, would needs be a stickler and interpose in
" behalf of the tenants; and to that purpose issued out a commission to some
" gentlemen of the barony of Kendal (whom I list not to name, most of
" them being now in their graves) to treat with her about composing that
" difference at Appleby-castle. When they came there, she used them with
" all kindness and courtesy, but told them plainly she would never refer any
" of her concerns in that kind to the protector or any person living, but leave
" it wholly to the discretion of the law; adding further, that she that had re-
" fused to submit to king James on the like account, would never do it to
" the protector, whatever hazard or danger she incurred thereby.

" Another instance of the care she took to preserve her rights, was as fol-
" loweth: There had been anciently paid for 400 years continuance, to the
" castle of Skipton, 800 boon hens yearly, and the like to the castle of
" Appleby, by the tenants, besides their rents. One Murgatroyd, a rich
" clothier of Hallifax, having bought a tenement near Skipton, was to pay
" one hen; which being demanded of him, he absolutely refused the payment
" of it. Her ladyship was resolved not to lose that hen, being her ancient
" right, and the loss of all the rest depending upon that. Being forced to bring
" an action against him at the assizes at York, she recovered the hen, though
" it cost her 200*l*, and Mr. Murgatroyd as much. And I believe Sir John
" Otway and Sir Thomas Stringer got in fees in that cause 40 *l* each of
" them.

" A great estate God had blessed her with, and given her withal a noble
" heart and an open and liberal hand, to do good generally to all.

" A great esteem she had for grave divines and learned men, as may ap-
" pear by these three following examples. Dr. Henry King, late bishop of
" Chichester, had been for some years chaplain to her first husband Richard
" earl of Dorset: Upon whose death, he not having any considerable prefer-
" ment, this lady settled a rent charge upon him of 40 *l* a year, out of her
" jointure lands in Sussex. The like to Dr. Brian Duppa, who had also been
" her first lord's domestic chaplain, who died bishop of Winchester. The
" like annuity or rent charge she also gave to Dr. George Morley, chaplain to
" her second husband, who was also her godson, and is now bishop of Win-
" chester. Many years she duly paid these rent charges, till in the late cala-
" mitous times having all taken from them, these reverend persons were forced
" to go over sea, and hard put to their shifts to live, so as they made their
" application to her ladyship to send them a sum of money in lieu of these
" rent charges, for their subsistence abroad; which she willingly consented
" to, and paid 1000 *l* upon that account.

" One strange and unexampled piece of charity she did, which few ladies
" would have done. Her husband the earl of Dorset had two bastard daugh-
" ters;

" ters; whereof one died in her minority, the other she married to one Mr. " Belgrave a divine, bestowed a portion on her, and preferred him to a living " in her gift in Sussex, worth 140*l* a year.

" Colonel Charles Fairfax, uncle to the late general Fairfax, was her great " friend upon all occasions. He had many children, and but a small estate. " When he sent his son Henry to Oxford, she allowed him 40*l* a year to- " wards his maintenance in Queen's college, till he came to be a fellow, and " he is now a worthy divine and highly preferred *.

" An extraordinary care she took, and was at a very great charge in the " searching of ancient records in the tower of London, the Rolls, and other " places, that any way concerned her ancestors; wherein she employed Mr. " Roger Dodsworth, grandfather to Mr. Dodsworth that now liveth at Crosby " Ravensworth. These records, containing the lives and deaths, marriages, " burials, with other memorable things of all her progenitors for 400 years, " she caused to be fairly ingrossed in three great large books, one of the Ve- " teriponts, one of the Cliffords, and one of the earls of Cumberland. And " in the margin is expressed where the originals are to be found.

" She was a woman of excellent parts both natural and acquired. Of an " happy memory, and a solid and sound judgment. She was well versed in " the holy scripture, which she was able to quote upon any sudden occasion. " The psalms of David appointed for the day she constantly read, and had " three or four chapters read to her by some of her women daily. She and " her family received the sacrament at least four times in the year; and if she " removed to some other of her houses, then also with a sermon. She had " in the worst of times the liturgy of the church of England duly in her " own private chapel, where she never failed to be present at it, though she " was threatned with sequestration: Yet by means of her honourable friends " and relations in both houses of parliament she always escaped it.

" In what castle soever she then lived, every Monday morning she caused " ten shillings to be distributed among 20 poor housholders of that place; " besides the daily alms which she gave at her gate to all that came.

" All the groceries, spices, stuffs, and the like, which she used in her house, " all wines, malt, hay, corn, and straw for her stables, she bought of neigh- " bours and tenants near the place of her then residence, paying always ready " money when they came for it. So as she was a great help and support to " those parts. Seldom had she any thing from London, being desirous the " country might receive benefit by her.

" She could give a good account of most histories that are extant in the " English tongue. Indeed she was an indefatigable reader, and had a library " stored with very choice books, which she read over, not cursorily, but with " judgment and observation.

* Here seems to have been some mistake. There was never any of this name fellow of that college. One *Anthony Fairfax* was entred in that college in 1627, but he never came to be fellow. One of the fellows of Magdalen college in the said university, in king James the second's time, was Dr. *Henry Fairfax*; who was probably the person here spoken of by Mr. Sedgwick.

" Exceeding

" Exceeding temperate was ſhe in her diet, never drank wine when ſhe was " paſt 80 years of age, excepting ſometimes a little wine glaſs of ſack mixed " with water. Nor did ſhe ever take phyſick in her life, as I have heard her " oftentimes ſay.

" She wore, in her latter days, always very plain and mean apparel, indeed " far too mean for her quality. A petticoat and waiſtcoat of black ſearge was " her conſtant wear, nor could any perſuade her to wear others.

" She kept always two gentlewomen, who wore better cloaths by far than " their lady. And four landry maids, ſome of her tenants daughters, to whom " ſhe gave good wages; and to any of them that married with her conſent, ſhe " gave 50*l* towards a portion, beſides what their parents gave them; and moſt " of them this day live happily and contentedly.

" Her books of account were moſt exactly kept. Beſides which, ſhe kept " in a large folio paper book a diary or journal, wherein ſhe cauſed to be en" tered the occurrences of the day, and all ſtrangers that came to her houſe, " whether upon viſits or buſineſs.

" On the 23d of March 1675, this moſt worthy lady yielded to nature, in a " good old age, and left a bleſſed and happy memory behind her."——So far Mr. Sedgwick, who dates his manuſcript Dec. 10, 1682 *.

* On a pillar in Kendal church, in the pulpit ile, next under the chancel, is the following monumental inſcription:

M. S.
Viri vere generoſi
Plurimiſque nominibus deſideratiſſimi,
Georgii Sedgwick.
Qui,
omnibus cultioris humanitatis dotibus
abunde ornatus,
Honorabilli^mo. D. D^r. Philippo
Comiti Penbrockienſi,
Celeberrimæ deinde illius viduæ
Amanuenſis ſibi locum meruit:
Cujus familiâ,
(qua nemo famulus non floruit)
Annis pariter atque opibus auctus,
(monente munificentiſſima dominâ,
partis feliciter fruendis ſedem
ſenectuti ſuæ comparare)
Fundum, huic municipio vicinum, emit,
dictum Collinfeild;
Ubi plus tribus luſtris,
Singulari in pauperes charitate,
Amicitiâ in proximos,
Erga omnes benevolentiâ,
Notis omnibus charus et amabilis vixit,
nec paucioribus flebilis obiit,
decimo die Junii,
Anno { Salutis humanæ } 1685
{ Ætatis ſuæ } 67.

The

The Cliffords *arms* are; Checky Or and Azure, a fess Gules.—The *crest*: Out of a ducal coronet Or, a wyvern rising Gules.—*Supporters*: Two wyverns Gules, with wings expanded Azure.

We proceed next to the issue and posterity of the said countess. After the death of her younger daughter *Isabella* countess of *Northampton* as aforesaid, without surviving issue; her elder daughter MARGARET remained sole heir of the Clifford family. Which *Margaret* was married to JOHN lord TUFTON, afterwards earl of THANET; and brought with her into that family the inheritance of the Cliffords her ancestors.

Tufton is said to be a corruption of Toketon †; for by that name the family was called till Edward the third's time.

The first that we meet with was *Elphege de Toketon*, lord of the manor of *Toketon* in Rainham in the county of Kent, and of another manor of the same name in the parish of Northiam in the county of Sussex, in the reign of king John. Who had a son,

Osmere de Toketon; who had a son,

William de Toketon; whose son and heir was,

John de Toketon; who had a son,

Roger de Toketon; who had another

Roger; who in the 36 Ed. 1. married Julian sister of Sir John de Champaigne knight. And here the pedigree seems to be somewhat confused, occasioned by a multiplicity of collaterals, the family being then very numerous. The next in descent seems to have been,

John de Toketon; and next to him,

Simon de Toketon, or *Tufton*; for now the name began to be diversified. His son and heir was,

William Tufton, who lived in the reign of king Henry the fourth. He had a son,

William, who was living in the reign of Edward the fourth. His son and heir was,

Nicholas Tufton, who died in the 30 Hen. 8. leaving a son and heir,

John Tufton, then seated at Hothfield in Kent: who in the 4 Eliz. was sheriff of that county, and died about five years after. His son and heir was

John Tufton; who was sheriff of the same county in the 18 Eliz. and was knighted by king James in the first year of his reign, and made baronet by the same king at the first erection of that dignity. His son and heir was,

Sir *Nicholas Tufton* baronet; who in the 2d year of king Charles the first was made lord Tufton of Tufton in Sussex, and two years after was created earl of Thanet. He was father of *John*, who married *Margaret* daughter of the lady *Anne Clifford* as aforesaid; with whom begins the first generation of the *Tuftons* in Westmorland.

† Collins's Peerage.

1st Generation

1st Generation of the Tuftons in Westmorland.

JOHN, fecond earl of Thanet, was eldeft furviving fon and heir of earl *Nicholas*, by his wife the lady Frances, daughter of Thomas earl of Exeter. Which *John*, in the year 1629, married the aforefaid *Margaret* daughter of *Richard Sackville* earl of Dorfet by his wife the lady Anne Clifford. By whom he had fix fons, *Nicholas*, *John*, *Richard*, *Thomas*, *Sackville*, and *George*. Of whom the firft four, and a fon of the fifth, became fucceffively earls of Thanet. *George*, the fixth, being with his brother *Sackville* at the prince elector palatine's court in the year 1667, when the old duke of Loraine invaded that prince's country, they offered their fervices to attend that prince in his war, when this *George Tufton* engaged in refcuing the faid prince out of an ambufcade, with about 20 other gentlemen, feveral of whom were killed, and the faid *George* received a wound, of which he languifhed and died three years after.

The faid earl John by his faid wife had alfo fix daughters: *Anne*, who died young; *Margaret*, married to George lord Coventry; *Frances*, married to Henry Drax of Bofton in the county of Lincoln efquire; *Cecilie*, married to Chriftopher lord Hatton; *Mary*, married to William fon and heir of Sir William Walter of Sarefden in the county of Oxford baronet; and *Anne*, married to Samuel Grimfton fon and heir of Sir Harbottle Grimfton baronet, mafter of the rolls.

The faid earl John had alfo feveral brothers and fifters; of whom, *Chriftian* the youngeft fifter was married to *William Milward* of Chilcote in the county of Derby efquire, fon and heir of Sir *Thomas Milward* of Eaton in the fame county knight.

This earl John died in the year 1664; and his countefs furvived him about 12 years.

In the year 1676 (being the year in which fhe died) fhe devifed the Clifford eftate to *John* her fecond fon in tail, with remainders to *Richard*, *Thomas*, and *Sackville*, her other younger fons.

2d Generation.

In purfuance of his mother's will as aforefaid, JOHN the fecond fon entred upon and enjoyed the premiffes. And in three years after, his elder brother earl *Nicholas*, who married Elizabeth fecond daughter of Richard Boyle earl of Burlington, died without iffue; whereby John fucceeded alfo to the paternal title and inheritance, becoming thereby the fourth earl of Thanet. This earl *John* died within lefs than a year after his brother Nicholas, and unmarried; whereby the honour and eftate devolved upon the third brother *Richard*.

RICHARD TUFTON, fifth earl of Thanet, died alfo unmarried, three years after his brother *John*, *viz.* in 1683; and was fucceeded by the fourth brother *Thomas*.

Thomas Tufton, sixth earl of Thanet, married Catherine daughter and coheir of Henry Cavendish duke of Newcastle. Which Thomas, as heir to his grandmother Anne, baroness of Clifford, Westmorland, and Vesey, being intitled to those baronies, brought his claim into the house of lords. Whereupon their lordships came to this resolution, Dec. 12, 1691, That Thomas earl of Thanet is the sole lineal and right heir to Robert de Clifford, first summoned to parliament as *lord de Clifford*, by writ dated Dec. 29, in the 28 Ed. 1. And that the said title and barony of lord Clifford doth of right belong to the said earl of Thanet and his heirs.

By his said wife he had three sons, who all died in their infancy. And five daughters; (1) *Catherine*, married to Edward viscount Sondes, son and heir of Lewis earl of Rockingham. (2) *Anne*, married to James earl of Salisbury. (3) *Margaret*, married to Thomas Cooke esquire, afterwards lord Lovel, viscount Cooke, and earl of Leicester; which Margaret, in the year 1734, was declared baroness Clifford, as heir to the lady Anne Clifford. (4) *Mary*, married to Anthony earl of Harold, only surviving son of Henry duke of Kent; afterwards, to John earl Gower, her second husband. (5) *Isabella*.

The said earl *Thomas* levied a fine, and thereupon settled the estate on the next *heir male* of the family, viz. *Sackville* eldest surviving son of his brother *Sackville* fifth son of *John* second earl of Thanet aforesaid; and died in the year 1729.

3d Generation.

Sackville Tufton, seventh earl of Thanet, was son and heir of *Sackville* aforesaid, fifth son of earl John, by his wife *Elizabeth* daughter and sole heir of *Ralph Wilbraham* of Newbottle in the county of Northampton esquire, second son of Sir *Thomas Wilbraham* of Woodhey in the county of Chester baronet. The said Sackville the father had five other sons, and six daughters; viz. *John*, who died an infant. *Wilbraham*. Another *John*, who died at the age of 34. *Richard*, who died young. *Thomas*. *Elizabeth*, who died an infant. *Catherine*, who died unmarried. *Elizabeth*. *Christian*. *Margaret*. *Mary*.

This earl *Sackville* (the son) married the lady *Mary Savile*, younger daughter and coheir of *William* marquis of *Hallifax*: And by her had issue *John*, who died before his father, and unmarried; and *Sackville* the present earl: And two daughters, *Mary*, married to Sir William Duncan baronet, physician to his majesty king George the third; and *Charlotte*.

This same earl Sackville, differing with his tenants in Westmorland about their fines after the death of earl Thomas, after a long contest in chancery, a trial at bar in 1739 was directed, to be by a special jury of the county of Middlesex *, on the two following issues, *viz.*

* In which cause eleven witnesses were produced by the tenants from Westmorland, whose ages together amounted to a thousand years.

1. Whether

1. Whether by the custom of the respective manors of Burgham, Appleby, Burgh under Stanemore, Pendragon, Kirkby Stephen, Sowerby nigh Burgh, Winton, King's Meburn, Langton, Mallerstang, Knock, Sowerby, East Stanemore, South Stanemore, Scattergate and Burrels, Woodside, Moorhouses, Bondgate, Burgh Over and Burgh Nether, on the *death of the last general admitting lord*, a reasonable fine, to be assessed at the will of the lord, not exceeding two years value, be payable; or any other, and what fine?

2. Whether by custom of the said manors, on the *death or alienation of the tenant*, a reasonable fine, to be assessed at the will of the lord, not exceeding two years value, be payable; or any other, and what fine?

The verdict of the jury was, that such fines according to the yearly value, were not payable: But that,

1. By custom of the said manors and every of them, *on the death of the last general admitting lord*, a fine to be assessed at the will of the lord, not exceeding ten pence for every penny old rent, commonly called a ten-penny fine, is payable. And,

2. That by custom of the said manors and every of them, *on the death or alienation of the tenant*, a reasonable fine, to be assessed at the will of the lord, not exceeding seventeen pence for every penny old rent, commonly called a seventeen-penny fine, is payable.

And the same was decreed accordingly by the lord chancellor Hardwicke.

And by consent, as to other matters in dispute, it was referred to Robert Fenwick and Joseph Taylor esquires, and such other third person as they should appoint, to settle the same; who made an award, and the same was inserted accordingly in the decree, *viz.*

(1) That the tenants hold their tenements according to the ancient custom of tenant-right, and as customary estates of inheritance, descendible from ancestor to heir, under certain ancient yearly rents, and such general and dropping fines as are settled and ascertained by the order in this cause.

(2) By the custom of the said manors, upon all admittances where the ancient rent exceeds 1 *s*, 3 *s* and no more is payable to the steward for every single admittance; and where one tenant hath several admittances at the same court, and the ancient rent of any one of them exceeds 1 *s*, then 3 *s* is payable for the first admittance, and 6 *d* for every other; where the ancient rent doth not exceed 1 *s*, then 1 *s* only is payable for every single admittance; and where one tenant hath several admittances at the same court, and the ancient rent in one of them exceeds 1 *s*, in such case 1 *s* only is payable for the first, and 6 *d* for every other.

(3) That the tenants have a right to open quarries within their own estates or in the wastes of the manor, and get stones for building or repairing their houses or fences or other necessary uses upon their estates, without licence of the lord or his steward; but may not open quarries, or get stone out of quarries in lease or opened by the lord, without such licence.

(4) That the tenants have right to cut up, take, and carry away turf, peat, heath, furze, and bracken or fern, upon the wastes, for fuel and thatching, without such licence.

(5) That the tenants have right to plow and make ſuch huſbandry of their lands as they think fit, without ſuch licence.

(6) That the tenants have a right to leaſe or demiſe their tenements for any term not exceeding three years.

(7) That all abſolute ſales or alienations ought to be by deed poll or indented; and the ſame to be preſented at the next court, in order for the purchaſer to be admitted on payment of a dropping fine. Femes covert intereſted in lands alienated, to be examined privately by the ſteward.

(8) That the tenants may mortgage for any term not exceeding three years, without licence or fine; but when the mortgagee is admitted, he ſhall pay a dropping fine.

(9) That the tenants may, without licence or fine, exchange lands lying intermixed in common fields, for lands of equal value in the ſame manor; ſo it be with the approbation of the lord or his ſteward.

(10) That the tenants may cut down and fell underwood growing on their reſpective tenements; and may cut down and uſe any other wood or timber for repair of their tenements, hedge boot, plough boot, cart boot, eſtovers, and other neceſſary uſes, provided the ſame be ſet out by the lord or his ſteward. (the ſame to be without fee) in 20 days after requeſt in writing atteſted by one witneſs, and if not ſet out within that time, the tenants may cut down and uſe the ſame.

(11) That the lord may ſell timber, provided he leave ſufficient for repairs, neceſſary boots, and eſtovers.

4th Generation.

SACKVILLE TUFTON, eighth earl of Thanet, ſon and heir of *Sackville* by his wife the lady Mary Savile, married Mary daughter of lord John Sackville ſecond ſon of Lionel duke of Dorſet, and hath iſſue Sackville lord Tufton, and another ſon, and alſo a daughter which is the eldeſt child.

The arms of the earls of Thanet are; Sable, an eagle diſplayed Ermine, within a bordure Argent. The Creſt: on a wreath, a ſea lion ſejant. Supporters: two eagles, their wings expanded Ermine.

OF APPLEBY IN GENERAL.

NO certain derivation of this word hath hitherto been agreed upon. Without having recourſe to the Roman name *Aballaba* (which Mr. Horſley doubts whether it was the Roman name of this place, but rather thinks this was the Roman *Galacum)* we chuſe to adopt a more obvious derivation, by referring it the fruit of that name. And if this place was indeed the Roman *Aballaba*, yet the Romans did not ordinarily impoſe new names, but only modified the names they

they found at the feveral places according to their own idiom. So that we may fuppofe fomething of the like pronunciation had been here before the Roman times; and perhaps we may afcend fo high as the Hebrew tongue for its origin. *Appel*, *abel*, *afel*, is common to the Saxon, Belgic, Danifh, and other northern languages; and, by univerfal confent, hath been appropriated to particularize the forbidden fruit. *Abel*, or as the Hebrews foften it *avel*, (by a tranfmutation frequent in all languages of the letters *b*, *f*, and *v*) fignifies *forrow*, *mourning*, and *woe*. And it is exactly agreeable to the figurativenefs of that language, to transfer the word to this fruit upon the aforefaid confideration. Our Englifh-Saxon word *evil* feems to fpring from the fame fource; and a *doer* of *evil* for the fame reafon is contracted into *devil*. *Malum*, to fignify an apple, may poffibly have been received into the Latin tongue from the like caufe.—The name is not peculiar to this place. There is an Appleby in Derbyfhire, another in Lincolnfhire, an Appleby Magna and Parva in Leicefterfhire, and others in other places. So there is *Applethwaite*, *Applegarth*, *Appleton*, and the like, of the fame derivation.

This town was anciently of large extent. *Burrels*, or *Burrals*, which is now near a mile diftant from the town, means nothing but the *borough walls*, or walls of the *burgh* or town. And there have been ruins of buildings plowed or dug up at two or three miles diftance from the town as it now ftands. The Romans undoubtedly had a ftation here. But the infcriptions which are to be found about the fchool-houfe are not Roman, but copied from Roman infcriptions in other places by Mr. Bainbridge the fchoolmafter, and fome of them altered according to his own fancy.

This place continued to be confiderable long after the Roman times, even until the reign of king Henry the fecond. But in the 22d year of that king's reign, it was furprized by William king of Scots, and utterly deftroyed. But he did not keep it long, himfelf being taken prifoner foon after at Alnwick. King Henry fined Gofpatric fon of Orme (as was obferved before) in the fum of 500 marks for delivering it up, and the other officers in other fums according to their rank.

And afterwards, in the 12 Ric. 2. it was fo totally burned down and wafted by the Scots, that it was not able fo much as to pay the fee farm rent to the crown, and never afterwards in any confiderable degree recovered from that fatal overthrow. Infomuch that by three feveral inquifitions, one in the 7th, another in the 25 Hen. 8. and the third in the 2 and 3 Ph. and Mary, concerning the arrears of 20 marks ancient rent due to the crown, the jurors find, that the town was very much diminifhed and ruinated, fo that they were wholly incapacitated to pay the faid yearly rent; that on St. Stephen's day, in the year 1388, the faid town was burned by the Scots, and from that time had been repairing, but that the greateft part ftill lay in ruins: Whereupon it was ordered, that inftead of the aforefaid fum of 20 marks, they fhould pay for the future no more than two marks or 26*s* 8*d* yearly. And they obtained quietus's in the exchequer accordingly.

What

What ſtill remains of it is an handſome ſmall town, containing between 70 and 80 families, conſiſting principally of one broad ſtreet, terminated on the north by the church, and riſing by an eaſy aſcent to the caſtle on the ſouth; with two handſome croſſes or obeliſks, one at each end. On the upper croſs is this inſcription,

Retain your loyalty.
Preſerve your rights.

The ſhambles and town hall in the middle of this ſtreet greatly incommode it. If theſe were taken away, and removed to more proper places; the ſtreet, from its natural ſituation and openneſs, would be very grand and elegant.

At the upper end of this ſtreet as aforeſaid ſtands the CASTLE aloft; having the river Eden underneath it many fathoms perpendicular on the eaſt, and on the other ſides encompaſſed with an high wall, and a deep ditch.

There is no doubt but there was a caſtle here in the Roman times. But the greateſt part of the building hath been often defaced and broken down, in the wars between England and Scotland. And particularly much hurt was done thereto by the Scots in the ſeveral reigns of Richard the ſecond and Henry the fourth. After which, in Henry the ſixth's time, Thomas lord Clifford built the greateſt part of it as now ſtands, being after the faſhion of thoſe times.

In the weſtern part of this caſtle is placed *Cæſar's tower*, which ſtands apart from the reſt of the caſtle; and probably received its name from ſome of the later emperors.

The aforeſaid lady Anne Clifford repaired the ſame, and built fair new ſtables there; and the whole continues in very good condition to this day *.

Appleby hath been a TOWN CORPORATE of very ancient time. But their charter of incorporation is loſt; and they are now only a town corporate by preſcription. They have had indeed many charters and renewals thereof, which are yet extant; but theſe are only grants of privileges and immunities, and not of incorporation.

King Henry the ſecond, upon his reſtoring the town, after its deſtruction by the Scots as aforeſaid, granted to them by his charter the ſame privileges which he had granted to the city of York juſt before †. For which charter they paid into the exchequer the ſum of 40 marks.

What

* Dr. Todd ſays, In the year 1641, the lady Anne Clifford fortified this caſtle for the king, and putting as great a number of ſoldiers in it as it could contain, gave the government of it to Sir Philip Muſgrave, who held it out till after the battle of Marſton Moor, whereby all the northern part of England was loſt. In the year 1648, Mr. Whitlock (p. 343.) gives an account, that this caſtle was garriſoned for the king; and that on the 16th of October in that year it ſurrendered to the parliament forces, and that therein were taken 5 knights, 25 colonels, 9 lieutenant colonels, 6 majors, 46 captains, 17 lieutenants, 10 cornets, 3 enſigns, and 1200 horſe.

† Henricus Dei gratia, rex Angliæ, dux Normanniæ et Aquitaniæ, et comes Andegaviæ; archiepiſcopis, epiſcopis, abbatibus, comitibus, baronibus, juſticiariis, vicecomitibus, et omnibus miniſtris

What thoſe privileges were, appears from the York charter; and are the very ſame which king John afterwards granted ſpecially to the town of Appleby, *viz.* " a freedom from toll, ſtallage, pontage, and laſtage throughout " England, except in the city of London." He granted to them alſo the borough or town of Appleby, rendring to the ſheriff the rent due for the ſame, one moiety at the feaſt of St. Michael, and the other at Eaſter *.

There are many *Inſpeximus's* and confirmations of the ſaid grants by the ſucceeding princes.

In the 14 Ed. 1. the king, reciting an *Inſpeximus* in the 16 Hen. 3. reciting the charter of John, confirms the ſame, with this addition, " that although " they had been wont to pay their fee farm rent by the hands of the ſheriff, " they might, if they thought fit, pay the ſame into the exchequer by the " hands of their own bailiffs."

In the 5 Ed. 5. there was another confirmation; with this clauſe, " that " whereas king Edward the ſecond, in the 5th year of his reign, had taken " into his hands the town of Appleby for 60*l* in arrear of their fee farm rent; " the now king Edward the third, in conſideration of the fine by them paid " to him on that account, reſtores the town to them, to hold by the ſaid farm " as aforeſaid."

In the 3 Cha. 1. there is another confirmation; reciting a charter of James the firſt, another of Elizabeth, another of Henry the eighth, which recited the charters of Edward the firſt, Henry the third, and king John; and confirming the ſame.

niſtris et fidelibus ſuis, Francigenis et Angligenis totius Angliæ, ſalutem. Sciatis me conceſſiſſe, et præſenti charta confirmaſſe Burgenſibus meis de Appelbia omnes libertates et liberas conſuetudines habendas, quas Burgenſes mei de Eboraco habent. Quare volo et firmiter præcipio, quod prædicti burgenſes mei de Appelbia habeant bene et in pace, libere et quiete, plenarie et integre et honorifice, omnes eaſdem libertates et liberas conſuetudines, quas Burgenſes mei de Eboraco habent, ſicut eas illis conceſſi et præſenti charta confirmavi. Et prohibeo ne quis eos inde diſturbet. Teſtibus hiis; Hugone Murdach', Randulpho de Glanvill, Willielmo de Stutevill, Roberto de Stutevill, Michaele Belet', Willielmo de Bending, et aliis. Apud Richemund'.

* Johannes Dei gratia, rex Angliæ, dominus Hyberniæ, dux Normanniæ et Aquitaniæ, et comes Andegaviæ; archiepiſcopis, epiſcopis, abbatibus, comitibus, baronibus, juſticiariis, vicecomitibus, et omnibus miniſtris et fidelibus ſuis, ſalutem. Sciatis nos conceſſiſſe, et præſenti charta confirmaſſe, burgenſibus noſtris de Appelbi, omnes libertates et liberas conſuetudines habendas, quas burgenſes noſtri de Eboraco habent. Quare volumus et firmiter præcipimus, quod prædicti burgenſes noſtri de Appelby habeant bene et in pace, libere et quiete, plenarie et integre et honorifice, omnes libertates et liberas conſuetudines, quas burgenſes noſtri de Eboraco habent; ſicut rex Henricus pater noſter eas illis conceſſit, et charta ſua rationabiliter confirmavit: et prohibemus ne quis eos inde diſturbet. Præterea dedimus et conceſſimus eiſdem burgenſibus noſtris de Appelbi, *libertates et quietantias de thelonio, et ſtallagio, et pontagio, et leſtagio*, per totam terram noſtram Angliæ, quantum ad nos pertinet, præterquam in civitate Londinenſi. Conceſſimus et eis burgum de Appelbi tenendum in manu ſua, reddendo inde firmam quam debent vicecomiti noſtro de Weſtmerland apud Appelbi, ſcilicet medietatem ad feſtum ſancti Michaelis, et alteram medietatem ad Paſcha. Teſtibus, Guafrido Filio Petri Comite Eſſex', Willielmo Briweir', Hugone Bard', Willielmo de Stutevill, R. Conſtabulario Ceſtriæ, Hugone de Nevill, Symone de Pateſhill. Dat' per manus Symonis Wellenſis Archidiaconi, et Johannis de Gray'. Apud Ebor' 26 die Marcii, anno regni noſtri primo.

But

But these are only still confirmations of the aforesaid privileges of freedom from tolls, stallage, pontage, and lastage; and not at all any grant of incorporation.

Yet notwithstanding, it is in fact evident, that they were governed by a mayor and other corporation officers, perhaps as early as any other corporation in the kingdom.

In the reign of king Henry the third, a lease of lands at Appleby, by the abbot and convent of Wederhale to Robert son of Godfrey, was for the greater notoriety published in the county court, and in the chapter, and in the *burgmote* of Appleby; and sealed (amongst others) with the seals of John de Veteripont, of Walter de Ulvesby official, and the *common seal of the burgesses of Appleby* *. Which said John de Veteripont died about the 26th year of that king's reign, *viz.* in 1241.

By a deed without date, Richard de Apelby clerk granted to Robert son of the said John de Veteripont (which Robert died before the end of that king's reign) a messuage in the town of Apelby, between the messuages of Robert de Goldington and Emma daughter of Barnard: To hold of Idonea daughter of John son of Thomas, to him and his heirs for ever; rendring for the same for all secular service 4 *s.* Witnesses, Master William de Goldington then *mayor* [*majore*] of Apelby, Robert de Goldington and John Bretton *provosts* of the same [*praepositis* de Apelby], and divers others.

In the 6 Ed. 1. before the justices itinerant in Cumberland, there was an agreement between the *mayor* of Appleby, claiming to be "quit from paying "toll throughout England by charter except within the city of London," and Thomas son of Lambert de Multon; whereby the said Thomas granted for himself and his heirs, that the townsmen of Appleby aforesaid should be quit of toll, ferryings [transversagiis], stallage, and other mercantile charges within his liberty of Egremond †.

In the act of parliament of the 13 Ed. 1. st. 3. c. 1. concerning the acknowledging of a statute merchant, where in the English it is said that the merchant shall cause his debtor to come before the mayor of *London* or some chief warden of a city or of another good town; in the original French it is that he shall cause him to come before the mayor of *Appleby*—"face venir sun "dettur devaunt le meyre de *Appelby* †."

From all which it is clear, that there was a mayor of Appleby of very ancient time. And this solves a question which hath sometimes been made, whether (amongst other things) the mayor by the charter of incorporation had the power given to him of a justice of the peace. That office was not instituted till the reign of Edward the third. In the first year of Edward the third, power was given to the crown to appoint keepers of the peace. In the 18 Ed. 3. power was given to the justices of the peace of hearing and determining, which they now enjoy. Charters before the 1 Ed. 3. could not refer to an office which did not then exist. Charters granted between the 1st and

* Registr. Wetheral.

† Machel from Dugd. MS.

and 18th of Ed. 3. (as some such there are) conferred upon the mayor or others the power of keeping the peace, and no more. After the 18 Ed. 3. the king granted by charter the power also to hear and determine, which ever since hath been annexed to the office of justices of the peace. So that what power the mayor of Appleby may have in this respect, must have been granted since the 18th of Edward the third.

The town of Appleby being granted to the burghers as aforesaid by king John in the first year of his reign; the said king afterwards granted (as hath been set forth) to Robert de Veteripont Appleby and Brough, together with the sheriffwick and rent of the county of Westmorland. Which grant to Robert de Veteripont being subsequent to the grant to the burghers, hereby it came to pass, that neither the borough nor the services thereof passed to Robert de Veteripont. Yet in respect of the general words of the Veteripont charter, which would have passed the borough, if the same had not been before granted to the burgesses, the Veteriponts (we find) made claim to the services of the borough. In the 4 Ed. 1. the burgesses of Appleby brought a special writ against Roger de Clifford and Isabella his wife and Roger de Laburne and Idonea his wife, reciting, that whereas the foresaid burghers are tenants of our lord the king, and hold nothing of the aforesaid Roger and Isabella, Roger and Idonea, the aforesaid Roger and Roger do not permit the said burghers to grind their corn at such mills as they shall judge most convenient for them to make choice and use of, nor permit them to take stallrent in all markets and fairs at the said town, nor customs of such merchants as traffick there, as they and their ancestors in time past were accustomed to do; and distrain them day by day to compel them to do fealty to the said Roger and Roger for their tenements in the town aforesaid as if they were their homagers, of whom they hold not any thing at all, nor of any other but our lord the king; to the great damage of our lord the king and the aforesaid burghers. And Roger and Isabella, Roger and Idonea, by the attorney of the said Isabella and Idonea, appeared, and freely acknowleged, that they do require fealty of the aforesaid burghers, for their tenements in the town aforesaid; for they say, that the aforesaid burghers hold of them, and not of our lord the king; for they affirm, that king John, grandfather of our now lord the king, gave the aforesaid town of Appleby to one Robert de Veteripont, great grandfather of the said Isabella and Idonea, whose heirs they are, by a certain charter which they produce; and which doth testify, that the aforesaid king gave to the said Robert, Appleby and Burgh under Stanemore, with the services of all his free tenants in Westmorland, excepting those who hold by knights service: And they say, that the aforesaid Robert and all his heirs successively, from the time of making the aforesaid charter, were in seisin of the fealty of the burgh of Appleby, by the tenants which hold in the aforesaid village, as lords of the village aforesaid. And the said burghers, for our lord the king, say, that whatever charter the said Roger and Roger produce under the name of the said king John, the said Robert ancestor of the said Isabella and Idonea never by the said charter did obtain any seisin of the borough of Appleby, nor his heirs succeeding him had any right or lordship in the aforesaid borough, but that the burghers aforesaid were answerable to our lord the king, and never did fealty to the said Robert or his heirs by reason of their tenements: But they say, that whereas they hold the said borough of our lord the king at the fee farm rent of 20 marks yearly to be paid, they and their ancestors have done fealty to the said Robert de Veteripont and his heirs, by four burghers, by the community of the said town to this chosen and sworn, to answer to the said Robert and his heirs, as sheriffs, and not as lords of the aforesaid borough; and if they have done to them any other fealty, it was by distress, and not of right. And thereupon issue is joined. And because the said Roger and Roger are sheriffs of Westmorland in fee, whereupon the knights and freeholders of the said county are suspected, therefore it is ordered by the court, that inquiry be made of the premisses by jurors of the counties of Northumberland, Cumberland, and York: who find, that neither Robert de Veteripont, nor any that succeeded him as heir, ever had seisin of the borough of Appleby in which the burghers dwell, but that king John gave to the said Robert *Old Appilby* where the *Bondmen* dwell [*Vetus Appilby ubi Villani manent*], and Burgh under Stanemore, with the appurtenances; which lands king John had in his hands, by reason of the trespass committed by Hugh de Moreville: They find also, that the said king John gave to the said Robert the sheriffwick and rent of the county of Westmorland, with the services thereof of all the tenants of the king, except those that hold by knights service: And as to the fealty done to the said Robert and his heirs by the burghers of Appilby for the said borough, they find, that the same burghers never did fealty to the said Robert or his heirs for the said borough, except by two bailiffs chosen by the community of the said borough, so as to be responsible to him for the rent of the said borough, as sheriff in fee, and not as lord of the borough: They find also, that if the said burghers at any time have done any fealty to them, it was by distresses and force, and not by their will. And judgment was given for the burgesses plaintiffs, against the defendants *.— And this perhaps might be the reason of specially inserting in their next charter (as hath been shewed) that they may pay the said rent either to the sheriff for the use of the king, or immediately into the exchequer.

The town having obtained success in the contest touching their tenure, thought also to have set on foot a title by franchises, which belonged to the sheriffs in point of jurisdiction; as, the returns of writs, and pleas of Withernam. Whereupon in the 7 Ed. 1. the burghers of Appleby come and present, that king John gave them such liberties as the citizens of York; and that the said king John gave to Robert de Veteripont the sheriffwick of Westmorland, who first hindred the burgesses to use returns of writs and pleas of Withernam: and in pursuance of that claim, in the 14 Ed. 1. the sheriff of Westmorland was commanded to permit them to have returns of all the king's writs, and to make summons and attachments, and that he should make returns to the burgesses of writs to be executed in that town. The sheriff appeared and averred, that the bailiffs of that town never had returns of writs.

* Dugd. MS.

But

But the bailiffs appeared not to avouch their franchises, and thereupon they were amerced.

After this again, on the other hand, the sheriffs began to question the burgesses. For in the 15 Ed. 1. Isabella and Idonea sued William de Goldington, John his brother, Thomas Brayton, and other burgesses of Appleby, for that whereas attachments, appeals of death, and other felonies, ought to be sued before the king's justices by writs, or before the sheriff and coroners in the county court, the defendants held appeal against John de Apulby for the death of Nicholas Straingé, and caused him thereupon to be attached and imprisoned; and though Isabella, as sheriff of Westmorland, had come personally and brought the king's writ of *supersedeas*, yet the bailiffs held their court of Appleby: And this they declare, to their damage of 1000 *l.* The defendants appear, but could not defend it. And judgment was given for the plaintiffs; and the town's liberty seized, and afterwards replevied.

So much of their ancient grants and charters——

In the time of Oliver Cromwell, they seem to have had a charter imposed upon them, restrictive probably of their former privileges; for they had been firm in their attachment to the royal cause. To which purpose the reverend Thomas Machel, speaking of the plunderings and devastations which Appleby had sustained in former ages, adds, "And if you seek for a later instance, "you may find one in the height of Cromwell's tyranny; for when those "bloody regicides, which made the very name of an Englishman odious in the "world, were not content to bury their malice with that most pious and innocent king whom they most barbarously murdered, but would farther proceed "to proscribe his son and proclaim their lord and sovereign a traytor, no man "there (either by reward or threatning) could be induced to act or to appear "in so horrid a villainy. The mayor withdrew himself, and the bailiffs "(whose office it was) threw up their commissions, though but poor men, "insomuch that the soldiers were glad to have recourse unto a fellow in the "market, an unclean bird, hatched at Kirkby Stephen, the nest of all traytors, who proclaimed it aloud, whilst the people stopped their ears and "hearts, having nothing open but their eyes, and those even filled with tears. "What should I speak of those perpetual persecutions which the neighbouring gentlemen, who are aldermen of the town, underwent for their loyalty to "the king? I think I need no other argument both for their acting for the "king and their faithful perseverance, than their constant sufferings, sequestrations, and imprisonments; from which they were never free one fortnight "together, during the unhappy usurpation of that cruel tyrant. And the "townsmen were not far behind this gallant example of their noble leaders; "who when captain Atkinson came down from the castle with his musketeers "to chuse a Roundhead mayor, and clapped his hand on his sword, saying, "*I'll do it by this* *, yet made resistance; for they then conferred the office (to

* This captain Atkinson who was of Winton in this county, was afterwards hanged, for being concerned in Kaber Rigg plot.

" prevent bloodſhed) on a moderate man, who had acted on neither ſide, " except in bearing that office before; and ſo he was mayor two years to- " gether. And though Oliver, through captain Atkinſon's means, in order " to make himſelf more abſolute, gave a charter to this ancient corporation, " which was rather impoſed than accepted of, yet they preſerved their old " one to the laſt. And when the firſt gentleman, whoſe name I neither need " nor am willing to mention *; after his many refuſals in Oliver's time ac- " cepted the place on the king's return, he would not handle the ſtaff of au- " thority, nor ſuffer the oath of office to be adminiſtred unto him, till he had " ſent for Oliver's charter, and in the face of the court cut it in pieces with " his own hands, and then looking about he eſpied ſome taylors, and caſt it to " them, ſaying it ſhould never be a *meaſure* unto him. What ſhould I ſpeak " of thoſe great acclamations and expreſſions of joy which the people could " not ſmother, at the news of the king's return? What, of that wonderful " pomp and ſolemnity (the like whereof was never ſeen in thoſe parts) upon " his coronation, when there were almoſt as many bonefires as houſes, and two " ſtately high ſcaffolds at each end of the town, hung with cloth of arras and " gold; whither, after ſervice done at the church, the counteſs of Pembroke, " with the mayor, aldermen, and all the other gentry of the county aſcended, " with I know not how many trumpets, and an imperial crown carried be- " fore them, where they proclaimed, prayed for, and drank the health of the " king upon their knees; the aged counteſs ſeeming young again to grace the " ſolemnity. The expences of that day were very conſiderable. For through- " out the town was kept open houſe, after the example of that noble coun- " teſs, who thought not her gates then wide enough to receive her gueſts, " which before had been too wide for receiving armies of ſoldiers."

Finally, whatever charters had before been granted to this corporation, as ſuch, were (amongſt many others throughout the kingdom) ſurrendered to king James the ſecond, and were then loſt, or have not ſince been heard of. And the ſaid king James, July 3d, in the firſt year of his reign, incorporated them *de novo*; ſetting forth, that whereas they had ſurrendered to him all their franchiſes and liberties concerning the electing and appointing of perſons to the offices of mayor, recorder, aldermen, common council, coroner, ſerjeant, ſword-bearer, bailiffs, and chamberlains of the corporation, he therefore grants to them that they ſhall be a body corporate, by the name of mayor, aldermen, and capital burgeſſes of the borough of Appleby; that one of the burghers ſhall be mayor, that there ſhall be a recorder, that twelve of the burgeſſes (beſides the mayor) ſhall be aldermen, that ſixteen of the capital burgeſſes ſhall be of the common council, that there ſhall be a coroner, ſword-bearer, ſerjeant at mace, two chamberlains, and two bailiffs. John Atkinſon, gentleman, to be the firſt mayor. Thomas earl of Thanet, recorder. Sir Chriſtopher Muſgrave knight, Edward Muſgrave and Hugh Machel eſquires, Andrew Cole, John Atkinſon, Thomas Warcop, John Lawſon, Richard

* Hugh Machel eſquire, brother of the ſaid Thomas.

Jackſon,

Jackſon, John Coniſton, Thomas Carleton, John Hall, and Philip Machel, gentlemen, to be the firſt aldermen. Thomas Carleton, gentleman, town-clerk. To exercise their office for ſuch time and in ſuch manner as had before been uſed. Vacancies to be ſupplied as had been uſual in the ſaid borough for 20 years next before. The mayor, in caſe of ſickneſs or reaſonable cauſe of abſence, may with the aſſent of three aldermen appoint one of the aldermen to be his deputy. The recorder alſo may appoint a deputy during his pleaſure. With a power reſerved to the king, to diſplace any of theſe at his pleaſure. He grants them a fair on the ſecond Thurſday in April, to continue for two days, at any convenient place within the borough or the liberties or precincts thereof. He grants to them courts leet, view of frankpledge, fairs, markets, waifs, eſtray, deodands, goods of felons and fugitives, felons de ſe, of perſons put in exigent and outlawed, and all other things as they had formerly enjoyed; paying the farm to the king as heretofore. With a reſtrictive clauſe, that neither the mayor, aldermen, nor any of the burgeſſes ſhall interrupt or moleſt any of the king's juſtices, ſheriff, or other bailiffs or miniſters within their borough.

About two years after this, the king iſſued a *Quo warranto* againſt this amongſt other corporations; who being not willing to diſpute a title with the king, though they had received their charter from himſelf ſo lately before, reſolved to return it, which they did on the 4th of June 1688, under their common ſeal; to the effect following; "We the mayor, aldermen, and capital burgeſſes of the borough of Appleby in the county of Weſtmorland, "in all humble obedience to his majeſty, do by theſe preſents grant, ſurrender, and yield up, to the king, his heirs and ſucceſſors, all the powers, "franchiſes, and liberties whatſoever and howſoever to be uſed or exerciſed "by us, by any right, title, or intereſt veſted in us, by any charters, letters "patent, cuſtom, or preſcription, concerning the electing, nominating and "appointing of any perſons into the offices of the ſaid borough; and humbly "beg of his majeſty to accept of our ſurrender, and with all ſubmiſſion implore his grace and favour to regrant to us the naming and chuſing of the "ſaid officers, and the ſaid liberties and franchiſes, or ſo many of them, and "in ſuch manner, as his majeſty in his great wiſdom ſhall judge moſt meet "for the government of the ſaid borough, and with ſuch reſervations, reſtrictions, and qualifications, as his majeſty ſhall be pleaſed to appoint."

No further charter was ever granted. But the ſaid king by his proclamation, for reſtoring corporations to their ancient charters, bearing date Oct. 17, 1688 *, declares, that the reſignation of this (amongſt many other charters) was never inrolled, and conſequently the reſignation was void; and if ſo, the charter ſo far ſtood good. But then the ſame declaration extends to the former ſurrender likewiſe, that the ſaid former ſurrender was alſo never inrolled. And it ſeemeth to be holden (as we have ſpoken more at large in treating of the Kendal charter) that a charter granted in conſideration of a void ſurrender is alſo void. And the conſequence of all this will be, that the borough of

* Appendix, N° xxxix.

Appleby

Appleby subsists as an ancient corporation by prescription, without any known written charter now in force.

And in virtue of this prescriptive right, the corporation at present consists of a mayor, twelve aldermen, a recorder, sixteen common councilmen with a sword-bearer and serjeant at mace, two chamberlains, and other officers. The common council chuse the mayor, and the mayor chuses all his officers. They have power to arrest for any sum without limitation: To acknowledge statutes merchant before the mayor: To take toll both in fairs and markets: To seize felons goods, waifs, estrays, forfeitures, and escheats. All which belong to the mayor. He takes place, by immemorial custom, of the judges of assize: Which may have arisen possibly from the contests as above mentioned between the sheriff and the town; and this may be one reason perhaps, why the owners of the castle do not seem to have exerted themselves at any time, to procure for the corporation a charter from the crown, with fuller and more explicit powers and privileges.

Their ARMS, according to Mr. Bloome, are, Gules, three crowned lions passant guardant Or. The crest, in a coronet a salamander Proper. The supporters, two dragons Gules. Motto, *Nec ferro nec igni.*

Their common *seal* has on one side in an antique shield the arms aforesaid, viz. three cowned lions passant guardant, in pale. The shield is embellished with branches and *apples* thereon (which, by the way, agrees with our derivation of the name of this place). The legend round is, *Sigillum communitatis burgi de Appilby:* And on the reverse, St. Laurence laid at length naked, with his hands across, on a gridiron; which is supported by two persons at each end, the one covered, the other uncovered. Underneath the gridiron is a representation of burning coals. Above, appears a banner displayed, towards the head, bearing the arms of the borough; towards the feet, is an angel, receiving in a sheet or cloth a small figure reprenting the head and uplifted hands of St. Laurence. The legend round is *Hic jacet Laurencius in craticula positus.*

They have also a *small seal*, which represents the virgin Mary crowned, sitting on a throne, with the child Jesus at her breast. Underneath the throne is a figure in a suppliant posture, with hands and face uplifted. The legend round is, *Sigillum commune beatæ Mariæ virginis de Appelby.*—This seems to have been one of the chantry seals; for there was a chantry of St. Mary both in the church of St. Laurence and the church of St. Michael.

Besides these, the mayor has a small seal, for acts which he may singly do as mayor.

This borough sends two members to PARLIAMENT *.

The ASSIZES for the county are held at this town, as is natural to suppose; the castle being the place of the sheriff's residence: And the judges for

* For a list of the Burgesses, see the Appendix, N° xxxiv.

time

time immemorial have been entertained there at the expence of the sheriff; which might perhaps spring originally from the hospitality of the noble family of the Cliffords.

The SESSIONS OF THE PEACE are also held at this place. In former times, there were disputes between the justices residing in the bottom of Westmorland, and those residing in the barony of Kendal; these latter thinking it hard to travel so far as Appleby to a quarter session: And each of them proclaimed sessions to be held in their respective parts of the county. To prevent which confusion, it was referred to the judges of assize in the year 1676, who recommended, and it hath been the rule ever since, that the justices shall meet at Appleby on Monday in the sessions week, and summon juries in the bottom for matters arising there; and then adjourn to Kendal on Friday in the same week, and summon juries in the barony for matters arising there: And that at Midsummer, when the days are long, they shall hold their session alternately at Appleby and Kendal for the whole county, on Tuesday (that no person need to travel on Sunday to go to the sessions); and shall summon half the jury or juries out of the bottom and half out of the barony; and that this being for the whole county, there shall then be no adjournment.

At the west end of the bridge stands the old GAOL; a little, mean, incommodious building; without one inch of ground out of doors, wherein the prisoners might receive fresh air. Though the prisons of ancient times were generally in the castles, yet this gaol, from the monkish inscription over the door, seems not to be very modern; viz.

"Porta patens esto nulli claudatur honesto."

Now lately, viz. in the year 1771, hath been erected on the other side of the river a new gaol, with a yard, and other conveniences; which, when finished, will be a much more comfortable habitation than the former to the miserable inhabitants. And adjoining hereunto, new court houses are intended to be erected, wherein to hold the assizes and sessions.

At the east end of the bridge stands the HOUSE OF CORRECTION, tolerably convenient for the purpose: with a garden backwards towards the river.

Towards the high end of the town, on the east side, in an healthy and pleasant situation, stands an HOSPITAL for 12 widows and a mother, founded by Anne countess of Pembroke in the year 1653.

In her statutes for governing the same, which bear date on May 16th in that year, it is ordered, that prayers be said duly every morning in the chapel of the hospital by the vicar of Appleby: The doors of the hospital to be shut every night at 8 in the winter, and 9 in the summer, and not opened till 7 in the morning in winter, and 6 in the summer: The court to be swept once in every week, and the kennels and watercourses about it to be kept clean: If any difference arise among them, the same to be determined by the major part of themſelves and the vicar; and if they cannot end it, then to be referred to the owner of the caſtle and the mayor of the corporation.

For maintenance of the ſaid hoſpital, ſhe purchaſed the manor of Brougham, and the late diſſolved hoſpital of St. Nicholas nigh Appleby; and by deed bearing date Mar. 27, 1654, between the ſaid counteſs of the one part, and Sir Charles Howard, Sir Francis Howard, Sir Philip Muſgrave, Sir John Lowther, Sir William Townſhend, Sir George Fletcher, Sir Thomas Sandford, Chriſtopher Liſter, Robert Hilton, and the mayor of Appleby for the time being, of the other part, reciting, that whereas ſhe had built an hoſpital at Appleby for 13 poor women, and had purchaſed certain lands in Brougham and St. Nicholas, of the yearly value of about 100 *l*, which ſhe is reſolved to ſettle not only for the maintenance of the ſaid poor women, but alſo for the yearly payment of 4 *l* to the poor of the pariſh of Brougham, ſhe therefore grants to the ſaid Charles Howard and the other truſtees, all that the late diſſolved hoſpital of St. Nicholas, and all that the manor and lordſhip of Brougham, in truſt, to pay to each of the ſaid poor widows reſident in the ſaid hoſpital (except the mother) 6 *l* a year, and to the mother 8 *l*, and 8 *l* yearly to the parſon of Appleby in caſe he officiate every day in the week (except Sunday) in the chapel of the ſaid hoſpital, otherwiſe to ſuch perſon as the heirs of the ſaid counteſs lords of the caſtle and manor of Appleby ſhall appoint ſo to officiate. The reſidue to be kept in bank, for repairing the houſe, and defraying the charges of the truſtees. When 8 of the truſtees ſhall be dead, the ſurvivors to convey to other ten perſons of worth and quality inhabiting in the ſaid county, to be nominated by the heirs of the ſaid counteſs lords of the caſtle and manor of Appleby, or by their guardians in caſe of minority; and in default thereof for the ſpace of 6 months, then the ſurvivors or major part of them to make election both of feoffees, widows, mother, and chaplain, and ſo *toties quoties*.

About 8 years after this, *viz.* in 1661, the ſaid counteſs (having diſdained, as it ſeemeth, to apply to the Protector) obtained from king Charles the ſecond letters patent for eſtabliſhing the ſaid hoſpital, by the name of the hoſpital of *St. Anne* of Appleby: The counteſs to name the firſt mother and ſiſters; and afterwards, upon the death, or expulſion for any crime or cauſe, of any of them, the ſaid counteſs and her heirs, lords of the caſtle and manor of Appleby, to appoint another: And they alſo to be viſitors of the ſaid hoſpital, and have power to correct and expel for immorality or other cauſe; and, with the conſent of the lord chancellor, or of the archbiſhop of York for the time being, to have power to make ſtatutes for the government of the ſaid hoſpital, and diſpoſition of the lands, goods, and revenues thereof; the ſaid revenues not to exceed the ſum of 100 *l* yearly.

In the year 1687, July 6th, Thomas earl of Thanet, by writing under his hand and ſeal, (by virtue, as it ſeemeth, of his viſitatorial power as aforeſaid) reciting that great abuſe had been practiſed in the hoſpital, as well in ſharing amongſt the mother and ſiſters the 6 *l* a year appointed for the repair of the houſe [being part of the aforeſaid ſurplus, which was then 8 *l* a year], as

 alſo

alſo in diſpoſing money falling due during vacancies, and that the ſame ought to be accounted part of the public money of the ſaid hoſpital, for providing a ſtock to be uſed on emergent occaſions,—orders, that ſuch houſe and vacancy money be put into a cheſt for ſuch public uſe, and no part be made uſe of without the direction of himſelf, his heirs, or their ſteward or receiver at Appleby caſtle; and that a yearly account be made thereof, and allowed and ſigned by the ſteward.

Here is a good MARKET every Saturday, for corn and other proviſions; and a fair yearly on St. Laurence's day. And alſo a fair every Whitſun-eve and Whitſun-monday; and on the Saturday every fortnight for cattle from Whitſun-eve till Michaelmaſs. And alſo king James the ſecond's fair is held on the ſecond Thurſday in April and the day following.

At the entrance of the churchyard, there is a convenient and decent market houſe or cloiſter; which fronts to the market place, and was built chiefly at the expence of Dr. Thomas Smith biſhop of Carliſle; unto which alſo Dr. Barlow biſhop of Lincoln gave 10 *l.* For this, the corporation pays a rent of 5 *s* yearly to the vicar, in conſideration that part of the ſaid building was erected upon the churchyard.

In the year 1598, the market was removed to Gilſhaughlin, on account of the plague; in which year, between Aug. 1. and Mar. 25. there died in Appleby, Scattergate, Colby, and Colby Leathes, 128 perſons.

OF THE PARISH OF ST. LAURENCE IN APPLEBY.

APPLEBY is divided into two pariſhes; of St. *Laurence*, and St. *Michael.*

The pariſh of St. *Laurence* is bounded on the Eaſt by St. Michael's, commonly called *Bongate* pariſh; on the South-eaſt and South, by Ormeſhead and Aſby pariſhes; on the Weſt, by Croſby Ravenſworth and Morland pariſhes; and on the North, by the ſaid pariſhes of Morland and St. Michael's: And contains in the whole about 160 families, all of the church of England.

The church (as the name imports) was dedicated to *St. Laurence*; which was the original of the fair at Appleby on that ſaint's day, and the ſame feaſt of St. Laurence is for the like reaſon in ancient writings appointed for the payment of rents in places thereabouts.

It is a vicarage, valued in the king's books at 9 *l* 5 *s* 2½ *d.*

It was given by Ranulph de Meſchines, as is aforeſaid, together with the church of St. Michael, to the abbot and convent of St. Mary's York;

with two parts of the tithes of all his demesne lands on both sides of the river Eden, which grant was confirmed by king Henry the first *.

Afterwards the same was confirmed by Athelwald first bishop of Carlisle; and afterwards by Hugh his successor, under the following limitations: That the house of Wetheral, in the name of the said abbey, possess the same to their own use; but saving nevertheless the pension usually paid thereout to the abbey; and that the said abbey do present fit persons to be vicars thereof, to be sustained out of the revenues of the said church, so as that such vicar receive thereout six marks yearly, he paying all episcopal and archidiaconal charges †.

Afterwards, in the year 1247, the same was confirmed by Silvester bishop of Carlisle ‡; and in the year 1251, judging the six marks aforesaid to be insufficient,

* Henricus rex Angliæ, &c. Thurstano Archiepiscopo Eborum, et omnibus fidelibus et ministris suis de Westmerland et de Cumberland, salutem. Sciatis me concessisse et confirmasse Richardo abbati et conventui Sanctæ Mariæ de Eboraco, ecclesias de Appelby, sc. Sancti Michaelis et Sancti Laurentii, et terras earum, cum decimis de dominicis ejusdem villæ ex utraque parte aquæ; et decimas de dominico de Mebrau, et de Salchild; sicut carta R. Meschin testatur. *(Regisstr. Wetheral.)*

† Hugo Dei gratia Karliolensis episcopus, venerabilibus fratribus in Christo Roberto Abbati et conventui Sanctæ Mariæ Eborum, salutem æternam in Domino. Cum plerumque contingat, ut per incuriam negligenter administrantium in ecclesiis, vel (quod pejus est) per dilapidationem perperam agentium officium prælatorum, in eis alienationes possessionum et rerum ecclesiasticarum in enormem fiant læsionem piorum locorum, atque ea quæ ad sustentationem pauperum et peregrinorum et deservientium in eis devotione fidelium sacris cœnobiis conferuntur, in usus alios qui potius salutem animarum impediant quam promoveant minus licite transferuntur: Cum autem, vacante sede Karleolensis ecclesiæ, multa in eodem episcopatu sint perpetrata, et quæ fieri debuerant improvidenter omissa: Nos, reformationi matricis ecclesiæ non solum vacare studentes, verum et aliarum universitati et præcipue religiosorum utilitati providentes, optamus aliena revocare, collapsa reparare, et quod negligenter a matricibus ecclesiis sunt separata annuente Domino ex injuncto nobis officio cupimus resarcire. Propterea, karissimi fratres in Christo, attendentes devotionem vestram et religiositatem et caritativam in recipiendis hospitibus liberalitatem quam indesinenter habundantius exhibetis; concedimus vobis, ut ecclesias de Apelby Sancti Michaelis et Sancti Laurentii, quas vobis in proprios usus prædecessor noster felicis memoriæ Adelwaldus Karliolensis episcopus cum omnibus libertatibus et pertinentiis earundem vobis concessit, sicut in originalibus literis quas ab eodem episcopo recepistis et habetis plenius continentur, vobis nihilominus de communi assensu capituli nostri Karleolensis præsenti scripto perpetuo confirmamus habendas et pacifice possidendas in usus proprios: Salvo jure diocesano. Ita tamen, ut domus de Wetheral nomine universitatis vestræ easdem in proprios usus possideat. Salvis tamen consuetis pensionibus quas de eisdem ecclesiis percipere consuevistis. Et ministraturi in eis nobis et successoribus nostris vicarii idonei a vobis præsententur, qui de bonis ipsarum ecclesiarum congruam recipiant sustentationem; ita, scilicet, quod vicarius in ecclesia Sancti Michaelis recipiat v marcas, et vicarius in ecclesia Sancti Laurentii percipiat vj marcas: Et ipsi vicarii jura episcopalia et archidiaconalia persolvent, et honeste ecclesiis deservient. Hiis Testibus, B. Priore Karl'. Magistro Ada Offic'. Domino Willielmo Capellano. *(Registr. Wetheral.)*

‡ Universis sanctæ matris ecclesiæ filiis, &c. Silvester Dei gratia Karleolensis episcopus, salutem in Domino. Noverit universitas vestra, Nos communi consilio de assensu capituli nostri ecclesiæ Sanctæ Mariæ Karl', concessisse, confirmasse, et ratas habere concessiones, confirmationes, &c. quas venerabilis pater Hugo Dei gratia Karl' episcopus prædecessor noster fecit abbati et conventui Sanctæ Mariæ Ebor', super ecclesiis de Appelby Sancti Michaelis et Sancti Laurentii, et de Kirkeby Stephan, et de Morland, tenendis et habendis in proprios usus integre et plenarie, cum omnibus capellis

ſufficient, he taxed the ſaid vicarage as follows: *viz.* the whole altarage, with all the tithes of hay and mills, with the manſion-houſe and other houſes on the weſt part of the church, with the waſte ground thereabout: with 20 acres of land, and the whole common of paſture and of wood belonging to the ſaid abbey. And alſo all the tithes of Hoffe, namely, of meal 10 ſkeps, of corn 5½ ſkeps, and of malt 5 ſkeps [*de farina decem eſkeppas, de frumento quinque eſkeppas et dimidium, et de braſeo quinque eſkeppas*]. And foraſmuch as 48 acres of land in the field of Appleby had been given to the church aforeſaid for finding a chaplain to do ſervice every day in the chapel of the caſtle at Appleby, and 37 acres in the field of Hoffe had been given to the church aforeſaid for ſervice to be done in the chapel of Hoffe three days in every week, it ſhall be in the option of the abbot and convent, whether they will keep (by the prior of Wetheral) the ſaid lands with the burden aforeſaid, or aſſign them with the ſaid burden to the vicar: And the vicars of St. Laurence ſhall not pay for the future the 20*s* penſion which they had formerly paid to the vicar of St. Michael's *.

The ſucceſſion of incumbents (ſo many as have occurred to us) is as follows;

In 1070, *Radulphus*, chaplain to Ranulph de Meſchiens the patron, was rector of the church of St. Laurence Appleby †.

About the year 1210, *Roger Dean*, in a bull of pope Gregory the ninth, is mentioned as parſon of the church of Appleby ‡.

In 1225, there was a diſpute between *William* abbot of St. Mary's York, parſon of the church of St. Laurence in Appleby, plaintiff, and Robert ſon of Godfrey defendant, concerning divers lands in Appleby §.

About the year 1230, one *Jurdan*, vicar of St. Laurence Appleby, was witneſs to an exchange of lands at Appleby, for inlargement of the church-yard ‖.

After

capellis et pertinentiis ſuis. Concedimus etiam et confirmamus et ratas habemus omnes donationes et confirmationes penſionum, libertatum, procurationum, et aliorum beneficiorum eccleſiaſticorum, quas idem venerabilis pater prædeceſſor noſter fecit abbati et conventui prædictis, ſicut in ipſius chartis ſuper hiis confectis p'enius continetur, et ſicut temporibus prædeceſſorum noſtrorum habuerant. Et in hujus rei teſtimonium et confirmationem præſenti ſcripto ſigillum noſtrum una cum ſigillo capituli noſtri appoſuimus. Teſtibus Dominis Waltero de Rudham, Willielmo de Swyneford, Henrico de Kingtun; Magiſtris Rogero Pepin, Johanne de Aſkeby; Domino Gilberto de Kyrketun, Domino P. de Petricurta, Nicoloa Spigurnel, et aliis. Actum Lundon' xij Kal. Marcii. Anno Domini m.cc.xl°. Septimo. (*Regiſtr. Wetheral.*)

* Regiſtr. Wetherel. † Todd. ‡ Todd. § Regiſtr. Wetherel.

‖ Omnibus has literas viſuris vel audituris, Mr. Willielmus de Goldington de Apelby, ſalutem. Noverit univerſitas veſtra me conſenſu totius villæ de Apelby dediſſe et confirmaſſe Deo et eccleſiæ Sanctæ Mariæ Eborum, nec non priori et monachis de Wederhale, unam placeam terræ in villa de Apelby, illam ſcilicet quæ jacet inter terram Hugonis Tinctoris et terram Petri Arbridil in Schiteregate in villa de Apelby, libere et quiete ab omni ſervicio ad villam de Apilby pertinente in perpetuum: Pro quadam parte crofti ſui quæ in dicta villa extendit ſe a parte orientali eccleſiæ Sancti Laurentii a ſiniſtris verſus aquam de Edene, quam dicti prior et monachi ad augmentum cæmeterii noſtri dederunt. Ego vero Willielmus et hæredes mei warrantizabimus, &c. In cujus rei teſtimonium,

After him we find *William de Kyrketon*, vicar of Appleby, one of the commiſſioners for ſetting out the boundaries of certain lands at Kirkby Thore, belonging to the monks of Holme *.

In 1303, a writ was iſſued againſt *Walter de Doncaſtre*, vicar of St. Laurence, for 17 marks †.

In 1307, Sir *Stephen de Popilton* was inſtituted into this vicarage, upon the preſentation of the abbot and convent of St. Mary's York: Saving to them their uſual penſion ‡.

In 1332, Sir *John de Carleton* was preſented by the ſaid abbot and convent, and thereupon inſtituted and inducted. By an inquiſition thereupon it appears, that this Sir John was immediate ſucceſſor to Sir Stephen above mentioned §.

In 1359, ſentence was given at York againſt Sir *William Colyn* vicar of St. Laurence, who had endeavoured to throw the charges of ſerving the chauntry in the caſtle upon the prior and convent at Wedirhall.

In 1379, Sir *Robert Baynes* was preſented and inſtituted.

In the town cheſt of Appleby, there is a releaſe in the year 1399, from *Thomas de Brunby* vicar of St. Laurence in Appleby, to Richard Pathenal chaplain, of three burgages in Appleby.—And in the year 1406, the ſaid Sir *Thomas de Brunby* was cited to York, on the like neglect as of Sir William Colyn above mentioned, in not ſerving the chauntry in the caſtle; and, upon his not appearing before the judge of the prerogative court of the ſaid abbot and convent, was excommunicated; and the excommunication was to be read in the pariſh churches of St. Laurence and St. Michael in Appleby, and in other churches and public places within the dioceſes of Carliſle and York, every Sunday and Holiday ſo long as the ſaid abbot and convent ſhould require, and not to ceaſe until he ſhould comply and make ſatisfaction to the judge and parties ∔.

And in the year 1466, another difference happened to ariſe, between Sir *Richard Appleby* perpetual vicar of the pariſh church of Appleby and the ſaid abbot and convent, concerning the providing of neceſſary furniture for the ſaid chapel, namely, a book, chalice, and veſtments, which were then wanting; (the family of Clifford being then turned out of all, and the caſtle in the hands of the grantees of the crown:) but this was at length compromiſed by William Peteman LL. D. and William Langton LL. B. arbitrators indifferently choſen, who awarded, that the ſaid Sir Richard the vicar, ſo ſoon as

nium, ſigillum meum, una cum ſigillo communitatis de Apelby, &c. appoſui. Hiis teſtibus, Magiſtro Rogero Pepin, Richardo decano de Morland, Jurdano vicario Sancti Laurentii de Apelby, Waltero vicario Sancti Michaelis de Apelby, Johanne et Roberto tunc cappellanis, Richardo Maunſell, Galfrido de Inge, Johanno Clerico de Apelby, et aliis.

* Regiſtr. Holme. † Nicolſon. ‡ Id.

§ What is here mentioned, and elſewhere throughout within this county of Weſtmorland and dioceſe of Carliſle, concerning the preſentation and inſtitution of the ſeveral incumbents in their reſpective pariſhes, is (where not otherwiſe expreſſed) generally taken from biſhop Nicolſon's extracts from the regiſters of the biſhops of Carliſle at Roſe.

∔ Regiſtr. Wetheral.

conveniently

conveniently might be, ſhould at his own coſts provide one veſtment and chalice, and the abbot and convent a maſs book; and if any of theſe ſhould fall into decay, or be loſt or deſtroyed, the ſaid Sir Richard ſhould repair and make them good during his incumbency *.

In 1518, Sir *Richard Garnett*, vicar of St. Laurence, was witneſs to an agreement for the chantry prieſt to teach a ſchool in Appleby.

In 1526, Sir *Henry Hartley*, vicar of St. Laurence, was commiſſary to Roland Threlkeld then official to the archdeacon of Carliſle.

In 1541, after the diſſolution of the abbey, the rectories of St. Laurence and St. Michael, and the advowſon of the vicarage of St. Laurence, and all tithes parcel of Wetheral, were granted to the dean and chapter of Carliſle. After which, the firſt incumbent that we have met with was Dr. *Hugh Sewel*, on whoſe reſignation in 1573, inſtitution was given to *Lancelot Manfield*, who was preſented by Ralph Sewel of Culgaith and John Sewel of Ouſby, to whom the dean and chapter had made a grant of this turn.

In 1582, on the death of Lancelot Manfield, *Chriſtopher Walker* was inſtituted, on the preſentation of Richard Dudley of Yanwath eſquire, aſſignee of the biſhop of Durham and others, aſſignees of John Sewel, aſſignee of the dean and chapter.

In 1624, on the death of Chriſtopher Walker, *William Crakanthorp* was inſtituted, on the preſentation of the dean and chapter.

In 1628, *John Scott* ſucceeded William Crakanthorp.

In 1636, on the death of John Scott, *Edward Guy*, M. A. was inſtituted on the preſentation of the vicedean and chapter.

In 1653, the counteſs of Pembroke, in her ſtatutes for the hoſpital, orders prayers to be read there by Mr. *Anthony Shaw*, vicar of Appleby.

In 1656, Mr. *Ambroſe Rowland*, vicar of St. Laurence, was one of the truſtees in the ſettlement of an eſtate at Temple Sowerby by Anne counteſs of Pembroke for divers public uſes as will hereafter appear.

In 1661, *James Buchanan*, ſon of one of the prebendaries, was inſtituted.

He was ſucceeded by *Michael Hodgſon*; in what year we have not found.

In 1681, on the death of Michael Hodgſon, *Gabriel Smalwood* was inſtituted; on whoſe tombſtone in the churchyard is this epitaph:

" Hic mortale ſuum carniſque exuvias depoſuit Gabriel Smalwood, M. A.
" eccleſiæ hujus vicarius deſideratiſſimus: Qui, bonis quotidie pauperibus
" elargitis, tandem (quæ ſola jam reſtabant donanda) Deo animam, terræque
" corpus reddidit, Martii die 7mo, A. D. 1698. Ætatis ſuæ 48."

On whoſe death, in the ſaid year, *James Lamb*, M. A. was inſtituted, on the preſentation of the dean and chapter.

In 1720, on the death of James Lamb, *John Chriſtopherſon*, B. D. was inſtituted, on the like preſentation.

In 1758, on the death of John Chriſtopherſon, *Sandford Tatham*, M. A. was inſtituted.

* Regiſtr. Wetheral.

The CHURCH of St. Laurence was burned down in the 22 Hen. 2. when the town was taken by the king of Scots; and rebuilt, by the said king Henry, a is supposed, about two years after.

In the year 1655, the same being much in decay, the lady Anne Clifford at her own expence took down all the timber, and the walls of most part of the chancel, where a vestry was heretofore, and rebuilt the same without one; and instead thereof, a vestry was taken out of the west end of the church. A quire also was taken down, which projected towards the town, and had belonged to the Warcops of Colby and the Colbys their anceftors. In which reparations the countess expended near 700*l.*

In the inside of this church, at the south end of the communion table, is a noble monument within high iron grates; on the south side of which monument is this legend:

"Here lyeth interred the body of the lady Margaret Russel, countess dowager of Cumberland, youngest child of Francis Russel second earl of Bedford, married to George lord Clifford third earl of Cumberland. She lived his wife 29 years, and died his widow at Brougham-castle the 24th of May 1616, 10 years and 7 months after his deceafe. She had issue by him two sons, Francis and Robert, who both died young; and one daughter, the lady Anne Clifford, married to Richard Sackvil, third earl of Dorset; who, in the memory of her religious mother, erected this Monument, A. D. 1617."

Upon the north side of the same monument:

> "Who faith, love, mercy, noble constancy,
> "To God, to virtue, to distress, to right,
> "Observ'd, express'd, shew'd, held religiously,
> "Hath here this monument: Thou seest in sight,
> "The cover of her earthly part; but, passenger,
> "Know heaven and fame contains the best of her."

Within the iron grate, in the east end of the north ile, is a yet more noble marble monument, which bears the following epitaph:

"Here lies, expecting the second coming of our lord and saviour Jesus Christ, the dead body of the lady Anne Clifford, daughter and sole-heir to George Clifford, third earl of Cumberland, by his blessed wife Margaret Russel countess of Cumberland. Which lady Anne was born in Skipton-castle in Craven the thirtieth of January (being Friday) in the year 1590, as the year begins on Newyear's-day; And, by a long continued descent from her father and his noble ancestors, she was baroness Clifford, Westmerland, and Vesey, high sheriffess of the county of Westmerland, and lady of the honour of Skipton in Craven aforesaid. She married, for her first husband, Richard Sackvil earl of Dorset; and for her second husband, Philip Herbert earl of Pembroke and Montgomery; leaving behind her only two daughters that lived, which she had by her first husband; the eldest Margaret countess of Thanet, and the younger Isabella countess of North-

ampton.

" ampton. Which lady Anne Clifford, countess dowager of Pembroke, Dor-
" set, and Montgomery, deceased at her castle of Brougham, the 22d day of
" March, in the year of our lord 1675, christianly, willingly, and quietly;
" having before her death seen a plentiful issue (by her two daughters) of 13
" grandchildren. And her body lies buried in this vault."

Above this, on another tablet of black marble, is the pedigree and coats of arms of her progenitors, beginning at the first Robert de Veteripont.

For the keeping of these monuments in repair, and other uses, the said countess purchased an estate at Temple Sowerby, and by deed bearing date Feb. 2. 1656, conveyed the same to Sir John Lowther and Sir Thomas Sandford baronets, Robert Hilton and Lancelot Machel esquires, Robert Branthwaite esquire mayor of Appleby, John Thwaites, John Thwaites the younger, John Smith, Thomas Yare, Edmund Guy, John Lowson, and Thomas Rowlandson, aldermen, the reverend Ambrose Rowland vicar of Appleby, and the vicar of Appleby for the time being, in trust, for the great respect which she bears to the corporation of Appleby, by reason of her dear and blessed mother who lies interred in the church there, that they cause the rents and profits of the said estate (which was then let at 6*l* a year) to be employed by the mayor, with the consent of the other trustees or four of them, for the repairing and decent keeping the tomb in the quire of the church at Appleby, where her said mother lies interred, and one other tomb which she the said countess was then preparing to be set up for herself; and for the repair of the grammar school house, and the moot hall or court house, both in and belonging to Appleby aforesaid; and likewise for the repair of Appleby bridge. On the death of trustees, the survivors to chuse others.

Belonging to the church of St. Laurence were anciently two CHANTRIES.

1. The chantry of the *blessed virgin Mary*; founded by the family of *Goldington*, and endowed by them with revenues in the town and elsewhere, for celebrating divine service at the altar of St. Mary in the church aforesaid, for the mayor, bailiffs, and commonalty, and for the souls of the founders and their ancestors, and all faithful people, and especially of those who should be in any wise benefactors to the said chantry.

In the 14 Ed. 1. there is a deed of confirmation from Ralph de Irton bishop of Carlisle and John de Goldington; from whence it appears, that there were divers rents assigned for the maintenance of a chantry priest in the church of St. Laurence, charged upon 15 persons by name, which were to be as a security for raising 5½ marks yearly: If these should not be sufficient, then he charges other rents on the houses of 13 other persons. And if the said John de Goldington shall improve the said rent, the overplus above the said 5½ marks shall remain to himself and his heirs.

In the 31 Hen. 6. on a dispute about a way to the water at Rutter-beck, which had been granted by the lords of the manor of Ormeshead to the tenants of the chantry of St. Mary in Appleby; between Sir John Lambe, chaplain, otherwise called the chantry priest of the chapel or chantry of our lady

3

lady in Appleby, and Robert Langhorne, Thomas Sowerby, John Warthecupp, and Robert Smith, for themſelves and all the reſidue of the ſaid Sir John's tenants in the town of Appleby, of the one part, and John Barton eſquire lord of the manor of Ormſide, of the other part; the ſame was referred to the arbitration of Sir William Stowe, knight, and commander of the mount of St. John, Sir Robert Lowther of Lowther knight, Richard Riſtwald of Appleby gentleman, and Rowland Barton of Newcaſtle upon Tyne clerk: Who awarded, that the ſaid Sir John's tenants in Appleby ſhall have eaſment and liberty of driving their kine (but no other cattle) with a herd, at noon time, during the ſummer ſeaſon only, over the weſt end of Braidmyre ſike, and ſo over Braidmyre to Rutter-beck; and the ſaid herd to drive them within the compaſs of a ſhot of a burdbolt of the Birk-hill dike; and the ſaid kine to ſtay in the ſaid Rutter-beck, until the ſaid herd might ſet two ſpecks on his ſhoes; and then to drive them back again the ſame way: and the ſaid tenants to pay for the ſame, on the feaſt of St. Dunſtan yearly, for every cow 2*d.* *

About 2 years after, the ſaid John Barton eſquire made a rental for the watergate of the cows of the tenants in Appleby; by which it appears, that the number of tenants was 77, and the number of cows 95. †

2. The other chantry in the church of St. Laurence was founded by *Robert Threlkeld*, by the name of the chantry of *St. Nicholas*; and endowed alſo with ſeveral burgage houſes in Appleby.

In the 4 Ed. 3. there was a licence from biſhop Roſs to Robert Threlkeld to aliene in mortmain, with an Inſpeximus of letters-patent of the ſaid king granting licence of alienation to the ſaid Robert of lands in Appleby of the yearly value of 3*l* 4*s* 7*d*, which he held of the king in burgage by the farm of 2*s* 10*d*, which farm is called *Danegeld:* As appears by inquiſition taken by John de Lowther eſcheator general in the northern parts. ‡

Beſides this chantry of St. Nicholas, there was alſo an *hoſpital* of St. Nicholas in the pariſh of St. Michael; as will appear in its place.

There was alſo a CHAPEL in Appleby, as appears by a deed in the 23 Hen. 6. whereby Robert Warcop, mayor, and the burgeſſes of Appleby, granted to John Marſhall chaplain, a certain ruinated chapel upon the weſt end of the ſtone bridge of St. Laurence in Appleby; to hold the ſaid chapel to the ſaid John and his ſucceſſors. The ſaid John to repair the ſaid chapel at his own expence. They grant alſo a licence to him to repair a certain chamber or oratory over the ſaid chapel. To pay a yearly rent of 2*d* to the mayor and burgeſſes, if demanded ‖.——This ſeems to be the very ſame which is now the old gaol; having to this day much more the appearance of a monkiſh cell than a priſon. The revenues thereof perhaps did ariſe from the charity of paſſengers.

* Machel. † Id.

‡ From the evidences in the town cheſt. ‖ Town cheſt.

The

The mention of the *chantries* naturally introduces the account of the SCHOOL. The ſchool, as now eſtabliſhed, is not ancienter than the reign of queen Elizabeth: But there was ſome kind of a ſchool before.

In the 31 Hen. 6. John Marſhall, vicar of St. Michael's, ſold to Thomas lord Clifford a burgage houſe in Appleby, deſcribed to be on the weſt ſide of the ſtreet called Kirkgate, extending in length to a certain narrow lane called *School-houſe gate.*

The chantries ſometimes were given all to one perſon, in conſideration of his teaching ſchool. It was probably upon this account, that in the 19 Ed. 4. the mayor and burgeſſes granted (as appears by their deed) to Thomas Whinfell chaplain, the chantry of the bleſſed virgin Mary, which Thomas de Goldington and John his ſon and their anceſtors had founded in the church of St. Laurence; together with the chantry of St. Nicholas in the ſaid church; and alſo the chantry founded by Sir William Engliſh in the church of St. Michael.*

In the 7 Hen. 8. there was an indenture of agreement, between Sir Richard Garnett vicar of St. Laurence, and Sir Leonard Langhorn chaplain of the chantry of St. Mary; whereby the ſaid chaplain, for the ſtipend of 7 marks, covenanted to officiate and teach ſchool; the ſaid chaplain to have alſo the orchard and all the fruits of it, with hay to feed an horſe.

And more fully, by indenture in the 10 Hen. 8. June 6, 1518, the mayor, bailiffs, and commonalty of the borough of our lord the king of Appleby in the county of Weſtmorland grant unto Leonard Langhorne the chantry of the bleſſed virgin *Mary* in the church of St. Laurence in the borough aforeſaid, with all the lands, tenements, rents and ſervices thereto belonging; to have and to hold the ſame during his life, to celebrate divine ſervice at the altar of St. Mary in the church aforeſaid, according to the rules of the eſtabliſhment and foundation of the ſaid chantry: And further, conſidering that the ſaid chantry is not ſufficient for the ſuſtenance of one chaplain; they give him power to hold two other chantries, namely, the chantry of *St. Nicholas* in the ſaid church of St. Laurence, and the chantry late of William Ingliſh in the church of St. Michael in Appleby aforeſaid. On the other part, the ſaid Leonard Langhorne covenants to teach one grammar ſchool in the borough aforeſaid, during the time that he ſhall enjoy the ſaid chantries. It is further covenanted, that in caſe of ſickneſs or infirmity or pilgrimage, they ſhall excuſe his attendance on the ſaid ſchool during ſuch time. And if it happen that the tenements or rents of the ſaid chantry of St. Mary, by the wars of the Scots or other misfortunes, be waſted or dilapidated; then the ſaid Leonard ſhall be excuſed from officiating and teaching as aforeſaid, until the ſame ſhall be ſufficiently repaired or reſtored. Witneſſes of this agreement, Henry Salkeld mayor, Richard Garnett vicar, Roland Machel, Hugh Machel, Edmund Machel, John Helton, William Gyllat, Thomas Harryſon, and others.†

In the valuation in the firſt fruits office in the 26 Hen. 8. there is this Item; "The chantry or grammar ſchool in the town of Appleby is worth yearly in

* Town cheſt.

† Machel.

the mansion house and one close 8 *s*, in rents and farms of divers burgages lying within the town of Appleby 4 *l* 3 *s* 3 *d*. In the whole 4 *l* 11 *s* 3 *d*."

In the 1 Ed. 6. By a return made by Sir Thomas Wharton knight and other commissioners of king Edward the sixth, to inquire of all colleges and chantries and their revenues vested in the king by act of parliament in that year, in the counties of Westmorland and Cumberland, it is certified, as to Appulbye, that there is a stipendiary used to celebrate mass and other divine service in the parish church there, and to keep a free grammar school. Edward Gybson incumbent and schoolmaster there hath a clear yearly revenue of the same for his salary 5 *l* 19 *s* 10 *d*. The goods and ornaments belonging to the same be valued at 2 *l* 1 *s* 8 *d*.

In the next year, the king granted to William Warde gentleman, and Richard Venables esquire, the revenues of the chantry at Appleby, to the amount of 5 *l* 11 *s* 8 *d* a year, payable by 47 different persons. To hold of the king as of his manor of Greenwiche, by fealty only, in free socage.

Queen Mary, in consideration probably of the loss sustained by the school from the dissolution of the chantries, granted to the said school 5 *l* 10 *s* 8 *d* yearly, charged upon the rectory of Crosby Ravensworth. And there was a decree in the exchequer, in the 3 & 4 Ph. and Mary, for the payment of one year's arrear thereof to Edward Gybson schoolmaster.

Finally; queen Elizabeth, by letters patent, in the 16th year of her reign, established a free grammar school in Appleby, of the foundation of the burghers there; to have ten governors, of whom when any shall die, the survivors or the major part of them then dwelling within the town of Appleby shall chuse another of the inhabitants or freeholders of the town of Appleby aforesaid, into the place of him so dying. The governors to appoint a master and usher; and make statutes and ordinances from time to time; and take lands and possessions, so as they exceed not the clear yearly value of 40 *l*. The first governors were Barnaby Machel, John Hartlay, Rainold Hartlay, Leonard Smith, Robert Bland, John Smith, William Bland, John Pelter, Cuthbert Pelter, and John Robinson.

In the 21 Eliz. In consideration of 300 *l* (240 *l* of which had been given by the will of Dr. Miles Spencer, and the rest made up by other benefactions) Robert Bowes of Aske in the county of York esquire granted a rent charge of 20 *l* a year, upon the manor and demesne called Newton Garths in the county of Durham.

In the 31 Eliz. Rainold Hartley ordered by his will, that if the governors of the school, within 5 years after his decease, should purchase the close lying on the back side of the school-house, his executors should give 40 *l* towards it; and if they should not make such purchase, but build a new school house, then his executors should give 6 *l* 13 *s* 4 *d* towards the rebuilding thereof.

In the 1 Jac. Christopher Walker, vicar, with consent of the bishop and the dean and chapter, granted to Reginald Bainbrig and his successors, a parcel of land 27 ells in length and 10 in breadth, to build a school upon, which had before belonged to the priory of Wetheral, lying between the mansion-house of the chantry of the virgin Mary on the north, and a burgage of George earl of Cumberland called Pear-tree garth on the south, and to the highway on the west; paying to the grantor and his successors yearly 6*d* at Martinmass.

The said Reginald Bainbrig purchased of Miles Hartley for 40*s* the Pear-tree garth, lying between the street leading from the church to the school on the south side, and a burgage late of the prior of Wetheral on the north: which by his will in the 4 Jac. he devised to the school. He also gave by his will all his books to the school (on paying 6 *l* to his executors), and also all the materials which he had provided for building a school-house.

In 1661, Dr. Thomas Smith, then prebendary of Carlisle, procured a lease of the tithe corn of Drybeck to be granted by the dean and chapter to the schoolmaster of Appleby; for which he pays to the dean and chapter 3 *l* 3 *s* 4 *d* yearly.

In 1671, an indenture was executed, between Sir Richard Sandford baronet, Richard Brathwaite esquire, Robert Hilton esquire, Lancelot Machel esquire, John Thwaites, Thomas Carleton, Leonard Smith, William Smith, gentlemen, Robert Dover, and John Nanson, yeomen, governors of the free grammar school of Appleby, of the one part; and the provost and scholars of Queen's college in Oxford, of the other part; whereby the said governors, in consideration of the great love and affection of the reverend Dr. Thomas Barlow provost of the said college (afterwards bishop of Lincoln), Dr. Thomas Smith prebendary of Durham (afterwards bishop of Carlisle), and Mr. Randal Sanderson rector of Weyhill in Hampshire, manifested by the gift of 380 *l*, do grant and set over all their power of nominating a schoolmaster unto the said provost and scholars, that they and their successors shall and may at all times hereafter appoint a schoolmaster; and that the said governors and their successors shall still have and retain the corrective power as formerly over such master as shall by the said provost and scholars be elected, the better to continue the said master in his due observance and regards towards them. And the said provost and scholars do for them and their successors covenant and promise to and with the said governors and their successors, that within 6 weeks after notice of the removal or death of a schoolmaster, they will take care to send a fit person for the supply of the said place.

In pursuance of which agreement, benefactions were given to more than the amount of the above consideration; the said Dr. Smith gave 200 *l*, Mr. Sanderson 300 *l*, and Dr. Barlow 100 *l* and some books: Sir John Lowther of Lowther baronet gave also 100 *l*. All of whom had been Appleby scholars. Dr. Smith was born at Whitwall in the parish of Asby; Mr. Sanderson, at Regill in the parish of Crosby Ravensworth; and Dr. Barlow, at Lang-gill in the parish of Orton.

Of the said money, 500 *l* was lent to Richard Brathwaite esquire, one of the said governors; who in consideration thereof mortgaged his estate at Burtergill, and charged the same with an annuity of 30 *l*, payable at Martinmass and Whitsuntide to the schoolmaster of Appleby; this being the legal interest at that time. Another 100 *l* was let out upon bonds. And of the remaining 100 *l*, 60 *l* was paid to Mr. Robert Edmundson, schoolmaster, for resigning his place; and 40 *l* reserved towards the building of a dwelling-house for the head

head master of the school. Which, together with the wall about the court or garden wherein the house stands, was built in the same year, and the overplus of the charges above the said 40 *l* was jointly paid by the said Dr. Smith and Mr. Sanderson.

In the year 1676, the said Mr. Sanderson gave 30 *l*, to be expended in planking the floor of the school, renewing the tables and seats, inlarging the windows on the back side of the school, and cieling the chambers in the first loft.

In 1684, the governors purchased the demesne lands of New-hall within the manor of Sandford, with some small tenements thereto belonging, of Thomas Warcop and his son George, for 500 *l*, being part of the said benefactions.

The abovesaid agreement, whereby the governors transfer to the college their right of nominating a schoolmaster, is undoubtedly void in law. But it is so manifestly for the advantage of the school and neighbourhood, that it seems to have been thought unnecessary to be at the expence of an act of parliament to confirm it. Elections by a number of feoffees or the like are frequently controuled by some leading person, and more especially in parliamentary boroughs, where merit is not always the principal thing regarded; for there are other ends to serve. And we need go no further perhaps for an example, than this instance before us. For notwithstanding that queen Elizabeth by the charter of foundation had appointed all the ten governors of the school to be chosen out of the inhabitants or freeholders, that is, persons who have a freehold estate [*de inhabitantibus vel liberis tenentibus*] in the town of Appleby; yet at the time of this agreement, we find four of the governors (first named) not inhabiting within the town, and (so far as appears from a list of the burghers taken upon the occasion of an election of members of parliament not long after) three of them having not then any estate in the town, and the fourth not so much as would make a vote, having only what they called half a burgage. And the school, it seems, was conducted accordingly: for they gave the schoolmaster 60 *l* to resign. And into his place was elected Mr. *Richard Jackson*, schoolmaster of Kendal, who had before been schoolmaster of Bampton; one of the most eminent teachers of his time.

He was succeeded by *Jonathan Banks*, B. A. in 1686, nominated by the college; on whose death in 1721, *Thomas Nevinson*, M. A. succeeded on the like nomination.

On the cession of Mr. Nevinson, succeeded the present schoolmaster *Richard Yates*, M. A. nominated also by the college; who hath executed that office for the space of 50 years*, with honour, ability, assiduity, and learning; who hath instructed two generations of gentlemen and others, not only in the town and neighbourhood, but from many other parts of the kingdom; and furnished during that time near half the foundation of Queen's college aforesaid; who, together with classical precepts, hath been always solicitous, by his example and every method of instruction, to recommend the practice of virtue and religion.

* viz. at this present writing in 1773.

In

In the year 1720, March 26, Thomas earl of Thanet gave to the provost and scholars of the said college 1000 *l*, which they employed towards building the said college, in consideration that they shall pay 40 *l* a year, or legal interest, as exhibitions for five poor scholars, who have had their education for three years immediately before their going to the university in the free grammar school of Appleby. None to be intitled to any share therein who were not born in Westmorland. And none to hold an exhibition after he hath left the college, or taken the degree of master of arts; keeping all terms, and doing all public exercises, during that time. Especial regard being always had, if equally deserving, to such as shall be sons of any of the tenants of the said earl or his family, within the manor and parishes of Appleby, Brough, Brougham, and Kirkby Stephen, or any other of his manors in the said county. The nomination of the said scholars to be in the said earl during his life, and of the provost and scholars afterwards. In case there shall be a failure of such poor scholars from Appleby school, then and not otherwise, and during such time only, the said exhibitions shall be given to other poor scholars in the said college to be nominated as aforesaid, provided they were born in the said county, and had their education in any other school of the said county.

Besides these, the lady Elizabeth Hastings, by her will dated Ap. 24, 1739, devised her manors, lands, and hereditaments in Wheldale in the West Riding of the county of York, to the provost and scholars of Queen's college in Oxford; out of which 140 *l* a year shall be applied for five exhibitions of poor scholars of 28 *l* each. But they shall receive for the first four years (from Pentecost preceding the election) only 20 *l*, the other 8 *l* to be laid up in the college chest, 20 *l* of which to be paid at the middle of the 5th year, and 20 *l* more at the end of it, to those that have taken their bachelor's degree. The schools of Leeds, Wakefield, Bradford, Beverley, Skipton, Sedbergh, Rippon, Sherborn, Appleby, Heversham, St. Bees, and Penrith, to have each a privilege of sending one poor scholar every five years to the place of nomination; the master to send with him a certificate that he hath distinguished himself above the rest of the same rank in his school for morals and learning; is well grounded in the principles of the church of England, hath competent parts and remarkable industry, and hath applied himself to the reading of Greek authors at least four years. The boy to carry likewise a certificate of his age from the register, signed by the minister and churchwardens. Every candidate to enter upon his 19th year, and none to stand after his 21st is compleated. Copies of that part of the will to be read to the candidates four times in the two last years antecedent to the election. The rectors of Berwick, Spofforth, and Bolton-Percy, and the vicars of Leeds, Ledsham, Thorp-Arch, and Collingham, to meet every five years at the best inn in Abberford, on Thursday in Whitsun week, before eight in the morning. The boys to be there the night before. To begin exercise by eight; the same to be, part of an oration in Tully, not exceeding eight or ten lines, to be translated into English; and part of one of Demosthenes, about the same number of lines, into latin; and two or three verses of the latin testament into greek: This for the forenoon. In the afternoon, two subjects; one of practical divinity out of the catechism,

catechism, on which to give their thoughts in latin, in not fewer than eight lines, nor more than twelve; the other, a thesis for two distichs of verses: All to be on one fair sheet of paper signed by the boys. The electors to return ten of the best, signed by them, to the provost and fellows, who shall out of them chuse eight. The names of the eight to be written on distinct pieces of paper, rolled up, and put into an urn or vase by the provost. The five whose names are first drawn, to be elected. If any of them marry, or go into orders, before the expiration of five years, his exhibition from thence to cease. The provost and fellows may deprive an exhibitioner for misbehaviour. The vicar of Ledsham to give notice three months beforehand to the schoolmasters; for which he shall have 1 *l*, and 9 *l* more for the election charges. And the boys shall have for travelling from the Yorkshire schools 5 *s*, and from the others 10 *s*. If any school shall send none for four elections, the provost and fellows shall put in another school in the same county. The overplus of the estate to be given by the provost to the best deserving, for residing the sixth year; or may be added to increase the exhibitions.

COLBY.

Descending from Appleby towards the west, at about a mile's distance, we arrive at the village of Colby.

It appears to have been held of ancient time by a family of the name *de Colby*, and from them to have come by an heiress to the family of *Warcop*.

In the 22 Hen. 2. we find one *William de Colby*, who was one of those officers that were fined by the said king, for delivering up Appleby castle to the king of Scots. Which *William* seems to be the same who in the register of Wetheral priory is styled *William de Breton* lord of *Colleby*, who in the said king's reign confirmed a grant of lands to the said priory.

In an inquisition in the reign of king Henry the third, concerning waste made in the lands of Robert son of John de Veteripont during his minority by the prior of Carlisle who had the wardship of the said Robert granted to him, the name of one of the jurors is *Hugh de Colleby*. Which said *Hugh de Colleby* was witness to a grant of lands at King's Meburn by John son of Walter de Ravensby to the priory of Wetheral.

In the 8 Ed. 2. by the inquisition *post mortem* of Robert de Clifford, the jurors find, that *Thomas de Colleby* held *Colleby* of the said Robert on the day on which he died; the wardship of whom, when it should happen, was worth 13 *l* 16 *s* 8 *d* a year; and the cornage of the said vill 6 *s* 10 *d*.

In the 16 Ed. 3. *Hugh de Colleby* had a letter of attorney from William de Corbrigg and John de Berewys, to give possession of the manor of Berewys to Thomas de Berewys.

By an inquisition in the 18 Ed. 3. it was found, that *Margaret de Colby* held the manor of Colby.

In the 15 Ric. 2. after the death of Roger de Clifford, the inquisition finds, that *Thomas de Mallerstang* and *Margaret* his wife, as of the right of the said *Margaret*,

Margaret, held the manor of Colby, by homage and fealty and the cornage of 6*s* 10*d*. So that here it went off with a daughter.

In the 4 Hen. 4. Maud widow of Roger de Clifford died seised in dower of the rents and services of *Thomas* son of *William de Warthecopp* and *Margaret* his wife, as of the right of the said *Margaret* (so that this *Thomas* seems to have been her second husband), for the manor of Colbie.

In the 31 Hen. 6. *Thomas Warcopp*, vicar of Kirkby Stephen, as of the right of *Margaret* mother of *Katherine* late wife of the said *Thomas*, held the said manor of Thomas de Clifford. And after him *Thomas Warcop* of Colby, son of *Thomas Warcop* vicar of Kirkby Stephen.

By an inquisition of tenants holding by knights service of Henry earl of Cumberland in the 18 Hen. 8. it is found, that *Thomas Warcopp* of Colby held the manor of Colby by the cornage of 6*s* 10*d*.; yielding wardship, marriage, and relief, and suit to the county court; and that the said manor heretofore belonged to *Hugh de Bello-campo*.

In the 33 Hen. 8. *Thomas Warcop* of Colby and *Barnaby* his son and heir apparent, exchanged a tenement in Colby for lands elsewhere.

In the 1 and 2 Ph. and Mary, *Barnaby Warcopp* held the said manor *.

In Mr. Machel's time, in the reign of king Charles the second, there was one *Thomas Warcop* of Colby gentleman, who (he says) was the principal of the family, but it was then gone to decay. He had 22 children; but the name and family at Colby is now totally extinct.

The Warcops sold most of the tenements to freehold; and the rest that were not then able to purchase have been since infranchised.

Ranulph de Meschines gave a carucate of land at Colby to the priory of Wetheral in 1086 †.

And in the reign of king Henry the second, Emsand son of Walter granted to God and the abbey of St. Mary's York and the monks of Wederhale a carucate of land at Colleby. Which grant William Beeton lord of Colby cousin and heir of the said Emsand confirmed, to God and the monastery of St. Mary's York, and to Clement the abbot and his successors and the monks there serving God and St. Mary, for the health of his soul and of Emma his wife and his father and mother and all his ancestors and successors. Witnesses Robert archdeacon of Carlisle, Murdach dean (rural) of Appleby, William de Lowther, Adam de Musegrave, Gospatric son of Orme, Torphin de Wateby, Thomas de Hellebeck, Gamel de Sandford, Adam son of Uctred of Botelton, Alan son of Torphin de Alneston, Waldeve de Kirkeby Thore, William de Appilby, Copsi the Moorward, and others. And the same was also confirmed by king Henry the second ‡.

* All the extracts of the inquisitions *post mortem* of the Cliffords, here and elsewhere, are taken from copies made from the evidences at Appleby and Skipton castles by Mr. Machel and Mr. Bird.

† Machel.

‡ Registr. Wetheral.

The

The biſhop of Carliſle hath ſome tenants at this place, who pay an annual rent of 3*l* 6*s* 8*d*.

The priory of Carliſle alſo had ſome lands lying between Colby and Bolton, given to the ſaid priory by Uchtred and Ada his heir; which were confirmed by king Henry the ſecond.

BARWISE.

Turning Southward from Colby, we come to the demeſne and hall of Berwise. In the reign of king Henry the third, we find one *Alan de Berwys*, a man of conſiderable note. He was one of the witneſſes to a charter of John de Veteripont to the inhabitants of Kirkby Thore, to be free from the demands of the foreſters. And he was one of the jurors to inquire concerning the waſte committed by the prior of Carliſle in the lands late of the ſaid John, during the minority and wardſhip of his ſon.

In the 40th year of the ſaid king, Thomas Vipont, biſhop of Carliſle, by virtue of a mandate from pope Alexander the 4th, granted to this Alan de Berwys, by reaſon of his diſtance from the pariſh church, and inundations in the winter ſeaſon, a licence to build a chapel on his own ground there; and he was to endow the ſame, and might receive benefactions for the ſame alſo from others: The chaplain to take an oath of obedience to the vicar of the mother church.

He ſeems to have had ſeveral ſons. To one of them, *Alan*, he gave all his lands in Slegill; whoſe deſcendents continued there for five generations.

John de Berewyſe and *Henry* his brother, who ſeem to have been other two ſons, were witneſſes to a deed of a meſſuage in Appleby, from Richard de Apelby to Robert de Veteripont ſon of John.

In the 27 Ed. 1. *John de Berewiſe* ſon of John de Berewiſe granted lands in Aſkeby to William ſon of Simon de Brampton.

In the 30 Ed. 1. *William de Berewys* repreſented the borough of Appleby in parliament.

In the 7 Ed. 2. *Alexander de Berewiſe* repreſented the ſaid borough.

In the 16 Ed. 3. *Thomas de Berewiſe*, ſon of *Euſtace de Berewyſe*, being then come of age, had livery of the manor of Berewyſe. In the next year we find him ſtyled *Sir Thomas de Berewiſe.*

In the 34 Ed. 3. *Thomas de Berewiſe* repreſented the county of Weſtmorland in parliament.—And this is the laſt of the name that hath occurred.

How the eſtate came to the *Roſſe's*, whether by marriage or otherwiſe, we have not found.

But in the 12 Hen. 7. we find one *Thomas Roos* at Barwyſe; who obtained a diſpenſation to marry Elizabeth Blenkinſop of Hellebeck, his couſin in the 4th degree.

They had a ſon *Thomas Roos* of Barwiſe eſquire, who died in the 35 Hen. 8.

It is ſaid, the laſt of this name forfeited the eſtate, by ſtealing a ſilver chalice out of the church *.

Afterwards it came into the hands of Sir *John Sudwick:* Who ſold the ſame to Sir *John Boyer.*

Lady *Boyer* ſold the ſame to *Reginald Dobſon* of Dufton; who had a ſon *Reginald Dobſon*, who had two daughters, *Elizabeth* married to Robert Brathwaite of Warcop eſquire, and *Milcah* married to Cuthbert Collingwood of Newcaſtle upon Tyne merchant. And *Barwiſe* was ſold to *John Stephenſon* of Newcaſtle aforeſaid merchant; who ſold the ſame in 1748 to *Thomas Carleton* of Appleby eſquire, who had only two daughters, the younger of whom was married to George Stephenſon of Warcop eſquire, and died without iſſue; the elder daughter *Elizabeth* was married to John Metcalfe of Bellerby in the county of York eſquire, and hath iſſue now living, *Elizabeth*, *John*, and *Thomas.*

HOFF AND DRYBECK.

From Barwiſe advancing towards the South-eaſt, we arrive at HOFF and DRYBECK; which finiſhes our perambulation of the pariſh of St. Laurence.

DRYBECK is a ſmall village, conſiſting of about ten families, in the manor of *Hoff:* ſo called from a ſmall rivulet running by it, which in the ſummer ſeaſon is dry.

HOFFE *(Offa)* was a frequent name among the Saxons, and poſſibly the village might receive its name from the owner, in like manner as the owner often received his name from the place he lived at.

There was one *William de Offa* witneſs to a deed of a meſſuage in Appleby, from Richard de Apelby to Robert ſon of John de Veteripont, in the reign of king Henry the third.

Nevertheleſs, before this time, namely, in the reign of king Henry the ſecond, Sir Hugh Morvil was in poſſeſſion thereof, from whom it deſcended to his two daughters coheirs, *Ada* married to Thomas de Multon, and *Joan* married to Richard Gernon; which Joan had a daughter and heir Ada married to Richard Boyvil and afterwards to William de Furnival. Thus by an inquiſition in the 55 Hen. 3. it is found, that Ada then widow of William de Furnival deceaſed, held a moiety of a certain manor called Off, beyond Trent, in the county of Weſtmorland; and that Helwiſe her daughter, wife of Euſtachius de Balliol, was her next heir, aged 23 years. But the whole afterwards, by failure of iſſue of this younger branch, came to the Multons, deſcendents of Sir Hugh Morvil's elder daughter Ada.

In the 20 Ed. 1. Sir *Hugh de Multon* of Hoffe was a juror at Appleby, in a cauſe between the king and the abbot and convent of St. Mary's York, concerning the advowſon of the two churches in Appleby. Which Sir Hugh was not of the direct line, but probably a younger brother of the family.

* Machel.

By an inquisition in the 3 Ed. 2. it was found, that the heir of *Thomas de Multon*, then under age, held Hoff of Robert de Clifford lord of Westmerland.

And in the 8 Ed. 2. after the death of the said Robert, it was found, that the heir of *Thomas de Multon* of Gillesland held the manor of Hoff and Drybeck; the wardship whereof was worth 30*l* a year, and the cornage 9*s* 2*d*.

This heir of *Thomas de Multon* was a daughter, *viz.*

Margaret de Multon of Gillsland; who was married to *Ranulph de Dacre*, and brought with her the inheritance into the family of Dacre.

By an inquisition in the 18 Ed. 3. it was found, that *William Dacre* held the manor of Hoffe and Drybeck.

In the 10 Hen. 5. after the death of John lord Clifford, the inquisition finds, that *Thomas de Dacre* held of the said John, on the day on which he died, the manor of Hoff.

In the 17 Hen. 6. *Thomas de Dacre*, lord of Gillsland, made a settlement of his estates, and amongst the rest, of the manor of Hoff, and all his lands and tenements in Drybeck and Appleby.

In the last year of king Hen. 6. *Ranulph de Dacre* being slain in the battle of Towton Field, his estates were confiscated, but were restored to his brother *Humphrey* by king Edward the fourth; amongst the particulars whereof, is the manor of Hoff.

In the 1 Hen. 7. after the death of the said Humphrey, the inquisition finds, that Humphrey Dacre lord of Dacre and Gillsland held of Sir Thomas Thweng knight (who was probably a grantee of the crown, after the attainder of John lord Clifford) the manor of Hoff; and that *Thomas Dacre* was his son and heir, of the age of 18 years on the feast of St. Catherine then last past.

Which Thomas Dacre had a son *William*, who had issue *Thomas*, *Leonard*, *Edward*, and *Francis*. *Thomas* had a son *George*, who died in his infancy; and three daughters, *Anne*, *Mary*, and *Elizabeth*; of whom, *Mary* died unmarried, *Anne* was married to Philip earl of Arundel, and *Elizabeth* to the lord William Howard, both of them sons of Thomas duke of Norfolk. The intailed estates came to their uncles in tail male; all of whom were attainted of treason and banished upon account of the affair of Mary queen of Scots. Which intail continued till the tenth year of king Charles the first, when *Ranulph* son of *Francis*, the last in the intail, died without issue.

During the time of these estates being in the crown, queen Elizabeth in the 33d year of her reign demised to Richard Southwaite gentleman the woods, underwoods, and trees growing in Hoff Lun wood, in the manor of Hoff and Drybeck, in four several copses; *viz.* Greenbank coppice or hag, 20 acres; Howgill coppice or hag, 20 acres; Bradland bank, 30 acres; Foddering-land hag, 12 acres; for the term of 21 years: paying for the same 40*s* yearly.

And in the 35th year of her reign, the said queen granted the *herbage* and *hay ground* of Hoff Luyne wood, parcel of the manor of Hoff and Drybeck, being parcel of the lands and possessions of Leonard Dacre esquire, attainted

of

of treason,—to Thomas Yaire, Miles Yaire, and Anne Yaire, and their assigns, for the term of their lives, or till surrender or forfeiture; for which they paid a fine of *6 l 8 s 4 d*, and a yearly rent of *3 l 6 s 8 d*. And after the death of each who died tenant thereof, *30 s* to be paid in the name of an heriot.

Note, *Lun, Llwyn*, is British; and signifies a wood or grove.

In the 44 Eliz. the said queen granted (amongst other particulars) the manor of Hoffe and Drybeck, to Edward Carill, John Holland, John Cornewalleys, and Robert Cancefield, esquires, until and so long as there should be an heir male of the body of Francis Dacre esquire late attainted of treason in full life.

Finally, *William Williams*, who had been steward at Greystock castle, purchased this manor, and died leaving four daughters coheirs; the eldest was married to Sir Edward Hassel knight, the second to *John Winder* esquire counsellor at law, the third to Mr. Relph of Cockermouth, and the fourth to Dr. Gibbon dean of Carlisle. The said John Winder with the second daughter had Hoff; and had issue *Williams Winder* esquire, who devised the same to his kinsman *Edward Milward* esquire grandson by his mother's side to the said Dr. Gibbon, and son of the reverend Thomas Milward rector of Marton and of Kirkby Thore.

There was anciently a *chapel* at Hoff, wherein a chaplain was to officiate three days in every week; for which, as appears from bishop Silvester's endowment of the vicarage as aforesaid, 37 acres of land were assigned in the field of Hoff.

The sum of *18 s* a year was payed out of Hoff to Shap abbey, for and in name of alms corn.

The hospital of St. Leonard's York had two oxgangs of land in Drybeck. (*Dugd.*)

At the south end of the old bridge at Hoff, is a place which in Mr. Machel's time was called Douglass-ing; where, it is said, a battle was fought between the Scotch and English. At which time Appleby was burned. Bones of dead men have been dug up near the old bridge stead.—Perhaps this may refer to the 13 Ric. 2. in which year, in the month of November, when the Englishmens barns were full, and their yards or barnekins well stored with provisions for the winter, the Scots, under the conduct of the earl of *Murray* and the lord *Douglas*, entred into England, and burned the country of Gilsland, kept on their journey to Burgh under Stanemore, and so through Westmorland and Cumberland, and after much spoil and waste made in all the countries and parts aforesaid, with many prisoners and great riches, they returned into their own country. *Drake's Historia Anglo-Scotica*, 84.

PARISH OF ST. MICHAEL'S APPLEBY.

PASSING over the bridge, we come to the other parish in Appleby, namely, that of ST. MICHAEL, which now is scarcely deemed part of Appleby, and goes commonly by the name of *Bongate* parish. *Bongate*, properly so called, is the street where the *villani* or *bondmen* inhabited, who were attendent upon the castle to execute the servile and laborious offices.

Thus by the inquisition aforesaid, on occasion of the dispute between the town and the owners of the castle, it was found, that king John did not grant to Robert de Veteripont the town of Appleby then properly so called, but *Old Appleby* where the *bondmen* inhabit.

This parish is bounded on the east by the parishes of Romaldkirk and Warcop; on the south, by the parishes of Warcop and St. Laurence Appleby; on the west, by the parishes of Kirkby Thore and Marton; and on the north, by the parishes of Kirkby Thore, Marton, and Dufton; and contains in the whole about 145 families, all of the church of England.

It is a vicarage, valued in the king's books at 20*l* 13*s*. 9*d*.

Ranulph de Meschines gave this church to the abbot and convent of St. Mary's York: Which grant was confirmed by king Henry the second. And the same was confirmed and appropriated to the said priory by Athelwald first bishop of Carlisle; whose appropriation was confirmed by his successor Hugh, under the following limitations; namely, that the cell of Wetheral possess the same to their own use, saving to the said abbey their usual pension; and that they present a fit vicar to the same, and allow him a stipend of 5 marks, he discharging all episcopal and archidiaconal charges.

It seems, after this, that the bishops of Carlisle claimed the patronage of the advowson; whereupon pope Gregory by his bull in the year 1239 confirmed the patronage to the priory of Wetheral *.

Nevertheless, in the year 1248, the abbot and convent granted the patronage of the said vicarage to the then bishop of Carlisle and his successors; saving to the said abbot and convent the pension accustomably paid to them out of the same by the prior of Wederall. Which vicarage at the same time was taxed at 20 marks †.

In 1256, *Walter Feadwell* was vicar; as appears by an instrument in that year by Thomas Vipont bishop of Carlisle executed at Bewley, on a reference to him by the abbot and convent of St. Mary's York, ordaining, that the vicar and his successors shall have for their portion the tithes of lambs and wool, all oblations, Lent offerings, the tithes of flax, gardens, the whole white tithes, of colts, calves, sacramental offerings, the tithes of hay throughout the whole parish, of mills, alehouses, marriages, mortuaries, the tithe of pigs, and all tithes and oblations to the altarage happening howsoever, and a moiety of the

* Regist. Wetheral. † Id.

arable and meadow land; alſo all the tithes ariſing from the hoſpital of St. Nicholas in the ſaid pariſh; and certain tofts and crofts therein ſpecified *.

In the year 1291, there was a diſpute between king Edward the firſt and the abbot of St. Mary's York, concerning the advowſon of the church of St. Laurence in Appleby and the church of St. Michael in Appleby in Bondegate; the king affirming that king Henry the ſecond preſented to the ſame Adam and John his clerks: But the jurors find, that the abbot had more right in the ſaid advowſons than the king. The names of the jurors were, Thomas de Culwene, Hugh de Multon of Hoffe, William de Stirkeland, John de Roſſegill, R. le Englays, Richard de Preſton, knights; Jo. Mauſchael, William de Crakenthorp, Richard de Muſegrave, Jo. Fraunceis of Cliburn, Richard de Warthecop, and Richard Tyrel.

In 1302, one *Richard de Bradewood* was vicar; who being accuſed of nonreſidence, and having made his purgation, had thereupon letters of remiſſion granted.

In 1339, on the death of Richard de Bradewood, *Henry de Appleby* was collated by biſhop Kirkby.

In 1362, *Richard de Aſlackby* was collated by biſhop Appleby.

In 1369, the ſame biſhop collated *John de Merton*; who in the ſame year was preſented by the provoſt and ſcholars of Queen's College in Oxford to the vicarage of Burgh under Stanemore, upon an exchange agreed on between him and *John Raynald* vicar there.

In 1452, one *John Marſhall*, vicar of St. Michael's, ſold to Thomas lord Clifford a burgage in Appleby.

* Omnibus Chriſti fidelibus ad quos præſens ſcriptum pervenerit, Thomas permiſſione divina Karliolenſis eccleſiæ miniſter humilis, ſalutem in Domino ſempiternam. Ad univerſitatis veſtræ notitiam volumus pervenire, quod cum inter viros religioſos abbatem et conventum Sanctæ Mariæ Eborum, per fratrem Thomam de Scyreburn monachum et Galfridum de Grangiis procuratores ſuos et priorem et monachos de Wederal perſonaliter comparentes ex una parte, et Walterum de Feadwelle perpetuum vicarium ecoleſiæ Sancti Michaelis de Appelbi perſonaliter comparentem ex altera parte, ſupra taxationem vicariæ ejuſdem eccleſiæ coram nobis eſſet actitatum: Nos, de communi conſenſu utriuſque partis, non obſtante taxatione aliqua prohibiti, vicariam memoratæ eccleſiæ taxavimus in hunc modum: viz. Quod prædictus Walterus et ſucceſſores ſui qui miniſtraturi ſunt in dicta eccleſia habeant nomine vicariæ omnes agnos, lanam, omnimodas oblationes, decimas quadrageſſimæ, lini, ortorum, totius albi, pullorum, vitulorum, denariorum venientium cum pane benedicto, decimas fœni totius parochiæ, molendinorum, cerviſiæ, et ſponſalia, mortuaria, decimas porcellorum, et omnimodas decimas et obventiones ad altaragium qualitercunque contingentes, et medietatem totius terræ arabilis et prati. Ita tamen quod tota terra arabilis et pratum per viros fide dignos, ad hoc ex utraque parte communiter electos, in duas equales partes dividantur, et ſorte dirimantur. Item, dictus vicarius et ſucceſſores ſui habebunt totam decimam provenientem de hoſpitali beati Nicholai in eadem parochia; et omnes toftos et croftos a domo Attini uſque ad domum Roberti Wa'di ex auſtrali parte dictæ eccleſiæ continuatos. Et dictus prior habebit omnes toftos et croftos reſiduos ſimiliter ad eccleſiam pertinentes, cum capitali meſſuagio. In cujus rei teſtimonium, una cum ſignis dictorum prioris et vicarii, mutuis ſcriptis utriuſque partis, ſigillum noſtrum apponi fecimus. Datum apud Bellum Locum in craſtino annunciationis dominicæ. Anno Domini M.CC.L.VI°.

Et ſciendum eſt, quod dictus vicarius et ſucceſſores ſui omnia onera ordinaria conſueta et debita ſuſtinebunt. Ex præcepto autem epiſcopi et de conſenſu partium, poſt conſignationem hujus literæ fuit iſta clauſula appoſita. *(Regiſtr. Wetheral.)*

In

In 1561, *John Smith*, chaplain to bishop Best, was collated to the vicarage of *Bondgate*, being then vacant by non-payment of the queen's subsidy by *George Lancaster* the late incumbent.

In 1569, on the resignation of John Smith, *Gregory Scot*, chancellor of the diocese, and prebendary of Carlisle, was collated by the same bishop.

In 1576, on Gregory Scot's death, *Thomas Burton* was collated by bishop Barnes.

In 1579, *Thomas Fairfax* was collated by bishop May.

In 1582, on the resignation of Thomas Fairfax, *William Porter* was collated by the same bishop.

In 1611, on the death of William Porter, *John Teasdale*, M. A. was collated by bishop Robinson. And after him, one *John Spencer*, M. A.

In 1634, *Robert Symson*, M. A. was collated by bishop Potter, and in the same year also to Ormshead.

In 1661, on the resignation of the said Robert, (who seems to have held through all the changes of times, and was afterwards presented to Marton, probably upon this resignation) his son *Barnaby Symson*, M. A. and sometime fellow of Queen's college in Oxford, was collated; who also afterwards succeeded his father at Ormeshead, and lastly at Marton. He continued rector of this parish and Marton upwards of 50 years; and dying in 1712, was succeeded in this parish by *James Cock*, B. A. being collated by bishop Nicolson.

In 1738, on the death of James Cock, *John Hill* was collated by bishop Fleming.

The before-mentioned countess of Pembroke, amongst her other benefactions, raised this *church* out of its ruins. In remembrance whereof, the following inscription was cut in wood between the chancel and the body of the church: "The right honourable the lady Anne Clifford, countess dowager of Dorset, "Pembroke, and Montgomery, repaired this church, A. D. 1658."

There is a large vault on the north side of this church, the ancient burying place of the Hiltons of Hilton in this parish.

Belonging to this church was anciently a *chantry* founded by Sir William English.—In the town chest of Appleby there is a lease in the 7 Ed. 4. granted to John Dey of a tenement and garden in Appleby, by Sir James Harrington patron and John Winton chaplain of the chantry of Sir William Englys knight.

And in the next year there is a lease of a burgage in Appleby to Gilbert Brown, granted by the said John Winton, styled chaplain of the chantry of the virgin Mary in the church of St. Michael Appleby.

Part of the tenements in Bongate are freehold; but the greater part customary.

Proceeding northwards from Bongate, we ascend *Battlebarrow*, which sufficiently denotes from whence it derived its name. But what particular battle was fought there, no tradition informs us. In some of the Latin instruments, this street is called *Vicus del Fyte.*

At the furthest part thereof, on the west side, is an house which was built out of the ruins of an ancient *friery*, that stood behind the opposite row of houses, where the ground adjacent still carries that name. And it seems to have been dedicated to the virgin Mary, because there is a well that springs out of those grounds called Lady-well. They were of an order of white friers; and the friery was founded in the year 1281, by the lords Clifford, Percy, and Vescy *.

In a bill of expences of the funeral of one Guy Nelson, about the reign of king Henry the eighth, are these Items: To sex priestes 2*s* 2*d*. For proving the testament 3*s* 4*d*. Making it 4*d*. Item, to the prior of freers for fraternyte 1 *d* †.

In the 28th of the same king, Thomas Blenkinsop of Helbeck esquire gave by his will 6*s* 8*d* to the fryars of Appleby.

After the dissolution, in the 35 Hen. 8. the king granted to Christopher Crakanthorpe of Newbiggin esquire, the house and site of the late priory of Friers Carmelites, commonly named the white friers within the town of Appleby, with two gardens and one orchard by estimation an acre and an half, and the toft late the cemitery of the said late priory by estimation one rood, and other lands in the parish of Bongate belonging to the said priory to the amount of 20 acres or thereabouts. The purchase money for this, and Hale Grange, and the manor of Hardendale and Wasdale, was 255 *l* 3 *s*.

Advancing further towards the north west, in the way to Crackenthorp, we came to the ground called *St. Nicholas*; which belonged of old to a little *hospital* of that name: It stood where the farm-house stands now.

John de Veteripont gave this hospital to the abbey of Shap. Which donation was confirmed by Walter bishop of Carlisle; upon condition, that they should maintain there three lepers commonly called lazars for ever ‡.

In the 5 Ric. 2. Roger de Clifford gave licence to the monks of Hep, to inclose a piece of ground in the fields of St. Nicholas.

* Tanner, 588. † Id.

‡ The hospital also of St. Leonard nigh Kendal was established for the maintenance of lepers. This disorder seems to have prevailed in certain countries and at certain times more than others. Anciently in this realm, there was a legal provision for removing of lepers apart from the rest of the society; there being in the register of Writs the form of a writ *De leproso amovendo.* Perhaps the greater cleanliness of modern times may have contributed to abate the rigour of this distemper; as also the change of food, by the disuse in a great measure of salted provisions. At the time of these charitable institutions, there were few or no inclosures in this realm, except only for deer; and no hay or other provender laid up for the fattening of cattle in winter: but they killed and salted their cattle and sheep at the beginning of winter, before they became leen upon the common pasture. In some parts of the kingdom, and particularly in this county, there are yet some remains of this practice in salting up about Martinmass-tide their beef for winter provision; and perhaps this may be one reason of the itch or scurvy sometimes prevailing amongst the poorer sort of people: as in an higher degree, in long sea voyages, the necessary use of salted provisions occasions dreadful ravages by the scurvy.

After

After the diſſolution, king Henry the eighth, in the 36th year of his reign, granted to Thomas lord Wharton, all that the hoſpital of St. Nicholas nigh Appleby, with all the poſſeſſions and revenues thereto belonging.

In the 12th year of king James, Philip lord Wharton and Sir Thomas Wharton knight his ſon and heir apparent, for the conſideration of 700*l*, ſold to Iſrael Fielding of Starforth in the county of York gentleman, all that the late diſſolved hoſpital, farm, or grange, of St. Nicholas near Appleby, late belonging to the monaſtery of Shap, and all the meſſuages and lands thereto belonging, or enjoyed therewith for 40 years next before.

And in the year 16.2, Anne counteſs of Pembroke purchaſed the ſaid farm of William Fielding eſquire; and ſettled the ſame upon her hoſpital at Appleby as aforeſaid.

CRACKENTHORP.

Deſcending further, on the north ſide of the river Eden, we come to Crackenthorp, which ſeems to have received its name from ſome rookery there; for *crake* to this day, amongſt the country people, is uſed to ſignify a rook or crow.

The Machels ſeem to have continued and reſided at this place, longer than any one family of note at any other place in the county. Above the degree of yeomen always; and ſeldom or never aſcending to the degree of knight. Eſquires or gentlemen conſtantly; and peculiarly remarkable in all generations for a brave and martial ſpirit: To which, even their family name might ſome little contribute. The name was frequently written of ancient time *Mau chael*, *Malchael*, and when latinized *Malus Catulus*. And the reverend Thomas Machel (whom we have often had occaſion to mention with honour in theſe memoirs, and who was a younger brother of this family) obſerves, that before the holy war they ſealed with a ſingle Indian dog (as he calls it), *ex graco et tigride nato*; in a rampant poſture, having a forked tail: and were called *Mali Catuli*, either becauſe the firſt of that name had deſtroyed ſome ſuch noxious beaſt, or (which indeed is more likely) was generally of a warlike diſpoſition.

The ſaid Thomas Machel goes farther, and ſuppoſes that they may be deſcended from the Catuli amongſt the ancient Romans. But, without the help of conjecture, it is evident, that this was a name at the time of the conqueſt. In thoſe parts of Weſtmorland and the adjoining places which we have had occaſion to take notice of, as mentioned in Domeſday, we find, "*In Loneſdale et Cocreham habuerunt* Ulf *et* Machel *duas carucatas terræ ad geldum.*" This the ſaid reverend gentleman would have been pleaſed to have diſcovered, in honour of the antiquity of his name. Whether *Ulf* and *Machel* had any cognation, we cannot preſume to determine. *Ulf* is no other than *Wolf* latinized, which is a name ſtill in uſe; and the impreſſion of the ſeal at Crackenthorp which Mr. Machel deſcribes, bears a ſtriking reſemblance of that animal.

Mr. Machel ſuppoſes that *Whelp-caſtle* at Kirkby Thore might receive its name from this family; and that the family of *Whelpdale* alſo may poſſibly have

have some connexion therewith. And there is indeed (besides the name) this resemblance, that the three greyhounds (improperly, as it seemeth), which the Machels now bear instead of the aforesaid fierce animal, are the arms also of the family *de Whelp-dale*.

There was one *Liulf (L'Ulf)* of Kirkby Thore, who gave lands there to the abbey of Holme Cultram in the reign of king Henry the second.

Also one Waldeve son of Gamel son of *Whelp* gave lands there to the said abbey.

And there is a confirmation by king Henry the second of a grant of lands at Crackenthorp to the priory of Carlisle, which had been given by *Halth le Malchael* and Eva his wife. Which particle *le* seems to imply that *Malchael* (Malus Catulus) is a surname descriptive of the person; as when we say *Ulf le Malchael* (for instance), it will signify in plain English *Wolf that mischievous whelp*.

There is no regular pedigree or succession of the Machel family. They were very numerous, and dispersed into many branches: which dissipated partly the estate, and renders it impossible at this distance of time to deduce the inheritance in a direct lineal succession. What follows we have digested in chronological order, chiefly from the copies or extracts of the family writings made by the said Mr. Thomas Machel, which take up near half of his fifth volume.

1. The first of the name that hath occurred at Crackenthorp is the said *Halth de Malchael*, who (together with his wife as aforesaid) gave to the priory of Carlisle, probably at the foundation thereof, 15 acres of land by the bank of Truttebeck, and a meadow of the land of Crackenthorpe in Ellertker upon the banks of Hedene and of Trutteheck. And there was a grant also to the same priory, by *Humphrey Malchael*, of one third part of the church of Lowthere.

2. About the 26 Hen. 2. *Willielmus Malus Catulus* grants to *Galfridus Malus Catulus* certain lands at Crackenthorp, rendring to him yearly one pound of pepper or eight pence; and doing for the same foreign service to the king as much as appertaineth. And if the said *Galfridus* or his heirs shall forfeit to any one in word or deed that is not blodwite, they shall pay 6*d*, and make satisfaction to the party injured: And if it be blodwite, they shall pay 12*d*, and also make like satisfaction.

3. Towards the latter end of the same king's reign, *John Mauchael* was witness to a grant of lands to the abbey of Holm Cultram, by Adam son of Liulf of Kirkby Thore.

About the same time *Galfridus Malus Catulus* granted lands at Crackenthorp to Alexander de Crackenthorp.

4. In the 7 Ric. 1. There was an exchange of lands at Crossebi and at Loudre, between Henry de Withenton and Galfridus Malkael.

5. In the time of the said Richard the first, *Roger Machel* (whom the Machels claim to be of this family) was lord keeper of the great seal, and was drowned on the coast of Cyprus, as he attended the king to the holy land.

 It

It is ſaid, there is a place at Crackenthorp called from him Rogerheved, Roger-head or hill.

6. *John Mauchael* was witneſs to the grant of the advowſon of the church of Kirkby Thore by Adam de Kirkby Thore to Robert de Veteripont, who lived in the reign of king John.

And the ſaid *John Mauchael* (as it ſeemeth) was witneſs to a grant of lands at Appleby by John de Veteripont ſon of the ſaid Robert to Norman de Redman.

7. In the reign of Hen. 3. *William Mauchael* granted to his brother *Alexander Mauchael* certain lands at Crackenthorp: And on the ſeal of this grant is the aforeſaid rampant beaſt (of whatever ſpecies it might be).

8. In the reign of the ſaid king Henry the third, *John Mauchel* ſon of Alexander made an agreement with *William* ſon of *William de Crackenthorp*, concerning the moulter of the corn-mill there.

9. In the reign of Ed. 1. *John Mauchel* of Crackenthorp was witneſs to ſeveral deeds executed at the county court at Appleby. And in the 20 Ed. 1. he was a juror at Appleby between the king and the abbot and convent of St. Mary's York, concerning the advowſon of the two churches at Appleby.

10. By an inquiſition in the 3 Ed. 2. and another in the 8 Ed. 2. it appears, that *Thomas Mauchell* then held Crackenthorp under the Cliffords; the wardſhip whereof, when it ſhould happen, was *13l 6s 8d* a year, and the cornage *6s 10d*.

11. In the 43 Ed. 3. by inquiſition, *John Mauchall* then held Crackenthorp.

12. In the 20 Ric. 2. *John Mauchell*, granted lands at Crackenthorp to his ſon *William*, on his marriage with Margaret daughter of William de Thorneburgh.

13. In the 10 Hen. 5. By inquiſition after the death of John lord Clifford, *John Machell* ſon of *William* then held the manor of Crackenthorp; which *John* died in the 1 Ed. 4. leaving a ſon and heir *John*, being then above the age of 21 years.

14. In the reign of king Henry the ſixth, two of the Crackenthorps of Newbiggin were ſlain in the battle of Towton-field, amongſt many of the northern nobility and gentlemen. And it is probable the Machels of Crackenthorp then ſuffered likewiſe; for we find a pardon by king Ed. 4. of this ſame *John Maychell*.

15. In the 1 Hen. 8. there is a like pardon of *Hugh Machell* ſon of *John*; which although very full and comprehenſive, including treaſons, murders, and other felonies, yet ſeems to have been only upon a particular occaſion, namely, on account of the eſcape of one Henry Parker; for he is ſtyled in the ſaid pardon Hugh Machell of Crackenthorp gentleman, otherwiſe called Hugh Machell one of the manucaptors of Henry Parker.

This *Hugh* had a brother *Guy Machell*, which *Guy* ſeems to have been the elder brother. In the 5 Hen. 8. there was an indenture made between the ſaid *Guy* and *Hugh*, that "if it fortune oder of theme to be ſpendit in the

"king's warres now at this tyme in his noble vayege, or at any oder syke lyke
" vayege, that then the overliver of theme shall suffer [*i. e.* forbear] to mak
" any entre to any part of the londs and tenements that was his broder's so
" being spendit, unto the space of two yers then next ensuing; so that all
" the fermes and profetts shal cume and be peassabilly receyved to the behuf,
" fynding, and seting-of the pure childrin that are cummyn of him so spendit
" and faderless; in symblable maner as their fader *John Machell* dyd unto his
" childrin."

In the same year the said *Hugh* had beaten the chantry priest of Appleby; and there is an award thereupon, setting forth, that whereas Sir Henry Smyth the chauntry priest of Appleby was beaten, hurt, and maimed by *Hugh Machell* of Crakanthorp gentleman, and the said parties had bound themselves by their faith and troth to abide the award of Sir Stephen Ellis parson of Skipton, Ambrose Crackenthorp of Howgill esquire, Sir Alexander Hall vicar of Morland, and John Tillotson bailiff of Carleton in Craven, the said arbitrators do thereupon award, that the said Hugh shall pay to the chantry priest 40*s* a year [a large sum in those days] during his life, the payment to be made in the church of St. Laurence Appleby upon the altar of St. Nicholas the confessor, or to the said Henry in Appleby when the payment is ready: Provided, that if the said Hugh or any for him can provide a better thing for the said Sir Henry, of which the said Sir Henry shall hold him contented, then the said payment from thenceforth to cease.

In the 7 Hen. 8. the aforesaid *Guy* farmed Colby Layths; and he had a dispute with the vicar of Appleby concerning the tithes, which was compromised by the mediation of *Dr. Machel* prebendary of York.

In the 10 Hen. 8. the mayor, bailiffs, and commonalty of Appleby grant to Leonard Langhorne chaplain, in consideration of his teaching school there, two chantries in the church of St. Laurence and one in St. Michael's; to which grant were witnesses (amongst others) *Roland Machell*, *Hugh Machell*, and *Edmund Machell*.

In the 11 Hen. 8. there is an entry of several payments made by Sir Richard Garnet, vicar of St. Laurence Appleby, to *Roland Machell*, *Edmund Machell*, *Nicolas Machell*, *Brian Machell*, and *Jacob Machell*.

In the 13 Hen. 8. there is a submission to an award, between Thomas Harryson of Appleby yeoman, and *Hugh Machell* of Crakanthorp gentleman, upon all matters depending in traverse between the said parties, concerning the distribution of the goods and chattels of the said Sir Richard Garnet deceased.

In the 21 Hen. 8. *Guy* suffered a recovery to cut off the intail; and there was a settlement to *Guy* for life, to *Hugh* his brother for life, then to *Thomas* son of *Guy* and his heirs for ever, of the estates at Crakanthorp, Kesliff, Appulby, and Brampton in Westmorland, and at Lasingby and Kirk Ouswald in Cumberland. This settlement was contested by *Richard* son of *William Machell*, cousin and heir (as he set forth in his claim) of *John Machell* deceased, But it was decreed against him.

In the 22 Hen. 8. there was an award between the said *Guy* and *Hugh*, by Thomas Dudley and Richard Briscow esquires, Robert Clibborne and Ambrose Machell gentlemen, with the umpirage of Thomas Blenkinsop and Gilbert Wharton esquires; concerning an island supposed to belong to and go in lease always with the mill, and for the killing and hurting of divers swine of the said *Guy* by the children and servants of the said *Hugh*, for eating and destroying the corn and grass of the said *Hugh*: Which said arbitrators, having first determined concerning the island, proceed as to the swine, and award, that the said *Hugh* shall for the said trespass lay down before the arbitrators the sum of 3*s* 4*d*, for the use of the said *Guy*; and for the more amity to be had between the parties, they do award, after the receipt of the said sum of 3*s* 4*d*, that the said *Guy* shall give back again the said sum to the said *Hugh*; and for all other trespasses in corn or grass, or any unkindly or unlawful words spoken by the said *Guy* or *Hugh*, or by the wives of the said *Guy* and *Hugh*, or any of their children, they do award the same clearly to be laid aside, without any amends or report thereof to be made in reproach or hurt of any of them.

Two years after this, there was another arbitration between the said parties about the mill, by the right reverend Richard Ewynwod abbot of Shape, William Pykering esquire, Robert Clibburne and John Hoton gentlemen: Who by their award determine certain disputes about the mill at Crackenthorp, which *Hugh* had in lease from *Guy*; and that both the said parties release to each the sureties of the peace which they had each against the other.

In the 28 Hen. 8. the said *Guy* made his will; which, as it shews perfectly the fashion and manner of those times, is here inserted at length: "In the
" name of God, Amen. The 24th day of the month of October, year of
" our Lord God 1536. I Guy Machell of Crackenthorpe, sick of my body,
" whole and perfect of my remembrance, in this manner and form following
" make my last will and testament. First, I give and bequeath my soul to
" almighty God, to our blessed lady clean virgin, to all the company of
" heaven; and my body to be buried within the church of St. Michael of
" Appleby. Also I give and bequeath for the portion of my mortuary 3*s* 4*d*.
" Also I give and bequeath for my forgotten tithes, my soul to be discharged
" of the church 20*d*. Also, if the said gift and legacy for the portion of
" my mortuary be not sufficient to the vicar, then I will, on inventory of all
" my goods to be made by four sworn men prized and valued, that which the
" law requireth to be fully and truly paid. Also I give and bequeath to my
" son *Thomas Machell* my best jack *. Also I give and bequeath to my son
" *Henry Machell* my best steel coat, with my best sword. Also I give and be-
" queath to my son *Edward Machell* my other steel coat, with one other sword.
" Also I give and bequeath to my son *Leonard Machell* one basaerd †. Item,
" I give and bequeath to my son *Guy Machell* one little sword. The residue

* *Jack*, was a kind of defensive coat armour worn by horsemen in war, not of one solid piece, but of several square pieces of steel, scaled fish-like, and covered over with leather. Leather doublets, being less and lighter, are called *jackets*, a diminutive from *jack*.

† *Basaerd*; a poniard, or dagger.

" of

" of all my goods, moveable and unmoveable, not given and bequeathed be-
" fore, my funeral expences and debts paid, I give and bequeath to my wife
" *Margaret Machell*, and to my sons *Henry Machell*, *Edward Machell*, *Leonard*
" *Machell*, *Guy Machell*, *Wylfryde Machell*, *Gyllys Machell*, *Myghtfell Machell*,
" *Robert Machell*, and to my daughter *Anne Machell*; whom I order and make
" my true executors, to dispose for my soul's health, as they think best to
" please God and comfort to my soul. Also I will that all my goods move-
" able and immoveable remain whole together, under the government and
" rule of my wife Margaret, without any division, parts, or portions, till the
" youngest of my forenamed sons come and be of perfect age and discretion;
" and then by the sight of friends the goods left and unspended to be divided
" by even portions to my wife, sons, and daughter aforenamed. Also I make
" and order supervisors of this my will the right honourable the lord Henry
" earl of Cumberland, his honourable son lord Henry Clifford, and my right
" worshipful friend Sir Thomas Ch——— knight; desiring of them all to see
" that my wife and sons aforenamed executors be not hurt ne harmed with
" wrongs; but that they help and aid them in right, for the love of God, as my
" great trust is therein. Records of this my last will and testament, Thomas
" Hyll, John Shepperth, Henry Nelson, with others more."

16. *Guy* died soon after the making of this will. And within a year afterwards, the aforesaid Dr. *(Henry) Machell* died at Donnington: And *Hugh Machell* his brother claimed his effects as next of kin.

In the 30 Hen. 8. On a dispute between *Hugh Machell* of Crakanthorp gentleman, and John Richardson of Scattergate; a commission was issued out of chancery, directed to *Ambrose Machell*, Henry Barton, and Thomas Rose, gentlemen, to make inquiry and settle the dispute about a house in Batelbarghe.

In the 38 Hen. 8. a marriage settlement was made by *Hugh* who had the estate for life, and *Richard Machell* who had the reversion after *Hugh*'s death. *Richard Machell*'s son *John* was to marry *Elinore Machell* daughter of *Hugh*, if the law of the church would permit. The marriage took effect, and they had some lands settled upon them at Crakanthorp and Laysenby.

17. In the 2 and 3 Ph. and Mary, there was a dispute between the said *Richard* and *Henry Machell* his brother. *Richard* distrained the goods of *Henry* and of divers others, for greenhue, boon days, and other services. This produced several riotous and tumultuous proceedings. Whereupon Henry, by *supplicavit* to the court of chancery prayed sureties of the peace against the said *Richard Machell* gentleman, *George Machell*, *John Machell*, *John Machell* the younger alias *Colston*, and five others. These differences were afterwards referred to Thomas Sandefurthe, Richard Salkelde, Thomas Fallowfelde, and Thomas Wybarr, esquires.

In the next year, the said *Henry Machell* had a suit in the court at York for the northern parts, against *George Machell*, *Barnaby Machell*, *Nicolas Machell*, and four others, for ploughing up his ground and other riotous proceedings: Which dispute also was compromised by arbitration; and the defendants were bound not only to abide the award of the arbitrators, but also in the mean

 time

time not to meddle with any ground within the tenement of the ſaid *Henry Machell*, nor otherwiſe to moleſt him concerning the ſame *.

18. In the 4 and 5 Ph. and Mary, *Richard Machell* of Caldbeck in the county of Cumberland gentleman, by indenture, bargained and ſold to Richard Lowther of Lowther eſquire, the wardſhip, cuſtody, and marriage of *Hugh Machell* ſon and heir of *John Machell* deceaſed; and if the ſaid *Hugh* ſhall die before the ſaid Richard Lowther ſhall have beſtowed him in marriage, or before he accompliſh his full age of 21 years; then the ſaid Richard Lowther to have the wardſhip, cuſtody and marriage of *Anthony Machell*, one other of the ſons of the ſaid John Machell deceaſed; and if Anthony ſhall die, then of the next heir of the ſaid Anthony; and ſo from one to another, until the ſaid Richard Lowther ſhall have had the marriage and other full profits, according to the meaning of the ſaid indenture. The ſaid Richard Lowther to have and enjoy the manor and manſion-houſe at Crackenthorp and other eſtates in Cumberland and Weſtmorland of him the ſaid Hugh, during the ſaid time, paying to the ſaid Richard Machel 10*l* yearly, and to find and provide for the ſaid Hugh, or ſuch other as aforeſaid during the ſaid time, ſufficient and convenient meat, drink, apparel, and other neceſſaries meet and requiſite to the ſtate and degree of the ſaid Hugh and ſuch other as aforeſaid, as to reaſon ſhall appertain, at the diſcretion and worſhip of the ſaid Richard Lowther.

19. In the 16 Eliz. *Barnaby Machell* was appointed in the charter of foundation one of the firſt governors of Appleby ſchool.

20. The next of the family that hath occurred was *Lancelot Machel* eſquire. He had two ſons, *Hugh* the elder; and *Thomas* above mentioned, who was ſometime fellow of Queen's college in Oxford, fellow of the royal ſociety, rector of Kirkby Thore, and chaplain in ordinary to king Charles the ſecond.

27. *Hugh Machel* of Crackenthorp eſquire, ſon and heir of Lancelot. His brother Thomas records of him, that though he was of little ſtature, yet he inherited the family ſpirit, of which he gives two inſtances: The one was at

* It is matter of curioſity to obſerve the form of addreſs to that court: —— "To the King and queen, &c. In moſt humble manner complaining, ſheweth unto your highneſs and your ſaid council, your daily orator Henry Machell of Crakynthorpp in your county of Weſtmorland gentleman, that whereas your ſaid orator is lawfully poſſeſſed, of the dimiſſion and leaſe of one Thomas Machell, of and upon one houſe or tenement called Ryecloſe houſe, with certain arable land, meadow, paſture, and common, with the appurtenances, in your county aforeſaid, for the term of certain years yet enduring; ſo it is, moſt dread ſovereign lord and lady, that about the feaſt of St. Luke the evangeliſt laſt paſt, in the third and fourth years of your majeſtie's reigns, one George Machell of Crakynthorpp in your county aforeſaid gentleman, accompanied with divers other perſons by his commandment and procurement, to the number of ſix perſons and more to your ſaid orator unknown, unlawfully aſſembled together in riotous manner, againſt your grace's laws and peace; and, in the night ſeaſon, did not only enter to one parcel of arable land called Windyke, and the ſame with ploughs rive up and plow unmanured, ſo that the ſame is deſtroyed this year that it cannot bear corn, but alſo on the morrow after with like force came again with many other perſons in like riotous manner, and broke open the walls and doors of the ſaid Ryecloſe houſe, and the goods therein caſt out at the doors and ſpoiled; to the perilous example of all ſuch like offenders, and the extreme loſs and damage of your ſaid orator, to the value of 20 marks. May it therefore pleaſe your majeſties to grant your grace's letters miſſive unto the ſaid George Machell perſonally to appear to anſwer the premiſſes, for the love of God and charity."

Brough,

Brough, when was he yet but young. Upon Mr. T——'s offering to fend a challenge by him unto his father, Hugh took him in hand himfelf, and beat him fo as to end the controverfy without further trouble. The other inftance was near Marton church, in the year 1688; where being challenged by his coufin W. S. he broke his adverfary's fword in the combat, and thereupon threw away his own, ran in upon his adverfary, ftruck up his heels, and gave him that life which he would not afk.

28. *Lancelot Machel* efquire, fon of Hugh. He was humane, gallant, honourable, and univerfally refpected; and died at Crackenthorp in the year 1767, in the 88th year of his age; having been many years fheriff of the county under the right honourable the earl of Thanet.

He was fucceeded by his fon and heir,

29. *Richard Machel*, M. A. the worthy rector of Afby and of Brougham, now living (*viz.* in 1775); who has a fon and heir apparent *Lancelot*, and other children.

The *arms* which they now bear (wherein they have deviated from the original, as having little connexion with the *Malus Catulus* of old) are; Sable, three greyhounds courant Argent, collared Or.

The *manor houfe* is an handfome building, beautifully fituate, with fair fields behind it down to the river Eden.

At a place called *Chapel-hill*, there are the ruins of an ancient *chapel* dedicated to St. Giles. And there is ftill a place called *Chapel-garth*, and a well adjoining called *Chapel-well*. This chapel muft have been very convenient to the neighbourhood, by reafon of their diftance from the mother church. Probably it might be fupported from part of the tithes, whilft the monafteries fubfifted. The oblations at the faid chapel in the 26 Hen. 8. were valued at 15*s* a year.

Nigh the way-fide, between Crackenthorp and Kirkby Thore, on the fouth of the ancient Roman way, is a large Roman *camp*, 300 yards in length, and 150 yards in breadth; having three entrances on each fide and at each end, with bulwarks before them. And at about a bow-fhot diftance, further by the way-fide, is a fmall *fort*, called *Maiden-hold*; which feems to have been as a guard houfe or watch tower belonging to the camp; and by its name may poffibly have fome relation to the *Maiden-way* at Kirkby Thore, and *Maiden-caftle* upon Stanemore *.

At a place called Machel's bank, about ten yards from the Roman way, were difcovered by fome workmen cafting a ditch, three *urns*, with burnt bones and afhes therein; contiguous to each other, in a triangular form, in the middle of a round pit of clay made for the purpofe, about a yard deep, with the fides perpendicular. And herein they were compaffed and covered

* Machel.

with

with burnt bones and black ashes, to within a foot of the surface of the ground, the remainder being closed up with earth. The urns were of a blackish sort of clay, but softer than earthen pots are wont to be, for the sherds would not ring. In the two largest were ashes and bones; but in the least, ashes only. And about 40 or 50 yards distant from the former, by the way-side also, was found a pit of like form, full of ashes and bones without any urns; which gave occasion to the said Mr. Thomas Machel to conjecture, that urns were a mark of distinction, for persons of superior quality.

HELTON BACON.

Towards the north-east from *Crackenthorp*, we came to HELTON, by way of distinction called *Helton Bacon* (there being another *Helton* in the Parish of Askham). We cannot derive the name of this village from any *hill*, for of ancient time (so far as our materials extend) it is invariably written *Helton*. *Helle* signifies to *pour out*; as *Hellebeck* probably had its name from the torrent of water rushing down there. Which also may have been the case here at this place. But the present *artificial* torrent at *Helton Bacon*, by hushing (as it is called) for getting lead ore, is not of any antiquity (so far as we can find), and seemeth not to have been practised in Westmorland till of late years. How far a right of *hushing* can be now established, independent of usage and prescription, it is not our province to inquire. But certain it is, that the thick mud, running down into the pure limpid stream of Eden, pollutes the water for many miles in its descent, and renders it less wholsome to the cattle and also to the king's subjects, and banishes the fine trout for which Eden has been famous for ages.—But it is possible the word *Helton* here may have been only a contraction of *Hellerton*; for one of the first families of note which we find here did bear that name.

In the partition of the inheritance between the two daughters and coheirs of the last Robert de Veteripont in the 14 Ed. 1. were assigned to Idonea the younger daughter, the homage and services of *Thomas de Hellerton*, *Robert de Bacon*, and others, for the manor of Helton.

In the 8 Ed. 2. after the death of Robert de Clifford, the inquisition finds, that *Robert Bacon* and the heirs of *Andrew de Hellerton* then held *Helton*; the wardship whereof, when it should happen, was worth *13l* a year, and the cornage 13*s* 8*d*. This *Andrew de Hellerton* had the same by grant from his cousin *Thomas de Hellerton*. *Robert Bacon*, the owner of the other moiety, shews clearly how this Helton came by the name of *Helton Bacon*.

The said heirs of *Andrew de Hellerton* were probably daughters. For in the 43 Ed. 3. *William L'Engleys* and *John de Appleby* held the *Hellerton* moiety, and *Adam Bacon* the other moiety.

In the 4 Hen. 4. *William Whapelote* and *Ellen* his wife in the right of the said *Ellen*, and *Adam Bacon*, held the manor of Helton Bacon.—And from henceforth we hear no more of *Bacon*. But after this we find the manor in the hands of the *Heltons*; who came hither from Burton in the parish of Warcop,

cop, but probably (ſo far as one may judge from the name) had originally ſprung from this place.

In the 10 Hen. 5. after the death of John lord Clifford, *Richard Riſtwald* and *John Helton* held the manor of Helton Bacon.

In the 31 Hen. 6. *Richard Riſtwald* and *Thomas Helton* held the ſame. And two years after, we find *Thomas Helton* of Helton (by way of diſtinction, as it may ſeem, from Helton of Burton) was one of the coroners for the county of Weſtmorland.

In the 16 Hen. 7. *Richard Reſtwolde* (by way of ſettlement) conveyed to *John Withers*, *Chriſtopher Bainbridge*, *Nicholas Mayowe*, and *Richard Newport*, clerks, a moiety of the manor of Hilton Bacon.

And in the 16 Hen. 8. the ſurvivor *John Withers* conveyed the ſame to *Edward Hilton* of Bleachyndon in the county of Oxford clerk; who in the ſame year granted the ſame in truſt to *John Pantrie* and *Ambroſe Hilton* of Oxford clerks, *John Whelpdaile* of Penrith and *Richard Rigg* of Little Strickland gentlemen.

In the 19 Hen. 8. the ſaid *Edward Hilton* granted the ſame to *Robert Hilton* of Burton, and the ſaid truſtees releaſed their intereſt therein to the ſaid *Robert Hilton* accordingly.

In the 1 and 2 Ph. and Mary, *Thomas Helton* held the manor of Helton Bacon.

Next, we come to the pedigree certified at Sir William Dugdale's viſitation in 1664*, which proceeds as follows:

1. *Robert Hilton* of Hilton Bacon, in the reign of queen Elizabeth, married a daughter of Thomas Blenkinſop of Helbeck eſquire; and by her had iſſue, (1) Thomas. (2) Anthony, who died unmarried. (3) John Hilton of Gainsford in the county of Durham.

[*N. B.* Here ought to come in another *Thomas* (according to a pedigree by Sir Daniel Fleming, which ſeems more authentic) who married the widow of Brackenberg, whoſe maiden name was Bainbridge.]

2. *Thomas Hilton* of Hilton Bacon married Jane daughter and coheir of Reginald Hartley of Appleby; and died about the year 1632. They had iſſue, (1) George, who died unmarried. (2) Thomas. (3) Katherine, married to Brian Garnet of Kendal.

3. *Thomas Hilton* of Hilton Bacon married Elizabeth daughter of Thomas Sandford of Aſkham eſquire; and died in 1645. They had iſſue, (1) Robert. (2) Thomas. (3) George Hilton of Bongate. (4) Martha, married to Robert Collingwood of the county of Durham.

4. *Robert Hilton* of Hilton Bacon eſquire, aged 45 at the aforeſaid viſitation. He married Mary daughter of John Hilton of Hilton-caſtle in the county of Durham, commonly called baron Hilton. They had iſſue, John, Thomas, Robert, Elizabeth, Alice, and Mary.

* The pedigrees here and elſewhere, which were delivered in at Dugdale's viſitation, we have from Mr. Machel, who had them from Dugdale.

John the eldest died without issue; for in the 28 Cha. 2. *Robert Hilton* of Durham esquire and Mary his wife and *Thomas Hilton* of Murton gentleman, son and heir apparent of the said *Robert*, infranchised divers customary tenements in Brackinber, Hilton Bacon, Ellerholme, and Bongate. Others of the tenements were infranchised by the Hiltons at different times. And finally, the manor itself and demesne were sold in the year 1696, to Sir John Lowther of Lowther: Except some lands which came by mortgage to lawyer Fletcher; and except a long lease of the royalties which had been granted to the duke of Bridgewater.

The *arms* of Hilton are; Sable, 2 saltiers in chief, and 3 annulets, 2 and 1, Argent. The crest: On a wreath, a demigriffin.

The ancient *manor house* is now much in ruins.

Anciently, here was a *chapel*, about a quarter of a mile from the village; which is now intirely demolished.

MURTON.

Next unto *Helton*, further towards the east, is MURTON, that is, the *Moor-town*. There are many places of this name in the kingdom. *Morvil* is the same latinized.

By the inquisition *post mortem* of the first Roger de Clifford, in the 11 Ed. 1. it is found, that he held in the right of his wife Isabella, in the vill of Morton, one capital messuage of the value of 2*s* yearly, and one carucate of land in demesne, which contains in it 120 acres of arable land, of which every acre was worth 8*d*. yearly (saving the service of the lords of the fee); 16 acres of meadow, worth 12*d* an acre yearly; 5 acres of wood, worth 6*d* an acre, without waste: That there were six free tenants who paid 9*s* 4*d* yearly, and did suit at the court there from three weeks to three weeks: That he had there ten bondmen, each of whom held one oxgang of land, for which he paid 5*s* 11*d* yearly for all services and burdens; except the aid at the feast of St. Michael, which was 26*s* 8*d*. And that the perquisites of his free court in the said vill were worth yearly 2*s*. And he held all the premisses of Baldwin Wak, by homage and foreign service.

But in the next king's reign, we find the manor of Morton in the hands of the Musgraves of Musgrave, in which it continued for many generations. In the 8 Ed. 2. after the death of Robert lord Clifford, it appears, that Thomas Musgrave, then under age and in wardship, held of the said Robert, Great Musgrave and Morton; the wardship whereof was worth 42*l* a year, and the cornage for both 1*l* 12*s* 4*d*.

And so it continued in the Musgraves all along, till the 11th year of king James, when Sir Richard Musgrave of Hartley-castle knight sold the same to

Thomas Hilton of Hilton; who removed from Hilton to the manor houſe there.

The ſaid houſe, called Murton-hall, is ſituate under a high mount called Mellfell; and near to the remarkable hill, like a pyramid, called Murton Pike. It was a good old houſe and convenient; a ſpring of water running through it.

There was a chapel here formerly; the place being diſtant about three miles from the pariſh church.

Part of the demeſne lands were ſold by the Hiltons to lawyer Fletcher of Strickland: The reſt of the demeſne and manor were ſold to Sir John Lowther the purchaſer of many eſtates and manors in this county: in whoſe poſterity the ſame ſtill continue.

LANGTON.

Southwards again from Murton, and north-eaſt from Bongate, is LANGTON, which now lies chiefly in demeſne. It was purchaſed by Robert de Veteripont of Ada daughter of John Tallebois and widow of Robert de Cliveland, unto whom it had deſcended from her mother.

It ſeems to have been anciently well inhabited; and the name itſelf implies it, *Long-town*. And there ſeems to have been a church or chapel here, ſo far as we may judge from names; for there is a place called *Kirkbergh*, which is, and from ancient time hath been, held free and independent of the manor, except only the payment of 2*s* cornage.

By an inquiſition after the death of Roger lord Clifford in the 1 Ed. 3. it was found as follows:—At Langeton, the ſite of a certain manor burned by the Scots, worth nothing yearly for want of tenants, and by reaſon of the deſtruction made by the Scots. And there are 30 acres of demeſne land, which lie untilled for the reaſon aforeſaid, the herbage whereof is worth yearly 18*d.* Thirty oxgangs of land, which lie untilled for the cauſe aforeſaid, the herbage whereof is worth 15*s* 6*d* a year. Sixteen acres of demeſne meadow, worth yearly 3*s* and no more, for the too great abundance of meadow and paſture in thoſe parts. Four cottages, which yield yearly 2*s*. One water mill, worth yearly 13*s* 4*d*. Pleas and perquiſites of the court of Appleby and Langton, worth yearly 4*s*.

And after the death of John lord Clifford, in the 10 Hen. 5. the inquiſition finds, that at Langton there are 10 meſſuages, worth nothing in iſſues above repriſes; 40 oxgangs of land, at 3*s* 4*d* each; fourſcore acres of meadow, at 6*d* each; water mill, 13*s* 4*d*; one fulling mill, 6*s* 8*d*; one hundred and fourſcore acres of paſture at one penny each.

PARISH OF DUFTON.

DUFF was anciently a name in Scotland, and perhaps also in England. *Macduff* is a name well known; which means the son of *Duff*. And it is not improbable that *Dufton (Duff's town)* might be so called from some person of that name.

The parish of Dufton is bounded on the East by the parishes of Middleton in the county of Durham, Romaldkirk in the county of York, and Brough in the county of Westmorland; on the South, by the parish of St. Michael's Appleby; on the West, by the parish of Marton; and on the North, by the parish of Alston in the county of Cumberland, and the said parish of Middleton. It contains in the whole about 63 families.

It is a rectory; valued at 19*l* 2*s* 6*d* in the king's books.

The church is dedicated to St. Cuthbert.

The patronage of this rectory was of ancient time in the barons of Graystock, and from them by marriage came into the family of Dacre, being also at the same time lords of the manor of Dufton; and the advowson still continues appendant to the said manor.

The first of the Graystocks that we have met with, who had any connection with Westmorland, was *Thomas* baron of Graystock, who married Christian daughter of the first Robert de Veteripont. And it is not improbable, that this might introduce him to Dufton and other places in Westmorland. For in the next generation but one, we find Dufton clearly in the hands of the Graystocks, and attended with circumstances which imply that it had been in the family for some time before.

By the inquisition *post mortem* of Robert de Clifford in the 9 Ed. 2. it appears, that *Ralph* son of *William de Graystock* held of the said Robert the villages of Dufton, Brampton, Bolton, and Yanewich; the wardship whereof (when it should happen) was worth 100 marks *per annum*, and the cornage 25*s* 6*d*.

By the inquisition after the death of John lord Clifford in the 10 Hen. 5. it is found that *John de Graystock* son of *Ralph* held the manors of Dufton, Brampton, Bolton, and Yevenwith of the same John lord Clifford, with the same cornage as before.

Again, in the 31 Hen. 6. it is found by inquest that *Ralph* baron of Graystock held of the lord Thomas de Clifford, Yanwith, Bolton, Brampton, and Dufton; and that Lancelot Threlkeld held Yanwith of the said Ralph, Nicolas Radcliff held Bolton, and Thomas Lancastre held Brampton, and that Dufton was in the hands of the said baron himself.

In the 4 Ed. 4. after the death of the second John de Clifford, this *Ralph* baron of Graystock held the same.

In the 2 Hen. 7. after the death of Ralph baron of Graystock, the inquisition finds, that the said Ralph died on Friday next after the feast of Pentecost in the 2 Hen. 7. That on the day on which he died, he was seised of Duffeton

Duffeton and the advowſon of the church there, holden of Henry lord Clifford, as of his manor of Appilby, by the ſervice of rendring to the ſaid lord 25*s* 6*d* yearly for cornage, and by ſuit to the county court at Appilby yearly from month to month: That *Elizabeth* is his kinſwoman and heir, namely, being daughter and heir of Robert Grayſtock knight, ſon and heir of the aforeſaid Ralph.

This *Elizabeth* was married to *Thomas* lord *Dacre* of Gilſland, and brought with her the inheritance into that family. By an inquiſition of knights fees in Weſtmorland in the 18 Hen. 8. it appears, that *William Dacre* knight, lord of Dacre, held then the manor of Dufton. And by a like inquiſition in the 1 & 2 Ph. & Mary, he appears then alſo to have held the ſame.

This family of Dacre ended in daughters coheirs. For *George* lord Dacre dying unmarried, the inheritance came to his three ſiſters. Of whom, *Anne* the eldeſt was married to *Philip Howard* earl of *Arundel*, eldeſt ſon of *Thomas* duke of *Norfolk*. And in the partition of the eſtate, Dufton fell to her purparty. She had a ſon and heir *Thomas* earl of *Arundel*; who had a ſon and heir *Henry* earl of *Arundel*, in whoſe time a leaſe of the lordſhip of Dufton for 99 years was granted to Sir *Chriſtopher Clapham* knight, in which leaſe the clauſe prohibiting waſte having been omitted, he cut down all the wood called Dufton wood, and ſold it for more than the whole purchaſe coſt him. The remainder of the term, and afterwards the perpetuity of the eſtate, was purchaſed by *John Winder* of Lorton in Cumberland, counſellor at law; who was ſucceeded by his ſon and heir *Williams Winder* eſquire; who, dying without iſſue, deviſed the ſame to the preſent owner *Edward Milward* eſquire, ſon of the reverend *Thomas Milward*, M. A. rector of Marton and of Kirkby Thore.

The ſucceſſion of *incumbents* hath been as followeth:

In 1293, Sir John de Grayſtock knight preſents one *Henry de Waleys* to the rectory of Dufton on the 30th of January, upon a vacancy by the death of Sir *Robert* the laſt rector there, who died on the Monday before St. Paul's day in the year aforegoing: Whereupon a *jus patronatus* was ordered, and (in the mean time) the cure committed to *William Boukes*. The conteſt ſeems to have been long, for the ſaid Henry had not inſtitution given before the firſt of July in 1298. And the iſſue of the cauſe appears in an entry of fines levied in the 27 Ed. 1. Between *Ralph* ſon of *William de Grayſtock* complainant, and *John* ſon of *William* deforciant, concerning the manor and barony of Grayſtoke in the county of Cumberland and the advowſon of the church there, and the manor of Dufton with the appurtenances and the advowſon of the church of the ſame manor in the county of Weſtmorland: The ſaid *John* acknowledged the right to be in the ſaid *Ralph* after the deceaſe of him the ſaid *John*, and he ſubmitted to hold of the ſaid *Ralph* during the life of him the ſaid *John*, and after his death the premiſſes to remain to the ſaid *Ralph* and his heirs.

In 1315, *Matthew de Redman* rector of Dufton had a diſpenſation of abſence, for the better following his ſtudies, for three years.

In

In 1324, *Roger de Kendal* (then only an acolite) was instituted into the rectory of Dufton, on a presentation by king Edward the second (in right of his ward William lord Graystock).

In 1340, on the resignation of Sir *William Hawys* rector of Dufton, *Robert de Helton* was instituted on a presentation by the lord Ralph de Nevil (who married the mother of the said William lord Graystock).

In 1366, *William* son of *Robert de Threlkeld* was instituted on a presentation by king Edward the third in right of his ward Ralph lord Graystock; on the death of *William de Brampton*, whose will was proved at Rose in that year, whereby he bequeathed his body to be buried in St. *Cuthbert*'s church at Dufton.

In 1412, *Robert Coldall* was rector of Dufton; who in that year surrendred certain lands to Ralph baron of Graystock.

In 1449, a writ of possession of the manor of Dufton and advowson of the church there was granted to Sir John Graystock knight, alias John lord of Graystoke, during the minority of Elizabeth daughter of Robert son of Sir Ralph Graystock.

In 1566, on the death of *Roland Threlkeld* rector of Dufton, Sir *John Dent* clerk was instituted upon the presentation of the lady Elizabeth Dacre widow.

In 1575, on the death of the said John Dent, Sir *Christopher Walker* was instituted on a presentation by queen Elizabeth (in right of her ward George lord Dacre).

In 1615, on Walker's death, institution was given to *Richard Burton*, M. A. presented by the assignee of a grant of this avoidance from Anne countess dowager of Arundel.

In 1661, Sept. 27, *Simon Webster* was presented by Sir Christopher Clapham knight.

In 1675, on Simon Webster's death, *James Buchanan*, M. A. was instituted upon a presentation by the said Sir Christopher Clapham.

In 1680, James Buchanan dying, *John Lindsey* succeeded; but his presentation and institution are not entred in the register.

Upon the death of John Lindsey in 1728, *Williams Gibbon*, M. A. was instituted on the presentation of Williams Winder esquire.

In 1736, on the resignation of Williams Gibbon, *Thomas Milward*, M. A. was presented by the same patron.

In 1762, Mr. Milward resigning, *William Kilner* clerk was presented by the same Williams Winder esquire.

Christopher Walker, by his will in 1670, gave 40 *l*. the interest thereof to go to a schoolmaster at Dufton, to be appointed by the rector, the lord's bailiff, and six sufficient men of the town of Dufton.

And *Michael Todd* by his will charged his lands at Knowle Green in the parish of Staines in the county of Middlesex with 4 *l* a year to a schoolmaster, to be approved of by the minister and churchwardens; 5 *l* to be distributed on on Michaelmaſs day yearly to the poor of the ſaid pariſh; 4*l* for binding out two poor boys, natives of the ſaid pariſh, apprentices yearly; 10*s* a year for a ſermon on the Sunday after Michaelmaſs day, and 20*s* yearly to 20 poor men who ſhall attend at the ſaid ſermon and divine ſervice.

PARISH OF MARTON.

I. *Pariſh of Marton.*
II. *Manor of Marton.*
III. *Manor of Brampton.*
IV. *Manor of Knock.*

I. PARISH OF MARTON.

DESCENDING from Dufton towards the weſt, we come to the pariſh of MARTON, which was anciently written *Merton*; and Mr. Machel ſuppoſes the ſame to be ſo called from a *mere* or lake at the north end of the town. It is commonly called *Long Marton*, not from its extraordinary length, as it ſhould ſeem, (for many other villages in the bottom of Weſtmorland are longer;) but more likely by way of diſtinction from ſome other place of the ſame name. But of ſuch other there is at preſent no appearance, unleſs we ſuppoſe *Murton* and *Marton* to have had originally the ſame appellation. It is once, in the biſhop's regiſter, called *Merton Parva*. But there is no judging what theſe places were formerly, by what they are now; nor yet what they were formerly at different periods. For the Scots made ſtrange alterations often in a very ſhort time. Even *Langton* (we have ſeen), which ſeems to have been called the *Long town* by way of eminence, is now no town at all: and we have ſhewed the reaſon of it.

The pariſh of Marton is bounded on the eaſt by the pariſh of Dufton, on the ſouth by the pariſh of St. Michael's Appleby, on the weſt by the pariſh of Kirkby Thore, and on the north by the pariſh of Alſton in the county of Cumberland: and contains in it three manors or lordſhips, viz. *Marton*, *Brampton*, and *Knock*; and in the whole about 173 families.

The church, according to Dr. Todd, is dedicated to St. *Margaret* and St. *James.*—Perhaps St. *James* may be the tutelar ſaint of the *church*. St. *Margaret* had a *quire* there dedicated to her, as appears by the laſt will and teſtament of Sir John de Morelaunde hereafter mentioned.

It is a rectory, valued at 21*l* 15*s* 7½*d* in the king's books; in the patronage of the right honourable the earl of Thanet, by hereditary deſcent from the Veteriponts and Cliffords.

In

In the reign of king Henry the ſecond, about the year 1170, we find one *John de Hardcla* rector of *Meretun*; who witneſſed a confirmation of grants to Shap abbey by Bernard biſhop of Carliſle.

In 1298, *William de Coumb*, rector of Merton, becoming blind; the biſhop appointed Mr. William Bouk to be his coadjutor. And the ſaid William de Coumb reſigning the next year, the lady Ydonea de Leyburn widow preſented *John de Medburn* a minor, who was to allow to the reſigning rector ſuch a penſion for life as ſhould be thought reaſonable by the ordinary. The biſhop committed the cuſtody of this infant to William de Brampton a prieſt; directing him to diſpoſe of the profits of the rectory in ſuch manner, as to provide for the ſupply of the cure, and the education of the ſaid John in ſome public ſchool of learning.

In the year 1330, being the 4 Ed. 3. that king, being in poſſeſſion of the eſtate of Thomas de Wake lord of Lydel, preſented *Thomas de Herewood* to the vacant rectory of Merton: by what title we have not found.

In the next year, we find one *Ralph de Malton* rector of Merton; who had a diſpenſation of abſence for two years, by reaſon of his attendance on the earl marſhall.

In 1334, Sir *John de Morelaund* prieſt was preſented by Robert de Clifford; and, on an inquiſition *de jure patronatus*, had inſtitution given to him. This ſame Sir John de Morelaunde, who is ſtyled rector of the church *de Parva Merton*, had a diſpenſation for 3 years abſence granted to him, and the like for 2 years afterwards.

In 1358, on the death of the ſaid Sir John de Morelaunde, inſtitution was given to Sir *William de Loundres*, preſented by Sir Thomas de Muſgrave knight, in right of his wife Iſabel relict and dowager of Robert de Clifford. On the ſame day, the laſt will and teſtament of the ſaid Sir John de Morelaunde was proved at Roſe; whereby he bequeaths his body to be buried in St. *Margaret*'s quire at Merton; his larger ſalver *(mazerium majorem)* to the friers Carmelites at Appleby, and his leſſer to the ſaid lady Iſabel de Clifford; and to the prior and convent of Carliſle 100 *s*, for the praying for his ſoul and the ſouls of his kindred.

In 1362, the ſaid William de Loundres exchanged his living of Merton for the rectory of Adyngham in the dioceſe of York, with the conſent of the patrons and ordinaries: whereupon Sir *Robert de Wolſelay* was preſented to the rectory of Merton.

In 1369, *John Donkyn*, parſon of Merton, was a truſtee in the ſettlement of ſeveral eſtates in Weſtmorland.

In 1393, *Henry Kirkby*, parſon of Merton, was witneſs to an agreement concerning the chapel of Brougham.

In 1465, which was the 5 Ed. 4. the king granted to Anne his ſiſter the manor of Merton and the advowſon of the church there; the ſame being then in the hands of the crown by the attainder of John lord Clifford.

In 1476, *Edward Wherton*, rector of Merton, was a truſtee in the ſettlement of the Wibergh eſtate at Clifton.

In 1562, on the death of *William Bury* rector of Merton, *George Bury*, M. A. was instituted, on the presentation of Henry earl of Cumberland.

In 1577, Mr. *John Baynes* was instituted, on the presentation of Thomas Burton clerk and others, assignees of Anne countess of Cumberland.

In 1591, *Richard Burton* was presented by George earl of Cumberland.

In 1640, on the death of Richard Burton, *Henry Hutton*, M. A. son of judge Hutton (a native of Penrith) was instituted; but no mention is made in the register of the presenting patron. He was also prebendary of Carlisle, and was ejected from his prebend by Cromwell's commissioners *, and seems to have died soon after.

The next incumbent seems to have been *Lancelot Lowther*, son of Sir Christopher Lowther of Lowther. Which Lancelot died in 1661, being very old; it being then 54 years after the death of his father, who died at the age of 77.

On the death of Lancelot Lowther, *Robert Symson*, M. A. was instituted, on the presentation of Anne countess dowager of Dorset, Pembroke, and Montgomery: Who was succeeded by his son *Barnaby Symson*. On whose death in 1712, *Christopher Grandorge* was instituted on the presentation of Thomas earl of Thanet.

In 1726, on the death of Christopher Grandorge, *Robert Leyborne*, M. A. was presented by the same patron.

In 1730, on the resignation of *John Middleton*, S. T. P. Sackville earl of Thanet presented to the said rectory the present incumbent † *Thomas Milward*, M. A. a gentleman of consummate natural and acquired endowments. He is descended of Sir Thomas Milward before mentioned of Eaton in the county of Derby knight, whose son and heir William Milward of Chilcote in the same county esquire married Christian daughter of Sir Nicolas Tufton first earl of Thanet, by whom he had a son Thomas, father of the present rector of Marton, who also at the same time is rector of Kirkby Thore ‡.

The *church* is situate in the fields of Brampton, at a considerable distance from both Marton and Brampton; for the equal accommodation (as it seemeth) of both the said villages.

On the south side of the church, is an ile called Knock porch; built probably, as it may seem from the Cliffords arms in the window, by the patron for the use of the inhabitants of Knock; who had anciently a chapel near Dufton, in a place which still bears the name of Chapel Flatt.

Besides the arms of the Cliffords, there are in the windows of the chancel the arms of Graystock, Dacre, Lancaster, and Wharton; all of whom, in their several ages, had possessions in this parish.

* Walker's Sufferings of the Clergy. Part 2d, page 10.

† *N. B.* He died in 1775.

‡ In 1775, on the death of the said Thomas Milward, his son *Joseph Milward*, M. A. was instituted on a like presentation by Sackville earl of Thanet.

II. MANOR OF MARTON.

The manor of Marton appears to have belonged to the Veteriponts. And by an inquisition of waste suffered by the prior of Carlisle, whilst he was guardian of the last Robert de Veteripont, in the reign of king Henry the third, it was found, that at Merton certain sheepfolds *(bercaria)* of fourscore feet in dimension were alienated by the prior, and the park destroyed by dogs and nets, and want of inclosure; that the little vivary was destroyed, so that there was taken from thence as much as could be taken by nets; and the great vivary much impoverished of great fish.

In the partition of Marton between the two daughters of the said Robert, each of their shares was estimated at 13*l* 3*s* 5½*d*: Besides the advowson of the church, which was estimated at 40 marks, when it should be vacant.

In the 43 Ed. 3. the heirs of *Thomas de Wake* held the manor of Merton of Roger de Clifford, by homage and fealty, and 8*s* 6*d* cornage.

In the 15 Ric. 2. after the death of the said Roger de Clifford, *John de Holland* knight held the same.

In the 10 Hen. 5. *John de Gray* knight and *Margaret* his wife, as of the right of the said *Margaret*, held the same in like manner.

In the 31 Hen. 6. *Thomas Gray* knight, and afterwards in the same year *Thomas Salinger* knight held the same.

In the 18 Hen. 8. it was in the hands of the king: By what title we have not found.

Finally, this manor, like many of the rest, came into the hands of the *Lowthers*, in which family it still continues.

III. MANOR OF BRAMPTON.

Brampton is a long straggling village, about a mile eastward from Marton.

There were several of the name *de Brampton* of ancient time; but none, so far as we have found, that was lord of the manor.

In the 3d, and again in the 8 Ed. 2. we find *Ralph* son of *William de Graystock* held of the Cliffords, Brampton, Dufton, Bolton, and Yanwich; the wardship whereof, when it should happen, was worth yearly 100 marks, and the cornage 1*l* 5*s* 6*d*.

In the 10 Hen. 5. Sir *John de Graystock* knight held the same as above.

After this, we find Brampton in the name and family of *Lancaster*, who are said to have been a younger branch of the Lancasters of Sockbridge. We find one *John de Lancaster*, who held Brampton in the reign of Edward the fourth; his son *John* held the same in the reign of Henry the seventh; and *Edward Lancaster* in the reign of Henry the eighth.

The

The *Lancasters* held the same immediately of the *Graystocks*, and the *Graystocks* held over of the *Cliffords*. Thus, on a *Quo Warranto* brought against Henry lord Clifford in the 19 Hen. 7. the said lord Clifford set forth, that John Lancaster died seised of the manor of Brampton in the 10 Ed. 4. his son and heir John being then 30 years of age: That John Lancaster the elder held the same of John late baron of Graystoke, by knights service, to wit, homage, fealty, and scutage, namely, twenty shillings when scutage runs at forty shillings: That the said baron of Graystoke held the same *ultra* of Henry lord Clifford by the like services: That the said John Lancaster the elder died in the homage of the baron, and the baron died in the homage of the said lord Clifford, the son and heir of the said baron being then 22 years of age, who paid to the said lord rent, homage, fealty, relief, and all other services.

This family of *Lancaster* ended in three daughters, in the reign of queen Elizabeth; the eldest of whom was married to *Birkbeck* of Hornby; the second to *Backhouse* of Morland; and the third to *Wharton* of Kirkby Thore. And thereupon the manor became parted into three portions. Mr. *Birkbeck* exchanged his share with Henry earl of Cumberland for lands at Hornby; which part still continues in his descendent the present earl of Thanet. The descendents of Mr. Backhouse enjoy the second part. And the third part, which belonged to the Whartons, hath been sold to the tenants.

The ancient *manor house*, called Brampton-hall, was built anew by *Thomas Burton* esquire, grandson of Richard Burton aforesaid, rector of this parish; which Thomas Burton was a justice of the peace for this county in the time of Oliver Cromwell, and was afterwards knighted by king Charles the second for divers services he had performed (though an Oliverian) to the royal party. The said Sir Thomas Burton sold the same to the ancestor of the present *George Baker* of Ellemore-hall esquire, who sold the same to divers of the inhabitants, who demolished the hall, leaving only so much remaining as was sufficient for fitting up a farm house.

IV. MANOR OF KNOCK.

KNOCK, anciently called *Knock Shalcock*, is a little village about a mile north from Marton. It belonged, amongst the rest, to the Veteriponts and Cliffords; and the first family that appears to have held the same under the Cliffords were the *Boyvils*.

In the 8 Ed. 2. *John de Boyvile* held Knock Shalcock; the wardship whereof was worth 13*l* 6*s* 8*d*, and the cornage 3*s* 4*d*.

In the 2 Ed. 3. *John de Boyvile de Knoke* held two parts of the manor aforesaid of Roger de Clifford; *Robert* his son and heir being then 16 years of age.

In the 43 Ed. 3. *John de Rookeby* held the manor of Knock Salcock.

In the 15 Ric. 2. *William de Soulby* held the same.

In the 10 Hen. 5. *Thomas de Rookby*: And after him, *John Rookby* held the same; who had a daughter and heir *Joan* married to *John Lancaster* of Howgill knight, who in the 31 Hen. 6. held the manor of Knock in right of his said wife.

The said *John Lancaster* of Howgill died without issue male, leaving four daughters coheirs. And in the partition of the estate, Knock was in the share appointed for *Christian* and *Elizabeth*; the former of whom was married to Sir *Robert de Harrington*, and the latter to *Robert Crackenthorp* esquire.

After this, we find the manor of Knock in the Clifford family, perhaps by purchase from the said coheirs; in which family it still continues in the person of the present earl of Thanet.

The abbey of Shap had some lands here, given by John de Veteripont; which were parcel of the demesne.

PARISH OF NEWBIGGIN.

THE parish of Newbiggin (*New-building*; *big* being a word not yet quite out of use, signifying to build) is a small parish about three miles in compass, surrounded by the parish of Kirkby Thore, except only on the north where it joins to the parish of Kirkland in Cumberland, being separated therefrom by a small rivulet, which descends from the mountain *Crossfell* (one of the highest mountains in the north, so called probably from a cross erected thereupon by way of boundary between two parishes or lordships) which rivulet from its first rising, until it fall into the river Eden, divides the two counties of Westmorland and Cumberland.

This parish contains only the township of Newbiggin, and part of the hamlet of *Hale*, the grange whereof belonged heretofore to the abbey of Holm Cultram. Thus in the 10 Hen. 5. after the death of John lord Clifford, the inquisition finds, that the abbot of Holme then held the grange of Hale, paying for the same yearly 13*s* 4*d*.

The *church* is dedicated to St. Edmund; and is a rectory, valued at 4*l* 14*s* 9*d* in the king's books, in the patronage of the lord of the manor. It has only about 11 acres of glebe land; and the tithe corn, it is said, of the whole parish belongs to the lord of the manor by prescription, under the yearly rent of 9*l* 6*s* 8*d*, and an horse grass to the rector: By what right, we presume not to determine. From the smallness of the parish, and the comparative largeness of the prescriptive rent, there is no room to suppose this to be a very ancient composition. And it hath no benign aspect towards the patron, in prescribing terms to his presentee. Which yet is a case that frequently happens, where the lord of the manor is patron of the advowson.

In 1759, Mrs. Deborah Crackenthorp gave 200*l*, whereby to procure an augmentation by the governors of queen Anne's bounty; wherewith an estate was purchased at Kirkoswald, now of the yearly value of 20*l*.

The parsonage house is but an indifferent building; which stands at the north-west end of the village near the church.

The first grant that we meet with of the manor of Newbiggin (with the advowson appendant) was from *Gamel* son of *Whelp*, to

1. *Robert*, *dapifer de Appleby*; who thereupon assumed the name of *Robert de Newbiggin*. Which grant *Waldeve* son of *Gamel* confirmed by deed to *Laurence* son of the said *Robert*.

2. This *Laurence*, who lived in the reign of king Hen. 2. married a Wharton; which is ancienter than any account that we have met with of the Whartons of Wharton (much more, of the Whartons of Kirkby Thore). But at our first account of the Whartons of Wharton, in the reign of Edward the first, they were then a considerable family. So that this account (which in the present pedigree is chiefly taken from a manuscript of Sir Daniel Fleming) may likely enough be right.

This *Laurence* son of *Robert de Newbiggin* gave lands at Newbiggin to the abbey of Holm Cultram, by the metes and bounds in the grant specified *.

He had issue,

3. *John de Newbiggin*, who married a Blennerhasset. Who had issue,

4. *John*, who married a Barton. One of the witnesses to the grant of the advowson of the church of Kirkby Thore by Adam de Kirkby Thore to Robert de Veteripont, in the time of king John or Henry the third, is *John de Newbiggin* (probably this same John). Who had issue,

5. *Thomas*, who married a Vaux. And had a son,

6. *Robert*, in the reign of Ed. 1. who married Agnes a daughter of Wackerfield.

By an inquisition after the death of Robert de Clifford, who died in the 7 Ed. 2. the jurors find, that Robert de Newbigging then held the manor of Newbigging; the wardship whereof was worth 10 *l*, and the cornage 20 *d*.

* Laurencius filius Roberti senescalli de Neubyginge, præsentibus et futuris, Salutem. Sciatis me dedisse et præsenti charta confirmasse Deo et Sanctæ Mariæ de Holme et monachis ibidem Deo servientibus, in liberam, puram, et perpetuam eleemosynam, pro salute animæ meæ et sponsæ meæ, totam illam terram de Sparstanerig, et illam quæ est subtus Sparstanerig, infra illas divisas; sc. A petra illa quæ stat super ripam fossati super Trebrigge, usque ad petram quæ stat juxta duas spinas, et sic per transversum usque ad spinam quæ stat ad superius caput terræ; et a capite terræ ascendendo per sicum usque ad grisam petram quæ est ad inferiorem partem Ruchokes: Et ab illa petra in transverso usque ad magnam et latam grissam petram quæ jacet super Sparstanerig: et ab illa petra in transversum usque ad gilam quæ est inter Sparstanerig et Castellerig: Et inde ascendendo per prædictam gilam usque ad rivulum qui est ad superius caput de Sparstanerig: Et sic descendendo per ipsum rivulum usque in fossatum monachorum subtus Warthebeck: Et inde descendendo per fossatum usque ad petram desuper Trebrigge juxta duas spinas. Hanc prædictam terram tenebunt monachi per divisas prænominatas, bene et in pace, integre et plenarie, libere et quiete ab omni servicio terreno, consuetudine, et exactione seculari. Et ego et hæredes mei warrantizabimus prædictis monachis prædictam terram contra omnes homines in perpetuum.

And by another grant he conveys to them—totam partem meam et quicquid ad me et hæredes meos pertinet de marisco inter me et monachos infra fossatum quod monachi fecerunt divisam consensu meo inter Newbiginge et illos; et communem pasturam trecentis et sexaginta ovibus, et viginti vaccis, et uni tauro, et triginta bobus, in campo de Newbiginge, in omnibus locis ubicunque mea propria averia pascunt et averia totius villæ de Newbiginge. (*Registr. Holme.*)

And

And in the same year, Robert de Newbigging presented Sir *Thomas de Newbigging* to the rectory there, who was instituted thereupon; saving to the church of Kirkby Thore the yearly pension of 3*s* of old time due and accustomed.—Accordingly in an account of the profits of the rectory of Kirkby Thore in the year 1575, we find amongst the receipts 3*s* paid to the rector of Kirkby Thore out of the rectory of Newbiggin. By which it seemeth, that Newbiggin is a parish carved out of the parish of Kirkby Thore; or, to speak more properly, that this was originally no more than a chapel of ease, and that this payment (as was common in such cases) was reserved as an acknowledgment of the superiority of the mother church.

And besides the aforesaid pension, the rector of Newbiggin was bound to perform altar service at the church of Kirkby Thore two days in the year, on which days, the rector of Kirkby Thore was to find a dinner for the said rector of Newbiggin and his dog.

The said Robert de Newbiggin had a son and heir,

7. *Robert de Newbiggin*, who married Emma a daughter of Threlkeld; and in the 10 Ed. 2. made a settlement of his estate, to him and his wife Emma during their lives and to the heirs of their bodies, remainder to his own right heirs. This Robert was the last of the male line of the name *de Newbiggin*, having only a daughter,

8. *Emma de Newbiggin*, who about the 5 Ed. 3. was married to *Robert de Crackenthorp*, supposed by the reverend Thomas Machel to have been a younger brother of the Machels of Crackenthorp, who thereupon took the arms of Newbiggin, as was usual on the marriage of heiresses. And the family pedigree seems to confirm this account, by attributing the same arms both to Newbiggin and Crackenthorp. Nevertheless, there seems to be some cause of doubt in this matter. For although it might be not improbable that one of the family of Machel should take the name *de Crackenthorp* (for there are many instances of local names thus assumed), yet it is not likely that Robert would altogether relinquish his own family arms, nor was it usual in like cases; but rather he would quarter the arms of Newbiggin with his own paternal arms of Machel. And in fact, the Crackenthorps bore the same arms before this match with Newbiggin (for this Robert was not the first of the name) which they bore afterwards. In an ancient roll of arms in the heralds office of the knights that attended king Edward the first in his expedition into Scotland, are the arms of Crackenthorp, the same as they are now, *viz.* Or, a cheveron between three mullets pierced Azure.

In the reign of king Hen. 3. we find at Crackenthorp one *William de Crackenthorp* son of *William*, who made an agreement with John Mauchel about the mill there.

In the 18 Ed. 1. the said John Mauchael and *William de Crackenthorp* were witnesses to a grant of lands at Sandford, by John de Sandford to John de Helton. At the same time, *William de Crackenthorp* (as appears upon the division of the barony of Westmorland between the two daughters of Robert de Veteripont) held a third part of the manor of Brougham, probably by marriage of a coheiress.

7 And

And again in the 8 Ed. 2. after the death of Robert de Clifford, the inquisition finds, that *John Godbert*, *William Crackenthop*, and *Henry de Reddings* then held the manor of Brougham.

It is probable, that *Robert de Crackenthorp*, who married the heiress of Newbiggin, was son of this *William*.

In the 13 Ed. 3. the said *Robert de Crackenthorp* presented to the rectory of Newbiggin one *John de Hale*, on a vacancy by the death of the aforesaid Thomas Newbigging.

And three years after, he presented one *Gilbert de Tindale* to the said rectory, being void by resignation. And soon after he died; leaving, by his said wife Emma de Newbiggin, a son and heir,

9. *William de Crackenthorp*; who in the 18 Ed. 3. together with *John Tyndal* and *John Trotter*, held the manor of Brougham.

In the 38 Ed. 3. *William de Crackenthorp* presented one *Thomas de Appleby* to the rectory of Newbiggin, being vacant by the resignation of *Robert de Appleby*.

And in the 41 Ed. 3. on the resignation of Thomas de Appleby, the said *William* presented one Sir *Robert de Merton*.

In the 49 Ed. 3. the said *William* made a settlement of his estate (perhaps on the marriage of his son); in which settlement, Robert de Merton, rector of the church of *St. Edmund* of Newbiggins, is a trustee.

In the same year, Robert de Merton resigned his living, and Sir *John de Culwen* was presented and instituted. And presently he exchanged, with *Roger de Kirk Oswald*, for the vicarage of Bromfield; whereupon the said Roger was presented by the said William de Crackenthorp, and instituted.

In the 15 Ric. 2. after the death of Roger de Clifford, the inquisition finds, that *John de Tyndall* and *William de Crackenthorp* held two parts of the manor of Brougham.

The said *William*, by his wife who was of the name of Grimston, had a son and heir,

10. *John de Crackenthorp*, who married a daughter of Brisco. In the 5 Ric. 2. during his father's life-time, he served for the county of Westmorland in parliament; and was allowed, for his charges during his attendance for twenty days, 12*l*.

In the 9 and 13 Ric. 2. he was again returned for the same county.

In the 16 Ric. 2. he served again for the same county, and had an allowance of 18*l*, for 28 days attendance.

In the 21 Ric. 2. he appears to have been under sheriff of the said county.

And in the 1 Hen. 4. he was knight of the shire for the said county, and had an allowance of 26*l* 16*s* 0*d* for sixty-three days attendance.

He had a son and heir,

11. *John de Crackenthorp*, who married a Blencow.

This John had a brother *William*, who in the 18 Ric. 2. was elected one of the knights of the shire for Westmorland, and had 19*l* 12*s* 0*d* allowed for 49 days. In the 21 Ric. 2. he was again returned for the same county. In the

1 Hen.

1 Hen. 4. he served in parliament for the borough of Appleby. In the 3 Hen. 4. he served for the county. And again in the 4 Hen. 4. and had an allowance of 28 *l* for 71 days. In the 7 Hen. 5. he was elected burgess for Appleby; and in the 3 Hen. 6. he served for the county. He married a Sandford; and died in the 17 Hen. 6.

Robert de Crackenthorp, another brother, married one of the coheirs of the last Lancaster of Howgill. Which *Robert*, in the 1 Hen. 5. served for the county of Westmorland in parliament, and had allowance of 16 *l* for 40 days. In the 3 Hen. 5. he was again returned for the same county. And again in the 5 Hen. 6.

The said *John de Crackenthorp* by the inquisition *post mortem* of John de Clifford in the 10 Hen. 5. appears to have held the manor of Newbiggin, and one third part of the manor of Brougham. He died in the 14 Hen. 6. leaving a son and heir,

12. *John de Crackenthorp*, who married a Leyburn. In the 5 Hen. 6. we find this John, who is called John de Crackenthorp the younger (his father being then living), receiver to the lady Elizabeth (Piercy), widow of John lord Clifford, of her revenues in Westmorland.

Thomas Crackenthorp, brother of this *John*, in the 27 Hen. 6. served the office of sheriff for Cumberland; and in the 29 Hen. 6. represented the county of Cumberland in parliament. The said *Thomas*, as also his brother *James*, engaging on the part of the house of Lancaster against that of York (as did almost all the northern nobility and gentry) in the then civil wars, were slain in the great battle of Towton-field, together with their general John lord Clifford.

In the 31 Hen. 6. *John Crackenthorp de Newbiggin*, together with two others, appears by inquisition to have then held the manor of Brougham: from which special designation of the place, there can be no doubt but that the Crackenthorps of Brougham and Newbiggin were the same family.

The said *John* died in the 6 Ed. 4. leaving a son and heir,

13. *John de Crackenthorp*, who married a Musgrave.—In the 20 Hen. 7. *John Crackenthorp*, *William Bird*, and *John Burgham* held the manor of Brougham.

In the 4th, and again in the 5th of Hen. 8. *John Crackenthorp* was sheriff of Cumberland.

In the 18 Hen. 8. he, and two others, held the manor of Brougham.

The said *John*, besides his son and heir *Christopher*, seems to have had a younger son *William*, to whom he gave the said third part of the manor of Brougham: For in the 1 and 2 Ph. and Mary, *Margaret* widow of *William Crackenthorp* and *John* their son and heir held the third part of the said manor of Brougham. And after this, we find the name no more at Brougham.

14. *Christopher Crackenthorp* of Newbiggin esquire, son and heir of John, married a daughter of Blenkinsop of Helbeck.

In the 26 Hen. 8. he built the hall or manor-house at Newbiggin, as appears by this inscription, cut in stone over the hall door:

Christofer

Christofer Crakenthorp men did me call,
Who in my tyme did builde this hall,
And framed it as you may see,
One thousand five hundred thirty and three.

In the 35 Hen 8, this Christopher, for the sum of 255*l* 3*s*, purchased of the crown the grange and tenement called *Hale-grange*, with the appurtenances, in *Kirkby Thore*, late belonging to the monastery of Holm Cultram; with lands in *Kirkby Thore* and *Newbiggin*, belonging to the said monastery, to the amount of 182 acres in the whole; and also the house and other possessions of the late priory of *Friers Carmelites*, commonly named White Friers, in Appleby; and the whole manor of *Hardendale* and *Wasdale*, late belonging to the monastery *de Bellalanda*, otherwise *Byland* in Yorkshire. The *Hale* revenues were extended at 4*l* 3*s* 4*d* a year; the *Friery* at 26*s* 8*d*; and the *Byland* possessions at 8*l*. To hold of the king *in capite* by the 20th part of one knight's fee; and paying to the king yearly for *Holm Cultram* 8*s* 4*d*, for the *Friery* 2*s* 8*d*, and for *Byland* 16*s*.

The said Christopher had a younger son *John*, who was founder of the family of the Crackenthorps at Little Strickland.—His eldest son and heir was,

15. *Henry Crackenthorp* esquire; who in the 27 Eliz. presented to the rectory of Newbiggin one Sir *Roland Vaux*, on the death of Sir *Giles Robinson* the last incumbent.

This Henry had four wives. First, he married a Dalston. His second wife's name was Sandford. His third wife's name was Carnaby, of Halton-tower in Northumberland. The fourth was Winifred sister of Sir Christopher Pickering knight; by whom he had issue, (1) Christopher, his eldest son and heir. (2) William. (3) Richard, a clergyman, who married Mary lady Honywood of Mark's Hall in Essex: he was chaplain to king James the first, and died in 1624. (4) Henry. (5) Anne, married first to John Pennington of Seaton esquire, and after him to Sir Richard Sandford of Howgill-castle. (6) Frances, married to one Mr. Laithes. (7) Winifred, married to Sir William Hutton's eldest son, and afterwards to Mr. Warcop a clergyman. (8) Barbara, married to Sir Richard Fletcher of Hutton.

16. *Christopher Crackenthorp* esquire, son and heir of Henry. He married Mary daughter of Sir James Bellingham of Levins knight; and by her had issue, (1) Henry, who was slain in the fight at Wigan, upon the entrance of king Charles the second into England, before the battle at Worcester: He married a Featherston, but died without issue. (2) Richard, who succeeded his father. (3) Robert, who died unmarried. (4) Frances, married to one Darcie of York. (5) Isabel. (6) Dorothy, married to John Philipson of Calgarth esquire. (7) Elizabeth, married to Birkbeck of Orton.

17. *Richard Crackenthorp* esquire, second son and heir of Christopher. He married to his first wife Mary daughter of Sir Christopher Dalston of Acornbank knight; and by her had issue, (1) Henry, who died young. (2) Christopher, who succeeded his father. (3) John. (4) Thomas, whose posterity, after failure of issue male from his brother Christopher, succeeded to the inhe-

 ritance

ritance in tail male. (5) William. (6) Mary. (7) Barbara.—To his second wife he married Lettice daughter of one Lowgher a clergyman in Staffordshire, and relict of Thomas Denton of Warnell esquire; and by her had (8) George. (9) James. (10) Richard. (11) Francis. (12) Lettice.

In confirmation of the above account, there is in the family a long scroll of escutcheons, beginning with the arms of Newbiggin single, (supposing the arms of Newbiggin and Crackenthorp to have been the same, which we have shewn, nevertheless, to be somewhat doubtful) then, Newbiggin impaling Wharton, Blennerhasset, Barton, Vaux, Wackerfield, Threlkeld, Grimston, Brisco, Blencow, Sandford, Leyburn, Musgrave, Blenkinsop, Pickering, Bellingham, Fetherston, and Dalston. It seems to have been drawn about the time of Dugdale's visitation, which was in the year 1664.

18. *Christopher Crackenthorp* esquire, second son and heir of Richard. He married Anne daughter of Robert Rawlinson of Cark-hall in Cartmell in the county of Lancaster esquire. He was of the age of 32 at the time of Dugdale's visitation aforesaid. He left issue, (1) Richard. (2) Robert. (3) Christopher, of the six clerks office, who married a daughter of Sir William Glyn of Broadlane in the county of Flint baronet, and died without issue. (4) Mary.

19. *Richard Crackenthorp* esquire, son and heir of Christopher, married Deborah eldest daughter and coheir of Samuel Mottram of Thorp-hall in the county of Lincoln esquire; and had issue, (1) Mottram. (2) Henry, who died an infant. (3) Deborah, who died unmarried. (4) Anne, now widow of Adam Askew of Newcastle upon Tyne, M. D. who after the death of her brothers and sister without issue, remaineth heir general of the Crackenthorp family, but by the intail on the male issue was excluded from the inheritance.

This Richard, in 1698, on the death of *Thomas Dawson* rector of Newbiggin, presented to the said rectory *Thomas Jackson*, B. A.

20. *Mottram Crackenthorp* esquire, son and heir of Richard, died unmarried. And here the male branch in the direct line failing, we go back to *Thomas* aforesaid, fourth son of Richard at N° 17. Which Thomas married Mary younger daughter of Threlkeld of Melmerby, and had issue Christopher, Richard, and Mary.

21. *Christopher Crackenthorp* of Newbiggin esquire, son and heir of Thomas, married Dorothy second daughter of William Sandford of Askham esquire, and died without issue.

The said Christopher in 1731, presented *Richard Smith* to the said rectory.

He was succeeded by his brother,

22. *Richard Crackenthorp* esquire, who married Dorothy daughter of Edward Crewe of London; and had issue, Richard, Christopher, Mary, Susan, Dorothy, Anne, Catharine, John, James, and Thomas; most of whom died young.

23. *James Crackenthorp* of Newbiggin esquire, the only surviving son of Richard, succeeded his father, and married Anne second daughter of George Vane of Long Newton in the county of Durham esquire, and died without

ſſue; and in him the name of Crackenthorp of Newbiggin was extinct. He deviſed the inheritance to his widow during her life, and after that to his ſiſter Dorothy wife of William Cookſon of Penrith eſquire and the heirs male of her body, in defect thereof to the reverend Adam Aſkew ſecond ſon of Dr. Adam Aſkew of Newcaſtle upon Tyne aforeſaid.

The *arms* (as aforeſaid) of the Crackenthorps are; Or, a cheveron between three mullets pierced Azure: The creſt; on a wreath Or and Azure, an holly tree ſprig or buſh proper.

The *manor houſe* ſtands at the north end of the village; and was built (or rather rebuilt) by Chriſtopher Crackenthorp as aforeſaid, in the reign of king Henry the eighth.

The *church* is but ſmall, being in proportion to the pariſh. In the eaſt window, in Mr. Machel's time, were the Cliffords arms: And in the ſouth window next unto it, a monk with a paſtoral ſtaff, probably deſigned for St. Edmund. There is an ile on the north ſide, which belongs to the lord of the manor and patron of the living; and ſeems to have been the ancient burying place of the family. But in the year 1686 there was another place aſſigned; and on the ſouth wall was put up this diſtich, in the ſame ſtyle of poetry as the inſcription over the hall-door:

This place is aſſigned here as you ſee
For the patron of the church interred to be.

The pariſh conſiſts of only about 31 families in the whole, whereof diſſenters 3.

Upon the rocks, at a place called Crawdundale in this pariſh, were formerly found characters and ancient inſcriptions, all of which are now obliterated and mouldered away by length of time. Mr. Camden takes notice of one, the former part whereof was not legible, but in the other part was to be ſeen the name of *Varronius commander of the 20th legion*; and another, in which was the name of *Ælius Lucanus commander of the 2d legion*. The 20th legion, he ſays, was quartered at Deva, now called Weſt-Cheſter; and the 2d legion was quartered at Iſca, now Caerleon, in Wales; and might be drawn into theſe parts, for the defence thereof. The exact time hereof is not eaſily to be ſet down; yet in order to the pointing out the very time, Mr. Camden obſerves, that there was to be ſeen in a rock near adjoining, in capital letters, the name of *Cneius Octavius Cotta, conſul*, (CN. OCT. COT. COSS.) yet in all the conſular rolls he owns he could meet with no ſuch name.

[Upon the whole, if this account of the above mentioned inſcriptions were not ſupported by ſo reſpectable an authority, one might be tempted to conclude that ſome part thereof might be owing to ſtrength of imagination. It is a ſoft, red, mouldering ſtone. And if an inſcription, which was legible in Camden's time, is not now at all to be found; it ſeemeth as unlikely, that an inſcription made in the Roman times ſhould continue to the days of Camden. And it is not impoſſible, but that the whole might be the work of the ingraver who cut the inſcription over the hall door, or the amuſement of ſome labourer at a vacant hour in quarrying ſtones in the rock there.]

PARISH OF KIRKBY THORE.

I. *Pariſh of Kirkby Thore.*
II. *Manor of Kirkby Thore.*
III. *Manor of Temple Sowerby.*
IV. *Manor of Milburn.*

I. PARISH OF KIRKBY THORE.

KIRKBY THORE is ſo called from a temple anciently dedicated to the great idol of the Pagan-Saxons, called Thor; which was of more eſtimation among them, than any of the reſt of their idols. This was majeſtically placed in a very ſpacious hall, and there ſet as if he had repoſed himſelf upon a covered bed. On his head this idol wore a crown of gold, and round in compaſs above and about the ſame, were ſet or fixed 12 bright burniſhed golden ſtars; and in his right hand he held a kingly ſcepter. He was eſteemed the god of thunder; and every Thurſday was weekly dedicated unto his peculiar ſervice, from whence that day received its name.

Mr. Camden ſuppoſes this place to be the *Gallagum* of the Romans; but Mr. Horſley with more probability fixes the *Gallagum* at Appleby, and proves this place to have been the Roman *Brovonaca*.

This pariſh is bounded on the Eaſt by the pariſhes of Dufton and Marton; on the South, by the pariſhes of St. Michael's Appleby, Morland, and Cliburn; on the Weſt, by the pariſh of Brougham; and on the North, by the pariſhes of Kirkland, Newbiggin, and Alſton: And contains about 146 families; whereof, diſſenters 6.

The church is dedicated to St. Michael. It is a rectory, valued in the king's books at 37*l* 17*s* 11*d*. The patron is the right honourable the earl of Thanet, by hereditary deſcent from Robert de Veteripont, who purchaſed the ſame of the then lord of the manor. The original purchaſe-deed is ſtill at Appleby caſtle, whereby Adam ſon of Waldeve of Kirkby Thore grants to Robert de Veteripont the advowſon of the church of Kirkby Thore, with all the liberties and dignities to the ſaid church belonging, as well in the chapels of Soureby and Millebúrn, as in lands and other poſſeſſions.

Biſhop Nicolſon takes notice of a remarkable inſtance in the year 1280, of biſhop Irton's faithful adherence to the right of his ſovereign in oppoſition to the then faſhionable uſurpations of the ſee of Rome, in the caſe of proviſions

4 to

to vacant benefices, in the very first year of his prelacy; for he then certifies the bishop of Bath and Wells, then lord chancellor, that there had been no divine service in the church of Kirkby Thore in eight years past, by reason of a papal interdict; which being for not admitting a foreigner to a provision, and the church under a lay patronage, he hopes the king will resent it. (Pryn. tom. 3. p. 1231.) But it is observable, that though the bishop here admits the papal provisions to benefices under lay patronages to be incroachments on the royal authority, yet he says nothing of the like disposal of those that are the property of ecclesiastical patrons, who were supposed to be more the pope's subjects than the king's; for in truth he himself held his bishoprick by a papal provision, without the king's consent.

In the year 1343, one *Roger de Clifford* was rector of Kirkby Thore; who being grown very old and infirm, had one Sir Thomas Paytesun (a priest) assigned to him for an assistant, both in spirituals and temporals.

And two years after, *Ralph de Brantingham* was presented to the vacant rectory of Kirkby Thore, by king Edward the third, in right of Robert son and heir of Robert lord Clifford, then an infant, and the king's ward.

In 1354, on the resignation of one *Thomas de Riplyngham*, the said king presented *Adam de Hoton* in right of the said Robert, being not yet of age.

In 1362, on the death of the said Adam de Hoton, *William de Corbrigg* was presented by Roger de Clifford lord of Westmorland. The same year this William had licence of absence for a year to pursue his studies, and letters dimissory for orders. The like licence was afterwards renewed to him for three years. The said William appears to have been rector in 1335, which was the 48 Ed. 3.

In the reign of king Henry the sixth, *Roger de Crackenthorp* (one of the Newbiggin family) was rector.

In the reign of Edward the fourth, *Henry Wherton*, a younger son of Gilbert de Wherton lord of the manor of Kirkby Thore, was rector.

In 1526, 18 Hen. 8. *Richard Evenwode*, abbot of Shap, was presented by Henry earl of Cumberland, on the resignation of *Richard Rawson*, to whom he was to pay a yearly pension of 30*l*. during his life.

In this Richard Evenwode's time, who was both abbot and rector, this church narrowly escaped an appropriation to Shap abbey. The writings were drawn, the money advanced, all requisite consents obtained, and nothing prevented the completion thereof but the dissolution of the abbey *.

The

* The following is a copy of the instructions given by Evenwode to his agent in the said business of the appropriation:

"Articles of instructions from th' abbot of Shapp to Thomas Jolye concerninge th' appropriation of Kirkbythore.

Imprimis, the saide abbott doth sende to the same Thomas four deids unsealed concerninge the same appropriation.

Item, an other instrument sealede by the jentylmen churche wardens and other of the said parishinge in the name of th'ole parishinge.

Item, to remembre my lorde of Cumberlande, for sealinge of his deide of graunte under the seall of his armes for your going upon.

Item,

The great bell at Kirkby Thore, which is the largest in the county, (but hath been burst long ago) is said to have been brought thither from Shap abbey: Which, by reason of the connexion at that time of the rector of Kirkby Thore with the abbey, is not improbable: And the steeple at Kirkby Thore seems not to have been made for such a bell.

Richard Evenwode seems to have been succeeded by *Michael Crackenthorp*; which Michael died in the 11 Eliz. 1568.

On Michael Crackenthorp's death, *Robert Warthcoppe* was instituted on the presentation of Henry earl of Cumberland.

On his resignation, in 1597, institution was given to *Thomas Warcop*, M. A. on the presentation of George earl of Cumberland.

In 1629, Mr. *Lancelot Lowther* (son of Sir Christopher Lowther of Lowther), on the presentation of Francis earl of Cumberland, was instituted to the rectory of Kirkby Thore, together with the chapels of Milburn and Sowerby. He was also made rector of Marton towards the beginning of the civil wars. He was ejected from Kirkby Thore *, but seems to have had interest to keep Marton, of which place he died rector in 1661.

He was succeeded at Kirkby Thore by Mr. *Thomas Warcop* of the family of Warcop of Colby †. Which Mr. Warcop died during the usurpation.

Mr. Warcop was succeeded by *William Walker*, M. A. of Christ's college in Cambridge; who had been some time schoolmaster of Giggleswick in Yorkshire ‡.

On the death of William Walker in 1677, *Thomas Machell*, M. A. was instituted on a presentation by the honourable Thomas Tufton, brother of Ni-

Item, to remembre my saide lord (forsomiche as my lorde busshop of Carlioll comith nott down) to write a lovinge letter for sealing of his deide, and for the redy expedition and settinge forwardes of such busynes as apperteinyth to him in that behalf.

Item, a like letter to Mr. William Hogyll archdicon of Carlioll, for the sealing of such wrytynge as belongyth to his office.

Item, to remembre all other writings nott yit maide nor sealed, eyther by the kyng's highnes, my lorde of Canterbury, or any other necessary or requisit to be hade in the premisses.

Item, I do send you by my servant this berer, the residue of the fyne to the kyng's highnes for the same Kirkbythore, 40*l*.

Item, I do send you, over and beside the saide fyne, with this same berer, for discharging other chargies as sealinge of writyngs with other necessaries appon your discretion to be payede and laide down, appon a rakynnyng thereof to be maide by you of the same, 10*l*.

Item, that ye remembre to thanke Mr. Hughes for his payns hertofor takyn in these premises, and desire him of his goode continuance in the same; and accordinge to Mr. Blenkansope promess and yours, he shall have such a nagge as I truste shall content him, to be delyvered at such tyme as you thincke goode to sende for the same.

Item, desieringe you to remembre a proviso to be obteyned, that I may have and perceyve the fruits of the same Kirkbythore duringe my lif natural, in discharge of my pension.

Per me

Ricum Abbate."

* Walker's Sufferings of the Clergy. Part 2d, page 299.

† Machel.

‡ The *fiat* for his testimonial from the college is yet extant, signed by persons most of them eminent in their day: "Apr. 19, 1651. We are content that Mr. William Walker have a testimonium "according to the usual form for masters in arts. R. Widdrington. H. More. Hu. Bethel. "Will. Owtram. G. Rust. J. Sedgwick. Dan Bull." (Bound up in Mr. Machell's collection.)

cholas

cholas Tufton then earl of Thanet. This is that Thomas Machell, whom we have ſo often had occaſion to mention with honour, for his large collection of materials relating to the hiſtory and antiquities of Weſtmorland.

On the death of Thomas Machell in 1699, *Edmund Wickens*, M. A. was inſtituted on a preſentation by the ſaid Thomas Tufton then earl of Thanet.

In 1722, on the death of Edmund Wickens, *Carleton Atkinſon*, M. A. was inſtituted on the preſentation of the ſame patron.

In 1762, on the death of Carleton Atkinſon, *Thomas Milward*, M. A. rector of Marton as aforeſaid, was inſtituted on the preſentation of Sackville earl of Thanet.

In 1775, on the death of Thomas Milward, *Gilpin Gorſt*, M. A. was inſtituted on a preſentation by the ſame patron.

II. MANOR OF KIRKBY THORE.

1. The firſt lord of the manor of Kirkby Thore that we have met with was *Whelp*, who lived about the reign of king Stephen or Henry the ſecond. From him probably, or one of his anceſtors, *Whelp-caſtle* had its name.

2. He had a ſon *Gamel*. Which *Gamel* had a ſon,

3. *Waldeve*; who granted divers lands at Kirkby Thore and Hale to the abbey of Holm Cultram; with common of paſture for 400 ewes, 20 rams, and the lambs of the firſt year; and as many oxen, ſows, and horſes, as they ſhall need for their houſhold and tillage; and for ſix cows, one boar, and their young till one year old *. Which grant was confirmed by Lyulph ſon of Lyulph, who ſeems to have held one fourth part of the manor under the ſaid *Waldeve*; for in his charter of confirmation he ſtyles the ſaid *Waldeve* his lord.

* Univerſis Sanctæ Matris Eccleſiæ filiis tam preſentibus quam futuris, Waldevus filius Gamelli, ſalutem. Sciatis, quod ego voluntate et conſenſu hæredis mei et aliorum hæredum noſtrorum, conceſſi et hac præſenti charta mea confirmavi, Deo et Sanctæ Mariæ et monachis de Holme, in campo de Kyrkeby Thore terram illam quæ dicitur Toſtes et Hale, et omnem terram et mariſcum infra foſſatum monachorum ſubtus Sparſtanerig; præter terram eccleſiæ, et terram Roberti de Broy quam dedit monachis prædictis in eſcambio. (With many other parcels of lands, ſetting forth their reſpective abuttals and boundaries.) Habebunt etiam communem paſturam quadringentis ovibus et viginti multonibus cum ſectis ſuis unius anni, communiter cum vicineto de Kyrkebythore; et tot bobus et vaccis et equis quot opus habuerint ad terram ſuam excolendam, et domum ſuam tenendam, et opera ſua facienda; et ad ſex ſues, et unum verrem, cum ſectis ſuis unius anni. Et quando monachi adducent averia ſua ad nundinas vel ad forum, habebunt liberum acceſſum et receſſum cum illis in prædicta paſtura. Et accipient lignum, et turbas, et petas, et omnia alia neceſſaria cum vicineto de Kyrkebythore. Et donationem Lyulphi, et donationem Thomæ Extranei, et donationem Arnaldi et Fulconis, ſicut in eorum chartis continetur, hac mea charta confirmo. Hæc omnia prædicta concedo et do prædictis monachis in liberam, puram, et perpetuam eleemoſynam, pro ſalute animæ meæ et ſponſæ meæ et anteceſſorum meorum, libere, quiete, et honorifice; nominatim a cornagio, et multura, et omni ſeculari ſervicio, conſuetudine, et exactione. Et ego et Adam hæres meus, et cæteri hæredes noſtri warrantizabimus hanc donationem; et acquietabimus de cornagio et omni forenſi ſervicio, contra omnes homines in perpetuum. *(Regiſtr. Holme.)*

And

And by another charter he releases to the said abbey all his right and claim, as lord of the manor, in certain lands therein specified given to the said abbey by Laurence de Newbiggin †.

4. This *Waldeve* had two sons *Adam* and *Alan*. *Adam* the elder brother, by his charter confirmed to the said abbey his father's grants ‡.

This is that *Adam de Kirkby Thore* who granted the advowson of the church to Robert de Veteripont as aforesaid.

His younger brother *Alan de Kirkby Thore* granted also to the said abbey divers lands at Kirkby Thore, which grant was confirmed by *Adam* his lord and brother *.

This *Adam de Kirkby Thore* the elder brother had a son,

5. *Gilbert de Kirkby Thore*, who confirmed the grants of his grandfather and father †; and granted other lands at Kirkby Thore to the said abbey, by his charter bearing date in the year 1247, being the 32 Hen. 3.

The said *Gilbert* was living in the 14 Ed. 1. and confirmed divers other grants of lands at Kirkby Thore given to the said abbey (for there seems to have been an emulation which of them should contribute most). Particularly, *Lyulph* son of *Lyulph* aforesaid gave divers lands there; as did also *Adam* son of the said *Lyulph*, with the assent of his lord *Adam* son of *Waldeve*. And *Robert*

† Universis Sanctæ Matris Ecclesiæ filiis tam præsentibus quam futuris, Waldevus filius Gamelli filii Whelp, salutem. Sciatis me dedisse, concessisse, et hac præsenti charta mea confirmasse, consensu et assensu Adæ hæredis mei, Deo et Sanctæ Mariæ et Monachis de Holm-Coltram, totum rectum et totam calumniam quam habui ego et hæredes mei in Sparthanerig, &c. pro salute animæ meæ et hæredum meorum, et pro animabus patris mei et matris meæ, et omnium antecessorum et successorum meorum, in liberam, puram, et perpetuam eleemosynam, quietam et solutam a nobis et ab omnibus serviciis nostris. *(Registr. Holme.)*

‡ Omnibus Sanctæ Matris Ecclesiæ filiis, præsentibus et futuris, Adam filius Waldevi de Kyrkebythore, salutem. Noverit universitas vestra me, pro Dei amore et salute animæ meæ et omnium antecessorum et successorum meorum, concessisse et præsenti charta mea confirmasse Deo et ecclesiæ Beatæ Mariæ de Holme et monachis ibidem Deo servientibus, in puram et perpetuam eleemosynam, omnes donationes quas Waldevus pater meus eis dedit, in terris cultis et incultis, in pasturis, turbariis, et in omnibus aliis rebus in territorio de Kyrkebythore, sicut chartæ patris mei testantur. *(Registr. Holme.)*

* Sciant omnes tam præsentes quam futuri, quod ego Alanus filius Waldevi de Kyrkebythore, voluntate et consensu Adæ domini mei et fratris mei, dedi et concessi et hac præsenti charta mea confirmavi Deo et Sanctæ Mariæ et monachis de Holm, in liberam, puram, et perpetuam eleemosynam, viii acras terræ in territorio de Kyrkeby Thore, et medietatem marisci ad capita earum, scilicet, juxta tres acras versus Soureby. Et ego et hæredes mei warrantizabimus has prædictas acras terræ cum prædicto marisco prædictis monachis contra omnes homines in perpetuum, liberas, quietas, et solutas, ab omni seculari servicio, consuetudine, et exactione. *(Registr. Holme.)*—— And there is a like grant by the said Alan of a toft and croft at Kirkby Thore to the said abbey.

† Omnibus Sanctæ Matris Ecclesiæ filiis, Gillebertus filius Adæ de Kyrkebythore, salutem. Noverit universitas vestra, me pro salute animæ meæ et antecessorum et successorum meorum, concessisse et hac præsenti charta confirmasse Deo et Sanctæ Mariæ et monachis de Holm, in liberam, puram, et perpetuam eleemosynam, omnes donationes quas Waldevus avus meus eis dedit, et omnes alias donationes quas dictus Waldevus et Ada pater meus eis chartis suis confirmaverunt, in terris cultis, et incultis, in pasturis et turbariis, et petariis et in omnibus aliis rebus et communiis in territorio de Kyrkebythore, quietas ab omni seculari servicio, sicut chartæ prædicti Waldevi avi mei et Adæ patris mei testantur. *(Registr. Holme.)*

de

de Broy released to them certain rights and claims which he had there; and made an exchange with them of divers lands, whereof the *Maiden way* is expressed to be one of the bounder marks ‡: And *Amabil* daughter of *Robert de Bereford* executed to the said abbey a like release.

Also *John de Veteripont* gave certain lands there to the said abbey; and the said *John*, as lord of Westmorland, of whom this manor was holden in chief, granted to the inhabitants of Kirkby Thore freedom from *pulture* of his foresters in Westmorland, and from finding testimony to his foresters which is called *witnessman*; and that if they shall be found guilty of offences in hunting or vert, they shall not be called to account for the same in any of his courts of the forest, but only in the county court.

6. After *Gilbert*, the next that we find was *John de Kirkby Thore* (probably son of *Gilbert*); who in the 8 Ed. 2. after the death of Robert de Clifford, is found by inquisition to have held of the said Robert the manor of Kirkby Thore; the wardship whereof, when it should happen, was valued at 10*l* a year, and the cornage thereof was 32*s* 6*d*.

In the 9 Ed. 2. and again in the 14 Ed. 3. *John de Kirkby Thore* was knight of the shire for Westmorland.

7. In the 43 Ed. 3. and also in the 15 Ric. 2. *John de Kirkby Thore* held the manor of Kirkby Thore.

8. So, in the 10 Hen. 5. *John de Kirkby Thore* held the same.

9. In the 31 Hen. 6. it is found by inquisition as follows: *Gilbert de Kirkby Thore* heretofore held 3 parts of Kirkby Thore, and paid yearly for cornage 19*s* 10*d*; and owed wardship, marriage, and relief. And now *John de Kirkby Thore* holds the same 3 parts by all the services aforesaid; and makes fine by suit to the county court, notwithstanding that the lord of Westmorland released to one of his ancestors the said suit.—And *Robert de Berford* heretofore held immediately the 4th part of the same vill of Kirkby Thore, and paid yearly for cornage 12*s* 8*d*, and owed wardship, marriage, and relief. And now *Ralph Pudsay* knight, lord of Berford upon Teys, holds immediately the same 4th part, by the services aforesaid. And *John Wherton* holds the said 4th part of the said knight, by all the services aforesaid *.

And this is the first introduction of the *Whartons* to Kirkby Thore. They claim to be descended from a younger branch of the *Whartons* of Wharton-hall; which probably may be true (although they do not clearly make out the connexion): And to this day they bear the arms of the *Whartons* of Wharton, viz. Sable, a manch Argent; with a crescent above the manch, by way of distinction of the younger branch: The crest; On a wreath, a bull's head erased.

1. This *John Wharton* we assume as the first of that family at Kirkby Thore. In the 17 Ed. 4. we find Margaret daughter of John Wharton of Kirkby Thore esquire married to William son of Thomas Wybergh of Clifton esquire.

‡ De Maydengate usque ad domos predictorum monachorum.

* Rawlinson.

2. Next unto John, we find *Gilbert Wharton* of Kirkby Thore esquire, who had a younger son Henry (as we observed before) rector there. And in the reign of Henry the seventh, *Gilbert Wharton* of Kirkby Thore was, with others, collector of the subsidy in Westmorland.

3. In the 14 Hen. 7. we find *John Wharton* of Kirkby Thore esquire, probably son of Gilbert.

4. This John had a son *Gilbert*: For in the 4 Hen. 8. *Gilbert*, son and heir of John Wharton of Kirkby Thore, did (by way of settlement) grant to Thomas Warcop of Colby esquire and others, all his manors, demesnes, lands, tenements, rents, and services, in Kirkby Thore, Brampton, and elsewhere in Westmorland; and all his lands, tenements, rents, and services, in Cumrewe, and Aleby-field in Gilsland, one close called Bartyn Park in the barony of Graystocke with one tenement contiguous thereunto, and also the reversion of all his lands and tenements in Glassenby and elsewhere, in the county of Cumberland; to the use of Katherine his wife during the minority of his son and heir *John*, and after her decease to the joint heirs of himself and the said Katherine, remainder to his own right heirs.

In the 18 Hen. 8. the said Gilbert appears to have held 3 parts of Kirkby Thore as aforesaid. And Thomas Pudsey of Bereford upon Teis held the 4th part, which 4th part the said Gilbert held of Thomas Pudsey.

And twenty years after this, we find the said Gilbert and his son John both living. For in the last year of the reign of Hen. 8. *John Wharton*, son and heir apparent of *Gilbert Wharton*, was trustee in a marriage settlement of a daughter of Hugh Machel to the son of Richard Machel gentlemen, both of Crackenthorp.

5. In the 18 Eliz. we find *John Wharton* esquire in a list of subscribers to the building of Temple Sowerby bridge. And this *John* probably had a son,

6. *John Wharton* of Kirkby Thore esquire; for in the pedigree of the Whartons of Kirkby Thore, certified at Sir William Dugdale's visitation in 1664, the first in the list (except two *Johns* in the reign of Hen. 7.) is *John Wharton* esquire, who married Cicely daughter of Sir Nicholas Thornburgh of Celshed in the county of Lancaster knight, and died (as is there said) in 1600. [Indeed, these heraldic pedigrees, especially at any considerable distance of time, are generally very imperfect, and contradicted for the most part by records, where we have been so fortunate as to meet with such. It was impossible for the heralds to judge in most cases of their authenticity, and the person certifying the same might not be perfectly acquainted with the antiquities of his family.—The Sir Nicholas Thornburgh here mentioned should have been Sir William Thornburgh, who was of Selside in Westmorland.]

7. The abovesaid *John*, by his wife Cicely Thornburgh, had a son and heir *Thomas Wharton* esquire; who married to his first wife, Frances daughter and coheir of Reginald Hartley of Appleby esquire: by whom he had issue, (1) John. (2) Henry, who died unmarried. (3) Richard, who also died unmarried. (4) Anne, married to Thomas Birkbeck of Orton. (5) Mary, married to Richard Lancaster of Sockbridge esquire. (6) Dorothy, who died unmarried. (7) Jane, married to Thomas Lowther of Rosetrees in Cumberland.

land. He married to his second wife, Bridget daughter of Robert Teasdale of Dufton, widow of Jeffrey Wybergh of Bolton. He died in 1620.

8. *John Wharton* esquire, son and heir of Thomas, married Katherine daughter of Christopher Wyvill son and heir apparent of Sir Marmaduke Wyvill of Constable Burton in the county of York baronet, and by her had issue John, Stephen, Henry, Christopher, Philip, Thomas, Mary, Isabel, Jane, and Petronilla. He died in 1648.

9. *John Wharton* esquire, son of John, married Anne daughter of Richard Crackenthorp of Little Strickland gentleman. He was of the age of 37 at Dugdale's visitation aforesaid; and had then three daughters, Bridget, Jane, and Anne. And it seemeth that he had no more children afterwards. For he cut off the intail, and (to raise portions for his daughters) sold the estate to his cousin *Humphrey Wharton* of Gilling esquire, barrister at law.

10. The said *Humphrey Wharton* had issue only one son, *viz.*

11. *Humphrey Wharton* of Gilling esquire, who married a daughter of Byerley of Grainge in the county of Durham esquire, and by her had issue Humphrey, Robert, Christopher, and Anthony, and three daughters. Of the sons, Humphrey, Robert, and Christopher, died without issue, and the fourth son Anthony succeeded to the inheritance.

12. *Anthony Wharton* of Gilling esquire married a daughter of Sir William Hickes of the county of Essex, and by her had issue (1) William. (2) Anne, who married and died leaving issue two daughters, *viz.* Anne married to John Hall Stephenson of Skelton castle in Cleveland esquire, and Frances married to William Farquharson esquire. (3) Margaret. (4) Mary.

13. *William Wharton* of Gilling esquire succeeded his father, and died without issue, leaving coheirs the present owners his sisters Margaret and Mary and the daughters of his sister Anne.

The *hall* or *manor house*, as also most part of the present town (Mr. Machel says), have been built out of the ruins of *Whelp Castle*; of which there are now scarce any remains. The main body of it hath stood (as may be conjectured, he says, from the ruins under ground) in a place called the *Burwens*, on a rising ground, at the bank of the rivulet called Troutbeck, and not far from the river Eden. The square inclosure, called the High Burwens, seems to have been the area of it, containing 8 score yards in diameter, now ploughed and cultivated; and the outer buildings, mantle, and gardens, to have run down along the said rivulet at least as far as the fulling-mill, and possibly further, beyond the high street or Roman way; thence up the west side of the said street about 8 score yards, and thence up again in a straight line to the west angle of the said area. For in all these places the vestigia of it may be discovered, by conduits under ground; subterraneous vaults; fair pavements of floors made with flags; tiles, and slates, with iron nails in them, by which they have been fastened: but principally, by the foundations of walls, both of brick and stone; as also by coins, altars, and urns, with other fictilia, often found thereabouts.

 The

The said Mr. Machel, in the year 1687, in a search there, found amongst the rifled foundations a fourfold wall, made up of four walls jumped together, and as it were united into one. They were made of hewn stone, each wall being two foot and four inches thick, so that the whole was nine foot and four inches. The outermost wall was strongly cemented to the very foundation with the best Roman mortar, seeming to be a composition of lime, gravel, and brick. The other three had their foundations first laid in clay, and then in a coarser sort of lime. And underneath all, was a pavement of cobble stones, to make the foundation more firm and durable.

In another part he found an altar FORTVNAE SERVATRICI.

Some leaden pipes also were found; and a drain made through the quadruple wall to carry off the water.

There were also found divers chambers, or arched vaults, under ground; with floors flagged with stone, or paved with brick. The bricks for the pavement were generally about ten inches square, and two inches deep: though some were a foot square and 2½ inches deep.

All which do loudly proclaim the same to have been Roman: As also the ancient Roman way, which branches off here, called the *Maiden-way*; and terminates at Caervorran in Northumberland near the Picts wall, for the length of near 20 miles, through fells, wastes, and moors. Along which street, it is generally thought, were placed those stations and mansions mentioned by Antonine in the ninth Itinerary.—And it is observable, that the gill at the other end of the *Maiden-way* near Caervorran is called *Glen-Whelp* (now by corruption *Glen Welt*).

There was an ancient *well* discovered by the said Mr. Machel, at the low end of the town near the bridge, by the side of the great Roman way leading from Appleby to Carlisle. In which were found urns, and several curious fine earthen vessels; the cusp of a spear; and sandals, whose soles were stuck full of nails, and sewed together, not with thread, but with leather: Most of which were carefully preserved, designed, and described in a letter from the said Mr. Machel to Sir William Dugdale, and printed in the Philosophical Transactions Apr. 20, 1684.

Mr. Horsley takes notice of the following inscription found here:

DEO BELATVCAD	Deo Belatucadro
RO: LIB: VOTV	libenter votum
M FECIT	fecit
IOLVS	Iolus *.

There is a close called *Meadow Powes* at Kirkby Thore, charged with 3*l* 6*s* 8*d* yearly to several charitable uses, particularly to the poor of Warcop and Bleatarn: Which, on a dispute in the year 1672, was decreed to be paid, by Humphrey Wharton esquire, purchaser of the said close †.

Some few years ago, the horn of a *moose deer* was found at the depth of about four feet from the surface of the earth; which was discovered by the river

* Horsl. 298. † Cases in the time of lord chancellor Finch, page 81.

washing

washing away the bank near the conflux of Troutbeck and Eden. Which is now in the possession of John Dalston of Great Salkeld esquire, in his large collection of natural curiosities.

In the said lordship of Kirkby Thore, is a freehold estate called *Spittle*; which name indicates the same to have belonged to some of the religious houses. It is about half a mile north-west from the church.

Nigh unto which is *Hale* aforesaid; part in the lordship of Kirkby Thore, and part in the parish of Newbiggin.

III. MANOR OF TEMPLE SOWERBY.

Below Kirkby Thore, and adjoining thereto on the north-west, lies TEMPLE SOWERBY; so called by way of distinction, from its having belonged heretofore to the Knights Templars: for there are two Sowerbys in the bottom of Westmorland, the other being called *Brough Sowerby*.

Before this place was granted to the Templars, it seems to have been called Sowerby only, without any other name of distinction. And we find several persons deriving their name from thence, as *Adam de Soureby*, *William de Soureby*, *Hugh de Soureby*, and others. But whether any of this name, or who else, were then lords of the manor, hath not appeared to us.

The Knights Templars became first established in England about the reign of king Stephen, who began his reign in the year 1135. When or by whom this manor was granted to the Templars, we have not found. The lords of this manor claim and exercise for themselves and their tenants, several privileges which heretofore belonged to the Knights Templars, who had large possessions in this kingdom; which privileges were granted to them by a charter of king Henry the third. Which said king, for the love of God, and for the health of the soul of king John his father, and of the souls of all his ancestors and successors, grants to the fraternity of the Knights Templars as follows: "That they shall hold all their possessions, with all liberties, free customs and quietances, in wood and in plain, in meadows and pastures, in waters and mills, in ways and paths, in lakes and ponds, in marshes and fisheries, in granges and woods, with soc, and sac, and tol, and theam, and infangthief, and outfangthief, and hamsoken, and grithbrich, and blodwite, and fledwite, and flitwite, and ferdwite, and hengwite, and leirwite, and flemenefrith, and fines for murder and robbery, forstall, ordell, and oreste: That they shall be free from aids of kings, sheriffs, and their officers, and from hidage, and carucage, and danegeld, and horngeld, and armies, and wapentacs, and scutages, and tallages, lestages, stallages, shires, and hundreds, pleas, and plaints, ward, and wardpeny, and averpeny, and hundredpeny, and borethalpeny, and thethingpeny, and from the works of castles, parks, bridges, inclosures, and from all caringe, sumage, and navage, and buildings or other works about the king's houses; neither shall

" their

"their woods be taken for any such works, nor the corn or other goods of "them or any of their tenants for the furnishing provisions for any such castles: "And that they shall have their assart lands within the forest free from the "regard and view of the foresters: And they and their men, and the goods "of every of them, shall be free from toll in all fairs and markets, and pas- "sages of bridges, ways, and of the sea, throughout the whole realm: And "if any of their men shall be adjudged to forfeiture of life or limb, or shall "fly and not stand to judgment, or shall be found guilty of any offence which "incurs forfeiture of goods and chattels, either in the king's court or in any "other; the said goods and chattels shall belong to the said fraternity, and the "king's officers shall not seize them: Waif also, found in the fee of the "Templars, shall belong to the said fraternity: And if any of their tenants "shall forfeit their fee, the said brethren may enter thereupon immediately, "notwithstanding that the king hath used to have in the fees of felons and "fugitives the year, day, and waste: Amerciaments for offences also they shall "have:—Saving to the king the judgment of life and limb. And if any of "the liberties aforesaid shall by continuance of time go into disuse, they shall "nevertheless enjoy the same in time following *."

Other privileges the lords of this manor have sometimes asserted, which are clearly without foundation; such as appointing overseers of the poor, surveyors of the highways, and the like; which offices did not exist till some hundreds of years after the granting of the above mentioned privileges, nor till after the dissolution of the Templars, Hospitallers, and every other of the religious societies.

The Templars were dissolved in the year 1312; and, eleven years after, their possessions were by act of parliament given to the Knights Hospitallers. In the intermediate space, we find Temple Sowerby held by Robert lord Clifford by way of escheat. For by an inquisition after the death of the said Robert, who died in the year next after the dissolution of the Templars, we find that the said Robert died seised in his demesne as of fee, of certain tenements in Temple Sowerby, as his escheats, by the dissolution of the Templars; which he held of the king *in capite* by knights service: And there were there 16 oxgangs of land in the hands of tenants at will, which paid yearly 3*l* 4*s* 0*d*. Eight cottages 20*s*. One water mill worth yearly 4*l*. Pleas and perquisites of the court 6*s* 8*d*.

This manor, by the said act of parliament, being transferred to the Hospitallers, continued in their hands till the dissolution of the religious houses in the reign of king Henry the eighth. Which said king, by letters patent bearing date July 15, in the 35th year of his reign, granted to *Thomas Dalston* esquire (together with the manors of Brundholme, Uldale, Caldbeck-Upperton, and Kirkbride, late parcel of the possessions of Henry Percy earl of Northumberland, and divers other possessions in Cumberland, late belonging to the monastery of Holme) the whole manor of Temple Sowerby with the appurtenances in the counties of Westmorland and Cumberland, late belonging to the

* 2 Dugd. Mon. 558.

priory

priory of St. John of Jerufalem, and parcel of the poffeffions of the late preceptor of the mount of St. John Baptift in the county of York: Except and referving all mines of lead and coal within the faid manor.

Which faid *Thomas Dalfton* was the eleventh in defcent from the firft of that name of Dalfton in Cumberland; and was the common anceftor of the Dalftons both at Dalfton and Temple Sowerby: And with him therefore we begin our pedigree of the Dalftons at Temple Sowerby.

1. *Thomas Dalfton* of Dalfton efquire had two wives: By the former wife he had iffue who continued the defcent in the direct line at Dalfton. By his fecond wife, who was daughter and coheir of Thomas Carlifle, he had iffue,

2. *Chriftopher Dalfton* of Uldale efquire; who married Mabel daughter of Sir John Lowther of Lowther. This Chriftopher, about the 16 Eliz. had a difpute with the tenants of Temple Sowerby concerning their cuftom of tenant right; whereupon it was decreed by the lord prefident and council at York for the northern parts, with the confent of the faid Chriftopher, that for the ending of controverfies, a divifion fhould be made of the feveral meffuages, lands, and tenements in Temple Sowerby, by arbitrators chofen for that purpofe; who did thereupon award, that the tenants fhould have their houfes and buildings, tofts, crofts, garths, and orchards to their feveral meffuages and tenements belonging, with the moiety or one half of all their arable lands, meadows, feedings, commons, pafture, and other the premiffes to their feveral meffuages and tenements appertaining; and the faid Chriftopher Dalfton thereupon to make them leafes of their feveral meffuages, lands, and tenements for 1000 years, referving the rent of four marks yearly, every one to pay according to the rate and quality of his farmhold.

The faid Chriftopher had iffue,

3. *Thomas Dalfton* of Uldale efquire. He married Jane daughter of one Philips of Brignall in the county of York. He died in 1611; leaving iffue,

4. Sir *Chriftopher Dalfton* of Acorn Bank, who was knighted by king James in the year 1615, upon his return from his progrefs into Scotland. He married Anne daughter of Sir William Hutton of Penrith; and by her had iffue, (1) John. (2) Thomas Dalfton of Oufeby, who married Anne daughter of Richard Nevinfon of Newby efquire. (3) Mary, married to Richard Crackenthorp of Newbiggin efquire. (4) Dorothy, married to Sir William Carleton of Carleton-hall. (5) Barbara, married to James Bellingham fon and heir of Alan Bellingham of Levins efquire. (6) Anne, married to John Whelpdale of Penrith gentleman. (7) Sufanna, married to Edward Nevinfon of Newby efquire.

5. *John Dalfton* of Acorn-bank efquire, fon and heir of Sir Chriftopher, married Lucie daughter and heir of Richard Fallowfield of Great Strickland efquire; and by her had iffue Chriftopher, Thomas, John, George, William, and Charles; and five daughters, Elizabeth married to Anthony Ducket of Grayrigg efquire, Frances married to Thomas Warwick of Warwick in Cumberland, Jane married to William Howard, Dorothy, and Margaret.—Thus ftood the pedigree at Dugdale's vifitation in 1664.

The faid John died in 1692, at the age of 86 years.

In

In the chancel of Kirkby Thore church upon a mural monument, on a brass plate, is inscribed this epitaph:

" Subtus reconditur depositum mortale Johannis Dalston de Acornbank infra comitatum Westmoriæ armigeri, filii Christophori Dalston equitis aurati. Dum in vivis erat, magnum se præbuit virtutum omnium exemplar, feræ posteritati imitandum. Paternum genus duxit a Roberto de Dalston, fratre Huberti de Vallibus et consanguineo Radulphi de Micenis; cui Will. 1. conquestor dictus, Cumbriam dedit. Primam juventutem humanioribus literis imbuit collegium reginæ Oxoniæ; juris vero municipalis scientia hospitium Grayense quod Londini est. Patriæ restitutus, officia justiciarii ad pacem, Locum tenentis deputati, vicecomitis Cumbriæ, et nuntii ad parliamenta de Burgo Aballaba, bene et fideliter gessit. Bello civili, quod exarsit A. D. MDCXLI, a partibus regiis fortiter stetit; pro ea, perduellionum rabie, gravia passus. Publicis negotiis maxime idoneus, intra privatam vitam se continuit: satius ducens, hospitalitatem inter vicinos colere; rem familiarem augere; sibi suisque sapere. Matrimonio accepit Luciam filiam unicam et hæredem Richardi Fallowfield arm. de Melkinthorp intra agrum Westmoriæ, quæ maternum stemma habuit de familia de Lowther de Lowther-hall. Ex illa suscepit filios filiasque Christophorum, Thomam, Georgium, Willielmum, Carolum; Elizabetham, Franciscam, Janam, Dorotheam, Margaretam. Annorum et bonorum operum satur, animam Deo resignavit, apud prædium suum de Millrigg, 13 die Aprilis mensis, A. D. MDCXCII, cum vixisset annos 86."

6. *Christopher Dalston* of Mill-rigg esquire, son and heir of John, married Bridget daughter of Sir Henry Fletcher of Hutton baronet; and by her had issue John, Christopher, and Henry.

7. *John Dalston* of Acorn-bank esquire, son and heir of Christopher, married Lucy only daughter of James Cook of Stockton merchant; and by her had issue John and Christopher.

In the old chapel at Temple Sowerby, before the same was taken down and rebuilt, was the following monumental inscription:

" Here lies John Dalston of Acorn-bank esquire, a justice of the peace and " deputy lieutenant for the counties of Westmorland and Cumberland. He " was son and heir of Christopher, who was son and heir of John, who was " son and heir of Sir Christopher, who was son and heir of Thomas, who was " son and heir of Christopher, who was third son of Thomas de Dalston of Dalston-hall. He married Lucy the only daughter of James Cook of Stockton " merchant, by whom he had issue John and Christopher: John survived " him. He died in the 44th year of his age, 1° Jan. Anno Regni Reginæ " Annæ sexto, Annoq; Dom. 1707."

8. *John Dalston* of Acorn-bank esquire, son and heir of John, died unmarried; and was succeeded by the next heir of the family, *viz.*

9. Sir *William Dalston* knight, son of Henry third son of Christopher above mentioned at N° 6. Which Sir William dying unmarried, was succeeded by his sister and heir,

10. *Mary*,

10. *Mary*, wife of *William Norton* efquire, who hath four daughters now living.

The paternal *arms* of this family are the fame with thofe of the Dalftons of Dalfton, *viz.* Argent; a cheveron ingrailed, between 3 daws heads erafed, Sable; armed, Or: With a crefcent for the younger brother charged upon the cheveron. The creft; Out of a ducal crown Or, a falcon's head Proper.

The ancient manor houfe is *Acorn-bank* before mentioned, fo called from the afcent towards it being heretofore covered with oak wood, of which there are yet to be feen ftumps of prodigious thicknefs. It is a neat houfe, much improved by the late John Dalfton efquire; and the wood being now cleared away from before it, there is an extenfive and delightful profpect of the country all about, except only towards the north.

The *chapel* at Temple Sowerby is lately rebuilt, in a very handfome manner. In the year 1338, there is an entry in the bifhop's regifter of a confirmation of an old award made by Ralph de Irton bifhop of Carlifle, between the parifhioners of Kirkby Thore and the inhabitants of Temple Sowerby; whereby it is declared, that the latter are and fhall be (as they have ever been) free from contributing any thing towards the repairs of the church, belfrey, or churchyard walls at Kirkby Thore: Saving that if hereafter it fhall be thought neceffary to inlarge the nave or body of the church, they fhall then bear a third part of the expence.—This order was revived in bifhop Kirkby's time, and he and his fucceffors are made guarantees of it.

In the valuation in the firft fruits office in the 26 Hen. 8. the chapel of Temple Sowerby is rated at 20*s*, by a penfion from the rector of Kirkby Thore.

In the year 1656, Anne countefs dowager of Pembroke purchafed of Edward Nevinfon of Newby efquire, for the fum of 110*l*, an eftate at Temple Sowerby, the profits whereof to be employed in keeping in repair the two tombs of her mother and herfelf in Appleby church, in repairing the fchool at Appleby, the moot hall, and the bridge.

The *bridge* below Temple Sowerby over the river Eden was rebuilt in the year 1575; towards which, there was a fubfcription of the gentlemen and other principal inhabitants of the county; more particularly of thofe within (what were then called) the Eaft and Middle Wards.

The faid bridge being carried away by an inundation in the year 1748, the fame was then again rebuilt at the expence to the county of 550*l*. In taking up the frames under the old pillars, and digging deeper for a fure foundation, the workmen found another frame underneath; both the frames of good oak, not in the leaft decayed.

IV. MANOR OF MILBURNE.

North-east from Temple Sowerby and Kirkby Thore, lies the manor of MILBURNE, so called probably from a water mill on the rivulet there. This is the most northern village in the county; and is divided from Blencarne in Cumberland by the water called Blencarne beck, which taketh its course by Newbiggin, Acorn-bank, and so into Eden, and divides all along in its course these two counties.

Milburne contains in it *Kirkhouse*, a small hamlet holden of the rectors of Kirkby Thore (unto which the name seemeth to refer), wherein the chapel is situate; *Gullom Holme*, another small hamlet; *Milburne* and *Grange*, two handsome villages; which are all holden of *Howgill-castle*, the ancient seat of the lords of the manor.

The first account that we have of this particular manor, is in the reign of king John; which said king granted to *William de Stuteville* the *Forest of Milburne*.

Afterwards *Nicholas de Stuteville* granted to *Robert de Veteripont* the whole village and grange of Milneburne, as William de Stuteville or his ancestors had held the same.

The said Robert granted part thereof to Shap abbey; namely, the whole village of the grange of Milneburne.

In the 3 Ed. 2. we find that earl *Patrick* of *Dunbar* held Milneburne of the Cliffords; that is, that part of it which had not been granted away to the abbey. And at the same time, Thomas de Haltecło and Adam Garnet held the residue (probably in the name of the abbey), rendring for the same 4 *l*.

And in the 8 Ed. 2. we find the same earl Patrick holding Milneburne; of which the wardship was rated at 6 *l* 13 *s* 4 *d*, and the cornage was 21 *s*. 8 *d*.

In the 43 Ed. 3. it was found by inquisition, that *Bertrine de Johnby* and *Robert de Vallibus* had held the manor of Milneburne of one Patrick earl of Dunbar; which Patrick held the same of Robert de Clifford, and the said Robert de Clifford held the same of the king *in capite* by knights service. And afterwards the said earl Patrick forfeited the same to king Edward grandfather of the present king, for adhering to Robert de Bruce king of Scotland, enemy of our lord the king.

After this came in the family of the *Lancasters* (perhaps by grant from the crown after the said forfeiture). In order to deduce which family, we must recur to the ancient barons of Kendal. *William de Lancaster* the third of that name, baron of Kendal, had a bastard brother (as we mentioned before), whose name was *Roger*. This *Roger de Lancaster* had three sons, *John*, *William*, and *Christopher*. From *Christopher* the youngest issued the family of the Lancasters of Sockbridge. *John* the eldest, by the name of John de Lancastre of Holgill, in the 1st and again in the 2d of Ed. 3. was chosen to represent the county of Westmorland in parliament. He died in the 8 Ed. 2. without issue male; whereupon his estate went over to the next heir male of

 the

the family, namely, to *John de Lancaster*, son of the second brother *William*. This *John de Lancaster* died in the 25 Ed. 3. and was succeeded by his son,

Sir *William de Lancaster* of Howgill knight. This Sir William, in the 33 Ed. 3. had a licence from the bishop of Carlisle for a chaplain for that year in his family. He died in the 22 Ric. 2. leaving issue,

Sir *William*; who died in the 8 Hen. 4. leaving issue,

Sir *John de Lancaster* of Howgill knight. In the 8 Hen. 4. and again in the 9 Hen. 5. he represented the county of Westmorland in parliament.

In the 10 Hen. 5. by the inquisition *post mortem* of John lord Clifford, the jurors find, that *John de Lancastre* held the manor of Milneburn, by the cornage of 21*s* 8*d*; and also divers lands and tenements there, for which he paid 4*l* for all services. This Sir *John* died in the reign of Hen. 6. leaving four daughters coheirs, 1. *Christian*, married to Sir Robert de Harrington knight. 2. *Isabel*, married to Sir Thomas le Fleming of Coniston knight. 3. *Margaret*, married to Sir Matthew de Whitfield knight. And, 4. *Elizabeth*, married to Robert de Crackenthorp esquire, a younger brother of the Crackenthorps of Newbiggin. And in the partition of the estate, in the 16th year of the same king, *Christian* and *Elizabeth* were to have the manors of Depedale, Blencoyne, Holgyl, and Knock Salcok, and the lands there, as also in Milneburn and Lowenthwaite; and *Margaret* and *Isabel* were to have the manor of Rydal, and all the lands and tenements in Rydal and Loughrigg.——The arms of these Lancasters were; Argent, two bars Gules, on a canton of the second a lion passant guardant Or.

In the division between *Christian* and *Elizabeth*, *Howgill* fell to *Elizabeth*, who thereupon brought the same in marriage to *Robert de Crackenthorp*.

This *Robert* had a son *Ambrose Crackenthorp* esquire; which Ambrose was one of the arbitrators in the 5 Hen. 8. between the chantry priest of Appleby and Hugh Machel of Crackenthorp gentleman, concerning the said Hugh's beating the said chantry priest. The said Ambrose died without issue male; and was succeeded by his brother,

Anthony Crackenthorp of Howgill esquire; who had only three daughters, *Anne*, *Margaret*, and *Cicely*.

Of whom *Anne* the eldest, who had Howgill for her purparty, was married to Sir *Thomas Sandford* of Askham knight; and thereby brought this manor to the *Sandfords*.

This Sir *Thomas Sandford*, by his wife *Anne Crackenthorp*, had a son *Thomas* who succeeded him at Askham; a second son *Henry*, who married Agnes daughter of Gervase Strickland; and a third son, *viz.*

Richard Sandford esquire, who removed to Howgill-castle. He married Anne daughter of John Warriner of Helsington, and by her had 18 children; of whom, the eldest was,

Sir *Thomas Sandford* of Howgill knight; who died without issue: And was succeeded by his brother,

Sir *Richard Sandford* of Howgill knight; who married Anne daughter of Henry Crackenthorp of Newbiggin esquire, and widow of Pennington of Seaton. He had issue,

 Sir

Sir *Thomas Sandford* baronet; who married Bridget daughter of Sir George Dalſton of Dalſton knight, and had iſſue Richard, George, William, Anne, Elizabeth, and Catharine, beſides ten other children who died young.

Sir *Richard Sandford* baronet, ſon and heir of Sir Thomas, married Mary daughter of Sir Francis Bowes knight, and had iſſue Mary and Richard. He was murdered at London, Sept. 8, 1675, by Henry Symbal and William Jones, who were executed for the ſame; of which there was a printed account in the year 1680.

Sir *Richard Sandford* baronet, ſon of the laſt Sir Richard, was born (it is ſaid) in the very ſame hour in which his father died. He died unmarried; and was ſucceeded by his ſiſter and heir,

Mary; who was married to *Robert Honywood* of Mark's Hall in Eſſex eſquire, and had iſſue *Richard*, *John*, and *Philip*. *Richard* left iſſue a ſon, who died in his minority. *John* died without iſſue. Whereupon the inheritance deſcended to the third brother, the preſent owner, *viz.*

Philip Honywood eſquire lieutenant general of his majeſty's forces.

Howgill castle, which is the manor houſe, is a fair building, which ſtands high on the ſkirts of the mountains in the eye of the country, and hath a large proſpect to the ſouth and ſouth-weſt; but is ſhut up by mountains on the north. The walls were formerly, and ſome of them are yet, 10½ foot thick (which exceeds the dimenſion of the Picts wall, which was only 8 or 9 foot). And underneath the dwelling-houſe (to which they aſcended by ſtairs on the outſide) were vaults and cellars, arched over with ſtone; which was the common way of building in the northern parts, whilſt they were in continual apprehenſions of the Scots; and ſerved not only to the uſe which they are now put to, but to keep their horſes and cattle ſecure.

In this manor, near to a place called *Green Caſtle* (which is a round fort with deep trenches about it, on the ſouth end of Dunfell) was an *altar* found with this inſcription, DEO SILVANO.

In the mountains are outburſts of *coals*, which the country people ſometimes pick out for burning lime. There is alſo *lead* ore, which diſcovers itſelf in the banks of rivulets.

Beſides the *chapel*, there ſeems to have been a *chantry* at Milburne. For Robert de Veteripont gave Milburne Grange aforeſaid to Shap abbey, for the purpoſe of eſtabliſhing a chantry *(pro cantaria facienda)*; and the chapel was there before, as appears from the grant of Adam de Kirkby Thore to the ſaid Robert. But it is not unlikely, that this nevertheleſs might be intended as an augmentation to the chapel; and that for the ſaid benefaction, the abbot and convent ſhould find a chaplain, who, beſides the ordinary ſervice, ſhould alſo pray (as uſual) for the ſouls of the founder and his kindred. And it ſeemeth, that out of the ſaid grange the abbey was to pay for the purpoſe aforeſaid 4*l* yearly, that being the ſum ſpecified in the inquiſition in the 3 Ed. 2. aforeſaid:

 Which

Which was a confiderable fum in thofe days. And this could not be any fum payable to the Cliffords as lords paramount of the manor; for the whole cornage of the whole manor was only 21*s* 7*d*.

But if this was the cafe, the abbey had found fome means to throw this charge upon the rector; for in the valuation in the firft fruits office, in the 26 Hen. 8. the chantry at Milburne is faid to be worth yearly 4*l*, in a penfion by the rector of Kirkby Thore.

And in the reign of queen Elizabeth this appears to have been advanced further; for in the accounts of the profits of the rectory in the years 1572 and 1573, there is fet down as a deduction, to Sir John Spedding curate at Milburne, for each year 4*l* 13*s* 4*d*.

This chapel hath been twice augmented by the countefs dowager Gower, with 200*l* each time, which procured 400*l* from the governors of queen Anne's bounty, wherewith lands were purchafed in Dillaker, Firbank, Howgill, and Bolton, of the prefent yearly value of 34*l*.

In the faid chapel, in what is called the Sandford ile, there is a monument of Anne wife of Richard Sandford of Howgill-caftle efquire aforefaid, who had 18 children, and died Jan. 29, 1605.

PARISH OF BROUGHAM.

Paffing over the river Eden, we come to the parifh of BROUGHAM; at the north-weftern extremity of the county; which we fhall treat of under the following heads:

I. *Parifh of Brougham.*
II. *Manor of Brougham.*
III. *Brougham Caftle.*
IV. *Whinfell Park.*
V. *Hornby.*
VI. *Winderwath.*
VII. *Woodfide.*

I. PARISH OF BROUGHAM.

BROUGHAM, *Burg-ham* (or Caftle-town), was the *Brovacum* of the Romans, where they had a company of *Defenfores*; and many Roman antiquities have been found here. Mr. Horfley mentions an altar which was found here in 1602, near the confluence of the rivers Eamont and Lowther; with this infcription:

IMP.

IMP.	Imperatori
C. VAL	Cæſari Valerio
CONST ANTINO	Conſtantino
PIENT	Pientiſſimo
AVG.	Auguſto.

And another, taken notice of by Burton and Gale; which Mr. Horſley reads thus:

DEABVS MATRIBVS	Deabus Matribus
TRAMAR. VEX. GERMA	Tramarinis vexillatio Germa-
NORVM PRO SALVTE	norum pro ſalute
RP. V. S. L. M.	Reipublicæ, votum ſolvit libens merito.

The *pariſh* of Brougham is bounded on the eaſt by the pariſh of Kirkby Thore; on the ſouth, by the pariſhes of Clibburn and Clifton; on the weſt, by the pariſhes of Barton and Penrith; and on the north, by the pariſh of Edenhall.

It is a *rectory*, valued in the king's books at 16*l* 10*s* 7½*d*; in the patronage of the earl of Thanet.

The *church* of Brougham ſtands in a beautiful ſituation, nigh the river Eamont, at a great diſtance from any inhabitants; one half of the village having been purchaſed (as will appear afterwards) by the owners of Whinfell park, to inlarge their boundary on that ſide; after which, for the eaſe and benefit of the inhabitants of the oppoſite part, on that ſide next unto the caſtle, the *chapel* ſeems to have been erected. Of which remaining part, Mr. James Bird, about a century ago, purchaſed a conſiderable number of tenements, to make room for his demeſne. So that now there are not much above 20 families in the whole pariſh.

The church is vulgarly called *Ninekirks*, ſuppoſed to have been dedicated to *St. Ninian*, a Scottiſh ſaint, to which kingdom probably this church did belong at the time of the dedication: It is ſometimes called the church of *St. Wilfrid*: Thus one Thomas de Derby, rector of Brougham in the reign of king Edward the third, bequeathed his body to be buried in the church of *St. Wilfrid de Burgham*. And in the year 1637, Sir Robert de Wolſlay, rector of Merton, in his will requeſted, that his body might be interred in the church of *St. Wilfrid de Burgham*, and bequeathed 26*s* 8*d* to purchaſe a book for the ſaid church. So that we muſt either ſuppoſe that the Scots had one tutelar ſaint of the church, and the Engliſh another; or rather perhaps that this latter is the ſaint of the *chapel*, which indeed is not ſo properly a chapel of eaſe under the mother church, as another church (as it were) within the ſame pariſh; for there is not the rector to officiate in the pariſh church, and a curate in the chapel, but the rector officiates in both at different times and on different occaſions.

In the year 1393, it is ſaid that there was an agreement between Thomas Reding lord of the manor of Brougham, and Edward Skelling then rector, concerning

concerning frequent prayers to be had in the chapel of Brougham; that from thenceforth all manner of facraments of the church fhall be adminiftred at the chapel of Brougham, except burial; that on Chriftmafs-day in the morning fhall be fong and mafs at the chapel, then after to go to the church to the high mafs and offering; on eafter-day in the morning at the chapel mattins with refurrection and one foling mafs for fervants and old aged perfons and fick perfons, and all the refidue to go to the church to the high mafs (and fo of the reft). That the parfon fhall find two feargies afore St. Wilfrey, on his own proper cofts. For which fervices, Thomas Reding, lord of the manor, gave to the chapel at Brougham and parfon of the church and his fucceffors, one tenement as it lies at the weft end of Brougham, with the garths about the chapel, within the precincts of the wall and no farther, with the woods and waftes and all the commodities within belonging; with one acre of land arable on the fouth fide, as the plough head goes no farther *.

This church and chapel being both much in decay, the countefs of Pembroke, in the years 1658 and 1659, pulled them wholly down and rebuilt the fame, more handfomely and ftrongly, all at her own coft.

There was a difpute in bifhop Nicolfon's time, concerning the repair of this chapel. Mr. Bird, the owner of the houfe and demefne adjoining, contended that the rector ought to repair the fame; for that it was built (he alledged) at the rector's requeft to the bifhop, on conditions to that purpofe. It is indeed much nearer to the parfonage houfe than the church itfelf is, and whilft the town of Brougham had a being, was more convenient for the greateft part of the parifh. But the village being demolifhed, and the lands fwallowed up in that demefne, and none being likely hereafter to dwell at the caftle, the owners of that demefne are chiefly accommodated by it. The lands about it, formerly the parfon's, were alfo exchanged (for others nearer to the reft of the glebe) into the demefne. So that the owner of the demefne the bifhop thought moft juftly liable to the repair (unlefs it fhould be thought fit to let the chapel go down).

One Gilbert de Burgham in the time of king John or Henry the third, gave half of the village of Brougham, with the *advowfon* of the church there, to his lord *Robert de Veteripont*, of whom he held in Drengage, that the other half might be free from that fervice. And the heirs of the faid Robert have held the advowfon ever fince.

In the year 1310, which was the 4 Ed. 2. one *Robert de Appleby* was inftituted to the rectory of Burgham, on the prefentation of Sir Robert de Clifford knight.

* This account was taken from the papers of Thomas Brougham efquire: Whereof bifhop Nicolfon fomewhat doubts the authenticity; perhaps his reafon might be, becaufe there are fome incumbents of churches mentioned as witneffes, who are not to be found in the bifhops regifters of thofe times. The witneffes are, William Engane and Mald his wife, William Hill his chaplain, Thomas Britton parfon of the church of Caldbeck, Thomas Mercer chaplain, John Wefton chaplain, William Hornby, Henry Skelling de Brougham, Stephen Meyburn chaplain, Thomas Whinfell chaplain, Henry Kirkby chaplain parfon of Merton, John Pray vicar of Morland [There was one John del Bray, vicar of Morland about that time], Edward Skelling parfon of Brougham, Richard Tyndall, John Tyndal, Simon Hawell, William Haywell, and others.

In

In 1355, Sir *Thomas*, rector of Brougham, was (amongst others) required by the bishop to pronounce the greater excommunication against certain persons who had broken up a paved way, and committed other outrages in the church-yard of Penrith.—And two years afterwards, we find a dispensation granted to *Thomas del Close* (probably the aforesaid Sir *Thomas* rector of Brougham), to be absent from his living, so long as he attends on the lord Clifford.

In 1362, on the death of Thomas del Close, *Thomas de Derby* was instituted on the presentation of Roger de Clifford lord of Westmorland.

In 1365, on the resignation of Thomas de Derby, *John de Merton* was instituted to the said rectory of Brougham, on the presentation of the said Roger de Clifford—And two years after, on the resignation of the said John de Merton, the aforesaid *Thomas de Derby* was presented *de novo*, and reinstituted.

In 1393, *Edward Skelling* is said to have been rector, when the aforesaid composition was made concerning the chapel.

In the year 1575, one *John Wansford*, rector of Brougham, was deprived; and was succeeded by *Thomas Burton*, on the presentation of Henry Appleton of Rose gentleman, grantee of that turn from Anne countess dowager of Cumberland.

In 1583, on the resignation of the said Thomas Burton, institution was given into the rectory of *Browgham*, alias *Ninekyrkes*, to *Cuthbert Bradley*, on the presentation of George earl of Cumberland.

In 1624, on the Death of Cuthbert Bradley, *Christopher Beecroft* was instituted, on the presentation of Francis earl of Cumberland, and Henry lord Clifford his son and heir apparent.

In 1629, *William Crackenthorp* was instituted on the presentation of the said Francis earl of Cumberland.

In 1644, *Arthur Savage*, M. A. was dispossessed of this living, and about three years after he got it again, and kept it till the year 1655, but without receiving any of the profits all that time, except for one year *.

In 1664, one *Anthony Savage* resigned the rectory of Brougham, whereupon *Samuel Grasty*, M. A. was presented by Anne countess dowager of Dorset, Pembroke, and Montgomery.

In 1680, *Rowland Borrow*, M. A. was instituted on a presentation by Richard earl of Thanet.

In 1708, *John Atkinson*, M. A. was presented by Thomas earl of Thanet.

In 1713, *Carleton Atkinson*, M. A. was presented by the same patron.

In 1722, on the cession of Carleton Atkinson to Kirkby Thore, *William Preston* clerk was presented by the said Thomas earl of Thanet.

In 1770, on the death of William Preston, *Richard Machel*, M. A. was presented by Sackville earl of Thanet.

* Walker's Sufferings of the Clergy, part 2d, page 372.

II. MA-

II. MANOR OF BROUGHAM.

Having finished the matters relating to the church, we proceed next to the history of the *manor*.

In the 22 Hen. 2. *Odard de Burgham* was one of those officers (being the third in command) who were fined for delivering up Appleby-castle to the Scots; and was then probably lord of this manor.

For, in the next generation, in the time of king John, or beginning of the reign of king Henry the third, we find *Gilbert de Burgham* (son of *Odard* as it may seem) who sold the advowson as aforesaid to *Robert de Veteripont* his superior lord.

The next account that we have of it is in the reign of king Edward the first, when it appears to have been divided into three parts; for in the partition of the Veteripont inheritance between the two daughters of the last Robert de Veteripont, Idonea the younger daughter had assigned to her the homage and service of *Christiana de Burgham*, *William de Crackenthorp*, and *Henry Rydin*; which two last seem to have married two sisters of *Christiana*.

In the 8 Ed. 2. after the death of Robert de Clifford, the inquisition finds, that *John Godberd*, *William Crackenthorp*, and *Henry de Reddings*, then held the manor of Burgham; of which manor, the wardship when it should happen was rated at 3 *l* 6 *s* 8 *d*, and the cornage 13 *s* 6 *d*.

In the 11 Ed. 3. *John de Redding* and Agnes his wife suffered a recovery of lands in Burgham.

In the 18 Ed. 3. after the death of Robert de Clifford son of the aforesaid Robert, *William de Crackenthorp*, *John Tyndal*, and *John Trotter* held the manor of Burgham.

In the 43 Ed. 3. by an inquisition after the death of one *John Cuthberd* [perhaps a descendent of *Godberd* above mentioned; for the name, in the transcript, at such a distance of time may easily be mistaken] it appears, that the said John Cuthberd held of Roger de Clifford lord of Westmorland, in the town of Brougham, the third part of the manor of Brougham and 40 acres of land, by cornage, and by the service of paying yearly for *puture* of the foresters of the said Roger 2 *s* in money, and 3 quarters and 3 bushels of oats, and by the service of paying yearly to the maintenance of the king's bailiff for the time being 10 *d*: And that *John Fernesyde* was his heir.

In the 2 Ric. 2. there is a bounder roll of the manor, which is set forth as having been then agreed upon by the assent of Roger de Clifford and *John Burgham*.

In the 15 Ric. 2. after the death of the said Roger de Clifford, the inquisition finds, that *John de Tyndal* and *William de Crackenthorp* held two parts of the manor of Burgham, by the cornage of 13 *s* 6 *d*.

In the 17 Ric. 2. the aforesaid composition concerning the service to be performed in the chapel is said to have been made by *Thomas Reding* lord of the manor of Brougham.

In the 10 Hen. 5. after the death of John de Clifford, the inquisition finds, that *John de Lancastre* and *Katherine* his wife, and *John de Crackenthorp*, held two parts of the manor of Burgham, as in the right of the said Katherine and John de Crackenthorp. The third part, in the 16 Hen. 6. was given by *Johan Teasdale* widow, to *Henry Bird*, in marriage with her daughter *Johan*.

In the 31 Hen. 6. *John Burgham*, *John Crackenthorp de Newbiggin*, and *John Byrde* held the vill of Burgham.

In the 10 Hen. 7. by an inquisition on a Quo Warranto it was found, that *John Burgham* died seised of the manor [*i. e.* one third part, as it seemeth] of Burgham, and was succeeded by his son *John Burgham*.

By a rental of the estate of Henry lord Clifford in the 20 Hen. 7. *John Crackenthorp* paid for suit of county for Burgham 11 *s*, *William Byrde* for the same 1 *s*, and *John Burgham* for the same 11 *s*.

By a rental of Henry earl of Cumberland in the 18 Hen. 8. *Christopher Burgham*, *John Crackenthorp*, and *William Bird* held Brougham, by the cornage of 13 *s* 6 *d*.

In the 1 and 2 Ph. and Mary, *Margaret* wife of *William Crackenthorp*, and *John* their son and heir, *Thomas Burgham*, and the widow of *Henry Byrde*, held Burgham.

This *Thomas* had a son *Henry*; who (as appears from the parish register) had a son *Thomas*; which Thomas son of Henry was last in the male line of that branch at Brougham. He died in the 5 Ja. 1. leaving two sisters coheirs; of one of whom (Margaret) there is a monument in the church at Kirk Oswald, by which it appears that she died two years after her brother.

At this time, one third of the manor remained in the name and family of *Bird*; one other third part had been sold a few years before, namely, in the 4 Ja. 1. to *Agnes* widow of *William Fleming* of Rydal esquire, which was afterwards purchased by *James Bird*; the other third part was sold to *William Wright* a farmer at the castle houses, whose son *Alexander* sold the same to *James Browne* of Martindale one of Oliver Cromwell's captains, who sold to the countess of Pembroke, who in the year 1654 settled the same, together with the hospital of St. Nicholas, in trustees, for the maintenance of her hospital at Appleby, and to pay 4 *l* yearly to the poor of the parish of Brougham; reserving to herself and her heirs owners of Appleby castle, all rights, dues, and payments, whether it be netegeld, foster hens, serjeant oats, or other due.

And two years after this, the said countess caused a fair stone pillar to be erected by the way-side nigh Brougham, with this inscription, "This pillar "was erected, A. D. 1656, by the right honourable Anne countess dowager "of Pembroke, and sole heir of the right honourable George earl of Cumberland; for a memorial of her last parting in this place with her good and "pious mother, the right honourable Margaret countess dowager of Cumberland, the 2d of April 1616. In memory whereof, she also left an annuity of 4 *l*, to be distributed to the poor within this parish of Brougham, "every 2d day of April for ever, upon the stone here by. Laus Deo."

Finally, in the year 1676, by indenture between James Bird of Brougham gentleman of the one part, and the honourable John Tufton of Bolebrooke in in the county of Sussex esquire (grandson of the said countess), John Dalstone of Milrigge, in the county of Cumberland esquire, Thomas Dalstone of Penrith in the said county of Cumberland esquire, and Samuel Grasty of Brougham aforesaid clerk of the other part, setting forth, that whereas the said John Tufton had granted to the said James Bird all that the manor or third part of the manor of Brougham, heretofore the lands of William Wright and James Browne gentleman, or of one of them, and which the late Anne countess dowager of Pembroke purchased of him the said James Browne, and also divers other customary messuages and tenements, parcel of the said manor or third part of the said manor as aforesaid, with all mines, quarries, rents, fines, boons, services, and other appurtenances (excepted nevertheless the capital messuage and demesne lands called Hospital lands, parcel of the said manor); He the said James Bird grants an annuity or rent charge of 4*l*, issuable out of certain lands at Yanwith therein mentioned, to be yearly paid on March the 25th at the chapel of Brougham, and distributed by the minister and churchwardens of the parish of Brougham on the 2d day of April yearly amongst the poor people of the said parish of Brougham, at a certain pillar lately erected in a place there called Winter Close, by the said late countess dowager of Pembroke deceased.

So that now the manor of Brougham, which for about 350 years had been held separate in three divisions, became again united in the name and family of *Bird*.

This family came from Burd Oswald in Gillesland, and first got footing at Brougham in the reign of Hen. 6. as aforesaid, by marriage of the heiress of the owner of one of the three divisions. There is no certain pedigree of the family. The last of the name at Brougham was the aforesaid James Bird, who was steward to the earl of Thanet. He made a considerable collection of matters relating to the tenures of the several manors holden under the lords of Westmorland, chiefly from the evidences at Appleby castle; of which one copy now remaineth at Rydal hall: Other collections he made relating to divers matters of antiquity in both the counties of Cumberland and Westmorland, unto which bishop Nicolson sometimes refers; which, it is feared, are now all lost.—This James Bird had nine sons, who all arrived at man's estate; yet he died without an heir male. And the estate was sold to John Brougham esquire of a younger branch of the ancient family of that name in this place, who had removed to Scales in Cumberland, and by this purchase returned to Brougham.

We have met with no authentic account of the pedigree of this family of Brougham. There was a pedigree of the Scales branch certified at Sir William Dugdale's visitation of Cumberland in 1665; but it was respited for exhibiting the arms and proofs. It consisted only of four generations, of *Peter*, *Henry*, *John*, and *Henry*; and amongst these, *John*, (who is said to have married a Fleming) is evidently mistaken; for that gentleman's name was *Thomas*.

According to our account of the manor, as above set forth, an history, though not a regular pedigree, of the family, may be deduced as follows:

22 Hen. 2. *Odard de Burgham* was an officer at Appleby caftle under Gofpatric fon of Orme.

In the next generation *Gilbert de Burgham* was lord of the manor of Burgham, and gave one half (as aforefaid) of the village to have the other freed from Drengage.

About the 14 Ed. 1. *Chriftiana de Burgham* held a third part of the faid manor.

In the 35 Ed. 3. *John de Burgham* was fheriff of Weftmorland under Robert lord Clifford.

2 Ric. 2. *John Burgham* had part of the manor.

31 Hen. 6. *John Burgham* had a third part.

10 Hen. 7. *John Burgham* died, and was fucceeded by his fon *John*.

18 Hen. 8. *Chriftopher Burgham* held a third part.

1 and 2 Ph. and Mar. *Thomas Burgham* held the fame.

In the 5 Eliz. *Henry Brougham* was in poffeffion of the family eftate at Brougham, and had a fuit in chancery with Thomas Bird concerning fome lands called Newlands. In the 10 Eliz. he conveyed fome lands to the faid Thomas Bird.

In the 27 Eliz. *Thomas Brougham* was in poffeffion, having in that year fold certain lands at Brougham to Thomas Anfon. In the 28 Eliz. he fold fome lands to James Bird; and in the 5 Ja. 1. he died, leaving two fifters coheirs.

Next we come to the pedigree certified to Sir William Dugdale; which, with fome neceffary alterations made by Sir Daniel Fleming, is as follows:

Peter Brougham of Scales (or rather, as it feemeth, of Blackhall; for the eftate at Scales was not in the family till the time of Peter's fon Henry, who purchafed it of the Southaiks) was of a younger branch of the Broughams of Brougham, and probably was younger fon of the laft Henry.

Henry Brougham of Blackhall gentleman, fon of Peter. He married firft a daughter of Wharton of Kirkby Thore, and by her had iffue a daughter Jane married to Aglionby. To his fecond wife he married Catherine daughter of Fallowfield of Melkanthorp, and by her had iffue,

Thomas Brougham of Scales gentleman; who married Mary daughter of Daniel Fleming of Skirwith efquire, and by her had iffue Henry, Toby, Thomas, Chriftopher, William, John, and a daughter Agnes married to Anthony Wybergh of Clifton gentleman.

Henry Brougham of Scales gentleman, fon and heir of Thomas, married Mary daughter of William Slee of Carlifle merchant; was of the age of 37 at the time of the aforefaid vifitation; and had iffue Agnes, Thomas, Henry, William, Jane, Barnard, John, Mary, Matthias, Peter, George, and Samuel.

Of thefe, all the fons, except Peter and Samuel, died without iffue. John the fifth fon, commonly called commiffioner Brougham, purchafed the eftate of James Bird's grandchildren, and by his will intailed it upon his four nephews, according to feniority, and their iffue male; *viz.* Henry Richmond Brougham, and John Brougham, fons of his brother Peter; and John and Henry, fons of his brother Samuel. Of whom, Henry Richmond Brougham died

died in 1749 without iſſue; his brother John died before him: John ſon of Samuel died in 1756, without iſſue male; whereby the eſtate came to his brother, the preſent owner, Henry Brougham eſquire.

The *arms* of Brougham are; Gules, a cheveron between three luces Argent.

III. BROUGHAM CASTLE.

The CASTLE of Brougham, ſeparate from and independent of the manor, hath been all along held by the Veteriponts, Cliffords, and their deſcendents.

After the death of John de Veteripont, during the minority of his ſon, who was ward to the prior of Carliſle, we find by an inquiſition then taken, that the ſaid prior had ſuffered the walls and houſe of Brougham to go to decay for want of repairing the gutters and roof; that a certain bercary (or ſheepfold) was fallen down for the length of fiveſcore feet, for want of ſupport; that the timber was alienated; and one forge reduced to nothing by the neglect of repairs.

The firſt Roger lord Clifford built the greateſt part of this caſtle; over the inner door of which he placed the aforeſaid inſcription, "This made Roger."

By the inquiſition after the death of Robert ſon of the ſaid Roger, it was found, that he died ſeiſed of the caſtle of Brougham, with eightſcore acres of arable land, worth yearly 4*d* an acre; and 40 acres of meadow worth 12*d* an acre: That he had no meſſuages there, but only three coterells (for that he was not lord of the vill), each of which coterells was worth 12*d* yearly: That he had there alſo one water mill, worth 20*s* yearly.

Roger de Clifford, grandſon of the ſaid Robert, built the greateſt part of this caſtle next unto the eaſt, where he cauſed his own arms, together with thoſe of his wife Maud Beauchamp daughter of the earl of Warwick, to be cut in ſtone. There is a pond called Maud's Pool, which bears her name to this day. By an inquiſition after her death, in the 4 Hen. 4. the jurors find, that the caſtle of Brougham and demeſne thereto belonging were worth nothing, becauſe they ſay it lieth altogether waſte, by reaſon of the deſtruction of the country made by the Scots; and that the whole profit of the caſtle and demeſne is not ſufficient for the reparation and ſafe keeping of the ſaid caſtle.

By the inquiſition after the death of John de Clifford, in the 10 Hen. 5. the jurors find, that belonging to the ſaid caſtle there is a certain rent of 20 quarters of oats, and 30*s* ſterling to be received yearly out of the vills of Clyburne, Wynanderwath, and Brougham: Which rent, as well of oats as of money, together with the cuſtody of the office of head foreſter of Whinfell, are granted to Chriſtopher de Moreſby for life, the reverſion to Thomas ſon and heir of the ſaid John de Clifford and his heirs. And they ſay, that to the ſaid caſtle belong 22 quarters of oats to be paid yearly out of the manor of Clyfton.

Francis

Francis earl of Cumberland entertained king James the first at this castle on the 6th, 7th, and 8th of August in the year 1617, in his return from his last progress into Scotland.

The said castle having been again desolated in the civil wars, Anne countess of Pembroke repaired the same, and caused the following memorial thereof to be cut in stone in capital letters: "This Brougham castle was repaired by the "ladie Anne Clifford, countesse dowager of Pembrooke, Dorsett, and Mont-"gomery, baronesse Clifford, Westmerland, and Vesie, ladie of the honour "of Skipton in Craven, and high sheriffesse by inheritance of the countie of "Westmerland in the yeares 1651 and 1652, after it had layen ruinous ever "since about August 1617, when king James lay in it for a time in his journie "out of Skotland towards London, until this time.

"Isa. Chap. 58. Verse 12.

"God's name be praised."

Since her time this castle hath partly gone to decay, and partly been demolished by the owners; and now lies totally in ruins.

IV. WHINFELL PARK.

Together with the castle, hath been enjoyed the ancient park and chace called *Whinfell.*

In the division of the patrimony between the two daughters of the last Robert de Veteripont, the elder daughter's share hereof is described to be, half of the forest of Qwynnefel, in herbage, agistment, wood sold, and all other issues, worth 23*l* 3*s* 3½*d* *per annum*; and the younger daughter's share half of the forest of Qwynnefel on the outside of the park and coney warren lying towards Wynanderwath, worth also 23*l* 3*s* 3½*d* *per annum.*

By the inquisition after the death of Robert de Clifford in the 8 Ed. 2. the jurors find, that he died seised of one park inclosed, the herbage whereof was worth yearly 5*l*, and the herbage without the park (with the agistment and other profits in the wood of Quinfell) 7*l* 3*s* 4*d*, turbary 4*s*, pleas and perquisites of the court 13*s* 4*d*.

In the 10 Hen. 5. after the death of John de Clifford, the jurors find, that belonging to the said castle there is a wood called the Outewod of Whinfell, containing 140 acres of wood worth 2*d* an acre *per annum*, and 40 acres of pasture worth 1*d* an acre; which are called Blauncheland, Goryneholme, and Barrykholme.

There were here anciently oak trees of prodigious growth, particularly three that were called the Three Brothers; the skeleton of one of which yet remaineth, about 13 yards in circumference, a considerable way from the root.

John de Veteripont gave to the priory of Wetheral, for the health of the soul of himself and of Sibil his wife, 20 cart loads of fire wood yearly out of his forest of Wynfel.

In the time of the first Robert de Clifford, in the year 1333 or 1334, Edward Baliol king of Scotland came into Westmorland, and stayed some time with the ſaid Robert at his caſtles of Appleby, Brougham, and Pendragon. And during that time, they ran a ſtag by a ſingle greyhound out of Whinfell park to Red Kirk in Scotland and back again to this place; where, being both ſpent, the ſtag leaped over the pales, but died on the other ſide, and the greyhound attempting to leap, fell, and died on the contrary ſide. In memory of this fact the ſtag's horns were nailed upon a tree juſt by, and (the dog being named Hercules) this rythme was made upon them:

Hercules kill'd Hart a-greeſe,
And Hart a'greeſe kill'd Hercules.

And the tree to this day bears the name of Hart-horn tree *. The horns in proceſs of time were almoſt grown over by the growth of the tree, and another pair was put up in their place.

A court-leet is held within this foreſt, by the ſtyle of the court of the manor of *Oglebird*; but from what original we have not been able to diſcover: Nor hath the word occurred in any record or other evidence that hath fallen under our notice; ſave only, that one of the incloſures belonging to the eſtate purchaſed by the counteſs of Pembroke at Temple Sowerby, is called *Oglebird* bank.

V. HORNBY.

Within this pariſh of Brougham is Hornby, which continued for a conſiderable time in the name of the *Birkbecks*: having been granted in the 6 Ed. 6. by Henry earl of Cumberland to *Edward Birkbeck*.

In the 3 and 4 Ph. and Mary, *Edward Birkbeck* of Hornby gentleman was a truſtee of a third part of the manor of Brampton, for the uſe of the family of Backhouſe of Morland.

The pedigree certified at Dugdale's viſitation in 1664, was as follows:

1. *Thomas Birkbeck* of Hornby, gentleman, married a daughter of a younger branch of the Lancaſters of Sockbridge; and had a ſon and heir,

2. *Edward Birkbeck* of Hornby eſquire; who married Bridget daughter of John Calvert of Cockeram in the county of Lancaſter. [Of this family, and probably ſon of this Edward, was *Simon Birkbeck*, an eminent preacher, who was educated at Queen's college in Oxford, and was afterwards vicar of Gilling in Yorkſhire. He was author of a book, which was much valued by Mr. Selden and other learned men, called *the Proteſtants Evidence*, ſhewing, that for 1500 years after Chriſt, the fathers and guides of Chriſt's church taught as the church of England now doth; which was printed at London in

* So ſay the counteſs of Pembroke's memoirs, and other hiſtorical anecdotes. But from the improbable length of the courſe, we would rather ſuppoſe, that they ran to *Nine Kirks*, that is, the church of Ninian the Scottiſh ſaint, and back again; which from ſome parts of the park might be far enough for a greyhound to run. And *before* this time, there was a place in the park denominated from the *hart's horns*; which ſeem therefore to have been put up on ſome former occaſion, perhaps for their remarkable largeneſs. For one of the bounder marks of the partition aforeſaid between the two daughters of the laſt Robert de Veteripont is called *Hert-horn ſike*.

1635, and after in 1657.]—The said *Edward Birkbeck* died about the year 1634; leaving a son and heir,

3. *Henry Birkbeck* of Hornby esquire; who married Ellen daughter of George Poole of Wakebridge in Derbyshire, who had issue,

4. *Thomas Birkbeck* of Hornby esquire, aged 23 at the time of the said visitation.

The *arms* of Birkbeck are; Argent, a fess chequy Or and Sable, between three lions heads erased Gules.

VI. WINDERWATH.

On the right hand of the Roman way leading towards Penrith, at the distance of about two furlongs, stands WINDERWATH HALL within the precincts of this parish, although the said hall and the demesne belonging thereto are in the parish of Clibburn. And this is a case which happened sometimes at the building of churches, when the lord of the manor or other person who built the same had lands lying in another district. This hall and demesne were sold by George earl of Cumberland to Thomas Brathwaite of Warcop esquire; one of whose descendents sold the same to Mr. Wyvill, in whose posterity it still continues.——The arms of Wyvill are; Gules, 3 Cheveronells braced vaire: On a chief Or, a mullet pierced of 5 points Sable.

VII. WOODSIDE.

A little beyond Winderwath hall, on the same side of the road, is WOODSIDE, a small hamlet belonging to Brougham castle. After the death of John de Clifford in the 10 Hen. 5. the jurors find, that the said John died seised of the village of Woodside, containing 5 messuages, worth nothing yearly above reprises; and 24 acres of arable land, and 9 acres of meadow, worth 6*d* each.

PARISH OF BARTON.

I.

THE parish of BARTON, at least a great part of it, anciently belonged to the barony of Kendal, and was in the hands of the *Lancasters* barons of Kendal; a branch of which family removed into this parish, and settled at Sockbridge, and continued there for many generations, until that branch ended in daughters; and the posterity of the eldest of those daughters enjoy the manor of Sockbridge, and divers other possessions in the said parish to this day. It seemeth therefore necessary, before we proceed to a particular description

description of the parish and the several divisions thereof, to deduce the genealogy of that family; whereby what followeth will be better understood.

1. After the direct male line of the *Lancastres*, barons of Kendal, was determined on the death of *William de Lancastre* the third of that name; we find a bastard brother of the said William, whose name was Sir *Roger de Lancastre*, unto whom the said William his brother (as aforesaid) gave Barton and Patterdale. He married Philippa eldest daughter and coheir of Hugh de Bolebeck in the county of Northumberland, and died in the 19 Ed. 1. leaving issue John, William, and Christopher.

2. *John de Lancastre*, son and heir of Roger. In the 22 Ed. 1. he was summoned to attend the king into France, in his wars there. In the 25th of the said king, he was employed in an expedition against the Scots. In the 33d year of the said king, he presented John son of Sir Hugh de Lowther to the rectory of Barton. His wife's name was Amora. He died in the 8th year of king Edward the third, without issue male; and part of the inheritance went over to Sir John de Lancastre of Howgill, son of his second brother William, from whom descended the Lancastres of Howgill. From Christopher the third brother did descend the Lancasters of Sockbridge, of whom we speak.

This *Christopher* married Joan daughter of Sir Hugh Lowther of Lowther knight. And by her had issue,

3. *Gilbert de Lancastre*; whose wife's name was Elizabeth.—In the 12 Ed. 2 he levied a fine of his manor and lands in Strickland Ketel, Sockbridge, andHarteshopp.

In the 5 Ed. 3. there was an exchange of lands at Thrimby between the prior of Watton and Sir Hugh Lowther, to which one of the witnesses was Sir Gilbert de Lancastre.

He died before his father; and left issue,

4. *William de Lancastre*; who married Margaret daughter of Thomas Warcop of Smerdale esquire. They had issue,

5. *Thomas de Lancastre*; who married Christian daughter of Hugh Salkeld of Rosgill esquire: and by her had issue William, Hugh, Robert, James, Gilbert, and Edward.

6. Sir *William de Lancastre* knight, son and heir of Thomas, married Margaret daughter of Sir Thomas Strickland. In the 14 Hen. 6. he was escheator on the inquisition *post mortem* of John duke of Bedford, grantee of the Richmond fee, parcel of the barony of Kendale. He was also sheriff of Westmorland. He had issue only a daughter, Mabel, married to Sir Hugh Lowther. He was succeeded in the intailed estate by his brother,

7. *Hugh de Lancastre*; who married a daughter of Betsham of Betsham, and by her had issue,

8. *Christopher Lancaster* esquire; who married Eleanor daughter of Thomas son of Sir Richard Musgrave. They had issue 5 sons, Thomas, William, Edward, Stephen, and Nicholas: and 4 daughters, Margaret, married to John Boost of Penrith; Isabel, married to one Shipton of London; Jane, married to Christopher Lancaster of Deepdale; and Elizabeth, married to John Hodgson of Barton.

9. *Thomas Lancaster* esquire, son and heir of Christopher, married a Laybourne, and had issue only two daughters. He was succeeded by his brother,

10. *William Lancaster* esquire; who had a son,

11. *Lancelot Lancaster* esquire: Which Lancelot had 3 wives. By his first wife Anne, daughter of Nicholas Harrington of Eubarhall, he had issue, (1) Edmund. (2) Elinour, married to Richard Cleyburne. (3) Anne, married to John Wharton. By his second wife, Margaret, daughter of Thomas Rookby of Morton, he had (4) Thomas. (5) George. (6) Ambrose. (7) Grace, married to James Harrington of Woolocks in Cumberland. (8) Joan, married to Thomas Dykes. By his third wife, Winifred, he had, (9) A son, whose name doth not appear. (10) William. (11) Lancelot. (12) Frances, married to one Turner. (13) Francis. (14) Simon. (15) Anne. This Lancelot, in the 33 Hen. 8. was a joint purchaser of the rectory of Barton.

12. *Edmund Lancaster* esquire, son and heir of Lancelot, married Margaret daughter of John Middleton esquire; and was living when the pedigree was certified at an herald's visitation in 1575. He had issue Lancelot, Richard, Frances, and Margaret.

13. *Lancelot Lancaster* esquire, son and heir of Edmund. He married Frances Tankard eldest daughter of Thomas Tankard esquire of Yorkshire, in the reign of king James the first. By indenture dated Aug. 10, in the 21st year of that king, this Lancelot, and Christopher son and heir of Richard Lancaster deceased late brother of the said Lancelot, in consideration of 489*l* 9*s* 1*d*, did covenant to convey, by fine or otherwise, their manor of Strickland Roger, unto Hugh Barrow of Skelsmergh and Matthew Philipson of Strickland Roger yeomen and their heirs.—This Lancelot died without issue; and was succeeded by the said Christopher as next heir, being the son of his younger brother Richard deceased: *viz.*

14. *Christopher Lancaster* esquire (of Crake-trees); who married Elizabeth daughter of Thomas Tankard esquire, son of the above-named Thomas Tankard: By whom he had no issue male. But he left 4 daughters; (1) *Frances*, married to Sir Christopher Lowther of St. Bees and Whitehaven baronet, younger brother of Sir John Lowther of Lowther: This Sir Christopher paid the other sisters portions, and had the estate. (2) *Elizabeth*, married to William Hutton of Penrith and Gale. (3) *Barbara*, married to Mr. Davyes of Winder. (4) *Mary*, married to Mr. Highmore of Cumberland.

The arms of these Lancasters were; Argent, two bars Gules, on a canton of the second a lion passant guardant Or.

II.

Having thus deduced the family of the Lancasters, which had such large connexions with this parish, we proceed to give an account of the PARISH itself.

It

It is bounded (beginning at the middle of the river Eamont over against the church, and descending down the river) by the parishes of Dacre and Penrith in the county of Cumberland on the West and North, to the place where the river Lowther runs in. Thence, ascending the river Lowther, it is bounded on the East by the parish of Brougham up to Lowther bridge. Thence bounded further on the East by the parishes of Clifton, Lowther, Askham, and Bampton. On the South, and again towards the West, by the parishes of Kendal and Gresmere in the barony of Kendale, and by the parishes of Crosthwaite and Greystock in Cumberland; and contains in the whole about 115 families, whereof there are only three or four dissenters.

The church is dedicated to St. Michael; and is a vicarage, valued in the king's books at 11*l* 1*s* 0½*d*; in the patronage of Sir James Lowther baronet.

It was given by the aforesaid Sir John de Lancastre son of Roger to the priory of Wartre in Yorkshire, to which it was afterwards appropriated; and on the dissolution was granted by the crown to Thomas earl of Rutland, who sold the same to Lancelot Lancaster aforesaid and Michael Hudson, in whose descendents or assignees respectively the same still continues.

In the year 1304 (which was the 33 Ed. 1.) upon the death of *William de Corbrigge* rector of Barton, *John* the son of Sir *Hugh de Lowther* knight (as is aforesaid) was presented to the said rectory by the aforesaid Sir John de Lancastre son of Roger. And upon a *jus patronatus* issued and an inquisition thereupon taken, the jurors find, that the said rectory is worth *communibus annis* 40*l* a year, besides the portion which the prior and convent of Wartre have in the same, which is taxed at 12*l*: And so they say, that it is portionary, but not pensionary. They find also, that Roger de Lancastre, father of the said John, presented to the same next before. They find further, that the person presented is free and legitimate, and that he is 14 years of age and nigh 15, and probably is learned as far as his age will permit, and hath the first tonsure. At the next ordination, this John de Lowther was ordained Acolite. Four years afterwards, and before he had any other orders conferred upon him, he was instituted notwithstanding his minority, having a dispensation for the same from pope Clement the fifth. Seven years after this, being then subdeacon, he was allowed by the bishop to follow his studies abroad for three years.

In the year 1318, the appropriation of the church of Barton by the said Sir John to the priory of Wartre was confirmed by the bishop of Carlisle; on condition, that the vicar have a full third of the whole revenue and bear all ordinary charges, the prior and convent bearing the extraordinary. And there was a reservation to the bishop of the collation to the vicarage. But nevertheless, two years after this, on the resignation of the said John de Lowther, the bishop did not collate; but the prior and convent presented *Gilbert de Sandale*, and the bishop instituted him thereupon, and in the instrument of institution calls them the true patrons.

And two years after this, *viz.* in 1322, on the resignation of the said Gilbert de Sandale, *William de Elvington* was instituted on the presentation of the said prior and convent.

 In

In 1336, on William de Elvington's resignation, the prior and convent presented one of their own canons *William de Kyrkton*.

In 1345, on his resignation, *John de Fenton* was presented and instituted as before.

In 1354, on the resignation of one *John de Sherborn*, the prior and convent present *Robert de Ferby*. And in the same year, on his resignation, *John de Wystow* was instituted.

In 1361, *William de Newton* was presented and instituted as before.

About the year 1422, the prior and convent presented William Spenser the *cellerarius* of their convent to the vicarage of Barton*.

In 1476, *Robert Wresyl* was vicar of Barton.

In 1541, Lancelot Lancaster of Sockbridge esquire, and Michael Hudson of Barton gentleman, purchased (as aforesaid) the rectory of Barton; and upon a vacancy in 1566, there was a dispute between the said Lancelot and George Hudson son of the said Michael concerning the presentation, by which it may seem that at the time of the purchase it had not been settled between them whether they should present jointly or by turns, or which of them should present first. But the bishop, on this vacancy, collated Sir John Hudson clerk by lapse, through the default or neglect (as is set forth) of George Hudson of Barton gentleman, the true patron of the said church.

In 1581, Adam Abbot was admitted curate of Patrickdale in this parish, on the nomination of the said Sir John Hudson the vicar, with the approbation of Edmund Lancaster esquire and George Hudson gentleman, proprietors of the rectory, according to a late compromise to that purpose.

In 1608, on the death of the said John Hudson, *Lancelot Dawes*, M. A. was instituted, on the presentation for this turn of John Fetherston gentleman; yet at the same time George Hudson clerk was presented by Edmund Lancaster of Sockbridge and Thomas Carleton of Carleton esquires, claimants for the same turn. He died in 1653, and was succeeded by

Timothy Roberts, a Welchman; who was ejected after the Restoration for Nonconformity.

The male line of the Lancasters failing in the next generation, the Lancaster moiety of the advowson came to Sir Christopher Lowther as aforesaid, on his marriage with one of the daughters; and the house of Lowther is now in possession of the whole.

In 1660, *John Harrison* was presented by Sir John Lowther of Whitehaven.

On the death of Mr. Harrison in 1705, *Richard Stainton* clerk was instituted on the presentation of the said Sir John Lowther.

In 1734, on the death of *Richard Stainton*, *Richard Jackson*, M. A. was presented by Sir James Lowther of Whitehaven baronet.

In 1738, on the death of Richard Jackson, *William Lindsey*, M. A. was presented by the same patron.

* Dugd.

In

In 1753, *Joseph Wilson*, clerk, was instituted on a presentation by the same patron.

In 1759, on the death of Joseph Wilson, *John Cowper*, M. A. was instituted on a presentation by Sir James Lowther of Lowther baronet.

The CHURCH is a low but large building, having two rows of pillars in the body of it. In the middle, between the body of the church and the chancel, is a fair stone tower, but with low, flat battlements.

Over the porch, on the outside, cut in stone, is an escutcheon with 3 harts heads.

In the chancel, above the communion table, are 5 rows of escutcheons, 7 in each row; many of which are now defaced, and others perhaps only put in for ornament or to fill up the number; but amongst them were to be seen in Mr. Machel's time the arms of Arundel, of Percy earl of Northumberland quartering Lucy, of Dacre, Lowther, Lancaster, Strickland, Threlkeld, Machel, Moresby, Orpheur, Crackenthorp.

Upon a brass plate in the chancel is the following inscription:

"Hic jacet Francisca Dawes, filia Thomæ Flecher de Strickland, armigeri, "natu maxima; perquam charissima quidem et perdilecta uxor Lanceloti "Dawes de Barton-Kirke, generosi. Quæ huic mundo, spe multo melioris, "23° Feb. valedixit: Anno ætatis suæ 23. Annoque Dni 1673.

"Under this stone, reader, inter'd doth lye
"Beauty and virtue's true epitomy.
"At her appearance the noone-son
"Blush'd and shrunk in 'cause quite outdon.
"In her concenter'd did all graces dwell:
"God pluck'd my rose, that he might take a smel.
"I'll say no more: But weeping wish I may
"Soone with thy dear chaste ashes com to lay.

"Sic efflevit maritus."

Towards the east end of the south ile, near to the chancel, is a grave stone with a fillet of brass inscribed, "Here lyeth William Lancaster son of Chris-"topher: On whose soul Jesu have mercy."—Probably the same William as above at N° 10.

Opposite to this are painted the arms of Stapleton impaling a defaced coat, and the arms of Lancaster.

On the south side is an ile, which has been divided into two; in the lower of which, now belonging to Winder, is a monument inscribed W D, for William Davyes, who was buried here in 1674.

On the north side of the quire and of part of the body of the church is the Lancaster ile, formerly the burial place of the Lancasters of Sockbridge.

The VICARAGE HOUSE, about 200 yards from the church, is an handsome building, erected in 1637 by Dr. Lancelot Dawes vicar of this parish, who

was

was alfo rector of Afby, and prebendary of Carlifle. He was born in this parifh, educated at Queen's college in Oxford where he was fellow, and afterwards took the degree of doctor of divinity in one of the Scotch univerfities.

The faid Dr. Dawes purchafed the Hudfon moiety of the rectorial tithes; which defcended to his nephew Thomas Dawes; whofe fon Lancelot fold part thereof (*viz.* the tithes of High Barton) to his brother John, who fold the fame to Edward Haffel efquire. The other part (*viz.* the tithes of Yanwath and Bridge, Patterdale, and Martindale) the faid Thomas Dawes fold to Thomas Whelpdale efquire, who fold the tithes of Patterdale to Mr. George Mounfey, and the reft remain to his daughter Elizabeth married to John Richardfon efquire during her life, and after her deceafe to her children.

There is a *penfion* of 6 *l* a year paid to the bifhop out of this rectory by the impropriators.

The hofpital of St. Leonard York had two carucates of land in *Bart nhevel* (the fame probably which is now called High Barton).

Belonging to this parifh is a *charity* of 200 *l*, bequeathed by the will of Mrs. Dudley of Yanewith; half of the yearly intereft of which fhe fettled as an augmentation of the vicar's falary, the other half to be diftributed amongft the poor.

The SCHOOL at Barton was founded by Gerard Langbaine, D. D. provoft of Queen's college in Oxford, a native of this parifh, and the aforefaid Dr. Lancelot Dawes, in the year 1649.

Dr. Langbaine gave to it 30 *l*. He alfo purchafed an eftate at Culgaith of the then value of 20 *l* a year; 10 *l* whereof were to go to bind out two apprentices within Barton parifh, the reft to the ufe of the fchool.

Dr. Dawes gave 25 *l*; and alfo 20 *s* yearly to the faid fchool, out of the tithes of the eftate called Barton-kirk.

Dr. Adam Airey, principal of Edmund Hall in Oxford and native alfo of this parifh, gave the intereft of 100 *l*.

And the parifhioners contributed (befides their labour) 46 *l* 6 *s* 8 *d*; to be applied towards building of the fchool, and the intereft of what remained to go to the ufe of the fchoolmafter.

And they entered into an agreement in writing amongft themfelves, in order to prevent confufion, that the feven men named in the faid agreement and their heirs fucceffively fhould be governors of the fchool, *viz.* Mr. Lancelot Dawes, Mr. Francis Siffon, Mr. William Davis, Stephen Mounfey, William Smith, Lancelot Smith, and William Langbaine.

Yet in the year 1675 we find thefe governors, Sir John Lowther of Sockbridge baronet, Sir John Lowther of Lowther baronet, Daniel Fleming of Rydal efquire, John Harrifon vicar of Barton; William Dawes fenior, Theodorus Siffon, William Smith fenior of Bowerbank, George Mounfey fenior, Thomas

Thomas Winter, gentlemen; William Smith of Potshousfcale, William Sisson of Crostormount, and William Smith of Brow, yeomen *.

Finally, Dr. William Lancaster, provost of Queen's college aforesaid, (a native also of this parish) added a further augmentation to the schoolmaster's salary †.

III.

Concerning the *manor of Barton*; we find several of old time of the name *de Barton*, who seem to have been a considerable family in this parish, but not lords of any of the manors that we can find.

In the 15 Ed. 2. Robert de Barton was one of the jurors upon the inquisition on the forfeiture of Roger lord Clifford.

And in the 19 Ed. 2. Robert de Barton was knight of the shire for Westmorland.

And there was a family of Bartons at Ormshead; whose arms were, Azure, a bend within 3 harts heads Or; which seems to argue that they sprung from Hartsop in this parish.

The lords of this manor of very old time were the Lancasters barons of Kendal; one branch of which family (as we have shewed) settled at Sockbridge. But the manor of Barton went out of the name of Lancaster, to the Multons of Gilsland. With the heiress of Gilsland it came to the Dacres.

Thus in the 36 Ed 3. by an inquisition after the death of Margaret de Dacre (who was the said heiress) the jurors find, that the said Margaret held, together with Ralph de Dacre her husband, the manor of Barton.

And so it descended, together with the castle and manor of Dacre, in the eldest hereditary line of the Dacres until the reign of king Charles the second, when Barbara and Anne daughters and coheirs of Thomas earl of Sussex sold the same to Sir Christopher Musgrave of Edenhall baronet, who again sold the same to Edward Hassel esquire the present owner.

In the 17th year of king John, William de Lancastre, baron of Kendal, obtained a grant of a market at Barton ‡.

IV.

A considerable part of ULLESWATER, from the middle eastward, is within the manor of Barton. It has its name probably from *Ulf*, a name frequent in old time: *Lyulf (L'Ulf)* was the first baron of Graystock, to whom this lake did belong. It is a large mere of 7 or 8 miles in length, and of a great breadth and depth, wherein is great store of fish; as perch, trouts, grey trouts (some very large, even a yard long, and thick in proportion), pikes, case, chars, eels, and skellies. Divers persons have fisheries therein, for which they pay yearly a quit-rent.

* Machel. † Todd. ‡ Denton.

The

The water which supplies this lake, at its highest source, springs at Kirkston-fell in the manor of Hartsop. Thence it runs, on the east side of Hartsop-hall, into a lough about a quarter of a mile over called Broad-water, bearing the name of Hartsop beck till it comes there; and further (after having received Haifwater) till it be out of Hartsop lordship. Then it receives Deepdale beck, which comes eastward into it, and some other rills, and from thence carries the name of Deepdale beck till it comes to Goldrel bridge near Patterdale chapel, where Grisedale beck comes in from the west, and there it receives the name of Eamont. Thence it runs northward about a quarter of a mile into this great lake. In the course of which lake there are three remarkable islands; 1. Cherry island, so called from a cherry tree anciently growing there, distant from the head of Ulleswater about a mile and a half. 2. Wallholme, over against Stybarrow; so called from its having been anciently walled about; distant from Cherry island about two bowshots. 3. House-holme, about a quarter of a mile below; so called probably from some house thereon formerly. From hence the water turns in a bow above two miles to a crag near How-Down. Thence directly north-west to Dun-Mallard, 3 miles in length, and in breadth near one mile. And there the lake ending, the river re-assumes its name; and so running by Sockbridge, Yanwath, Brougham castle, and Hornby, it empties itself into the river Eden.

V.

At the head of the said water, above Patterdale, lies the manor of HARTSOP, probably so denominated from abounding with deer anciently.

Hartsop hall, the ancient manor house, is a little old building, wherein here is nothing very remarkable, save that in the parlour in the plaister there is an escutcheon of three harts heads caboshed, the same as over the porch at Barton church *. Which are undoubtedly the arms of the family that this place belonged to, which probably ended in a daughter married into the Lancaster family; for these arms are quartered with the Lancasters of Sockbridge at Sockbridge hall.

Hartsop is of the marquis fee, parcel of the barony of Kendal aforesaid. Thus amongst the escheats in the 12 Eliz. it is found, that the manors of Hartsop and Strickland Roger, Ladyford, and certain lands in Skelsmergh, were holden of the marquis of Northampton in socage, and by the yearly rent of 26*s* 8*d*, by Edmund Lancaster. And in the 15 Ja. after the death of the said Edmund, the inquisition finds, that he died seised of the premisses, holden as aforesaid, and that Lancelot Lancaster was a son and heir, being then of full age.

There is fine blue slate got here; which may be transmitted into the country by boats down Ulleswater.

A mile from Hartsop hall is *Aisdale*, where is a tarn called Haifwater, which affords trouts, skellies, and eels.

* Machel.

VI.

Descending by the water from Hartsop, we come to PATTERDALE, so called probably from St. *Patrick*, to whom the chapel seems to be dedicated. For in the bishop's register it is called *Patrickdale*, on the admission of Adam Abbot to be curate as aforesaid. And nigh unto the chapel is a well called St. Patrick's well.

This dale is also part of the ancient barony of Kendal. And in the 31 Hen. 3. William de Lancastre infeoffed the aforesaid Roger de Lancastre in 200 acres of his demesne land in Patricdale worth yearly 4*l*, one miln worth 60*s*, and herbage and pannage worth 14*s*, and the rent of free tenants to the value of 28*s* 10*d*. The said Roger had also the service of Gilbert de Lancastre, who held by knights service by the tenth part of one knight's fee; and the service of Walter de Lancastre, who held also by the tenth part of one knight's fee. The said William afterwards gave to the said Roger the whole forest of Westmorland; except Feusdale, and Swartfell, and the head of Martindale, which the said Roger had by a former grant.

The *chapel* is about ten miles south-west from the parish church. It hath about ten acres of glebe land worth about 8*l* a year; and one third part of the tithes of Patterdale, worth about 8*l* a year more; and the interest of 200*l* alloted to this chapel by the governors of queen Anne's bounty in the year 1743, and not yet laid out in a purchase of lands. Out of this revenue there is a deduction of 4*l* a year paid to the vicar of the parish, who is obliged to preach in the chapel four times a year; and 6*s* yearly to the rector of Graystock.

The *hall* belongs to Mr. John Mounsey, whose ancestors purchased the same of the Threlkelds in whom it had continued for many generations. This Mr. Mounsey and his forefathers for time immemorial have been called kings of Patterdale, living as it were in another world, and having no one near them greater than themselves. The hall is an handsome little house, with a court and orchard, and terras walk at the door, from whence the ascent to the house is by several steps. It fronts to the chapel towards the south. On the west side of it are vast rocks and mountains.

North from the hall is a little gill called *Glenridden*; from the Scotch word *glen* which signifies a gill or hollow, and *Ridden* the name of the river which runs there with a precipitate course into Ulleswater.

Near to Glenridden lieth *Glencune*, a little farther to the north; as much as to say, a glen in a corner; *cune*, *coyn*, or corner, being one and the same thing.

Nigh the chapel, towards the west, lies a little hollow or gill, which they call *Grisedale*, and the tenants there (who are only about 8 or 10) are called in the court rolls as of the *forest* of Grisedale. Grise is a common name for swine, and it may well seem to have taken its name from being frequented by wild boars, which are beasts of the forest. Unto which, the large rock called *Stybarrow*, on the west side of Ulleswater, may have some allusion.—And perhaps there have been deer alſo in this dale; for there is a place in it called *Glemara Park.*—In the head of the dale, is a rocky mountain called *Eagles-crag*; and eagles to this day frequent and breed in the mountains thereabouts.

Higher up, about a mile ſouth from the chapel, is *Deepdale*, ſo called from its ſituation; where there are about ten families, who hold of Grayſtock caſtle in Cumberland.

VII.

MARTINDALE is ſo denominated probably from another ſpecies of beaſts of venary, namely, the *martern*, valuable for its fur. Manwood, in his Treatiſe on the Foreſt Laws, which was firſt publiſhed in the reign of queen Elizabeth, ſpeaking of the martern, ſays, of theſe we have no great number in the foreſts on the ſouth ſide of Trent, but yet in the county of Weſtmorland in Martendale there are many. This place is ſeparated from Patterdale by an high hill called *Berndale* (probably from the like cauſe).

In the rental of queen Katharine's eſtate in the barony of Kendal in the 28 Cha. 2. the tenants in *Borebank* near Ulleſwater ſtand charged with a rent of 11*s* 10*d*, as of the marquis fee.

Martindale has a ſmall *chapel*, about 5 miles diſtant from the church towards the ſouth-weſt. The ancient endowment whereof is 2*l* 15*s* 4*d* yearly paid by the inhabitants. In 1682, Richard Birket, curate there, left by his will 100*l* to this chapel, in the hands of 4 truſtees, and as theſe die away, others are to be choſen by the ſurvivors: 50*l* whereof were added to an augmentation of 200*l* by lot given by the governors of queen Anne's bounty, and an eſtate purchaſed therewith in Martindale; and the other 50*l* remain in the hands of the truſtees. The curate has a little houſe alſo, with about 4 acres of land. The whole revenue of the chapel amounts at preſent to 17*l* a year.

Mr. Machel, whoſe account was taken about 100 years ago, ſays, that the curate is always put in by the vicar's appointment, or by his approbation.

But amongſt the Eſcheats in the 39 Eliz. it is found, that Anthony Yatts yeoman was ſeiſed, in the bailiwick and chapelry of Martindale within the barony of Barton, of all the tithes there, together with the title of donation and nomination of the ſtipendiary prieſt in the chapel of Martindale, which he purchaſed of Edward Stanhope eſquire in the 35 Eliz. and which the ſaid Edward Stanhope purchaſed of Robert Cheyney gentleman and Winifred his wife and others in the 29 Eliz. And in the 10 Cha. 1. it was found, that William Buſher died ſeiſed of two parts in three to be divided of the ſaid tithes, donation, and nomination; and that Anne wife of John Davis was his daughter and heir.

The manor, like as of Barton, came from the Multons by marriage to the Dacres; and now by purchaſe belongs to the aforeſaid Edward Haſſel eſquire.

Here is a kind of foreſt, repleniſhed with red and fallow deer; and there are tenants who are bound to aſſiſt the lord in hunting and turning the red deer on the tops of the mountains to the foreſt, whom they call *ſtrones*; and they

 have

have for their pains 8*d* for every four of them in ale or other liquor. They are to appear upon summons; and if they do not, they are finable for it at the court baron *.

There hath anciently been a family *de Martindale* (and there are many yet of the name): Their arms were; Argent, a bend Azure, 2 bars Gules.

VIII.

POOLEY, a village at the foot of Ullefwater, taketh its name undoubtedly from that great pool or lake. It is pleafantly fituate; having, befides the embellifhments of wood and water, a great acceffion of beauty from *Dun-mallard* hill (fo called from the refort of wild fowl thither from the lake) on the oppofite fide of the water in the county of Cumberland, belonging to the aforefaid Edward Haffel efquire, who hath a fair eftate near adjoining. Unto this hill Pooley is connected by an handfome ftone bridge lately erected, where anciently was only a ftank for ftopping the water for the fake of fifhing, and a paffage on the furface of the ftank.

Here feems to have been formerly a fmall market for fifh. There is yet a fair ftone crofs, with fteps or feats about it, on the top of which are the Dacres arms. This crofs was repaired by the earl of Suffex, as appears by this infcription on the weathercock, "Thomas earle of Suffex, May 2, 1679."

The village contains about ten families; moft of whom purchafed their tenements to freehold of the earl of Suffex about a century ago.

IX.

The manor of SOCKBRIDGE contains in it the hamlets of *Sockbridge*, *Tirrel*, and *Thorp*.

The village of *Sockbridge* lies weft from the church, and contains about 15 families. The tenants purchafed themfelves free of Sir John Lowther of Sockbridge, as did alfo thofe of *Tirrel* and *Thorp*.

Here was born the aforefaid Dr. Lancafter, vicar of St. Martin's in the Fields, and provoft of Queen's college in Oxford, to which college he was a great benefactor. He was fometime fchool-mafter at Barton, before his admiffion into the faid college.

Sockbridge hall ftands north from the river Eamont about a bow-fhot, and as much eaft from the village of Sockbridge. It is in a low fituation, there being three defcents into the court-yard, before you enter the hall. It is built quadrangular. And over the hall-door is a flender old tower.

On the ceiling, in plaifter work, in the old dining room, are the arms of Lancafter quartering Hartfop; and impaling Tankard, *viz.* a cheveron charged with 3 annulets between three efcalops; and another coat, *viz.* a cheveron charged with three flower-de-lis.

* Machel.

Tirrel, a little south-east from Sockbridge, contains about ten families.

And the village of *Thorp* is a little west from Sockbridge, and contains about 4 or 5 families.

X.

The hamlet of *Winder* (so called perhaps from its height and exposure) is part of it in the manor of Sockbridge, and part in Barton. It is distinguished into High and Low Winder (but both of them high enough).

Winder is of the Marquis Fee, parcel of the barony of Kendal. Amongst the Escheats in the 10 Ja. it is found by inquisition, that Lancelot Davies died seised of one capital messuage called Low Winder, and 4 messuages and tenements in Low Winder, and one messuage at Borebank, holden of the king as of his castle of Kendal, by knight's service. And the like is found in the 13 Cha. after the death of John Davies.

In like manner amongst the Escheats in the 10 Cha. William Sisson is found by inquisition to have holden in High Winder one capital messuage called Selleron, and 6 other messuages and lands, of the king as of his manor of Kendal called the Marquis Fee; which said premisses the said William Sisson purchased of Edward Lancaster and Lancelot Lancaster.

XI.

A little below Sockbridge, on the same side of the river Eamont, is YANWITH or YANWATH (perhaps so called from some *wath* or ford there, by way of distinction from the village called the *Bridge* a little below).

This is the only manor within this large parish of Barton, that appears to have been held under the Cliffords lords of Westmorland; and consequently all the rest of the parish seems to have constituted no part of the barony of Westmorland, but to have been part of the large barony of Kendale, even all that which belonged to the Lancasters as aforesaid.

In the 8 Ed. 2. after the death of Robert lord Clifford, Ralph son of William baron of Graystock held the manor of Yanewith.

In the 10 Hen. 5. John de Graystock held the manor of Yevenwith by the cornage of 8*s* 6*d*.

In the 4 Ed. 4. Ralph baron of Graystock held the same. That is to say, these Graystocks held the same of the Cliffords, as mesne or intermediate lords; for others at the same time held the same of the Graystocks: one moiety thereof being holden by the *Threlkelds*, and the other by the *Lancasters*.

So early as the reign of king Edward the first, *Henry Threlkeld* obtained a grant of free warren in the manor of Yanwith. And in the 40 Ed. 3. *William Threlkeld* paid a relief for a moiety of Eanwath, which he held of the barony of Graystock.

In the reign of king Henry the sixth, the *Lancaster* moiety came also to the *Threlkelds*. For in the 6th year of that king, the four daughters and coheirs of of Sir John de Lancaster of Howgill, in consideration of the sum of 20*l* paid to each of them, sold to Sir *Henry Threlkeld* knight a moiety of the manor of Yanwith. The last of which name was Sir *Lancelot Threlkeld* of Threlkeld in Cumberland, son of that Sir Lancelot who married the heiress Vescy widow of John lord Clifford in the reign of king Edward the fourth. He died without issue male, leaving three daughters coheirs.——The arms of Threlkeld were; Argent, a manch Gules.

Grace, one of the said daughters, was married to *Thomas Dudley*, of a younger branch of a family of Dudleys in the south, and with her he had the manor of Yanwath. He had issue,

Richard Dudley, who married Dorothy daughter of Edmund Sandford of Askham esquire; and by her had issue.

Edmund Dudley, who married Catherine daughter and coheir of Cuthbert Hoton of Hoton John esquire (Sandford of Askham, and Huddleston, marrying the other two coheirs). He had issue, Richard, a priest: Thomas, who succeeded him: John a lawyer, who married the bastard daughter of Sir Christopher Pickering, who was afterwards married to Cyprian Hilton of Burton esquire: Another son, called Henry; and six daughters.

Thomas Dudley, son of Edmund, married a daughter of Middleton of Carlisle; and had issue, Edmund who died without issue, Christopher, Mary, and Catharine.

Christopher Dudley, son of Thomas, married first Elizabeth daughter of bishop Snowden; to his second wife he married Agnes daughter of Daniel Fleming of Skirwith gentleman, by whom he had a daughter Mary who died young. And having no issue surviving, he sold the manor of Yanwath and Eamont-bridge to Sir John Lowther baronet about the year 1654, in whose posterity it still continues.

The arms of these Dudleys were; Or, a lion rampant with his tail forked Vert, lingued and armed Gules. (With a crescent.)

The village of *Yanwath* contains about 12 families, most of them customary tenants, doing suit and service of court at Yanwath hall.

The said hall stands at the north end of the village, a little on the west side of it, on a high bank by the river Eamont. It is quadrangular; hath an agreeable prospect; and at a distance hath the appearance of a small castle. Over the gate there hath been a chapel. And at the south corner there hath been an handsome tower, with turrets and battlements.

About a mile south from the hall, at the end of Yanwath wood, opposite to Lowther hall, is an ancient round fortification, called *Castle Steads*.

Eamont bridge is a small village, containing about 12 families, most of them customary tenants It is so called from a fair stone bridge over the river Eamont; deriving its name from two Saxon words, *ea* which signifies water; and *munt*, a hill or mountain: this river descending from a most remarkably mountainous country.

In the reign of king Hen. 6. there seems to have been a general contribution towards the building, or perhaps rather rebuilding of this bridge. In the register:

gifter of Thomas Langley bifhop of Durham (in the poffeffion of the dean and chapter of Durham), who was alfo lord chancellor, and cardinal, and (as it feemeth) the pope's legate, there is an indulgence of 40 days, to any of his diocefe, or of other diocefes, whofe diocefans fhould confirm the fame, who fhould contribute towards the building of this bridge *.

Near this vill, are two curious monuments of antiquity. One on the fouth fide thereof, called *Maybrough caftle*, almoft in the fhape of an horfe fhoe, having the entrance on the eaft fide leading into an area 88 yards in diameter. It hath confifted of one fingle rampier of ftones, of which the rubbifh now lies loofe in ruins, partly grown over with wood. Many of the larger ftones were taken away in the reign of king Hen. 6. for the repairing of Penrith caftle. Near the middle, towards the weftern part, is a large ftone, upwards of three yards in height: formerly, there have been feveral others. It feems to have been, like many other circular inclofures, a place of worfhip in the times of the ancient Druids.

The other is at the fouth-eaft end of the village, by the way fide on the left hand in going to Penrith, called the *Round table*; being a round trench, with two entrances oppofite to each other at the fouth and north. The diameter of the circle within the ring is about 120 feet. It feems to have been a jufting-place. The country people call it king Arthur's round table. And perhaps the knights, after jufting and exercife, might dine here.

PARISH OF CLIFTON.

CLIFTON is faid to have been fo called from two very remarkable *cliffs* above which it ftands, on the eaft fide of the river Lowther; one, of hard ftone like marble, about half a mile fouth-weft from the church; the other, of a fine free ftone, about half a mile weft from the church, and is called *Cat-fcar*, from a number of wild cats frequenting that place formerly.

The parifh is bounded on the north and eaft by the parifh of Brougham, on the fouth by the parifh of Lowther, and on the weft by Yanwath in the parifh

* Univerfis fanctæ matris ecclefiæ filiis, ad quos præfentes literæ pervenerint, Thomas permiffione divina Dunelmenfis epifcopus, falutem in omnium falvatore. Inter cætera opera pietatis, conftructioni pontium, viarum, et calcetorum fubvenire, ex quibus folutis et difruptis feu confractis eveniunt frequenter difpendia corporum, et pericula animarum, opus caritativum non modicum reputamus. De Dei igitur omnipotentis immenfa mifericordia ac beatiffimæ virginis Mariæ matris fuæ, ac beatorum Petri et Pauli apoftolorum ejus, et fancti Cuthberti patroni noftri confefforis gloriofi, omniumque fanctorum meritis et precibus confidentes, omnibus parochianis noftris, et aliis quorum diocefani hanc noftram indulgentiam ratam habuerint, de peccatis fuis vere pœnitentibus, contritis, et confeffis, qui ad conftructionem novi pontis lapidei fuper et de ultra aquam de Amot in parochia de Penreth Karliolenfis diocefeôs aliqua de bonis fibi a Deo collatis grata contulerint, feu quovis modo affignaverint fubfidia caritatis, quadraginta dies indulgentiæ concedimus per præfentes pro noftro beneplacito duraturas: Datas apud manerium noftrum de Aukland quinto die Aprilis Anno Domini 1425, et noftræ confecrationis 19.

of

of Barton (from which it is separated by the river Lowther); and contains about 42 families, 5 whereof are dissenters.

The church is dedicated to St. Cuthbert; or as some say, to St. Nicholas.

The *parish* and *manor* are commensurate (for it contains but one manor). It is a rectory, valued in the king's books at 8*l* 3*s* 4*d*, and is in the patronage of the bishop of Carlisle.

In the year 1303, bishop Halton collated Mr. Peter Tillioll to the vacant rectory of Clifton: saving to the prior and convent of Wartre the accustomed yearly pension of one mark.—When this pension was given, the smallness of the parish (rendered more inconsiderable by the incursions of the Scots) probably saved it from a total appropriation, as in several other like cases; whereas the large ones seldom escaped, such as Kendal, Kirkby Lonsdale, Kirkby Stephen, Brough, St. Laurence's and St. Michael's Appleby, Morland and Barton, which last was appropriated to this same priory of Wartre.

In 1314, on the resignation of *Henry de Carliol*, rector of Clifton, *T. de Caldebeck* was collated by the same bishop.

In 1317, on his resignation, the said bishop Halton collated *William de Ribbeton*, who was not ordained deacon till four years after.

In 1354, *Thomas de Salkeld* was collated by bishop Welton.

In 1359, *Peter de Morland* was rector of Clifton.

In 1376, *Robert de Merton*, rector of Clifton, resigned in order to an exchange with the rector of Newbiggin; whereupon *John de Merton* was collated by bishop Appleby.

In 1465, on the resignation of *Thomas Byre*, Sir *Richard Shaw* was collated by bishop Scroop.

In 1566, on the death of Sir *Thomas Ellerton* rector of Clifton, *John Wybergh*, M. A. was instituted by bishop Best, on a presentation by Thomas Carleton gentleman and Thomas Wilson yeoman, who claimed as assignees under a grant made by bishop Oglethorp.

In 1583, on the death of John Wybergh, *Edward Maplett*, M. A. was collated by bishop May.

In 1632, on the death of *John Fletcher* rector of Clifton, *Robert Symson*, M. A. was collated by bishop Potter.

In 1634, on the cession of Mr. Robert Symson to Bongate, *John Winter*, M. A. was collated by the same bishop: He was ejected by Cromwell's commissioners, but outlived the storm, and was restored in 1660.

In 1668, on the death of John Winter, *Rowland Burrowes*, B. A. was collated by bishop Rainbow.

In 1707, on the death of Rowland Burrowes, *Jeremiah Seed* was collated by bishop Smith.

In 1722, on Mr. Seed's death, *Jeffrey Bowness*, B. A. was collated by bishop Bradford.

In 1735, on the death of Mr. Bowness, *Curwen Huddleston*, M. A. was collated by bishop Fleming.

In 1769, on the resignation of Curwen Huddleston, *Wilfrid Huddleston*, B. A. was collated by bishop Law.

The

The *church* is but ſmall, being in proportion to the pariſh. On the north ſide is an ile belonging to the hall.

The *parſonage houſe* is a ſmall building; but hath a fine proſpect from it towards the north.

The MANOR of Clifton, by deed without date, was given by Sir *Hugh de Morville* to *Gilbert Engaine*, and his heirs, about the time of king Henry the ſecond. Witneſſes of which grant were, Thomas ſon of Goſpatric, Thomas de Ellaber, Gervaſe d'Aincourt, Adam de Ireby, Roger de Beauchamp, Adam de Solvil, Hervice Niger, Adam de Thoreſby, Richard Fitz-Adam, and Robert de Levington.

By another deed without date, *Gilbert Engaine* of Clifton grants to Thomas Niger of Carliſle and Chriſtian his wife and their heirs, half a carucate of land, being four oxgangs, at Clifton; free from ſuit of court, moulter, and pannage: paying one penny rent at Chriſtmaſs. Witneſſes, Radulph de Notyngham ſheriff of Weſtmorland, Sir Thomas de Hellebeck, Sir Robert de Aſkeby, Sir John de Moreville, Sir Robert de Yanewith, Odard de Bruham, and Henry de Tirrel.

In the 14 Ed. 1. *Henry Engaine* held Clifton; and in the 3 Ed. 2. *Gilbert Engaine* held the ſame.

And again in the 8 Ed. 2. after the death of Robert de Clifford, the inquiſition finds, that *Gilbert Engayne* held of the ſaid Robert on the day on which he died, the manor of Clifton; the wardſhip whereof, when it ſhould happen, was worth 26 *l* 19 *s* 4 *d*; and the cornage 16 *s* 4 *d*.

Which ſaid *Gilbert*, in the ſame year, ſettled his manor of Clifton, except ſix meſſuages and 20 acres of land in the ſaid manor, to the uſe of himſelf for life, remainder to *Gilbert* his ſon and *Joan* his wife and the iſſue of their bodies, remainder to his own right heirs.

In the 12 Ed. 2. Robert de Aſkeby and Margaret his wife grant to *Gilbert* ſon of *Richard Engayne* of Clifton, a toft and croft and all their land at Clifton, to hold during his life, of Margaret de Aſkeby their daughter, by the rent of a roſe on the nativity of St. John Baptiſt yearly: Witneſſes whereof were, Sir Hugh de Lowther, Sir John de Roſegill, knights, and others *.

In the 21 Ed. 3. *Gilbert de Engayne*, ſon of *Gilbert*, ſettles his whole village of Clyſtone upon *Henry* his ſon and *Joan* his wife, daughter of Robert Lowther of Halton in Northumberland, and their iſſue; in defect thereof, to his own right heirs.

In the 31 Ed. 3. *Gilbert* ſon of *Gilbert D'engayne* granted to Roger de Clifford lord of Weſtmorland, by indenture, the ſervices of John Richardſon and ſeveral others by name, with their bodies and all that belonged to them *(cum eorum corporibus et eorum ſequela)* for the life of the ſaid Roger, and to the heirs of the ſaid Roger during the life of the ſaid Gilbert if the ſaid Roger die before him.

This was the ſervice of *Drengage*, which exiſted chiefly in this corner of the county, for executing (as it ſeemeth) the ſervile and laborious offices at

* Several of theſe inſtruments were copied by Mr. Machel from the evidences at Clifton hall.

Brougham castle. In the 3 Ed. 2. on an inquisition of the king's tenants *in capite* who held by cornage, it is found moreover, that Gilbert Engaynne, Adam de Coupland, the heir of Geoffrey Fitz-Henry, William Tilia, Robert de Sowerby, and Hugh Tilia, held divers tenements in Clibburne, Clifton, Lowther and Melkanthorp, by the service of *drengage*. And at Brougham, we have seen, that one half of the manor was given to free the other from that service.

The said *Gilbert D'engayne* son of *Gilbert*, was the last of the name in the direct line, having only a daughter, named *Eleanor*; who, in the 38 Ed. 3. was married to *William de Wybergh* of St. Bees; and thereby brought the manor of Clifton into the name and family of *Wybergh*.

In the 38 Ed. 3. on the Monday next after Palm Sunday, *Gilbert* son of *Gilbert D'engaine* of Clifton grants to *William Wybergh* and *Elianore* his wife, their heirs and assigns, one yearly rent of 24 *l* out of his lands at Clifton.

And in the same year, *William Engayne* grants to *William de Wybergh* one moiety of the manor of Clifton, which he had by the grant of *Gilbert* his brother, to hold during the life of the said *Gilbert*.

And by another deed in the same year, *Gilbert* releases and quits claim to *William de Wybergh*, his heirs and assigns, all his right and claim in one moiety of the manor of Clifton with the appurtenances, which *William* his brother had by his gift for the term of the life of the said *Gilbert*. He grants also to the said *William de Wybergh* all his bondmen with all belonging to them (*omnes bondos et nativos meos et eorum sequelam*).

Again, in the 40 Ed. 3. *Gilbert de Engaine* gives to *William Wybergh* and *Elianore* his wife, and the heirs of their bodies lawfully begotten, his whole moiety of a moiety of the manor of Clifton, in demesne and in services, with the services of *free tenants*, and with the *bondmen* (*cum nativis et eorum sequelis*), to the said moiety of the moiety of the said manor belonging. [Where we may observe, that the *free tenants* (*liberi tenentes*) were not what are now called *freeholders*, as seised of a freehold estate, in opposition to tenant-right; but only that they were not bondmen or villeins of the lord holding in drengage.]

The arms of the *Engaines* were; Gules, a bend wavy, with six crosses fitchet, Or, three above and three below.

At the east end of the chancel are three little windows. In the middle window is a crucifix. In one of the other is the portrait of a woman in a posture of devotion, and underneath are the said arms, and writ above *Helynor Ingayne*. In the third window, in Mr. Machel's time, was a man leaning his cheek on his right hand, and holding a book in his left; and above, the arms of Fallowfield of Great Strickland.

In the 4 Ric. 2. the said *Elianor*, being then a widow, made a settlement of the estate; for in that year there is a deed, wherein John de Dufton chaplain grants to *Elianore* who had been the wife of *William de Wybergh* and to *Thomas de Lowther* of Ascome, their heirs and assigns, his manor of Clifton, with the rents and services, milns, meadows, woods, and other appurtenances, which he had by the gift of the said *Elianore*.

In the 14 Ric. 2. *William Engain* (uncle of the said Elianore) grants to *William Ferreur* of Clifton and his heirs, all his lands and tenements, wood, pasture, and the like, at Clifton. And in the same year, *Thomas de Lowther* of Ascome (aforesaid) releases the same to *Ferreur*. Which said *William Ferreur* was second husband of the said *Elianor*. For in the next year, by the inquisition *post mortem* of Roger de Clifford, it is found, that *William Ferreur* and *Elianor* his wife, as of the right of the said *Elianor*, held of the said Roger, on the day on which he died, the manor of Clifton.

In the 10 Hen. 5. after the death of John de Clifford, the inquisition finds, that *William Wybergh* (probably son of *Elianor* by her former husband) then held the manor of Clifton: And finds also, that the said John de Clifford held at Clifton, in his demesne as of fee, one messuage and 16 acres of land, worth yearly 12*s*.

In the 31 Hen. 6. *Thomas Wybergh* held Clifton of Thomas de Clifford as of his barony of Westmorland, by homage and fealty, and 16*s* 4*d* cornage, and other services and rents reckoned amongst the services of the castle of Burgham.

In the the 17 Ed. 4. *Thomas Wybergh* on his son *William's* marriage with Margaret daughter of John Wharton of Kirkby Thore esquire, settles on the issue of the said marriage, a tenement in Clifton then in possession of Thomas Raper, one acre of land in Clifton called *drengage* acre, and one parcel of demesne land there. This *Thomas Wybergh* died in the 19 Hen. 7. leaving his son and heir *William* then 30 years of age.

In the 5 Hen. 8. a contract was entred into between the said *William* and Geoffrey Lancaster of Melkanthorp gentleman, that *Thomas* son and heir of *John Wybergh* son and heir of the said *William* should marry Elizabeth daughter of the said Geoffrey.

In the 18 Hen. 8. *Thomas Wybergh* esquire held of Henry earl of Cumberland the manor of Clifton by the cornage as before, owing also wardship, marriage, relief, and suit to the county court; owing also further by the custom of the castle of Burgham twenty-two quarters and an half of oats issuing out of the manor aforesaid, which custom is called *Dringage*, and was rented at divers times as the same could be sold.

In the 28 Hen. 8. an award was made by Henry earl of Cumberland, between Sir John Lowther knight and *Thomas Wybergh* gentleman, concerning certain lands which the said Thomas Wybergh had inclosed; by which it was awarded, that the said Thomas should hold the same inclosed as before.

In the 4 Ed. 6. *Thomas Wybergh* esquire exchanged some lands at Clifton with the said Henry earl of Cumberland.

In the 5 Eliz. on a dispute concerning the boundary of the manor of Lowther, an indenture of agreement was made between Richard Lowther of Lowther esquire and *Thomas Wybergh* of Clifton esquire, setting forth the bounder marks particularly: And they further covenanted, that each of them in their own respective lordships will permit and suffer so much of the moor as laid uninclosed to lie so for ever, and not to inclose any part of the moor, wastes, or common of Lowther or Clifton, but that it shall lie as free common of pas-ware, for the beasts and cattle of the inhabitants of both the towns and lordships as well of Clifton as of Lowther from thenceforth for evermore, without let, interruption, or disturbance of either party.

This family suffered much in the civil wars in the reign of king Charles the first. The manor was mortgaged to Sir John Lowther, and never afterwards redeemed. But the hall and demesne still remain to the Wyberghs.

In the year 1651, *Thomas Wybergh* esquire of St. Bees was in the list of delinquents (as they were called) whose estates were ordered to be sold by an ordinance of Cromwell's parliament in that year.

This *Thomas* was succeeded by his son *Thomas Wybergh* esquire, who died in the year 1670.

He also was succeeded by his son *Thomas*.

Who also had a son *Thomas*.

Who had another *Thomas*; who married *Mary* daughter and heir of Christopher Hilton of Burton esquire, and by her had 22 children. He died in 1753, and was succeeded by his eldest surviving son,

William Wybergh esquire; who dying in 1757, was succeeded by his son and heir,

Thomas Wybergh of Clifton esquire now surviving.

The arms of *Wybergh* are; Sable, three bars Or, with three mullets of the second, two in chief and one in base.

The *hall* or manor house stands on the other side of the highway opposite to the church. It appears to have been a strong, old building, turreted; in a pleasant situation, with fair fields on every side. It seems to have been built by the Engaines, there being (in Mr. Machel's time) on the latches of some of the doors the arms of Engaine, and the same were formerly carved in wood over the dining room chimney, but now removed.

The *village* of Clifton contains about 25 families; besides which there are about 7 straggling houses at *Clifton Dikes*.

Anciently, amongst other services, they paid a boon service, which was, to go to St. Bees with man and horse, to fetch salt from thence, or other necessaries, once in every year. For which, most of them would compound with the bailiff for half a crown, when he went to warn them, which was sometimes in the depth of winter. But some would rather chuse to go, and then they had 18*d* a piece of the lord, and bread and cheese and ale when they returned. The last that went was Henry Penrith *, who brought salt from St. Bees to Lowther, at the summons of Sir John Lowther, unto whom the manor was mortgaged.

The manor having come to the said Sir John by virtue of the said mortgage, the tenants paid a fine to him on the death of the mortgagor; and Thomas son of the said mortgagor dying, Sir John demanded another fine upon his death; which the tenants contesting, the matter was compromised, and the tenants paid 1000*l.* for an infranchisement; that is, to be free from all fines for the

* Machel.

 future,

future, but to pay their ancient rents; and it was agreed that the commons ſhould be incloſed, the tenants to have two thirds of the ſame (paying 2 *d* an acre), and the lord to have one third.

Clifton moor is memorable in hiſtory, on account of a ſkirmiſh between William duke of Cumberland and the rebels in the year 1745; wherein about 15 were killed on both ſides: in which lieutenant colonel (now lieutenant general) Honywood of Howgill caſtle was taken up for dead, having received ſeveral dangerous wounds in his head after his ſcull-cap was beaten off, his hat having before been cut through nine times.

Dr. Todd makes mention of a fountain near the bank of the river Lowther in this pariſh, of chriſtalline limpid water, ſtrongly impregnated with ſteel, nitre, and vitriol, which was of great benefit to perſons afflicted with ulcers and ſore eyes, and ſcorbutic complaints.

I.

PARISH OF ASKHAM.

ASKHAM ſeems to have been ſo called from ſome proprietor thereof in ancient time of the name of *Aſke*; for ſuch a name there was. So late as the reign of king Henry the eighth, Sir *Robert Aſke* of Yorkſhire is recorded in hiſtory for heading an inſurrection; and that ſame Sir Robert ſeems to have had ſome connexions in Weſtmorland, for he had a daughter married to Sir Robert Bellingham of Burneſhead. 'Tis true, this place of ancient time was moſt commonly, and in the moſt authentic inſtruments, written *Aſcum* or *Aſcom*. But this was only by way of accommodation to the latin idiom, rejecting the letter *k*; for they ſeem to have underſtood juſt ſo much of pure latin, as to know that it did not admit the letters *k* and *w*. *Aſcom* is the *home* or habitation of *Aſke*. The Saxon is *ham*; which, ſuffixed to the name of a place, ſeems generally to denote one of the more conſiderable towns or villages, of which *hamlet* is a diminutive.—*Aſkeby* (now *Aſby*) in the ſame county ſeems to be of the like derivation. Others derive the name of this place from the Saxon *Eſc*, which ſignifies an *hazel nut*; with which fruit this place even to this day remarkably abounds. And the word *Aſcum*, in the old law latin, ſignifies a boat; ſo denominated from its reſembling a nut ſhell.

The *pariſh* of Aſkham is bounded on the Eaſt by the pariſhes of Lowther and Bampton, on the South by the pariſh of Bampton, on the Weſt by the pariſh of Barton, and on the North by the pariſhes of Barton and Lowther; and conſiſts of about 81 families, all of the church of England, except only one or two.

The church is dedicated to St. Peter, perhaps in alluſion to the rock on which it is founded.

It is a vicarage, in the patronage of the owner of the hall and demesne. It was valued in the 26 Hen. 8. at *6l 0s 0d*. The clear yearly value, as certified to the governors of queen Anne's bounty, *31l 16s 0d*.

This church was granted to the monastery of Wartre in Yorkshire, and the appropriation thereof to the said monastery was confirmed by pope Innocent the fourth in the year 1245. The canons of Wartre had also half a carucate of land at Askham *. After the dissolution, the same was granted to Thomas earl of Rutland; who sold the rectory and advowson to Lancelot Lancaster and Michael Hudson; and they, for the sum of *256l 2s 3d*, in the 34 Hen. 8. conveyed the same to Thomas Sandford esquire of Askham; whose descendent William Sandford esquire sold the rectory to Sir John Lowther of Lowther in the year 1680, but reserved the advowson of the vicarage.

In the year 1295, which was the 24 Ed. 1. one *Richard de Seterington*, canon of Wartre, was vicar of Ascom: On whose resignation *William de Malton*, another canon of the same house, was presented by the prior and convent; to whom institution was given, on condition that (according to the order of the said prior) he should have always resident with him another brother of the same order. For where the revenues would bear it, it seemeth to have been not unusual to quarter upon the incumbent one other or more of the convent. Thus at Morland we find three rectors at one time.

In 1346, upon the death of *John Claworth* vicar of Ascom, *Robert de Dale*, a canon of Wartre, was presented by the said prior and convent.

In 1359, the said Robert resigns; and *John de Wyntringham*, another canon of the same house, was presented by the said prior and convent.

In the year 1366, which was the 40 Ed. 3. one *Robert de Ferriby* appears to have been vicar of Askham. And in 1375, *Henry de Holme*.

In 1380, *John de Merton*, canon of Wartre, was presented by the prior and convent.

In 1437, *John Danby* was vicar.

In 1448, *Robert Wresyl*; who was afterwards vicar of Barton.

In 1563, on the death of *Thomas Watter*, institution was given to *John Airay*, on the presentation of *Thomas Sandford* esquire.

In 1573, John Airay died. In whose time Thomas Sandford esquire granted the presentation on the two next avoidances to John Middleton of Farlam in the county of Cumberland gentleman, in consideration of the good counsel and advice given to him the said Thomas Sandford in his causes. And Mr. Middleton presented *John Simpson*, who received institution thereupon. This John Simpson died in the year 1604; and upon this vacancy, there is a case stated, and the opinion of Sir Edward Coke thereupon. The case states the death of Middleton before the avoidance, and that he had by his will given the next turn back again to the heirs of Thomas Sandford; that the heirs had refused the bequest; and one of the questions is, whether the executors of Middleton should present, or it would fall to the bishop. On the margin of this query, Sir Edward writes, " The presentment of the executors is good in

* Burton's Monast. Ebor. 381.

law,

law, and the bishop ought to allow of it." However, the living was suffered to lapse, and the bishop thereupon collated Thomas Warwick, M. A.

In 1611, on Mr. Warwick's resignation, *John Hutchinson* was instituted, on the presentation of Christopher Teasdale purchaser of this turn.

In 1635, John Hutchinson resigns, and *Lancelot Hutchinson* is instituted, on a presentation by king Charles the first, in right of Thomas Sandford a minor, his ward. This Lancelot was ejected during the usurpation of Oliver Cromwell, and was succeeded by *Christopher Langborne*. Which Christopher was ejected in his turn after the Restoration, and Lancelot Hutchinson reinstated.

In 1678, *Joseph James*, master of arts of one of the universities of Scotland, was presented by William Sandford esquire.

In 1681, Joseph James resigns; and *Thomas Bell*, master of arts of Scotland, was presented by William Sandford esquire.

In 1690, the said Thomas Bell was deprived, for not taking the oaths to king William and queen Mary; and *David Bell*, master of arts of Scotland, brother to the said Thomas, was instituted on the presentation of the same William Sandford esquire.

In 1695, on the cession of David Bell to Kirklinton, *John Sisson*, B. A. was presented by the same patron.

John Sisson died within a year after, and *Jeremy Seed*, B. A. was presented by the same patron.

In 1707, on the cession of Jeremy Seed to Clifton, *Archer Chambers*, M. A. was presented by the same patron.

In 1711, on the death of Archer Chambers, institution was given to *Lancelot Sisson* clerk on the presentation of the same patron.

In the same year, on the cession of Lancelot Sisson, *Jeffrey Bowness*, B. A. was instituted on the presentation of the same patron.

In 1723, on the cession of Jeffrey Bowness to Clifton, *William Milner*, master of arts of Scotland, was instituted on the presentation of the said William Sandford esquire, being the ninth vicar presented by the same patron.

The CHURCH is a small old building, with two little bells. Upon the timber in the body of the church, are the letters ED, TS, 1593; for Edmund Dudley and Thomas Sandford who probably gave timber for the repair thereof. And upon one of the coupling beams are the letters J B, supposed to mark the timber contributed by John Bradley of Knipe.

At the entrance into the chancel, lies a large grave stone; under which, in digging a grave, was found a stone coffin, and on the covering this inscription JOHES DE CLAWORTH, who (as appears above) was vicar there, and died in 1346.

On the south side is a large ile belonging to the hall. Under an arch in the said ile is an old monument, whereon is now only legible WILS DE SANFORD (lord of the manor, who died in the 5 Hen. 5.)

There is also a *chapel* in the hall or ancient manor house.

The *vicarage house* was built by Lancelot Hutchinson vicar, in the reign of king Charles the first.

II.

II.

OF THE MANOR OF ASKHAM.

The first account that we meet with of this manor is in the reign of king Henry the third, when Sir *Thomas de Helbeck* (lord of the manor of Helbeck) received the same in exchange for divers lands holden by knight's service *.

He had a son *Thomas de Helbeck*, who also had a son *Thomas de Helbeck*, who in the 3 Ed. 2. appears by inquisition to have held the manors both of Helbeck and Ascom.

But soon after, we find this manor gone out of the name of Helbeck; for in the 8 Ed. 2. after the death of Robert de Clifford, the inquisition finds, that *Robert de Swineburne* then held the manor of Ascom, by homage and fealty, and 50*s.* 9*d* cornage. And the wardship thereof, when it should happen, was estimated at 20*l.*

In the 46 Ed. 3. *Robert de Swynburn* conveyed the same to William de Sandford senior clerk, William de Sandford junior clerk, Thomas Bannay, and Edmund de Sandford; who all joined in a conveyance in the 48 Ed. 3. to William Colynson; which William Colynson reconveyed the same in the 49 Ed. 3. to the said *Edmund de Sandford* in fee. Which Edmund was founder of the family of the Sandfords both at Askham and Howgill. He was younger brother of *William de Sandford*, lord of the manor of Sandford in the parish of Warcop, descended of a family of the same name, who had been lords of the manor there, for several generations, at least from the reign of king Richard the first. And with this Edmund we begin our pedigree of the Sandfords of Askham.

1. The said *Edmund de Sandford* married Idonea, daughter and heir of Sir *Thomas English (L'Engleys)* lord of Little Asby, of an ancient family there: by which he came not only to the manor of Little Asby, but also to a moiety of the manor of Helton, and a large estate in land at Askham, which she inherited from her father. All which was previous to the purchase made by her husband of the manor of Askham.

He had by his said wife five children, *viz. William, Robert, John*, a daughter *Joan* married to Robert Brette esquire, and another daughter *Idonea* who seems to have died unmarried.

He died in the 50 Ed. 3. His wife survived him, and married to her second husband Sir Thomas Ughtred knight, and to him had issue William and Margaret. She survived her second husband also; for in the 10 Hen. 4. there is a bond from *Idonea Ughtreth*, late wife of *Thomas Ughtreth* knight, to *William Sandford* knight her son for performance of covenants.

In the 2 Hen. 5. there is a will of the said Idonea, in which she constitutes two executors, *viz.* Robert Brette esquire, who married her daughter Johan; and her son *John Sandford*, brother of the said *William*: And therein she charges

* Machel, from the Blenkinsop evidences at Helbeck.

her

her son Sir *William Sandford*, and that he shall charge his sons, and sons sons after him, to provide a fit priest to celebrate divine service in the church of Ascome for ever, for the souls of their benefactors and of all faithful people departed this life; on pain of her blessing or malediction. It is dated at Cranesle in the county of Northampton (probably where her second husband had resided).

And there is also a schedule of her estate in Westmorland, as followeth: "I dame Edone Sandforth" [by which it appears, after the death of Ughtreth, that she occasionally re-assumed the name of Sandforth) "makyth my "remembrance of all my landys in Westmerland, the wyche ys myn herritake: "yat is to say, the tone halfe off the towne off Helton Flechane wyth the "purtenance, yat is to say, Helton-dall wyth the skewegh. Item, lond in "Carholond. Item, lond in Butterwyke. Item, the manor of Knype. "Item, Satrow parke, wyth the browne more. Item, the Depeynge. Item, "the Court yard, wyth the Rodebanke, and the schaype cott; and halfe the "mylne of Helton. Item, Stockthwayte and Wythwath. Item, two acrs "of lond in the Whale that lyeth by the beke. Item, a barwayne at Helton "towne head. And these parcells above sayd ys myne anerytance be my "lord my fader the whych my lady my graname guaffe my fader and to hys "hayres. Item, I have in Ascome eight oxgangs of lond, and halfe the "mylne longyne to the same, the wych my lord my fader purchase of Syr "Hew of Lowther, and gauffe it to me. Item, as tochyng the mannor and "the londes and the towne of Ascome, the wych that my lord my husband "and I purchesed of Syr Robert Swyneborne that cost us eight hondreth "marks and fifty, of the wyche my therde as I hade in Syr Thomas Ughtred "dayes: and for these londes of Ascome the chyld suld be ward gyff the law "will, and for noe nother londes that myne is."——In this schedule, the manor of Little Asby is not mentioned: And for that, (being held by knight's service) an infant heir would have been subject to wardship. Probably, it was settled upon the marriage of her son William. It is certain it was then in the family, and after several generations was given to a younger brother who removed to Howgill, in whose posterity it still continues.

She was living five years after this; for in the 7 Hen. 5. she made another will (her son *William* being then dead), wherein she bequeathed "her body "to be buried in the church of St. Peter in Leycester, and to the said church "her principal legacy, being her best vestment, by name a mantle: To Idonea Sandford she bequeathed her best black bed with the appurtenances: "To the mother of Robert Brette, all her gowns and curtles: To Johan her "daughter one vessel of silver, without a cover: To the said Idonea all her "chests and jewels: And to Robert Sandford her heir those 8 oxgangs of "land, and half of the mill in Ascome, which her father bought of Sir Hugh "de Lowther; upon condition that he find one chaplain to celebrate mass "for the soul of her father and her ancestors in the chapel of St. Mary of Ascome; and if he find one, then a certain distribution of 10 s for the soul of "her father aforesaid and their ancestors; but if he will not so do, then the "said oxgangs to be sold, and the money thence arising to be applied for the "finding

"finding a chaplain and making distribution as aforesaid."——Which chapel then stood nigh unto the hall, distinct from other buildings.

Before we take our leave of *Edone Sandford*, it occurs to observe a sort of pride frequently in the heiress of an ancient family, in recounting the titles and estates of her ancestors. She considers herself as possessed of all the blood of all her progenitors. And this excites a laudable effort to perpetuate the name, by works of magnificence or of charity. Dame *Helene Engayne* at Clifton had her portrait and name depicted in one of the church windows, in token (no doubt) of her having been a benefactress there. And in an higher sphere, the lady Anne countess dowager of Pembroke will be memorable at Appleby for generations to come.

The arms of *English* were; Sable, 3 lions rampant, caud inflexed, Argent.

2. Sir *William de Sandford* of Askham knight, son of Edmund and Idonea. In the 15 Ric. 2. after the death of Roger de Clifford, the inquisition finds, that William de Sandford then held the manor of Askham.

In the 9 Hen. 4. William de Hoton in Foresta and William de Bolton quit claim to Sir William de Sandford knight, of all their right which they had in the manor of Askham, with the mill there, and other lands elsewhere.

This Sir William died before his mother, about the 5 Hen. 5. for in that year there is a receipt for rent given by her to his executors William de Hoton in Foresta de Inglewod, Hugh de Salkeld de Rosgill, John de Lancastre de Brampton, and William de Wybergh.

He died without issue, and was succeeded by his brother,

3. *Robert de Sandford.* That this Robert was younger brother of William, we find, for that at Little Asby about that time, one Thomas Dalamore held the manor of Little Asby in right of his wife, late wife of William Sandford elder brother of Robert Sandford esquire; and that she had the same in jointure with her said late husband, the reversion thereof belonging to the said Robert.

This Robert succeeded his brother about the 5 Hen. 5. as aforesaid, and his mother Idonea 3 or 4 years after. For in the 8 Hen. 5. he appears to have been possessed of all the lands, tenements, rents, reversions, and services, left by lady Ughthrich, with the appurtenances in the county of Westmorland.

In the 10 Hen. 5. after the death of John lord Clifford, Robert de Sandford held the manor of Ascome.

He married Elizabeth Thornburgh; and died in the 28 Hen. 6.

4. *Thomas Sandford* esquire, son and heir of Robert, married Margaret Musgrave, and died in the 2 Hen. 8.

5. *William Sandford* esquire, son and heir of Thomas. He married Mabel daughter of Sir Christopher Curwen knight, lord of the manor of Bampton and Knipe Patrick, and died before his father.

6. *Edmund Sandford* esquire, son and heir of William. He married Elizabeth Warcop; and by her had issue, Thomas; Dorothy, married to Richard Dudley of Yanwith; Joan, married to William Thwaites of Unerigg; and another daughter, who died unmarried. He died in the 9 Hen. 8.

7. Sir *Thomas Sandford* knight, son and heir of Edmund, married Anne one of the three daughters and coheirs of Anthony Crackenthorp of Howgill, brother of Ambrose Crackenthorp, whose father married a Lancaster; whence they quarter the coat of the Lancasters of Howgill. Which Sir Thomas, besides his eldest son Thomas, had a younger son *Richard Sandford* esquire, who removed to his mother's inheritance at Howgill, and was founder of the family of the Sandfords of Howgill. He had also a daughter Dorothy, married to Alan Bellingham of Helsington esquire, who had issue Sir James Bellingham father of Sir Henry Bellingham of Levins.—He died in the 6 Eliz.

8. *Thomas Sandford* of Askham esquire, son and heir of Sir Thomas by his wife Anne Crackenthorp. He married Anne, eldest daughter of Cuthbert Hutton of Hutton John; who bore, Gules, a fess between three Cushions Argent, tasseled, Or.—The said Thomas began the building at Askham-hall in the back court, which was afterwards finished by his executors. Over the gate, on a tablet, are the arms quarterly of Sandford, English, Crackenthorp, and Lancaster; and underneath, this inscription in capital letters curiously raised.

Thomas Sandford esquyr
For thys paid meat and hyr;
The year of oure saviour
XV hundrethe seventy foure.

He died in the same year.

9. *Thomas Sandford* esquire, son and heir of Thomas, married Martha daughter of Sir John Witherington knight; whose arms were, quarterly Argent and Gules, a bend Sable on the first and fourth.—They had issue John, Edmund, Elizabeth, Anne, Martha, Dorothy, and Margaret. He died in the 7 Ja. 1.

10. *John Sandford* esquire, son and heir of Thomas, married Mary only daughter of Edward Aglionby of Carlisle esquire; and died in the 5 Cha. 1. He had issue,

11. *Thomas Sandford* esquire; who was a captain in the army of king Charles the first, in the year 1648. He married Elizabeth eldest daughter of William Orpheur of Plumland-hall otherwise called High Close, esquire. The Orpheurs bear; Sable, a cross with a mullet in dexter point Argent. He died in the 31 Cha. 2.

12. *William Sandford* esquire, son and heir of Thomas, married first Mildred one of the daughters and coheirs of Sir Willoughby Rookeby of Murtham and Skyres in the county of York baronet; and she dying without issue was buried at Askham, where a handsome monument is erected to her memory. He afterwards married Dorothy daughter and sole heir of George Smalwood of Upleatham esquire, by Dorothy the last and sole heiress of the Colthirst family, and by her had a son William, who died in his minority; and several daughters, the eldest of whom, *Mildred*, was married to *William Tatham* of Overhall in the county of Lancaster esquire, to whom she had (besides several

other

other children) her eldest son and heir *William Tatham* esquire a very learned and eminent counsellor at law, who died in 1775 unmarried.

The paternal arms of Sandford are; party per cheveron Sable and Ermine, two boars heads in chief coupy Or.

III.

OF THE MANOR OF HELTON FLECKET.

This place hath received this descriptive denomination, to distinguish it from another Helton in this county which was called *Helton Bacon* from a family of the name of *Bacon*, owners thereof. Probably this Helton also might be denominated from the owner; but this hath been more early than we have any notice. Anciently it was written *Fleckan*, *Flecben*, sometimes *Fleckam*.

In the partition of the Veteripont inheritance between the two daughters of the last Robert, in the 14 Ed. 1. the homage and services of *Robert de Morvill*, for the manor of *Helton Flecban*, were assigned to the younger daughter Idonea.

Which *Robert de Morvill* died in the 18 Ed. 1. and this manor was divided between his two daughters and coheirs *Margaret* married to *Wessington*, and *Idonea* married to *English*.

The *Wessington* moiety proceeds as follows: In the 8 Ed. 2. after the death of *Robert de Clifford*, the inquisition finds, that *Walter de Wessington* held the same; the wardship whereof was worth *6 l 13 s 4 d*, the cornage *16 s 4 d*. In the 31 Ed. 3. *William de Wessington* and *Alice* his wife levied a fine of a moiety of the manor of Helton Flechan, to the use of *William Wessington* (probably their son). Sir Daniel Fleming says, it belonged afterwards to *Mallory* and *Norton*; and finally came by purchase to the house of Lowther.

The account which occurs to us of the *English* moiety is thus: *Idonea* the younger daughter of Robert de Morvill, being married to *Robert English* lord of Little Asby, had a son *William*, who had a son *John*, who had a son *Robert*, who had a son *Thomas*, which *Thomas* in the 13 Ed. 3. obtained a grant of free warren at Helton Flecham, with licence to impark the wood of Satron.

The said *Thomas* had an only daughter and heir *Idonea* married to *Edmund de Sandford* as aforesaid; in whose name and family this moiety continued, till the last of the name at Askham, William Sandford esquire, sold the same to Sir John Lowther in 1680.

PARISH OF LOWTHER.

LOWTHER undoubtedly hath its name from the river. The word is British, and signifies clear water. So *Lauder*, a river in Scotland, gives name to *Lauderdale*.

The *river* Lowther springs in Wet Sleddale in the parish of Shap, and runs along by Shap abbey, Rosgill hall, through the parish of Bampton, by Askham and Lowther halls, Clifton hall, Round table, and at Brougham castle falls into Eamont, where it loseth its name, and is carried along with the river Eamont into Eden.

The *parish* of Lowther is bounded on the east by the parish of Morland; on the south by the parishes of Shap, Bampton, and Askham; on the west, by the parishes of Askham and Barton; and on the north, by the parish of Clifton; and contains about 72 families, all of whom (except only one dissenter) are of the church of England.

It is a rectory, valued in the king's books at 25*l* 7*s* 3½*d*; and is in the patronage of Sir James Lowther baronet.

Before we proceed to the several particulars relating to this parish, it is necessary to give some account of the family which derived their name from hence.

I.

FAMILY OF LOWTHER.

I. THE first of the name of *Lowther* that we have met with, appear in a grant of lands at Kirkby Thore, by Liulf son of Liulf of Kirkby Thore to the abbey of Holm Cultram, in the reign of king Henry the second. To which grant, amongst other persons of considerable note, are witnesses WILLIAM DE LOWTHER, and THOMAS DE LOWTHERE.

And to a grant by W. Breton of a carucate of land at Colby to the abbot Clement and the fraternity of the abbey of St. Mary's York, the Witnesses are, Robert archdeacon of Carlisle, Murdac dean (rural) of Appleby, *William de Lowther*, Adam de Musgrave, Gospatric son of Orme, Torphin de Wateby, Thomas de Hellebeck, Gamel de Sandford, Adam son of Uchtred de Botelton, Alan son of Torfin, Waldeve de Kirkby Thore, William de Appilby, and Copsi Maureward. (The said Clement was made abbot in the 32 Hen. 2.)

II. To a deed of Lands at Slegill, without date; amongst others, are witnesses Sir THOMAS DE LOWTHER and *Alan de Berwys*; which Alan appears to have lived in the reign of king Henry the third. So that it is not improbable, that this Sir *Thomas* was the *Thomas* above mentioned, and son of the said *William*. And about the same time, *Thomas de Lowther* was witness to the foundation

dation charter of a chantry in the chapel at Great Strickland hall: And to an agreement between the prior of Wetheral and Alexander de Windsor concerning Morland wood *.

III. The next that we meet with, was Sir GERVASE DE LOWTHER knight, who lived in the reign of the same king Henry the third †. About the same time, *Gervase de Lowther* archdeacon of Carlisle often occurs.

IV. Next we come to a pedigree certified at an herald's visitation of Yorkshire in 1585, and at a visitation of Westmorland in 1627 ‡. Both which pedigrees begin with Sir HUGH DE LOWTHER knight, who was attorney general in the 20 Ed. 1. and knight of the shire in the 28 Ed. 1. and again in the parliament holden at Northampton in the 33 Ed. 1.

He married a daughter of Sir Peter de Tilliol of the county of Cumberland knight; and by her had issue, 1. *Hugh*, his son and heir. 2. *Thomas*, who was one of the jurors on the inquisition *post mortem* of Alexander king of Scotland in the 21 Ed. 1. who found, that he died seised of the manors of Penrith, Soureby, Langwetheby, Salkild, Carlatton, and Scotby; which he held of the king of England *in capite*, rendring for the same yearly one soar hawk at the castle of Carlisle, and doing to the king of England for the same homage and fealty: And that John de Balliol was his next heir, of the age of thirty years.

The said Sir *Hugh* was afterwards justice itinerant and escheator on the north side of Trent, and in the 5 Ed. 3. was made one of the justices of the court of king's bench.

V. Sir HUGH DE LOWTHER, son of the last Sir *Hugh*, according to both the aforesaid pedigrees, married a daughter of Lucy lord of Cockermouth. In a pedigree of this family at Rydall hall, it is said that he married Margaret daughter and heir of William de Quale. Perhaps both may be right; as one of these two might be his second wife. It is certain, the Lowthers, next after their paternal coat, quarter the arms of Whale; *viz.* Ermin, a canton Azure, charged with a cross upon 3 stares Argent.

This Sir Hugh de Lowther, taking part with Thomas earl of Lancaster and other nobles, who resented the haughtiness and pride of Piers de Gaveston earl of Cornwall, the great favourite of Edward the second, had the king's pardon with the said earl of Lancaster and others of great quality, for taking arms, and being concerned in the death of the said Piers de Gaveston, or any others whatsoever, according to a special provision in the parliament held at Westminster in the 7 Ed. 2. whereby it was enacted, that none should be called to account for the death of the said Piers de Gaveston.

In the 17 Ed. 2. he was one of the knights of the shire for Cumberland; and the year following this Hugh de Louthre and Richard de Denton were commissioned to array and have ready all men at arms in the county of Cumberland, an invasion being threatned by the French king, who with a great

* Registr. Wetheral. † Collins's Peerage. ‡ Machel.

 army

army had entred the duchy of Gascony; and on the 17th of November in the same year, he and John de Lancastre of Holgill were commissioned to array all men at arms in the county of Westmorland, and to be in readiness to attend the king, who determined at Easter to go in person against the French, who had taken several towns in his duchy of Guyenne.

In the 13 Ed. 3. he was again commissioned to array all men at arms in the counties of Westmorland and Cumberland, the king then going beyond the seas.

In the 14 Ed. 3. he served for the county of Westmorland, in the parliament held at Westminster.

In the 15 Ed. 3. he was again returned one of the knights for the county of Cumberland, to the parliament held at Woodstock, and with Peter de Tylliol the other knight had a writ for 19*l* 12*s* to be levied on the county for their expences in attending 49 days.

In the 17 Ed. 3. he served for the same county, wirh John de Orreton; and in the year following was elected with Henry de Malton.

He was sheriff of the county of Cumberland in the 26, 27, 28 Ed. 3. And in the 33d, and again in the 46 Ed. 3. he was returned one of the knights for the county of Westmorland *.

VI. The next in the aforesaid pedigrees is Sir Robert de Lowther knight; who married Margaret daughter and heir of William Strickland bishop of Carlisle.

At the same time was *John de Lowther* (younger brother, as it seemeth, of the said Robert), who in the 50 Ed. 3. was returned one of the knights for the county of Westmorland, and in the indenture is styled John son of Hugh de Louthre. He was also returned for the same county with James de Pickering to the parliament held at Gloucester in the 2 Ric. 2. and the year following with William de Threlkeld to the parliament held at Westminster.

There was also another brother *William*; who in the 14 Ric. 2. with Sir Thomas Colville and Sir John Etton knights, William Selveyn, Henry Van-Croypole, and Simon Ward, obtained the king's licence to challenge certain persons of the kingdom of Scotland, to exercise feats of arms. And thereupon the king appointed John lord Roos to fix a camp, and to be judge in the said exercise. In the 2 Hen. 4. this *William de Louthre* was sheriff of Cumberland, as also in the 8th year of the same king.

The said Robert de Lowther was one of the knights for Cumberland, in the parliament held at Westminster in the 17th of Ric. 2.

In the 2 Hen. 4. he was again elected for Cumberland. And in the 5 Hen. 4. he served for that county, together with his brother William.

In the 8 Hen. 4. he was chosen, with John de Skelton, knight for Cumberland: And in the same year was in commission with William Osmonderlowe, William Stapilton, and the sheriff of Cumberland, to levy an aid in the said county, for making the king's eldest son a knight, and the marriage of the

* Collins.

king's

king's eldest daughter, *viz.* 20*s* out of each knight's fee, and 20*s* for every 20*l* land held in socage, according to an act of parliament in the 21 Ed. 3.

In the 2 Hen. 5. he was chosen with Sir William de Leigh, and in the 5 Hen. 5. with Sir Peter de Tilliol, knight for Cumberland.

He died in the 9 Hen. 6. and the following epitaph was inscribed on a brass plate on Lowther church to his memory:

Moribus expertus, et miles honore repertus,
Lowther Robertus jacet umbra mortis opertus,
Aprilis mense decimante diem, necis ense
Transit ad immense celestis gaudia mense.
Mille quadringentis ter denis, mons morientis,
Annis, viventis escas capit omnipotentis.

His widow survived him a considerable time. For in the 22 Hen. 6. *Margaret*, who had been the wife of Robert Lowther knight, demanded against Isabella who had been the wife of John Barton the manor of Ormeshead and lands in Great Asby. He had issue, 1. *Hugh*. 2. *Anne*, married to Sir Thomas Curwen of Workington knight. 3. *Mary*, married to Sir James Pickering of Killington knight. 4. *Elizabeth*, married to William Lancaster.

VII. Sir Hugh Lowther knight, son and heir of Robert, married Margaret daughter of John de Derwentwater. He served in his father's life-time under that victorious monarch king Henry the fifth, and was in the famous battle of Agincourt, there being with him *Geffrey de Louther* and *Richard de Louther*. He was sheriff of Cumberland in the 18 Hen. 6. and seems to have died not long after.

VIII. Sir Hugh Lowther knight, son and heir of *Hugh*, married Mabil daughter of Sir William Lancaster of Sockbridge. In the 27 Hen. 6. he was representative in parliament of the county of Cumberland together with Sir Thomas Curwen.

In the 31st year of this king's reign, there was one Sir *Robert Lowther* knight, an arbitrator between the chantry priest of Appleby and the lord of the manor of Ormshead, concerning a watergate to Rutter beck. Which Sir *Robert* seems to have been brother or uncle of this Sir *Hugh*.

In the 34 Hen. 6. the said Sir *Hugh* was sheriff of Cumberland.

He died in the 15 Ed. 4.

IX. Sir Hugh Lowther knight, son and heir of the last Sir *Hugh* by his wife Mabil Lancaster, married Anne daughter of Sir Lancelot Threlkeld by Margaret Bromflet heiress of Vescy and widow of John lord Clifford.—And with this Hugh, and not before, comes in the pedigree certified by Sir John Lowther at Sir William Dugdale's visitation in 1664.

In the 22 Ed. 4. dame *Mabil Lowther* and *Hugh Lowther* her son demised Newton Miln for 21 years to John Fleming of Rydal esquire.

In the 17 Hen. 7. this Hugh was made one of the knights of the Bath, at the marriage of prince Arthur, eldest son of the said king.

He died about the second year of king Henry the eighth; leaving issue, *John*, *Lancelot*, and *Robert*; and two daughters, *Joan* married to the said John Fleming esquire, and *Mabil* married to John Leigh esquire.

X. Sir John Lowther, knight, married Lucy daughter of Sir Thomas Curwen of Workington.

In the 4 Hen. 8. he was arbitrator in a dispute between the abbot of Furness and the aforesaid John Fleming of Rydal esquire. He was sheriff of Cumberland in the 7 Hen. 8. the 34 Hen. 8. and the 4 Ed. 6.

He had a son *Hugh*; and a daughter *Mabil*, married to Christopher Dalston of Uldale esquire.

XI. Sir Hugh Lowther knight, son and heir of Sir *John*, by his wife Lucy Curwen. He married Dorothy daughter of Henry lord Clifford; and by her had issue, 1. *Richard*. 2. *Gerard*, a bencher in Lincoln's-inn. 3. *Margaret*, married to *John Richmond* of High-head castle esquire. 4. *Anne*, married to Thomas Wybergh of Clifton esquire. 5. *Frances*, married to Sir Henry Goodyer of Powlesworth knight. 6. *Barbara*, married to Thomas Carleton of Carleton esquire.

He died before his father, and his eldest son succeeded his grandfather Sir John; *viz.*

XII. Sir Richard Lowther knight. He married Frances daughter of John Middleton of Middleton hall esquire. He was several times sheriff of Cumberland. He was also lord warden of the West Marches, and thrice commissioner in the great affairs between England and Scotland. In the 11th year of queen Elizabeth, when Mary queen of Scots fled into England, and arrived at Workington; queen Elizabeth, on notice thereof, sent orders to this Sir *Richard Lowther* to convey her to Carlisle. But whilst that princess was in his custody in the castle of Carlisle, he incurred the queen's displeasure by permitting the duke of Norfolk to visit her.

He had issue by his wife Frances Middleton 8 sons and 7 daughters; *viz.* 1. *John*, who died before his father, without issue. 2. *Christopher*. 3. *George*, who died without issue. 4. *Gerard*, who was chief justice of the common pleas in Ireland, and died without issue. 5. *Hugh*, a captain in the army, in the time of queen Elizabeth and king James. 6. *Richard*, who died without issue. 7. *Lancelot*, one of the barons of the exchequer in Ireland. 8. *William*, who married Elianor Welbery of Ingleton in Yorkshire; from whom descended the Lowthers of Ingleton. The daughters were, 1. *Anne*, married to Alexander Fetherstonhaugh of Northumberland esquire. 2. *Florence*. 3. *Frances*, who died young. 4. *Margaret*, who died unmarried. 5. *Dorothy*, who died young. 6. *Mabel*, who also died young. 7. *Frances*, married to Thomas Clyburne of Clyburne esquire.

On

On a mural monument in the family burying place in Lowther church is the following inſcription:

Sir Richard Lowther knight ſucceeded Henry lord Scroop in the office of lord warden of the Weſt Marches; and was thrice a commiſſioner in the great affairs between England and Scotland all the time of queen Elizabeth. And after he had ſeen his children to the fourth degree, given them virtuous education and means to live, advanced his brothers and ſiſters out of his own patrimony, governed his family and kept plentiful hoſpitality for 57 years together, he ended his life the 27th of January, A. D. 1607. Ætatis ſuæ 77.

XIII. Sir Christopher Lowther knight, ſecond ſon and heir of Sir *Richard*, by his wife Frances Middleton. When king James the firſt came into England, on his acceſſion to the crown, he was waited on by Mr. Lowther with a gallant company from the borders of Scotland to Newcaſtle; where the king conferred upon him the order of knighthood.

In the 15th year of the ſame king, he was in a ſpecial commiſſion with the lord William Howard, Philip lord Wharton, and others, for repreſſing all murders, robberies, and other diſorders, on the borders of Scotland. He was alſo in all other commiſſions, concerning the government of the counties of Cumberland and Weſtmorland.

He married Eleanor daughter of Sir William Muſgrave of Hayton in Cumberland; and by her had iſſue 8 ſons and 4 daughters, *viz.* 1. *John*, who ſucceeded him. 2. *Gerard*, a captain, ſlain in the wars againſt the Turks, in the king of Poland's ſervice. 3. *Richard*, barriſter at law. 4. *Chriſtopher*, rector of the church of Lowther. 5. *William*, clerk of the warrants of the common pleas in Ireland. 6. *Lancelot*, rector of the church of Marton; who married Eſther Pearce of the city of Dublin, and by her had *Chriſtopher Lowther* of Colby Laithes; who had a ſon *Gerard Lowther* rector of Bowneſs, father of *Henry Lowther* now rector of Aikton, whoſe ſon and heir apparent *William Lowther*, is the preſent rector of Lowther. 7. *Robert Lowther*, alderman of London, who married to his firſt wife Margaret daughter of Thomas Cutler of Steinburgh in Yorkſhire; his ſecond wife's name was Holcroft, by whom he had two ſons, firſt, *Anthony*, who had iſſue Sir *William Lowther* of Maſk baronet, who by his wife Catherine daughter and heir of Thomas Preſton of Holker eſquire had iſſue Sir *Thomas Lowther* of Holker baronet, who by his wife Elizabeth daughter of William Cavendiſh duke of Devonſhire had iſſue Sir *William Lowther* of Holker and Whitehaven baronet, who died unmarried: The other ſon of Robert was *John Lowther*, who married the widow of George Preſton of Holker eſquire, and died in 1697. 8. *George Lowther*.—The daughters were, 1. *Eleanor*, married to Richard Fallowfield of Strickland hall eſquire. 2. *Anne*. 3. *Frances*, who died young. 4. *Frances*. Beſides theſe, the ſaid Sir Chriſtopher had a natural ſon Sir *Gerard Lowther*, who was one of the judges in Ireland.

XIV. Sir John Lowther knight, eldeſt ſon of Sir *Chriſtopher*. He was one of the knights for the county of Weſtmorland in the 21ſt year of king

James the first, as also in three parliaments in the reign of Charles the first; in the last of which, *John Lowther* esquire his eldest son was elected with him. He was one of his majesty's counsel at York for the northern parts.

He married Eleanor daughter of William Fleming of Rydal esquire; and by her had issue 3 sons and 2 daughters. The sons were,

1. *John*, who succeeded him.

2. *Christopher*, who was created baronet in 1642. His father purchased for him the estate at St. Bees and Whitehaven. He married one of the coheiresses of the Lancasters of Sockbridge; and by her had issue Sir *John Lowther* of Sockbridge, afterwards of Whitehaven, who served in parliament as knight of the shire for Cumberland, from the 31st year of king Charles the second till that king's death. He was one of the commissioners of the admiralty in the reign of king William. He married Jane daughter of Webley Lee esquire, and besides 3 daughters, *Elizabeth*, *Catharine*, and *Jane*, had issue *Christopher*, who had a daughter Frances married to Richard Lamplugh of Ribton esquire; and another son the late Sir *James Lowther* of Whitehaven baronet, who died unmarried.

3. *William*, from whom are descended the Lowthers of Swillington.

The two daughters were, *Agnes* married to Roger Kirkby of Furness in Lancashire esquire; and *Frances* married to John Dodsworth of Thornton Watlass in the county of York esquire.

This Sir *John Lowther* of Lowther died in 1637, and was succeeded by his son,

XV. Sir John Lowther knight, who in the year 1640 was created a baronet of Nova Scotia. He was a great sufferer for the royal cause in the reign of king Charles the first; and during the usurpation lived retired, but was one of the knights for Westmorland in that parliament which restored king Charles the second.

He married to his first wife, Mary daughter of Sir Richard Fletcher of Hutton, and by her had issue 5 sons and 6 daughters. The sons were, 1. *John*, 2. *Richard*, who died young. 3. *Richard*, grandfather of the present Sir James Lowther baronet. 4. *Christopher*, a Turkey merchant in London. 5. *Hugh*, a merchant in London.—The daughters were, 1. *Mary*, who died young. 2. *Eleanor*, married to Sir Christopher Wandesford of Kirklinton in the county of York baronet. 3. *Barbara*, married to John Beilby of Grange in the county of York esquire. 4. *Anne*. 5. *Mary*, married to Edward Trotter of Skelton castle in the county of York esquire. 6. *Frances* married to Sir Thomas Pennyman of Ormesby in the said county baronet.

To his second wife he married Elizabeth daughter of Sir John Hare of Stowe Bardolfe in the county of Norfolk knight, and widow of Woolley Leigh esquire; and by her had issue seven children, *viz.* *Ralph*, who was father of John Lowther member for Pontefract in 1722; *William*, counsellor at law; *Robert*, the third son; and four daughters, *Mary*, *Anne*, *Elizabeth*, and *Margaret*, which last was married to Sir John Aubrey of Llantrithed in the county of Glamorgan baronet.

XVI. John Lowther of Hackthorp esquire, eldest son of the last Sir *John*, married to his first wife Elizabeth daughter and coheir of Sir Henry Bellingham of Levins baronet; and by her had issue, 1. *John*, aged 9 at Dugdale's visitation aforesaid in 1664. 2. *Mary*, married first to George Preston of Holker gentleman; afterwards to John Lowther esquire one of the commissioners of the revenue in Ireland.

To his second wife he married Mary, daughter of William Withens of Eltham in the county of Kent esquire; and by her had issue *William Lowther* esquire, who was member for the city of Carlisle in the parliament holden in the 2d year of William and Mary, and died soon after unmarried.

This *John Lowther* of Hackthorp died in his father's life-time; and his elder son *John* afterwards succeeded to the family estate.

XVII. Sir John Lowther of Lowther baronet, grandson and heir of the last Sir *John*, was born at Hackthorp hall, and educated at Appleby school (to which he was a considerable benefactor) and afterwards at Queen's college in Oxford.

He married Catharine daughter of Sir Henry Frederic Thynne, sister of Thomas viscount Weymouth.

He was chosen one of the knights for Westmorland in the parliament that met at Westminster on the 8th of March 1678, which being dissolved in July, and a new one called to meet on the 17th day of October following, he was again elected for the said county. Which parliament, after several prorogations, did not sit to do business till the 21st of October 1680, when falling on the popish plot, and bringing in a bill for disabling James duke of York from inheriting the crown, it was dissolved on the 18th of January the same year. The dissolution of these two last parliaments put the nation into some ferment, and obliged his majesty to call another to meet at Oxford the 21st of March in the same year: but this change of place very much displeased the major part of both houses, who apprehended some arbitrary designs in it; and Sir John Lowther, with most of the old members, being chosen, proceeded with the same zeal upon the bill of exclusion: whereupon they were dissolved seven days after their meeting. This was the last parliament called by king Charles. And in that called by king James, Sir John Lowther was again elected; as he was also in the convention parliament that settled the crown on the prince and princess of Orange, and in all other parliaments whilst he was a commoner. He had the courage to concert with his friends, the revolution brought about by king William; and on his landing in the west, secured the city of Carlisle, and procured the counties of Westmorland and Cumberland to appear in his interest.

For all which services, on king William's accession, he was constituted vice-chamberlain of his majesty's houshold, and sworn of his privy council, five days after their majesties were proclaimed. Also on the king's appointing the lords lieutenants of the several counties, he made him lieutenant of the county of Westmorland in the year 1689. In the year following, he was appointed one of the lords of the treasury. In 1696, he was advanced to the dignity of viscount and baron, by the style and title of baron Lowther of Lowther and viscount Lonsdale. In 1699 he was made lord privy seal, and was twice one of the lords justices for the government of the kingdom during his majesty's absence.

He died in the year 1700, of the age of 45 years; leaving issue three sons and five daughters. The sons were, 1. *Richard.* 2. *Henry.* 3. *Anthony*, one of the commissioners of the revenue in Ireland, chosen representative for Cockermouth in 1714, and afterwards knight of the shire for Westmorland: He died in 1741, unmarried.—The daughters were, 1. *Mary*, married to Sir John Wentworth of North Elmsal in the county of York baronet. 2. *Elizabeth*, married to Sir William Ramsden of Byrom in the same county baronet. 3. *Jane*, who died unmarried in 1752. 4. *Margaret*, married to Sir Joseph Pennington of Moncaster in the county of Cumberland baronet. 5. *Barbara*, married to Thomas Howard of Corby in the said county of Cumberland esquire.

XVIII. Richard Lowther, second viscount Lonsdale, died at Lowther of the small-pox, unmarried, in the year 1713, being the same year in which he came of age.

XIX. Henry, third viscount Lonsdale, succeeded his brother *Richard*. In the year 1715 he was constituted *custos rotulorum* and afterwards lord lieutenant of the counties of Westmorland and Cumberland. In 1717 he was made one of the lords of the bed chamber. On the accession of king George the second, he was appointed constable of the tower of London, and lord lieutenant of the hamlets thereof. He was afterwards lord privy seal. And having gone through several offices of state with dignity and honour, he died in the year 1750 unmarried, universally esteemed and lamented, being a nobleman of most eminent abilities, integrity, learning, piety, affability, benevolence, and every public and private virtue.

In him the title of viscount Lonsdale and baron Lowther was extinct. But in that of baronet, and in the estate, he was succeeded by the present Sir *James Lowther* baronet, son of *Robert*, son of *Richard*, son of *John*, the common ancestor of them both.

The said *Richard*, second son of John the common ancestor, resided at Maul's Meburn, and was chosen member for Appleby in 1688 and 1690. He married Barbara daughter of Robert Pricket of Wresal castle in the county of York esquire, and had issue *Robert* his son and heir; *Christopher*, who married Anne only daughter of Sir John Cowper cousin german to the lord chancellor Cowper; *Richard*, a captain on the Irish establishment; and a daughter *Eleanor*, married to Dr. Barnard a physician at York.

Robert Lowther of Maul's Meburn esquire, eldest son of Richard, was sometime storekeeper of the tower, and in 1716 was appointed captain general and governor in chief of the island of Barbadoes. He married Catharine only daughter of Sir Joseph Pennington baronet by Margaret his wife fourth daughter of John viscount Lonsdale. He died in September 1745; leaving issue, (1) *James*. (2) *Robert*, knight of the shire for Westmorland in 1763. (3) *Margaret*, married to Henry lord Barnard, now earl of Darlington. (4) *Catharine*,

(4) *Catharine*, married to lord Harry Paulet, now duke of Bolton. (5) *Barbara*, unmarried.

XX. Sir James Lowther of Lowther baronet, son and heir of Robert Lowther of Maul's Meburn esquire, by the death of his father, and of Henry viscount Lonsdale, and of Sir William Lowther baronet, became possessed of the three great inheritances of Maul's Meburn, Lowther, and Whitehaven.

He was chosen knight of the shire for Westmorland in 1761; was elected for the same county, and also for Cumberland, in 1774; is lieutenant and custos rotulorum, and colonel of the militia, of both the said counties.

In 1761, he married the lady Mary Stewart, daughter of John earl of Bute, by Mary Wortley Montague only daughter of Edward Wortley Montague, ambassador to Constantinople; and as yet hath no issue *.

The *Arms* of Lowther, as certified by Sir John Lowther at Dugdale's visitation aforesaid, are; 1. Or, six annulets, 3, 2, and 1 Sable: by the name of Lowther. 2. Ermin, a canton Azure, charged with a cross upon three stares Argent; by the name of Quaile. 3. Argent, a lion rampant Sable; by the name of Stapilton. 4. Gules, three fishes Or; by the name of Lucy. 5. Sable, three escalops within a bordure ingrailed Argent; by the name of Strickland. 6. Sable, three covered cups Argent; by the name of Warcop. 7. Sable, three martlets volant Argent. - - - - - 8. Or, two bars Gules, and on a canton Gules a mullet of the first; by the name of Lancaster.

The *Crest*: On a wreath, a griffin passant Argent.

II.

MANOR AND ADVOWSON.

The MANOR and ADVOWSON seem never to have been intirely separated, and therefore our account of them jointly will be most intelligible, as they will mutually tend to illustrate each other.

So early as the reign of king Henry the second, the manor seems to have been divided into three parts, and consequently the appendent advowson. For *Humphrey Machel*, in that king's reign, granted to the priory of Carlisle a third part of the church of Lowther; which grant the said king confirmed: Upon which account the rector of Lowther paid yearly to the said priory 26*s* 8*d*, which pension is now paid to the dean and chapter. In the year 1649, it was given in upon oath to Cromwell's commissioners, that the dean and chapter of Carlisle had right to a third part of the possessions of the church of Lowther, and likewise of presenting to it every third turn. Hereupon a controversy arose (as had done before in 1609 with Sir Christopher Lowther) between that collegiate body and Sir John Lowther. But on inquisition and

* The latter part of this pedigree is chiefly taken from the Baronetage, vol. 1. p. 453. Edit. 1771.

examination

examination of witnesses it appeared, that whatever right of presentation the dean and chapter might have had originally, they never had so much as once presented to the rectory. A caveat had been entred of the like nature by queen Elizabeth in 1579, claiming right to a third presentation invested in the late dissolved monastery of Watton, but it had no effect *.

In the 6 Ed. 1. one of the three parts seems to have been divided into two by means of two coheirs, one married to *Robert de Morvil*, and the other to *Gilbert de Whiteby*: the two remaining parts belonging to the priory of *Watton*, and *William de Stirkland*. For in that year, in an assize, an agreement was made between the prior of *Watton*, *Robert de Morvil* and *Alice* his wife, *Gilbert de Whiteby* and *Henry* son and heir of *Christian* wife of the said *Gilbert*, and *William de Stirkland*, concerning the advowson of the church of Lowthre.

Accordingly, in the 3 Ed. 2. we find the manor in four hands; for in that year, the heir of *John de Coupland*, *Henry de Haverington*, *Simon de Alve*, and the prior of *Watton* held Lowther under the Cliffords.

In the 8 Ed. 2. the family of *Lowther* appear to have one fourth part, probably by purchase from the said *Simon de Alve*; for by an inquisition in that year, after the death of Robert lord Clifford, it appears, that *Adam de Coupland*, *Henry de Haverington*, *Hugh de Lowthre*, and the prior of *Watton* then held *Lowthre*; of each of whom (except the prior) the wardship was worth 40*s*, and the cornage of the whole 20*s* 4*d*.

Not long after we find the advowson in two hands, and so the same seems to have continued till after the dissolution of the monasteries. In the 14 Ed. 2. the bishop in his ordinary visitation finding *William de Capella*, rector of Lowther, so aged and extravagant, that he was unfit for the discharge of his cure and management of his ecclesiastical revenues, assigned *William de Kendale* clerk to be his guardian and assistant. And two years after, upon the death of the said *William de Capella*, an agreement was made between *Walter de Styrkland* and the prior of *Watton*, by which the present vacancy was given to the said prior, and thereafter to the said *Walter* and his heirs alternately with the prior and his successors.

In the 7 Ed. 3. there was an exchange of lands between Sir *Walter de Stirkland* and Sir *Hugh de Louther*; whereby Sir *Walter* conveyed also to Sir *Hugh* his moiety of the advowson of the church of Lowther. But that seems to have been only for the next avoidance; for the *Stricklands* continued in possession of that moiety long after.

In the 36 Ed. 3. on the death of Sir *Thomas de Hurworth* rector of Louthre, Sir *Thomas de Stirkland* knight presented Mr. *Walter de Wells* priest, who was instituted thereupon.

In the 40 Ed. 3. Sir *Thomas de Stirkland* conveyed his lands of Levenes, Helsyngton, and other places, with the advowson of the church of Lowther, to trustees (by way of settlement).

In the 3 Ric. 2. Sir *John Bone* was rector of Lowther; having in that year from the bishop a dispensation of absence.

* Todd.

In

In the 10 Hen. 5. after the death of John lord Clifford, Sir *Robert Lowther* knight appears by inquisition to have then held the whole manor of Lowther, paying cornage 20*s* 4*d*.

In the 4 Hen. 6. Sir *Robert de Louther* knight, in pursuance of a grant to him made by Sir *Thomas de Stirkland* knight, presented *John de Raby* chaplain to the rectory of Lowther, who was thereupon instituted.

In a rental of the Clifford estate in the 31 Hen. 6. it is expressed, that John de Coupland, Adam de Haverington, Simon de Alve, and the prior of Watton heretofore held *Lowther-William* and *Lowther-John*, by homage and fealty and 20*s* 4*d* cornage; and that *Hugh de Lowther* now holds the same by the same service.—Which distinction of *Lowther-William* and *Lowther-John* is also observed in a rental of Henry earl of Cumberland in the 18 Hen. 8.

In the 5 Ed. 4. the next avoidance of the rectory of Lowther was granted by the prior and convent of *Watton* to *John Wherton* esquire and others. Whereupon the said John presented one *John Wherton* clerk, who was thereupon instituted, in the place (as it seemeth) of one *Thomas Cleveland* deceased; for in the same year the will of *Thomas Cleveland*, late rector of Lowther, was proved by the commissioners of the archbishop of York, during the vacancy of the bishoprick.

In the next account which we have met with of the advowson, the *Strickland* moiety appears to be in the family of *Lowther*; the same having been purchased, together with the manor of Hackthorp, by Richard Lowther esquire. And in the 22 Eliz. a caveat being entred against the admission of any clerk presented on the next vacancy on the behalf of queen Elizabeth claiming right of a third presentation lately invested in the dissolved monastery of *Watton*; a like caveat was entred by *Christopher Lowther* gentleman, son of *Richard*. And soon after, on the death of Mr. *Anthony Garnet*, institution was given to *Thomas Fairfax*, S. T. B. on the presentation of the said *Richard Lowther*.

And in the 29 Eliz. on the resignation of Mr. *Fairfax*, *Leonard Lowther*, M. A. was instituted on the presentation of the said *Richard Lowther*.

In the 7 Ja. 1. on the death of Mr. *Leonard Hudson* alias *Lowther*, the dean and chapter of Carlisle claimed (by caveat) the patronage; but institution was given to *Christopher Lowther*, B. A. on the presentation of Sir *Christopher Lowther* knight.

In the 14 Cha. 1. it was found by inquisition, that two parts of the manor of Lowther were holden of Francis earl of Cumberland by the service called *Noltgeld*, paying yearly to the said earl 20*s* 4*d*; and by the service called *Serjeant food*, paying 10*s* yearly: And that the third part was holden of Robert Strickland esquire, paying yearly one hawk or 6*d* *.

In the 16 Cha. 1. *John Teasdale* was rector of Lowther; he being in that year a contributor to the building of the school there.

In 1676, on the death of *William Smith* rector of Lowther, *Richard Threlkeld*, B. A. was instituted on the presentation of Sir *John Lowther* baronet.

In 1694, *Richard Holme*, M. A. was presented by the same patron.

* Rawlinson.

In 1738, on the death of Richard Holme, *Hugh Robinson*, M. A. was presented by *Henry* viscount *Lonsdale*.

In 1763, on the death of Hugh Robinson, *Henry Lowther*, M. A. was instituted on a presentation by Sir *James Lowther* baronet.

In 1769, on the resignation of Henry Lowther, *William Lowther*, B. A. was instituted on a presentation by the same patron.

The village of Lowther heretofore was considerable, consisting of the hall, the church, the parsonage house, and 17 tenements, messuages, and cottages, all which messuages and tenements were purchased by Sir John Lowther in the year 1682, and pulled down and demolished to inlarge his demesne, and open the prospect to his house, for they stood just in the front of it *. After he had removed the village, he likewise (with consent of the bishop and incumbent) pulled down the parsonage house, which was a very mean one, and built a better, with out-houses suitable, in a more convenient place; and exchanged the lands and other revenues belonging to the church, greatly to the advantage of the incumbent. He also, in 1685, pulled down and rebuilt a great part of the hall, and much improved that which was left standing. Lastly, in the year 1686, he pulled down all or most of the church, and rebuilt it in a much better form, with a cupola in the middle, and furnished the same very elegantly, and inriched it with noble communion plate. The hall was unfortunately burned down about the year 1720, little remaining thereof except the bare walls, and two large wings that escaped the flames. The present owner Sir James Lowther baronet is preparing to rebuild the hall in a still more magnificent and commodious manner.

The reverend Thomas Robinson, rector of Ousby, in his Essay towards a natural history of Westmorland and Cumberland, printed in the year 1709, speaking of Lowther hall, says, "It is not only by the elevation of the ground "freed from those fogs and waterish frosts, which in the spring mornings draw "down to the rivers, and so corrupt the air as to harbour flies and other "noisome insects, or else by the intensity of the cold kill the fruit in the "blossom; but is also so much below and at such a distance from the moun-"tains, that all those fierce and rapid blasts of wind, occasioned by the de-"clivities of the mountains, are either spent or strike a level before they reach "it. Yet this situation hath so much advantage from the mountain winds, "as that they brush and fan the air, and preserve it from stagnation and cor-"ruption. It is not only fenced from violent winds by all kinds of forest "trees of nature's own production, but adorned and beautified by such fo-"reign trees and winter greens as are raised by human art. It hath by nature "such a gradual ascent to the house, as makes the avenue to it most noble "and magnificent. Its situation is upon a limestone rock, which doth not "only secure the foundation, but so fertilizes the earth and soil, as to make "it proper for gardens, orchards, terras-walks, and other most delightful "conveniences. The demesne and parks, which surround the house, are of

* Machel.

"the fame fertile foil, producing rich and plentiful crops of grafs and corn. "The elevation of its fituation gives it a moft curious landfkip of woods, "waters, mountains, rocks, towns, churches, and caftles, which entertain the "eye with a delightful profpect. Thofe thick and pleafant copfes of wood "and trees by the fides of the river Lowther, near two miles in length, do fo "multiply, refract and reflect the fun beams, that it enjoys as warm, and a "more fragrant air, than the lower dales and vallies."

There is a fmall SCHOOL at Lowther which was endowed by Sir John Lowther and his uncle Richard, whofe donations are regiftred at large in the parifh regifter book in the year 1638. And a fchool-houfe was built by them and the aforefaid John Teafdale the rector in 1640.

There was another fchool of a more ample foundation fet on foot by John vifcount Lonfdale, for the benefit of all the northern counties. But being only in its probationary ftate, it was thought fit by the late lord Lonfdale to be difcontinued.

III.

MANOR OF WHALE.

WHALE is a fmall village in the parifh of Lowther, about a mile fouth from the church, confifting of about 8 or 10 families, with two or three ftraggling houfes on Whale moor.

It was anciently held by a family of the name *de Whale*. In the 7 Ed. 1. *John de Whale* was a juror on the inquifition *poft mortem* of Peter de Bres.

In the 8 Ed. 2. it was found by inquifition, that *Richard le Fraunces* held of Robert de Clifford, on the day on which he died, Meburn Maud and Quale; the wardfhip for both being 40*s* yearly, and the cornage 33*s*.

And in the 10 Hen. 5. after the death of John de Clifford, *Richard Vernon* held Meburn and Whale, by the like cornage of 33*s*.

Finally; this, like as many others, was drawn within the vortex of the houfe of Lowther, from age to age purchafing, and never felling again.

IV.

MANOR OF HACKTHORP.

About a mile and an half fouth-eaft from the church, is the village of HACKTHORP, containing 13 or 14 tenements. The hall is at the fouth end. Over the court door are the Lowther arms, unto which family it now belongs.

It was never held of the Cliffords; but was anciently part of the patrimony of the barons of Kendal.

In the reign of king Henry the third, Ralph de Aincourt releafed to William de Lancaftre and his heirs his right in 50*s* of land, in which he was bound unto him by the charter of William de Lancaftre his grandfather, for the quit-claim which the said William made to the said Ralph of the service of Gamel de Hakethorpe. The said William released to Ralph de Aincourt and his heirs the service of the said Gamel in Drengage and other services *.

In the 35 Ed. 3. Sir Thomas de Stirkland (who held under the barons of Kendal) had a licence from the crown to impark his woods at Hackthorp and other places, for his good services in the parts of France.

It was purchased of the Stricklands by the Lowther family as aforesaid: And in the 14 Cha. 1. it was found by inquisition, that the Manor of Hackthorp and advowson of the church of Lowther were holden of the king as of his manor of Kirkby in Kendale, called the Marquis Fee, by knights service; and were worth by the year five marks †.

V.

MANOR OF MELKANTHORP.

About two miles eastward from the church is the village of *Melkanthorp*, which anciently seems to have belonged to a family of that name.

In the 8 Ed. 1. *Galfridus de Melcanthorp* was constable of Roger lord Clifford of his castle of Appleby.

In the 3 Ed. 2. by an inquisition of tenants in Westmorland who held by cornage, it was found, that *Margaret de Ros* then held Melkanthorp, paying 5*s* cornage. Whether she was a daughter of the Melkanthorps, or she was the Margaret de Ross who then held Kendal castle, hath not appeared to us. The latter is more probable; for Melkanthorp was not holden of the Cliffords lords of Westmorland, but was parcel of the manor of Kendal called Marquis Fee.

Melkanthorp afterwards came to the Musgraves; then to the Fallowfields; and by marriage of the heiress of Fallowfield to the Dalstons of Acorn Bank; who sold the same to Sir John Lowther.

The arms in Melkanthorp hall (which is the manor house of Great Strickland) are, *Musgrave*, quartering *Ward* and *Stapleton*. 2. *Fallowfield*. 3. *Dalston*, impaling *Fallowfield* ‡.

* Machel from Dugdale. † Rawlinson. ‡ Machel.

PARISH

PARISH OF MORLAND.

I. *Pariſh of Morland.*
II. *Manor of Morland.*
III. *Great and Little Strickland.*
IV. *Thrimby.*
V. *Newby.*
VI. *Slegill.*
VII. *King's Meaburn.*
VIII. *Bolton.*
IX. *Buley.*

I. PARISH OF MORLAND.

The pariſh of Morland (*Moor-land*) is bounded on the Eaſt by the pariſhes of Kirkby Thore and St. Michael's Appleby, being ſeparated from them by the River Eden; on the South-eaſt by the pariſh of St. Laurence Appleby; on the South, by the pariſh of Croſby Ravenſworth; on the South-weſt, by the pariſh of Shap; on the Weſt and North-weſt, by the pariſhes of Bampton and Lowther; and on the North, by the pariſh of Cliburn: And contains about 271 families; all of the church of England, 7 only excepted.

The church of Morland (according to Dr. Todd) is dedicated to St. Laurence.

It is a vicarage, in the patronage of the dean and chapter of Carliſle, valued in the king's books in the 26 Hen. 8. at 11 *l* 18 *s* 1½ *d*. The clear yearly value, as certified to the governors of queen Anne's bounty, 45 *l*.

Ketel ſon of Eldred ſon of Ivo de Talebois baron of Kendal, gave this church and two carucates of land at Morland, to the abbot and convent of St. Mary's York *; which grant was confirmed firſt by Athelwold, and afterwards by Hugh, biſhops of Carliſle: Which ſaid Hugh granted and confirmed the ſame to the ſaid abbey, for the proper uſe and ſuſtenance of the monks of the houſe of *Wetheral*, a cell of the ſaid abbey: The abbot and con-

* Chetellus filius Eltredi omnibus audientibus vel videntibus literas has, tam futuris quam præſentibus, ſalutem. Notum ſit vobis, me dediſſe et conceſſiſſe, conſilio amicorum meorum, deo et eccleſiæ ſanctæ Mariæ Eborum et monachis ibidem deo ſervientibus eccleſiam de Morland, cum omnibus ſuis pertinentiis, et eccleſiam de Wirchington, et duas carucatas terræ in eadem villa, et unum molendinum et omnia quæ ad eum pertinent, in liberam, puram, et perpetuam eleemoſynam, pro anima mea, et hæredum meorum, et pro animabus omnium parentum meorum, et omnium fidelium defunctorum. Quapropter concedo et præſentis chartæ teſtimonio confirmo, ut ſit præfata eleemoſyna quieta et illibata, et ab omni terreno ſervicio abſoluta, uſibus prædictorum monachorum in perpetuum. Teſtibus Chriſtiana uxore mea, Willielmo filio meo, et multis aliis. (*Regiſtr. Wetheral.*)

 vent

vent to appoint a vicar, and to allow him yearly 100*s*.—Other lands at Morland were given to the said abbot and convent of St. Mary's York and to the prior and monks of *Wederhale*, by Henry Legate and Peter his brother †.

The cell of Wetheral seems about that time to have been overstocked. For in the time of bishop Bernard (who was intermediate between the said bishops Athelwold and Hugh) we find three incumbents at Morland all at one time; for, to the confirmation by the said bishop Bernard of the grants by Thomas son of Gospatric to Shap abbey (about the year 1170), amongst other witnesses, there are *Gilbert*, *Walter*, and *Thomas*, rectors of the church of Morland.

And about the year 1230, *Richard de Agmeta* was vicar of Morland, and at the same time there was one *Thomas* parson of Morland.

In 1234, *Michael*, vicar of Morland, was witness to a composition about Morland wood *.

In the year 1313, king Edward the second presented Sir *John de Warwyke*, deacon, to the vicarage of Morland; the abbacy of St. Mary's York being then vacant.

In 1316, on the death of the said Sir John, the abbot and convent present Mr. *Henry de Rillington*; who is instituted, with a reservation of 4 marks yearly pension to the said patrons.

In 1332, one Sir *Henry*, vicar of Morland, being accused and cited for keeping (contrary to the constitutions of Otho and Othobon) a concubine named Emma Hall [Emma de Aula], had his absolution and dismission.

In 1334, Sir *Henry de Appleby* vicar of Morland, and Sir *Richard de Haverington* vicar of the prebendal and collegiate church of Derlington in the diocese of Durham, with the consent of their respective patrons and ordinaries, exchange their livings; whereupon Sir Richard de Haverington is instituted to Morland.

In 1362, on the death of Sir Richard de Haverington, the abbot and convent present Sir *John Murrays*, priest, who is instituted.

In the next year after, he exchanges with Sir *William de Laysingby*, for the rectory of Welbery in the diocese of York.

In 1368, Sir William de Laysingby makes a new exchange with Sir *John Bray* vicar of Helmesley in the diocese of York; to which the abbot and convent, patrons of Morland, give their consent. This same Sir John, by the name of *John del Bray* (John of the brae), appears to have been vicar in 1383.

In the year 1424, there was a dispute between Sir *John Richemont* vicar of Morland and the prior of Wetheral, concerning the oblations in St. Mary's chapel of *Wythe* within the parish of Morland, and half an acre of land lying upon *Litel Aynesbergh*, and abutting on the common of *Banc*, within the territory of the vill aforesaid; which was referred to the arbitration of the abbot of St. Mary's York. Who awarded the same to the prior; unless it should appear, from the records of the abbey, that by real composition at any time, the oblations in the said chapel had been given to the vicar ‡. [The place

† Registr. Wetheral. * Idem. ‡ Idem.

where this chapel stood seems to have been nigh the river Lyvennet at about the middle way between Morland and King's Meaburn, in a place now called Chapel Garth, belonging to the vicarage.]

In 1513, Sir *Alexander Hall*, vicar of Morland, was (amongst others) an arbitrator, in a case of assault and battery, between Hugh Machel of Crackenthorp gentleman, and Sir Henry Smith chantry priest at Appleby *.

In the year 1563, on the death of *John Blythe* vicar of Morland, *George Nevil*, D. D. was instituted; being presented by Marmaduke Peers, to whom this avoidance had been granted by the abbot and convent of St. Mary's York, before the dissolution.

In 1567, on the death of Dr. Nevil, *Thomas Warwick* clerk had institution, by virtue of a grant from the dean and chapter of Carlisle.

In 1624, *William Hall* was instituted, on a presentation by the dean and chapter.

In 1660, *Piercy Burton* was instituted.

In 1668, on the death of Piercy Burton, *John Hutchinson*, M. A. was instituted.

In 1679, *Michael Hudson*.

In 1680, *William Atkinson* had institution.

In 1720, on the death of William Atkinson, *James Rickerby*, M. A. was presented by the dean and chapter, and instituted thereupon.

In 1743, after the death of James Rickerby, on a dispute between dean Bolton and the chapter concerning the dean's negative voice, this vicarage was suffered to lapse, and *John Brown*, M. A. was collated. The said John Brown was author of the Essay on the Characteristicks, and other ingenious writings.

In 1757, on the cession of John Brown, *Daniel Brocklebank* was instituted, on a presentation by the dean and chapter.

In 1773, on the death of Daniel Brocklebank, *John Jackson* clerk was instituted on the like presentation.

The *church* at Morland is a fair large building, with two rows of pillars, three in each row; with a tower steeple, and three good bells.

The south ile of the said church, heretofore belonging to Thrimby Grange, was given up by the last viscount Lonsdale, as useless to him; and is now made use of by the parishioners in common. There is another small ile, on the north side of the chancel, belonging to Great Strickland hall; which hall and manor having some time belonged to the Dalstons of Acorn Bank, the ile from thence still retains the name of Dalston's porch.

* Chart. Machel.

II. MANOR

II. MANOR OF MORLAND.

The manor of Morland was never held of the Veteriponts or Cliffords; but belonged to the barons of Kendal. *Ketel* ſon of *Eldred* ſon of *Ivo* aforeſaid was both lord of the manor and patron of the advowſon.

William de Lancaſtre, the firſt of that name, grandſon of the ſaid *Ketel*, granted the manors of Heverſham, Grayrigg, and Morland, in frank marriage with his daughter *Agnes*, to *Alexander de Windeſore* ſon and heir of *William de Windeſore*. In the time of which *Alexander*, a partition was made of the wood at Morland, between him and the prior of Wetheral *.

The ſaid *Alexander Windeſore* had a ſon *William de Windeſore*; who had a ſon *Alexander de Windeſore*, who in the 11 Ed. 2. levied a fine of the manors of Grayrigg and Morland. This laſt *Alexander* had a ſon *William*, who in the 25 Ed. 3. is found by inquiſition to have held the manor of Morland of William de Coucy, by cornage, wardſhip, and relief. In the 36 Ed. 3. he had a grant of a market and fair at Morland (which, if ever ſet on foot, have been long ſince loſt by diſuſe). In the 49 Ed. 3. by the inquiſition after the death of Joan de Coupland, it appears that he then held the manors of Ha-

* Omnibus Chriſti fidelibus ad quorum notitiam præſentes literæ pervenerint, W. Prior de Wederhale et Alexander de Wyndeſore ſalutem æternam in domino. Noverit univerſitas veſtra, quod de communi et unanimi aſſenſu mei et domini Alexandri de Wyndeſhover, boſcus de Morland, qui ad nos utroſque pertinebat in communi, partitus eſt in hunc modum: viz. Quod totus boſcus propior villæ de Morland, qui vocatur Linſtouc, remanebit domino Alexandro et hæredibus ſuis in perpetuum, uſque ad quendam ſiketum qui dividit Mechilrig et Linſtouc, ſicut curſus illius ſiketi ſe extendit in longum inter boſcum de Mechilrig et Linſtouc. Totus autem boſcus qui dicitur Mechilrig, et totus boſcus a Mechilrig verſus orientem. remanebit priori et ſucceſſoribus ſuis in perpetuum uſque ad aquam de Lyvennet. Ita quod licebit dicto Priori et ſucceſſoribus ſuis includere partem ſuam pro voluntate ſua, et redigere ad culturam ſicut melius ſibi viderint expedire ſine impedimento aliquo prædicti Alexandri et hæredum ſuorum. Similiter autem licebit predicto Alexandro et hæredibus ſuis includere partem ſuam pro voluntate ſua, et redigere ad culturam ſicut melius ſibi viderint expedire, ſine impedimento dicti Prioris vel ſucceſſorum ſuorum. Ita tamen quod dictus Alexander et hæredes ſui habebunt communam herbagii, ad propria animalia tantum, in boſco prioris et ſucceſſorum, quantum remanebit incultum, ſine nocumento dicti Prioris et ſucceſſorum ſuorum. Et dictus prior et ſucceſſores ſui habebunt communam herbagii tantum in boſco Alexandri et hæredum ſuorum, quantum remanebit incultum, ſine nocumento dicti Alexandri et hæredum ſuorum. Dictus autem prior et ſucceſſores ſui reſpondebunt libere tenentibus ſuis de parte ſua boſci. Et dictus Alexander et hæredes ſui reſpondebunt libere tenentibus ſuis de parte ſua boſci. Sciendum eſt autem, quod quædam pars boſci de Morland in prædicta partitione non continetur, viz. Boſcus à via de Appeltreholme, ſicut eſt in pendenti condorſi, uſque ad Amſelbergile. Et iſte boſcus in perpetuum erit communis dicto priori et ſucceſſoribus ſuis, et dicto Alexandro et hæredibus ſuis, ad eſtoveria ſua capienda ibidem. Nec aliquis ſine altero aliquid inde dare poterit vel vendere. Et uterque perſona tactis ſacroſanctis juraverunt, quod nunquam venient per ſe vel per alias perſonas contra tenorem iſtius ſcripti. Et ut iſta partitio ex utraque parte rata et ſtabilis ſit in perpetuum, Prior pro ſe et ſucceſſoribus ſuis, et dominus Alexander pro ſe et hæredibus ſuis ſigilla ſua hinc inde huic ſcripto appoſuerunt. Hiis teſtibus, Domino J. de Veteriponte, Domino R. Priore et W° Official' Karl: Thoma Filio Wilhelmi, Thoma Filio Johannis, Will° de Daker, Waltero de Stirkeland, Johanne Mauchael, Roberto de Aſkeby, Thoma de Louther, Alano Pincerna, Roberto de Neuby, Michaele et Waltero vicariis de Morland et de Appelby, Waltero de Meburn, Adamo de Soureby, Johanne de Neubigging, et aliis. *(Regiſtr. Wetheral.)*

verſham,

versham, Grayrigg, and Morland, by homage and fealty and the service of 13*s* 4*d* yearly, as of the manor of Kirkby in Kendale.

This said last *William de Windesore* had a daughter and heir *Margery*, who was married to *John Ducket* esquire, which first brought the family of *Ducket* into Westmorland, who settled at Grayrigg, and continued there for 12 generations. The manor of Morland doth not appear to have come to the *Duckets*. And whether indeed the *Windsors* had the whole manor of Morland is uncertain. Probably they had not. It seemeth that *Ketel* aforesaid, together with the church and lands there, gave part of the manor to the aforesaid abbey. For the monks of Wetherall, and since the dissolution the dean and chapter of Carlisle, have enjoyed the greatest part of the said manor; and the assignees perhaps of the *Windsors* the other part. Accordingly, there seem to have been two manor houses, one called *Low Hall*, which belonged formerly to the *Musgraves*, who are said to have had one third part of the lordship, and the dean and chapter the other two thirds *; the other called *Broadfold*, holden of the dean and chapter by the family of *Backhouse*, which continued at Morland for several generations.

By a rental of the possessions of the cell of Wedyrhall, when Richard Esyngwalde was prior there in the 6 Hen. 7. 1490, there appear to have been 21 tenants to the said priory at Morland, paying in the whole the yearly rent of 11*l* 10*s* 10¾*d*; besides 90 acres of demesne.

In the 9 Eliz. there is a licence to *Robert Bowes* and *Eleanor* his wife, to alienate Morland to *Simon Musgrave*.

And in the 13 Eliz. *John Southaic* gentleman appears to have been seised of a moiety (as it is there called) of the manor of Morland, with 100 acres of wood, which he purchased of *Simon Musgrave* and *Julian* his wife.

And by inquisition in the 34 Eliz. it appears, that *Lancelot Backhouse* gentleman (son of *Henry*, son of *Robert*) died seised of a moiety of the manor of Morland, and also of the wood and underwood commonly called Morland wood, containing by estimation 50 acres; which he held by feoffment from *John Southaic* esquire: And also one pasture called Woodhouse Close; one parcel of meadow adjoining to the said close; one acre of arable and meadow called Stanelands: Of all which he died seised in the manor of Morland. And also of one third part of the manor of Brampton; and of one third of one messuage and one cottage in Dufton; both of which, at Brampton and Dufton, he had by deed indented of Briget Backhouse widow his grandmother, dated Feb. 2. in the 3 and 4 Ph. and Mary, made to Edward Birkbeck of Hornby gentleman, and John Backhouse clerk, to the use of the said Briget for life, remainder to Henry Backhouse and his heirs male, remainder to Gilbert and his heirs male, remainder to Anthony and his heirs male, remainder to the right heirs of the said Briget for ever. The jurors further say, that the said Lancelot held the said moiety of the queen *in capite*, by the service of the 20th part of one knight's fee; that it is worth yearly 22*s*. And that the said third part of the manor of Brampton, and other the premisses at Dufton, he held

* Machel.

of

of our said lady the queen, as of her manor of Dufton by fealty and suit of court, and rendring for the same yearly one third of a pound of pepper, one third of two pence for the third part of a pound of cumin, and one third of two shillings for all services; and is worth yearly 3*l* 10*s*. And that *Robert Backhouse* was his brother and heir, then aged 21 years.

This family of *Backhouse*, like many others, ended in a daughter; married to Isaac Eels esquire. Their arms were; Or, a cross bend, erminois. Crest: an eagle displayed, Vert; with a serpent wavy, Proper, inflexing its head and tail towards the eagle.

III. GREAT AND LITTLE STRICKLAND.

STRICKLAND (*Stirkland*) gave name to the family of *Strickland*, which continued here for many generations, and afterwards removed to Sizergh. They held likewise of the barons of Kendal, and not of the barons of Westmorland.

About the time of the reign of king Henry the sixth, a family of the name of FALLOWFIELD succeeded at Strickland, whether by purchase from the Stricklands, or how otherwise, we have not found.

The first of the name of *Fallowfield*, that hath occurred in Westmorland, was *Nicholas de Fallowfield*, who in the 10 Hen. 5. was one of the jurors on the inquisition *post mortem* of John de Clifford.

In the 34 Hen. 6. *Thomas Fallowfield* esquire was a juror on the inquisition *post mortem* of Thomas de Clifford.

And to bring the name home to Great Strickland, in the first year of queen Mary, we find a bond of indemnity to one of the Wyberghs of Clifton, executed by *Thomas Fallowfield* of Great Strickland esquire, and *Edward Fallowfield* gentleman his son and heir. In which year also *Thomas Fallowfield* represented the county of Westmorland in parliament.

In the reign of king James the first; *Richard Fallowfield* of Strickland hall, esquire, married Hellen daughter of Sir Christopher Lowther of Lowther knight: Who had a daughter and heir *Lucy Fallowfield*, married to *John Dalston* of Acorn Bank esquire; who brought with her a large accession of fortune to that family. The said *John Dalston* had a son *Christopher*, who sold the estate to Sir *John Lowther*, in whose posterity it still continues.

The arms of Fallowfield were; Sable, three escalops Or *.

At Little Strickland, there was a family of CRACKENTHORPS for several generations. They descended, by a younger branch, from the Crackenthorps of Newbiggin. The common ancestor was *Christopher Crackenthorp* of Newbiggin esquire, who in the time of king Henry the eighth married a Blenkinsop of Helbeck; and by her had issue *Henry*, who succeeded to the inheritance at Newbiggin; and a younger son *John*, who settled at Little Strickland.

* Machel.

This

This *John Crackenthorp*, by his wife Mabel Cowper, had iſſue *Chriſtopher* his eldeſt ſon; and a ſecond ſon *Richard Crackenthorp*, D. D. the famous logician, who was chaplain in ordinary to king James the firſt, a profound divine, a ſubtle canoniſt, and replete with all the learning of thoſe times.

Chriſtopher, ſon and heir of *John*, married Barbara Ward of Yorkſhire; and by her had iſſue *Richard*, *Thomas*, and *Frances*.

Richard, ſon and heir of *Chriſtopher*, married Elizabeth Fairer of Warcop tower; and by her had iſſue *Chriſtopher*, *Anne*, *Grace*, *Barbara*, *Elizabeth*, and *Mary*.

Chriſtopher, ſon and heir of *Richard*, married Jane daughter of Andrew Huddleſton of Hutton John eſquire; and by her had iſſue *Richard*, *Andrew*, *William*, *Jane*, and *Anne*.

Richard, ſon and heir of *Chriſtopher*, married Elizabeth daughter of John Wilſon of Spittle. He ſold the eſtate at Little Strickland to Mr. John Pattinſon of Thrimby: And had iſſue, beſides ſeveral other children, the reverend *Gilbert Crackenthorp*, now living (1775), the late worthy ſchoolmaſter of the free grammar ſchool of Kirkby in Kendale.

In the reign of king Charles the ſecond, THOMAS FLETCHER eſquire, barriſter at law, reſided and had a good eſtate at Little Strickland. He was recorder of Appleby in 1692. He was anceſtor by a daughter and coheir to Sir Fletcher Norton knight the preſent ſpeaker of the honourable houſe of commons.

In the reign of king Henry the third, Sir Walter de Stirkland knight had a licence from Hugh biſhop of Carliſle, to keep a domeſtic chaplain in his family within the pariſh of Morland.

IV. THRIMBY.

THRIMBY is a ſmall village in this pariſh, conſiſting only of about ſix families. Moſt of the lands were bought up by John viſcount Lonſdale.

It ſeems to have belonged anciently to a family who received their name from thence. In the 4th year of king John, there was an agreement between the prior of Watton and *William de Tyrneby*, concerning a carucate of land, together with paſture for 1000 ſheep at Tyrneby *.

And

* Hæc eſt finalis concordia, facta in curia domini regis apud Appelby, die Jovis proximo poſt feſtum ſancti Michaelis, anno regni regis Johannis quarto, coram dominis J. Norwicenſi epiſcopo, Hugone Bardulf, Johanne de Geſtelinges, Magiſtro Rogero Arundell, Willielmo filio Ricardi, juſticiariis, et aliis fidelibus domini regis ibidem præſentibus: Inter Robertum priorem de Watton conquerentem, et Petrum canonicum ſuum poſitum loco ipſius inde ad lucrandum vel perdendum, et Willielmum de Tyrneby, de warrantia chartæ unius carucatæ terræ cum pertinentiis, et de paſtura mille ovium in Tyrneby. Unde placitum fuit inter eos in prædicta curia, ſc. Quod prædictus Willielmus recognovit prædictam carucatam terræ cum pertinentiis et paſturam eſſe jus et perpetuam eleemoſynam prædicti Roberti prioris, habendas et tenendas ſibi et ſucceſſoribus ſuis de prædicto

Willielmo

And a dispute arising between the priory of Watton and the rectors of the church of Morland, concerning the tithes of their lands within the said parish, as well of the lands which they had in their own hands, as of those which were let to farm; the same was referred to commissioners appointed by authority of the pope: who awarded, that the prior and convent of Watton should pay to the rectors of Morland for ever, the tithe of the corn of all their lands in the parish of Morland let or to be let to farm; except one carucate of land which they held in demesne, for the tithes whereof they should pay to the church of Morland for ever and the rectors there, one mark of silver yearly †.

In the 13 Joh. one of the witnesses to a charter of Shap abbey is *William de Thirneby*.

In the next reign, *John* son of *William de Thirneby* gave to the priory of Wederhale certain lands at Thirneby, with a grange thereupon.

Afterwards, Thrimby appears to have belonged to the *Harringtons*. Thus amongst the Escheats in the 25 Ed. 3. *John de Haverington* held of the king *in capite* the manor of Thirneby, as of the fee of Coucy (afterwards called the Richmond fee) ‡.

In the rental of queen Katharine's lands in the 28 Cha. 2. Sir John Lowther stands charged with a yearly rent of 13*s* 4*d* for lands in Thrimby, parcel of the said Richmond fee.

The tithes of Thrimby, which heretofore belonged to the priory of Wetheral, belong to the dean and chapter. A lease of which tithes was given as a legacy to the vicars of Dacre in succession. Which tithes being diminished greatly by the purchased lands being laid into Lowther park, and the lease being suffered to expire, the said John viscount Lonsdale gave to the dean and chapter 200*l* for the same, whereby they obtained the further sum of 200*l* from the governors of queen Anne's bounty, wherewith an estate was purchased for the use of the vicars of Dacre.

The *chapel* of Thrimby was quite deserted and fallen to decay, until the same was restored by the above mentioned Thomas Fletcher esquire; who by deed bearing date Feb. 2. 1681, granted to Richard Crackenthorp of Little Strick-

Willielmo et hæredibus suis in perpetuum, per servicium viginti solidorum reddendorum inde annuatim pro omni servicio. Præterea, prædictus Willielmus concessit prædicto Roberto priori et successoribus suis, totam culturam quæ fuit Gilberti de Lancastre, et jacet proxime bercariæ prædicti Roberti prioris, versus Austrum: Et quinque acras in cultura sua de Witerick propinquiores prædictæ bercariæ versus Occidentem jacere incultas ad communem pasturam averiorum suorum et totius villæ de Tyrneby in perpetuum. Præterea idem Willielmus concessit prædicto Roberto priori et successoribus suis exitum prædictæ bercariæ qui est versus Orientem super terram suam ad latitudinem quinque perticarum, secundum quod longitudo totius curiæ prædictæ bercariæ extendit versus Austrum. Præterea Willielmus concessit prædicto Roberto priori et successoribus suis, pascere bona sua de rivulo qui currit extra et per medium curiæ grangiæ suæ pro voluntate et placito suis, in quantumcunque ipse Willielmus vel hæredes sui concedere possint. Et sciendum est, quod prædictus Willielmus vel hæredes sui non possint a modo aliquid colere infra metas vastæ prædictæ pasturæ de Tyrneby: Nec ipse vel hæredes sui possint attachiare alicujus hominis averia ad eandem pasturam, nisi solummodo sua propria averia et hominum suorum de prædicta villa de Tyrneby. *(Registr. Wetheral.)*

† Registr. Wetheral. ‡ Rawlinson.

land

land gentleman, James Webster clerk son and heir apparent of James Webster of Thrimby gentleman, and divers others in trust, an annuity or rent charge of 10*l*, out of his messuage, tenement, and lands, known by the names of Bryam tenement, High Sandriggs, and Low Sandriggs, for a chapel and an English and grammar school to be taught in the chapel. The curate and schoolmaster to be chosen by the trustees; the person to be chosen to be an unmarried man, and to continue so during the time he officiates, unless a dispensation thereof be obtained from the major part of the trustees under their hands and seals. When four trustees only shall be left, they shall convey to eight others, four to be in Thrimby, and four in Little Strickland. Children in Little Strickland and Thrimby, whose parents live upon day-labour, to be taught gratis.

This chapel has received twice by lot 200*l* of the augmentation by queen Anne's bounty; with which sum of 400*l* an estate was purchased, called Stonygill, in the parish of Crosby Ravensworth.

To avoid the inconvenience of teaching in the chapel, a new schoolhouse hath been lately erected.

V. NEWBY.

There are many places of the name of NEWBY (which means no more than *New town*); and therefore this, by way of distinction, and from the nature of its situation, is called *Newby Stones*.

This manor also appears to have had no connection with the barony of Westmorland under the Cliffords. There were anciently many of the name *de Newby*, who seem to have been lords of this manor.

In the 10 Hen. 8. one *Richard Vernon* of Nether Haddon in the county of Derby held of the king *in capite* 16 messuages and 300 acres of land in Newby.

He was succeeded by his son *George Vernon* esquire; of whom, *Richard Nevinson* of Kemplees yeoman rented a messuage at *Newby in the Stones*, together with a wood called Newby wood, and a parcel of ground called *Forty penny farmhold*. In the 4 and 5 Ph. and M. the said *Richard Nevinson* appears to have been possessed of certain lands and tenements, rents and services, in Newby Stones; which he settled on *Richard* his son and the heirs male of his body, remainder to *Stephen* his second son and the heirs male of his body, remainder to his own right heirs: Thomas Sandford of Askham and Thomas Blenkinsop of Helbeck esquires being trustees in the settlement *.

The pedigree of *Nevinson*, as certified at Dugdale's visitation in 1664, is as followeth:

1. *Richard Nevinson* of Kemplees, died about the fifth year of Philip and Mary (seised, as it seemeth, of the manor of Newby). He had issue, (1) *Richard*, who died without issue male. (2) *Stephen*, who succeeded by virtue of

* Machel from the evidences at Helbeck.

the intail. (3) *Marian*, married to Rowland Robinſon of Newby in the 3 and 4 Ph. and M.

2. *Stephen Nevinſon*, ſecond ſon of Richard, had a ſon *Richard*, and a daughter *Jane* married to Richard Bowerbank.

3. *Richard Nevinſon* of Newby eſquire, ſon and heir of Stephen, married one Mayplate of Cumberland, and by her had iſſue, (1) *Edward.* (2) *Stephen*, ſurnamed The Long, who died unmarried. (3) *Anne*, married to Thomas Dalſton of Ouſeby eſquire, ſecond ſon of Sir Chriſtopher Dalſton of Acorn Bank knight. (4) *Elizabeth*, married to Thomas Lough of Blencarn.—The ſaid Richard died in the 13 Cha. 1. and by inquiſition it was found, that he died ſeiſed of one capital meſſuage, 20 acres of arable land, 5 acres of meadow, and 15 acres of paſture, in Newby Stones; one moiety thereof in poſſeſſion, the other moiety in reverſion after the death of Stephen Nevinſon, holden of the king *in capite*, by the 100th part of one knight's fee: his heir being within age.

4. *Edward Nevinſon* of Newby eſquire, ſon and heir of Richard, married Suſanna daughter of Sir Chriſtopher Dalſton of Acorn Bank knight. Which Edward was of the age of 40 years at Dugdale's viſitation aforeſaid.

This family claimed to be deſcended from a family of that name of conſiderable account in the South. And a reſpite was entred by Sir William Dugdale, for further proof of the connexion between the two families, but no further proof was made.

The ſaid Edward Nevinſon, by his wife Suſanna Dalſton, had iſſue, (1) *John.* (2) *Richard*, a merchant in Kendal. (3) *Chriſtopher.* (4) *Edward*, a vintner in London. (5) *Thomas.* (6) *Anne*, married to Hugh Machel of Crackenthorp gentleman, ſon and heir apparent of Lancelot Machel of Crackenthorp eſquire. (7) *Margaret*, married to one Walton a tanner in Penrith. (8) *Elizabeth.*

5. *John Nevinſon* of Newby eſquire, ſon and heir of Edward, married Elizabeth Garth of Hedlam in the county of Durham; and by her had iſſue, (1) *William.* (2) *Elizabeth*, married to Mr. Thomas Dawes of Barton Kirk.

6. *William Nevinſon* of Newby eſquire, ſon and heir of John, married Mary ſiſter of the late general Stanwix; and had iſſue, *Stanwix*, *William*, *John*, *Thomas*, *James*, *Elizabeth*, and *Mary*.

7. *Stanwix Nevinſon* of Newby eſquire, ſon and heir of William, married firſt Elizabeth ſiſter of Francis Blake of Twiſel caſtle in the county of Northumberland eſquire; and to his ſecond wife married Julia daughter of John Gaſkarth of Penrith eſquire; and dying without iſſue, gave the eſtate to his widow.

The *arms* of Nevinſon are; Argent, a cheveron, charged with a mullet, between three eaglets diſplayed, Azure. The Creſt; a leopard paſſant, collared Or, the tail Sable.

The hoſpital of St. Leonard's York had lands at Newby, given by the aforeſaid Ketel, ſon of Eldred, ſon of Ivo de Talebois, baron of Kendal.

VI. SLE-

VI. SLEGILL.

SLEGILL, *Sleagill*, probably hath its name from *sloe* trees (vulgarly pronounced *slea* trees) having grown there. This seems to have been esteemed anciently part of Newby; for in the time of Edward the second, we find a lease from John Prodhom and Joan his wife of lands at Slegill *in the hamlet of Newby*. And Slegill, as the other manors before mentioned within this parish, was not held of the Cliffords, but was part of the barony of Kendal.

This manor, in the reign of king Henry the third, and for some time after, appears in the hands of divers persons who received their name from the place.

There was one *Gilbert de Schleagyle*, who gave a messuage with the appurtenances to the priory of Wetheral. And Thomas de Morland appears to have held lands at Slegill of *Gilbert de Slegill*.

After him, *Robert de Slegill* was witness to a grant of lands at Meburn Regis by John son of Walter de Ravensby to the priory of Wetherall.

By a deed without date, *Adam de Slegill*, son of *Robert de Slegill* grants to John de Staffole and Alice his wife and their heirs, his *manor* of Slegill, with the appurtenances; together with the service of one barbed arrow by Robert le Spencer for his lands in Slegill, and with the service of one race of ginger by William Prodhom.

The Slegill arms were, a greyhound catching an hare.

Amongst the Escheats in the 13 Cha. I. it is found by inquisition, that *William Fayrer* died seised of 12 messuages and tenements in Slegill, in the tenure of divers customary tenants there, holden of the king as of his manor of Kendal called the Marquis Fee, by knights service.

The *Blenkinsops* of Helbeck had considerable possessions here; as also had the abbot and convent of *Shap*.

In the 30 Hen. 8. there is a grant by Richard Evenwode abbot of Shap and the convent there, to Thomas Blenkinsop of Helbeck esquire, his heirs and assigns, of a watercourse running across a close of theirs at Slegill called Milneflatte, to the water mill of the said Thomas, as shall be most convevient; rendring to them for the same two pence of silver yearly at the feast of Pentecost, if demanded.

In the year 1670, *William Mawson* gentleman, with consent of the dean and chapter, gave a lease of the tithes of Slegill to the vicarage of Penrith.

VII. KING'S MEABURN.

KING'S MEABURN, as then belonging to the crown, was so called by way of distinction from *Maud's Meaburn*, which belonged to Maud wife of the first Robert de Veteripont, sister of Sir Hugh de Morville; the one was *Meaburn Regis*, the other *Meaburn Matildæ*.

This

This manor, together with the rest of the barony of Westmorland, was granted by king John to the said Robert de Veteripont, in whose posterity it still continues.

In the partition of the estate between the two daughters of the last Robert de Veteripont, Isabella de Clifford had three fourths of this manor, and her sister Idonea de Laybourn the other fourth; the whole together valued at 50*l* 6*s* 3*d*.

In the 18 or 19 Ed. 1. John Crombwell and Idonea his wife, widow of Roger de Laybourn, granted to Stephen son of William de Meburne and his heirs, six acres of land to be measured out of their moor of King's Meaburne, at the north end thereof; paying to them and their heirs yearly, for all services, six shillings.

In the 1 Ed. 3. after the death of Roger lord Clifford, the inquisition finds, that he died seised, at King's Meaburne, of a capital messuage, the herbage whereof was worth by the year 3*s*; in demesne lands 217 acres by the greater hundred, all which lie uncultivated, by reason of the want of tenants, and the destruction made by the Scots, the herbage whereof is worth by the year 21*s* 5*d*; twenty-two acres of meadow, worth 22*s*; rent of one free tenant, 2*s* 8*d*; forty-eight oxgangs in the hands of tenants at will, worth yearly 4*l* 16*s*; sixteen cottages, worth yearly 16*s*; water mill, 50*s*; pleas and perquisites of court, 3*s*.

Sir Hugh de Morvil gave two oxgangs of land in Meburn to the priory of Carlisle; which king Hen. 2. confirmed; expressing the same to consist of 32 acres in Meburn Field, and the meadow at the head of two corn lands, and common of pasture for the cattle of their men, which they had in the days of Waldeve.

The priory of Wetheral had some lands at King's Meaburn; and there is a grant in the register of the said priory of a parcel of ground there, whereon a grange or farm house was erected, by John son of Walter de Ravensby: Witnesses of which grant were, Robert de Ravenswithe, and Thomas de Derwentwater, knights; John de Helton, Robert de Slegille, Alan le Butiler, Walter de Boulton, Hugh de Colleby, and others.

VIII. BOLTON.

Bolton was variously written in ancient times; as, *Boeltbun*, *Beeltun*, *Boveltbun*, *Bothelton*: From all which it may be conjectured that it received its name from the owner, *Bothel*, *Bovel*, *Boel*, or the like. *Bovel*, and *Bolt*, are names yet in use in Westmorland. *Bothwell*, in Scotland, is a name well known.

In the 8 Ed. 2. after the death of Robert lord Clifford, *Ralph* Baron of *Graystock* son of *William*, held Dufton, Bolton, Brampton, and Yanewith; the wardship whereof, when it should happen, was estimated at 100 marks, and the cornage of the whole 25*s* 6*d*.

In

In the 20 Ed. 2. *John de Derwentwater* held the manor of Bolton. For the Derwentwaters held the same of the Graystocks as mesne lords, the Graystocks holding immediately of the Cliffords.

In the 11 Ric. 2. there was a writ of inquiry, concerning a breach of privilege of parliament, by an enormous riot and forcible entry committed in Bolton, upon the goods, lands, servants, and tenants of Sir *John de Derwentwater*, one of the knights of the shire for Cumberland, whilst he was sitting in parliament.

In the 15 Ric. 2. after the death of Roger de Clifford, the inquisition finds, that *Ralph de Graystoke* held of the said Roger, on the day on which he died, the manor of Bolton.

In the 10 Hen. 5. after the death of *John de Clifford*, *John de Graystock* held the same.

In the 31 Hen. 6. it is found by inquisition, that *Nicholas Radcliff* then held Bolton of *Ralph* baron of *Graystock*, as the said baron held the same of Thomas de Clifford.

At the dissolution of the abbey of Shap, it appears that the said abbey had a rent out of Bolton of 16*d* a year, paid by Sir *Cuthbert Ratcliffe* knight.

In the 1 and 2 Ph. and M. *George Ratcliffe* knight held Bolton of *William* lord *Dacre*, as the said lord *Dacre* held the same of Henry earl of Cumberland.

Afterwards, the *Fletchers* of Hutton purchased the *manor* of Bolton, in which family it still continues. *Jeffrey Wybergh*, a younger brother of the Wyberghs of Clifton, purchased the hall and demesne; whose son *Thomas Wybergh* sold the same to his father's sister Mrs. *Dorothy Halton*, widow of Mr. *Miles Halton* who had been steward at Graystock castle; who gave the same to her younger son *Miles Halton*; who had a daughter and heir *Dorothy* married to *Edward Birket*, M. A. prebendary of Carlisle, whose son *Henry Birket* esquire now enjoys the same.

King Henry the second confirmed to the priory of Carlisle certain lands lying between Bolton and Colby, which were *in calumnia* (debateable lands) with common of pasture and other easments there, given by Uchtred and Adam his heir.

The priory of Wetheral had five tenements in Bolton of the yearly rent in the whole of 2*l* 11*s* 8*d*.

And in the year 1326, an inquisition was taken in St. Laurence's church in Appleby, before Robert de Southaic official of bishop Ross, upon this question, Who ought to furnish the chantry in the chapel of Bolton? The substance of the evidence was, that the ancestors of Sir John de Derwentwater founded the said chantry, and when there wanted vestments or other ornaments in the said chantry, the lord and his bailiff distrained the goods and chattels of the tenants of the prior of Wederhal in Bolton, and kept the same; and that on complaint thereof by the tenants to the prior, the prior distrained the vicar to find a chaplain; and that whatever might be between the prior and vicar, the lord and his bailiff kept the diftrefs, till all the faid things were provided. But whether the land was fpecially charged in the firft endowment to find the fame, the witneffes knew not *.

Before the augmentation by the governors of queen Anne's bounty, the revenues of the chapel were certified to amount to 4 *l* 10 *s* a year: Which did arife from 3 *l* a year paid by the vicar of Morland, and 30 *s* a year arifing from the produce of the chapel yard, furplice fees, and the tithes of garths in Bolton, and of chickens, eggs, ducks, hemp, and flax, throughout the lordfhip of Bolton. In the year 1754, this chapel received an augmentation of 200 *l* by lot, with which an eftate was purchafed in the parifh of Orton. And in the year 1761, the lady Gower gave 200 *l*, being part of a charity of her father Thomas earl of Thanet; whereupon other 200 *l* were obtained from the governors of the faid bounty of queen Anne; with which fum of 400 *l* an eftate was purchafed at Bolton.

Towards raifing a falary for a *fchoolmafter* at Bolton; James Hanfon of Bolton yeoman, in the year 1721, by his will gave 40 *l*. And Elizabeth Hanfon his widow 10 *l*. Jofeph Railton of London, by deed in the year 1762, gave 40 *l*. William Bownefs of Bolton, by deed in 1762, gave 50 *l*. And Michael Richardfon of Suthamftead Abbots and Suthamftead Banifter in Berkfhire, D.D. by his deed in 1765, gave 50 *l*. in all 190 *l*. The intereft thereof to be applied to the ufe of a fchoolmafter.

IX. BULEY.

Eaftward from Bolton, and about a mile and an half weft from Appleby, is a pleafant feat belonging to the bifhop of Carlifle, called Buley castle, on the fouth fide of Eden, oppofite to Crackenthorp. It was formerly controverted, but is now agreed to be in Morland parifh.

It was fo called, from its being built by, or belonging unto John Builly, whofe daughter and heir Idonea was married to the firft Robert de Veteripont.

It is now a mean ruinous building; but anciently the bifhops fometimes refided here. Several ordinations have been held at this place. And divers confirmations of charters and other publick acts are dated from hence. Perhaps at fuch times efpecially, when the bifhop was defirous to be removed out of the way of the Scotch incurfions.

* Regiftr. Wetheral.

PARISH

PARISH OF CLIBURN.

CLIBURN, *Cleburn*, *Cleyburn*, seems to derive the name from its situation. *Burn* is a rivulet or brook. And there is in the soil here a course of *clay*, which discovers itself in the channel and banks of the rivulet called *Leeth*, which runs on the west side of the village, and falls into *Lyvennet* below Cliburn mill.

The parish is bounded on the east, south, and west, by the parish of Morland; and on the north, by the parishes of Lowther, Clifton, and Brougham; and contains about 36 families, all of the established church.

The church is dedicated to St. Cuthbert. It is a rectory, in the patronage of the bishop of Carlisle; rated in the king's books at 9*l* 1*s* 5½*d*: the clear yearly value, as certified to the governors of queen Anne's bounty, 40*l* 10*s*.

This, though it still continues a rectory, was appropriated to the abbey of St. Mary's York. And the reason why it continued a rectory most probably was, because the parish was so small, that the revenues thereof would do little more than maintain an incumbent to perform the duty. And this might be a reason why the advowson, on a dispute, was given up to the bishop of Carlisle, and a small pension only reserved to the abbey; for they could not both maintain a vicar, and receive any thing considerable for themselves.

The appropriation was early. By whom, hath not appeared to us. But it was confirmed by Athelwold first bishop of Carlisle, who came to the see in the reign of king Henry the first.

In the time of Walter Mauclerk, fourth bishop of Carlisle, the abbot and convent aforesaid, on an arbitration, were ordered to give up the perpetual advowson of the church of Cliburn, to the bishop and his successors.

And accordingly, in the year 1284, the said abbot and convent granted to Silvester bishop of Carlisle and his successors, the advowson of the church of Cliburn; Saving to the said abbey the usual pension *.

Which pension at first was 10*s* yearly; as appears from the acknowledgment of *Nicholas Malveysin*, rector of Cliburn about that time †.

In

* Universis Christi fidelibus, ad quos præsens scriptum pervenerit; Thomas abbas et conventus beatæ Mariæ Eborum salutem in Domino. Noverit universitas vestra, nos unanimi consensu capituli nostri dedisse et concessisse venerabili patri et domino Silvestro Dei gratia Karliolensi episcopo suisque successoribus, jus patronatus ecclesiæ de Cliburne; salvis nobis antiquis et consuetis pensionibus de eisdem. Et nos et successores nostri dicto episcopo et suis successoribus advocationem dictæ ecclesiæ contra omnes homines in perpetuum warrantizabimus. In cujus rei testimonium præsenti scripto sigillum capituli nostri duximus apponere. Datum apud Ebor' octavo Idus Maii, anno domini millesimo ducentesimo quadragesimo octavo. *(Regiſtr. Wetheral.)*

† Omnibus Christi fidelibus ad quorum notitiam præsens scriptum pervenerit; Nicolaus Malveysin, rector ecclesiæ de Cliburn, salutem æternam in domino. Noverit universitas vestra quod ego teneor solvere annuatim abbati et conventui sanctæ Mariæ Eborum et monachis de Wederhal decem solidos nomine pensionis prædictæ ecclesiæ de Cliburn, sc. medietatem ad Pentecosten, et medie-

In the year 1302, *Peter Tillioll* was collated by bishop Halton, with reservation of a pension of one mark of silver yearly, payable to the prior and convent of Wederal.

In 1309, *Simon de Laton* had the rectory, and was allowed to let it to farm, to enable him to pay his proportion of a subsidy granted by the spiritualty, for the relief of the holy land.

In 1317, one *John de Burdonne* was rector.

In the year 1342, one Sir *Henry de Resse* was rector of Cliburn; to whom a licence of absence was granted by the bishop.

In 1556, *Edward Knype* was presented to the rectory of Cliburn by king Philip and queen Mary, the bishoprick being then vacant. He was also rector of Warcop. And by his will, dated in 1574, he bequeathed a sum of money for the purchase of 20 nobles yearly for ever of quit rent, to be distributed amongst his poor relations and the poor parishioners of Warcop and Cliburn.

On the death of the said Edward Knype in the year following, *Richard Phaer* was collated by bishop Barnes.

In 1577, on the death of Richard Phaer, *Christopher Witton* was collated by bishop Story.

In 1587, Christopher Witton resigns, being to be collated to the rectory of Scaleby; and *William Meye*, M. A. (probably a relation of the bishop) was collated by bishop Meye.

On William Meye's death, in 1625, *Richard Fleming*, M. A. was collated by bishop Senhouse.

In 1639, on his death, *Timothy Tullie*, M. A. was collated by bishop Potter.

In 1673, on the cession of *John Ardrey* rector of Cliborn, *William Fenwick* was collated by bishop Rainbow.

In 1687, on the death of William Fenwick, *Nathanael Spooner* was collated by bishop Smith.

In 1688, on the cession of Nathanael Spooner, *Richard Shepherd* was collated by the same patron.

In 1739, on the death of Richard Shepherd, *Marmaduke Holme* was collated by bishop Fleming.

In 1760, on Marmaduke Holme's death, *Robert Stephenson* was collated by bishop Osbaldiston.

The *church*, in proportion to the extent of the parish, is very small.

The *parsonage house* is situate near adjoining to the churchyard. It is an old building, but in a pleasant situation, by the side of the Leeth.

The MANOR of Cliburn became early divided into CLIBURN TALEBOIS and CLIBURN HERVEY. *Cliburn Talebois* derived its name from the owners, a

tatem ad festum sancti Martini in hyeme. Et ad hoc fideliter faciendum sacramento meo me obligavi. In cujus rei testimonium præsenti scripto sigillum meum apposui. Hiis testibus; Magistris Roberto de Saham, Rogero Pepin, Johanne de Popelton, Gilberto de Lincoln, Waltero de Gaugy, Johanne Malet, Johanne de Yvetot, Henrico Teutonico, Roberto Rupe, T. de Karl' clerico, et aliis. *Id.*

branch probably of the ancient family of *Talebois* barons of Kendal. *Cliburn Hervey* seems also to have received its denomination from the owner; but it had gone out of that name before the commencement of any of our accounts.

In the 14 Ed. 1. in the partition of the Veteripont inheritance between the two daughters and coheirs of the last Robert, the homage and service of *Lucas Talebois* were assigned to Idonea the younger sister, for *Cliburn Talebois*.

In the 8 Ed. 2. *Lucas Talebois* held of *Robert de Clifford* one moiety of the manor of Cliburn; the wardship whereof was valued at 13*l* 6*s* 8*d*, and the cornage was 12*s* 4½*d*.

In the 43 Ed. 3. *Walter de Talebois* held the manor of Cliburn Talebois.

In the 15 Ric. 2. *Walter de Talebois* in like manner held the same.

Again, in the 10 Hen. 5. *Walter de Talebois* held the manor of Cliburn Talebois and also Kirkeber, by the cornage of 14*s* 4½*d*.

After this, we no further meet with the name of *Talebois*. It ended in a daughter *Elizabeth*, married to *Robert le Franceys* of Cliburn *; of an ancient family there; for in the 20 Ed. 1. there was one *John Franceys* of Cliburn, who was a juror at Appleby in a cause between the king and the abbot and convent of St. Mary's York, concerning the advowson of the two churches at Appleby.

The said *Robert* and *Elizabeth* had a son and heir *John le Franceys* de Clyburne.

How long this moiety continued further in the name of *Franceys* doth not appear. It became at length united (after the tenants had been most of them sold free by one or other of the intermediate lords) with the HERVEY moiety, which we proceed next to deduce.

In the 8 Ed. 2. by the inquisition *post mortem* of Robert de Clifford, the jurors find, that *Walter de Tylia*, *John de Staffoll*, and *Robert de Sourby* (trustees probably in a settlement) held a moiety of Cliburn, by the cornage of 7*s* 8½*d*.

In the 43 Ed. 3. *Robert de Cliburn* held the manor of Cliburn Hervey. Which *Robert* also at that time was lord of the manor of Bampton Cundale.

In the 7th and again in the 10th of Ric. 2. *Robert de Cliburn* was knight of the shire for Westmorland.

In the 15 Ric. 2. *Thomas* son of *John de Warthecopp* and *Margaret* his wife, widow of *John Cliburn*, as of the right of the said *Margaret*, held the manor of Cliburn Harvey; the reversion thereof, after the death of the said Margaret, to go to *Roland Cliburn* son and heir of the said John Cliburn and Margaret.

In the 34 Hen. 6. after the death of Thomas lord Clifford, one of the jurors upon the inquisition was *Roland Cliburn* esquire.

In the 23 Hen. 8. *Robert Cliburn* was arbitrator in a cause between Guy and Hugh Machel.

The next that we meet with was *Richard Cliburn* esquire; who repaired or rebuilt the hall in the reign of queen Elizabeth: as appears by the following

* Dugd. MS.

inscription over the hall door (which, by the way, is not an original composition, but borrowed as is usual among poets, from the inscription before mentioned, over the hall door at Newbiggin;)

Richard. Clebur. thus. they. did. me. cawle.
who. in. my. time. builded. this. haule.
1577.

Thomas Cliburn of Cliburn esquire, son and heir of Richard, married Frances daughter of Sir Richard Lowther of Lowther knight. And this is the last of the name of *Cliburn* that hath occurred to us. Not improbably, it ended, like most of the rest, in daughters.

The *hall* and manor, after passing through several hands, became mortgaged at last to Sir *John Lowther* of Lowther, surnamed *The Rich*; whose posterity still enjoy the same.

The arms of Cliburn are: Argent, a chief; and three chevronels brased; in bass, Sable.

Within this parish is a tenement, now belonging to Sir James Lowther baronet, called *Gilshaughlin* (from rubbish shoveling down), where the market was held in the year 1598, when the plague raged at Appleby.

Belonging to this parish is *Winderwath*, though intercepted from it by the upper part of Whinfell forest, which is in the parish of Brougham; so as Winderwath is no where contiguous to the rest of the parish. It was sold by George earl of Cumberland to one of the *Brathwaites* of Warcop; who sold it to Mr. *Wyvil*, in whose posterity it still continues.

PARISH OF BAMPTON.

I. *Parish of Bampton.*
II. *Bampton Patric.*
III. *Bampton Cundale.*

I. PARISH OF BAMPTON.

THERE is a Bampton in Cumberland, which Mr. Denton calls *Villata Bembæ* or *Bombæ*, which seemeth to argue that the place hath received its name from the owner. And to this purpose it is remarkable, that the little hamlet in Bampton, next adjoining to the church, is to this day called *Bombey*.

This parish is bounded on the East by the parishes of Lowther, Shap, and Morland; on the South, by the parish of Shap; on the West, by the parishes of of Barton and Askham; and on the North, by the parishes of Askham and Lowther: and contains about 140 families, all of the church of England, one only excepted.

The whole parish is but one township or constablewick, and probably of ancient time hath been but one manor, when it received the name of Bampton. But so early as any account hath occurred to us, Bampton was divided into two parts, *Bampton Patric* and *Bampton Cundale*; both so called from their respective proprietors.

Within Bampton there is a place called *Knipe*, which is often spoken of as distinct from Bampton; as where it is said *Bampton and Knipe Patrick*, *Bampton and Knipe Cundale*. *Knipe* is so called from its situation. It signifies the top of an hill or rock. The Saxon word is *knap*. In the gospel, where the Jews led our Saviour to the *brow of the hill* whereon their city was built (in order to cast him down headlong), the Saxon expresseth it by the *knap of the munt*. The Islandic word is *gnype*. *Nab* is a word of the like derivation, signifying the top and outermost verge of a steep hill. Thus, opposite to Knipe, towards the east, we find *Hardendale Nab*.

The *church* of Bampton is dedicated to St. Patric. It is a vicarage in the patronage of the crown (ever since the dissolution of monasteries); and is rated in the king's books at *7l 5s*; the clear yearly value, as returned to the governors of queen Anne's bounty, *8l 13s 4d*. And in the year 1750 it was certified at *33l*.

It was appropriated to the abbey of Shap, about the year 1170.—Amongst the writings at Crackenthorp hall, there is a confirmation of this appropriation, together with that of the church of Shap, to the said abbey, by Robert bishop of Carlisle, in the year 1263: With a grant to the abbot and convent, in respect of the smallness of their revenues, that they may officiate in the said churches by two or three of their own canons, one of whom to be presented to the bishop as vicar, to be answerable to the bishop in spirituals; and another to be answerable to the abbot and convent in temporals. Yet so, that in each church they have one secular chaplain, to hear confessions, and execute such other matters, as cannot so properly be done by their own regular canons. Dated at *The Rose* (apud la Rose) on the morrow of St. John Baptist, 1263. And the confirmation thereof by the prior and chapter of Carlisle bears date on the day following *.—In 1287, the same was confirmed, in like form, by Ralph de Irton bishop of Carlisle.

In the year 1300, *Roger de Barton* was instituted to the vicarage of Bampton, on a presentation by the abbot and convent of Heppe; and the vicarage was taxed at *8l 6s 8d*, wherewith the vicar was to maintain himself and one secular priest: the abbot and convent to sustain all other charges ordinary and extraordinary, and subsidies granted or to be granted. To make up which sum of *8l 6s 8d*, the vicar was to receive all the obventions, altarages, and small tithes; except the tithes of wool and lamb and corn.

* Machel.

In

In 1309, on the resignation of Roger de Barton, the prior and convent present another of their canons, *John de Appleby*.

In 1358, one *John de Hauville* was vicar of Bampton; on whose resignation, the prior and convent present *John de Merland*, who is instituted thereupon.

In the year 1362, *John de Askeby* was vicar of Bampton. By his will he bequeathed his body to be buried in the quire of St. Patric of Bampton; and gave also 2*s* to the chapel of St. Thomas of the church of Bampton. Of which chapel or oratory we have found no footsteps remaining.

Three years after this, we find one *Gilbert Rakit* vicar.

In 1369, *John de Bampton* was instituted, on the presentation of the abbot and convent.

After the death of the said John in 1379, the bishop issues a commission, in favour of *William de Wicliff* then vicar, to inquire of such dilapidations as the executors of John may be liable to.

In 1382, on the resignation of William de Wicliff, *William de Sutton* canon of Heppe was presented and instituted.

In the year 1539, there is a lease of the corn tithes of the parish of Bampton, from the abbot and convent of Heppe, to Sir *Edward Harper* vicar of Bampton.

In 1565, *John Harrison* was presented by Richard Salkeld esquire, by grant from the abbot and convent before their dissolution.

Two years after this, on the death of John Harrison, institution was given to *Roland Winter*, presented by queen Elizabeth.

In 1580, on Roland Winter's death, *Christopher Symson* clerk was instituted on the same title.

On the death of Christopher Symson, in 1586, *Barnabas Scott* had the like presentation and institution.

In 1641, on the death of one *James Atkinson* vicar of Bampton, *Matthew Wilkinson*, M. A. was presented by king Charles the first, and instituted thereupon.

In 1672, *Thomas Knott* was presented by king Charles the second.

In 1698, on Thomas Knott's death, *Thomas Wearing*, M. A. was instituted on a presentation by king William.

In 1742, on Thomas Wearing's death, *William Stephenson* was instituted on a like presentation under the great seal.

In 1763, on William Stephenson's death, *William Langhorn* was instituted on a like presentation.

In 1775, on William Langhorn's death, *Thomas Kilner* was in like manner presented and instituted.

The *church* of Bampton is a neat elegant building; erected, where the old church formerly stood, in the year 1726.

Thomas Gibson, M. D. who was born at High Knipe in this parish, gave 200*l* to this church, whereby to procure an augmentation by the governors of queen Anne's bounty; which was laid out in a purchase of lands at Rossel Bridge

Bridge in the parish of Kendal. The said Dr. Gibson was fellow of the college of physicians, and physician general to the army. He was author of the book intitled Gibson's Anatomy. He married to his second wife a daughter of Richard Cromwell son of Oliver.

The *vicarage house* was rebuilt at the expence of the celebrated and very learned Dr. Edmund Gibson, bishop of London, a native also of High Knipe aforesaid, and nephew of the said Dr. Thomas Gibson. Which Edmund caused a monument to be erected in the church in memory of his father and mother, with this modest plain inscription:

Memoriæ Sacrum
Edmundi et Janæ Gibson,
Charissimorum Parentum,
Monumentum hoc posuit
Edmundus Episcopus Londinensis,
Anno Domini MDCCXLIII.

At the east end of the church on the outside is the following inscription:

M. S.
Thomæ Jackson, in vicinia nati,
Qui Scholam hanc, cui circiter annos
XLIV vigilantissime præfuit,
commendavit adeo,
ut non tenuis fuerit gloria
inter Bamptonias educatos numerari.
Utrumque docuit Gibsonum,
alterum Cl. Lincolniæ præsulem *,
alterum Coll. Reg. Oxon. præpositum †,
et aliquos plurimos, qui patriæ simul
et scholæ sunt ornamenta.
Obiit pridie Kal. Junii,
An: Dom: MDCCXIX.
Ætatis suæ LXIV.

At the other end of the church, on the outside, is the epitaph of Mr. Wearing the vicar, written by himself, leaving only a blank for the day and year of his death: In whose time the church and school were rebuilt.

Panditur elegantius denuo sanctuarium Dei:
Resurgunt ædes gratiis musisque sacratæ:
Instaurata omnia,
Thoma Wearing Vicario.
Vix dotatam, cum dirutam; tum auctam, ter amabilem
Unam hanc, unice, confarreavit ecclesiam,
Nec impar, nec appetentior, ille minister:

* The aforesaid Dr. Edmund Gibson, first bishop of Lincoln, afterwards of London.

† Dr. John Gibson, a native also of High Knipe.

Prisca

Prisca fide, patriis moribus, simplici munditia.
Bibliorum prius oraculis rite sciscitatis,
Liturgiæ, ceu Palladii, ad aras usque tenax;
Rationem Œconomiæ qualem qualem editurus,
Quod feliciter vortat, excessit:
Sicut egens, multos autem locupletans,
Tanquam nihil habens, et omnia possidens.
Ilicet, age, aude, ingredere actutum, mi tu,
Hac itur ad cœlum;
Nusquam alibi requies:
Ut simus potiundo, faxit Deus.
Natus 7 March 1647: Inductus 25 March 1699:
Denatus 30 August 1742.

In the year 1623, *Thomas Sutton*, D. D. a native of this parish erected a free grammar *school* at Bampton, and endowed the same with the sum of 500*l*, which was laid out in a purchase of tithes in that neighbourhood: Twelve of the principal parishioners and neighbours to be governors of the said school: The master to be a person in holy orders, and a licensed preacher.

In the year 1665, By indenture between Sir John Lowther of Lowther baronet, John Dalston of Acorn Bank esquire, Thomas Sandford of Askham esquire, George Fothergill of Orton clerk, John Bradley of Knipe gentleman, and Christopher Teasdale of Sockbridge gentleman, of the one part; and Richard Walker, Edmund Cleburne, Henry Nicholson, Robert Wright, Thomas Jackson, and Richard Mounsey, of the parish of Bampton, yeomen, of the other part: It is covenanted and agreed, that all the said parties shall be governors of the said school, and the six last named shall be trustees of the revenues, who shall nominate others when reduced to three, to whom the six first named or their heirs respectively shall convey the said tithes in trust as aforesaid; and when three of the first named shall die, their survivors shall in like manner chuse others: That the schoolmaster shall be a licensed preacher, or shall by covenant promise to preach or procure one to preach in the parish church once every 14 days, if he be in health: That the schoolmaster when chosen shall covenant by indenture, that if he be convicted of drunkenness, incontinency, or any other notorious crime, or be absent from the school above a month in a year without leave of the major part of the governors, or be so negligent, or of so bad deserving, that in the judgment of the major part of the said governors he be not fit to be schoolmaster; that then his election shall be void, and he shall have no longer any stipend there.

William Stephenson, rector of Laxton in Nottinghamshire, who also was born in this parish, gave by his will 150*l* to the church and school.

II. BAMP-

II. BAMPTON PATRIC.

In the moſt early account that we have met with of the MANOR of Bampton, we find the ſame divided into moieties as aforeſaid, diſtinguiſhed by the names of *Bampton Patric* and *Bampton Cundale*.

BAMPTON PATRIC ſeems to have received its ſurname from the owner *Patricius de Culwen*, who lived in the reign of king Henry the ſecond; from whom is deſcended the family of the Curwens of Workington.

This *Patricius* or *Patrick de Culwen* was younger ſon of *Thomas*, ſon of *Thomas*, ſon of *Goſpatrick*, ſon of *Orme*, younger ſon of *Ketel*, ſon of *Eldred*, ſon of *Ivo de Taleboís* baron of Kendal in the time of William the conqueror.

The elder branch of the family, from *Ketel*'s elder ſon *Gilbert*, continued the deſcent in the direct line of the barons of Kendal. From *Orme* the younger ſon aforeſaid deſcended the family of which we now ſpeak.

Orme married *Gunilda* daughter of *Goſpatric* earl of Dunbar: By whom he had a ſon called by his grandfather's name *Goſpatric*; and he was the firſt of the family who ſettled at Workington, by an exchange made between him and his uncle William de Lancaſtre baron of Kendal, of Middleton in Weſtmorland, for Lamplugh and Workington in Cumberland.—It is not impoſſible but that Bampton Patrick might receive its name from this *Goſpatric*. For it is to be obſerved, that very frequently of ancient time *Goſpatric* was written *Coſpatric*. Cos may ſeem to have been an abbreviation of *Comes*. And it is no abſurdity to ſuppoſe, in thoſe illiterate ages, that this *Cos Patricius* (Earl Patrick) of Dunbar, might eaſily degenerate into *Goſpatric*.

This *Goſpatric* ſon of *Orme* had a ſon and heir *Thomas*, who founded Shap abbey.

Thomas was ſucceeded by his ſon *Thomas*; who dying without iſſue, *Patric* his younger brother, of whom we now ſpeak, ſucceeded to the inheritance.

This *Patric*, during the life of his elder brother Thomas, had given to him, by his father, *Culwen* in Galloway, who thereupon took the name of *Patricius de Culwen*; and, Workington in Cumberland being their principal ſeat, thence came the name of the *Culwens de Workington*. Which name, in proceſs of time, degenerated into *Curwen*; for our anceſtors, who were a military people, delighted in rugged and harſh pronunciations: hence they introduced in like manner the letter *r* into the ſound of the word *Colonel*.

In the 8 Ed. 2. after the death of Robert de Clifford, the inquiſition finds, that *Gilbert de Culwen* [brother and heir of Thomas, ſon of the ſaid Patric] held of the ſaid Robert, on the day on which he died, *Bampton Patric* and *Gnype Patric*, and alſo the manor of *Hepp*; the wardſhip whereof, when it ſhould happen, was worth 52 *l*, the cornage 26 *s* 7 *d*.

Again, in the 43 Ed. 3. *Gilbert de Culwen* [grandſon of the ſaid *Gilbert*] held of the Cliffords the manor of *Gnypp*; and the ſaid *Gilbert de Culwen*, the abbot of *Hepp*, and *Robert de Cliburne*, held the manor of Bampton Patric, by homage and fealty, and the cornage of 13 *s* 4 *d*.

In the 15 Ric. 2. *Gilbert de Culwen* and *Robert de Cliborne* held Bampton Patryke and Knipe Patryke, by the cornage of 15*s* 9*d*.

In the 10 Hen. 5. *Christopher de Curwen* and *John de Cliburn* held the manor of Bampton Patric and Knype Patric, by the cornage of 15*s* 10*d*.

In the 1 Hen. 6. Sir *Christopher Curwen*, knight, purchased certain lands at Bampton Skewes; one of the witnesses to which purchase was *Edward Culwen* esquire.

By an inquisition in the 19 Hen. 7. it was found, that Bampton Patric and Knipe Patrick were holden by *Christopher Culwen* by knights service, to wit, by homage, fealty, and scutage, namely, for Bampton Patric, when scutage runs at ten pounds, 10*s*; and cornage 13*s* 4*d*: for Knipe Patric, when scutage runs at ten pounds, 4*s*; and cornage 17*s*. That the said *Christopher Culwen* died on the 6 Apr. 14 Hen. 7. And that *Thomas* his son and heir was of the age of 30 years at his father's death.

In the 18 Hen. 8. the heir of *Thomas Curwen* knight and *Thomas Cliburne* held the same.

Finally, we find the same in the name and family of *Warwick*; of whom *Francis Warwick* esquire sold the manor to the present owner Edward Hassel esquire; reserving the demesne, of which he died seised in 1772, and was succeeded by his sister Mrs. *Anne Warwick*.

III. BAMPTON CUNDALE.

We come next to the other part of Bampton, which belonged to the family *de Cundale*. Where that *dale* is, from whence this family received their denomination, hath not occurred to us. But that they communicated this their name to *Bampton Cundale* there can be no doubt.

So early as the reign of king Henry the second, we find *Henry de Cundale* (amongst other principal men of note) witness to a compromise between the abbot of Byland and others, concerning the boundaries of the manor of Bleatarn belonging to the said abbot and convent.

And in the 13th of king John, *Henry de Cundall* was one of the witnesses to the grants of the first Robert de Veteripont to Shap abbey.

In the 8 Ed. 2. after the death of Robert lord Clifford, *Henry de Cundale* held Bampton Cundale and Gnype; the wardship whereof, when it should happen, was worth 13*l* 6*s* 8*d*; the cornage 15*s* 3*d*.

In the 43 Ed. 3. the abbot of *Hepp*, *William de Hornby*, *Gilbert de Culwen*, and *Robert de Cliburne*, (probably as trustees) held the manor of Bampton Cundale, by the cornage of 15*s* 11*d*.—For now it seems to have gone off with a daughter of Cundale, married to Cliburn. For in the 15 Ric. 2. after the death of Roger de Clifford, the inquisition finds, that *Robert de Cliburn* and *Margaret* his wife, as in right of the said *Margaret*, held of the said Roger the manor of Bampton Cundale, by the cornage of 15*s* 3*d*.

In the 10 Hen. 5. *John de Clyburne* held the same.

In the 31 Hen. 6. *Roland Clyburn* held Bampton Cundale and Knipe, by homage and fealty and 15*s* 3*d* cornage, owing also for the same wardship, marriage, relief, and suit to the county court. And afterwards, in the same year, *John Cliburn* held the same: Which heretofore (as the inquisition sets forth) were held by *Ralph de Cundal*.

In the 19 Hen. 7. it was found by inquisition, that *John Clyborne* held Bampton Cundale of Henry lord Clifford, by homage, fealty, and scutage; when scutage runs at ten pounds, 10*s*; when more, more; when less, less: and the cornage of 15*s* 3*d*. That the said *John* died 8 Aug. 4 Hen. 7. And that *Thomas Clyborne* his son and heir was then 22 years of age.

In the 18 Hen. 8. *Thomas Clyborne* held the same, by the like services.

In the 1 and 2 Ph. and M. *Richard Clibburn* held the same, of Henry earl of Cumberland.

Last of all, this, like many other neighbouring places, came by purchase to the house of Lowther.

Within the bounds of this parish is a large lake called *Hawes-water* well replenished with sundry kinds of fish: Nigh unto which is *Measand* school, endowed by *Richard Wright* formerly of *Measand*, with the profits of an estate now let at about 24 *l per annum*, out of which is deducted yearly about 3 *l* for finding books for poor scholars and other out-payments.

PARISH OF SHAP.

I. *Parish and church of Shap.*
II. *Abbey and manor of Shap.*
III. *Rosgill.*
IV. *Thornthwaite.*
V. *Mardale.*
VI. *Swindale.*
VII. *Mosedale.*
VIII. *Wet Sleddale.*
IX. *Hardendale and Wasdale.*

I. PARISH AND CHURCH OF SHAP.

SHAP was invariably in ancient times written *Hep* or *Heppe*, most probably from the fruit of the bramble which still bears that name. By the common people that fruit is still pronounced *cheap*, from whence the transition to *Shap* is not difficult. Nor doth it at all derogate from this account, that there are at present few shrubs of that kind there; for the face of the country is totally altered since those ancient times; for all was then forest and wood, even so late down as the foundation of the abbey.

The pariſh of Shap is bounded on the Eaſt by the pariſhes of Morland and Croſby Ravenſworth; on the South, by the pariſhes of Croſby Ravenſworth and Orton; on the Weſt, by the pariſhes of Kendal, Bampton, and Barton; and on the North, by the pariſhes of Bampton, Lowther, and Morland: And contains about 182 families; all of the church of England except one or two.

The church is dedicated to St. Michael the archangel; as appears from the will of one Sir Thomas Tipping prieſt, bearing date in the year 1540 *.

It is a vicarage, rated in the 36 Hen. 8. at 8*l* 15*s* 7½*d*. The clear yearly value, as certified to the governors of queen Anne's bounty, 6*l*.

It hath ſince received an allotment of 200 *l* from the ſaid governors, wherewith an eſtate was purchaſed in Cumberland; and other 200 *l* in conjunction with 200*l* given by the counteſs dowager Gower, with which an eſtate was purchaſed in Stavely in the county of Weſtmorland.

About the year 1170, Thomas ſon of Coſpatric, founder of the abbey, gave the whole rectory of this church to the monks there; which was confirmed by biſhop Bernard, the portion of the vicarage to the ſaid church, conſiſting in the altarage, only excepted.

And amongſt the Blenkinſop writings at Helbeck, there was a confirmation of the churches of Hep and Bampton to the ſaid abbey, by Thomas de Veteripont biſhop of Carliſle, dated at Buley, on Sunday next before the nativity of the bleſſed virgin Mary, 1256. With a very fine oval ſeal two inches broad, with a biſhop in his mitre and robes, the right hand erect with a finger pointed up, and the left hand holding a croſier, circumſcribed with theſe words " Sigillum Thomæ Dei gracia Karleolenſis Epiſcopi †."

And the ſame were again confirmed in 1263, by the then biſhop and prior of Carliſle; with a grant to the abbot and convent to ſerve in the ſaid churches by two or three of their own canons, one of whom to be inſtituted as vicar, and another to be anſwerable to the ſaid abbey in temporals.

In 1295, on the death of fryer *Walter de Ditton* one of their canons, the abbot and convent *Vallis Magdalenæ de Hepp* preſent fryer *William de Kirkedal*, another of their canons, to the vacant vicarage of Hepp, who was thereupon inſtituted.

In 1319, *Thomas de Wynton*, canon of Hepp, was preſented and inſtituted.

In 1333, the abbot and canons had licence from biſhop Kirkby, to remove the body of Iſabella wife of William de Langleigh de Appleby, their pariſhioner, famed for having miracles done by it, to ſome proper place within the church or churchyard of Hepp; that the reliques might be reverenced by the people, with freer and greater devotion.

In 1342, on the reſignation of fryer *John de Richmund* vicar of Hepp, the abbot and convent preſent the abbot *John de Langeton*.

In 1397, Robert abbot of Hepp appealed to the pope, againſt Richard Pyttes vicar general of the biſhop of Carliſle, who had ſequeſtred the profits of the pariſh church of Hepp; alledging, that the ſaid benefice, except only

* Machel. † Idem.

the

the altarage ſettled on the vicar, was appropriated to him the ſaid abbot and his convent, and had been ſo for time whereof the memory of man was not to the contrary.

In 1514, the abbot and convent of Shap ſue for an half burgage in Cockermouth, bought by *Alexander Ynglish* late vicar of Shap, with money of which he had defrauded the ſaid monaſtery.

In 1574, after the death of Sir *John Whinfell*, vicar of Shap; Sir *John Brockbank* was collated, on a lapſe, by biſhop Barnes.

This vicarage being ſo very ſmall, few perſons have been willing to be at the expence of inſtitution and induction; but it hath been generally ſuffered to go in lapſe, and ſupplied by curates under a ſequeſtration. But having received augmentations by the governors of queen Anne's bounty, it hath ſince become neceſſary to have vicars canonically appointed. Accordingly, in 1759, William Langhorne clerk was preſented under the great ſeal; and on his death in 1775, James Holme clerk was preſented by Sir James Lowther baronet, and inſtituted thereupon.—The aforeſaid augmentations were, 200*l* which came by lot, wherewith a purchaſe was made of houſes and lands at Seathwaite in the pariſh of Croſthwaite, and two cattle gates on Seathaller or Wad-Fell; and 400*l*, whereof 200*l* was given by lady Gower, with which an eſtate was purchaſed in Stavely.

The *church* is a pretty large ancient building; with a ſquare tower, and three bells.

At the end of the ſouth ile, is a chapel or burying-place belonging to Roſgill hall.

II. ABBEY AND MANOR OF SHAP.

The ABBEY of Shap was transferred hither from *Preſton* in Kendale; perhaps for the ſake of the ſituation, which is in a lonely vale, on the weſt ſide of the river Lowther, about a mile weſt from the church of Shap, well adapted to the purpoſes of retirement and contemplation.

Thomas ſon of *Coſpatric* by his charter without date (which was about the year 1119, in the 20 Hen. 1.) gave to God and St. Mary Magdalene and the canons of Preſton of the order of Præmonſtratenſes, a portion of his lands at Preſton in Kendale, to build a manſion for the ſaid canons, to wit, his whole demeſne park there, and other lands, ſpecifying the reſpective metes and bounds. He grants to them alſo as much of his woods as they had a mind to take, and alſo the bark of ſuch wood as they ſhould cut down, without the view of his foreſters, and maſtage alſo for their hogs, and the tithe of his pannage: And liberty to grind at his mill moulter free, whenſoever they ſhould come, and as ſoon as the mill ſhould be empty *.

After-

* Univerſis ſanctæ matris eccleſiæ filiis, tam præſentibus quam futuris, qui has literas viſuri ſunt, vel audituri, Thomas filius Coſpatricii, ſalutem. Sciatis, quod ego dedi et conceſſi, et hac præſenti charta mea confirmavi, Deo et ſanctæ Mariæ Magdalenæ et canonicis de Preſton, qui ſunt de ordine

Afterwards, the ſame *Thomas* ſon of *Coſpatric*, on removing the ſaid monaſtery to Shap, granted to God and the church of St. Mary Magdalene of the vale of Magdalene, and the canons of the order of Præmonſtratenſes ſerving God there, all that his land which was *Karl* [that is, as it ſeemeth, which had belonged to his *carls* or huſbandmen, tenants at will] by theſe bounds; from the ford of *Carlwath*, aſcending by the river on the ſouth as far as *Langeſhabeck*, and ſo aſcending by *Langeſhabeck* to the road which comes from Kendale, and ſo following that road northwards till it come to *Staniraſe* nigh *Raſland*; and ſo by that road unto *Raſate*; and ſo going down on the other ſide of the hill, to the great ſtone where they were wont to ſtand to watch the deer as they paſſed [ubi homines ſolebant facere *leſtablie*; *ſtable-ſtand* was, where the men ſtood with bows or dogs ready to ſhoot or courſe; and tenants were in ſome places bound, at the ſummons of the lord, to aſſemble *ad ſtabliam faciendam*, which was called the *buckſtall*]; and ſo going down to the river *Lowther*, and further as far as the diviſion of *Roſgill* towards the eaſt; and ſo all along ſouthward by the top of the hill of *Creſkeld*, and ſo to *Alinbalike*. He grants to them alſo the vale, with *bruſh-wood* [which, by the way, countenanceth the notion of Heppe receiving its name from thence] in the eaſtern part over againſt their own, ſtretching along by the top of the hill to the houſe which formerly was *William King*'s, and ſo to the land which belonged to *Matthew de Hepp*, and ſo going down weſtward to the ſaid ford of *Karlwath*. He alſo grants to them paſture in common with his tenants at *Raſat*, and paſture at *Thamboord*, and at *Swindale* on both ſides (to the top of *Binbarb* on one ſide, and on the other ſide beyond *Thengeheved*), for 60 cows, 20 mares to run in the woods, and 500 ſheep, with their young till the age of three years; and

ordine Præmonſtratenſi, in liberam, puram, et perpetuam eleemoſynam, pro ſalute animæ et ſponſæ meæ, et omnium anteceſſorum meorum, unam portionem terræ meæ in Preſton in Kendale, ad faciendum quandam manſionem canonicorum, videlicet, totum dominicum parcum meum ſubtus Lackſloſt et in Lackſloſt, uſque viam quæ venit de Preſton Uthered; et inde ſequendo viam, uſque ad viam quæ venit de Holme; et ita ſequendo viam de Holme uſque ad ſicam qui venit de Haſildmire; et per ipſum ſicum uſque ad aquam quæ eſt diviſa inter duas Preſtonas; et ita aſcendendo uſque ad prænominatam viam de Lackſloſt. Præterea, dedi eis totam terram ſubtus viam de Wathſudden uſque Stainbrigge, et totam terram de Stainbrigge uſque ad Brackenthwait, ſicut ſylva dividit et planum, et ita uſque ad terram Ricardi filii Sigith, et ſic ad viam quæ venit de Stainbrigge uſque ad diviſam de Farleton; id eſt, totam terram quæ fuit Michaelis filii Helenæ; et ita ſequendo diviſam de Farleton, uſque in diviſam inter duas Preſtonas; et ita aſcendendo uſque ad prædictam viam de Wathſudden, excepto dimidio prato de Mireſbrigge, et decem acris apud Siggethwait, *ad ſalum eorum*. Et totam terram de ſurſum Wathſudden, ſcilicet ubi capella fuit infirmorum. Habebunt etiam de boſco meo, quantum capere voluerint, et nunc habuerint, ſine viſu foreſtariorum meorum; et cortices lignorum quæ preciduerint, ipſorum erunt. Concedo etiam eis liberam communiam infra metas de Preſton, cum omnibus aliis aiſamentis et libertatibus, quæ pertinent ad prædictam villam de Preſton, in boſco et in plano, in viis et in ſemitis, et in aquis et in molendinis; et paſturam porcorum ſuorum, ſive *plenagiorum*, et decimam pannagii mei. Et molent ad molendinum meum ſine multura, quando venerint, et tam [cito quam] mezca fuerit evacuata: *Et aquam proprium habuerint molendinarium, ad meum molendinum ceſſabunt hominum prænominatum.* Volo quod prædicti canonici habeant et teneant eadem in pace et plenarie et honorifice, in liberam, puram, et perpetuam eleemoſynam, ſine omni ſeculari ſervicio, conſuetudine, et exactione. Et ego et hæredes mei warrantizabimus eis hanc donationem, contra omnes homines in perpetuum. Hiis teſtibus, &c. 2 Dugd. Monaſt. 594. From an old copy then in the poſſeſſion of Sir James Bellingham.——Note, the words printed in Italics ſeem to have been miſcopied, being not (to us) intelligible.

for

for five yoke of oxen: And wood also for the abbey, for timber, fire, hedging, and other necessaries, without the controul of his foresters *.

This Thomas died Dec. 7. 1152, and was buried in this abbey.

Thomas, son of the said Thomas, confirmed his father's grants. Which Thomas son of Thomas married a sister, as it seemeth, of the first Robert de Veteripont. For after the death of this Thomas son of Thomas, his widow Johanna de Veteripont gave nine acres of land in the vill of Heppe to the abbot and canons of the vale of Magdalene at Heppe.

Afterwards, in the 13th year of king John, *Robert de Veteripont*, being then come into possession of the barony of Westmorland by the favour of that king, confirmed the aforesaid grant of Shap, and the grant also of Renegill, which had been made to the said abbey by Maud his mother and Ivo his brother; and he granted further to the said abbey the grange of Milneburn, and the tithes of all his mills in Westmorland, and of all the renewal of beasts in his forests in Westmorland taken by him or his men, by bows, dogs, or otherwise †.

John

* Universis sanctæ matris ecclesiæ filiis, præsentibus et futuris, chartam istam visuris vel audituris, Thomas filius Cospatricii sempiternam in domino salutem: Noverit universitas vestra, me dedisse, concessisse, et hac mea præsenti charta confirmasse, Deo et ecclesiæ beatæ Mariæ Magdalenæ de valle Magdalenæ, et canonicis Præmonstratensis ordinis ibidem Deo servientibus, totam terram quæ fuit Karl, scilicet per has divisas; de vado de Karlwath, ascendendo per Lowther apud Austrum, usque ad Langeshabeck, et sic ascendendo per Langeshabeck, usque ad semitam quæ venit de Kendale, et sic sequendo semitam illam versus aquilonem, usque dum veniat ad Stanirase juxta Rasland: Et ita per semitam illam usque ad Rasate, et sic descendendo extra montem, usque ad magnum lapidem ubi homines solebant facere Lestablie; et ita descendendo usque in Lowther, et sic ascendendo per Lowther, et ultra, usque ad divisas de Rosgill penes orientem, de longo in longum apud Austrum per supercilium montis de Creskeld, et sic usque in Alinbalike. Præterea, dedi eis vallem cum brusula in orientali parte contra suam, tendens in longum per supercilium montis usque ad domum quæ fuit quondam Willielmi King, et ita usque ad terram quæ fuit Matthei de Hepp, et sic descendendo versus occidentem, usque ad prædictum vadum de Karlwath. Dedi etiam eis communem pasturam cum hominibus meis qui manent in Rasat, et pasturam in Thambord, et in Swindale ex otraque parte, usque ad supercilium montis desuper Bimbarh, et ex altera parte de Swindale, ultra Thengeheved, ex utraque parte, ubi voluerint, et opus fuerit, possint die ac nocte, infra dictam pasturam moram facere, et ad abbatiam, et ad vaccariam suam, cum necesse fuerit, ire, et redire, cum libero introitu et exitu. Hanc prædictam pasturam dedi eis et concessi, scilicet, vaccis sexaginta, et equabus sylvestribus viginti, et quinque centum ovibus, cum sequela trium annorum, et quinque carucatis boum. Præterea dedi eis turbariam, et petariam, et quareriam, ubicunque invenire poterint in territorio villæ de Heppe, et viam liberam, eundo et redeundo ad turbariam et petariam et quareriam prædictam, et ad abbathiam suam. Dedi etiam eis licentiam capere nemora, ad abbathiam suam, in bosco meo, ad ædificandum, et comburendum, et claudendum, ubi melius voluerint, et invenire poterint, et cætera necessaria, sine visu forestariorum, cum omnibus communibus, easiamentis, et libertatibus, prædictæ villæ de Heppe pertinentibus. Hæc omnia supradicta dedi Deo et prædictis canonicis, habenda et tenenda, in puram, liberam, et perpetuam eleemosynam, pro salute animæ meæ, et sponsæ meæ Graciæ, et hæredum meorum, et omnium antecessorum et successorum meorum. Et ego et hæredes mei warrantizabimus omnia supradicta prædictis canonicis, contra omnes gentes imperpetuum. Hiis testibus, &c.——2 Dugd. Mon. 594.

† Omnibus sanctæ matris ecclesiæ filiis, præsentibus et futuris, Robertus de Veteriponte, salutem. Noverit universitas vestra, me dedisse et confirmasse Deo et beatæ Mariæ Magdalenæ de valle Magdalene, &c. sedem et locum prædictæ vallis Magdalenæ, in territorio villæ de Heppe, cum omnibus pertinentiis et rebus suis, quæ continentur in chartis Thomæ filii Cospatricii, et in chartis Thomæ filii Thomæ filii sui, quas de prædictis omnibus habent: Et totam villam de Renegill, cum omnibus pertinentiis

John de Veteripont, son of the said Robert, gave the hospital of *St. Nicholas* nigh Appleby to the said abbey; whose grant was confirmed by Walter Mauclerk bishop of Carlisle, so as the said abbot and convent should maintain three lepers in the said hospital for ever.

The same *John de Veteripont* gave to the canons of Hepp, a parcel of his demesne land in the field of Knock Salcock.

Robert de Veteripont, Son of John, gave to the said abbey four marks yearly out of his rents at Ascome and Milneburn: And there is a writ in the 19 Ed. 2. setting forth the said grant, and that the said rent had come into the hands of the king by reason of the forfeiture of Roger de Clifford, and therefore commands the king's constable of the castle of Appleby to pay the arrears thereof to the said abbey.

Ralph son of *Adam de Bothelton* gave certain lands at *Bolton*, as did also *Adam* son of *William de Derwentwater*, *Uctred* son of *Simon de Bothelton*, *Henry de Threlkeld*, and *Walter* son of *Thomas de Bothelton*, divers other lands there, by several grants.

They had also divers possessions at *Gargrave* in *Craven*.

They had the appropriated church of *Johnston* in *Annandale*; which was confirmed to them by *Edward Baliol* king of Scots, in the year 1332.

Roland de Thornburgh granted to them a messuage in Kendale; which was confirmed to them by *William* son of *Walter de Lindesay*.

Adam son of *Hughtred* gave lands in *Hegnyp* (i. e. *High Knipe*).

Sir *Robert de Askeby* knight gave several parcels of land at *Ormeshead* †.

William de Hoff, by deed without date, gave to the said abbey a messuage in *Skiterigate* in Appleby.

In the 31 Hen. 3. *Thomas* son of *Henry de Redeman*, for the health of his soul and of the souls of his father and mother and ancestors and posterity, confirms to the said abbey, two oxgangs of land in the vill of *Apelby*, which *Norman* his brother bequeathed with his body to the said abbey: Which said lands *Norman* had by the gift of John de Veteripont; and into which he the said *Thomas*, after the death of *Norman*, had entry as next heir. Rendring for the same to him the said Thomas, his heirs and assigns, three barbed ar-

nentiis suis, &c. sicut etiam charta Matildæ matris meæ, et confirmatio Yvonis fratris mei, quas inde habent, melius testantur. Dedi etiam dictis ecclesiæ et canonicis villam totam Grangiæ de Milleburn, sicut monachi de Holme melius eandem villam aliquando tenuerunt, cum Grangia vocara fuit, cum omnibus pertinentibus et rebus, &c. quam villam Nicholaus de Stuttevill mihi dedit, et charta sua confirmavit, quam chartam habeo, et prædictis canonicis dedi, &c. Dedi etiam dictis canonicis omnes decimas mihi pertinentes omnium molendinorum meorum de tota Westmeria, et omnes decimas novationis bestiarum, quæ captæ erunt de cetero in omnibus forestis meis in Westmeria, per me vel per homines meos, de dominico vel de maneriis meis, sive per arcus, sive per canes, &c. Testibus, Gilberto filio Rogeri filii Reinfredi, Wydone de Hellebec, Willielmo filio Ranulphi, Eudone de Bellocampo tunc vicecomite Westmariæ, Henrico de Redeman seneschallo de Kendall, Radulpho Daincourt, Anselmo de Furnesio, Henrico de Cundall, Willielmo de Morvilla, Willielmo Anglico, Willielmo de Thirneby, Johanne de Hardcla, Alano Pincerna, Waltero de Meburn, et aliis. Datum apud Cliburne, anno 13° regis Johannis, 8° Kal. Maii, die Sabbati. 2 Dugd. Mon. 594.—From the Register of Shap Abbey, heretofore in the possession of the lord William Howard of Naworth; but which now seems to be lost.

† From several collections made by bishop Nicolson.

rows one penny yearly at the feast of St. Laurence, and doing for the same foreign service ‡.

In the 43 Ed. 3. *Margaret* wife (or rather widow) of Sir *Hugh de Lowther*, gave all her lands in Westmorland to the said abbey (which after a course of near 400 years came back into the family by their purchase of the abbey possessions.)

Besides these and many other grants of lands, the abbey had the rectories and advowsons of the churches of *Warcop*, *Bampton*, and *Shap*.

They had also the MANOR of Shap. This manor appears of ancient time to have belonged to the *Culwens* (of the family of *Culwen*, corruptly *Curwen*, of Workington) held under the Cliffords lords of Westmorland. In the 8 Ed. 2. *Gilbert de Culwen* held the said manor. In the 34 Ed. 3. *Gilbert*, grandson of the said *Gilbert de Culwen*, knight, released to the said abbey all his right in certain lands and tenements in Shap, which he had of the infeoffment of Hugh de Lowther knight, and which the said Hugh had of Thomas de Preston: The deed is sealed with a frett, and chief charged with a crescent. In the 10 Hen. 5. we find the manor itself held jointly by the *abbot of Hepp* and *Christopher Curwen:* And afterwards the whole manor appears in possession of the abbey, by gift (no doubt) of the *Curwens*.

The state of the *revenues* of this abbey at the dissolution, will best appear from the particulars of the grant thereof by the crown to the *Wharton* family. King Henry the eighth, in the 36th year of his reign, granted (together with the monasteries of *Gisburn* and *Rival* in Yorkshire) the monastery of Shap, to Sir *Thomas Wharton* knight, lord *Wharton*, and the heirs male of his body, to hold of the king by the service of the twentieth part of one knight's fee, and paying for the whole into the court of augmentations 41 *l* 11 *s* yearly; with the reversion thereof in the crown. Afterwards, king James the first, in the ninth year of his reign, for the faithful service of Sir George Wharton, knight of the Bath, late deceased, [which Sir George was killed in a rencounter by Sir James Stuart] and other considerations, granted to *Philip* lord *Wharton*, and *Thomas Wharton* knight, son and heir apparent of the said *Philip* and brother of the said *George*, the reversion and remainder. The particulars whereof are as follows:

" The house and site of the monastery of *Shappe*, and the demesne and manor of Shappe, and all the tithes of corn, hay, wool, lambs, and other tithes whatsoever yearly accruing of and in the said site and demesne lands of the said monastery; and all the messuages, lands, tenements, and hereditaments, in the tenure and possession of *Antony Knevett*, *John Plumer*, *Hugh Platt*, *Thomas Ayraye*, *Richard Smith*, *William Dockere*, *John Cowperthwaite*, the wife of *William Hayton*, *Richard Hayton*, *Richard Whinfell*, *Robert Whinfell*, *John Robinson*, *John Walker*, *Thomas Dockere*, *Edward Alexander*, *Richard Hayton*, *William Ayraye*, *John Castells*, *John Robinson*, *Thomas Crakill*, the wife of *William Hebson*, the wife of *Miles Wetherhed*, *John Dockere* of Rigg, the wife of

‡ Machel, from the Evidences at Helbeck.

——— *Sanderson* or wife of *Richard Dockere*, *Roland Stewardson*, *Thomas Hayton*, *Thomas Thomson*, *Edward Ayraye*, *Henry Ayraye*, *Richard Robinson*, *John Cloudsdale*, *John Alexander*, *John Barwick*, *Robert Alexander*, *John Lowther*, *Thomas Dockere*, *John Robinson*, *Hugh Hayton*, *Henry Platt*, *John Greenhewe*, *William Smythe*, the wife of *Richard Robinson*, *Richard Lowther*, *Robert Haggerd*, *William Robinson*, the wife of *Thomas Robinson*, *James Brokebank*, and *John Stevenson*, or their assigns:

And also all that the grange of *Renegill*; with the rents and services of divers tenants there, and the messuages, tenements, and other hereditaments, in the tenure of divers other persons, to the number of 22 in the whole:

In *Keilde* and *Thornshappe*; divers tenements in the tenure and possession of *Alexander Dokree*, *Richard Robinson*, *Robert Wellis*, *Richard Barwike*, *Ralph Morthwaite*, the wife of *William Hogerd*, *Hugh Whitehead*, *Richard Hayton*, *Roger Hayton*, *William Hayton*, *John Dobson*, the wife of *John Mathew*, *Hugh Lowther*, *Thomas Dokree*, *Robert Brian*, and *William Mathew*:

In *Taleburgh*, *Racete*, and *Rosegill*; messuages and tenements, in the tenure of *John Hogeson*, *William Moreland*, *Richard Arais*, *Thomas Whitehead*, *Richard* his son, *William Lancastre*, *Roger Mesand*, *Robert Gibson*, *Henry Cowperthwaite*, *John Hayton*, and *Thomas Salkelde*:

In *Carebullen* in the parish of Bampton, and in *Knipe*; messuages and tenements in the tenure of *William Hudson*, *Robert Hudson*, *William Walker*, *Alexander Burgis*, *William Mateson*, *Hugh Baxter*, *John Baxter*, *William Hudson*, *Hugh* his son, *John Wilkinson*, and *William Horne*:

In *Preston* in Kendale; thirteen messuages and tenements:

In *Hutton Yate* and *Farleton*; seven:

And the lands called *Laurence* lands, in *Crowforth* in the said county of Westmorland:

Tenants in *Great Ashby*; *Margaret Myre*, and *George Myre* her son, and *William Unthanke*:

In *Malde's Meborne*; *John Willan*, *Thomas Addison*:

In *Wynandermere*; *Isaac Dixon*:

Helton dale; *John Holme*:

Hardling; *William Wilkinson*:

Beggarthwatt; *Thomas Langhorne*:

Terrel; *Christopher Idle*:

Frostermouth; *Roland Martyn*:

At *Bolton*; a messuage and tenement in the possession of *John Benson*, and a rent of 16*d* issuing out of the lands of *Cuthbert Ratcliffe* knight, 8*d* out of the tenement of *Richard Gibson*, 8*d* out of the tenement of *John Dent*, and 3*d* out of the tenement of *Edward Allayne*:

At *Brampton*; a rent of 4*d* and divers services there, and also 53*s* 4*d* which *Henry* then earl of *Cumberland* ought to pay for and in the name of alms called *Almes-corne*:

And at *Malde's Meborne*, 22*s*; which *John Fletcher*, *Lancelot Milner*, *Robert Hogeson*, and *Richard Winter* ought to pay yearly for and in the name of alms called *le alms corne*, issuing out of the said vill of *Malde's Meborne*:

At

At *Hoffe Lone*, 18*s*; which *Richard Yare*, *Robert Wilson*, *John Richardson*, and *Richard Richardson* ought to pay yearly for and in name of alms called *le almes corne*, issuing and to be delivered out of the vill of *Hoffe Lone*:

Also all that corn called almes corn to the said monastery of Shap belonging [that is, corn in kind, as it seemeth, and not in money] which they the said *Henry* earl of *Cumberland*, *John Fletcher*, *Lancelot Milner*, *Robert Hogeson*, *Richard Winter*, *Richard Yare*, *Robert Wilson*, *John Richardson*, and *Richard Richardson* ought to render yearly:

One tenement at *Ellerker*, in the possession of *John Allon*:

One tenement and cottage at *Sandford*, in the tenure of *Robert Bolland*:

At *Halkerthwaite*; divers messuages and tenements:

At *Whayle*; a yearly rent of 6*d* and services issuing out of the lands and tenements of *John Lowther* knight:

At *Knipe*; a rent of 6*d* out of the lands of *Edmund Bradley*, and 13*d* out of the lands of the heirs of *Stephen Salkeld*:

At *Roselands*; a rent of 2*d* and services issuing out of the lands of *William Hegberd* and *Thomas Hegberd*:

At *Appleby*; one messuage and tenement in the tenure of *Leonard Smithe* or his assigns:

And also all that late hospital of *St. Nicholas* nigh Appleby, and all the possessions and revenues thereof:

Reserved and excepted out of the said grant, *Sleddale Grange*, *Milborne Grange*, and all those lands in *Rosegill* in the tenure of *Thomas Salkeld*, and the several lands and tenements in *Slegill*, *Melkenthorpe*, and *Great Strickland*; and except also the lead, and bells, in and upon the church and site of the said late monastery, the leaden gutters and pipes, and lead in the windows; and excepting and reserving to the king and his successors all the aforesaid rent of 41*l* 11*s*, the payment thereof to commence, after the heirs male of the body of the said *Thomas* lord *Wharton* shall be extinct, or the aforesaid tail in the premisses shall be determined."

This abbey and the said revenues thereof continued in the *Wharton* family till the time of the late duke, when the same were sold together with their other estates and manors in Westmorland to *Robert Lowther* esquire, father of the present owner Sir *James Lowther* baronet.

The said abbey was not exempt from the ordinary jurisdiction: On the contrary, the abbots were admitted by the bishop of the diocese; unto whom, at the time of their admission, they swore canonical obedience. Thus in the year 1379, *Robert Marescball* the abbot made oath before bishop Appleby, that he would pay reverence and due subjection to the said bishop and his successors and to the apostolic see (saving the privileges of his order) *.

And in the absence of bishop Kite, in the year 1519, at the request of the said bishop, the abbots of Cockersand and Welbeck confirm the election of

* Ego Robertus Mareschall, abbas monasterii de Hepp, ordinis Praemonstratensis, subjectionem et reverentiam secundum regulam sancti Augustini, tibi patri episcopo tuisque successoribus canonice substituendis, et ecclesiae tuae Karliolensi et sacrosanctae sedi apostolicae (salvis privilegiis ordinis mei) me exhibiturum promitto, et manu mea subscribo. *Regist. Ap.*

the abbot of Shap; and on the 25th of March following, in the cathedral church of Durham, the said abbot received solemn benediction by the suffragan of that see, with the ceremonies of the pastoral staff, sacerdotal girdle, and ring *.

In Henry the eighth's Valor in the 26th year of his reign, there is an Item of 10*s* a year *oblations in stipite* at the said abbey. Perhaps this might be for fuel, in *stumps* of trees grubbed up, after the wood was destroyed.

This abbey was valued at the dissolution at 154*l* 7*s* 7½*d* a year; yet it was not dissolved in the 27 Hen. 8. amongst those which were rated under 200*l*: And the reason might be, because the act in that year speaks of those which contained under the number of 12 persons, whereas in this abbey there were 20 religious. Or perhaps Henry earl of Cumberland, the patron thereof, who was highly in favour with that king, might have interest to save it in that first attack.

The said abbey was not surrendered till the 14th of January in the 31 Hen. 8. and therefore was amongst those whose surrenders were confirmed by the act of parliament in that year; and being one of the privileged orders, its possessions were amongst those which were capable of being discharged from tithes. And yet it hath never been inserted in any of the lists of monasteries dissolved in that year; and the reason hath been, because those lists contain only such houses as were valued at 200*l* a year or upwards.

The last abbot was *Richard Evenwode*, as he subscribed his name to several instruments yet extant; but he surrendered the abbey by the name of *Richard Baggot*: whether he was illegitimate, and subscribed by the name of his mother or reputed father promiscuously, or it was done intentionally that the surrender thereby might be void, or how otherwise this happened, hath not appeared to us. He was living in the first year of queen Mary, and enjoyed a pension of 40*l* a year. And of the canons and officers there were then surviving 13 persons, each of whom had pensions as follows: *Hugh Watsonne, Robert Barlonde, John Addison, Edward Michael*, and *Edmund Carter*, 6*l* each; *Martin Mackarethe, John Dawstone*, and *Richard Mell*, 5*l* each; *John Bell*, 5*l* 6*s* 8*d*; *George Ellerston, Anthony Johnson, John Rode*, and *Ralph Watsonne*, 4*l* each.

Amongst the writings at Crackenthorp, there is a testimonial of one Thomas Sawleman clerk, in the year 1444, with the *common seal* of the abbey, partly defaced. There appears to be St. Mary Magdalen with a crosier in her right hand, and part of the legend . . . . . DALENE . . . ET CONVENTU . . . . †.

The taxation to be paid at Rome for admission to the dignity of abbot was 100 florins of gold; as appears from a copy of the "Regestum taxæ in impetrandis ecclesiis patriarchalibus, metropolitanis, cathedralibus, et conventualibus, per totum orbem persolvendæ," in the British Museum, Harl. MSS. Nº 1850. Amongst which are, *Canterbury* archbishopric 10000 florins of gold, *York* 10000, bishopric of *Durham* 8000, *Winchester* 12000, *Carlisle* 1000.— A florin of gold seems to have been about the value of an English crown.

* Nicolson. † Machel.

And

And confidering the diminution in the value of money, thefe florins might now be reckoned as pounds.

The church of the abbey appears to have been a fpacious building. The tower thereof at the weft end is yet ftanding; on the eaft part whereof are the marks where the roof of the church hath adjoined to it. Nigh thereunto is a little farm houfe, which hath formerly been fome of the offices. Juft below the abbey are the ruins of an old bridge, the pillar whereof in the midft of the water is yet remaining. About half a mile to the north eaft is a farm houfe called the Grange, which belonged to the abbey, with fpacious fields adjoining.

There were alfo fome lands at Shap which belonged to the abbey of *Byland* in Yorkfhire, given by the aforefaid Thomas fon of Cofpatric to God and St. Mary *de Bellalanda*: He granted alfo to the faid abbey of Byland pafture for 500 fheep in Heppe and Heppefhow.

In the year 1687, June 24, Philip lord Wharton procured a charter for a market at Shap weekly on Wednefday, and three fairs yearly, *viz.* on the 23d and 24th of April, the 1ft and 2d of Auguft, and the 17th and 18th of September.

And on the 14th of December in the faid year, the faid lord Wharton, in confideration of one year's cuftomary rent paid by the tenants of the faid manor, granted to them and their heirs to be free from toll in the faid market and fairs.

Towards the fouth end of the village of Shap, near the turnpike road, on the eaft fide thereof, there is a remarkable monument of antiquity; which is an area upwards of half a mile in length, and between 20 and 30 yards broad, encompaffed with large ftones (with which that country abounds) many of them three or four yards in diameter, at 8, 10, or 12 yards diftance, which are of fuch immenfe weight that no carriages now in ufe could fupport them. Undoubtedly this hath been a place of Druid worfhip, which they always performed in the open air, within this kind of inclofure, fhaded with wood, as this place of old time appears to have been, although there is now fcarce a tree to be feen (*Shap-Thorn* only excepted, planted on the top of the hill for the direction of travellers). At the high end of this place of worfhip, there is a circle of the like ftones about 18 feet in diameter, which was their *fanctum fanctorum* (as it were) and place of facrifice. The ftone is a kind of granite, and when broken appears beautifully variegated with bright fhining fpots like fpar. The country people have blafted and carried away fome of thefe ftones, for the foundation ftones of buildings. In other places, fome have cut thefe ftones (but with difficulty) for milftones. When polifhed, they would make beautiful chimney-pieces.

III. ROS-

III. ROSGILL.

Within the parish of Shap, is the manor of ROSGILL or ROSKGILL; probably not so called from any shrub of that name growing there, as we have before supposed of Shap and of Sleagill; but rather from *Rhôs* or *Rose*, which in the British signifies a moist valley or dale.

In the reign of king Henry the third, we find *John de Rosgill* witness to a grant of lands at Thrimby to the priory of Wetheral.

In the 20 Ed. 1. *John de Rossegill* knight was one of the jurors in a cause between the king and the abbot of St. Mary's York, concerning the advowson of the two churches at Appleby.

In the 5 Ed. 3. Sir *John de Rossegill* was witness to an exchange of lands, between Sir Hugh de Lowther and the prior of Watton.

In the 18th of the same king, *Robert de Rossegill* is the first in the list of jurors upon the inquisition *post mortem* of Robert de Clifford.

The last of the *Rosgills*, whether this *Robert* or another, had a daughter and heir *Christian*, who in the reign of Richard the second was married to *Hugh de Salkeld* of Corby-castle, who first brought in the *Salkelds* to Rosgill. Which Hugh was knight of the shire for Westmorland during the whole reign of king Richard the second, and part of the reign of king Henry the fourth.

In the 8 Ed. 4. there is a deed of lands at Ormside, to *Thomas Salkeld* junior, lord of Rosgill: Witnesses whereof, William Salkeld, Roger Salkeld.

In the 3 Hen. 8. there is an indenture between the abbot and convent of Shap and *Richard Salkeld* of Rossgill, son and heir of *Thomas Salkeld* of Corby esquire.

In the 26 Hen. 8. *Thomas Salkeld* held lands at Rosegill of the said abbot and convent.

In the 3 and 4 Ph. and Mary, *Richard Salkeld* of Rosegyll esquire was one of the arbitrators in a dispute between Richard and Henry Machel of Crackenthorp.

In the 8 Eliz. *Richard Salkeld* esquire presented a vicar to the church of Bampton, by virtue of a grant which had been made of that turn by the abbot and convent before their dissolution.

In the 7 Cha. 1. by inquisition after the death of *Richard Salkeld*, it is found that he died seised of a moiety of the manor of Rosegill, holden of the king *in capite* by knights service; and that *Dorothy Morley* is his sister and sole heir: Which *Dorothy* was married into the family of *Christian* of Ewanrigg in Cumberland, in whom the demesne still continues, but the manor was sold to Sir John Lowther, ancestor of the present owner Sir James Lowther baronet.

The arms of Salkeld were; Vert, a fret Argent.—In the east window of the quire of the church at Shap, are the arms of Clifford and of Salkeld.

IV. THORN.

IV. THORNTHWAITE.

THORNTHWAITE was anciently a large forest. It is part in the parish of Shap, and the other part in the parish of Bampton. It anciently belonged to the *Curwens* aforesaid, until Sir *Henry Curwen* sold the same to the lord *William Howard* of Naworth; who gave it to Sir *Francis Howard* his younger son; whose son and heir *Francis Howard* of Corby esquire enjoyed the same in the reign of king Charles the second. By a daughter of which family it came to *Francis Warwick* of Warwick-briggs esquire, who sold the greatest part to the present owner *Edward Hassel* of Dalemain esquire, retaining the other part, which still continues in the *Warwick* family.

V. MARDALE.

This division is part of the forest of *Thornthwaite*, and lies part in the parish of Shap, and part in the parish of Bampton. The *chapel* of Mardale is in the parish of Shap: the present revenue whereof is about 26*l* *per annum*, being the produce of three allotments of queen Anne's bounty of 200*l* each, and of 75*l* contributed by several different persons.

VI. SWINDALE.

This also is part of *Thornthwaite* forest; which extended wide in these uncultivated places. It may have received its name, either from the situation, as *Swin* signifies inclining or crooked; so there is *Crookdale* in this same parish of Shap: Or it may be so called from wild boars having frequented there; as there are *Grisedale*, *Boredale*, *Stybarrow*, in the neighbouring parish of Barton; and *Wildboarfell* in Ravenstondale. *Hogherd* (we have seen) was a name in this parish, now corruptly written *Hoggart*, or (as varied by the late excellent painter of that name who was of Westmorland extraction from Kirkby Thore) *Hogarth*.

At this place is a small chapel, which was built by the inhabitants to answer the purpose both of school and chapel. There was a small endowment for a schoolmaster, and he was permitted to read prayers on Sundays. By an allotment of queen Anne's bounty, the chapel and school together are now worth about sixteen or seventeen pounds a year.

VII. MOSEDALE.

MOSEDALE, *Moss-dale*, is a wild, bleak, *mossy*, and mountainous dale; but profitable for fine blue slate: which, since it was found out (which is not a century ago), hath quite altered the face of the country as to building. It is a beautiful, dry, clean, light covering; and, in Weftmorland, by reafon of its vicinity, cheaper than thatch, becaufe durable. Much of it, by land-carriage, is conveyed over Stanemore into the counties of Durham and York.

This dale alfo is the property of the faid Edward Haffel efquire.

VIII. WET SLEDDALE.

South-weft about a mile and an half from Shap is the hamlet of SLEDDALE *Slea-dale*, diftinguifhed from another *Sleddale* in the barony of Kendale by the name of *Wet Sleddale*; for if any rain is ftirring, the air fcoops it furprifingly into the hollow of that dale.

We have obferved before, that Sleddale Grange belonged to the abbey of Shap. In the year 1360, there is a remarkable circumftance in the bifhop's regiftry relating to this grange. Complaint being made of fome unknown perfons riotoufly breaking into the houfes and grange of the abbot and convent of Hepp at Sleddale, and committing feveral diforders there; the bifhop iffues out his mandate to the dean (rural) of Weftmorland, and to the rector of Lowther, the vicars of Hepp, Morland, and Crofby Ravenfwath, to denounce the greater excommunication, at the time of high mafs, when the greateft number of people fhould be gathered together, the bells ringing, and the candles lighted and put out, againft the faid rioters.

IX. HARDENDALE AND WASDALE.

Next we come to the manor of HARDENDALE and WASDALE *(Wafte dale)*. This manor belonged to *Byland* abbey in Yorkfhire. By whom it was given, we have not found. *Thomas* fon of *Cofpatric* (we obferved before) gave fome lands at Shap to this abbey, and it is not unlikely that he gave alfo Hardendale and Wafdale.

After the diffolution, king Henry the eighth, in the 35th year of his reign, granted to *Chriftopher Crackenthorp* of Newbiggin efquire, and his heirs, the manor of *Hardenefdale* (otherwife *Hardendale*) and *Wafdale*; together with the meffuages, tenements, and other hereditaments, in the tenure and poffeffion of *Thomas Sanderfon*, *Michael Sanderfon*, *John Kytchyn*, *Henry Copertbwaite*, *William Kytchyn*, *John Sanderfon*, *William Lowes*, *William Atkynfon*, *Thomas Robynfon*, *Chriftopher Winter*, *Simon Lykbarry*, *John Lykbarry*, *Richard Pullo*, *Richard Wafshington*, *Thomas Byrkhead*, *Edward Lowther*, and *Miles Howe*, lying and being in Hardendale and Wafdale; together with all knights fees, efcheats, reliefs, heriots, court leet and view of frankpledge, affize of bread, beer, and ale, waifs, eftrays, free warren, and all other rights in Hardendale, Wafdale foot, and Wafdale head: Paying to the king, his heirs and fucceffors, 16*s* yearly into the court of augmentations.

The faid manor ftill continues in the pofterity of the faid Chriftopher, in like manner as the Newbiggin and other eftates.

At

At Hardendale was born the learned Dr. John Mill, principal of Edmund Hall in Oxford, celebrated for his edition of the New Testament in Greek, in which are collected the various readings of abundance of different manuscripts.

Opposite to Wasdale foot, but in the parish of Crosby Ravensworth, by the side of the river Birkbeck, was discovered some few years ago a spaw water, now known by the name of *Shap well*, to which in the summer season is a considerable resort. It is impregnated with sulphur, and smells like rotten eggs or the barrel of a musket just fired: And hath been found serviceable in scorbutic disorders.

PARISH OF ORTON.

I. *Parish of Orton.*
II. *Manor of Orton.*
III. *Langdale.*
IV. *Tebay.*
V. *Bretherdale.*
VI. *Birkbeck Fells.*

I. PARISH OF ORTON.

ORTON is nothing but a contraction of *Overton*; the situation of which place sufficiently shews its derivation. There are many places in England of the same name. Sometimes this place was distinguished by the name of *Sker-Overton*, from the scar under which it stands.

It is bounded on the East by the parishes of Asby, Crosby Garret, and Ravenstondale; on the South, by the parish of Sedbergh in the county of York, and the parish of Kendal; on the West, by the said parish of Kendal; and on the North, by the parishes of Shap, Crosby Ravensworth, and Asby: And consists of about 360 families, all of the church of England, except one quaker family.

The church is dedicated to *All Saints*. It is a vicarage, in the gift of the land-owners within the parish; so that there are about 240 patrons; who, to avoid confusion, keep the advowson in the hands of trustees, who are bound to present according to a majority of votes upon an election-day. It is rated in the king's books at *16l 17s 3½d*.

This church was appropriated to the priory of Conishead [Conyng's-heved] in Lancashire, in the reign of king Henry the second; and there is a confirmation thereof by John Bartholomew, prior of Carlisle, in the time of Hugh third bishop of Carlisle.

The person who gave the same to the said priory was *Gamel de Penigton*; as appears by the confirmation thereof by king Edward the second in the 12th year of his reign: who, reciting the several grants which had been made to the said priory, confirms the same, and amongst the rest "the grant which "Gamel de Penigton made to the canons of the said place, of the churches "of Penigton, Molcastre, and Sker-Overton, with the appurtenances *."

There is another recital in the said confirmation, of an acre of land in Overton, called *Frerebiggins*, given by Alan son of Alan de Penigton, to the canons of the said place.

And another recital of two acres and an half and thirty perches of land in Overton, given by Thomas de Musgrave.

The place called *Frerebiggins* probably received its name from having belonged to the *friers* or brethren of the said priory. For there are no footsteps remaining of any other religious society, which had any possessions within the manor of Orton. Below *Frerebiggins*, there is a place called *Frere-mire*; and there is a parcel of turbary called *Frere-moss*, which probably was given by the Penigtons, lords of the manor, together with the lands at *Frerebiggins*, to the said priory. There were two messuages and tenements belonging to the church and priory (which are mentioned in the valuation in the twenty-sixth year of king Henry the eighth), of which there are no traces any where now to be found, except only at the said *Frerebiggins*. The vicar hath about nine acres of land there still, but no dwelling-house. The rest were probably alienated by the priory, as was very frequently done by the religious houses, on the apprehension of their approaching dissolution; and there was no law to restrain them.—There is indeed a place called *The Chapel*, about half a mile south from the church: But that seems only to have been for the sake of receiving the oblations of persons resorting to a well there, called Lady-well; which was reported to have salutary effects in divers maladies. And there are many wells throughout the country, to which the superstition of those times attributed the like virtues; that is to say, in plain English, they were efficacious in all cases wherein cold water in general is so.

The first vicar that appears upon record after the church was given to the priory was Sir *Richard de Bernard Castle*; who, in the year 1293, was presented to the vacant vicarage of Ovyrton by the prior and convent of Conyngsheved; unto whom institution was thereupon given by bishop Halton.

In 1302, one *Henry*, whose surname is not recorded, was vicar of Overton, being presented in the spiritual court, and cited for incontinency; whereupon he became bound to the bishop in 20 marks, to be forfeited, if thereafter he should be charged and convicted of incontinency with any woman.

In 1338, on the death of *Thomas de Appleby* vicar of Overton, the prior and convent of Conyngsheved present one of their own canons, *Richard de Wessington*; for whose institution the bishop grants a commission, notwithstanding his being a canon regular.

* 2 Dugd. Mon. 424.

In 1373, one Sir *Robert de Berdesbay* was vicar of Overton; on whose death, the prior and convent of St. Mary's de Conynges-heved presented Sir *Thomas Bell*, one of their own canons.

In the year 1455, *William Birkbeck*, vicar of Overton, was a trustee in a marriage settlement of Thomas Blenkinsop of Helbeck esquire, of certain lands which the Blenkinsops had at Overton.

In 1534, one *Thomas Lorde* appears to have been vicar of Overton.

In 1573, on the death of *Philip Machel* vicar of Overton, institution was given to Mr. *Robert Corney*, on a presentation by queen Elizabeth, in right of her duchy of Lancaster (after the dissolution of the priory of Conishead).

In 1594, upon the death of the said Robert Corney, a caveat was entred by Gerard Lowther esquire, high sheriff of the county of Cumberland, in claim of the right of presentation of Sir John Puckering lord keeper of the great seal. But in about a fortnight after, the bishop granted instituion to *Henry Atkinson*, M. A. presented as before by queen Elizabeth in right of her duchy of Lancaster.

In 1595, Mr. Atkinson being dead, *John Corney*, M. A. was instituted on a presentation in the same form as before by queen Elizabeth.

During the incumbency of this John Corney, the rectory and advowson were purchased of the crown, by Francis Morice of the city of Westminster esquire, and Francis Phelips of the city of London gentleman (who purchased divers other rectories, for the sake of making an advantage in selling them again). They sold the rectory and advowson of the parish of Orton, in the year 1618, to the said John Corney, Edmund Branthwaite, and Philip Winster, for the sum of 570*l*, in trust for the land-owners within the parish; and these three conveyed to 12 feoffees in trust, to present upon an avoidance such person to the vicarage, as shall be chosen by a majority of the land owners at a meeting to be appointed by the said feoffees within three months next after the avoidance; and in trust, when the number shall be reduced, to convey to other feoffees to be chosen by such majority as aforesaid. And so it still continues.

Nevertheless, notwithstanding the said purchase, in the year 1637, a caveat was entred by one Edward Newburgh, claiming to be called on the death or resignation of John Corney. And in 1639, a like caveat was entred (Mr. Corney being not yet dead) by Thomas Barlow, M. A. Edward Birkbeck, and others, on behalf of themselves and other parishioners, claiming right of presentation.

In 1643, Mr. Corney being then dead, and the living vacant, the parishioners renewed the caveat last mentioned; but the bishop's register book, and episcopacy, failing here (says bishop Nicolson), we cannot hence learn the issue.

The event was this: The civil wars then raging, each party attempted to have a vicar of their own side. Some few of the inhabitants, who were of the parliament party, took upon themselves of their own accord (without any election or application to the feoffees in trust), to present one *Alexander Fetherstonhaugh*,

stonhaugh, a chaplain in the parliament army; who obtained institution: but the parish by force kept him out of possession.

The marquis of Newcastle, who commanded the king's majesty's forces in the northern parts, recommended one Mr. *Lowther* then in Ireland.

The land owners, according to the rule established amongst them, elected one *George Fothergill*, and the feoffees presented him accordingly to the bishop for institution. And at the same time they excused themselves to the marquis of Newcastle, purging themselves of a charge of disaffection which had been imputed to them, and beseeching his excellency, that the election which they had duly made might stand firm and unalterable, notwithstanding his excellency's commendatory letters in behalf of Mr. Lowther.

The bishop not giving institution to their presentee, they sent to him a messenger, with a letter, which shews somewhat the spirit of the times, and the contempt into which the episcopal office had then fallen. They address his lordship (or rather, his *grace*, for archbishop Usher then held the see of Carlisle in *commendam*) thus, "May it please you, Sir."—And after expressing their wonder, that notwithstanding Mr. Fothergill had waited on the bishop, with a presentation in form, the bishop had not admitted him but instituted another, they intreat him either to institute Mr. Fothergill, or to send answer by the bearer why he refused; "that so (say they) we may take such further course, as *law and present authority* shall afford."

But the bishop having instituted Mr. Fetherstonhaugh as aforesaid, the parish filed their bill in equity, and at length Mr. *George Fothergill* became established on the election of the land owners as aforesaid. In 1662, he was ejected for not complying with the act of uniformity; but afterwards conformed, and was presented to the living of Worsop in Nottinghamshire.

On this vacancy, *Roger Kenyon* was elected, and thereupon presented by the feoffees. He died in 1703, at the age of 85; having been married to his wife (who survived him) 60 years.

On the death of Roger Kenyon, *Thomas Nelson*, M. A. was elected and presented as before, and instituted thereupon.

In 1736, on the death of Thomas Nelson, *Richard Burn*, A. B. was elected, presented, and instituted in like manner. He was born at Winton in this county, and educated at Queen's college in the university of Oxford, which university afterwards conferred upon him the honorary degree of Doctor of laws. He was author of two books, one on the office of a Justice of the peace, the other on Ecclesiastical law. He was one of his majesty's justices of the peace for the counties of Westmorland and Cumberland, and was made by bishop Lyttelton chancellor of the diocese of Carlisle.

The *church* is a large old building, with a tower steeple, and four pretty large bells. They were cast at Nottingham, by John Wolley bell-founder, in the 21 Hen. 8. For which he had (carriage included) 76*l*, by the hands of Thomas Blenkinsop, Lancelot Lancaster, Lancelot Lowther, esquires, John Thornborrow, Rowland Thornborrow, and Oliver Crosby, yeomen, in the

the name of all the parishioners: The bass bell to be like in sound to the third bell of the abbey of Shap, and the other three solemn and sweet consonant thereunto. As appears by an indenture bearing date the fourth of April in that year. But the bells have all or most of them been since re-cast.

The people come regularly to church, five, six, or seven miles, every Sunday. And the modern practice of appropriating seats hath not yet obtained in this church. All the seats, except the vicar's, are repaired at the public expence; and no one of the parishioners hath a right to any particular seat. The contrary practice is extremely full of inconvenience in many places; particularly in the metropolis, where one may frequently see most of the congregation standing in the alleys, whilst the pews are locked up, the owners thereof being in the country, or perhaps in bed.

The *vicarage house* is much improved by the present incumbent; who hath lived to see wood of his own planting grown up to shelter it, which it stood much in need of.

There are two *schools* in the parish. One at *Tebay*, founded by Robert Adamson of Blacket Bottom in Grayrigg gentleman, in the year 1672, and endowed by him with the estates called Ormondie Bigging and Blacket Bottom of the clear yearly value of about 24*l.*

The other school is at *Greenholme*, founded by George Gibson of the same place gentleman, in the year 1733, and endowed by him with 400*l* original Bank stock, worth now yearly about 22*l.*

II. MANOR OF ORTON.

The first lord of the manor of whom we have any account, was the aforesaid *Gamel de Penigton* (for such, most probably, he was), who gave the church to the priory of Conishead as aforesaid in the reign of king Henry the second. The churches were most commonly appendant to the manors. And that this family had considerable possessions at Orton, appears not only from what hath been already observed, but also from an ancient grant without date, by *Alan* son of *Alan* son of *Benedict de Penigton* to his uncle *Simon* son of the said *Benedict*, of all that moiety of *Keldelith* (including one capital messuage and tenement called The Raine), to hold to him and his heirs by the payment of 2*s* rent yearly for all services and demands; doing for the same to the king foreign service as much as appertaineth: Witnesses of which grant were, Ralph de Beethom, Gilbert de Croft, Michael de Furneis, Robert de Bonville, William son of Waldeve, Simon de Cartmell, Alan son of Orme, Alan son of Gilbert, Walter de Mulcaster, David his brother, Thomas prior of Conishead, Alan parson of Pulton, T. parson of Heversham, Adam chaplain of Oldinham, T. chaplain of Ulverston, R. chaplain of Kirkby, and others.

Note, *Keldelith* is what is now by contraction called *Kelleth*; and is derived of two Saxon words, *keld* which signifies a well or spring, and *lyth* which signifies

nifies light or soft. There is a stream near Kendal called *Light-water*, of the same import.

In our next account of the manor, it appears to be divided into moieties, so early as the reign of king Edward the first, whether by daughters coheirs, or by purchase, or how otherwise, we have not found. In the 6 Ed. 1, we find clearly the manor of Orton in the hands of the *Dacres* of Dacre in Cumberland, and the *Musgraves* of Musgrave in this county. For in that year, *Ranulph de Dacre* obtained a grant to himself and his heirs, as also to *Thomas Musgrave* and his heirs, of a market on the Wednesday every week, and a fair yearly on the eve, day, and morrow of the apostles Simon and Jude *at their manor of Overton*; and from henceforward it continued divided into moieties, until the whole became united again by purchase of the inhabitants from the several owners of the respective moieties. The *Dacre* moiety continued intire; but the *Musgrave* moiety became further divided. These moieties were not separated by metes and bounds, but the owner of each moiety had tenants interspersed throughout the whole manor, and the division appears to have been made according to the respective quantities of the lord's rents. But for ease and convenience this manor of very ancient time was divided into two townships or constablewicks, now known by the names of *Orton Lordship* and *Raisbeck Lordship*; and the division was as follows: "As a certain syke between Overton and the hamlet of Rayssebeck runs through the middle of Freermire down into the Bibeck, and by the middle of the Bibeck down into the water of Tybay, and so going up the middle of the water of Tybay to the Scoddigate of Hanskew as Boudirdal beck falls into Tybay. And so going up by the boundaries of Raustindall, Crosseby Gerard, and Little Askeby, and the aforesaid hamlet of Rayssebeck in the vill of Overton aforesaid, to the top of the Sker, by the right metes and boundaries between Great Askeby and the Grange thereof and the aforesaid hamlet unto the Hundehow, and so going down from the Hundehow by the nearest way into the aforesaid sike, running through the middle of Freermire. Witnesses of which division were Sir Michael de Harclay, and Sir John de Rossgill, knights; John de Helton, Richard de Warthecopp, Henry de Warthecopp, Alan de Keldelyth, Robert son of Thomas de Langdall, and others *."—The first of which witnesses is known to have lived in the latter end of the reign of king Henry the third, and the former part of the reign of king Edward the first.

There are four other lordships in the parish, *viz.* of *Langdale*, *Tebay*, *Bretherdale*, and *Birkbeck Fells*, part of which last is in the parish of Crosby Ravensworth.

(1) *Of the* Dacre *moiety of the manor of Orton.*

After *Ranulph de Dacre* aforesaid, who obtained the charter for the market, we find by an inquisition in the 3 Ed. 2. concerning the free tenants in Westmorland

* Copied by the reverend Thomas Machel from the writings then in the possession of Edward Birkbeck of Coatflat-hall gentleman.

morland who held by cornage tenure, that *William de Dacre*, son of the said *Ranulph*, then held a moiety of the manor of Overton.

Again, in the 8 Ed. 2. after the death of Robert de Clifford, the inquisition finds, that *William de Dacre* held of the said Robert, on the day on which he died, a moiety of the manor of Overton, and a moiety also of the manor of Waitby; by homage and fealty, and 12*s* 6*d* cornage: And that the wardship thereof, when it should happen, was worth by the year 40*l*.

In the 43 Ed. 3. on an inquisition of tenants holding in free tenancy of Roger de Clifford, the jurors find, that *John de Dacre* held the manor, (as it is there called) of Overton-Dacre, by the cornage of 5*s* 1*d*.

In the 15 Ric. 2. after the death of the said Roger, the inquisition finds, that *William de Dacre* held a moiety of the manor of Overton, by homage and fealty, and cornage 5*s* 1*d*.

In the 10 Hen. 5. after the death of John de Clifford, the inquisition finds, that Elizabeth mother of the said John held in dower the rents and services of divers tenants; and amongst the rest, of *Thomas Dacre* knight, for the manor of Overton.

In the 17 Hen. 6. the said Sir *Thomas Dacre*, lord of Gillesland, made a settlement of his estate at Overton.

In the 7 Hen. 7. the inquisition after the death of *Humphrey de Dacre* finds, that the said *Humphrey* held (amongst other particulars) jointly with Mabel his wife, to him and the heirs of his body, a moiety of the manor of Overton.

And by an inquisition in the 19 Hen. 7. the jurors find, that *Humphrey Dacre* lord of Dacre was seised in his demesne as of fee, of and in a moiety of the manor of Overton, with the appurtenances; and that the said moiety was holden of the king *in capite* by knights service, and 12*s* 6*d* cornage; and by the service of doing suit at the county court of the said lord the king from month to month at his castle of Appleby: And that the said Humphrey died seised thereof on the first day of August in the 6th year of the reign of the said king Henry the seventh; and that *Thomas Dacre*, then 16 years of age, was son and heir of the said *Humphrey*.

The said *Thomas* lord Dacre had a son *William*, who in the 18 Hen. 8. (as appears by inquisition) held of Henry earl of Cumberland a moiety of Overton, by the cornage of 5*s* 1*d*; owing also to the said earl for the same, wardship, marriage, and relief, and suit to the county court.

The said *William* lord *Dacre* had a son *Thomas*; who had a son *George*, who died without issue; whose two surviving sisters and heirs were married to *Philip* earl of *Arundel* and the lord *William Howard*, both of them sons of Thomas duke of Norfolk.

And in the 12th year of king James the first, *Anne* countess dowager of *Arundel* (her husband *Philip* earl of *Arundel* being then dead), *Thomas* earl of *Arundel* her son, the lord *William Howard* of Naward and the lady *Elizabeth* his wife, *John Cornewallis* of Sohom in the county of Suffex esquire, and *Robert Cansfield* of London esquire, (which two last were lessees of the crown of the Dacre estates, being then under an escheat by the attainder of the heirs male of the Dacres upon occasion of the affair of Mary queen of Scots) in consideration of the sum of 1840*l* 5*s* 10½*d*, conveyed to Edmund Branthwaite gentleman, Thomas Birkbeck, James Birkbeck, and Thomas Powley, yeomen, (in trust for themselves and the rest of the tenants) the said moiety of the manor of Overton, and also the moiety of two water corn milns, parcel of the said moiety, and the several tenements following; to wit, fifteen tenements in Orton, two at Chapel, three at Streethouse and Scarside, seven at Raisbeck, four at Sunbiggin, five at Kelleth, Coatgill, and Langdale, two at Tebay, one at Rounthwaite, nine at Coatflat, five at Scales, three at Bousfield, and three at Park *, of the yearly finable arbitrary rent in the whole of 28*l* 18*s* 9½*d*, with some small quantities of free rent.—Except and reserving eight acres of land of the yearly rent of 8*s* in Kelleth, then in the tenure of Philip Hewetson; and a yearly rent of 2*s* then paid by one Gilbert Atkinson of Howgill for freeledge of common upon East Grain and Middle Grain in Langdale fells, which had then for time immemorial been paid as part of or appurtenant to the said moiety; and except one sheep heath upon Langdale fells, holden of the then Philip lord Wharton, under the yearly rent of 8*s*.

(2) *Of the* MUSGRAVE *moiety of the manor of Orton.*

Next after *Thomas de Musgrave* aforesaid, who lived in the reign of king Edward the first, we find *Richard de Musgrave* holding a moiety of the manor of Overton, together with the manors of Crosby Gerard and Little Musgrave; whilst at the same time *Thomas de Musgrave*, then a minor, held the manor of Great Musgrave. So that this *Richard* must have been of a collateral branch of the family, probably uncle of the said minor. This *Richard de Musgrave* sold part of this moiety in the 29 Ed. 1. to *Adam de Henecastre*, with whose daughter *Avicia* the same came in marriage to Sir *Thomas de Helbeck*; and by marriage of the heiress of *Helbeck*, both that and the manor of Helbeck came to the *Blenkinsops*.

In the 19 Ric. 2. *Thomas de Blenkinsop* of Helbeck settled upon his son William and Maud his wife upon their marriage, half of his demesne in the village of Overton, with one place in the said village called Rasegill-hall, with 16 tenements there in the hands of tenants at will, reserving to himself the mill and moulter.

In the 33 Hen. 6. another *Thomas Blenkinsop* of Helbeck (for there were fourteen generations of Blenkinsops at Helbeck, and ten of them of the name of Thomas) had, upon his marriage with his wife Katharine, settled on the issue of the said marriage, all the lands aforesaid at Overton, together with certain lands in the village of Tebay: William Birkbeck vicar of Overton, and Richard Warton chaplain, being trustees in the settlement.

* This account of the particulars is taken from a rental of George lord Dacre, when under the guardianship of Thomas duke of Norfolk.

In

In the 10 Ed. 4. another *Thomas Blenkinsop* appears by inquisition to have been seised of the said moiety; his son *Thomas* then being 33 years of age.

In the 24 Hen. 8. *Thomas Blenkinsop* of Helbeck esquire, on his going to serve the king's majesty against the Scots, made his will, and thereby constituted his brother Richard Blenkinsop, and his two uncles George, and John (a priest), together with his cousin Sir Richard Leigh priest, trustees of his moiety of the manor of Overton, to take up the rents thereof, which were 13*l* or thereabouts, to be employed to the best advantage towards the use of his daughters, for so many of them as should come to years.

In the 14th year of queen Elizabeth, *Thomas Blenkinsop* of Helbeck gentleman, son and heir of Thomas, had livery of his lands from the court of wards; and, amongst other particulars, were, half of a water mill, and 29 messuages in Coteflat, Gaisgill, Tebay, Ellergill, Langdale, and Flakebrigg; besides other ten held in socage, by fealty and rent of one pepper-corn.

The last of the Blenkinsops who held this moiety, was *Thomas Blenkinsop* of Helbeck esquire, son of *Henry*, who in the year 1630, together with Anne his wife and Elizabeth his mother, for the sum of 565*l*, sold the same to trustees for the use of the tenants; consisting of seventeen tenements in Raisbeck, eight in Sunbiggin, seven in Kelleth, three at Raisgill-hall, and five at Coatflat; of the yearly finable arbitrary rent of 11*l* 18*s* 5½*d*, and 4*s* 9*d* mill rent: reserving the water mill at Coatflat, valued at 40*s* a year. It appears they were papists; for there was a covenant of indemnity for the sum of 20*l* a month, or two thirds of the profits of the lands, to be forfeited for their recusancy in not resorting to church.

The other share of the *Musgrave* moiety appears to have been in the hands of the Warcops of Smardale. The last of whom, *viz. Thomas Warcop* of Smardale esquire had two daughters coheirs, married to *John Dalston* of Dalston in Cumberland esquire, and *Talbot Bowes* of Egleston abbey in the county of York esquire; who in the 34 Eliz. for the sum of 400*l*, sold their moiety (as it is called) of the manor of Overton to *George Birkbeck* and *Robert Whitehead* of Orton and *George Sharp* of Scales; consisting of one moiety of Raisgill-hall mill, and 56 tenements of the yearly finable arbitrary rent of 10*l* 16*s* 6*d*.

The said three purchasers conveyed to *Edward Branthwaite*, *Oliver Birkbeck*, and *Roger Ward*, in trust to reconvey to them their several shares agreed on; of whom, *George Birkbeck* had (besides his own estate) 32 tenants, in Orton, Bousfield, and elsewhere within the manor, together with the moiety of the mill; *Robert Whitehead*, 11 tenants; and *George Sharp*, 6; with a rateable part of the wastes, and other manerial rights. All the three purchasers, or their heirs or assigns, in process of time, have sold most of the respective tenements to freehold. And the whole manor is now become reunited in the hands of the freehold purchasers; and is conveyed from time to time to lords of the manor in trust, for the sake of keeping courts leet and baron for the convenience of the tenants.

The *market* at Orton, by the charter of king Edward the first, was to be on Wednefday *; which charter, in the year 1655, was confirmed by Oliver Cromwell. And in 1678, the faid Oliver, lord protector of the commonwealth, reciting a writ of *ad quod damnum* iffued, and an inquifition thereupon taken before Anne lady Clifford countefs of Pembroke and Montgomery, Sheriffefs of the county of Weftmorland, grants to the inhabitants of the town of Overton and their fucceffors, licence and power to hold within the faid town one fair yearly upon Friday before Whitfunweek, and alfo a fair in every fortnight; the firft of the faid fairs to begin on Wednefday next after Whitfunweek, and to continue till the day of Simon and Jude following; with a court of pypowders, and power to take tolls. The feal is about fix inches in diameter. On one fide are the arms of the commonwealth, with this motto underneath, *Pax quæritur bello:* And circumfcribed, *Magnum figillum Reipublicæ Angliæ, Scotiæ, et Hiberniæ, &c.* On the reverfe, Oliver in armour on horfeback, and circumfcribed thus, *Olivarius, Dei Gratia, Reipublicæ Angliæ, Scotiæ, et Hiberniæ Protector.* And Oliver's *Friday* fair, has by ufage transferred the fortnight fairs, and even the market alfo, to *Friday*; on which day the market is now kept weekly.

It is not certain where the ancient *manor houfe* of Orton ftood. It feems to have been near to the church, on the fouth fide thereof, where are ruins to be feen of old buildings: And the hill afcending to the church on that fide is to this day called Hall-hill brow.

Raifgill hall, fituate on the rivulet called Raifbeck, nigh where it falls into the river Lune, is the houfe where the Blenkinfops kept their courts; but they always inhabited at Helbeck.

About a mile fouth eaft from Sunbiggin in this mancr is a lake called *Sunbiggin Tarn*, furnifhed (befides eels) with a red trout not unlike char: Where wild ducks alfo frequent and breed. The moors are generally furnifhed with *groufe* or moor game. And Orton fcar is famed for *dotterels*.

Upon the higheft part of Orton fcar is the *beacon*, which hath been a building about three yards long within, and two yards and an half wide. It com-

* Rex archiepifcopis, &c. falutem. Sciatis nos conceffiffe et hac charta noftra confirmaffe, dilecto et fideli noftro Ranulpho de Dacre, quod ipfe et hæredes fui et dilectus et fidelis nofter Thomas de Mufgrave et hæredes fui, imperpetuum habeant unum mercatum, apud manerium fuum de Overton, in comitatu Wefmorlandiæ, fingulis feptimanis per diem Mercurii, et unam feriam ibidem fingulis annis per tres dies duraturam, videlicet, in vigilia, et in die, et in craftino fefti apoftolorum Simonis et Judæ, nifi mercatum illud et feria illa fint ad nocumentum vicinorum mercatorum, et vicinarum feriarum. Quare volumus et firmiter præcipimus, pro nobis et hæredibus noftris, quod prædicti Ranulphus et Thomas, et eorum hæredes, imperpetuum habeant unum mercatum apud manerium fuum prædictum, fingulis feptimanis per diem Mercurii, et unam feriam ibidem fingulis annis per tres dies duraturam, videlicet, in vigilia, in die, et in craftino fefti apoftolorum Simonis et Judæ, cum omnibus libertatibus et liberis confuetudinibus ad hujufmodi mercatum et feriam pertinentibus, nifi mercatum illud et feria illa fint ad nocumentum vicinorum mercatorum et vicinarum feriarum, ficut prædictum eft. Hiis teftibus, &c. Data per manum noftram apud turrim London' nono die Januarii.

municates with the beacons of Penrith, Stanemore, and Whinfell (in the barony of Kendal). And by means of these beacons, when watches were kept up, intelligence might be conveyed thirty or forty miles in a few minutes.

Behind the scar, opposite to Raisbeck, about half a mile on the east side of the way as one goeth towards Asby, is a place called *Castle Folds*, in a situation exceeding well contrived, whereunto to draw their cattle in case of a sudden inroad of the Scots, of which notice was immediately communicated by the beacons. In which place the cattle would be secure, until upon the alarm given, the country might rise against the invaders. It is in a solitary place, not likely to be sought after or found, and situate in a large tract of naked rocks, the soil being washed off by the rains, and not easily accessible. The place hath been strongly walled about, and contains an area of about an acre and a half; and at the highest corner there hath been a fort, about seven yards square within, by way of shelter for the keepers, and as a kind of citadel to retire to, if the outworks should be taken.

Nigh Raisgill hall, there is a tumulus, or British sepulchre, in a regular circle near 100 yards in circumference, rising gradually from the extremity to about the height of three yards in the middle. It is composed of loose stones thrown together promiscuously; and in digging lately was found one very large stone supported by one other large stone on each side; and underneath the same was an human skeleton, with the bones of several others round about.

III. LANGDALE.

LANGDALE carries its own derivation along with it. This manor was never held of the Cliffords; for it was granted away before by king Henry the second, and confirmed by king John *, to the priory of Watton in Yorkshire.

In the 36 Hen. 3. there was a grant of free warren in Watton and Stancton in Yorkshire, and in Ravenstondale and Langedale in Westmorland, to the said priory.

* Johannes Dei gratia, &c. Sciatis nos concessisse, et hac charta nostra confirmasse Deo et Sanctimonialibus de Watton, in puram et perpetuam eleemosynam, totam Langedale, cum omnibus pertinentiis suis, et totam terram et pasturam inter ipsam Langedale et Burtresdale bec, sicut aquæ qua vocatur Tybbey descendit; ad faciendum inde omnem voluntatem suam, pro salute nostra, et pro animabus omnium antecessorum nostrorum. Quare volumus et firmiter præcipimus, quod prædicti Sanctimoniales totam terram illam habeant et teneant, et pasturam, bene et in pace, libere et quiete, integre, plenarie, et honorifice, in bosco et plano, in pratis et pasturis, in aquis et molendinis, in viis et semitis, et in omnibus aliis locis, et aliis rebus ad eas pertinentibus, et cum libertatibus et liberis consuetudinibus suis, sicut charta regis Henrici patris nostri rationabiliter testatur. Testibus, Guilielmo Filio Petri Comite Essexiæ, Hugone Bardolf, Willielmo de Stuteville, &c. Datum per manus S. Wellensis Archidiaconi, et J. de Gray, apud Doncastriam 28° die Martii anno regni nostri primo. 2 *Dugd. Mon.* 801.

After the dissolution of the monasteries, this manor was granted to the Wharton family; and, together with other of the Wharton estates, was purchased in the late duke of Wharton's time, by Robert Lowther of Maulds Meburn esquire, whose son and heir Sir James Lowther baronet now enjoys the same.

IV. TEBAY.

The manor of TEBAY comprehends the vills of *Ellergill*, *Gaisgill*, *Tebay*, *Rounthwaite*, and *Borrowdale*.

In the reign of king Edward the second, there was one *William de* ELLERGILL, who conveyed a capital messuage at Ellergill (which possibly may have been the ancient manor house) to Richard de Blenkinsop, the first of that name and family at Helbeck.

And about the same time, Richard son of *Robert de* GAISGILL conveyed to the said Richard de Blenkinsop divers lands and tenements there. And these made part of the Blenkinsops' estate in this parish, though not in the manor of Orton.

Of very early time, one *Radulph de* TYBAI was witness to a grant of lands at Kirkby Thore, to the abbey of Holm Cultram.

After him there was one *Herbert de Tibbay* who had lands at Tebay, but not the manor, at least not all of it; for it seems to have been parcelled out amongst several owners. The family of *Hastings* of Crosby Ravensworth had part. So had the family of *English* of Little Asby. And a small part was held under the Veteriponts and Cliffords, by the rent of 5*s* for all services.

In the 2 Joh. Geoffrey Fitz Peter and Roger de Bellocampo, sheriffs of Westmorland, accounted in the exchequer for 100 marks, paid by *Herbert de Tibbay*, *Robert* his son, and *Hugh de Hastings*, for lands in Tibbay.

In the 2 Hen. 3. Hugh de Hastings had a grant of free warren in Tibbay and Crosby.

In the 31 Ed. 1. and again in the 14 Ed. 2. *Henry Threlkeld* (of Crosby Ravensworth) had a grant of free warren in Tebay and Rounthwaite.

And in the 12 Ed. 3. *William English* had a like grant of free warren, with licence to impark 100 acres of land there.

In the 15th year of the same king, a fine was passed in the exchequer of the manors of Tibbay and Runthwaite; to hold to *William English* knight for life, remainder to *William* his son and the heirs male of his body, remainder to his sister Julian in fee.

In the 3 Ed. 2. the heir of *Thomas de Hastings* held of Robert de Clifford two carucates of land in Tybay, by the rent of 5*s*.

So in the 15 Ric. 2. after the death of Roger de Clifford, *Richard de Restwold* and *William de Querton* held divers lands in Tibay, by the rent of 5*s* for all services.

In like manner in the 10 Hen. 5. after the death of John de Clifford, the inquisition finds, that *Henry de Wherton* and *Richard Ristwould* held of the said John, on the day on which he died, lands and tenements in Tybay, by fealty and the rent of 5 *s*.

This *Henry de Wherton* was then lord of the manor of Wharton, and lived at Wharton hall. How the *Whartons* came to the whole manor of Tebay, we have not found. The same came from the *Whartons* to the *Lowthers* as aforesaid, in which family it still continues.

At a small distance from the village of Tebay northwards, in a place called Castle-green, is part of a round mount, with a trench on the outside, called *Castle-bow*; part of it hath been washed away by the river Lune. Opposite to which, is another hill called *Castle-bow* nigh Greenholme on the south-west side of the river Birkbeck. They seem to have been used for batteries, to command the passes in both places.

In the 7 Hen. 7. *Humphrey de Dacre* died seised of lands in ROUNTHWAITE. And the *Dacres* and *Blenkinsops* had some possessions also in *Tebay*. This seems to be the reason why some part of the land tax hath been paid all along from these places into the manor of Orton. For generally, in assessments to the subsidies (to which the land tax succeeded), where a man's estate lay in several contiguous townships, he was rated for the whole in the division where he inhabited, or where the main part of his estate lay. And the annual land tax acts still provide, that every place shall pay in that division where it paid in the 3 and 4 W. and Mary, when the land tax first commenced.

BORROWDALE hath its name from the river Borrow, which empties itself into Lune at Borrow-bridge. On the South, about 100 paces from the bridge, but within the parish of Kendal, are the ruins of a castle, which hath been moated about, and from the thickness and strong cement of the walls yet remaining, seems to have been a place of considerable strength. It is most advantageously situated, to command the whole passage through the mountains there.

V. BRETHERDALE.

BRETHERDALE is commonly said to have had its name from three brothers who inhabited there some 200 years ago. But that is only an imagination. It had this name long before; or rather, the name whereof this is a corruption, and sufficiently indicates its own derivation, namely, *Brere* (*i. e.* Brier) *dale*. And the countenance of the place to this day is correspondent thereunto. Therefore the two other brothers should be *Hepp* and *Sleagill*.

This place belonged to the abbey of Byland (de Bellalanda) in Yorkshire; being probably given to the same by the aforesaid Thomas son of Cospatric.

In the reign of king Edward the first, we find the abbot de Bellalanda holding of the two daughters of the last Robert de Veteripont, Asby Grange and Breredale, by the rent of 31 *s* 11½ *d* for all services.

In the 31 Hen. 6. the ſaid abbot held of Thomas de Clifford a certain paſture called Breredale, paying for the ſame a white rent [*de alba firmi*] of 5*s* for all ſervices.

In the 18 Hen. 8. the ſaid abbot held of Henry earl of Cumberland a certain paſture called Bretherdale, in ſocage; and paid yearly for the ſame 5*s*.

After the diſſolution of the monaſteries, the *Whartons* purchaſed this manor, which is now in the family of Lowther, as the others before.

VI. BIRKBECK FELLS.

The lordſhip of BIRKBECK FELLS is within the *manor* of Croſby Ravenſworth, and part of it alſo within the *pariſh* of Croſby Ravenſworth, where it is treated of more at large.

Moſt of the pariſh of Orton is in the Eaſt Ward; but Birkbeck Fells is in the Weſt Ward; and a ſmall part of the pariſh, namely, ſo much thereof as is in Fauſide Foreſt is in Kendal Ward.

PARISH OF CROSBY RAVENSWORTH.

I. *Pariſh of Croſby Ravenſworth.*
II. *Manor of Croſby Ravenſworth.*
III. *Manor of Mauld's Meburn.*
IV. *Manor of Regill.*

I. PARISH OF CROSBY RAVENSWORTH.

THERE are many places of the name of CROSBY, which imports no more than *Croſs-town*, or church town: And they are commonly diſtinguiſhed by ſome additional deſcription; which from vulgar pronunciation, and ignorance of languages and etymology in former ages, have been variouſly written. Amongſt all the variations of the additional name of this place, that of *Ravenſworth* is the moſt unlikely to be the true one. It was never anciently written *Ravenſworth*, nor is it eaſy to conjecture, from whence that termination could ariſe. *Ravens*, at ſuch a place, are eaſily accounted for. It was moſt frequently written *Ravenſwath*, as if ſo called from ſome ford there before the erection of the bridge: ſometimes *Ravenſwart*, and *Ravenſthwaite*; unto which laſt, the ſituation of the place ſeemeth well to accord; for *thwaite* ſignifies a level ground incloſed with hills or wood: Hence the words *Brackenthwaite*, *Sievythwaite*, *Rounthwaite*, *Oxenthwaite*, and the like. The common people pronounce it *Ravenſide*, which in ſound comes neareſt to *Ravenſthwaite*.

And

And there hath been a family from very ancient time at this place of the name of *Thwaite*.

This parifh is bounded on the Eaft by the parifhes of St. Laurence Appleby, and Afby; on the South, by the parifhes of Afby and Orton; on the Weft, by the parifhes of Orton and Shap; and on the North, by the parifhes of Shap and Morland: and contains about 158 families, all of the church of England.

It is not very certain, to whom this church was dedicated. According to the account of *Randall Sanderfon*, M. A. who was born in this parifh, it was dedicated to St. Laurence. The reverend Thomas Machel fays, it was dedicated to St. Leonard; whether this might be confounded with the hofpital of St. Leonard at York, which had lands here, cannot without further evidence be afcertained.

It is a vicarage, valued in the king's books at 7*l* 13*s* 4*d*. The clear yearly value, as certified to the governors of queen Anne's bounty, 35*l* 12*s* 7*d*. In 1721, Colonel James Grahme gave 200*l*, which with 200*l* given by the governors of queen Anne's bounty was laid out in lands at Lazingby, of the prefent yearly value of 20*l*.

Torfin de Alverftain, fon of *Uctred*, fon of *Gofpatric*, gave this church, with two carucates and 140 acres of land at this place, to the abbey of Whitby in Yorkfhire. Whofe grant was confirmed by *Alan* fon of *Torphin*, about the 20 Hen. 2. and by *Thomas de Haftings* fon of *Thomas de Haftings* and grandfon of the faid *Alan*; and alfo by Athelwald firft bifhop of Carlifle, by Robert archdeacon of the fame fee, and by Roger archbifhop of York. And the fame was afterwards appropriated to the faid abbey, by Bernard bifhop of Carlifle, referving out of the profits thereof 5*l* for a vicar to celebrate therein. Which alfo was confirmed by feveral fucceeding bifhops, and by the popes Gregory the ninth and Honorius the third. Walter bifhop of Carlifle afterwards conftituted a perpetual vicar therein, and allotted to him the altarage, and 20 acres of land with two tofts, paying to the monks of Whitby twenty fhillings *per annum*; and they were alfo to have the tithe of wool and lamb of the whole parifh, with two parts of the tithe hay of the whole village of Meburn: The vicar to bear all ordinary burdens, fynodals, and archidiaconal procurations; and the abbey the extraordinary.—And the faid *Thomas* fon of *Thomas de Haftings* freed the monks and their tenants from fuit to his mill there, and gave them leave to grind their corn where they thought beft *.

The priory of Wetheral (under the abbey of St. Mary's York) had alfo fome poffeffions in this parifh, given by *Ranulph de Mefchines*; and this church paid a penfion of 3*l* 6*s* 8*d* yearly to the faid abbey, which fince the diffolution of monafteries is paid to the dean and chapter of Carlifle.

After the diffolution, the rectory and advowfon were purchafed by the *Bellinghams* of Levins and Garthorne; which, together with the family eftate of the Bellinghams, were fold by *Alan Bellingham* efquire to the aforefaid colonel *James Grahme*; with whofe daughter and fole heir *Catharine*, the fame went by

* Burton's Monafticon Eboracenfe, 71, 2.

marriage

marriage to *Henry Bowes Howard* earl of Berkshire; who sold the rectory to the *Lowther* family; but the advowson continues in the hands of *Henry* now earl of Suffolk and Berkshire, grandson and heir of the said *Henry Bowes*.

There is a tradition of a friery having been here, adjoining to the north side of the churchyard. And there seems to be some remembrances of it, in the names of Monk garth, Monks barn, and Monks bridge. It might perhaps be some small house belonging to the said abbey of Whitby, or to some other religious house; for this parish had large connexions with divers other religious houses. The hospital of St. Leonard at York, as aforesaid, had divers lands here. The whole manor of Regill belonged to the abbey of Shap. And at Maulds Meburn there were lands belonging to four or five different religious societies.

In the year 1303, one *William de Insula* was vicar of Crosby Ravenswath; who in that year became bound to the bishop in the sum of 10*l*, to reside upon his benefice, and to live soberly and continently.

In 1361, *John de Linton* was vicar; on whose death, the abbot and convent of Whitby presented Sir *Robert de Threlkeld*, who was thereupon instituted.

And on the death of the said Sir Robert in the year following, *John de Regill* was instituted on the like presentation.

In the year 1572, bishop Barnes collated, on a lapse, Sir *Christopher Witton* clerk, to the said vicarage, being vacant by the neglect of Sir *Roland Thwaits* the last incumbent to subscribe the 39 Articles. But he seems to have been restored. For in 1576, *Thomas Burton*, LL. B. the bishop's chancellor, gave institution, on the death of *Roland Thwaits*, to *Edward Smyth* clerk, presented by one Richard Bacon of London, baker; by virtue of a third or fourth assignment of a grant made of the next avoidance, by the abbot and convent of Whitby, in the year next before their dissolution.

In 1597, on the death of the said Edward Smyth, institution was given to *William Willaine*, M. A. on the presentation of *Thomas Bellingham* of Garthorne gentleman.

In the year 1617, July 24, bishop Snowden, upon a pretended lapse, collated *Matthias Braddel*; but afterwards, on the 14th of October in the same year, he gave institution to *William Willaine* clerk, presented by Sir *James Bellingham* knight. (It seemeth that this William was son of the aforesaid William, and therefore by the canon law incapacitated to succeed his father; and that he had afterwards obtained a dispensation.)

In the time of Oliver Cromwell, *William Curwen*, M. A. appears to have been vicar, and by Oliver's commissioners ejected; but restored on the restoration of king Charles the second in 1660 *.

On the death of the said William Curwen in 1685, *William Wilkinson* clerk was presented by *Alan Bellingham* esquire, and instituted thereupon.

In 1708, on the death of William Wilkinson, *James Watson* clerk was instituted on a presentation by *James Grahme* esquire.

* Walker's Sufferings of the Clergy, Part ii. p. 226.

In

In 1747, on the death of James Watſon, *George Williamſon* clerk was inſtituted on a preſentation by *Henry Bowes Howard* earl of Suffolk and Berkſhire and *Catherine* his wife (daughter and heir of the ſaid *James Grahme*).

The *church* is a fair building, having a ſquare ſteeple or tower, with three bells. On the north ſide is an ile, belonging to the hall or ancient manor houſe.—The *churchyard* is a fine piece of *thwaite* or level ground, containing about two acres of land.

Belonging to this pariſh are ſeveral charities.

The reverend *Edward Holme*, M. A. gave 100*l*, which was laid out in lands at Scarſide in the pariſh of Orton; the produce thereof to be diſtributed in two-penny wheaten loaves weekly to poor people reſorting to the church on Sundays.

Edward Thwaites yeoman gave a rent charge of 4*l* 5*s* 0*d* out of Hill tenement; whereof 50*s* to be diſtributed amongſt the poor, 5*s* for a ſermon on the day of diſtribution, 20*s* to the ſchoolmaſter yearly, and 10*s* to buy books for poor ſcholars.

Thomas Addiſon yeoman gave 30*l*, the produce whereof to be diſtributed in penny loaves to poor women of the lordſhip of Croſby Ravenſworth.

They have alſo an ancient poor ſtock, in land or other ſecurities, of 3*l* 17*s* 6*d* yearly, for the poor of the whole pariſh.

And for the poor of the lordſhip of Croſby Ravenſworth ſolely 1*l* 8*s* 4*d*.

For the poor of Regill 4*s* 7*d*.

For the poor of the lordſhip of Maul's Meburn 2*l* 3*s* 8*d*.

John Knott by his will in 1734 gave an eſtate at Maul's Meburn, to the uſe of the poor of the ſaid lordſhip, and to pay 5*l* yearly to the ſchool of Croſby Ravenſworth, and 5*s* yearly for keeping dogs out of the church on Sundays: But after much money ſpent upon the litigated point how far owners of eſtates in the lordſhip and truſtees of the charity could be witneſſes to the will; the matter was at length compromiſed with the heir at law, for the ſum of about 100*l* to the charity.

II. MANOR OF CROSBY RAVENSWORTH.

The firſt lord of this manor of whom we have any account, was the aforeſaid *Torphin de Alverſtain*, who gave the church to the abbey of Whitby, in the reign of king Henry the firſt.

He had a ſon *Alan*, who confirmed his father's grant, in the reign of king Henry the ſecond.

This *Alan* ſon of *Torphin* had a ſon *Thomas de Haſtings*, who alſo had a ſon *Thomas de Haſtings*, who confirmed the ſaid grant as aforeſaid.

The next that we meet with was *Hugh de Haſtings*, who in the 2 Hen. 3. had a grant of free warren in Croſby Ravenſwath and Tibbay.

In the ſame king's reign, *Hugh de Haſtings* appears to have held the manor of Croſby Ravenſwath of John de Veteripont ſon of Robert. He alſo held the manor of Northallerton in Yorkſhire.

In the 8 Ed. 2. after the death of Robert de Clifford, the inquisition finds, that *Nicolas de Hastings* held of the said Robert, on the day on which he died, the manors of Crosby Ravenswath and Nateby, by homage and fealty, and *27s 2d* cornage. The wardship whereof, when it should happen, was estimated at 40*l*.

In the 43 Ed. 3. *Ralph de Hastings* held in like manner as before the manor of Crosby Ravenswath.

In the 10 Hen. 5. after the death of John de Clifford, the inquisition finds, that *Richard Hastynges* held the manors of Crosby Ravenswath and Nateby, by the aforesaid cornage of *27s 2d*.

By a feodary in the 31 Hen. 6. it appears, that *Edward Hastyngs* knight then held the manor of Crosby Ravenswath, by the cornage of *13s 7d*; subject also to wardship, marriage, relief, and suit at the county court: And *Lancelot Threlkeld* knight held the same of the said *Edward*. And henceforth we hear no more of *Hastings*.

The arms of *Hastings* were; Sable, a manch Argent.

This family of *Threlkeld* (whose principal residence was at *Threlkeld* in Cumberland) had considerable possessions in Westmorland, and particularly at Crosby Ravensworth, long before this time. For in the 32 Ed. 1. and again in the 13 Ed. 2. *Henry Threlkeld* had a grant of free warren at Yanwith, Crosby Ravenswath, Tebay, and Rounthwaite; and in the 5 Hen 4. *William Threlkeld* of Crosby knight, cousin and heir of *William Threlkeld* knight, father of *William Threlkeld* of Ulvesbye, son of *John*, son of *William*, paid his relief for two parts of the moiety of the manor of Ulvesbye.

This *Lancelot Threlkeld* knight was son of Sir *Lancelot* by Margaret daughter and heir of Henry Bromflett lord Vescy, widow of the aforesaid John de Clifford.

This Sir *Lancelot* the son was wont to say, he had three noble houses; one for pleasure, Crosby in Westmorland, where he had a park full of deer; one for profit and warmth, wherein to reside in winter, namely, Yanwith nigh Penrith; and the third, Threlkeld, well stocked with tenants to go with him to the wars.

He had three daughters coheirs; one married to *Thomas Dudley*, with whom he had Yanwith; the other two were married to two brothers, *Pickerings*, younger sons of Sir *James Pickering* of Killington in Westmorland. One of these two brothers with his wife had Threlkeld; the other brother, *viz. James*, had, with *Elizabeth* the eldest sister, Crosby Ravensworth.

The arms of *Threlkeld* differed only in colour from those of *Hastings*; being, Argent, a manch Gules.

In a feodary of Henry earl of Cumberland, in the 18 Hen. 8. it appears, that *James Pickering* esquire, as in the right of *Elizabeth* his wife, one of the daughters and coheirs of Lancelot Threlkeld knight, held of the said earl the manor of Crosby Ravynswath, by the cornage of *13s 7d*, owing also to the said earl for the same wardship, marriage, relief, and suit to the county court.

James was succeeded by his son *William Pickering* esquire; who in the 23 Hen. 8. was an arbitrator, together with Thomas Dudley of Yanwith and Christopher Threlkeld of Melmerby esquires, in a cause between Guy and Hugh Machel of Crackenthorp.

The said *William* had a son *Lancelot*, who about the 10 Eliz. married a daughter of Thomas Blenkinsop of Helbeck esquire. He appears to have been living in the 41 Eliz. and was succeeded by his son and heir, *viz.*

Thomas Pickering of Crosby esquire; who in the reign of king James the first sold the manor and part of the demesne to Sir *John Lowther* of Lowther knight.

The arms of *Pickering* were; Ermine, a lion rampant Azure, crowned Or.

The said Sir *John Lowther* gave the said estate in marriage with his daughter *Frances* to *John Dodsworth* of Thornton Watlass in the county of York esquire. He was a younger brother of the family of that name there. He had issue *John Dodsworth* of Crosby esquire, who died without issue, having devised this estate to Mr. *Francis Bayly* his faithful servant and steward, second son of Dr. Bayly of Penrith. Which *Francis* married Mrs. Mary Purley of Lincolnshire; by whom he had issue *Margaret Bayly*; which *Margaret* sold the premises to *Robert Lowther* of Mauld's Meburn esquire, father of the present owner Sir *James Lowther* baronet.

The *hall* is an ancient tower house, near adjoining to the west end of the church, and overshaded with trees. Formerly there hath been a moat about it. In the tower, where they enter, are two windows, one above the other, of no mean workmanship. Above the door, are the letters I D, for John Dodsworth, who repaired the tower, and cut these letters in the old work. There is a coat of arms, quarterly, of eight; which seems to have been put up by the Pickerings.

A little eastward from the churchyard is the *school*; a neat little building, but supported only by a small salary of 7 or 8 *l* a year, by money out at interest.

The *park* where Sir Lancelot Threlkeld kept his deer, lies a little southward from the hall and village adjacent, and is now called *Crosby Gill*. It was sold off from the rest of the demesne, by the last of the Pickerings, to *Edward Wilson* of Heversham hall gentleman; with whose kinswoman *Jane*, daughter of *Thomas Wilson*, it was given in marriage to *Robert Rawlinson* barrister at law, son of *William Rawlinson* of Colton in Lancashire by his wife Margaret daughter of Walter Curwen of Mireside.

Which said *Robert*, by the death of his mother's brother without issue, inherited a fair estate at Mireside, Carke, and Cartmell. By his wife Jane Wilson, he had issue a son *Curwen Rawlinson*, and four daughters, *Anne*, *Katharine*, *Eleanor*, and *Jane*; which two last died without issue.

Curwen Rawlinson esquire married Elizabeth only surviving child of Nicolas Monk bishop of Hereford and brother to George Monk first duke of Albemarle, son of Sir Thomas Monk of Potheridge in Devonshire, son of Anthony Monk esquire, son of Thomas Monk esquire by Frances Plantagenet daughter and coheir of Arthur Plantagenet viscount Lisle, son of king Edward the fourth. He had issue two sons, *Monk*, and *Christopher*: *Monk* died unmarried, and the inheritance descended to his younger brother *Christopher*.

The said *Christopher Rawlinson* was a gentleman of learning, and well skilled in antiquities. In the year 1698, being then gentleman commoner of Queen's college in Oxford, he published an elegant edition of king Alfred's Saxon version of *Boethius de Consolatione Philosophiæ*. He made also a large collection of matters relating to the counties of Lancaster and Westmorland, particularly that part which is called the barony of Kendal, from the Escheators books and other evidences: From which, Sir Daniel Fleming extracted so much as concerns the county of Westmorland; which extracts make a part of the valuable collection of manuscripts at Rydal hall. This *Christopher* also died unmarried; and thereby the estate descended to the issue of Curwen Rawlinson's two sisters *Anne* and *Katherine*.

Of whom, *Anne* was married to *Christopher Crackenthorp* of Newbiggin esquire; who had issue *Richard*; who had issue *Mottram*, *Deborah*, and *Anne*. *Mottram* died unmarried; and thereupon one moiety of *Crosby Gill* descended to his said two sisters: Of whom, *Anne* was married to Dr. *Adam Askew* of Newcastle upon Tyne, who received one half of the said moiety; and *Deborah*, dying unmarried, devised her half part of the said moiety to Dr. *Anthony Askew* of London, son and heir of the said Adam Askew by his said wife Anne Crackenthorp.

Katherine, the other sister of Curwen Rawlinson, was married to *Roger Moor* of Middleton serjeant at law; who had issue *Roger*, *Anne*, *Mary*, and *Katherine*. Of whom, *Roger* died without issue, and his moiety descended to his three sisters; *viz.* *Anne*, married to William Aylmer vicar of Warton; *Mary*, married to Charles Blake; and *Katherine* (who only had issue) married first to Mr. Rigg of Hawkshead, and afterwards to George Dixon. And all the three sisters, being widows, devised their shares respectively of the said moiety to the said *Katherine*'s grandchildren, two of whom enjoy the same at this time, *viz.* *Fletcher Rigg* esquire two shares, and his sister *Jane* (married to Mr. Edward Moore) one share.

The park wall hath been about three yards high, as appears by several parts thereof yet standing. And there is a farm house in the middle upon an eminence, which is yet called The Lodge. In this park also was plenty of black game.

Near the head of Crosby Gill, springs the river *Lyvennet*, at a place called Black-Dub, where king Charles the second, when he came in with the Scots in the year 1651, rested and dined, and drank of that water. Thence it runs to to Crofby, and paffing under Monks bridge near the church, runs down through Maud's Meburn, and from thence by King's Meburn, Wood head, Cliburn, and Julian Bower in Whinfell park, into the river Eden.

Above the head of Crofby Gill on the eaft fide, nigh the way leading from Crofby Ravenfworth, is a remarkable heap of ftones called *Penburrock*; which from its name muft needs be ancient. *Pen* is Britifh, and fignifies an head or fummit; *burrock* is Saxon, and fignifies an heap of ftones. And probably it hath been a *tumulus* or burying place in the time of the ancient Britons.

The lordfhip of *Birkbeck Fells* is in this manor, although the greateft part of the faid lordfhip is within the parifh of Orton.

In the reign of king James the firft, there was a difpute (as we have fet forth at large in treating of the barony of Kendal) between the lords of manors and their tenants, the lords claiming an abfolute eftate in the tenements, and the tenants infifting upon an inheritance therein according to the cuftom of the manor. After various litigations, divers lords and their tenants came to a compromife. And particularly in the manor of Crofby Ravenfworth, Sir John Lowther of Lowther knight, and John Lowther of Hackthorp efquire his fon, by their deed fetting forth, that whereas the tenants claim to be feifed of their feveral meffuages and tenements with the appurtenances, to them and their heirs, under certain rents, fines, boon days, works, and other fervices; and whereas there have been divers queftions and differences, between the faid lords and tenants, touching the validity of their faid cuftomary eftate which they claim as aforefaid; and whereas the faid tenants have agreed to pay forty years ancient rent for fettling and confirming their eftate; they therefore confirm to the faid tenants their eftate, to defcend acccording to the common law, except that the eldeft daughter or fifter fhall inherit; paying only two rents for a fine: referving neverthelefs the freehold eftate therein, and fuit of court, and fuit of mill. But releafing to the tenants all fervices of plowing, harrowing, fhearing, raking, peat leading, farm hens, and falt.

Which laft Item was from a demand, after Sir John Lowther had purchafed St. Bees and Whitehaven, of the tenants going there once a year and fetching falt and other neceffaries to Lowther; as the Wyberghs of Clifton, when they had St. Bees, had required the like boon of their tenants at Clifton.

But in the conclufion, moft of the tenements in this manor have been fold to freehold; the lord referving only the royalties, and fuit of mill after the twentieth multure, and power to inclofe 200 acres of the common to be fet out by a majority of the tenants; and the rent of 6*d* an acre, if the tenants fhall agree to inclofe the common.

There are three or four houfes on the eaft fide of the village of Crofby, called *Bank and Row*; which are within the manor of Garthorne, moft of which manor is within the parifh of Afby: It belonged to the Threlkeld branch

branch of Pickerings, and was sold by Sir *Christopher Pickering* to Sir *James Bellingham* of Over Levins, from whose descendent *Alan Bellingham* it was purchased by Colonel *James Grahme* as aforesaid, and from him descended to the present earl of *Suffolk* and Berkshire.

III. MANOR OF MAULD'S MEBURN.

Until *Maud de Veteripont*'s time, the whole tract, including both the *Meburns*, and the space between called *Meburn Field*, went by one general name of *Meburn*. It was often anciently written *Medburn*; which seemeth to indicate, that it received this name from the *burn* or rivulet (of Lyvennet) running all along down the *middle* of the vale.

The said Maud, who was sister to Sir Hugh Morvil, being married to William de Veteripont as is before mentioned, carried this estate to her said husband in frank marriage; and after the forfeiture of Sir Hugh Morvil, the other part of Meburn being taken into the king's hands, these two divisions became distinguished by the several names of King's Meburn and Maud's Meburn, or Mauld's Meburn (Meburn Matildæ).

The said William de Veteripont gave four oxgangs of land at Meburn to the friers of the hospital of St. Peter (otherwise called the hospital of St. Leonard) at York: Maud his wife (amongst others) being witness to the said grant.

Ivo de Veteripont, son of the said William and Maud, and brother of Robert, gave to the said hospital lands at Meburn circumscribed by these limits; *viz.* "From the nether or lower head of Undercot gill, unto the sike which is in the upper head, and so all along by the same sike southwards unto the ditch by the highway-side which leads from Appleby to Tibbay, and so nigh unto the public way or street westwards unto the boundary of Crosby, and thence unto the boundary of Askeby, and on to Keldheved, and thence towards the east between the boundaries of Meburn and Askeby unto the mills, and unto the ground which the said Ivo had before given to the aforesaid hospital."

Robert de Veteripont, son of Ivo, gave to the abbey of Shap 22*s* yearly to be paid out of Meburn in the name of *alms corn*.—After the dissolution of the abbey, in a rental of the Wharton estates (who had a grant of the possessions of the said abbey) *John Fletcher* and others, tenants of the demesne lands commonly called Meburn hall, stand charged for alms corn, formerly paid to the said abbey, 26*s* 8*d*.

There were several persons of the name *de Meburn* in those days, but none of them lords of the manor.

After the death of *Maud*, her son *Ivo* held Meburn; which *Ivo* had a son *Robert*, who in the 27 Hen. 3. granted this manor to *John le Frauncey*s; as appears by a record in that year, setting forth, that Robert de Veteripont son and heir of Ivo de Veteripont, recognized that he had given to *John le Frauncey*s *ceys* son of *Hugh le Franceys* the whole manor of Meburn which is called Maud's Meburn, to hold to him and his heirs, rendring yearly for all services one pound of cumin. (This payment was to Ivo: But there were other services to be performed to the barons of Westmerland, paramount lords of the fee.)

The said *John le Franceys* granted on the other hand, that Johan, daughter of the said Ivo, should peaceably have and hold the several lands and tenements granted to her by her father, with the services of villains and bondmen.

In the 41 Hen. 3. *Philip le Frauneeis* had a grant of free warren in Westmorland and Cumberland.

This *Philip* seems to have had a son *Gilbert*, whose son *Richard le Franceis* married a daughter of Sir Michael de Harcla. For in the 6 Ed. 1. the king seised the lands of Sir Michael de Harcla, until it shall appear by what right and title *Richard le Frauneeis* son and heir of *Gilbert le Frauneeis* married the daughter of Sir Michael de Harcla, being then the king's ward.

In the 35 Ed. 1. *John le Frauncéys* was a juror on the inquisition *post mortem* of Margaret de Ross.

In the 8 Ed. 2. after the death of Robert de Clifford, the inquisition finds, that *Richard le Fraunces* held of the said Robert, on the day on which he died, the manor of Meburn Maud and Whale, by homage and fealty, and the cornage of 33*s*. And that the wardship thereof, when it should happen, was worth 40*s*.

In the 15 Ed. 3. one *Isabella de Vernon* held Meburn. By which there seems to be little doubt, but that the family of *Frauncéys* had ended in a daughter married to Vernon.

In the 43 Ed. 3. *Richard Vernon* held the manor of Medburn.

In the 15 Ric. 2. and again in the 10 Hen. 5. *Richard de Vernon* held Meburn Mauld and Whale, by the cornage of 33*s*.

In the 31 Hen. 6. *William Vernon* held the same.

In the 1 and 2 Ph. and Mary, *George Vernon* held Meburn Maud and Whale, by the like services.

From this time we have no further account till the reign of king James the first; when in the 12th year of that king, a settlement was made of this manor of Meburn, upon *John Lowther* of Lowther esquire and Elianor his wife, daughter of William Fleming of Rydal esquire.

The ancient manor house seems to have been where the hall now stands. But the lands were so parcelled out amongst the religious societies, that there seems to have been scarce any demesne left. The last mentioned *John Lowther* esquire, afterwards Sir John Lowther, purchased there eight tenements, which make up the present demesne. From him it descended to his son Sir *John*, who gave the same to his second son *Richard*, who was succeeded by his eldest son *Robert*, father of the present owner Sir *James Lowther* baronet.

At Meburn town head was born LANCELOT ADDISON, son of *Lancelot Addison*, which *Lancelot* the son was educated at Queen's college in Oxford, passed many years in his travels through Europe and Africa, and joined, to excellent natural endowments, a great knowledge of letters and things, of which several books

books published by him are ample testimonies. He was rector of Milston in the county of Wilts, and afterwards became archdeacon of Coventry and dean of Litchfield. He married to his first wife Jane daughter of Nathanael Gulston esquire, and sister of Dr. William Gulston bishop of Bristol; and by her had issue, *Joseph* his eldest son, *Gulston* governor of Fort St. George, *Lancelot* fellow of Magdalen college in Oxford, and three daughters, Jane, Anne, and Dorothy. To his second wife he married Dorothy daughter of John Danvers of Shakerston in the county of Leicester esquire. In the churchyard of the cathedral of Litchfield is the following epitaph:

Hic jacet Lancelotus Addison S. T. P. hujus ecclesiæ decanus, nec non archidiaconus Coventriæ; qui obiit 20 die Aprilis, Ann. Dom. 1703. *Ætat. suæ* 71.

And on the inside of the cathedral is the following cenotaph or memorial of him:

P. M. Lanceloti Addison, agro Westmorland' oriundi, in collegio reginæ Oxon' bonarum literarum profecti, diutinis per Europam Africamq; peregrinationibus rerum peritia spectabilis, hujus tandem ecclesiæ decani et Coventriensis archidiaconi. In primis nuptiis duxit Janam Nathan' Gulston armigeri filiam, et Guillielmi Gulston episcopi Bristoliensis sororem: in secundis, Dorotheam Johan' Danvers de Shakerston in agro Leicestriensi armigeri filiam, funere mariti de se optime meriti nuper plorantem. Ex Jana tres filios, totidemq; filias suscepit, Josephum, Gulstonum arcis sancti Georgii gubernatorem, Lancelotum collegii Magdal' Oxon' socium, Janam et Annam prima juventute defunctas, et Dorotheam unicam ex tot liberis superstitem. Obiit A. D. 1703. *Ætat.* 71.

JOSEPH, the eldest son, had his first education at the Charterhouse, from whence he was removed to Queen's college in Oxford aforesaid. He had been there about two years, when the accidental sight of a paper of his verses occasioned his being elected into Magdalen college in that university. He employed his first years in the study of the old Greek and Roman writers, whose style and manner he caught, and retained to his dying day. He first distinguished himself by his Latin compositions in the Musæ Anglicanæ. His first English publication was a copy of verses to Mr. Dryden, which was followed by a translation of Virgil's fourth Georgic, of which Mr. Dryden makes honourable mention in the postscript to his own translation of all Virgil's works. Also the Essay upon the Georgics, which is prefixed to Mr. Dryden's translation, was furnished by Mr. Addison.—He had a pension from the government of 300*l* a year, to support him in his travels through several parts of Europe. An account whereof he published on his return; in which, instead of the usual topics of the customs and policies of the several governments, reflections on the genius and manners of the people, maps of their provinces, or measures of the buildings, he presented a journal of classical observations, with remarks on the present picture of the country, compared with the landskips drawn by the poets seventeen hundred years ago, this being a most engaging kind of criticism, which convinces at first sight,

 and

and ſhews the vanity of conjectures made by antiquarians at a diſtance.—His tragedy of Cato and other dramatic pieces, and the ſhare which he had in thoſe periodical publications, the Tatler, Spectator, and Guardian are known to every one, and will remain an eternal monument to his memory.

His firſt public employment was that of Commiſſioner of Appeals, in which he ſucceeded the celebrated Mr. Locke. Afterwards he was made under-ſecretary of ſtate, which office he held under Sir Charles Hedges and the earl of Sunderland. His next advancement was to the poſt of ſecretary to the marquis of Wharton when he went lord lieutenant into Ireland; where alſo he had the poſt of keeper of the records given to him, with an advanced ſalary. Upon the death of the queen, he was made ſecretary to the lords juſtices; and on the earl of Sunderland's going into Ireland, he was again made ſecretary for the Iriſh affairs; and ſoon after, one of the lords commiſſioners of trade. Finally, he was advanced to the poſt of one of his majeſty's principal ſecretaries of ſtate; but on his health declining, he reſigned the ſame, and died of an aſthma and dropſy in the year 1719, in the 49th year of his age. He left behind him one only daughter by the counteſs of Warwick, whom he married in the year 1716.

IV. MANOR OF REGILL.

This place of old time was invariably written *Renegill:* From what original, is not certain. Perhaps it was from the name of the owner. *Rene* was a name in the time of William the Conqueror, and long after. The firſt of the anceſtors of king William the third who came to be prince of Orange, was *Rene de Naſſau.*

The aforeſaid Maud de Veteripont gave half a ploughland of her demeſne in Renegill in frank marriage with her daughter Chriſtian to Robert ſon of Derman: Which land was called Hynthorneham.

Afterwards ſhe gave to her ſon Robert the whole vill of Renegill; he rendring to her for all ſervices one hawk. Which he was to hold of Ivo his brother. Ivo confirmed the ſame to Robert and his heirs, in the 9th year of king John.

And in the 13th year of the ſame king, the ſaid Robert granted to the abbey of Shap the whole vill of Renegill with the appurtenances; which he expreſſeth as granted to him by Maud his mother, and confirmed by Yvo his brother.

After the diſſolution, the revenues of the abbey of Shap were granted by the crown in the 36 Hen. 8. to Thomas lord Wharton; and the particulars of Renegill were as follows:—Divers rents and ſervices iſſuing out of the lands and tenements of the heirs of *William Hilton*, the heirs of *William Howgill*, the heirs of *John Medburn*, and of the wife of *Roland Herdſon*; and all meſſuages, mills, tofts, cottages, lands, tenements, meadows, paſtures, and other hereditaments, in the tenure or occupation of *Thomas Winter* and *Richard* his ſon, *Henry Dun*, *John Blamire*, *John Colſtane*, *Thomas Furneſs*, *Roland Furneſs*,

John Willain, Thomas Hugill, Thomas Blamire, William Robinson, William Adison, John Adison, Thomas Stable, the wife of *Richard Lowis, John Adison, Richard Mathews,* and *Roland Hogeson.*

The Whartons sold Regill Grange and half of the demesne, to Dr. Lancelot Dawes of Bartonkirk; and the other half to Sir John Lowther, who afterwards purchased the whole. And finally, whatsoever remained in the hands of the Whartons, which had belonged to the said Abbey, was purchased in the time of the late duke of Wharton by *Robert Lowther* of Meburn esquire, whose son and heir Sir *James Lowther* baronet now enjoys the said possessions.

There was here anciently a *chapel* or oratory: of which there are some remembrances, in the names of chapel garth, chapel lands, and the like.

Here was born Mr. *Randall Sanderson,* some time fellow of Queen's college in Oxford, and rector of Weyhill in Hampshire; who gave 100*l* for the founding and endowing a free school at Regill. He was also a considerable benefactor to the school at Appleby, where he was educated.

PARISH OF ASBY.

I. *Parish of Asby.*
II. *Asby Winderwath.*
III. *Asby Coteford.*
IV. *Little Asby.*
V. *Garthorne.*

I. PARISH OF ASBY.

ASBY was anciently written *Askeby,* probably from the same origin as *Askham* before mentioned.

This parish is bounded on the East by the parishes of Ormshead, Warcop, and Crosby Garret; on the South, by the parishes of Crosby Garret and Orton; on the West, by the parish of Crosby Ravensworth; and on the North, by the parishes of Crosby Ravensworth and St. Laurence Appleby: And contains about 72 families, all of the church of England.

The church is dedicated to St. Peter; and is a rectory, valued in the king's books at 23*l* 13*s* 4*d*: in the patronage of Walter Fletcher of Hutton in the Forest in the county of Cumberland esquire.

In the reign of king Henry the third, we find one *Adam* parson of Askeby witness to a deed of lands there.

In the year 1298, 27 Ed. 1. one *Richard le English* was parson of Asby, who in that year gave one messuage and six acres of land in Great Asby, for making a chantry in the chapel of St. Leonard of Little Asby.

In

In the same year, *William de Brampton* was presented to the rectory of Askeby, by Sir Robert de Askeby knight.

In the year 1319, on the death of William de Brampton, *William de Keldesyke* was instituted, on the presentation of the said Sir Robert de Askeby.

In 1345, on William de Keldesyke's death, *Thomas de Anant* was instituted, on the presentation of Sir Hugh de Moriceby knight, who married the daughter and heir of the said Sir Robert de Askeby. This Thomas de Anant gave by his will 100 marks to the town of Newcastle upon Tyne, and 50 marks to the parish of Askeby.

In 1374, on the death of Thomas de Anant, *Stephen de Meburn* was instituted on the king's presentation in right of the heir of Christopher Moriceby then in wardship of the king.

In 1563, Sir *Percival Kirkbryde* was instituted, on a presentation from Michael and John Kirkbryde, who derived their title from the lady Anne Knevet, widow of Sir Henry Knevet of East Horseley in the county of Surrey.

In 1572, on the deprivation of Percival Kirkbryde (probably for not subscribing the 39 articles) institution was given to *John Barnes*, presented by John Vaughan of Eskrig in the county of York esquire, and the lady Anne his wife.

In 1578, *Thomas Fairfax*, S. T. B. was instituted by his proxy Hugh Sewel, who took the usual oaths in his name; on a presentation by Lancelot Pickering esquire.

In 1593, on removal of Mr. Fairfax to Caldbeck, Mr. *Oswald Dykes* was instituted.

In 1618, *Lancelot Dawes*, M. A. was instituted on the king's presentation, upon a suggestion of simony, and a mandate was issued to the archdeacon to induct him. This Lancelot Dawes built the greatest part of the parsonage house at Asby. He was also vicar of Barton, and prebendary of Carlisle.

In 1661, *George Tibbold* was presented by Sir George Fletcher baronet.

In 1694, *Henry Fleming*, M. A. on the death of George Tibbold, was presented by the said Sir George Fletcher.

In 1728, on the death of Henry Fleming, *Joshua Burrow* was presented by all the coheirs of the said Sir George.

In 1739, on the death of *Joshua Burrow*, *Richard Machel*, M. A. was presented by Thomas Pattenson esquire, purchaser of that turn.

The *church* of Asby is an ancient building, with three bells.

There was heretofore a *chantry* in this church, dedicated to the virgin Mary, founded by Robert de Askeby in the year 1299.

A little below the church eastward, rises a large spring called St. *Hellen's well*. It has been neatly seated round; and (no doubt) in antient time, like the rest, did not want its miracles.

Near to the church also eastwards, is a small *school-house*, built (as the inscription over the door sets forth) by George Smith, merchant taylor and citizen of London, in 1688. He endowed it with 20*s* a year, leaving also a legacy of 10*l*, the intereſt whereof (then ſuppoſed to be 12*s*) was to be diſpoſed of on St. George's day yearly for ever, 6*s* to the poor of the pariſh, 5*s* to be ſpent in ale by the feoffees of the ſchool, and the remaining ſhilling to purchaſe a foot-ball for the ſcholars. Dr. Thomas Smith biſhop of Carliſle, who was born at Whitewall in this pariſh, beſtowed (amongſt many other deeds of charity) 100*l* upon this ſchool.

The abbey of Shap had three tenements in Great Aſby; which at the time of the diſſolution were in the poſſeſſion of William Unthanke, Margaret Myre, and George Myre, or their aſſigns.

II. ASBY WINDERWATH.

It ſeemeth that anciently all the *Aſkebys* (which now make three diſtinct manors) were one undivided intire manor. Afterwards, the ſame became diſtinguiſhed into *Little Aſby* and *Great Aſby*. *Little Aſby* ſeems to have been originally the principal place; for in ancient writings we ſometimes find it ſtyled *Old Aſkeby (Aſkeby Vetus)*. *Great Aſkeby* became again divided into moieties, *Aſkeby Wynanderwath* and *Aſkeby Cotesford*.

There is a *Winanderwath* in the pariſh of Cliburn, and *Winandermere* in the barony of Kendal. But from whence any of them derived their name, we have not certainly found; moſt likely, from the name of the owner.

The lords of *Aſkeby Winanderwath* (who alſo were patrons of the advowſon) ſo far as we are able to go back, were of the name *de Aſkeby*.

In the reign of king Henry the ſecond, *William* ſon of *Robert de Aſkeby*, and *Gilbert* and *Adam* his brothers, were witneſſes to a grant of lands at Blaterne to the abbey of Byland.

In the reign of Richard the firſt, Sir *Robert de Aſkeby* knight (probably ſon of *William*) was witneſs to divers inſtruments.

The next of the family ſeems to have been *Gilbert*. For in the reign of king Henry the third, *Robert* ſon of *Gilbert de Aſkeby* granted to Adam ſon of Hugh de Soureby and Idonea daughter of William de Cotesford (kinſwoman of the ſaid Robert) in frank marriage, four acres of his demeſne land of Winanderwhat, within the vill of Winanderwhat and without, namely, three acres and an half in Sulewhatſite, and half an acre nigh the bank which goes down from the foreſt upon Rokeraithe; and granted alſo, that they might grind their corn growing on the ſaid lands at his mill of Winanderwhat moulter free, or carry the ſaid corn to be ground elſewhere without doing ſuit to his ſaid mill. Witneſſes to the ſaid grant were (amongſt others) Robert de Cotesford, Geoffrey de Cotesford, William Engliſh, and Adam parſon of Aſkeby.

In the 14 Ed. 1. *Robert de Aſkeby* held the manor of Great Aſkeby of the two daughters and coheirs of the laſt Robert de Veteripont.

In the 28 Ed. 1. *Robert* ſon of *Henry de Aſkeby* founded the chantry of the virgin Mary aforeſaid in St. Peter's church at Aſkeby.

This *Robert* was knight of the ſhire for Weſtmorland in the 30 Ed. 1.

In the 3 Ed. 2. on an inquisition of lands in Westmorland held by cornage, it was found, that *Robert de Askeby* held a moiety (as it is there expressed) of Great Askeby and Winanderwath, and one carucate of land in Winton.

In the 7 Ed. 2. the said *Robert* was again knight of the shire for Westmorland.

In the 8 Ed. 2. after the death of Robert de Clifford, the jurors find, that *Robert de Askeby* held a moiety of Askeby Winderwath; the wardship whereof was worth 10*l*, the cornage 19*s*.

In the 12 Ed. 2. *Robert de Askeby* and *Margaret* his wife granted to Gilbert son of Richard Engayne of Clifton, a toft and croft and all their land at Clifton, to hold during his life of *Margaret de Askeby* their daughter, by the rent of a rose on the nativity of St. John Baptist.

This *Margaret de Askeby* was their only child; who carried the inheritance by marriage to Sir *Hugh de Moresby* knight; who in the 2 Ed. 3. and again in the 10 Ed. 3. was knight of the shire for Westmorland.

In the 11 Ed. 3. there was a grant of free warren to *Hugh de Moresby* in Winanderwath and Askeby.

In the 16 Ed. 3. a fine was levied between *Hugh de Moresby* and *Margaret* his wife complainants, and *Robert de Askeby* deforciant, of the manor of Wynanderwath and of a moiety of the manor of Rookby; to hold to the said *Robert* for life, remainder to the said *Hugh* and *Margaret* and the heirs of their bodies, remainder to the right heirs of the said Robert in fee.

Two years after this, the said *Hugh* appears to be dead; for in the 18 Ed. 3. a fine was levied of the manor of Great Askeby, between *Christopher de Morisby* and *Isabel* his wife of the one part, and *Margaret* wife of *Hugh Morisby* of the other part; to hold to the said *Christopher* and *Isabel* and the heirs of their bodies, remainder to the heirs of the said *Margaret* in fee.

In the 28 Ed. 3. amongst the escheats in Cumberland, it is found, that *Christopher Moriceby* held a moiety of the manor of Distington, and the manor of Moriceby in Cumberland, and the manor of Askeby in Westmorland.

In the 43 Ed. 3. *Christopher Moresby* held of Robert de Clifford the manor of Askeby Wynanderwath.

In the 47 Ed. 3. the king presented a clerk to the rectory of Askeby as aforesaid, in right of the heir of *Christopher de Mericeby* then in ward to the king.

This heir was a daughter *Anne*, married to Sir *James Pickering* of Killington knight. Which *Anne*, by a rental of Henry earl of Cumberland in the 18 Hen. 8. appears to have then held a moiety of Askeby called Wynanderwath, and one carucate of land in Wynton.

This *Anne*, to her husband Sir *James Pickering*, had a son and heir Sir *Christopher Pickering*, who had an only child *Anne*; which *Anne* was thrice married, first to Sir *Francis Westby*, secondly to Sir *Henry Knevett*, and thirdly to *John Vaughan* esquire.

In the 6 Eliz. there was a presentation to the rectory of Asby (as is above mentioned) by virtue of a title derived from the lady *Anne Knevet*, widow of Sir *Henry Knevet*.

And

And in the 15 Eliz. there was a preſentation to the ſaid rectory, by *John Vaughan* eſquire and the lady *Anne* his wife.

Six years after this, we find the advowſon in the hands of *Lancelot Pickering* eſquire, of the family of that name at Croſby Ravenſworth and Garthorne; ſo that he ſeemeth to have purchaſed the manor, with the advowſon appendent. And Sir *Richard Fletcher* of Hutton (in whoſe family it ſtill continues) purchaſed the ſame of the *Pickerings*.

III. ASBY COTESFORD.

This had its name of diſtinction evidently from the owner.

At the ſame time that *William de Aſkeby* was witneſs to divers inſtruments, ſo alſo was *Richard de Cottesford*, in the reign of king Henry the ſecond.

In the firſt year of king John, Gilbert Fitz-Reinfred, ſheriff of Weſtmorland, accounted in the exchequer for 3*l* paid by *Hugh de Cottesfurth* for lands in Aſby after the death of his uncle.

In the 14 Ed. 1. *Peter de Cotesford* held Aſkeby Cotesford of the two daughters of Robert de Veteripont.

In the 8 Ed. 2. *John de Cottesford* held a moiety of Great Aſkeby; the wardſhip whereof was worth by the year 6*l* 13*s* 4*d*; the cornage 4*s* 2*d*.

In the 43 Ed. 3. *John de Cotesforth* held the manor of Aſkeby Cotesforth.

In the 15 Ric. 2. *Stephen de Cotesford* held the ſame.

In the 31 Hen. 6. *John de Cotesford* held a moiety of Aſkeby called Aſkeby Cotesford, by homage and fealty, and 4*s* 2*d* cornage; owing alſo for the ſame, wardſhip, marriage, and relief.

In the 4 Ed. 4. *John de Cotesford* was one of the jurors on the inquiſition *poſt mortem* of John de Clifford; and this is the laſt of the name that we have met with.

This manor came afterwards to the *Muſgraves*, and paſſed with a daughter and heir to Dr. *Bouchier*, who ſold the ſame to the preſent owner *Roger Pindar* gentleman.

There are two eſtates in this pariſh which go by the name of *Grange*; one of them went along with the manor of Aſby Cotesford; the other belonged to the abbey of Byland in Yorkſhire, but by whom it was given we have not found.

IV. LITTLE ASBY.

To a deed of lands at Crackenthorp, in the reign of king Henry the ſecond, three of the witneſſes are, *William de Aſkeby*, *Richard de Cotesford*, and *Richard Engliſh* [L'Engleys]: who were ſeverally lords of the three Aſkebys.

In the 4th year of king John, there was an agreement between Robert le Scot and *Richard le Engleys*, concerning half a carucate of land, with the appurtenances, in Old Aſkeby.

In

In the 13th year of the same king, *William English* was witness to a grant of Robert de Veteripont to Shap Abbey.

In the 20 Ed. 1. Sir *Robert le Engleys* was a juror at Appleby in a cause between the king and the abbot of St. Mary's York.

In the 2d, 4th, and 5th of Ed 2. *Robert L'Angleys* knight represented the county of Westmorland in parliament.

In the 2 Ed. 3. *William L'Englishe* and *Elena* his wife levied a fine of the manor of Little Asby and lands in Great Asby, to the use of the said *William* and *Elena* and the heirs of their bodies, remainder to *Robert* brother of the said *William* and the heirs of his body, remainder to *Thomas* another brother, remainder to *John Dawney* and the heirs of his body, remainder to the right heirs of the said *William*.

In the 12 Ed 3. there was a grant to *William Englishe* to impark 100 acres of land in Kirklevington in the county of Cumberland, 100 acres elsewhere in the said county, 100 acres at Tibbay and Runthwaite in the county of Westmorland, and 100 acres at Assmudeby in the county of York.

In the 15 Ed. 3. a fine was passed of the manors of Tybbay and Runthwaite, to the use of *William L'Englishe* knight for life, remainder to *William* his son and the heirs male of his body, remainder to *Julian* his sister.

In most of the parliaments from the 12 Ed. 2. to the 22 Ed. 3. *William Lengleys* was knight of the shire for Westmorland.

In the 34 Ed. 3. *John* son of *Robert L'Engleys* made a settlement of his estate at Little Asby; Henry de Sandford, parson of Crosby Gerard, being a trustee in that settlement.

In the 43 Ed. 3. on an inquisition of knights fees in Westmorland, it was found, that *Robert Lenngleys* then held Little Asby.

The said *Robert* had a son *Thomas English* knight, who died before his father, and was the last of the name at Little Asby. He had issue only a daughter, *viz.*

Idonea English, who was married to *Edmund de Sandford*, a younger brother of Sir *William Sandford* of Sandford in the parish of Warcop knight.

The said family of *English* had considerable possessions in the parish of Askham. And *Idonea* removed with her husband to Askham; and they were the founders of the family of *Sandford* both at Askham and Howgill. She married to her second husband Sir *Thomas Ughtred:* And in the 15 Ric. 2. we find, that *Thomas Ughtred* and *Ydonia* his wife, as of the right of the said *Ydonia*, held the manor of Little Askeby, by homage and fealty and the cornage of 2*s* 10*d*.

In the 10 Hen. 5. after the death of John de Clifford, the inquisition finds, that *Robert de Sandeford* held the same. Which *Robert* seems to have been second son of the said *Edmund* and *Idonea*, his elder brother *William* having died without issue. For by an inquisition of the services of knights and others, free tenants, holding of Thomas de Clifford as of his barony of Westmorland, in the 31 Hen. 6. it is found, that *Robert Engleys* heretofore held Little Askby, and paid for the same *ad cornagium* 2*s* 10*d*, and owed wardship, marriage, re-chief, and suit to the county court. And now *Thomas Dalamore* esquire holds the same, as of the right of *Margaret* his wife, late wife of *William Sandford* elder brother of *Robert Sandford* esquire, which *Margaret* had the same vill in jointure with the aforesaid *William* her late husband, the reversion thereof belonging to the said *Robert*.

Soon after this, we find *Thomas Sandford* (son of the said *Robert*) holding the same by the like services.

In the 18 Hen. 8. *Thomas Sandford* of Askham esquire held the same. Which *Thomas* had two sons; *Thomas*, the elder, who continued at Askham; and *Richard*, the younger, who had Howgill; unto which younger branch acceded also little Asby, and continued in the Sandfords of Howgill till failure of issue male, when the same was transferred by marriage of *Mary* daughter and heir of Sir *Richard Sandford* of Howgill baronet to *Robert Honywood* of Mark's hall in Essex esquire; whose son, lieutenant general *Philip Honeywood*, now enjoys the same.

At Little Asby was a *chapel*, dedicated to St. Leonard; unto which *Richard le English*, parson of Asby as aforesaid, gave a messuage and 6 acres of land for the establishing a chantry therein.

In digging of peats within this manor, nigh the East end of Sunbiggin tarn, about 40 years ago, were found the horns of two large bulls, jumped together in the posture of fighting; one of them probably having pushed the other into the mud, where they had both sunk. The rest of the skeletons could not be recovered, by reason of the water oozing in. One pair of these horns was carried to Howgill castle, where they are yet to be seen.

V. GARTHORNE.

This manor seems to have belonged to the hospital of St. Leonard's York. At least part of it did; for in the 9 Ed. 1. the said hospital had a grant of free warren in Docker and Garthorne. And it doth not appear to have been held at any time of the Veteriponts or Cliffords.

A small part of it is in the manor of Crosby Ravensworth. It belonged heretofore to the *Pickerings*, and was sold by Sir *Christopher Pickering* of Ormshead in the reign of king James the first to Sir *James Bellingham* of Over Levins. Sometimes a branch of the family of *Bellingham* resided at Garthorn hall. *Alan Bellingham* esquire, in the reign of king Charles the second, sold the same to colonel *James Grahme*, ancestor of the present owner Henry earl of Suffolk and Berkshire.

PARISH OF ORMSIDE.

ORMSIDE is a corruption (as most of the names of places and persons have been corrupted in ignorant times) of *Ormes-head*, or (which is the same) *Ormeshevd:* And had its name probably from some owner of the name of *Orme*. *Orme*, governor of Appleby castle (father of Cospatric), who lived in the reign of king Henry the second, we have often had occasion to mention. That this place had its name from him, we cannot affirm: but rather it seems to have been from some other of the name before that time.

This parish is bounded on the East by the parish of Warcop; on the South, by the parishes of Warcop and Asby; on the West, by the parish of St. Laurence Appleby; and on the North, by the parishes of St. Laurence and St. Michael's Appleby.

Who the church was dedicated to, we have not found. It is a rectory, in the patronage of the bishop of Carlisle; rated in the king's books at 17*l* 17*s* 3½*d*. The clear yearly value, as certified to the governors of queen Anne's bounty, 40*l*.

This church was appropriated to the abbey of St. Mary's York. And in the year 1248, the abbot and convent granted to the bishop of Carlisle the advowson of Ormesheved; reserving to themselves their usual pension out of the same.

In the year 1294, *William de Gosford*, priest, was collated to this rectory by bishop Halton.

In 1321, *John de Morland* was collated by the same bishop.

In 1343, Sir *Robert de Risindon* appears to have been rector of Ormesheved; a dispensation being then granted to him of absence for three years upon account of study.

In 1362, Sir *John de Grete*, chaplain, was collated by bishop Welton; and two years after had a dispensation of absence, by reason of his attendance on the lord Clifford.

In 1367, Sir *Robert Bix*, chaplain, was collated to the vacant rectory of Ormesheved by bishop Appleby.

In 1406, one of the trustees in a settlement of the manor of Ormesheved made by John de Barton of Ormesheved and Alice his wife, was *Richard de Colleby*, parson of the church of Ormesheved.

In 1565, on the death of Sir *Christopher Parker*, rector of Ormeshead, Mr. *Richard Towlson* was collated by bishop Best.

In 1569, on the death of Richard Towlson, the same bishop collated Sir *John Watson* clerk.

In 1571, Mr. *John Barnes* was collated by bishop Barnes.

In the next year, on his resignation, the same bishop collated Mr. *John Corry*.

Three years after this, on Mr. Corry's resignation, the same bishop collated Mr. *Lancelot Manfield*.

In 1582, on the death of Lancelot Manfield, Sir *John Braythwaite* clerk was collated by bifhop May. And in the year 1585, this John Braythwaite refigned his rectory, before a public notary and other witneffes. But the bifhop feems not prefently to have accepted his refignation, for no fucceffor was appointed till two years after, when the fame bifhop collated *John Hudfon* clerk.

In 1591, on the death of John Hudfon, the faid bifhop May collated *Richard Burton*, M. A. in deacon's orders.

In 1635, on the refignation of Richard Burton, *Robert Symfon*, M.A. was collated by bifhop Potter.

In 1661, *Barnaby Symfon*, M. A. was collated by bifhop Sterne.

He was fucceeded by *John Symfon* clerk; on whofe death, *Thomas Nicolfon*, A. B. was collated by bifhop Waugh, in 1726.

And in the next year after, on the ceffion of Thomas Nicolfon, *William Nicolfon*, M. A. was collated by the fame patron.

In 1731, on the death of *William Nicolfon*, *Thomas Cautley* clerk was collated by the fame bifhop.

In 1762, on the death of Thomas Cautley, *William Prefton*, M. A. was collated by bifhop Lyttelton.

The *church* of Ormfide, as alfo the parifh, is but fmall. It ftands near unto the hall. It hath a tower fteeple, with two little bells. There is an ile on the north fide belonging to the lord of the manor.

In the MANOR of Ormfide there are two hamlets or villages, diftinguifhed by the names of *Great Ormfide* and *Little Ormfide*, perhaps after *Little Ormfide* was parted from the reft of the manor.

GREAT ORMSIDE is pleafantly fituate, on the fouth fide of the river Eden; and contains about 20 families.

The firft perfon of note that we have found with certainty at Ormfide, was in the reign of king John, namely, *John de Ormefheved*, who, together with Robert de Boell, in the 4th year of the faid king, was appointed to receive poffeffion of Appleby caftle, in behalf of Robert de Veteripont, to whom the king then firft granted the fame during his pleafure. The writ for delivery thereof was thus: "The king, &c. To W. fon of Peter, &c. Know ye, that "we have committed to our trufty and well beloved Robert de Veteripont "our caftles of Apelby and Burgh, and the whole bailiwick of Weftmerland, "with all their appurtenances, to be kept by him during our pleafure. And "therefore we command you, that without delay you deliver up to Robert de "Boell and *John de Ormefheved* ferjeant (fervienti), of the faid Robert de Ve"teripont, on the behalf of the faid Robert de Veteripont, the faid caftles "and the whole bailiwick of Weftmorland, with all things thereunto belong"ing." And the like writs were directed to all the tenants of the honour of Apelby and Burgh and the whole bailiwick of Weftmorland to be obfervant of him during fuch time.

In the 8th year of the fame king, when Maud the daughter of Torphin de Wateby granted to the faid Robert de Veteripont all her lands in Weftmorland,

land, one of the witnesses to the confirmation thereof by her second husband Philip de Burgo, was *John de Ormesheved then sheriff of Westmorland* (under the said Robert de Veteripont).

In the 36 Hen. 3. to a grant of lands at Appleby by the last Robert de Veteripont to one Richard Clerke during his life, one of the witnesses was *Robert* son of *Guy de Ormesheved.*

In the 14 Ed. 1. *John de Ormesheved*, son of *Robert*, lord of the manor of Ormesheved, granted to *John* his son and heir, certain lands in Ormesheved, abutting on the lands of Simon son of *Robert* son of Eudo de Ormesheved; and also lands in Little Ormesheved, together with the homage and services of John de Rosgill for his lands there. Witnesses; Michael de Harcla then sheriff of Westmorland, John de Terriby, and others.

In the same year, *John de Vescy* held part of the manor of Ormesheved of the two daughters of Robert de Veteripont. By the inquisition it should seem that he held the whole manor, but it appears clearly afterwards that he held but a moiety; and the inquisitions often express the whole instead of a part.

In the 3 Ed. 2. *John de Derwentwater* held the manor of Ormesheved. And again, in the 8 Ed. 2. after the death of Robert lord Clifford, *John de Derwentwater* held the manor of Ormesheved; the wardship whereof, when it should happen, was worth 10 *l*; the cornage, 13 *s* 6 *d*.

And in the 43 Ed. 3. *John de Derwentwater* held the same. So in the 15 Ric. 2. and again in the 4 Hen. 4. *John de Derwentwater* held the said manor.

In the 8 Hen. 4. *John de Barton* and Alice his wife made the settlement aforesaid of the manor of Ormesheved.

In the 10 Hen. 5. *Nicolas de Radcliff* and *Elizabeth* his wife (daughter of *John de Derwentwater*) held the manor of Ormeshead, in right of the said *Elizabeth*.

In the 30 Hen. 6. there is a letter of attorney from Robert Warcop junior, *Thomas Barton* of Ormeshead, and Christopher Sourby chaplain, to Richard Martendall of Patterdale, to deliver seisin to *John de Barton* and Katherine his wife of lands in Ormeshead, Great Salkeld and Great Asby.

In the 31 Hen. 6. *Thomas Ratcliffe* held a moiety of Ormeshead immediately of Thomas de Clifford, called *Ormeshead Vescy*, because holden heretofore by *John Vescy*; and *John Barton* held the same of *Thomas Radcliffe*.

In the same year there was a dispute between *John Barton* of Ormshead esquire, and the chantry priest of the chapel or chauntry of our lady in Appleby, concerning a watergate and common of pasture on Ormshead moor; which was referred to Sir William Stowe knight and commander of the mount of St. John, Sir Robert Lowther of Lowther knight, Richard Ristwald of Appleby gentleman, and Roland Barton of Newcastle upon Tyne clerk: Upon which they made an award; the particulars whereof we have inserted in treating of the chantries at Appleby.

In the 18 Hen. 8. *Cuthbert Radcliffe* held the manor of Ormshead, and *Robert Barton* held the same of the said *Cuthbert*, as is supposed (so the inquisition expresseth it) as of the heirs of *Derwentwater*.

In the 20 Hen. 8. *Robert Barton* of Mekil Ormeshead esquire makes a settlement of his manors of Mekil Ormeshead and Littel Ormeshead, and his lands there, as also at Great Asby, Patterdale, Sandwyk, and Pullo, in the county of Westmorland, and his lands in Yorkshire and Northumberland, upon his cousin *Henry Barton* of Chempsforth in the county of Essex gentleman, remainder to *Thomas Barton* of Warcop, remainder to *Andrew Barton* of Smythylls in the county of Lancaster, remainder to *John Barton* of Whenby in the county of York in tail male, remainder to his own right heirs. And the said *Henry* covenants, that he shall not be married nor affied to no woman by the sacrament of matrimony, without the assent and consent of the said *Robert*.

In the 29 Hen. 8. there is a release by Isabella Hylton widow of Richard Hylton of Burton; one of the sisters and coheirs of the late *Robert Barton* of Ormeshead gentleman, to Robert Pulleyn gentleman, and Thomas Hilton gentleman son and heir of the late Robert Hilton of Burton gentleman, of all her right in the lands descended to her from her said brother in Westmorland, Cumberland, and Northumberland. Witness (amongst others) *Henry Barton* of Ormeshead.

In the 30 Hen. 8. there is an award between *Henry Barton* of Ormeshead gentleman, and divers other persons, concerning lands late belonging to *Robert Barton* deceased; wherein it is awarded, that Henry shall enjoy the manor of Mikil Ormeshead, and lands in Littel Ormeshead and other places.

In the 33 Hen. 8. there is an exchange of lands at Ormeshead, between Roland Hartley and *Henry Barton* of Great Ormeshead gentleman.

Finally, in the reign of queen Elizabeth, *Thomas Barton* (probably the next in the intail) sold the manor of Great Ormeshead, to Sir *Christopher Pickering* knight, of the family of the *Pickerings* of Crosby Ravensworth.

The said Sir *Christopher Pickering* died without ever having been married, and gave the manor of Ormside to *Frances* his natural daughter, who was married to *John Dudley* of Dufton esquire, of the family of the Dudleys of Yanwath: Who dying without issue by her, she married again to *Cyprian Hilton* of Burton esquire, who had with her the manor of Ormside: Rutter, which was part of the demesne, was sold to Mr. Williams of Johnby in Cumberland.

She had to her said husband *Cyprian Hilton*, a son *Christopher*; who had a son *Cyprian*; who had a son *Christopher*; who had a daughter *Mary*, married to *Thomas Wybergh* of Clifton esquire, in whose time the manor was sold to *George Stephenson* of Warcop esquire, who died intestate and without issue, and his estate descended to two coheirs, sisters of his father *John Stephenson* gentleman, and upon the partition thereof this manor came to the share of John Fawell of Temple Sowerby gentleman, grandson of Anne the elder sister, who in the year 1770 sold the same to Sackville earl of Thanet.

In the aforesaid north ile of the church is the burying-place belonging to the hall; wherein is one large grave stone, upon which are three inscriptions on so many plates of brass; *viz.* 1. The epitaph of Sir *Christopher Pickering* knight, who died Jan. 14, 1620; having been five times sheriff of Cumberland. 2. Of *Cyprian Hilton* esquire, who died Dec. 22, 1652. 3. Of *Cyprian Hilton*

Hilton esquire, who died Dec. 27, 1693; aged 34: and left three sons and five daughters.

The *hall* is an ancient tower house, built like the rest of the old houses in this country, as a place of defence. There is a well that springs under the kitchen within the house.

The tenants have been mostly purchased free, probably when part of the manor and demesnes were sold off.

In the year 1689, behind the church in the river Eden, on the south side next the hall, were found several vessels of brass, some of which seemed to have been gilt. The river exposed them by washing away the soil. They seemed not to be ancient. Upon one of them were the letters F D, supposed to stand for the name of Frances Dudley, widow of John Dudley aforesaid, and daughter of Sir Christopher Pickering. They were buried probably during the civil wars in the reign of king Charles the first.

Little Ormside, about half a mile south-east from the church, contains about eight or nine families. The tenants seem to have been purchased off from the manor of Ormside at large, and are now within the manor of Gathorne in the parish of Asby. But most of them, in like manner as of Great Ormside, have been infranchised.

In the said manor of Ormside is a single hall house called Breeks, about half a mile south from the church. There is a freehold demesne belonging to it, formerly sold off from the rest of the demesne by Thomas Barton esquire to his brother William; whose son Robert Barton sold it to John Pattenson attorney at law in Penrith, who had a son Thomas, who had a son Lancelot, father of the present owner Thomas Pattenson of Melmerby esquire.

PARISH OF RAVENSTONDALE.

THIS parish hath its appellation from a brook of the name of *Raven* running through it; in like manner as the village Renwick (Ravenwick) in Cumberland. It was commonly of old time written *Ravenstandale*: So there was *Stanmore* in the parish of Brough.

The parish is bounded on the East by the parish of Kirkby Stephen; on the South, by the parishes of Kirkby Stephen and Sedbergh; on the West, by the parish of Orton; and on the North, by the parishes of Crosby Garret and Kirkby Stephen: And contains about 225 families; whereof 59 are dissenters.

The church is said to be dedicated to St. Oswald *. It is a perpetual curacy, in the patronage of Sir James Lowther baronet.

* Machel.

The

The manor, with the advowson appendent, was granted by Torphin son of Robert, son of Copsus, to the priory of Watton of the order of Sempringham in Yorkshire. Which Torphin son of Robert seems to be the same person who gave the manor of Blaterne to the abbey of Byland, and who lived in the reign of king Henry the second. But the church was not appropriated to the said priory of Watton till the year 1336, *Gilbert de Wiggeton* the rector then resigning *.

The tenor of Torphin's grant is set forth in an account given to the reverend Thomas Machel, by Mr. Anthony Prockter curate of Ravenstondale and Mr. George Fothergill of Tarnhouse; as also in a manuscript written in the year 1645, by Anthony Fothergill of Trannahill, great grandfather of the late Mr. Anthony Fothergill of Brounber, whose account was taken from an office copy of the charter of donation remaining amongst the evidences in the tower or palace of the late abbey of St. Mary without the walls of York; which tower was blown up with gunpowder by Oliver Cromwell in the year 1644, and this with many other valuable charters belonging to the religious houses was thereby destroyed and lost. The said charter was (in English) as follows: "Know all men present and to come, that I Torphin son of Robert son of "Copsus have given, and by this my charter confirmed, to God and the "blessed virgin and all the holy men serving God in the monastery of Wat-"ton, all the whole vill of Ravenstandale, with that part of the vill called "Newbiggin, with the boundaries and limits thereof as well without the vill "as within; that is to say, from the head of Beversdale, as the water of "Beversdale runs till it comes into the water of Tebey; and from thence "by Hanscus to the Blea Tarn; and from thence into Rasett; and so to "Couling stones; and from Couling stones to Skeat beck runs into Smerdale "beck; and so by Smerdale beck till it comes to Smerdale Flatt; and from "thence till it come to the highest place on Ashfell; and so to Tarn wath "hole; and from Tarn wath hole, as Kirkby way goes, till it come at Scan-"dal water; and so going up that water into a path-way that goes to Mal-"lerstang searth; and then on the top of Wildboar fell to the head of the "water of Ulnedale; and as the water of Ulnedale runs till it come into the "water of Rothay; and as the water of Rothay runs till it come betwixt "Washingham and Keldon; and from thence to the head of Beversdale."

Newbiggin being particularly mentioned in this grant (which is a part of Ravenstondale) seems to have been in respect of a chapel which anciently stood there, at the north end of the village; which chapel probably was dedicated to St Helen, there being a spring near the same called St. Helen's well.

This order of Sempringham, unto which the priory of Watton belonged, was founded by St. Gilbert at a place of that name in Lincolnshire, in the year 1148. They had very large privileges granted to them by several popes and kings of this realm.

Pope Celestine the third, who came to the see in 1191, granted to them a privilege of exemption from payment of tithes of lands which they had in

* Todd.

their own cultivation, which being restrained by the general council of Lateran in the year 1215 to the tithes of such lands as they were in possession of before the said council, and divers spiritual judges refusing to admit their exemption, pope Honorius the third directed a special commission to the abbots of Kirkstede, Revesley, and Barlinges, to inforce by spiritual censures the said privilege of exemption, modified by the decrees of the said general council, that is, of such lands as they were in possession of before the said council, but not of lands acquired or to be acquired after the said council.

And king Henry the third, in the year 1225, being the eleventh year of his reign, reciting the privileges that had been confirmed to the said order by his father king John, extends the same to other houses of that order then newly established; and grants as follows:

"Henry by the grace of God, &c. Know ye, that we have taken into "our hand, custody, protection, and defence, the house of Sempringham, "and all the houses of that order [sixteen in number, of which Watton is "expressed to be one] together with the masters, priors, canons, and monks "of the said order, and all their servants, tenants, lands, and other possessions, as our own special and free alms. Wherefore we will and firmly "command, that they hold all their tenements well and in peace, freely and "quietly, and intirely, and fully, and honourably, in wood and in plain, in "meadows and pastures, in waters and fisheries and vivaries, in stream and "strand, in forests, in mills, and in ponds, in tofts, and crofts, and underwoods, in ways and in paths. And they shall be quit, as well themselves "as their men, in city and town, in markets and fairs, in the passage of "bridges and ports of the sea, and in all places throughout all England and "Normandy, and through all our lands and waters, from toll, and pontage, "and passage, and pedage, and lestage, and stallage, and hidage, and carucage, "and wardings, and works of castles and bridges and parks and walls and "trenches, and taxes, and tributes, and armies, and services in the forests in "all places where their possessions lie" [and particularly in Westmorland throughout the whole forest of Malrestang]; "and from all gelds, and danegelds, and woodgelds, and fengeld, and horngeld, and footgeld, and penygeld, and trithingpeny, and hundredspeny, and from miskenning, and from "thenage, and from headpeny, and buckstall, and trist; and from all fines, "amerciaments, and forfeitures, and aids, and wapentac, and cities, and "trithings, hundreds, and shires, and thenementale; and from murder, and "robbery, and conspiracies, and outlawry; and hamsoken, grithbreach, bloodwite, footwite, and forestal, and hengwite, and lairwite. And they shall be "free from scott, and wardpenny, and bordeshalfpeny; and from all carriage, and sumage, and navage, and building, and all other kinds of "work about the king's houses; and from all aids of sheriffs and their officers, "and scutage, and assises, and gifts, and summonses, and tallages, and frankpledges, and from borthevenlig, and all pleas, and plaints, and occasions, "and customs, and from their beasts to be taken by distress, and from all "earthly service and secular exaction. And their woods shall in no wise be "taken for the aforesaid works or any other. And they shall have their own "court and judicature, with sak, and soke, and thol, and theam, and infang-"thief, and outfangthief, and flemensfrith, and ordel, and oreste, within "time and without, with all other free customs, and immunities, and liber-"ties, and of all pleas, plaints, and quietances. And we do prohibit, that "no sheriff or officer, or other person, great or small, within their posses-"sions shall presume to take any man, bind, beat, slay, or shed blood, or "commit any other rapine or violence; or distrain their beasts on the lands "of their said possessions; nor detain any of their bondmen, fugitives, or "chattels; nor in any wise hinder their men coming to their mills; nor "trouble them or their men for any custom, service, or exaction, or any other "cause, in respect of their goods which their men can swear to be their own; "but they shall be quit of all customs and exactions and occasions, and ge-"nerally of all things in all manner of ways which do or shall belong to us, "our heirs and successors: Except only the jurisdiction of life and limb. "Also we grant to them in perpetual alms the amerciaments and forfeitures "of their men of all pleas wheresoever they shall be judged, whether in our "court, or in any other, so far as to us appertaineth. And if it shall hap-"pen that any of their men shall be condemned to death, or loss of limb, or "perpetual banishment, the aforesaid canons and monks shall have all their "chattels without any gainsaying: Saving to us by our officers the execution "of the judgment of life and limb. And if any person shall claim any thing "against any of the said houses in respect of their possessions, or vex or im-"plead them in any wise, we prohibit that they answer not for any thing, nor "enter into plea, and that no man cause them to be impleaded, unless before "us or our heirs, or before our justices itinerant."——And he extends the said privileges to three houses of that order then newly founded (that is, after the grant of king John's charter above referred to).

King Edward the third, by his charter in the 4th year of his reign, reciting the charter of king Henry the third *verbatim*, confirms all the aforesaid privileges, and further grants them a freedom from pannage and murage; extending the same to another house of that order then newly founded, called the house of St. Edmund of Cantebrigg.

And finally, king Henry the sixth, in the 16th year of his reign, reciting by Inspeximus the said charters of king Henry the third and Edward the third, confirms the same "by the advice and assent of the lords spiritual and tem-"poral in parliament assembled *."

By this it appeareth, that besides freedom from toll and other personal or pecuniary charges, they had also a privilege of sanctuary throughout their whole possessions, so that the sheriff or other the king's officer might not enter to apprehend any offenders, but they were to be tried before the steward of the manor by a jury of the tenants, and punished according to the sentence of that court: Except only in cases of life and member; and in such case they were

* These grants of privileges being more full and ample than any other we have met with, and withal the original charter from whence our copy was taken having been destroyed by blowing up the tower of St. Mary's at York as aforesaid, and no printed copy extant thereof that we know of, we have inserted a copy of king Henry the sixth's charter in our Appendix, N° II.

to be tried within the manor by commiſſioners (as it ſeemeth) to be appointed by the crown; and the priory was intitled to the goods of the felons attainted.

In purſuance of theſe grants, the aforeſaid manuſcript of Anthony Fothergill ſets forth, that if a murderer fled to the church or ſanctuary, and tolled the holy bell (as it was called), he was free; and that if a ſtranger came within the precincts of the manor, he was ſafe from the purſuer. And he adds, "Of our own knowledge, and within our own memory, no felon (though a "murderer) was to be carried out of the pariſh for trial. And one Holme, "a murderer, lived and died in Ravenſtondale; whoſe poſterity continued for "two generations, and then the family became extinct." And to this day there is a place within the lord's park, in ſight of the ancient highway leading from Kirkby Stephen to Kendal, called by the name of Gallow-hill.

Amercements for bloodſhed and other crimes not being felony were very frequent not many years ago, and the juriſdiction with regard to theſe offences undoubtedly ſtill continues, for no act of parliament hath taken it from them. The privilege of ſanctuary was aboliſhed in this as in all other places by act of parliament in the reign of king James the firſt, and many other of the aforeſaid privileges have been taken away by other acts of parliament, others have been loſt perhaps by diſuſe, and others have become obſolete by the alteration of circumſtances.

The lord of the manor hath ſtill the juriſdiction of probate of wills and granting letters of adminiſtration; which privilege is not mentioned in any of the aforeſaid ancient grants, being of prior origin to the inſtitution of the order of Sempringham. The juriſdiction of wills and adminiſtrations anciently belonged to the county court; in which court all cauſes of eccleſiaſtical as well as of temporal cognizance (not being criminal) were determined. Out of the county court, were derived the courts baron; and with theſe the juriſdiction of wills and adminiſtrations was transferred to many of the lords of manors; and their claim hath been more eſpecially favoured, where the manor belonged to any of the religious ſocieties.

In this manor the ſteward of the lord's court alſo adminiſters the oath of office to the churchwardens of the pariſh; but offences of eccleſiaſtical cognizance are inquirable only by the ordinary of the dioceſe. And in all other reſpects, as in granting licences of marriage, ordering and diſpoſing matters relating to the church, accounts of the churchwardens, and other particulars of eccleſiaſtical inquiry, this pariſh hath no peculiar exemption from the epiſcopal juriſdiction *.

The

* In the regiſter of Weſheral priory, there is an entry of a claim of privilege belonging to that priory, made by the abbot of St. Mary's York before Hugh de Creſſingham and others juſtices itinerant at Carliſle, in the 20 Ed. I. viz. "The abbot of St. Mary's York claimeth this liberty "and cuſtom, that all felons coming to his liberty of Wederhal, for felony committed *out* of his "liberty aforeſaid, and coming to the church of the aforeſaid liberty, and tolling a bell, and making oath before the bailiffs of the ſaid liberty that hereafter they will behave themſelves well and "faithfully, ſhall remain in that liberty within the boundaries thereof at their pleaſure: That is to "ſay;

The aforesaid king Henry the third, in the 36th year of his reign, granted to the monks of Watton a privilege of free warren in Watton and Stancton in the county of York, and in Ravenstondale and Langdale in the county of Westmorland.

In the 14 Hen. 8. a *Quo warranto* was issued against the prior of Watton, to shew why he claimed to have divers liberties in the manor of Ravenstandale and several other manors *.

And in the 27th year of the same king, John Kite bishop of Carlisle cited *ex officio* the prior and convent of Watton, to shew their title to the church of Ravenstandale; who, having made proof thereof, were discharged by the bishop from the said suit †.

After the dissolution of the monastery, king Henry the eighth granted the said church and manor to the archbishop of York during his life; and in the 38th year of his reign, Nov. 5. he granted the reversion thereof to Sir Thomas Wharton knight, lord Wharton; amounting, over and above certain reprises allowed in the particulars, to 93*l* 11*s* 8*d* yearly. For which, the said lord Wharton was to pay 935*l* 16*s* 8*d*, being ten years purchase, at three different payments, the first payment of 235*l* 16*s* 8*d* to be at the nativity of St. John Baptist next, 350*l* at Christmass then next following, and 350*l* at the next Christmass after ‡.

And by a rental of the particulars, it appears, that the park and demesne there were rated at 100*l* a year; and the rectory (including the profits of

" say; between the cross which is on the bank of Eden towards Cork-by, and the cross which is " by the chapel of St. Oswald on the side of the water of Eden next to Corkeby; and between the " cross which stands nigh the Loge upon the bank of the aforesaid water, and the cross which " stands nigh the sike of Waryewyke, and the cross which stands between the vill of Scotteby and " the Grange of the prior of Wederhale; and so by that rivulet to the cross which stands upon the " bank of the aforesaid rivulet nigh Cumquityn; and so from the aforesaid cross to the boundaries " of the prior of Wederhale and the vill of Cumquityn upon Lytiltwaite; and so from Lytiltwait " unto Lencraike, which is upon the bank of the water of Eden; and so unto Wederhale, and to " the aforesaid cross on the bank of Corkeby nigh the said grange of the prior." The case was, one Richard Gener (with two other persons) coming nigh unto the house of Roger son of Martin, and striking his dog, the said Roger came out of the house with a sword in his hand, and therewith struck the said Richard under the navel up to his heart, so that he instantly died of the wound. Upon this, the murderer fled to the liberty of the prior of Wederhale, and stayed there from Candlemass until Michaelmass, and upon the king's coming into these parts he fled into Scotland. And the abbot being called, came by his attorney, and pleaded that the aforesaid Roger came into his said liberty after the felony was committed, and tolled a certain bell in the church, and swore before the bailiffs of the liberty that for the future he would demean himself well and faithfully, so was admitted to stay there as long as he pleased, so that he went not out of the bounds of the said liberty; and that he and his predecessors had used that custom in the said liberty time out of mind. Which thing being put upon inquest, the jurors find, that the said abbot and his predecessors had used the said custom which the said abbot claimed time out of mind, and without interruption. It was therefore granted, that the said abbot go without day; saving the king's right, if he shall contest the same at any other time.—But in another plea, concerning the reception of William Provost of Wederhale and Matthew Symundeham, who killed Robert Schawel of Great Corkeby in the night-time in the fishery of Wederhale *within* the liberty aforesaid, the abbot declared, that he did not claim any refuge there for felons committing felony within the said liberty, but only for those who came for refuge for felony committed out of the said liberty.

* Dugd. MSS. † Nicolson. ‡ Harleian MSS. 7389. pag. 44.

weddings,

weddings, churchings, mortuaries, and burials) at 132*l* 19*s* 6½*d*. Outpayments to be disbursed, To Edward Mynese schoolmaster his stipend 20*l*. To Mr. Toppin curate, with 10*s* for an horse, his wages 8*l* 16*s* 8*d*. To the busshopp of Carlioll for synage money 4*s*.

The said rectory and manor continued in the family of Wharton till the late duke of Wharton's time, when the same were sold, together with the other Wharton estates in Westmorland, to Robert Lowther esquire father of the present owner Sir James Lowther baronet: Except the great and small tithes and oblations within this parish; which were sold to the inhabitants and landowners. For none of these tithes or other dues were ever set out for the use of a vicar, but the cure was supplied occasionally by regulars sent out from the monastery; and the church continues to this day, not a vicarage, but only a perpetual curacy.

To the *curate* there belongs a small thatched dwelling-house, with other like outhousing; and a garth and garden adjoining: The same being a messuage and tenement which heretofore belonged to one William Robinson schoolmaster of Ravenstondale, and on his dying without a will, escheated to the lord. Whereupon Philip lord Wharton gave the same for the use of the curate. To the said curate also belong two closes called Haber and Muffelgill, given by one Hodgson; one parcel of ground adjoining to the backside of the church, called the Orchard, given by the aforesaid Anthony Fothergill of Trannahill, and one Bovell and others in Ravenstondale. Half an acre of land, given by William Chamberlain of Waingarth. The whole glebe and houses are now worth about 18*l* a year. The ancient salary paid out of the rectory, 8*l* a year. The reverend William Morland of Winton (sometime rector of Graystock) gave to this church 100*l*, for which 5*l* interest was to be paid till some person would give more: Whereupon Mr. George Fothergill of Tarnhouse took the said 100*l*, and granted for the same a rent charge issuing out of his manor of Blaterne of 5*l* 1*s* a year. John and Isabel Fothergill of Brounber gave 20*l*, wherewith land was purchased, now let for 27*s* a year, for a sermon to be preached annually on the tenth day of August. There is another small benefaction of 5*l* given by Henry Fothergill of Newbiggin, the interest whereof to be given for a sermon to be preached yearly on St. Bartholomew's day. The whole revenue of the church (including surplice fees) is now worth about 35*l* a year.

The *church* was rebuilt in the year 1744, in an elegant manner. It hath a square tower steeple, with three bells. In the old church there were two rows of seats below the communion table, where (it is said) the steward and jury of the manor sate formerly, in their court of judicature. And the malefactors were imprisoned in a hollow arched vault, the ruins whereof are still to be seen, on the north side of the church.

There is also an handsome dissenting *meeting house* at Ravenstondale; for the support of which, Philip lord Wharton gave by his will the sum of 100*l*, to be laid out in a mortgage as soon as might be on some estate in Ravenstondale for three years, according to the laudable custom of that manor; the interest thereof to go for the benefit of Mr. Timothy Punchen the then diffenting minifter and his fucceffors for ever: And the fame to be laid out in a purchafe of lands as foon as might be convenient: Accordingly, in the year 1693, the fame was laid out on a mortgage in Ravenftondale, with a declaration of truft that the fame fhould enure for the benefit of the minifter, and the mortgage to be renewed every three years according to the cuftom of the faid manor. Befides this, one Mr. Pindar, a diffenting minifter at London, gave to the faid meeting houfe 30*l*. John Thomfon of Kirkby Stephen, hofier, 20*l*. Ifabel Langhorn 6*l*. James and Mary Fawcet 20*l*. George Murthwaite 10*l*. All which fums have been laid out in the purchafe of lands. There was alfo 100*l* in money, contributed by Chriftopher Todd and others; 20*l* of which hath been loft, and the reft is let out at intereft by the truftees. The reft of the falary is raifed by voluntary fubfcriptions. And the whole revenue of the meeting houfe raifes to the prefent minifter about 40*l* a year.

In the old church there was a fmall bell, called the Saint's bell, which was wont to be rung after the Nicene creed, to call in the diffenters to the fermon. And to this day the diffenters, befides frequenting the meeting houfe, oftentimes attend the fermon at church.

There was here alfo a *fchool*, endowed about the year 1668, by Thomas Fothergill, B. D. mafter of St. John's college in Cambridge (who was born at Brounber in this parifh) and others of his name and kindred. In the year 1758, a very good new fchool-houfe was built by the inhabitants and other contributors. Adjoining to the eaft end whereof was erected alfo a commodious dwelling houfe for the mafter; towards which, the reverend George Fothergill, D. D. principal of Edmund hall in Oxford, gave 10*l*; the reverend Thomas Fothergill, D. D. provoft of Queen's college in the faid univerfity, gave 20*l*; and the reverend Henry Fothergill, M. A. rector of Cheriton Bifhop in Devonfhire, gave 10*l*; all three brothers, born at Lockholme in this parifh. Towards the maintenance of a fchoolmafter, the aforefaid Philip lord Wharton gave a rent charge of 5*l* yearly out of his eftate at Raine in the parifh of Orton. There was alfo a large fchool ftock given by the founders of the fchool and others. With 140*l* of which ftock, a parcel of ground was purchafed at Blaterne, called Horngill, containing 84 acres, now worth about 20*l* a year, which in the year 1703 the truftees imprudently (and perhaps illegally enough) fold to Thomas Pattenfon of Breeks gentleman, and accepted for the fame a rent charge of 6*l* a year iffuing out of the faid Horngill and inclofure called Crowhill. Another eftate was purchafed at Foxell Rigg in the parifh of Sedbergh for 112*l*; which the truftees in like manner converted into an annuity of 5*l* a year. Another eftate at Bousfield in the parifh of Orton was purchafed for 195*l*, now let for 12*l* a year; which alfo, not many years ago, narrowly efcaped being converted into a rent charge or annuity; notwithftanding that, befides other illegalities, there is a fpecial claufe in the deed of fettlement, that the truftees fhall apply the rents and profits of the faid eftates for the ufe of the fchoolmafter, and fhall not make any leafe thereof for a longer term than 21 years. The continual decreafe in the value of of money, and consequently increase in the value of lands, renders all fixed sums in process of time extremely inadequate.—The whole revenue of the school at present amounts to about 30*l* a year.

The parish consists of four *Angles* (as they are called), but it is all one manor and constablewick. It is so long since the manor was given away to the priory, that there is no tradition remaining, where the ancient *manor house* stood. There is a pretty large *park*, lying north from the church, the wall whereof appears to have been about ten feet in height; but there is no remembrance of any deer having been kept there. It was walled about by Philip lord Wharton in the year 1660; the sum total of the expence thereof being 128*l* 16*s*, besides *love-boons*, that is, the voluntary labour of the inhabitants of the neighbouring townships, who went to get and to lead stones for the work. [From which kind of services most of the boons in the several manors probably had their original. And if there had been a park wall to be erected every year, it is not unlikely that a custom might have obtained of boon quarrying and leading stones.]

In the customs of this manor, betwixt lord and tenant, there is much remaining of the ancient military establishment. In order to ascertain these customs, it was agreed upon between Thomas lord Wharton the first purchaser and the tenants as followeth:

" Articles of the customary tenant-right of the whole lordship and parish of Ravenstondale in the county of Westmorland, which have been accustomed and used within the said lordship time out of man's memory. All which articles and customary tenant-right, I the lord Wharton, lord warden of the East and Middle marches of England for anenst Scotland, and captain of the king and queen's majesties town and castle of Berwick, am well contented and pleased withal. In witness whereof I have subscribed my hand the 6th day of October in the 3d and 4th years of our sovereign lord and lady king Philip and queen Mary.

First, It hath been and is accustomed within the said lordship, that at the exchange or entrance of any tenant, he pay unto the lord as much fine or grassom, as the whole year rent of the same tenement extendeth unto, and not above.

Item, It hath been accustomed within the same lordship, that all manner of felonies, murders, forfeitures, petty michers, and all other trespasses committed and done within the precinct of the said lordship's liberties of Ravenstondale, either by any of the inhabitants, or by any other foreign persons, be inquired upon by an indifferent jury taken and appointed by the lord or his officers within the lordship in that behalf.

Item, It hath been and is accustomed within the said lordship, that for all manner of contentions, variances, debates, demands, titles, claims, or tenant-right farm-holds, which have been, is, or shall be depending in controversy, between tenant and tenant, party and party, within the said lordship, be fully ordered, determined, and ended, by an indifferent jury and inquest taken and appointed

appointed by the lord or his officers there, by the assents and consents of the said parties within the said lordship in that behalf.

Item, It hath been and is accustomed, that none of the tenants or other persons shall improve, inclose, or take up any of the common pasture there, without licence of the lord and appointment of the jury taken and elect in that behalf.

Item, It is ordered and agreed, between the lord of the same lordship and the tenants there, that from henceforth they shall break or divide no farmholds.

Item, It hath been and is accustomed, that such a son as the father shall appoint, being able to serve the king and the lord, shall be set tenant of his father's tenement, before his death or after, agreeing with the lord after the custom there.

Item, It hath been and is accustomed within the said lordship, that if the tenant have no son but daughters, such a daughter as the father shall appoint, using herself honestly before the day of her marriage, shall have his tenement, agreeing with the lord after the custom there.

Item, It hath been and is accustomed, that where any tenant dieth without issue of his body lawfully begotten, it shall be lawful to the said tenant to assign or appoint his tenantright of the same tenement, to whom as shall please him, agreeing with the lord as appertaineth thereto in that respect."

The customs of the manor were further explained by indenture between Philip lord Wharton and the tenants, Feb. 12. in the 22 Eliz. as followeth:

"Imprimis, It is declared and agreed, that it hath been and is accustomed within the said manor, time whereof the memory of man is not to the contrary, that all the tenants which hold lands or tenements of the said manor, of ancient time by the laudable custom of tenantright, have possessed and enjoyed the same to them, their heirs and assigns; paying at the change of every lord, and at the change of every tenant, one year's rent for a fine, and not above, besides the rent which they pay to the lord: The fine to be paid according to the rent, and not according to the value as the same be let.

Item, That the late improved grounds shall pay, at the change of lord and tenant, eight years rent, besides the yearly rent, according to the rent they pay for the said new improved grounds. And the tenants to pay their fines on the change of the lord and tenant, as well for the old, as for the new, upon their admittances.

Item, That every person to whom any alienation of any of the said tenements shall be made, shall, at the court of the manor next following the said alienation, by himself or some other, give notice and knowledge thereof in the said court to him who shall keep the said court; and then shall take order there for the payment of his fine, according to the rate before expressed.

Item, That none of the tenants shall divide or sever their ancient and customary tenements, or the said new improvements, or any part of them, upon pain of forfeiture; unless they do first agree with the lord or steward or some other

other having authority from the ſaid lord ſo to do. In which agreement, it ſhall not be lawful for the lord to augment or increaſe any rent, either of the ancient cuſtomary tenements or of the new improvements, that ſhall be ſo divided; but ſhall divide the rents proportionably, according to the value of the land ſo divided. And this ſhall not be expounded or taken to be a change of a tenant, ſo as the lord ſhall have any fine in that reſpect for the portion ſo divided.

Item, That if any tenant ſhall die without iſſue of his body lawfully begotten, not having in his life by his will in writing, or otherwiſe by any lawful act done in the preſence of four of the tenants of the ſaid manor at the leaſt, aliened or beſtowed the ſame; what lands ſuch tenants ſhall die ſeiſed of ſhall eſcheat to the lord, as if ſuch tenant had been dead without heir general or ſpecial.

It is nevertheleſs declared and agreed, that any of the tenants, having no iſſue of his body lawfully begotten, and being of the age of ſixteen years, may by his laſt will in writing, or by any other lawful act done in the preſence of four of the tenants of the ſaid manor, give and bequeath his tenement to whom he will; the party to whom it ſhall be ſo given, paying upon his admittance 20 years rent for a fine, and not above: and the lord ſhall not refuſe to admit him, ſo that he be an able man to ſerve, and not notoriouſly known to be an enemy to the ſaid lord.

Provided, that a leaſe or demiſe of the manor, or of any tenement, for ſeven years or under, ſhall not be deemed any change of the lord or tenant, whereby any fine ſhall be due; yet any tenant may let his tenement for 21 years in poſſeſſion and not above, the leſſee to whom the ſame ſhall be let for 21 years or under, and above 7 years, paying to the lord a fine as for change of tenant, and giving knowledge of ſuch leaſe at the next court *."

By reaſon of the aforeſaid proviſion for keeping the tenements intire, the ancient military eſtate continues in many places in a great meaſure ſtill unaltered. And by this means, there was a ſufficiency kept up for the maintenance and ſupport of the ſoldier; and the children, except the eldeſt, migrated into other places. And ſo late as the time of biſhop Nicolſon's parochial viſitation in 1703, he was informed at Ravenſtondale by the churchwardens, that they had not had a beggar in the pariſh within the memory of man; and at the

* In Furneſs in the county of Lancaſter, we find the like cuſtoms declared and agreed upon in the reign of queen Elizabeth; amongſt which are the following particulars:—" Item, That no " perſon within this lordſhip make any fray, on pain of 6 s 8 d; nor blood ſtroke, on pain of " 3 s 4 d; nor ſhall unlawfully chide, on pain of 1 s; nor make tuxhill or hubbleſhowe, on pain " of 1 s; nor fold breake, on pain of 3 s 4 d. Item, That no perſon ſlander any juryman, nor any " that giveth evidence to a jury, nor call any perſon thief or perjured, or any woman whore, " except they will juſtify and make proof thereof on pain of 6 s 8 d. Item, Whereas dividing, " parcelling, and portioning of ancient tenements hath been a great decay and impoveriſhment of " the lord, and chiefly in hindering of the ſervice of her highneſs for horſes, and to the ſpoil and " waſting of her majeſty's woods, and occaſion of making a great number of poor people within " the lordſhip to the impoveriſhment of her highneſs's tenants; it is declared and agreed, that " none ſhall aliene any parcel of his tenement, but intirely, and not by parcels, otherwiſe the bar- " gain to be utterly void of every parcel ſo ſold."

ſame time, they added, that they had never a gentleman among them, except only the *curate* and *ſchoolmaſter*.

And this happy equality in a great meaſure ſtill continues. The moſt conſiderable family ſeems to have been that of Fothergill; which at preſent is very numerous.

In the reign of king Henry the eighth, at the famous rencounter at Sollom Moſs, Sir *William Fothergill* of Ravenſtondale was ſtandardbearer to Sir Thomas Wharton. His arms were; Vert, a ſtag's head couped, within a bordure inverted, Or.

In the reign of king Charles the ſecond, *George Fothergill* of Tarn-houſe eſquire (before mentioned) was clerk of the peace for the county of Weſtmorland. Which houſe was then the only ſlated houſe in this pariſh; whereas now, ſince the elegant covering of blue ſlate was diſcovered, moſt of the houſes in Ravenſtondale are ornamented with that cover. The aforeſaid arms are over the door at Tarn-houſe. In the old church, at the Eaſt end of the South ile were two monuments, with the following epitaphs:

1.

Here lieth the body of George Fothergill of Tarn-houſe eſquire, the Queen's Majeſty's receiver for Weſtmorland, Lancaſhire, and Cumberland. Who departed this life Apr. 26, 1681.

2.

Nov. 19. 1676, was interred under this ſtone, Julian the wife of George Fothergill of Tarn-houſe, ſecond daughter of Richard Skelton of Armathwaite caſtle in the county of Cumberland eſquire.

Thomas Fothergill aforeſaid of Brounber was maſter of St. John's college in Cambridge, and founder of the ſchool at Ravenſtondale as aforeſaid. And Mr. *Anthony Fothergill*, late of Brounber deceaſed, without any aſſiſtance from a liberal education, by the mere force of natural endowments, was the author of ſeveral conſiderable tracts, religious and controverſial: Unto whoſe ſon and heir Mr. *Thomas Fothergill* of Brounber we are obliged for ſeveral of the above particulars relating to this pariſh.

Dr. *George Fothergill* aforeſaid, principal of Edmund hall in Oxford, was one of the moſt eminent tutors of his time, whilſt he was fellow of Queen's college. He was a perſon univerſally eſteemed, pious, benevolent, learned, humane. Beſides his other benefactions, he gave 30 or 40 *l* towards the building of the new church in Ravenſtondale, and laid out near 20 *l* in a preſent to the ſame of communion plate. The ſeats, when finiſhed, were ſold, towards defraying the expences of the whole, to the ſeveral owners of the reſpective meſſuages and tenements within the pariſh. There were divers Quakers who refuſed to purchaſe. For theſe, the ſaid Dr. George Fothergill purchaſed; and ordered thoſe ſeats to be occupied by the poor of the pariſh, until ſuch time as the owners of the Quakers meſſuages ſhall pay the purchaſe money; which when they ſhall do, then the intereſt of that money to go to the poor.

He

He publiſhed in his life-time ſeveral ſermons preached before the univerſity upon particular occaſions; and left behind him a volume of ſermons, which are the exact picture of the author's life and manners.

His brother Dr. *Thomas Fothergill* aforeſaid ſucceeded him as tutor, and in every reſpect copied after ſo amiable an example, and is now the worthy provoſt of the ſaid college, and vice-chancellor of the univerſity.

The eldeſt ſurviving brother Mr. *Richard Fothergill*, enjoys the paternal eſtate at Lockholme; with whom the compiler of theſe memoirs eſteemeth it an honour to have been intimately acquainted.

At a place called *Raſate* (the word *raſe* meaning an hill or riſing ground) not far from Sunbiggin tarn, are two *tumuli*, in which have been found many dead mens bones; the bodies being laid round about the hills, with the heads all lying upwards towards the hill top, and the hands laid upon their breaſts.

In the high ſtreet, leading from Kirkby Stephen to Sedbergh, near Rawthey bridge, is a circle of large ſtones, ſuppoſed to be a monument of Druid worſhip.

At Ravenſtondale town head is a *tarn* or lough, which in Mr. Machel's time was well ſtocked with perches and eels.

About half a mile from the town head, in the year 1774, was found in digging peats, two foot below the ſurface, a copper veſſel, ſound and intire, the diameter whereof at the bottom is 8 inches, at the top 14 inches, in the wideſt part juſt under the neck 16 inches; the depth 18 inches; it contains about 8 gallons and an half. It is made of three plates of copper, neatly joined together, and hath been pretty much uſed as a fire veſſel. It is very ſlender; and therefore there are fixed ſix fillets of copper at equal diſtances, which reach up the ſides two inches and an half, and are turned down about as much upon the bottom. That part of the fillets turned over part of the bottom, is a good deal thicker than the other extremities which go up the ſides, and are ornamented with ridges, ſomewhat in the nature of fluting. The veſſel, when ſet down, reſts on the thicker part of theſe fillets, which keeps it ſteady, and the bottom from any wear or bulging. There is no iron in any part of it. Two ears or handles are fixed on the inſide, the tops of which are on a level with the edge of the veſſel; in each of which is a moveable ring. Theſe ears and rings are pretty ſtrong and maſſy, but of baſer metal. The whole is of excellent workmanſhip, and very elegantly finiſhed.

In this pariſh ſprings the river *Lon* or *Lune*, which in its courſe gives name to the country of *Lonſdale*, and empties itſelf into the ſea a little below *Lancaſter*.

PARISH OF CROSBY GARRET.

THE church of this place, standing on the top of a steep hill or mount, hath caused that sometimes the village is called *Crosby on the Hill*. Most commonly it is called *Crosby Garret*, supposed to be from a like reason, forasmuch as the highest rooms in houses are called *garrets*. But in reality, *Garret* is no other than a corruption of *Gerard*, for it was always anciently written *Crosby Gerard*, most probably from the name of the owner.

This parish is bounded on the East by the parishes of Musgrave and Kirkby Stephen; on the South, by the parish of Ravenstondale; on the West, by the parishes of Ravenstondale and Orton; and on the North, by the parishes of Asby, Ormside, Warcop, Musgrave, and Kirkby Stephen: And contains about 59 families; of which, dissenters 9.

The church is dedicated to St. Andrew; on whose festival they heretofore held their feast.

It is a rectory valued in the king's books at 19*l* 4*s* 4½*d*. The clear yearly value, as delivered in to the governors of queen Anne's bounty, 47*l* 2*s* 6*d*. The late rector and lord of the manor James Bird gave 200*l*, unto which the governors of queen Anne's bounty added 200*l*, wherewith land was purchased within the manor, which land the said Mr. Bird also infranchised.

It hath been all along in the patronage of the lord of the manor. And therefore the history of the church and of the manor will best go together, and conduce in some measure to illustrate each other.

The first account we have of either, is in the year 1296, 25 Ed. 1. when *William de Soulby* lord of the manor being then under age and in wardship to Isabella daughter of the last Robert de Veteripont, and then widow of Roger de Clifford, she the said Isabella, in right of her said ward, presented to the rectory of Crosby Gerard one *Thomas de Burgh sub Mora*, who was thereupon instituted by bishop Halton.

In the next generation, we find the manor of Crosby Gerard in the hands of the Musgraves, probably by marriage of the heiress of *Soulby* (for there was an heiress of *Soulby* at that time, namely, *Johan* daughter of the said *William de Soulby*). And in the 8 Ed. 2. after the death of Robert de Clifford son of the aforesaid Roger and Isabella, the inquisition finds, that *Richard de Musgrave* held of the said Robert, on the day on which he died, the manor of Crosby Gerard; the wardship whereof, together with Little Musgrave which he then also held, was worth 34*l* a year. The said *Richard* held then also a moiety of the manor of Orton. And the cornage for all the three was 26*s* 3*d*.

In the 28 Ed. 3. *Henry de Sandford* was rector of Crosby Gerard, having obtained in that year from the bishop a licence of absence for the better following of his studies; and three years after, the like grant was renewed to him, on condition that he should cause divine service to be performed by a chaplain in the oratory of Robert de Sandford his father at Sandford once or twice in every month.

In

In the 43 Ed. 3. *Peter Morland*, *John de Kabergh*, (probably as trustees in a settlement) and the prior of *Watton* held the manor of Crosby Gerard, paying 8 *s* 6½ *d* cornage.

In the 5 Ric. 2. on the death of the aforesaid Henry de Sandford, *John de Calve* was instituted to the rectory, on the presentation of *Thomas de Musgrave* knight.

In the 15 Ric. 2. *Thomas de Musgrave* and the prior of *Watton* held Crosby Gerard, by homage and fealty and 10 *s* 1 *d* cornage.

In the 10 Hen. 5. after the death of John de Clifford, *Richard Musgrave* held the manor of Crosby Gerard, by homage and fealty and the cornage of 10 *s* 1 *d*.

In the 31 Hen. 6. *Richard Musgrave* knight held three parts, and the prior of *Watton* the fourth part, of the said manor; paying cornage 8 *s* 6 *d*.

In the 38 Eliz. on the death of *Lancelot Shaw* rector of Crosby Gerard, *Richard Fallowfield* was instituted, on a presentation by Thomas Ambler of Kirkby Stephen yeoman, to whom this avoidance was granted by *Humphrey Musgrave* late of Hartley esquire and dame *Agnes* his wife.

In the 12 Cha. 1. on the death of Richard Fallowfield, *Edmund Mauleverer* was instituted on the presentation of Sir *Philip Musgrave* baronet. Which said Sir *Philip Musgrave* conveyed the manor and advowson to Sir *Richard Musgrave* knight, his eldest son; who had issue only two daughters, the elder of whom died an infant, and the other daughter (Mary) was married to *John Davison* of Blakeston in the county of Durham esquire.

In the time of Oliver Cromwell, *Christopher Jackson* was rector, who was ejected by the Bartholomew act in 1662; he lived afterwards retired in Ravenstondale, where he had a small estate*. He was succeeded by Thomas Denton.

In 1702, *Thomas Denton* dying, *Joseph Forster*, M. A. was presented by *Mary Davison* widow, mother and guardian of *Thomas Davison*; which *Thomas Davison*, when he came of age, sold the manor and advowson to *Thomas Gate* of Whitehaven gentleman.

In 1713, the said Thomas Gate presented *James Lamb*, M. A. to the rectory.

In 1717, *William Bird* clerk was presented by the same patron; who by his last will and testament devised the manor and advowson to the said William Bird.

In 1742, the said William Bird resigning, presented his son and heir apparent *James Bird*, M. A. to the rectory.

In 1763, on the death of James Bird, *James Fenton* clerk was presented by Richard Burn LL. D, Anne Coulston widow, and John Coulston gentleman, trustees under the will of the said James Bird.

In 1769, on the resignation of James Fenton, *William Bird*, B. A. son and heir of the said James Bird, was instituted on a presentation by the said Richard Burn and Anne Coulston.

* 2 Calamy's Account of Ministers ejected, pag. 753.

This manor having belonged of early times to the lords of Soulby, and afterwards to the Musgraves, who resided elsewhere; there is no tradition remaining where the *manor house* of Crosby Gerard stood.

Within the manor there are about 40 tenements, only two or three of them freehold, the rest customary, some by indenture at an eightpeny fine, and others arbitrary.

There is a small *school* at Crosby Garret, built at the expence of the inhabitants, and endowed from time to time by the charitable donation of divers persons *.

The

* The following account is inserted, as well for a memorial of the said benefactions, as by way of precedent for the like laudable purpose in other places:

		l.	*s.*	*d.*
1629.	Apr. 12. Given by Richard Fallowfield, parson of Crosby Garret, 3*l*. The use to go to the maintenance of a schoolmaster there; and when there is no schoolmaster, to be given to the poor. The said 3*l* to remain to the said use for ever	3	0	0
	Item, By Henry Robinson to the same use	0	6	8
	Thomas Wilson	0	13	4
	James Skaife, by an order, to the same use	0	10	0
	Margaret wife of James Richardson	0	6	8
	Margaret Skaife	0	13	4
	Thomas Johnson, by order,	1	0	0
	Edward Skaife	1	0	0
	John Skaife, parish clerk	0	10	0
	Overplus of the schoolhouse money, by consent	0	6	3
	Humphrey Bell	1	0	0
1648.	Given by John Symson of Sandford to the use of the school at Crosby Garret and Warcop 5*s* a year, to be paid one year to Crosby and another to Warcop: due to be paid every Candlemass out of the lands of Robert Peart and Bartholomew Skaife of Sandford. And for want of a school at Crosby, the said 5*s* to be paid to Warcop; and for want of a school at Warcop, to be paid to Crosby.			
1662.	Apr. 26. Given by ——— Richardson at his death, to the use of the school 2*l*; and for repairing the wood bridge in the way to Smerdale, 1*l*	3	0	0
1664.	June 7. Given by James Richardson bailiff, by his last will and testament for keeping a schoolmaster for advancing learning	2	0	0
1667.	Apr. 8. By Reginald Robinson, by his last will and testament, unto the school stock and poor of Crosby Garret, 10*s*; viz. 5*s* to each	0	10	0
1668.	By John Skaife by his last will, to the school stock for advancing learning 1*l*. To Smerdale wood bridge 10*s*	1	10	0
	Feb. 6. By general consent of all the inhabitants of Crosby Garret (except James Bell, Thomas Taylor, Thomas Robinson of Pots, and Henry Robinson) to the school-stock of Crosby Garret for the advancing of good learning 4*l* 4*s*, which they received of George Richardson of Mazin Slack for his privilege in the fell or common, and for a little parcel of ground for a garth beside his house. And it is the desire of the said inhabitants, that the said sum be employed for the maintenance of a schoolmaster for ever	4	4	0
1676.	July 6. Given by Elizabeth Robinson widow, and Reginald Robinson; administrators to the abovesaid Henry Robinson, to the school stock of Crosby Garret, 5*s* 4*d*; being the whole which the said Henry Robinson received and reserved as his part of George Richardson's money	0	5	4
	William Robinson, by his last will and testament	10	0	0

1682.

The manor of LITTLE MUSGRAVE is in this parish, though separated from *Great Musgrave* only by the river Eden. So far back as we have any account, this manor of Little Musgrave, as well as Great Musgrave, belonged to that ancient family which gave name to both places, and who still continue lords of both the said manors.

In the reign of king Charles the second, Sir Christopher Musgrave knight, and afterwards baronet, representative in parliament for the county of Westmorland, resided here during the life-time of his elder brother Sir Richard. There is an apartment in the house where they now keep court at Little Musgrave, which is yet called the lord's chamber.

K.

PARISH OF KIRKBY STEPHEN.

THE parish of Kirkby Stephen is bounded on the East by the parishes of Brough and Bowes; on the South, by the parishes of Grinton, Aisgarth, and Sedbergh, all of which (as well as Bowes) are in the county of York; on the West, by the parishes of Sedbergh, Ravenstondale, and Crosby Garret; and on the North, by the parishes of Crosby Garret, Musgrave, and Brough: And contains about 600 families; whereof, dissenters 12.

The church was dedicated to *St. Stephen*; and from thence the town and parish received their denomination.

It is a vicarage, valued in the king's books at 48*l* 19*s* 2*d*. In the time of William the Conqueror, it was in the patronage of *Ivo de Talebois* baron of Kendal; who granted the same to the abbot and convent of St. Mary's York. After the dissolution, the same came to the *Whartons* of Wharton; in which family the advowson continued till the late duke of Wharton's time, who granted the same to his steward *Matthew Smales* of Gilling in Yorkshire esquire; from whom it descended, after the death of the male issue, to his daughter *Jane*, wife of *Henry Chaytor* esquire of an ancient family at Croft in Yorkshire; who granted the same to their second son *Henry Chaytor*, LL. D. who also is the present incumbent.

		l.	*s.*	*d.*
1682.	Apr. 17. Given by Reginald Robinson, younger brother of the aforesaid Henry, unto the school stock, by his last will and testament, 10*l*; and 10*l* more, the use thereof to be distributed every year at Easter to the poor of the parish	20	0	0
1683.	Apr. 7. Given by James Bell, by his last will and testament, 50*s* to the use of the school, and 50*s* more to the poor — — —	5	0	0
1684.	Given by Thomas Bowland by his last will and testament 40*l* to the use of the teaching schoolmaster of Crosby Garret for ever, and 40*l* to the use of the poor — — — — —	80	0	0

Ivo

Ivo de Talebois aforesaid, in the year 1088, gave this church of Kirkby Stephen, and three carucates of land there, and his tithe, to the said abbot and convent of St. Mary's York.

And *Athelwold* first bishop of Carlisle, who came to the see in 1133, confirmed the grant thereof; on condition that the monks should allow to the priest officiating a sufficiency to maintain himself and pay the synodals. And the same was afterwards confirmed by king Henry the second.

After this, *Hugh* bishop of Carlisle, in the reign of king Henry the third, confirmed the same to the said abbot and convent; so as that they present a perpetual vicar to the same, and allow him yearly 100 *s.* *

Not long after, there arose some disputes between *Walter* bishop of Carlisle, and the said abbot and convent, touching the said church; which were referred to the prior of Carlisle and other arbitrators. The sum of their award was this: That the church of Kirkby Stephen, with all its appurtenances and chapels (namely, with the chapel of Burgh, and if there be any others which ought to be called chapels) should be ceded to the said abbey for ever; saving the vicarage as here-under taxed: viz. that the said vicarage, which by the bishop's predecessors had been taxed at 100 *s*, shall enjoy the whole altarage, with all the appurtenances of the said church and its chapels, except the tithes of the sheaves of corn and pulse not being in the tofts and gardens [*decimis garbarum bladi et leguminis extra toftos et ortos*]; and also eight oxgangs of land, and one competent manse; and shall pay yearly to the said abbey 20 *s.* The vicar to sustain all burdens and archidiaconal charges. But the payment of the said pension was not to take place, till after the death of *John Ferentine* the then rector.

In the year 1292, *Thomas de Capella* was vicar here, and a rigorous disciplinarian. *Prynne Chron. Vind.* Vol. 3. p. 485.

* Hugo Dei gratia Karliolensis episcopus, Omnibus Christi fidelibus has literas inspecturis vel audituris salutem in Domino. Quoniam ex officio nobis injuncto, subjectorum nostrorum, et maxime religiosorum, tenemur utilitati providere, et eorum bona augere et consovere; Noscat universitas vestra, quod nos, divina ducti pietate, de assensu capituli Karliolensis ecclesiæ, concedimus et præsenti pagina confirmamus Deo et ecclesiæ sanctæ Mariæ Eborum, et monachis ibidem Deo servientibus et in posterum servituris, ecclesias de Kirkby Stephan et de Morland, cum omnibus capellis ad eas pertinentibus, et cum omnibus aliis pertinentiis suis in proprios usus ipsorum, habendas et possidendas imperpetuum. Ita scilicet, quod ecclesia de Kirkby Stephan cum suis pertinentiis cedat in usus proprios dictorum monachorum Ebor', ad sustentationem pauperum et peregrinorum; et ecclesia de Morland cum suis pertinentiis in usus proprios monachorum domus de Wederhale, quæ est cella ecclesiæ sanctæ Mariæ Ebor', ad eorum sustentationem. Decedentibus vero vel cedentibus personis vel rectoribus prædictarum ecclesiarum qui nunc in eis sunt constituti; liceat præfatis monachis libere et sine alicujus contradictione vel impedimento eas sibi in usus proprios retinere. Ita tamen quod in eis vicarios idoneos constituant nobis et successoribus nostris præsentandos, qui de proventibus ipsarum C solidos singuli ipsorum de singulis ecclesiis percipiant in perpetuum, curamque animarum a nobis et successoribus nostris percipere et de spiritualibus providere teneantur. Ut autem hæc nostra concessio et confirmatio perpetuæ firmitatis robur obtineat, hoc præsens scriptum sigilli nostri impressione duximus communire. Datum 13 Kal. Novembris, anno incarnationis Domini MCCXX°. (*Registr. Wetheral.*)

In

In 1304, the said Thomas de Capella exchanged this vicarage for that of Arthureth, and Sir *Thomas de Leycester* was thereupon presented by the aforesaid abbot and convent.

In 1318, on the death of the said Thomas de Leycester, Mr. *Henry de Rillington* was instituted on the like presentation.

And the said Henry dying in the year after, Sir *John de Boted* succeeded in like manner.

In 1336, *John de Bowes* was instituted on the like presentation by the abbot and convent. And upon an inquisition then taken, the ancient valuation of the vicarage was found to be 110*s*, and the new 26*l* 13*s* 4*d*.

In the year 1354, the bishop, having proceeded *ex officio* against this John de Bowes, for incontinence with Margaret Wyvill and others, and for that contrary to the constitutions he publickly kept the said Margaret as a concubine, and having heard his defence, certifies that the said vicar is not liable to the penalties in the constitutions, but is sufficiently corrected for any crime proved against him, and ought not to be further molested.

In 1362, on the death of the said John de Bowes, the abbot and convent presented Sir *John de Danby*, who was instituted thereupon.

In 1376, *Peter de Morland* was instituted on the like presentation.

In 1386, on the death of Peter de Morland, Sir *John de Bruddesford* was instituted.

In 1422, we find one *Thomas Warcop* vicar of Kirkby Stephen; for by the inquisition *post mortem* in that year of John de Clifford, it is found, that *Thomas Warcop* vicar of Kirkby Stephen in the right of Katherine his wife, and Christopher Berdesey in the right of Margaret his wife, daughters and co-heirs of Robert Sanford esquire, held of the said John the manor of Sanford. Which *Thomas Warcop* had a son *Thomas Warcop* of Colby.

In 1539, the said abbey of St. Mary's York was surrendered to the king; and the revenues thereof in this parish of Kirkby Stephen appear from the account in the augmentation office to have been as follows: "Of lands, "tenements, and cottages in Kirkby Stephen, 9*l* 5*s* ½*d*. In Nateby 4*s*. In "Winton 20*s*. And for the farm of the rectory, with the tithe of divers "small villages within the parish, namely, of the farm of the tithe sheaves of "Kirkby Stephen 12*l*. In Hartly and Soulby 11*l* 6*s* 8*d*. Wharton and "Nateby 4*l* 8*s* 8*d*. Winton, Kaber, and other places 22*l*."

In 1547, king Edward the sixth granted to Sir Richard Musgrave of Hartley knight, the rectory of Kirkby Stephen, with the advowson of the vicarage. And in the next year, the said Sir Richard, in consideration of 471*l*, granted to Thomas lord Wharton all the said rectory and advowson, except the tithes of corn and hay of Hartley, Soulby, and Cayber. And it was covenanted, that the said Sir Richard Musgrave, his heirs and assigns, should enjoy all the tithe of hay, wool, and lamb, and other things whatsoever, within the demesne lands, town field, hamlet, or precinct of the manor of Hartley against the vicar and his successors; and in consideration thereof, that the lord Wharton should have the tythes of corn and hay of Cayber before excepted; which were to return to Sir Richard Musgrave in case of failure of the tithe of wool and lamb at Hartley *.

In 1562, *Peter Vaux* was instituted to the vicarage; who granted a lease to the lord Wharton his patron of the revenues of the vicarage for 40*l* a year; which kind of lease the patrons seem to have exacted of the incumbents for a long time together. For, above 40 years after this, viz. in the year 1605, we find a rental made by Philip lord Wharton of his whole estate, in which the particulars relating to the church of Kirkby Stephen, including the vicarial revenues, are as followeth; viz. In profits of the tithe barn of Kirkby Stephen, 46*l* 8*s* 4*d*. In profits of Winton tithe barn 36*l*. In profits of tithe calves and broken tithes thereof, 3*l* 6*s* 8*d*. In profits of the tithe wool 40*l*. In profits of the tithe lambs and odds thereof 30*l*. In profits of the oblations and other duties collected at Easter 16*l*.—To be paid out thereof to the vicar his rent (the value of the glebe included, not reckoned in the above particulars) 48*l* 19*s* 2*d*.—Which was the very sum that the vicarage was rated at in the king's books; of which the patrons seem to have availed themselves, by a kind of simoniacal contract with their presentees.

In 1563, on the death of Peter Vaux, Sir *Parcevil Wharton* clerk was instituted on the presentation of Edward Wharton patron for that turn only, by grant from Thomas lord Wharton.

In 1568, on the death of Percevil Wharton, Sir *John Swinbank* clerk was instituted, on the presentation of John Rigg of Little Strickland gentleman, on a like grant for that turn.

In 1620, one *Anthony Wetherell* appears to have been vicar, who was supposed to be author of the remonstrance by the tenants against the lords claim before mentioned of an absolute estate in their tenements.

In the time of Oliver Cromwell, *Francis Higginson* appears to have been vicar. He was very active against the Quakers, who sprang up at that time; and writ two very notable pamphlets against them †.

In

* Bp. Nicholson.

† As these discourses of Mr Higginson are extremely scarce (for we have not found more than one printed copy thereof) it may not be amiss to preserve some of the contents of the same.

From these it appears, that the Quakers at their first setting forward committed various kinds of extravagances and disorders; which probably, if they had not been opposed, would more readily have subsided. But the ministers, justices of the peace, constables, and others, followed these people about, disputed with them, bound them over to the peace, procured them to be indicted, and by such opposition rendered the sect considerable. Mr. Higginson produceth instances of these people running about the streets, foaming, and bellowing out such like expressions as these, "Repent, repent; Wo, wo! The judge of the world is come!" Some of them stood naked upon the market cross, on the market days, preaching from thence to the people. Particularly, he mentions the wife of one Edmund Adlington of Kendal who went naked through the streets there. And two others of the society, a man and a woman, who called themselves Adam and Eve, went publickly naked; and when examined concerning the same at the assizes, the man affirmed that the power of God was upon him, and he was commanded so to do.

Many of them in their assemblies, sometimes men, but more frequently women and children, or they who had long fasted, would fall down suddenly as in an epileptic fit, and there lie groveling upon the ground, struggling as it were for life, and sometimes more quietly as if they were just expiring. Whilst the agony of the fit was upon them, they would foam at the mouth, their

lips

In 1663, *Joshua Stopford*, M. A. was instituted on a presentation by Philip ord Wharton.

In

lips would quaver, their flesh and joints would tremble, and their bellies swell like a blown bladder. In such fit they continued sometimes an hour or two, and when it left them, they roared out with a voice loud and horrible. All which easily accounts for the name of *Quakers* being given to them.

In their preaching, they called themselves, "The way, the truth, and the life." One James Milner declared himself to be God and Christ: For which blasphemy being imprisoned at Appleby, and the wife of one Williamson coming to see him there, she professed herself publickly to be the eternal son of God. And the men that heard her, telling her that could not be, because she was a woman, she answered, No, you are women, but I am a man.

They railed at the judges sitting upon the bench, calling them scarlet coloured beasts. The justices of the peace they styled "Justices *so called*;" and said there would be Quakers in England, when there should be no justices of the peace.

They made it a constant practice to enter into the churches with their hats on during divine service, and to rail openly and exclaim aloud against the ministers with reproachful words, calling them liars, deluders of the people, Baal's priests, Babylon's merchants selling beastly ware, and bidding them come down from the high places. One instance of this kind (ludicrous enough) happened at Orton. Mr. Fothergill, vicar there, one Sunday exchanged pulpits with Mr. Dalton of Shap, who had but one eye. A quaker stalking as usual into the church at Orton, whilst Mr. Dalton is preaching, says, Come down thou false Fothergill. Who told thee, says Mr. Dalton, that my name was Fothergill? The Spirit, quoth the Quaker. That spirit of thine is a lying spirit, says the other; for it is well known I am not Fothergill, but peed Dalton of Shap.

There was one justice Burton, who attended at Kendal, Kirkby Stephen, Orton, and other places, together with the ministers, to endeavour to suppress these disorders, and (amongst the rest) committed James Nayler of famous memory to Appleby gaol, for want of finding sureties for his good behaviour. Soon after this, Mr. Burton one night going home (to Brampton) from Appleby, was way-laid by four musketeers, two on each side of the lane, every one of whom discharged his musket at the justice as he passed along, but happily missed both him and his servant. It was not known who these four persons were. It was believed they were Quakers, some of the Quakers having given out before, that they would pick his skin full of holes. And they had not then taken up the principle of not bearing arms; for many of them, and Nayler among the rest, had been Cromwell's soldiers.

The said James Nayler, at the prosecution of Mr. Higginson, Mr. Fothergill, and other ministers, was indicted at Appleby for blasphemy, at the Christmass session in the year 1652. His examination thereupon was as follows:

Justice *Pearson*. Put off your hat.

James. I do it not in contempt of authority; for I honour the power as it is of God, without respecting mens persons, it being forbidden in scripture. He that respects persons, commits sin, and is convinced of the law as a transgressor.

Justice *Pearson*. That is meant of respecting persons in judgment.

James. If I see one in goodly apparel and a gold ring, and see one in poor and vile raiment, and say to him in fine apparel, Sit thou in a higher place than the poor, I am partial, and a judge of evil thoughts.

Col. *Brigs*. If thou wert in the parliament house, wouldst thou keep it on?

James. If God should keep me in the same mind I am in now, I should.

Col. *Brigs*. I knew thou wouldst contemn authority.

James. I speak in the presence of God, I do not contemn authority, but I am subject to the power as it is of God, for conscience sake.

Justice *Pearson*. Now authority commands thee to put off thy hat. What sayest thou to it?

James. Where God commands one thing, and man another, I am to obey God rather than man.

Col. *Benson*. See whether God commands it, or your own wills.

The indictment was read, wherein James was indicted for saying that Christ was in him, and that there was but one word of God, and the like.

In 1673, *John Rawlet*, M. A. was instituted on a presentation by the same patron. This Mr. Rawlet was author of a volume of divine poems; and of a book yet well known by the name of The Christian Monitor. His character as a most exemplarily pious and good man remaineth to this day.

In

Col. *Brigs*. Where wast thou born?

James. At Ardislaw, two miles from Wakefield.

Col. *Brigs*. How long livedst thou there?

James. Until I was married; then I went into Wakefield parish.

Col. *Brigs*. What profession wast thou of?

James. A husbandman.

Col. *Brigs*. Wast thou a soldier?

James. Yea I was a soldier between 8 and 9 years.

Col. *Brigs*. Wast thou not at Burford among the levellers?

James. I was never there.

Col. *Brigs*. I charge thee, by the Lord, that thou tell me whether thou wast or not.

James. I was then in the north, and was never taxed for any mutiny, or any other thing, while I served the parliament.

Col. *Brigs*. What was the cause of thy coming into these parts?

James. If I may have liberty, I will declare it. I was in the fields at the plough in barley seed time, meditating on the things of God, and suddenly I heard a voice saying unto me, Get thee out from thy kindred, and from thy father's house; and I had a promise given in with it: whereupon I did exceedingly rejoyce, that I had heard the voice of that God which I had professed from a child, but whom before that day I had never known. So I went home, and stayed there a good while; and not being obedient to the heavenly call, I was in a sad condition, as my friends know, and those that knew me wondered at me, and thought I was distracted, and that I would never have spoken nor eaten more.

Col. *Brigs*. (interrupting him). Friend, didst thou hear that voice thou sayest spake unto thee?

James. Yea, I did hear it.

Col. *Brigs*. Were there not some others besides thyself at plough with thee?

James. Yea, there were two more besides myself.

Col. *Brigs*. And did not they hear that voice as well as thyself?

James. No, friend; it was not a carnal voice, audible to the outward ear.

Col. *Brigs*. O then, I know what voice it was.

James. ——After I was made willing to go, I gave away my estate, and cast out my money, and I began to make some preparation, as apparel and other necessaries; but a while after, going agateward with a friend from my own house, having an old suit without any money, having neither taken leave of wife or children, nor thinking of any journey, the voice came to me again, commanding me to go into the west, not knowing whither I should go, nor what I was to do there; but when I had been there a little while, it was given me what I was to declare; and ever since I have remained, not knowing to-day what I am to do to-morrow.

Col. *Brigs*. Friend, you said, you gave away your estate, and cast out your money before you came forth: To whom did you give your estate and money?

James. I gave it to my wife.

Col. *Brigs*. Dost thou call that giving away thy estate, and casting out thy money? I should not much care if all my estate was so given away.—But what was the promise which thou saidst was given in to thee?

James. That God would be with me; which I find made good every day.

Col. *Brigs*. I never heard of such a call as thine in all my life.

James. I believe so.

Justice *Pearson*. Is Christ in you as a man, as you before affirmed?

James. Christ, God and man, is not divided. Separate God and man, and he is no more Christ. Christ God and man is every where.

Justice *Pearson*. Dost thou believe Christ, as he is man, to be in thee?

James.

In 1681, *Samuel Shaw*, clerk, was presented by the same patron, and instituted thereupon.

In

James. I witness him in me; and if I should deny him before men, he would deny me before my father which is in heaven.

Justice *Pearson*. How do you mean that Christ is in you? Do you mean that he is in you spiritually?

James. Yea, spiritually.

Justice *Pearson*. By faith, do you mean, or how else?

James. By faith.

Justice *Pearson*. Why, what difference is there then in this point between the ministers and you?

James. The ministers affirm Christ to be in heaven with a carnal body, but he is with a spiritual body.

Justice *Pearson*. Which of the ministers say so?

James. The minister, so called, of Kirkby Stephen.

Mr. *Higginson*. I confess I said, Christ was in heaven with a carnal body. I was willing to own a truth, though in coarse language. I look upon it as an unmeet expression, and should not have used it, had I not been drawn to it upon this occasion. Discoursing with Nayler at Mallerstang about the reality of Christ's human nature, I asked him whether he did believe that Jesus Christ, now glorified in heaven, was a true real man, as well as true God. When, according to his manner, he laboured to speak as ambiguously as he could, and would plainly affirm or deny nothing; urging him with the same question again, with some little alteration, I asked him, whether he did believe that Jesus Christ was now in heaven in a body of flesh; to which when I pressed him to answer plainly, Thomas Airey, one of Nayler's companions, said to me thus; Dost thou imagine that the body of Christ in heaven is a carnal body? To which I answered presently, thinking they had understood English language; Thomas, take the word carnal, not as it is used in the scripture, in opposition to that which is holy or spiritual, but according to its natural and proper signification, as it signifies fleshly, and so I believe the body of Christ in heaven to be a carnal body, that is (as I said) a body of flesh.

Col. *Brigs*. Wast thou not at a kirk about Sourby?

James. I was a member of an independent church at Wood church.

Col. *Brigs*. Wast thou not excommunicated for thy blasphemous opinions?

James. I know not what they have done since I came forth; but before, I was not to my knowledge.

Justice *Pearson*. How comes it to pass that your people quake and tremble?

James. The scriptures witness the same condition in the saints formerly; as David, Daniel, Habakkuk, and divers others.

Justice *Pearson*. Did they fall down?

James. Yea, some of them did so.

Justice *Pearson*. What sayest thou to the scriptures? Are they the word of God?

James. They are a true declaration of the word that was in them who spoke them forth.

Justice *Pearson*. Why dost thou disturb the ministers in their public worship?

James. I have not disturbed them in their public worship.

Justice *Pearson*. Why dost thou speak against tithes, which are allowed by the states?

James. I meddle not with the states. I speak against them that are hirelings. Those that were sent of Christ never took tithes, nor ever sued for any wages.

Justice *Pearson*. Dost thou think we are so beggarly as the heathens, that we cannot afford our ministers maintenance? We give it them freely.

James. They are the ministers of Christ who abide in the doctrine of Christ.

Justice *Pearson*. But who shall judge? how shall we know them?

James. By their fruits ye shall know them. They that abide not in the doctrine of Christ, make it appear they are not the ministers of Christ.

Justice *Pearson*. That is true.

This same Justice Pearson (to shew how catching is enthusiasm) afterwards turned Quaker, and writ a book against tithes.

 ——Such

In 1691, on the death of Samuel Shaw, *John Atkinson*, M. A. was instituted on a presentation by Thomas lord Wharton.

In 1733, on the death of John Atkinson, the right of presentation was contested, between Matthew Smales esquire by virtue of a grant from the late duke of Wharton, and Robert Lowther esquire, as purchaser of the said duke's estates in this parish. And on a *jus patronatus* issued and tried, the right was decreed to Mr. Smales, and his presentee *Henry Rycroft*, M. A. was instituted accordingly.

In 1746, on the death of Henry Rycroft, *Alderson Hartley*, M. A. was instituted, on a presentation by Henry Chaytor esquire and Jane his wife. Which Jane was daughter of the said Matthew Smales, to whom the advowson had come after the death of five brothers, sons of the said Matthew, without issue.

In 1755, on the death of Alderson Hartley, *William Fawcet* clerk was presented by the same patrons, and instituted thereupon.

In 1759, on the resignation of the said William Fawcet, *Henry Chaytor*, M. A. was instituted on the presentation of his father Henry Chaytor esquire.

The CHURCH is a large building, with a lofty tower steeple, and four bells. The church has two rows of pillars, six in a row, plain and round. On the north side is an ile projecting which belongs to Smardale hall.

And on the north side of the chancel is an ile belonging to Wharton hall; in which is a large monument of alabaster. On the table, which is six foot square, raised about three foot and an half from the ground, are three figures at full length, namely, of Thomas the first lord Wharton, in the middle; on the right side Elianor his first wife; and on the left, his second wife Anne. About the table, on the edges, beginning at the west end, is the following legend.

Thomas Whartonus jaceo hic, hic utraque conjux;
  Elionora suum hinc, hinc habet Anna locum.
En tibi, terra, tuum, carnes ac ossa resume;
  In cœlos animas, tu Deus alme, tuum *.

At

——Such was the rise of the Quakers. And as they could not probably have prevailed but by a preposterous (though well meant) opposition; so on the contrary, in these our days, we may see the happy effects of toleration. By letting them alone, they are coming about of themselves; and in the next generation most of their formal absurdities will be no more heard of.

* Under his head is the crest of the Wharton arms, viz. a bull's head (for in the days of coat armour something terrible was generally erected upon the helmet), which is supposed by the common people to represent the Devil in a vanquished posture: Under which notion a waggish schoolmaster once of that place thus paraphrased the above legend:

Here I Thomas Wharton do lie,
  With Lucifer under my head;
And Nelly my wife hard by,
  And Nancy as cold as lead:
Oh, how can I speak without dread!
  Who could my sad fortune abide,
With one devil under my head,
  And another laid close on each side!

This

At the east end,

Gens Whartona, genus; dat honores dextera victrix
In Scotos. Stapletona domus mihi quam dedit, uxor
Elionora fecit ter bina prole parentem:
Binam adimunt teneris, binam juvenilibus annis,
Fata mihi; dat nomen avi mihi bina superstes.
Anna, secunda uxor, celebri est de gente Salopum.

At the west end have been three coats of arms, now defaced; most probably, of the said lord Wharton and his two wives respectively.

On each side there are four niches, wherein have been the effigies of several persons, with their respective bearings; probably branches of the Wharton family.

On the south side of the chancel is a large quire belonging to Hartley castle. Under an arch in the south wall is a large gravestone with this inscription:

"Hic jacet Ricardus Musgrave, miles, juxta Elizabetham uxorem suam, "et Thomam filium et hæredem eorum; qui obiit ix°. die Mensis Novembris, "Anno Domini M° CCCC° lxiiii°. Cujus animæ propitietur Deus. Amen."

Betwixt the chancel and this quire, under the great arch, is the figure of a man in armour, with a sword at his right side, and something like a broken spear or truncheon at his left. Under his head, an old fashioned helmet, and a lion couchant at his feet, lying upon a table of stone, with nich-work on the sides. This is commonly said to be a cenotaph in memory of Sir Andrew Harclay earl of Carlisle. But by the annulets on the breast plate, it seemeth rather to have been for one of the Musgraves. The said Sir Andrew, for high treason, was degraded from his earldom and knighthood, and afterwards beheaded, and his head and quarters set up in different parts of the kingdom. It is not therefore likely, that his sword would have been represented on his monument, much less his coat armour on his breast. And his arms were, Argent, a cross Gules, with a martlet in the dexter chief point Sable *.

The

This consideration of *horns* generally used upon the crest, seemeth to account for what hath hitherto by no author or other person ever been accounted for; namely, the connexion betwixt *horns* and *cuckolds*. The notion of cuckolds wearing horns prevails through all the modern European languages, and is of four or five hundred years standing. The particular estimation of badges and distinction of arms began in the time of the crusades, being then more especially necessary to distinguish the several nations of which the armies were composed. Horns upon the crest (according to that of Silius Italicus,

Casside *cornigera* dependens infula———)

were erected *in terrorem*. And after the husband had been absent for three or four years, and came home in his regimental accoutrements, it might be no impossible supposition, that the man who wore the horns was a cuckold. And this accounts also, why no author of that time, when this droll notion was started, hath ventured to explain the connexion: For wo be to the man in those days that should have made a joke of the holy war; which indeed, in consideration of the expence of blood and treasure attending it, was a very serious affair.

* His sentence was, That he should be stripped of his earl's robes and ensigns of knighthood, his sword broken over his head, his gilt spurs hacked off from his heels, and that he should be drawn

The VICARAGE HOUSE hath been totally rebuilt by the present incumbent, and is beautifully situate on the west side of the river Eden. At the extremity of the garden, the fall from the rock is perpendicular many yards down to the river. From the top of which, is a prospect of Hartley castle, of the river in various points of view, and of all the open country towards the east.

Near to the vicarage, and almost adjoining to the east end of the church, is the SCHOOL; which was the ancient rectory house.

And by letters patent in the 8th year of queen Elizabeth, the said queen granted power to Thomas lord Wharton, to found a free grammar school at Kirkby Stephen, for the instruction of youth inhabiting there and in the neighbouring parts, and to settle also a yearly sum of *6l 13s 4d* for the relief of the poor. The governors of the said school to be eight in number; of whom the first were Thomas Musgrave and Thomas Warcopp esquires, Miles Skeyffe, Michael Wharton, Anthony Wharton, and Ambrose Lancaster, gentlemen, and Philip Machell and John Swynebancke clerks. On the death of a governor, the survivors to chuse another within six weeks: If they neglect within that time, then the archbishop of York to appoint one. The said Thomas lord Wharton to appoint a schoolmaster during his life; and to have power to make statutes for the government of the said school, so as they be not contrary to the said letters patent. After his death, the governors to appoint a schoolmaster within one month after a vacancy; if they neglect, then the said archbishop to appoint one. And after the said lord Wharton's death, the governors (with consent of the bishop of the diocese) may make statutes, so as they be not contrary to those of the lord Wharton. And for the aforesaid purposes, power was given to assign the mansion house of the rectory of Kirkby Stephen and other houses to the said mansion house belonging, and one rood of ground parcel of the said rectory, and the yearly rent of *26l 13s 4d*.

And in the 10th year of the said queen, the said lord Wharton settled upon the said school the parsonage house aforesaid with the houses and buildings about the same, and one garth on the backside of the said house towards the water of Eden; and *12l* a year to the schoolmaster, *26s 8d* a year to an usher to be appointed by the schoolmaster, and *6l 13s 4d* to two exhibitioners to be sent from the said school to Oxford or Cambridge or other university, to have each *3l 6s 8d* a year for seven years. The said several sums, making in the whole *20l* a year, to be paid out of the corn tithes of Kirkby Stephen and Winton. (Nothing appears to have been settled for the poor.)

In the year 1736, by a decree in chancery, the tithes of Kirkby Stephen were discharged from the said payment, and the whole *20l* a year decreed to be paid by Robert Lowther esquire, purchaser of the residue of the Wharton estates in Westmorland.

drawn to the place of execution and there hanged by the neck, his heart and bowels taken out of his body, burnt to ashes and winnowed, his body cut into four quarters, one to be set upon the principal tower of Carlisle castle, another on the tower of Newcastle upon Tyne, a third upon the bridge at York, and the fourth at Shrewsbury, and his head upon London bridge: All which was performed accordingly.

During the confuſion in the late duke of Wharton's affairs, no regular ſchool having been kept for eleven years, the ſum of 220*l* (being the ſtipend which had accrued during that time) was decreed to be laid out for the future benefit of the ſchool: part whereof was expended in repairs of the ſchool and ſchoolmaſter's houſe, part was laid out in a purchaſe of lands, and the remainder continues in South ſea annuities in the public funds, and the intereſt applied for the purpoſes of the original donation.

There is alſo a rent charge paid to the ſchoolmaſter of 6*l* a year out of an eſtate at Nateby, in conſideration of 100*l* given to the owner of the ſaid eſtate by Sir Thomas Wharton knight, brother to Philip the third lord Wharton *.

Moreover, by deed bearing date Oct. 7. 1623, between John Knewſtubb of Cockfield and John Gauden of Mayſand in the county of Eſſex of the one part, and the maſter, fellows, and ſcholars of St. John's college in Cambridge of the other part, they the ſaid John Knewſtubb and John Gauden grant to the ſaid maſter, fellows, and ſcholars an annuity of 11*l*, to be paid forth of certain lands called Squires in the pariſh and fields of South Minſter and Steeple in Eſſex, to be diſpoſed of as followeth; 20*s* yearly to the college, and 10*l* for the exhibition of two poor ſcholars commonly called ſizers, to either of them 5*l*. One of them, to be a ſcholar born and brought up in the pariſh of Kirkby Stephen, and of Mr. Knewſtubb's name and kindred, and for lack of ſuch, any other that hath been one whole year in the ſchool of Kirkby Stephen; and for lack of ſuch, to be taken forth of the ſchool of Appleby. The nomination of which ſcholar to be always by the vicar and ſchoolmaſter of Kirkby Stephen, ſubſcribed with both their hands, and ſent to the maſter and fellows of the ſaid college. And the ſaid 5*l* to be paid yearly, till the ſaid ſcholars be of ſtanding to take the degree of maſter of arts, and be capable of or have for their better maintenance a ſcholarſhip. And the other 5*l* to a ſcholar born in the pariſh of Cockfield, or elſe forth of the ſchool of Sudbury, or of Bury, in Suffolk. With the like limitations in reſpect to his kindred †.

This John Knewſtubb was born at Kirkby Stephen, fellow of St. John's college aforeſaid, and rector of Cockfield, where he died in the year next after eſtabliſhing theſe exhibitions. He was the author of "A confutation of "monſtrous and horrible heresies taught by Henry Nichols, and embraced of "a certain number who call themſelves the Family of Love." He alſo publiſhed a ſermon and lectures on the 20th chapter of Exodus. At Cockfield is the following monumental inſcription:

Humillimus pientiſſimusq; Dei ſervus, Johannes Knewſtub, hujus eccleſiæ de Cockfield per annos xlv *vigilantiſſimus et fideliſſimus paſtor, nutricius eccleſiæ et ſcholarum ſingularis; Chriſtianæ veritatis, ſalutiferæ evangelii doctrinæ, veræ*

* The original grant whereof the author of theſe memoirs hath ſeen in the hands of the late Mr. Atkinſon, vicar; but it is now ſaid to be loſt.

† From an account in Mr. Machel's collection, in the hand-writing of Mr. George Fothergill of Tarn-houſe, who was then one of the governors of the ſchool.

puræque

puræque religionis contra Antichristum Romanum ejusque emissarios, acerrimus assertor et propugnator: Nullis hujus sæculi procellis succumbens, fortiter adversus omnes casus humanos, pro divini numinis gloria, summa cum tolerantia restitit. Tandem senio confectus, lxxx° *ætatis anno, ex hac miserrima vita in cælestem patriam, pie sanctèque migravit,* xxix° *Maii, anno reparatæ salutis* 1624.

Kirkby Stephen is a considerable *market town*; noted for the sale of a great number of stockings, knit there and in the neighbourhood. In the 25 Ed. 3. Roger lord Clifford obtained a grant for a market on Friday weekly, and two fairs yearly, one on St. Mark's day and the morrow after, and the other upon St. Luke's day and the morrow after, at his manor of Kirkby Stephen *.

And king James the first, by his charter bearing date the 10th day of March in the third year of his reign, granted to George earl of Cumberland (instead of the aforesaid market and fairs) one market on Monday in every week, and two fairs yearly, one on the Wednesday, Thursday, and Friday after Whitsuntide, and the other on two days next before the feast of St. Luke and on that feast day; with a court of piepowder, tolls, tallages, and other jurisdictions thereunto belonging.

II.

MANOR OF KIRKBY STEPHEN.

The manor of Kirkby Stephen, in the time of the said Roger lord Clifford, was all in the hands of the Cliffords, as parcel of the manor of Brough. Part of it hath been sold off; and it now belongs to three several lords, namely, the earl of Thanet as descendent of the Cliffords, Sir Philip Musgrave baronet, and Sir James Lowther baronet.

In the partition of the inheritance between the two daughters of the last Robert de Veteripont, in the reign of king Edward the first, we find that the manor of Kirkby Stephen was assigned to Idonea intire, except five acres of demesne land there. And the yearly value thereof was estimated at 39*l* 16*s* 9*d*.

The inquisition in the 8 Ed. 2. after the death of Robert de Clifford, finds, that at Kirkby Stephen he died seised of one capital messuage or manor house, worth by the year one shilling. Fifty acres of demesne land, worth 4*d* an acre. Several acres of meadow, worth 16*d* an acre. Certain marsh land held by Henry de Warthecop, worth by the year 8*s*. Six oxgangs of land worth by the year 9*l*. Ten messuages of cottagers, worth 1*s* each. One water miln, worth by the year 6*l*.

In the inquisition *post mortem* of Roger de Clifford, in the 1 Ed. 3. there is a like recital of particulars; and amongst the rest are, certain separate pastures called *Kyrkeby-cerne*, worth by the year 8*s*. There is no place now known by

* Dugdale MS.

such

fuch name. *Karne* is Britifh, and fignifies a *rock*. There is a romantic place, where the river Eden runs between Kirkby Stephen and Nateby, at *Stenkrith-bridge*, where there are numbers of rocks, with round holes therein, from one foot to fix or more in diameter, and deep proportionably from fix inches to one two or more yards. The largeft of thefe, juft above the bridge, is called *Coop-karnel hole*, by an evident derivation from *coop*, hollow, and *karn*, a rock. Whether thefe are the operations of nature or the effects of human labour hath been doubted. There are no other fuch any where to be found thereabouts, or elfewhere in the county, but only juft at this place, about 80 or 100 paces above and below the bridge. They cannot have been made by the river, for fome of them are higher than the river ever rifes, unlefs perhaps fometimes in an exceeding high flood. Dr. Borlafe, in his account of Cornwall, defcribes a rocky place formed exactly in the fame manner, and concludes it to have been a Druid place of worfhip, and the hollows to have been made for wafhings, purifications, and the like. The fituation here hath indeed, in other refpects, much the appearance of Druidifm; for it is well known that the Druids affected places of fhade and folitude. To look down from Stenkrith bridge into the cavities amongft the rocks, with wood hanging over, the water roaring by the depth of the fall, then foaming and as it were feeking a paffage, then hiding itfelf and appearing again from the gaping clefts below, is apt to infufe a kind of religious horror and veneration. Even the word *Stenkrith* hath in it fomething of Britifh. The *ftone* there hath a mixture of red, which colour the Britons expreffed by *rith*; as *Penrith* in Cumberland means *red-hill*.

It doth not appear where ftood the ancient capital meffuage or manor houfe above mentioned. There is a good houfe at a place called *Melbecks* (that is, between the brook which runs by it on one fide, and the river Eden on the other; *mel* being an old word which fignifies *between*; fo the paffage betwixt two doors is called *Meldoors*); which houfe, together with a confiderable eftate in land, belonged to an ancient family of the name of *Hartley* at this place. Of whom, *Hugh Hartley* gentleman married Jane daughter of Mr. Rowland Scaife of Blafterfield and Winton, and by her had iffue, 1. *Edward*. 2. *Agnes*, married to Mr. Thomas Raw of Kirkby Stephen. 3. *Ifabel*, married to Mr. Michael Wharton of Wharton Dikes.

The faid *Edward Hartley*, fon of Hugh, had a fon *Hugh*; who alfo had a fon *Hugh*; who had a fon *Edward*; who had a fon *Hugh*; who was fucceeded by his brother *Alderfon Hartley*, M. A. vicar of Kirkby Stephen as aforefaid; who, dying unmarried, was fucceeded in this inheritance by his eldeft fifter *Anne*, married to *Richard Yates*, M. A. fchoolmafter of Appleby as aforefaid.

III.

MANOR OF HARTLEY.

It would be difficult to form any derivation of this word, as it ftands corrupted in the prefent fpelling, framed from the found only. But the further we go back, the more the true derivation unfolds itfelf. The famous Sir Andrew, afterwards earl of Carlisle, was surnamed *de Harcla*; and in a few generations further back, the word was most commonly written *Hardclay*. And the soil of the place sufficiently indicates the reason of the name.

This manor for a long time continued in the name of *Hardclay*. In the first year of the reign of king Edward the first, there was a dispute concerning the manor of Dalston in Cumberland, between *Michael de Harclay* knight (father of the said Sir *Andrew*) plaintiff, and the bishop of Carlisle defendant; wherein the plaintiff derived his descent from *Hervicius*, who was seized of the said manor of Dalston in the reign of king Henry the first, who was succeeded by his brother *Robert*, who was succeeded by another brother *Walter*, who had a son *Michael*, who had a son *Walter*, who had a son *Michael*, who had a son *William*, who had a son *Michael* the present plaintiff.

Accordingly, in the reign of king Henry the second, to an agreement and compromise concerning the boundaries of the manors of Bleatarn and Musgrave, the names of two of the witnesses are, *Michael de Hardclay*, and *Walter* his son.

In the 6th year of king John, we find *Michael de Hardclay*, son of (the last) Walter.

In the 13th year of the same king, *John de Hardclay* was witness to Robert de Veteripont's grant to Shap abbey. Which *John* seems to have been a collateral, and not in the direct course of primogeniture.

In like manner, to a grant of lands and wood at Brampton, by Walter de Moreville to the said Robert de Veteripont, one of the witnesses was *John de Harclay*.

In the reign of king Henry the third, the grant of the advowson of the rectory of Kirkby Thore, by Adam de Kirkby Thore to the said Robert, was attested by *Michael de Hardclay*.

In the 14 Ed. I. in the partition of the inheritance between the two daughters and coheirs of the last Robert de Veteripont, mention is made of *Michael de Hardclay* holding the manor of Hardclay under them.

In the 8 Ed. 2. after the death of Robert de Clifford, the inquisition finds, that *Andrew de Harcla* held the manors of Harcla and Smerdale; and that the wardship of Harcla, when it should happen, was worth by the year 40 *l*; and of Smerdale, 6 *l* 13 *s* 4 *d*. And the cornage for them both 26 *s*.

In the 15th year of the same king, this *Andrew de Harclay* was created earl of Carlisle, to him and the heirs male of his body; which is the first record that mentions an intail of a title to the heir male. He was afterwards, in the reign of the same king, attainted, degraded, and executed for high treason as aforesaid; and his estates being forfeited to the crown, the manor of Hartley was granted by the said king to Nevil baron of *Raby*, who sold the same to Sir *Thomas Musgrave* of Musgrave knight, in whose posterity it still continues.

The family of Musgrave often resided at Hartley castle, during which time the castle was kept in good repair; and there was a park behind it well

replenished

replenished with deer. It was a noble building, standing upon an eminence, and overlooking the village of Hartley, the town of Kirkby Stephen, and many other villages. The late Sir Christopher Musgrave, father of the present owner Sir Philip Musgrave baronet, in a great measure demolished the same, and removed the materials of wood and lead for the reparation of his seat at Edenhall in Cumberland: and nothing now remains thereof, but the venerable ruins of part of the old walls.

There have at several times considerable quantities of lead been got within the manor of Hartley; and also a seam of coal hath been worked upon Hartley fell, being the seam of Stanemore coal diminishing gradually; but the profits thereof from time to time have not been thought sufficient to encourage the continuance of the working.

IV.

MANOR OF WINTON.

WINTON probably had its name from some remarkable battle fought there: for *win* in the Saxon signifies battle; and to *win* is still in use to denote victory in battle or otherwise. So there is *Winchester*, *Winwick*, *Winthorpe*, and the like.

This manor continued all along in the hands of the Veteriponts and Cliffords, as it doth in the possession of their posterity to this day; being parcel of the manor of Brough; without ever having been granted off to any inferior lord: Except some small parcels thereof, which are now held under divers inferior lords, part thereof also having been infranchised at different times.

In the division of the inheritance, in the reign of king Edward the first, between the two daughters and coheirs of the last Robert de Veteripont, we find that each of them had a moiety of the manor of Winton, the value whereof was then estimated in the whole at the yearly sum of 48 *l* 4 *s* 6½ *d*.

In the 8th Ed. 2. after the death of Robert de Clifford, the inquisition finds, that the said Robert de Clifford, on the day on which he died, held at Winton one capital messuage, worth yearly 1 *s*; 100 acres of demesne land, worth yearly 6 *d* an acre; 20 acres of demesne meadow, worth 1 *s* an acre yearly; that he had there also foreland and waste, worth yearly 5 *s*; 28 oxgangs of land, at 5 *s* a year each; 10 messuages of cottagers, worth each by the year 1 *s*; one water mill burnt, worth yearly 4 *l*; that there were also free tenants there, who paid yearly 6 *s* 4¼ *d*; and that Henry de Warthecop held there certain marshy grounds, for which he paid yearly 8 *s*.

In the 10 Hen. 5. after the death of John de Clifford, the inquisition finds, that the said John, on the day on which he died, held at Winton 20 messuages, worth nothing in all issues above reprizes (by reason of the destruction made by the Scots); 40 oxgangs of land, worth yearly 3 *s* 4 *d* each; 80 acres of meadow, worth yearly 6*d* each; 600 acres of pasture, worth yearly 1*d* each; and the water mill, worth yearly 13*s* 4*d*.

The capital messuage or manor house above mentioned seems to have been that which is now called the *hall*, at the upper end of the town. This hall belonged heretofore to the name and family of Scayfe; which appears to have been of ancient standing in this and the neighbouring places. So early as the reign of Ed. 2. *John Scayfe* (in the 6th year of that king) served in parliament as burgess for Appleby; and again in the 1st and in the 2 d of Ed. 3. In the 17 Ed. 3. *Thomas Scayfe* represented the said borough in parliament. In the 4 Ed. 4. *Thomas Scayfe* was a juror on the inquisition *post mortem* of the second John de Clifford. In the 8 Eliz. *Miles Skeyffe* was constituted one of the first governors of Kirkby Stephen school. There was one *major Scaife* in Oliver Cromwell's time, who obtained a considerable share of the sequestred estates. The last of the family in the direct line, Mr. *Robert Scaife*, sold Winton hall to Mr. *Gerard Andrews*; whose daughter and heir Mrs. *Bowes Andrews* the present owner was married to *Bartholomew Dixon* gentleman, and hath no issue.

The *school* is an handsome little building, which was erected in the year 1659, at the expence of several of the principal inhabitants and land-owners, but chiefly of the reverend William Morland, M. A. who was bred at Jesus college in Cambridge, was made schoolmaster of Kirkby Stephen in the year 1630, and in 1639 was instituted to the rectory of Graystock in Cumberland, and ejected in 1650 by Cromwell's commissioners, and afterwards restored on the return of king Charles the second.

In 1681, Robert Waller of Winton yeoman granted divers parcels of freehold land in Kaber to four feoffees in trust for the use of the schoolmaster.

And in the year 1722, Richard Munkhouse of Winton gentleman, gave by his will, for the better endowment of the said school, the sum of 100*l*; provided the feoffees, within 3 months after his decease, should grant the sole nomination of a schoolmaster on all future vacancies unto his brother Thomas Munkhouse gentleman and his heirs for ever. He also gave 10*l* towards the repairs of the said school, and 40*s* for making a garden on the waste ground thereto adjoining. In pursuance whereof, there are two stones put up in the front wall of the schoolhouse, setting forth both the said benefactions, and the consent and agreement of the feoffees, that Mr. Thomas Munkhouse and his heirs shall have the nomination of a schoolmaster, reserving to themselves a power of displacing him (that is, for neglect, or immorality, or such other cause for which a schoolmaster by the laws of this realm may be deprived).

Mrs. Dorothy Munkhouse, widow of the said Mr. Thomas Munkhouse, by her will in the year 1755 gave the legal interest of 50*l* for ever, for providing 6 loaves of Maslin bread, to be distributed in Kirkby Stephen church every Sunday throughout the year, to six poor persons residing within the parish; and appointed her son Richard Munkhouse esquire, his heirs and assigns, sole trustees of the said charity.

IN

IN Kirkby Stephen churchyard is a monumental inſcription, which from the ſtrain of modeſty, filial piety, and unaffected ſimplicity with which it is adorned, we have thought not unworthy of our notice:

1762.

To the memory of the reverend Joſeph Langhorne of Winton and Iſabel his wife.

Her, who to teach this trembling hand to write
Toil'd the long day, and watch'd the tedious night,
I mourn, tho' number'd with the heavenly hoſt;
With her the means of gratitude are loſt.

John Langhorne.

This is that John Langhorne, D. D. who hath favoured the public with many elegant productions both in proſe and verſe; particularly,

Fables of Flora.
Effuſions of friendſhip and fancy: Being letters to and from ſelect friends. 2 Vols.
Letters between Theodoſius and Conſtantia. 2 Vols.
——— between St. Evremond and Waller. 2 Vols.
——— on the eloquence of the pulpit.
——— on religious retirement.
Life and writings of Collins.
Sermons before the honourable ſociety of Lincoln's Inn. 2 Vols.
Poems. 2 Vols.
Solyman and Almena.
Origin of the Veil.
Frederic and Pharamond.
Precepts of conjugal happineſs.
Verſes in memory of a Lady.
A diſſertation hiſtorical and political on the ancient republics of Italy.
The country juſtice, a poem: In two parts.
Plutarch's Lives: Tranſlated from the Greek. 6 Vols. This laſt in conjunction with his brother William Langhorne, M. A.

They both were natives of this place. Their father died when they were very young; and the mother, the ſaid Dr. Langhorne in one of his poems thus further pathetically laments:

Ah ſcenes belov'd! ah conſcious ſhades,
That wave theſe parent-vales along!
Ye bowers where fancy met the tuneful maids,
Ye mountains vocal with my Doric ſong,
Teach your wild echos to complain
In ſighs of ſolemn woe, in broken ſounds of pain.

For her I mourn,
Now the cold tenant of the thoughtleſs urn——
For her bewail theſe ſtrains of woe,

For

For her these filial sorrows flow,
Source of my life, that led my tender years,
With all a parent's pious fears,
That nurs'd my infant thought, and taught my mind to grow.

* * * * * *

O best of parents! let me pour
My sorrows o'er thy silent bed,
There early strew the vernal flower,
The parting tear at evening shed——
Alas! are these the only meed
Of each kind thought, each virtuous deed,
These fruitful offerings that embalm the dead?

Then, fairy-featur'd Hope, forbear———
No more thy fond illusions spread:
Thy shadowy scenes dissolv'd in air,
Thy visionary prospects fled;
With her they fled, at whose lamented shrine,
Love, gratitude, and duty mingled tears,
Condemn'd each filial office to resign,
Nor hopeful more to soothe her long declining years.

THIS village also the compiler of these memoirs boasts as the place of his nativity.

V.

MANOR OF KABER.

From what original this place derives its name, doth not sufficiently appear. It was always anciently written *Kabergh*. *Bergh*, it is well known, means *town*. Perhaps the other component of the word may have been the name of the owner: for *Kay* is a name yet not uncommon.

In the reign of king Henry the second, we find a person of considerable note, of the name of *Robert de Kabergh*.

In the reign of king John, *Robert* son of *Robert de Kabergh* was a witness to divers instruments.

In the 8 Ed. 2. after the death of Robert de Clifford, the inquisition finds, that *Alan de Kabergh* held of the said Robert, on the day on which he died, the manor of Kabergh, by homage and fealty, and the cornage of 17*s* 8*d*.

In the next king's reign, we find the same or part thereof in the name of *Rookby*. For in the 9 Ed. 3. *Thomas de Rookby* obtained a grant of free warren in Kabergh. And in the 31st of the same king, *John de Rookby* levied a fine of the moiety of the manor of Kabergh. Or rather, this seems to denote the village of Rookby, as being part of the manor of Kaber at large.

 Soon

Soon after this, we find Kaber in the name of *Fulthorp*, in which name it continued a long time.

In the 43 Ed. 3. *Roger de Fulthorp* held the same.

In the 15 Ric. 2. *William de Fulthorp*.

In the 17 Hen. 6. *Thomas Fulthorp*, who was one of the justices of the court of common pleas, held the manor of Kabergh.

In the 31 Hen. 6. *Alan Fulthorp* held the same; who was succeeded by his son *Christopher Fulthorp*.

Thus by the inquisition of Quo Warranto aforesaid against Henry lord Clifford in the 19 Hen. 7. it appeared, that *Alan Fulthorp* held the manor of Kabergh of him the said Henry, by homage and fealty, and the cornage of 17*s* 8*d*; and when scutage ran at 40*s*, then paying for the same 40*s*; and when at more, more; and when at less, less: And doing suit from month to month at the county court of our lord the king at his castle of Appleby. That *Christopher Fulthorp*, son and heir of the said *Alan*, succeeded his father therein.

In the 24 Hen. 8. there is a receipt by Ambrose Middleton gentleman, feodary of Henry earl of Cumberland, of the sum of 100*s*, for the relief of *John Fulthorp* esquire son and heir of *Christopher Fulthorp* esquire, for the manor of Kabergh holden of the said earl by the service of one knight's fee, as of his castle of Appleby.

In the 1 and 2 Ph. and Mary, *Thomas Fulthorp* held the same.

Afterwards, the same appears to have been in the possession of *George Wandesforth* of Kirklington in the county of York esquire; who in the 2 Jam. 1. conveyed the manor of Kaber to *Robert Wadeson* of Yafforth in the said county yeoman; and in the 15th year of the said king, *John Wadeson* of Yafforth aforesaid esquire, afterwards Sir *John Wadeson* knight, in consideration of the sum of 1200*l*, sold the manor of Kaber to Robert Jackson of Brough, Thomas Robinson of Naitby, Robert Hindmore of Kirkby Stephen, and Anthony Fothergill of Trannahill in Ravenstondale, in trust for the inhabitants and land owners.

The ancient *manor house* stood where a barn hath been lately erected by the owner Mr. Thomas Granger. And behind it are two small inclosures, which still go by the name of the Orchards.

There is a small *school* at Kaber, erected by one Thomas Waller and the rest of the inhabitants, and endowed by the said Thomas Waller with the sum of 133*l*, the interest whereof then amounted to 8*l* a year, as appears by the following inscription over the school door:

A yeoman of this town did live
Till he was old, and then did give
Unto this school the yearly sum
Of eight pounds for each year to come.
That children might be taught therein,
Behaviour and good discipline.

His

His name, his age, and day of death,
May all be feen here underneath.
Thomas Waller the donor. He died October the 17th, 1689. In the 79th year of his age.

In 1727, Miles Munkhoufe of Starrow gave 5*l* to the faid fchool. And in 1744, George Petty of Kaber by his will gave 20*l*.

After the reftoration of king Charles the fecond, in the year 1663, there was an intended infurrection of the republican party, and feveral for that purpofe affembled at a place called Kaber-Rigg. But being prevented by the vigilance of the militia officers, they difperfed, and feveral of them were apprehended; and in March following, captain Atkinfon and divers others of them were condemned and executed at Appleby for high treafon †.

VI.

MANOR OF SOULBY.

The name of this place in ancient time was moft commonly written *Sulleby*: whether from the name of the owner, or how otherwife, we have not found. But that the owners, in after time, received their name from the place, there is no doubt.

In the reign of king John, one of the witneffes to the grant of the advowfon of the church of Kirkby Thore by Adam de Kirkby Thore to Robert de Veteripont, was *Henry de Sulleby*.

To a grant of lands at Brampton by Walter de Morvil to the faid Robert de Veteripont, one of the witneffes was *Robert de Sullebi*.

To a grant of privilege to the men of Kirkby Thore, by John fon of the faid Robert de Veteripont, one of the witneffes was *Henry de Sulleby*.

In the 36 Hen. 3. a fettlement was made, by *Richard* fon of *Henry de Suleby*, on the marriage of *Robert* his eldeft fon with Alice eldeft daughter of Sir Thomas de Hellebeck. Witneffes whereof were, Sir William de Dacre, John de Moreville, Thomas de Mufgrave then fheriff of Weftmorland, William parfon of Crofby Gerard, Robert his brother, Henry de Standley, William de Warthecop, and William de Soureby.

The next we meet with was *William de Souleby*, who had a fon and heir in wardfhip to Ifabella de Clifford; in whofe right fhe prefented to the rectory of Crofby Gerard, in the 25th year of the reign of king Edward the firft.

But it feems that this fon died foon after, and was fucceeded by his fifter *Johan* then alfo under age. For we find the wardfhip of the body and land of *Johan*, daughter and heir of *William de Sulleby*, committed to John de Helton and

† Flem.

Agnes

Agnes his wife; rendring a reasonable rent during her minority, to John St. John and Thomas Penerell, executors of the last will and testament of the said Isabella, widow of Roger de Clifford.

And soon after, we find the manor of Soulby in another name and family. For in 3 Ed. 2. on an inquisition of tenants in Westmorland who held by cornage tenure, it was found, that *Thomas Musgrave* of Musgrave, who was then under age, held the manor of Soulby. And at the same time, Thomas Bowet held four oxgangs of land in Soulby and Warcop, for which he paid 6*d* cornage.

In 8 Ed. 2. *Thomas de Hellebeck* held a moiety of Soulby. The wardship of the said manor, when it should happen, was estimated at 30*l* a year; the cornage 13*s* 4*d*.

In the 32 Ed. 3. Sir *Thomas Musgrave* obtained a charter of free warren, in his demesne lands at Soulby.

In the 15 Ric. 2. *Thomas de Musgrave*, *William de Wharton*, and *William de Styrkland*, held the manor of Soulby.

In the 10 Hen. 5. *Richard Musgrave*, and *Henry de Wharton* held the manor of Soulby, the cornage whereof was then said to be 11*s* 4*d*. And at the same time *William de Lowther* held 4 oxgangs in Soulby, and 16 acres in Warcop, of the yearly cornage of 6*d*. And *William de Styrkland* held divers lands and tenements at Soulby, of the like yearly cornage of 6*d*.

From henceforth, the manor of Soulby seems invariably to have continued in the name and family of *Musgrave*; except only two or three tenements which are holden of Smardale hall, and seem to be those which had been granted off separate as abovementioned.

The *hall* or manor house, seems to have been in the grounds now called Hall-garths. And there are lands called the demesne, now held in tenancy.

The *chapel* of Soulby was built at the cost of Sir Philip Musgrave baronet, lord of the manor, in the year 1663; and in the same year was consecrated by bishop Stern. In the act of consecration it is set forth, that the said Sir Philip Musgrave and his heirs and assigns, lords of the manor of Hartley castle, shall repair the said chapel from time to time: That the inhabitants of Soulby, in token of their subjection to the mother church, shall three times in the year at least, of which Easter to be one, repair to the mother church, and there hear divine service, and receive the sacrament: That the said Sir Philip Musgrave during his life, and after his death his heirs and assigns, lords of the manor of Hartley castle, shall have power from time to time to nominate a fit minister, to be approved and licensed by the bishop: So as that the said Sir Philip Musgrave, and his heirs and assigns as aforesaid, shall maintain the said minister or curate, and allow him at least 20*l* a year, at Christmass, Lady day, Midsummer, and Michaelmass, by equal portions: And if the chapel shall continue void for six months, or if the curate for six months together shall not perform divine service, the bishop shall have power to nominate a curate for that turn: And reserving to the bishop power of visiting the same, as other chapels within his diocese.

This chapel is now worth upwards of 50*l* a year, arising from lands in the neighbourhood, part settled thereon by the patron and founder, and part purchased by queen Anne's bounty, towards the obtaining whereof the lady Gower gave 200*l* from a charitable fund established by her father Thomas earl of Thanet.

VII.

MANOR OF SMARDALE.

Smere is the ancient name of that sort of grass now called clover, and is a word not yet quite out of use in that respect. And in old times, this place was most commonly written *Smeredale.*

This manor was anciently in the family of the name *de Smeredale*, who came to it by purchase from *Thomas de Helbeck* in the 20 Ed. 1.

Afterwards, we find it in the possession of Sir *Andrew de Harclay*; for in the 8 Ed. 2. after the death of Robert de Clifford, the inquisition finds, that Sir *Andrew de Harclay* held Harclay and Smerdale; that the wardship of Harclay was worth 40*l* a year, and of Smerdale 6*l* 8*s* 4*d*; and the cornage for them both 26*s*.

But after his attainder, this manor came again into the family of *Smerdale*; which family, like many of the rest, ended in a daughter, who was married to a younger brother of the Warcops of *Warcop*.

In the 15 Ric. 2. after the death of Roger de Clifford, the inquisition finds, that *Thomas* son of *John Warcop*, in the right of *Katherine* his wife, held of the said Roger the manor of Smerdale, by homage and fealty and the cornage of 13*s* 4*d*.

In the 31 Hen. 6. *Thomas Warcop* of Lamberset held the manor of Smerdale; and afterwards, in the same year, *Reginald Warcop* held the same. Which *Reginald* died in the 8 Hen. 7. as appears by inquisition, *Edward Warcop* his son and heir being then 24 years of age.

Which *Edward Warcop* married Anne daughter of Thomas Layton, and by her had issue,

John Warcop of Smardale; who by a rental of Henry earl of Cumberland in the 18 Hen. 8. appears then to have held Smardale of the said earl. He married Anne daughter of Jeffrey Lancaster of Crake-trees; and had issue,

Thomas Warcop of Smardale, who lived in the reign of queen Elizabeth, and married Elizabeth daughter of Rowland Thornburgh, and by her had issue two daughters coheirs. *Frances* the elder was married to Sir *John Dalston* of Dalston in Cumberland knight, with whom he had Smardale. *Agnes* the younger was married to Talbot Bowes of Egleston abbey esquire, second son of Sir George Bowes.

And

And here ended the name of *Warcop* of Smardale. Their arms were the ſame as thoſe of the Warcops of Warcop, viz. Sable, three covered cups Argent: with a creſcent for diſtinction of the younger houſe.

And thus the manor became transferred to the family of DALSTON, in which it ſtill continues.

The ſaid Sir *John Dalſton* of Dalſton was ſon of *Thomas*, from whom deſcended by a younger ſon the Dalſtons of Acorn Bank. Which *Thomas* was ſon of *John*, ſon of *Robert*, ſon of *Henry*, brother of *John*, ſon of *John*, ſon of *Henry*, ſon of *Simon*, ſon of *Henry*, ſon of *Adam*, ſon of *Henry*, ſon of *Reginald*, ſon of *Robert* (brother to Hubert de Vallibus firſt baron of Gilſland) to whom Ranulph de Meſchiens gave the barony of *Dalſton*, and who thereupon took the name *de Dalſton*.

In the deſcending line, the ſaid Sir *John Dalſton* had a ſon *John*, father of *George*, father of *William*, father of *George*, brother of *John*, father of *Charles*, father of Sir *George Dalſton* baronet, who died in 1765, leaving only an infant daughter *Elizabeth*.

The arms of *Dalſton* are; Argent, a cheveron ingrailed, between three ravens heads eraſed Sable, billed Or. The creſt; Out of a ducal crown Or, a falcon's head Proper.

Smardale *hall* is an ancient building, which was conſiderably repaired by the late Sir George Dalſton, who inhabited there for ſome time.

There hath been anciently a *chapel*, at a little diſtance from the hall weſtward; where is a well yet called Chapel-well, which ſprang up within the chapel.

VIII.

MANOR OF WAITBY.

This place was ſometimes anciently written *Wadeby*, ſometimes *Waldeby*; which ſeems to indicate its true derivation. *Waldeve* was a name not uncommon; ſo that *Waldeby* may probably ſignify the ſame as *Waldevi locus*, or *Waldeve's (Waltheof's)* ſeat or habitation.

King John, in the 5th year of his reign, granted the wardſhip of Hugh ſon of Jernegan to Robert de Veteripont; and Maud, widow of Henry Jernegan releaſed her dower in Karthorp near Tanfield in Yorkſhire to the ſaid Robert, who had the cuſtody of her ſon by the ſaid king's grant. Which Maud was daughter and heir of *Torphin de Wadeby*; and granted all her lands in Weſtmorland to the ſaid Robert, in the 8th year of that king. She was afterwards married to Hugh de Burgh her ſecond huſband, who confirmed the ſaid grant.

 Not

Not long after this, the manor of Waitby appears to have been divided into moieties, probably by the means of daughters coheirs.

About which time lived one *Gilbert de Wateby*, perhaps of a collateral branch of the family of *Torphin*; who was witness to many grants and other instruments, by the style and title of *Gilbert de Wateby Clericus*; by which it seemeth that he was the conveyancer.—After him, we find no other of the name *de Wateby*.

In the 3 Ed. 2. *William de Dacre* held a moiety of the manor of Wateby, as also of Orton, the cornage whereof was 12*s* 6*d*.

In the 8 Ed. 2. *Henry de Warthcop* appears to have had the other moiety of Wateby, together with the manor of Warcop; the wardship whereof was 30*l* a year, and cornage 17*s* 8*d*.

In the 11 Ed. 3. a fine was levied of a moiety of the manor of Waitby by *Robert Parving*; to hold to the said Robert for life, remainder to Adam Peacock and the heirs male of his body, remainder to the right heirs of the said Robert in fee.

In the 43 Ed. 3. *William de Dacre* levied a fine of a moiety of the manor of Waitby. And in the same year it is found by inquisition, that *Robert Parvings*, *Elena Huthwayt*, and *William de Thwayts*, held the manor (perhaps the other moiety of the manor) of Waitby.

In the 15 Ric. 2. and again in the 4 Hen. 4. *William de Strykland* held a moiety of the said manor, the cornage thereof being 7*s* 5*d*.

In the 10 Hen. 5. *William de Lowther* held a moiety of the manor of Waldeby, by the cornage of 7*s* 5*d*. And *Ralph* earl of *Westmorland* held the other moiety, together with the manor of Warthecop, by the cornage as aforesaid of 17*s* 8*d*.

In the 31 Hen. 6. *George Nevil* knight, lord *Latimer*, held a moiety of Waitby called *Waitby-Agnes* [which argues that it had been formerly divided between coheirs], and which (as the inquisition expresseth) *Richard Warcop* formerly held: And at the same time *Thomas Beauchamp* held the other moiety.

In the 19 Hen. 7. *Thomas Blenkinsop* held a moiety of the manors of Wateby and Orton; and *Thomas*, father of the said *Thomas* (as the inquisition sets forth) died seised thereof in the 10 Ed. 4.

In the 18 Hen. 8. *John Bell*, *John Hoton*, the heirs of *Thomas Musgrave*, and *Thomas Lancaster*, in right of their wives, daughters and coheirs of *Thomas Beauchamp*, held a moiety of the manor of Wateby; and *Geoffrey Lancaster* the other moiety.

After this, we have met with no further particular account, till the reign of king James the second; when Sir *John Lowther* of Sockbridge, who married one of the coheirs of *Lancaster*, sold the lands, consisting of 33 tenements, to freehold.

And in 1713, his son *James Lowther* of Whitehaven, esquire, sold the *manor* to *Richard Munkhouse* of Winton gentleman, from whom the same descended to the present owner Richard Munkhouse of Winton esquire.

The

The *fchool* at Waitby was built in the year 1630, by Mr. James Highmore clothworker in London, who was born at Waitby; for the benefit of the inhabitants of Waitby and Smardale. And the fum of 400*l* was given by him for that ufe, and for the ufe of the poor widows of thofe places; twelve twopenny loaves being ordered by his will to be diftributed every funday to twelve widows, being 60 years of age and upwards.

In a rental of the eftates of Philip lord Wharton, in the latter end of the reign of queen Elizabeth, there is a place called *Abbot-hall* at Waitby, then in the tenure of the wife of James Hindmore, (which probably had belonged to fome of the religious houfes,) holden of the faid lord Wharton: And the vicar of Kirkby Stephen held there of the faid lord certain improved lands upon Withbar and Calf clofe, of the yearly rent of 9*s*.

IX.

MANOR OF NATEBY.

From whence *Nateby* had its name, we have not found. Perhaps it might be, from the *Nativi* or bondmen inhabiting there, attendent upon the caftle of Pendragon; even as *Bondgate* was fo called from its being the place of habitation of the fervile tenants of the caftle of Appleby. And the *Drengage* tenure was the like of divers inhabitants of places adjacent to the caftle of Brougham.

In the 8 Ed. 2. after the death of Robert de Clifford, the inquifition finds, that *Nicolas de Haftinges* then held the manors of Nateby and Crofby Ravenfwath; that the wardfhip of the fame, when it fhould happen, was worth 40*l* a year; and the cornage for them both 27*s* 2*d*.

In the 43 Ed. 3. *Ralph Haftinges* held the manor of Nateby of Robert de Clifford, by homage and fealty, and cornage of 13*s* 7*d*.

In the 10 Hen. 5. *Richard Haftinges* held the fame in like manner.

In the 18 Hen. 8. *Thomas Wharton* held the fame of Henry earl of Cumberland; which heretofore (as the inquifition expreffeth it) was held by the heirs of *Nicholas Haftings*.

After this, the fame continued in the *Wharton* family all along.

In the year 1693, *Philip*, lord *Wharton* and *Thomas Wharton* his fon convey to truftees a clofe of pafture called Naitby Birkett, parcel of a leafe commonly called there Naitby leafe, then in the poffeffion of *Hugh Wharton* gentleman or his affigns at the yearly rent of 16*l* 10*s*, and formerly at the rent of 22*l*: And all that clofe of meadow and pafture called Low Field in Ravenftonedale, late belonging to Robert Waller, which came to the faid Philip lord Wharton by forfeiture on the attainder of the faid Robert Waller, containing fix acres: for the ufe of a licenfed diffenting meeting houfe in Swaledale.

 Finally

Finally, this manor of Nateby, together with the other Wharton eſtates in Weſtmorland, came by purchaſe to Robert Lowther eſquire, father of the preſent owner Sir James Lowther baronet.

X.

MANOR OF WHARTON.

WHARTON was anciently written *Wherton*, and when transferred into the barbarous latin of thoſe days *Querton*; for in the place of the letter *W* they frequently ſubſtitute *Q*, ſometimes *G*, as when for *war* they ſay *guerra*: But whether this place may have had its name from ſome battle fought there, can be only matter of conjecture.

So early as the reign of king Edward the firſt, there was a family of note at this place of the name of *Wharton*. One of whom married a daughter and coheir of Philip Haſtings of Croglin in Cumberland; whereby the Whartons obtained part of Croglin, as afterwards they got the whole. And it is remarkable, that the Haſtings' arms were the ſame as thoſe of the Whartons; or rather it may ſeem, that the Whartons took their arms at that time; viz. in a field Sable, a manch Argent.

Accordingly, in the next king's reign, we find, that *Henry de Quherton* preſented one W. de Edenhall to the rectory of Croglyn.

And by an inquiſition in the 3 Ed. 2. we find that *Henry de Querton* (the ſame perſon) held of Robert de Clifford the manor of Querton, by the cornage of 6*s* a year.

And in the 23 Ed 3. we find one Piers Tylliol holding his tenement at Croglin of *Hugh de Wharton*.

And in the laſt year of the ſame king, *Hugh de Querton* preſented to the rectory of Croglin aforeſaid.

In the 15 Ric. 2. and again in the 4 Hen. 4. *William de Wherton* held the manor of Wherton, under the cornage aforeſaid of 6*s*.

In the 2 Hen. 5. *Richard de Wherton* ſerved in parliament as burgeſs for Appleby. And the 5 Hen. 5. *Richard de Wherton* ſerved as member for the county.

In the 10 Hen. 5. *Henry de Wharton* held the manor of Wharton of John de Clifford.

Notwithſtanding the indubitable authenticity of the preceding account, nothing of all this is taken notice of in the pedigree certified at the heralds viſitation in 1585. But the ſame begins with,

1. *Thomas Wharton*, who in the 31 Hen. 6. held the manor of Wharton of Thomas de Clifford. About which time alſo begins the pedigree of the Whartons of Kirkby Thore, with one *John*, probably a younger brother of this family. The ſaid *Thomas* married (as the pedigree ſets forth) a Lowther of Lowther. And by her had iſſue,

2. *Henry Wharton*; who married Alice daughter of Sir John Coniers of Hornby, knight, who had iſſue,

3. *Thomas*; who married Agnes daughter of Reginald Warcop of Smerdale: And by her had iſſue, (1) *Thomas*. (2) *Chriſtopher*. (3) *Joan*, married to John Fulthorp of Hipſwell. (4) *Florence*, married to Thomas Forſter of Ederſton.

4. Sir *Thomas Wharton* knight, advanced by king Henry the eighth to the dignity of baron, for the ſignal defeat which he gave to the Scots at Sollom-moſs.

He married to his firſt wife, Eleanor, daughter of Sir Bryan Stapleton of Wighill knight; and by her had iſſue, (1) *Thomas*. (2) Sir *Henry Wharton* knight; who married Joan, daughter of Thomas Maliverer of Allerton, who after his death married to her ſecond huſband Robert lord Ogle. (3) *Agnes*, married to Sir Richard Muſgrave knight. (4) *Joan*, married to William Pennington of Moncaſter eſquire. Beſides theſe, he had two other children who died in their infancy; as appears from the inſcription at the eaſt end of his monument aforeſaid in Kirkby Stephen church.—To his ſecond wife he married Anne daughter of George earl of Shrewſbury; and by her had no iſſue.

5. *Thomas*, ſecond lord Wharton, married Anne daughter of Robert Devereux earl of Suſſex; and died in 1572, leaving iſſue *Philip* and *Thomas*.

6. *Philip*, third lord Wharton, married to his firſt wife, Frances daughter of Henry Clifford earl of Cumberland; and by her had iſſue, (1) Sir *George Wharton* knight of the Bath; who married Anne daughter of John Manners earl of Rutland, but died without iſſue, being ſlain in a rencounter by Sir James Stuard knight, in 1609. (2) *Thomas*; who married Philadelphia daughter of Sir Robert Cary knight: this Thomas died in his father's life time, leaving iſſue Philip who ſucceeded to the title and inheritance. (3) *Franciſca*, married to Sir Richard Muſgrave baronet. (4) *Margaret*, married to Thomas lord Wooton. (5) *Eleanor*, married to William Thwaytes of Long Marſton in the county of York eſquire. The ſaid Philip, third lord Wharton, married to his ſecond wife Dorothy daughter of ——— Colbie, and relict of ——— Tamworth; and by her had a ſon *Henry*.

7. *Philip*, fourth lord Wharton, ſon of Thomas, and grandſon of Philip the third lord. He was active againſt the royaliſts, and colonel of a regiment of horſe, in the reign of king Charles the firſt; but was not aſſenting to that king's death and the abolition of the government.

He was thrice married; firſt, to Elizabeth daughter of Sir Rowland Wandesford of Pickhay in Yorkſhire, and by her had a daughter *Elizabeth* married to Robert lord Willoughby of Ereſby, and after to Robert earl of Lindſey.

His ſecond wife was Jane daughter of Arthur Goodwin of Upper Winchendon in Buckinghamſhire; by whom he had (1) *Thomas*. (2) *Goodwin*. (3) Colonel *Henry Wharton*; who died at Dundalk in Ireland, of the ſickneſs which ſwept away great part of duke Schombergh's army. He was a brave bold man. In the reign of king James the ſecond, when Tirconnel was made governor:

governor of Ireland, he affumed the habit of a player, and fung before the king in the playhoufe the famous party fong of Lillibullero. (4) *Margaret*, married to major Dunch of Pufey in Berkfhire. (5) *Mary*, married to William Thomas of Glamorganfhire efquire. (6) *Philadelphia*, married to Sir George Lockhart of Carnwath.

His third wife was Anne daughter of William Carr efquire, groom of the chamber to king James the firft; by whom he had a fon *William*, who was killed in a duel by Mr. Wolfey.

8. *Thomas*, fifth lord Wharton, fon of Philip. He was very active in bringing about the revolution; and afterwards in oppofing the Tory miniftry in queen Anne's time. For which fervices, he was made vifcount Winchendon and earl of Wharton, and laft of all marquis of Wharton.

He married to his firft wife a daughter of Sir Henry Lee of Dichley in Oxfordfhire, by whom he had no iffue. To his fecond wife he married Lucy daughter of lord Lifburne, and by her had iffue, (1) *Philip*. (2) *Jane*, married to John Holt of Redgrave in Suffolk efquire, and afterwards to Robert Coke efquire. (3) *Lucy*, married to Sir William Morice baronet.

9. *Philip*, fixth lord Wharton, and fecond marquis of that name. He was about 17 years of age at the death of his father. He was a perfon of unbounded genius, eloquence, and ambition: had all the addrefs and activity of his father, but without his fteadinefs: violent in parties, and expenfive in cultivating the arts of popularity; which indeed ought to be in fome meafure charged to his education under fuch a father, who (it is faid) expended 80,000*l* in elections, an immenfe fum in thofe days; by which the eftate became incumbered, and the fon was not a perfon of œconomy enough to difengage it. In a word, if the father and fon had been one degree higher in life, and lived in Macedonia at the time of Philip and Alexander; they would have done juft as Philip and Alexander did.

The young marquis fet out in the world a violent Whig, and for his extraordinary fervices, in parliament and out of it, was created *duke* of Wharton. After that, he fet up in oppofition to the miniftry, then became a Tory, then a Jacobite, then a rebel to his king and country, and accepted a commiffion in the king of Spain's army againft Gibraltar.

He married Martha daughter of major general Holmes; which being not adequate to his father's defigns and expectations, it is thought haftened his father's death (for he died within fix weeks after): By her he had a fon, who died in his infancy. He afterwards married a maid of honour of the queen of Spain, who furvived him, but had no iffue by him.

He died at the age of 32, in a Bernardine convent in a fmall village in Spain, where the charitable fathers hofpitably took him in; and was buried in the fame poor manner in which they bury their own monks. †

† It is thought fit here to fubjoin Mr. Pope's account of this extraordinary perfon; being one of the moft finifhed characters in all Pope's works:

"Wharton, the fcorn and wonder of our days;
Whofe ruling paffion was the luft of praife:

Born

The *arms* of the Whartons, as aforesaid, are; Sable, a manch Argent. The crest; On a wreath, a bull's head erased.—And king Edward the sixth, in recompence of the services of the first Thomas lord Wharton, granted to him an augmentation of his paternal coat, viz. a border ingrailed Or, charged with legs of lions in saltire gules, armed Azure.

The *village* of Wharton was demolished long ago, to make room for the park and demesne; and the tenants dispersed to Wharton Dikes, about half a mile off, to the south west.

The *hall* is now in ruins and desolate, inhabited by no human creature but a poor hind. The estate was purchased by Robert Lowther of Mauls Meburn esquire, father of the present owner Sir James Lowther of Lowther baronet.

XI.

FOREST OF MALLERSTANG.

Before the grant of the barony of Westmorland to Robert de Veteripont, the forest of Mallerstang (with the rest) belonged to Sir *Hugh de Morvill*; and there is a large round hill yet called Hugh Morvill's seat, where Anne countess of Pembroke erected a stone pillar, and upon one of the stones is this inscription, A. P. 1664.

The castle of Mallerstang, called *Pendragon castle*, is said to have been built about the the time of Vortigern, by *Uter Pendragon*. Who this *Uter* was,

Born with whate'er could win it from the wise;
Women and fools must like him, or he dies.
Tho' wond'ring senates hung on all he spoke,
The club must hail him master of the joke.
Shall parts so various aim at nothing new?
He'll shine a Tully, and a Wilmot too.
Then turns repentant, and his God adores,
With the same spirit that he drinks and whores:
Enough, if all around him but admire,
And now the punk applaud, and now the friar.
Thus with each gift of nature and of art,
And wanting nothing but an honest heart;
Grown all to all, from no one vice exempt;
And most contemptible, to shun contempt;
His passion still, to covet gen'ral praise;
His life, to forfeit it a thousand ways;
A constant bounty, which no friend has made;
An angel tongue, which no man can persuade;
A fool, with more of wit than half mankind;
Too rash for thought, for action too refin'd;
A tyrant to the wife his heart approves;
A rebel to the very king he loves;
He dies, sad outcast of each church and state,
And, harder still, flagitious, yet not great."

 may

may be difficult to ascertain. There was a family of the name of *Ughtred* of ancient time. And during the time of the Saxons in England before the Norman conquest, there was a famous warrior of the name of *Uchtred* son of *Waltheof* earl of Northumberland; who with a much inferior army gave the Scots under their king Malcolm a most signal overthrow: for which victory king Ethelred gave to *Uchtred* his daughter the princess Elgiva in marriage, and with her the counties of Northumberland and York for a portion.

Pendragon seems not to be properly the surname of a man, but an epithet only, describing his warlike quality. *Pen*, it is well known, signifies a mountain, or something that is great; and *dragon* in all ages hath been applied to military persons. This *Uter Pendragon*, tradition reports, in order to fortify this his castle, endeavoured to draw the river Eden round it, but to no purpose; which occasioned this proverb,

Let Uter Pendragon do what he can,
Eden will run where Eden ran.

After the death of John de Veteripont, in the reign of king Henry the third, the wardship of his son Robert, during his minority, was committed to the prior of Carlisle, who suffered great waste to be committed in the estates of the said Robert; and particularly, on an inquisition thereof taken, it was found, that the vale of Mallerstang was much decayed by the multitude of vaccaries, and chiefly by the archery of Roger the forester, and other archers of Lounsdale, by default of the prior and for want of keeping. Also, purprestures were made in many places within the forest, and in the boundaries of the forest, by sufferance of the said prior after he took upon him the guardianship.

After the death of Roger de Clifford, in the 11 Ed. 1. it was found by inquisition, that the forest of Mallerstang, in herbage and agistment and all other issues, was worth yearly 44 *l* 7 *s* 6 *d*.

In the 8 Ed. 2. the jurors find, that in the vale of Mallerstang there is one castle called Pendragon, with a vaccary held by Andrew de Harcla of the rent of 6 *d* a year, and six vaccaries more worth 20 *s* a year each, agistment worth 6 *d* year, turbary 6 *s* 8 *d*, pleas and perquisites of court 13 *s* 4 *d*.

In the 1 Ed. 3. the jurors find, that belonging to Roger de Clifford deceased was the castle of Pendragon, together with the forest of Mallerstang to the same belonging; that the buildings in the castle cannot be extended, for that the costs of maintaining the same exceed the profits thereof: That in the said forest there are divers vaccaries and other profits of herbage in the hands of tenants at will, who pay yearly at Martinmass and Whitsuntide 30 *l*.

In the 15 Ed. 3. the Scots burned this castle to the ground.

In the 36 Ed. 3. the king granted to Roger de Clifford in fee, the vaccary called Southwaite in the forest of Mallerstang.

In the reign of king Edward the fourth, during the attainder of Henry lord Clifford, part of the estate was granted to Sir William Parr of Kendal castle; and after the death of Sir William, his son Thomas being under age and in wardship

wardſhip of the king, the ſaid king granted to Lancelot Wharton the office of bowbearer of Mallerſtang in right of his ſaid ward †.

Over the entrance of the caſtle gate is this inſcription, "This Pendragon caſtle "was repayred by the lady Anne Clifford, counteſſe dowager of Pembroke, "Dorſett, and Montgomerie, baroneſſe Clifford, Weſtmerland, and Veſcie, "high ſheriffeſſe by inheritance of the county of Weſtmerland, and lady of "the honour of Skipton in Craven, in the year 1660; ſo as ſhe came to lye "in it herſelf for a little while in October 1661, after it had layen ruinous "without timber or any covering, ever ſince the year 1541. Iſaiah, Chap. "lviii. Ver. 12 ‡.

"God's name be praiſed."

She built alſo the bridge over the river Eden nigh the caſtle.

The caſtle was afterwards demoliſhed by Thomas earl of Thanet about the year 1685.

The ſaid counteſs alſo repaired and endowed the *chapel*, as appears by the following inſcription in the chapel porch:

"This chapple of Mallerſtang, after itt had layne ruinous and decayed "ſome 50 or 60 years, was newe repayred by the lady Anne Clifford counteſſe "dowager of Pembrooke, Dorſett, and Montgomery, in the year 1663; "who alſoe endowed the ſame with lands which ſhe purchaſed in Cawtley near "Sedbergh, to the yearly value of eleaven pounds for ever."—This eſtate ſhe gave for maintenance of a perſon qualified to read prayers and the homilies of the church of England, and to teach the children of Mallerſtang dale to read and write Engliſh, in the chapel there.

The ancient ſalary is about 9*l* 10*s* yearly. And in the year 1714, Thomas earl of Thanet gave 200*l*, wherewith an augmentation was procured from the governors of queen Anne's bounty, and an eſtate purchaſed in Garſdale. And in 1762, the counteſs dowager Gower gave 200*l* (being part of a charitable fund of her father the ſaid Thomas earl of Thanet) wherewith another bounty was procured, and an eſtate purchaſed nigh Sedbergh. And in 1772, ſhe gave other 200*l*, and thereby obtained another augmentation, wherewith an eſtate was purchaſed adjoining to the laſt above mentioned.

† Mach. from Dugdale.

‡ The words are: *And they that ſhall be of thee ſhall build the old waſte places; thou ſhalt raiſe up the foundations of many generations; and thou ſhalt be called, the repairer of the breach, the reſtorer of paths to dwell in.*——Biſhop Rainbow, in his funeral ſermon of this lady, pitched upon a text no leſs appoſite, viz. Prov. 14. 1. *Every wiſe woman buildeth her houſe.*

I. PARISH OF BROUGH.

THE parish of Brough was anciently part of the parish of *Kirkby Stephen*, even as *Gresmere* and *Windermere* were parts of the parish of Kendal. For parishes in England were not set out all at once, but the boundaries became ascertained by usage, or special agreement, or the extent sometimes of the founder's estate.

Ivo de Talebois gave the church of Kirkby Stephen to the abbot and convent of St. Mary's York: The said abbot and convent granted the advowson of the vicarage of Kirkby Stephen to the bishop of Carlisle and his successors: And the bishops, in consequence thereof, claimed also the patronage of the *chapel of Burgh*.

On the other hand, *Robert de Veteripont*, having obtained a grant of *Appleby and Burgh*, with their appurtenances (*cum appendiciis*, with their *appendages*); his posterity claimed the patronage of Brough, as appendant to the manor.

A third claim was put in by the crown, asserting that the patronage thereof had never passed out of the crown by virtue of the said grant, but that it still remained in the crown.

To this purpose there is a very notable record *, in the 15 Ed. 1. On an assise of *Darrein presentment*, the king claimed the presentation against Isabella and Idonea, daughters and heirs of Robert de Veteripont; setting forth, that king Henry the third, father of the present king, presented last to the church one William de Clifford, by whose cession the church is now vacant. The said Isabella and Idonea on their own behalf set forth, that the manor of Burgh, with divers lands there, did heretofore belong to Hugh de Morvil, who forfeited the same, and thereupon they came into the hands of king Henry the second; and after his death, into the hands of king Richard (the first), who presented one Thomas Bowet: After king Richard's death, the same came into the hands of king John; who granted to Robert de Veteripont, ancestor of the said Isabella and Idonea, Appleby and Burgh, with all their appurtenances: That to the said Robert de Veteripont succeeded his son John: That the said John de Veteripont dying, his son Robert (father of the said Isabella and Idonea) being then under age and in custody of king Henry the third, and the church then becoming vacant, the said king Henry the third presented thereto one Peter de Chamberi: That the said Robert de Veteripont dying, and the church then again becoming vacant by the death of the said Peter de Chamberi, the said Isabella and Idonea being then under age and in custody of the said king; he the said king Henry the third, in the name of his said wards, did present one William de Clifford, by whose cession the church is now again become vacant: And they further say, that in the first presentation of the said king Henry the third, one *W.* (Walter Malclerk) bishop of Carlisle, by reason of the custody of the lands of the said Robert de Veteripont son of

* Machel from Dugd. MSS.

John being then in his hands, together with the advowson of the church aforesaid, by a grant from the said king until the said Robert should be of full age, opposed himself to the said presentation; and that the said king by his letters disclaimed any thing to himself by virtue thereof, but only in the name of the said Robert: And in like manner, on the second presentation by the said king, Roger de Clifford and Roger de Leyburn having the custody of the lands of the said Isabella and Idonea by a like grant from the crown until they should come of age, the said king by his letters testified, that they gave their assent to the said presentation for that turn, saving to them their right when the church should again become vacant: And thereupon the said Isabella and Idonea, by virtue of the said grant from king John, who gave to the said Robert de Veteripont the said manor and lands with all their appurtenances, insist upon their right to present; because the advowson, though not specially mentioned in the grant, was appendant to the said manor. But by the court: Forasmuch as in the said grant no mention is made of the advowson, but only *Burgh with its appurtenances*; in such grant of the king, it is presumed, that he retained to himself the advowson, and did not grant the same. And judgment was given for the king.

Which judgment is very remarkable; and proceeds upon the distinction, that although in the case of a common person the grant of a manor *with the appurtenances* passeth an advowson appendant to such manor, yet in the case of the king it is otherwise, and the advowson doth not pass without being specially named. And this shews, that the statute of *Prerogativa Regis* made in the next king's reign (17 Ed. 2. c. 15.) was not introductory of a new law as to this matter, but only declaratory of what the law was before: Which enacteth, that "When our lord the king giveth or granteth land or a manor "with the appurtenances, without he make express mention in his deed or "writing of knights fees, advowsons of churches, and dowers when they fall, "belonging to such manor or land, then at this day the king reserveth to "himself such fees, advowsons, and dowers; albeit that among other persons "it hath been observed otherwise."

And in pursuance of the aforesaid judgment, the crown continued in possession of this advowson (though not without further contest both by the bishop and the posterity of the said Robert) until king Edward the third, at the instance of his chaplain *Robert Eglesfield*, who was rector of this church and founder of Queen's College in Oxford, granted the same to the said college; in the patronage of which college it still continues.

The parish of Brough is bounded on the East by the parishes of Romaldkirk and Bowes in the county of York; on the South, by the parish of Kirkby Stephen; on the West, by the parish of Musgrave; and on the North, by the said parish of Romaldkirk: And contains about 210 families, all of the church of England.

The church is dedicated to St. Michael; and is a vicarage, valued in the king's books at 8 *l* 18 *s* 9 *d*.

 The

The ſucceſſion of incumbents, ſo far as we have any account, hath been as follows:

So early as the reign of king Richard the firſt, we have found *Thomas Bowet*, preſented by that king, as in poſſeſſion of the advowſon after the forfeiture of Sir Hugh de Morvil; and without any oppoſition, ſo far as appears, from the abbot and convent of St. Mary's York, to whom the church of Kirkby Stephen did then belong. But during the incumbency of Thomas Bowet, we find a diſpute between the ſaid abbot and convent on one part, and Walter Malclerk biſhop of Carliſle on the other part, concerning the church of Kirkby Stephen; which was referred to the prior of Carliſle and other arbitrators, who awarded, that the church of Kirkby Stephen with all its appurtenances (namely, the *chapel* of *Burgh* with its appurtenances, and if there be any other which ought to be called chapels) ſhall be ceded to the ſaid abbey; that after the ceſſion or death of Thomas Bowet, the chapel of Burgh ſhall accrue to its mother church of Kirkby Stephen, without any impediment of the biſhop of Carliſle.

However, in the next biſhop's time, in the year 1248, which was the 34th year of king Henry the third, the abbot and convent (ſo far as concerned the diſpute between them and the biſhop) granted to Silveſter biſhop of Carliſle and his ſucceſſors the advowſon of the church of Burgh.

Nevertheleſs, the biſhop's claim did not take place; for on the death of Thomas Bowet, the ſaid king Henry the third preſented the aforeſaid *Peter de Chamberi*, Robert de Veteripont ſon of John being then under age and the king's ward, though the king had granted the cuſtody of the lands of the ſaid Robert to the biſhop as aforeſaid.

On the death of Peter de Chamberi, the ſaid king Henry the third preſented *William de Clifford*; the two daughters and coheirs of the ſaid Robert being then under age, and the king's wards.

On the ceſſion of the ſaid William de Clifford, the right of preſentation was conteſted as aforeſaid between king Edward the firſt and the ſaid two daughters of Robert de Veteripont; which ended in favour of the king's title. And *John de Langton* ſeems to have been then preſented by the king. For in the 33 Ed. 1. *John de Langton*, rector of Burgh, reſigns his living, on being made biſhop of Chicheſter; and thereupon the king preſented *Hugh de Burgh*, and Robert de Clifford knight preſented *William de Corby*. On a *jus patronatus* iſſued, the jurors ſay, that the church is vacant by the reſignation of John now biſhop of Chicheſter; that the king laſt preſented the ſaid John to the ſaid church; that the ſaid church is penſionary to the biſhop of Carliſle in 20*s* yearly; that concerning the right of patronage they are in doubt; for that Adam de Ulveſby, ſteward of the biſhop, appeared in taking the inquiſition, and produced a charter of the abbot and convent of St. Mary's York, which teſtifieth, that the ſaid abbot and convent had granted the patronage of the ſaid church to Silveſter biſhop of Carliſle and his ſucceſſors; and that Nicholas de Grendon, bailiff of the ſaid Robert de Clifford, appeared alſo, and propounded *ore tenus* in the name of the ſaid Robert, that he the ſaid Robert is the

the true patron, for that king John granted to the ancestor of the said Robert the manor of Burgh with the appurtenances. The result was, that *Hugh de Burgh*, the king's presentee, was instituted.

The next incumbent seems to have been *William de Northwich*. For on the death of William de Northwick, rector of Burgh, in the 8 Ed. 3. 1332, the king presented the above mentioned *Robert de Eglesfield*; which Robert was founder of Queen's college in Oxford as aforesaid, for the education and emolument chiefly of persons born within the two counties of Westmorland and Cumberland: a most beneficial institution, as those two counties above all others were over-run with ignorance and barbarism, occasioned by the perpetual hostilities which existed between the neighbouring borderers on both sides; and which hath been productive of infinite advantage, not only to the said two counties, but to the kingdom in general, in furnishing many able and learned men for the service both of church and state. In honour of whose memory, we have thought fit to lay together all that hath occurred to us concerning the family of *Eglesfield*. They were of *Eglesfield* [Eagles-field], a small village in Cumberland, from whence they derived their surname.

So early as the reign of king Henry the third, we find in the 44th year of that king, a suit at law, between *Adam* son of *Richard de Eglesfield* plaintiff, and *Henry de Eglesfield* defendant, concerning a mill in Eglesfield: which implies, that the family were then lords of the manor; for the mills generally in ancient time belonged to the lords of manors, being erected by them for the use of their tenants; and it seemeth, that the tenant, without the lord's permission, could not erect a mill; most of the tenants being bound by their tenure to grind their corn at the lord's mill.

The next account that we have is in the 1 Ed. 3. in which we find, that *Robert de Eglesfeld* held the manor of Ravenswyke. And this probably is the same *Robert de Eglesfield* [or, as the name is spelt in the bishop's register, *Eglesfeld*], of whom we now speak. Dr. Todd says, he was son of *John Eglesfield* by *Beatrix* his wife; which probably may be true: but he doth not cite his vouchers. As to the other particulars here mentioned, we have undoubted authority; the same being extracted from the Escheators books for Cumberland, as copied by Mr. Denton.

In the 12 Ed. 3. there was a grant of free warren to *Robert Eglesfield*, in the manors of Eglesfield, Dregg, and Ravenwyke.

In the 14 Ed. 3. it is found by inquisition, that *Robert Eglesfield*, granted the hamlet of Ravenwyke to the provost and scholars of Queen's college [*Aula Reginæ*] in Oxford, holden of the king *in capite*, by homage and fealty and the rent of 2*s* 8*d* to be paid yearly into the exchequer at Carlisle. And the inquisition further finds, that the said Robert held 40 marks of land and rent in the manors of Eglesfield and Dregg, of Anthony Lucy (lord of Cockermouth) by fealty and 6*s* 8*d* yearly.

In the 32 Ed. 3. *John Eglesfield* [heir general, probably, of the family] infeoffed Roger Kirkbride and John Browne chaplains in lands at Langholme, Castle Carrock, Gamelsbie, Cringledyke, Hetherford, Burgh, Crookdaik, Eglesfield, Newton, and Kirkbampton, to the use of *John* his son and heir.

In

In the 35 Ed. 3. *John de Eglesfield* appears to have been lord of Langholme, and to have had lands at Crookdaik, Eglesfield, and Kirkbampton.

In the 39 Ed. 3. *John de Eglesfield* held the manor of Eglesfield, by homage, and 6*s* 8*d* cornage; the extended value thereof being ten marks.

In the 44 Ed. 3. Maud widow of John de Ribbeton held lands in Eglesfield, of *John de Eglesfield* lord thereof.

In the 22 Ric. 2. *John Eglesfield* held in free tenancy the manor of Eglesfield, of the castle and manor of Cockermouth, by the service of 6*s* 8*d*.

In the 9 Hen. 8. *Gawin Eglesfield* esquire was high sheriff of the county of Cumberland.

In the 34 Hen. 8. from a general feodary for Cumberland, compiled in that year from the rolls of the court of wards and liveries, it appears, that *Richard Eglesfield* then held the manor of Eglesfield of our lord the king as of his castle of Cockermouth, by homage and fealty, and 6*s* 8*d* cornage, and the service of witnesman in five villages to be performed; that he held also the manor and village of Alingburghte; and divers messuages, lands, and tenements in Dreigg in Coupland in the said county of Cumberland, of the king as of his castle of Egremont, by knights service, homage, fealty, suit of court, 6*s* 8*d* cornage, and 12*d* for seawake, and puture of the serjeants.

In the 5 Ed. 6. *Richard Eglesfield* esquire was high sheriff of the said county of Cumberland. And this is the last of the name and family that we have found at Eglesfield *.

The said *Robert de Eglesfeld*, on his presentation to the rectory of Burgh, was instituted in the person of *Adam de Eglesfeld* his proxy. He was ordained priest in the cathedral church of Carlisle in Lent following. The right of presentation, at this vacancy, was contested by Robert de Clifford in the courts at Westminster, and judgment given for the king. In 1342, the profits of the rectory were sequestred by the bishop, for the non-residence of the said *Robert de Eglesfield*; whereupon the king sent a writ of relaxation, the said *Robert* being employed in attendance upon the king's person.

In the year 1344, the church was appropriated, by pope Clement the sixth, to the provost and scholars of the said college; and an account was then taken of the value of the living, which was then rated at 53*l* 16*s* 7*d*, though in the time of William de Northwick (the inquisition says) it was sometimes worth 100*l* a year: whereof the vicar was endowed with the manse and glebe, with lands at Helbeck, the tithes of hay of Helbeck and Sourby, Great Burgh and Little Burgh (the tithes of hay of Staynesmore being excepted, which were to remain to the college); the tithes of mills, milk, calves, colts, and prescriptions for the same; the tithes of flax, hemp, Lent fines, mortuaries, oblations, obventions, and all small tithes (except the tithes of wool and lamb). The vicar to sustain all charges ordinary and extraordinary, and to pay the pension of 20*s* yearly to the bishop, and to maintain the roof of the chancel.

The next after Robert Eglesfield that we find was *John Rainold*, vicar of Burgh; who in the year 1369 made an exchange with *John de Merton* vicar of

* For a list of the provosts of Queen's college, see the Appendix, N° III.

St.

St. Michael's Appleby; and the provost and scholars thereupon presented the said John de Merton to the vicarage of Brough.

The next that we have found was of the name of *Raisbeck*; who in the year 1506 opposed the establishing of a chapel at Brough, as will appear.

The next that hath occurred to us is *Thomas Rigg*, whose epitaph was depicted in one of the windows in the chancel, legible in bishop Nicolson's time all but the date: "Orate pro anima magistri Thomæ Ryge, quondam vicarii istius "ecclesiæ; et pro animabus parentum, benefactorum, parochianorum suorum, "ac omnium fidelium defunctorum: Quorum animabus propitietur Deus." He appears to have been living in 1532.

In the year 1537, 28 Hen. 8. after Ask's rebellion in that year, we find a vicar of Brough, but his name is not mentioned, in a letter from the duke of Norfolk to the king—"Aglianby, I doubt not, or now hath shewed your "highnes what was done att Carlisle. And thoughe none were quartered, "because I knewe not your pleasure therein before; yett all the threescore and "fourteene be hanged in cheaines or ropes uppon gallowes or trees, in all suche "townes as they did dwell in. And whereas your majesty would have send the "vickar of Perith to you; it is not of Perith, but of Brughe, that your grace "doth meane, for there is none suche: for whome I have sent to my lorde "of Cumberland, for I lefte him in his keepinge. And also I have for "doctor Towneley, and doubt not within three daies to have them both with "me, and soe shall send them up †."

In 1568, we find *Lancelot Shaw*, M. A. vicar of Brough.

In 1594, *Roger Salkeld*, M. A. was presented by the provost and scholars, on the death of *Lancelot Shaw*.

In 1611, *David Heckstetter*, S. T. B. was instituted, on the death of Roger Salkeld.

In 1623, on David Heckstetter's death, *William Richardson*, S. T. B. was instituted.

In 1664, *Christopher Harrison*, M. A. was instituted, on the presentation of the provost and scholars.

In 1695, *Joseph Fisher*, M. A. was instituted, on the death of Christopher Harrison. He was afterwards archdeacon of Carlisle.

In 1703, on the death of Joseph Fisher, *Francis Thomson*, S. T. B. was instituted; who died in the year 1735. His wife, who was widow of the said Joseph Fisher, died two years after him. They had two sons; the elder, John Thomson esquire, now one of his majesty's justices of the peace for the county of Westmorland: The younger son, William Thomson, M. A. late fellow of the said college, rector of Southweston and Hampton Poyle in the county of Oxford, was author of a volume of elegant poems published in the year 1757. The said William Thomson caused two epitaphs to be ingraved in the chancel of Brough church in memory of his parents; which, being much above the common run of monumental inscriptions, and withal extremely characteristic of the persons described, are here inserted:

† From the lords answer to the tenants remonstrance concerning tenantright. MS.

1.

Dear to the wise and good, by all approv'd,
The joy of virtue, and heaven's well belov'd!
His life inspir'd with every better art,
A learned head, clear soul, and honest heart.
Each science chose his breast her favourite seat,
Each language, but the language of deceit.
Severe his virtues, yet his manners kind,
A manly form, and a seraphic mind.
So long he walk'd in virtue's even road,
In him at length, 'twas natural to do good.
Like Eden *, his old age (a sabbath rest!)
Flow'd without noise, yet all around him blest!
His patron, Jesus; with no titles grac'd,
But that best title, a good parish priest.
Peace with his ashes dwell. And, mortals, know,
The saint's above; the dust alone below.
The wise and good shall pay their tribute here,
The modest tribute of one thought and tear,
Then pensive sigh, and say, "To me be given,
"By living thus on earth, to reign in heaven."

2.

Here rests a pattern of the female life,
The woman, friend, the mother, and the wife.
A woman form'd by nature, more than art,
With smiling ease to gain upon the heart.
A friend as true as guardian angels are,
Kindness her law, humanity her care.
A mother, sweetly tender, justly dear,
Oh! never to be nam'd without a tear.
A wife, of every social charm possest,
Blessing her husbands, in her husbands blest.
Love in her heart, compassion in her eye,
Her thoughts as humble, as her virtues high.
Her knowledge useful, nor too high, nor low,
To serve her maker and herself to know.
Born to relieve the poor, the rich to please,
To live with honour, and to die in peace.
So full her hope, her wishes so resign'd,
Her life so blameless, so unstain'd her mind,
Heaven smil'd to see, and gave the gracious nod,
Nor longer would detain her from her God.

* The river Eden runs not far from Brough.

The

The said Francis Thomson was succeeded by *Thomas Hodgson*, M. A. on the the presentation of the provost and scholars in 1735.

In 1768, on the death of Thomas Hodgson, *Thomas Barnett*, M. A. was instituted on the like presentation.

The CHURCH at Brough is a pretty large handsome ancient building. The *steeple* is not so old; having been built about the year 1513, under the direction of Thomas Blenkinsop of Helbeck esquire. There are in it four excellent bells, by much the largest in the county, except the great bell at Kirkby Thore. Concerning these bells at Brough, there is a tradition, that they were given by one *Brunskill*, who lived upon Stanemore, in the remotest part of the parish, and had a great many cattle. One time it happened that his bull fell a bellowing, which in the dialect of the country is called *cruning* (this being the genuine Saxon word to denote that vociferation). Whereupon he said to one of his neighbours, Hearest thou how loud this bull crunes? If these cattle should all crune together, might they not be heard from Brough hither? He answered, Yea. Well then, says Brunskill, I'll make them all crune together. And he sold them all; and with the price thereof he bought the said bells: (Or perhaps he might get the old bells new cast and made larger.)—There is a monument in the body of the church, in the south wall, between the highest and second windows; under which it is said the said Brunskill was the last that was interred.

At the south end of the communion table is this inscription: "Here lyes "Mr. Gabriel Vincent, stuart to the right honourable Anne Clifford, countess "dowager of Pembroke, Dorset, and Montgomery, and chief director of "all her buildings in the north; who died in the Roman tower of Brough "castle, like a good christian, the 12th of February 1665, looking for the "second coming of our saviour Jesus Christ."

The *pulpit* is of stone. There was heretofore an handsome *reading desk*, given by Sir *Cuthbert Buckle* knight, vintner in London, who was born upon Stanemore in this parish, and was lord mayor of London in the year 1593. His name was upon the desk thus: "By Cuthbert Buckle, Anno Domini "1576."—He also built a bridge upon Stanemore, which still bears the name of *Buckle's bridge*; and gave 8 *l* a year to a school upon Stanemore.

There was a *chantry* in this church founded in king Henry the third's time, by Thomas son of Thomas de Musgrave; who granted certain lands and tenements to God and St. Mary the virgin and to his chapel of Burgh under Stanemore, and to Sir William de Askeby chaplain, and his successors serving God there, whom he and his heirs should present to the said chapel. To which grant was witness (amongst others) Sir Michael de Harclay.

But it seemeth that the presentation to this chantry was soon after transferred to the family of Helbeck. For in the next king's reign, 19 Ed. 1. Thomas de Hellebeck presented Sir Eudo de Appleby to the chantry in the town of Burgh, which had been founded and endowed by Sir Thomas Musgrave knight, and unto which the said Thomas presented William de Askeby.

The altar of this chantry was in the north ile, called our Lady's ile, or Lady-porch.

Adjoining to which ile, from the east end thereof towards the vestry, was a little quire, called the closet, which belonged to the Blenkinsops of Helbeck; for the erecting of which, Thomas Blenkinsop esquire by his will in 1522 gave four marks, and also lime and other necessaries.

The *painting* in the *windows* of this church hath in former times been very extraordinary. The reverend Thomas Machel, who had a peculiar taste that way, took a particular account of so much as was remaining thereof about the year 1675, which was as follows, beginning with the east window in the chancel, and so going round by the south, west, and north.

In the east window of the chancel, three lights; 1. The virgin Mary. 2. The crucifix. 3. The other Mary. Above the crucifix, had been the Cliffords arms, part of the chequer remaining. Under all, the aforesaid epitaph of Thomas Ryge.

In the next window in the chancel, southward; three lights: 1. At the top, an escutcheon Azure, with the hands and feet of our saviour saltier-wise Argent, and an heart in fess point Gules: They are the five vulnera, in honour of which the papists keep a festival. In the middle of the said light, the lady Mary, with a crown on her head, in a blue robe, under which some children kneeling before St. Michael; and underneath, this scroll, "Ora pro nobis sancte Michael." St. Michael was pictured with green wings, a scarlet robe above a white one (as St. Mary had also), and a pair of scales in his right hand, in one scale something like a lion or dragon [perhaps to signify the devil, with whom the scripture represents Michael to have contended]; in the other scale the bible or mass book. Underneath, in a roundel, the resurrection of Christ. 2. The virgin Mary praying, in the same robes as the former, with yellow hair; with St. Michael behind her. Above her head, our saviour with a globe in his left hand. The rest defaced. 3. In the middle of this light, a bishop with a book in his right hand, and a crosier in his left. Above him, an escutcheon, with all the instruments of our saviour's persecution. Underneath, in a roundel, Queen's College arms; and on a scroll wrapped about the wreath "Meus Jesus est amor."

In the second south window in the chancel, over the door, two lights; 1. The virgin Mary, with our saviour in her right arm, and a scepter in her left hand: Underneath, this coat of arms; Argent, a cross Sable, and on a scroll wrapped about a rod in a roundel "Karlio . . . . [for some of the bishops]. 2. St. George. The rest defaced.

In the third south window in the chancel, 1. Edward the Confessor. 2. Nothing. Above both, T. R. for Thomas Rigg. Underneath, a fragment of the same inscription as before.

In the body of the church, in the highest south window, in diamond squares, J H S. The rest defaced.

In the second south window, two lights; 1. St. Peter, and under him the virgin Mary and a boy praying, with this scroll from his mouth, "Mater Dei!" And

And under them both, "Sancta Maria ora pro nobis." 2. Our saviour in a sitting posture.

In the third south window, which is below the pulpit, three lights; 1. St. John. Underneath, St. Michael in white, with yellow edgings and yellow wings: In the one scale the child Jesus; in the other, a like animal as before. 2. The virgin Mary, with Christ in one hand, and a scepter in the other. Underneath, a monk in white praying, with this scroll, "Fili Dei miserere mei." 3. Defaced. Under all, "Orate pro anima domini Thomæ Rud, qui istam fenestram fieri fecit."

In the fourth south window: All saints, their picture and names. With the scaling ladders from the seven sacraments.

In the fifth south window, two lights; 1. St. John Baptist. 2. St. John the evangelist, with a cup.

In the steeple window; St. John, with a cup. And in a little vacancy, the Musgrave arms.

In the west end window of the north ile, the letter R, for Rigg.

In the first north window beginning from the west end, two lights; 1. A saint defaced. 2. Another saint, with this inscription, "St. John Gryzostem;" with a fur about his neck, and a red cope with a cross.

In the second north window, two lights; 1. Defaced. 2. St. John of Beverlay.

In the third north window, two lights; 1. The angel Gabriel, saluting the virgin Mary; from his mouth this scroll, "Ave, graciæ plena, dominus tecum." 2. The virgin Mary; the Holy Ghost ascending, and Christ with a cross descending. The scroll, "Ecce fiat mihi secundum voluntatem tuam." Above all, an escutcheon Or, with an hammer and pair of pincers Sable.

In the fourth north window, three lights; 1. St. John Baptist. 2. Defaced. 3. St. John the evangelist, with a cup.

In the Blenkinsop quire, the north window, three lights; 1. The virgin Mary, or rather St. Katharine, though she be crowned, for she has in her left hand a Katharine wheel. Above, the Blenkinsop arms, quartering Salkeld, Vaux, and Helbeck. 2. A bishop, with a crosier. Above, the Blenkinsop arms. 3. St. Michael.

At the vicarage house, on the right hand of the gate, is cut in stone J H S; and underneath, T. R. for Thomas Rigg, who built it and the wall.

In the parlour were the college arms, and an eagle, with this motto, "Nosce teipsum." In the hall, bishop Robinson's arms impaled to Carlisle; *viz.* 1. Carlisle. 2. Robinson; Azure, a pike bend-wise Argent. On a fess of the second, a red rose between two roundlets Gules.—Eagles, in several parts; being the arms of *Eglesfield*.

At the further Brough, there was a *chapel* or *oratory*, founded by John Brunskill (probably the same who gave the bells) in 1506. Unto whom, Thomas Blenkinsop esquire of Helbeck gave the ground called Gibgarth, on condition that he should build a chapel there; and also an *hospital*, with two beds in it for travellers and other poor people; and maintain and repair the same fame for ever: paying to him and his heirs a *d* rent at Pentecoft yearly. And on defect of fuch maintaining and repairing the faid chapel, hofpital, and beds; the land to revert to the faid Thomas and his heirs.

In purfuance whereof, he the faid John Brunfkill founded an oratory or chapel, dedicated to our lady St. Mary the mother of Chrift, and to St. Gabriel the archangel; who, as Roger bifhop of Carlifle and Richard abbot of Shap did by writing under their hands and feals affirm, wrought many fair and divers miracles by the fufferance of our lord God. Two priefts were eftablifhed to fing and to pray in the faid chapel for evermore, for the fouls of all the benefactors of the faid chapel that were departed from the world, and for the welfare of them that were living. One of the faid priefts was to teach grammar, the other to inftruct children willing to learn finging, freely without any falary from them. The foundation of this chapel was confirmed both by the bifhop of Carlifle and the archbifhop of York; and yet was afterwards oppofed by the vicar of Burgh, who conceived himfelf much prejudiced thereby, and particularly in refpect of the oblations which were given from him to the faid chapel. Whereupon he fet up the crofs, and lighted up candles in the church at mid-time of the day, caufed the bells to be rung, and curfed with bell book and candle all thofe that fhould receive any oblations of them that reforted to the faid chapel, or fhould give any encouragement unto the fame. Brunfkill the founder complained to the archbifhop's court at York againft the vicar Mr. Rafebeck, and obtained a fharp citation againft him, cenfuring him as an abandoned wretch and inflated with diabolical venom for oppofing fo good a work. Notwithftanding which, Mr. Rafebeck appealed to the pope; and an agreement was made between the founder and him, by a compofition of 20*s* yearly to be paid to Mr. Rafebeck and his fucceffors vicars of Burgh.

Thus the chapel continued till the diffolution of the religious houfes. And the prieft that taught to fing being removed, the other that taught grammar was thought fit to be continued as mafter of a free fchool. And by the commiffioners Sir Walter Mildmay and Robert Keylway efquire, order was taken, and a fund fettled for this purpofe. So that a falary of 7*l* 11*s* 4*d* was to be paid yearly to the mafter of the fchool by the king's auditors, they receiving all the rents and revenues which formerly belonged unto it as a chapel, and which were given to it by the founder and other benefactors.

This is all the endowment which it hath at prefent, except a convenient dwelling houfe and garden, which were given by one of the fchoolmafters Mr. John Beck. But it was formerly very bountifully endowed by feveral benefactors; as Henry earl of Cumberland, Edward Mufgrave of Hartley efquire, William Mufgrave fon of Richard Mufgrave of Brough, Thomas Blenkinfop efquire, Hugh Newton, and divers others, who gave lands in Brough, Stanemore, Moreton, Yanewith, Mekil-Strickland, Bampton Cundale, and Mekil-Afhby, all in Weftmorland; and in Penrith in Cumberland; and Weft Laton in Yorkfhire; and Bernard-caftle in the county of Durham.

The governor thereof, whilft a chapel, was the abbot of Shap for the time being. Since the diffolution, that power feems to be in the king.

In the years 1527 and 1532, there are two acquittances from Thomas Rige vicar of Burgh, for the half yearly payment of 10*s* composition money paid to him by the abbot of Shap commendatary of the chapel of St. Mary in the parish of Burgh. By which it seemeth, that the abbot himself then held the chapel in commendam.

At the dissolution, the valuation thereof, as appears from the Valor in the first fruits office, was as follows: "The grammar school of Burgh is worth, " in a mansion house with divers tenements and burgages in the town of Burgh " 119*s* 10*d*; one tenement in the town of Laton upon the moor 20*s* 20*d*; " one tenement in the town of Bernard-castle 18*s*: In the whole 7*l* 19*s* 6*d*.— " Reprises: A free rent yearly paid to the earl of Cumberland, five pence " and half a farthing.

" The singing school of Burgh is worth in rents and farms of divers bur- " gages in the town of Burgh 10*s*; one tenement in the town of Mauldes " Meburne 11*s*: In the whole, 21*s*. In oblations within the chapel of St. " Mary Burgh 79*s*. Total 100*s*."

By which it may seem, that there had been some embezilments or alienations, perhaps by the worthy governors the abbots, of which they seem to have been capable enough, as we have found one of them solemnly certifying miracles to have been performed in the said chapel, another in all probability holding the chapel himself. Or perhaps they might draw to the abbey such of the revenues as were most convenient, as at Yanwath, Strickland, Bampton, and Asby.

Opposite to the cross, in the said further Brough, on the right hand as one goes towards Stanemore, behind a house, was a well covered over with a milstone, at the eye of which they took up the water, which was called St. Mary's (or St. Winifred's *) well. Perhaps it got the name of St. Mary's after founding of the chapel. Many came hither on pilgrimage in the times of popery, and the vicar of Burgh had a diploma from the pope (the aforesaid Christopher Harrison the vicar said he had seen it) to receive the oblations of all pilgrims there. Which oblations, by reason of the vicinity of the chapel, and the distance from the mother church, would be likely to fall into the hands of the chaplain. And this might be one principal reason of the vicar's opposing the establishment of a chapel there.

There is now no chapel in the parish of Brough, except only the chapel of *Stanemore*. In the year 1594, Cuthbert Buckle aforesaid by his last will and testament gave an annuity of 8*l* charged upon his estate at Spittle, towards the maintenance of a *schoolmaster* at Stanemore, to be employed in teaching children to read, write, cypher, and cast account. The heir at law contested the devise, but in 1600 a decree was obtained in favour of the school, and the heir was required to convey the said annuity to trustees for the use of the school. The inhabitants erected a schoolhouse at their own expence, and pur-

* Most of the particulars relating to this chapel, Mr. Machel had from the reverend Mr. Harrison the then vicar.

chased

chased three roods of land for liberty for the scholars. After the building of the schoolhouse, the same (in consideration of the great distance from the parish church) was consecrated by bishop Robinson in the year 1608, and became a chapel, in which the schoolmaster was to officiate as curate on Sundays and holidays, as well as to teach the children on the other days. Afterwards, in the year 1699, Thomas earl of Thanet repaired the chapel, and built a schoolhouse near adjoining. He inclosed also a large parcel of waste ground, called Slape Stones, then of the yearly value of 10*l* or thereabouts, and granted the same to 14 persons in trust that the rents and profits of the said close be paid to the schoolmaster and curate as an augmentation of his former salary of 8*l*. The said schoolmaster and curate to be appointed by the said earl, his heirs and assigns, lords and owners of the manor of Brough. When six trustees die, the survivors are to chuse others. There is to be no service at the chapel in the afternoon on Easter-day, but the inhabitants are to repair to the mother church, and there hear divine service, and receive the sacrament. And in the forenoon of every first Sunday in May, June, July, and August, there shall be no service in the chapel, but the inhabitants shall repair to the mother church.

The said earl gave 200*l*, with which, together with the augmentation by queen Anne's bounty of other 200*l*, an estate was purchased at Raisgill hall in the parish of Orton, for the use of the curate.

And the countess dowager Gower, one of the daughters of the said earl, gave 200*l*, with which and with 200*l* of queen Anne's bounty, an estate was purchased nigh the chapel, and infranchised by the present earl in 1762.

The trustees of the Slape Stones pasture took it in their heads to keep the same in their own possession, descending (as it were) from father to son, and paid to the curate 10*l* or 12*l* a year, and afterwards advanced to the present curate 15*l* a year; and on a bill filed against them in the chancery in the year 1764 in the name of the attorney general at the relation of the present earl of Thanet the patron and James Fenton curate, they swore in their answer they believed it was not worth more. In the end, in the year 1770, it was decreed, that they should deliver up possession to the curate, who immediately advanced the pasture to 35*l* a year, although under the discouragement of having gates broken down, cattle killed or maimed, and other enormities committed in the night-time; and it is now let at 38*l* a year. And a new set of trustees was appointed by the court.

John Bracken, curate of the chapel, by his will in 1754, gave 20*l*, the interest whereof to be applied for repairing and finding books for the chapel; 5*l*, the interest whereof is to be given yearly to poor housholders within the chapelry; and 5*l*, whereof the interest is to be applied to purchase books for poor children at the school.

There is also a poor stock belonging to the parish of Brough, of about 67*l*. Of which, 50*l* was given by Mr. Richard Bovel of London; the rest was contributed by others in small sums.

II. OF

II. OF THE MANORS OF BROUGH, STANEMORE, AND SOWERBY.

These three manors having continued all along in the hands of the Veteriponts, Cliffords, and their descendents, and never been granted off to any inferior lords; what we have to say concerning one, will generally be applicable to them all.

All *Stanemore* is not in the parish of Brough. South Stanemore is in the parish of Kirkby Stephen; and the most eastern part of it is in the parish of Bowes in Yorkshire, the boundary of the two counties being also the boundary of the parishes.

Brough is commonly expressed by the description of *Brough under Stanemore*, to distinguish it from other places of the same name, of which there are many. It is commonly divided into two parts, which anciently were denominated Over Brough and Under Brough, Great Brough and Little Brough, but now most commonly Church Brough and Market Brough.

This place was the *Verteræ* of the Romans, where in the decline of the empire a Roman captain resided, with a band of the *Directores*. But now the name is turned into *Brough*, or more properly *Burgh*. For (to note it once for all) in the time of the later emperors, little castles, meet for warlike occasions, and furnished with store of corn and other provisions, began to be termed *Burgi*, by a new name, which, after the empire was translated into the east, the Germans and others seem to have borrowed of the Greek word Πυργος. Hence also came the name of *Burgundians*, because they inhabited *Burghs*, for so in that age they used to call those dwelling places which were planted here and there along limits and marches.

That this *Burgh* was *Verteræ*, there seemeth to be no doubt; because the distance thereof from *Lavatræ* (which is *Bowes*) of the one side, and from *Brovacum* (which is *Brougham*) of the other side, being reduced into Italian miles, doth exactly agree with Antoninus's measures; and for that the Roman way leadeth through this place from Bowes to Brougham.

From Brough to Bowes eastward, the road leadeth over the ridge of fells already mentioned. And, to see the difference of times, it is curious to observe how Sir Daniel Fleming described the same not 100 years ago (no doubt, from his own experience): "Here," says he, "beginneth to rise that high, "hilly, and solitary country, exposed to wind and rain, which because it is "*stony* is called in our native language *Stane-moor*; over which is a great (but "no good) road, the post passing twice every week betwixt Burgh and Bowes, "and coaches going often that way, though with some difficulty and hazard "of overturning and breaking. All here round about is nothing but a wild "desert, unless it be an homely hostelry or inn, in the very midst thereof, "called the *Spittle* on Stanemore, for to entertain wayfaring people." The badness of the road (which perhaps was indeed the worst hard road in England) contributed to render all the rest more dismal; and in stormy weather it was the more vexatious, as the traveller could make no ſpeed. But now, from ſome of the worſt, it is by reaſon of the turnpike road carried that way become nearly as good as the beſt road in the kingdom. And (to note the improvement of commerce and correſpondence) inſtead of twice a week, the poſt goes ſix times a week to and from Brough.

The *Spittle* aforeſaid was a charitable inſtitution, and belonged to Marryke abbey in Yorkſhire; and after the diſſolution, the tenants thereof applied it to the purpoſe of an inn. But ſince the turnpike road was made, it is become uſeleſs in that reſpect, as there is no need for the traveller to halt between Brough and Bowes; for whereas before it took up ſix hours in travelling thirteen miles, the ſame can now be performed with more eaſe in an hour and an half.

Spittle houſe is in Yorkſhire.

On the top of Stanemore, on the Weſtmoreland ſide, is the fragment of a croſs, which we call *Rerecroſs (Rear-croſs*, a croſs reared or ſet up), and which the Scots call *Roycroſs*, as much as to ſay, the King's croſs; which Hector Boetius the Scotiſh writer recordeth to have been erected as a mear ſtone or boundary between England and Scotland, what time as king William the conqueror granted Cumberland unto the Scots, on this condition, that they ſhould hold it of him as his tenants, and not attempt any thing prejudicial or hurtful to the crown of England.

A little lower, upon the Roman way, ſtood a ſmall ſquare fort of the Romans, which at this day is called *Maiden-caſtle*. From whence, it is reported, the ſaid highway went, with many windings, along what was called the *Maiden way*, as far as to Caervorran in Northumberland.

In the reign of king Henry the third, we find one Adam de Slegill *foreſter* of Stainmore, under the Veteriponts.

After the death of John de Veteripont, during the long minority of his ſon Robert, we find an account of great waſte committed or ſuffered by the prior of Carliſle, to whom the king had granted the cuſtody of the ſaid Robert, after Adam de Slegill had left the foreſtry of Stanemore. And, amongſt the reſt,——Item, the tower of Burgh is decayed, and the joiſts are rotten, and moſt part of the houſe is brought to nought, by default of the prior keeping the ſame.

In the 8 Ed. 2. after the death of Robert de Clifford, it was found by inquiſition, that the ſaid Robert, on the day on which he died, held the caſtle of Appleby and barony belonging to the ſame caſtle; and (amongſt other particulars) the caſtle of *Burgh under Stayneſmore*, part of the ſaid barony, with the precinct of the trenches thereof, the herbage of which was worth yearly 6*s* 8*d*. Two hundred acres of demeſne land, 22 whereof at the leaſt were worth yearly 9*d* each. An hundred and ten acres of meadow, each of which worth by the year 12 *d*. Two parks, the herbage whereof, with all iſſues, was worth by the year 100*s*. Alſo free tenants, who paid yearly 17*s* 2 *d*. Alſo twenty oxgangs of land, worth each by the year 4*s*. Ten tofts coterell, worth yearly 6*d* each. One bakehouſe, with the profits of meaſuring the corn of the village, 20*s*. One water miln burned, worth yearly 6*l* 13*s* 4*d*.

Alſo

Alſo the conſtableſhip [of the caſtle] worth yearly 40*s*. Alſo the profits of the fairs, worth by the year 10*s*. [And this was before any grant of a fair that wen ow know of.]—Alſo, in the Lower Burgh, 24 tofts and an half, which are burned, each whereof pays yearly 12*d*. Alſo, upon *Stainemore*, ten vaccaries which are burned; each whereof, with the meadow adjoining, worth by the year 10*s*. And five vaccaries not burned; each whereof, with the meadow adjoining, worth by the year 20*l*. Alſo, Alan de Cabergh, Nicholas de Muſgrave, and Geoffrey de Teſedale held there four cloſes of new improvement, of the yearly rent of one hundred and fifteen ſhillings and one farthing. Agiſtment there, worth yearly 10*s*. Pleas and perquiſites of the court 13*s* 4*d*.—The ſum total, 49*l* 18*s* 4¼*d*.———Alſo at *Sowreby* nigh Burgh; One capital meſſuage, worth by the year 12*d*. Fourſcore acres of demeſne land, worth yearly 8*d* each. Sixteen acres of meadow, worth yearly 18*d* each. Two free tenants, who pay yearly 7*d*. Sixteen oxgangs of land, worth yearly 5*s* each. Ten meſſuages coterell, worth by the year 12*d* each. One water miln, worth yearly 40*s*. One vaccary, worth yearly 26*s* 8*d*.—The, ſum total, 11*l* 15*s* 7*d*.

In the 10 Hen. 5. after the death of John de Clifford, the inquiſition finds that at *Burgh* he died poſſeſſed of eleven meſſuages called vaccaries, to wit, the vaccaries of Knolhow, Skrythergill, Calfhowelade, Aldpark, Swynſty-wath, Mouthowlake, Thornethowegayll, Burghway, Severyg, Strykeſcales, Hegerſcale, and one park called the Old Park; worth in the whole by the year 10*l* 10*s* 10*d*. And that Elizabeth his mother held the caſtle and manor of which the ſaid vaccaries and park are parcel; and alſo the vaccaries of Newhall, Ramſon, Burwanthwayt, and Mekilthwayt; together with 9*s* rent, iſſuing out of a meſſuage called the vaccary of Oxenthwayt; and alſo the vill of *Soureby*, parcel of the ſaid caſtle and manor; and the ſervices of divers tenants of *Great Burgh* and *Little Burgh*, who paid to her yearly 10*s*.

The *caſtle*, in the year 1521, was by caſualty ſet on fire, two years before the death of Henry lord Clifford, ſurnamed the Shepherd, a little while after he had kept a great chriſtmaſs there, ſo as nothing was left but the bare walls. And ſo it lay, till rebuilt by the lady Anne Clifford, counteſs dowager of Dorſet, Pembroke, and Montgomery, in the year 1661.

The roof of the old tower had been contrived, not raiſed in the middle, to throw the water out at the ſides, but higheſt at the extremities, with a gutter in the middle, to receive the rain water.

And the lower windows or lights in the tower are framed with a turn in the wall, ſo as to let in the light, but to prevent an arrow ſhot from without from flying in a direct line; ſo that a perſon on the inſide might ſtand facing the window, without incurring any danger.

This tower, except the bare walls, was demoliſhed, and the timber ſold, by Thomas earl of Thanet, about the year 1695, when he was repairing Appleby caſtle; and the whole caſtle of Brough now lies totally in ruins. But the tower, having been built upon an eminence, and the walls ſtrong and well cemented, and therefore yet ſtanding for the moſt part, the whole preſents to the eye a kind of venerable magnificence, the very ruins adding to the solemnity of the prospect.

Robert lord Clifford, in the 4 Ed. 3. obtained of that king a charter for a *market*, upon Thursday every week at his manor of Burgh under Stanemore; and a *fair* yearly, to continue for four days, *viz.* two days before the feast of St. Matthew, on that feast day, and the day next following. Which charter king Edward the sixth, in the third year of his reign, by Inspeximus confirmed. The market is very inconsiderable; but the fair, held on the place called *Brough hill* (though not for four days, but for two of those days annually) is very remarkable for the sale of large numbers and quantities of cattle, horses, cloth, hardware, shoes, saddles, and many other sorts of merchandise.

III. MANOR OF HELBECK.

Helbeck, by a kind of delicacy of the modern proprietors, is styled *Hilbeck*, as if so denominated from the *hills* adjacent. But it was of ancient time invariably written *Hellebeck*; not from any infernal idea (for it is a pleasant situation enough), but from the water pouring down, expressed by the Saxon word *helle*, which is a word not yet out of use to signify the pouring out of any liquid: as *heling* signifies inclination or leaning aside, as when sailors say the ship *heeleth*.

Helbeck belonged for a considerable time to a family of that name; which ended in a daughter. And this brought in the family of *Blenkinsop*, which continued there for many generations, and probably is not yet extinct, for there are still several of the name thereabouts; but the family sold the estate a good many years ago, which after various shiftings of owners, now rests in John Medcalf esquire, grandson of Thomas Carleton late of Appleby esquire deceased.

The *Blenkinsops* were a considerable family, and had a large collection of writings, not only relating to themselves, but of several other kinds, as divers originals belonging to Shap abbey and other places, which as it is not known how they came by the same, neither is it known what became thereof, and in all probability they are all now totally lost, except what hath been preserved thereof by copies taken and extracts made by the reverend Thomas Machel, who had free access to the same, and whose collection therefore in that respect is extremely valuable.

Family of Helbeck.

1. So early as the reign of king Henry the second, to a grant by Maud de Veteripont to her son the first Robert de Veteripont, of lands at Renegill, two of the witnesses were *Thomas de Hellebeck* and *Wido* (Guy) his son.

And to a deed about the same time of lands at Clifton by Gilbert de Engain, amongst other witnesses is Sir *Thomas de Hellebeck*.

2. To the aforesaid Robert de Veteripont's charter to the abbot and convent of Shap, in the 19th year of king John, *Wido de Hellebeck* was one of the witnesses.

And to the grant of the advowson of Kirkby Thore, by Adam de Kirkby Thore to the said Robert de Veteripont, one witness (amongst the rest) was Guido de Hellebeck.

3. The next that we meet with was *Robert de Hellebeck*, probably son of Guy.

To the grant of Langeton to the aforesaid Robert de Veteripont by Ada daughter of Talebois, one of the witnesses was *Robert de Hellebeck*.

Which said Robert de Hellebeck was collector of the aid, in the reign of king Henry the third.

4. The next was Sir *Thomas de Hellebeck*; who was a witness to a grant of lands at Appleby in the 36 Hen. 3. by the second Robert de Veteripont to Richard Clerke.

This Sir Thomas held lands in Richmondshire and Westmorland by knights service, namely, for the fourth part of one knight's fee; also by an exchange made, he obtained Ascom and some lands at Suarraby, which he held by the like service.

And with him beginneth the Blenkinsop account of this family, except for one *Hamon* said to be father of this Thomas; which most probably is a mistake: not only because the circumstance of time seems to point out this Thomas to be son of Robert abovementioned, but also because *Hamon* is a name that hath not occurred in any of the evidences of those times. But from hence downwards, the Blenkinsop pedigree is very circumstantial, and seems to have been taken from their family writings.

5. Sir *Thomas de Hellebeck*, son of the last Sir Thomas, lived in the time of king Edward the first. He married Avicia daughter of Adam de Henecastre, and with her had lands in Little Stirkeland, Overton, Sunbiggin, Raisbeck, Cotflat, and Keldlyth. To all which, Richard de Musgrave quitted claim in the 29th year of that king.

He had issue, (1) Thomas, (2) Edmund; who married Isabel de Slikeburne, a widow, in the year 1326. He had some lands and privileges granted to him by his father in the lordship of Helbeck. And he had a son called Edmund. (3) Alice, married to Robert, eldest son of Sir Richard, son of Henry de Suleby, having for her portion 110 marks. Upon which marriage, Sir Richard de Suleby settled all his demesne lands, rents, homage, and services thereunto belonging, which he had in Appleby. (4) Alane, who was a clergyman, and had given by his father to him and his heirs, one messuage and two oxgangs of land in Helbeck. (5) Isabel, married to Patricius de Castlecaroke, who had for her portion lands at Sunbigin, Rasebeck, Keldelith, and Coatflat, with half of the fulling mill there. (6) Margaret, married to William de Lancastre, who had for her dower lands in Stirkeland in Kendale.

6. Thomas

6. *Thomas de Hellebeck* eldest son of the last Sir Thomas, by inquisition in the 3 Ed. 2. appears to have then held by knights service Hellebeck and Ascum. In the 8 Ed. 2. he was knight of the shire.

And this Thomas was the last of the name in the direct male line; having only a daughter *Isabella*, who soon after this was married to *Richard de Blenkinsop*. For in the 8 Ed. 2. after the death of Robert de Clifford, the inquisition finds, that *Thomas de Hellebeck* held a moiety of Soulby; and that *Richard de Blenkinsop* held part of Hellebeck, and *Isabel de Slekeburne* held divers tenements there.

By which it appears, that Hellebeck was then gone from Thomas de Hellebeck to Blenkinsop, in marriage with his daughter Isabella. The *Isabel de Slekeburne* who had some tenements there, was wife to Edmund aforesaid, younger brother of this Thomas. And the reason why this said Thomas appears to have had a moiety of Soulby, was upon account of his sister Alice as aforesaid having been married to Robert de Soulby, so that Thomas held the same probably as trustee upon the marriage settlement.

The arms of Hellebeck were; Gules, 6 annulets Or, with a bordure ingrailed Argent.

Family of Blenkinsop.

I. The first of the family of Blenkinsop that came to Helbeck, by marriage of the heiress of that house, was Richard de Blenkinsop, younger brother of *Robert de Blenkinsop*, unto whom Edward king of Scots gave all the lands and tenements of Ughtertyre with the appurtenances, to the value of 20 marks yearly, which had come into the hands of the said king by the forfeiture of Sir John Sainclere, in the 7th year of his reign.

Thomas de Hellebeck, on the marriage of his daughter to the said Richard, settled upon them and the heirs of their bodies the whole manor of Helbeck; except the lands and tenements held by Isabel de Slicburn and Edmund her son, and one messuage in the possession of William son of Hugh, of the yearly rent of 10*s*, which Alan de Hellebeck paid for the lands which he had in the said village. He was coroner of Westmoreland in the 19 Ed. 2. He died towards the beginning of the reign of king Edward the third; for in the 5th year of that king, we find the said Isabella styled widow. They had issue,

II. Thomas de Blencansop, who appears to have been very young at his father's death, for he came not of age till the 19 Ed. 3. *his* letter of attorney to take possession of his estate at Helbeck being dated in that year; upon the seal whereof were 6 annulets within a bordure ingrailed, and writ about thus, *S. Thome de Blencansop*. He had issue a son,

III. Thomas de Blencansop esquire (the first that appears with that addition). This Thomas, upon his marriage, had all the lands at Helbeck,

Overton, Soulby, and Brampton, ſettled upon him and Katherine his wife. He had the office of conſtable of Brough caſtle granted to him and his heirs, for 600 years, with all its appurtenances, eaſments, and commodities, by Roger de Clifford lord of Weſtmorland. The grant was dated at the caſtle of Burgh on Sunday before the feaſt of St. James the apoſtle, in the 4 Ric. 2.—In the 11th year of the ſame king, he repreſented the county of Weſtmorland in parliament.

IV. William de Blenkansop eſquire, ſon of the laſt Thomas. He married Maud, daughter of Richard de Salkeld, and had then ſettled upon them by the ſaid Thomas a moiety of his whole demeſne in the village of Overton, with one place in the ſame village called Raiſgill hall, with 16 tenements held by tenants at will, reſerving the mill and moulter; his ſon Robert de Blenkanſop, and Richard Talbot of Burgh, being attornies to deliver poſſeſſion. This ſettlement was dated in the 19 Ric. 2.

In the 9 Hen. 5. he was knight of the ſhire for Weſtmorland.

In the 10 Hen. 5. after the death of John de Clifford, the inquiſition finds, that William de Blenkenſop then held the manor of Helbeck, paying 6*s* cornage. And he appears to have been living above 20 years after this.

V. Thomas Blenkensop eſquire, ſon and heir of William. He was the firſt who took the name without *de* annexed. And about this time, to wit, in the reign of king Henry the ſixth, it ſeems to have become general, to leave out that particle of deſignation of the place, except where by reaſon of a vowel following it was incorporated and become part of the word, as Danvers, Doiley, and the like.

In the 1 Hen. 6. he repreſented the county of Weſtmorland in parliament, his father being then living; for he is ſtyled Thomas ſon of William Blenkenſopp.

In the 25 Hen. 6. his father conveyed to him the ſite and manor of Helbeck for the term of his life, paying for the ſame yearly 10 marks.

VI. Thomas Blenkinsop eſquire, ſon and heir of Thomas. He had ſettled upon him on his marriage with his wife Katharine, all the lands aforeſaid at Overton, and certain lands in the village of Tebay, in the 33 Hen. 6. William Birkbeck vicar of Overton, and Richard Warton chaplain, being truſtees in the conveyance.

He appears alſo to have had lands and tenements in Kyrkeby upon Wyſke in Yorkſhire, of 40*l* rent.

VII. Thomas Blenkinsop eſquire, ſon and heir of Thomas and Katharine. About the 9th year of king Edward the fourth, he married Margaret daughter and coheir of Richard Salkeld of Corby eſquire.

This Thomas articled with John Brunſkill in the 7 Hen. 7. for the building of St. Mary's chapel at Burgh.

By an inquiſition of Quo Warranto in the 19 Hen. 7. againſt Henry lord Clifford, the jurors find, that Thomas Blenkinſop was ſeiſed of the manor of Helbeck

Helbeck with the appurtenances in his demesne as of fee, and being so seised held the said manor of Henry lord Clifford by knights service, namely, by homage, fealty, and scutage, that is to say, when scutage runs at 40*s* for each knight's fee, then to pay 40*s*; when more, more; and when less, less; and by the cornage of 6*s*; and by the service to do suit at the court of our lord the king in the county of Westmorland, from month to month, at the king's castle of Appleby: And that the said manor is worth 40*l* above reprises: That the said Thomas died in the 18th year of king Hen. 7. Thomas his son and heir being then 17 years of age: That the said Henry lord Clifford had received all the issues and profits of the said manor during the minority of the said Thomas the son, and married the said heir to Elianor daughter of Robert Leygh esquire, and received the profits of the said marriage.

VIII. THOMAS BLENKINSOP esquire, son and heir of Thomas, by his wife Margaret Salkeld. In the 16 Hen. 8. he was employed in the king's wars against the duke of Albany, and set forward the 19th of October in the said year; having made his will, and appointed Sir Thomas Rigg vicar of Brough together with his wife (if he should die before his return) executors in trust for his younger children. But he returned, and lived to make another will.

In recompence of his good and laudable service to Henry earl of Cumberland, warden of the west marches towards Scotland, he was gratified, by the donation of the said Henry, with the custody, wardship, and marriage of William Skarburgh son and heir of Richard Skarburgh gentleman of Glosburn in Yorkshire, in the 17 Hen. 8.

He paid 10*l* a year to Sir William Bastoign in the county of Bedford knight, out of Little Corby and Warwick Briggs, in the right of dame Elianor his wife.

He took care about the repair of the church of Brough, and building the the steeple there.

He was under-sheriff of Westmorland in the 21 Hen. 8.

IX. THOMAS BLENKINSOP esquire, son and heir of Thomas, by his wife Elianor Leigh. By articles of marriage in the 24 Hen. 8. it appears that this Thomas was married to Magdalene youngest daughter of Sir Edward Musgrave of Hartley, having settled upon them 20 marks yearly, in consideration of 100*l* portion; and in case of his father's second marriage, the young couple were to live either at Corby or Helbeck, as they should think fit.

He gave 26*s* 8*d* towards the building of the bridge at Brough; whence it is, that his arms are placed thereupon, together with the Clifford's, who most probably were also contributors thereunto.

By his will, in the 37 Hen. 8. upon his going to serve the king against the Scots, he left his brother Richard Blenkinsop, and his two uncles George and John a priest, together with his cousin Sir Richard Leigh priest, in trust, to receive

receive the rents of his estate at Raisbeck in the lordship and parish of Overton (in case he should die in that expedition) to be employed for the use of his small children, daughters, so many of them as should come of age.

He left issue three sons, 1. Thomas. 2. Charles, to whom he gave an annuity of 10 *l*. 3. Matthew, steward to the lord Wharton. And several daughters; one of whom was married to William Farrand of Carleton hall near Skipton esquire; another daughter, Margaret, married to Hugh Machel of Crackenthorp esquire; another to Thomas Bellingham of Gaythorn esquire; another to John Aglionby of Carlisle esquire; and another to Lancelot Pickering of Crosby Ravensworth esquire: Each of whom had 100 *l* to her portion.

X. THOMAS BLENKINSOP esquire, son and heir of Thomas, by his wife Magdalene Musgrave. In the 2 and 3 Ph. and M. he married Margery, one of the daughters of William Wykeliffe of Wykeliffe in the county of York esquire. His father Thomas settled upon them, on the marriage, his whole part and share of the castle or manor of Corby, with all lands, tenements, and hereditaments whatsoever in Corby, Warwykebrigs, Caldecotes and Caldecote banks, Eglanby, and Murthwaite, except half the fishing of Corby upon the river Eden, and three parts in four of the water mill at Corby; and also all and every his burgages, messuages, lands and tenements in the city of Carlisle.

In the 9 Eliz. he purchased of John Appleby of Torpenhow in Cumberland gentleman, divers messuages, lands, and tenements at Ellergill in Tebay. The deed of bargain and sale (in pursuance of the statute of the 27 Hen. 8.) was inrolled at the quarter sessions at Appleby, before Henry Crackenthorp, Richard Dudley, and William Gylpinge esquires, justices, and John Myddleton clerk of the peace.

He died in the 13 Eliz. leaving issue, 1. Thomas. 2. Henry. 3. Francis. 4. Barbara, married to Robert Ward of Bowes esquire. 5. Katherine, married to John Warcop of Warcop esquire. And three other daughters, who died unmarried.

XI. THOMAS BLENKINSOP esquire, son and heir of Thomas, by his wife Margery Wykeliffe. This Thomas is the seventh of the name, in a direct regular succession. He was of the age of 34 years at the death of his father, as appears by inquisition, and had livery of his lands on the 20th of May, in the 14th year of queen Elizabeth.

XII. HENRY BLENKINSOP esquire, son and heir of the seventh Thomas last mentioned. He was under age at his father's death, and in ward to Sir Simon Musgrave of Edenhall. There was paid to the crown for the fine of his marriage 40 *l*; for which the said Sir Simon and others were bound, in the 21 Eliz.

He married Elizabeth daughter of Thomas Tankard of Burrowbrigg in Yorkshire, having with her 500 *l* portion. Upon which marriage, all the paternal estate of the Blenkinsops was settled on them and their heirs male.

He ſold his part of Corby, with other lands in Cumberland, to the lord William Howard and others, for 770*l*, in the third year of king James.

He died in the 11th year of the ſaid king; having had iſſue, 1. Katherine, who died unmarried. 2. Dorothie, a nun at Liſbon. 3. Jane, married to Thomas Bird of Colby. 4. Thomas, his ſon and heir. 5. Frances, who died unmarried. 6. Elizabeth, who died alſo unmarried. 7. Mary, married to Robert Cawell of Bolton in Lancaſhire gentleman.

XIII. Thomas Blenkinsop eſquire, ſon and heir of Henry. He was under age when his father died, and by that means became ward to the counteſs of Cumberland; for whoſe compoſition was paid 200 marks.

In the 16th year of king James, he married Anne daughter of Sir Edward Oſbaldeſton of Oſbaldeſton in the county of Lancaſter knight. She had 600*l* for her portion.

This Thomas ſold the eſtates at Overton and Slegill to the tenants and others. He alſo ſold part of the manor of Helbeck, in the 13 Cha 1. to Richard Burton clerk; and in 1657, the ſaid Thomas Blenkinſop, Anne his wife, and Francis their ſon and heir apparent, conveyed the reſidue of the manor to Thomas Burton of Brampton eſquire, ſon of the ſaid Richard (which Thomas Burton was one of Oliver Cromwell's ſequeſtrators). The Blenkinſops were papiſts, and ſuffered much when in thoſe days the penal laws were put in rigorous execution.

The ſaid Thomas Blenkinſop was living when this account of the family was taken by Mr. Machel, about the year 1675. Mr. Machel deſcribes him as a venerable, well looking old gentleman. He had iſſue, 1. Francis. 2. Henry, who died an infant. 3. Mary, who died unmarried. 4. Elizabeth, who died alſo unmarried. 5. Thomas. 6. John, who died an infant. 7. Henry, who died alſo an infant. 8. Anne. 9. Dorothy. 10. Katherine.

XIV. Francis Blenkinsop eſquire, ſon and heir of Thomas, was, when the above account was taken, living with his father at Helbeck hall, and unmarried. And he is the laſt of whom we have any account. He ſold the hall and demeſne to major Scaife (another of Cromwell's ſequeſtrators) who was younger brother of a family of that name at Winton hall.

The arms of Blenkinſop were, Argent, a feſs between three garbes banded Sable; on the feſs a creſcent, for diſtinction of a younger houſe.

They had 22 tenants at Helbeck, who paid a finable rent of 19*l* 12*s* 9*d*. And 25 tenants at Brough, with a finable rent of 11*l* 5*s* 10*d*. And, amongſt them, had 53 boon days ſhearing; 21 boon days mowing, all but one in Helbeck; and 41 loads of boon coals.

In the year 1687, *Richard Burton* clerk, rector of Huntingdon in the county of Kent, conveyed the manor to *George Baker* of Crook in the county of Durham eſquire; and after various fines, recoveries and wills, *George Baker* of Ellemore hall in the county of Durham eſquire (grandſon and heir of the above George Baker) conveyed the ſame to Thomas Carleton of Appleby eſquire, who

who alſo in the year 1726 purchaſed the hall and demeſne. Which *Thomas Carleton* had two daughters, *Elizabeth* and *Dorothy*. The younger daughter *Dorothy* was married to George Stephenſon of Warcop eſquire, and died without iſſue. *Elizabeth*, the elder, was married to *John Metcalf* of Bellerby in Yorkſhire eſquire, and hath iſſue now living (viz. in 1773) two ſons and one daughter, namely, *John*, *Thomas*, and *Elizabeth*.

In the front wall of an houſe nigh the bridge (which houſe is now the Black Bull inn) are two coats of arms, ſome parts whereof are now defaced, but were diſtinguiſhable in Mr. Machel's time; being Helbeck impaling Blenkinſop, and Salkeld impaling Vaux. And above, the letters J H S | M, (*Jeſus hominum ſalvator. Maria.*) It was the court houſe for the tenants which the Blenkinſops had at Brough. Perhaps aforetime it might be the place of the chapel or oratory before mentioned.

PARISH OF MUSGRAVE.

MUSGRAVE, without queſtion, received its name from the family which reſided there for ſeveral ages, afterwards removed to Hartley caſtle, and finally ſettled and now continues at Eden-hall in Cumberland. *Muſgrave* is a name of office. *Grave* means governor, ſteward, or keeper. So the *ſheriff* is *ſhire-grave*: and there is *landgrave* amongſt the Germans; *palſgrave* (palace-grave); *margrave* or mark-grave, *marquis*, *marchiarum comes*, count or warden of the marches. And it is generally ſuppoſed, that *Muſegrave* and *Margrave* are the ſame. But, as there is not much likeneſs between the words, ſo it is certain that this family did not receive their name from being wardens of the marches againſt Scotland; for the name is much ancienter than the introduction of that office into the borders. The learned *Junius* quotes *Heſychius* as explaining the word *Muſe* to ſignify *domeſticum atrium*, the curtilage about the houſe: And in that ſenſe, it is eaſy to conceive the office of *Muſegrave*.

The pariſh of Muſgrave is bounded by the pariſhes of Rumaldkirk and Brough on the Eaſt; by the pariſhes of Kirkby Stephen and Croſby Garret on the South; by the pariſh of Warcop on the Weſt; and by the ſame pariſh of Warcop on the North: And contains in the whole about 38 families; all of the church of England.

The church is dedicated to St. Theobald. So in a deed of lands, in the 20 Hen. 7. Edward Crakenthorp is ſtyled rector of the church of St. *Theobald* in *Parva Muſgrave*, which was a miſtake of the writer for *Great Muſgrave*; for there never was a church at Little Muſgrave, which is a ſmall manor in the pariſh of Croſby Garret.

The ſaid church was appropriated to the abbey of St. Mary's York; but the pariſh, and conſequently the revenues, being ſmall, the abbot and convent could not maintain a vicar and fave much to themfelves out of the overplus: and therefore it continues a rectory, valued in the king's books at 16*l* 1*s* 11$\frac{1}{4}$*d*. The clear yearly value, as certified to the governors of queen Anne's bounty, 48*l*. The late rector Mr. Pindar gave 200*l*, to which the faid governors added other 200*l*, wherewith an eftate was purchafed at Orton in this county.

In the year 1248, the abbot and convent of St. Mary's York granted to Silvefter bifhop of Carlifle and his fucceffors, the patronage of the church of Mufgrave; faving to themfelves the ancient and accuftomed penfion out of the fame.

And about 40 years after, there was a difpute between the abbey and bifhop Halton about the patronage of this church, together with the tithes of Kirkby Stephen and other matters; which ended in an arbitration and compromife: by which, the faid bifhop and his fucceffors fhould have the patronage and advowfon of this church of Mufgrave.

In the quire of the church is a monument, with the figure of a fhaven monk graved in brafs, in his robes, holding up his hands in a praying pofture, and this infcription over his breaft, *Repofita fpes in finu meo*. And in four roundells, one at every corner, an angel with this label, *Mercy Jefu*. And under his feet, *Orate pro anima magiftri* Thomæ Ouds *quondam rectoris* . . . . . . *dominorum epifcopi et archdiaconi Carliolenfis officialis, qui obiit* xxii . . . . . This feems to have been earlier than any account of the rectors of Mufgrave in the bifhop's regifters; for *Ouds* is a name that hath not elfewhere occurred to us.

In 1298, *William de Burton*, rector of Mufgrave, had licence from the bifhop to go abroad and ftudy in foreign univerfities for fix years. He was afterwards promoted to the vicarage of St. Nicolas in Newcaftle upon Tyne.

In the year 1303, bifhop Halton collated to this rectory *Robert de Haloutan*, probably his kinfman; for fo the name was varioufly written.

In 1313, *John de Burdon* was collated by the fame bifhop; faving to the abbot and convent of St. Mary's York their ancient yearly penfion of 5*s*.

Four years after this, the faid bifhop collated *Thomas de Gouldington*, with the fame provifion.

In 1330, *Robert de Denham* was collated by bifhop Roffe, on an exchange with the faid Thomas de Gouldington for the prebend of Hotherden in the king's free chapel of Wolverhampton.

In 1337, Sir *Adam de Levirton* was collated by bifhop Kirkby.

In the next year, we find one *John de Brydkirk* rector of Mufgrave, who had a difpenfation of abfence by the faid bifhop Kirkby for three years.

In 1342, *John de Stoketon*, rector of Mufgrave, was confirmed (by patent) official of Carlifle, having formerly been invefted with that jurifdiction by delivery of the feal of the faid officialty.

After the death of John de Stoketon, one Sir *William de Sanford* was collated by bifhop Kirkby, but in what year doth not appear.

Next after him, was *William de Ellerton*; but on whofe collation or prefentation appeareth not.

These

These two are specified in a return to a writ of Certiorari sent by the king to the bishop in the year 1363; to which purpose also a monition had come from the pope's nuncio; and the ground of both was, on account of the detaining a provisionary pension assigned out of the said rectory by the pope to Robert Kerret.

In the year 1359, one *John de Soulby* brought a presentation from the king, who claimed by reason of the bishoprick being lately vacant and in the king's hands. At the same time, three writs of *scire facias* were served on the bishop, notifying that judgment had been given in the king's court at Westminster for his majesty both against the bishop himself, and also against Robert Kerret and William de Ellerton clerks. Hereupon a commission of inquiry *de jure patronatus* was issued; and the king's claim proving good, the said *John de Soulby* was instituted and inducted. And soon after, he had letters dimissory to all orders; as well the inferior, to which he had not yet attained, as the sacred orders. By his will he bequeathed his body to be buried in the churchyard of St. Andrew's Holborn.

In 1361, on the death of the said John de Soulby, Sir *Peter de Morland* was collated by bishop Welton.

In 1375, one Sir *Richard de Upton* was rector of Musgrave; who received absolution by the archdeacon of Carlisle, from a sentence of suspension incurred by his contumacy.

In 1490, in a rental of the revenues of the priory of Wederall, Sir *Edward Crakenthorpe*, rector of the church of Musgrave, is charged with a pension of 5*s* a year to the said abbey.

In 1556, *Thomas Anggreme* was presented to this rectory by king Philip and queen Mary, during the vacancy of the bishoprick.

In 1577, on the death of *John Birkbeck*, rector of Musgrave, *Jeoffrey Birkbeck* was presented by William Birkbeck of Gray's Inn gentleman, administrator of the goods and chattels of Henry Birkbeck late of Eamont bridge, assignee of Roger Schellet, who had a grant of that avoidance from bishop Oglethorp in the year 1558, confirmed by the dean and chapter.

In 1599, one Mr. *Barker* resigns the rectory of Musgrave; and *Bernard Robinson*, S. T. B was collated by (his brother) bishop Robinson.

On the removal of the said Mr Robinson to Torpenhow, in the year 1612; *John Spencer* was collated by the said bishop Robinson.

In 1634, on John Spencer's death, *William Dodding*, M. A. was collated by bishop Potter.

Three years after, on the death of Mr. Dodding, *John Vaux*, M. A. was collated by the same bishop.

In 1671, *John Ardrey* was collated by bishop Rainbow.

In 1684, on the death of John Ardrey, *Christopher Thornton*, M. A. was collated by the same bishop.

In 1719, on the death of Christopher Thornton, *Simon Pindar* clerk was collated by bishop *Bradford*.

In 1755, on the death of Simon Pindar, *Robert Hall* clerk was collated by bishop Osbaldiston.

In

In 1756, on the cession of Robert Hall, *Edward Knowsley* clerk was collated by the same bishop.

In 1775, on the death of Edward Knowsley, *William Paley*, M. A. was collated by bishop Law.

The *church*, as the parish, is but small. On the south side thereof, is a fair ile, having an arched door into it, and another arch by which it communicates with the church. Perhaps it belonged anciently to the family of Musgrave, but is now used by the parishioners in common.

The parsonage house stands about 50 yards west from the church. It is a good strong building, erected by Mr. Pindar; beautifully situated on the north bank of the river Eden. But both house and church are subject to inundation by an high flood. The outhouses were rebuilt by the late incumbent Mr. Knowsley.

The MANOR of Musgrave is still in the family which gave name to the place. It is called *Great Musgrave* (as there is nothing great or little but by comparison) to distinguish it from a less, which is parted from it by the river Eden, called *Little Musgrave*, which belongs also to the Musgraves, and lies (as was observed before) in the parish of Crosby Garret. They seem anciently to have been one intire manor, and apportioned into different parishes by reason of the inconvenience of the river running between.

The said family at this place hath been very ancient and very numerous; by reason of which, it is difficult, if not impossible, to investigate or distinguish the regular direct line. Besides that there were, in this as in all other places, persons surnamed from the place, who were no way related to the principal family there.

I. The first of the name that we have met with, was PETER MUSEGRAVE, who lived about the time of king Stephen: for in the next king's reign, *viz.* in the reign of king Hen. 2. we find a dispute between *Robert* son of *Peter Musegrave* and the monks of Byland, concerning the boundaries of the respective manors of Musgrave and Blaterne; which dispute was compromised and settled in the county court at Appleby, William Fitz-Hugh being then sheriff *.

II. ROBERT

* Hæc compositio pacis facta est inter Thorphinum filium Roberti et Robertum filium Petri, et monaches de Beghland et Wallenum de Wardcop et Robertum filium Fidis, de calumnia quam Robertus filius Petri habuit de communi pastura inter Blaternam et Musegravam. Quod pro pace ista remanebit Roberto filio Petri in proprium octoginta duæ acræ terræ, scilicet, A sp na super Hobergham in transversum del siic subtus Maurebergha usque ad ductum versus Musegravam. Et a prædicta spina totum remanebit monachis in proprium versus grangiam, et usque ad ductum juxta capellam per divisas quas fecerunt et perambulaverunt. Et averiæ Roberti Musegrave nunquam infra hás divisas intrabunt, nec averiæ monachorum infra proprium Roberti. Robertus etiam habebit unum exitum averiis de Musegrava super Maurebergham, inter culturam monachorum et vallem subtus Hobergha, a divisis quas fecerint et perambulaverint juxta pratum. Et inde habebit Robertus communem pasturam usque ad vivarium, et inde usque ad viam super Cressekelde quæ vadit versus Appelbi,

II. ROBERT MUSEGRAVE, son of *Peter*; with whom the dispute was about the boundary of the said manor of Musgrave as aforesaid.

Note, The manor adjoining to that of Blaterne is the manor of Little Musgrave, which being described by the general name of the manor of Musgrave, seems to confirm the conjecture aforesaid that the two Musgraves were heretofore one intire manor.

III. The next that hath occurred to us, was ADAM DE MUSEGRAVE, in the reign of king John; who (amongst other persons of principal note) was witness to a grant of wood and turbary at Sandford, by William de Sandford to the first Robert de Veteripont.

IV. In the next king's reign was THOMAS DE MUSEGRAVE. For in the 36 Hen. 3. to a grant of the last Robert de Veteripont of lands to Richard Clerke of Appleby, one of the witnesses was *Thomas de Musegrave* then sheriff of Westmorland, that is, under-sheriff to the said Robert. And this Sir Thomas (as he was afterwards called) was one of the executors of the last will and testament of the said Robert.

In the 6 Ed. 1. Thomas de Musgrave and Ranulph de Dacre obtained a charter for a market at their manor of Orton.

V. The next that occurs was RICHARD DE MUSGRAVE. In the 14 Ed. 1. in the partition of the Veteripont inheritance between the two daughters and coheirs of the last Robert de Veteripont, the homage and service of *Richard de Musgrave* were assigned to Idonea the younger daughter.

VI. THOMAS DE MUSGRAVE was the next in succession. In the 3 Ed. 2. on an inquisition of tenants in Westmorland who held by cornage, it was found that *Thomas de Musgrave*, who was then under age, and in wardship, held Great Musgrave, Moreton, Souleby, half of Rookby, and part of Sandford. And at the same time *Richard de Musgrave* held Little Musgrave and Crosby Gerard. This Richard seems to have been of a collateral branch of the family; who had a brother Robert that conveyed lands to him in Soulby.

Appelbi, et usque ad quadrariam, et inde usque ad caput vivarii per divisas quas perambulaverunt et fecerunt. Totum hoc erit in communem pasturam averiis de Musegrava et averiis monachorum: Sed monachi arabunt culturam juxta fossatum molendini usque ad vivarium, sicut perambulaverunt et divisas fecerunt. Et habebunt culturam suam super Maurebergh et pratum in proprium sicut habuerunt ante istam compositionem, et nihil amplius ibi arabunt. Et averiæ de Musegrava in his locis nunquam intrabunt. Et Thorphinus et Robertus coram comprovincialibus affidaverunt, quod ipsi et hæredes eorum tenebunt hanc compositionem fideliter et sine malo ingenio in perpetuum. Sed si contigerit quod averiæ de Musegrava intrent in proprium monachorum, dabunt unum denarium pro 20 averiis secundum consuetudinem provinciæ. Similiter dabunt monachi, si averiæ eorum intrent proprium Roberti. Hæc compositio facta fuit in curia domini regis apud Appelby coram Willielmo filio Huei ballivo, et Murdaco decano, et Thoma de Hellebec, et Thoma filio Cospatricii, et Roberto de Kabergh, et Johanne Tailleboys, et Conano de Aske, et Willielmo de Ascheby, et Richardo Anglico, et Henrico de Cundale, et Stephano de Tyrnaby, et Rogero Winkenel, et Roberto filio Richardi, et Willielmo de Lathes, et Thoma fratre ejus, et Hyberto Clerico, Michaele de Harclay, et Waltero filio ejus, et cæteris probis hominibus qui tunc fuerint ibi præsentes.

In

In the 8 Ed. 2. after the death of Robert lord Clifford, the jurors find exactly the same again, that the said *Thomas*, who was then also under age, held the same as above, by cornage for the whole of 45*s* 10*d*. And that *Richard de Musgrave* held Crosby Gerard, Little Musgrave, and a moiety of Overton. And this *Richard* had a son *Robert*, who came of age in the 10 Ed. 3. and had livery of his lands in Crosseby, Overton, Little Musgrave, Soulby, and Kirkby Stephen.

This *Thomas de Musgrave* in the 19 Ed. 3. married Isabella de Berkeley, widow of John lord Clifford; and she continued his wife 17 years, dying in the 36 Ed. 3. and leaving the said *Thomas* her husband surviving.

He was returned to serve as knight of the shire for Westmorland in the 14, 15, 17, and 18 Ed. 3. And after his marriage with Isabella de Berkeley, *viz.* from the 24 to the 47 Ed. 3. he was summoned to parliament amongst the barons.

In the 20 Ed. 3. he was associated with the bishop of Carlisle and others in guarding the western marches towards Scotland.

In the same year upon the invasion made by David Brus king of Scotland, the said Sir Thomas having put himself in arms with the barons of those parts, was one of the commanders in the van of the army which gave battle to the said king near Durham, where his whole army being utterly routed, that king with divers of his nobles was taken prisoner. He was afterwards one of the commissioners for treating with the Scotch commissioners concerning the releasing their said king.

In the 21 Ed. 3. he was made governor of Berwick upon Tweed, as also sole justiciar throughout all the lands in Scotland whereof king Ed. 3. was then in possession.

In the 24 Ed. 3. he obtained of the king a remission of all the profits of two parts of the castle and manor of Skipton, for the time he and his wife had held the same during the minority of the infant heir her son by her former husband Robert lord Clifford; and also for his good services had a grant of 100 marks *per annum* to be received out of the exchequer.

In the 26 Ed. 3. upon danger of an invasion by the French, he was joined in commission with Thomas lord Lucie to array all the men at arms in the counties of Cumberland and Westmorland for the defence of the adjacent sea coasts.

In the 27 Ed. 3. he was associated with Ralph lord Nevil and the same Thomas lord Lucie in the wardenship of the west marches.

In the 32 Ed. 3. the said Sir *Thomas* obtained a charter for free warren in all his demesne lands at Musgrave and other places, with power to impark his woods called Hevenings in Musgrave, containing 200 acres. [Note, *hevening*, *heyning*, means freed, spared, or forborn; so winter heyning in forests was, when the cattle were not to be put in.]

In the 42 Ed. 3. he was constituted escheator for the counties of York, Northumberland, Cumberland, and Westmorland.

In the 46 Ed. 3. he was appointed, with the bishop of Carlisle and others, to the office of warden of the west marches. 6

In

In) the 47 Ed. 3. he was again made governor of Berwick. So likewise in the 49 Ed. 3. for one year. And in the 50 Ed. 3. for three years more; about which time he seems to have died, for in the parliament which was holden in that year we do not find him again summoned amongst the barons.

In his time Harcla came into this family, which having been forfeited in the reign of king Ed. 2. by the attainder of Andrew de Harcla governor of Carlisle, was granted to Sir Hugh de Lowther for life, remainder to Ralph de Nevil baron of Raby, under the yearly rent of 100*s*; which Ralph sold the same to the said *Thomas de Musgrave*. And king Ed. 3. in the 34th year of his reign confirmed the same to the said Thomas and his heirs, and remitted the rent; and granted to him his special licence to rebuild and fortify the castle at Harcla, which had been burnt by the Scots.

VII. Sir THOMAS DE MUSGRAVE, son and heir of Sir Thomas, married first Margaret daughter of Sir William Ross of Yelton in Yorkshire (probably the same Sir William Ross who was owner at that time of Kendal castle), and with her had Hubterswell and Cowen Wood in that county. And to his second wife he married Mary daughter of John Vaux, relict of Thomas Holland earl of Kent. In the 37 and again in the 43 Ed. 3. he was returned to serve in parliament for the county of York, in which he probably then resided (being during his father's life-time) on his former wife's estate there.—In the 5 Ric. 2. he presented a clerk to the rectory of Crosby Garret; and in the 8 Ric. 2. he died.

VIII. Sir THOMAS DE MUSGRAVE knight, son and heir of the last Sir *Thomas*, married Elizabeth daughter and one of the coheirs of Sir William Fitzwilliam of Sprotsburgh in Yorkshire; whose Arms were, Lozenges, Argent and Gules.

In the 16 Ric. 2. he was sheriff of Cumberland, and in the 1 Hen. 4. he was knight of the shire for Westmorland; and died in the tenth year of that king.

IX. Sir RICHARD DE MUSGRAVE knight, son, grandson, and great grandson of the three Thomas's respectively next above. His wife's name was Elizabeth, who died in the 3 Hen. 5.

The Musgraves, next to Fitz-William, quarter, Argent, 3 mullets Sable; which seem to belong to this Elizabeth (whose sirname we have not been able to recover); for none of the other families with which they were connected did bear these arms.

In the inquisition *post mortem* of John lord Clifford, 10 Hen. 5. the jurors find, that Sir *Richard de Musgrave* knight held the manors of Great Musgrave, Hartley, Crosby Gerrard, and Murton. And he is the first in the list of jurors who took that inquisition.

X. THOMAS MUSGRAVE esquire, son and heir of Sir *Richard*, married Joan daughter of the lord Dacre, and died in the 21 Hen. 6. His widow appears to have been living in the 34 Hen. 6. He had issue *Richard* his son and heir, and *Elizabeth* married to Henry Wharton.

XI. Sir Richard Musgrave, knight, married Elizabeth daughter of Sir Thomas Betham of Betham knight, and sister of Sir Edward Betham. He was one of the jurors on the inquisition *post mortem* of John lord Clifford in the 4 Ed. 4. And dying in the year after, he was buried in Kirkby Stephen church, as appears from his epitaph there above mentioned. He had issue, 1. *Elizabeth*, married to Thomas Gayt. 2. *Isabel*, married to Thomas Middleton of Middleton hall esquire. 3. *Thomas*. 4. *Margaret*, married to Thomas Elderton. 5. *Elianor*, married to William Thornburgh. 6. *Mary*, married to Thomalin Warcop. 7. *Richard*, who married Mary one of the two daughters and coheirs of Sir William Stapleton, and widow of Sir William Hilton. 8. *William*, to whom William lord Dacre, warden of the west marches, in the 25 Hen. 6. paid 100*l* for the repairs of Bewcastle. 9. *Agnes*, married to Robert Warcop. 10. *John*, who died without issue.

XII. Thomas de Musgrave, son and heir of *Richard*. He married Johanna the other daughter and coheir of Sir William Stapleton, by Margaret his wife; and with her he had Edenhall. The Arms of Stapleton are; Argent, 3 swords in triangle with the points outward Gules.

He died in the 9 Ed. 4. and had issue *Richard*, *John*, *Nicholas*, and *William*; from whom did descend the four families of Edenhall, Musgrave hall (or Fairbank), Hayton, and Crookdake: And four daughters; *Margaret*, married to John Sandford; *Elianor* married to Christopher Lancaster; *Mary*, married to Nicolas Ridley; *Isabella*, married to John Crackenthorp of Newbiggin esquire.

XIII. Sir Richard Musgrave knight, son and heir of *Thomas*. In a feodary of knights and others holding in free tenancy of Thomas de Clifford in the 31 Hen. 6. *Richard Musgrave* knight held Great Musgrave of the said Thomas, by homage and fealty, and 4*s* 2*d* cornage.

In the 8 Hen. 7. there was a dispute between the bishop of Carlisle and this *Richard*, concerning the patronage of the church of Musgrave.

He married Johan daughter of Thomas lord Clifford; and by her had *Edward*, *Thomas*, *John* a clergyman, and *Jane*.

XIV. Sir Edward Musgrave of Harclay knight, son and heir of *Richard*. In the life-time of his father, he was styled of Caterlen. In the 5 Hen. 8. he was sheriff of Cumberland with John Crackenthorp esquire. He was again in that post alone, as likewise in the 19 Hen. 8. In the 33 Hen 8. he and his son Sir William exchanged some lands with Sir Thomas Wharton of Wharton.

His first wife was Alice daughter of Thomas Radcliffe esquire, by whom he had *Mary* married to John Martindale, and *Margaret* married to John Heron of Chipchase. His second wife was Johan daughter and coheir of Sir Christopher Ward of Gryndall in the county of York knight, by whom the

Musgraves

Musgraves had Gryndall; out of which she gave by her will in the year 1540 to Katharine Allon her old servant a sufficient living for term of her life. (The arms of Ward are; Azure, a cross moline Or.) By his said second wife he had issue, 1. *William*. 2. *Edward*, who died without issue. 3. *Simon*. 4. *Elizabeth*, married to John Nevill lord Latimer. 5. *Magdalene*, married to Thomas Blenkinsop of Helbeck esquire. 6. *Johan*.

From this Sir *Edward* the eldest line failed in the third generation, and the inheritance came back to *Simon* the third son above mentioned.

XV. Sir *William Musgrave* of Harclay knight, son and heir of Edward, married Jane daughter of Sir Thomas Curwen.

In the 24th, and again in the 33 Hen. 8. he was sheriff of Cumberland.

In the 34 Hen. 8. he was charged by the king's letter to find 60 horse and 40 foot; and assisted Sir Thomas Wharton in that memorable defeat of the Scots at Sollom Moss.

In the 35 Hen. 8. he had the king's licence to settle his lands in Raughton, Gateskell, Brackinthwaite, Stocklewath, and Sebreham in Cumberland, upon John Musgrave gentleman for life, remainder to Adam, John, and Ingram, sons of the said John, successively in tail male, remainder to the heirs male of the body of the said John the father.

He had issue an only child, *viz.*

XVI. Sir Richard Musgrave knight, who came of age, and had livery of his lands, in the 37 Hen. 8.—In the 3 Ed. 6. he purchased of the king the rectory and advowson of the church of Kirkby Stephen, and sold the same again to Thomas lord Wharton, except the tithes of corn and hay of Hartley, Soulby, and Kaber.

He married Anne daughter of the said lord Wharton, and died in the 2 and 3 of Philip and Mary, at Edenhall. His widow afterwards was married to Humphrey Musgrave of Hayton esquire.

The said Sir *Richard* had issue, 1. *Thomas*, who died before his father, unmarried, in the 13th year of his age, in the 7 Eliz. 2. *Eleanor*, married to Robert Bowes of Aske in the county of York esquire; who died without issue.

And here the direct line failing, we go back as aforesaid to *Simon* third son of *Edward*.

XVII. Sir Simon Musgrave, knight, in the 11 Eliz. was sheriff of the county of Cumberland. He married Julian daughter of William Ellerkar of Yorkshire, and by her had issue, 1. *Christopher*. 2. *Thomas Musgrave* captain of Bewcastle, who married to his first wife Ursula daughter and coheir of Sir Reginald Carnaby and widow of Sir Edward Witherington: To his second wife he married a Scotch woman *. 3. *Richard Musgrave* of Norton Conyers, who

* Concerning this Thomas we have met with an anecdote, which is curious, as it exhibits to us the form and manner of proceeding to the ancient trial by battel; viz. " It is agreed between Thomas " Musgrave

who married Jane daughter of Sir John Dalston knight. 4. *John*, who married Isabel daughter of Thomas Musgrave of Hayton esquire. 5. *Anne*, married to Sir Nicolas Curwen of Workington.

XVIII. CHRISTOPHER MUSGRAVE esquire, eldest son of Simon, married Jane daughter of Sir Henry Curwen of Workington, and sister to Sir Nicholas. He died before his father; and left issue, 1. *Richard*. 2. *Julian*, married to Thomas Skelton of Armathwaite esquire. 3. *Mary*, who died unmarried. 4. *Margaret*, married to Francis Whitfield of Whitfield esquire.

XIX. RICHARD MUSGRAVE esquire, son and heir of Christopher son of Simon. He represented the county of Westmorland in parliament in the 1 Ja. 1. and at the coronation of that king was made knight of the Bath, and in the ninth year of that reign was created baronet. At his age of 14 he married Frances daughter of Philip lord Wharton. He died at Naples in Italy in the 13 Ja. 1. and lies interred in the cathedral church there. He left issue

" Musgrave and Lancelot Carleton, for the true trial of such controversies as are betwixt them, to " have it openly tried by way of combat before God and the face of the world, to try it in Canonby " holme before England and Scotland, upon Thursday in Easter week, being the 8th day of April " next ensuing, A. D. 1602, betwixt nine of the clock and one of the same day; to fight on " foot; to be armed with jack, steel cap, plaite sleeves, plaite breeches, plaite sockes, two basslaerd swords, the blades to be one yard and half a quarter of length, two Scotch daggers or dorks " at their girdles; and either of them to provide armour and weapons for themselves according to " this indenture. Two gentlemen to be appointed on the field to view both the parties, to see that " they both be equal in arms and weapons according to this indenture; and being so viewed by the " gentlemen, the gentlemen to ride to the rest of the company, and to leave them but two boys, " viewed by the gentlemen to be under 16 years of age, to hold their horses. In testimony of this " our agreement, we have both set our hands to this indenture, of intent all matters shall be made " so plain, as there shall be no question to stick upon that day. Which indenture, as a witness, " shall be delivered to two gentlemen. And for that it is convenient the world should be privy to " every particular of the grounds of the quarrel, we have agreed to set it down in this indenture " betwixt us, that knowing the quarrel, their eyes may be witnesses of the trial.

" The grounds of the quarrel:

" 1. Lancelot Carleton did charge Thomas Musgrave before the lords of her majesty's privy " council, that Lancelot Carleton was told by a gentleman, one of her majesty's sworn servants, " that Thomas Musgrave had offered to deliver her majesty's castle of Bewcastle to the king of Scots, " and to witness the same, Lancelot Carleton had a letter under the gentleman's own hand for his " discharge.

" 2. He chargeth him, that whereas her majesty doth yearly bestow a great fee upon him as " captain of Bewcastle, to aid and defend her majesty's subjects, therein Thomas Musgrave hath " neglected his duty; for that her majesty's castle of Bewcastle was by him made a den of thieves, " and an harbour and receipt for murderers, felons, and all sorts of misdemeanors. The precedent was, Quintin Whitehead and Runion Blackburne.

" 3. He chargeth him, that his office of Bewcastle is open for the Scotch to ride in and through, " and small resistance made by him to the contrary.

" Thomas Musgrave doth deny all this charge, and saith that he will prove that Lancelot Carleton " doth falsly bely him, and will prove the same by way of combat, according to this indenture. " Lancelot Carleton hath entertained the challenge, and so by God's permission will prove it true as " before, and hath set his hand to the same.

THOMAS MUSGRAVE.
LANCELOT CARLETON."

——What the event of the combat was, we have not found.

by

by his ſaid wife, 1. *Mary*, who died unmarried. 2. *Philip*, who ſucceeded him.

XX. Sir PHILIP MUSGRAVE baronet was of the age of ſeven years at the death of his father Sir Richard. He married Julian, youngeſt daughter of Sir Richard Hutton of Gouldſborough in Yorkſhire, one of the juſtices of the court of common pleas: Which Julian died in the year 1659, and was buried at Edenhall.

He was returned one of the knights of the ſhire for Weſtmorland, in the parliament which met Apr. 3, 1640, and again in the November following. In 1644, he was made commander in chief for Cumberland and Weſtmorland by a commiſſion from the marquis of Newcaſtle, and was alſo made governor of Carliſle. At the reſtoration of king Charles the ſecond, he was choſen to repreſent the county of Weſtmorland in parliament. He was much conſidered by that king on account of his ſervices and ſufferings *, and by him was again made governor of Carliſle, which place he held during his life. He had a warrant for creating him baron Muſgrave of Harcla caſtle, but declined taking out the patent. He had a grant of the tolls of the city of Carliſle, which continued in his family till the union. He died in 1677, and was buried at Edenhall, where is the following monumental inſcription:

Æ. M. S.

Philippus Muſgrave *baronettus, Proſapia antiqua* Muſgraveorum *in hoc agro oriundus, Decus gentilitium, quod hæres legitimus acceperat tanquam poſſeſſor boni nominis, ſua virtute auctum ad poſteros tranſmiſit. In bello civili* Caroli I. *auſpicia ſequebatur, potens conſilio, opibus, manu. Regias partes, fortuna deſerente, non deſeruit. Poſt bonorum amiſſionem, et capitis proſcriptionem, de cauſa optima tardiſſime deſperavit. Ob merita egregia, et ob fidem conſtantiſſime patri præſtitam, ſibi ſervatam,* Carolus II. *cum diu circumſpiceret ei honorarium, ut judicium ſimul et adfectus oſtenderet,* Carlioli *donavit præfectura, contra ingentem aliorum ambitum, idem petentium præmium. Vixit annos ſeptuaginta. Deceſſit* Æra X[ti] 1677. Feb. 7.

Chriſtophorus Muſgrave *Fil. Nat. Sec. Eq. Aur. parenti indulgentiſſimo Pietatis ergo P.*

By his ſaid wife Julian Hutton he had ſeven children: 1. *Richard.* 2. *Philip*, who died at Paris in the 20th year of his age unmarried. 3. *Chriſtopher.* 4. *William*, who died at the age of one year. 5. *Simon*, who at the age of 30 years was drowned in ſwimming for divertiſement. 6. *Thomas*, fel-

* Mar. 14, 1648-9. Reſolved, [by Cromwell's parliament] That Charles Steuart eldeſt ſon of the late king, James ſecond ſon of the late king, John earl of Briſtol, William earl of Newcaſtle, Sir William Widdrington, George lord Digby, Sir Philip Muſgrave, Sir Marmaduke Langdale, Sir Richard Greenville, Sir Francis Dodington, the earl of Worceſter, Sir John Winter, Sir John Colepeper, Sir John Byron, and George duke of Buckingham, ſhall be proſcribed as enemies and traytors to the commonwealth, and ſhall die without mercy wherever they ſhall be found within the limits of this nation, their eſtates confiſcated and forthwith employed for the uſe of the commonwealth. *Parliamentary Hiſt. v.* 19. *p.* 58.

low

low of Queen's college in Oxford, afterwards archdeacon of Carlisle, and prebendary of Durham, and finally dean of Carlisle. 7. *Frances*, married to Edward Hutchinson of Wickham abbey in the county of York esquire.

XXI. Sir Richard Musgrave baronet, eldest son of the said Sir Philip, married Margaret daughter of the aforesaid Sir Thomas Harrison; and by her had issue, 1. *Margaret*, who died in her infancy. 2. *Mary*, married to John Davison of Blakeston in the county of Durham esquire.

And here the male line of this branch failing, the next in succession was,

XXII. Sir Christopher Musgrave knight, and afterwards baronet, brother of the said Sir *Richard*. He was educated at Queen's college in Oxford, and afterwards in Gray's Inn. For his loyalty to the royal party, he was committed to the Tower, where he continued a long time prisoner before the restoration. After his father was made governor of Carlisle by king Charles the second, he was made captain of a company of foot, afterwards governor of Carlisle, and was chosen representative of the said city in parliament. He was also by the said king Charles the second made lieutenant general of the ordnance, and by queen Anne was made one of the tellers of the exchequer. He served in the first session of parliament after the Revolution for the university of Oxford, which he afterwards declined for the county of Westmorland. He was eminent for his great abilities and experience in parliamentary affairs, and died member of parliament for the said county in the year 1704.

He married to his first wife Mary daughter and coheir of Sir Andrew Cogan of Greenwich knight; and by her had issue, 1. *Philip*. 2. *Christopher*, who died unmarried. 3. *Mary*. 4. *John*. 5. *Richard*. (Which three last died young.) 6. *Joseph*, who served in parliament as representative for Cockermouth in 1713. 7. *Simon*, who died in the East Indies. To his second wife he married Elizabeth daughter of Sir Thomas Franklyn of Willsdon in the county of Middlesex knight; and by her had issue, 1. *Joseph*. 2. *Thomas*. 3. *George*, who had three sons; *Joseph*, who married Jane eldest daughter of the present Sir Philip Musgrave of Edenhall baronet; *Thomas* and *George*. 4. *Elizabeth*, married to John Wyneve of Brettenham in the county of Suffolk esquire. 5. *Dorothy*, married to James Hawley of Brentford in the county of Middlesex esquire. 6. *Mary*. 7. *Frances*. 8. *Anne*. 9. *Barbara*. (Which four last died unmarried.)

He died at London July 29, 1704, and was buried in St. Trinity in the Minories, near his eldest son Philip, who died before him.

XXIII. Philip Musgrave esquire, eldest son of Sir *Christopher*, married Mary eldest daughter of George lord Dartmouth; and by her had issue, 1. *Barbara*, married to Thomas Howard of Corby esquire. 2. *Christopher*.

He died July 2, 1688, and was buried near his father-in-law the lord Dartmouth in the chapel of Trinity Minories near the Tower of London, and to his memory a monument was erected in the parish church of Edenhall, with this inscription:

To the memory of Philip Musgrave *esquire, eldest son of Sir* Christopher Musgrave *of* Edenhall *in the county of* Cumberland *knight and baronet, by* Mary *his first wife daughter of Sir* Andrew Cogan *of* Greenwich *in the county of* Kent *baronet; who having had all the advantages of education at home and travel abroad, was qualified at the age of 25 years to serve his majesty king Charles the second as clerk of the council, and one of the principal officers of the ordnance, and his country also in parliament.*

XXIV. Sir CHRISTOPHER MUSGRAVE baronet succeeded his grandfather Sir *Christopher*. He was born in London in 1688; had his education at Eaton school, and at Christ Church college in Oxford. He succeeded his uncle *Christopher Musgrave* esquire as clerk of the council in 1710. He represented the city of Carlisle in the last parliament of queen Anne, and the county of Westmorland in 1722.

He married Julia daughter of Sir John Chardin knight; and from her brother Sir John Chardin baronet who died without issue, her son Sir Philip Musgrave baronet became possessed of Kempton Park in Middlesex in the year 1746. The Chardin Arms are; Argent, a cheveron with a dove in base Azure, and 2 red roses in chief.

He died in the year 1735, at the house of his friend and kinsman Henry Fleetwood of Penwortham in the county of Lancaster esquire, and was interred (according to his own desire) in the chancel of the parish church there, where his son Sir Philip Musgrave caused a monument to be erected to his memory.—By his said wife he had issue, 1. *Philip*. 2. *Christopher*, fellow of All Souls college in Oxford, and rector of Barking in Essex. 3. *Hans*, lieutenant colonel in his majesty's forces. 4. *Chardin*, provost of Oriel college in Oxford. 5. *Mary*, married first to Hugh Lumley esquire of the kingdom of Ireland, and secondly to John Pigot esquire of the same kingdom of Ireland. 6. *Julia*, married to Edward Hassel of Dalemain esquire. 7. *Barbara*, married first to John Hogg esquire of Scotland, and secondly to the lord chief baron Idle. 8. *Anne*, married to Henry Aglionby of Nunnery esquire. 9. *Elizabeth*, married first to Edward Spragge of Greenwich in Kent esquire, and secondly to John Johnston of the city of London esquire. 10. *Charlotte*, who died unmarried. 11. *Dorothy*, married to William Wroughton clerk.

XXV. Sir PHILIP MUSGRAVE baronet, the present owner of the family estate, married Jane daughter of John Turton of Orgreave in the county of Stafford esquire; and by her hath had issue, 1. *Jane*, married, as aforesaid, to Joseph Musgrave esquire. 2. *Julia*, who died young. 3. *Mary*, also dead. 4. *Elizabeth*, married to Heneage Legge of Idlicote in the county of Warwick esquire. 4. *Charlotte*. 6. *Dorothy*. 7. *Henrietta*. 8. *John Chardin*. 9. *Frances*. 10. *Christopher*.

The paternal Arms of Musgrave are; Azure, 6 annulets Or, 3, 2, and 1. The Crest: Two arms in armour Proper, gauntled, and grasping an annulet Or.

PARISH

PARISH OF WARCOP.

I. *Parish of Warcop.*
II. *Manor of Warcop.*
III. *Manor of Sandford.*
IV. *Manor of Burton.*
V. *Manor of Bleatarn.*

I. PARISH OF WARCOP.

THE *cups* in the arms of *Warcop* seem to have been assumed from a misapprehension of the name of the place; for it was never anciently written *Warcup*, but *Wartbecoppe*, and sometimes *Wardecop*. *Coppe* signifies the top of an hill. Which hill, no doubt, is the place where the *tower* or manor house stood, upon a rising ground ascending from the river Eden. Whether the former part of the word might be from a *wath* or ford over the river there before the bridge was erected, or rather from *ward* being kept there, cannot now with any precision be determined.

The parish of Warcop is bounded on the East by the parish of Musgrave; on the South, by the parishes of Crosby Garret and Kirkby Stephen; on the West, by the parishes of Asby, Ormeshead, and St. Michael's Appleby; and on the North, by the parish of Romaldkirk in the county of York: And contains about 117 families; all of the church of England, except one or two.

The church is dedicated to *St. Columbe*; by contraction, *St. Combe*. Thus in the year 1380, Thomas de Sandford bequeathed, according to the custom of those times, to the vicar of Warcop 20*s* (which kind of legacy afterwards obtained the name of *mortuary*) for his forgotten tithes, and his body to be buried in the churchyard of *St. Columbe*. And in 1526, *Edward Hilton* rector of Blechingdon by his last will and testament (hereafter mentioned) bequeathed a legacy for an obit to be performed in *St. John*'s ile or porch in the parish church of *St. Combe* of Warcop.—This saint is not in the Kalendar of saints in the Romish church, having never been canonized at Rome. He was the apostle of the Picts, and settled in one of the Hebrides islands, in the sixth century.

It is a vicarage, in the patronage of the lord of the manor; valued in the king's books at 9*l* 5*s* 3½*d*; and returned to the governors of queen Anne's bounty at the clear yearly value of 45*l*.

This church was appropriated to the abbey of Shap, by Robert de Clifford, in the reign of king Edward the first. Which appropriation bishop Halton confirmed, in consideration of the poverty and ruined estate of the said abbey, occasioned by the incursions of the Scots: reserving to himself and his succeſſors a yearly penſion of 4 *l*, to be paid by equal portions at Whitſuntide and Martinmaſs.

The laſt rector, before the appropriation, was one *Robert de Muſgrave*; unto whom we find a writ directed in the year 1310, concerning a diſpute about a farm in Great Ormeſheved.

On his death, the firſt vicar, preſented by the abbot and convent, in the year 1311, was *William de Warthecoppe* their late abbot.

In the year 1320, *Hugh de Hoveden*, prieſt, and canon of Heppe, was preſented by the ſaid abbot and convent.

In 1359, one frier *Nicholas de Preſton* was vicar; who was excommunicated for neglect of paying his yearly penſion to the biſhop and to the abbey, and on his diſcharging the ſame was abſolved.

In 1574, *Edward Knype* was vicar of Warcop and rector of Clybburn; who by his will bequeathed a ſum of money for the purchaſe of 20 nobles yearly of quit rent for ever, to be diſtributed amongſt his poor relations and the poor pariſhioners of Warcop and Clybburn for ever by equal portions.

On the death of the ſaid Edward Knype in the year following, Sir *David Jack* clerk was inſtituted, on the preſentation of Edward Warcopp of Warcopp eſquire. So that now the advowſon was come into the hands of the lord of the manor, by purchaſe probably from the grantee of the crown, after the diſſolution of the abbey.

In 1585, on the reſignation of David Jack, Sir *Nicholas Deane* was inſtituted, on the preſentation of Joſeph Warcop gentleman.

On the ceſſion of Nicholas Deane to Bromfield in the year 1589, Sir *Robert Robſon* clerk was inſtituted on the preſentation of John Warcop of Warcop gentleman.

In 1597, on the death of Robert Robſon, Sir *Anthony Jaques* clerk was inſtituted, on the preſentation of Thomas Brathwaite of Warcop eſquire.

In 1625, on the death of Anthony Jaques, *George Martin*, B. A. was inſtituted on the preſentation of king Charles the firſt in the right of George Brathwaite eſquire his ward.

In 1643, on the death of *John Hawton*, vicar of Warcop; *John Vaux*, M. A. was inſtituted on the preſentation of colonel Richard Dacre, grantee probably of the ſaid king for that turn, in right of Richard Brathwaite eſquire then in wardſhip to the king.

And in the ſame year, *Edward Mawſon*, M. A. was inſtituted on the preſentation of the ſaid king in right of his ſaid ward.

In 1663, *Charles Crow* clerk was inſtituted on the preſentation of Richard Brathwaite eſquire.

In 1714, on the death of *Richard Ward* vicar of Warcop, *Matthew Lamb*, B. A. was inſtituted on the preſentation of Richard Brathwaite, eſquire.

In 1735, on the death of Matthew Lamb, *Matthias Ward* was inſtituted on the preſentation of Robert Brathwaite eſquire.

The *church* is ſmall, with two little bells. On the ſouth ſide there is a porch, which belonged formerly to Warcop Tower (the ancient manor houſe). It was given up by one of the owners, Mr. Fairer, to the inhabitants for their own use, on condition of their repairing the same. On the north side is another ile, belonging to the owner of Burton hall in this parish, being probably that which in the will of Edward Wilton hereafter mentioned is called *St. John*'s porch.

The *vicarage house* hath been anciently moated round, including the garden, orchard, and outhouses; with a draw-bridge at the entrance: the necessity whereof is apparent, as it is situate by the road side out of Scotland.

II. MANOR OF WARCOP.

So early as the reign of king John, we find *William de Warthcop* witness to a grant by the first Robert de Veteripont to Robert son of William de Sandford.

And to a grant of lands at Morland to the priory of Wetheral, one of the witnesses was *William de Wardecop*.

In the time of John de Veteripont son of the aforesaid Robert, there is a grant to the lord of the manor of Warcop (without naming him), and to the lords of Sandford, Burton, and Helton, by the said John de Veteripont, of "*freedom* from pulture of the foresters, and from all things that he, his "ancestors, or heirs, or his foresters might or could take or demand at any "time by occasion of the said pulture, by the testimony of his verderers or "other officers of the forest: But if any forfeiture should incur by reason "of any trespass committed in the forest, or of vert or venison, the foresters "should apply to the lords of the said towns, and demand of them *wytnesman*, "and the said lords shall find to the foresters *wytnesman*."

After the death of the said John de Veteripont, who died in the 26 Hen. 3. his son Robert, then a minor, was committed to the custody of the prior of Carlisle, who suffered great waste to be done in his lands in Westmorland; and one of the jurors to inquire of the said waste was *William de Warthecopp*.

After the death of the said Robert de Veteripont son of John, who died in the 49 Hen. 3. one of the commissioners appointed for making partition of his lands between his two daughters was *Richard de Warthecop*.

In the 20 Ed. 1. *Richard de Warthecop* was a juror in a cause at Appleby, between the king and the abbot and convent of St. Mary's York.

To a grant of lands at Ormeshead about this time, by Robert son of Robert son of Gamel de Sandford, two of the witnesses were *Richard de Warthecopp* and *Henry* his son.

In the 8 Ed. 2. after the death of Robert de Clifford, the inquisition finds, that *Henry de Warthecop* held of the said Robert, on the day on which he died, the manor of Warthecop and half of Wateby; the wardship whereof was worth 30*l*, the cornage 17*s* 8*d*.

And

And in the ſame year, as alſo in the 10 Ed. 2. he was knight of the ſhire for Weſtmorland.

The next was *Thomas de Warthecop*, who in the 3d and again in the 4 Ed. 3. repreſented the ſaid county of Weſtmorland in parliament.

In the 5. Ed. 3. To a deed of lands at Breeks from Hugh de Ormeſheved to Adam de Appelby, one of the witneſſes is *Thomas de Warthecopp* then ſheriff of Weſtmorland.—And there ſeems to have been a ſucceſſion of ſeveral of the name of *Thomas*.

In the 50 Ed. 3. *Thomas de Warthecopp* was knight of the ſhire for the ſaid county.

So in the 4 Ric. 2. and in the 8 Hen. 4. the 9 Hen. 4. the 2 Hen. 5. and 8 Hen. 5. *Thomas Warthecopp* was choſen repreſentative of the ſaid county.

And about this time the family was become much diffuſed and multiplied. For there was then a branch of this family ſettled at Smardale, by marriage of the heireſs there. In the 10 Hen. 5. after the death of John de Clifford, in taking the inquiſition, *Robert de Warcop* was eſcheator for the king; and *Thomas Warcop* of Lambertſeat, and *Thomas Warcop* of Colby (who married the heireſs there), were two of the jurors. There was then alſo one *Thomas Warcop* of Warcop, who held divers lands there, but he was not lord of the manor; for the inquiſition finds, that *Ralph* earl of *Weſtmorland* then held the manor. There was alſo one *Thomas de Warcop* about that time who married a coheir of Sandford.

After this, we find nothing particular concerning the Warcops of Warcop for ſeveral generations. Probably they had been great ſufferers, as moſt of the northern gentry were, in the civil wars between the houſes of York and Lancaſter. And the manor ſeems to have been forfeited, and granted to the *Nevils*. By an inquiſition of knights fees in the 31 Hen. 6. it appears, that *George Nevil* knight, lord of Latymere, held Warcop. In the 18 Hen. 8. *Richard Nevil* lord of Latymere held the ſame. And in the 24 Hen. 8. *John Nevil* lord of Latymere, ſon and heir of the ſaid Richard, held the ſaid manor. And in the 1 and 2 Ph. and M. *George Nevil* held the ſame.—After this, we find the manor come back into the name of Warcop. And in the 17 Eliz. *Edward Warcop* of Warcop eſquire preſented David Jack as aforeſaid to the vicarage.

In the 28 Eliz. *Joſeph Warcop* gentleman preſented Nicholas Deane to the vicarage.

In the 32 Eliz. *John Warcop* gentleman preſented to the vicarage Robert Robſon clerk. And this is the laſt of the Warcops who was lord of the manor there. The name and family was not then extinct, nor perhaps is yet, for there are ſeveral of the name in divers parts of the county. But there are none of any conſiderable note; nor can they perhaps derive their pedigree from any of the aforeſaid branches of this ancient family.—Here therefore we leave the name Warcop of Warcop.

Their arms were; Sable, three cups with covers Argent.

We come next to the family of *Brathwaite* of Warcop. The last mentioned *John Warcop* sold the manor to *Thomas Brathwaite* esquire (afterwards Sir Thomas), the eldest in the direct line of the Brathwaites of Ambleside in the barony of Kendale. His father *Robert Brathwaite* esquire of Ambleside (son of *Richard*) purchased the manor of Burneshead; which, being the larger estate, he gave to this his eldest son *Thomas*, who afterwards purchased Warcop: And with him therefore we begin our pedigree of the Brathwaites of Warcop.

1. Sir *Thomas Brathwaite* of Burneshead and Warcop, knight, married Dorothy daughter of Robert Byndlose of Helsington; and by her had issue, (1) *Thomas*, his eldest son and heir. (2) *Richard*, to whom he gave Burneshead, and from him descended the Brathwaites of Burneshead. And five daughters, *Agnes*, *Alice*, *Dorothy*, *Mary*, and *Anne*, all married.†

2. Sir *Thomas Brathwaite* of Warcop, knight. He married Elizabeth daughter of Sir John Dalston of Dalston, by his wife one of the coheirs of

† This Thomas had a grant of a crest to the ancient arms of the family, as followeth:—— To all and singular as well nobles as others, to whom these presents shall come, to be seen, read, or heard; Edmund Knight esquire, alias Norroy principal herald and king of arms of the north parts of this realm of England from the river of Trent northwards, sendeth greeting: Whereas anciently from the beginning, the valiant and virtuous acts of worthy persons have been commended to the world in all ages with sundry monuments and remembrances of their good deserts, and amongst which the chiefest and most usual hath been the bearing of signs and tokens in shields called arms, being the evident demonstrations and testimonies of prowess and valour, diversly distributed according to the qualities and deserts of the persons meriting the same; which order, as it was prudently devised in the beginning to stir and kindle the hearts of men to the imitation of virtue and nobleness, even so hath the same been and yet is continually observed, to the end that such as have done commendable service to their prince or country, either in war or peace, might thereby receive due honour in their lives, and also leave the same in succession to their posterity for ever: And whereas Thomas Brathwait of Warcopp in the county of Westmorland gentleman, son and heir of Robert Brathwait of Ambleside in the county aforesaid gentleman, which Robert was the son of Richard Brathwait in the said county gentleman, who was descended of an ancient house and family long time bearing arms, that is to say, Gules, on a cheveron Argent three cross croslets fitchee Sable; and yet not knowing of any crest or cognizance meet and lawful to be born without prejudice or offence to any other person or persons: For accomplishing whereof, and finding no crest unto the same (as commonly to all ancient arms there belongeth none), I the said Norroy king of arms, by power and authority to me committed by letters patent under the great seal of England, have assigned, given, and granted unto the said Thomas Brathwait gentleman, to his said ancient arms, by way of increase, for his crest or cognizance, as followeth; that is to say, upon the helme on a torse white and black, a greyhound couchant Argent, his collar and lyne Gules, mantled Gules, double Argent. Which said arms and crest, and every part thereof, I the said Norroy king of arms do by these presents assign, give, and grant, allow, ratify, and confirm unto the said Thomas Brathwait and to his posterity for ever; and the same to enjoy, use, and bear, and also shew forth with their due differences according to the law of arms, at all times, in shield, coat armour, or otherwise, at his and their liberty and pleasure, without impediment, let, or interruption of any person or persons. In witness whereof, I the said Norroy king of arms have signed these presents with my hand, and put thereunto the seal of mine office, this 22d day of November, in the 34th year of the reign of our most gracious sovereign lady Elizabeth by the grace of God queen of England, France, and Ireland, &c. &c. in the year of our Lord God 1591.

EDMUND KNIGHT, alias
Norroy Roy d'Armes.

the

the last Warcop of Smardale. They had issue, (1) *George.* (2) *Dorothy,* married to Sir Thomas Dacre of Abbey Lanercost in Cumberland.

3. *George Brathwaite* of Warcop, esquire. He married Winifred daughter of Sir Richard Fletcher of Hutton. They had issue, (1) *Richard.* (2) *Barbara,* married to Christopher Hilton of Burton and Ormeshead esquire. (3) *Elizabeth,* married to Thomas Tempest of Stella in the county of Durham esquire.

4. *Richard Brathwaite* of Warcop, esquire, married Mariana daughter of James Chaloner of Gisbrough in the county of York esquire (one of king Charles's judges); and by her had issue, (1) *George,* who was six years of age at the time of Dugdale's visitation in 1664: He was afterwards captain in the army, and died without issue. (2) *Richard,* who on the death of his elder brother without issue succeeded to the inheritance. (3) *Mariana,* married to John Ogle of Newcastle upon Tyne esquire, to whom she had issue Sir Chaloner Ogle knight, rear admiral of the blue. (5) *James,* a captain in the army, who died without issue.

5. *Richard Brathwaite* of Warcop, esquire, married Elizabeth daughter of Sir Robert Booth knight, chief justice of the king's bench in Ireland; and by her had issue, (1) *Richard,* who married Dorothy daughter of Thomas Carleton of Appleby gentleman, and died before his father, without issue. (2) *Robert.* (3) *Henry.* (4) *Thomas.* (5) *George.* (6) *William.* (7) *Elizabeth.* (8) *Mary.* (9) *Lucy.*

6. *Robert Brathwaite* of Warcop, esquire, married Elizabeth daughter and coheir of Reginald Dobson of Barwise gentleman, and had issue, (1) *Richard,* now captain in the royal navy. (2) *Elizabeth,* who died an infant.

The said Robert Brathwaite by his will devised the manor of Warcop, with the demesne lands thereto belonging, and also the tithes of Warcop and Bleatarn, and the advowson of the vicarage, to Cuthbert Collingwood of Newcastle upon Tyne merchant (who married the other coheir of Reginald Dobson) to be sold for the purposes in the said will mentioned; and the same were accordingly sold to Thomas Carleton of Appleby esquire; who gave the same as a marriage portion with his younger daughter Dorothy to George Stephenson esquire; which George Stephenson dying without issue, the premisses came to coheirs sisters of his father John Stephenson gentleman; and upon a partition thereof, the manor of Warcop acceded to Elizabeth wife of William Preston clerk, rector of Brougham; whose son and heir William Preston, M. A. rector of Ormshead now enjoys the same (1776).

Warcop-hall is an handsome commodious building, elegantly situate on a rising ground. It was greatly improved, and much of it rebuilt, by the said George Stephenson.

But this was not the ancient manor house; for that was at the place which is now called *Warcop tower:* which was heretofore a large building, though there is now nothing thereof remaining but a small farm house and outhouses.

About

About 100 yards south-east from the village of Warcop, was a *castle*, which appears to have been a large building, and to have taken up more than one acre of ground. Mr. Machel says, that he had seen some part of the walls dug up, which were 15 foot thick, and of fair hewn stone, well cemented with lime and sand. And there was a tradition, he says, that the stones of the steeple of the church at Kirkby Stephen (which was built about the year 1606) were fetched from thence. The place where the castle stood still goes by the name of *Castle-hill*.

At about 200 yards distance south-eastward from the castle, is a place in the common field called *Kirksteeds*, where have been found wrought free stones; from which, and from the name thereof, it is supposed, that in this place heretofore there hath been a chapel.

Near the old Roman way, upon a place called Brough-hill, where the annual fair is holden, in casting up the new turnpike road, were found in a direct line at equal distances three Roman securis's or hatchets, not made of iron and steel, but of a much heavier metal like bell-metal.

III. MANOR OF SANDFORD.

West from Warcop, lies the manor of *Sandford*, on the north side of the river Eden; which probably had its name from some *ford* over that river, the soil being remarkably sandy all thereabouts.

In the reign of king John, there is a grant by *William* son of *Robert de Sandford*, to Robert de Veteripont, of his wood of Sandford and all the turbary of the said town, in consideration of his being discharged from homage and service, and of the sum of ten marks in silver and one palfrey; describing the boundaries as follows: "Beginning from Creskeld-beck where it falls "into Coupmanebeck, and so going up through the middle of Erthusegill "to a place where Rouche-beck falls into the said Creskeld-beck, and so "going up Rouche-beck into Tonwode mire which lies between the aforesaid "wood of Sandford and Humfreyshevcd, and so from Humfreyshevcd going "up to the sike which falls from the rock of Burton, and so to the way "which goes from Sandford towards Burton, and then going down north-"wards to the corner of the field of William son of Simon, and so going up "by the side of the said field towards the south to the head of Swinesete, "and so going along between the improved land and the wood which encom-"passeth Scalestedes mire, descending westward to the brook which is called "*Sandwath* just at the going out of Sandford, and so taking in the whole "turbary from Sandford aforesaid to Coupmane-beck: Paying to him and "his heirs 3d yearly at the feast of St. Laurence. Witnesses; *Reimund de* "*Derneford* then sheriff of Westmorland, *Guido de Hellebeck*, *Thomas* son of "*Reimund*, *Adam de Musegrave*, *Roger de Bethun*, *Thomas* son of *William* son "of *Reimund*, *William* son of *Simon*, *William de Morvil*, *Galfridus de Wateby*, "*Robert* the forester, *Nicolas de Ribles*, and others."

Afterwards, the said Robert de Veteripont regranted the same by the same metes and bounds to *Robert de Sandford*, son of the said *William*, for the sum of of 20 *l* paid to him in his necessity (as the charter expresseth it), that is, probably, when he went with the crusade into the holy land. Witnesses of which grant were, *Reimund de Derneford* sheriff of Westmorland, *Thomas de Helbeck*, *William Morvil*, *Thomas Bowet*, *Robert de Askeby*, *William de Warthecopp*, *Matthew de Rosgill*, *Geoffrey de Wateby*, *Adam Musgrave*, *William Chartney*, and others.

After the death of John de Veteripont son of the said Robert, it was found by inquisition, that the prior of Carlisle, guardian of the heir during his minority, had suffered great destruction to be made in the underwoods of Sandford.

In the 14 Ed. 1. in the partition of the inheritance between the two daughters of the last Robert de Veteripont, Idonea the younger daughter had allotted to her the homage and service of *Richard de Sandford*.

In the 18 Ed. 1. there is a grant from *John* son of *John de Sandford* to John de Helton; Witnesses whereof were, Richard de Warthecop, Henry his son, John Mauchael, William de Crakenthorp, Thomas de Helton, Thomas son of James de Morton, William de Neuby, and others.

In the 10 Ed. 2. *Robert de Sandford* was knight of the shire for the county of Westmorland.

In the 15 Ed. 2. Sir *William de Sandford* represented the said county in parliament. He had a younger brother *Edmund*, who removed to Askham; and was the founder of the family of that name both at Askham and Howgill. There was also at that time one Sir *Robert de Sandford*, probably son of the said William, who served in parliament for the said county, from the 16 Ed. 2. to the 9 Ed. 3. in eleven different parliaments.

In the 6 Ed. 3. *Simon de Sandford* served in parliament as burgess for the borough of Appleby.

In the 9 Ed. 2. *William de Sandford* served for the said borough.

In the 12 Ed. 3. *Thomas de Sandford* served in parliament for the county of Westmorland.

In the 14th, 17th, and 18th of Ed. 3. *Robert de Sandford* was knight of the shire for the said county.

In the 15 Ed. 3. *Thomas de Sandford* and *William de Sandford* served as burgesses for Appleby.

In the 20 Ed. 3. *William de Sandford* and *Thomas de Sandford* represented the county: and in the same year *Simon de Sandford* served for the borough.

In the 22 Ed. 3. *Thomas de Sandford* was knight of the shire.

In the 24 Ed. 3. *Robert de Sandford* served for the said borough; as also in the 26 Ed. 3. And in the 28 Ed. 3. he served for the county.

In the 30 Ed. 3. *Robert de Sandford* appears to have held the manor of Sandford. He had a son Henry, who was rector of Crosby Gerard; which Henry had a licence from the bishop of Carlisle to be absent from his church, on condition that he should cause divine service to be performed once or twice in every month in his father's oratory at Sandford.

In the 35th, and again in the 37th of Ed. 3. *Thomas de Sandford* was knight of the shire.

In the 43 Ed. 3. by an inquisition of knights fees, it is found, that *Thomas de Sandford* then held Sandford of Roger de Clifford, by homage and fealty, and 3*s* 4*d* cornage.—Which Roger de Clifford granted and confirmed to this Thomas and Isabel his wife common of turbary in Sandford; so as they and their tenants pay their accustomed yearly rent of one halfpeny for every cart load in Sandford myre.

In the 12 Ric. 2. *Robert de Sandford* was knight of the shire.

In the 15 Ric. 2. by the inquisition *post mortem* of Roger de Clifford, it is found, that *Robert de Sandford* then held the manor of Sandford.

In the 4 Hen. 4. after the death of Maud de Clifford, the inquisition finds, that *Robert de Sandford* held the same of her as part of her dower and jointure.

In the 1 Hen. 5. *Robert de Sandford* served in parliament as burgess for Appleby.

In the 10 Hen. 5. after the death of John de Clifford, the jurors find, that *Christopher Berdesey* and *Margaret* his wife, and *Thomas de Warthecopp* and *Katherine* his wife, held the manor of Sandford, as of the right of the said *Margaret* and *Katherine*.—From whence it is clear, that this eldest branch of the family of Sandford (in like manner as almost all the other great families) ended in daughters.

By an inquisition of knights fees in the 31 Hen. 6. it appears, that *Thomas Warcop* vicar of Kirkby Stephen as of the right of *Katherine* his late wife, and *Christopher Berdesey* as of the right of *Margaret* his wife, daughters and coheirs of *Robert Sandford* esquire, held the same.—And afterwards, in the same year, *Thomas Warcopp* of Colby son of *Thomas Warcopp* late vicar of Kirkby Stephen as of the right of *Katherine* wife of the said vicar, and *Christopher Berdesey* and *Margaret* his wife as of the right of the said *Margaret*, held the same, by homage and fealty, and 3*s* 4*d* cornage.

In the 18 Hen. 8. *Thomas Warcop* of Colby, son and heir of *Edward Warcop*, held Sandford of Henry earl of Cumberland.

In the 1 and 2 Ph. and Mary, *Barnaby Warcop* held the same.

In the next generation, the same went off again with daughters coheirs. For in the 34 Eliz. *John Dalston* of Dalston esquire and *Frances* his wife, and *Talbot Bowes* of Eglestton Abbey in the county of York esquire and *Agnes* his wife, daughters and coheirs of *Thomas Warcop* of Smardale esquire deceased, sold to the several tenants their tenements at Sandford to freehold, with a respective proportion of the wastes, mosses, and commons.

And in the 23 Cha. 2. Sir *Thomas Brathwaite* of Warcop knight, and *Elizabeth* his wife (daughter of the said John Dalston by his wife Frances Warcop as aforesaid), sold to *Andrew Wharton* of Gray's Inn esquire the *manor* of Sandford, with the soil, profits of courts, waifs, strays, deodands, felons goods, escheats, rents, boons, and the like.

And the said *Andrew Wharton* sold the demesne and rents to the several inhabitants and land owners.

We

We have not found to whom the rectorial *tithes* of Sandford were immediately granted after the diſſolution of the monaſteries. In the year 1678, they were in the poſſeſſion of Thomas Gabetys eſquire of Croſby Ravenſworth, who ſold the ſame to William Crook of Coppal in the county of Lancaſter gentleman; and in 1700, Samuel Crook of the ſame place gentleman, and Mary Crook widow his mother, ſold the ſame to ſeveral of the inhabitants, who afterwards ſold out to the reſt.

The *hall* or manor houſe was ſold by the ſaid Andrew Wharton to Richard Fawcet; in which houſe there was anciently a chapel, as appears by the aforeſaid licence of abſence to Henry de Sandford.

There was a tenement and cottage at Sandford which belonged to Shap abbey; which, at the time of the diſſolution of the abbey, was in the poſſeſſion of one Robert Bolland.

Nigh to Sandford field corner, on the right hand of the road leading from Warcop towards Appleby, not far from the Roman way, are three or four Tumuli. The largeſt of which is 91 paces in circumference, the next 86, the next about 40, the other a ſmall one almoſt defaced. And near the ſame was a circle of ſtones, almoſt at equal diſtances, in diameter about 50 paces; which are now removed, being made uſe of in building.

The largeſt of theſe *tumuli* was opened in the year 1766, at the deſire of Dr. Charles Lyttelton biſhop of Carliſle and preſident of the Antiquarian ſociety, by the reverend William Preſton of Warcop hall aforeſaid; who gave to his lordſhip the following account: "Agreeable to your lordſhip's directions, I yeſterday finiſhed cutting through the largeſt of the barrows or "tumuli upon Sandford moor. Though I employed 6 or 8 men, it took us "up three whole days. We drove a level, and for ſome time found nothing "worth taking notice of. At laſt a workman going to the very top of the "barrow, and beginning to dig there, about half a yard below the ſurface "threw out a ſmall piece of a veſſel, upon which we examined every thing "with great care, and immediately found a ſmall urn or veſſel, ſet in a "large one. It contained ſomething white like aſhes, as much as might be "laid upon a ſixpence, which the wind ſoon diſperſed. On one ſide of the "urn, but a little deeper, lay a two-edged ſword, with a curious carved hilt, but "almoſt deſtroyed with ruſt. Its breadth is nearly two inches and a half; "its length, ſomewhat more than two feet. On the other ſide lay the head, "as it ſeemeth, of an halbert or ſome ſuch inſtrument, together with ſome "other things which I cannot explain. Underneath theſe, about a yard "deeper, we came to what at firſt appearance reſembled a vault, but on a "nearer examination proved to be nothing but a vaſt heap of ſtones of "various kinds, ſuch as are not to be found on that moor or near it. In "clearing the place of theſe, we found nothing, till at the very bottom, "and as near as we could gueſs exactly under the urn, we came to a ſquare "place about 4 feet in length and 2 in breadth. In this was laid ſome

" rich black mould, about 3 inches deep, and amongſt this were many " human bones, which evidently appeared to have been burned. Under " this was nothing but ſolid gravel. The ſtones had been piled up in form " of a pyramid, and the diameter of the ground they covered was about " 6 or 7 yards, and the depth we ſunk, eſpecially in the center, ſomewhat " more than ſix."

Near to theſe Tumuli is a ſmall camp, with a ſingle trench; and at a ſmall diſtance upon another hill is another camp of about the ſame dimenſions.

On the right hand of the road, going towards Appleby, near Coupland beck bridge (as it is commonly called, but the name of it in the ancient evidences is *Coupman beck*) hath been a round fortification or caſtle, the diameter whereof within the walls was 40 paces, and the thickneſs of the walls (including the rubbiſh) about ten yards. The ſtones of a red colour, and ſtrongly cemented with lime and ſand.

Over againſt the ſaid fortification, but nearer to the bridge, is a ſquare, which ſeems to have been the place where an hoſpital formerly ſtood. That ſuch hoſpital there was, appears from the partition made of the inheritance of the laſt Robert de Veteripont between his two daughters; for in the ſhare of Iſabella was, the *advowſon of the hoſpital of Coupmanbeck.* And in a deed without date of a moiety of the manor of Helton from Thomas to Andrew de Hellerton, one of the bounder marks is, from ſuch a place down to the *hoſpital of Coupmanbeck.*

IV. MANOR OF BURTON.

North from Coupland beck bridge, at the ſkirt of *Roman fell*, (as it is now called, not for any particular reaſon deducible from the time of the old Romans, for the ancient name of it was *Rutmanfell*) lies the hamlet of *Burton.* This, like many of the reſt, was heretofore in the hands of a family denominated from the place. We find ſeveral of the name *de Burton* in the reign of king Henry the third.

But ſoon after, it came into the name of *Helton*, probably by marriage of the heireſs of *Burton*; whoſe arms were, Argent, a bend wavy Sable.

In the 20 Ed. 1. by a deed dated at Burton, *William de Helton* granted certain lands at Ormeſhead to *Thomas de Helton*: Witneſſes whereof were, Henry de Threlkeld ſheriff of Weſtmorland, Henry de Warthecopp, Thomas de Warthecopp, Richard de Blenkinſop, Hugh de Ormeſheved, and others.

In the 8 Ed. 2. by the inquiſition *poſt mortem* of Robert de Clifford, it is found, that *William de Helton* held of the ſaid Robert on the day on which he died, the manor of Burton; the wardſhip whereof, when it ſhould happen, was worth 10*l* yearly, and the cornage 13*s* 4*d*.

In the 43 Ed. 3. *William de Helton* held the manor of Burton.

In the 50 Ed. 3. *William de Helton* served in parliament as burgess for Appleby.

In the 2 Ric. 2. *John* son of *John de Hilton*, by a deed dated at Burton, made a settlement of certain lands and tenements, rents and services, in the vills of Sandford and Hilton Bacon, upon *Agnes de Hilton* (his daughter, as it seemeth) and the heirs of her body, remainder to *Thomas* son of *John de Hilton* and the heirs of his body, with remainders over.

In the 15 Ric. 2. after the death of Roger de Clifford, the inquisition finds, that *William de Hilton* and *Agnes* his wife held the manor of Burton, as of the right of the said *Agnes*.—So that here it had gone off with the said Agnes, married probably to one of the same family.

In the 12 Hen. 4. *John de Helton* represented the borough of Appleby in parliament.

In the 10 Hen. 5. after the death of John de Clifford, the inquisition finds that *William de Helton* held the manor of Burton, by homage and fealty, and 13*s* 4*d* cornage.

In the 15 Hen. 6. *Robert Helton*, son and heir of *William Helton*, son and heir of *William Helton*, son and heir of *Thomas Helton*, brother and heir of *William Helton*, made a settlement of certain lands at Ormeshead and Great Asby.

In the 31 Hen. 6. *William de Helton* held the manor of Burton of Thomas de Clifford, by the like services as before.

Next we come to a pedigree certified at Dugdale's visitation in 1664. Which pedigree nevertheless, although it consisted only of 6 generations, seems (as most of the other Heraldic pedigrees, when compared with the inquisitions *post mortem* and other authentic documents) to be very imperfect. However, the pedigree (such as it is) runs thus:

1. *Christopher Helton* of Burton esquire, in the reign of Ed. 4. married Margaret daughter of Thomas Marshall of Kirk Oswald: And had issue,

2. *Richard Helton* of Burton esquire; who married Isabel daughter of John Barton of Ormeshead esquire: And had issue,

3. *Andrew Helton* of Burton esquire; who married Alice daughter of John Aglionby of Carlisle; and by her had issue (1) *John* (2) *Winifred*, married to Leonard Musgrave of Johnby in Cumberland. (3) *Julian*, married to an Irish lord, and afterwards to a sea captain.

4. *John Hilton* of Burton esquire, son and heir of Andrew, married Mary daughter and coheir of Saxton of Byham hall in Essex; and died about the year 1630. He had issue, (1) *Cyprian*. (2) *George*, who married Jane daughter of Fletcher of Dovenby in Cumberland. (3) *Johan*, who died unmarried.

5. *Cyprian Hilton* of Burton esquire, son and heir of John, married Frances daughter and sole heir † of Sir Christopher Pickering of Ormeshead, and

† So says the pedigree; but she was bastard daughter of Sir Christopher Pickering, who having no other child, and never having been married, gave to his said daughter the manor of Ormeshead. Her mother's name was Todhunter, Sir Christopher's milkmaid at Threlkeld. The said Frances was first married to John Dudley a lawyer, to whom she had no issue. *(Flem.)*

with her had the manor of Ormeshead. He died in 1649; and had issue, (1) *Christopher*. (2) *John Hilton* of Stanemore, who married Isabel daughter of John Farer of Warcop Tower. (3) *Andrew*, who died without issue. (4) *Mary*, married to William Farer of Warcop Tower.

6. *Christopher Hilton* of Ormeshead esquire, son and heir of Cyprian, married Barbara daughter of Thomas Brathwaite of Warcop esquire; and was of the age of 36 at the aforesaid visitation.—So far the pedigree.

But, intermediately, in the 18 Hen. 8. by an inquisition of knights fees holden of Henry earl of Cumberland, it appears, that *Robert Hylton* then held the manor of Burton. And in the same year, by the will of Edward Hilton clerk, whereby he devised a cottage at Helton Bacon to charitable uses, *Robert Hilton* of Burton and his heirs are made trustees of that charity ‡.

In

‡ In the naym of God, Amen. In the zere off our lorde God MCCCCCXXVI, and in the xviith zere of the reynge off our sovereyn lord kynge Henry the viiith, the xxth day of February; I Edwarde Hilton clerke parson off Blechesdon in the counte of Oxfordeshyre, hoyll of mynde, mayks my wyll under this manere: As concernynge the dysposition of my cotage, meys, or tenement in Helton Baken in the counte of Westmerland, in whiche latly dwellede John Johnson, and of and in all thyngs to the seyde cotage pertenynge or belongyng; Fyrst, I wyll that John Pantre, Ambros Hilton, clerks, John Whelpdall of Penrethe in the counte of Comberlande, and Rychard Rygge off Lytyle Strykland in the counte of Westmerland, gentylmen, my feoffers whichy stands feoffede, possessede, and seasede in my seyde cotage or tenement, with all thyngs theireto appertenynge or belongynge, for thys use, that they or anny off them shall provyde helpe, and they, their herrys or assygnes shall doo anny thynge expedient or necessary for fulfyllynge, observynge, or kepynge of this my wyll, at anny convenient tym they or anny of theym shal be requirede by the provest of the Qwen's college in Oxforde for the tyme beynge, or by his certayn assigne or assyngnes, at any tym herafter, or by the vicar of Warcope for the tym beyng, or his certayn assigne or assygnes. Morover, I will that the seide vicar off Warcope for the tym beyng, and on off the churchemen or churchewardens off Warcope, and an other churcheman or churchewarden off Burton, in the forseide counte of Westmerland, as shal be thoght necessary or expedient by the seyde vycare, shal have the seyde cotage or tenement, and tak, reseve, and perseve zerly for evermor all rentts, profetts, revenys, or anny other thyngs to the seyde cotage or tenement appertenynge or belongynge, of my forseyde feoffes their herers or assignes, or of the tenande or occupyer of the seyde cotage, to thys use and entent; that is to say, that the seyde vycare, churchemen or churchewardens so chosyng for the tym beyng, with the forseyde rentts and profetts growyng and comyng of the seyde cotage or tenement, with anny thynge theirto pertenyng or belongyng, shall finde, observe and keppe an annyversary or obite zerly for evermore the xv day of July, with Placebo and Dirige over evyne, and v masses to be songe or seyde the forseyde xv day of July, one de quinque Vulneribus, another de Natwitate Johannis, another de Sancta Trinitate, another de Annunciatione beatæ Mariæ, with a collect, secret, and post communion at every masse ut in die annyversario, and the hye masse of Requiem in die annyversario to be songe or seyde in Seynt John's porche, at the alter of Seynt John within the paryssyshe churche of Seynt Combe of Warcope. Excepte the sayd xv day of July fortune to falle off Sonday, then I wyll the seyde obite or annyversary shall be kepedde within thre days after, as shall be thoght convenient by the seyde vycare for the tym beynge. In whyche obite or annyversary the forseyde vycare and pryst shall pray specially for the sowlls off the sayd Edward Hilton, hys father Christopher Hilton, and hys mother Margaret wyff to the sayde Christopher, and for the sowlls of hys bretheryne and sisters, hys fryndds and benefactors, and for the sowlls of all the predecessors and successors of the forsaid Christopher Hilton, and for all crysten sowlls. Morover, I wyll that seyd rentts and profetts growyng or comyng of the seyde cotage or tenement, with anny thyng theirto pertenyng and belongynge, shall be distributte and dysposede as herafter folowethe: The forseyd vycar of Warcope beynge present to have viii^{d}, and every on of the other iiii pryst to have vi^{d}, and to have

In the 19 Hen. 8. the ſaid Edward Hilton clerk granted to *Robert Hilton* of Burton eſquire and his heirs, a moiety of the manor of Helton Bacon.

In the 1 and 2 Ph. and M. upon an inquiſition of knights fees in Weſtmorland; it is found, that *Thomas Helton* then held the manor of Burton.

Accordingly, in Sir Daniel Fleming's pedigree of his family, he makes *Andrew*'s father *Thomas*, who married Anne Wharton of Kirkby Thore; and *Thomas*'s father *Robert*, who married a Hartley: Which ſeems to agree with theſe inquiſitions. And in the 29 Hen. 8. there is a releaſe from Iſabella Hylton, widow of *Richard Hylton* of Burton, to *Thomas Hylton* gentleman ſon and heir of the late *Robert Hylton* of Burton gentleman, of her right in certain lands deſcended to her from her brother Robert Barton of Ormeſhead gentleman. So that it ſeemeth, that *Robert* and *Thomas* ſhould have come in (and ſo the chronology ſeems to require) after *Chriſtopher* at N°. 1. and that *Richard* at N°. 2. was not of the direct line, but came in by ſpecial agreement.

The aforeſaid *Chriſtopher Hilton*, at N°. 6. in the pedigree, had a ſon and heir,

7. *Cyprian Hilton* of Ormeſhead eſquire; who married Abigail only child of Hugh Wharton eſquire of a younger branch of the family of Wharton of Wharton-hall.

In 1684, the ſaid Cyprian and Abigail his wife infranchiſed divers cuſtomary tenements in Hilton Bacon.

He died in 1693, leaving the ſaid Abigail his widow, and nine children, viz. *Chriſtopher*, *George*, *Margaret*, *Barbara*, *Hugh*, *Elizabeth*, *Mary*, *Abigail*, and *John*. Which *John* had ſeveral ſons, who died young; and 7 daughters, the eldeſt of whom, Mary, was married to Daniel Robinſon eſquire, now ſheriff of the ſaid county (unto whoſe learning and critical knowledge in antiquities we have been much obliged in our inveſtigations in this part of the

have to drynke ymonge theym viii[d]; alſo the paryſhe clerke to have for ſyngyng and miniſteryng at the alters and helpyng at maſſes ii[d], and to ather churcheman or churchewarden, on of Warcoppe and another of Burton, beyng preſent at the ſeyd maſſes ii[d]; and to v chyidrynge helpyng at the ſeyd maſſes v[d]; and to v poyr neydſull pepyll v[d]; and for breyd and hale to be ſpent within the forſeyd porche of Seynte John, after the Dirige, v[d]. And alſo I wyll that v[d] be offerydde, that is to ſay, after the Offertory of every maſs i[d]. And alſo to the ſeyce vycar or his corete to pray for the ſowlls before reherſyde upon Sondays iiii[d], and v[d] for v tapers to ſtande uppon the herſe in tym of Dirige and maſſes. The recedew of the ſeyde rentts or profetts comyng of the ſeide cotage or tenement to be gevyng and diſtribute to poyr and neydſull pepyll of the forſeyde paryſhe of Warcoppe. Alſo I wyll that thys my preſent wyll be regeſtraytt in the regeſture of my lord buſſhope off Karlyll for thentent that iff anny herafter ſhuld lett or hynder this my wyll, that they ſo lettyng or hyndryng ſhall be called afor my ſayd lorde or his officers, and they ſo lettyng or hyndryng to be chargyt by my ſeyde lorde or his officers by corporal hothe or other cenſurs off churche, that they ſhall not from thensforthe lett or hynder this my preſent wyll, nor wythedraw anny dewte to the forſeyde cotage or tenement pertenyng or belongyng; and in caſe their be any dewty wythedrawn, that they ſhall reſtore it agane under the payn of curſyng, or off other cenſurs off the churche. And for thentent that thys my wyll may be better obſervede and kepyde, I mayk Robert Hilton off Burton in Weſtmerland and his heirs for evermore to be ſupervíſors and overſeers that thys my wyll be well and trewly obſervyde and kepede in tym to com, accordynge as is above expreſede. In witneſſe whereoff, &c.

county),

county), and hath issue Mary, Janet, John, Anne, Elizabeth, Christopher, and Anthony.

8. *Christopher Hilton* esquire, son and heir of Cyprian, married Mary daughter of John Pattenson of Penrith gentleman; and had issue Cyprian, Mary, and Abigail. Of whom, Cyprian and Abigail died in their infancy.

9. *Mary Hilton*, daughter and sole heir of Christopher, was married to *Thomas Wybergh* of Clifton esquire, and had issue 22 children; of whom, the eldest surviving son *William*, dying in 1757, left issue a son and heir *Thomas Wybergh* esquire, now lord of the manor of Burton.

The arms of Hilton are; Sable, 2 saltiers in chief, and 3 annulets, 2 and 1, Argent. The crest, On a wreath, a demigriffin.

At this place was born *Christopher Bainbridge*, educated at Queen's college in Oxford, afterwards dean of York, bishop of Durham, and at length archbishop of York. He was sent ambassador to Rome by king Hen. 8. where he acquitted himself so much to the pope's satisfaction, that he created him cardinal of St. Praxis; but he did not long enjoy this honour, for quarrelling with his steward Rivaldus de Monena an Italian, and caning him for his faults, the revengeful Italian poisoned him, and he died at Rome July 14, 1511, and was there interred.

V. MANOR OF BLEATARN.

South from Warcop, on the opposite side of the river Eden, is the village of *Bleatarn*; so denominated from the *tarn* and marshy ground thereabouts.

This manor was granted to the abbot and convent of Byland in Yorkshire of the Cistertian order, in the reign of king Henry the second. And there are divers charters yet extant, granted in the same king's reign (as appears from the names of several of the witnesses) with the seals very compleat and perfect, now in the possession of Mr. James Richardson of Birks within the said manor, whereby divers lands at Warcop and Bleatarn are granted and confirmed to the said abbey.

The first is by *John Taillebois*, of all his lands which Robert son of Torphin had given to him and his heirs, on the west side of the river Eden. Witnesses whereof are, *Robert archdeacon of Carlisle, Murdach dean (rural, of Westmorland), Henry chaplain of the archdeacon, Robert chaplain of Appleby, Umfrey Malus-catulus, Michael de Hardcle*, and others.

The second is by *Torphin* son of *Robert*, of a moiety of the lands at Warcop on the west side of the river Eden, comprehended within the boundaries therein particularly specified †.

The

† Eboracensi archiepiscopo et toti capitulo sancti Petri, et omnibus sanctæ ecclesiæ filiis, Torphinus filius Roberti, salutem. Sciatis me dedisse, et hac mea charta confirmasse, Deo et monachis sanctæ

The third is, by *Walleve de Bereford*, of the fourth part of the other moiety, describing the very same boundaries.

The fourth is, by *Thorphin* son of *Robert*, and *Robert* his brother; being a confirmation of grants made to the said abbey by *Walleve de Bereford*, *Robert* son of *Thorphin*, *John Tailebois*, and *Richard* son of *Ketel*. Witnesses whereof were, *William* son of *William*, *Thomas de Hellebeck*, *Robert*, son of *Peter*, *Conan de Asc*, *William* son of *Robert de Ascabi*, *Gilbert* and *Adam* his brothers, *Richard English*, *William* his son, *Robert de Helton*, *Richard* son of *Maud*, *Gilbert* his son, *Robert* son of *Copsy*, and *John* his brother.

About which time we meet with the record abovementioned, of a cause depending in the county court at Appleby, between the aforesaid *Thorphin* son of *Robert* and the monks of Byland of the one part, and Robert son of Peter Musegrave and his tenants of the other part, concerning common of pasture between Blatarne and Musgrave. And the same was compromised in the court there, and it was settled, that there shall remain to Robert son of Peter 82 acres, *viz.* from the thorn, upon Hoberghe, across the sike under Maureberghe, to the way towards Musegrave; and from the said thorn the whole shall remain to the monks towards the Grange, and to the way nigh the chapel, and the cattle of Robert shall never enter within these boundaries, nor the cattle of the monks within the property of Robert. Also Robert shall have one outgate for the cattle of Musegrave upon Maureberghe, between the culture of the monks and the vale under Hoberghe, and from thence to the Tarn, and from thence to the way upon Cressekeld which goes towards Appleby, and to the place where four ways meet, and from thence to the head of the Tarn. All this shall be in common pasture for the cattle of Musegrave and the cattle of the monks. But the monks shall plow the culture nigh the mill dam unto the Tarn, and shall have their culture upon Mureberghe, and the meadow in property, as they had before this composition, and shall plow nothing more there; and the cattle of Musegrave therein shall never enter. And Thorphin and Robert were sworn *coram provincialibus*, that is, in open

sanctæ Mariæ de Bellalanda, in perpetuam eleemosynam dimidium terræ illius de Wardecop, quæ comprehenditur per has divisas ab occidentali parte Edenæ: Scilicet, sicut vadit siic ille qui descendit de Faldebergha, et transit per medium Skermund, et intrat in Edenam; et inde sicut Edena currit usque ad vetus fossatum quod est divisa inter Ormesheved et Wardecop; et inde sicut ipsum fossatum ascendit et vadit ultra Thurgarberch, et descendit in Hornegile; et sic sursum per Wulvesdale beck usque ex adverso divisarum quas ostendi monachis a Wulvesdale beck versus orientem usque ad Cressekeldas; et a Cressekeldis sicut rivulus ipse currit a Cressekeldis et cadit in rivulum qui venit de Blaterna; et inde sursum contra ipsum rivulum usque ad propinquiorem vallem quæ est ab occidente de Faldebergha; et inde per fundum vallis ejusdem usque ad prædictum siic de Skermund. Dimidium ergo totius terræ quæ infra has divisas continetur dedi et confirmavi Deo et sanctæ Mariæ et prædictis monachis in perpetuam eleemosynam, propriam, liberam, solutam, et quietam ab omni terreno servicio et exactione seculari, pro salute animæ meæ et patris et matris meæ et omnium meorum. Ego quoque coram capitulo sancti Petri Eboraci hanc donationem confirmavi, et affidavi quod hanc terram, quam eis dedi in perpetuam eleemosynam, liberam de me et de hæredibus meis fideliter tenebunt, et warrantizabo contra omnes homines ego et hæredes mei. Hiis testibus, Roberto decano Eboracensi, Johanne filio Letholdi, Bartholomeo archidiacono et toto capitulo sancti Petri quorum nomina ex altera parte chartæ descripta sunt, Murdaco decano Westmerland, Roberto filio Willielmi de Kernebi, Thoma de Colevilla, Gaufrido de Daivilla, Roberto clerico de Manefeld, et aliis multis qui ex altera parte descripti sunt.

court,

court, that they and their heirs would obferve this agreement. And if the cattle of either of them fhould trefpafs beyond their limits, they were to pay to the party injured one penny for 20 cattle according to the cuftom of the country. Witneffes whereof were, *William Fitz-Hugh* fheriff, *Murdach* the dean, *Thomas de Hellebec*, *Thomas fon of Gofpatric*, *Robert de Kabergh*, *John Toillebois*, *Conan de Afke*, *William de Afkeby*, *Richard Englifh*, *Henry de Cundale*, *Stephen de Tyrnaby*, *Roger Winkenel*, *Robert* fon of *Richard*, *William de Lathes*, *Thomas* his brother, *Hubert Clerk*, *Michael de Harclay*, *Walter* his fon, and other good men †.

There is alfo another charter, which from the names of the witneffes appears to have been in the reign of Hen. 3. whereby *Thomas de Fenton*, fon and heir of *Richard de Fenton*, confirms to the faid abbey one carucate of land in Warcop called *Plowlande*, which *Richard* fon of *Ketel* gave to the faid abbey: Witneffes whereof were, *Ralph de Daker*, *Thomas de Mufegrave*, *Richard de Geringes* then fheriff of Weftmorland, *Thomas de Helebeck*, and *Robert de Afkeby*, knights; *William de Wardcop*, *Geoffrey de Melkinthorp*, *John de Hormefheved*, *Robert de Hormefheved*, and *John de Helton*.

And there is an inclofure at Plowlands which ftill bears the name of Chapel mire.

The abbey of Byland was furrendered to the crown in the 30 Hen. 8. by John Leedys, alias John Allenbrig; and in the 38 Hen. 8. Nov. 4, the king for the confideration of 2100*l* 11*s* 0*d* granted to *Margaret Symfon* widow, *Anthony Bellafis* clerk, and *William Bellafis* efquire (amongft other particulars) the demefne and manor of Blaterne, and all the lands there called Hornegill garthes, formerly in the tenure of *Henry* earl of *Cumberland*, and late in the tenure of *Richard Bellafis* deceafed, former hufband of the faid *Margaret* and father of the faid *William*, and then in the tenure of the faid *Margaret* as executrix in truft for the faid *William* her fon. This *Richard* was fteward of the faid manor to the faid abbot and convent, and before the furrender obtained a grant of the fame for 61 years. On *Margaret*'s death, it furvived to *Anthony* and *William*; and on *Anthony*'s death without iffue, the whole came to the faid *William*, who was fucceeded by his fon Sir *William Bellafis* knight, father of *Brian Bellafis* efquire, father of Sir *William Bellafis* knight, father of *Richard Bellafis* efquire, who had a fon *William Bellafis* efquire, who in the 22 Cha. 2. fold the manor to *Nicholas Salvin* of Croxdale in the county of Durham gentleman, who in the 25 Cha. 2. fold the fame to *George Fothergill* of Tarnhoufe in Ravenftondale gentleman; which *George Fothergill* fold the fame to Sir *Chriftopher Mufgrave* of Hartley caftle baronet, anceftor of the prefent owner Sir *Philip Mufgrave* baronet.

In the 44 Eliz. there was a fuit in the court of York for the Northern parts, between *John Pulleine* of Scotton in the county of York plaintiff, and the tenants of Blaterne defendants; of the record of which caufe the aforefaid Mr. James Richardfon hath an exemplified copy: By which it appears, that in civil caufes that court did not much differ in the form and manner of proceed-

† From a copy taken by Mr. George Fothergill of Tarn houfe.

ing

ing from the high court of chancery. The addreſs is, "To the Queen's "moſt excellent majeſty, and her honourable counſel eſtabliſhed in the north "parts." The plaintiff in his bill ſets forth, that Richard Bellaſſes of Morton in the county of Durham eſquire, then lately deceaſed, had granted to him the plaintiff a leaſe of a moiety of the manor of Blaterne, for the term of 40 years, if he the plaintiff ſhould ſo long live: That the tenants hold their tenements to them and their heirs, according to the cuſtom of tenant-right uſed and allowed within the ſaid manor, by paying to the lord thereof certain yearly rents; and by doing her majeſty's ſervice upon the borders of England anenſt Scotland, when and as often as they ſhall be thereunto required by the lord warden of the weſt marches: And that every tenant, by cuſtom of the ſaid manor, ought to pay a reaſonable fine and greſſom, on the change or alteration of lord or tenant: That the plaintiff had demanded a reaſonable fine arbitrable according to the moiety of their ſeveral rents, after the rate of 7 years fine according to the quantity of their rents; and that the defendants had refuſed to pay the ſame. The tenants anſwer, as to the fines, that they had no ſuch cuſtom; but that on the death of the lord or tenant, they were to pay a god's-penny only, and nothing on change of lord by alienation or leaſe. Unto which there is a replication, and rejoinder, and an examination of witneſſes upon interrogatories. And finally, upon examination and deliberate hearing of the cauſe, in the preſence of learned counſel on both ſides, it is ordered by the court (in reſpect that the witneſſes were ſo contrary and repugnant one to another, that the court could not conveniently determine concerning the cuſtom), that the cauſe be referred to be tried by the due courſe of the common law, and not to be returned hither and heard in this court hereafter in equity, becauſe the tenants refuſe to abide the arbitrary † order of this court, or of any other indifferent commiſſioners to whom the court would have referred it, but the defendants obſtinately and wilfully affirmed in open court, that they would be ordered no otherwiſe than by her majeſty's laws. And the court order the manner in which the cauſe ſhall be brought to iſſue at the common law. Nevertheleſs, the right honourable Philip lord Wharton is required by this honourable court, to call the plaintiff and defendants before his lordſhip, and to end the matter arbitrarily betwixt them if he can; and if his lordſhip cannot conveniently ſo do, then the parties may proceed at the common law as aforeſaid. But Mr. Pullein dropt the ſuit, and nothing farther was done.

But in the 18 Cha. 2. there was a ſuit at law between the laſt *William Bellaſis* aforeſaid and the tenants, concerning the fines; which by the recommendation of Sir Chriſtopher Turner judge of aſſize was referred to the arbitration of Sir John Lowther; who awarded, that they ſhould pay a ſevenpenny fine, on change of lord by death, and on change of tenant by death or alienation: That in caſe of a widow, the fine for that part which ſhe holds (viz. a

† That is, by way of arbitration.

moiety) ſhall not be paid till her death, marriage, or miſcarriage. And by conſent the ſame was decreed in the court of chancery accordingly.

The ſaid abbey had a cell of monks here at Bleatarn. Their buildings appear to have covered a pretty large parcel of ground.

About 30 years ago, in digging amongſt the rubbiſh, was found an arched vault, ſuppoſed by the workmen to have been an oven, out of which they took more than 40 cart loads of ſtones.

About 2 years ago, in a ſmall brook, which hath waſhed or run near to the walls of the abbey, were found the ſide poſts and part of a ſluice or lock, which ſeems to have been placed there for laying under water four or five acres of ground above the ſame; which parcel of ground yet goes by the name of the Tarn, and a large field thereto adjoining is called Tarn Moor.

At a ſmall diſtance eaſt from the abbey, are the veſtiges of two large fiſh ponds; near to which, about 60 years ago, were dug up ſeveral pieces of leaden pipes, ſuppoſed to have been for conveying water to the ſaid fiſh-ponds.

A little ſouth-eaſtward from the ſaid ponds, is a large parcel of ground, now common, which appears to have been incloſed with an high earthen fence and a ditch on each ſide, part of which fence yet remains; and the ſame goes by the name of the Abbey park.

ADDENDA;

ADDENDA.

VOL I.

Page 66. *Kendal cottons.*

AS a ſpecimen of the large trade carried on in Kendal cottons, it appears from the cuſtom-houſe books at Liverpool, that in one year, viz. 1770, there were exported to America from that port only between three and four thouſand pieces; namely,

To Barbadoes	—	120 pieces
Dominique	—	30
Jamaica	—	810
St. Kitts	—	40
Newfoundland		194
New York	—	80
Virginia and Maryland		2693

Carolina 640 yards; which may be about 40 pieces more. So that the total will be 3500 pieces and upwards exported from this port only in one year.

Page 73. *Kendal Bells.*

In the year 1774, theſe bells were altered from a peal of ſix to eight. The firſt, ſecond, third, and ſixth were new caſt; the ſixth having been burſt, and not having been quite tunable with the reſt. The fourth and fifth of the old ſet remain as they were, and are the ſeventh and eighth of the preſent peal. One of theſe bells is ſaid to have been brought from the abbey of Shap; which, if any, was probably this ſixth: not only from its being diſproportioned in ſound from the reſt; but from the inſcription on the fourth old bell, which imports that the third, fourth, and fifth were repaired or recaſt by the pariſh, but ſaith nothing of the ſixth.

A D D E N D A.

The inſcriptions on the ſeveral bells, in their order as ranged at preſent, are as follows:

1. Our voices ſhall with joyful ſound
Make hills and vallies eccho round.

2. Such wond'rous power to muſic's given,
As elevates the ſoul to heaven.

3. While thus we join in chearful ſound,
May love and loyalty abound.

4. Ye ringers all that prize your health and happineſs,
Be ſober, merry, wiſe, and you'll the ſame poſſeſs.

5. In wedlock bands,
All ye who join with hands,
Your hearts unite;
So ſhall our tuneful tongues combine
To laud the nuptial rite.

6. On the ſixth bell is the following memorative inſcription:
In the year 1774, theſe bells were re-caſt from a peal of ſix to eight, by the direction of
Thomas Strickland }
Thomas Scariſbrick } Aldermen.
John Wilſon, M. A.
Brian Wilſon
William Strickland
James Wilſon of Lambrigg, And
Henry Shepherd of Patton. A committee appointed by the pariſh veſtry.
Thomas Symmonds, D. D. vicar.

7. (Which was the fourth in the old peal.)
Has tres campanas
Jam tota Parœcia ſanas
Reddidit, ut quarta
eſt tertia quinta ſimul.
Third, fourth, and fifth, and all may toll,
O'th' pariſh charge without controul.

8. (Which was the fifth in the old peal.)
Me ſonus nolæ memorem tubæ facit.

Their

Their weight is,

		Cwt.	Qs.	lb.
1st.	—	8	0	4
2d.	—	8	1	20
3d.	—	9	1	0
4th.	—	10	2	11
5th.	—	14	0	15
6th.	—	15	3	0
7th.	—	19	3	9
8th.	—	25	0	15

Page 74. *Kendal chantries.*

In the year 1553, the following penſions were paid to thoſe that had been the incumbents of chantries:

	l	s	d.
St. Mary's chantry to Adam Sheparde incumbent —	3	6	8
St. Anthony's chantry to Robert Baſe — —	3	4	4
St. Chriſtopher's chantry to John Garret —	2	14	7
St. Thomas Becket's Altar chantry to Alan Sheparde —	4	13	4
St. Leonard, alias le Spittle, chantry to Geffry Baynebridge	4	4	0

Page 75. *Docwra hall.*

Docwra hall had its name from a reſpectable family that reſided at the ſame a long time, but which now ſeems to be totally extinct. At Lilly Hoo in Hertfordſhire is the following monumental inſcription, on the north ſide of the chancel:

"M. S.

"Beati mortui qui in Domino moriuntur.

"Here lieth the body of *Thomas Docwra* the elder eſquire, lord of this
"town and patron of this church, deſcended of the ancient family of
"the *Docwras* of *Docwra Hall* in Kendal in the county of Weſtmorland,
"nephew and heir unto the right honourable Sir *Thomas Docwra* lord
"grand prior of the knights of St. John of Jeruſalem. He had to
"wife Mildred Hales of an ancient family in Kent, a grave and virtuous
"matron, with whom he lived 52 years, having been juſtice of the
"peace 40 years, and high ſheriff of the ſhire Anno 23 Eliz. beloved
"and reverenced for his gravity, wiſdom, piety, juſtice, and hoſpitality;
"he died in his houſe at Putteridge by him built, in the 84th year of
"his age, Anno Dom. 1602, leaving four ſons and two daughters."

Page 83. *Kendal charities.*

Henry Wilkinson of Kendal clerk, in 1598, devifed his houfes to be fold, and the money to be put out at intereft, and the produce thereof diftributed in the churchyard by the churchwardens on the fecond of February yearly to the poor of the town of Kendal.

Nicholas Bateman, gentleman, gave 10*l*; to be lent out yearly to fome young tradefman without intereft, except only that he fhall pay for the fame 3*s* 4*d* to the ufe of the church and for writing the bond.

Christopher Woodburne of Kendal, in 1723, gave by his will 8*l* yearly, to put out four poor boys apprentices, the fame to be paid to the mafter on their binding; and alfo 10*s* to each to find them fhirts and cravats.

Page 108. *Old Hutton Chapel.*

On the north-eaft fide thereof is the following infcription:

Twelve loaves each Sunday in this houfe are given,
Twelve for to feed: Praife they the Lord of Heaven.
Ex dono Thomæ Robinfon, integerrimi viri,
Pauperibus et capellæ hujus maxime munifici,
Roberto grandævo et benigno patre nati,
Cujus vita fine macula, fine labe peracta,
Non quifquam pietate prior, nec amantior æqui.
1706.

Page 127. *Brathwaites of Burneshead.*

In the parifh church of Catterick in Yorkfhire, is the following epitaph of *Richard Brathwaite* of Burnefhead efquire, and of Mary his fecond wife daughter of Roger Croft; by which it appears that Sir *Strafford Brathwaite* their fon, who was killed in an engagement with an Algerine man of war, was buried at Tangier.

Juxta fitæ funt
Ricardi Brathwait
de Burnefhead in comitatu
Weftmorlandiæ armigeri, et
Mariæ ejus conjugis reliquiæ.
Ille quarto die Maii Anno 1673
denatus eft: Hæc undecimo Aprilis 1681
fupremum diem obiit. Horum filius
unicus, Strafford Brathwait eques

auratus

auratus, adversus Mauros christiani
nominis hostes infestissimos fortiter
dimicans, occubuit: Cujus cineres
Tingi in Mauritania Tingitana
humantur.
Requiescant in pace.

Page 129. *Burneshead chapel.*

After the death of the reverend William Smith curate of Burneshead in the year 1776, the appointment of a curate to the chapel was contested, not by the vicar against the chapelry, but by the people amongst themselves. The owners of messuages, lands, and tenements within the chapelry, charged with, or chargeable to the payment of chapel salary, asserted the right of electing a curate to be in themselves. The tenants of such of the said messuages, lands, and tenements as were let to farm, claimed a right of voting, by virtue of their actual paying such salary so charged upon the estates demised to them. Each party had a majority in their own way. The land owners presented to the vicar their candidate the reverend William Barton to be by the said vicar nominated to the bishop in order to obtain his lordship's licence, who did thereupon nominate him accordingly. The tenants presented to the bishop their candidate the reverend John Jackson, setting forth their claim, and praying him to be admitted. Four caveats were entred at Chester; and the parties (according to custom in like cases) became violent and exasperated. The bishop, in order to get rid of the caveats with as little trouble to himself as might be, and to save charges to the parties, intimated, that if no suit should be commenced within the six months, so as that the curacy should fall in lapse, he would license the said Mr. Barton. Upon this the land-owners acquiesced. And upon the lapse, Mr. Barton was licensed accordingly.—Upon the merits, it doth not seem that there could have been any doubt as to the legality. For whatever right of election the land-owners may claim by custom against the vicar, there is no such custom for the tenants or farmers against their landlords.

By the improvement of the rents of lands, it is said that this curacy is now worth 70*l* a year.

Page 132. *Stricklands.*

Richard Newby of Strickland Roger, by his will in 1616, gave 40*l*: The interest of 10*l* thereof to be distributed yearly to the poor of Grayrigg; the interest of other 10*l* thereof to the poor of Lambrigg; the interest of 6*l* 13*s* 4*d* thereof to the poor of Docker: and of 13*l* 6*s* 8*d* (being the residue of the said 40*l*) to the poor of Strickland Roger and Strickland Ketel.

Page 164. *Fleming.*

There is a ſmall miſtake in ſtyling Sir Daniel Fleming *baronet*. He was only *knight*. His ſon Sir William Fleming was the firſt baronet of the family, being ſo created in the year 1704, with remainder to the iſſue male of his body, and in defect thereof to the iſſue male of his father Sir Daniel Fleming.

Page 179. *Undermilbeck.*

Anthony Garnet of the Barkerknott in Undermilbeck, who died in the year 1774, gave by his will a legacy of 60*l* to the overſeers of the poor of Undermilbeck, in truſt to place the ſame out at intereſt, and the produce ariſing therefrom to be by them laid out in bread, a part or portion whereof is to be diſtributed by them every Sunday amongſt the poor of Undermilbeck who attend divine ſervice.

Page 185. *Windermere water.*

This lake, with regard to the fiſheries, is at preſent divided into three *cubbles* (as the people call them, which in Mr. Machel's time were called *cables*; but from what foundation either of the words is derived we have not found). The firſt cubble or diviſion, being the high end of the lake, contains one fiſhing. The ſecond cubble or diviſion, being the middle part of the lake, contains five fiſhings. The third cubble or diviſion, being the low end of the lake, contains ſix fiſhings.

In the year 1774, the houſe called Holme-houſe in the middle of the great iſland in this lake was demoliſhed, in order to be rebuilt and enlarged; in the place whereof, a very curious edifice hath been erected by Mr. Engliſh the preſent owner: which having attracted the attention of travellers and other viſitants of the lake, it is thought proper here to give ſome account thereof.—The building is a perfect circle fifty-four feet in diameter. The roof thereof is a dome, ſlated with fine blue ſlate got in the neighbourhood. The walls of this building are built of a blue flint ſtone, which came from a place called Hacklerigg, the property of Dr. Atkinſon. The ſtones which are raiſed from the quarry are very large. There are ſeveral ſtones in the building which are twenty-two feet in length, and a great number fifteen feet. The building is four ſtories high, excluſive of the garrets, which are in the roof, which is ſomewhat remarkable it being a dome: the ſaid garrets are lighted from the roof, but it doth not in the leaſt affect the outline of the building. The principal rooms are lighted by Venetian windows, and are

are fo placed as to have a view on each end of the lake. The principal entrance is under a portico fupported by fix columns and two pilafters fix foot in height exclufive of the bafe and capital. The columns ftand on pedeftals fix foot in height, and continue all round the building; which form the area for the lower part of the building, which is nine foot below the furface of the ground, and contains the kitchens, brewhoufe, fervants hall, cellars, and other offices. The afcent into the above-mentioned entrance is by two flights of circular fteps as high as the pedeftal, where there is a large landing before the hall door. The whole building is intended to be very elegantly finifhed, with mahogany doors, window-frames and every other article fuitable thereto. The pedeftal part ftands upon a fquare plan, and the proprietor propofes planting different kinds of trees in clumps, at a certain diftance from each angle, which will form four viftas from the building. The height from the ground floor to the cieling is fixteen feet. From the fecond floor to the cieling, fourteen feet and fix inches in height. From the third floor to the cieling, ten feet in height. From the fourth floor to the cieling, eight feet and fix inches in height. The principal rooms are feventeen feet fix by twenty-two feet, and continue the fame from the ground floor to the top of the building.—In cutting a large drain on the weft part of the building, which is to take away the wafh from different parts the building to the lake, were found feveral pieces of lead and old iron, and a great number of old bricks. About fix feet deep in the earth, they dug through feveral old drains. And a chimney was found in its perfect ftate. They found at the fame time feveral pieces of old armour. In levelling the ground on the north part of the building, they dug through a beautiful pavement, curioufly paved with pebbles of a fmall kind. They alfo dug through feveral curious gravel walks.

Page 204. *Redmans of Over Lewins.*

Of this family, moft probably was *Richard Redman*, D. D. perhaps a younger brother of *Matthew Redman* (fon of *Richard*) who was knight of the fhire in the 20th Hen. 6. This Dr. Redman was zealous in the intereft of the houfe of York, whereupon he was promoted by king Edward the fourth to the fee of St. Afaph in the year 1468. In 1471, he was made abbot of Shap. In the reign of king Henry the feventh, he became intangled in the affair of Lambert Symnel, and on that account incurred the king's difpleafure, and by him was complained of to the pope; who by a bull, dated Jan. 9, 1487, commiffioned the archbifhop, with the bifhops of Winchefter, Ely, and Exeter, to inquire into that matter, and to tranfmit the refult of it to Rome. It is fuppofed that he acquitted himfelf to the king's fatisfaction, as he was in 1492 appointed by him one of the commiffioners to treat of peace with the Scots, and in the year after was made one of his privy council. In 1495, he was promoted to the fee of Exeter; and in 1501, was tranflated to Ely; which promotion having enjoyed not full four years, he died Aug. 4, 1505, at Ely

Ely House in Holborn, and was burried in his own cathedral church of Ely, where a sumptuous monument is erected to his memory. By his last will he gave considerably to his old monastery of Shap, several legacies to all the religious houses in the diocese of Ely, 100 marks to the cathedral, and the like sum to be distributed to the poor on the day of his burial.

Page 205. *Bellinghams of Helsington and Over Levins.*

In the parish church of Catterick in Yorkshire, is the following epitaph of *Grace* daughter of *Alan Bellingham*:

"Gracia, Belingamii filia, vidua Cliburni, Gerardi Lowtherii uxor,
"lectissima fœmina, summæ pietatis, invictæ patientiæ, charitatis
"in pauperes maximæ, verborum parcior, eximiæ prudentiæ, sin-
"gularis in maritos obsequii, mortis adeo memor, ut septem hujus
"peregrinationis suæ annis nunquam proficisceret, quin linteum
"sepulchrale circumferret. Obdormivit in Domino, Anno Ætatis
"suæ 36. 1594."

Page 224. *Betham.*

It hath appeared, that our conjecture was right, concerning the manor of Betham not having been forfeited by Sir Thomas Betham in consequence of the battle of Bosworth field. For it continued in the family by a female heir a long time after that, and did not come into the Derby family until the reign of king Charles the second. And the succession of that ancient family of Betham, which we often find mentioned in the occurrences of those times, so far as we have been able to recover the same, hath been as follows:

I. The first that we meet with was Ralph de Betham, who was witness to the foundation charter of Cockersand abbey. This Ralph, for the health of his soul, and the soul of his wife Ingaretha, gave a salt work, with two patellæ, in Betham, to the abbey of Furness, in the reign of king Hen. 2.

II. Thomas de Betham, son and heir of Ralph, married Amuria, one of the four daughters and coheirs of Richard Fitz-Roger lord of Wood Plumpton in Lancashire, by his wife Margaret daughter and heir of Dunstan Banister; by whom he had two sons, *Ralph* and *Roger*. *Ralph* the elder, in the 17th year of king John, (amongst other sons or daughters and heirs of divers mesne lords holding under the barons of Kendal) was delivered as an hostage to the said king, for the future fidelity of Gilbert son of Roger Fitz-Reinfred and of William his son, who had joined with the rebellious barons. The said Thomas appears to have been living in the 26 Hen. 3. being in that year a witness, amongst others, to a grant of lands by Sir John Fleming of Beckermet.

III. The faid RALPH DE BETHAM, elder fon of Thomas, fucceeded his father; and by his wife Felicia had a fon and heir, viz.

IV. THOMAS DE BETHAM, who was knight of the fhire for Weftmorland in the 30 Ed. 1. and again in the 2, 4th, and 5th of Ed. 2. In the fourth year of the fame king Ed. 2. he obtained a charter for a market and fair in Betham. His wife's name was Emma, who furvived him; for in the 7 Ed. 3. Joan wife of John le Tours lord of Lowick, and daughter of Sir John le Fleming, had fettled on her the reverfion of what Emma de Betham then held in dower. By his faid wife Emma, he had iffue a fon *Robert*, and two daughters *Eleanor* and *Helwife*.

V. Sir ROBERT DE BETHAM knight, fon and heir of Thomas, had, by Maud his wife, a fon and heir, viz.

VI. THOMAS DE BETHAM, who married Parnel daughter of Sir Robert de Burton knight, and fifter and at length fole heir to Anthony de Burton lord of the manor of Burton, who died without iffue. By his faid wife Parnel, he had iffue *Ralph*, *Thomas*, and *Robert*.

VII. Sir RALPH DE BETHAM, knight, fon and heir of Thomas, in the 8 Ed. 3. had a grant of free warren in Betham. In the 20 Ed. 3. writs were directed to Ralph de Betham, together with Thomas de Rofs of Kendal caftle, to fend their prifoners from their caftles to the tower of London. In the 49 Ed. 3. Ralph de Betham knight held of Joan de Coupland the manor of Burton with the appurtenances, by homage and fealty and the fervice of 32*s* yearly, as of her manor of Kirkby in Kendale. The faid Ralph de Betham, by Alice his wife, had iffue,

VIII. ROBERT DE BETHAM, father of,

IX. JOHN DE BETHAM; who in the 8 Hen. 4. reprefented the county of Weftmorland in parliament. He married Margaret fifter of Sir William Tunftal knight, and by her had iffue,

X. Sir THOMAS DE BETHAM knight, to whom, in the 3 Hen. 5. a commiffion of array was iffued and directed, to mufter all men of arms. In the 3 Hen. 6. he reprefented the county of Weftmorland in parliament; and appears to have been living in the 22 Hen. 6. He had iffue two fons, *Edward* and *Roger*, and a daughter *Elizabeth* married to Sir Richard Mufgrave of Hartley caftle knight.

XI. Sir EDWARD BETHAM knight, fon and heir of the laft Sir Thomas, married Joan daughter of William Nevil lord Faulconberg and earl of Kent, but had no iffue. Whereupon the eftate devolved upon his brother *Roger*.

XII. Roger de Betham, brother and heir of Edward, had an only child Anne, who in the reign of king Ric. 3. was married te Sir Robert Middleton of Leighton, son of Sir *Geoffrey Middleton* a younger son of *John Middleton* of Middleton hall esquire, and thereby brought a great addition of fortune into the Middleton family of Leighton. The said Sir Robert Middleton, by his said wife Anne the heiress of Betham, had issue a son, viz.

XIII. Thomas Middleton of Leighton esquire, who married Johan daughter of Sir Thomas Strickland knight; and, dying in the 8 Hen. 8. left issue,

XIV. Gervase Middleton esquire, who married a daughter of Kirkham of Northamptonshire; and died in the 1 Ed. 6. leaving issue by his said wife,

XV. George Middleton esquire; who married Margaret daughter of Sir Christopher Metcalf, and by her had issue,

XVI. Thomas Middleton esquire; who married Katharine daughter of Sir Richard Houghton of Houghton Tower, and by her had issue,

XVII. Sir George Middleton of Leighton, baronet; which dignity he obtained for his services to king Charles the first. He was a great sufferer in the royal cause, having been subjected to sequestrations and severe compositions. He married Frances daughter and heir of Richard Rigg of Little Strickland esquire, and by her had issue Mary and Katharine. And these two causes seem to have effected the dismembring of the estate, namely, the impoverishment of the family by sequestrations, and the succession of coheiresses. And about this time the manor of Betham came into the Derby family.

Mary, the elder daughter of Sir George Middleton, was married to Somerford Oldfield esquire of the county of Chester, who had issue George Middleton Oldfield esquire, who came to live at Leighton, and left two daughters coheirs; the elder was married to Albert Hodgson esquire, and the younger to one of the Fletchers of Hutton hall in Cumberland, and died without issue. The said *Albert Hodgson* engaged in the rebellion in 1715, and his estate was confiscated.—What became of Katharine, the other daughter of Sir *George Middleton* we have not found.

What were the arms of Betham is not certainly agreed. Mr. West (whose knowledge in matters of that kind is unquestionable), in his Antiquities of Furness abbey, says, that the arms of Betham were; Argent, a chief dancette Sable. In the heralds office, the arms of Betham are; Or, three flower de lys Argent: And these latter were depicted in a window of the gallery

gallery of the old Hall at Leighton, expresly by the name of Betham †. And yet on the monument in Betham church, whereon are the effigies of a man and woman cut in stone, which undoubtedly hath been erected in memory of some of the Betham family, amongst the several escutcheons found there, the flower de lys do not appear. Our account of this monument, which we gave in the body of the work, was copied from Mr. Machel's manuscript, who though he personally visited the several places, yet here he had not the opportunity of a thorough examination. For by the floor of the chancel having been raised about a foot and an half above the level of the body of the church, the monument was half buried. The present worthy vicar hath had the curiosity to examine it to the bottom, and the arms thereon appear as follows (beginning at the head of the man on the south side, and so going eastward). 1. A raguled cross. 2. Six annulets, three, two, and one. 3. Escalops, two and one. 4. A saltier ingrailed. 5. On the north side, at the foot of the woman; A chief indented, or otherwise a chief dancette, but it doth not evidently appear which of the two. 6. A lion's head guardant. 7. A cross lozengeed. Under the head of the lady, there is a vacancy large enough for another coat, but there is none, nor doth it appear that any hath been defaced. Now here are neither the flower de lys, nor the chief dancette (unless the coat at No. 5 be so; which is at least doubtful). Nor have we found to whom the first coat, under the head of the man, did belong. The second is *Musgrave*. The third, *Strickland*. The fourth, *Middleton*. The fifth, most probably *Burton*, whose coat was a chief indented. The sixth, *Fitz-Roger*. And the seventh, *Croft*. If we could suppose that the vacancy beneath the head of the lady was left for the flower de lys or other arms of Betham to be engraved afterwards, and that the bearing at No. 1 was assumed by the Middletons of Leighton to distinguish them from the other branch of the family at Middleton hall (a thing not without example), all the rest might easily be accounted for. It is clearly not the monument of the last Sir Thomas Betham and his lady (as is commonly supposed), but is more modern, and seems to have been put up by Thomas Middleton of Leighton esquire, in memory of his father Sir Robert Middleton, and his mother Anne heiress of the family of Betham.—They were connected with the *Musgraves*, by a daughter of Sir Thomas Betham.—This Thomas Middleton's wife was a daughter of *Strickland*.—*Middleton*, on our supposition of the arms being changed, may represent the ancient stock at Middleton hall.—*Burton*, by marriage of the heiress there, was a quartering

† The arms painted in glass in the said gallery, evidently in Sir Geoffrey Middleton's time, are these; 1. *Middleton*: Argent, a saltier ingrailed Sable. 2. *Croft*: Lozengee, Argent and Sable. 3. *Coigners*: Argent, a manch Or. 4. *Yealand*: Argent, three ravens heads erased proper. 5. *Auranches*: Argent, a cross Gules. (These three last were quarterings of Croft, whose heiress Sir Geoffrey Middleton married. The following were quartering of Betham.) 6. *Betham*: Or, three flower de lys Argent; placed in the same manner as the arms of France. 7. *Burton*: Or, a chief indented Azure. 8. *Fitz-Roger*: Argent, a lion rampant guardant Or, armed and langued Gules. 9. *Banister*: Argent, three cheverons Gules. (Which last was a quartering of Fitz-Roger, who married the heiress of Dunstan Banister.)

of Betham.—*Croft* was a quartering of Middleton, from Allison Croft one of the two coheirs of James Croft of Dalton esquire, and grandmother of this same Thomas Middleton.

Page 237. *Burton.*

The manor of Burton, about the time of king Edward the second, came to the family of Betham, by marriage of Sir Thomas de Betham with Parnel daughter of Sir Robert de Burton and sole heir of her brother Anthony de Burton who died without issue; and by marriage of the heiress of Betham, it came to the Middletons of Leighton; and by a coheiress of that house, to the Oldfields of Cheshire; who sold to Thomas Benison of Hornby esquire; whose daughter and heir was married to John Fenwick esquire; whose brother and heir Thomas Fenwick esquire sold the same to Thomas Pearson esquire the present proprietor.

END OF THE FIRST VOLUME.

ERRATA.

VOL. I.

Page 8 line 11. for *personality*, read personalty.
52 — 31. for *charge*, read change.
143 — 6, 7. for *Undermillbeck*, read Applethwaite.
157 — 15, for *march*, r. manch.
179 — 2. for *Berkthwaite*, r. Birthwaite.
23. for *Fulbarrow*, r. Falbarrow.
184 — 32. dele *de*.
258 — 35. for 1621, r. 1691.
260 — 19. for *to*, r. by.
311 — 14. for Ed. 5. r. Ed. 3.
381 — line penult. for *caringe*, r. cariage.
391 — 14. r. and no farther.
473 — 1. r. or one penny.
490 — 3. for 1678; r. 1658.
518 — 26. after *Sceat beck*, add *as Sceat beck.*
597 — 26. for *patri*, r. patriæ.

VOL. II.

16 — 3. for *fewer*, r. sewer.
79 — 27. r. Thornton East, Westwood.
300 — line penult. for *published*, r. re-published.

Lightning Source UK Ltd.
Milton Keynes UK
UKHW020026010720
365831UK00010B/319